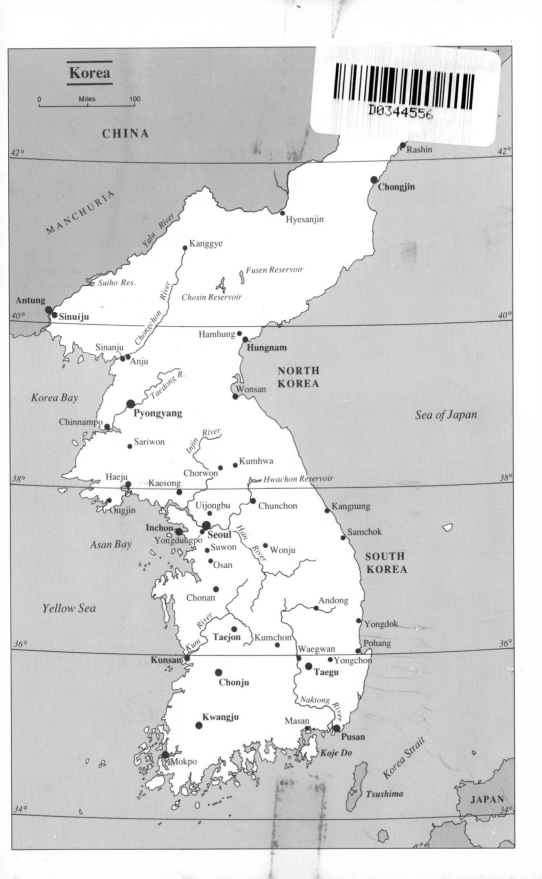

# Korea

0     Miles     100

CHINA

MANCHURIA

42°

Rashin

Chongjin

Hyesanjin

Yalu River

Kanggye

Fusen Reservoir

Suiho Res.

Chosin Reservoir

Antung

40°   Sinuiju

Chongchon River

Hamhung

Sinanju

Hungnam

Anju

NORTH KOREA

Taedong R.

Wonsan

Korea Bay

Sea of Japan

Chinnampo

Pyongyang

Sariwon

Injin River

Kumhwa

Chorwon

38°   Haeju    Kaesong

Hwachon Reservoir

Ongjin

Uijongbu

Chunchon

Kangnung

Inchon

Seoul

Samchok

Yongdungpo

Han River

Asan Bay

Suwon

Wonju

SOUTH KOREA

Osan

Yellow Sea

Chonan

Andong

Yongdok

36°    Kum River    Taejon   Kumchon    Pohang

Kunsan

Waegwan

Yongchon

Chonju

Taegu

Kwangju

Naktong River

Masan

Pusan

Koje Do

Mokpo

Korea Strait

Tsushima

JAPAN

34°

42°

40°

38°

36°

34°

| DATE DUE | | | |
|---|---|---|---|
| | | | |
| | | | |
| | | | |
| | | | |
| | | | |
| | | | |
| | | | |
| | | | |
| | | | |
| | | | |
| | | | |
| | | | |

# BOOKS BY CLAY BLAIR

Nonfiction

*The Atomic Submarine and Admiral Rickover*
*The Hydrogen Bomb,* with James R. Shepley
*Beyond Courage*
*Valley of the Shadow,* for Ward M. Millar
*Nautilus 90 North,* with William R. Anderson
*Diving for Pleasure and Treasure*
*Always Another Dawn,* with A. Scott Crossfield
*The Voyage of Nina II,* for Robert Marx
*The Strange Case of James Earl Ray*
*Survive!*
*Silent Victory: The U.S. Submarine War Against Japan*
*The Search for J.F.K.,* with Joan Blair
*MacArthur*
*Combat Patrol*
*Return from the River Kwai,* with Joan Blair
*A General's Life,* with Omar N. Bradley
*Ridgway's Paratroopers*

Fiction

*The Board Room*
*The Archbishop*
*Pentagon Country*
*Scuba!,* with Joan Blair
*Mission Tokyo Bay,* with Joan Blair
*Swordray's First Three Patrols,* with Joan Blair

# THE
# FORGOTTEN
# WAR

# THE
# FORGOTTEN
# WAR

## America in Korea 1950-1953

# CLAY BLAIR

**Times** BOOKS

Grateful acknowledgment is made to *The Saturday Evening Post* for
permission to reprint an excerpt from the article, "How Do Our Negro Troops
Measure Up?" by Harold H. Martin from the June 16, 1951, issue of *The
Saturday Evening Post.* Copyright © 1951 by Curtis Publishing Co. Copyright
renewed. Reprinted by permission.

The photographs in this volume were obtained from the National Archives.

Library of Congress Cataloging-in-Publication Data

Blair, Clay, 1925–
The forgotten war.

Bibliography: p.
1. Korean War, 1950–1953—Campaigns. 2. Korean War,
1950–1953—United States. I. Title.
DS918.B53 1988   951.9′042   87-40195
ISBN 0-8129-1670-0

Designed by Robert Bull Design

Manufactured in the United States of America

24689753

First Edition

For my progeny:
Marie Louise, Clay III, Sibyl, Kemp, Robert, and Christopher.
And for Joan's: David and Christopher West.

# FOREWORD

The United States has fought nine major wars, four in the twentieth century. Of these conflicts, the war in Korea, 1950–1953, ranks among the most important, yet is the least remembered. There is no monument in Washington commemorating its valorous dead. To the several generations born since it was fought, the "Korean War" is little more than a phrase in history books.

The war was a traumatic and momentous chapter in American history. It was a big, long war, during which nearly 6 million men and women served in the armed forces. Americans fought in Korea nearly three times as long as they had fought in World War I and almost as long as they had fought in World War II. The first year of combat was brutal and bloody, often surpassing the toughest battles of any war in American history. Total American casualties in Korea were heavy: 33,629 killed and 103,284 wounded.

The impact of the war on the United States government and society was profound. This war:

• Greatly intensified hostilities between the West and Communist-bloc nations, especially the newly founded People's Republic of China, delaying for decades a normalization of relations between Washington and Peking.

• Gave powerful impetus to a massive nuclear and conventional arms race between the United States and the Soviet Union, which transformed America from an ill-armed democracy into the militaristic state which exists today.

• Gave root to the notion that the "spread of communism" in the Far East could be contained by "limited" American military power, which led to American military intervention in Vietnam.

ix

• Fostered a national climate which strengthened the appeal of McCarthyism and similar repressive ideologies and unseated the Democratic party, which had held the White House for twenty years.

These larger aspects of the Korean War have been explored elsewhere, although a definitive study is wanting. This book is mainly about the war itself: the men who fought it; the action on the battlefields; the policy disputes between President Harry S. Truman and General Douglas MacArthur and others, which directly or indirectly influenced the conduct of the war.

\* \* \*

The United States embarked on the war in Korea to rescue the newly established Republic of Korea (ROK) from Communist invaders, first the North Koreans, then the Chinese. Fighting under the aegis and flag of the United Nations, the United States and South Korea were eventually supported by eighteen other Western nations, fourteen of which contributed combat forces and four of which contributed only small noncombatant medical contingents.

Although the air and naval forces of the contributing nations were important, the burden of the war in Korea, like all wars in history, was borne by the infantry. The ROK Army started with eight infantry divisions and added more as the war progressed. The United States provided seven divisions, six Army and one Marine. The British Commonwealth (United Kingdom, Canada, Australia, New Zealand) contributed one division. Turkey sent one brigade. France, the Netherlands, Greece, Belgium, the Philippines, Thailand, and Colombia each provided one battalion.

\* \* \*

The three-year infantry war in Korea may be divided into two distinct phases: one year of dramatic and far-reaching maneuver, which has been dubbed the "Blitzkrieg," followed by two years of static, positional warfare at or near the 38th Parallel, which has been dubbed the "Sitzkrieg." The first phase, or year, may be further subdivided into five parts: the North Korean invasion of South Korea, the expulsion of North Korean forces from South Korea, the United Nations invasion of North Korea, the Chinese intervention in the war and invasion of South Korea, the expulsion of Chinese forces from South Korea and stalemate at the 38th Parallel. The second phase, or two years, consisted mostly of massive artillery duels near the 38th Parallel and futile (but costly) infantry struggles over a few hills or thousands of yards of terrain, while armistice negotiations proceeded over a tortuous course.

This book is a close study of the first year of the war, covering the period June 25, 1950, to about June 25, 1951, when the final battle lines were drawn.

The highlights of the final two years are summarized in the last chapter. Inasmuch as combat actions in the second phase had little or no bearing on the outcome of the war, these are subordinated to the political aspects which arose in the armistice negotiations or elsewhere.

\* \* \*

More particularly this book is about the United States Army infantry operations in Korea. The Army furnished about 86 percent of American infantry manpower in the war; the Marine Corps, about 14 percent. The battlefield death toll was directly proportional: 86 percent in the Army (29,367) and 14 percent in the Marines (4,262). Army veterans of the Korean War would contend that the Marine Corps publicity was inversely proportional to the manpower committed and deaths sustained: 86 percent for Marines and 14 percent for the Army. Whether the contention is true or not is difficult to say. In any event, this book is the other way around: 86 percent of the space is devoted to the Army infantry operations; 14 percent to the Marines and other UN infantry.

The first year of the Korean War was a ghastly ordeal for the United States Army. For various reasons, it was not prepared mentally, physically, or otherwise for war. On the whole, its leadership at the army, corps, division, regiment, and battalion levels was overaged, inexperienced, often incompetent, and not physically capable of coping with the rigorous climate of Korea. These "human factors" are explored at close quarters for the first time, not for the purpose of adding "color" or sensationalism but rather to provide some insight into numerous failures on the battlefield which have not hitherto been explained.

Two other "human factors" are probed in detail: the representation of West Point graduates among the various levels of command and the performance of black troops in combat. The reasons for doing so are twofold. First, notwithstanding the "democratization" of the Army officer corps by an infusion of Army Reserve and National Guard officers, West Point was—and still is—the principal source of leadership for the professional Army. It seemed worthwhile to measure the presence and influence of West Pointers in Korea and, where possible, to assess their performances. Secondly, the Army officially and categorically condemned the performance of black units in Korea and, partly as a result, took the historic step of desegregating the entire Army in October 1951. Recently black activists have countercharged that the alleged poor showing of many black units in Korea did not occur because blacks were cowardly or incompetent, as the Army implied, but because too many of the white officers who led the black units were cowardly or incompetent racists.

The heart of this book is battle narrative, stripped of hyperbole and tears and critically analyzed. It depicts the Army infantry in Korea at its best as well as its worst. For the several generations of younger readers to whom the "Korean War" is merely a phrase, I hope this account will be eye-opening and instructive. For older readers I hope that the narrative and analysis will stir memories and perhaps answer questions that still nag. For those who were there, and wrought victory from defeat, I salute you, and I ask forgiveness for the errors of commission and omission that plague all who dare reduce the chaos of the battle to a neat and comprehensible story.

CLAY BLAIR
Washington Island,
Wisconsin
1984–1987

# CONTENTS

xiii

## PART THIRTEEN: Red China Checked

# PART ONE

# Eve of War

# WASHINGTON:
# 1949-1950

I

On January 20, 1949, Harry S. Truman strode onto an elaborate stand in front of the United States Capitol and was sworn in for his first full term as president of the United States.

That chilly day in Washington Truman stood at the pinnacle of his personal power and popularity. In the previous November's presidential elections, despite major defections in the Democratic party and an apparently invincible Republican opponent, Thomas E. Dewey, Truman had not only won an upset victory for himself but also delivered a Democratic majority to both the Senate and House. Never before in American politics had there been such a personal triumph. Truman was appropriately deemed the "wonder man" of American politics.[1]

Truman had many noble qualities. He was decent, honest, foursquare, close, and loyal to his family and determined to do the right thing. He came from humble circumstances—a Missouri farm—where he had acquired a habit of thrift or, in a grander phrase, fiscal conservatism. He had a good ration of common sense. He could spot a city slicker a mile away. Although he had not gone beyond high school, he had improved on his education by prodigious reading in history and biography. He was physically fit and, at age sixty-four, still mentally keen and receptive to new ideas. Professionally he was a dedicated, loyal Democrat—a strict party man—who had slowly climbed the ladder to the Senate, from which Franklin D. Roosevelt had plucked him to be his vice presidential running mate in 1944. Innately modest and at times self-deprecating, Truman had not sought the White House. When it suddenly

3

and unexpectedly came to him on Roosevelt's death on April 12, 1945, Truman likened it to being hit by a load of hay and asked one and all to pray for him.

He had all these fine qualities—and more—but he had one fatal weakness as president and commander in chief: He had little or no grasp of grand strategy or military power. Worse, he did not concede that weakness. On the contrary, he fancied that with one or two exceptions he knew more about the military and grand strategy than all his generals and admirals put together.[2]

He held most professional military officers in contempt. After he had returned to private life, he said: "You always have to remember when you're dealing with generals and admirals, most of them, they're wrong a good deal of the time. . . . They're most of them just like horses with blinders on. They can't see beyond the ends of their noses. . . ." Half to three-quarters of all generals were "dumb." Besides that, he said, "No military man knows anything at all about money. All they know how to do is spend it, and they don't give a damn whether they're getting their money's worth or not. . . . I've known a good many who feel that the more money they spend, the more important they are." The "worst offenders" were the admirals, Truman said. The basic fault of both generals and admirals was the education they received at West Point and Annapolis: "It seems to give a man a narrow view of things."[3]

These harsh words may have sprung from an adolescent rejection. As a youngster of thirteen or fourteen Truman read widely in military history and fantasized a military career so grand, he wrote, it would "make Napoleon look like a sucker." By the time he was graduated from high school, the fantasy had hardened to a "wild desire" to go to West Point. However, as luck would have it, Truman was born with "terrible" eyesight (flat eyeballs), and as a consequence, his application to West Point (and later Annapolis) was turned down. That not only shattered his adolescent dreams but denied him the easiest way to get a free college education. From that time onward he was hostile to the professional military establishment and appeared to have a deep, perhaps even unconscious, desire to scold and punish it.[4]

Notwithstanding this rejection, Truman remained attracted to the military and at age seventeen joined a local National Guard artillery unit as a private. Since most guardsmen then (as now) tended to hold the Regular Army establishment in contempt, Truman may have felt right at home in this environment. He did well, advancing first to corporal, then to sergeant, and when his unit was mobilized for service in France in World War I, the men elected him (as was the custom) a lieutenant. In France he was promoted to captain and named to command Battery D, 129th Artillery Regiment of the 35th Division, which he ably led in combat.

His experience and close contact with the Regular Army establishment hardened his earlier contempt for it. His letters to his future wife, Bess, from that period are laced with acid comments about West Pointers. They were "ornamental and utterly useless" fops, he wrote, who sat close to the throne and to whom "promotion comes easy." He would "not trust 'em with a pair of mules or any surplus cash" because they would either lose the mules or sell them and use the money to buy whiskey. Anyone who would want to make the Army a career in peacetime was "certainly off in his upper works." In a remarkable foreshadowing of one of his future roles, in 1919 he wrote from France: "For my part I want to be [in civilian life] where I can cuss 'em all I please when I please, and you can bet there are some in this man's Army who are going to get cussed and more if they fool around me when I get out. I'd give my right arm to be on the Military Affairs Committee of the [United States] House [of Representatives]."[5]

In the period between the world wars Truman continued his close ties to the Army. He remained in the Army Reserve, going to summer camp every year. He eventually rose to full colonel and command of an artillery regiment. Perhaps in part to enhance his political career, he founded—and com- manded—the Missouri Reserve Officers Association. He was also an enthusi- astic member of the American Legion. These continuing military activities did not, however, diminish his disdain for the Regular Army establishment or elevate or broaden his strategic vision.

When World War II broke into full fury, Truman was a United States senator newly elected to his second term. As such he created an instrument which enabled him to "cuss" the regular military establishment on a grand scale. He founded and chaired a special Senate subcommittee to investigate "waste" and "duplication" and "fraud" in military procurement. Then (as now) it was a fertile field for a senator, especially one with a chip on his shoulder. He rooted the field with diligence and zeal, publicly flailing generals, admirals, and defense executives. He later boasted that his efforts had saved the nation $15 billion and uncounted lives on the battlefield. The claims would be difficult to confirm or assess, but the very existence of what became known as the Truman Committee probably exerted a positive influence on defense procurement and manufacturing. In any event its work made Truman famous.

Journalists and some historians were to assert that this wartime investigat- ing work in military procurement significantly elevated and broadened Tru- man's strategic vision and grasp of the military. However, a contrary case could be made: that a prolonged submersion into the world of machine tools, assembly-line schedules, steel quotas, turgid defense contract clauses had the effect of narrowing Truman's strategic vision. One thing is certain: The experi- ence powerfully reinforced Truman's conviction that all military men were fiscal idiots, that many engaged in budgetary legerdemain, and that a few were downright crooks.[6]

The journalistic acclaims heaped on the Truman Committee led in part to Roosevelt's decision to choose Truman as his vice presidential running mate in 1944. Then and in the postelection period one would have thought that

Roosevelt would have drawn Truman close into his high inner circle to elevate and broaden his strategic vision. Quixotically, Roosevelt did not. He foolishly isolated Truman from most grand strategy and foreign policy making, even after Truman had been sworn in as vice president. When Truman succeeded Roosevelt as commander in chief of the most powerful military force in the history of the world, he still had the military vision of a National Guard artillery colonel and an American Legionnaire who knew a lot about military procurement. He wrote that he had never even heard of the nation's most expensive single defense outlay: the atomic bomb.[7]

Early in his role as commander in chief Truman signaled his contemptuous attitude toward the military—the Army in particular—by his choice of senior Army aide and adviser in the White House. He had his pick of the many young, brilliant, and dedicated West Point strategists who had emerged in World War II. Instead, he chose a fat, sloppy old Missouri National Guard and American Legion crony, political fixer, and influence peddler, Harry H. Vaughan, who had campaigned in Truman's behalf during Truman's tough and close race for reelection to the Senate in 1940. Truman had first brought Vaughan to Washington to serve as an aide on his Senate investigating committee. After Pearl Harbor Vaughan had volunteered for active duty, but following injury in a plane crash, he returned to serve Truman as military aide thereafter. Although Vaughan's military credentials were slight to nonexistent and he was utterly lacking in strategic vision, Truman promoted him first to brigadier, then to major general. As one of Truman's closest friends and advisers Vaughan wielded enormous influence in military matters. To the Army, Harry Vaughan was not merely an embarrassment but an insult.[8]

\* \* \*

Truman's trench-level military outlook combined with his fiscal conservatism and contempt for generals and admirals had led him to weaken gravely the armed forces of the United States during his first, inherited term as commander in chief. He chose this course notwithstanding the almost day-by-day intensification of Soviet bellicosity and adventurism in the postwar years and the onset of the cold war. Moreover, the weakening continued unabatedly despite Truman's own ever-tougher cold war foreign policy, which clearly demanded substantial military strength to give it credibility.[9]

The president's sins against the military in his first three years and nine months were legion. The first and without doubt the gravest was his decision to impose unrealistic—even crippling—budget ceilings on the Pentagon which were based not on strategic considerations but on what Truman himself decided the country could afford.

Truman was determined that in the postwar years America must maintain a balanced federal budget and reduce the $250 billion national debt, all without incurring new federal taxes. The Pentagon threatened these fiscal objectives by recommending a minimum postwar "austerity" budget of about $15 billion a year. In order to stay on his fiscal course, Truman arbitrarily cut the Pentagon budget by a third—to about $10 billion a year—and turned a deaf ear to repeated pleas from his military chiefs for more. In fact, his unannounced goal was to cut the Pentagon budget even more drastically: to about $6 or $7 billion a year.[10]

One rationale for these crippling military cuts was a revolutionary new cold war policy known popularly as "foreign aid." The theory was that American money given to certain countries would prime economic pumps, speed up recovery, and make these countries less vulnerable to an external or internal Communist takeover, thereby reducing the need for military protection from America. This concept, which Truman eagerly embraced, led to foreign aid grants in the immediate postwar years totaling about $10 billion, most of it for the Marshall Plan. In the long term, foreign aid worked as designed in many countries; however, to view foreign aid as a viable or realistic substitute for American military power was, to say the least, naïve.

The severe budget ceilings on the Pentagon compelled a drastic postwar reduction in America's standing forces and in the quality and quantity of its armament. At the end of World War II America had 12 million men and women in uniform. By December 1948, at the end of Truman's first term as commander in chief, the standing forces had shrunk to a mere 1.5 million men and women. It had slight combat effectiveness and was everywhere in desperate need. For example:

*Army.* The Army of World War II numbered 6 million men and nearly 100 superbly equipped and trained divisions. When the war was over, a nationwide clamor arose to "bring the boys home." Notwithstanding the new global responsibilities that had befallen America, Truman caved in to political pressures and allowed a frenzied and disgraceful demobilization to occur. Within a matter of a few months the great wartime American Army was reduced to a few regular cadres processing incoming, unhappy draftees, most of whom were assigned to clerical or occupational duties in Germany and Japan.

No one wanted to maintain a big postwar American Army sustained by a draft that unfairly favored the affluent. After careful study, outgoing Army Chief of Staff George C. Marshall recommended that America maintain a standing Army of about 700,000 professionals, backed up by universal military training (UMT). Under UMT all physically qualified Americans would serve in an arm of the military for about one year of training, then go into a Reserve force which, in theory, could spring to arms within a matter of days.

UMT was a sensible and fair policy for a democracy, an extension or sophisticated version of the early militia of the colonial era. However, there was not a prayer that Congress would approve UMT or anything like it in peacetime, especially on the heels of an all-out world war. Nonetheless, Truman sincerely and passionately—and naïvely—embraced UMT for at least two main reasons. First, he believed universal military service would foster a democratization of the Army, diluting the influence of the West Point professionals. Secondly, it would save huge sums of money, enabling him to reach his goal of a $6 or $7 billion Pentagon budget.[11]

Truman pursued the UMT fantasy energetically all through his first term and allowed the unpopular draft to expire in 1947. As a consequence, by March 1948 the Army had dwindled to 530,000 men and was, as Chief of Staff Omar N. Bradley wrote, "in a shockingly deplorable state." It had "almost no combat effectiveness" and "could not fight its way out of a paper bag." There was only one division—the 82d Airborne—that could be remotely described as combat-ready.[12]

During the 1948 cold war scare, when Moscow overthrew the Czechoslovakian government and sealed off Berlin, Bradley persuaded Truman to reinstate the draft and build the Army to about 850,000 men, manning twelve ready divisions, backed by six National Guard divisions in a high state of readiness. However, by the end of 1948, when the Berlin crisis had been countered by the Berlin airlift and no other immediate threats were on the European horizon, Truman cut the Army back to 677,000 men, manning ten divisions, and passed the word that even deeper cuts lay in store.

*Navy.* The Navy of World War II was the mightiest seagoing fighting force in the history of the world. It consisted of 40 aircraft carriers, 24 battleships, 24,000 aircraft, manned by 3.3 million men, plus a Marine Corps of 480,000 men. Outgoing Chief of Naval Operations Ernest J. King recommended a postwar Navy of about 550,000 men manning about 400 ships, including 15 aircraft carriers and a Marine Corps of about 100,000 men.

In contrast with his predecessor Roosevelt, who favored the Navy, Truman held it and its stepchild, the Marine Corps, in utmost disdain and showed no inclination to soften his views or try to understand the role of sea power. His views no doubt sprang from his Army background. During the thirties, when Roosevelt was lavishing money on the Navy, the Army and its ancillaries, the National Guard and Reserve, suffered grievously by comparison. Truman believed not only that the admirals were the "worst offenders" when it came to handling money but also that the Navy and Marine Corps had established powerful and dangerous "propaganda" machines to support their reckless profligacy.[13]

By December 1948 Truman had savaged the Navy. It consisted of 429,000 men, manning 289 combatant vessels, including 11 aging aircraft carriers; the Marine Corps, 86,000 men. For future security of the seas the Navy had proposed construction of a fleet of modern aircraft carriers capable of handling new jet fighters. Truman had reluctantly approved the keel laying of one such vessel; but its future—indeed, the future of the entire Navy—was in serious doubt, and a mutiny was afoot in the senior naval staff.

*Air Force.* The Army Air Forces of World War II numbered 218 groups with 68,400 aircraft and 2.3 million men. Outgoing chief airman Henry H. ("Hap") Arnold recommended a postwar force of seventy groups, manned by 400,000 men.*

There was little doubt that air power had changed the character of warfare. World War II had shown that no nation could wage war successfully without absolute control and mastery of the skies. But the war had also disproved some extreme claims of the airmen—for example, that cheap, easy victories could be achieved by air power alone. Notwithstanding the immense and relentless strategic air offensive against Germany, it had still been necessary to mount a huge and costly Allied ground offensive to destroy the Wehrmacht.

Truman also distrusted the airmen. He demeaned them as "glamour boys" who made wild claims. He believed their planes were exorbitantly—and needlessly—expensive. Despite the recommendations of several blue-ribbon committees and others, which seconded Arnold's concept of a seventy-group Air Force, Truman categorically rejected it as excessively expensive and continued to oppose it with all his might and main. By June 1947 the Air Force had shrunk to thirty-eight groups, of which—scandalously—a mere eleven were operationally effective. During the 1948 Berlin crisis, when the airmen got Truman off the hook, the existing thirty-eight groups were brought up to near full strength and Truman authorized an additional ten. However, when Congress voted an extra billion for sixty-six groups, Truman, insistent that the Air Force be held to forty-eight groups, stubbornly and imperiously "impounded" the money. Moreover, he allowed the Air Force (and Army) only a pittance for research and development of ballistic missiles.

* * *

Truman's second greatest sin against the military was in permitting the nation's stockpile of atomic bombs to deteriorate to deplorably weak levels. Owing to the president's demobilization of America's conventional forces and his failure to persuade the Congress to adopt UMT, Pentagon planners were virtually compelled to shape a nuclear strategy (which would later be called "massive retaliation") to hold the huge conventional Russian military forces in check. However, owing to postwar problems incurred in plutonium production and the lassitude (and even hostility) toward weapons design and assembly prevalent at the Los Alamos Scientific Laboratory, between February 1946 and April 1948 there were only about a dozen atomic bombs in the stockpile and

---

*An Air Force bomber group consisted of 30 planes; a fighter group, 75 planes. A seventy-group Air Force would comprise a total of 6,869 fighters and bombers.

thirty-two Air Force B-29 bombers equipped to deliver them. These labora-tory-produced bombs were unassembled; it took twenty-four men two days to prepare one weapon for combat.[14]

During his first term as president Truman remained appallingly indifferent to nuclear strategy and the state of the nation's atomic bomb stockpile. One historian of the subject, David Rosenberg, wrote: "During 1945 and 1946 President Truman devoted little attention to atomic energy matters beyond his efforts to establish the AEC [Atomic Energy Commission] and promote Ber-nard Baruch's plan for international control of atomic energy by the United Nations." Truman, Rosenberg went on, was not even informed of the size of the stockpile until April 1947, two years after becoming president. Moreover, Rosenberg asserted, at least two more years went by before Truman was "thoroughly briefed" on the intricacies of nuclear strategy.

In April 1947, when he discovered how small the stockpile was, Truman was "shocked," Rosenberg wrote. Even so, he did little or nothing to correct the deficiency. Although the Pentagon requested an urgent buildup to 400 atomic bombs, one year later, in April 1948, there were still only 50 atomic bombs in the stockpile, all of them laboratory-built implosion bombs of the type dropped on Nagasaki. By December 1948 Los Alamos scientists had finally produced a new and more efficient atomic bomb design—delivering a bigger bang for less fissionable material—but there were still only about 100 old-fashioned Nagasaki-type bombs in the stockpile and a like number of Air Force bombers to deliver them.

*  *  *

Truman's third sin, also viewed as a way to save Pentagon money, was to impose a radical (but unworkable) "unification" on the armed forces, much against the will of the Navy and Marine Corps. In theory "unification" had some merit and appeal. During World War II there had been several glaring communications breakdowns between the Army and Navy (notably when the Japanese attacked Pearl Harbor and during the 1944 invasion of Leyte) and numerous procurement snafus (notably the failure of the Navy to produce sufficient LSTs, or landing ship, tanks). Unification was conceived to correct these communications and planning weaknesses and, above all, to avoid "du-plication" and "waste" and thereby to provide a more efficient military estab-lishment at less cost.

The Army urged unification in the postwar years for two principal rea-sons: to gain greater control over the Navy, on which it wholly depended to go places, and to curtail drastically the Marine Corps, which it viewed as a duplication of its ground and air forces. The Army enlisted the support of the airmen by promising their long-sought "independence" as a separate service within the "unified" military establishment. Convinced from his wartime experiences as a procurement gadfly that unification would save the nation billions, Truman embraced the idea as passionately as he did UMT, and he rushed unification legislation to Congress in December 1945.

His timing could not have been worse. Only four months earlier the Navy and Marine Corps had successfully concluded the war in the Pacific and were at the peak of public esteem. Taking advantage of the nation's adoration, the admirals and Marine Corps generals fought unification as defiantly, valorously, and skillfully as they had fought the Japanese. One war hero after the next took the witness stand to punch holes in Truman's proposal. Navy and Marine Corps partisans in Congress rose in defense of the two services, mocking and vilifying Truman and the Army and airmen for daring to suggest they might have fought more bravely and effectively had they been directed by some nebulous central authority in the Pentagon.

The unification law finally passed by the Republican-controlled Eightieth Congress in 1947 was a stiff defeat for Commander in Chief Truman. It created a National Military Establishment with a secretary of defense, as Truman had asked, but the act was so watered down and toothless as actually to be counterproductive and, in the eyes of many, harmful. The office of secretary of defense had no real power or control and no staff, not even a legal deputy. In such a loose administrative environment the admirals and Marine Corps generals were free to continue fighting tighter unification. And they did so with a vengeance, throwing the new organization into utter turmoil.

Adding to the confusion and turmoil was Truman's quixotic choice to be the first secretary of defense, James V. Forrestal. He was a former Ivy League Wall Street investment banker and a Republican who, as secretary of the Navy, had initially been a vigorous opponent of unification but who finally accepted it. Forrestal was highly esteemed for his intellect, dedication, and patriotism, but he was a moody, emotionally unstable, apolitical workaholic who could not make decisions or lead men. Although Truman delegated heavy responsibility to Forrestal, he did not really like him or have faith in him and did not back him up, either publicly or privately. Burdened beyond all reason and overly immersed in too much detail, by December 1948 Forrestal was close to a severe emotional breakdown.[15]

## II

After his inauguration in 1949 Truman, psychologically reinforced by his political victory and now in control of Congress, conceived a new and even more drastic shake-up of the armed forces. This plan was motivated principally by fiscal conservatism. He continued to be obsessed by a conviction that there was enormous fat, waste, and duplication in the Pentagon.

Although never formalized on paper or publicly proposed as a package, his plan would entail the following four major steps.

First, he would replace the indecisive intellectual James Forrestal with an impressive, forceful executive who would not hesitate to knock (or cut off) heads in the Pentagon and put a stop to the interservice wrangling, rampant disloyalty, and budget flimflams.

Secondly, he would impose firmer unification on the armed forces by persuading Congress to enact legislation transforming the unworkable National Military Establishment into a true executive department, comparable to State, Treasury, Commerce, etc. The legislation would significantly increase the legal powers of the secretary of defense and establish a chairman of the Joint Chiefs of Staff (JCS). The chairman would be chief military adviser to the secretary of defense and preside over meetings of the JCS, guiding its deliberations toward firm and unanimous budgets, force levels, and missions, producing in the process a more economical military establishment.

Thirdly, pending enactment of this legislation, Truman would bring aboard five-star General Dwight D. Eisenhower, then president of Columbia University (but by law still on active duty, subject to recall by the president), to "preside" over the JCS. Truman's purpose was to enlist Eisenhower's enormous prestige in formulating a tight, unified defense budget. The JCS "guideline" would be $14.5 billion, but secretly Truman planned to cut that figure by $2.5 billion—down to about $12 billion.

Fourthly, America would proceed with due speed to align itself militarily in a mutual defense pact with the nations of Western Europe, the proposed North Atlantic Treaty Organization (NATO). The idea for this historic treaty had been conceived by Europeans. Truman looked upon it with favor, in part because it would enable the United States to reduce its military presence in Western Europe and hence save money. As the organization was initially envisioned, America would not contribute any substantial ground forces to NATO but mainly existing air and sea power—principally an atomic bomb air offensive. By backing the NATO treaty, Truman hoped to hurry along a German peace treaty, enabling the 100,000-odd American army of occupation forces to withdraw. To launch NATO, Truman would have to fork out about $1 billion in military hardware to the treaty nations under a newly conceived funding device known as the Mutual Defense Assistance Program (MDAP). However, that seed money would be cheaper in the long term than the overhead (salary, benefits, retirement pay, etc.) that would be incurred by a large and continuing American military ground force in Europe.

\* .\* \*

Unaware that he was being "used" in White House budget maneuvering, Eisenhower arrived in Washington in January 1949 to take up his duties as JCS "presiding officer." He was shocked by all he saw and heard, but especially by the almost complete absence of control and direction over the armed forces from Commander in Chief Truman. In his diary Eisenhower wrote that Truman "has to show the iron underneath the pretty glove" and "lay down the law" and "get tough—and I mean tough." He had to urge the president to back him and Forrestal to the "hilt." But he doubted that Forrestal had the strength to carry on. He was mired in detail and overworked, and he "looked badly [*sic*]."[16]

Overall, Eisenhower found, the military posture and readiness of the armed forces were deplorable. "We're suffering," he noted in his diary. He blamed this on Truman's obsessive budget cutting. In his diary he recalled how he had futilely "pleaded" for a $15 billion Pentagon budget in the early postwar years. He went on: "Now inflation has raised the cost of everything so much even the $15 billion begins to look inadequate."

Eisenhower began work with the JCS on a $14.4 billion budget on January 24. His cohorts were Air Force Chief of Staff Hoyt S. Vandenberg; the chief of naval operations (CNO), Louis E. Denfeld; and Eisenhower's successor as Army chief of staff, Omar Bradley. He knew Vandenberg and Bradley well; both had worked closely with him in the defeat of Germany, Bradley as commander of all American ground forces in Europe, Vandenberg as commander of the Ninth (Tactical) Air Force. He did not know Denfeld, who had spent most of World War II in Washington as a personnel expert and whose naval combat experience was limited to a few months in the Pacific at the end of the war.[17]

By this time the budget squeeze and unification squabbling had led to all-out bureaucratic war between the Air Force and Navy. Vandenberg and Denfeld were scarcely on speaking terms. Vandenberg—fighting for a seventy-group Air Force—wanted to mothball all of the Navy's aircraft carriers and cancel construction of the big new carrier. Denfeld, stoutly defending his aircraft carriers, insisted that the Air Force be held to forty-eight groups. Eisenhower, supported by Bradley, sought the middle ground (a "balanced force") of eight or ten aircraft carriers (but not to include the big new carrier), more money for the Air Force (but not for seventy groups), and a well-equipped and "ready" Army of not fewer than ten divisions.

After six weeks of tedious, tense negotiations Eisenhower became gravely ill and was forced to bed. The tension had brought on a severe recurrence of a digestive problem from which he had suffered for years (later diagnosed as ileitis). On advice of his physician, Eisenhower gave up smoking (four packs a day) and the pressures of Washington and took a prolonged vacation. For all practical purposes, this ended Eisenhower's association with the Truman administration's military budget process. The loss was great. Had Eisenhower been able to carry on, it is just possible that with his great prestige he could have solved the Air Force–Navy impasse and persuaded Truman not only to support a $15 or $16 billion budget but to make up past "deficits" as well.

In the meantime, the armed forces were in greater disarray than ever. One reason was that James Forrestal, burdened with the tasks of shepherding new legislation through Congress to create the Department of Defense, had a complete mental breakdown. He fell into a deep depression and was afflicted with acute paranoia. He insisted his telephones were tapped and that Communist agents and others were out to assassinate him. Truman, acting out of decency, loyalty, and compassion, had hoped to keep Forrestal in office until May 1, but at about the time Eisenhower fell ill and left, the president decided that Forrestal, too, had to be replaced immediately.*

## III

Truman had already chosen Forrestal's successor: Louis A. Johnson. He was a huge, forceful man, standing six feet two inches tall and weighing 250 pounds. His ambition and gall were commensurate with his height and weight. His goal was nothing less than to replace Truman in the White House in 1953.[18]

Then fifty-eight years old, Louis Johnson was a West Virginia lawyer-politician-millionaire with long ties to the military. He had served with the Army in France during World War I, from which he emerged as a major. During the peacetime years he had been active in the Army Reserve and in veterans' organizations, rising to the rank of colonel and serving a high-profile term as national commander of the American Legion. In the late 1930s President Roosevelt, in return for political favors, had appointed him to the then prestigious post of assistant secretary of war. But Johnson had turned out to be such a disruptive conniver and publicity seeker that Roosevelt had been forced to remove him from that post. In World War II he had served as Roosevelt's "personal emissary" to India and in several other minor posts.

His star began to rise again during the Truman administration. In the 1948 presidential campaign Johnson remained loyal to the president in what every pol and political pollster had deemed a lost cause. Appointed chief of campaign finances, Johnson allegedly donated $250,000 to the campaign personally and managed to wheedle an astounding $2 million more from hesitant or reluctant donors. As a payoff for this remarkable feat—so the story went—Truman had given Johnson the job he wanted most: secretary of defense. Johnson made little secret of the fact that he intended to use that position as a stepping-stone to the presidency.

---

*On May 21 Forrestal committed suicide.

Omar Bradley, who came to know Johnson well, later wrote: "I doubt seriously if Johnson knew much about military strategy or weapons systems." He had kept a commission in the Army Reserve, rising, like Truman, to colonel, but he had not served in a responsible military position since the late 1930s. His grasp of grand strategy was on a par with that of his American Legion cohorts Harry Truman and Harry Vaughan. Moreover, Johnson was a man of action, not a thinker, and therefore not much inclined to deep study of tedious JCS or State Department strategy papers.[19]

No written record has turned up describing Truman's private instructions to Johnson. However, a fairly accurate summary would be as follows: First, Johnson would bash Pentagon heads and make unification really work. The legislation soon to emerge from Congress creating the Department of Defense would greatly strengthen his hand. Secondly, he would force the JCS to produce a unified strategy and budget along the lines Eisenhower had been pursuing: more weight to the Air Force, less to the Navy, and no supercarrier. Thirdly, he would impose a maximum budget ceiling of $12.3 billion, cutting away all the "fat," and, if necessary, would further reduce the force levels in the Army.

Johnson formally took office on March 28. His first major move was dramatic and brutal: Without any prior notice to Denfeld or to Secretary of the Navy John L. Sullivan, he issued an order canceling the Navy's big carrier, USS *United States,* already in preliminary stages of construction. Shocked and angry, Secretary Sullivan resigned in protest while outraged admirals went to full battle stations. When Johnson announced plans to face them down by crashing a quiet farewell ceremony for Sullivan, his senior aide was appalled: "You can't do that! When Al Capone kills them in Chicago, he sends them flowers, but he doesn't go to their funeral." Johnson brazenly barged into the ceremony anyway. The admirals, the aide recalled, "looked daggers at him." One of them later characterized him as a "criminal."[20]

Johnson next turned his sights on the Army. It had originally built the Pentagon solely for itself and its then big stepchild the Army Air Forces. Hence the offices for the Army secretary and chief of staff (and the Air Force leaders) were lavish and conveniently located. In the early months of unification Forrestal had shoehorned the senior naval staff into the Pentagon, but in keeping with his introvertish nature, he had been satisfied to settle himself and his small staff in a "cubbyhole." Covetously eyeing the office suites of the Army's senior leaders, Johnson peremptorily claimed them, settling his huge bulk into the Army secretary's enormous and elegantly furnished office.[21]

This was a humiliating and perhaps deliberately intended display of power and arrogance, but it was insignificant compared with the next insult Johnson inflicted on the Army. By coincidence, when Johnson took office, Army Secretary Kenneth C. Royall had just resigned, and one of Royall's assistants, the able North Carolina tobacco and publishing millionaire and patriot Gordon Gray, was temporarily "acting" secretary of the Army. Gray, too, had made plans to return to civilian life and was merely filling in so that the Army's civilian leadership position would not be vacant. Johnson disliked and distrusted Gray because he had been informed (erroneously) that Gray had not contributed a dime to Truman's 1948 campaign. Even so, when Johnson could not get another man he wanted for the secretaryship, he offered the job to Gray. But Gray, who had already committed himself to a deanship at the University of North Carolina, firmly declined.

What happened next was almost incomprehensible. Apparently insulted by Gray's refusal or incapable of accepting a denial, Johnson hurried over to see the president and formally proposed Gray as Army secretary, assuring Truman that Gray wanted the job "so bad he could taste it." Truman, who admired Gray, was delighted. He promptly announced the appointment and sent Gray's name to the Senate for confirmation. When Gray learned what had occurred, he was astounded and furious and immediately met with Truman to explain he had made other commitments. When Truman agreed to "take the rap" for this public gaffe—tell the Senate he had made a mistake and withdraw the appointment—Gray, in order to spare the president public humiliation, volunteered to serve as secretary for a brief or "respectable time." When Gray privately confided all this to Army Chief of Staff Omar Bradley, the latter felt "immensely disquieted." Later he wrote that "What it boiled down to was that Johnson, for whatever reason, had lied to Truman. . . ."[22]

There was plenty for Johnson to do in the Pentagon—enough work to break a normal man—but Johnson soon began to wield his mace beyond his own bailiwick. Truman noted in his diary with mixed perplexity and acerbity:

Something happened. . . . Louis began to show an inordinate egotistical desire to run the whole government. He offended every member of the Cabinet. We never had a Cabinet meeting that he did not show plainly that he knew more about the problems of the Treasury, Commerce, Labor, Agriculture than did the Secretaries of those departments. . . . He never missed an opportunity to say mean things about my personal staff. . . . He is the most ego maniac [sic] I've ever come in contact with—and I've seen a lot.[23]

In particular, Johnson clashed spectacularly with Truman's new secretary of state, the strong-minded, urbane, Ivy League intellectual hawk Dean Acheson. As one of Truman's recent biographers put it, "Their relationship grew steadily worse. The time came when the two were hardly on speaking terms. . . ." As a result, "Johnson reduced relations between the Department of State and the Department of Defense to the most formal liaison," forbidding even personal or friendly social contact.[24]

In time Johnson's behavior became so bizarre and erratic that many senior administration officials began to believe that Johnson, too, was emotionally unstable. In his diary Truman bluntly attributed Johnson's behavior to "a pathological condition." In his memoir Dean Acheson agreed, writing that the evidence was persuasive that Johnson was "mentally ill." Omar Bradley concurred. In his autobiography he described the Forrestal-Johnson succession this way: "Unwittingly, Truman had replaced one mental case with another."[25]

\* \* \*

In May, having been in office about six weeks, Johnson unveiled Truman's new budget ceiling of $12.3 billion. The news, Bradley observed with understatement, came as a "profound shock." Casting aside all the tedious JCS position papers, Johnson himself dictated budget shares and force levels. He gave the Air Force most: $4.4 billion for forty-eight groups, of which fifteen would be composed of strategic bombers capable of delivering atomic bombs. The Army got $4 billion, but its manpower was again cut—from 667,000 with ten divisions to 630,000 and nine divisions. The Navy got the least: $3.9 billion for 238 combatant vessels, including seven World War II-vintage fleet carriers. From a distance Eisenhower complained in his diary: "Of course the results will not show up until we get in serious trouble. We are repeating our own history of decades—we just don't believe we ever will get into a real jam."[26]

That summer of 1949 Congress, as expected, enacted Truman's legislation creating the Department of Defense. The law contained his request to provide a "legal" chairman of the JCS. Still anxious to have Eisenhower's prestige behind his military budget, Truman offered the post to him. But Eisenhower, aware of the new $12.3 billion ceiling, firmly declined to have anything further to do with the Truman administration and continued to gripe in his diary about Truman's string of broken promises.

Truman next turned to Omar Bradley. In their attempts to create a distinctive public "image" for Bradley, who was innately modest, shy, and colorless, his public relations officers had painted the fifty-six-year-old four-star general as an amiable "Missouri school teacher" or the "GI's general," or, in the postwar years, the "nicest guy in Washington"—a general who never raised his voice or swore or gave unreasonable orders. He was indeed a warm, decent, likable, and considerate man and, in private, an amusing one. But he was far from being the cookie pusher of his press clippings. Nor had he been a "GI's general." More accurately he had been a "general's general" and a man of concealed but intense and steely ambition who had climbed higher and faster in the European Theater of Operations (ETO) than anyone else except Eisenhower. In the scramble Bradley had been ruthless toward his less gifted peers and utterly intolerant of the mediocre. As a result, he had sacked more generals than any other American commander in World War II.[27]

Earlier Bradley had confided to Eisenhower that he wanted "no part" of the JCS chairman's job. But he changed his mind and accepted it for several reasons. By that time the Navy had openly mutinied against Johnson, the Air Force, and the strategy of nuclear retaliation, and Bradley was deeply concerned that this rebellion might tempt Moscow to take advantage of America's military disarray. He believed that he and a middle-of-the-road Army successor on the JCS could provide the necessary moderating influence to prevent a calamity. Secondly, he believed that in his elevated position he might be able to persuade Truman and Johnson to appreciate the need for the larger twelve-division Army he had proposed in 1948. Thirdly, Truman and Johnson probably promised him a fifth star. Bradley was not rank-happy—far from it—but a fifth star would guarantee him a higher lifetime pay and certain other attractive emoluments.[28]

Upon accepting the post, Bradley then had to deal with the difficult and sensitive problem of recommending his successor as Army chief of staff. It was difficult because the war had produced so many outstanding Army generals who deserved the honor and promotion to four stars. In mulling this over, Bradley decided to "dip down" and choose a "younger" man—that is, someone about two years junior to him from the West Point class of 1917. In so doing, he would, in effect, encourage the retirement of the "older" group—his peers or seniors—and open paths for promotions for younger, more energetic and deserving generals, thereby infusing the Army with renewed zeal and boosting morale in the senior officer corps.

In the class of 1917 there were three men who stood head and shoulders above all others: Mark Wayne Clark, Joseph Lawton ("Joe") Collins (both fifty-three years old), and Matthew Bunker ("Matt") Ridgway (fifty-four). Early in the selection process, Bradley eliminated Mark Clark, who had commanded Fifth Army and later the Fifteenth Army Group in the Italian campaign and already had four stars. Bradley did not like Clark; he considered him a lightweight, self-serving egotist. Moreover, on analysis, Clark's conduct of the Italian campaign was now being sharply and publicly criticized, especially by Texans, whose 36th National Guard Division had been twice massacred, first at Salerno, then at the Rapido River, near Monte Cassino. Texas was an Army stronghold, politically and otherwise; the Army could not further alienate the state and its powerful congressional delegation, which now included House Speaker Sam Rayburn.[29]

This left Collins and Ridgway, both superb, much-decorated corps commanders in the ETO, whose battlefield performances were beyond reproach. Collins had commanded the famous VII Corps, spearhead of Bradley's First Army at Utah Beach and for the remainder of the war. Eisenhower and Bradley considered Joe Collins the most gifted and dependable of the dozen corps commanders in the ETO, and on VE day Collins was at the top of their lists for promotion to Army commander and four stars. In the postwar years Collins had served Eisenhower and Bradley in the Pentagon trenches, first as the Army's architect of unification, then as chief of public relations, finally as Bradley's vice chief of staff. Not far behind in their estimation was Matt Ridgway, who had organized, trained, and led the Army's elite paratrooper forces, first as commander of the famous 82d Airborne Division in Sicily, Italy, and Normandy, then as commander of XVIII Airborne Corps (incorporating three American airborne divisions, the 82d, 101st, and 17th), which, in a ground role, had been outstanding in helping contain the German break-through in the Bulge. In the postwar years Ridgway had ably served first in the sensitive post of Eisenhower's personal representative to the United Nations, then in the Caribbean as commander in chief of the first "joint" field command.

Of the two men, Ridgway was superior in intellect, executive ability, command presence, and forcefulness. However, he had three negatives for those times: He had had no experience in the postwar Pentagon trenches, he was an unflinching idealist who was almost incapable of compromise, and he had recently experienced a highly controversial second divorce and third marriage. Because of these factors, and others, Bradley decided on the following plan. He would try to work out a deal in which both Collins and Ridgway could be chief of staff, first Collins, then Ridgway. Collins would serve a "bobtail" term of three years, retiring in 1952. Meanwhile, Ridgway would be brought into the Pentagon to serve as Collins's deputy chief of staff for administration, the Army's "general manager," a job that would provide him the necessary Pentagon experience and seasoning to qualify him to replace Collins.[30]

When the Bradley and Collins appointments were announced in August 1949, there was not universal rejoicing within the Army establishment. There were whispers that both generals had "sold out" to the despised Louis Johnson, thereby "politicizing" the JCS. The Collins appointment was especially controversial. Although Bradley had attempted to assuage the "older group" by appointing Wade H. ("Ham") Haislip (West Point, 1912) Collins's vice chief of staff, many of that faction were hurt and resentful; their sun had clearly set. The succession of Eisenhower, Bradley, Collins convinced others that the "ETO clique" had "taken over the Army," and those generals who had fought elsewhere (Italy, the Pacific, China-Burma-India) were to be left out in the cold. The large faction of Mark Clark loyalists, stoutly defending his controversial generalship, was really irked. No less so were the elite, vocal, and devoted Ridgway fans, who were not privy to Bradley's future plans for their hero.[31]

Besides, many did not share Eisenhower's and Bradley's personal admiration for Collins, whose apt nickname was Lightning Joe. These critics believed

Collins was too talky and superficial, that he tended to deal with the surface rather than the substance of issues, that he was lacking in humility and was publicity-hungry. Others believed that while his "can do" mind-set had been indispensable in wartime, his relentless optimism and impulsiveness were not necessarily the best traits for a chief of staff in a cold war, where confrontation usually demanded the most tedious and cautious analysis. Still others resented the public way Collins displayed his Catholicism. False—and damaging— rumors spread in the Protestant Army that Catholics would get favorable treatment.

## I V

In late August 1949, two weeks after Bradley had settled into his new post as JCS chairman and Joe Collins had replaced him as Army chief of staff, the Pentagon received its most jarring blow since World War II. A hastily impro- vised and highly secret Air Force airborne "detection net," designed to pick up radioactivity from a Russian atomic bomb explosion in the atmosphere, reported unmistakable evidence of such an explosion. In a twinkling—and long before American scientists had forecast—the "backward" peasants in Russia had achieved the impossible and America had lost its "atomic monop- oly." Since the "net" had only recently been established, there was no way of knowing with absolute certainty whether the Russians had exploded other atomic bombs earlier. Conceivably they had and now possessed a stockpile comparable to the modest American stockpile. Whatever the exact case, the astute Senator Arthur H. Vandenberg—uncle of Air Force Chief of Staff Hoyt Vandenberg—aptly characterized the implications: "This is now a different world."[32]

This news arrived at a profoundly awkward time for Commander in Chief Truman and his zealous military budget cutter Louis Johnson. At the time Truman had just decreed yet another cut in the forthcoming military budget and Johnson was gearing up to enforce it. No specific figures had been an- nounced, but Pentagon rumor had it that Johnson intended to cut yet another billion, from the ruinous $12.3 billion to a catastrophic $11 billion. The shock- ing and scary news from Russia would almost certainly make further cuts in the military budget difficult to justify to Congress and to the public.[33]

It was a moment in history for Harry Truman to stand tall: to proclaim a "different world" strategically, to abandon his petty conviction that he was still being budgetarily flimflammed by the generals and admirals, and to pro- nounce a dramatic turnabout in his national security programs. He did not elect that course. He did the opposite. He—and Louis Johnson—dishonestly or stupidly pooh-poohed the Soviet explosion as not a bomb but more likely a "laboratory accident." Although the scientific evidence indicated otherwise, in his public announcement of the discovery Truman refused to use the word "bomb," limiting himself to an ambiguous "atomic explosion." Later, in response to a reporter's question, he actually expressed doubt that the Russians had the technological know-how to build an atomic bomb.[34]

Behind the scenes, rightly believing the Pentagon would use the explosion as justification for bigger military budgets, Truman stubbornly resisted all such suggestions. His orders to Louis Johnson remained unchanged: Cut. However, the generals, admirals, and hawkish scientists, such as Edward Teller, did manage to push the president into making two major decisions, both designed to increase the size and power of America's nuclear stockpile:

One, in response to an urgent plea from the JCS, first conveyed to the White House on May 26, the president on October 17 finally authorized a significant production increase in numbers and types of fission bombs. "At the time he took this action," the historian Rosenberg wrote, "Truman had never received a thorough briefing on atomic strategy from the JCS." The JCS laboriously and slowly prepared an oral briefing, but Truman's vacation and then the Christmas holidays delayed the presentation until January 10, 1950. On that date, almost five full years into his presidency, Louis Johnson and Omar Bradley finally introduced field artilleryman Truman to the intricacies of nuclear strategy.

Two, following a heated moral and technical debate among the nuclear physicists and pushed by a strong recommendation from the JCS, Truman on January 31, 1950, authorized research on a much more powerful "hydrogen" or fusion bomb. Six weeks later, on March 10, 1950, again on the recommendation of the JCS, he approved a "crash" program for the hydrogen bomb, to be carried out "as a matter of highest urgency."[35]

\* \* \*

While these decisions were under consideration, the long-festering mutiny in the Navy broke into the open with unabated fury. Led by the naval aviators, it began in September with a series of press leaks which again directly and savagely attacked unification, the administration's strategy of nuclear retaliation, Louis Johnson, the Air Force, the B-36 bomber, and, by implication, the president himself. Johnson's new secretary of the Navy, Francis P. Matthews, was overwhelmed by the fury and utterly powerless to contain it.

The mutiny led to a sensational congressional investigation by the House Armed Services Committee. To make its case, the Navy paraded an impressive lineup: statements from five-star Admirals Ernest King and wartime Pacific Fleet commander Chester W. Nimitz; personal appearances by Pacific War heroes Raymond A. Spruance, Thomas C. Kinkaid, Arthur W. Radford, Captain Arleigh A. Burke, and dozens of other admirals and Marine Corps generals. Of these, Radford, then commander in chief of the Pacific Fleet, was the most forceful and outspoken witness.

The gist of the Navy's case against unification was as follows. Johnson and the JCS (where the Navy was "outvoted") were wrongly tailoring the American military establishment to a single strategy of an "atomic blitz." That strategy was wrong because an atomic blitz would neither deter nor win a war, and moreover, the use of atomic weapons was immoral. Dependence on the B-36 bomber to deliver the atomic blitz was a bad gamble because the plane had so many deficiencies it was "useless defensively" and "inadequate offensively" and thus was an unwise investment. Even if some B-36s were able to reach Soviet targets, Air Force pilots would not be able to drop bombs accurately enough to be effective, and besides that, the explosive power of atomic bombs was far less than advertised and not likely to inflict decisive damage on the enemy or break his will to resist.[36]

The Navy's case was hypocritical and dishonest. The JCS was not gearing the defense of the West solely to an atomic blitz. New JCS war plans in the works were being shaped around a NATO defense of Western Europe at the Rhine River. The atomic blitz was a vital element of the plan but not the sole element. Moreover, in JCS debates, Denfeld had endorsed these new war plans, and he (and other B-36 critics) were well aware that new and greatly improved Air Force jet bombers (B-47; B-52) were coming along to replace the B-36. In denigrating the power of the atomic bomb, the Navy based its data and case on the obsolete Nagasaki bomb, ignoring the new fission bomb designs, which yielded at least twice the power of the Nagasaki bomb. As for morality, the Navy's principal aim in the mutiny was to restore funds and authorization for its canceled supercarrier, which was designed specifically to launch big aircraft capable of carrying atomic bombs and thus give the Navy a continuing, vital role in the nuclear age.

This open mutiny was one of the sorriest spectacles in American military history. There had never been anything like it. Even the Billy Mitchell revolt of the 1920s was, by comparison, decorous and low-key. Fundamentally the fault was Truman's. Had he exercised firmer and enlightened leadership as commander in chief, the mutiny could never have occurred. His choice of political cronies Johnson and Matthews (who even conceded publicly he knew nothing about the Navy) to fill the leadership vacancy he created was a serious error in judgment. Rather than defuse the ticking bombs in the Navy, they ignited them, Johnson by sins of commission, Matthews by sins of omission.

The "rebuttal" witnesses on behalf of unification were principally Louis Johnson, Air Force leaders Stuart Symington and Hoyt Vandenberg, and, finally, Omar Bradley. Of the four, Bradley was by far the most forceful and impressive. Outraged by the dishonesty and hypocrisy of the Navy's case and by the crybaby complaints of the admirals about sagging morale in the Navy and Marine Corps, and deeply worried about the damage the Navy was causing in the military establishment, Bradley uncharacteristically got out the whip and gave the Navy and Marine Corps a severe public lashing. In this, his most famous public utterance to date, Bradley labeled the admirals a bunch of "fancy Dans." He excoriated and ridiculed them for every argument they had advanced before the hearing. Moreover, he raised questions about Denfeld's qualifications as a leader and military strategist. This tough speech rang down the curtain and put an end to the hearings—and the mutiny. In effect, Omar Bradley pulled Truman's fat out of the fire and filled the military leadership vacuum Truman had allowed to exist for all too long.[37]

As Bradley had implied, what was required was a long-overdue housecleaning in the top levels of the Navy, with new, able civilians and admirals to take command and restore discipline and morale. On the uniform level this was done. Johnson sacked Denfeld and replaced him with the most intelligent and respected admiral in the Navy, aviator Forrest P. Sherman, a Pacific War hero and an early architect of unification, who had remained aloof from the mutiny. But Johnson, probably with an eye to the 1952 political convention, where Frank Matthews would again exercise power in the Nebraska delegation, retained him as Navy secretary, even though Matthews was by then thoroughly despised and an object of ridicule ("Rowboat Matthews") throughout the Navy. Like Truman's Army aide Harry Vaughan, Matthews was not only an embarrassment but an insult.

*　*　*

On the heels of these events yet another setback with profound military consequences for America occurred. In China on October 16 Chiang Kai-shek's Nationalist forces were finally and decisively defeated by the Communist forces of Mao Tse-tung. In Peking the victorious Mao rightly claimed a momentous and historic victory and established the People's Republic of China. The remnants of Chiang's routed army retreated to Formosa, a big island about 100 miles off the coast of China. Mao claimed sovereignty over Formosa as well and publicly vowed to evict Chiang from the island.

The civil war in China had been raging for decades. During World War II, when Japan attempted to conquer all China, Chiang and Mao temporarily buried the hatchet in order to meet and repel the Japanese in a common effort. In the postwar years, however, the Chinese civil war resumed with renewed fury. Although Chiang had been a prominent anti-Axis ally in World War II, Truman wisely made the decision to stay out of that Asian civil war, limiting assistance to Chiang to military and economic aid.

The Communist victory threatened America's military strategy in the Far East in an important but little understood way. In its grand strategy deliberations, the JCS had decided (as in World War II) that should Moscow launch

World War III, first priority would go to the defense of Western Europe, second to the Far East. America would fight a "defensive" war in the Far East until Western Europe was secure. It would hold an offshore "defensive perimeter" which ran (north to south) from the Aleutian Islands through the home islands of Japan (the key bastion) to the Ryukyu Islands (Okinawa) to the Philippines. Formosa was not included because America had "bypassed" it in World War II and had not established military bases there.

After Mao's victory in mainland China the JCS had now to assume that the Chinese Communists would finish off the Nationalist government by invading Formosa. A Formosa under Chinese Communist military control would interpose a dangerous hostile salient in America's offshore defensive perimeter. Soviet bombers, based on Formosa, could easily attack Okinawa, the Philippines, and American naval forces plying between those places and Japan. In a phrase of the times, Formosa was like an "unsinkable aircraft carrier" perfectly positioned to threaten America's strategic offshore perimeter.

The "problem" of Formosa led to an intense debate within the Truman administration. Louis Johnson believed that overt military aid should be given the Nationalists on Formosa to repel a Communist invasion, possibly including American "occupation forces." The JCS equivocated. At first it stated that given the military budget squeeze (the "present disparity between our military strength and our global obligations") and possible further budget squeezes lying ahead, "the strategic importance of Formosa does not justify overt military actions" or occupation. However, in December 1949, the JCS, under pressure from Johnson and others, about-faced and recommended a "modest, well-directed, and closely-supervised program of military aid" to Formosa (and Indochina as well), "integrated with a stepped-up political, economic, and psychological program pursued energetically." In other words, overt military assistance to Chiang.[38]

Dean Acheson adamantly opposed Johnson's position for several reasons. First, Acheson had decided that the most advantageous long-term China policy for America was to adopt a conciliatory attitude toward Peking in the hope of "splitting" the Chinese and the Russians, bringing the Chinese back into the American orbit. Further aid to the Nationalists on Formosa would undermine that policy. Secondly, Acheson believed that Chiang Kai-shek was a corrupt and detestable anachronism and wanted nothing to do with him. Thirdly, Acheson had serious doubts that the Chinese Communists had the necessary naval capability to mount an invasion of Formosa.

These debates, which greatly intensified the Johnson-Acheson feud, were resolved by the president in a sweeping new Far East policy paper, issued on December 30, 1949. In effect, Acheson won hands down. America would maintain a conciliatory policy toward Peking in the hope that "serious frictions would develop between the Chinese communist regime and Moscow."

68001

There would be no more aid for Chiang; continuing aid might work to the benefit of the Communists by rallying anti-Communist sentiment in China to Peking. It would also subject America to charges of "imperialism." In newspaper jargon, the decision became Truman's "hands-off" Formosa policy.

The policy enraged a powerful anti-Truman bloc in Congress and the media. The bloc was composed of a dozen right-wing senators, led by Robert A. Taft, Joseph R. McCarthy, William F. Knowland, and William E. Jenner; plus publishers Henry Luce and William R. Hearst; and others, colloquially and collectively called the "China Lobby." It had been urging Truman in the postwar years to take more aggressive action to "save" China from communism. When Chiang was routed, it blamed the "loss" of China on the Truman administration for being "soft on communism." The bloc regarded Truman's hands-off Formosa policy as the ultimate betrayal of an old friend and ally, and it flayed Truman and Acheson without restraint. Louis Johnson secretly allied himself with the bloc, connived with the senators to abet their attacks on his bureaucratic enemy Dean Acheson, and even passed state secrets to the Nationalist ambassador in Washington.[39]

## V

The explosion of the Russian atomic bomb and the defeat of Nationalist China forces persuaded Dean Acheson that a "different world" had indeed arrived. He was soon convinced that America must change course: arm rather than disarm. Working closely with Paul Nitze, chairman of the State Department's Policy Planning Staff, Acheson initiated the drafting of a massive new policy paper (National Security Council No. 68, or NSC-68) designed to persuade Truman and Johnson—indeed, the entire administration—that America must commence a dramatic rearmament program to meet the new threats being posed by Moscow. Ironically, at the very time Acheson conceived this top secret paper he was under violent public attack by right-wing critics for being "soft on communism."[40]

When Louis Johnson got wind of NSC-68, he was naturally outraged. The recommendations he knew it would contain ran counter to his budget-cutting policies and every public statement he had made about the adequacy of national security. If adopted, the paper would, in effect, make him look the fool. Contrarily, the JCS welcomed NSC-68 as a godsend. Covertly the Joint Chiefs supported Nitze in every conceivable way, leading Bradley to write later: "The JCS unequivocally supported NSC-68, creating a rare, awkward and ironic situation in which the three military chiefs and their chairman were more closely aligned with the views of the Secretary of State than with the Secretary of Defense."[41]

When the paper was finally finished, Acheson sent a copy to Louis Johnson and asked Johnson to bring Bradley and meet him at State on March 22, 1950, to discuss its contents. When Johnson and Bradley arrived, one of the most bizarre scenes in the history of government ensued. As Nitze launched an oral briefing on the paper, Acheson wrote later, Johnson suddenly exploded. Acheson described the scene: "Suddenly he lunged forward with a crash of chair legs on the floor and fist on the table, scaring me out of my shoes. No one, he shouted, was going to make arrangements for him to meet with another cabinet officer and a roomful of people and be told what he was going to report to the President. Who authorized these meetings contrary to his orders? What was this paper, which he had never seen?" Acheson tried to calm him, but Johnson, "gathering Bradley and other Defense people, stalked out of the room," leaving Acheson and his aides "in shocked disbelief." The Defense-State liaison officer, Major General James H. Burns, "put his head in his hands and wept in shame."

When Acheson reported this shocking incident to Truman, the president was dismayed. He probably made the decision that day that Johnson must be replaced; but his debt to Johnson was large, and he did not pursue the search for a new defense secretary with any vigor. However, he privately laced into Johnson, with the result that when NSC-68 reached Johnson's desk on April 6, signed by Acheson, the JCS, and other senior strategists, Johnson put his signature on it without pause. As Acheson aptly commented, "Johnson was not left in a strong offensive position."[42]

The paper was presented formally to the National Security Council on April 25. It was discussed and, as Acheson (wrongly) put it in his memoir, "became national policy." In fact, NSC-68 was in no way "implemented." When Truman asked the JCS for a cost estimate ("I will not buy a pig in a poke," he wrote the Pentagon), the chiefs came back with a figure of about $40 billion a year. In the existing fiscal climate, Acheson later conceded with masterful understatement, it was "doubtful" that such vast expenditures would be seriously considered by the Truman administration, and they were not. In sum, Acheson had "won" an internal academic exercise, but the Truman-Johnson pinchpenny views on military spending continued to prevail.[43]

\* \* \*

In the meantime, Congress received Truman's fiscal year 1951 military budget, Johnson's first fat-cutting $12.3 billion\* effort. Johnson proudly

---

\*The exact figure was $12,333,294,000 for the armed services. To this was added a request for $800 million for administration of the new Department of Defense, for a grand total of $13,133,-294, usually shortened to "$13 billion." The budget still held the Air Force to forty-eight groups, the Navy to 238 combatant ships (including 7 fleet carriers), but country slicker Bradley had and deceitfully boasted to Congress that his austerity program was providing "significantly more powerful military forces within the same dollar requirements." In a famous, oft-quoted, and silly remark, Johnson crowed that if the Russians hit America at 4:00 A.M., America's atomic bombers would strike back by 5:00 A.M.[44]

The military chiefs found themselves in a tough moral dilemma. They did not agree in the slightest with Truman's budget or Johnson's braggadocio. But Johnson was the civilian authority to whom they owed obedience and loyalty. They had either to support his orders or to resign. None elected to resign; they unanimously supported the Johnson budget.

This moment may have been the nadir of JCS history. Omar Bradley set the tone. He testified that "frankly, considering the intelligence estimates that we have available and realizing the amount of money which our economy can stand for defense is a presidential responsibility, I am in complete agreement with that ceiling." The budget did not give the chiefs all they wanted, he conceded, and there were vulnerabilities; but it was a "sound part of a long range program" designed to give "sufficient emphasis" to the vulnerabilities so that the "effectiveness is maximum, the risk is minimum within a few years." However, if there were a "critical change" in the intelligence estimates, Bradley assured Congress, he would "not hesitate" to ask for more. Later he added: "I emphasized in my statement—maybe I did not emphasize it sufficiently—that the eventual strength of our country depends upon its industrial capacity. We must not destroy that by spending too much [on the military] from year to year." Still later Bradley testified: "We must not spend the country into economic collapse."[45]

In his autobiography Bradley wrote that the president's military budget cutting "was a mistake, perhaps the greatest of Truman's presidency." He went on: "My support of this decision—my belief that significantly higher defense spending would probably wreck the economy—was likewise a mistake, perhaps the greatest mistake I made in my postwar years in Washington."[46]

The three military chiefs—Joe Collins, Hoyt Vandenberg, and Forrest Sherman—echoed Bradley's testimony. Of the three, Collins was the most obsequious and dishonest. When questioned about the Army's manpower cut from 677,000 to 630,000, he airily dismissed the cut by rationalizing that fewer men could be better equipped. Collins later testified glibly: "The $13 billion we get has been arrived at by a process of cross checks and evaluation and in my judgment it represents a sound and well balanced program as well as men and human frailties can foresee in the future."[47]

In truth the American Army was once again in dreadful shape. In June

coaxed Truman and Johnson to increase the Army's "tactical" divisions from nine to ten. The total authorized manpower, still supported by a draft, was 1.5 million.

1950 it was far below its previously authorized strength of 677,000. It actually numbered only 591,000. Of these, 360,000 were in the United States, and 231,000 were overseas: 108,500 in the Far East; 94,300 in Europe; the rest in Hawaii, Alaska, or the Caribbean. Furthermore, Johnson's new fiscal year 1952 budget guidelines would reduce authorized strength from 630,000 to 610,900, the ten divisions to nine, probably reducing actual strength to the disastrous 1948 level of 560,000 and, if the draft was again allowed to lapse (as planned), perhaps below that.[48]

The total of ten "tactical" divisions then authorized was egregiously misleading. In order to stay within budget, Collins had been forced to deactivate one battalion of three in each division's three infantry regiments and one of three firing batteries in each of the four divisional artillery battalions. Inasmuch as Army doctrine and training were rigidly based on the concept of three-battalion regiments, and no substitute doctrine had been (or could be) promulgated, the deactivation gravely impaired—even crippled—the combat capability and "readiness" of the divisions.

As a whole, the Army was not well trained or well manned. In 1948, owing to the shortage of funds, "basic training" had been cut to a mere eight weeks. The cycle was increased to fourteen weeks in March 1949, but that did not include specialty or "branch" training. The 1948, 1949, and 1950 "peacetime" drafts, which provided a total of 300,000 men, had filled the Army with all too many disgruntled, indifferent, or even hostile soldiers. (For the affluent the draft was not difficult to evade.)

Nor was the Army combat-minded. Most enlisted Army volunteers of that era had not joined to fight. An Army general put it this way in 1951: "In an attempt to fill their quotas, our recruiting officers had painted a rosy picture: 'Join the Army and see the world.' 'Have fun in Japan.' 'Good pay. Many benefits.' . . . Recruiters didn't stress the obligations of a soldier."[49]

Stockpiles of matériel left over from World War II were deteriorating, and the budget cutting had seriously retarded the procurement of new equipment and research and development for ever better equipment. A new heavy tank, the Patton, had been introduced, but in June 1950 the Army had only 310 Patton tanks—all in the States. The inadequate World War II 2.3-inch antitank bazooka had been superseded by the new and adequate 3.5-inch bazooka; but in June 1950 there were only a few on hand, and none had been sent to the Far East. The Army's new "general manager," the deputy chief of staff for administration, Matt Ridgway, later put it this way: "We were, in short, in a state of shameful unreadiness."[50]

\* \* \*

From his post as president of Columbia University Eisenhower suddenly and unexpectedly spoke out, throwing the military budget proceedings into a tizzy. He stated it was his "conviction" that the United States had "already disarmed to the extent—in some instances even beyond the extent—that I . . . could possibly advise." Invited to appear before a Senate Appropriations subcommittee, Eisenhower proposed that at least a half billion dollars be added to the Pentagon budget. When challenged by reporters, Truman baldly asserted that there were no "fundamental differences" between his views and Eisenhower's. However, almost immediately Louis Johnson asked Congress for an additional $350 million. Impressed by Eisenhower's testimony, the House boosted this figure to $383 million. Led by Republican Henry Cabot Lodge, the Senate went dramatically further: On June 21 it voted a whopping $2.5 billion increase—to $15.6 billion.

Truman and Johnson viewed this stampede with utmost concern. While Truman laid plans to fight the Senate increase, behind the scenes Johnson formally gave the JCS money guidelines for the fiscal year 1952 military budgets. Perhaps influenced by Congress or Eisenhower, Johnson's total was not the rumored cut to $11 billion. Nonetheless, it was yet another cut: to $12,164,000,000. At a press conference, when asked if he planned an increased military budget for the following year, Truman replied testily: "The Defense budget next year will be smaller than it is this year, and we are continually cutting it by economies. And we are not alarmed in any sense of the word."[51]

By June 25, 1950, Harry Truman and Louis Johnson had all but wrecked the conventional military forces of the United States. The fault was Truman's alone. Acting out of an expressed belief that his grasp of strategy and military power was superior to that of his "dumb" and "wrong" and spendthrift generals and admirals who wore blinders and couldn't see beyond their own noses, he had allowed his obsessive fiscal conservatism to dominate his military thinking and decisions. If there was also a deep-seated unconscious need to continue to "cuss" and punish the military establishment for its early rejection of him, he had succeeded. Moreover, he had set the stage for even more grievous punishment, should it be called upon for an emergency.

# TOKYO AND SEOUL: 1949-1950

I

At the end of World War II the United States had incurred many military commitments in the Far East, but none more overriding than the occupation of Japan. The Russians, who entered the Pacific War at the eleventh hour, were deliberately frozen out of Japan. The British and French contributed token occupation forces but soon withdrew most of them. The upshot was that Japan became an exclusively American fiefdom, ruled by a benevolent proconsul, five-star General of the Army Douglas MacArthur. His military mission was twofold: to disarm and demilitarize Japan and, at the same time, to defend it against possible attack by the Russians, who were not pleased at being excluded from an occupation role.[1]

\* \* \*

Douglas MacArthur, approaching his seventies, was a legendary and intensely controversial world figure. One of his recent biographers, William Manchester, summed him up:

He was a great thundering paradox of a man, noble and ignoble, inspiring and outrageous, arrogant and shy, the best of men and the worst of men, the most protean, most ridiculous, and most sublime. No more baffling, exasperating soldier ever wore a uniform. Flamboyant, imperious, and apocalyptic, he carried the plumage of a flamingo, could not acknowledge errors, and tried to cover up his mistakes with sly, childish tricks. Yet he was also endowed with great personal charm, a will of iron, and a soaring intellect.[2]

Since his graduation from West Point in 1903 MacArthur's career had been spectacular. As a heroic frontline brigadier general in World War I he had won two Distinguished Service Crosses and an unprecedented seven Silver Star medals. In the late 1920s and early 1930s he had been chief of staff of the Army, serving both Presidents Herbert Hoover and Roosevelt. Upon his "retirement" he had accepted a prestigious, high-paying job as military adviser to Philippine President Manuel L. Quezon. When the Japanese were on the threshold of launching the Pacific War, Roosevelt had recalled MacArthur to active duty as commander of the American forces in the Philippines. Early in World War II MacArthur had won the Medal of Honor for his heroic but futile defense of Bataan and Corregidor, a promotion to four stars, and command of the Southwest Pacific Theater. By the end of the war he had been promoted to five stars and named to command the proposed massive amphibious invasion of Japan. In the postwar years he wore two hats: supreme commander for the Allied Powers (SCAP) in Japan and commander in chief of all American naval, air, and ground forces in the Far East (CINCFE).

Along the way MacArthur had generated so many legends and so much controversy that it would remain difficult to separate fact from fiction and objectively assess his ability as a military commander. Reflecting one school, Manchester wrote that "unquestionably he was the most gifted man-at-arms this nation has produced." But more recent and meticulous scholarship by MacArthur biographer D. Clayton James and military historian Ronald H. Spector has thrown this widely held view into serious doubt. Spector, in his brilliant history of the Pacific War, judged that "despite his undoubted qualities of leadership, MacArthur "was unsuited by temperament, character, and judgment for the positions of high command which he occupied throughout the war."[3]

As America's proconsul in Japan MacArthur had assumed the air and power of a head of state. His dealings with Washington were carried out with kingly disdain and loftiness. Shortly after the war was over, he had insulted and antagonized President Truman in several ways, notably by refusing Truman's "invitation" (tantamount to an order) to return to Washington for honors and consultations. Worse, he had overtly encouraged his own nomination as a Republican candidate for the presidency in 1948, aligning himself with Truman's political rivals and critics. He did not trust the Department of State or Dean Acheson. For a long time he had all but barred State from Japan.

Truman and Acheson, in turn, distrusted MacArthur. For Truman, MacArthur was the archetype of all he held in contempt in the Regular Army establishment. In his diary Truman excoriated him as "Mr. Prima Donna, Brass Hat, Five Star MacArthur," a "play actor" and "bunco man." Truman scribbled on: "He's worse than the Cabots and Lodges—they at least talked with one another before they told God what to do. Mac tells God right off.

It is a very great pity to have stuffed shirts like that in key positions." In his autobiography Omar Bradley wrote that Truman continued to voice similar sentiments about MacArthur all through the postwar years, but he shrank from a politically hazardous public confrontation with or condemnation of MacArthur—at least for the time being.[4]

MacArthur lived a remarkably insulated and circumscribed life, shuttling back and forth on a clockwork schedule between his Spartan office in the Dai Ichi ("Number One") Building and his comfortable well-staffed home in the American Embassy. He had no close personal friends. His professional confidants, with one exception, were those men who had served him before or during World War II, known collectively as the "Bataan Gang." He seldom left Tokyo for any purpose. He took little or no interest in the momentous political upheavals and wars in China and Southeast Asia. He had given no indication that he would ever "retire."

The exception among his professional confidants was Major General Edward M. ("Ned") Almond, MacArthur's chief of staff and, by virtue of his position, the second most powerful American in Tokyo. Ned Almond was a brilliant human dynamo. Eisenhower, in 1948, rated him as one of the half dozen ablest men in the Army. Almond's mind inspired awe and fear; his energy evoked humor. One admirer, John H. Chiles, said: "He could precipitate a crisis on a desert island with nobody else around." Another, Maurice H. Holden, said: "When it paid to be aggressive, Ned was aggressive. When it paid to be cautious, Ned was aggressive."[5]

Almond's early Army career had been highly promising. Born in Luray, Virginia, in 1892, he was graduated from the Virginia Military Institute (VMI) in 1915 and one year later obtained a Regular Army commission. In World War I he won a Silver Star Medal commanding a machine-gun battalion in France. During the peacetime years his climb up the career ladder was steady and sure. He was early selected for the Command and General Staff School (1928), the Army War College (1934), voluntarily attended the Army Air Corps Tactical School, qualifying as an observer (1939), and the Naval War College (1940). When World War II broke out, he was among the first of his peers to be promoted to general and the first to achieve every infantryman's dream: command of a division.

The problem was the division. Fellow VMI graduate George Marshall assigned Almond to command the 92d Infantry Division, one of three divisions composed of blacks commanded mostly by white officers. After training the division for a year and a half at Fort Huachuca, Arizona, Almond took it to Italy in late 1944. The division failed in combat and had to be broken up and reorganized.[6]

Almond was not blamed for the failure of his black troops in combat. There was a long-standing and widespread belief in the strictly segregated U.S.

Army that "Negroes won't fight." The performance of Almond's 92d Division merely served to reinforce that belief. However, by his taking on the assignment, Almond's highly promising career had been sidetracked, and as a result, he had fallen far behind his contemporaries. Moreover, he had suffered terrible personal grief. His only son, Edward M., Jr., a West Pointer (1943), had been killed in action in the ETO, as had his only daughter's husband, West Pointer (1942) Thomas T. Galloway.[7]

Despite these professional and personal setbacks, Almond emerged from the war in high repute and with ambition still intact. However, there was not much hope that before mandatory retirement he could catch up with his contemporaries, some of whom were three- or four-star generals. In 1946, seeking a change of scenery and faces, he asked for duty in the Far East and was assigned to MacArthur's general headquarters (GHQ) in Tokyo as G-1, or personnel expert. Owing to the pell-mell postwar demobilization and re-staffing problems in the Far East, this ordinarily humdrum assignment proved to be a monumental challenge. Almond handled it with high competence and loyalty, thereby gaining MacArthur's utmost confidence. As a result, when MacArthur's chief of staff, Paul J. Mueller, was rotated home in January 1949, Almond, who was the most senior and capable general on the GHQ staff, replaced him. Almond thus became the first "outsider" (or "European Theater general") to penetrate MacArthur's inner circle. But it was a dead-end job. With the promotion of his junior, Joe Collins, to Army chief of staff, there was no future in the postwar Army for Ned Almond and, owing to Collins's intense dislike of Almond, probably only a slim chance of a third star on retirement.[8]

Although MacArthur kept very close watch over GHQ business, he disliked dealing directly with the staff or attending meetings. Other than the shrunken Bataan Gang, he saw very few staffers face-to-face. The standing staff joke was that "on a clear day in Tokyo you could see Mount Fujiyama; on a *very* clear day you could see MacArthur." Not untypical was the case of his adjutant general Richard M. Levy. During his two and a half years at GHQ he saw MacArthur exactly twice: the day he reported for duty and the day he left. This deliberate reclusion gave MacArthur's chief of staff Almond far more "power" than men in similar jobs elsewhere. Everything in GHQ had to go through Almond, who then briefed MacArthur, adding his own recommendations, which MacArthur usually followed.[9]

* * *

To carry out his military missions, MacArthur had retained one of his two wartime armies, the Eighth, commanded by Robert L. Eichelberger. In the frenzied postwar demobilization Eighth Army lost most of its veteran fighters and wartime strength. But MacArthur had maintained its organizational structure with four divisions. These divisions, all of which had fought in the Southwest Pacific, were the 1st Cavalry ("dismounted," or regular infantry), the 11th Airborne, and the 24th and 25th Infantry divisions. To heighten the American presence and ensure internal security, Eighth Army's divisional, regimental, and battalion headquarters were scattered all over Japan. From 1945 to 1949 Eighth Army was strictly an occupational force; it was not equipped and did not train for battle. Its mere presence was believed to be sufficient to deter a Russian attack on Japan.[10]

When Eichelberger was rotated home in September 1948, he was replaced as commander of Eighth Army by another "European general," three-star Walton Harris Walker, who was nicknamed Johnnie for the scotch whiskey. Walker was an "older" West Pointer (1912), three years senior to Eisenhower and Bradley and four years senior to Ned Almond. He had been an outstanding corps commander in George Patton's Third Army in the ETO, where he won his third star, but because of his seniority, he, like Almond, had little chance of rising further in the postwar Army. He came to Japan, one close admirer remembered, anticipating a "nice, cushy time, beautiful quarters and easy duty" before retirement.[11]

Walker was born in 1889, in the small farming town of Belton, Texas, son of a dry goods merchant. He entered West Point in 1908 and, as a first classman (senior) had "hazed" plebes Bradley and Eisenhower. Later, in 1916, Walker and Eisenhower had served in the same regiment on the Mexican border, where they became close friends and hunting companions and where both were hit and nearly killed by the same lightning bolt during a thunderstorm. In the mid-twenties they renewed their friendship at the Command and General Staff School. There Walker became close friends with another classmate, who was one of Eisenhower's closest cohorts, Leonard T. ("Gee") Gerow. These would prove to be important associations, but Walker's big "break" came in the mid-thirties, when he was assigned to be executive (exec) officer (second-in-command) of an infantry brigade commanded by George Marshall, who formed a high opinion of Walker. When Marshall became Army chief of staff in 1939, Walker was serving as exec of the Army's Washington "brain trust," the War Plans Division, which was then commanded by Gee Gerow.[12]

After the war had erupted in Europe, Marshall chose World War I tanker George Patton to organize the Army's armored forces. Patton tried his best to recruit his old associate Eisenhower, who had served with him in a tank outfit after World War I. Eisenhower was eager to join Patton, but Gee Gerow wanted him in War Plans and eventually got him as an understudy. Ultimately Eisenhower replaced Gerow as chief. In this shuffle Walker escaped from War Plans and got the job Eisenhower wanted: command of one of Patton's armored brigades, with a promotion to brigadier general. After America had entered the war, Walker shot up the ladder to command of an armored division (and promotion to two stars), then an armored corps, the XX, which went into Normandy with Patton's Third Army.[13]

Walker's XX Corps was often at the spearhead of Third Army's blazing drive through France and Germany. Patton, who did not lightly bestow praise, commended him: "Of all the corps I have commanded yours has always been the most eager to attack and the most reasonable and cooperative." In his diary Patton, who kidded Walker about his tendency to put on weight, jotted: "In spite of being fat, Walker is good . . . a very fine soldier [who] has never yet complained about any order he has received." In a letter to Marshall recommending Walker for three stars, Eisenhower, who rated Walker almost on a par with Collins and Ridgway, said that Walker "has constantly led his corps with exemplary boldness and success. He is a fighter in every sense of the word, whether in pursuit or in more difficult conditions of attack against fortified positions."[14]

After the war, when Eisenhower replaced Marshall as chief of staff, he remained close to Walker and gave him the best job he had open: command of Fifth Army in Chicago. In 1947 the Walkers (and Gerows) were among the few old Army friends who were invited to the wedding of Eisenhower's only son, John S. D. (West Point, 1944). After Bradley had replaced Eisenhower as chief of staff, he was no doubt influenced by Eisenhower when he offered Walker command of Eighth Army for his final tour.

Johnnie Walker was no intellectual giant, nor did he pretend to be. He was a capable, experienced, spit-and-polish field general. His command style was Pattonesque: tough, aggressive, occasionally overserious and pompous. Short in stature (five feet eight inches), he bulged at the waist and was constantly trying out and discarding diets. Although affable in private, he seldom smiled in public, leading *Time* magazine to describe him as bulldoggish and "grim-faced."

Unlike his idol George Patton, Walker was not an inspiring troop leader. Many thought it was because Walker was innately shy or felt inferior because of his height. In public, perhaps in compensation, he "stuck his chest out and strutted like a pouter pigeon," one of his senior ETO commanders recalled. But it didn't come off; it wasn't imposing. Nor was he capable of charming the press to enhance his "image." On the contrary, in the presence of reporters he was stiff and taciturn and sometimes hostile.[15]

He had one memorable eccentricity: He was a speed demon to the point of recklessness. No one doubted the rumors that his driver was an ex-auto racer. His adjutant at Fifth Army in Chicago, Thomas J. Marnane, who also served him in Japan, remembered: "I worried, as did everyone else, that he'd kill himself in a car wreck. Even in Chicago he'd have his driver going sixty, seventy miles an hour." The eccentricity prompted much amateur psychological analysis in Eighth Army. Some believed that Walker, like Patton, had a "death wish." Marnane speculated that it was overcompensation, for his short stature. "Maybe the faster he drove, the taller he looked in his own mind."[16]

From the outset Johnnie Walker's relationship with Douglas MacArthur and GHQ was distant and cool, and it remained that way. Perhaps Walker, no diplomat, disliked MacArthur and could not—or would not—disguise his feelings. Perhaps he was intimidated by MacArthur's soaring intellect and oratorical eloquence or put off by his obsessive thirst for the limelight. Or having served and idolized Patton, perhaps Walker found all other bosses somehow lacking.

Complicating this relationship was an almost instantaneous clash between Walker and MacArthur's chief of staff, Ned Almond. Since Walker was senior to Almond by one star, he may have resented Almond's influence with MacArthur or at least Almond's apparent determination to isolate MacArthur from everyone, including Walker. Possibly Almond was jealous of and resented Walker's appointment to command Eighth Army, a job Almond himself qualified for in terms of seniority and may have wanted. Whatever the reasons, there was no chemistry whatsoever between the two men, and the initial clash soon escalated into such bitter hostility that they could not communicate with civility.

One of Walker's senior staff officers, John H. ("Mike") Michaelis, described the Almond-Walker relationship as "horrible." He recalled: "I'd be in Walker's office briefing him, and the phone would ring. 'Walker, this is Almond.' Mind you, that is a two-star talking to a three-star. Almond would say, 'I want you to do so-and-so.' And Walker would ask, 'Is this Almond speaking or Almond speaking for MacArthur?' They just couldn't get along." Thomas Marnane, who became the secretary of the Eighth Army general staff, remembered: "Almond was impossible. Very snotty. He'd call me up and chew me out about [absurdly] small things, like there being no [sewing] thimbles in the PX [post exchange]. I soon developed a very low opinion of him. He gave Walker a bad time."[17]

## II

The occupation of Japan was a big drain on Army resources in the postwar years. As Truman cut military budgets deeper and deeper, the Army was hard pressed to support MacArthur with adequate forces. Complicating this problem was another, closely linked: the occupation of nearby South Korea.

Japan had annexed the Korean peninsula after the 1904–1905 Russo-Japanese War. The United States had seldom professed more than slight strategic, political, or economic interest in Korea. World War II compelled Washington to alter that outlook to a degree. When Japan finally surrendered, Korea would be "liberated" from the Japanese yoke and something had to be done. Accordingly, at the Cairo meeting of the Allied heads of state in November 1943, President Roosevelt endorsed a vague policy that would ensure a "free and independent Korea." This policy was refined at the Big Three meeting in Yalta in early 1945. There Roosevelt, Soviet Premier Joseph Stalin, and Britain's Prime Minister Winston S. Churchill agreed that after hostilities had ceased, Korea should become an Allied trusteeship, administered by the victorious Big Four powers, including China.

At the Potsdam meeting in late July 1945 Truman and Stalin briefly discussed Korea's future, but America took no concrete action until Russia entered the war against Japan on August 8, 1945, simultaneously invading both Manchuria and Korea. The swift movement of Soviet troops into northern Korea raised the possibility that Moscow intended to seize control of the whole peninsula. Confronting that unwanted possibility, the Pentagon hurriedly produced a plan to rush American troops into southern Korea to block the Soviet advance. A Pentagon Army colonel looked at a school map for "thirty minutes" and with complete disdain for terrain, or established lines of communication or trade or indigenous political institutions and jurisdictions or property ownership, proposed slicing the Korean peninsula in half at the 38th Parallel. Moscow accepted the partition without objection.*[18]

America had not really prepared for an occupation role in Korea. Still fearing the Soviets might overrun the whole peninsula, the Pentagon ordered the closest American Army troops at hand, XXIV Corps on Okinawa, commanded by Major General John R. Hodge, to rush to southern Korea. On September 8, 1945, Hodge led his advance troops ashore at the small, cramped seaport of Inchon, which served Korea's largest city, Seoul. There Hodge learned that the Russians had halted at the 38th Parallel, as agreed, and were accepting the surrender of Japanese forces in the northern sector. He breathed more easily and began accepting the surrender of Japanese forces in the southern sector.

Believing the trusteeship idea to be a valid long-term solution for Korea and beset by a host of postwar problems, Washington continued to show little real interest in Korea. It delegated responsibility for Korean matters to MacArthur. But MacArthur, who was also burdened with pressing postwar problems in occupied Japan, had little time for Korea. He hurriedly and thoughtlessly issued a harsh "occupation" decree which seemed more applic-

---

*The division gave the Russians 48,000 square miles and a population of 9 million; the United States, 37,000 square miles and a population of 21 million.

able to a defeated Japan than to a "liberated" Korea. To make matters worse, John Hodge unwisely decided to leave the Japanese colonial government—and the despised Gestapo-like, Japanese-dominated national police force—temporarily in place in the southern sector until he and his Russian counterpart could set up a proper all-Korean government, according to the four-power trusteeship concept.[19]

The Koreans were shocked and outraged by these hasty, insensitive Allied decisions. For thirty-five years they had been virtually enslaved by the Japanese. They had assumed that Allied "liberation" would mean just that: They would be free to form their own peninsula-wide government according to the mandate of the people. To them the proposed Allied trusteeship merely meant continued and prolonged occupation and oppression by another set of colonialists. They therefore adamantly opposed the trusteeship, fomenting political chaos throughout the peninsula, especially in the American sector, where energetic leftist agitators equated trusteeship with fascism and pro-Japanism. The Soviet occupiers consolidated a hold on the minds of the leftists in both sectors by propagandizing that the trusteeship was purely an invention of the American imperialists, and they may well have surreptitiously supported the leftists in the American sector with money, arms, and promises.

There was another large problem. The Japanese had developed and exploited Korea as a single economic entity. In the northern sector, which was rich in minerals and sites for hydroelectric plants, they had concentrated "heavy" industry and manufacturing. In the southern sector, which was suitable for agriculture, they had encouraged the long-standing cultivation of rice and other staples. Hence in commerce the North depended on the South for food and the South on the North for manufactured goods. The early expulsion of the Japanese industrialists and technocrats and the division of the peninsula at the 38th Parallel soon led to a complete disruption of normal patterns of manufacturing, commerce, and trade and, inevitably, to economic chaos, which leftist agitators also hastened to exploit.

John Hodge was a highly capable, blunt-spoken field general, but he was ill suited for an occupation command. He had no prior experience in politics or economics and small grasp of the Asian mentality and Korean language. Moreover, he disliked and distrusted Koreans, whom he described as "the same breed of cat as the Japanese." His ill-conceived decision to keep the despised Japanese colonial government—and national police—in power was overruled by Washington but not before Hodge had been thoroughly reviled and undermined by the leftists. In reaction to these attacks from the left and to ever-increasing anti-American propaganda and hostility from the Soviet sector, Hodge aligned his occupation government with wealthy conservative, anti-Communist political factions in the South and promoted Koreans who had served as underlings to the Japanese in the police force to top positions.

Since the leftists viewed most conservatives and Korean policemen as Japanese collaborators and traitors, they were further antagonized.

The upshot was a gradual freeze-out of centrists and leftists from positions of influence in the emerging southern Korean government and police. Inasmuch as the Soviets were embarked on a diametrically opposed course—freezing out conservatives—a political polarization was under way in Korea that would make it virtually impossible to form a single Korea-wide government as envisioned in the trusteeship idea. In sum, the political and economic realities and occupational decisions on the scene in both sectors of Korea were consigning the trusteeship to an early grave.

John Hodge saw this reality early and clearly. After a mere three months of occupation duty he became implacably opposed to the trusteeship and urged Washington to abandon it and pursue some other more realistic policy. His own recommendation was dramatic and drastic: that both America and Russia withdraw occupation forces from Korea simultaneously and "leave Korea to its own devices and an inevitable internal upheaval for its self-purification." Washington clung to the trusteeship idea, but at a foreign ministers' meeting in Moscow in December 1945 it was agreed that Korea-wide elections would be pushed more vigorously, with the aim of establishing a single, stable Korean government and terminating the trusteeship within five years.[20]

During all this turmoil and chaos MacArthur remained indifferent to Korea. He imperiously declined repeated pleas from Hodge to visit Seoul and work his famous magic on the Oriental minds there. He turned a deaf ear to Hodge's repeated requests for guidance and advice. "Use your own best judgment as to what action is to be taken," MacArthur replied to one such request. "I am not sufficiently familiar with the local situation to advise you intelligently, but I will support whatever decision you may take in this matter." When Hodge finally ran out of patience and asked for a transfer to other duty, MacArthur would not approve it. He advised Hodge to take a forty-five day leave in the States and "forget Korea" temporarily.[21]

Early in the occupation Hodge felt the impact of Truman's pell-mell demobilization and postwar military economies. A few months after VJ day his big battle-hardened three-division XXIV Corps had dwindled to a force of but 45,000 men, many of them green draftees. In the existing political and economic chaos of southern Korea this American force was not sufficient to maintain law and order. To offset his manpower losses, Hodge doubled the Korean police in his sector to 25,000 men and equipped them with captured Japanese weapons, American jeeps, and a modern communications network. At the same time he proposed the creation of a 50,000-man "army" to augment the police in difficult situations and to serve as a deterrent to a possible hostile attack from the northern sector. Believing an "army" as such might provoke a Korean "arms race," MacArthur and the JCS disapproved the proposal, suggesting as a substitute a Filipino-like "constabulary" of about 25,000 men, organized along military lines with regiments and battalions and equipped with light machine guns and mortars.

Hodge founded the Constabulary with minimum fanfare in early 1946. It drew most of its initial officer cadre (forty of sixty men) from a group of Koreans who had been conscripted into the Japanese armed forces in World War II and who were in leftist eyes "pro-Japanese." The Constabulary was soon a preserve for such Koreans, evoking first verbal attacks, then infiltration from the leftists. As a result of these attacks and police jealousy, the Constabulary got off to a wobbly start and had to be "purged" of leftists and "Communists." But by the end of 1946 it numbered about 20,000 men, who were being trained in military fundamentals by Hodge's men.

Meanwhile, during 1946 the problems in Korea multiplied. By then (if not earlier) Moscow had made the decision to subvert any and all attempts to unify Korea under a single government and retain the northern sector as a puppet or satellite state, in part to have a buffer on its own border. Accordingly, the Soviets sabotaged Korea-wide election talks, propagandized relentlessly against the American occupation forces (still insisting that the hated, inflammatory trusteeship was an American invention), and abetted leftist agitators in the southern sector. In the fall these leftists provoked the worst crisis of the American occupation: a massive revolt of workers, farmers, and peasants— virtually a full-scale revolution—which forced Hodge to resort to massive military countermeasures to restore order. In these brutal clashes the police and embryonic Constabulary were put to the ultimate test. Both emerged triumphant—and more powerful.[22]

\* \* \*

The ever-shrinking American Army, trying to make do on a shoe-string budget, began to view South Korea with utmost disdain, if not contempt. When in early 1947 Hodge insisted that the American Army must keep at least 45,000 men in South Korea to carry out the occupation mission, Secretary of War Robert P. Patterson, desperately looking for ways to save money, recommended to Forrestal that the Army pull out of South Korea at the earliest practicable date. The JCS, which then included Army Chief of Staff Eisenhower, provided the military justification. Reversing all previous views, it declared that the United States "has little strategic interest in maintaining the present [U.S.] troops and bases in Korea." In the event of hostilities in the Far East, the JCS went on, the 45,000 troops in Korea "would be a liability" and could not be sustained there without "substantial reinforcements prior to the initiation of hostilities." Moreover, the JCS argued, in the event the United States elected to launch offensive operations against the continent of Asia (a remote contingency), it "most probably would by-pass the Korean peninsula."

In the event the Communists swallowed up South Korea and threatened Japan and other American strategic interests in the Far East, "neutralization by air action would be more feasible and less costly than large scale ground operations."[23]

At first, then Secretary of State George Marshall did not agree. However, in September 1947 the Russians, who were still scuttling all attempts to unify Korea by any means, surprisingly proposed to withdraw their occupation forces from North Korea, provided America did the same in South Korea. Believing this proposal offered a new "opportunity" to solve the Korean problem, Marshall and his closest advisers gave the matter "close study." On September 29 Marshall decreed that "ultimately the U.S. position in Korea is untenable even with expenditure of considerable U.S. money and effort." The following month one of his top advisers, George F. Kennan, chairman of the State Department's Policy Planning Staff summed up the department's conclusion on Korea:

There is no longer any real hope of a genuinely peaceful and free democratic development in that country. Its political life in the coming period is bound to be dominated by political immaturity, intolerance and violence. Where such conditions prevail, the communists are in their element. Therefore we cannot count on native forces to help hold the line against Soviet expansion. Since the territory is not of decisive strategic importance to us, our main task is to extricate ourselves without too great a loss of prestige.[24]

By the time Bradley relieved Eisenhower as Army chief of staff in early 1948, the occupation of Japan and South Korea had become a huge—and expensive—Army headache. Some figures Bradley confronted tell the story. On paper the Army's authorized strength was 560,000; its actual strength was 552,000. On paper MacArthur's authorized strength, mainly for the occupation of Japan and South Korea, was about 124,000,* of which 40,000 were then designated for South Korea. Owing to the shrinkage of the Army and other factors, MacArthur's actual strength was about 114,000 men—10,000 short. He had compensated for his shortage by steadily robbing the South Korean occupation force, reducing it to 30,000 men, and was demanding that his ground forces be brought up to authorized strength without delay. Because the

---

*This figure does not include 28,000 Philippine Scouts, which MacArthur provided to support the new Philippine government and for which the Army was paying. Counting the Scouts, MacArthur's authorized Far Eastern strength was actually about 152,000 men. MacArthur was also responsible for the occupation of Ryukyu Islands (Okinawa), the Marianas (Guam, Saipan), and the Bonin Islands (Iwo Jima), which required about 15,000 men and which were included in his 152,000-man authorization. This left about 60,000 men for Eighth Army and administrative duties in Japan.

JCS was then facing further budget cuts, it had to inform MacArthur that the shortage could not be made up and that furthermore, his authorized strength would be cut again—to 106,000 men, of which no fewer than 30,000 had to remain in South Korea.[25]

The economic strain imposed by the occupation of South Korea led the Truman administration, in March 1948, to declare a new policy whereby Army forces could be withdrawn from there. Basically Truman's new policy dumped the "Korean problem" into the lap of the United Nations. Working through the UN, Washington would: (1) continue to press for Korea-wide elections and political unification through the auspices of the UN; (2) when that failed, support an independent government elected in the southern sector only; (3) withdraw the 30,000-man Army occupation force at the earliest possible time after the creation of the Republic of Korea; (4) give South Korea a hefty economic grant to strengthen its chaotic economy; (5) proclaim continuing moral support for South Korea but not regard anything that occurred there (such as a North Korean invasion and takeover) in the future as a casus belli.[26]

When confronted with this paper, one of its architects, Omar Bradley, a man noted for his moral conscience, had some second thoughts. Would the United States in fact callously look the other way if North Korea invaded South Korea? Bradley asked the JCS staff to restudy possible options in that eventuality. In so doing, the staff reiterated the now-unequivocal JCS view that Korea was of "little strategic value to the United States" and that unilateral commitment of U.S. military force in Korea would be "ill advised" and "impracticable." However, as a "last resort," the staff study suggested, the UN might counter a North Korean invasion with a "police action," carried out by "an international [military] force" to which the United States might contribute "units." Still troubled, Bradley requested that the JCS forward this paper to the president for further discussions, but his fellow chiefs talked him out of that, owing to the "predominantly political tenor" of the study.[27]

In Korea Hodge and most of his men silently cheered the withdrawal policy. The Army occupiers hated South Korea. It was a miserably poor, primitive, mountainous place with few paved roads or amenities. Although the country was situated in a temperate zone,* the climate was peculiarly inhospitable: jungle hot and steamy in the rainy season (June to September) and arctic cold in winter. The rice paddies, situated in the narrow valleys and draws among the endless hills and ridges, were fertilized by stinking human feces.

---

*If superimposed on the east coast of the United States at the 38th Parallel, South Korea would extend roughly from Washington, D.C., to Atlanta; North Korea from Washington to about Boston.

Personal communications were difficult; few Koreans spoke English, and fewer Americans spoke Korean. One Army general wrote that he was revulsed by "the squalor, the stench, the sea of human misery and the lack of beauty and comfort."[28]

Washington lost no time in implementing the new policy. On its urging the United Nations "adopted" Korea and formally proposed free elections to establish a unified Korean country and government. As expected, North Korea boycotted the elections. Voting in May 1948, the South Koreans elected a National Assembly, which in turn established the Republic of Korea (ROK), with its capital in Seoul. North Korea responded by creating a Soviet-style government called the Democratic People's Republic of Korea, with its capital in Pyongyang.

The two Korean governments were launched with sharply contrasting leaders. In South Korea it was an eccentric seventy-three-year-old, right-wing, militant anti-Communist, Syngman Rhee, who had lived for forty years in America as an exile and lobbyist for Korean independence. In exile Rhee had earned three college degrees (B.A., George Washington University, 1907; M.A., Harvard University, 1908; and a Ph.D., Princeton University, 1910) and had adopted the honorific "Doctor." Returning to Seoul in 1945, Rhee had ridden the chaotic South Korean political roller coaster with masterful skill, but fundamentally he drew his major support from the Americans and Korean conservatives.

In North Korea it was a taciturn, ill-educated thirty-six-year-old Kim Il Sung, who was also an exile, but one of a different stripe. In about 1932, at age twenty, Kim left Korea and joined a guerrilla force which harassed Japanese troops in Manchuria and North Korea all through the 1930s. During World War II, it is believed, he was recruited by Chinese or Soviet Communists to fight the Japanese openly in Manchuria, rising to lead a roving band of about 400 men. He may have attended Soviet military schools in Moscow. After the war he returned to northern Korea under the aegis of the Soviets and was promoted—and greeted—as a returning hero. Aligning himself with Communist political action committees in the Soviet sector (and possibly abetting Communist activities in the South), Kim rose swiftly to a commanding position among the leaders in northern Korea.[29]

In their respective inaugural addresses both Rhee and Kim deplored the division of Korea, and each vowed to reunite the peninsula under his own government. MacArthur chose this ceremonial occasion to pay his very first visit to South Korea, and in his public comments he supported Rhee's determination to unify the country. "An artificial barrier has divided your land," he told the Korean Assembly in warlike tones. "This barrier must and shall be torn down. Nothing shall prevent the ultimate unity of your people as free men of a free nation." In an aside to Rhee (overheard by reporters) MacArthur blithely—and grandly—promised Rhee continuing military support: "If Korea should ever be attacked by the Communists, I will defend it as I would California." These bellicose statements, which directly contravened the new Truman policies on South Korea, caused no little consternation in Washington.[30]

Itching to withdraw militarily from South Korea, Washington next turned to the task of creating a ROK military force to help fill the vacuum created by the departing American troops. Rhee and Hodge wanted a six-division ROK Army of no less than 100,000 men with a possible reserve of another 100,000. MacArthur, still fearing a Korean "arms race," continued to oppose a ROK "Army" as such. He suggested a less provocative plan to double the strength of the South Korean Constabulary from 25,000 to 50,000 men and to provide it with "heavy weapons" (including some obsolescent artillery) from American units withdrawing from Korea and from other sources. Although they fully recognized that a 50,000-man paramilitary Constabulary was insufficient force to maintain external security in South Korea over the long term, the JCS and Truman approved this plan.[31]

In September 1948, soon after Rhee and Kim had assumed control of their respective governments, American and Russian troops began withdrawing from South and North Korea. Among the first American soldiers to leave was John Hodge, who by that time completely distrusted and despised Syngman Rhee, whom he considered a devious, emotionally unstable, brutal, corrupt, and wildly unpredictable leader. Upon leaving South Korea, Hodge described his three years there as "the worst job I ever had." At Rhee's request the JCS agreed to leave one American regimental combat team* in South Korea until about June 1949.[32]

As stipulated by Washington, the forces departing South Korea left behind certain gear to equip the 50,000-man ROK Constabulary: 100,000 small arms (rifles; pistols); 51 million rounds of ammo; transport (trucks; jeeps) for 40,000 men; mortars, antitank bazookas and guns; machine guns, and about 100 obsolete 105-mm "snubnose" howitzers (the discarded "infantryman's cannon" of World War II). Owing to Washington's fear that Rhee might invade North Korea (as he had often threatened), tanks, motorized artillery, and aircraft were deliberately withheld from the ROKs.[33]

The Russians completed troop withdrawals from North Korea by the end of 1948. They, too, left behind an indigenous military force: the North Korean People's Army (NKPA), or, in Korean, *In Min Gun*. The Russians were far

---

*The regimental combat team (RCT), evolved in World War II, was a self-contained fighting unit composed of one regiment of infantry, reinforced by a battalion of artillery, a company of tanks, and other special elements.

more supportive than the Americans, showing no qualms about a Korean arms race or fear that North Korea would invade South Korea. From the start Russian advisers had designed the NKPA to be a tough, mobile, fully equipped army of about 135,000 men, supported by an air force. When the regular Russian troops left, the NKPA comprised about ten divisions, one of them an embryonic armored division to be equipped with about 150 T-34 Russian tanks. The NKPA was also furnished a full array of light and heavy artillery, including powerful Russian-built 120-mm howitzers, some of which were motorized.[34]

The growth of the NKPA—and Kim's increasingly bellicose statements—alarmed Syngman Rhee and his government. Rhee pleaded with Washington for help in converting his Constabulary to a full-scale and well-equipped army with tanks, heavier artillery, and a supporting air force. But Tokyo and Washington, still wary of fostering a Korean arms race and of the possibility that Rhee might launch a "preemptive war" on North Korea, held back. In the face of this indifference, in late 1948 the Rhee government, more or less on its own, officially converted the 50,000-man Constabulary to a ROK Army and drew plans to build its strength rapidly to 100,000 men. Of this number, 65,000 would man eight infantry divisions, 35,000 would staff headquarters and service units. Each ROK division would thus consist of about 8,000 men, slightly less than the strength of an NKPA infantry division and about half the strength of an American division.

Soon after Truman's inauguration in 1949 Rhee renewed his demands on Washington for military help. His shopping list was formidable: tanks; mobile artillery; aircraft (some 350 to start a ROK Air Force); etc. These latest requests arrived while Eisenhower was "presiding" over the JCS in his futile effort to produce a unified military budget. Now aware of the growing power of the NKPA, the JCS reappraised America's military commitment to South Korea. It concurred in Rhee's plan for an eight-division ROK Army and recommended additional American gear to equip the added 15,000 ROK GIs. However, still fearing that Rhee might invade North Korea, the JCS refused to endorse his request for tanks, mobile artillery, or aircraft. On March 23, 1949, about the time Eisenhower and Forrestal left the Pentagon and Louis Johnson took over, Truman approved these JCS recommendations.[35]

In addition, the JCS and Truman approved a proposal to leave behind American military "advisers." Known formally as the Korean Military Advisory Group (KMAG, pronounced "kay-mag"), the outfit would be composed of about 500 officers and enlisted men, commanded by Brigadier General W. Lynn Roberts, who had been in Korea for about one year, serving in a similar capacity during the occupation. Roberts officially launched KMAG on July 1, 1949, after the departure of the last American occupation troops.

With these developments, in the summer of 1949, Washington relieved

MacArthur of all further responsibilities for South Korea and delegated them to the State Department. It was represented in Seoul by a young but experienced "Korean hand," Ambassador John J. Muccio, who had a thorough grasp of the Byzantine South Korean politics but only a slight knowledge of military affairs. Since State now reigned supreme in South Korea, KMAG was placed administratively under Muccio, and Lynn Roberts thereby became chief military adviser not only to Rhee and the ROK Army but to Muccio as well.[36]

## III

During 1948 and 1949, while the withdrawal from South Korea was in progress, Washington launched a reappraisal of America's occupation policies in Japan. The State Department planners, led by George Kennan, concluded that an economically revitalized, unfettered Japan could be America's strongest and most useful ally in containing the march of communism in the Far East. Accordingly, a number of "harsh" occupation policies, including some which had tended to dampen Japanese industrial production, were rescinded. In addition, Washington gave Japan a half billion dollars in foreign aid to prime its economic pump and began discussions aimed at framing a peace treaty which would enable America to withdraw its occupation forces.[37]

There was one large military problem. When it adopted its new liberal postwar constitution, Japan specifically and legally rejected militarism. Its government would not ever again authorize the establishment of armed forces. This radical decision (cheered by many at the time) caused deep concern among America's military planners. If America signed a peace treaty and withdrew its occupation forces, Japan, the key bastion in America's strategic Far East offshore defensive perimeter, would be left utterly defenseless. It would create a power vacuum into which the Russians or Chinese Communists might attempt to move, either by subverting the Japanese government or by outright invasion. For this reason, and others, the JCS opposed an early Japanese peace treaty and hoped that Japanese leaders could be persuaded to create a low-profile (or even secret) military force sufficiently powerful at least to defend Japan against an external attack.[38]

The new and lenient attitude toward Japan had a profound impact on Johnnie Walker's Eighth Army. In the spring of 1949, when MacArthur issued a new directive relaxing the stern character of the occupation, it relieved Eighth Army of many policing and administrative duties which had kept its men busy. In effect the new policy left thousands of men in Eighth Army with nothing to do. In order to head off the certain trouble the devil would make for all those idle hands, MacArthur decided Eighth Army must transform itself into a hard, combat-ready force. The languorous, travel-poster Army life in Japan would come to an abrupt end.

These orders came as a challenge to Walker and his Eighth Army staff. The responsibility for executing them in detail fell on the shoulders of Walker's chief of staff, Eugene ("Gene") M. Landrum, who had likewise come to Japan for a "cushy" final tour before retirement.

Landrum was an affable officer of many talents, but his reputation was checkered. Born in 1891 in Pensacola, Florida, he graduated from public high school and enlisted in the Army in 1910 as a private. Six years later he won a commission and, during his World War I tour in the Philippines, married the daughter of the American governor-general. During the peace-time years he had advanced easily and steadily, completing courses at the Command and General Staff School (1933) and Army War College (1936). When World War II started, he was a full colonel and the chief of staff of an infantry division.[39]

Landrum's World War II service was a roller-coaster ride: hero one minute, bum the next. It began in Alaska, where Landrum was a brigadier general serving as a senior staff officer to the Army theater commander. In May 1943, when the Allies mounted an invasion of the island of Attu to eject the recently arrived Japanese occupiers, the American 7th Infantry Division commander, Albert E. Brown, was relieved of command for lacking aggressiveness. Gene Landrum was appointed the new division commander and led the Attu campaign to a successful conclusion. He emerged from this experience with a chestful of medals, a second star, and a bright future.[40]

During the Allied invasion of Normandy Landrum came over Utah Beach as a "spare" division commander in Joe Collins's VII Corps. When the poorly trained 90th Infantry Division bogged down in the Cotentin Peninsula, Collins relieved the commander and substituted Landrum. But Landrum was not able to repeat his Attu stellar performance; the 90th Division continued to fail. Landrum, Collins wrote, "unfortunately . . . did not quite measure up," and Collins—perhaps too precipitously—relieved him, and Omar Bradley sent him back to the States. Marshall gave Landrum a second chance—command of a new division destined for duty in the ETO—but Eisenhower refused to accept him back in his command, and the division went overseas without Landrum.[41]

After the war, busted back to colonel, Landrum wound up as G-1 of Walker's Fifth Army headquarters in Chicago, where by date of rank he was senior to everyone on the staff. Johnnie Walker took a shine to Landrum, believing (as had Patton) that Landrum had been unfairly treated by Collins in Normandy. Although Walker still had his loyal wartime chief of staff, William A. Collier, in tow, Landrum gradually began to displace Collier in performing the duties of Fifth Army chief of staff and, eventually, Collier went off to South Korea to join John Hodge's staff. When Walker was offered command of Eighth Army, he invited Landrum to come along as his chief of staff, probably with the hope of repromoting him to general before Landrum's retirement.[42]

\* \* \*

At the time MacArthur issued orders for Eighth Army to transform itself into a combat-ready force, it still numbered four divisions (1st Cavalry, 7th, 24th, and 25th), but it was a "bastard" organization. The Truman-Johnson economy measures had forced the deactivation of its two corps headquarters (I and IX) and one battalion in each of its twelve regiments, save one. The exception was the 24th Regiment of the 25th Division, to which most black combat troops were assigned, in keeping with the Army's segregationist policies of that era. (Because of the large number of blacks in Japan, the 24th Regiment not only had three battalions but was also about 10 percent overstrength.) In addition, economies had dictated that each Eighth Army division deactivate 4 field artillery batteries, 4 antiaircraft batteries, 100 antitank guns, and most of its armor.*

On paper, an American infantry division at full war strength numbered about 18,800 men. Owing to the budget restrictions, however, three of Eighth Army's four divisions each were authorized only 12,500 men; the 25th (to which all blacks were assigned) 13,500. On paper, the 1st Cav, 7th, and 24th divisions were thus about 6,000 men short of full war strength; the 25th, about 5,000 men short. In reality, because of the limits on personnel, rotation policies, and other factors, the 1st Cav, 7th, and 24th divisions numbered only about 11,300 men each and were thus about 7,000 men short of full war strength. The 25th Division, numbering 13,000 men, was 5,500 men short of full war strength. On the whole, none of the four divisions was capable of laying down more than 62 percent of its normal infantry firepower.[44]

The GIs of Eighth Army were a variegated lot. Many of the senior noncoms were conscientious career soldiers who had joined the Army in the 1920s and 1930s. They had fought in World War II and looked forward to retirement after twenty or thirty years' service. Many were World War II volunteers or draftees who had chosen to make the Army a career and had eight or nine years' total service. There were some postwar volunteers, lured into the Army with promises of foreign travel and good pay. But too many

---

*Usually an infantry division included one battalion of seventy-seven tanks (older Shermans or the newer Pershings or variants of each) plus a tank company (twenty-two tanks) in each regiment, to form armor-infantry teams. For economy reasons and to avoid damage to the roads in Japan, the Eighth Army divisions were restricted to one company of old M-24 Chaffee light tanks, which were used primarily for ceremonial purposes. The few Shermans and Pershings or variants in Japan were stored in warehouses.[43]

Eighth Army GIs were 1948 and 1949 draftees of low caliber and motivation. It was later established that nearly half the GIs in Eighth Army (43 percent) ranked in the two lowest categories in Army aptitude and classification tests.

In occupied Japan these GIs, whether married or single, had found a not unpleasant life. Most Japanese were docile and cooperative and, outwardly at least, appeared to welcome their conquerors. A warm companionship between the Japanese and the GIs evolved. Since most Japanese were economically destitute, many were eager for domestic housework, and it was not uncommon for a first sergeant and his family to have one or two servants. Drugs (principally alcohol) were plentiful and cheap—and widely abused. Black-marketeering of all kinds throve, enabling many unscrupulous GIs to enhance their incomes substantially.[45]

To provide a rationale and plan for transforming Eighth Army into a combat-ready force Johnnie Walker and Gene Landrum had to conceive a theoretical "threat." Accordingly, it was assumed that Russia, staging from Sakhalin, would invade Japan's northernmost "home" island, Hokkaido, while Communist fifth columnists and saboteurs created internal chaos. The American war plan (remarkably similar to MacArthur's 1941 plan for defending the Philippines against Japanese invasion) was to stop the Russians "at the beaches." Air Force bombers, staging from Okinawa, would atom-bomb the Russian invasion forces. Eighth Army ground forces would "defend" Hokkaido (and other "home" islands) from invasion and ensure the security of key communications facilities, GHQ, ordnance depots, and so on.[46] No consideration was given to the possibility of a "limited" or "little" war. In particular, no serious planning was ever done for a defense of South Korea by Eighth Army. That place had been "written off" strategically by the JCS and lay outside America's strategic offshore defensive perimeter.[47]

* * *

The Eighth Army training program was launched with a blizzard of paperwork and orders. The headquarters staff was not excluded. The assistant G-3, Mike Michaelis, remembered with amusement: "General Walker called an 'alert' and moved the headquarters to the field. It was a top secret CPX [command post exercise] which envisioned a Russian invasion of Hokkaido. Until then combat preparations had been almost negligible. The CPX was a disaster. It took almost three days for them to get the tents set up. The people had no place to sleep. There was no lighting, no communications. They couldn't get the meals together. It was god-awful. But by June 1950 we'd done this so many times that the headquarters was adequately trained to go into the field."[48]

Several factors significantly impeded training in Eighth Army. First was the excessively high turnover rate: 43 percent annually. Most battalions were not only understrength but also like a revolving door. Many of the new arrivals had not been adequately trained in fundamentals, let alone in squad, platoon, company, or battalion exercises. Second was the lack of open space for large training maneuvers in crowded Japan. For the most part such exercises were limited to the confines of small regimental posts. Third was an acute shortage or the complete absence of combat equipment. Much of what the Army had, a master sergeant wrote, was "not even field-worthy; nearly all of it was worn or old." Vehicles in use since World War II were falling apart or inoperable. Ammunition stored since VJ day had badly deteriorated. Portable field radios had corroded and become useless. Mortars had rusted from lack of use or careless maintenance. So grave were these deficiencies—and so deaf was the Pentagon to requests to correct them—that MacArthur had been compelled to send salvage teams back to the Pacific battlefields (Operation Roll-up) to recover rusty abandoned equipment, which was refurbished in Japanese-ope-rated facilities.[49]

Nonetheless, Walker established a rigid, graduated field training schedule and demanded it be adhered to. It called for completion of company-level training by December 1949, battalion-level by May 1950, regimental-level by July 1950, and divisional-level by December 1950. Along the way some units would receive specialized training in amphibious landings and air transporta-bility (even though MacArthur had few troop carrier aircraft). Ultimately all units would undergo joint training with the Air Force providing close air support to ground forces.[50]

To make certain divisions did not evade his orders, Walker closely moni-tored progress in the field. Teams of inspectors, supervised by his G-3, William H. Bartlett, toured Japan, pouncing unannounced. A member of one team, Edgar R. Luhn, remembered: "Our team was composed of about fifty-eight men—forty officers and eighteen enlisted men. We had our own train to travel and live in. We'd go to a battalion and stay with it about three weeks, inspect it from A to Z. In one outfit we found two-thirds of all rifles broken. We sent these to ordnance to be rebuilt and requisitioned new ones. In another outfit we could not find one single vehicle fit to run. After we'd finished our inspec-tions, we held a critique with all the unit officers. General Walker would fly in and address them. Sometimes he'd get so heated I was afraid he'd shatter the podium."[51]

Notwithstanding this close supervision, Walker was not able to adhere to his training schedule. It had called for completion of battalion-level train-ing by May 1950. Joe Collins later wrote that even by June 25, 1950, "few units of the Eighth Army had reached a satisfactory level of battalion train-ing. . . ." Moreover, because of the wide dispersion of Eighth Army units and the rampant turnover, there was no sense of cohesion, esprit, or unit pride, even at regimental level, let alone the army level.[52]

## IV

In South Korea Lynn Roberts, chief of KMAG, had initiated a training program for the ROK Army which, by a remarkable coincidence, ran almost exactly parallel to that of Walker's Eighth Army.

Then fifty-nine years old, Roberts had been "passed over" for promotion to two stars, and as a result, he faced mandatory retirement in July 1950. His Army career had been undistinguished. He was a West Pointer (1913) who was an infantryman in World War I and a tanker in World War II. In the latter war many of his classmates were two-star generals commanding divisions, and two were corps commanders. But by December 1944 Roberts was still only a colonel commanding a combat unit of the 10th Armored Division. He finished the war with one star, serving as assistant commander of the 4th Armored Division.[53]

Having been passed over and facing retirement, Roberts might well have sat back and enjoyed himself. But he elected the opposite course. Like Johnnie Walker, Roberts seemed suddenly obsessed with a kind of messianic zeal to field a credible army in the one year of active service he had left.

He, too, faced a difficult challenge. By this time the ROK Army had grown to about 100,000 men. As planned, 35,000 were assigned to headquarters and service outfits and 65,000 to the eight infantry divisions authorized and equipped by Washington. The American equipment, supplies, and spare parts were running out at an alarming rate, and there was little hope for substantial replacements from Washington. Rhee provided some uniforms, ammo, and other gear from newly established South Korean factories, but this placed a heavy strain on the chaotic economy. The upshot was not only inferior equipment but also a chronic shortage of everything from beans to bullets— especially bullets. The embryonic, untrained ROK units were wasting millions of rounds of ammo in operations against bandits and guerrillas all over South Korea.[54]

There was another serious problem: the uneven quality and integrity in the ROK Army officer corps. This was led by the thirty-six-year-old chief of staff, Major General Chae Byong Duk, who was five feet five inches and weighed an unmilitary 250 pounds. The majority of ROK officers were patriotic and dedicated, but the corps became a haven for too many venal opportunists who used their newly acquired power for personal gain. Among this element theft, bribery, blackmail, and kickbacks were commonplace.[55]

The ROK enlisted manpower was also a problem. It was mostly raw, and the majority was illiterate. There were no military phrases in the Korean language, such as "sector," "zone," "phase line," "regiment," "squad." A language had to be improvised, and the result was usually cumbersome or faintly comical: A machine gun became "a-gun-that-shoots-very-fast," and a vehicle headlight became "a-candle-in-a-shiny-bowl." Such transliterations made radio communications, encoding, or written instructions a nightmare. Oriental pride, or "face," greatly complicated and often undermined the training. An inexperienced or incompetent ROK noncommissioned officer (NCO) who gave an incorrect or foolish order could not openly admit to a mistake, nor could he be "advised" or "corrected" in the traditional direct American Army way without disastrous "loss of face."[56]

After conducting army-wide tests, Roberts and his men decided they had to start training from scratch, beginning with squad-level marching drills and individual qualification on the rifle range. The plan was to progress gradually from squad-level training to platoon-level, then on up the line to company-, battalion-, and regiment-level, and finally to division-level training. This plan was vastly complicated by the fact that the eight infantry divisions of the ROK Army were already deployed in the field.[57]

Roberts did his utmost. He established several technical schools and sent his advisers to serve with the various regiments and battalions to begin and oversee basic training. But progress was slow. In KMAG's first six months— July through December 1949—fewer than half the men in the sixty-seven ROK battalions qualified in using the M-1 rifle. Only thirty battalions had progressed from squad- to platoon- to company-level exercises. Less than one-third of the battalions were sufficiently advanced to begin battalion-level exercises. Even so, Roberts remained unflinchingly optimistic.[58]

In all this nothing was more vitally important than the tactical disposition of the four ROK divisions at the 38th Parallel. Whether they were adequately trained or not, it was believed the mere presence of these divisions could provide a deterrent to an NKPA invasion. Accordingly, KMAG personnel applied tedious hours of study to the "traditional" or "likely" invasion routes and advised ROK dispositions accordingly.

The invasion route finally deemed most "likely" was the Uijongbu Corridor. This is a broad valley on the west side of the peninsula, with a good road network leading straight south from the border to Seoul. Near the 38th Parallel the valley is narrow and the hills provide good defensive positions. Here was placed what was believed to be the best-trained ROK division, the 7th. It was disposed with two regiments on the line and one in reserve, fifteen miles behind the "front." In event of invasion, the ROK 2d Division, assigned to antiguerrilla missions near Taejon (about 120 miles south), would rapidly move forward to reinforce the 7th Division at Uijongbu. The ROK 1st Division was placed close on the left (or west) flank of the 7th, near Kaesong. The ROK 6th Division was positioned to the right of the 7th, in the more mountainous terrain of mid-Korea, near Chunchon. The other ROK division, the 8th, was assigned to the "least likely" invasion route: the extreme east coast, which is dominated by the rugged Taebaek Mountain range.[59]

Despite the vital nature of the missions, the four divisions were seldom maintained on a "war footing." The regiments and battalions were not kept at full strength or on full combat deployment. Commanders frequently rotated units rearward for training, rest and recreation, parades or for other purposes. Although the war plan called for two regiments on the line and one in reserve, the opposite was usually the case. Commanders freely granted passes and furloughs, and some were reluctant to impose strict discipline. The senior officers were as often away with their families or attending to their private businesses as they were in their command posts (CPs).

Across the border the NKPA, advised by a Russian KMAG, was progressing at a far faster rate. By the end of 1949 it had grown, as planned, to about 135,000 men, one-third of them tough combat veterans of the Chinese civil war. The units had completed regimental-level training and were moving on to divisional exercises. The armored division had trained extensively with its Russian-built T-34 tanks. Staff planners, assisted by the Russians and working in secrecy (and maintaining strict radio silence) drew detailed plans for an invasion of South Korea.[60]

Meanwhile, tension along the 38th Parallel was extreme; the border area was like a war zone. Almost nightly the North Koreans infiltrated South Korea with strong infantry patrols, probing ROK positions, taking prisoners, or simply wounding and killing. The ROKs retaliated with their own patrols. Often the opposing patrols met in the dark and had firefights. Both sides were heavily engaged in numerous clandestine activities, infiltrating intelligence agents, assassins, and political provocateurs into each other's territory. Not infrequently both sides engaged in heavy artillery duels, as if preparing for a full-scale invasion. In the last six months of 1949 KMAG had officially logged an astounding 400 "border incidents."[61]

Even so, the ROK Army remained almost casually disposed and ill equipped to meet any threat from the north. While Roberts's KMAG made some progress, by early 1950 it was clear that his training schedule could never be met. Then came a series of public statements—bombshells—from Washington that seriously undermined the morale of KMAG, the Rhee government, and the ROK Army.

The first was President Truman's emphatic declaration, delivered on January 5, 1950, that the United States had adopted the hands-off Formosa policy. To Rhee and his Seoul government, Chiang represented the most militant indigenous anti-Communist force in this sector of the Far East. Rhee did not doubt that Peking would now soon move militarily against Formosa. Once Formosa had been taken, it was not unlikely that Moscow or Peking, or both, would goad the NKPA into attacking South Korea. In that event, would Washington also abandon South Korea?

The answer to that question appeared to have been contained in a second bombshell, delivered a week later by Dean Acheson. At a press conference, principally called to explain and clarify the hands-off Formosa policy, Acheson, who tended to be theatrically professorial (and at times patronizing), unwisely digressed to describe publicly the concept of America's offshore strategic defensive perimeter in the Far East. Although he did not specifically mention South Korea, his remarks contained the clear implication that it lay outside the perimeter.[62]

Acheson had apparently not intended to make a public declaration implying a hands-off South Korea policy. His discussion related mostly to America's position toward the two Chinas. The "defensive perimeter" description was only tangential to his main points, and it was hardly noticed—except, of course, in Seoul (and perhaps, as was later charged, in Pyongyang). Rhee and his government—and KMAG—minutely studied the Acheson transcript with mounting anger. However, when the South Korean ambassador to Washington privately expressed his concern over his country's "apparent exclusion" from Washington's "defensive plans" in the Far East, he was reassured and told not to believe everything he read in the newspapers.[63]

The third bombshell came one week after Acheson's remarks. In a gesture apparently designed to "punish" Truman (or maneuver for a bargaining position), the China bloc in Congress, which had consistently backed the Rhee government, voted down a small ($10 million) supplemental economic aid bill for South Korea. This action by his former stout supporters in Congress bewildered and dismayed Rhee. However, it proved to be but a short-lived crisis. After intense administration lobbying the bill was reintroduced—and passed—the following month, after it had been "sweetened" with a rider granting further (but small) economic aid to Chiang.

Then came the worst bombshell of all: a published Q and A interview with Democratic Senator Tom Connally, who was a friend of the administration and who held the prestigious position of chairman of the Senate Committee on Foreign Relations. Asked by the editors of *U.S. News & World Report* if the United States would seriously consider abandoning South Korea, Connally replied: "I am afraid it is going to be seriously considered because I'm afraid it's going to happen, whether we want it or not." In response to a follow-up question asking if Korea was not an "essential" part of America's defensive strategy, Connally replied: "No. . . . I don't think it is very greatly important."[64]

The Connally interview caused such great dismay in Seoul that Acheson and Muccio were compelled to make public statements containing implied denials that Washington would ever abandon South Korea. But these statements did little to calm the Seoul government. Rhee bitterly and sarcastically complained privately to the American chargé d'affaires in Seoul that Connally's remarks were "an open invitation to the communists to come down and take over South Korea." He wondered how a man "in his right senses" could make "such an irrational statement."[65]

These depressing public utterances were paralleled by a series of equally discouraging secret messages to KMAG from the Pentagon, then coping with the drastic Johnson budget cuts. First came an order which directed Roberts to prepare for a "gradual curtailment" of KMAG activities in South Korea and to halve his staff (from about 500 to 250) by the end of 1950. Next came news that a desperately needed $10 million supplementary military aid bill had been shelved pending further "study" by a Pentagon survey team, which would take months. Finally came word that Roberts's intended replacement, Major General Frank A. Keating, had retired rather than take the KMAG job and no replacement had as yet been found. "KMAG's future," its official historian wrote, "was at best dubious."[66]

*　*　*

At about the time these statements were coming out of Washington, General Roberts commenced a puzzling enterprise. He launched a carefully orchestrated publicity campaign to convince the world that the ROK Army was a superb outfit, capable of meeting any test the North Koreans could impose. His motives for fostering this deception have never been explained. KMAG speculation centered on the following possibilities. The campaign was disinformation designed to offset the quixotic statements coming out of Washington and to intimidate the North Koreans and deter an invasion; rhetoric to justify Washington's apparent decision to disengage militarily from South Korea; cunning distortions to convince Washington that military and economic aid to South Korea had been a good investment and therefore more money and matériel should be allocated; an intentional—or unintentional— need to exaggerate his own personal achievement in his final assignment in the Army in the hope of getting another star upon retirement; a combination of all the above.

Whatever his motives, Roberts was remarkably successful. Assisted by the American ambassador, John Muccio, his first step was to persuade Washington to encourage more VIPs and journalists to visit South Korea. When they began arriving in increasing numbers, Roberts artfully stage-managed the visits and proselytized unabashedly. The visitors were wined, dined, and briefed in Seoul, then escorted to the "field" to see the ROK Army in "action." The field maneuvers were executed by handpicked ROKs, who had been carefully rehearsed about what to do and say.[67]

Glowing reports on the ROK Army were soon flowing into Washington. Republican Senator H. Alexander Smith wrote that the ROKs were "thoroughly capable of taking care of Southern Korea in any possible conflict with the North." Republican Senator William F. Knowland, usually a severe critic of Truman's Far East policies, submitted a similar appraisal. After a visit to South Korea Ambassador-at-large Philip C. Jessup wrote Acheson that he had been "impressed with the smartness of the Korean troops in drill." William C. Foster, deputy administrator of the Economic Cooperation Administration (ECA), gushed: "The rigorous [ROK] training program has built up a well-disciplined force of 100,000 soldiers, one that is prepared to meet any challenge by North Korean forces." Even MacArthur and his staff in Tokyo were apparently taken in. MacArthur urged Army General Leland S. Hobbs, an outstanding division commander in the ETO, to inspect Korea. After the visit Hobbs "went away enthusiastic about the work of KMAG and the Korean Army. . . ." Journalist-author John Gunther, in Tokyo to write a book on MacArthur, was told by GHQ (as he wrote) that if war came in Korea, "the South Korean forces ('The best Army in Asia') could wipe out the North Koreans with no difficulty."[68]

The campaign reached a climax of a sort with a story in the June 5, 1950, issue of *Time* magazine by Far East correspondent Frank Gibney. After a visit to Korea he wrote that thanks to KMAG, the "Americanized" ROK Army was "hard-working" and "first rate." He went on: "Most observers now rate the 100,000-man South Korean Army as the best of its size in Asia . . . and no one now believes that the Russian-trained North Korean Army could pull off a quick, successful invasion of the South without heavy reinforcements."[69]

The official and secret reports on the tactical capabilities of the ROK ground forces by Roberts and Muccio during the spring of 1950 were uniformly upbeat, often glowing. In March 1950 Roberts told the Pentagon that the North Korean troops were definitely "inferior" to the ROK troops. The following month Muccio, addressing a large group of State Department officials in Washington, boasted that progress in training the ROK Army had been "heartening" and had "kept pace" with the North Koreans. In cables to State in May and June of 1950 Muccio described the ROK Army as "superior" to the NKPA in "training, leadership, morale, marksmanship, and better small arms equipment, especially M-1s [rifles]. . . ." On June 23 Muccio's assistant in Seoul, Chargé Everett F. Drumwright, in a cable to State, crowed: "The [South] Korean Army, in particular, has made enormous progress during the past year."[70]

Roberts and Muccio did, however, concede there were some soft spots in the ROK Army: the lack of heavy artillery, antiaircraft defense, and a ROK Air Force. Concurrently with the campaign to tout the ROK Army, they commenced a campaign within a campaign to persuade Washington to help fill these gaps. In the spring of 1950 Roberts's reports to the Pentagon and the press and Muccio's cables to State suddenly began to stress the danger of the NKPA heavy mobile artillery and especially the NKPA Air Force, then estimated to consist of perhaps 100 Russian-built propeller-driven fighters and bombers. North Korean air power, Roberts warned the Pentagon, gave the NKPA a definite edge in the overall balance of military power. In a similar vein, Muccio warned State that North Korean air power could have an "adverse effect" on "actual military operations" and "morale." Both men urged Washington to reverse earlier JCS decisions and help field a ROK Air Force and provide the ROK Army with heavy artillery, antiaircraft weapons, and tanks. But Washington, still fearing Rhee would invade North Korea, remained coolly indifferent.[71]

The net effect of the Roberts campaign was to create the impression that the ROK troops were the best in the Far East and lacked only air power and heavy artillery to be completely invincible. As KMAG internal reports showed, this was far from the truth. There were continuing grave, fundamental weaknesses in the ROK Army, and by June 15, 1950, it was still far from being trained. Only about 25 percent of the ROK Army (sixteen of sixty-seven battalions) had completed battalion-level training and was ready to move on to regimental exercises. Moreover, the widespread corruption in the infrastructure and profligacy in the field had seriously sapped the efficiency and staying power of the ROK Army. The original stockpile of 51 million rounds of small-arms ammo had dwindled to 19 million. Owing to the careless use and loss of spare parts, "35 percent of the vehicles" were out of commission, leaving only 2,100 trucks and jeeps. For the same reasons, "10 to 15 percent" of the weapons were "unusable."[72]

Beyond that, the gravest threat to the ROK Army was not the dubious 100-plane NKPA Air Force but rather its awesome force of 150 Soviet T-34 tanks. In the Roberts campaign in the spring of 1950 the Soviet tanks were scarcely mentioned—and never stressed—either publicly or privately. Tanker Roberts had fostered the belief that Korea was "not good tank country," and apparently for that reason he was not overly concerned about the NKPA armored forces. For an experienced tanker like Roberts, who knew firsthand the terror that German panzer divisions had evoked among some tankless American infantry in the Bulge, his apparent indifference to the NKPA armored forces was simply inexplicable.[73]

## V

The ROK 1st Division, anchoring the left flank of the four-division force deployed at the 38th Parallel, had placed its 12th Regiment at Kaesong, the ancient capital of all Korea. One of its senior KMAG advisers was Army Captain Joseph R. Darrigo, aged thirty. He was a conscientious, competent adviser, one of the few in KMAG who liked duty in Korea.

By late June 1950 Darrigo had been at the 38th Parallel for almost six months, a "record" tour in the revolving-door KMAG. He rightly believed that he had become an expert on the ROK Army and the opposing NKPA. Darrigo's perception of the situation was starkly clear. The NKPA was without any doubt preparing for invasion at any moment. His war warnings had made no discernible impression on KMAG or Seoul. Despite all his tactful prodding, his outfit—and the ROK Army—was still not properly alerted and disposed for battle. There was still no sense of alarm or urgency. Half or more of the 1st Division troops were on pass or furlough; only one rifle company of Darrigo's 12th Regiment was deployed at the parallel.[74]

During the month of May 1950 Darrigo's deep concern intensified. From January to May "border incidents" had continued unabatedly. During one week, March 3 to March 10, there had been eighteen "incidents," as well as twenty-nine major guerrilla raids in South Korea. But in May border incidents and guerrilla raids suddenly dropped off sharply, North Korean civilians were evacuated from the border zone, and the NKPA mysteriously removed the railroad tracks leading from Kaesong north to Pyongyang. In early June Radio Pyongyang began broadcasting propaganda ostensibly aimed at fostering a peaceful unification of Korea. Darrigo's well-developed military instinct led him to believe that all these signs, especially the sudden lull in enemy aggression, probably meant the NKPA was making final preparations and troop dispositions for an all-out attack on South Korea, but his analyses and alerts continued to make no impression on KMAG or the Rhee government.[75]

One reason was that Darrigo's alerts were probably lost in the Niagara of similar war alerts from South Korean and American intelligence sources. Since Rhee was prone to cry wolf, the alerts were not believed in Tokyo and Washington. In an analysis in March 1950 MacArthur's G-2 (intelligence chief), Charles A. Willoughby, cabled the Pentagon that he foresaw continued guerrilla and psychological warfare in Korea but that "there will be no civil war in Korea this spring or summer." At about the same time Joe Collins's G-2 in the Pentagon, Alexander R. Bolling, wrote that "Communist military measures in Korea will be held in abeyance pending the outcome of their programs in other areas, particularly Southeast Asia." Dean Acheson later stated that intelligence specialists in Tokyo, at the Pentagon, at the Central Intelligence Agency (CIA), and at State were "in agreement that the possibility for an attack on the Korean Republic existed at that time but they were all in agreement that its launching in the summer of 1950 did not appear imminent."[76]

By this time Darrigo was sharing his house with his young, newly arrived KMAG assistant, Lieutenant William E. Hamilton. On Saturday afternoon, June 24 (Korean time), Hamilton decided he would drive down to Seoul to "pick up supplies" and, perhaps, enjoy a night on the town. When Darrigo went to bed that night he felt distinctly lonely; he was the only American Army officer at the 38th Parallel.[77]

At about three-thirty on Sunday morning Darrigo was jarred awake by the crash of close artillery fire. He sat bolt upright and listened intently. At first he believed it to be the South Koreans firing their 105-mm snub-nosed "infantry cannons" at NKPA positions. But as the noise increased in fury, he realized it was not South but North Korean artillery. Moreover, it was not the usual sporadic harassing border fire. It was heavy, continuous, and alarming.

Was this *it?* Darrigo asked himself. *Invasion?*

He pulled on his trousers and ran outside to get a better look. He could see the muzzle flashes reflected on low-lying dark clouds, which presaged the onset of the rainy season. The guns were close and seemingly firing without letup. Then he heard a tattoo of small-arms fire, the unmistakable advance of infantry. Bullets whined all around him and thudded into the stone house.

Darrigo grabbed his shirt and shoes and jumped into his jeep, his Korean houseboy on his heels. Still shirtless and shoeless, he drove the jeep down twisting, dusty roads, south toward downtown Kaesong. In the middle of town at a traffic circle he stopped suddenly, mouth agape. Pulling into the railroad station was a fifteen-car North Korean train, jammed with infantry—some hanging on the sides. Sometime during the evening the NKPA had relaid the railroad tracks!

The train—and the large numbers of NKPA soldiers—was proof to Darrigo that this was no "rice raid" or minor border incident. It was obviously a meticulously planned, highly professional military attack, the real thing. And like Pearl Harbor, he thought, it had come on a Sunday morning without warning. The NKPA movement by train into Kaesong had cannily outflanked Darrigo's thinly deployed 12th Regiment. The outfit did not stand a chance, and there was no way Darrigo could get back to its CP to offer his advice.

The North Korean soldiers—a full infantry regiment—detrained and almost immediately spotted Darrigo. They opened fire with Russian-made rifles, carbines, and pistols. With bullets whistling all around the open jeep, Darrigo sped out of Kaesong, southbound. Like a Paul Revere, he drove through the night to spread the alarm. Thirty minutes later he reached headquarters of the ROK 1st Division, located in a heavily fenced compound just south of the Imjin River near Munsan. Unable to raise the sleeping headquarters guards, Darrigo doggedly and noisily rammed the jeep against the heavy wooden gate until he got a response.

The young (thirty-year-old) commander of the ROK 1st Division, Colonel Paik Sun Yup, was able and dedicated. Unfortunately he and his KMAG adviser, Darrigo's immediate boss, Lieutenant Colonel Lloyd H. Rockwell, were in Seoul for the weekend. However, Paik's headquarters quickly found and alerted Paik, and he in turn found and roused Rockwell. Shortly after dawn both men joined Darrigo at the 1st ROK Division headquarters.[78]

When Paik began issuing orders, his three regiments were disposed as follows. The 12th was at the parallel near Kaesong, outflanked by the train-borne NKPA soldiers and apparently overrun. The 13th was about fifteen miles east of Kaesong and the 11th was in reserve near Seoul. Paik ordered the 11th to move rapidly forward to positions behind the Imjin River. For the next two days the 11th and 13th ROK regiments would fight valiantly at the Imjin in a vain attempt to hold back nearly two full NKPA divisions, whose attack was led by a battalion of T-34 Russian tanks.[79]

This NKPA attack was powerful and determined, but the main attack came as expected, in the Uijongbu Corridor. Two full NKPA divisions, each spearheaded by forty T-34 tanks and other mechanized vehicles and supported by 120-mm howitzers, hit the ROK 7th Division. The ROKs reeled, recovered, then mounted a surprisingly stout defense. As planned, Seoul ordered the 2d Division to move rapidly forward from Taejon to reinforce this critical corridor. But the 2d could not get there in time. The 7th was forced to give way. It fell back on Uijongbu, thereby exposing the right flank of Paik's 1st Division, which was holding along the Imjin River, and forcing Paik to fall back toward Seoul.

Farther east, in the hills of mid-Korea, elements of two other NKPA divisions simultaneously struck the ROK 6th Division. As with Paik's 1st, only two regiments were on the line; but as it happened, he had not issued any weekend passes, and these regiments were at full strength. Besides that, the ROK 6th Division had unusually good artillery units. Its forward elements, some fighting from concrete pillboxes, held, giving the commanders time to rush the reserve regiment forward from Wonju, forty miles south. The division inflicted harsh casualties on the NKPA regiments and might have held longer, but the collapse of the ROK 7th Division at Uijongbu exposed its distant left flank, also forcing it to withdraw.

There were two other subsidiary D day NKPA attacks on the extreme flanks. West of Paik's 1st Division, on the Ongjin peninsula, which juts into the Yellow Sea, a strong NKPA force attacked the lone 17th ROK Regiment, commanded by Paik's younger brother. One ROK battalion was overrun and decimated, but the other two evacuated as planned (the ROKs correctly did not consider the peninsula defensible) on three LSTs. On the opposite side of Korea, on the mountainous east coast bordering the Sea of Japan, the NKPA simultaneously hit the widely dispersed and understrength ROK 8th Division, both frontally and by multiple amphibious assaults on its coastal flanks. Caught in a well-executed land-sea envelopment, the division was powerless to mount an effective defense, and was soon forced to withdraw.

During these well-planned and well-executed quadruple assaults the

NKPA Air Force was out in full force, about 100 planes. Some of the bombers attacked Seoul and its airport, Kimpo, causing panic among the civilians. Some of the fighters bombed and strafed ROK Army forces. But the NKPA Air Force's contribution to the battle was slight. Contrary to the predictions of Roberts and Muccio, the ROK soldiers did not panic; they all but ignored the planes. Of far greater menace and effectiveness were the Russian T-34 tanks. The NKPA made a mockery of Roberts's judgment that Korea was "not good tank country." The T-34s rolled southward, easily and relentlessly, creating terror and panic among most ROK units. But not all. About ninety of Paik's 1st Division troopers died valiantly in suicidal attempts to destroy the tanks with satchel charges and other makeshift explosive devices.

Seventy-two hours after the NKPA invasion had begun, it was obvious to Joe Darrigo and his KMAG cohorts that the battle to stop the NKPA invasion was lost. The causes for this disaster were numerous, but the main ones were Truman's inability to grasp grand strategy—to back American foreign policy with adequate military power—and his battery commander's view that he was a victim of Pentagon budget flimflams. South Korea obviously required a continuing American military presence to ensure its survival until the embryonic ROK Army had matured and been properly equipped. Truman's crippling cuts in the Army's budget had compelled a premature American withdrawal from South Korea, leaving that new and unstable nation ripe for conquest. The inexplicable and ill-advised public statements by Acheson and Connally in the spring of 1950 may well have encouraged Moscow and Pyongyang to proceed when they did. The timing may also have been prompted by the status of training in the ROK and American Eighth armies. Further delays would have confronted the NKPA with a better-trained ROK Army and, should America intervene (as MacArthur had promised Rhee he would) a better-trained Eighth Army. Whatever the case, considering the strategic situation that existed, an NKPA invasion on June 25, 1950, was bound to succeed.

# PART
# TWO

# Drawing a Line

# MOMENTOUS
# DECISIONS

## I

The news of the NKPA invasion of South Korea first reached Washington via a United Press wire service story from Seoul. It arrived in the early evening of Saturday, June 24 (eastern daylight saving time is thirteen hours "behind" Seoul time), followed shortly thereafter by a secret cable alert from Ambassador Muccio. Many governmental officials, including President Truman and Secretary of State Dean Acheson, were away for the weekend. Louis Johnson and JCS Chairman Omar Bradley had only just arrived back that day after a grueling flight from Tokyo. Bradley was sick in bed with an intestinal "bug."[1]

At about 9:20 P.M. Acheson telephoned Truman, who was in Independence, Missouri, to say that while the reports were still fragmentary, the news from South Korea appeared to be "serious." He suggested that as a first step the United States should summon the United Nations Security Council into emergency session the following day, Sunday, and press for a condemnation of North Korea, together with a demand for a cease-fire and an NKPA withdrawal to the 38th Parallel. Truman approved this suggestion, and later that night Acheson set the machinery in motion at the Department of State.[2]

The news came as a shock. Believing that communism was a worldwide monolith controlled by Moscow, Washington assumed that North Korea would not invade South Korea except on the specific orders of Joseph Stalin. Up to this point in the cold war Stalin had not resorted to overt military hostilities to achieve the apparent Kremlin aim of communizing the world. What did this resort to force portend? All-out war? If so, why begin in South Korea? Was the invasion merely a military feint designed to draw the West's

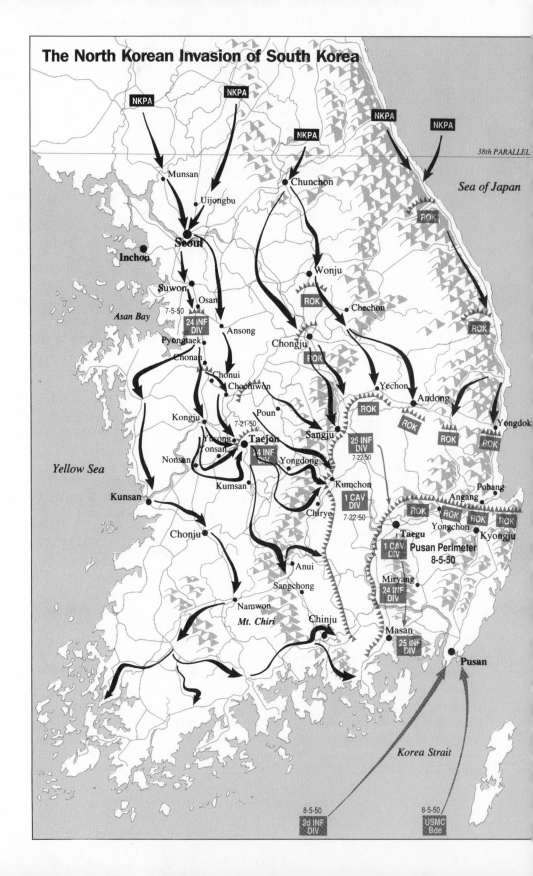

military forces into the maw of Asian mainland? Would the real Soviet move come in Western Europe? The Middle East?[3]

As Truman mulled these questions, his dander rose. The United States had been pushed around for five years. Truman had worked tirelessly to achieve a thaw in the cold war and to build the United Nations into an effective forum for settling international disputes. As he saw it, Stalin had worked just as tirelessly to prevent a thaw and to subvert the United Nations. Raw, naked military aggression in South Korea, a new country sponsored and supported by the United Nations, was the ultimate Stalinist subversion and affront.[4]

Truman's recent biographer Robert J. Donovan wrote that he "had an appetite, too much of a one, really, for unhesitating decision." The NKPA invasion, Donovan asserted, "was a blow [which] he felt personally" and which had "uncapped his ample reserves of anger and righteous indignation." Even before returning to Washington to consult with his chief foreign policy and military advisers, Truman had made up his mind. "We are going to fight," he said to his daughter, Margaret. "We can't let the U.N. down," he told an aide. To another, he said: "By God, I'm going to let them have it."[5]

Truman was foremost a political animal, and his decision to get tough with Moscow was no doubt strongly influenced by this background. He had won a stunning political victory in 1948, but ever since then his popularity had been slipping. The China Lobby had firmly implanted the idea that the "loss" of China to communism was Truman's fault because in foreign policy he was "soft on communism." Senator Joseph R. McCarthy had recently launched the shameful era that would bear his name, charging that Truman was "soft on communism" domestically as well, that the federal government was infested with Communist spies, fellow travelers, and pinkos. The recent sensational trials of Judith Coplon, Alger Hiss, and the British-employed nuclear physicist Klaus Fuchs (which led to exposure of the American Rosenberg-Gold-Greenglass "atomic spy" network) had lent credence to McCarthy's charges. In the existing domestic political climate the "loss" of South Korea to communism would have been politically catastrophic for Truman and the Democratic party.[6]

Dean Acheson, then a prime target of the McCarthyites for "harboring" and "coddling" Communists in State and for publicly defending Alger Hiss, also reacted hawkishly. In fact, he emerged in the Korean crisis as the most ardent hawk in the administration. His position, which amounted to an abrupt turnabout, has not been satisfactorily explained. To be sure, it reflected the views of the president. However, Acheson consistently exceeded Truman in bellicosity. His reaction may have been partly political: to avert the inevitable domestic outcry over another "loss" to communism. It may have been partly personal: to disprove the charges of his critics that he personally was soft on communism. It may have been partly bureaucratic: to force the implementation of his cherished but pigeonholed rearmament program contained in NSC-68 and, as an offshoot, increased aid to NATO. It may have been partly guilt: State, solely responsible for South Korea, had not provided it adequate military backup in response to KMAG's imprecations, and Acheson himself had, by implication, publicly written off South Korea.

Acheson advised Truman to stay put in Independence on Sunday, June 25, until better information could be obtained and analyzed. Meanwhile, the senior leaders at the Pentagon and State rushed to their offices that Sunday. Louis Johnson and Omar Bradley had a prior commitment to attend an aircraft carrier demonstration that afternoon in Norfolk with Forrest Sherman. However, before leaving, Bradley conferred in the Pentagon with Army Chief of Staff Joe Collins, who had rushed back from his Chesapeake Bay weekend retreat, and others. Collins had a special responsibility that day. Earlier the secretary of defense and the JCS had "divided up" responsibility for possible theaters of war. The Army had been appointed "Executive Agent" for the Far East. The secretary of the Army and the Army chief of staff were thus responsible for assessing the situation there and for making recommendations to the JCS and Louis Johnson.[7]

The Army had a brand-new secretary, Frank Pace, Jr., who had replaced Gordon Gray on April 19. When he took office, Pace was only thirty-seven years old, the second youngest man in the history of the Army to hold that post. He was a tall, skinny, glib, handsome, glad-handing, wealthy lawyer-politician from Arkansas who (the rumors went) would help Louis Johnson's 1952 presidential bid in the South. A graduate of Princeton, Pace had been an Air Force transport pilot in World War II. After the war he had become a rising star in the Truman administration, serving an apprenticeship in the Justice and Post Office departments before moving over to the Bureau of the Budget. There he soon became right-hand man to Budget Director James E. Webb, a dedicated fiscal conservative who was the administration's foremost advocate for cutting Pentagon budgets. In early 1949, when Truman appointed Webb to be undersecretary of state to Acheson, young Pace had replaced Webb as budget director and, as such, had been an important adviser to Louis Johnson in the latter's fiscal assault on the Pentagon. As secretary of the Army Pace was in a good position to continue advising Johnson on ways to cut the "fat" out of the Army.

The Paces were attractive, social, and much sought as dinner guests in Washington circles. When the first alert came from Seoul that Saturday night, they were at columnist Joe Alsop's for an elegant dinner, along with Assistant Secretary of State for Far East Affairs Dean Rusk. Pace was known as a "quick study," but, as he later conceded, "I wasn't a military expert at all." He had not been on the job long enough (a mere two months) to have developed a grasp of the Army or grand strategy. Like Navy Secretary Frank Matthews and the newly appointed Air Force secretary, Thomas K. Finletter, Pace was a babe in the cold war woods. During the Korean crisis his contribution was to be slight.[8]

In an entirely different class was Joe Collins's "general manager," the able, experienced, tough-minded paratrooper hero Matt Ridgway. When the alert came, he had been off on a long weekend boondoggle—his first break from his man-killing Pentagon job in nine months—in Pennsylvania, "inspecting" the 28th National Guard Division. His attractive new young wife, Mary Princess (nicknamed Penny), who had recently given birth to a son, Matthew, Jr., had accompanied him. They had rushed back to their Fort Myer quarters, and by Sunday morning Ridgway was back at his Pentagon desk. From that moment onward Ridgway, by virtue of his job and the force of his personality, became Collins's principal adviser and executive for the Army's role in the Korean War.[9]

Ridgway may well have been the most outspoken hawk in Washington. He had first encountered Russians in the ETO when his XVIII Airborne Corps met them face-to-face near the Baltic Sea at the end of the war. There, despite the celebrations and exchange of gifts and vodka toasts, Ridgway had developed a deep distrust of the Red Army and the Kremlin. This distrust had been intensified during his two-year postwar tour as Eisenhower's personal representative at the United Nations, where almost daily he had to confront Soviet diplomatic intrigues, intransigence, and duplicity. He had formed an unflinching belief that the Kremlin's principal postwar aim was to conquer America— and the world—and his well-reasoned top secret reports to Eisenhower making that case, which circulated all through government, had been influential in hardening Washington's attitude toward Moscow in 1946 and 1947.[10]

When the alert from Seoul was telephoned to Ridgway in Pennsylvania, his first thought was that the NKPA invasion of South Korea might well be "the beginning of World War III . . . Armageddon, the last great battle between East and West." He rushed back to the Pentagon and directed his senior assistants to keep a sharp eye out for Soviet military movements in Western Europe and the Middle East. He urged Collins—and Omar Bradley— to recommend to Truman that the nation go to "immediate partial mobilization," reasoning thus: "If we take this action and war does *not* come, we have lost money. If we do not take it and war *does* come, we risk disaster."[11]

* * *

All that day, Sunday, Washington planners and policymakers huddled in urgent conferences. These early discussions were influenced to no small degree by the Roberts-Muccio view that the ROK Army was the best army in Asia and could handle the NKPA. That belief was reinforced that day by a memo from Bradley to the JCS. During his recent trip to Tokyo he had spent nearly an hour on June 20 in conference with Lynn Roberts, who was in Tokyo on his way home to retirement. In this private soldier-to-soldier talk, Roberts had assured Bradley the ROK Army could "meet any test the North Koreans imposed on it." Bradley memoed the JCS for planning purposes: "After my talk with General Roberts, I am of the opinion that South Korea will not fall in the present attack unless the Russians actively participate in the action."[12]

The confidence in the ROKs was reinforced by an urgent cable from John Muccio. Owing to the departure of Roberts (not yet replaced) and KMAG Chief of Staff W. H. Sterling Wright (in Tokyo, also preparing to go home), Muccio had assumed the role of military adviser to the ROK Army. "Ammunition is critically needed," he wrote, "to meet situation. . . ." He had simultaneously asked MacArthur to ship him a ten-day supply immediately and begged Acheson to "back up" his request. Not to do so would be "catastrophic," he went on, concluding on this upbeat note: "I am confident that if adequately supplied, ROK security forces will fight bravely and with distinction."[13]

Confidence in the ROK Army was further reinforced that day by MacArthur's G-2, Charles Willoughby. It was contained in the first telecon* between Collins and Ridgway in the Pentagon and Willoughby in Tokyo. When Collins and Ridgway queried Willoughby about the situation in South Korea, Willoughby conceded that it was a major NKPA invasion aimed at conquering South Korea but that the ROK Army was withdrawing with "orderliness," the morale of the South Koreans was "good," and the Rhee government was "standing firm." Nonetheless, Willoughby "said," GHQ was proceeding with a prearranged contingency plan to evacuate American personnel (women and children first) by ship from Seoul's seaport, Inchon, with appropriate air and naval protection.[14]

This first telecon contained a historically fascinating sidelight. Without consulting Truman, that day both GHQ, Tokyo, and the Pentagon decided independently to respond affirmatively to Muccio's request for a ten-day supply of ammo for the ROK Army. When he received the request, MacArthur ordered his chief of staff, Ned Almond, to load two ships immediately. In the telecon Collins asked Willoughby if he was correct in assuming Tokyo was meeting Muccio's request. Willoughby replied: "We are meeting emergency

---

*A telecon, or teletype conference, was conducted by displaying, on both ends, a blowup of the typewritten questions and answers on a big, movielike screen. This way of communicating enabled large numbers of assistants to sit in the auditorium with the major participants and thereby obtain an instant picture of the situation, thinking, and decisions. Besides Collins and Ridgway, there were twenty other officers observing the exchange in the Pentagon, including the entire uniformed upper echelon of the Army. MacArthur's absence on the Tokyo end was taken for granted; Willoughby, a Bataan Gang veteran, obviously spoke for him.

request for ammunition." The two ships would be escorted by air and naval vessels. Thus the Pentagon and GHQ, Tokyo, had made the decision to project American military power into South Korea without presidential authorization.[15]

The misplaced confidence in the ROK Army was even further reinforced later that day in a heroically optimistic cable from Muccio. He reported that while the "hard-fighting ROK ground forces" had been surprised and "knocked off balance," they had "made a gallant comeback by midnight and seem to have stabilized situation." He went on to say: "I can give assurances that Korean GIs have given extremely good account of themselves, and I am confident they will not be found wanting in the tests to come. But it is obviously essential that we give them not only adequate but sustained aid."[16]

All these misleading reports about the ROK Army caused the Pentagon initially to reach unrealistic conclusions on what might be needed to "save" South Korea. "Outside" ground forces would not be required; American air and sea power, backing the ROK Army, would be sufficient.

## II

Truman returned to Washington that Sunday evening, June 25. En route he summoned his chief Pentagon and State advisers to a meeting that night at Blair House, the president's temporary home and office during the renovation of the White House. Thirteen senior officials gathered at Blair House for a fried chicken dinner and urgent talks. Of the thirteen, the majority—eight—were from the Pentagon. These included Louis Johnson and Omar Bradley, returned from the aircraft carrier demonstration in Norfolk, the three service secretaries—Frank Matthews, Frank Pace, and Tom Finletter—and the three military chiefs—Collins, Vandenberg, and Sherman.[17]

Confident that the ROK Army would push back the NKPA, the Pentagon contingent had a larger Far East worry that night: Formosa. Recently the Chinese Communists had taken Hainan Island and had amassed 200,000 troops on the mainland opposite Formosa. The Pentagon advisers believed that the NKPA invasion in Korea might possibly be a feint to divert attention and resources from a Chinese Communist invasion of Formosa. Johnson and Bradley, armed with a long and eloquent study paper from MacArthur urging American support for Formosa, took advantage of the crisis atmosphere to push for a reversal of the Truman-Acheson hands-off Formosa policy. On Johnson's instructions, the ailing Bradley read the entire MacArthur paper, and Johnson recommended (as the JCS had the previous December) that an American survey team be authorized to go to Formosa to find out what was required to maintain the security of the island.[18]

This opening thrust was quickly deflected, and the discussion properly turned to the larger picture: Stalin and the Kremlin. What did Stalin's decision to resort to "raw aggression" portend? Bradley speculated. He did not think Stalin was "ready" for global war; the Kremlin was probably "testing" America's spiritual resolve to its containment rhetoric. However, Bradley went on, this major escalation in the cold war was a "moral outrage" which the United States and United Nations could not countenance. To knuckle under in this test, he said, would be tantamount to "appeasement." One act of appeasement could lead to further acts and hence almost inevitably to global war. "We must draw the line somewhere," Bradley concluded, and Korea "offered as good an occasion for drawing the line as anywhere else."[19]

All fourteen men present, including most emphatically President Truman and Dean Acheson, were of like mind. All the prior policies set forth in various position papers, reached after years of careful study—that South Korea was of little strategic importance and should not be a casus belli—were summarily dismissed. On June 24, 1950, South Korea had suddenly become an area of vital importance, not strategically or militarily (as Acheson would write in his memoirs) but psychologically and symbolically. Stalin had chosen that place to escalate cold war to hot war. The line would be drawn. South Korea would be supported, not because its conquest would directly threaten America's vital interests but because a failure to meet Stalin's challenge there would be so morally derelict it might fatally damage America's prestige and lead to a collapse of the free world's will to resist Communist aggression in places that really counted.

The conferees next wrestled with these questions: How much help? What form should it take? There was a stingy approach to the problem: Minimize, not maximize, the commitment. Finally, they agreed on the following steps, to be carried out with utmost haste under the "guise of aid" to the UN, which that day had condemned the NKPA invasion and invited "all members" to help the ROKs.

• MacArthur would proceed (as he was already doing) with sending "ammunition and equipment" to the ROKs in order to help "prevent the loss" of Seoul.
• MacArthur would rush a "survey party" to South Korea to find out what other military aid the ROKs might need to hold Seoul.
• MacArthur would provide "such naval and air action" as was necessary to prevent the loss of Seoul partly under the guise of ensuring "safe evacuation of United States dependents and non-combatants."
• The Navy's Seventh Fleet, then at Subic Bay in the Philippines, would proceed to Sasebo, Japan, to augment MacArthur's thin naval forces.[20]

The White House announcements of these decisions were deliberately understated. There was no indication or implication that America was embarked on the road to war. America was merely humanely responding to a United Nations request for limited assistance to South Korea. So informed, the American public reacted favorably. To most citizens Korea was a blank spot on the map. But wherever Korea might be, Truman was correct: Joe Stalin and his Communist minions had been shoving the free world around long enough. A line had to be drawn someplace.[21]

\* \* \*

Misled by Roberts and Muccio, MacArthur and his GHQ continued to take a casual view of the situation in South Korea. On the first day of the alert Acheson's special representative John Foster Dulles, who was in Tokyo working on the Japanese peace treaty and who had recently visited South Korea, called on MacArthur to express his concern. Curiously MacArthur told Dulles the exact opposite of what his G-2, Willoughby, had told the Pentagon: that the NKPA attack was "not an all-out effort" to subjugate South Korea. He went on to assure Dulles confidently that the ROK Army "would gain victory." In a memo describing this encounter and his ensuing experience in Tokyo, Dulles wrote that two full days elapsed before GHQ realized the NKPA attack was "serious."[22]

On the following day, June 26 in Tokyo, MacArthur received the four-point directive which had been drawn up and approved at the Blair House meeting. Since he had already ordered the ammunition to be sent to South Korea and alerted his air and naval forces to provide protection for the evacuation of the 2,000 American civilians from Seoul and could do nothing about the Seventh Fleet except await its arrival, that left only one unfulfilled item: dispatching the "survey party" to South Korea to find out what was going on and determine what else the ROKs might need. The very same afternoon MacArthur chose a GHQ section chief, Brigadier General John H. Church, to command the party (twelve other officers and two enlisted men) and told him to go to Korea immediately.[23]

John Church was then only several days shy of his fifty-eighth birthday, older even than JCS Chairman Omar Bradley. He was "homey" and "frail" and sick, almost crippled by arthritis. To relieve the agonizing pain, he kept a bottle of whiskey close at hand. Although far from well, Church was not lacking in courage. As a young lieutenant in World War I he had twice been wounded leading infantry units in the trenches. In World War II, as chief of staff of the crack 45th Infantry Division, he had been in the thick of the fighting in Sicily, at Salerno, at Anzio (where he temporarily commanded an infantry regiment), and in southern France. Later, as assistant division commander (ADC) of Alex Bolling's 84th Infantry Division in the ETO, he had fought in

Holland and Germany, where he was wounded for the third time. In the two world wars Church had won a DSC and two Silver Stars for heroism, plus a host of other medals.

To many, however, it seemed that Church's time had come and gone, that to send him off to yet another war at his age and in his poor state of health was unfair and unwise. MacArthur, who had turned seventy in January, apparently did not share that view. One result was that by and large, Army officers sent to Korea were older and, in some cases, less robust than their World War II counterparts.[24]*

*       *       *

While the Church party was en route by air to Seoul's Kimpo Airport, Truman met a second time with his advisers at Blair House on the night of June 26, Washington time. The news from South Korea was still fragmentary, but what was there, Joe Collins reported, was now "bad." The ROK Army was crumbling. The Rhee government had apparently abandoned Seoul to the NKPA. The fat little ROK Army chief of staff, General Chae, Collins said, had "no fight left in him." Truman, almost in despair, said, "I don't want to go to war," but he insisted that America had to do all in its power to help the South Koreans. American military aid had to be escalated.[25]

For the first time there was serious talk of committing American ground forces. Louis Johnson and Omar Bradley cautioned against that step. Bradley said (and Collins agreed) that if American ground forces were committed to South Korea, there would have to be a general "mobilization," including a call-up of the National Guard and Reserves, so the Army could meet its commitments elsewhere. Bradley suggested that it might be preferable to wait a "few days" before doing that. The president and Acheson agreed, and the conferees decided to inform MacArthur explicitly that the use of American ground forces in South Korea was "not authorized."

Before this second Blair House meeting, George Kennan had reached the conclusion, based in part on ambassadorial intelligence reports, in part on intuition, that Moscow would probably limit overt aggression to the Far East but that it might be multipronged. As Johnson and the JCS had been warning, Formosa could be a "likely" target. Kennan's views, together with those of the

---

*At the time of the Normandy invasion Eisenhower was fifty-three, Bradley fifty-one. Army Chief of Staff George Marshall (then sixty-three) believed strongly that younger men should command in the field, but seniority and other factors tied his hands. Hence the three American Army commanders at Normandy were considered "old": Courtney Hodges (First), fifty-seven; George Patton (Third) fifty-eight; William H. Simpson (Ninth) fifty-six. Fifth Army commander Mark Clark and his classmate Joe Collins (in line for ETO Army command), both forty-eight, more nearly fitted Marshall's age criterion.

JCS, had caused Acheson to regard the Formosa problem with greater concern. Conceivably Chiang might even take advantage of the crisis to stage a "return to the mainland," fatally exacerbating the military crisis in the Far East.

Hence, that night and later the ever-hawkish Acheson began to view Korea and Formosa as a related problem. He therefore recommended that Formosa be "neutralized" by American sea power. Truman and the other conferees agreed to this and to several other, more bellicose measures:

- Air Force and Navy planes operating over South Korea in support of the evacuation of American civilians through Kimpo Airfield and Inchon would be directed to go "all-out" in "fullest" support of the ROK Army, but operating only *south* of the 38th Parallel.
- The Seventh Fleet would be diverted from its destination (Sasebo, Japan) to the Formosa Strait, where it would prevent a Communist attack on Formosa or a Nationalist attack on the mainland. A special carrier task force would be sent to Japan in lieu of the Seventh Fleet.
- MacArthur would be placed in command of all American forces operating in, over, or around South Korea as well as of the Seventh Fleet at Formosa.[26]

## III

En route to Kimpo Airfield, the John Church party received a warning that Kimpo might be in enemy hands. Accordingly, the pilot diverted to an airfield at Suwon, about twenty miles south of Seoul. By the time the plane landed, at 7:00 P.M. on June 27, Korean time, the JCS had delegated MacArthur command of all American forces then in South Korea, and MacArthur had radioed Church that his party would henceforth bear the more imposing—and martial—title "GHQ Advance Command (ADCOM)."[27]

Church found South Korea in utter chaos. The Rhee government had indeed abandoned Seoul. Rhee was temporarily in Suwon but preparing to withdraw to Taejon, a railroad hub sixty-five miles south of Suwon. KMAG had disintegrated; its personnel were evacuating with the civilians or straggling all over Korea. The road south from Seoul was jammed with fleeing ROK soldiers, thousands of refugees, and a few reporters and photographers. The fleeing ROKs had hastily and stupidly blown the bridge over the Han River, just south of the city of Seoul. In so doing, the ROKs had cut off thousands of their own troops and most of their heavy weapons, transport, and supplies.[28]

Having been misled about the quality of the ROK Army, Church was flabbergasted to find it in total rout. He later wrote that he attributed the collapse to "lack of leadership . . . rather than fear." In the fighting most of the ROK officer corps, never strong to begin with, had melted away. Many ROK soldiers were eager to stand and fight, but they didn't know how or where; they were leaderless. The worst offender was the fat little ROK chief of staff, General Chae, who had abandoned Seoul with Rhee, leaving his troops to fend for themselves.[29]

Church had come to South Korea merely to gather facts, but the circumstances he encountered led him to upgrade his role drastically. In effect, John Church assumed command and direction of the tattered ROK Army and the defense of South Korea. As he and his staff saw the situation, the best—indeed, the only—option left was to throw up a strong defense on the south bank of the Han River. During that night all effort was directed toward that single laudable, but very ambitious, objective. However, by dawn on June 28 (his birthday) Church realized that in view of the paucity of ROK infantry and a complete lack of heavy weapons, the objective was beyond his capability.[30]

That morning he conveyed the bad news to MacArthur by radio. He told GHQ, Tokyo, that the ROK Army was incapable of restoring the status quo ante bellum in South Korea. In order to recapture Seoul and reestablish ROK positions at the 38th Parallel, Church said (as he wrote later) that "it would be necessary to employ American ground forces." The response to this momentous conclusion was a cryptic message from Tokyo informing him that a "high-ranking" officer would arrive at Suwon on the following morning if the airfield was usable. Realizing that the "high-ranking" officer could only be MacArthur, Church told GHQ that so far Suwon was still in friendly hands but to exercise utmost caution.[31]

Early the next morning, June 29, MacArthur, wearing his famous stained World War II campaign hat and carrying his equally famous corncob pipe, flew to Suwon with a planeload of staff and some reporters. By this time the gravity of the situation in South Korea had finally begun to sink in at GHQ, and MacArthur was in a hawkish mood. En route he decided on a course of action that would, for the second time, exceed his authority and directives and considerably intensify the scope and degree of the American commitment to the war. Calling his air chief, General George E. Stratemeyer, into private conference, MacArthur directed him to launch his Far East Air Force (FEAF) across the 38th Parallel to bomb North Korean airfields. Without objection Stratemeyer immediately radioed his headquarters from MacArthur's plane: "Take out North Korean airfields immediately. No publicity." Perhaps anticipating the incredulity this order might evoke at FEAF headquarters, Stratemeyer added: "MacArthur approves."[32]

This impulsive order was not only a brazen overstepping of MacArthur's authority but also foolish. The NKPA Air Force was not a big threat in the Korean War. The big threat was NKPA tanks. What was needed most at that crucial moment was a concentration of American air power at the Han River, where the NKPA armor was massing to cross. MacArthur's order had the effect of gearing almost the whole of Stratemeyer's air power for an attack in the wrong direction. Later that day John Church persuaded MacArthur to rescind the order and concentrate American air power at the Han River. However, the stream of conflicting and changing orders to FEAF had the effect of diluting the air attacks at the Han, and they were deemed to be of limited success.[33]

MacArthur and his party, which included his chief of staff, Ned Almond, remained on the ground in South Korea for about eight hours. The day commenced with a briefing in Church's ADCOM headquarters, which was attended by Rhee, Muccio, Chae, and others. Rhee summed up the situation well: "We're in a hell of a fix." After lunch MacArthur decided that he wanted to see the Han River battlefield with his own eyes. Accordingly, the party piled into "broken-down cars" and proceeded northward on the Seoul highway, against a tide of thousands of fleeing refugees and ROK soldiers. Observing the ROK soldiers closely, MacArthur pronounced a harsh judgment on the ROK Army: "I haven't seen a single wounded man yet."[34]

When the motorcade neared the south bank of the Han River, MacArthur got out and climbed a hill for a better view. Beyond the river he could see dense smoke arising from Seoul, now occupied by the NKPA. While enemy mortar shells fell close, MacArthur later wrote, he reached two momentous conclusions: American ground forces must be committed immediately to save South Korea, and an amphibious envelopment at Inchon, or some such site on Korea's west coast, would ultimately be needed to defeat the NKPA. That evening he told both John Church and a news correspondent, Marguerite Higgins of the *New York Herald Tribune,* that he would recommend to President Truman that American ground forces be immediately dispatched to South Korea.[35]

Recent meticulous scholarship by military historians D. Clayton James and Ronald H. Spector has shown that MacArthur, acting impulsively, made a number of judgmental and tactical errors in World War II which needlessly expended hundreds of American lives. But those lapses could be classed as minor compared with his decision to recommend the commitment of American ground forces in support of South Korea at this time. It was one of the most ill-conceived decisions in the history of the professional American military establishment.[36]

The decision was wrong for two principal reasons. First, it would commit American GIs to fighting Asians on the Asian mainland. Most professional military men had, as Forrest Sherman later put it, "grown up believing that course should be avoided if possible." The historical correctness of this generalization had been amply borne out in World War II, when the Allies had bogged down in miserable, costly, and largely fruitless military campaigns in Burma and China. Secondly, it would entail the use of Eighth Army troops, who were, in terms of training and equipment, pitifully unprepared for battle.[37]

Even if Eighth Army had been in a superb state of readiness and training, there was certain to be great risk and loss of life in the initial baptism of fire. Army experience in World Wars I and II had shown that except in rare cases, "every unit breaks on initial contact" with the enemy, as one four-star general and Army chief of staff put it. Flinging untrained, understrength, ill-equipped Eighth Army units into a fluid, crumbling front in South Korea would deny them the recommended opportunity to face enemy fire gradually and build the essential confidence and camaraderie required of a successful fighting unit.[38]

In reaching this decision, MacArthur may have been strongly influenced by the military superiority complex endemic in the American Army in 1950. The Army had only recently destroyed the Axis in a series of magnificent campaigns spread all over the globe. Owing to this superior attitude and to the Roberts propaganda campaign, MacArthur did not hold the NKPA in high regard; on the contrary, he was contemptuous of it. He was guilty of grossly underestimating the capabilities of the enemy.

\* \* \*

While MacArthur was in South Korea, Eisenhower, who was in Washington for a routine physical examination, called at the Pentagon on June 28, Washington time. He had hoped to confer with Omar Bradley, but by then Bradley's intestinal bug had forced him to bed in his quarters. In lieu of Bradley, Ike met with Collins, Haislip, Ridgway, and their principal assistants. He was astonished by the complacency and indecisiveness he found, he wrote in his diary. He gave Collins and his assistants a five-star chewing out. "My whole contention," Ike went on in his diary, "was that an appeal to force cannot, by its nature, be a partial one. This appeal, having been made, for God's sake, get ready! Do everything possible under the law to get us going. Remember in a fight (our side) can never be too strong. I urged action in a dozen different directions . . . even if it finally came to the use of the A-bomb (which God forbid)."[39]

Matt Ridgway made notes on Ike's chewing out: "General Eisenhower dropped in . . . [and] stated in most vigorous language and with great emphasis his feelings that we ought at once to begin partial mobilization; perhaps reinforce our European forces by a division or two; publicly increase our security measures throughout the country; at once remove the limitation placed on MacArthur to operate south of the 38th Parallel; even to consider the use of one or two atomic bombs in the Korea area, if suitable targets could be found."[40]

Few men knew MacArthur as well as Eisenhower, who had served directly under him twice—in the War Department from 1930 to 1932 and in Manila from 1935 to 1939. In a remarkably prescient and candid aside, Eisenhower warned that MacArthur was ill suited to run the Korean War. "In commenting upon General MacArthur," Ridgway jotted in his desk journal, "Ike expressed the wish that he would like to see a younger general out there, rather than, as he expressed it, 'an untouchable' whose actions you cannot predict, and who will himself decide what information he wants Washington to have and what he will withhold."[41]

Bradley wrote later that Ike's visit to the Pentagon had made a profound impression on Joe Collins and his staff. What Eisenhower had urged, in effect, was all-out mobilization—a maximizing of military force. Following his visit, the Army high command became increasingly hawkish and, notwithstanding the majority view in the JCS, began drawing plans for committing American ground forces in South Korea.[42]

* * *

After his arduous trip to South Korea MacArthur returned to his home in Tokyo for a good night's sleep. While he slept, the JCS, now receiving a continuous stream of reports from various sources in Korea and Japan, began to realize that with the ROK Army disintegrating, it was doubtful that American air and sea power alone could save South Korea. During that day—June 29, Washington time—the full JCS concluded, reluctantly, that if South Korea were to be saved, the use of some American ground forces could probably not be avoided much longer.[43]

Two purely military considerations pushed the chiefs closer to committing limited American ground forces that day. The first was the need to ensure the safety of the airfield at Pusan. It and the field in Suwon (which might be lost at any hour) were the only two air installations in South Korea capable of handling the big four-engine C-54 Air Force transports which were now being employed to bring in emergency supplies of ammunition to the ROKs and to evacuate American stragglers. The second consideration was the need to ensure the safety of the South Korean seaports of Pusan and Chinhae (twenty miles east of Pusan), which the American Navy was using as unloading points for ammo and supplies.[44]

That same afternoon, June 29, at 5:00 P.M., the Blair House conferees met again. By then the news from South Korea was grim. The ROKs were fleeing in disarray; John Church would almost certainly have to abandon Suwon soon. In order to maintain a "foothold" in South Korea in the Pusan area, the JCS recommended unlimited air and naval attacks against North Korea—north of the 38th Parallel—and the defensive deployment of one American RCT and certain communications and service troops in the Pusan-Chinhae area, to protect the airfield and ports.[45]

Without hesitation the president approved the JCS recommendations. Shortly afterward the JCS cabled MacArthur new authorizations, which greatly increased the American commitment in Korea:

• MacArthur's air forces could now operate beyond the 38th Parallel against "purely military" targets such as air bases, depots, tank farms, troop columns, and the like. However, he was to exercise "special care" to ensure that American aircraft stayed "well clear" of Manchuria and the Soviet Union.

• MacArthur could send "essential" communication and service units and "such Army combat and service forces" as required to ensure the retention of the "general area Pusan-Chinhae." Although not specified in the order, these "combat" forces were later limited to one RCT, to be used only in a defensive role.

The decision to authorize formally unlimited air and naval action in North Korea carried with it the possibility of a Soviet counterreaction: air, ground, or naval intervention in Korea. Mindful of this threat, the conferees deliberated what instructions should be given MacArthur in that event. President Truman later recalled that the instructions Louis Johnson had drafted carried an implication that (as Truman put it) "we were planning to go to war against the Soviet Union." Truman was in a mood to take "every step necessary" to push the NKPA back to the 38th Parallel, but he did not want to become so "deeply committed" in Korea that America "could not take care of other situations as might develop."[46]

The upshot was a considerable toning down of Johnson's draft message to read:

The decision to commit United States naval and air forces and limited army forces to provide cover and support for South Korean troops does not constitute a decision to engage in war with the Soviet Union, if Soviet Forces intervene in Korea. The decision regarding Korea, however, was taken in full realization of the risk involved. If Soviet Forces actively oppose our operations in Korea, your forces should defend themselves, should take no action to aggravate the situation, and you should report the situation to Washington.[47]

Notwithstanding these warlike steps, Truman publicly continued to downplay the gravity of the Korean crisis and the extent of American intervention. At a press conference that afternoon he declared emphatically that "we are not at war." One reporter, searching for a terse way to characterize the situation, asked if it could be described as a UN "police action." The president agreed, perhaps a little too hastily and certainly to his everlasting regret, that the phrase was apt.[48]

## IV

While the Blair House conferees slept that night, June 29, MacArthur arose early on the morning of June 30, Tokyo time, and went to the Dai Ichi Building. There he polished his report on his visit to South Korea and cabled it to the Pentagon, addressed to the JCS via the Department of the Army, the executive agency and communications channel for all Korean War matters. The report arrived at the Pentagon shortly before midnight, June 29. Alerted by a duty officer, Joe Collins got out of bed and went to the Pentagon to read it.[49]

MacArthur began by describing his visit to Suwon and the Han River battlefront, painting a lugubrious picture. He went on to excoriate the ROK Army. It was "in confusion" and "had not seriously fought" and "lacked leadership" and had "absolutely no system of communications." It now numbered no more than "25,000 effectives" and was "entirely incapable of counter action." Every effort had been made to establish a defense of the "Han River line" and the Seoul–Suwon "corridor," but "the result is highly problematical." If the NKPA advance continued further, it would "seriously threaten the fall of the Republic."[50]

His conclusion was galvanizing:

The only assurance for the holding of the present line, and the ability to regain later lost ground, is through the introduction of U.S. ground combat forces into the Korean battle area. To continue to utilize the forces of our Army and Navy without an effective ground element cannot be decisive. . . . Unless provision is made for the full utilization of the Army-Navy-Air team in this shattered area our mission will at best be needlessly costly in life, money and prestige. At worst it might even be doomed to failure.

Included in this report was a sketchy (one-sentence) outline for deploying and utilizing the American ground forces. As a first step MacArthur would "immediately move" one American RCT into the Han River line or the Seoul–Suwon corridor. While this force blocked the southerly advance of the NKPA, MacArthur would rush "a possible" two full American infantry divisions to South Korea. These would then be deployed for an "early counter offensive," presumably designed to destroy the NKPA or at least to push it back beyond the 38th Parallel.

This historic plan, ringing with boldness, deserves closer scrutiny than it has hitherto received. The crux of the plan—deployment of an RCT in the Seoul–Suwon Corridor in time to dig in and block the NKPA—was simply preposterous. The NKPA was already crossing the Han River and driving south on Suwon, scattering the remnants of the ROK Army before it. There was no RCT in Japan in a sufficient state of readiness to "rush" to South

Korea. An RCT would have to be improvised. Since there was insufficient airlift in Japan to bring over the heavy equipment of an RCT, most of it would have to go by sea. All this would take time—far too much time to do the job MacArthur had in mind.

MacArthur's glib assurance of an "early offensive" by two full American divisions was no less preposterous. All the problems faced in getting a single RCT to South Korea would be multiplied enormously by moving two full divisions. Moreover, the two green divisions would land in South Korea in the teeth of an onrushing hostile army flush with victory. Even if they survived, it would take weeks or months to regroup and launch a "counter offensive."

This fantastical MacArthur plan bore an eerie likeness to another fantastical plan he had conceived ten years before for the defense of the Philippines from a Japanese attack. Like the South Korean plan, the earlier plan had drastically underrated the enemy and overrated his own forces. There were also certain tactical similarities, such as an early and aggressive confrontation with an advancing enemy without a scheme for defense in depth. The Philippine plan had failed under the weight of overwhelming Japanese superiority, forcing MacArthur into his famous perimeter defense in Bataan and Corregidor. Events in South Korea were to follow a remarkably similar course.

As Joe Collins pondered MacArthur's report, he was well aware of its profound implications: that notwithstanding all previous decisions to avoid an American war against Asians on the Asian mainland at all costs, MacArthur was urging just that and proposing to do it with troops that were not sufficiently trained or equipped for combat. Yet Collins raised no objections. On the contrary, he enthusiastically embraced this proposal which went far beyond the JCS decision of that day to limit the American ground forces to a defensive role near Pusan.

Seldom in American history had there been an occasion fraught with greater peril or demanding more thoughtful analysis. A more prudent man than Collins might have felt compelled to summon the full JCS to the Pentagon for one last discussion on so momentous a matter. But not "Lightning Joe," the man noted for speed and snap judgments in tight corners. He decided to take matters into his own hands, and in the dark of that night he embarked on a course that was to hasten America into full-scale war in Korea.

Collins had a well-developed sense of history and public relations, honed by a postwar tour as the Army's chief publicist. Fully conscious of the historic nature of the moment, he decided to confer person to person with MacArthur by telecon. As he and his advisers gathered in a darkened room before the movie screen, Collins wrote later, "the air was fraught with tension."[51]

From the outset Collins let MacArthur know that he was in his corner. He dutifully stated the obvious—no doubt for the record—that MacArthur's request to introduce American ground forces into combat in South Korea would require "presidential approval." This would take "several hours," Collins said, because Truman would want to confer carefully with his top advisers. But more to the point, Collins reminded MacArthur that he, MacArthur, already had authorization to move one RCT to the Pusan area. Would that authorization not permit "initiation of movement" per MacArthur's plan pending approval of its entirety? Collins asked. There was no suggestion whatsoever that the president was likely to disapprove MacArthur's plan.[52]

MacArthur was not satisfied with this bureaucratic dallying. Cutting straight through to the core of the matter, he said that while the movement of one RCT to Pusan established the "basic principle" that American ground combat forces could be deployed in South Korea, it did not give him "sufficient latitude for efficient operations" or, in fact, satisfy his specific request to move an RCT into the battle area. "Time is of the essence," MacArthur prodded, "and a clear cut decision without delay is imperative."

Collins capitulated at once: "I will proceed immediately through Secretary of Army to request presidential approval your proposal to move RCT into forward combat area. We will advise you as soon as possible, perhaps within a half hour."

After stepping from the telecon room, Collins found a phone and called Frank Pace. He relayed the gist of MacArthur's request, added his own enthusiastic approval, and urged Pace to telephone the president immediately. It was now about 5:00 A.M. on June 30. The president was "up and shaved." In response he unhesitatingly approved the movement of one RCT to the combat zone but reserved decision on the larger commitment—the two full divisions—until he could confer with the Blair House group. Pace relayed all this to Collins, who, in turn, teleconned MacArthur: "Your recommendation to move one RCT to combat area is approved. You will be advised later as to further buildup."[53]

At no time during this long telecon did Collins or anyone else raise questions about the state of training in Eighth Army or the validity or feasibility of MacArthur's fantastical deployment plan. However, it is clear from several polite peripheral questions that Collins (or a stand-in) put to MacArthur that there was considerable unease over it. For example, Collins asked MacArthur if he intended to move the RCT by air, and if so, could he airlift the RCT's heavy equipment and artillery? If this question were read another way, the Pentagon was saying that for his plan to succeed, MacArthur *had* to move the RCT by air, and since it would be impossible to move the RCT's heavy equipment by air, the plan would fail.

Collins concluded his end of the telecon with a fawning and dissembling salute: "Everyone here delighted your prompt action in personally securing first hand view of situation. Congratulations and best wishes. We all have full confidence in you and your command."

Having thus committed American ground forces into the Korean War, Collins telephoned his JCS colleagues at about 5:30 A.M. to tell them what he had done. The official JCS historians recorded with masterful understatement that at least one of them, Forrest Sherman, "felt some unease." In fact, they all were shocked, not only because they had not been consulted but also because of the grave implication of the decision. Bradley, who had consistently opposed committing American ground forces to South Korea, later wrote in his autobiography that he had been "deeply concerned." Even so, not Bradley or Sherman or Vandenberg protested the decision formally, then or later. Sherman came to believe it was a "sound" decision; Bradley wrote that "in a sense, it was unavoidable and inevitable."[54]

Several hours later—at 8:30 A.M.—the JCS convened in Louis Johnson's office to discuss MacArthur's larger request for the commitment of two American divisions to South Korea. There was no dissent; the commitment of the RCT to combat almost automatically entailed further commitment. Louis Johnson stunned the conferees—and threw the discussion into chaos—by declaring that deployment of the two divisions did not require presidential approval; that as secretary of defense he had full authority to authorize the deployment. The chiefs dealt with this bizarre pronouncement by ignoring it.[55]

At about nine-thirty that morning, June 30, the president once again convened the Blair House group. Bradley produced a draft of the JCS message to MacArthur, authorizing the deployment of the two divisions. Truman read the message, then astonished the conferees by stating, in effect, that Washington should not limit MacArthur to two divisions, that he should be authorized to deploy "any and all ground forces under his command" necessary to get the job done. There was no dissent.

The president then presented the conferees with another startling proposal. The day before he had received an offer from Chiang Kai-shek, volunteering 33,000 infantrymen for the defense of South Korea. The president was inclined to accept the offer because it would lend an international (and Oriental) flavor to the rescue of South Korea. Acheson and the JCS strongly opposed the idea for two reasons. First, introduction of Chinese Nationalist troops into the Korean War might give the Chinese Communists an excuse to enter the war in support of the NKPA or might provoke an attack on Formosa. Secondly, the JCS had little faith in the quality and equipment of the Nationalist infantry and believed that properly outfitting it for combat in Korea and shipping it there would put a serious drain on MacArthur's already overstrained resources.

At the suggestion of Forrest Sherman, Truman approved the imposition of a naval blockade of Korea. The instructions for the blockade were not included in the cable to MacArthur that day; they were delayed about twenty-four hours. They specified that MacArthur would use such means available to him to "suppress seaborne traffic to and from North Korea and to prevent movement by sea of forces and supplies for use in operations against South Korea." In carrying out the blockade, MacArthur would take care "to keep well clear of the coastal waters of Manchuria and USSR."

After this Blair House meeting the Pentagon group returned to Johnson's office to recast the instructions to MacArthur to reflect Truman's view that no limits be placed on the commitment of MacArthur's available ground forces. The discussion proved to be more complicated than at first envisioned because MacArthur's long-standing, primary military mission was to protect Japan. The matter was finally resolved with this cable: "Restrictions on use of Army Forces imposed by JCS . . . are hereby removed and authority granted to utilize Army Forces available to you as proposed . . . [in your report]. . . . Subject only to requirements for safety of Japan in the present situation which is a matter for your judgment."[56]

The Pentagon group then rushed back to the White House for an 11:00 A.M. meeting to brief the leadership of the Senate and House. Despite considerable advice to the contrary, Truman had decided to continue downplaying the crisis and not to ask the Congress for a formal declaration of war; he would continue publicly to describe—and demean—Korea as a "police action." This decision came back to haunt Truman, but that day the congressional leadership backed his decisions almost unanimously. Only one member of Congress—Truman's "enemy" Republican Senator Kenneth S. Wherry—expressed disapproval. Wherry believed Truman should have consulted Congress before committing Americans to war in Korea.[57]

Later that day the White House issued a terse statement to the press, outlining the major decisions the president had taken over the preceding two days. It stated that the Air Force had been authorized to attack "specific military targets" in North Korea "wherever militarily necessary" and that a naval blockade had been imposed for "the entire Korean coast." However, the extent of the commitment of American ground forces was not forthcoming, presumably for security reasons. The White House merely said: "General MacArthur has been authorized to use certain supporting ground units." But the press was not misled. Within an hour or so of the release the *Washington Evening Star* appeared on newsstands with a banner headline: U.S. SENDS GROUND TROOPS INTO KOREA.[58]

The die was cast; there was no turning back. America was committed to waging air, sea, and ground war against Asians on the Asian mainland. America was intervening in a Korean civil war, not because its strategic interests in the Far East were threatened but because Washington had to show Moscow that "raw aggression" was unacceptable, that a line had to be drawn.

This momentous decision was arrived at in a mere six days. One of the more curious aspects about it was that no one in a high position in the Truman administration opposed the decision. All the senior men who helped shape it—Truman, Acheson, Johnson, the JCS, MacArthur—appeared to be trying to outdo the other in bellicosity and haste.

# 4

# FANTASTICAL
# DEPLOYMENTS

## I

After Truman had authorized MacArthur to use "any and all" ground forces at his command "subject only to requirements for safety of Japan," GHQ conceived a far more sophisticated—and yet more fantastical—plan to administer a quick and cheap coup de grace to the NKPA. In addition to the two American divisions that would be deployed into the teeth of the onrushing NKPA per the original plan, a third division would land amphibiously behind the NKPA at Seoul's cramped seaport, Inchon. This amphibious landing would sever the NKPA line of communications and "trap" it between American "pincers."[1]

Contrary to later descriptions, Inchon was neither a "brilliant" nor an extraordinary concept. It could be classified as standard Army doctrine for peninsular warfare, wherein an overextended enemy force, lacking air and sea power, becomes ever more vulnerable on its flanks. It was doctrine that in World War II led to Allied landings first at Salerno, then at Anzio during the peninsular campaign in Italy. The Pentagon, which produced war plans for every conceivable contingency, had only recently (June 19, 1950) approved and distributed a plan known as SL-17, which assumed a NKPA invasion, a retreat to and defense of a perimeter at Pusan, followed by an amphibious landing at Inchon. Its author, Donald McB. Curtis, later remembered that in the "week of June 26, 1950," GHQ "urgently requested" fifty copies of SL-17, and he asserted that "this is where General MacArthur got his idea for the Inchon landing."[2]

The grand plan (Operation Bluehearts) as conceived by Ned Almond and the GHQ staff was as follows. The 24th Infantry Division, based on the southernmost Japanese home island (Kyushu) that was closest to South Korea, would go into battle first. It would land at Pusan about July 2, then proceed immediately toward Suwon to block the NKPA drive down the western sector of the peninsula and provide inspiration for the routed ROK Army in that area. The 25th Division would follow immediately and deploy in the center of the peninsula to backstop and inspire the ROK forces in that area. The 1st Cav Division would carry out the amphibious landing at Inchon about July 20. While the 1st Cav was landing at Inchon the 24th Division would attack north, closing the pincers.[3]

On paper, Bluehearts seemed to make good sense. Its centerpiece—the quick, surprise amphibious landing at Inchon—would employ modern air and naval weapons unavailable to the NKPA, and a technique of warfare the NKPA had not been trained to confront. It would bring to bear the fullest possible weight of MacArthur's slim military resources in the shortest possible time.

In reality, Bluehearts was absurd. It was a highly complex military maneuver that demanded at the very least well-trained, well-led, well-equipped, and combat-experienced infantry. Eighth Army was in no way prepared to carry out such a demanding and risky task. As Ned Almond later conceded, the Army was merely "40 percent combat effective." That estimate may have been on the rosy side.[4]

Nonetheless GHQ proceeded to issue orders for Bluehearts in a perfect frenzy. Customary and ordinary military prudence and common sense were thrown to the four winds. When Almond gave the 1st Cav its marching orders he told the division commander to expedite the Inchon landing "to the utmost limit"; otherwise the only thing the 1st Cav would hit on landing would be the "tail end of the 24th Division" as it passed northbound through Seoul. The 1st Cav drew its weapons in a frenzy and made plans to board ship in Yokohama. Its men were led to believe they would return "in a matter of a few weeks."[5]

No man knew better the grave weaknesses of Eighth Army than Johnnie Walker. Yet he raised no objections to the GHQ orders. One reason was that Walker knew well that neither MacArthur nor Almond trusted him. As the Army's general manager, Matt Ridgway, put it later: "MacArthur did not have confidence in Walker. . . . Their relations were very strained at the time. He had even considered relieving Walker of command." Had Walker expressed serious objections to Bluehearts he would probably have found himself out of a job, a ruinous end to a long and distinguished career.[6]

Thus the mad momentum at GHQ was adopted by Eighth Army headquarters in Yokohama without reservations. All orders emanating from GHQ, however unrealistic, were carried out without question and with utmost urgency.

## II

Of the four divisions in Eighth Army the one chosen to enter combat first, the 24th, was the least combat-ready—officially and optimistically rated at 65 percent. Only two of its two-battalion regiments (21st and 34th) were actually on Kyushu; its third (19th) was temporarily on Honshu at a training area. The division's total strength on June 27 was only slightly greater than a NKPA division: 11,242 men. To beef it up for battle, GHQ immediately stripped 2,108 noncoms from the other three divisions and rushed them to the 24th. Other sources would provide another 2,615 men, bringing the total number to 15,965 men. This "levy" severely sapped the strength of the other two divisions programmed for battle. The 1st Cav, for example, lost 750 senior noncoms, leaving only master and first sergeants in its infantry companies and artillery battalions.[7]

The 24th Division was commanded by a "can do" general, William F. Dean, who seemed ideally suited for the frenetic job at hand. At age fifty Dean was the youngest of the four division commanders in Eighth Army and the only one who had commanded troops in combat. He was also the only one of the four who knew South Korea well.[8]

Born in Carlyle, Illinois, in 1899, Dean was a big (six-foot, 210-pound), bluff field general, a fighter and an impressive leader. From his high school days Dean had set his sights on West Point, but he had not been able to get an appointment. Determined to make the Army a career, Dean enrolled at the University of California, Berkeley in a prelaw course and joined the ROTC. A mediocre student, Dean was graduated after five years (1922) minus a law degree, but he obtained an ROTC commission (1923) and went on permanent active duty. He married Mildred Dern, niece of wealthy Utah politician George H. Dern, who was a U.S. senator, then governor, then Franklin D. Roosevelt's secretary of war from 1933 until his death in 1936. The Deans had two children, June (who married an Air Force officer, Robert Williams) and William, Jr., who was preparing to enter West Point with the class of 1954.[9]

Perhaps assisted by his uncle-in-law's high positions, Dean climbed the peacetime Army career ladder steadily, attending both the Command and General Staff School and the Army War College (1940). But when World War II commenced, he was stuck for all too long in various desk jobs. Finally, in late 1943, he was promoted to brigadier general and assigned to the ETO-bound 44th Infantry Division as assistant commander. An act of bravery during a training exercise nearly denied him combat. When a flamethrower hose broke loose and engulfed the operator in fire, Dean leaped to rescue the operator and, in the process, was himself so badly burned that doctors declared his left leg would have to be amputated. Hearing this, Dean "went AWOL" from the hospital, sailed for France, rejoined his division, and limped into battle in late 1944 with a hawthorn cane. The 44th Division surgeon kept Dean going; the leg did not fully heal until after the war.[10]

Dean was thoroughly competent and apparently fearless on the battlefield. Early in the action he won a DSC for personally leading a platoon through a withering German artillery barrage. When the division commander was wounded and invalided home, the corps commander, Ham Haislip, promoted Bill Dean (then forty-five years old) to the top job. In tough fighting near Mannheim and Heidelberg, during which his hair turned from blond to white, Dean led the division well. After Germany had surrendered, the division was selected for the invasion of Japan, but the Japanese surrendered before it set sail for the Pacific.[11]

In the postwar years Dean, by then a two-star general with a promising future, was assigned to duty with American occupation forces in South Korea. He served as a deputy commander to John Hodge until August 1948, when the occupation command was dissolved and Hodge went home. Thereafter Dean was made commander of the 7th Infantry Division and as such withdrew it to Sapporo, on Hokkaido, Japan. From May to October 1949 he put in a tour on Walker's Eighth Army staff but hated every minute of it. When a "sudden transfer" left the 24th Division without a commander, Dean talked Walker into giving him the job.

Dean's one-year tour in South Korea, he later wrote, had been "interesting and troubling." Wearing several "hats," he had been the senior American adviser to the police and constabulary, along with other jobs. He had traveled widely in South Korea, picked up a "few words" of the Korean language, observed at close hand the Byzantine political scene, and got to know Rhee and other governmental and military figures. However, he had no love for the place. He did not want—or expect—ever to return to South Korea and was as surprised as everybody else when the war alert reached his 24th Division headquarters in Kokura.[12]

Notwithstanding his rank and bright future in the Army, Dean remained unpretentious and a touch self-deprecating. An aide remembered that whenever possible and practical, Dean preferred to walk rather than ride in staff cars (the local Japanese nicknamed him Aruku Shoko, or Walking General). He had "no hang-ups about status," the aide remembered. He was "his own best shoeshiner." "Always much more of a doer than a talker," the aide recalled, Dean was at root a simple, down-to-earth soldier who saw most issues in blacks and whites and was put off by "hypocrisy" and "self-proclaimed paragons of virtue who kicked their dogs when they thought no one was looking."[13]

The 24th Division staff, like that of most divisions in Japan, was a mixed bag. Dean's ADC (in case of incapacitation, his immediate successor) was fifty-eight-year-old Brigadier General Pearson Menoher, a West Point classmate (1915) of Eisenhower and Bradley's who, during World War II, had been chief of staff of Ham Haislip's XV Corps. As such he had often given Bill Dean orders. Menoher's position as Dean's ADC was largely honorary, perhaps a returned favor from Dean. He was really too old and senior to replace Dean in combat. The artillery commander was Brigadier General Henry J. D. Meyer, fifty, another West Pointer (1919) and "superb soldier" who had commanded the 45th Division artillery in combat in the ETO. Unfortunately for Dean, Meyer was on leave in the States. The chief of staff of the division was Meyer's West Point classmate William J. Moroney, fifty-two, a regimental commander in the Pacific during World War II who was now a "drunk" and a "weak spot."[14]

\* \* \*

Dean's forces immediately at hand on Kyushu, the 21st and 34th regiments, were in no way prepared for war. Of the two outfits, the less ready in every respect was the 34th Infantry.

Earlier in the year the 34th had performed so poorly in its readiness tests that Johnnie Walker had sacked its commander. The new leader was Jay B. Lovless (University of Montana, 1925), most recently an Eighth Army logistician. In World War II George Marshall had recommended that no regimental commander in the Army should be more than forty-five years old. Lovless was then forty-nine, merely one year younger than Dean. In World War II (at age forty-three) Lovless had been named commander of the 23d Infantry Regiment in Normandy on D plus ten and had commanded it well through VE day, earning a DSC. But that was one war back; Lovless was now well over Marshall's recommended age limit for regimental command. Moreover, he had shortcomings as a battle leader: According to his senior assistant, Lovless was a "martinet" who was "a nervous, highstrung, impatient, dictatorial type of officer."[15]

Lovless had worked hard to shape up the 34th in his brief tour as commander, but the difficulties were nearly insurmountable. The regiment was physically fragmented: The HQ was in Sasebo; the two battalions were five miles away in the countryside.\* Under the tough Lovless regime one of the battalions was always in the training area, but it was located forty miles from the billeting area "on top of a mountain and so cut up," Lovless wrote, "that

---

\*A normal infantry battalion was a powerful force and a key maneuver element of the regiment and division. It consisted of about 900 men, divided into three rifle companies (of three platoons), each composed of about 200 men, plus one heavy-weapons company of about 166 men, manning 81-mm or 4.2-inch mortars, 75-mm recoilless rifles, and .30- and .50-caliber machine guns. These forces were directed by a battalion commander and a sizable staff, which included the battalion exec, the S-1 (personnel), S-2 (intelligence), S-3 (plans), and S-4 (logistics), grouped into a headquarters company, plus other supporting units.

it was impossible to conduct a satisfactory battalion exercise." On Lovless's recommendation, Dean had approved a consolidation of the 34th at an area near Hiroshima, but this had not yet been done. In May the two battalions had been tested individually. "Detailed results were not known," Lovless wrote, but it was believed the scores were still far from satisfactory. Moreover, "the 34th had never trained or practiced as an entire regiment."

There was a chronic shortage of "qualified, trained officers," Lovless added. Two key men, the regimental exec, William T. Ramsay, and the commander of the 1st Battalion (or 1/34), Lawrence G. Paulus, forty-six, were in Lovless's view, "not satisfactory." Ramsay had "had no troop or staff duty" in the infantry; the 1/34 commander, Paulus, was "an artilleryman with no infantry troop training." Lovless had urged their replacement, but apparently because the Pentagon had assigned them to their jobs, Dean had been reluctant to ask for a change.

In the judgment of the regimental S-3 (plans), John J. Dunn, a tough-minded former enlisted man who won a DSC in World War II, the equipment provided the 34th was "a national disgrace." He wrote that "between 25 and 50 percent of our small arms were unserviceable." The regiment had not been supplied the new 3.5-inch antitank bazooka; it was still equipped with the 2.36-inch bazooka of World War II, which Dunn believed to be "worthless." Nor had the supporting artillery been provided with new armor-piercing "shaped-charge" antitank ammo, technically known as high-explosive antitank or HEAT. There was an acute shortage of 81-mm and 4.2-inch mortars. Moreover, what little mortar ammo there was on hand "was so old and corroded" that "eight out of ten shells fired failed to explode." The .30-caliber machine-gun barrels were "worn out and not accurate" and lacked aiming lights and chronometers. Until very recently the 34th had only one-third of its "required vehicles," such as trucks and jeeps, and it got more only because Lovless had connections in the logistic command. Owing to a shortage of Army-issue shoes and boots, many men in the 34th were forced to wear tennis shoes.

For all these reasons, and more, on June 30, 1950, the 34th Infantry was still in poor shape. One of Dean's senior officers put it this way: "The morale and spirit of that regiment was [sic] not good."[16]

The other regiment at hand, the 21st Infantry, was commanded by West Pointer (1924) Richard ("Dick") W. Stephens. At forty-seven, he, too, exceeded George Marshall's recommended age limit for regimental commanders. Stephens had not before led troops in battle; in World War II he had been chief of staff of the 30th Infantry Division in the ETO. His exec remembered that Stephens was "built like a bull and getting heavy around the middle" and losing his hair. He was "unconventional in many respects" and a "real character" who was "certainly outspoken in his relations with seniors" and who "loved his evening martinis." Between Lovless and Stephens, Bill Dean much preferred Stephens.[17]

The 21st was slightly ahead of the 34th in its training cycle. Both of Stephens's battalions had "passed" battalion-level readiness tests; the 1/21 had even had some air transportability training. However, the 21st's exec, forty-year-old Charles F. ("Fritz") Mudgett (University of North Dakota, 1933), an able World War II battalion commander in Italy, remembered that the regiment had not maneuvered as a unit and was "unprepared for war." He wrote in retrospect that it was "rather sad, almost criminal, that such understrength, ill-equipped and poorly-trained units were committed. . . ."[18]

Bill Dean well knew his division was in no way prepared for combat, but he raised no objections to Johnnie Walker. In view of the existing frenzy, had he done so it is likely he would have been relieved of command, if not by Walker, then by GHQ. Dean rationalized his indifference to the welfare of his men by saying he believed the division's mission in South Korea would be "short and easy." He subscribed to the prevailing American view that his division, however ill trained and ill equipped, had merely to make an appearance on the battlefield and the NKPA would melt into the hills.[19]

That conviction spread all through the 24th Division, dangerously and cruelly misleading the men. Platoon leaders soft-soaped their men with Truman's euphemistic terminology: "You've been told repeatedly that this is a police action, and that's exactly what it's going to be." Dean's men were soon boasting that "as soon as those gooks see an American uniform they'll run like hell." The belief grew that in no time at all the division would return to its soft billet in Japan—and to great glory.[20]

Yet, deep down, Bill Dean must have suspected rougher times than he let on. Soon after the alert he requested that Eighth Army send him three combat-experienced men to shore up the command in the 34th Regiment. Two of these men had fought with Dean in the 44th Division in the ETO: Robert R. Martin (Purdue University, 1924), forty-eight, and Robert L. ("Pappy") Wadlington, forty-nine. The other, Harold B. ("Red") Ayres, thirty-one, then serving in the 25th Division, had won a DSC in Italy and was reputed to be the "best battalion commander in the Far East." Pappy Wadlington replaced the exec; Ayres would replace the 1/34 commander. Robert Martin, who had commanded a regiment in Dean's 44th Division in the ETO, would be near at hand should Lovless fail.[21]

\* \* \*

Walker's initial orders to Dean, telexed on the night of June 30, reflected the frenzy in the Eighth Army staff. Dean was to fly his division headquarters and one infantry regiment (of two battalions) to Pusan; the heavy gear, such as artillery, trucks, ammo, and food, was to follow by ship.

In issuing these orders, GHQ apparently overlooked or dismissed some hard-learned airborne lessons of World War II: that the Air Force disliked and disdained troop carrier operations and gave them lowest priority in equipment and personnel; that all airborne movements into unfamiliar territory depended on nearly ideal flying weather for success; that air movement of troops and their equipment (recoilless rifles; bazookas; mortars; machine guns; ammo; field radios; jeeps) demanded sturdy runways and well-organized ground support and fuel supplies at both the departure point and destination; that aircraft in the Far East suitable for use as troop carriers were severely limited in numbers, load capacity, and range.[22]

To spearhead this mission Dean chose Dick Stephens's 21st Regiment. However, on analysis the original plans had to be discarded. Owing to the budget cuts, FEAF had only about two dozen C-54s in Japan. Up to then these had been employed in flying emergency ammo to South Korea and evacuating personnel, and as a result of this hard use, many planes were undergoing maintenance and repairs. Inasmuch as a C-54 could hold only fifty men (fewer with heavy gear), it would take many days—perhaps even a week—to assemble all the serviceable planes and lift the designated divisional units to South Korea. Moreover, the weather was so bad—heavy rains and low ceilings—the Air Force could not absolutely guarantee the delivery of so much as a single squad.[23]

In view of these factors, it would have been prudent to abandon the "airlift" altogether, but this was out of the question. GHQ had specified "air movement," and in the existing climate no one was willing to challenge GHQ. The airlift plans were therefore hurriedly scaled down to meet operational realities. Only a single "combat team" of about 450 men would be flown to Pusan; all the rest of the division and its equipment would go by ship.

Since Stephens's 21st Regiment had already been chosen for the air movement, the "combat team" would come from his outfit, drawn from either the 1/21 or the 3/21. There was no hesitation over this decision. The 1/21 commander, West Pointer (1939) Charles B. ("Brad") Smith, thirty-four, had ably commanded an infantry battalion on Guadalcanal. The 3/21 commander, West Pointer (1922) Delbert A. Pryor, had not before led troops in combat, was too old for the job (forty-four), and was, in the words of the 21st exec, Fritz Mudgett, "physically unfit."[24]

At 8:05 A.M. on July 1 Brad Smith, leading a convoy of 440 men through a torrential downpour, arrived at the Air Force base outside Itazuke, Kyushu.* Bill Dean was there to greet the force and wish the men well, but he had

---

*Task Force Smith was composed of about half a battalion: two rifle companies (B and C) which were beefed up with riflemen from Pryor's 3/21, two composite heavy-weapons platoons, equipped with four 75-mm recoilless rifles, four 4.2-inch mortars, and four 60-mm mortars.

bad news. So far FEAF had managed to provide only six C-54s for the airlift. More were on the way—maybe. Meanwhile, they would have to make do with what they had.[25]

Notwithstanding the downpour in Japan and the reportedly unfavorable weather in South Korea, Smith and his men immediately began to load and board the aircraft. At 8:45 A.M. the first C-54 was airborne. Minutes later a second aircraft, carrying Smith and a slimmed-down 1/21 headquarters, took off. The flight to Pusan took only one hour, but it concluded with more bad news: The field at Pusan was closed on account of bad weather. Both planes were forced to return to Japan, a maddening anticlimax for Smith's keyed-up men.

Later in the day the weather improved, and the airlift commenced anew. Six planeloads of infantry got to South Korea before bad weather again closed the Pusan field. The next morning the airlift resumed, but then a new problem arose: The big heavy C-54s were tearing up the flimsily built runways at Pusan. By noon, when Smith and 406 men had been delivered, the Air Force forbade any further operations of C-54s into there. Until steel matting to reinforce runways could be rushed to South Korea, future airlifts would be restricted mainly to smaller C-47 transports (the military version of the DC-3), which could carry only eighteen soldiers. As a result, Smith had to leave behind nearly half his heavy firepower: two 75-mm recoilless rifle teams and two 4.2-inch mortar teams.[26]

Meanwhile, Bill Dean was trying to get to South Korea by air. He was aboard one of the C-54s denied permission to land at Pusan on July 2. After returning to Japan, he got in a C-45 (a small twin-engine "executive" aircraft) with the goal of landing farther north at Taejon. But by the time the plane reached the Taejon area it was too dark to find the small, poorly marked airfield, and once again Dean was compelled to return to Japan. After a few hours' sleep he was airborne again, on the morning of July 3. This time he found South Korea blanketed by a dense fog. Determined to find Taejon at any cost, the pilot dropped down to wave-top level over the Yellow Sea, flew in beneath the fog and mist, and found the objective. Dean wrote: "I never thought I'd have so much trouble in getting to a war."[27]

\* \* \*

Owing to budget cuts in the U.S. Navy, the units of the 24th Division which moved to South Korea by ship had to scrounge transportation. The commander of the 34th Regiment, Jay Lovless, was lucky. He found some ships at the Navy base in Sasebo and embarked on the night of July 1—the first day of the vaunted airlift—arriving in Pusan the following evening, July 2, with some elements of the division's 52d Field Artillery Battalion (or

FAB)* commanded by West Pointer (1931) Miller O. Perry. Thus the 34th—not the 21st, as intended—became the "first" full (as then constituted) regiment to reach South Korea. The remainder of Stephens's 21st and some artillery elements, embarking at Moji and Sasebo, had a very hard time finding ships. At Sasebo, Fritz Mudgett remembered, he had to commandeer three "filthy" Japanese freighters, recently employed in returning Russian-held Japanese POWs from Manchuria, plus two LSTs, on "loan" to the so-called Japanese Defense Force. "It was a hell of a way to go to war," Mudgett wrote.[28]

*  *  *

At Pusan on the evening of July 2 Task Force Smith boarded a train and headed north, arriving at Taejon the following morning, July 3, just ahead of Bill Dean. By that time the NKPA had forced John Church and his ADCOM headquarters to retreat from Suwon to Taejon. When Smith reported to Church, the latter was still brimming with confidence, or overconfidence. He put his reedy finger on a map at Osan, a village south of Suwon, and laconically told Smith that all that was really required to stop the NKPA were some American GIs—men who would not run from tanks—to bolster the ROK Army.[29]

While Smith jeeped north to reconnoiter the terrain at Osan, a tired and frustrated Bill Dean arrived at Taejon and, as instructed by GHQ, took command of all American forces in South Korea from the tottery John Church. Studying the poor maps available, Dean rashly conceived a new and far more elaborate blocking plan. He put his finger on the village of Pyongtaek, just south of Osan on the Seoul–Pusan highway. As Dean saw it, Pyongtaek was the key real estate. North of Pyongtaek the advancing NKPA was confined to a fairly narrow corridor between Asan Bay, an arm of the Yellow Sea, and the mountains to the east, where there were few roads. South of Pyongtaek the Korean peninsula opened up and spread westward, offering solid flat ground for a NKPA flanking movement. If he could hold at Pyongtaek, Dean figured, the NKPA could be bottled up in the narrow corridor north of the village and denied the opportunity to spread west.[30]

The tactical scheme Dean evolved was as follows. Task Force Smith, reinforced by a battery of Perry's 52d FAB, would take the positions chosen by John Church north of Pyongtaek near Osan, on the main Seoul–Pusan highway. Brad Smith would give the NKPA a bloody nose. Meanwhile, the

---

*An Army division of 1950 was authorized four artillery battalions of about 500 men each, manning 18 howitzers (in three batteries, A, B, C) per battalion. Three of the artillery battalions directly supported the three infantry regiments with 105-mm howitzers. The fourth artillery battalion, equipped with longer-range 155-mm howitzers (in three batteries, A, B, C), provided additional support to any or all three regiments or to other divisions nearby.

two battalions of Jay Lovless's 34th, which had arrived in Pusan the night before, would move forward as soon as possible to man the Pyongtaek "front." The 1/34 would dig in on the north side of Pyongtaek at a "river" (actually a stream) crossing. The 3/34 would occupy Ansong, a village about eleven miles directly east of Pyongtaek, where subsidiary north-south and east-west roads crossed, to hold the right flank in the foothills. In the event Task Force Smith could not hold, it would fall back through Osan to Pyongtaek, reinforcing the 1/34. As other 24th Division infantry units arrived in Pusan—mainly the rest of Brad Smith's 1/21 and Delbert Pryor's 3/21—they would rush north to reinforce this front.

While this scheme displayed an appropriate "can do" spirit for the Eighth Army spearhead, on analysis it could be characterized as foolhardy. It committed piecemeal three green, ill-equipped understrength battalions to the defense of three objectives eleven miles apart with scant or no communications between the units and only the haziest notion of how they might consolidate in event of a setback. A more prudent plan would have been to postpone the confrontation with the NKPA by one or two days at another, more defensible site, such as the Kum River, about thirty miles farther south. The postponement would have given Dean time to bring up his two "full" infantry regiments (comprising four battalions), the 21st and 34th, and one or two battalions of artillery. These regiments could have been deployed in consolidated positions behind the Kum River, linked to each other and to a divisional CP by a working communications net.

In drawing his plan, Dean, still convinced his mission would be "short and easy"—that the NKPA would bolt at the sight of American uniforms—overlooked or ignored a cardinal lesson of World Wars I and II: that even well-trained, well-equipped American divisions were skittish until bloodied. A consolidated line behind the Kum River, providing a sense of cohesion, would have minimized the insecurity as these ill-equipped and green troops entered battle for the first time.[31]

Dean's plan later was rationalized with the argument that it was necessary to meet the enemy in this forward-thrusting fashion in order to "buy time" in which to get the remainder of the 24th Division and the full 25th Division to South Korea. However, a consolidated Kum River line might well have "bought" more "time" with less risk and fewer casualties.

\* \* \*

As these plans were being translated into field orders, yet another American general arrived in Taejon. He was West Pointer (1918) George Bittman Barth, commander of the 25th Infantry Division artillery. He had come to fill in temporarily for Dean's artillery commander, Henry Meyer, who was rushing back from leave in the States. Barth, then fifty-two, was qualified as both an infantryman and artilleryman. He had made a splendid record in World War II first as chief of staff of the crack 9th Infantry Division in North Africa and Sicily, then as a courageous regimental commander in the trouble-plagued 90th Infantry Division, which Gene Landrum had briefly commanded in the Cotentin. Barth had helped "save" the 90th Division (suffering a severe battle wound in the process), and for that he had earned the everlasting gratitude (plus a DSC) of VII Corps commander Joe Collins.[32]

The arrival of Barth raised the total number of senior Army ground commanders at the front in South Korea to five: four generals (Dean; his ADC, Pearson Menoher; Church; and Barth) and one colonel (Lovless). All were onetime European Theater commanders who were accustomed to fighting vast, mobile land battles across well-defined fronts, backed up by massive concentrations of artillery and good field communications. They tended to be "roadbound." None had ever fought Asians. None had experience in guerrilla or "limited" warfare.[33]

Since Bill Dean had insufficient artillery to justify a full-time job for Barth, he asked Barth to go to the Pyongtaek-Ansong "front" to serve as his "eyes and ears." Barth promptly jeeped forward and found Task Force Smith, which had been reinforced by the 52d FAB commander, Miller Perry. Perry had in tow one firing battery of six 105-mm guns. Barth shared Dean's admiration for Brad Smith: "Young, clean cut and vigorous, Smith was my man from the minute I saw him. He probably had no more real idea of what lay ahead than I did, but his quiet confidence gave the assurance that his men would give a good account of themselves in their first fight," even though Smith's force was "pitifully weak."[34]

As Task Force Smith moved north on the highway, bucking a sea of fleeing refugees and ROK soldiers, the men began to gripe. Like other American GIs before them, they found South Korea to be a miserable place. It was raining hard and, owing to some atmospheric fluke, cold. The rain had turned the dust, which layered all of South Korea, to sticky mud. The stink of human feces in the rice paddies was almost unbearably revolting. The headlong flight of the ROK soldiers was infuriating.[35]

Yet morale in Task Force Smith was high. As Barth wrote later, the GIs had an "overconfidence that bordered on arrogance." When they came upon a group of ROK engineers who were preparing some bridges for demolition to stop the march of NKPA tanks, Barth and Smith angrily upbraided the ROKs for cowardice and threw the explosives into a river. "No thought of retreat or disaster entered our minds," Barth wrote.[36]

By early morning on July 5, Task Force Smith was dug in on the Seoul–Pusan highway a little north of Osan. However tenuous, the line against Joe Stalin had been drawn. There were in total 540 Americans: 17 officers and 389 enlisted men in Brad Smith's infantry; 9 officers and 125 enlisted men in Miller

Perry's artillery battery. Of Smith's group of 406, whose average age was twenty or slightly less, about 1 in 6 had been in combat before.[37]

Smith's force, however, was not adequately equipped to fight T-34 tanks. It lacked the most effective portable antitank weapon: land mines to plant in the road. There were ten 2.36-inch bazooka teams in all, but this small-caliber bazooka had proved to be inadequate against German tanks in World War II. Owing to budget cuts, few of the new armor-piercing HEAT shells had reached Eighth Army. Perry had but six rounds—one-third of the total supply on Kyushu.[38]

Smith had been told that he could count on the Air Force for "close air support." However the "glamour boys" of the Air Force, flying out of Japan in World War II workhorse F-51 Mustang prop planes and the new fast but short-legged F-80 jets, had not been much help and, on occasion, had been harmful. In the budget squeeze the Air Force had given close air support a low priority. Many pilots were not trained for it. The bad weather had forced the cancellation of many missions. There was little coordination between Air Force and Army ground units, no means, as yet, to call the fighters for a "surgical strike" on specific targets. As a result, on July 3, after the fog had cleared, friendly fighters strafed and bombed ROK forces at Pyongtaek and Suwon, destroying a nine-car ROK ammo train, the Pyongtaek depot (and half the town), the Suwon depot, and thirty ROK trucks. More than 200 ROK soldiers—and uncounted civilians—had been killed in these uncoordinated and careless air attacks.[39]

\* \* \*

Meanwhile, Jay Lovless had been assembling his 34th Regiment (1,981 men) at Pusan for the move north. Pappy Wadlington had taken over as the new exec; Lawrence Paulus had relinquished command of the 1/34 to Red Ayres, who flew from Japan to Pusan on a plane with the 21st commander, Dick Stephens, assumed command of the 1/34 without having met Lovless, and went ahead to Pyongtaek to scout positions.[40]

In Pusan a KMAG officer was detailed to brief the officers of the 34th for battle. One of the 34th's platoon leaders, West Pointer (1948) William B. Caldwell, recalled the briefer's absurd remarks: "He explained to us that he had been in Seoul when the North Koreans attacked on the twenty-fifth of June. He had to swim the Han River to escape the North Koreans. But now he felt very confident and comfortable: As soon as the flag and the troops of the U.S. Army were in position, it would stop this sort of rabble organization of the NKPA. He described it as a group of young soldiers, many of them teenagers, oftentimes without weapons, who were ill-trained and lacked combat capability. I remember how incongruous his remarks seemed in view of the fact that he had barely escaped with his life."[41]

The 34th entrained at Pusan and began moving north on July 4: The train stopped in Taejon, where Lovless had a heated confrontation with Dean. As the regimental S-3, John Dunn, remembered it, when Dean unfolded his plan to deploy Lovless's 1/34 at Pyongtaek and his 3/34 eleven miles away at Ansong, Lovless, believing the plan was bad for all the obvious reasons, "protested in a very spirited manner." Lovless argued that he would be "much more effective if he was allowed time to get his regiment together to fight as a unit."[42]

This was apparently the first time any senior officer in Eighth Army had raised a question about the soundness of its plan of operation. John Dunn thought Lovless was "basically sound in his thinking," but Dean was disappointed by his negative attitude. Dean elaborated on his plan, "giving numerous reasons" for his decisions, Dunn wrote, but when Lovless remained unconvinced, Dean, "becoming a bit exasperated [,] said 'I want a battalion up there' and that ended the discussion."[43]

On this sour note Lovless continued north and established his CP at Songhwan, six miles south of Pyongtaek. Red Ayres, whom Lovless had still not met, took formal command of the 1/34 in Pyongtaek and dug into position. Later in the day David H. Smith, commanding the 3/34 (less the regimental reserve, L Company), detrained and went northeast to Ansong. The 63d FAB, commanded by Robert H. Dawson, whom Lovless did not know either, had orders to move north from Pusan as rapidly as possible to support the 34th, but it was delayed in unloading its gear at Pusan and in finding transportation north. As a result, the 34th deployed for battle with no artillery support. Moreover, it had no internal communications. Such unit radios as were available and operating would not reach from the regimental CP at Songhwan to Pyongtaek or Ansong or from the 1/34 CP at Pyongtaek to the 3/34 CP at Ansong.

Nor was there any immediate help to be had from the rest of Dick Stephens's 21st Regiment, coming by ship. Through no fault of Stephens's, it was lagging. First to arrive were the other two companies (A and D) of Brad Smith's 1/21. They went north, but when they got to Chonan (south of Lovless's CP), unknown to Lovless or to Brad Smith, Bittman Barth, who had no tactical responsibility or authority, told them to halt and dig into defensive positions two miles south of Chonan, for reasons never made clear. Red Ayres or David Smith could have used these two companies to reinforce their thin positions. Unknown to Lovless or Red Ayres, these quixotic orders left Smith's 1/21 divided between Osan and Chonan with Ayres's 1/34 interposed at Pyongtaek and the 34th's CP at Songhwan, with no communications between any of the units. Meanwhile, Dick Stephens, his staff, and Delbert Pryor's 3/21 were still in Pusan trying to find transportation north.[44]

When Red Ayres took command of the 1/34 at Pyongtaek, he was not a little appalled, by both Dean's blocking plan and the pitiful state of his outfit. He later wrote: "Dean and Barth acted as if they were deploying corps against numerically inferior forces instead of three weak, poorly-armed battalions against divisions of well-armed and well-trained and well-supported NKPA forces. . . . Dean's impression that this [Pyongtaek] was a strong position with its left flank secured by the Yellow Sea was erroneous."[45]

## III

At 7:30 A.M. on July 5 Brad Smith spotted a column of eight NKPA tanks advancing south on the highway toward his position. It was another cold, miserable, rainy day; he could expect no help from the Air Force.[46]

Behind the lead column of eight tanks were twenty-five more—in all, thirty-three. The formation constituted a regiment of the NKPA 105th Armored Division, which was blazing a path for the NKPA's 4th Infantry Division, coming behind on the highway in trucks and on foot in a vast snaking column six miles long. The NKPA was confident that the bad weather protected it from air attack but was unaware that American infantry lay in wait.

One mile to the south of Smith's position Bittman Barth stood watching near Miller Perry's six 105-mm howitzers. Barth recorded that at 8:16 A.M., when the NKPA had drawn to about a mile from Smith's positions, Perry gave the order to open fire. Husbanding the six rounds of HEAT they had, the gunners used conventional high-explosive (non-armor-piercing) shells. There were no hits, no damage to the tanks was seen; nor did the tanks even hesitate. Barth watched the oncoming tanks with mounting unease—instinct told him a disaster was in the making—then climbed into his jeep and sped south to Pyongtaek to alert Red Ayres and his 1/34.

Brad Smith remained cool and steady as the big clanking tanks rolled ever closer through the rain and mist, occasionally firing their powerful 85-mm guns. He passed the word to the teams on the 75-mm recoilless rifles not to fire until the tanks came within 700 yards. Meanwhile, his bazooka teams, having taken advantageous positions, readied their weapons and waited. The two heavy (4.2-inch) mortar teams, positioned on the reverse slope of a hill, made final adjustments on their weapons.

When the lead tanks closed to 700 yards, Smith signaled the recoilless-rifle teams to open fire. Each team scored "direct hits"; but the conventional shells, some of which may have been duds, did no discernible damage, and the tanks came on relentlessly. When the tanks were almost abreast of the infantry, the bazooka teams opened up at point-blank range (fifteen yards). One team fired twenty-two rockets at the "weaker" rear armor of a T-34, but still the tank did not stop. Nor did the others.

Miller Perry now decided to fire his Sunday punch—the six rounds of HEAT. These, or a combination of these and bazooka fire, seriously damaged the two lead tanks, forcing them off the highway. One burst into flames. The three-man crew climbed out, two men with arms raised in surrender, the third defiantly firing a burp gun. His fire killed an unidentified American machine gunner—the first American casualty of the war.

What was most startling—even stupefying—to the Americans in this encounter were the boldness and skill of the NKPA tank crews. They had not turned tail as expected. They appeared to be unfazed by the American fire. The other six lead tanks proceeded southward on the highway, first shooting up Smith's truck park, then attacking Perry's artillery positions. Unaccustomed to being "invaded" by an enemy, some of the artillerymen panicked. But not the cool Miller Perry. He grabbed a bazooka and boldly attacked a tank at close range and stopped it. In the process Perry was hit in the leg. Another artillery bazooka team stopped another tank.

In all, the American infantry and artillerymen knocked out four of the thirty-three NKPA tanks. The remaining twenty-nine clanked through Task Force Smith and continued south along the highway to Osan. Shaken but resolute, Smith and Perry remained in position to meet the oncoming NKPA infantry. At about 11:30 A.M., when the lead trucks closed to about 1,000 yards, Smith, as he reported later, "threw the book at them." Some trucks were hit and burst into flames, but swarms of well-disciplined NKPA infantry continued the advance on foot, boldly attacking Smith's shrinking perimeter frontally and then on both flanks, circling behind him.

Again the American soldiers were dumbfounded. One of them later wrote: "Instead of a motley horde armed with old muskets, the enemy infantry were well-trained, determined soldiers and many of their weapons were at least as modern as ours. Instead of charging wildly into battle, they employed a base of fire, double envelopment, fire blocks on withdrawal routes, and skilled infiltration."[47]

By about 2:30 P.M. it was clear to Smith that his position was hopeless. He gave the order to withdraw, a difficult maneuver in daylight while under heavy enemy attack. It did not go well. When the troops heard the withdrawal order, discipline broke, and many men panicked and "bugged out" for the rear, throwing away BARs (Browning automatic rifles), machine guns, ammo, M-1 rifles, carbines, helmets, boots, and even shirts as they plunged wildly into stinking, slippery rice paddies, chased by burp-gun fire. Under the circumstances, Smith had no alternative but to leave behind his dead and about thirty severely wounded men on litters, who were tended by a brave corpsman who refused to flee.[48]

Making his way to the rear, Smith was surprised to find the wounded Perry still courageously at his post, manning five of his six surviving guns. The artillerymen removed the sights, aiming circles and breech locks from these five guns—rendering them useless—and joined the infantry withdrawal toward Osan. There Smith and Perry found most of the artillery trucks undamaged and formed a convoy. Since the NKPA tanks lay between them and Ayres's 1/34 at Pyongtaek, they followed a secondary road southeast to Ansong, where David Smith's 3/34 was outposting the flank. Along the way they picked up stragglers.

In this historic, heroic, but utterly futile confrontation Task Force Smith had been wiped out in a few hours. In total, Smith and Perry lost about 185 men killed, wounded, captured, or missing. The force had not, as designed, given the NKPA a bloody nose but merely a tweaking. It had not stopped the armored group at all and had only slightly delayed and inconvenienced the NKPA infantry. It would require five days for Smith to round up and reequip his stragglers and integrate them with his other men. The effective fighting power of one of Dean's three battalions had been squandered, all to no purpose.

Worse was the psychological impact of the defeat on the remainder of Dean's men. The reality of this disciplined, apparently fearless enemy came as a severe shock to all. As one soldier put it, "News of the delaying action at Osan had an unhealthy effect as it grapevined through the rank and file of the 24th Division. . . . It planted a doubt in many minds about the effectiveness of our tactics and weapons . . . [and] swollen by rumor . . . the doubt ate like a cancer into the combat morale of all troops moving to the front."[49]

\* \* \*

After his hasty withdrawal from Perry's artillery position that morning, Bittman Barth arrived at Pyongtaek to alert the 1/34 commander, Red Ayres, whom he had not yet met. By that time Ayres had fully deployed the 1/34—all strangers to him—for battle: A and B companies on the highway north of Pyongtaek; C Company in reserve in the village. Barth informed Ayres of the oncoming tanks, correctly guessing that Smith probably could not hold, and exceeding his authority as Dean's observer, Barth ordered Ayres to send a bazooka patrol north toward Osan to intercept the tanks. He also brought up the regimental reserve (L Company) to provide (as he thought) protection for the withdrawal of Miller Perry's valuable artillery pieces.

In response, Ayres dispatched the regimental I and R (intelligence and reconnaissance) platoon, commanded by Charles E. Payne, "a dapper fast-talking" veteran of the Italian campaign. It was accompanied by an infantry unit commanded by William Caldwell, who remembered:

We went looking for tanks from Pyongtaek and found one. Lucky for us it was stuck on a railroad track; it couldn't move to train its guns. We moved very close and fired our 2.36 rocket launcher. Every round we had was a complete dud. I sent back for more bazooka teams. They fired many shots at this stranded tank—pot shots—but every single round we shot was a dud. Battalion sent up some mortars, to no avail. Our 2.36 rocket launchers were completely ineffective because of the faulty ammo.[50]

This miniexpedition was accompanied by a small contingent of brave war correspondents, including *Life* photographer Carl Mydans and Marguerite Higgins, whose presence in the war zone was not welcomed by the senior commander because of her sex. Higgins wrote with a note of astonishment and alarm what was already well known in the Army: that even with good ammo the 2.36 bazookas were "no match for Soviet tanks unless they scored a lucky hit from very close range." She also wrote, incorrectly, that Private Kenneth Shadrick, who was killed in this action, was the "first casualty" of the war, an error that was widely published in America.[51]

\* \* \*

After dark that night, July 5, Bill Dean jeeped forward from Taejon to Pyongtaek to confer with Barth and Ayres. He remained in Pyongtaek with Barth and Ayres for several hours, awaiting word on the fate of Task Force Smith. Smith's makeshift convoy, consisting of eighty-six stragglers, "without shoes, hats, or much of anything else," had pushed on from Ansong to Lovless's CP at Songhwan, where Smith dropped off some wounded men before going on south to Chonan. Since Dean had not stopped to see Lovless, whose CP was within a few yards of Dean's route north, or established any kind of communication with him, Dean remained unaware that Brad Smith was safe in Chonan.[52]

Dean remained in Pyongtaek until one o'clock in the morning, futilely speculating on the outcome of Task Force Smith. He finally decided that the lack of any word and Payne's and Caldwell's encounter with the tanks north of Pyongtaek could only mean the rumors were true: Smith and his force had been wiped out. Finally, Dean returned to his CP in Taejon (again without stopping to see Lovless, from whom he would have learned that Brad Smith was safely in Chonan), arriving so late that he got but one hour's sleep that night.[53]

Shortly after Dean left Pyongtaek, Miller Perry arrived at Ayres's CP from Ansong. He gave Barth and Ayres a calm and dispassionate account of the action at Osan—the first official report—laying heavy stress on the power, discipline, and courage of the NKPA. This middle-of-the-night report galvanized Barth and led him to take tactical command and to make some radical changes in Dean's blocking plan.[54]

As Barth now saw it, the Pyongtaek–Ansong "line" was too thin and too widely dispersed to hold against the kind of enemy power Perry had described. He conceived a new plan: consolidation of the 34th at Chonan, ten miles south of Pyongtaek on the Seoul–Pusan highway. Barth briefed Ayres on the plan and gave him new orders. Ayres was to blow the highway bridge over the "river" north of Pyongtaek, hold the village as long as he reasonably could without endangering the battalion, then withdraw to Chonan to link up with the 3/34 and the two companies of Brad Smith's 1/21 already dug in there. The decision about when to withdraw would be entirely up to Ayres, but "under no circumstances" was he "to end up like Brad Smith," which Ayres took to mean "chewed to pieces."

There may have been a misunderstanding between Barth and Ayres over these new orders. Barth later claimed that what he meant to convey to Ayres was that the 1/34 should withdraw south toward Chonan, but in order to buy more time, the battalion should fight a delaying action at two separate and specific places between Pyongtaek and Chonan. If this was really what Barth intended to convey, he was at fault for not making his orders clearer and more specific. Ayres later claimed that he had no such understanding.

At 1:30 A.M. Barth left Pyongtaek and jeeped south to Songhwan to brief Jay Lovless on the new plan. Lovless found it not a little odd that this complete stranger from another division was giving his reserve (L Company) and his battalion commander Ayres direct and detailed tactical orders. However, inasmuch as Lovless found the new plan more closely in line with his original desire to fight his regiment as a consolidated unit, he raised no objections and quickly dispatched a messenger to David Smith's 3/34 CP in Ansong, ordering him to withdraw to Chonan. David Smith, who had already learned about the power of the NKPA from both Brad Smith and Perry, lost no time in executing these orders. The 3/34 would "tie in" with the two companies (A and D) of Brad Smith's 1/21, which Lovless learned for the first time had already dug in at Chonan.

Meanwhile, the 34th Regiment's S-3, John Dunn, awoke from a dead sleep to find the CP in a great state of excitement. He volunteered to go to Pyongtaek to establish a liaison with Ayres and assist him however he could. Lovless, echoing Barth's new plan and orders, told Dunn to tell Ayres to "hold as long as he could but not to lose the battalion and then fall back to a position in the vicinity of Chonan." Since these plans represented a radical change from those insisted upon by Bill Dean in the heated meeting at Taejon on July 4, Dunn asked Lovless to repeat them. After Lovless had done so, adding that the regimental reserve (L Company) should cover the 1/34 withdrawal, Dunn set off for Pyongtaek in a jeep. He arrived about daylight on July 6, another wet, cold, overcast day, decidedly unfavorable for close air support. On the way north Dunn passed about ten of Brad Smith's men "going south without shoes or weapons."

At about that time the lead tanks and infantry of the NKPA reached the blown bridge north of Pyongtaek. Ayres was on the scene commanding his A and B companies, which were dug in south of the bridge on either side of the road. His battalion was less well armed than Task Force Smith's: no artillery; no mines; only a "few" 4.2 mortars "with limited ammo" and two obsolete 57-mm and one 75-mm recoilless rifles. As the NKPA infantry swarmed south around the stopped tanks, firing at the Americans, the green men stared numbly, only about half of them finding the wit to fire back. Some who did found their M-1 rifles to be useless. A sergeant later reported that twelve out of thirty-one of the rifles in his platoon were "defective."

Returning to his CP, Ayres found John Dunn in conference with the battalion exec, Leland R. Dunham. Dunn relayed to Ayres the orders from Lovless to "hold as long as possible but not to lose his battalion and then [to] fall back to the vicinity of Chonan." The decision about when to fall back was entirely up to Ayres. Ayres described the power of the oncoming NKPA—two columns of infantry, each "nearly a mile long"—and the stunned reaction of his men and said he could probably hold out no more than an additional hour. When Dunn responded that he could not see how one hour's resistance would help the overall situation in any way and that furthermore, he believed a delay might put the battalion "in an impossible situation," Ayres "picked up the telephone" and gave his outfit the order to withdraw to Chonan.

Able battalion commanders were rare in Eighth Army in the early days of the Korean War. To perform this complex job properly required years of professional schooling and command, intelligence, coolness under fire, and the gift of leadership. Although Red Ayres was a complete stranger and had commanded the 1/34 only twenty-four hours, he had made a fine impression. Dunn later wrote that Ayres "was a brave, outstanding combat leader—one of the coolest men under fire I have ever seen." The 1/34 platoon leader William Caldwell agreed with that assessment. He remembered that Ayres "was certainly a tremendous individual—an outstanding leader and professional soldier."[55]

For all his professionalism, however, Red Ayres could not prevent a disgraceful bugout in the 1/34 and its "covering" force, the reserve L Company. When the withdrawal order reached company level, discipline broke down. To one GI the masses of enemy soldiers "looked like the entire city of New York" coming at him. Under increasingly heavy fire the Americans fled the battlefield, many leaving behind all their heavy weapons, rifles, and carbines. On the long, uneasy retreat south to Chonan the men of 1/34 and L Company discarded ponchos, helmets, ammo belts, rifles, and wet, pinching shoes. When it finally reached Chonan, one Army historian wrote, the 1/34 "was a shabby-looking outfit" with "no organization." In effect, another battalion had been squandered.[56]

When the men of 1/34 first began drifting into Chonan, Barth, who was there, professed to be astonished—and angry—with Ayres because the 1/34 had not mounted the delaying actions he claimed he had ordered. He later wrote of Ayres: "I probably could have stopped him and gotten his battalion on a [delaying] position north of Chonan by dark." But this is problematic. In view of the general panic in the 1/34 and L Company that afternoon, it is not likely that either Ayres or Barth could have stopped the men between Pyongtaek and Chonan to face NKPA tanks and infantry. Ironically, the NKPA did not immediately and vigorously pursue beyond Pyongtaek that day.[57]

While the 1/34 and L Company retreat was in progress, David Smith was withdrawing the 3/34 from Ansong to Chonan. Although the 3/34 had not yet been fired upon by the enemy and was never in real danger like the 1/34, its withdrawal also turned into undisciplined flight. Smith was showing signs of exhaustion. To Pappy Wadlington, he "was incapable of accepting or carrying out orders." On the road from Ansong to Chonan his men also abandoned ammo, weapons, helmets, shoes, and other gear.[58]

Simultaneously with these withdrawals, Lovless decamped his CP at Songhwan and reestablished it in the rear, near Chonan. War correspondents Carl Mydans and Marguerite Higgins, who had been sleeping on the CP floor and were not notified, awoke to find the Songhwan CP completely deserted. Higgins later wrote: "In the coming days I saw young Americans turn and bolt in battle, or throw down their arms cursing their government for what they thought was embroilment in a hopeless cause. . . . It was routine to hear comments like 'Just give me a jeep and I know what direction to go in. This mama's boy ain't cut out to be no hero.' "[59]

# IV

When the sleepless Bill Dean learned that the 34th Regiment had withdrawn to Chonan, he was furious. He climbed into his jeep at Taejon and sped north to Lovless's CP near Chonan. There ensued a stormy meeting with Barth, Lovless, Dunn, and the two battalion commanders, Red Ayres and David Smith. Dean heatedly demanded to know who had authorized the withdrawal. Bittman Barth and Jay Lovless remained mute, Lovless waiting for Barth to accept responsibility for the orders. When no one spoke up, Red Ayres broke the awkward silence and took full responsibility for the withdrawal of his 1/34. In so doing, he attempted unsuccessfully to set Dean straight on one point: The battalion had not bugged out, as word had it. It had withdrawn in accordance with "sound principles enunciated in military manuals."[60]

But there was no reasoning with the enraged and frazzled Bill Dean that night. Notwithstanding arguments from Lovless, Dunn, and Ayres to the contrary, he remained adamantly convinced that his original blocking scheme at Pyongtaek-Ansong had been the correct one and that he had been, in effect, betrayed by his own officers. He sent Bittman Barth packing—back to Taejon—and made up his mind to sack Jay Lovless the minute Robert Martin arrived in Taejon. Had there been spare battalion commanders with combat experience at hand, he might well have sacked Red Ayres and David Smith on the spot. Before storming out of the CP to return to Taejon, Dean gave Lovless orders to attack north at dawn the following morning, July 7, with the reserve L Company, reestablish contact with the NKPA, and then fight a delaying action back to Chonan.

These orders were not received with great enthusiasm. By then the 34th, consolidated at last (and tied in with the other unbloodied half of Brad Smith's 1/21) had begun digging in south of Chonan in what Lovless considered pretty fair defensive terrain. Advance elements of Robert Dawson's (understrength) 63d FAB were now detraining at Chonan, joining elements of Miller Perry's 52d FAB, to reinforce these positions. To attack out of these consolidated positions with green troops and ineffective antitank weapons—and with no tanks—merely for the sake of reestablishing contact with the oncoming NKPA or to gain and hold Chonan and then to mount a complex delaying action seemed foolhardy. Red Ayres later wrote that he thought the orders were "ridiculous," that Dean, "in stress," was acting out of "emotion" rather than "sound tactics."[61]

Nonetheless, orders were orders, and on the morning of July 7 Jay Lovless sent Charles Payne's I and R Platoon and the regimental reserve, L Company, heading north toward Chonan. As this force was moving cautiously forward, a message came from Bill Dean in Taejon to reinforce the attack with David Smith's full—and as yet unbloodied—3/34. Although Lovless had greatest misgivings over these orders, he complied, and the 3/34 moved north behind the I and R Platoon and L Company. The regimental S-3, John Dunn, jeeped forward to offer whatever help he could.

That same morning, at about ten, Robert Martin, on orders from Dean, arrived at Lovless's CP. He had no helmet or weapon and was still wearing street shoes. He had obviously come to relieve Lovless of command of the 34th, but he had no orders to that effect from Dean. He accompanied Lovless in the command jeep all that day, as Lovless sped around to the CPs of the 1/34, the 3/34, and the newly arrived 63d FAB.[62]

Payne's I and R Platoon, making contact with the NKPA north of Chonan, was ambushed and badly shot up. Escaping the trap, Payne withdrew. Hearing the news, David Smith quickly found some good defensive positions and ordered his 3/34 to break off the attack and dig in on the roadside. While this was going on, John Dunn volunteered to lead L Company forward to rescue some of Payne's men who had been trapped. However, before Dunn could get going, the 3/34's S-3, West Pointer (1943) Boone Seegers, came south on the road and reported he had already rescued them.[63]

At about this time David Smith lost complete control of his 3/34. The battalion panicked and bugged out. Dunn, who could find neither Smith nor his exec, was appalled and disgusted. "The standard of our officer corps," he wrote, "hit a new low. Cynicism and self interest had replaced duty and honor among too many of our so-called leaders."

Others agreed, although in less harsh words. The 1/34 platoon leader William Caldwell wrote that while there were many acts of individual bravery on the part of the men, "I feel that whenever we had a breakdown that it was often-times due to the lack of leadership we had on the part of some of our young leaders and the lack of appreciation of what was happening possibly on the part of some more senior." The 3/34 operations sergeant, Charles W. Menninger, a combat-hardened veteran of the 3d Infantry Division, wrote:

The thing that stands out in my mind was that there appeared to be little or no communications, and very little leadership, the feeling that it was "every man for himself." . . . We NCOs were left behind to sit around the so-called CP while the officers were out running around in jeeps, doing what the enlisted personnel were supposed to be doing. . . . The attitude of superior officers at the beginning was all wrong.[64]

John Dunn and others managed temporarily to stop the bugout of the 3/34, but late in the afternoon, in the face of what appeared to be renewed NKPA pressure, it bugged out again. At about the same time the division's aged ADC, Pearson Menoher, and the frail John Church arrived at Lovless's CP, which had been combined with that of Ayres's 1/34. Menoher handed Lovless an order from Bill Dean formally relieving Lovless of command, with instructions to turn over the 34th to Robert Martin. Lovless, professionally ruined, accepted this not unexpected blow stoically. He generously gave Martin his .45 pistol, web belt, canteen, and first-aid kit, then left the CP and ran into John Dunn coming in to report the latest disgrace of the 3/34. Lovless deflected Dunn's report, saying, "Explain it to the general," and walked away.[65]

Robert Martin listened attentively to Dunn's report, then asked, "Will the regiment take orders from me?" Dunn was quite startled. He had no idea who Robert Martin was, but he replied yes. Thereupon Martin ordered Dunn to take command of the 3/34 and "put it back on that position."[66]

Dunn raced out to stem the retreat. By that time the road was thronged with wild-eyed, thoroughly panicked southbound infantry, who had been joined by artillerymen and service troops. In an extraordinary display of leadership, Dunn turned the whole mass around and headed it back north to reoccupy its positions. That done, Dunn and the S-3, Boone Seegers, rounded up some 3/34 officers, got in two jeeps, and drove ahead of the troops to set an example. Moments later the jeeps were ambushed. Both Dunn and Seegers were badly wounded, Seegers mortally, Dunn in three places, including a severed artery. They crawled or were lifted out of the jeep and struggled into brush. "The officers who were not hurt," Dunn wrote later, "did absolutely nothing to aid the wounded."[67]

A 3/34 rifle company had been advancing up the road behind Dunn and Seegers. When its men heard the enemy fire, they went to ground and formed a skirmish line, halfheartedly returning the enemy fire. The wounded Dunn crawled up on a knoll, where he had a good view of the action. Stanching the flow of blood, he estimated the number of NKPA soldiers to be at most forty. The Americans were so close he could recognize the officers and hear them giving orders. "They could easily have walked right through the few scattered enemy in the area but the officers made no effort to have the men advance." Then, with sinking heart, Dunn heard the company commander yell, "Fall back! Fall back!" Dunn and Seegers were abandoned, Seegers to die that night, Dunn to be captured and imprisoned for thirty-eight months. He wrote: "To think that a regular American unit commanded by professional officers, out-numbering the enemy ten to one . . . would abandon their own people and leave the field in possession of a few trained monkeys was nauseating."[68]

Following this latest disgrace, Robert Martin came on the field and took command of the 3/34. He stopped and temporarily steadied the men and ordered them to dig in for the night, proclaiming grandly that "as long as I'm in command, this regiment will not withdraw another inch." At daylight the following day, July 8, the NKPA, led by five or six tanks, hit Chonan. In the street fighting that ensued early that morning, Martin, manning a bazooka like an infantryman, attacked a tank at point-blank range. Simultaneously the tank fired off a round from its 85-mm gun and cut Martin's body in half. He had commanded the 34th Regiment for fourteen hours. Sergeant Menninger commented: "When I say that the regiment lacked proper leadership, I can point to the fact that this Colonel Martin was killed in the street fighting a T-34 instead of being where he could direct the movement of the troops."[69]

Upon Martin's death, Bill Dean wrote, the 3/34 disintegrated and bugged out again, this time in earnest. Its nominal commander, David Smith, was medically evacuated. Many of its officers were killed, wounded, or captured. Among the wounded was Walter P. ("Pinky") Meyer, who had married Lovless's daughter on the day the regiment sailed from Sasebo. The 34th's exec, Pappy Wadlington, temporarily commanding the regiment, placed the senior functioning 3/34 officer, Newton W. Lantron, in command of the battalion's 150 to 175 known survivors. One of the survivors, Sergeant Henry Leerkamp, remembered: "Major Lantron was a rare combination of a good peacetime and good wartime officer. He was cool under fire and steadied the troops. . . . When some of the men left their positions and ran to the rear . . . Major Lantron, with pistol out, stood in the road and stopped them."[70]

Dean's impetuous orders to throw the green, ill-equipped 3/34 into an attack at Chonan against NKPA tanks and infantry was, as Red Ayres observed, "ridiculous." The 3/34 had not delayed the NKPA significantly. The attack had lost, among others, three of the regiment's ablest men—Robert Martin, John Dunn, and Boone Seegers—and consigned scores of men to the hell of NKPA POW camps for years.

\* \* \*

On July 7 Johnnie Walker flew into Taejon for his first visit to the battlefield. There was no hint of criticism then or later about Dean's brash deployment plan. As Walker's chief of staff, Gene Landrum, recalled, Walker admired Dean unreservedly. He was just what Walker wanted: "a fighter and a doer." Walker believed that American forces could win only by relentless and continuous attacks, which would throw the NKPA off-balance, that every opportunity to attack should be seized.[71]

The next day, July 8, Walker and Dean jeeped forward to the hills overlooking Chonan, where they watched the 3/34 bugout. A "sweating officer" of the 3/34 came to tell Dean of Robert Martin's futile heroism—and ghastly death. Dean put Martin in for a DSC—the first to be awarded in the Korean War.[72]*

Dean laid the blame for the failure of his blocking plan not on its design but on the 34th Regiment. He was "quite bitter about the 34th Infantry," Dick Stephens wrote, and became determined to "instill a will to fight in that regiment." Since the exec, Pappy Wadlington, temporarily commanding the 34th's survivors, was too old and "too weak" to continue as top man, and there was no logical replacement in South Korea, Dean asked Walker to send a new regimental commander from Japan.[73]

The same day—perhaps at Walker's suggestion—Dean got off a personal letter to MacArthur which revealed that Dean's initial belief that his mission in South Korea would be "short and easy" had been shattered. "I am convinced," Dean wrote MacArthur, "that the North Korean Army, the North Korean soldier and his status of training and the quality of his equipment have been underestimated." Its armored force, in particular, was formidable. Dean's men could not stop the T-34 tank with the 2.36 bazooka or ordinary high-explosive 105-mm artillery shells. They urgently needed the new 3.5-inch

---

*Brad Smith and Miller Perry later received DSCs for the action at Osan.

bazooka, HEAT shells, and 90-mm antitank guns, which were slightly more powerful than the T-34's 85-mm gun, and tanks with 90-mm guns. Moreover, Dean wrote, "The two-battalion regimental organization with which we are operating does not lend itself to effective combat." He asked for additional infantry battalions to bring his division up to "regular triangular organization" and urged that other regiments heading for South Korea be so organized.[74]

Before Walker returned to Japan that day, he and Bill Dean reviewed options. It was decided that the city of Taejon, where Dean had located the 24th Division CP, was now the key real estate and that an all-out effort would be made to hold it for as long as possible. The major elements of Dean's 24th Division—the surviving units of the 21st and 34th regiments plus the newly arriving 19th Regiment—would consolidate where they might have been more effectively deployed in the first place: in a defensive line along the meandering Kum River, north of Taejon.[75]

\* \* \*

The task of setting up a Kum River line with the NKPA in close, hot pursuit and with such slim American forces was difficult. It was further complicated by the geography and road network. South of Chonan, where the 3/34 had been routed, the Seoul–Pusan highway divided, one fork going to Kongju, one to Chochiwon, before it reunited near Taejon. This compelled Dean to divide his thin forces to fight delaying actions on both forks. He assigned Pappy Wadlington's shattered 34th the Kongju fork; Dick Stephens's 21st, the Chochiwon fork, which was believed to be the main line of advance of the NKPA.[76]

This difficult delaying mission would be Dick Stephens's introduction to combat in Korea. Owing to the heroic, but futile, fight of Brad Smith's 1/21 at Osan, Stephens initially had only one and a half battalions to deploy against the NKPA: Delbert Pryor's 3/21 and A and D companies of Smith's 1/21 (less Smith, for the time being). Stephens courageously led Smith's two companies, together with some 1/21 fillers who had arrived from Pusan, to a forward position in Chonui, north of Chochiwon on the highway, and dug in. Pryor, as ordered, deployed his 3/21 in Chochiwon. Stephens was backed up by a battery of the newly arrived 11th FAB (equipped with 155-mm howitzers), commanded by Ben E. Allen, and a reduced company of M-24 Chaffee light tanks—lightly armored reconnaissance vehicles mounting a 75-mm cannon— and some combat engineers.[77]

With scarcely a pause the NKPA attacked the Stephens force at Chonui on the morning of July 10. Concealed by a heavy ground fog, T-34 tanks led the enemy formation. At 8:00 A.M. the fog lifted to reveal a swarm of NKPA tanks and infantry advancing frontally and on both flanks. Inspired by the presence of Stephens, these green Americans fought stoutly for about three hours—until about 11:00 A.M.—then began to buckle and flee. Stephens tried to stop the flight, but it was useless; the familiar American stampede through the stinking, slippery rice paddies was not to be stopped. The panic was intensified when two Air Force F-80 jets mistakenly strafed Stephens's men with machine guns and Ben Allen's 11th FAB also mistakenly bombarded them with 155-mm shells.[78] Later Dick Stephens commented:

There was no incentive for our men to fight well except strong leadership and high unit spirit. They saw no reason for the war . . . [and] had no interest in a fight which was not even dignified by calling it a war. . . . It took strong leadership and a very high spirit to get them to put their hearts in it. It was a bitter fight in which many lives were lost and we could see no profit in it except our pride in our profession and our units as well as the comradeship which dictates that you do not let your fellow soldier down.[79]

Falling back on his main positions at Chochiwon, Stephens ordered Delbert Pryor to launch his 3/21 on a counterattack toward Chonui. But West Pointer Pryor was unable to carry out these orders—and was soon evacuated as a nonbattle casualty (NBC). He was replaced as battalion commander by Carl C. ("Cliff") Jensen, thirty-eight. The 21st's exec, Fritz Mudgett, remembered with resentment that Del Pryor "failed when the chips were down" and wound up in a desk job in Tokyo, "far removed from combat."[80]

Backed by the four light tanks, Cliff Jensen led the 3/21 counterattack. The tanks "performed poorly." The division G-3, West Pointer (1934) James W. Snee, remembered: "The division had back orders two years old for recoil oil, so the tank 75-mm guns had never been fired. When the guns were fired in Korea, it was done by lanyard and promptly blew off the tank turrets." Two of the tanks were lost, but one got a lucky hit on a T-34 and disabled it.[81]

Jensen regained a ridge south of Chonui—no small achievement—but was unable to advance farther. On the recaptured ground his men discovered a grisly and outrageous sight: six dead American POWs, hands tied behind their backs, each shot in the back of the head. The discovery of this atrocity infuriated Jensen and his men and spurred them to fight with a savagery and purpose theretofore lacking.

That same afternoon the Air Force finally came through with meaningful help to the infantry. A flight of F-80 jets, dipping down through the overcast at Pyongtaek (twenty-five miles north), found a juicy target: NKPA tanks and trucks lined bumper to bumper on the highway. While maneuvering to attack this target, the jets summoned help. In typical Air Force hyperbole FEAF described the attack as "one of the decisive air-ground battles of the entire conflict." The combined air power that afternoon claimed to have destroyed an estimated 38 tanks, 7 half-tracks, and 117 trucks and to have killed a "large number" of NKPA soldiers.[82]

On the following day, July 11, Dick Stephens consolidated his blocking line at Chochiwon. Brad Smith arrived with the other half of his 1/21, and for the first time in Korea Smith had the 1/21 in one piece. Stephens deployed it "in reserve" just to the south of Jensen's 3/21.

That morning, again concealed by ground fog, the NKPA hit Jensen's 3/21 in what the official Army historian Roy E. Appleman described as "one of the most perfectly executed coordinated enemy assaults of the war." In a matter of a few hours the 3/21 was encircled and shattered. Jensen was killed; most of the battalion staff was captured or missing. Only 150 of the 667 men in the 3/21 escaped that day to Brad Smith's lines. (Later another 172 straggled in.) Yet another battalion had been squandered.[83]

Onward came the NKPA 3d Division, like a great relentless flood. On July 12 it skillfully attacked Brad Smith's newly integrated 1/21, which was composed of many green replacements. Smith held for about two hours. Then, for the second time, he was overwhelmed and forced to give orders to withdraw. This time the withdrawal, steadied by Smith, was "orderly." Moving one company at a time by truck, Smith fell back behind the Kum River. That evening, when Smith found time for a head count, he had but 325 men, including 64 from the 3/21.

These actions of the 21st Regiment at Chonui and Chochiwon and the FEAF attack at Pyongtaek delayed the NKPA at least two days and possibly three. However, the cost to the 21st was ghastly: Of its 2,400 men, 1,400 were dead, wounded, or missing, including Cliff Jensen and most of the 3/21. Even so, Bill Dean was pleased by the fighting spirit the regiment had demonstrated by comparison with the 34th, and he awarded Stephens a DSC for his brave frontline, foxhole leadership. Moreover, war correspondents who witnessed the action showered praise on Stephens and made him temporarily famous. One, Keyes Beech, wrote that notwithstanding Stephens's age, girth, and lack of charisma, he "fought with grace and ease under the most trying conditions."[84]

Meanwhile, Pappy Wadlington, still temporarily commanding the 34th, withdrew it down the fork to Kongju, pursued by the NKPA 4th Division. The 34th's principal surviving force was Red Ayres's 1/34, reorganized and partly reequipped while the 3/34 was being mauled at Chonan. Wadlington was backed by some batteries of Robert Dawson's 63d FAB, four newly arrived light tanks, and some combat engineers. Three of the four tanks were lost, but Wadlington got the shattered 34th and the 63d FAB guns behind the Kum River with minimal casualties, a tribute to the professionalism and courage of Red Ayres, who commanded the rear guard.[85]

By the early hours of July 12 the remnants of Stephens's 21st and Wadlington's 34th regiments were at last digging in behind the Kum River, backed up by artillery batteries of 11th, 52nd, and 63d FABs. The infantry forces were wretchedly weak: Brad Smith's mauled 1/21 on the right, plus a few stragglers from the shattered 3/21; Red Ayres's 1/34 on the left, plus a few stragglers of Lantron's 3/34. Replacements and fillers were rushing north from Pusan to the 34th, but as yet there were none for the 21st. Consequently, Dean decided to pull the 21st to the rear and replace it with his fresh but green 19th Infantry, then arriving in the battle zone from Pusan.

\* \* \*

So ended the first week of American ground combat in Korea. It had not gone well for the Americans. Under cover of foul weather the NKPA had advanced an impressive fifty air miles from Suwon to the Kum River, suffering only moderate casualties. It had shattered or disorganized two American regiments comprising four infantry battalions plus several artillery batteries and supporting units. Perhaps 3,000 Americans were dead, wounded, missing, or captured. In their panicky bugouts the Americans had left enough weapons, equipment, and ammo on the battlefields to fit out one or two NKPA regiments.

The Americans had achieved little in this piecemeal and disorganized waste of precious lives and equipment. At most they delayed the NKPA a total of three, possibly four, days. Notwithstanding Army claims to the contrary, these delays were not in any way decisive to the American forces and might well have been matched at less cost by a consolidated and cohesive defense behind the Kum River. Moreover, the collapse of these ill-trained, ill-equipped, ill-led, and thinly disposed American units in first combat was a psychological victory of incalculable dimensions to the NKPA. In combat, as elsewhere, success breeds success.

**PART**
# THREE

# Retreat to the Pusan Perimeter

# TAEJON LOST

## I

The power and professionalism of the NKPA and the lackluster performance of the 24th Division came as a terrific shock to GHQ, Tokyo. It soon became evident that the proposed amphibious landing of the 1st Cav at Inchon was a pipe dream. The division was redirected to land at or near Pusan to reinforce the 24th and 25th divisions. In addition, MacArthur bombarded the Pentagon with urgent requests for additional troops, both for service in Korea and to provide for the defense of Japan, which had been virtually denuded by the commitment of three divisions to Korea and manpower levies on the other to reinforce them. Between July 2 and 10 MacArthur requested:

• A Marine Corps RCT, then, rather, the full 1st Marine Division, based in California.[1]
• The full 2d Infantry Division, based at Fort Lewis near Tacoma, Washington.
• An RCT from the 82d Airborne Division, based at Fort Bragg, North Carolina.[2]
• Eleven infantry battalions, to bring the four divisions of Eighth Army up to full strength.
• Eleven artillery batteries, to bring the artillery battalions of the four divisions to full strength.
• Thousands of individual fillers, to bring other units up to strength and to replace battle casualties.
• An armored group of three medium tank battalions.

119

- A brigade of Army combat engineers.
- Two corps headquarters.

The requests were accompanied by steadily escalating rhetoric. On July 7 MacArthur reported that he was confronted by an "aggressive and well trained professional army" which had "demonstrated superior command of strategic and tactical principles" in the drive south of Seoul. By July 10 he had judged the situation to be "critical." Expressing doubt that the Americans could hold the southern tip of Korea, MacArthur requested, in addition to the foregoing, "a field army of four full divisions and component services."[3]

These cables and telecons "jolted" the JCS, which until then was still vastly underrating the NKPA. MacArthur's urgent requests for massive ground reinforcements raised many thorny questions, among them: Even if the ground forces could be scraped together, how deep should America commit itself on the Asian mainland to what could conceivably be a Russian diversion or feint as a prelude to an all-out assault on Western Europe or the Middle East? Was the fiscally conservative president now willing to spend the vast sums of money required and take the political risk of partial or full mobilization to "draw a line" against Joe Stalin in Korea?[4]

All three military services were hard pressed to reinforce MacArthur, but none more so than the Army. It was then composed of but ten "tactical" divisions: four in Walker's Eighth Army, one in Germany (1st Infantry) to give the embryonic NATO some substance, and five (2d and 3d Infantry, 2d Armored, 11th and 82d Airborne) in the so-called General Reserve. Of the five in the General Reserve, one division (2d Armored) was deemed unsuitable for deployment in a "police action" in a place which was "not good tank country," and two (3d Infantry, 11th Airborne) were pitifully understrength, being composed of but two regiments of two battalions. Only two divisions (2d Infantry, 82d Airborne) of the five in the General Reserve could be classed as anywhere near ready for deployment to Korea, but the 82d was ruled out because it was highly trained for special missions and lacked the proper weapons and equipment required for sustained ground combat.[5]

In addition to these ten tactical divisions, the Army had about eleven independent tactical regiments or RCTs scattered here and there. These included one (29th) in MacArthur's command on Okinawa, guarding SAC bases; one (5th) in Hawaii; one (65th) in Puerto Rico, whose principal mission was to protect the Venezuelan oil fields; one (14th) in Camp Carson, Colorado, on standby to join another RCT in Alaska should trouble arise there; one (33d) in Panama; and a half dozen elsewhere. These regiments also had been reduced to two battalions each; most were nowhere near authorized strength.[6]

Without a partial call-up of the National Guard or the Army's Organized Reserve components, there was no way to meet MacArthur's request for eleven infantry battalions, plus an additional army of four divisions, plus fillers. There were only eighteen understrength infantry battalions in the General Reserve. To fulfill MacArthur's requests would require the deployment of the entire General Reserve (plus everything else that could move) to the Far East, leaving the United States, Alaska, Hawaii, Puerto Rico (and the Venezuelan oil fields), and the Panama Canal Zone completely vulnerable.[7]

In order to acquaint MacArthur personally with these realities, and to make an independent assessment of the situation in South Korea, Truman ordered that two members of the JCS go to Tokyo and Korea. Soldier Joe Collins and airman Hoyt Vandenberg were the logical nominees. They departed in great haste on July 10.[8]

The temporary absence of Joe Collins left the Army's general staff in the hands of Ham Haislip and "general manager" Matt Ridgway. Inasmuch as Haislip's presence was required in the JCS "tank," at the White House, and on Capitol Hill, he was away from his office most of the day, leaving Ridgway, already hollow-eyed from lack of sleep, the "man in charge." On Ridgway's shoulders fell the considerable burden of deciding how to do everything possible to help MacArthur without so stripping the United States and its possessions of military power as to invite a Soviet attack or a fifth column takeover.

Early in the Korean crisis Ridgway had rightly concluded that some degree of mobilization—calling up the National Guard or the Army's Organized Reserve—would be required, and he had been urging that course without stint. But the JCS, perhaps reflecting Truman's desire to downplay the crisis or save money, continued to oppose mobilization. Joe Collins believed calling up the Guard was inadvisable because of the possible adverse "impact upon the economy and morale" and because Guard units would require extensive training (overtaxing limited Army facilities) before they could be classed as combat-effective. Consequently Ridgway and the general staff were initially compelled to choose reinforcements for MacArthur from the meager Army forces already in existence. In short, they would have to gut the General Reserve.[9]

Ridgway recommended that the following forces be dispatched to MacArthur as soon as possible:

• The entire 2d Infantry Division for combat in South Korea, increasing numbered American divisions there to four.
• The two battalions of the 29th Regiment on Okinawa (but not the headquarters) and the three battalions of the 5th RCT in Hawaii (either independently or as an RCT) to bring the regiments of the 24th or 25th divisions to full strength.
• Two battalions plus three battalion "cadres" of the 3d Infantry Division to flesh out the 1st Cav and 7th Infantry divisions.

• An airborne RCT, not from the "untouchable" 82d Airborne Division as MacArthur requested, but from the far less effective, understrength 11th Airborne Division.

• Three tank battalions, eleven 105-mm artillery batteries, a brigade of combat engineers, and other support units.

• Individual fillers, both experienced and inexperienced, from any and all units, except the 82d Airborne, to go by air where possible.

• Several 3.5-inch bazooka instruction teams, with weapons and ammo, to go under highest priority by air.[10]

These recommendations were promptly approved (in some cases by the president), and by July 10—as Bill Dean was withdrawing into the Kum River line—Ridgway had placed all units on alert for movement to the Far East. In total, the Army had met, to the best of its ability, most of MacArthur's initial requests for organized combat units: the 2d Infantry Division; an airborne RCT; seven infantry battalions required to bring the three divisions already committed to combat in Korea up to strength,* plus three battalion cadres for the uncommitted 7th Infantry Division; and tank, artillery and engineer units. The transfers gutted the General Reserve, leaving only the 82d Airborne Division intact. The large and complicated matter of supplying MacArthur an additional four-division field army with all supporting components plus a full Marine Corps division was left for discussion among MacArthur and Collins and Vandenberg.

These initial commitments to GHQ were carried out while the Army was still trying to operate under the crippling Truman-Johnson manpower and budget ceilings. But the march of events soon swept away the ceilings. In a mere ten days the authorized strength of the Army climbed from 630,000 to 740,000, a force level to be achieved by extending the tours of those men already on active duty, by a larger draft, and by a call-up of certain individuals in the Organized Reserve. At the same time the JCS requested an $11 billion supplemental appropriation, bringing the total for the 1951 fiscal budget year to $22,651,000,000. Louis Johnson rejected the request as "too high." However, by that time Johnson had become a discredited nonperson whose out-of-cadence opinions counted for nothing. Truman swiftly overruled him and sent the bill to Congress.[11]

Despite the energy and enthusiasm Matt Ridgway had brought to fulfilling MacArthur's initial requests, his eyes and the eyes of many of his staffers remained fixed on Western Europe for signs of other, perhaps more cata-

---

*The 25th Division, with a surplus of black troops, was short only two infantry battalions, not three.

strophic Soviet moves. In a memo Ridgway reminded one and all that MacArthur's responsibility was "local" compared with that of the JCS, that it was possible that if all MacArthur's requests were met, it might "dangerously deplete or even exhaust our presently available resources in certain critical categories," and that the Pentagon should not yield to the temptation to give MacArthur "a book of blank checks, just because he is presently front stage in what may after all prove to be a mere 'affair of outposts.' "[12]

## II

Joe Collins and Hoyt Vandenberg arrived in Tokyo on the morning of July 13, the day after Bill Dean had emplaced his 19th and 34th regiments behind the Kum River. They went immediately to the Dai Ichi Building, where they met with MacArthur, Ned Almond, Johnnie Walker, and others, including four-star Admiral Arthur W. Radford, who had survived the 1949 "Admiral's Revolt" and was now the commander in chief of the Pacific Fleet, with headquarters in Pearl Harbor, Hawaii.[13]

MacArthur, who by date of rank was fourteen years senior to Collins and twenty years senior to Vandenberg and who outranked both by a star (five to four), staged a dazzlingly dramatic briefing. Pacing his small, Spartan office, puffing thoughtfully on his pipe, he was, Collins remembered, "cool and poised" and spoke with "confidence and élan" in "vigorous and colorful language" as though, Collins wrote, "addressing not just his immediate listeners but a larger audience unseen."

On the strategic level MacArthur did not believe Moscow wanted all-out war but would provide maximum "underground" support to the North Koreans through China and Manchuria. The challenge should be met by the United States without "delay or halfway measures." He wanted a "maximal effort." He urged his JCS visitors to "grab every ship in the Pacific and pour the support into the Far East." Admittedly America held a poor hand in the Far East, but long experience had convinced him that "it is how you play your poor hands rather than your good ones which counts in the long run." A decisive Communist defeat in Korea would check the spread of communism everywhere.

On the tactical level MacArthur cautioned Collins and Vandenberg (and the greater unseen audience) not to underestimate the "toughness, skill and leadership" of the NKPA (as GHQ had done). Now that three American divisions had been committed to South Korea, he was confident the situation would ultimately be "stabilized." He reiterated his recently expressed view that two full-strength field armies comprising eight divisions and supporting components would be required in Korea. To provide for the security of Japan, he urged that the Japanese police force be converted to a constabulary of four divisions, equipped with American gear.

His grand plan for defeating the NKPA was as follows. He would first "isolate the battlefield" by closing off NKPA supply routes at the China and Russia borders with American air power. For this purpose he would need additional Air Force medium and heavy bombers and another Navy task force. This air operation provided a "unique opportunity" for using atomic bombs, MacArthur said, but he did not pursue this drastic suggestion in detail. After the battlefield had been isolated and stabilized, MacArthur went on, his intention was not merely to drive the NKPA back across the 38th Parallel but rather to "destroy" it. This he would do by reviving the recently canceled Inchon amphibious landing plan, designed to trap the NKPA in giant pincers between those forces and an attacking Eighth Army. The Inchon landing would be carried out by the oncoming 2d Infantry Division and the Marine Corps RCT already promised him and then embarking or preparing to embark in the States, plus the airborne RCT. After the NKPA had been destroyed, the problem would be to "compose and unite Korea," and that might require American occupation of the entire peninsula.[14]

Joe Collins demurred from these Delphic pronouncements on several counts:

First, he refreshed MacArthur on the general American war plan. As in World War II, American grand strategy put Europe first, the Far East second. America had made new commitments to the defense of Western Europe, to NATO. These commitments must be honored.

Secondly, Collins doubted that MacArthur's requests for two field armies comprising eight full divisions could or would be met. He could guarantee the eight infantry battalions and artillery batteries required to bring the three divisions already in Korea up to strength, the three battalion cadres for the 7th Division, armor and engineers, the full 2d Division, the airborne RCT, replacements, and possibly a full Marine division, but beyond that he could not go. The General Reserve, already gutted, could not be reduced further.

Thirdly, although he approved of an amphibious landing behind the NKPA in principle, Collins had strong reservations about the chosen site, Inchon. That cramped port had huge (thirty-plus-foot) tides and treacherous currents and was dominated by a fortified island, Wolmi. Moreover, the troops advancing inland on Seoul would immediately have to cross the formidable Han River.

This was the first indication to Douglas MacArthur that the Truman administration could not—or would not—go all out in his support in the Far East; that insofar as possible the conflict in Korea would be handled with a minimum of force; that personally MacArthur was to be shortchanged, as he believed he had been in World War II. MacArthur and Ned Almond were furious—but they concealed their anger. MacArthur said he well understood the reasoning behind America's war plans, but he questioned the wisdom of saving fire-fighting equipment for one quiescent district while another district was burning uncontrollably. America would win in Korea or lose everywhere.[15]

*    *    *

From Tokyo Collins and Vandenberg flew to Korea in a C-47 with Johnnie Walker—a six-hour trip. By that time Walker had established Eighth Army headquarters in Taegu, a large city with good communications facilities and an airstrip, fifty-five air miles northwest of Pusan and sixty-five miles southeast of Taejon. A "tired and greatly worried" Bill Dean jeeped rearward from Taejon to Taegu in order to meet with Collins and Walker. Owing to the need to fly out of Taegu before dark, Collins and Vandenberg stayed only one hour.[16]

The military overview in South Korea as presented to Collins and Vandenberg that evening, July 13, by Eighth Army briefers was not altogether reassuring.[17]

• On the "western front" at the day-old Kum River line, the NKPA 3d and 4th Infantry divisions (and possibly another, the 2d) were preparing to renew the assault and had already commenced a withering artillery barrage. Dean's newly arrived 19th Regiment had relieved the shattered 21st on the river, backed up closely by Miller Perry's 52d FAB and more deeply by Allen's 11th and the 13th FABs. On the left of the 19th was the reorganizing 34th Regiment, backed up closely by Dawson's 63d FAB. Dean still had no faith in the 34th. The 1st Cav Division, redirected from Inchon to southern Korea, would land on July 18 and immediately move up to reinforce the 24th Division in Taejon. Walker believed with its help he might stabilize the western front. But he desperately needed extra infantry battalions to bring the regiments up to strength, fillers and replacements, the bigger 3.5-inch bazookas and other antitank weapons, and, not least, greatly improved close air support from FEAF.

• On the "central front," directly north of Taegu, the NKPA was driving south from Wonju along two parallel corridors, aiming for Sangju and Ansong. In this rugged mountainous area the organized remnants of the ROK Army, perhaps comprising the equivalent of three or four divisions (no one knew for certain), were conducting a delaying action but did not appear capable of making a firm stand anywhere north of Taegu. A concerted NKPA push in these corridors could cut off and trap Dean in Taejon. To avoid that catastrophe—and to put backbone in the ROK Army—Walker was directing the newly arriving 25th Division to reinforce that sector.

• On the "eastern front"—the Sea of Japan seacoast—the NKPA advance had been desultory, slowed in part by an ill-advised diversion of NKPA forces westward into the Taebaek Mountains, mudslides on the coastal highway, and the notable resistance of the ROK 23d Regiment. Nonetheless the NKPA had advanced as far south as Yondok, threatening Pohang, a seaport which Walker intended to develop as an alternate to the overtaxed Pusan and the site of a FEAF fighter strip. Two battalions of ROKs had been directed to Pohang. They would be supported by American engineers and antiaircraft units.[18]

Notwithstanding the precarious situation on all three fronts, Walker was sanguine. He might be forced to abandon Taejon, but he did not intend to yield Taegu. The situation would gradually turn in his favor: Every mile the NKPA advanced cost it dearly in blood and equipment and took it that much farther from its supply base. Contrarily, each mile Eighth Army yielded tended to consolidate it into a smaller perimeter which was more easily defended. If the Pentagon rushed the requested men and equipment to Korea, Walker believed he might be able to hold a perimeter until such time as the planned Inchon landing relieved the pressure on Eighth Army.

Collins and Vandenberg returned to Tokyo, where they again conferred with MacArthur, then flew back to Washington, where they arrived on July 14, Washington time. They briefed the JCS, Louis Johnson, and President Truman. The tenor of the briefing, reflecting the views of Johnnie Walker and MacArthur, was upbeat. Walker could probably hold a perimeter until some kind of amphibious landing somewhere (but, it was hoped, not Inchon) behind the NKPA could be mounted. Collins did not believe MacArthur would require two American field armies comprising eight full divisions to defeat the NKPA; however, he endorsed MacArthur's request to increase the Marine Corps RCT to a full division to assist the 2d Infantry Division in the proposed amphibious envelopment.[19]

Over the next two weeks, to meet MacArthur's demands for ground manpower, the JCS and, when required, President Truman approved the following measures, many of them highly controversial.

• A comb-out of all Army headquarters, depots, posts, stations, service installations, and military schools. This produced 7,350 fillers during July (the majority flown to Korea) and was to yield 17,205 more in August.
• A call-up of individuals in the Army's volunteer Reserve and inactive, nonvoluntary Reserve. This produced 25,000 men immediately and another 135,000 over the next eleven months.
• The mobilization of ninety-two National Guard and Army Organized Reserve units. This produced four National Guard divisions (28th; 40th; 43d;

45th), two RCTs (196th; 278th), twenty-two antiaircraft battalions, six engineer battalions, and two artillery battalions.*
• A call-up of the entire organized Marine Corps Reserve, 138 units comprising 33,500 men.[20]

Notwithstanding these drastic steps, the JCS continued to view MacArthur's proposed amphibious landing at Inchon with deepest misgivings and was reluctant to provide him with further major forces to carry it out. Forrest Sherman stubbornly opposed committing a full Marine division to the Far East. He yielded only after repeated and heated cables from MacArthur. When paratrooper Matt Ridgway informed Joe Collins that an RCT from the 11th Airborne Division could not be trained and equipped in time for Inchon even on a "crash" schedule, Collins struck it from the Inchon operation and, in spite of repeated protestations from MacArthur, refused to make it or, as suggested, a substitute RCT from the "untouchable" 82d Airborne Division, available.[21]

# III

Johnnie Walker and Bill Dean had great faith in Dean's green 19th Infantry Regiment, which had taken up positions on the Kum River with the 34th. Historically the 19th was famous for its stand in the Civil War battle at Chickamauga, where it well earned its sobriquet "The Rock of Chickamauga." Its men proudly called themselves "Chicks." Upon graduation from West Point, Walker had served first with the Chicks in Texas, later joined by young Eisenhower. In the mid-1930s Bill Dean had served a two-year hitch with the Chicks in Hawaii.[22]

One reason for the optimism was the 19th's commander, a brainy, highly regarded West Pointer (1927), Guy Stanley ("Stan") Meloy, forty-seven. Like Stephens of the 21st, Meloy had not ever commanded troops in battle. He, too, had been chief of staff of an infantry division in the ETO, the 103d, which had often fought side by side with Dean's 44th in Seventh Army and Haislip's XV Corps. Beginning in early 1945, Meloy's boss, the 103d's commander, had been the tough-minded Army hero of Bastogne: Anthony C. ("Tony") McAuliffe, former artillery commander of the 101st Airborne Division, who had spurned a German demand for surrender with the most famous Allied cry of defiance in World War II: "Nuts!"[23]

By the time the 19th Regiment relieved the 21st Regiment on the Kum

---

*The Air Force and Navy also mobilized Reserve and Air National Guard units: the Air Force called 130,000 men to active duty; the Navy, 165,000.

River, the fluke cold wave had passed and the Korean weather had returned to normal for mid-July: blazing hot and jungle humid. The summer days were sixteen hours long: 5:00 A.M. to 9:00 P.M. The enervating weather, long daylight hours, stink of the rice paddies, and utter lack of any creature comforts were a rude shock to the Chicks.[24]

More so was the rude introduction to combat. The Americans had blown the Kum River bridges and dug in on the south bank, but the river did not stop the NKPA artillery, mortars, tank and machine-gun fire. It was vicious and accurate and seemingly without respite. Stan Meloy judged it to be as intense as the worst the Germans had thrown at his 103d Division in the ETO. The majority of the Chicks, green to combat, were terrified.[25]

* * *

On the day after Collins's visit to Taegu, July 14, the NKPA assault on the Kum River line began with a powerful attack by the 4th Division on the left, in Pappy Wadlington's 34th sector at Kongju. The regiment was deployed thus: Newton Lantron's newly reorganized and reinforced 3/34 at the river; Red Ayres's 1/34 behind in reserve; and, farther south, batteries of Robert Dawson's 63d FAB. The preparatory artillery barrages had been so intense that Wadlington had lost one whole "company" (forty men comprising K) of the 3/34, plus his own S-2 and S-3 to "battle fatigue." The loss of K "company" left Wadlington with only two companies at the river.[26]

At 8:00 A.M. the NKPA swarmed across the river on barges or wading or swimming. Lantron called for artillery fire from Dawson's 63d FAB and Ben Allen's more distant 11th FAB, but the response was desultory or ineffective or worse. (The 63d's commander, Dawson, temporarily felled by a "blood infection," was being evacuated, relieved by William E. Dressler.) One of Lantron's 3/34 companies (I) held, but the other (L) abandoned its position and fled to the rear. Subsequently Lantron relieved the L Company commander.[27]

The NKPA, "squealing like a bunch of Indians," swarmed through the hole left by L Company southward to the positions of the 63d FAB. Within two hours Dressler was dead in his foxhole and his entire understrength outfit was wiped out. The NKPA captured all ten 105-mm howitzers (half of them serviceable) plus large amounts of ammunition, about seventy vehicles, and miscellaneous other weapons. At day's end 136 men of the 63d were dead or missing, 86 of them captured by the NKPA.[28]

On Bill Dean's orders Pappy Wadlington had gone to the rear that day to scout deeper defensive positions. At about 4:00 P.M., when he returned to his CP and learned of this latest disaster in the 34th, he gave orders for Red Ayres's 1/34, which was in reserve behind the 3/34, to attack and, if possible, to recapture the 63d's artillery pieces and gunners before dark. Ayres jumped off at about 5:00 P.M.; but while approaching the 63d FAB site, he ran into heavy enemy fire, and as instructed, he withdrew the 1/34 without having achieved anything. After dark Lantron's outflanked I Company decamped and escaped to the rear.

The action that day was another decisive victory for the NKPA. It had swiftly crossed a river in the face of an American defense, shattered yet another American infantry battalion, overrun and captured most of a field artillery battalion, and beaten back Red Ayres's counterattack. Moreover, the collapse of the 34th Regiment laid bare the entire left flank of Stan Meloy's green 19th Infantry.[29]

Late that afternoon Bill Dean, having been apprised of the 34th's collapse, sent an encouraging message to Wadlington and Meloy: "Hold everything we have until we find out where we stand—might not be too bad—may be able to hold—make reconnaissance—may be able to knock those people out and reconsolidate." But these words were scarcely on the way when an entirely new threat to Taejon appeared to be developing. Intelligence reported that the ROKs on the "central front" were giving way in panic, possibly opening the way for the NKPA to attack Taejon from the northeast. To meet this new threat, Dean ordered Stephens's regrouped 21st Regiment (1,100 men) to deploy to Okchon, due east of Taejon, to prevent an encirclement which might cut off the 19th and 34th.[30]

The collapse of Wadlington's 34th Regiment left only Stan Meloy's Chicks holding the Kum River line. Initially Meloy had deployed the Chicks thus: the 1/19, commanded by Otho T. Winstead, thirty-five, at the river; the 2/19, commanded by Thomas M. McGrail, forty-one, in reserve, except for its E Company, which held the extreme east flank on the river. The Chicks were supported by the 13th FAB, commanded by Charles W. Stratton, two batteries of Perry's 52d FAB and Ben Allen's 11th FAB. When the 34th melted away Meloy was compelled to commit McGrail's reserve 2/19 to fill the void on his left, holding merely one rifle company (F) to serve as regimental reserve.[31]

In the early-morning hours of July 16, in complete darkness, the NKPA 3d Division, backed by heavy artillery, tank, and machine-gun fire, crossed the Kum River and hit Meloy's Chicks. Winstead's 1/19 absorbed the initial blow. Winstead urgently requested Allen's 11th FAB to fire flares to light up the battlefield, but owing to a communications foul-up, there was an agonizing delay. During it hundreds of NKPA got across the river and overran and outflanked Winstead's 1/19 position. Meloy, who stood side by side with Winstead in the thick of this fighting, urgently summoned reinforcements from his thin reserve, then bravely led a counterattack, during which the 1/19's exec, John M. Cook, the S-1, Alan Hackett, and the S-3, Wayne B. Macomber, were killed.[32]

Meloy believed that this counterattack might have temporarily stabilized the situation and that he could hold the line at least until dark. But he was overly optimistic; the NKPA had outflanked him in the thin seam between the 19th and 34th. The NKPA infantrymen moving to the rear soon attacked Perry's 52d FAB position and threw up a strong roadblock behind the buckling 1/19. Learning of this, Meloy and his S-3, Edward O. Logan, twenty-eight, gathered a pickup force to break the roadblock and headed south about noon. In the fight to break the block, Meloy was severely wounded in the calf by shell fragments and was no longer capable of commanding, but he refused evacuation. To succeed him temporarily Meloy bypassed his inexperienced (West Point, 1940) exec, coast artilleryman Homer B. ("Chan") Chandler, and chose the 1/19's commander, infantryman Otho Winstead.[33]

Winstead inherited a confused and disintegrating flock of Chicks. At that point his former outfit, the 1/19, now commanded by Robert M. Miller, was flying apart and trying to withdraw but was thwarted by the roadblock at the rear. Perry's 52d FAB was under heavy attack; the more rearward 11th and 13th FABs were loading up and pulling out. In the left (or west) sector Tom McGrail and his 2/19 forces were falling back under vicious fire, bypassing the roadblock to the west, as instructed by Meloy. Leaving Logan to try to break the roadblock, Winstead went forward to steady the 1/19 and probably to find some way of evacuating the wounded Meloy around the roadblock. Shortly thereafter Winstead was killed by enemy fire.[34]

Apprised of this latest disaster, Bill Dean came forward from Taejon, leading a minirescue force: two light tanks and four antiaircraft (A/A) vehicles.* South of the roadblock Dean met the regimental S-3, Ed Logan, and the 2/19 commander, Tom McGrail, both of whom had skirted around it with various forces. Logan volunteered to lead the rescue team against the roadblock, but Dean chose McGrail for that mission, ordering Logan to the rear to find and prepare a new defensive line in front of Taejon.

While this discussion was going on, the exec, Chan Chandler, came barreling south on the road in a jeep, leading four other jeeps loaded with wounded, all of which had run the roadblock. In this perilous journey all the wounded men had been hit again one or more times; Chandler himself had been struck in the leg. Chandler continued going south and was eventually evacuated, along with other wounded Chicks, to a hospital in Japan, where he was to remain for forty-five days before rejoining the regiment.[36]

---

*Two of these vehicles were M-16 half-tracks mounting four interlinked .50-caliber machine guns (Quad 50s). The other two were M-19, fully tracked vehicles, mounting two interlinked 40-mm Bofors automatic cannons (Twin 40s). Developed—or overdeveloped—in World War II as A/A weapons to fend off prop planes, they were obsolete A/A weapons in the jet plane age. However, in Korea, these weapons, each with terrific firepower, proved to be highly useful in supporting the infantry. Hence A/A battalions were to be much in demand.[35]

McGrail climbed in a jeep and led the minirescue team up the road to break the roadblock. It soon came under heavy NKPA machine-gun fire. All four A/A vehicles, on which McGrail was counting heavily, were knocked out with 90 percent casualties. The two light tanks fired off all their ammo and then withdrew. McGrail managed to crawl away from his wrecked jeep and escape south unhurt. Later in the day Dean named him to temporary command of what was left of the 19th. A second effort to break the roadblock, led by a tough and skilled company commander, Michael Barszcz, was called off just as Barszcz made contact with the NKPA.[37]

At about 6:00 P.M. the men who were caring for the wounded Meloy north of the roadblock decided to run the gauntlet. They put Meloy in a surviving light tank and set off, leading about fifteen other vehicles, including a rig towing one of Perry's 105 howitzers. The tank and trucks ran the block without major damage or casualties. However, south of the block the tank carrying Meloy broke down. The tank crew tried to flag down a truck to pick up Meloy, but disgracefully, all fifteen vehicles in the convoy sped around the tank, leaving the wounded regimental commander to fend for himself. Lucky for Meloy, Mike Barszcz, who was then breaking off his attack, came upon Meloy and provided help and protection. Soon thereafter Tom McGrail's S-3, Kenneth J. Woods, came up and put Meloy in a truck and escorted him to safety. Meloy (who won a DSC for his actions that day) eventually wound up in the same hospital with his exec, Chandler. When he recovered from his wounds, Meloy was rotated to the States to continue an exemplary professional career, which earned him four stars.[38]

The shattered Chicks ran, straggled, or marched to the rear by various routes. Dean directed the bulk of them to the division CP area, which had displaced easterly about thirty miles, from Taejon to Yongdong. There Tom McGrail was able to collect and reorganize his 2/19, and it became the 24th Division reserve. Fortunately the NKPA, busy regrouping and making plans and celebrating another big victory—and bringing tanks across the Kum River—did not press the attack on Taejon for another two days.

Dean was to boast in his memoir that the celebrated Chicks "did a lot of killing and made the enemy pay full price for the ground won," but the historical data do not support him. The NKPA suffered hardly at all; the Chicks were thoroughly mauled. Of some 900 men on the river line when the NKPA attacked on July 16, only half that number could be found the next day. Winstead's 1/19 alone suffered a shocking 43 percent casualties: 388 of 785 men. Seventeen of its senior officers were dead. Miller Perry's 52d FAB lost eight of its nine howitzers, all its ammo, and most of its vehicles.[39]

## IV

Walker and Dean had hoped to hold Taejon, but the disaster at the Kum River line—too late with too little—and the shift of Stephens's 21st east to Okchon to meet a possible NKPA threat there left Taejon virtually wide open to the NKPA. Dean finally and reluctantly conceded as much, and on the morning of July 18 he gave orders to evacuate the city completely on the following day. However, at noon that day, July 18, Johnnie Walker came up to Taejon to announce that the 1st Cav Division was then landing in Pohang. If Dean could hold Taejon two more days—until July 20—that would give Walker time to bring the 1st Cav overland to reinforce the 24th and perhaps to stop the NKPA drive and "stabilize" the battlefield.[40]

By that time Bill Dean was a walking zombie, and his judgment may have been impaired. As he put it later, "I was too close to the trees to see the forest. . . ." The 24th Division, Dick Stephens wrote later, "could no longer be called an effective fighting force." All three regiments had been shattered. The 19th was even less effective and as Dean saw it, the 34th wouldn't fight. Yet Dean assured Walker he would hold at Taejon as requested. He later conceded that his decision was a "big error."[41]

Aside from a natural desire to help Walker in every possible way, two factors probably strongly influenced Dean's unfortunate and unwise decision. First, he was still determined to make his 34th Regiment "fight." Its repeated failures reflected adversely on division commander Dean. Walker had hand-picked a new, fresh, young commander for the 34th—its fourth in the space of a week—and Dean may have believed the new man could provide the requisite leadership. Secondly, the 3.5-inch bazooka instruction team had arrived in Taejon from the States, bringing weapons and ammo. If this weapon performed as advertised, the 34th might neutralize the T-34 tanks. If so, Taejon could become an electrifying turning point in the war.[42]

The new commander of the 34th was Charles E. Beauchamp (pronounced bo-shamp), a West Pointer (1930), who until then had been commanding the 32d Regiment of the 7th Division in Japan. To assist in the challenge confronting him, Beauchamp brought the 32d's S-3, William T. McDaniel, a West Pointer (1941) to be S-3 of the 34th.[43]

Beauchamp, at age forty-two, was the youngest regimental commander in Korea so far, and the greenest. During World War II he had not served with a combat unit. He had fought the war in the ETO in rear-area staff jobs, specializing in logistics. After the war he requested a troop command but did not get it until March 1950, when he took over the 32d Infantry. He had spent the postwar years on the staffs of the Infantry School, the Armed Forces Staff College, and the Army's Counter-Intelligence School. He remembered that Walker had ordered him to Korea because "I was younger than most of the regimental commanders in the Far East." He had never met Bill Dean.[44]

In his debut to combat, Beauchamp, like Martin, Stephens, and Meloy, was full of fire and brimstone, determined to make the 34th fight. Later he wrote: "We could have withdrawn on the night of July 19/20 with probably no losses. I feel that to some extent I influenced General Dean to stay on the 20th. I felt very confident on the evening of July 19th that we could hold the enemy out of Taejon another day and believe I so told General Dean."[45]

By the time Beauchamp took command of the 34th, Dean had conceived a crude plan for holding Taejon two more days. The 34th Regiment, supported by batteries of the 11th, 13th, and 63d FABs (in all 4,000 men), would meet and block the NKPA in the northwest sectors near the airstrip, where the 34th CP was located. Lighter forces were deployed southwest and south; one company (L) would block the road from Nonsan. The division Reconnaissance Company, temporarily attached to the 34th, would block due south on the road to Kumsan. Since Dean was still greatly concerned about the reported NKPA drive from the northeast (through the retreating ROKS, on the "central front"), he left Stephens's battered 21st in the Okchon area, considerably east of the city along the Taejon–Taegu road, to hold an exit through which the 34th could withdraw. The shattered 19th remained in the Yongdong area as division reserve.[46]

The NKPA plan for capturing the city was designed to take advantage of the weaknesses in this defensive deployment. The 3d Division would attack frontally, as Dean expected, down the main Seoul–Pusan highway from the northwest. But there would be no attack from the northeast at Okchon. Moreover, unknown to Dean and not expected, the 4th Division was to mount a sophisticated encircling attack from the southwest through Nonsan and Kumsan, where the American defenses were weakest. Beauchamp unwittingly played into his enemy's hands when he (unknown to Dean) ordered the division Reconnaissance Company, which was blocking south on the Kumsan road, to pull into the city to reinforce the 34th directly. This, as Dean wrote later, not only made the division "blind as to what the enemy was doing on the south flank" but also considerably thinned out its southern defense.[47]

The NKPA attack on Taejon began on the morning of July 19. As expected, the 3d Division hit hard with artillery and tanks from the northwest at Yusong, where Red Ayres's 1/34 was dug in on the main highway. Two of Ayres's outposted platoons were flanked and cut off, but the rest of the battalion held on for the better part of the day, supported by the guns of the 11th and 13th FABs, emplaced at the rear, and by sporadic (and largely ineffective) FEAF air strikes. However, by 2:00 P.M. Ayres, seeing that his position was growing perilous, recommended to Beauchamp that the regiment withdraw into the city that night. This recommendation was not well received by the gung ho Beauchamp, who rejected it forthwith.[48]

That day Ayres did not, as expected, have 3.5-inch bazookas to fight the T-34 tanks in his sector. The platoon leader William Caldwell remembered: "We had sent people from the First Battalion back to the division headquarters to receive instructions and weapons. Unfortunately, on July nineteenth, as these people were returning to battalion in a two-and-a-half-ton truck, the truck overturned, and the weapons and certain teams were lost. Later in the day one three-point-five-inch rocket launcher was delivered to A Company, First Battalion, and it was effectively used on the following day. How many others were lost, I don't know."[49]

Almost simultaneously with the attack on the 1/34, the NKPA's 4th Division, which had gone south to Nonsan, then circled east, struck with unexpected force at the 34th block at Yonsan, manned by L Company of Newton Lantron's 3/34. To bolster the line, Beauchamp rushed forward part of the division Reconnaissance Company, then put in a call for help to the division CP at Yongdong. Dean, who became "worried," ordered the division reserve, the 2/19, temporarily commanded by its exec, Glyn W. Pohl, into Taejon as backup for Beauchamp. Since Pohl had broken his eyeglasses and was "virtually blind," McGrail reassumed command of the 2/19 and gave Pohl command of the reorganizing 1/19. Dean himself rushed ahead of the 2/19 to Yonsan with two light tanks. When McGrail and the 2/19 got to Yonsan and entered the fight, McGrail found Dean directing the tank fire like a platoon leader.[50]

Although Beauchamp welcomed Tom McGrail's 2/19 at Yonsan, there was still a gap of one mile between it and Ayres's 1/34. Platoon leader William Caldwell remembered: "It was impossible to establish what would be considered a normal defensive position of contact between units and interlocking fires. We had no unending defense line. There were wide gaps between units and within units. This left units with open flanks. The enemy, with predominance in numbers and vehicles, always had the initiative. Invariably he struck down roads into our positions with tanks and infantry in close support. When those forces were stopped, he made wide envelopments around both flanks, often overrunning the artillery units in the rear, disrupting command posts and even attacking medical units. In addition to this, he sent large numbers of men posing as refugees through and around our lines with rifles, machine guns, and mortars hidden in 'refugee' bundles. These 'refugees' then assembled in large groups at predesignated areas back of our positions and struck from the rear."[51]

The various thinly linked elements of the 34th and McGrail's 2/19 soon found themselves under severe and relentless pressure. After dark Beauchamp withdrew his exposed CP and artillery, but not his infantry, closer to the city. At about 10:00 P.M. the battlewise Red Ayres, rightly convinced that his 1/34 was being encircled by tanks and infantry, again proposed to Beauchamp that the infantry withdraw into the city. Even though by that time Beauchamp had received reports of roadblocks on the Kumsan and Okchon roads—indicating a massive encirclement from the southwest and south—he again rejected withdrawal of the infantry as inappropriate.[52]

Bill Dean, perhaps nearly crippled by exhaustion, could not be found. He had not returned to the division CP at the end of the day. In effect, command of his division devolved temporarily to his ADC, Pearson Menoher. Later Dean himself shed no light on his whereabouts that night. He wrote:

I was forward of my own headquarters on the night of July 19. . . . I went to sleep to the sound of gunfire . . . [and] awoke very early, although I had been short of sleep for almost a month. . . . The situation was so confused that I could not even be certain we still held a solid line northwest of the city; and very few important command decisions were made at the time. Very few of the things I did in the next twenty-four hours could not have been done by any competent sergeant—and such a sergeant would have done some of them better. . . .[53]

\* \* \*

On the following day, July 20, the NKPA 3d and 4th divisions encircled, overran, and utterly shattered the American infantry standing before Taejon. In effect, the 34th Infantry and McGrail's attached 2/19 ceased to exist as organized fighting units. The battalions flew apart; little groups of soldiers fought incohesive and desperate battles to escape the trap.

Red Ayres's 1/34 was hit first. In darkness, about 3:00 A.M., NKPA armor and swarms of infantry came down the highway and overran the battalion. As small-arms fire slammed into his CP, Ayres sent a warning to Beauchamp by messenger, then ordered his men to evacuate. Ayres led one party out into the night; his exec, Leland Dunham, led another. Both independently headed south. After dawn these two fleeing groups merged in Tom McGrail's 2/19 sector and continued heading south.[54]

Upon receiving Ayres's report, Beauchamp jumped in his jeep and raced out in darkness to the 1/34 area, presumably to steady the battalion. On the way he nearly collided head-on with a T-34 tank, which sprayed the jeep with machine-gun fire. Grazed by a bullet, Beauchamp leaped out into a ditch and retreated on foot. In due course he met up with a 3.5-inch bazooka team. He led the team back down the road and found the tank. In the first known instance of a 3.5-inch bazooka victory, the team got close, fired, set the tank on fire, and captured its crew.[55]

Returning to his command post, Beauchamp, still unaware that the 1/34 had disintegrated and evacuated and deeply worried about reports of a penetration between it and McGrail's 2/19, called on his regimental reserve, New-ton Lantron's 3/34. He ordered Lantron to attack with two "companies" into the gap between what he supposed was the 1/34 and 2/19 "line." Lantron complied, but his force (the skeletal K and M companies) ran head-on into six T-34s and an estimated battalion of NKPA infantry which forced the task force to retreat in disarray. Lantron himself soon "disappeared" from the 3/34 CP in a jeep. He was believed to be dead, but as was discovered much later, he was captured by the North Koreans. When Lantron was declared missing several hours later, Beauchamp named M Company commander Jack E. Smith, who turned twenty-nine that day, to reorganize and lead the remnants of the 3/34.[56]

McGrail's 2/19 came under heavy attack at dawn—about the time Red Ayres and Leland Dunham were retreating through its sector. The attack was led by T-34 tanks, accompanied by considerable infantry. Out of contact with Beauchamp's CP, knowing that the 1/34 had disintegrated, and believing that the NKPA had got behind him and cut off his line of retreat into Taejon, McGrail gave orders for his 2/19 to evacuate its positions and head south in the general direction that the Ayres and Dunham groups had gone. These orders uprooted the last organized American resistance before Taejon. In this headlong flight McGrail, too, "disappeared" for a while, but he was to survive and escape to friendly lines.[57]

*   *   *

Bill Dean appeared at Beauchamp's CP early that morning, soon after Beauchamp had led the successful 3.5-inch bazooka attack against the T-34. The two senior commanders, unaware of the disaster taking place at the "front," calmly discussed and agreed upon an orderly withdrawal of the 34th that night to Okchon. During these discussions Beauchamp got the wrong impression that Dean had ordered Stephens's 21st Infantry to come west from Okchon and cover the withdrawal of the 34th. At that time Dean appeared to be completely rational; however, several hours later, when a messenger arrived at Beauchamp's CP from McGrail's disintegrating 2/19 to report the attack and ask for orders, Dean patted him on the back and said superciliously: "My boy, I am not running this show, Beauchamp is."[58]

To many, Dean's behavior appeared to be bizarre. For the moment, at least, his world narrowly focused down to an obsessive desire to fight T-34 tanks, as Robert Martin and Beauchamp had done. Leaving overall military operations in the hands of Beauchamp and his staff, he set out into the city on his hunting trip, leading two 2.36-inch bazooka teams. They soon found a tank, but the gunner missed repeatedly and finally ran out of ammo. Report-edly a frustrated Dean then emptied his .45 pistol at the tank. Later he joined a 3.5-inch bazooka team which also found a tank. Dean and the team stalked it through the city streets for several blocks until they found a good firing position on the second floor of a building. Under Dean's direction the team fired three rounds. All hit. As the tank burst into flames, Dean cried exultingly: "I got me a tank!"[59]

After this little triumph Dean returned to Beauchamp's CP. The two senior commanders, still apparently not aware of the disaster that was taking place all around them, sat down for a lunch of heated C rations and again discussed the withdrawal. Dean, revising his earlier plan for a night withdrawal, now believed it should begin immediately, in daylight. Beauchamp fully concurred and relayed the orders to his S-3, William McDaniel, who dutifully put the orders in writing and sent them off by messenger to the CPs of Red Ayres, Jack Smith (newly commanding the 3/34), and Tom McGrail. Of these men, only Smith, still holding a thin guard not far from the besieged 34th Infantry CP, received the orders and could comply.[60]

Now that Dean had officially ordered the withdrawal, Beauchamp deemed that his most urgent responsibility at the time was to make certain the route east to Okchon remained open. Accordingly he jumped into his jeep and sped through the city to the Okchon highway, where he still believed (erroneously) he would find Stephens's 21st closing up to hold the exit. To his dismay, Beauchamp found no sign of Stephens or his men, merely four light tanks of the division Recon Company. Climbing a hill, Beauchamp saw swarms of NKPA infantry advancing from the south to the northeast, apparently with the intent of blocking the Okchon road. Beauchamp tried to mount a defense of the road with the tanks, some A/A half-tracks, and retreating truckborne infantry, but to no avail. In an effort to hurry Stephens forward (as he thought), Beauchamp drove east to Brad Smith's 1/21 CP. There he learned to his further dismay that Smith had no orders to move into Taejon to cover the 34th's withdrawal. Beauchamp desperately telephoned the division CP to get this vital operation started, but Pearson Menoher—anxious to get a clear picture of the situation and word of Bill Dean—ordered Beauchamp to report to the division CP immediately.[61]

Faced with the harsh realities of combat in Korea, Beauchamp may have regretted his earlier optimism about holding Taejon and urging Dean not to withdraw the 34th on the night of July 19–20. Years later he said: "It was just criminal to send our troops into battle manned and equipped the way they were. When I took over, the Thirty-fourth's two battalions were down to about half strength, and many of these were green fillers. . . . It was just lucky that any of us got out of there alive."[62]

Back in Taejon at Beauchamp's decamping CP, Bill Dean was mystified— and angered—by Beauchamp's disappearance. Believing that Beauchamp had foolishly left his CP to go forward to reestablish contact personally with Ayres or had bugged out, Dean turned over command of the withdrawal to his old

ETO cohort, the 34th's exec, Pappy Wadlington, and the new S-3, William McDaniel. By that time Jack Smith had withdrawn the remnants of the 3/34 (L Company plus) close to the regimental CP. These infantrymen—the only remaining organized infantry in the 34th—established a perimeter to cover the loading and withdrawal. In so doing, L Company suffered 70 percent casualties: 107 of 153 men.[63]

The NKPA, meanwhile, had encircled Taejon from the southwest and established blocks on the Okchon and Kumsan highways. Learning of the block on the Okchon highway (but not of that on the Kumsan highway), Dean radioed Menoher at the division CP in Yongdong to "send armor" to break it. Shortly thereafter Beauchamp departed the division CP with five light tanks, going west through Stephens's 21st Infantry sector. Along the way Beauchamp came across about sixty fleeing riflemen of the 3/34 and turned them around to help. There was no offer of assistance from the 21st Regiment, which, unknown to Beauchamp, was then making withdrawal plans of its own. By the time Beauchamp's puny, nervous force reached the block, the NKPA was well dug in, and it easily repulsed Beauchamp's well-intentioned but lackluster attack. Beauchamp soon conceded his effort was hopeless and returned to the division CP.[64]

By this time many men of the 24th Division were fleeing Taejon. Among them was Sergeant George D. Libby of Company C, 3d Engineer Combat Battalion, who left in a crowded two-and-a-half-ton truck. NKPA fire disabled and stopped the truck at a roadblock, killing or wounding every man in the truck except Libby. Simultaneously tending to the many wounded and firing at the NKPA with a carbine, Libby held out until an artillery tractor came on the scene. Placing one of the wounded in the cab of the tractor, Libby positioned himself so that he shielded the driver from NKPA fire. While the tractor crashed the roadblock, Libby sprayed the NKPA with carbine fire, killing or wounding several. The tractor got through the block safely, but Libby, severely wounded in the arms and legs, died from loss of blood. For this selfless act he was awarded the Medal of Honor—the first of the Korean War.[65]

At about 6:00 P.M. Bill Dean gave the order to evacuate the 34th Regiment CP, which by then was under heavy attack. Pappy Wadlington and McDaniel (who had courageously salvaged some valuable 155-mm howitzers of the 11th FAB and rendered the rest inoperative) had organized a large convoy of trucks and other vehicles. While the pitiful remnants of Jack Smith's 3/34 covered, the miscellaneous troops at the CP boarded the trucks and moved out into the flaming, chaotic streets of Taejon, which were now infested with NKPA tanks and soldiers.[66]

It was a wild ride through a hail of enemy fire. Some jeeps and trucks spun out of line and crashed. Others got lost. Wadlington's jeep made a wrong turn into a cul-de-sac. He was forced to abandon the jeep under fire and eventually escaped on foot. After unsuccessfully exploring for various exits from the city, Dean mistakenly turned his jeep due south, down the Kumsan road. He soon ran into a NKPA block. He and his aide, Arthur M. Clarke (a pilot), abandoned the jeep and took to the hills with a group of stragglers who were hoping to infiltrate south or southeast to friendly lines after dark. Many were wounded; Dean and Clarke helped them along as best they could. About midnight Dean wandered off into the dark to get some water from a stream, fell down an embankment, hit his head, and went out like a light. When he awoke, he could not find Clarke or the others. He later met up with Lieutenant Stanley Tabor of McGrail's 2/19 and they wandered the hills for the next several days, dodging NKPA patrols. On about July 25 Dean and Tabor were surprised by an enemy patrol and, in a hair-raising escape into the rice paddies, became separated. Tabor was captured on August 4 and died in captivity.[67]

Bill Dean wandered the hills and back roads of South Korea, assisted occasionally by friendly Koreans, for a total of thirty-six days, trying to get to friendly lines. Emaciated and barely able to stand, he was captured in a village thirty-five miles south of Taejon by a "gang" of civilians and turned over to the police on August 25—a week or so after his son, William, Jr., entered West Point as a plebe. He was the NKPA's highest-ranking POW, but for reasons still not clear, the NKPA kept his capture a secret until December 18, 1951. Some American POWs were brainwashed and became propaganda tools for the Communists, but Bill Dean remained adamantly "unbreakable" throughout his nearly three years of incarceration. He was repatriated on September 3, 1953.[68]

Six months after the fall of Taejon, on January 9, 1951, President Truman authorized the Medal of Honor for Bill Dean's personal heroism on July 20 and 21 and presented it to his wife, Mildred Dern Dean, at a White House ceremony. Much later, when he learned of this award, Dean wrote: "There were heroes in Korea, but I was not one of them. There were brilliant commanders, but I was a general captured because he took a wrong road. . . . In the fighting I made some mistakes. . . . I lost ground I should not have lost. I lost officers and fine men. I'm not proud of that record, and I'm under no delusions that my weeks of command constituted any masterly campaign." He was "humbly grateful" for the Medal of Honor. "But I came close to shame when I think about the men who did better jobs—some who died doing them—and did not get recognition. I wouldn't have awarded myself a wooden star for what I did as a commander. . . ."[69]

## V

The hundreds of men of the 34th Regiment and McGrail's 2/19 who were cut off or trapped in Taejon and withdrew or escaped to the hills southward all had hair-raising adventures as well. Many senior officers, including Ayres, McGrail, and Jack Smith, made it out, but others did not. Ayres's 1/34 exec, Leland Dunham, was shot in the neck and killed on the Kumsan road. The 34th's new S-3, William McDaniel, was captured and probably murdered in captivity for his defiance to torture and brainwashing.[70]

Probably the largest 34th Regiment group was led out by the 1/34 platoon leader William Caldwell and the 1/34 S-3, Sidney M. Marks, a tough World War II paratrooper. Caldwell remembered: "The first battalion was decimated. I ended up on the high ground south of Taejon with Marks and three other officers and about two hundred men, many of them wounded. We had no maps, no communications, no ammo, except that on our backs, no food, no water, no vehicles. We headed south, then west, moving rather ponderously because of the injured and wounded. On the third day without food, men went into the fields and dug up potatoes and vegetables and ate them raw, a distressing sight.

"On the third or fourth night Marks and I, who were in superb condition, were elected to go ahead of the main party and try to find friendly forces and get help—transportation. We finally managed to reach a ROK headquarters, where we were refused help until Marks threatened to create an 'international incident.' The ROKs relinquished three trucks, and we shuttled the men to the ROK headquarters. The ROKs would do nothing more for us, nor would the [American] Army command in Pusan, which we raised by landline. We then commandeered a train and went due south to Yosu, on the coast, cooking our first edible food—eggs—in the engine boiler and washing them down with sips of sake and beer, the first purified liquid we'd had since Taejon. At Yosu we commandeered a boat, loaded our troops, and sailed for Pusan, where we were issued new gear and sent back into the line—every soldier in that group now a fighter."[71]

During the chaotic night of July 20–21, as the 34th and 2/19 were fleeing Taejon, Dick Stephens, still at Okchon with his 21st Infantry, became increasingly uneasy. His standing orders were "to hold at all costs." But with the NKPA in control of Taejon and blocking the Okchon road and without doubt making plans to encircle and overrun his thin position, these orders now seemed suicidal. The 24th's ADC, Pearson Menoher, temporarily commanding the division, agreed, and he authorized Stephens to pull out. At dawn on July 21 Stephens and surviving elements of Miller Perry's 52d FAB pulled back fifteen miles to the division CP area at Yongdong, joining Glyn Pohl's

1/19. The next day Wadlington, Red Ayres, and Tom McGrail, leading little bands of 34th Regiment survivors, arrived in Yongdong.[72]

Of all the "mistakes" Bill Dean had made as commander of the 24th Division, none had been greater than his decision to attempt to hold Taejon an extra day. The cost was frightful. Of the 4,000 Americans deployed in defense of the city with the 34th, 1,150 (30 percent) were dead, wounded, or missing and presumed dead, the vast majority (874) in the last category. Red Ayres's 1/34 had suffered about 28.5 percent casualties (203 of 712 men); the captured Newton Lantron's 3/34, about 38.4 percent (256 of 666); Tom McGrail's 2/19, about 29.5 percent (211 of 713). The 11th, 13th, and 63d FABs suffered similar heavy casualties and lost most of their 105-mm and 155-mm howitzers.[73]

\* \* \*

So ended the second week of American ground combat in Korea. The NKPA had gained another twenty-five air miles (from the Kum River to Okchon), making the total gain for the two weeks seventy-five air miles. Yet another American regiment, the 19th, had been chewed to pieces; the 34th Infantry had been mauled for the third time—this time decisively. The loss of 24th Division equipment over the two weeks, according to the Army historian, was sufficient to equip a full American division.[74] The loss included a total of thirty-one 105-mm howitzers and five 155-mm howitzers.

For the 24th Infantry Division these two weeks had been a ghastly time, one of the greatest ordeals in Army history. By July 22 at Yongdong its surviving commanders could account for only about half the men committed to Korea: 8,660 of 15,965. More than 2,400 men—including Bill Dean—were missing, and most of them were dead. The toll on senior commanders had been heavy: three regimental commanders (Martin killed; Meloy wounded and evacuated; Lovless sacked), one regimental exec (Chandler, wounded and evacuated), two regimental S-3s (Dunn severely wounded and captured; McDaniel captured and to be murdered), five battalion commanders (Cliff Jensen and Otho Winstead killed; Newton Lantron captured; Delbert Pryor and David Smith medically evacuated), and numerous other field-grade officers dead, wounded, missing, or sacked. One FAB commander (Dawson) had been temporarily evacuated as a NBC; another (Dressler) had been killed.[75]

By all rights the 24th had well earned a ticket home, or at least back to Japan, for extensive rest and recuperation (R and R), remanning, refitting, and retraining. But MacArthur and Walker, irrevocably committed to their fantastical strategy, could not afford that humanity. What was left of the 24th was desperately needed to hold the shrinking American perimeter. The 24th would be remanned, refitted, and recommitted on the spot. Perhaps then believing Bill Dean would reappear at any hour to resume his duties, on July 22 Johnnie

Walker gave command of the 24th to the frail, sickly, fifty-eight-year-old John Church, who since the arrival of the Eighth Army headquarters at Taegu and the deactivation of ADCOM no longer had a job.

The decisive victory of the NKPA at Taejon with its heavy American casualties caused deep consternation and a drastic change of plans at GHQ, Tokyo. For the second time GHQ was compelled to postpone the Inchon amphibious landing. The 2d Infantry Division and the Marine RCT then under orders to carry it out were diverted, as the 1st Cav had been earlier, to land at Pusan to reinforce the 24th, 25th, and 1st Cav divisions. But MacArthur, still believing an early Inchon landing was the key to victory, did not abandon the concept. He laid new plans to carry it out with other forces.[76]

# 6

# "STAND OR DIE"

## I

While the 24th Division was undergoing its terrible ordeal, two other Eighth Army divisions arrived in South Korea: the 25th, followed by the 1st Cav, which had been diverted from the ill-conceived amphibious assault at Inchon.

Advance elements of the 25th Division had landed at Pusan from July 10 to 12, while the 24th Division was withdrawing behind the Kum River. These forces could have provided vital reinforcements for the 24th Division in the battle for Taejon, but they had to address another serious problem the NKPA then posed. Despite some unexpectedly heroic delaying action by the ROKs on the "central front," the NKPA was pushing steadily south toward the major road and rail hub Taegu, where Walker had established Eighth Army headquarters. If the ROKs in that sector buckled and the NKPA captured Taegu, the American forces west of the city would be cut off and trapped, and Pusan would be exposed and probably lost as well, dashing any hope of evacuating American survivors.

As Walker viewed the unfolding situation, it was thus absolutely vital to hold Taegu. The plan he evolved was as follows. Most of the 25th Division's forces would be deployed directly north from Taegu to backstop the ROK forces on the "central front." In addition, some division elements would occupy and hold Pohang, the seaport east of Taegu on the Sea of Japan. This would provide an uncontested landing area for the 1st Cav Division or an alternative evacuation port for American forces should Pusan be lost. While the 25th Division held to the north, the 1st Cav, upon landing at Pohang, would proceed at top speed directly west on the Taegu–Taejon road to reinforce the 24th Division.

\* \* \*

The 25th Infantry Division was commanded by William B. ("Bill") Kean, who celebrated his fifty-third birthday on July 9. Born in Buffalo, New York, Kean was a "bobtailed" West Pointer who had entered the academy in June 1917 and been graduated on a crash schedule on November 1, 1918, too late for World War I. Recalled as "student officers" the following month, these cadet shavetails were regraduated in June 1919, after only two full years at the academy. During the peacetime years Kean, who stood near the bottom of his West Point class, had been selected for the Command and General Staff School, but not for the Army War College.[1]

Kean's professional career seemed to be going nowhere. But in 1939 he had the good fortune to be assigned to work for Omar Bradley in the G-1 section of the War Department. Bradley was impressed by Kean's tough-minded candor, analytical talent, and indefatigability. Early in World War II, when Marshall assigned Bradley to straighten out a troubled National Guard division, Bradley chose Kean (whom he kiddingly called "Captain Bligh") for his chief of staff. Thereafter Kean remained chief of staff to Bradley as Bradley shot up to power and fame. After the St.-Lô breakout, when Bradley moved up to be Twelfth Army Group commander, Kean (by then a general), at Bradley's request, remained chief of staff of First Army, partly to keep a fire lit under its conservative, low-key new commander, Courtney H. Hodges. Kean remained in that hot seat until the end of the war. He weathered some tough times, notably in the Battle of the Bulge, when the German Sixth Panzer Army dealt First Army a terrible opening blow.[2]

After Germany was defeated, Hodges's First Army was selected to partici-pate in MacArthur's invasion of Japan. Hodges and Kean led an advance staff group to Manila to begin the planning and there met MacArthur. Following the Japanese surrender in mid-August 1945, Hodges returned First Army to its traditional home, Governors Island, New York, and later retired. In Sep-tember 1948, coincidental with Walker's arrival in Japan to take over Eighth Army, Army Chief of Staff Omar Bradley assigned Kean to command the 25th Division and gave him another star—a well-deserved reward for his loyal wartime cohort.

Kean's artillery chief, Bittman Barth, had preceded the division to Korea, serving as Bill Dean's "eyes and ears" at Osan and Pyongtaek. Barth's artillery exec, West Pointer (1931) William W. Dick, had this to say about his division commander:

Kean was a superb commander in every respect. Tough to serve under in peacetime but just the kind you want to be in charge in combat. A brilliant tactician, excellent manager and absolutely tireless, he was a no-nonsense, but absolutely fair man. He did not suffer fools gladly. His workday would have crushed nine out of ten

Secretary of Defense Louis A. Johnson, Chairman of the Joint Chiefs of Staff Omar N. Bradley, and Commander in Chief, Far East, Douglas MacArthur meeting in Tokyo on the eve of the Korean War.

President Harry S. Truman, his new Secretary of Defense George C. Marshall, and deputy defense secretary Robert A. Lovett.

Defense secretary Marshall and Secretary of State Dean G. Acheson.

The Joint Chiefs of Staff in 1950–1951 *(left to right):* Admiral Forrest P. Sherman, Bradley, Air Force General Hoyt S. Vandenberg, and Army General Joseph Lawton Collins.

Eighth Army commander Walton H. ("Johnnie") Walker in Korea, standing in his command jeep, holding the grab bar. The siren and flashing red light on the right fender were Pattonesque touches.

MacArthur's chief of staff and later commander of X Corps, Edward M. ("Ned") Almond, the most controversial senior commander in Korea.

Walker with 24th Infantry Division commander William F. Dean *(above, right),* who was captured, and his successor, the frail and aging John H. Church *(below, left).*

American soldiers soft from occupation duty in Japan were shocked and exhausted by the endless hills of Korea. For a modern, mechanized Army, mountainous Korea was the worst possible place to fight a war.

One soldier, having reached a vantage point on a hilltop, is confronted with more endless hills. Note the absence of tree cover typical of Korea.

Charles B. ("Brad") Smith, commander, 1st Battalion, 21st Infantry Regiment, led the first American troops into combat in Korea.

Smith's boss, Richard W. Stephens, commander of the 21st Infantry, fought with his men in the frontline foxholes and won a high award for valor.

Ned D. Moore, commander of the 19th Infantry Regiment, a combat-experienced paratrooper, rushed from Japan to Korea to replace a wounded commander.

Charles E. Beauchamp replaced the commander of the 34th Infantry Regiment, who had been killed after fourteen hours on the job. The 34th Infantry was virtually wiped out at Taejon.

Nearing the enemy. A black soldier mans a 3.5-inch bazooka. These rocket-firing weapons were effective not only for knocking out Russian-built NKPA tanks, but also for blasting enemy bunkers.

Artillery support. The sturdy and reliable 105-mm howitzer, towed by tractors to the combat zone, ultimately provided the UN infantry a decisive edge against the Communist "hordes."

Engaging the enemy. Reaching a ridgeline on high ground, the infantry attack with fixed bayonets.

GIs capture and burn yet another Korean village. ''Mission accomplished''—at least for one day.

Aftermath. The terrible destruction of homes, villages, towns, and cities, which left millions of Koreans refugees.

When Champeny was wounded in September 1950, he was succeeded as commander of the 24th Infantry by one of the youngest regimental commanders in Korea, John T. Corley, thirty-six, who earned a place in the *Guinness Book of World Records* by winning eight Silver Star medals.

Tanker Welborn C. ("Tom") Dolvin. Dolvin's 89th Tank Battalion arrived in Korea to support the 25th Division.

In addition to added firepower, Dolvin's "Easy Eight" Sherman tanks sometimes provided the infantry a lift to the combat zone.

Hobart R. (''Hap'') Gay, commander of the 1st Cavalry, which was the third American division to land in Korea. Hap Gay was George Patton's chief of staff and closest confidant in World War II.

Hallett D. Edson commanded the 8th Cav when it was badly shattered at Unsan.

Gay's artillery chief and his successor as commander of the 1st Cav Division, Charles D. Palmer *(left),* with 5th Cav commander Marcel G. Crombez. Showman Crombez wears two well-taped grenades on his chest harness, the traditional yellow scarf of the ''old cavalry,'' and a bayonet in its belt sheath.

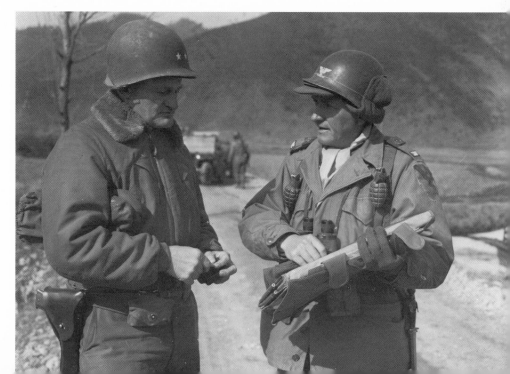

Hill's successor, Charles C. ("Chin") Sloane, who willingly accepted individual black replacements in the 9th Infantry and thereby initiated informal "integration" of the Eighth Army.

Sloane's able 2d Battalion commander, Cesidio V. ("Butch") Barberis, who "integrated" his outfit and who was later recommended for a Medal of Honor.

Sloane's 3d Battalion arrived in Korea staffed mostly with blacks. Its white commander, D. M. McMains *(center),* led the battalion until he was wounded.

younger men. Having served under five division commanders during World War II and Korea, I would rate him at the top.[3]

In contrast with Bill Dean, Bill Kean had an ADC who was fully qualified and physically able to replace him. He was Vennard Wilson (Tulane University, 1917), fifty-four, who had been in the job since 1948. A cavalryman/tanker and ordnance specialist who had served with the AEF in World War I, Wilson had ably commanded the independent 106th Cavalry Group in the ETO from Normandy to Germany. Bittman Barth wrote: "He was so unassuming that few people realized the scope and quality of his work. He not only knew his infantry but also was an expert in armored tactics."[4]

The three regiments of Kean's division—the 24th, 27th, and 35th—had been stationed in the southern part of the main Japanese home island of Honshu. The 24th Regiment, which served as a collecting unit for blacks, had three overstrength battalions; the 27th and 35th, but two. The latter two outfits had been gutted to provide part of the levy to beef up the 24th Division. William Dick remembered: "We were not well prepared to fight. . . . We were short units and short key officers and noncoms and short of equipment. Most vehicles were old and in bad shape, having been salvaged from Pacific battlefields and rebuilt in Japan."[5]

Kean received formal orders to embark the 25th Division for Korea on July 5. By then it was widely scattered: Elements of the 35th Regiment had moved to Kyushu to replace the 24th Division; the 24th and 27th regiments were at various posts on Honshu.[6] Kean chose his 27th "Wolfhound" Regiment to lead the division to Korea—but not its fifty-year-old commander, John W. Childs (Georgia Tech, 1921). Kean named Childs division chief of staff and gave command of the 27th to an "outsider," the Eighth Army assistant G-3, West Pointer (1936) Mike Michaelis, a paratrooper hero of World War II. At thirty-seven Michaelis was ten years—or more—younger than most of the American regimental commanders in the early weeks of the Korean War.[7]

A cool, handsome, blue-eyed Californian, Michaelis had enlisted in the Army as a private in 1932 and later won an appointment to West Point. In World War II he was a paratrooper with the 502d Regiment of Maxwell D. Taylor's 101st Airborne Division. In the 101st's baptism of fire in Normandy, when the 502d's commander broke a leg and became mentally unstable, Taylor named Michaelis (then only thirty-two years old) to command the regiment and later promoted him to full colonel. Michaelis remained in command of the 502 until severely wounded in Holland. When he returned from the hospital during the Battle of the Bulge, Taylor promoted him to be chief of staff of the division. From 1945 to 1948 Michaelis served in the Pentagon, the last two years as senior aide to Army Chief of Staff Dwight Eisenhower, who singled out Michaelis as one of four lieutenant colonels in the Army "of Extraordinary Ability."[8]

Michaelis recalled: "After World War Two they reduced a lot of us former regimental commanders to lieutenant colonel, saying we were too young to be colonels. They gave command of the regiments to old fogeys who had never been in combat or, if they had, not as troop leaders. When the Korean War started, they hauled out some of us regimental commanders who had had combat experience. . . . Walker's chief of staff, Gene Landrum, called me into his office and said: 'Congratulations! You're in command of the Twenty-seventh Wolfhounds. Your plane leaves in forty-five minutes.' We'd just had our first child—a daughter. The only thing I had time to do was rush to the American Consulate with my wife and get our daughter certified so she wouldn't be a Japanese citizen. I put twenty-five dollars, a razor, and tooth-brush in my pocket and took off."[9]

Kean and Michaelis flew to Korea on July 8, in advance of the division's shipborne elements, in order to get the lay of the land. Jeeping forward to Bill Dean's CP in Taejon, they were shocked. "It was a horrifying picture," Mi-chaelis remembered. "They were getting whipped every place they turned. Everything seemed to be chaotic. The headquarters was filled with hundreds of troops. I don't know where they came from. It was so bad I forbade any of my troops to visit the Twenty-fourth headquarters until it got back on its feet."[10]

Michaelis's 27th Infantry landed at Pusan on July 10 and mated with the 8th FAB, commanded by Augustus T. ("Gus") Terry, Jr., to form the 27th RCT. In keeping with Walker's plan to hold Taegu and Pohang, the RCT was fragmented. The regimental headquarters, one artillery battery, and the 1/27, commanded by Gilbert J. Check, thirty-seven, went directly north from Taegu into the mountains near Uisong to backstop the desperately fighting ROKs in that sector. The 2/27, commanded by Gordon E. Murch, also thirty-seven, and another artillery battery went to Pohang to backstop the ROKs who were still slowly retreating down the east coast road and to ensure the safety of the port until the arrival of the 1st Cav Division.[11]

Before moving out, Michaelis assembled his officers and noncoms to pre-pare them for combat. He told them he wanted the men "stripped down," paratrooper-style, to weapons, ammo, water, rations. All else would be dis-posed of. "In other words, what they could put in a backpack—and that was it," Michaelis said later. In the postwar years he had assiduously studied Oriental fighting tactics and jungle warfare. He passed along what he had absorbed from these studies: Always take the high ground overlooking your position; have every man drink a full canteen of water in the morning, then refill the canteen to ensure a proper level of body fluids throughout the day. In conclusion, Michaelis said, Patton-like, "Remember, you're here to kill and not to be killed."[12]

As it happened, the ROKs at Uisong and along the east coast road put

up greater resistance than expected. The result was that the disparate 27th
RCT elements had slight or no contact with the NKPA for ten days or
more. This gave Mike Michaelis's Wolfhounds and Gus Terry's artillerymen
time to adjust mentally and physically to the abrupt shift from a peacetime
garrison to the battle zone and to the rigors of the South Korean terrain and
climate, time to assimilate newcomers, and time to carry out realistic training exercises.

* * *

The next of the 25th Division regiments to arrive in Korea was the
full-strength (three battalions) black 24th Infantry Regiment, which landed at
Pusan on July 12. It was mated with the black 159th FAB to form the 24th
RCT. The 159th was also at full strength (three firing batteries of six 105-mm
howitzers). Both black units were commanded by white officers: the 24th
Infantry by West Pointer (1923) Horton V. White, forty-nine; the 159th FAB
by Walter J. Preston. The principal subordinate elements (battalions; firing
batteries) were commanded by a mixture of white and black officers, but white
officers predominated in the senior positions. Attached to the RCT was the
black 77th Engineer Combat Company (ECC). Commanded by Charles M.
Bussey, a black fighter pilot in World War II, the 77th was also at full
strength.[13]

On paper, the 24th RCT was the strongest and best-equipped American
fighting force yet to reach Korea, but neither Walker nor Kean expected much
from it. They subscribed to the widespread view in the Army that "Negroes
won't fight." Walker's lack of confidence in these black troops may have in part
influenced his decision to employ the late-arriving 1st Cav, rather than the 25th
Division, to reinforce the 24th Division at Taejon.

* * *

The history of blacks in the Army was a long and shameful tale,
more or less paralleling black history in American civil life. The Army had
never wanted black soldiers. But in the Civil War, World War I, and World
War II political and other circumstances compelled it to accept large numbers of blacks. Inasmuch as the Army, like most of the nation, was racist
and practiced rigid segregation, the presence of blacks in its ranks
created enormous and expensive problems, such as providing "separate but
equal" living, training, and recreational facilities. It also posed delicate
and difficult questions about opening the professional officer corps to qualified
blacks.[14]

During the Civil War the Union Army took in 186,000 blacks. They were
assigned to sixteen segregated infantry regiments commanded by white officers. After the war, in recognition of the contribution of these blacks to the

Union victory, Congress decreed that the Army would indefinitely maintain four (segregated) regiments on active status: the 9th and 10th Cavalry and the 24th and 25th Infantry. This well-intended tribute had an unfortunate side effect. In the words of one black historian, the creation of these permanent black units "institutionalized segregation" in the Army, making it far more difficult to break down barriers.

During the mass mobilization for World War I the Army took in 404,000 blacks, of whom 368,000 were draftees. Most blacks were assigned to menial and demeaning "service units." However, in response to pressure from black activists and others, the Army, as an experiment, fielded two black infantry divisions, which in those days were composed of four regiments each. Commanded at the senior and most subordinate levels by white officers, these divisions were the 92d and 93d. Both divisions were sent to France with the AEF. The 92d, which saw little action, was assigned to the American Army; the 93d, which saw considerable action, fought with the French. The 92d was judged a failure; the 93d, barely successful. The allegedly poor performance of these two divisions gave rise to the view in the twentieth-century American Army that "Negroes won't fight."

In the years between the wars, when the professional Army shrank to about 140,000 men, the active-duty black population fell commensurately to about 4,000. Racism was rampant. Most blacks were assigned, on paper, to the congressionally mandated four black regiments: the 9th and 10th Cavalry, the 24th and 25th Infantry. In practice, however, most blacks were consigned to demeaning post duties such as collecting garbage, policing lawns, operating the laundries, driving trucks, providing senior officers domestic help ("orderlies"), or entertaining the troops with gospel songs. As in the civilian sector, blacks were denied opportunities for schooling and advancement. Black officers were a rarity.

The mobilization for World War II brought nearly 1 million black reservists, volunteers, and draftees into the Army. Most were assigned to segregated service units, and the Army hoped to keep them there and away from battlefronts. However, once again pressure from black activists and others, and the Roosevelt White House, compelled the Army (and Army Air Corps) to field numerous black combat units. Because of the spotty performance of the 92d and 93d divisions in World War I, the Army initially intended to restrict these ground units to regimental size or smaller. Accordingly, early in the war the 24th Infantry was sent independently to the Southwest Pacific Theater. However, the mounting outside pressure soon forced the Army to reverse itself and field three full-scale infantry divisions, which were commanded mostly by white officers: the 2d Cavalry (incorporating the 9th and 10th Cav regiments); the 92d and 93d (incorporating the 25th Infantry). In addition, the Army activated numerous independent battalion-size antiaircraft, antitank, tank, and artillery units—and even a token black parachute battalion, the 555th or "Triple Nickles."[15]

The performance of these black combat forces was uneven. Sent to North Africa, the 2d Cav Division was declared a complete failure. It was deactivated without seeing combat; its men were assigned to rear-area service units. Sent to the Southwest Pacific Theater, the 93d was employed principally to occupy rear areas and perform "service" chores. However, its 25th Infantry, temporarily attached to the Americal Division on Bougainville, did well in brief combat. A battalion of the independent 24th Infantry (the 1/24), which had spent most of its time performing "service" duties (as stevedores, etc.), also did well in brief fighting on Bougainville, while temporarily attached to the 37th Division. Reorganized as an independent unit, the full 24th Infantry later distinguished itself during mopping-up operations on Guam and Saipan.

Of all these black outfits, the 92d Division, commanded by Ned Almond, was the most conspicuous—and controversial. It was committed piecemeal to combat in Italy in September 1944. First to arrive was its 370th RCT (called the 92d Combat Team), which pursued retreating Germans north of Rome with some success. However, when the Germans dug in behind the Arno River, the 370th bogged down. Arriving later, the division's 365th and 371st regiments did no better. To provide the division added punch (and replacements), Fifteenth Army Group commander Mark Clark gave it a fourth regiment, the 366th, patched together from independent black anti-aircraft units already in Italy. When all these measures failed to inspire the division, Clark broke it up. He withdrew the 365th, 366th, and 371st regiments into army and corps reserves and substituted two new regiments: the famous 442d, composed of Japanese-Americans, and the 473d, also newly created from deactivated antiaircraft units. The black 370th Regiment, restaffed by "The Most Capable" of the men in the 365th, 366th, and 371st, remained on the battle line with the 442d and 473d, but the latter two did most of the division's heavy fighting. Almond pronounced the 370th to be "reasonably safe" but only with "constant attention" and "careful leadership."

In contrast, many of the smaller black units did well in World War II combat. Notable among these in the ETO were the 761st Tank Battalion, the 969th FAB, and the 614th Tank Destroyer Battalion. All received Presidential Unit Citations for valorous performance. During the Battle of the Bulge, when Eisenhower faced an emergency shortage of riflemen, he created thirty-seven overstrength black infantry platoons, made up of volunteers and commanded by white officers. Thrown into combat with scant unit training, these 4,500 black riflemen performed as well as—and in some instances better than—the men in comparable white units. The success of these smaller black units (most commanded by white officers) in comparison with the larger units (divisions, regiments) persuaded many senior officers that if the Army were again forced to field black combat units in a major war, they should be no greater than battalion size.

The uneven performance of black units in combat was puzzling and frustrating. After World War II, when it became fashionable in the Army to analyze battle factors "scientifically," Army boards and committees studied the "Negro problem" endlessly and exhaustively. Ned Almond and a majority of white officers blamed the failures on their perception that blacks were stereotypically "Sambos" and "Uncle Toms": cowardly and lazy; prone to panic and hysteria; indifferent to or contemptuous of military discipline, customs, and tradition; and mentally inferior for modern warfare. Contrarily, blacks and a minority of senior white officers argued that the failures were due largely to the abysmally low caliber of white officers assigned to lead the blacks (most capable white officers avoided such assignments), to the general lack of education among blacks, and—not least—to the Army's institutionalized segregationist policy, which automatically relegated blacks to second- or third-class status, creating nearly insurmountable hostilities and undermining the will to fight. Reflecting on this last aspect in relation to the 92d Division, Mark Clark agreed: "The Negro soldier needed greater incentive and a feeling that he was fighting for his home and country and that he was fighting as an equal."[16]

In the minority view the solution to the Army's postwar "Negro problem" was simple: Educate the blacks already in the Army, integrate them into white units, and provide incentive by opening up all possible avenues of career advancement. But the senior Army staff was no more prepared for such a drastic step than American society as a whole. In 1948, when President Truman issued an executive order designed to encourage desegregation of the armed forces, the Army, which had strong emotional, economic, and political ties to the Deep South, fought the order by every conceivable stratagem. Justifying the Army's position, Chief of Staff Omar Bradley wrote Truman that it would be "hazardous" to employ the Army deliberately "as an instrument of social reforms."[17]*

When the Korean War broke out, the Army was still rigidly segregated and racist. Owing to the drastic shrinkage in its size and the majority view that large black units were undesirable, Congress had relieved the Army of its obligation to maintain four black regiments on active service. Of the four "traditional" black regiments, only the 24th Infantry (organic to the 25th Division) in Japan remained, and it survived mainly because its larger struc-

---

*There was one exception. In the postwar years 82d Airborne Division commander James M. Gavin, entirely on his own, integrated the personnel of the elitist 555th ("Triple Nickles") Parachute Battalion into his division.[18]

ture was required to absorb the many blacks in Japan and because Ned Almond wanted the blacks out of sight and in one place.

The 24th Infantry was thus a legacy of the shameful treatment of blacks in the U.S. Army. It was staffed with professionals from its pre-World War II days, from the 9th and 10th Cav, 25th Infantry, the 92d and 93d divisions, and a sprinkling of men from the Triple Nickles, other elitist World War II black battalions, and draftees.

\* \* \*

On arrival in Pusan on July 13 the 24th RCT entrained immediately for Kumchon, where it established its CP. Positioned to the left (or west) of the 27th RCT, its mission was to backstop the ROKs who were blocking the NKPA from seizing the road running from Kumchon north through Sangju to Hamchang to Yechon. Like the other Americans preceding them to Korea, the blacks of the 24th RCT were shocked by the heat and humidity, the filth and stench, and the awesome mountainous terrain. Many old pros—and some new ones—in the outfit were determined that the 24th would give a good account of itself, erasing forever from Army minds the hated and humiliating belief that "Negroes won't fight."[19]

In the view of most black professionals in the outfit, however, there was a serious obstacle to that goal. They believed that with few exceptions the white officers holding the senior positions in the regiment were of low caliber, or worse, completely unqualified by experience or training to lead troops in combat. These included the 24th's commander, Horton White (the only senior West Pointer in the regiment), and his exec. White had not hitherto commanded troops in combat. In World War II he had been G-2 of MacArthur's Sixth Army in the Southwest Pacific.

One of the two young black West Pointers (both 1950) in the 77th ECC, David K. Carlisle, later wrote a history in collaboration with the 77th's commander, Charles Bussey, about his outfit's service in Korea. In it Bussey remembered two shocking episodes on the day the 24th arrived at Kumchon. First, Horton White confided to Bussey that he was unable to command the regiment. "I'm too old for this," White told Bussey. "I didn't realize it until this morning, but soldiering is for young-uns. Mine is all behind me. I'll do the job as required while I'm here, but I'll have to pack it in soon."* Secondly, a key senior officer on 24th's staff, "a big, fat, lazy bastard," had a heart attack, which Bussey surmised was faked. The officer was immediately evacuated.[21]

---

*A fellow West Pointer who commanded a regiment in Korea concurred in White's self-evaluation: "White was an intelligence specialist who was not competent to lead troops."[20]

Hence the 24th RCT entered the battle zone with weak leadership at the top. Fortunately there was one capable, combat-experienced senior white officer in the 24th: Paul F. Roberts, thirty-four, who had been twice-wounded and often decorated (Silver Star Medal, etc.) in World War II. To strengthen the top leadership, White chose Roberts to be the regimental exec. Carlisle and Bussey remembered that Roberts was "tough as nails and sharp as a tack" and did "a superior job," which enabled White to "take things easy."[22]

The 24th RCT spent about a week in Kumchon acclimatizing itself and preparing for battle. Its task forces patrolled along its assigned road as far north as Yechon. During that time the ROKs fought surprisingly well, but the NKPA gradually pushed them southward. On about July 19 the NKPA seized Yechon, an important road hub. In response, Johnnie Walker ordered Bill Kean to counterattack and recapture the town. That first combat assignment of the 25th Division fell to the 24th RCT.

White gave the Yechon mission to a battalion combat team (BCT) built around the 3/24, commanded by Samuel Pierce, Jr. The 3/24 had earlier patrolled Yechon and knew the terrain. Moving up aggressively on July 20, the 3/24 BCT promptly encountered heavy NKPA mortar, machine-gun, and rifle fire. Deploying his three rifle companies (I, K, L) to the south and west of Yechon, and backed by the heavy-weapons company (M), Pierce bivouacked for the night, and planned a textbook assault on Yechon on the following day.[23]

He chose L Company to lead the assault. It was commanded by a black paratrooper, Bradley Biggs, who was an alumnus of the elite Triple Nickles. Biggs remembered that his outfit deployed smartly by the book. During the assault, it encountered NKPA machine-gun and mortar fire, which was answered in kind, but within an hour and a half "at most" his troops (and others) had recaptured Yechon. The town, blazing with fires, was shortly turned over to troops of the ROK Capital Division.[24]

The 77th ECC commander, Charles Bussey, had jeeped forward to bring mail to the engineers of his 3d Platoon, commanded by Chester J. Lenon, who were supporting the 3/24. Approaching Yechon, Bussey suddenly encountered a formation of several hundred NKPA troops, who were apparently attempting to outflank the 3/24. Rounding up some nearby engineers and infantry, Bussey set up two machine guns, and laid down a withering fire. Manning the weapons himself and ignoring two minor wounds, Bussey personally inflicted an awesome and ghastly slaughter on the advancing NKPA. Later Bussey and the men counted and buried 258 dead enemy.[25]

Bussey's extraordinary feat deserved a high award. Visiting the regiment, an immensely pleased Bill Kean gave him a Silver Star (and a Purple Heart for his wound) remarking at the ceremony that it was merely a "down payment" on a "bigger medal" to follow. The 77th's first sergeant, Roscoe C.

Dudley, interviewed witnesses to confirm the facts of the fight and then recommended Bussey for the Medal of Honor, as apparently Kean had intended. But somewhere up the line the medal was killed. Believing Army racism was the main reason, David Carlisle subsequently mounted a campaign through official channels in Washington to "upgrade" Bussey's Silver Star to the Medal of Honor, but he met with a cool reception.[26]

A war correspondent with the Associated Press and later with *Time* magazine, Tom Lambert, accompanied the 3/24 BCT assault on Yechon. His vivid dispatch, widely published in the States, rightly claimed that the fight at Yechon was the "first sizable American ground victory in the Korean War" and "a far different story" from the performance of Bill Dean's 24th Division. The 25th Division historian put it this way: "It was the first South Korean city restored to friendly hands by American troops. Although it was not a tremendous victory, many believed it symbolic of the liberation of South Korea." Two congressmen rose on the House floor to note the action and laud the 24th Infantry.[27]

The victory was reason for blacks to celebrate, but Yechon was not long remembered. Moreover, the Army later attempted to obliterate it from the official record. Notwithstanding Lambert's dispatch and the division history, Army historian Roy Appleman, in his account of the Korean War, sneered at the Yechon fight, expressing doubt there had been any action "at all" and suggesting that the NKPA had withdrawn from the town before the BCT got there. Believing this sneering account also arose from Army racism, David Carlisle (joined by other blacks) produced overwhelming evidence to substantiate the "victory" in an effort to persuade the Army to revise the official history, but again Carlisle met with a cool reception.[28]

*　*　*

The last of Bill Kean's 25th Division major combat elements, the 35th Infantry, arrived in Pusan on July 13. It was commanded by Horton White's West Point (1923) classmate, Henry G. ("Hank") Fisher, fifty. The 35th was mated with the 64th FAB, commanded by West Pointer (1932) Arthur H. Hogan, forty-two, to form an RCT.[29]

Although Hank Fisher was a year older than White—by George Marshall's reckoning too old for regimental command—his attitude was completely different from White's: He was itching for a fight. Fisher well knew how to fight and command troops. Like Mike Michaelis, he had successfully commanded an infantry regiment (the 317th of the 80th Division) through many months of tough fighting in the ETO.

The Army historian wrote that Fisher, "ruddy-faced and possessed of a strong, compact body," was a "fine example of the professional soldier." He was "one of the ablest regimental commanders in Korea," who possessed an "exact knowledge" of weaponry and tactics. One of Fisher's young West Point (1945) officers, Sydney B. Berry wrote:

He was a professional in the finest sense of the word. He set high standards for his soldiers and his regiment and saw to it that we lived up to his expectations for us. He drove us in training with a sense of urgency and purpose. . . . Because "Hammering Hank Fisher," as we called him, had trained us in a tough, demanding, professional manner, we won battles in Korea from the beginning. Indeed, combat seemed easier than training under Hammering Hank Fisher. Many of us survived because of the tough, effective training Colonel Fisher had provided us.[30]

Upon landing at Pusan, the 35th, like the 27th Infantry, was fragmented. Johnnie Walker ordered Kean to send the 1/35, commanded by West Pointer (1939) Bernard G. Teeters, thirty-five, to Pohang to relieve Michaelis's 2/27, so that the latter could rejoin its parent organization. Fisher, his regimental headquarters, and his 2/35, commanded by John L. Wilkin, Jr., forty-two, camped for a few days in a rear area near Kyongju. This brief interlude before battle provided Fisher and his men with time to adjust to Korea, assimilate fillers, and engage in training exercises.[31]

On July 20, when Taejon fell, Walker concluded that the NKPA threat to Taegu from the west and northwest was greater than the threat from the north, where the ROKs were still fighting with surprising vigor and élan. He therefore ordered Bill Kean to suspend his ROK "backstopping" operations and redeploy the 25th Division (less Teeter's 1/35 at Pohang) to face northwest, along the road from Kumchon to Hamchang. Mike Michaelis's 27th RCT would occupy the southernmost sector in front of Kumchon; White's 24th RCT, the center sector in front of Sangju (where Kean would place the division CP); and Fisher's 35th RCT, the northernmost sector in front of Hamchang. ROK forces near Yechon would cover the division's right flank; the 1st Cav Division, scheduled to attack west up the Taegu–Taejon road, would cover the division left flank.[32]

In hindsight, Walker's critics faulted him for a "leisurely" early deployment of the 25th Division. It had "loitered" around Taegu for ten days, doing nothing of real consequence (except to retake Yechon), while the 24th Division was being savaged at the Kum River and Taejon, ostensibly "buying time" so the 25th (which was already there) and the 1st Cav could land. In response to Walker's justification for the deployment—that he could not be certain the ROKs could hold the NKPA north of Taegu and holding Taegu was vital to his strategy—the critics pointed out that if Walker had taken the time to visit ROK units north of Taegu and Pohang and assess their commanders and their spirit, he would have known that the NKPA attack, bedeviled by mountainous terrain and supply problems, had slowed to a crawl and that the ROK forces were more dependable than heretofore assumed.[33]

## II

The 1st Cav Division began landing unopposed and piecemeal at Pohang on July 18. First came the 8th Cav Regiment, then the 5th Cav, and lastly, the 7th Cav, delayed en route by a typhoon.

Much was expected of the 1st Cav Division. Before it "dismounted" in World War II to become regular infantry it had had a long and colorful equestrian history. Since childhood MacArthur had been mesmerized by that history and by the outfit's songs ("GarryOwen"; "She Wore a Yellow Ribbon") and legends. During World War II and the occupation of Japan the 1st Cav had been his favorite—and favored—division. The famous 7th Cavalry Regiment (which had been commanded by George Armstrong Custer at Little Bighorn) had held the place of honor in Tokyo, providing color guards, bands, and "troopers," bedecked with yellow scarves for ceremonies and parades. Before the Eighth Army levy to beef up the 24th Division, the 1st Cav had been grandly rated at "84 percent" combat-ready. Initially it had been chosen for the starring role in the Inchon landing.[34]

The 1st Cav was commanded by fifty-six-year-old two-star General Hobart R. Gay, who was nicknamed Happy, shortened to Hap. Born in Rockport, Illinois, Hap Gay had been graduated from Knox College in 1917 and the same year received a commission in the cavalry. He commanded G Company in the 7th Cavalry Regiment, which during World War I was detailed to Mexican border patrols in Texas and New Mexico. Like many cavalrymen, Gay became an avid polo player. During a game in 1929 he was blinded in one eye, and because of that he was compelled to transfer to the Army Quartermaster Corps, in which he served until 1941.

Luckily for Gay, he had earlier met cavalryman George Patton. When Patton began drafting old calvarymen for senior posts in the Army's rapidly expanding armored corps, one-eyed quartermaster Hap Gay was among the first to get a call. Despite the fact that Gay had been sidetracked in quartermaster duties for eleven years and had attended neither the Command and General Staff School nor the Army War College, Patton appointed him to be chief of staff first of the 1st Armored Corps, next of Seventh Army, then of Third Army in North Africa, Sicily, and England and got him promoted to brigadier general. As such Hap Gay was Patton's closest professional cohort in World War II.[35]

During preparations for the Normandy invasion Gay suffered a temporary but traumatic career setback: He was sacked as Patton's Third Army chief of staff. The reasons are not clear. Gay claimed it was because he had deliberately withheld important orders to Patton during the Sicily campaign which would have canceled Patton's highly publicized career-enhancing capture of Palermo. However, Patton's diary suggests another reason. Eisenhower, Patton recorded, did not think Gay had sufficient "presence" to represent Patton at other high headquarters. Whatever the reasons, at Eisenhower's insistence Patton reluctantly replaced Gay but kept him in the wings of his Third Army headquarters. In early December 1944, just before the Battle of the Bulge, when Patton stood high with Eisenhower and could do no wrong, he persuaded Eisenhower to let him restore Gay to the job of Third Army's chief of staff. Eisenhower not only approved that proposal but also recommended Gay for promotion to two stars, writing Marshall that Third Army staff work under Gay had been "extraordinarily good." Gay was in the car accident with Patton in December 1945, when Patton was fatally injured.[36]

As George Patton's two chief lieutenants in World War II Johnnie Walker and Hap Gay became very close. Gay had been one of Walker's biggest boosters in Third Army headquarters. In his diary Gay had gushed: "General Walker is always most willing and cooperative. He apparently will fight any time, any place, and with anything that the Army Commander desires to give him." In September 1949, when command of the 1st Cav opened up, Walker got old cavalryman Gay for an honorary tour of duty before retirement.[37]

Besides service together in Patton's Third Army, Walker and Gay had another bond. Both had sons who had been graduated in the West Point class of 1946 and were headed for duty in the Far East. Walker's son, Sam Sims, who had chosen the infantry and become a paratrooper, was then on his way from the 82d Airborne for duty in his father's Eighth Army. Gay's son, Hobart, Jr., who had chosen the Air Force, was then on the way to fly with FEAF's 49th Fighter Bomber Group.[38]

As a troop commander Gay, like Walker, had adopted some of the techniques and mannerisms of his mentor, George Patton. He wore highly polished cavalry boots and carried a bamboo swagger stick with a silver hilt. "But he wasn't Patton," a senior 1st Cav officer remembered. Gay's chief of staff, West Pointer (1925) Ernest V. Holmes, forty-seven, an artilleryman who had spent most of World War II in Hawaii, recalled: "Gay was not a healthy or well man. I was told that he had a heart condition and was given command of the 1st Cav in Japan for rest and recuperation. However, there was nothing obvious about his illness nor did he ever miss a day's duty." Another senior 1st Cav officer said: "He was sort of old, but he took good care of himself."[39]

Gay's senior assistants were, like those in the 24th and 25th divisions, "European generals." The ADC was Frank A. Allen, Jr., fifty-four, a onetime cavalryman and World War II tanker who became Eisenhower's chief wartime public relations man at SHAEF and a Pentagon lobbyist in the postwar years. The artillery commander was the tough, able West Pointer (1924) Charles D. Palmer, forty-eight, who was descended from a long line of West Pointers and whose older brother, Williston B. Palmer (West Point, 1918), had commanded Joe Collins's VII Corps artillery in the ETO and in 1950 commanded the 82d

Airborne Division. Palmer had been chief of staff to Edward H. ("Ted") Brooks while he commanded the famous "Hell on Wheels" 2d Armored Division and later VI Corps in the ETO. Williston and Charles Palmer both went on to wear four stars, the only brothers in Army history to do so.[40]

\* \* \*

Johnnie Walker warmly welcomed the 1st Cav into Eighth Army. That it had been gutted of 750 key noncoms to beef up the 24th Division and now numbered only 11,000 men (7,500 men below full wartime strength) was apparently discounted. The old Third Army cohorts Walker and Gay were back in war harness, working another battlefield. Perhaps they believed the ghost of George Patton would make up for the deficiencies in manpower and equipment.[41]

As planned, Walker ordered Gay to attack directly up the Taegu–Taejon road, to the left (or south) of Kean's redeploying 25th Division. The 1st Cav would relieve the shattered 24th Division at Yongdong and block the NKPA advance toward Taegu astride the Taegu–Taejon road. What remained of the 24th Division would be withdrawn to Taegu, to constitute a reserve behind the 1st Cav and 25th divisions.

\* \* \*

The two-battalion 8th Cav Regiment was first into battle. It was commanded by Raymond D. Palmer (VMI, 1924), forty-nine. Hap Gay had assumed the regiment would be committed as a "full" and integrated unit, normally mated with the 99th FAB, commanded by Robert W. Holmes. But he was mistaken. As he had the 24th Division units, Walker fragmented the 8th Cav. The 1/8, commanded by Robert W. Kane, thirty-four, and temporarily supported by the 77th FAB and a few light tanks and A/A vehicles, would block the Taegu–Taejon road, loosely tying in with the 25th Division on its right. The 2/8, commanded by Eugene J. Field, forty-two, and supported by the 61st FAB, which was commanded by Alden O. Hatch, would deploy seven miles south of the 1/8 to block another road leading to Taegu from Muju. There would be no physical link between the 1/8 and 2/8. Gay protested the dispersion of his forces, but to no avail.[42]

While the 8th Cav was moving into its fragmented positions, Hap Gay rushed his two-battalion 5th Cav Regiment forward to provide a division reserve. The 5th Cav was commanded by a dashing old horse cavalryman, Carl J. ("Rosie") Rohsenberger, who was nearing his fifty-sixth birthday—far too old for regimental command—and was also almost totally deaf. Rohsenberger had entered the Army eons ago as a private and slowly worked his way up. He was a fighter, eager to make a mark in this unexpected conflagration in the evening of his career.[43]

Fortunately for Walker and Gay, the NKPA paused briefly after the capture of Taejon and Okchon. This provided John Church an opportunity to withdraw safely the shattered elements of the 24th Division through the 1st Cav positions. The division pulled back to Taegu and beyond for a well-earned respite. But the respite would not last long.

\* \* \*

By the morning of July 23 the NKPA was again on the move. Its 3d Division and armored elements, deploying on both roads leading eastward to Taegu, simultaneously struck the widely separated 1/8 and 2/8. Robert Kane's 1/8, equipped with 3.5-inch bazookas and backed by the steady and skilled 77th FAB, commanded by West Pointer (1933) William A. ("Billy") Harris, and A/A weapons, held stoutly on the Taegu–Taejon road. However, Eugene Field's 2/8, backed by Alden Hatch's 61st FAB, was promptly encircled and cut off.[44]

All that day and the next Hap Gay made desperate efforts to block the oncoming NKPA and to extricate Field's isolated and besieged 2/8. Rosie Rohsenberger was willing—even eager—to do all in his power to help, but the sudden shock of battle and his serious hearing impairment rendered him all but helpless.

There was yet another problem: The leadership in Rohsenberger's 1/5 was chaotic, or worse. The outfit had been brought to Korea by West Pointer (1931) Glenn F. Rogers, forty-three, but Rogers left almost immediately for KMAG. He was temporarily replaced by a 1/5 company commander, a former enlisted man who had won a battlefield commission in World War II. However, after merely two days he collapsed from heat and exhaustion, said he "couldn't go on," and evacuated himself as an NBC. He was replaced by the able regimental S-3, Charles J. Parziale, but he was wounded almost immediately and evacuated (he would return). A cool, newly arrived, decorated (two Silver Stars, two Purple Hearts) veteran of World War II, James M. Gibson, twenty-nine, named S-3 of the battalion, attempted to hold the headquarters together.[45]

In the fighting on July 24 Gene Field, the commander of the surrounded and besieged 2/8, wounded twice in World War II, was wounded again—this time very seriously—and his exec, Gerald Robbins, thirty-three, replaced him. Finally, during the night of July 24–25, the 2/8 split up and fought its way out of the trap. Field and Robbins got out but many 2/8 men (and seven of the eleven light tanks) were lost, together with many of the 2/8's vehicles, crew-served weapons, and other gear. In the attempted rescue and blocking actions Rohsenberger's 5th Cav incurred 275 casualties in the two battalions.[46]

For the cavalrymen this introduction to combat in Korea came as a rude shock. The heat and humidity were utterly enervating. "Front lines, as such, did not exist," the division historian wrote. The NKPA, commingled with thousands of fleeing refugees, infiltrated and attacked from the flanks and even the rear. Not even division artillery positions were safe. Artillerymen of Hatch's 61st and Holmes's 99th FABs, the historian wrote, "repelled enemy attacks in force that had the cannoneers fighting with small arms alongside their thundering artillery pieces." Owing to the enemy infiltration, planned withdrawals "became advances to the rear into even larger [enemy] forces."[47]

By daylight on July 25 the NKPA had overwhelmed or scattered three of the four infantry battalions of the 5th and 8th Cav. Of the four, only Robert Kane's 1/8 on the Taegu–Taejon road had held together. By that time the 7th Cav, commanded by West Pointer (1923) Cecil W. Nist, forty-nine, had landed at Pohang. Ordered to leave the 1/7 at Pohang to relieve Teeters's 1/35, Nist came up with his headquarters elements and the 2/7 to help the 5th and 8th Cavs. Flung willy-nilly into battle, the 2/7, commanded by Herbert B. Heyer, thirty-nine, buckled and began what the 7th Cav historian charitably characterized as "a chaotic withdrawal."[48]

In sum, except for Kane's 1/8 and the uncommitted 1/7, the 1st Cav Division failed in its first action. The fault was mostly Walker's for rushing the green, understrength, ill-equipped battalions pell-mell into the teeth of the oncoming enemy and especially for fragmenting the 8th Cav, which necessitated a major diversion of effort to rescue Field's 2/8. Had Walker adopted Hap Gay's plan to advance slowly and keep the regiments intact and in lateral contact, the introduction of the division to combat might have been less traumatic.

There was another problem. The regimental commanders Palmer, Rohsenberger, and Nist were "too old" and not experienced at leading troops in combat. The 7th Cav's S-2, William J. ("Mike") Cochrane, Jr., who had fought in the regiment in World War II, remembered: "The division and its regiments [in Japan] served as a place to give senior officers a 'going away present' before they went home and retired." Ray Palmer had served throughout World War II on Patton's headquarters staff; Cecil Nist had served as John Hodges's G-2 in XXIV Corps in the Southwest Pacific. The West Point artilleryman Billy Harris did not believe any of the three should have been allowed to command regiments in Korea. The division chief of staff Ernest Holmes explained: "I doubt if there was ever a thought given to the age or experience of the regimental commanders. We used what we had. There was little thought about an extensive conflict. Remember, we were [originally] supposed to land at Inchon and see the tail end of the North Koreans heading back north."[49]

By the end of the following day, July 26, the 1st Cav had steadied down and redeployed into better defensive positions. The infantry was backed by 105-mm artillery batteries and the 155s of the 82d FAB, commanded by Gerald N. Bench. But its "line" was "fluid," thin, and loosely held on all sides;

NKPA pressure was mounting dangerously. Moreover, Hap Gay faced a problem at his rear. From Taegu Johnnie Walker sent word that he was "disappointed" in the performance of the 1st Cav.[50]

* * *

On the right of the 1st Cav the NKPA simultaneously and massively struck Bill Kean's 25th Division, which had only just got into its new positions in the hills west of the Kumchon–Hamchang road. This assault was conducted by four fresh NKPA divisions (1st, 2d, 13th, and 15th), which had bypassed Taejon to the north and circled southeast through Poun.[51]

Mike Michaelis's two-battalion 27th Infantry Wolfhounds, in position northwest of Hwanggan, encountered the NKPA 2d Division's probing attacks on the night of July 23d. The Wolfhounds, supported by Gus Terry's superior 8th FAB, bit back with unusual, indeed even unprecedented, ferocity. Michaelis remembered his tactics: "One thing I learned about the North Koreans: If things did not go exactly as they had planned, they had to stop everything and call back the company and battalion commanders, set up a new pattern, then come out again. So, if you could destroy their initial onslaught, you had them. I came up with what I called the 'inverted snake procedure.' I would put one company astride the road leading into our positions, then take the high ground as far back as I could stretch, closing off the tail end. When the NKPA came down the road and bumped into the block, they'd start their usual probing on the flanks, forgetting [for the moment] the middle. I'd pull the middle back through and build up the flanks in the high ground. When finally you got down to the desperation point—in danger of losing your equipment and a lot of men—you broke contact and just hauled ass. That became our radio signal for withdrawal: How Able! How Able!"[52]

The full force of the NKPA 2d Division attack came upon the Wolfhounds in a ground fog early on July 24, led by six T-34 tanks. Gilbert Check's 1/27 was deployed forward to receive it, holding the high ground flanking the Poun road. Several tanks crashed through to Check's CP, raising Cain with 85-mm guns, but Check's men grabbed 3.5-inch bazookas and stalked at close range, knocking out three. When the fog cleared, Check called for an air strike. The three F-80 jets which responded each got a tank, for a grand total of six. Meanwhile, the Wolfhounds holding the high ground on the flanks repulsed the NKPA infantry in ferocious close combat.

Believing the NKPA might remount the attack that night in an effort to encircle the 1/27, Michaelis ordered Check to withdraw quietly through Gordon Murch's 2/27. The NKPA attacked as Michaelis foresaw, but not until daylight. They enveloped and closed on Check's abandoned positions directly in front of Murch's well-emplaced firepower. Enjoying a clear field of fire, Murch's men inflicted a slaughter on the NKPA before Michaelis ordered

Murch to "How Able" to the rear. The withdrawal was skillfully conducted under cover of the nine light tanks.[53]

The Wolfhounds were forced back on Hwanggan, but their fight on July 24 and 25 was a minor yet deeply stirring and important psychological victory for the Americans. For the first time in South Korea an American regiment had decisively delayed a full-scale NKPA attack, knocking out (with FEAF help) a total of six fearsome T-34 tanks in the process, and had then withdrawn by the book, intact and ready to fight on. As a result, the Wolfhounds—and Mike Michaelis—became overnight celebrities. Michaelis remembered: "The kids won a battle—won it big—and that was very important for the outfit. They developed that all-important confidence right away. In fact, they became so cocky they were almost intolerable."[54]

Much of the credit for this "victory" was owed to Michaelis himself. He was a young, thoroughly professional, highly capable, experienced troop leader, in superb shape, physically and mentally. Long in search of a battlefield hero, the press—Marguerite Higgins and the *Time-Life* team in particular—repeatedly flocked to his CP to publicize him in frontline dispatches. Michaelis did nothing to discourage this attention. "In World War Two I didn't play the press properly," he remembered. "In Korea I did. I had a sergeant to keep the press happy. He was a gem."[55]

\* \* \*

Horton White's 24th Infantry—fresh from the 3/24's victory at Yechon—was deployed on the right of the Wolfhounds at Sangju, backed by Walter Preston's steady 159th FAB. By that time White had delegated substantial tactical responsibility to his capable new exec, Paul Roberts.

On July 22 the 2/24, commanded by Horace E. Donaho, was ordered to patrol to the northwest of Sangju. It would maneuver with elements of the ROK 17th Infantry Regiment, now being advised by KMAG officer Joe Darrigo. The Army historian wrote that the 2/24's leading companies, E and F, were ambushed by NKPA and thereafter "began withdrawing in a disorderly manner." When Horton White hurried forward, the historian wrote, "he found the battalion coming back down the road in disorder and most of the men in a state of panic. He finally got the men under control."[56]

The Army historian went on: "The tendency to panic continued in nearly all the 24th Infantry operations west of Sangju. Men left their positions and straggled to the rear. They abandoned weapons on positions. On one occasion the 3rd Battalion withdrew from a hill and left behind twelve .30-caliber and three .50-caliber machine guns, eight 60-mm mortars, three 81-mm mortars, four 3.5-inch rocket launchers and 102 rifles."[57]

Some black officers who were present during the July combat at Sangju roundly disputed the historian's account. One who did so was the commander of F Company, Roger S. Walden, then twenty-eight. A pioneer black paratrooper and an alumnus of the Triple Nickles, Walden had joined the 24th Infantry earlier in the year, rising to command A Company of the 1/24 before the war broke out, after which he was assigned to command F Company. He remembered: "On the attack to the northwest from Sangju we had been assigned a line of departure (LOD). We headed up the road in a column of companies, E Company in the lead. Long before reaching the LOD E Company ran into an enemy roadblock. The men held up for thirty to forty minutes and the rest of the companies deployed to either side of the road to await developments. Shortly thereafter we were withdrawn to the rear, not in a state of panic—there was no panic whatsoever—to carry out a new task."[58]

The 24th Infantry suffered 323 battle casualties (27 killed; 293 wounded) at Sangju, but did not garner further laurels. To the contrary.* Whether true or not, word began to spread through the white Army that the 24th was not dependable, that the blacks were cowardly and would not fight. In the words of black paratrooper Bradley Biggs, the 24th was summarily "lynched" then—and later in the Army's official history. In defense Biggs and other able men in the outfit—Bussey, Carlisle, Walden—would charge that the failures in the 24th then and later were no worse than those in the white regiments and furthermore that most of the failures were due to the high turnover, incompetence, and racism of the white leaders in the 24th, "none of whom wanted to serve in the outfit in the first place," as Walden put it, and who regarded an assignment to the 24th as the "kiss of death" for their careers.[59]

These charges and countercharges would echo down through the years. Inasmuch as no historian has undertaken a dispassionate and objective study of the 24th Infantry in Korea, it is difficult to assess the pros and cons. However, even a cursory examination of the charges by the blacks who were present leads to the conclusion that the Army's official account is thinly researched, canted, insensitive, and utterly unreliable as "black history."

\* \* \*

The right (or north) sector of the 25th Division was occupied by Hank Fishers's 35th Infantry. Owing to the temporary detachment of Teeters's 1/35 to guard Pohang for the 1st Cav landing, Fisher at first had merely one battalion: Wilkin's 2/35, supported by artillery and a platoon of five light tanks. The division ADC, Vennard Wilson, who was designated tactical com-

---

*The black commander of A Company, Leon A. Gilbert, was court-martialed (under Article of War 75) for deserting his position and refusing a direct order to engage the enemy. Found guilty, Gilbert was sentenced to death, but President Truman commuted the sentence to twenty years of hard labor.

mander in this sector, further weakened Fisher's position by drawing off one company (F) to backstop the ROK forces in Fisher's right flank.[60]

The NKPA 1st Division began probing attacks in Fisher's sector on July 22. Under growing pressure, the ROKs on his right broke and fled, leaving Wilkin's green F Company alone and exposed. The NKPA infantry flanked F Company and brought it under fire from the rear, causing panic and a bugout. Most of the Americans escaped, but some were lost trying to get across a stream swollen by the incessant rain. In what the Army historian described as a "fiasco," F Company was thoroughly disorganized and sustained heavy casualties.[61]

The next day, July 23, the NKPA infantry, led by five T-34 tanks, hit Fisher hard. However, in an astonishing display of marksmanship, the 155-mm batteries of James V. Sanden's 90th FAB knocked out four of the five tanks with HEAT shells. (A timely FEAF air strike got the fifth.) This feat gave the depleted 2/35 heart, and it held its ground until later in the day, when yet another collapse of the ROKs on the right and growing lack of confidence in the 24th Infantry induced Bill Kean to pull the 35th south to help the 24th defend Sangju. By then Teeters's 1/35, relieved at Pohang, was en route to join Fisher, but Kean had to divert it to the left flank of the 24th Infantry, adjacent to the Wolfhounds, where the NKPA 2d Division was threatening to force a breakthrough at Hwanggan.[62]

By July 26 Bill Kean's entire 25th Division front was under massive and relentless NKPA attack. Michaelis's 27th and Fisher's 35th Infantry both performed well. White's 24th Infantry was viewed as a doubtful asset and, as a consequence, the overall effectiveness of the division was impaired. It could not maneuver as a three-regiment division without risk, and much of the energy of the 27th and 35th was expended in plugging holes created by alleged bugouts in the 24th Infantry. The Army historian wrote that Walker was "disappointed and upset" with the division and so informed Kean.[63]

# III

Owing to the weakness of Walker's forces, the failure of most of the 1st Cav Division, and growing doubts about the reliability of the 24th Infantry, Walker's plan to stand firm before Taegu appeared to be unrealistic. However, at this decisive point in its campaign, the NKPA made a ruinous mistake: It split off two of its best divisions, the 4th and 6th, to mount a wide envelopment of Eighth Army by going due south to the coast, then east through Chinju and Masan to Pusan.[64]

It was a ruinous mistake because it dispersed and diluted the power of the NKPA at the very time it should have been massing for a coup de grace at

Taegu. It violated the military principle of "concentration of force" at the main enemy, which in this instance was the weak and reeling Eighth Army. Had the crack NKPA 4th and 6th divisions reinforced the severely weakened NKPA 3d Division and the fresh NKPA 1st, 2d, 13th, and 15th divisions, which were maneuvering for the assault on Taegu, there is little doubt that they could have overrun Eighth Army and achieved a great victory.

\* \* \*

Walker detected the flanking threat almost immediately. To counter it, he reluctantly called on his only reserve, John Church's shattered 24th Division, which had been out of the fighting for only two days. Walker's plan was to create a new "front" in the south, west of the Nam and Naktong rivers, to block the NKPA drive on Pusan. The recently mauled 19th and 34th regiments would move immediately south, almost to the coast, and establish a north-south line running from Chinju to Kochang. The 21st Regiment, which had only just relieved the 7th Cav's 1/7 at Pohang and Yongdok, would remain temporarily in division reserve at Yongdok, but several thousand miscellaneous ROK troops in the southern area would be placed under Church's command.[65]

The Chicks of the 19th now had a new commander, West Pointer (1930) Ned D. Moore, forty-three, replacing the wounded Stan Meloy. Like Mike Michaelis, Moore was an alumnus of Max Taylor's 101st Airborne Division. In the airborne assaults of the 101st in Normandy and Holland, Moore had served on Taylor's headquarters staff as G-1. When the 101st was surrounded at Bastogne in the Battle of the Bulge, Moore, owing to the suicide of the incumbent, temporarily served as division chief of staff until Mike Michaelis recovered from the battle wounds he incurred in Holland. Moore had arrived in Japan in August 1948 and commanded a regiment of the 7th Infantry Division before moving on to the Eighth Army G-3 section. He had not ever directly commanded troops in battle; but he had been closely associated with elite, aggressive airborne infantry in combat (he was shot in the hand in Holland but refused evacuation), and he well knew what to do.[66]

Moore remembered: "When I reported to Walker in Korea, he told me he wanted me to take over the all-black Twenty-fourth Regiment. Nobody, including me, wanted command of the Twenty-fourth. When Meloy got hit at the Kum River, Walker told me to take over the Nineteenth, then temporarily commanded by Tom McGrail. I caught up with Bill Dean before the fall of Taejon and was in the division CP at Yongdong when the Thirty-fourth bugged out of Taejon. Then I was on my way to Chinju with the beat-up Nineteenth. I was 'temporarily attached' for weeks as commander, but when Meloy did not return, I became permanent—and thereby escaped command of the Twenty-fourth."

Johnnie Walker had a favor to ask of Ned Moore. Walker's son, Sam, was arriving from the 82d Airborne and needed a job. The older Walker had begun his career with the Chicks and apparently wanted Sam to carry on the family tradition. Would Moore take him?

"What kind of strings are you keeping on him?" Moore asked.

"Not a goddamned one," Walker replied. "He's just another infantry officer."

Moore took on this big responsibility, naming young Sam Walker commander of C Company in the 1/19. He remembered that Sam was "one of about fifteen kids in the regiment whose fathers had been my bosses."

As he set up his blocking position at Chinju, Ned Moore was simultaneously reorganizing and trying to reman the decimated 19th. He had no exec; that slot was being held open for the wounded Chan Chandler, who was expected to return. Meanwhile, the S-3, Ed Logan, was filling in as exec. West Pointer (1942) Elliott C. Cutler, Jr., a veteran of the ETO, replaced Logan as S-3. The 1/19 (down to about 300 men) was now temporarily commanded by Robert L. Rhea, forty. Tom McGrail had reverted to command of the 2/19 (about 300 men). Despite the heavy losses sustained among the junior officers, Moore found a few good, strong combat leaders still in place—for example, Mike Barszcz.[67]

On July 25, as he was girding for battle, Ned Moore received important—and generous—reinforcements, the first two of the eight individual battalions Matt Ridgway had ordered to Korea to bring the three divisions there up to strength. Moore was originally scheduled to get only one battalion, but owing to the sad state of the 19th and the importance of its new mission, Walker sent him two.

These two battalions had come from the 29th Infantry Regiment on Okinawa. Until alerted for movement on July 5, both units were at half strength (about 500 men each) and had received no field training other than simulated deployment to protect the Strategic Air Command (SAC) bases on Okinawa. Both had brand-new commanders with no prior combat experience. West Pointer (1929) Wesley C. Wilson, who was Ned Moore's age (forty-three) and a year senior to him at the academy, commanded the 1/29. Harold W. Mott commanded the 2/29.[68]

The battalions, strengthened by the addition of 400 draftees who had arrived in Okinawa from the States only the day before, had departed Okinawa on July 21 by ship. As Wilson and Mott understood the plan, the battalions would go first to Japan for six weeks of field training, then to Korea. But the urgency of the situation dictated direct movement to Korea—without field training. The 3/29's exec, Tony J. Raibl, thirty-nine, who acted as advance man for both battalions, protested these orders directly to Walker in Taegu, but to no avail. Upon landing at Pusan on July 24, both battalions were trucked to the 19th Regiment at Chinju so quickly that the men did not even have time to calibrate rifles, test-fire mortars, or clean the Cosmoline from the machine guns.

Upon receiving these reinforcements from Okinawa, Ned Moore, who was being "advised" by the fat, deposed ROK Army chief of staff, Chae Byong Duk, ordered Mott's 3/29 to advance west from Chinju to Hadong and make contact with the oncoming NKPA 6th Division. Mott, with Chae in tow, got his convoys moving in the early hours of July 26. The next day the NKPA 6th Division fell on the 3/29 in full fury and virtually inflicted a massacre. In all, the battalion suffered about 50 percent casualties; 403, including 349 missing (of whom 313 were later found dead). Chae and 3/29 company commanders Joseph K. Donahue and Hugh P. Milleson were killed; Mott, Raibl, the S-1, and William Mitchell, the S-2, were wounded; company commander Alexander E. Makarounis was captured. The senior surviving and unwounded officer, George F. Sharra, the combat-experienced commander of L Company (mostly comprised of raw recruits), took command and led the 3/29's fleeing survivors to safety. All of the battalion's weapons, vehicles, and other gear were lost.[69]

That same day, July 27, Moore sent the other Okinawa battalion, Wilson's 1/29, north out of Chinju toward Anui to replace Robert Rhea's 1/19, which was positioned at Anui to block the southerly movement of the NKPA's 4th Division and to link with the 34th Regiment at Kochang. The relief, carried out in the midst of a NKPA probing attack, was a shambles. Rhea's A Company, caught in a roadblock and not able to withdraw as planned, had to destroy its vehicles and flee into the hills. Wilson's ill-prepared B and D companies, entering combat for the first time, were cut off and riddled (215 casualties) and followed Rhea's men into the hills. After mounting several futile attempts to rescue his B Company, Wilson ordered a hurried withdrawal to Sanchong that night, thereby sparing his remaining two companies the total disaster that befell the 1/29.[70]

John Church and Ned Moore had displayed laudable aggressiveness in advancing to meet the enemy. However, the decision to commit the two, utterly green Okinawa battalions for this purpose was unfortunate, even callous. Serving almost as cannon fodder, the two units had incurred a shocking 618 casualties in a single day to little purpose.

*　*　*

Even though the NKPA had unwisely split off two fresh divisions from the drive on Taegu to make the flanking attack on Pusan, the gravity of the mistake was not yet apparent at Eighth Army headquarters. As a result, there was still utmost concern that Taegu might fall. The fresh NKPA 2d Division had joined the battered 3d Division in the advance on the Taegu–Taejon road. Six full-strength NKPA divisions were attacking the five depleted

ROK divisions on the north, central, and east fronts. Although the ROK Army continued to show improvement, it was steadily giving ground.

By July 26 Walker was forced to concede that holding operations by the 1st Cav and 25th divisions were no longer feasible. He therefore prudently—but reluctantly—warned Hap Gay and Bill Kean to prepare to fall back to the Naktong River, about ten miles west of Taegu. Although Walker absolutely forbade any talk of further withdrawals, the Eighth Army staff made secret plans to displace the American and ROK Army headquarters and Rhee government rearward to Ulsan or Pusan. The possibility of a complete evacuation from Korea—a Dunkirk—was now in the back of everybody's mind.[71]

Walker was still on a short tether to GHQ. Having made up his mind about what must be done, he telephoned Ned Almond to ask for a GHQ okay for the withdrawal. Almond—700 miles from the battlefield—was appalled by Walker's apparent defeatism and negative attitude. Almond stated that a general withdrawal of the 1st Cav and 25th divisions and a rearward move of Eighth Army headquarters to Pusan were sure to have a demoralizing effect on American and ROK GIs and would be viewed as the beginning of a "general debacle" that would almost certainly lead to a Dunkirk.[72]

After hanging up, Almond went immediately to see MacArthur. He relayed Walker's gloomy news and plans and urged MacArthur to go at once to Korea and put some ginger in Eighth Army. MacArthur agreed, and at about ten o'clock the next morning, July 27 (the day the Okinawa battalions were being slaughtered), MacArthur, Almond, some GHQ staffers, and selected news correspondents arrived in Taegu aboard MacArthur's plane, the *Bataan*.[73]

MacArthur, Almond, and Walker conferred in private for an hour and a half. As usual, MacArthur did most of the talking, speaking as much to the "unseen audience" and history as to Walker. He did not once allude directly to Walker's withdrawal plans. He spoke grandly and loftily of Eighth Army's role in history and the defeat of communism. Ultimate victory was near at hand. The 2d Infantry Division, the Marine RCT, and the Army's 5th RCT from Hawaii would be landing at Pusan soon, to reinforce Eighth Army. Yet another plan for an Inchon amphibious landing was taking shape, utilizing the 7th Infantry Division and the 1st Marine Division. Eighth Army *must* hold so that the larger schemes could unfold as designed. Eighth Army withdrawals must cease. There would be no Dunkirk in Korea.[74]

When he returned to the airport to enplane for Japan, MacArthur was "smiling and exuding confidence." He boasted to disbelieving reporters: "The enemy has lost his great chance for victory in the last three weeks. . . . This does not mean that victory passes to us instantly or without a long hard row and the most difficult struggle. That we will have new heartaches and new setbacks is inherent in the situation, but I have never been more confident in victory—in ultimate victory—in my life than I am now."[75]

After MacArthur had departed Taegu, a chastened Walton Walker put on hold his plans for the withdrawal of the 1st Cav and 25th divisions to the Naktong River; he did not follow up the earlier warning with a movement order. Nonetheless, withdrawals in that sector continued with tacit Eighth Army staff approval. During the night of July 28–29, Mike Michaelis, having incurred 323 casualties and under strong pressure from the NKPA 2d Division at Hwanggan, got permission from Bill Kean to pull back his Wolfhounds with cover provided by the nearby 7th and 8th Cav regiments. In turn, Hap Gay, fearing that the whole 1st Cav might be flanked, withdrew his division twelve air miles from Hwanggan to Kumchon. Bill Kean's 24th Infantry, now tightly bracketed by both the 1/35 and 2/35, pulled back into Sangju.[76]

Walker may or may not have approved of these withdrawals. Inasmuch as they conformed to his earlier plans, squelched by MacArthur and Almond, the likelihood is that he did approve. Nonetheless, he still had a GHQ pistol at his head and he therefore felt compelled to make a public pretense of conveying MacArthur's unrealistic and unreasonable orders that Eighth Army must absolutely hold in place.

On July 29 Walker called on Bill Kean at Sangju, Hap Gay at Kumchon, and John Church at Hyopchon to give them and their staffs a pep talk. Walker was inept at public relations, and his talk proved to be unfortunate. As paraphrased in Kean's CP journal, Walker, after describing the American ground reinforcements which would soon arrive, went on to say:

We are fighting a battle against time. There will be no more retreating, withdrawal, or readjustment of the lines or any other terms you choose. There is no line behind us to which we can retreat. Every unit must counterattack to keep the enemy in a state of confusion and off-balance. There will be no Dunkirk, there will be no Bataan. A retreat to Pusan would be one of the greatest butcheries in history. We must fight until the end. Capture by these people is worse than death itself. We will fight as a team. If some of us must die, we will die fighting together. Any man who gives ground may be personally responsible for the death of thousands of his comrades. . . . I want everybody to understand that we are going to hold this line. We are going to win.[77]

The exhortation would become famous—or infamous—as Walker's "stand or die" speech. Because it was inaccurate or silly in several respects, it was not well received. Contrary to Walker's assertion, there was a good line behind the division to which they could retreat: the Naktong River. In light of the NKPA infiltration and flanking tactics, it was silly to demand that American GIs not adjust to that smartly and give ground, as Michaelis had done.

In fact, the exhortation was pointless. Over the next several days the 1st Cav and 25th divisions were forced to fall back another fifteen miles. Simultaneously John Church's skeletal 24th Division, blocking the flanking drive of the NKPA 4th and 6th divisions on Pusan, was forced to give ground.

In the 24th Division's northern sector, near Kochang, Charles Beauchamp's 34th Regiment was hanging on—but barely. On July 29 the NKPA 4th Division fell on the 34th in a fury. Red Ayres's 1/34 and Jack Smith's 3/34 withdrew under the pressure, falling back toward Sanje. Simultaneously the elements of Charles Stratton's 13th FAB, supporting the 34th, panicked and bugged out. Church reinforced Beauchamp with the ROK 17th Regiment, which was still being advised by KMAG veteran Joe Darrigo, and with Dick Stephens's 21st Regiment (from Pohang-Yongdok), which consisted then mainly of Brad Smith's 1/21. But Stephens, Beauchamp, Smith, and Darrigo were not able to contain the attack. On August 1 Eighth Army ordered this conglomeration of units to pull back behind the Naktong River into defensive positions.[78]

This withdrawal left Ned Moore's Chicks, positioned farther south at Sanchong and Chinju, perilously overextended and exposed on the right (or north) flank. Accordingly that same day Eighth Army ordered Moore and his Chicks to abandon Sanchong and Chinju and withdraw east toward Masan. Moore complied, fighting a skilled and brave withdrawal (for which he won a DSC), but at Sanchong Wesley Wilson, commanding the attached 1/29 (from Okinawa), failed to get the word. As a result, he was cut off north of Chinju and had to withdraw through the mountains, a rugged and dangerous maneuver which fortunately was carried out without a single loss.[79]

It was soon evident to Walker that the shattered 24th "Division" was not nearly strong enough to block the drive of the NKPA 4th and 6th divisions on Pusan. Substantial reinforcements were en route by sea to Pusan (the full 2d Infantry Division; the Marine RCT; the Army's 5th RCT), but they might not arrive in time. This tight situation led Walker to take what would be described as a "great gamble": He would secretly and temporarily shift Bill Kean's 25th Division from the Taegu front to the southwest front to reinforce the 24th Division.[80]

A number of factors influenced Walker's decision to take this gamble: first, his knowledge that the NKPA had egregiously erred in splitting and diluting its forces on the Taegu front to threaten Pusan; secondly, perhaps as a consequence, the noticeable lessening in the NKPA pressure on Taegu; thirdly, the possibility of constructing and strengthening the Taegu front by simultaneously withdrawing the 1st Cav behind the Naktong River; fourthly, the increasing valor and success of the ROK forces; fifthly, the mobility of American forces.

The fifth factor was by no means last or least. The Taegu–Pusan road was in good shape. It was also paralleled by a railway. The distance between the fronts was less than 100 miles. With optimum and efficient utilization of the road and railroad, Kean could shift the entire 25th Division within a day or so. If a sudden crisis developed on the Taegu front, Kean could quickly shift the division back to Taegu. In military parlance, the "interior lines of communication" favored Walker.

Walker issued orders for the 25th Division redeployment on July 31. Kean and his men complied with astounding efficiency. While the 1st Cav held off the sluggish (and perhaps puzzled) NKPA west of the Naktong, the 25th Division withdrew into Taegu and boarded trucks and trains in great secrecy. By the evening of August 1 advance elements of the division (the Wolfhounds) were arriving in Masan. The 25th Division historian noted with pride and hyperbole that the secret shift of the division from the Taegu front to the southwest front was "one of the best executed and cleverest strategic moves in the history of the United States Army."[81]

Following the withdrawal of the 25th Division, Hap Gay commenced the retrograde movement of the 1st Cav to the Naktong River, per plan. Simultaneously ROK forces on Gay's right pulled back on the Naktong, to tie in with the Americans, in effect filling the gap left by the 25th Division. Rohsenberger's 5th Cav ably served as rear guard for the 1st Cav. After most of the division had crossed the Naktong, Gay blew the main highway and railroad bridges, killing "hundreds" of refugees who refused to obey his emphatic orders to stay clear.[82]

\* \* \*

All these redispositions, completed about August 2, compressed Eighth Army into what journalists labeled the "Pusan Perimeter." The label misleadingly implied a close-in, circular enclave at Pusan. In fact, the perimeter was quite large: an upright rectangle about 100 miles tall and 50 miles wide. It was bordered by the Naktong River on most of the left (or west), the Sea of Japan on the right (east), rugged mountains on the top (north), and the Korea Strait on the bottom (south).[83]

The Pusan Perimeter was not by any means an impregnable enclave. By the usual standards, the American forces were very thinly spread. But the Americans had the broad Naktong River and its valley before them and sufficient forces to block the roads over which NKPA tanks and mechanized artillery had to travel. Moreover, the American front was now clearly defined and more or less static. Thus the artillery and FEAF close air support could be utilized more effectively. The railway and road nets within the perimeter enabled the logisticians to bring supplies* from Pusan to the front quickly. All

---

*The flow of supplies into Pusan had increased, but it was far from sufficient to support three American and five ROK divisions. All units continued to suffer from shortages, particularly of ammo. The shortage was compounded by an earlier JCS decision, urged by Joe Collins, to support the French forces in Indochina. On August 1, 1950, an official Army historian wrote, there were supplies "sufficient to equip twelve infantry battalions" en route to Indochina.[84]

this gave the American forces for the first time increased feelings of security and a will to fight.[85]

Walker enjoyed another advantage: excellent communications intelligence (COMINT) from breaking some encoded NKPA radio transmissions. The full details of this operation remain classified, but a little background and a cursory outline of successes in Korea can be pieced together from unclassified material.

During World War II the Allied forces had benefited greatly from breaking German and Japanese military and diplomatic codes. In the postwar years Washington had directed code-breaking efforts against the Soviet Union and other Communist nations, but owing to a lack of funding, a shortage of qualified and highly motivated code breakers and linguists, bureaucratic inertia, infighting and other factors, it had not been able to duplicate the remarkable COMINT successes of World War II. Most encoded radio traffic out of Moscow was unbreakable.[86]

As a result of the effort directed toward Moscow and elsewhere, North Korean codes had of necessity been grossly neglected. A study conducted in June 1952 by George A. Brownell and others (the so-called Brownell Report) revealed that the State Department and Pentagon had ranked North Korea near the bottom (twelfth or lower) on its postwar code-breaking priority list. Hence, by the time the Korean War began almost nothing noteworthy had been achieved, and, Brownell reported, Washington had been "poorly prepared to handle Korean traffic."[87]

The upshot was that unlike the Army commanders of World War II, Johnnie Walker had no flow of decoded "strategic" enemy radio traffic from Washington to assist him. What he got, he had to acquire locally—"tactical" COMINT. In this effort, however, Walker's G-2 section was remarkably, even astoundingly, successful. One reason, a senior G-2 officer wrote, was that the NKPA was careless and had an "obvious lack of communications security." As a result, Eighth Army cryptographic specialists were able to "break into" the NKPA "tactical radio network" and "read" NKPA traffic. "They had a 'pad' which they changed weekly," a G-2 specialist explained. "It took only one day to break it, then we could read NKPA traffic for four or five days running." As a result of this tactical code breaking, plus the usual battlefield intelligence, the Eighth Army G-2 specialist wrote, "throughout July and August, every major enemy attack was known in advance. . . ."[88]

Possessing this advance knowledge proved to be a priceless asset for Walker. Alerted to enemy moves in advance, he was able to shift his few reserves within the Pusan Perimeter to key spots at the key times, further capitalizing on his favorable "interior lines of communication." Inasmuch as COMINT was ultra top secret and every effort was made to limit its distribution and conceal its output, only a handful of personnel in Eighth Army were aware of it. Those not "in the picture" would unwittingly praise

Walker for his seemingly uncanny—or even magical—ability to divine enemy intentions.

*  *  *

In arriving at the Pusan Perimeter, the Americans and ROKs had paid a ghastly price. By August 1 the American ground forces had incurred a total of 6,003 casualties, the majority (3,610) in the 24th Division. In all, 1,884 Americans were dead, 2,695 were wounded, 523 were missing, and 901 were POWs. This carnage was nearly three times that incurred in World War II on D day at bloody Omaha Beach (2,000) and nearly double the American casualties at Pearl Harbor (3,600) and twice those at Tarawa (3,000). To the Army's amazement, it was later confirmed that on this same date, August 1, ROK Army casualties stood at an appalling 70,000.[89]

No one in Taegu, Tokyo, or Washington yet knew it, but the NKPA had also sustained appalling casualties. On August 1 GHQ and the Pentagon estimated NKPA losses at 31,000 and 37,500 respectively. Later the Army discovered (also to its amazement) that the true figure was closer to 58,000. One reason for the gross underestimate was the tendency in Eighth Army to disbelieve or discount ROK Army estimates of casualties inflicted on the NKPA. Because of these heavy losses, by early August the ten combat divisions of the NKPA had been reduced to a total strength of but 70,000 men. The vaunted NKPA armored force had diminished from 150 to 40-odd T-34 tanks. Owing to complete, uncontested American air and sea supremacy and the NKPA's ever-lengthening and complex lines of communications, it could only barely supply its dwindling forces.[90]

Fed by the American intelligence underestimations of NKPA losses, press reports continued to describe the enemy in terms of "hordes" and "wave after wave" of men, who outnumbered the UN forces "four to one" or more. In actuality, on August 1 Eighth Army, with 45,000 men in the six ROK combat divisions and 30,000 men in the three American combat divisions, slightly outnumbered the NKPA combatant forces. Moreover, on that date long-awaited American reinforcements (the Army's 5th RCT, the Marine RCT, and the 2d Infantry Division) were beginning to arrive in Pusan. By August 4 Eighth Army frontline forces outnumbered NKPA frontline forces 92,000 to 70,000. Although as yet unperceived, this numerical advantage on the battlefield greatly strengthened the odds for a successful defense of the Pusan Perimeter.[91]

Thus, subtly and imperceptibly, the balance of power in South Korea was shifting to the battered Eighth Army. In splitting its forces for the wide flanking attack on Pusan in preference to a textbook massed attack on Taegu, the NKPA had seriously alarmed Eighth Army, but it had thrown away its best chance for a quick and decisive victory. In consolidating into what then (and later in many histories of the war) appeared to be a defensive, defeatist, and desperate "Custer's Last Stand" in the Pusan Perimeter, Johnnie Walker had in fact finally disposed Eighth Army in the most advantageous stance to defeat the NKPA ultimately.

## IV

In Washington the JCS continued to view the NKPA invasion of South Korea as a possible military feint in a larger Kremlin design. It kept a close watch on Western Europe, the Middle East, and particularly Communist China, which, notwithstanding the difficulties of consolidating a new government, had invaded Tibet and was supporting Ho Chi Minh in Indochina. The big concern was that Moscow might order Peking to intervene in the Korean War to assist the NKPA or that Peking, having assembled 200,000 troops opposite Formosa, might invade that island, as it had vowed to do, with or without encouragement from Moscow.

In late July an urgent intelligence report seemed to indicate that a Red Chinese invasion of Formosa was more than a mere possibility. The report stated that the Red Chinese had assembled a fleet of "4,000 vessels" on the mainland opposite Formosa. On July 27, believing an invasion could be imminent, the JCS sent MacArthur what amounted to a "war warning."[92]

The Truman administration policy toward Formosa was still to "neutralize" it: prevent a Communist invasion of Formosa or a Nationalist invasion of the Chinese mainland. In view of the apparent mounting Chinese Communist threat to the island, the JCS informed MacArthur, it had recommended drastic new steps: that the Nationalist Air Force be permitted to launch preemptive air strikes on the troop and ship concentrations and to mine the coastal waters on the mainland and that following a "survey" of the island, the administration provide the Nationalists such military aid as was necessary to repel a Communist invasion. The recommendations had not yet been approved; the JCS sought MacArthur's opinions.

MacArthur's views on Formosa were identical to those of Louis Johnson and Truman's right-wing critics. He believed that anyone in the Far East who was anti-Communist should be supported to the hilt by the Americans. The existing neutralization of Formosa placed a "restriction" on Chiang Kai-shek that was an "injustice" for which America might have to pay "a heavy military price" in the long run. He therefore concurred in the JCS recommendations to permit the Nationalist Air Force to attack the Communist troop concentrations and naval vessels on the mainland. He welcomed the idea of conducting a "survey" of the island and providing aid. He himself would lead the survey team.[93]

The chiefs were not political babes in the woods. They recognized, as MacArthur surely did, that a personal visit by him to Formosa could be—or would be—construed as a drastic shift in policy. Perhaps believing that the repercussions of the visit would build support for its own recommendations, the JCS followed up this exchange of cables with an equivocal suggestion. On the one hand, the JCS stated, inasmuch as its recommendations had not yet been approved, MacArthur might desire to send a "senior officer" to Formosa at this time, "proceeding later himself." On the other hand, the JCS stated, since the responsibility was MacArthur's, "he should feel free to go" himself.[94]

When Dean Acheson learned what the JCS had proposed and that Louis Johnson had approved, he raised "grave objections" to the main thrust: a preemptive Nationalist bombing attack on the Chinese mainland. That was simply "out of the question," Acheson declared. Even though the proposed attack was to be carried out solely by the Nationalists, the "responsibility of the United States would be manifest," and the result would be "at best a danger of estrangement of friendly governments and at worst war with Communist China." He still believed that a conciliatory policy toward Peking might someday swing China back into the American orbit.[95]

Truman was in a tight spot. Although he agreed with Acheson that bombing the Chinese mainland was out of the question, he could not stand idly by in the face of a possible Chinese Communist invasion of Formosa. He therefore authorized the military survey of the island, together with reconnaissance flights by Nationalist planes along the coast of China to find out the "imminence of any attack that might be launched against Formosa."[96]

MacArthur and the survey party enplaned at Tokyo on July 31. It was a massive group, requiring two C-54 aircraft. It included, in addition to Ned Almond, MacArthur's air chief, Stratemeyer, and his Seventh Fleet commander, Arthur D. Struble. En route to Formosa MacArthur, perhaps feeling the need for some dramatic military gesture, ill-advisedly and needlessly radioed the Pentagon that should the Communists launch an invasion of Formosa, he planned to send three FEAF F-80 squadrons to Formosa to destroy the invasion armada. Since this proposed action flagrantly exceeded MacArthur's existing authority, the JCS became alarmed. When another report asserting that the FEAF F-80s were already on Formosa and virtually in action arrived at the Pentagon, the chiefs were aghast. Although the latter report proved to be erroneous, the suspicion that MacArthur had made a "secret deal" with Chiang Kai-shek and could not be trusted persisted.[97]*

When the survey party landed in Formosa, MacArthur was greeted and

---

*In his memoirs, published in 1969, Acheson still insisted that MacArthur "had ordered three squadrons of jet fighters to Formosa without knowledge of the Pentagon."[98]

treated like a visiting head of state. Chiang, his world-famous wife, and a phalanx of Nationalist brass met the planes with appropriate pomp. MacArthur figuratively embraced the Nationalist regime for the news cameras by gallantly kissing Madame Chiang's hand. For the next two days MacArthur studied the Communist threat and Nationalist capabilities to repel it.[99]

Curiously, the immediate cause of the crisis and visit, the 4,000-vessel Communist armada, evaporated. MacArthur reported that the Pentagon-approved reconnaissance flights over the Chinese mainland showed no "undue concentration of forces," and on the basis of this intelligence MacArthur became satisfied "that Chinese Communists will not attempt an invasion of Formosa at the present time." The mystery was never solved. There are two likely possibilities: The Nationalists fabricated the crisis to encourage a change in American policy, or the Chinese Communists circulated disinformation in order to divert American attention from the NKPA at this critical time.[100]

The Nationalists reaped a rich propaganda harvest from MacArthur's visit. The net impression was that contrary to statements from Washington, the United States was, or was going to be, far more closely allied with the Nationalists militarily, in the struggle against communism in the Far East. Chiang himself publicly spoke of a "common cause" and of Taiwan and Washington's working "closely together," suggesting a significant change in policy. Wittingly or unwittingly MacArthur enhanced the Nationalist propaganda effort with a statement praising "my old comrade in arms" Chiang Kai-shek.[101]

The Pentagon, perhaps deliberately, did not inform Truman or Acheson that MacArthur had decided to go immediately to Formosa. First learning of it from press reports, Truman and Acheson were livid. MacArthur, in turn, professed to be absolutely astonished by all the "furor." He issued a statement declaring disingenuously that "this visit has been maliciously misrepresented to the public by those who invariably in the past have propagandized a policy of defeatism and appeasement in the Pacific." Truman was placed in the embarrassing position of having to say in response to questions at a press conference that "General MacArthur and I are in perfect agreement," as though MacArthur were an equal.[102]

Still fearing that MacArthur might have made a secret deal with Chiang or might otherwise exceed his authority with respect to Formosa, Truman felt compelled to place MacArthur on a tight rein. On August 4, at the president's direction, the JCS cabled MacArthur to say, in effect, that the original "neutralization" policy toward Formosa was still in force and that "only the President has authority to order or authorize military action against concentrations on the mainland." MacArthur promptly replied that he "fully understood" and that he was "operating meticulously" in accordance with the president's policy. He added that "under no circumstances" would he "extend the limitations of his authority" and hoped that neither Truman nor Johnson "had been misled by false or speculative reports from any source."[103]

Many people concerned with this minor but distracting episode had made mistakes in judgment. The JCS had begun the chain of errors by its flimsily based "war warning" to MacArthur and by acquainting him with its unapproved and foolish recommendations to allow the Nationalists to bomb the Chinese mainland and mine the coastal waters. The JCS had compounded that error by authorizing MacArthur's visit to Formosa without specific White House approval of the exact timing. MacArthur, in turn, had acted precipitously, and he had, as customary, overblown rather than underplayed his visit. Moreover, his premature radio message to the Pentagon about moving the F-80s to Formosa had served only to heighten distrust of him. Truman made mistakes by not exercising firmer control over what the JCS was telling MacArthur and by not issuing specific instructions to the Pentagon—and MacArthur—on the timing and scope of the visit.

What was most important about this episode was that it left Truman with a feeling of vast unease about MacArthur's loyalty and, if some sources can be believed, his mental stability. As Truman understated it in his memoirs, "The implication was—and quite a few of our newspapers said so—that MacArthur rejected my policy of neutralizing Formosa and that he favored a more aggressive method." As for MacArthur's mental stability, Truman allegedly told interviewer Merle Miller that there were times when he believed that MacArthur was "out of his head and didn't know what he was doing."[104]

# PART FOUR

# Defending the Perimeter

# 7

# PUSAN SAVED

I

In the early days of August the NKPA closed on the Pusan Perimeter with ten divisions. It mounted strong pressure on all fronts, but its main effort was directed in the southwest—the flanking attack of the 4th and 6th divisions designed to capture Masan and Pusan. It reinforced those divisions with the 83d Motorcycle Regiment, tanks, motorized artillery and other units, plus thousands of fillers. The goal was to capture Pusan by August 15—the fifth anniversary of the liberation of Korea from the Japanese. The NKPA 6th Division (10,000 men) staging out of Chinju would renew the drive along the Chinju–Masan road. To its north the NKPA 4th Division (7,000 men) would cross the Naktong and attack in concert toward Yongsan and Miryang, then turn south and link with the 6th Division for a joint attack on Pusan.

The NKPA decision to concentrate major strength in this sector had initially caused Johnnie Walker deep concern and led him to the hurried transfer of Bill Kean's 25th Division to reinforce John Church's skeletal 24th. But it was soon apparent that the NKPA strategy played into Walker's hands. It temporarily but decisively reduced pressure in the northwest sector against Taegu; it directed the main NKPA effort at what would prove to be Walker's main strength.

Perhaps unknown to the NKPA, powerful American reinforcements were then arriving, or about to arrive, in Pusan. These were the Army's 2d Infantry Division, the Army's 5th RCT, the Marine RCT, and the independent tank battalions. These forces comprised, in total, five regiments of infantry (fifteen battalions) at full or nearly full strength; six battalions of artillery; several tank

179

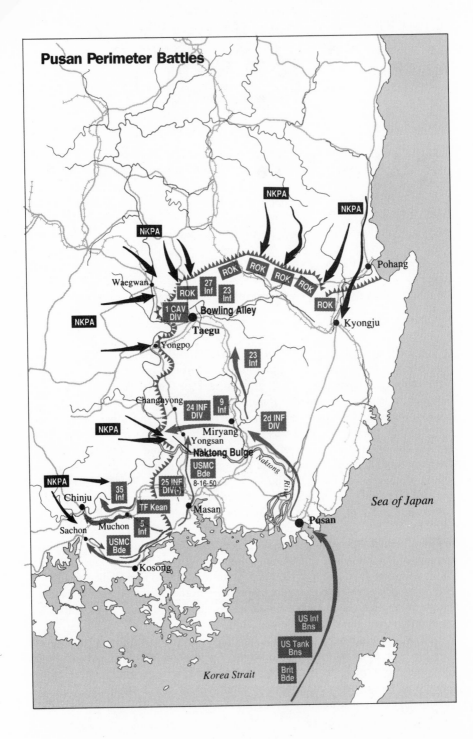

**Pusan Perimeter Battles**

NKPA

NKPA

NKPA

Pohang

Waegwan

ROK ROK ROK ROK

ROK
27
Inf
23
Inf

NKPA

1 CAV
DIV

Bowling Alley

ROK

Kyongju

**Taegu**

NKPA

Yongpo

23
Inf

Changnyong

24 INF
DIV

9
Inf

2d INF
DIV

NKPA

Miryang
Yongsan

**Naktong Bulge**

USMC
Bde
8-16-50

*Naktong River*

*Sea of Japan*

NKPA

35
Inf

25 INF
DIV(-)

Chinju

TF Kean

Masan

Sachon Muchon

5
Inf

USMC
Bde

**Pusan**

Kosong

*Korea Strait*

US Inf
Bns

US Tank
Bns

Brit
Bde

battalions; an A/A battalion; combat engineers and other support units, numbering in total about 30,000 men. Added to the 24th and 25th divisions, the reinforcements would bring the total American ground strength in the southwest sector to about 45,000 men—twice the strength of the NKPA forces attacking toward Pusan.

\* \* \*

Mike Michaelis's Wolfhounds led the 25th Division redeployment, arriving at Masan on about August 1. There Michaelis joined his old 101st Airborne Division cohort Ned Moore and the 24th Division commander John Church to draw up a battle plan—a blocking action designed to delay the NKPA until the 5th RCT and the Marine RCT arrived in the sector. Neither Moore nor Michaelis got much help or direction from Church or his ADC, Pearson Menoher, or anybody else on the 24th Division staff. Church was "a peculiar man," Moore remembered. He was "older, frail and sick a lot with arthritis." Michaelis wrote that Church "seemed lethargic" and that the 24th "was a whipped division with little initiative." His most "distinct impression" was the "inability of any of the division staff or command to issue a concise and positive order."[1]

The defense of Masan was complicated by a division in the Chinju–Masan road east of Chinju at Muchon. In effect, this division created two roads from Muchon to Masan, a "north road" and a "south road." Since the "north road" seemed the most likely route of the NKPA advance, Church had left Moore and his Chicks (2,335 men, including survivors in the 1/29 and 3/29 from Okinawa) astride it. Michaelis's vague instructions were to backstop Moore directly along the "north road." But Michaelis was deeply concerned about the "south road"; should the NKPA elect to take that route, it could outflank not only the 19th and 27th regiments but the whole of Eighth Army.

From Moore or his staff Michaelis gained the impression that the Chicks were "beaten" and not likely to mount a strong defense of the "north road." Hence the Wolfhounds were urgently needed there to backstop the Chicks. Yet some sixth sense told Michaelis that the "south road" could not be left unblocked. He therefore made the decision, entirely on his own, to redeploy his Wolfhounds from the "north road" to the "south road." He attempted to reach Church or Menoher for approval of this change, but owing to the poor—or nonexistent—communications, he was not successful. It was a bold gamble for Michaelis: If the NKPA ignored the "south road" and concentrated all its force against the Chicks, it was likely that the Chicks would collapse and flee, leaving the Wolfhounds cut off and trapped on the "south road" and the route to Masan-Pusan wide open.[2]

In preparation for this battle both Moore and Michaelis received significant reinforcements: a platoon each of six Sherman medium tanks, mounting

76-mm guns. These tanks, salvaged from World War II battlefields during Operation Roll-up and refurbished by the Japanese, comprised the advance elements of the 89th Medium Tank Battalion, which Eighth Army had activated in mid-July and assigned initially to the 24th Division. The battalion commander, Welborn G. ("Tom") Dolvin (West Point, 1939), thirty-four, who had fought in Italy and the ETO, remembered how his outfit was thrown together: "On July twelfth, while on the golf course, I got verbal word that my orders had been changed to Korea. I met a cadre of a hundred fifty-five men from the Second Armored Division in California on July seventeenth. We flew to Tokyo, arriving on July nineteenth, where we picked up another cadre of seventy men. My A Company left Tokyo by ship on July twenty-fourth and arrived in Pusan on July thirty-first. I flew over and met them on the dock at Pusan that day—a mere fifteen days after activation of the outfit. We left Pusan for Masan, joining the Nineteenth and Twenty-seventh regiments on the following day."[3]

In order to reestablish contact with the NKPA 6th Division and possibly to thwart its attack, Michaelis and Moore decided to launch independent tank-led probing attacks westerly on the morning of August 2. The plan was that these probes would meet at Muchon, just east of Chinju, where the road to Masan divided. Moore chose Wesley Wilson's depleted 1/29, the stronger of the two Okinawa battalions, to lead his attack; Michaelis chose Gilbert Check's 1/27.

Heartened by the presence of five Sherman tanks, Wilson's 1/29 jumped off in high spirits. However, the probe ran straight into an all-out NKPA attack and came to an abrupt halt. The fight that ensued was, in the words of the Army historian, a "disastrous spectacle." In the initial encounter one of Wilson's platoons was "almost annihilated" by swarms of flanking NKPA infantry. As the 1/29 fell back in confusion and fear, Moore, who was on the scene, committed Robert Rhea's 1/19, then Tom McGrail's 2/19, and finally the other Okinawa battalion, the skeletal 3/29. In the chaos of battle the American units inflicted heavy casualties on one another. Adding insult to this injury, FEAF fighters mistakenly strafed the Americans.[4]

Meanwhile, on the "south road," Gilbert Check's 1/27, led by six Sherman tanks, probed west toward the fork at Muchon. At first all went well. There was no sign of the enemy. Michaelis became worried that he had made a fatal error in judgment, that he would be court-martialed for disobeying orders. But near the fork Check's 1/27 ran into the flank of the NKPA 6th Division assaulting the Chicks on the "north road." Boldly and aggressively attacking (with help from FEAF fighters), Check laid into the NKPA truck convoys with heavy fire, forcing the motorized columns to turn about and flee to Chinju. In this important engagement Check and his men destroyed a dozen

NKPA vehicles, inflicted heavy casualties on the NKPA, and considerably eased pressure on the Chicks.[5]

While Check was fighting at Muchon, a substantial force of NKPA infantry slipped behind (or east of) him and threw a block across the "south road." Discovering this, Michaelis air-dropped a message to Check: "Return. Road cut behind you all the way. Lead with tanks if possible. Will give you artillery support when within range." Making a run for it with the surviving four of the six Sherman tanks in the van, and ably supported by Gus Terry's 8th FAB, Check made it back to the 27th CP at Chindong after dark.[6]

The next morning Michaelis thanked his lucky stars that Check had made it. A strong, undetected NKPA force—perhaps a full battalion—attacked the schoolhouse where he had located his CP. Decisively assisted by Check's battle-hardened GIs, Michaelis and the headquarters staff not only contained the attack but inflicted a slaughter on the NKPA, killing perhaps as many as 600. Two war correspondents—Marguerite Higgins and Harold H. Martin of the *Saturday Evening Post*—who were visiting the CP and were very nearly hit during the action, added to the Michaelis legend with laudatory stories. Martin characterized Michaelis in an article as "The Colonel Who Saved the Day."[7]

When the dust of battle had settled, it was clear that Michaelis's big gamble had paid off handsomely. The NKPA had chosen to take both roads to Masan. Michaelis's decision to block the "south road" may have indeed "saved the day" for Eighth Army or at any rate spared it a severe setback. Moreover, in the two actions Gilbert Check's 1/27 had dealt the North Korean 6th Division a telling blow, and it may well have saved the Chicks from another rout.

Johnnie Walker was elated. For the second time the Wolfhounds had won an important tactical—and psychological—victory. Michaelis had displayed outstanding initiative and battlefield savvy. Walker showered praise on him and gave him a battlefield promotion to full colonel (his second such promotion in two wars). Michaelis saw to it that Check got a DSC.[8]

An important factor in this victory was the debut of the 89th Tank Battalion. As Tom Dolvin put it, "Although admittedly deficient in training, this unit acquitted itself admirably in its first action. Losses were relatively high: six tanks and some personnel casualties. But the effect on the enemy was great. They were used to our light M-24s, which couldn't touch a T-34. But our medium Shermans with a 76 mm gun could knock out a T-34. That surprised them. After that engagement the enemy shifted his armored strength away from this sector."[9]

In the meantime, the rest of the 25th Division had arrived in Masan and the Army's 5th RCT had landed at Pusan. These three regiments were rushed to positions west of Masan: Henry Fisher's 35th to replace Moore's battered

Chicks on the "north road"; Horton White's 24th Infantry to the hills on the left of the 35th. The 5th RCT replaced the 27th on the "south road," freeing the Wolfhounds to serve as Eighth Army reserve, or "Fire Brigade."[10]

## II

After MacArthur's controversial trip to Formosa, President Truman, feeling the need to establish closer liaison with MacArthur, decided to send a personal representative to meet with him. Truman chose W. Averell Harriman, onetime governor of New York, Roosevelt's wartime ambassador to Moscow, Truman's ambassador-at-large for the Marshall Plan, and, since June 25, senior White House national security adviser and troubleshooter. Before Harriman took off for Tokyo on August 4, Truman, as Harriman recalled, gave him two messages for MacArthur: "One was: 'I want him to stay clear of Chiang Kai-shek and not to get us into a war with Mainland China.' The other was: 'I want to find out what he wants and, if it's at all possible to do it, I will give it to him.' "[11]

*  *  *

About this same time the JCS likewise felt a need for closer liaison with MacArthur. For one thing the JCS still had grave doubts about the proposed amphibious landing at Inchon, and the doubt was spreading far and wide. It seemed that MacArthur was being deliberately vague about the details of Inchon and the chiefs could not understand why. Accordingly, the JCS detailed Matt Ridgway and Air Force Deputy Chief of Staff for Operations (and acting Vice Chief of Staff) Lauris Norstad (West Point, 1930) to accompany Harriman to Tokyo, to brief MacArthur on JCS thinking and to find out what MacArthur was up to. The generals took along several subordinates to do legwork. In addition, Ridgway hand-carried a letter from Joe Collins to MacArthur, wishing him well and expressing the hope that MacArthur could win in Korea with the six-plus American divisions already in the Far East or on the way.[12]

The Harriman party landed in Tokyo on the morning of Sunday, August 6, Tokyo time. MacArthur met the plane, and the two principals drove to the Dai Ichi Building, trailed by a convoy of staff cars bringing the rest of the party. After attending the GHQ morning briefing, the party lunched with MacArthur and his wife at their home in the American Embassy. Later that day, while Ridgway and Norstad conferred with Almond and other GHQ staffers and made arrangements for a quick trip to Taegu, MacArthur and Harriman conferred for another two hours, mostly about the two Chinas.[13]

In a report he later submitted to Truman, Harriman made it clear that there was little hope that MacArthur would ever fully embrace the Truman-Acheson hands-off policy toward the Nationalists. As a soldier, MacArthur told Harriman, "he would obey any orders that he received from the President." MacArthur accepted the president's position on Formosa and would act accordingly but, Harriman added, "without full conviction." MacArthur, Harriman continued, "has a strange idea that we should back anybody who will fight communism" and that Washington should stop "kicking Chiang around" and support the rejected JCS recommendation to bomb Communist concentrations on the mainland and possibly support Chiang's dream of a "re-entry to the mainland." Moreover, MacArthur strongly opposed Acheson's conciliatory policy toward Peking, designed to draw China back into the American orbit.[14]

* * *

On Monday, August 7, Harriman, Ridgway, Norstad, and aides flew on to Taegu, where they met with Johnnie Walker and the Eighth Army staff and inspected some frontline units. All three visiting firemen were dismayed by what they found. Later, in a damning report, Ridgway wrote, in effect, that Walker's leadership of Eighth Army was abysmal. Ridgway found a "lack of force, acceptance of a mediocre staff and an unsound Base organization." Walker could not even name the "key commanders" in the ROK Army. Many of his senior staff officers appeared to be wanting in "energy and ability."[15]

The "mediocre" Eighth Army staff was presided over by Gene Landrum, who was nearing his sixtieth birthday. Ridgway's 82d Airborne Division had fought alongside Landrum's 90th Division in Normandy when Landrum failed and Joe Collins relieved him of command. Ridgway found it difficult to believe that Walker would rely on Landrum—too old and too weak for the task—at this critical time. Nor was Ridgway much impressed by Walker's chief of plans (G-3), artilleryman William Bartlett, fifty-one, whose three senior assistants were also artillerymen. Ridgway set wheels in motion which would result in early replacements for both Landrum and Bartlett and bring senior infantrymen into the planning section.[16]

The visitors closely scrutinized Eighth Army's senior field commanders. Ridgway had nothing to say about the division commanders, but he judged that "some" regimental commanders were "very poor." They were too old and lacked "combat experience and aggressiveness." He named no names, but undoubtedly he was referring to the three regimental commanders in the 1st Cav (Rohsenberger, Nist, and Palmer) and the 24th Infantry's Horton White. Although both Dick Stephens (21st Infantry) and Hank Fisher (35th Infantry) were considerably overage for regimental command, they were doing well, as were the "youngsters," Michaelis (27th Infantry), Beauchamp (34th Infantry), and Moore (19th Infantry). Replacements being sent by the Pentagon didn't help. "Three out of five were over fifty," Ridgway wrote.*

Eighth Army as a whole, Ridgway went on, suffered from "a lack of knowledge of infantry fundamentals," "a lack of leadership in combat eche-lons," and "the absence of an aggressive fighting spirit." The ROK forces, Ridgway concluded, "are doing better than the U.S. forces. They are imbued with the only offensive spirit observed in Korea." Ridgway elaborated: The junior officers were "good except for a lack of knowledge." However:

> [The] quality of soldier now engaged in Korea is not up to World War II stan-dards. [American troops are] easily stampeded. When attacked they do not re-spond with the fundamental infantry reaction to fire and movement, but instead call for artillery and air support and then withdraw if this does not suffice to interrupt the attack. Our troops do not counter-attack an enemy penetration. Our forces do not maintain outpost protection nor flank protection. Weapons are not properly emplaced to obtain a good field of fire. Troops take positions on tops of hills, apparently so they can be sure to see the enemy, and withdraw before he reaches them. . . . Our troops do not dig in and make no pretense at camouflaging their positions. They do not seek cover and concealment while moving by day. . . . They are visible to the enemy by terrestrial observation. . . . Signal communication within the front line regiments is poor . . . partly due to equipment which is in marginal operating condition. . . . Tactical air support of front line units is not satisfactory. . . .

Flying back to Tokyo that night, Matt Ridgway, a man of high principles, whom one of his close friends described as a "12th Century knight with a 20th Century brain," agonized. He believed that Walker's leadership of Eighth Army was so poor that he should be relieved of command. Years before (1921 and 1922), Ridgway had served closely with MacArthur at West Point, when MacArthur was superintendent of the academy and Ridgway was manager of athletics. From that experience Ridgway was well aware of MacArthur's weaknesses, but on the whole, he admired him. He thought MacArthur was a military genius, and he still had a deep sense of loyalty to him. For that reason, and others, Ridgway felt compelled to recommend Walker's immedi-ate relief to MacArthur. Yet to do so, Ridgway realized, was perilous. Walker had his back against the wall. His relief (and public disgrace) might further embolden the NKPA. MacArthur might misinterpret his motives and de-nounce Ridgway as a Truman lackey interfering with his operations or as a throat cutter trying to create a job for himself.[17]

In Tokyo Ridgway confided his inner thoughts to Harriman and asked for

---

*The average age of the nine regimental commanders in Eighth Army that day was forty-seven years. Rohsenberger at fifty-five was the oldest; Michaelis at thirty-eight, the youngest.

advice. Harriman (and Norstad) had also reached the conclusion that Walker should be relieved of command, but Harriman did not believe the suggestion should be made directly to MacArthur at this time, unless MacArthur himself opened the subject of "conditions in Eighth Army." It would be more prudent, Harriman suggested, first to talk the matter over with Collins, Bradley, Army Secretary Frank Pace, and others in Washington, including the president. Ridgway followed that advice with one exception. He expressed to MacArthur "in polite language" his view that the base organization was "unsound" and offered to send MacArthur an outstanding logistician, Paul F. Yount (who stood number one in the West Point class of 1930), to straighten it out. MacArthur apparently took no offense at this suggestion and "at once" accepted Ridgway's recommendation.[18]

Ironically, unknown to either Harriman or Ridgway, at this time MacArthur's confidence in Walker, steadily undermined by Ned Almond, had eroded almost completely. Had Ridgway forthrightly raised the matter of Walker's relief, MacArthur might very well have been receptive to the idea, notwithstanding the repercussions. A further irony was that MacArthur had decided that if he did relieve Walker, Ridgway was the best man in the Army to replace him. Had the change of command occurred at this time, events in Korea would very likely have taken a different and more favorable course for the American Army.[19]

On Tuesday morning, August 8, MacArthur again met with the full Harriman party, this time in his office at the Dai Ichi Building. For the next two and a half hours he told the group how he would win the war in Korea and what further assistance he would require from Washington to do it. Ridgway thought MacArthur's briefing was "brilliant." It was made, Ridgway wrote later, "with utmost earnestness, supported by every logical military argument of his rich experience, and delivered with all of his dramatic eloquence." Moreover, contrary to the prevailing view in Washington, Ridgway saw no evidence that MacArthur was being disloyal to Truman. "His recognition of authority superior to him, of his channels of command and of his sphere of responsibility was clear and unmistakable, and his loyalty to duly constituted superior authority was equally manifest."[20]

Time was working against America in Korea, MacArthur asserted. An early military victory was "essential." Any delay in achieving it increased the chances of "direct military participation" by Chinese Communist or Soviet forces and the possibility of a winter campaign when the weather in Korea was frigid—"comparable to my native state of Wisconsin"—and would result in heavy nonbattle casualties from frostbite. To achieve an early victory, MacArthur continued, American forces must launch "a coordinated offensive," mounted by Eighth Army and an additional, independent corps to land amphibiously at Inchon by September 25. And "once launched, this operation must be given every chance of success." MacArthur would personally "take in" the Inchon force and remain in Korea for two or three weeks, as necessary.

To carry out the coordinated offensive successfully, MacArthur continued, he really needed an "additional army of four divisions." However, he well understood the overall weakness in the General Reserve and that the four National Guard divisions called up would require extensive training and equipping. He therefore planned to carry out Inchon with merely two divisions, the 7th in Japan and the full 1st Marine Division. Since utilizing the 7th Division would utterly denude Japan of American fighting forces and leave Japan vulnerable to Soviet attack, it was "compelling" that he have the 3d Infantry Division (from the General Reserve) by September 15 to replace it, the full 1st Marine Division by the same date, and another Marine division (the 2d) by October 15. Moreover, MacArthur urgently required replacements for battle casualties. He was losing 1,000 men a week (a total of nearly 9,000 as of that date) and the Pentagon was "not even keeping up with my losses." The Pentagon should "treble trans-Pacific shipping."

Besides all that, MacArthur insisted, "every effort" should be made to secure troops from the other members of the United Nations at the earliest possible date. He suggested, among others, Britain, Canada, Australia, and "perhaps" even France. The British, he opined, could send troops from Hong Kong and Singapore in "1000-man increments" (battalions) without delay. "Has the great British Army sunk so low it can't afford one division?" he asked. (This challenge, soon relayed to London, produced almost immediate results. On August 24 the British two-battalion 27th Infantry Brigade in Hong Kong embarked for Korea.)

As for Formosa, MacArthur again asserted that he did not believe the Chinese Communists would launch an attack there. If they did, MacArthur said (as Ridgway noted), "I would go there and assume command, and deliver such a crushing defeat it would be one of the decisive battles of the world—a disaster so great it would rock Asia and perhaps turn back communism." Meanwhile, he repeated, America would be well advised to back the Nationalists, whose potential could be increased "enormously" with the military aid list GHQ was preparing.[21]

* * *

The Harriman party left Tokyo that same day and flew back to Washington. Every member was bedazzled and certain that MacArthur's plan for winning the war with an Inchon invasion was sound and should be backed by every resource the Pentagon could spare. Ridgway left convinced that MacArthur should have the 3d Infantry Division, even though it had already been gutted and was but a skeletal force. Harriman told Ridgway (as Ridgway noted) that "political and personal considerations should be put to one side and our government deal with General MacArthur on the lofty level of the great national asset which he is."[22]

By this time both Harriman and Norstad had decided that Ridgway should replace Walker as commander of Eighth Army in Korea. On return to Washington Harriman would recommend that change to Truman, Johnson, Bradley, Pace, and Collins. On the plane Norstad privately broached the subject with Ridgway, saying, "I think you ought to be in command here." Ridgway must have been flattered, but he replied: "Please don't mention that, it will look as though I was coming over here looking for a job and I'm not."[23]

In Washington Harriman turned in his and Ridgway's reports to Truman, Johnson, Bradley, and others. The overall effect was to build considerable support at the White House for MacArthur and the Inchon landing. But the JCS remained skeptical about an amphibious landing at Inchon. When Ridgway appeared before the chiefs to deliver MacArthur's request for the 3d Infantry Division to replace the 7th Division in Japan, he encountered doubt and debate. Subsequently it was decided that Collins and Forrest Sherman would go to Tokyo to examine the Inchon plan in greater detail before the JCS endorsed it. Owing to the deplorable state of the 3d Division, the chiefs seriously but briefly considered sending MacArthur the 82d Airborne Division. However, when Ridgway suggested the possibility of incorporating the Puerto Rican 65th Regiment into the 3d Division and other measures to provide the division greater strength, the chiefs accepted his ideas. Three days later, on August 11, Truman approved the transfer of the 3d Division from the General Reserve to the Far East, with the understanding that it would not be sent to Korea but be based in Japan, in effect replacing the 7th Division.[24]

Still very much concerned over the "leadership, organization and planning" in Eighth Army, Ridgway, as Harriman had suggested, met individually with Pace, Collins, and other top-level Army officials to convey his misgivings about Walker. Ridgway expressed the belief that Walker could hold the Pusan Perimeter but that he should be replaced before Eighth Army went on the offensive. Pace (perhaps influenced by Harriman), according to Ridgway's notes, "indicated his own conviction that a change ought to be made as early as possible but that he was uncertain as to the best method of making it." Thinking out loud about a replacement for Walker, Pace mentioned both Ridgway and West Pointer (1919) Alfred M. ("Al") Gruenther, fifty-one, then serving in the Army's upper echelons as deputy chief of staff for plans. Gruenther, who had been chief of staff to Mark Clark in Italy during World War II, had never led troops in combat.[25]

Joe Collins appeared less anxious to sack Walker. He told Ridgway that on his forthcoming visit to Tokyo to discuss Inchon with MacArthur, he would "visit Korea and, based on [sic] his observations at the time, would take up with MacArthur the question of Eighth Army command, Organization and

Staff." Should a change be necessary, Collins thought that either Ridgway or West Pointer (1915) James A. Van Fleet could replace Walker. Collins preferred Van Fleet because Ridgway was slated to replace Haislip as vice chief and because Ridgway might become "so involved I couldn't get you out." When Collins asked Ridgway what his "preference" might be, Ridgway replied that if America was headed for World War III (as still seemed likely to him), "I would prefer to fight in Europe."[26]

Meanwhile, Harriman proposed to President Truman that Ridgway replace Walker as commander of Eighth Army. Truman's reply was to "talk to Bradley about it." The upshot was that Bradley and Collins decided that if Collins determined on his forthcoming trip to Korea that Walker should be replaced and if MacArthur concurred in this decision, Ridgway would be proposed to MacArthur as Walker's replacement. However, Collins did not inform Ridgway of this decision.[27]

# I I I

The arrival of the fresh and powerful American ground reinforcements in Pusan led Walker to believe he could do more than merely hold the southwest front against the NKPA 4th and 6th divisions. With the new power coming into his command, he would destroy those NKPA forces by offensive actions, the first major American counterattack of the war.[28]

The overall plan for the southwest sector was as follows. John Church's weak 24th Division would remain on the defensive, dug in behind the Naktong River, and repel attacks of the NKPA 4th Division. It would then be relieved in place by the newly arriving 2d Infantry Division and resume its postponed remanning and reequipping. Farther south, at Masan, Bill Kean's 25th Division, reinforced by the Army's 5th RCT and the Marine RCT, would launch an offensive westward to Chinju—and beyond—designed to overrun and crush the NKPA 6th Division, after which Kean's forces would circle north to envelop the NKPA 4th Division opposite the 24th Division.

Bill Kean would be assigned four regiments (known as Task Force Kean) for the offensive. These were Hank Fisher's 35th, Horton White's 24th, and the newly arrived 5th RCT and Marine RCT. The 35th, 5th RCT, and Marine RCT would spearhead the offensive; the 24th would serve as reserve. Mike Michaelis's 27th Wolfhounds would not participate. They would remain in the Eighth Army reserve, should their services be urgently required elsewhere.

Kean's staff worked out the plan of maneuver. Fisher's 35th Regiment, which had recently relieved Ned Moore's Chicks on the "north road," would attack due west to the Muchon road fork. The Army's 5th RCT, which had relieved Michaelis's Wolfhounds on the "south road," would retrace the route of Gilbert Check's 1/27, linking with the 35th at Muchon. The Marine RCT would take a wide encircling route along the coast to Kosong and Sachon, then swing due north to Chinju, joining the 35th and 5th regiments for a combined assault on Chinju. Kean's 24th Regiment would provide security for the rear areas.

On paper, Bill Kean clearly had the edge. His 16,000-man task force outnumbered the reinforced NKPA 6th Division nearly two to one. His artillery was superior. His aggregate strength in medium tanks (about twenty-four) probably matched or exceeded that of the NKPA. He had substantial supporting air power; the NKPA had none. He was operating close to his supply base; the NKPA, vastly overextended, was short of ammo, gasoline, and everything else required to fight.

Offsetting these pluses were some significant minuses. Of the four infantry regiments in Task Force Kean, two (the 5th RCT and the Marine RCT) were green to combat; one (the 24th) was considered unreliable, and the other (the 35th) was comprised of only two understrength battalions, which had seen only about one week of hard combat. Moreover, the Americans were not yet physically accustomed to fighting in mountainous terrain and the blazing heat. They tended to be "roadbound" and to rely too much on mechanization and creature comforts. By contrast, the lean, hard soldiers of the 6th Division were among the most skilled and highly motivated combat veterans in the NKPA. They had not yet suffered a significant setback in the war. They had been told that the capture of Pusan would end the war and deliver all of Korea to the Communists.

* * *

Task Force Kean commenced operations on August 7. It began with an attack by Hank Fisher's 35th Regiment west along the "north road," led by John Wilkin's 2/35. For a while all seemed to go well. In a five-hour battle Wilkin's men destroyed two T-34 tanks and inflicted an estimated 350 NKPA casualties. By nightfall Fisher had closed on the high ground overlooking Muchon. There he dug in to await the arrival of the 5th RCT.

Unknown to Fisher, the NKPA had already got the tactical advantage. Several thousand NKPA troops had infiltrated into the empty, roadless hills between the "north" and "south" roads and were approaching the high ground overlooking the "south road," which the 5th RCT was to take to Muchon. In effect, the NKPA had secretly driven a wedge between the 35th and 5th RCTs.

The wedge struck Horton White's 24th Infantry, which was occupying the hills between the 35th and 5th regiments. The main force of the NKPA attack enveloped Sam Pierce's 3/24, which had earlier recaptured Yechon. During this action Private First Class William Thompson (of M Company), mortally wounded by grenades, heroically remained at his machine-gun position. He was later awarded a Medal of Honor, the second such award of the Korean War. However, Pierce was wounded, and the battalion lost cohesion. The Army historian wrote that the battalion stampeded, that the S-3, Christopher M. Gooch, was knocked down three times trying to stop the fleeing men, and that the battalion did not stop running until it reached Haman, four miles to the rear.[29]

This debacle resulted in the relief of Horton White. Kean sought a young, dynamic, and battle-experienced commander to replace White; but none (Ned Moore, for one) at hand wanted the job, and Walker was apparently reluctant to "punish" any promising officers with the command. As a result, the job went to Arthur S. ("Art") Champeny (Washburn College, 1912), who was to be fifty-seven years old on August 13—four years older than his division commander, Bill Kean.[30]

Although Champeny was clearly past his prime and not physically fit for the rugged duty in Korea, he was not without combat experience. In World War I he had won a DSC. In World War II he had commanded the 351st Infantry (of the 88th Division) in tough fighting at Monte Cassino in Italy. In the postwar years (temporarily a brigadier general) he had served two years in the Korean occupation under John Hodge, organizing and training the Korean Constabulary. He knew Korea and its people well.[31]

The appointment of Champeny to command the 24th RCT was a great disappointment to most of the capable white and black officers in the outfit. Engineer Bussey, who had been fond of Horton White and even felt sympathy for him, wrote that Champeny was not only an offensive bigot but professionally incompetent. In the Carlisle-Bussey history they disparagingly described one of Champeny's "harebrained" ideas, which, had Bussey carried it out, would almost certainly have resulted in many casualties in the 77th ECC. Bussey repeatedly cited Champeny as proof of the Army's seeming determination to saddle the 24th with unqualified or incompetent white officers.[32]

At about the time Champeny arrived, however, the 24th did receive one highly competent senior officer, and a West Pointer (1938) at that. He was John T. Corley, thirty-six, one of about two dozen experienced battalion commanders the Army had rushed to Korea by air. A West Point boxer, Corley was a legendary fighter. As a battalion commander in the 1st Infantry Division in North Africa, Sicily, France, and Germany, Corley had won a DSC, five Silver Star medals, and numerous other awards for heroism. A devout Catholic, Corley was the father of seven children. Although he was fully qualified by dint of experience to command the 24th Regiment, he was so eager to return to combat that he willingly replaced the wounded Sam Pierce as commander of the disorganized 3/24.[33]

\* \* \*

The 5th RCT began its attack along the "south road" simultaneously with the attack of Fisher's 35th on the "north road." From the outset nearly everything went wrong. A heavy coastal fog forced a cancellation of FEAF close air support and reconnaissance missions. The 1/5, commanded by John P. Jones, Jr., thirty-nine, which led the regiment, blundered and took a wrong fork. Instead of heading northwest for Muchon, the 1/5 headed down the coastal road assigned to the Marines.[34]

The 5th RCT was commanded by Godwin Ordway, Jr., forty-nine, grandson of a Union Army general and son of a colonel in the artillery. He was a handsome, dapper West Pointer (1925), a noted disciplinarian and paperwork demon. During World War II he had been chief of staff of the First Army's 29th Division, which in company with the 1st Division led the assault on Omaha Beach. Subsequent to the assault, Ordway had commanded one of the division's regiments in the fierce hedgerow fighting in Normandy. But this first troop command in combat was short-lived. Ordway got sick, was evacuated, and did not return to the division. He finished the war behind a desk in the G-3 section of Bradley's Twelfth Army Group. In the postwar years he had served in the Pentagon as a Latin America specialist. Matt Ridgway, who was the Army's leading Latin America specialist, had recommended Ordway for promotion to brigadier general, but Eisenhower had rejected the recommendation.[35]

Since onetime First Army Chief of Staff Bill Kean was thoroughly familiar with Ordway's brief, unrealized tour as a regimental commander in Normandy, he may not have been overjoyed to find Ordway in his division, again commanding a regiment. In any event, Kean was rightly infuriated at the 1/5's blunder in taking the the road assigned to the Marines. Thus Ordway launched operations under a cloud.

Meanwhile, owing in part to the spotty performance of the 24th Regiment, the NKPA infiltrators attained commanding positions in the hills overlooking the "south road" at Chindong and the road fork at Kogan. These infiltrators rained heavy fire on the "south road," delaying and disrupting the attack of Ordway's 5th RCT for two full days, further infuriating Bill Kean, who laid much of the blame on Ordway and, finally, exasperated, placed the 5th RCT under Marine control. It required the utmost efforts of all available forces on the "south road," including the Marines, to contain and eliminate the harassing fire of the infiltrators.[36]

The newly arrived Marine RCT, christened the 1st Provisional Marine Brigade, was a formidable combat unit—in all, 6,534 men. It consisted of the three-battalion 5th Marine Regiment ("Fifth Marines"), furnished with the new 3.5-inch bazookas; an artillery battalion with medium 105-mm howitzers from the 11th Marine Artillery Regiment; a tank battalion equipped with the M-26 Pershing (with a 90-mm gun); and supporting aircraft. The last consisted of three squadrons of the 33d Marine Air Group (with F-4U Corsair prop planes) and one squadron of four two-man Sikorsky helicopters—the first American helicopters to be sent to a war zone.[37]

The senior Marine was a brigadier general, Edward A. ("Eddie") Craig, fifty-three, ADC of the 1st Marine Division. In World War II Craig had commanded the 9th Marine Regiment ("Ninth Marines") on Guadalcanal and during the amphibious invasion of Bougainville and Guam, winning a Navy Cross and other decorations for heroism. The Fifth Marines were commanded by Raymond L. ("Ray") Murray (Texas A&M, 1935), thirty-seven. During World War II Murray had been a battalion commander in the Sixth Marines on Guadalcanal, Tarawa, and Saipan, winning a Navy Cross and other awards for heroism.[38]

The Army regimental commanders in Korea were jealous of these Marines, who arrived in Korea in a blaze of publicity. The majority of the Marine commanders and senior noncoms were combat-experienced infantrymen who had fought Orientals in the Pacific War. The ranks were filled with physically tough young men who had joined the corps to fight, not to sightsee. The Marines had superior firepower in squads, platoons, and companies. Moreover, in addition to its organic tank and artillery battalions, the Marine brigade had its own integrated, well-trained close air support. Whereas Army regiments still had to request FEAF close air support through a complicated, slow, and unsatisfactory chain of command, the Marines had support aircraft close at hand and virtually on instant call.

*       *       *

By August 9 Eddie Craig had got most of the mess on the "south road" cleared up, and Task Force Kean resumed operations with Ordway back in independent command of the 5th RCT. As originally planned, the Marines took the lightly defended coastal road southwest to Kosong and Sachon, and they made sensational advances. As also originally planned, Ordway took the road northwest to Muchon, to link with Fisher's 35th Regiment, but in contrast with the Marines, Ordway's operations ended in an epic disaster.[39]

By August 11 Ordway was making progress up the Muchon road. His 3/5, commanded by West Pointer (1935) Benjamin W. Heckemeyer, thirty-nine, bypassing or ignoring the NKPA in the hills, reached Muchon and, as planned, linked with Fisher's 35th and advanced four miles west on the "north road" toward Chinju. There the combined units, as planned, dug in to await the advance of the Marines north through Sachon. Walker and Kean were pleased: The 5th RCT was at last demonstrating the kind of aggressive spirit that Walker believed ultimately necessary to destroy the NKPA.[40]

The main body of the 5th RCT—the 1/5 and 2/5—was advancing more slowly. By August 11 it had only reached the village of Pongam, four miles northwest of Kogan. It was supported by a formidable supply train and collection of artillery: twelve 105s of John H. Daly's 555th (Triple Nickles) FAB, which had come from Hawaii mated to the 5th RCT, and six 155s of James Sanden's 90th FAB.[41]

That day the bypassed NKPA infiltrators in the hills fell on the main body of the 5th RCT and the artillery positions in a perfect fury. In a series of vicious tank-led attacks the NKPA created chaos among the Americans and seized the high ground dominating the road at a pass just north of Pongam. In the confused melee which ensued, both John Jones, commanding the 1/5, and the Triple Nickles' commander, John Daly, were wounded—Jones seriously. Refusing medical evacuation, Daly assumed command of the 1/5 until Ordway's S-2, Thomas B. Roelofs, forty-one, came up to replace Jones, who was evacuated.

By this time Bill Kean was under heavy pressure from Johnnie Walker to show some dramatic progress. The Marines were making the 5th RCT look like incompetent fools. Kean got on the radio and in no uncertain terms told Ordway to get cracking. But Ordway equivocated. The enemy had hit him in great strength; he dared not attempt the pass in daylight. Disbelieving Ordway's estimate of enemy strength (2,500 men), Kean, even though he was miles away, in effect assumed tactical control of operations. He later sent Ordway written orders to move his 2/5, supported by an artillery battalion, through the pass in darkness to link with the 3/5 and 35th Regiment at Muchon; the rest of the 5th RCT would remain at Pongam until dawn. Kean would hurry John Corley's 3/24 westerly through the hills to attack the NKPA confronting Ordway from the rear; simultaneously Ordway would take the rest of the 5th RCT through the pass in daylight.

When he received these orders, Ordway was dismayed. To him it seemed possibly "catastrophic" to fragment the 5th RCT while it was under such heavy enemy pressure. He tried—and failed—to reach Kean to get the orders rescinded. Having no other choice, Ordway complied with the orders and sent the 2/5 and a battery of the Triple Nickles led by Daly himself north through the pass in darkness. The 2/5, believing it constituted the advance guard of the main body, which would follow on its heels, moved smartly northwest— and beyond all communications with Ordway—seeking a linkup with the 3/5 at Muchon. Daly, wounded for the second time (and later awarded a DSC), was evacuated, replaced by Clarence E. Stuart.

Shortly after midnight the next morning, August 12, the NKPA again fell on the main body of the 5th RCT. At that time Ordway had the rest of his men deployed on the road in pitch-dark, preparing to advance through the pass after daybreak, as Kean had ordered. The new 1/5 commander, Roelofs, urged Ordway to move out—run the pass immediately—but Ordway, adhering to Kean's orders, remained in place for three critical hours, futilely trying to raise

Kean on the radio. Finally, at about 4:00 A.M., Ordway conceded that Roelofs was right and, notwithstanding Kean's orders to the contrary, passed the word to move out.

Ordway led the procession in his jeep. He went through the pass with no difficulty and soon caught up with his 2/5. Roelofs started behind him with the 1/5, most of his men advancing on foot. But behind the 1/5 an ambulance skidded into a ditch and blocked the road. This mishap created a massive traffic jam blocking the advance of the regimental supply trains and the artillery.

At dawn the NKPA, seeing that all this roadbound artillery was blocked and virtually helpless, attacked "suddenly and with devastating power." The artillerymen tried to shoot back, but the NKPA, firing from superior positions, shattered and overran the 555th and 90th batteries. The artillery batteries were hard hit: The 555th lost six guns; the 90th, five. About 300 artillerymen from the two outfits were dead, wounded, or missing. (Later it was found that the NKPA had murdered twenty captured men of the 90th.)

Learning of this disaster in his rear, Ordway hastened to send infantry to the rescue. Since Roelofs's 1/5 was under heavy attack near the pass and fragmented, it could provide little help. In desperation Ordway ordered the 2/5 to turn around and return to Pongam. Meanwhile, John Corley was attempting to bring his 3/24 from the west. But it was hopeless. Corley had only that day taken command, and his men had no heart for a fight. According to the Army historian they bugged out in droves; three of Corley's officers, attempting to stop the stampede, were killed or wounded.[42]

Kean's artillery commander, Bittman Barth, was nearby when the disaster occurred. When Barth called Kean to report it, Kean placed him in tactical command of the sector. It was decided that one of the three Marine infantry battalions would be hurried to Pongam to reinforce (or rescue) Ordway's 5th RCT. Barth would command the Marines as well as Ordway's 5th RCT and Corley's 3/24, badly scattered in the hills two miles short of Pongam.[43]

The 3d Battalion, Fifth Marines, supervised by regimental commander Ray Murray, operating in a helicopter, redeployed toward Pongam, late in the afternoon of August 12. The Marines, somewhat baffled by their orders to "attack to the rear," found the NKPA opposition slight (or nonexistent) and, like Kean, expressed skepticism at Ordway's estimate of enemy strength. Murray proposed to Barth an offensive action designed to clear the enemy from the area and rescue the men and guns of the 555th and 90th FABs. However, by that time Johnnie Walker, hard pressed by the NKPA in another sector, had ordered Task Force Kean to pull back to its original start line at Chindong and disband. The Marines assisted in Ordway's withdrawal.[44]

\* \* \*

So ended the operations of Task Force Kean. It fell far short of its main objectives of capturing Chinju, encircling the NKPA 6th Division, and attacking the NKPA 4th Division from the rear, but the operation was not without merit. The various components of the task force had inflicted severe casualties (an estimated 3,000) on the 6th Division and decisively interrupted its drive on Pusan. Marine close air support operating from two small ("jeep") aircraft carriers (*Sicily* and *Badoeng Strait*) had been particularly effective. In one noteworthy air attack on August 11 near Kosong, Marine Corsairs had wiped out most of the vehicles of the NKPA 83d Motorcycle Regiment and killed or wounded many enemy.[45]

The operation had also provided an opportunity to bloody two more RCTs on the offensive rather than on the defensive. The performance of the 5th RCT under Ordway was on the whole undistinguished and at times abysmal, but no more so than most Army regiments entering combat in Korea for the first time. Its men emerged from the experience chastened but wiser and determined to do better—much better. The Marines lived up to their advance ballyhoo; they proved themselves to be well-disciplined and well-led fighters. Like Michaelis's Wolfhounds, the Marines were to become one of Walker's dependable Fire Brigades.

The offensive had also given Bill Kean an opportunity to size up his regimental commanders. He continued to be well pleased with Hank Fisher in the 35th. He had sacked Horton White in the 24th, replacing him with Art Champeny. To no one's surprise, at the conclusion of this operation he also sacked Godwin Ordway.[46]

Bill Kean's choice to replace Ordway did cause surprise. He was the 2/5 commander, John L. Throckmorton, a cool and brainy West Pointer who stood high in the class of 1935. Throckmorton, thirty-seven, became the youngest regimental commander in Korea and the first battalion commander in Korea to move up to command a regiment.[47]

Born in Kansas City, Missouri, Throckmorton was the son of a recently retired Army colonel. At West Point he was a scrub football player and cadet battalion commander for three years and was very nearly selected for cadet captain. After graduation he fell under the influence of Bill Kean, who was "tough" but who significantly helped his early career. In Throckmorton's first troop assignment, Kean was his company commander. Later, while working under Bradley in the G-1 section of the War Department, Kean sprung Throckmorton from a teaching post (chemistry) at West Point and got him assigned to an infantry division. Still later, when Kean became chief of staff of Bradley's First Army, he drafted Throckmorton for his G-3 section, where Throckmorton remained for the rest of the war. During the peacetime years Throckmorton had been a member of the Army's celebrated Rifle Team, and in 1940 he was its coach. In the postwar years he qualified as a paratrooper.[48]

Until Korea Throckmorton had never commanded troops in combat, but he was a "quick study," brave under fire and extremely well organized. Both before and during Task Force Kean his 2/5 had performed with exceptional competence. The new job was a big challenge for young Throckmorton. The 5th RCT was by then in total confusion and disarray. Throckmorton began his command by insisting on some basics. He recalled: "The staff was exhausted. They had had no sleep and were not functioning properly. I *insisted* that every man get seven or eight hours' sleep every night. They did, and they improved a hundred percent. I was also concerned about the men. Their boots were shot. I got mad about that and raised hell at division. We got boots in a hurry."[49]

In time John Throckmorton transformed the 5th RCT into one of the best Army regiments in Korea.[50]

# IV

While Task Force Kean was mounting its offensive in the southern sector, John Church's 24th Division, holding defensive positions farther north along the Naktong River opposite the crack NKPA 4th Division, was undergoing yet another ghastly ordeal. It began on August 6, when the NKPA 4th (honored with the title "Seoul Division" for having captured the South Korean capital) unexpectedly launched a massive assault across the Naktong River into the 24th Division's positions at a bend in the river, which the GIs called the "Naktong Bulge."

In contrast with Task Force Kean, the 24th Division was pitifully weak and exhausted. Its total strength was 9,882 regulars. It grandly rated itself as 53 percent combat-effective, but 40 percent probably would have been closer to the mark. Its three infantry regiments (of two battalions) were gravely depleted. Ned Moore's 19th numbered but 1,910 men; Dick Stephens's 21st, 1,670; and Charles Beauchamp's 34th, 1,402. All regiments and other division elements were gravely short of tanks, weapons, ammo, and vehicles.[51]

The Naktong River "front" occupied by the 24th Division ran south-north from the confluence of the Nam and Naktong rivers to the village of Hyonpung. As the crow flies, the "front" was about twenty-two miles long, but in reality, the twisting course of the Naktong made it thirty-four miles. The front was manned, south to north, by Beauchamp's 34th Infantry, Stephens's 21st Infantry, and the attached ROK 17th Regiment (2,000 men), which was still being advised by Joe Darrigo. Moore's 19th Infantry was in division reserve near the division CP at Changnyong, about seven miles behind the river in the center of the division front.[52]

Owing to the acute shortage of manpower and the vast division frontage to be covered, the 34th and 21st were thinly dispersed along the river. Each of the two American regiments at the river had merely one battalion forward. The other battalions were immediately behind, in reserve. At the river the rifle and heavy-weapons companies were outposted on key hills. The division's four (depleted) FABs, two combat engineer battalions (3d and 14th), the division Recon Company and one battery of A/A vehicles, and the surviving Chaffee light tanks were scattered here and there along the front in support of the infantry.

In Beauchamp's southernmost 34th Infantry sector, the 3/34 (at 50 per-cent strength with 493 men) outposted the river, while Red Ayres's 1/34 (515 men) was in reserve. The 3/34 now had its fifth commander in a month of combat. The new man was one of the replacement battalion commanders flown to Korea, forty-one-year-old Gines Perez. Perez was a reservist who had made the Army a career after he had been called to active duty in 1941. During World War II, as exec of the 12th Cavalry Regiment of the 1st Cavalry Division, Perez had fought the Japanese in New Guinea and in the Philippines on Leyte and Luzon. Under his temporary command, the 12th Cav had dramatically liberated Santo Tomás University in Manila, where the Japanese had interned and starved about 3,900 Allied civilians.

When he arrived in Korea and reported to John Church's CP, Perez found administrative chaos. At first he was mistakenly assigned to command an artillery battalion; but after an awkward dinner with Church's artillery com-mander, Henry Meyer, the mistake was realized, and the next day Perez got himself properly reassigned to the infantry, drawing command of the 3/34. He remembered: "I didn't see any foxholes. I said [to the acting commander]: 'Don't you make foxholes here?' He said, 'Well, certainly, but the men have lost all their entrenching tools.' . . . I said '. . . I want to see some foxholes dug and I want to see at least one foxhole per man.' "[53]

During the early-morning hours of August 6 the NKPA 4th Division (7,000 men) crossed the Naktong and struck the 24th Division in an all-out attack. The main weight came in Perez's sector on his second night in com-mand. When he realized it was not a probing attack but the real thing, he tried to alert Ayres and Beauchamp by radio. Unable to raise them, he sent messen-gers, but they went astray. Seeing that he was being overrun and outflanked, Perez made the very hard decision to withdraw his CP. He told his staff that if the CP were not withdrawn, "we'd all be dead before noon."

Perez retreated eastward to Ayres's 1/34 CP. Finding Ayres asleep, Perez woke him and gave him the news. Ayers appeared not to believe him. As Perez recalled, Ayres "got up very leisurely and had breakfast." Perez went on: "They thought I was a newcomer [to combat], scared, and just bugging out." Beauchamp, now alerted, later told Perez: "We were watching you like a hawk. If what you said hadn't turned out [to be true] you were relieved."[54]

When it became clear that what Perez reported was true, Charles Beauchamp ordered Ayres to counterattack with his 1/34. Perhaps too hastily, Ayres sent his C Company, commanded by newcomer Clyde M. Akridge, hurrying forward by truck, while the other two came behind on foot. Rushed fragmented into battle, the battalion suffered a severe setback. Akridge's C Company was decimated; A and B companies were stopped in their tracks. Wounded three times, Akridge had to be evacuated. While bravely attempting to rescue the men of C Company, Ayres himself was trapped and cut off for hours. "He came out crawling on his belly," Perez remembered. Meanwhile, during the confused action that day Perez's 3/34 fled in all directions, as did Battery B of the 13th FAB, whose men left behind four or five howitzers and numerous vehicles.

John Church apparently was not fully apprised of the weight of the NKPA attack. Perhaps believing it was merely a strong probe, he ordered Ned Moore's reserve 19th Infantry to counterattack, clean out the NKPA, and restore the division's positions at the river by dark. In response, Moore sent Tom McGrail's 2/19 forward by truck and alerted Robert Rhea to prepare to follow with his 1/19. Both of the 19th's battalions, bedeviled by a shortage of trucks, conflicting information, and other factors, were slow to move up. It was late afternoon before McGrail's 2/19, supported by the division Recon Company, finally launched an attack. McGrail regained the sector abandoned by Perez's skittish I Company and attempted, without success, to put the I Company back on its position. Entering the fight at 6:00 P.M., Robert Rhea's 1/19 attempted an aggressive sweep to the river's edge but bogged down far short of it. The troops of the 34th and 19th Infantry and the Recon Company spent a fitful and scary night intermingled with NKPA on hilltops awaiting daylight.

To the right (or north) of this action, Dick Stephens's 21st Infantry went on full alert as well. Stephens had outposted the river with John H. McConnell's decimated 3/21 (360 men) and most of the 14th Engineer Combat Battalion (472 men), serving as infantry. Brad Smith's depleted 1/21 (540 men), less C Company, which was still at Pohang, was in reserve, reinforced by a company of the 14th Engineers. Fortunately for Stephens and his men, the NKPA activity in this northern zone was limited to strong patrolling, which the 3/21 repulsed with comparative ease.

Farther north yet, in the sector held by the ROK 17th Infantry Regiment, which served as the link between the 24th and 1st Cav divisions, all was quiet. Because the 17th was desperately required elsewhere to bolster diminishing ROK forces, Eighth Army pulled it out that day. To fill the gap it left, John Church organized Task Force Hyzer, named for a West Point (1937) engineer, Peter C. Hyzer, who commanded the 3d Engineer Combat Battalion. Task Force Hyzer (about 800 men) was composed of the 3d Engineers, a light tank company (less its tanks), and the division Recon Company. The requirement to deploy Task Force Hyzer to this northernmost sector to replace the ROKs seriously depleted Church's combat reserves in the center and southern sectors.

Disappointed by the 19th Infantry's counterattack, on the following day, August 7, Church ordered an all-out attack by the combined forces of the 19th and 34th to throw the NKPA back across the Naktong. However, Beauchamp's 34th (down to 1,000 men) was not able to contribute much. Red Ayres's 1/34 and Gines Perez's 3/34, both shattered, scattered, and isolated, were hard pressed merely to hold in place. On the right (or north), Moore's 19th achieved only partial success. Robert Rhea's 1/19 bogged down; some of its elements were thrown back. Howeyer, Tom McGrail's 2/19, the northernmost of the forces, actually reached the river, but its position was precarious. The extreme heat and humidity and the rugged terrain retarded these efforts as much as (or more than) the NKPA. Moore reported to Church that his men were "dropping out like flies" from the heat. By sunset the counterattack had run out of steam; the NKPA had not been ejected.

## V

By this time the 2d Infantry Division was disembarking in Pusan. Owing to the immediate need for reinforcements on the Taegu front and other factors, Johnnie Walker had vetoed the proposed plan for the 2d Division to relieve the 24th Division en bloc in the Naktong Bulge. However, in view of John Church's inability to clear the NKPA from the Naktong Bulge, Walker ordered the 2d Division to send forces to assist.

The 2d Infantry Division, composed of the 9th, 23d, and 38th regiments, was one of the most famous outfits in the Army. Owing to its outstanding performance in the ETO in World War II—especially in the Battle of the Bulge—it had been selected to be retained in the ever-shrinking postwar Army. But it too had felt the money pinch. When the division was alerted for duty in Korea in early July it was short 5,000 men. However, the ranks were hurriedly filled by various means before the division embarked and it arrived in Korea at full combat strength.[55]

The commander of the 2d Infantry Division was Laurence B. ("Dutch") Keiser, fifty-five. He was a West Point classmate (1917) of Joe Collins, Matt Ridgway, and Mark Clark. One of the few officers in that class to see combat in World War I, Keiser had been a sensation on the battlefield. At age twenty-three he was named to command an infantry battalion in the 5th Division and won a Silver Star for gallantry. But that was the last time Keiser commanded troops in combat. During World War II he served in Italy for five months as chief of staff of VI Corps under John P. Lucas, who was sacked at Anzio. He finished the war a brigadier general and chief of staff of the Fourth Army in Texas, lagging far behind his more illustrious classmates, who by then were wearing three and four stars.[56]

During his peacetime career Keiser had twice served with the 2d Infantry Division, and like many alumni of that famous outfit, he was drawn to it again. In November 1948, after a postwar tour with the Army's advisory group in China, Keiser joined the 2d Division at Fort Lewis, Washington, as ADC. In February 1950 Joe Collins promoted him to two stars and command of the division, a capstone to Keiser's thwarted career.

Keiser's chief assistants were the usual mixed bag of a peacetime Army division. His ADC, Joseph Sladen Bradley, fifty, was a West Point classmate (1919) of Bill Kean's. During World War II Bradley had served in the Southwest Pacific with the 32d Division as chief of staff and commander of an infantry regiment, winning a DSC, two Silver Star medals, and other awards. He made no secret of his desire to command a division. The artillery commander was Loyal M. Haynes (Knox College, 1917), fifty-five, who had fought with the AEF in France, but who manned Stateside desks throughout World War II. In the opinion of the senior officers in the division Haynes "was not physically and mentally up to the job." Nor was the very senior chief of staff, West Pointer (1916) Joseph M. Tully, who "went bananas" shortly after arriving in Korea and was replaced.[57]

As a division commander Dutch Keiser was not universally loved. Mike Michaelis put it bluntly: "Frankly, Dutch Keiser was a lousy commander." Keiser's new chief of staff, Gerald G. ("Gerry") Epley (West Point, 1932), promoted from division G-2, more or less agreed. Epley found Keiser "alert" and "lucid" and admired him personally, but "he wasn't the kind of commander a division should have. He rarely left his CP to visit units in the field. He communicated with his field commanders by telephone and sent Sladen Bradley [the ADC] out to serve as his eyes and ears."[58]

The first of the division's units to reach Pusan was the 9th ("Manchu") Regiment. Mated with the 15th FAB, commanded by John W. Keith, the 9th was a fully manned and equipped and powerful RCT. But it had two possible weaknesses: a "bastard" command setup and one all-black battalion.

Before its alert for duty in Korea the 9th had been commanded by West Pointer (1926) Charles C. ("Chin") Sloane, Jr., forty-eight. During World War II Sloane had been G-2 to Eisenhower and Mark Clark in London, North Africa, and Italy. More recently he had gained fame for conceiving the idea of a well-trained permanent "aggressor force" for Army war games, which had been publicized in *Life* magazine. After the 2d Division had been alerted, Dutch Keiser "recalled" many of his recently departed officers, Chin Sloane among them.[59]

Unknown to Keiser at the time he recalled Sloane, the Pentagon had sent him a batch of new senior commanders. Among them was a colonel, John G. Hill, fifty, who was directed to take command of the 9th Infantry. Hill had fought ably as an enlisted man in the AEF and afterward attended West Point (1924). But like Keiser, Hill had not commanded troops in combat in World War II. In the postwar years he had served four years in Europe as a senior staff officer. His son, John, Jr. (West Point, 1946), was then serving in the 7th Cav.[60]

Keiser was very fond of Sloane and angry that the Pentagon had forced on him these new commanders, especially Hill, whom he did not know and whom he ridiculed as a "damn staff officer" (dismissing Hill's long peacetime service with troops). The upshot was that Keiser appointed Hill commander of the 9th RCT and left Sloane as 9th regimental commander. It was an unwise and completely unworkable compromise which, in effect, gave the 9th dual or co-commanders.[61]

The 9th Infantry's black battalion was its 3d. It was composed of veterans of the deactivated 25th Infantry and other black outfits, plus a large number of postwar volunteers and draftees. Its commander was a capable, combat-experienced white, former National Guard officer D. M. ("Mac") McMains, thirty-nine. He had fought in the 112th Cavalry Regiment in the Southwest Pacific, rising to battalion commander and regimental exec. After the war he had returned to civilian life, but in 1948 he went on full-time active service, first as commander of the 3/9, then a year later (when it was decided all officers of the 3/9 should be black) as exec of the 9th Infantry.[62]

Shortly before the Korean War broke out, McMains was routinely transferred to the Far East. While on leave he suffered severe head and face injuries in an automobile accident which required hospitalization and plastic surgery. Upon receiving the war alert, Dutch Keiser recalled McMains to resume command of the 3/9 from the black officer who had succeeded him, H. Y. Chase. Notwithstanding his injuries, McMains was pleased to return to command the 3/9, which he had trained well. He and a new combat-experienced white exec, William H. Frazier, Jr., forty-two, had supervised its preparations for shipment to Korea and combat.[63]

No doubt owing to the perceived problems in Champeny's 24th Infantry, Eighth Army did not fully trust the 3/9. Upon its arrival in Pusan, Johnnie Walker decided not to commit it directly into hard combat. Instead, he ordered that the 3/9, plus one of Keith's 15th FAB batteries, a company of Shermans of the 72d Tank Battalion, engineers of the 2d Engineer Combat Battalion, and other forces, be sent to guard the FEAF airfield at Yonil, near Pohang. This task force was commanded by the ADC, Sladen Bradley, and Chin Sloane. In this way the 3/9 was introduced to combat in Korea gradually and the Hill-Sloane command problem was temporarily postponed. However, the deletion of the 3/9 left the 9th Infantry with merely two infantry battalions (and two supporting artillery batteries), a composition that would considerably penalize and confuse its leaders, who were accustomed to the standard three-battalion formation.[64]

\* \* \*

On the morning of August 8, while Ned Moore's 19th Infantry was engaged in yet another futile counterattack, John Hill jeeped forward to confer with John Church. The NKPA, Church said, had "busted right through" the 24th Division center. He wanted Hill to "attack at once," not later than 3:00 P.M. Hill protested: His troops had been on the road from Pusan all night; most were green; they needed a rest and time to steady down and get their bearings. Church gave Hill one extra hour. The two-battalion 9th Infantry would attack at 4:00 P.M. directly west into the NKPA, throw them out, and regain the Naktong River positions.

These vague and impetuous orders were ill considered and unfortunate. As it happened, unknown to Church, the NKPA had made a serious penetration farther south in the division's left sector, loosely held by Gines Perez's 3/34. These NKPA troops were moving eastward and would soon pose a serious threat to the division's rear and to its road net. In hurriedly committing the 9th Infantry, Church had blundered badly. As one professional analyst of the battle put it, "The result was to squander the 24th Division's only foreseeable major reinforcement in simply bolstering the center of the threatened sector, while the enemy continued to exploit an opening of major proportions on the division's left."

Harassed and rushed, Hill got his two battalions and Keith's artillery batteries in place and attacked late, at 4:45 P.M., in utterly strange terrain and with no overall picture of the friendly and enemy dispositions in his mind. The full-strength (850 men) 1/9, commanded by John E. Londahl, forty-two, attacked on the right. The full-strength 2/9, commanded by Fred L. Harrison, attacked on the left. Most of the men were green to combat; many were in poor physical condition. The intense heat and humidity came as a terrible shock and, as one Army historian put it, "slowed the advance to a crawl." Meeting heavy NKPA fire, Londahl's 1/9 recoiled and drifted northwesterly, away from the center of the fighting. Harrison's 2/9, advancing against lesser resistance, however, made fair progress. Even so, the 9th Infantry was soon compelled to stop, well short of the Naktong, having achieved very little.[65]

During that night (August 8–9) the NKPA exploited the penetration in Perez's 3/34 sector on the left (or south). But John Church, fixated on his center, continued to dismiss this growing threat. At dawn on August 9 he ordered John Hill's 9th Infantry to resume its attack toward the Naktong. Londahl's 1/9 and Harrison's 2/9 responded, but again the attack did not go well. Both battalions ran straight into a strong NKPA counterattack. Casualties in the 2/9 were heavy. The commander, Fred Harrison, lost a leg; his exec, Joseph A. Walker, assumed command of the battalion.[66]

By the morning of August 9 John Church was exhausted and nearly at wits' end. The heretofore ignored NKPA infiltrators closed in on the 24th Division CP at Changnyong, forcing it to displace fifteen miles to the rear, to Kyungyo. During this chaotic—and humiliating—displacement, Johnnie Walker flew in unannounced and raised all kinds of hell. Had he had a free hand, Walker probably would have relieved John Church of command. However, MacArthur had sent Church to Korea; he was thus "MacArthur's boy" and an untouchable. The upshot was a decision to mount an all-out coordinated division counterattack in the center at 5:00 P.M., employing all surviving forces of Hill's 9th, Moore's 19th, and Beauchamp's 34th Infantry. FEAF close air support and the 11th, 13th, and 15th FABs would "soften up" the NKPA prior to the jump-off.

The attack went off as scheduled, but it, too, utterly failed. Numbed with exhaustion, the survivors of the 19th and 34th regiments were simply incapable of further action. In Moore's 19th Regiment, an Army historian wrote, Tom McGrail's 1/19 (about 300 men) "did not even attempt to advance." Robert Rhea's 2/19 (about 280 men) made a feeble stab, but casualties from enemy fire and the heat continued to be heavy. Rhea and his S-3 were evacuated with heat prostration. The story in Beauchamp's shattered 34th Infantry was similar. Neither Red Ayres in the 1/34 (about 300 men) nor Gines Perez in the 3/34 (about 300 men) was able to mount any sort of offensive action.

The burden of the attack thus fell on the 9th Infantry. Londahl's 1/9 and Walker's 2/9 made a mighty effort but little progress. A platoon commander in the 9th Heavy Weapons Company, William R. Ellis, a veteran of combat in the ETO, remembered that then and later the "9th fought magnificently" in the Naktong Bulge and took grievous losses, especially among the officers. He wrote: "The original group of officers was gallant (far beyond those who followed) and far under-ranked as well. Most of the rifle company commanders were [only] first lieutenants, which was a disgrace in itself. They were forty-year-old, gray-haired World War II combat veterans—and still lieutenants in combat in 1950. I knew all of them and have regretted at times that I did not join them [in death] for they by-and-large died unknown and unrewarded for their bravery."[67]

* * *

During the night of August 9–10, the NKPA continued to exploit the penetration in the division's left (or south) sector. Scores, then hundreds of NKPA poured across the river, rushing eastward. Learning of this massive penetration, Beauchamp and Moore warned John Church and the division staff. To Beauchamp and Moore it appeared possible that the individual regiments, and even the 24th Division, might be encircled and lost. However, Church and his harassed staff, still in the process of moving the division CP rearward and therefore operating with limited communications, either did not get the word or chose to ignore it.

Church, meanwhile, had ordered yet another "all-out" attack in the division center. Essentially a duplication of the previous day's attack, it was mounted on August 10 by the survivors of the 9th, 19th, and 34th regiments. Again Hill's 9th carried the burden of the attack. Again Hill's casualties were frightful, especially in Walker's 2/9, where only one of his four companies had more than one officer left. Again results were disappointing. The 2/9, hit by a severe NKPA counterattack, was thrown back one mile.

That same morning, August 10, the NKPA, exploiting the penetration in the division's southern sector, closed in around the village of Yongsan, eight miles east of the Naktong. Below the village the NKPA established a roadblock which cut the division's main supply route (MSR) from the south. This dire circumstance finally compelled Church and the exhausted division staff to focus on this serious NKPA penetration. Since the NKPA was still not a serious threat in the division's northern sector, Church ordered Dick Stephens to send Brad Smith's 1/21 (less its C Company) and Peter Hyzer to send the division Recon Company to Yongsan to break the block. Meanwhile, Church also urgently requested that Johnnie Walker give him additional major reinforcements from the Fire Brigade, Michaelis's 27th Infantry Wolfhounds.

By the morning of August 11 the situation in the 24th Division sector was chaotic and desperate. Hundreds of the NKPA had swarmed through the southern sector to reinforce the earlier infiltrators near Yongsan and the roadblocks on the MSR south of the town. No area in the division rear was safe from enemy snipers or organized formations. Yongsan itself had come under heavy NKPA artillery fire. As a result, John Church was finally compelled to cease offensive operations toward the Naktong River to deal with the enemy in his rear. Every available unit was thrown into the task: Brad Smith's 1/21; the division Recon Company; engineers; F Company of Joe Walker's 2/9; even the division band.

Meanwhile, Michaelis's Fire Brigade 27th Infantry was mounting a rescue operation from the south. Chary of overcommitting this precious reserve, Johnnie Walker initially restricted Michaelis to one battalion combat team. Michaelis gave the task to Gordon Murch's 2/27, supported by a battery of Gus Terry's 8th FAB. Hurrying north toward Yongsan, Murch plowed into the flanks of the NKPA and soon found himself in a terrific fight. As he slowly crawled north, his 2/27 pushed the NKPA against Yongsan, increasing the pressure on the disparate elements of the 24th Division, which were barely holding on. Late in the day, when Murch bogged down, Walker authorized

Michaelis to commit another battalion, the 3/27. Recently organized and attached, the 3/27 (formerly the 3/29 from Okinawa) was commanded by another of the newly arrived combat-experienced battalion commanders, forty-one-year-old George H. De Chow.[68]

On August 12 Johnnie Walker again flew in to confer with John Church. He found complete chaos. The NKPA forces were swarming all over the MSR and had all but surrounded Yongsan. The three infantry regiments dug in facing the Naktong (9th; 19th; 34th) were desperately repelling new all-out NKPA assaults. Gordon Murch's 2/27 and George De Chow's 3/27 were coming up from the south toward Yongsan; but the Wolfhounds had run head-on into thousands of fleeing refugees, and progress was slow. Worse yet, every yard gained pushed more unwanted NKPA troops against Yongsan.

The situation convinced Walker that unless he committed further reserves, there was danger that the NKPA might capture Yongsan and continue east to Miryang and block the main Taegu–Pusan road and railway. He therefore reluctantly ordered 2d Division commander Dutch Keiser to provide a battalion combat team from another of his regiments, the 23d Infantry.

The 23d, like the 9th, also had a brand-new Pentagon-assigned commander, West Pointer (1929) Paul F. Freeman, forty-three. Freeman was an "old China hand." He had first served there with the 15th Infantry Regiment from 1933 to 1936. Three years later he returned to China as a language student and intelligence officer and was still in China when the Japanese bombed Pearl Harbor. As the Pacific War spread, he migrated to India, where he became G-4 to Joseph W. ("Vinegar Joe") Stilwell, and later organized Stilwell's commando team, which became famous in Burma as Merrill's Marauders. Returning to the Pentagon in mid-1943 as Stilwell's emissary, Freeman was drafted into the Army's war plans group. After working on the plan for the invasion of the Philippines, in late 1944 he joined the operation, serving as chief of staff of the 77th Division on Leyte and Luzon and the Sixth Army and I Corps G-3. On Leyte he had a brief tour of combat leadership when he led a two-company task force and "got shot at." After the war George Marshall invited him to join his China mission, but Freeman was "fed up" with China and declined, choosing instead duty in the Army's Latin America section, working with or under Matt Ridgway and Godwin Ordway.[69]

Upon the outbreak of the Korean War Freeman was ordered to command the 23d Infantry. Like John Hill, he was appointed RCT commander, leaving in place the incumbent regimental commander, West Pointer (1931) Edwin J. ("Ed") Messinger, forty-three, a noted athlete and paratrooper who had fought with the 17th Airborne Division in the ETO. However, unlike Hill, Freeman knew Dutch Keiser well from prior service and balked at this "bastard" command arrangement. Upon his arrival in Korea, the RCT title was abolished. Freeman took direct command of the regiment, and Ed Messinger was demoted to exec. In return, Freeman remained deeply loyal to Keiser and, almost alone among the senior officers of the division, defended Keiser's style of commanding from his CP. Thanks to the fine work of Messinger and others, Freeman found the 23d Regiment to be well trained and officered. Mated to the 37th FAB, commanded by West Pointer (1933) William H. Richardson, it arrived in Pusan ready for combat.[70]

When Freeman received Keiser's orders to provide a combat team to help rescue the 24th Division, he chose the 1/23. It was commanded by another new arrival to the division, West Pointer (1938) Claire E. Hutchin, thirty-four. Hutchin had never led troops in combat. During World War II he had been a Pentagon war plans officer; in the postwar period he had accompanied the Marshall mission to China. But Hutchin was fortunate to draw an able, combat-experienced exec, Cesidio V. ("Butch") Barberis, who had served in Walker's XX Corps in World War II.[71]

Led by Barberis, the 1/23 attacked toward Yongsan, in conjunction with the 2/27 and 3/27, on August 13. Like most American units newly committed to combat in Korea, the 1/23 had a rough first day. One Army historian wrote: "Unprepared for the heat and humidity of a Korean August and poorly conditioned for hill climbing, the men struggled slowly from one ridge to the next." Meanwhile, the combat-hardened 2/27 and 3/27 cracked through the NKPA and cleared the MSR and went into Yongsan. Later that day Hutchin himself led a patrol of his 1/23 into the town. Still later the rest of his battalion marched wearily in behind him. Credited with another smashing triumph ("saving the 24th Division"), the Wolfhounds withdrew that night for other missions. Hutchin's 1/23 remained to reinforce the division and to guard the MSR against further NKPA incursions.[72]

With his rear at last under control, Church refocused his attention on his "front." The situation there was still grave. In renewed, vicious attacks, wave after wave of stoic NKPA troops had inflicted further grievous casualties on the 9th and the ragged remnants of the 19th and 34th regiments. The 9th, bravely attempting to preserve its honor, was hit particularly hard. In E Company of Walker's 2/9 all the officers had been wiped out on five separate occasions. Throughout the regiment sergeants routinely commanded platoons in place of lieutenants. In all, on August 13 the 9th suffered 140 battle casualties and 59 nonbattle casualties, mostly from heat exhaustion. Ned Moore's 19th Infantry journal noted that the men of Londahl's 1/9 were "too exhausted even to remove their own dead."

Charles Payne of the 1/34 remembered the fighting:

Masses of gooks poured over the hills and through the gaps like a flood. Our people were fighting like seasoned troops but were just being overpowered. . . . Hour after hour we held the North Koreans off. . . . Time and time again the gooks rushed us. Each time we'd lose a man, the gooks would lose many. The ground was covered with their dead. We stacked our dead around us for protection. The battle seemed to go on forever.[73]

Determined finally to eject the NKPA from the 24th Division front, Church that night (August 13) ordered John Hill to take command of all the available infantry and launch yet another counterattack on the following day. Reeling with fatigue and lack of sleep, Hill summoned the no less exhausted Charles Beauchamp, Ned Moore, and Brad Smith to his CP. They drew plans which would employ all seven depleted infantry battalions (about 4,000 men), backed by all available artillery (five batteries, mounting thirty howitzers) and (they hoped) supported by FEAF close air. Hill also attempted to draw Claire Hutchin's newly arrived and powerful 1/23 (900 men) into this combined force. Butch Barberis remembered: "I stopped off at John Hill's Ninth Regiment CP and told him the MSR was clear and we would be happy to help evacuate his wounded, et cetera, et cetera. Hill was in quite a dither. In fact, in my estimation he was not in control of his faculties. He was quite irrational. He ordered me to position the battalion in the line. I explained we were not under his command but under Church's direct command. He was quite forceful in telling me that he was giving me a direct order and that I *would* comply with that direct order. I telephoned Church, and in short order he countermanded Hill and told me to maintain my vigil on the MSR and await further orders."[74]

The attack went off, per schedule, at dawn on August 14. It was raining hard. Because of that, no FEAF aircraft appeared, but the artillery laid down a ten-minute barrage. Again carrying the burden of the attack, John Hill's 9th Infantry occupied the center. Beauchamp's 34th and Brad Smith's 1/21 were on the left; Ned Moore's 19th was on the right. Joe Walker's 2/9 smartly took its first objective; but thereafter everything went wrong, and the attack fizzled out all across the front. The shattered 19th and 34th regiments were simply physically and mentally incapable of further offensive action. After an average gain of 500 yards against fierce NKPA resistance, Task Force Hill ground to a halt.

That day Johnnie Walker again flew in to see John Church. By that time John Hill had recommended to Church that his forces break off the attack and go over to the defensive. Inasmuch as Claire Hutchin's 1/23 had been sent north to reinforce Dick Stephens's weakened 21st Infantry and Task Force Hyzer, there were no other division reserves to commit to the battle. Walker, disgusted and furious, reached a drastic and, for the Army, a humiliating decision: He would commit Eddie Craig's Marine RCT to restore the 24th Division's front. To Church he delivered a scathing rebuke: "I want this situation cleaned up, and quick." Later that day Walker's senior field assistant and gofer (who held the title "Tactical Chief of Staff"), William A. Collier, fifty-four, flew down and gave the Marines marching orders, which, in effect, canceled the offensive of Task Force Kean toward Chinju.[75]

The Marines redeployed over the next two days, adding three powerful infantry battalions to the seven Army "battalions" committed to the Naktong Bulge. On August 17, under Church's command, the combined Marine-Army forces, backed up by carrier-based Marine close air support, scads of artillery, Marine Pershing tanks, and other support units, launched an all-out assault. By sunset the next day, August 18, Church had "decisively defeated" the NKPA 4th Division. The estimated 3,500 NKPA survivors fled back across the Naktong, and despite the reinforcements it received, the division would not recover from this major mauling. The fight, later named the First Battle of the Naktong Bulge, at long last was over.[76]

\*   \*   \*

The battle had been messy and nearly disastrous. It had cost the 24th Division and 9th Infantry Regiment terrible casualties. The diversion of the Marines to complete it was both galling and embarrassing to the Army.

Yet in the long term the First Battle of the Naktong Bulge proved to be one of the most decisive battles in the war against the NKPA. The utter destruction of the crack NKPA 4th Division came as a humiliating shock to the NKPA high command, which had publicly proclaimed the imminent fall of Pusan. It led the NKPA into more ruinous strategic blunders, perhaps in part to "save face." Still mindlessly (and publicly) intent on capturing Pusan, the NKPA rushed two more crack divisions, the 2d and 9th, to replace the 4th and reinforced the badly hurt 6th. The redeployment decisively weakened NKPA forces on the Taegu front, where Walker was weakest, farthest from his main supply base, and most vulnerable. In electing to focus the main fighting on the lower Naktong, rather than at Taegu, the NKPA continued to play into Walker's main strength at a place farthest from its own supply base. This flawed strategy ultimately proved to be the undoing of the NKPA.

# 8

# TAEGU SAVED

## I

During the action in the southwest sector of the Pusan Perimeter in the first two weeks of August the NKPA continued pressure on the Taegu front. However, the NKPA having split off four of its crack divisions (2d; 4th; 6th; 9th) to fight in the southwest sector, its strength at Taegu was greatly diminished.

Initially, only four NKPA divisions (1st; 3d; 13th; 15th) remained to mount the attack on the main axis from the northwest. Three of these divisions (1st; 3d; 15th) had been severely mauled in earlier fighting and probably were at no more than half strength (about 5,000 men). The 13th, activated in June 1950, was not well trained or battle-experienced. A fifth division (10th) was added to the Taegu front in early August. However, it, too, was green and had no combat experience, and furthermore, the Army historian wrote, it was saddled with "inept" commanders.[1]

Beyond that, the NKPA plan to take Taegu was not well conceived. Rather than concentrate the five divisions (about 35,000 men) for a massed attack along a single line of advance from the northwest, the NKPA spread them fanwise, across a forty-mile arc of the perimeter, to conduct, in effect, five separate attacks down several roads. None of the individual attacks had sufficient force behind it to exploit a breakthrough.

*   *   *

Walker had three divisions (about 35,000 men) defending the northwest sector: the 1st Cav and the ROK 1st and 6th divisions. The 1st Cav, dug

211

in behind the Naktong River directly west of Taegu, held a sector which stretched along the meandering Naktong, south to north, from Yongpo to Waegwan. The ROK 1st Division held a sector from Waegwan north along the Naktong to the town of Naktong. The ROK 6th Division continued the line eastward.[2]

In the 1st Cav sector there were two key sectors to defend: Waegwan, on the main Taejon–Taegu highway, where a secondary road from the southwest intersected, and, farther south, Yongpo, where a road from Koryong crossed the Naktong and continued in a northeasterly direction to Taegu. Hap Gay placed the two-battalion 5th Cavalry at Waegwan, and the 2/7 at Yongpo, which was not then under enemy attack. The two-battalion 8th Cavalry filled the gap between the 5th Cav and the 2/7. The 1/7 served as division reserve.

The 1st Cav was still a skittish division with poor and aged leadership at the regimental level. Hap Gay took one step to remedy that weakness: He sacked the 5th Cav's Carl Rohsenberger. Gay's ADC, Charlie Palmer, remembered: "Carl was willing and brave, but just too old and too deaf."[3]

To replace Rohsenberger, Gay and Palmer selected West Pointer (1925) Marcel Gustave Crombez, forty-nine. Born in Belgium, Crombez had enlisted in the Army as a private in 1919. Two years later he gained an appointment to West Point, where he had overlapped three years with Charlie Palmer. During World War II Crombez had missed out on the choice combat assignments, serving Stateside as a troop trainer and inspector for the Army Ground Forces. At the tail end of the war (1945) he finally got assigned to a combat command (108th Regiment, 40th Division) in the Pacific, but he saw no noteworthy action and received no awards. Temporarily promoted to colonel, he reverted to lieutenant colonel after the war. He commanded the 17th and 32d Infantry Regiments of the 7th Division in Korea during the Occupation, following which, in 1949, he got his eagles back.

Although at forty-nine Crombez was also "old" for regimental command, his benefactor, Charlie Palmer, believed him to be a "hell of a good field soldier" who could put backbone in the lackluster 5th Cav. Another senior 1st Cav commander shared that view. He remembered that Crombez was "an aggressive commander and he was respected." But not everyone in the 1st Cav Division agreed. Many viewed Crombez as an inept troop leader who was utterly insensitive to his losses and to the welfare of his men, an egotist and self-promoter who was in Korea principally to "get his ticket punched" as a combat regimental commander to better qualify himself for promotion to general. One West Pointer with the 5th Cav said: "Brave, yes. Professional, no." Another West Pointer said: "He was a sonofabitch."[4]

The Taegu sector was substantially strengthened by the arrival on or about August 7 of three American heavy tank battalions, which Matt Ridgway had sent directly from the States. These were the 6th (equipped with new Pattons), commanded by West Pointer (1935) John S. ("Red") Growdon; the 70th (Pershings, Shermans), commanded by William M. ("Bill") Rodgers; and the 73d (Pershings), commanded by Calvin S. Hannum.[5]

The commander of the 70th Tank Battalion, Bill Rodgers, forty-two, who had commanded a tank battalion in combat in the Southwest Pacific Theater, remembered how his outfit was slapped together and shipped to Korea:

At the Armored School at Fort Knox they called me in on Monday morning and said I had been named commander of the Seventieth and must leave with it for an unspecified overseas assignment on Friday morning. Five days! It was nothing more than a paper outfit, consisting of about two hundred men who were serving as demonstration troops for the school. We did not have a single item of equipment, no nothing!

The most urgent matter was to find tanks for our three tank companies. At that time they had placed a lot of [World War II M-26] Pershings up on concrete pedestals around Knox, to serve as monuments. We took these Pershings—we called them "monument tanks"—off the pedestals and used them to equip one company. We drew Shermans from the Rock Island Arsenal for the other two companies. Meanwhile, they were sending me tankers from all over; nobody knew anybody else. But we left by train on Friday morning as ordered. About one week later we sailed from California on a ship with two other tank battalions [the 6th and 73d], whose men had the same kind of hectic stories to tell. We landed at Pusan and went straight into combat, a complete bunch of strangers with no training, employing the [forty-four] Shermans and the [twenty-two] Pershing "monument tanks," which had a good 90mm gun, but many defects, to say the least, and were lacking some essential parts, such as machine guns.[6]

Notwithstanding the slap-dash manner in which these three tank battalions were assembled, the use of the flawed "monument" Pershings, and the lack of unit training, the tankers—and their 200-odd tanks—were a very welcome sight and greatly lifted spirits in the UN Forces at Taegu. Bill Rodgers's 70th Battalion was assigned to the 1st Cav immediately and would remain attached to the division. Red Growdon's 6th and Calvin Hannum's 73d battalions were placed in Army reserve near Taegu. Later, the 6th was attached to the 24th Division, but Hannum's 73d was withdrawn from the Pusan Perimeter and attached to the 7th Division for Inchon.[7]

* * *

The NKPA drive on Taegu began in the 1st Cav sector on August 9, merely a day or so after Crombez assumed command of the 5th Cav. The full but weak NKPA 3d Division crossed the Naktong in darkness south of Waegwan and struck hard in the sector held by the 1/5.[8]

That battalion finally had a permanent commander, Morgan B. Heasley, another recent arrival in Korea. Heasley had commanded a battalion in combat at the end of World War II, but he apparently had little stomach for another war. "Johnnie Walker was at the airport when Heasley arrived," West Pointer (1948) Harry A. Buckley, in the 1/5 A Company, remembered. "He said to Heasley: 'I'm sending you up to the river to die.' That welcome did not go over too well with Heasley."[9]

Heasley, however, had a flaw: a serious weakness for the bottle. "When he was sober he was good," the battalion S-3, James Gibson, remembered, "but he had a terrible drinking problem. He was drunk half the time he was in Korea." Crombez was aware of this weakness, yet curiously, he kept Heasley on the job. "Why he did was a big mystery no one ever solved," Gibson remembered. Buckley and others in the 1/5 would recall that Heasley, in fact, was merely a convenient figurehead; that the able Gibson tactically commanded the battalion in all but title.[10]

When the NKPA 3d Division hit the 1/5 it met a hot reception. Alerted in advance by intelligence, the 1/5 was waiting. It responded by lighting the night with brilliant flares and, by that light, delivered a hurricane of fire from well-emplaced large and small weapons. This heavy, concentrated fire, the Army historian wrote, "decimated" two of the three regiments of the NKPA 3d Division. By daybreak only about 1,000 NKPA troops remained in the hills east of the river, and owing to the heavy American fire, they were virtually stranded.[11]

To clean out the NKPA survivors—and reinforce the area against another attack—Hap Gay called on his reserve, the 1/7. This battalion was commanded by a forty-one-year-old West Pointer (1933), Peter Demosthenes Clainos, who was born in Greece and reared in New Hampshire. At West Point he had been a featherweight (129 pounds) boxing champ. He was still a featherweight and an intense, chain-smoking, combat-experienced fighter. During World War II he had trained a Greek battalion which wound up (minus Clainos) fighting in the Mediterranean Theater with British commandos. Clainos went on to command a battalion in the Pacific where he was wounded and won a Silver Star for heroism. He remembered: "When Korea started, Eighth Army took about forty percent of my men to fill out the Twenty-fourth and Twenty-fifth divisions. I landed in Korea at sixty-seven percent of my authorized strength. We were first assigned to backstop the ROKs at Pohang with heavy weapons—not troops. We gave the ROKs fire support and watched the fighting all around us from a hilltop for four days, rotating companies, to get the smell of gunpowder. This gradual initiation into combat proved to be invaluable training for the men; it built confidence.

"We were Hap Gay's favorite battalion. We became the so-called Palace Guard at Taegu. The press called us Clainos's Clouters or Clainos's Cavaliers. We were greatly reinforced with manpower, artillery, and tanks to make a battalion combat team. Whereas the normal battalion had eight hundred-plus men, I had fifteen hundred. It was a very powerful, self-contained force designed to clean out the enemy when he concentrated in force and broke through our thin lines."[12]

Over the next two days Clainos and his Clouters mounted a powerful and devastating counterattack in the 1/5 sector. Of the 1,000 NKPA troops that got across the Naktong, 700 were killed, wounded, or captured. The remaining 300 fled back across the river to find that the once-mighty 3d Division—victors at the Kum River and Taejon—had been reduced to a disorganized unit of barely 2,500 men. Its abortive attack on the 5th Cav, the Army historian wrote, had been a "catastrophe," and it could pose no further serious threat to Taegu.[13]

The next NKPA attack came at Yongpo, where the 2/7 faced the road from Koryong. The assault was mounted by the ineptly led, green NKPA 10th Division, which had only just arrived at Koryong. Its attack was probably planned to coincide with that of the NKPA 3d Division, but something went wrong. The 10th Division did not jump off until August 12, three days behind the 3d, a lapse that gave Hap Gay time to redeploy Clainos's Clouters.[14]

The 2/7 now had a new, aggressive, and battle-experienced commander. He was Gilman A. Huff, a former enlisted man who had won a battlefield commission and numerous medals for valor in the ETO. He was "a strange individual," Gay wrote, a "trial" and a "drunk" when resting but a "wonderful" fighter in war.[15]

The 2/7 was backed by the steady 77th FAB. Its commander, Billy Harris, was a West Point (1933) classmate of Pete Clainos and an aggressive and colorful officer. He was one of two sons of a retired Army major general and the nephew of West Pointer General Peter C. Harris, who had been the powerful adjutant general of the Army in World War I and afterward. Billy's older brother, Hunter, one year ahead of him at West Point, was a well-known Air Force bomber expert who had, in 1950, been selected as a brigadier general, and was to go on to four stars.

These high Army connections had probably saved Billy Harris from being washed out of West Point. In 1933, when he was a first classman (senior), standing high in his class, he developed such severe "stomach trouble" that the medical department recommended he not graduate. Learning of this, Army Chief of Staff Douglas MacArthur summoned Harris to Washington for a personal interview. Standing at attention, knees knocking, Harris made a good case for being allowed to graduate. "Do you think you're well enough to be an officer?" MacArthur asked.

"Yes, sir," Harris replied.

"I do too," MacArthur said, concluding the interview and dismissing Cadet Harris. "Go back to West Point."

In World War II, while older brother Hunter was gaining fame and glory in the Eighth Air Force, Billy was stuck in an ETO staff job, albeit one of the most fascinating and hush-hush in the theater. He was a senior American representative on the British-conceived deception plan for the Overlord invasion. Known as Fortitude, the plan was designed to convince Hitler and his generals that Overlord was a feint, that the real invasion would come at the Pas de Calais and in Norway. The job cleared Harris for Ultra (information from breaking the German military codes) and other high-level secrets, but it denied him a combat command. He finished out the war in the ETO on Omar Bradley's Twelfth Army Group intelligence staff and then spent three postwar years in the Pentagon, still suffering from a bad stomach.[16]

When the 10th Division crossed the Naktong River, it confronted first Gil Huff, next Billy Harris, and then Pete Clainos, who came up with his Clouters on August 14. These three tough, canny leaders inflicted yet another terrible slaughter on the NKPA. In its baptism of fire the 10th Division suffered 2,500 casualties. Its survivors were apparently so demoralized—or so ineptly led—that the division could not be used again in the attacks on Taegu. It would remain in defensive positions at Koryong.[17]

\* \* \*

These two victories were impressive achievements for the 1st Cav Division, but they were soon overshadowed by a serious setback in Crombez's 5th Cav sector. On August 14, a battalion of the NKPA 3d Division, supported by a few tanks and men of the NKPA 105th Armored Division, crossed the Naktong several miles north of Waegwan, then unexpectedly turned south and assaulted Hill 303, which dominated Waegwan.[18]

Hill 303 was occupied by Crombez's 2/5. It was commanded by West Pointer (1937) Paul T. Clifford, thirty-six, who had commanded a battalion in the ETO. He was an ambitious and able field commander in the Palmer-Crombez mold: tough and demanding and, many believed, "rash" and insensitive to his losses. The NKPA attack caught the 2/5 napping. By first light Clifford's G Company (and a platoon of mortarmen from H Company) had been cut off atop the hill. His F Company escaped encirclement by a hurried withdrawal.[19]

Marcel Crombez was humiliated and furious. The NKPA "capture" of Hill 303 gave the enemy not only the dominating terrain at Waegwan but also an opportunity to crow (on Radio Pyongyang) that the city had been "liberated" from the imperialist warmongers. Determined to regain the hill and city and rescue G Company and the mortarmen, Crombez counterattacked with all the force he could spare. Unfortunately the counterattack failed, but the survivors of G and H companies abandoned the hilltop in darkness and slipped through the NKPA lines to safety.[20]

Johnnie Walker and Hap Gay had no reserves to send Crombez. Walker called on FEAF for help. It responded in the early afternoon on August 17 with the most effective FEAF strike of the war: an awesome and dramatic air assault which wiped out the NKPA battalions and the supporting armor. In its wake Crombez attacked Hill 303 with another infantry-armor task force and by late afternoon the 5th Cav had regained Hill 303 and its lost honor.[21]

These actions at Waegwan and Hill 303, however, cost the 5th Cav heavy casualties. Many company and platoon commanders were killed or wounded; one soldier remembered that a platoon leader in B Company deliberately shot himself in the foot. Dozens of GIs were killed or wounded or fell exhausted from the heat. By the end of the action the combined strength of Clifford's F and G companies was merely sixty men.[22]

There was a grisly aftermath. After regaining the hill Clifford and his men found the bodies of twenty-six mortarmen of H Company. They had been captured and bound—hands tied behind their backs—then murdered with burp guns by the NKPA. Five American POWs had escaped to confirm the murders. When informed of these atrocities MacArthur broadcast a message to the NKPA high command decrying the "outrage," declaring he would hold the NKPA "criminally accountable under the rules and precedents of war."[23]

*   *   *

These actions of the 1st Cav Division, which resulted in the virtual destruction of two NKPA divisions (3d and 10th), were encouraging. It appeared quite possible that notwithstanding its terrible losses the division now had the grit to hold its sector until reinforcements could arrive. Walker's big worry was that the ROK 1st Division on the right of the 1st Cav would collapse, exposing the 1st Cav to encirclement from the rear.[24]

The ROK 1st Division had been under heavy attack for days by strong elements of three NKPA divisions: the half-strength 1st and 15th and the full-strength but green 13th (about 20,000 men in total). The ROKs were fighting valiantly, inflicting harsh casualties on the NKPA (1,500 in the 13th Division in one week), but they were outnumbered about two to one, and they were exhausted from weeks of unrelieved combat. By August 15 the NKPA in this sector had advanced to Tabu, a mere fifteen miles north of Taegu, causing near panic in that city.[25]

A sudden and entirely unexpected NKPA victory on the east coast heightened the panic in Taegu. In that sector the ROK 3d Division had held the lackluster NKPA 5th Division at bay for weeks. But on August 10 the NKPA 5th Division, linking with the NKPA 12th Division, had cut behind the ROK 3d Division and isolated it on the coast above Yongdok. Continuing this combined attack, the NKPA 12th Division had captured Pohang, thereby posing a threat to Taegu through the "back door."

Believing Taegu to be gravely threatened, Walker ordered emergency measures to save the city. First he shifted Eighth Army's Fire Brigade,

Michaelis's Wolfhounds, together with Paul Freeman's 23d Regiment (less Hutchin's 1/23, still temporarily attached to the 24th Division) from the Naktong Bulge sector to backstop the ROK 1st Division. Secondly, he persuaded FEAF to launch an unprecedented heavy-bomber attack (ninety-eight B-29s) on the "40,000" NKPA troops believed to be concentrating around the northwest front. Thirdly, he organized several regimental-size ROK task forces and rushed them to Pohang to reinforce the ROK 8th and Capital divisions, which were opposing the NKPA 5th and 12th divisions. Fourthly, he made arrangements with the Navy to evacuate the encircled ROK 3d Division and reland it near Pohang to join in a counterattack.[26]

*　*　*

As Michaelis and Freeman were moving their regiments north to Tabu to backstop the ROK 1st Division holding the Sangju–Taegu road the NKPA made another baffling move, possibly a grave tactical error. It withdrew its depleted 15th Division (about 5,000 men) from the Tabu sector and sent it eastward to reinforce the desultory NKPA 8th Division, which was directly north of Taegu, blocked by the ROK 6th Division, also fighting valiantly. This new dispersion of forces left only the half-strength NKPA 1st Division and the hard-hit NKPA 13th Division (about 13,000 men in total) plus a few tanks to continue the assault on Taegu from the northwest.[27]

Walker was well prepared to meet this diluted NKPA attack. The Wolfhounds, commingling with ROK 1st Division troops, who held the surrounding ridges, dug astride the road near Tabu. Paul Freeman's as yet unbloodied 2/23 and 3/23 went into position behind the Wolfhounds, both to backstop the Wolfhounds and to protect Terry's 8th and Richardson's 37th FABs.[28]

The NKPA 13th Division, leading the attack, collided with the Wolfhounds on the night of August 18. The Wolfhounds were fully prepared for a hard fight: high ground secure, mines laid, flares ready, all guns zeroed in. When the NKPA pulled into range, Michaelis let loose a hail of frightening and deadly effective fire. The fire caught and destroyed two NKPA tanks, a self-propelled artillery piece, and two trucks and killed or wounded perhaps 100 enemy troops. The NKPA pulled back to regroup.[29]

This scene was repeated night after night. Despite many tense moments caused by infiltrators, Michaelis and his three battalion commanders—Gilbert Check, Gordon Murch, and George De Chow—remained magnificently cool and refused to yield one yard of ground. Bit by bit they whittled down the strength of the NKPA 13th Division, inflicting about 4,000 casualties. The persistent and noisy onrush of the NKPA down this valley—or the hail of counterfire—reminded Michaelis's men of a bowling alley. Their highly publicized resolute stand was thus dubbed the "Battle of the Bowling Alley."[30]

On August 20 Johnnie Walker inspected the Wolfhound front. Surveying the NKPA carnage on the battlefield and the stout American positions, he declared grandly that Taegu "certainly is saved." And so it was—at least for the time being.[31]

Having failed to crack through frontally in the Bowling Alley, the NKPA sent its depleted 1st Division on a flanking movement to the east, down the Kunwi–Taegu road. Anticipating this attack, Walker had reinforced the road with a ROK task force. Nonetheless, the NKPA 1st Regiment overran the ROKs and broke into the rear, where Paul Freeman's 2/23 and 3/23 were guarding the 8th and 37th FABs. In a savage fight, led by the 2/23 commander, James W. Edwards, forty-one, a veteran of the ETO, and well supported by FEAF, one NKPA regiment was shattered and routed. In a skillful follow-up counterattack employing both his infantry battalions, Freeman trapped and decimated the regiment, thus ending all worries that either the NKPA 1st or the 13th Division could crack through to Taegu down the Bowling Alley without major reinforcements.[32]

Diluted by the transfer of four divisions to the southwest sector and by the transfer of the 15th Division to the central sector, the NKPA offensive in the northwest sector against Taegu thus ended in failure. The 1st, 3d, 10th, and 13th divisions had been severely shattered—the 3d almost beyond repair. Total NKPA casualties in this sector during August were probably close to 10,000.

These American victories in the northwest sector coincided with a ROK victory in the seesawing east coast sector. There the ROK Capital Division, supported by the relanded 3d Division and several ROK task forces, drove the NKPA 12th Division out of Pohang and "liberated" the port. Pursuing the retreating 12th Division northward into the mountains, the ROKs all but destroyed it, killing 3,800 men. The division was reorganized and remanned, utilizing several independent units as cadres, but it would not recover from this beating.[33]

## II

Joe Collins and Forrest Sherman arrived in Tokyo on August 21 to confer with MacArthur about the details of the Inchon landing. MacArthur arranged a full-scale briefing for late afternoon, August 23, giving them a chance to pay a quick visit to Korea, where, unknown to MacArthur, Collins was to assess Walker's ability to continue in command of Eighth Army.[34]

Collins and Sherman arrived in Taegu on August 22 and remained overnight. In addition to long and detailed talks with Walker and his staff, Collins toured the American sector of the perimeter in a light plane, stopping at the CPs of the principal units: Hap Gay's 1st Cav Division; Dutch Keiser's

2d; John Church's 24th; Bill Kean's 25th; and Eddie Craig's 1st Marine Brigade.

* * *

In the aftermath of Ridgway's earlier visit the "mediocre" Eighth Army staff had been strengthened. The chief of staff, Gene Landrum, had been replaced, although at Walker's request he remained in the headquarters. His replacement was Leven C. ("Lev") Allen, fifty-six (University of San Francisco, 1916), one of the smartest and most likable staff generals in the Army. After obtaining a commission in 1916, Allen had fought with Johnnie Walker in the 13th Machinegun Battalion in France, where he was wounded. Ably climbing the peacetime career ladder, Allen had attended the Command and General Staff School and the Army War College (1935). When World War II erupted he was serving in the war plans division with Walker and Gee Gerow. He had favorably impressed George Marshall and Omar Bradley. The latter chose Allen to replace him as Commandant of the Infantry School at Fort Benning in 1942 and in the following year to serve as his chief of staff in the vast Twelfth Army Group in the ETO. For outstanding performance in these two jobs Allen had been awarded two Distinguished Service medals and had gained an Army-wide reputation for fairness and coolness under pressure.[35]

The Eighth Army staff had been further strengthened by a new G-3, replacing William Bartlett. The new man was a senior colonel, John A. Dabney (University of Kentucky, 1926), forty-six, a brainy officer whose promising career had been (like Landrum's) thwarted by an unlucky assignment in World War II. Dabney had been chief of staff to Lloyd R. Fredendall, the general in charge of American forces (II Corps) at Kasserine Pass in North Africa when they were routed in their first battle with the Germans. In the wake of this disaster Eisenhower had sacked Fredendall, and his replacements (Patton temporarily, followed by Bradley) did not want Dabney. He had returned with Fredendall to the States, where he sat out World War II as G-3 of the Second (paper) Army. In the postwar years Dabney had helped establish the CIA, then transferred to Japan, first as commander of the 21st Infantry Regiment, next as a senior assistant in the G-3 section of GHQ.

Dabney was introduced to Johnnie Walker's love of speed in a traumatic fashion. He remembered:

One day I accompanied General Walker in a jeep convoy to inspect ROK units on the north front. On the return trip we were going like crazy down the road, Walker's jeep leading. A ROK truck, reacting to the siren in Walker's jeep, pulled off the road to let Walker's jeep pass. But before my jeep could pass, the truck pulled onto the road again. My jeep hit it head on, going sixty miles an hour. We were all thrown out. My steel helmet probably saved my life. I woke up in a M.A.S.H. unit. The doctor wanted to send me to a hospital in Japan, but

Walker sent word for him to sew me up and send me back. Forty-eight hours later, somewhat bruised and battered, I was back at my desk, doing the best I could.[36]

*   *   *

It was a time of momentary triumph for Walker and Eighth Army. In the previous three weeks Eighth Army had repulsed the NKPA 6th Division attack on Masan-Pusan and fought it to a standstill; destroyed the NKPA 4th Division during its attack on the Naktong Bulge; destroyed the NKPA 3d Division and decisively repulsed the NKPA 10th Division, in the upper Naktong River crossings; severely mauled the NKPA 1st and 13th divisions in the Bowling Alley; and, on the east coast, shattered the NKPA 12th Division and regained Pohang. For the moment the Pusan Perimeter was stabilized, and a lull had set in. The American troops were "weary," Collins found, but still "confident of their ability to hold the perimeter."[37]

One reason for the confidence was the impressive extent of the American buildup within the perimeter. By that time Eighth Army's infantry strength in all tactical units totaled 122,000 men, about half American, half ROKs. Both the Americans and the ROK divisions were backed up by about 24,000 "service" troops. Additional infantry units, comprising about 5,000 men, would arrive within the week: three American battalions from the States and the two British battalions from Hong Kong. The American tactical forces now included five tank battalions and some regimental tank companies (in all, about 500 tanks) and about twenty battalions of artillery (in all, about 360 howitzers). Additional equipment and supplies were now pouring into Pusan by air and ship at the rate of about 1,000 tons a day.[38]

Another reason for the confidence was the poor generalship and declining strength and professionalism of the NKPA. The North Korean strategy of spreading its forces around the whole of the perimeter for sporadic and uncoordinated attacks, rather than massing for a concerted offensive, had cost it dearly—perhaps 20,000 to 30,000 casualties in the August fighting. Intelligence sources indicated that the NKPA was running out of tanks, artillery, trucks, ammo, gasoline, and medical supplies.[39]

There were still, however, acute weaknesses on the American side. Although most American units had been bloodied and were steadying down and fighting with greater skill and spirit, battlefield leadership at the division, regimental, battalion and company level was still, on the whole, below standard and overage. Notwithstanding the increased flow of individual American replacements, there was still a dire manpower shortage. John Church's 24th Division was down to 10,000 men—40 percent understrength—and so exhausted it was no longer capable of sustained combat.[40]

In fact, Walker was in the process of drastically overhauling the 24th

Division. The aged and battle-weary ADC, Pearson Menoher, would be replaced by a vigorous, younger general: West Pointer (1927) Garrison H. ("Gar") Davidson, forty-six, a famous football player and head football coach at West Point from 1932 to 1938 who was married to Al Gruenther's sister. An engineer, Davidson had fought under Patton in North Africa and Sicily and with Patch's Seventh Army in France. After hostilities ceased, he had presided over the first German War Crimes Tribunal. He had come to Korea to prepare a defensive line (the Davidson Line) for the evacuation of Eighth Army through Pusan. Since that drastic course no longer appeared to be necessary, he was in need of a job and was deemed the ideal man to prop up the frail and sickly John Church.[41]

The three shattered regiments of the 24th Division—the 19th, 21st, and 34th—were also undergoing assessment and overhaul. In Ned Moore's 19th Infantry both battalion commanders—Robert Rhea (1/19) and Tom McGrail (2/19)—were transferred out, replaced by newly arrived, combat-experienced and decorated veterans: Morris J. Naudts, thirty-six, for Rhea and Oliver G. Kinney, thirty-seven, for McGrail. Both the 19th and 21st regiments received hundreds of replacements. Ned Moore remembered that among his fillers were about 100 blacks, volunteers or draftees, from Eighth Army service units. Moore scattered the blacks among his white rifle squads, where they performed as well as—and in some bases better than—the whites.[42]

The 34th Infantry, commanded by Charles Beauchamp, presented Walker with a difficult situation. Influenced by a stream of derogatory comments from Bill Dean, John Church, and others, Walker believed, perhaps unfairly, that the regiment lacked a will to fight and was beyond repair. (Of its 2,000 men who landed at Pusan, only 184 had survived.) In a harsh and drastic decision, with which Collins concurred, Walker decided to deactivate the regiment (and its normal artillery support, the 63d FAB) and replace it with Johnny Throckmorton's 5th Infantry and its attached 555th FAB.[43]*

The deactivation of the 34th Infantry yielded two "surplus" battalions in the 24th Division. Walker and Church utilized these to build the 19th and 21st regiments to conventional three-battalion units. Red Ayres's 1/34 went to Ned Moore's 19th Infantry to become the 3/19. Gines Perez's 3/34 went to Stephens's 21st Infantry to become the 2/21. Charles Beauchamp returned to Japan to resume command of the 32d Infantry in the 7th Division; the surviving 34th Infantry staffers either left Korea or went to the 19th and 21st as replacements.[44]

In addition, Red Growdon's newly arrived and attached 6th Tank Battalion, equipped with new Patton heavy tanks, gave the 24th Division added

---

*Officially the 5th Infantry and 555th FAB would remain designated an RCT "attached" to the 24th Division.

punch and confidence. West Pointer Growdon was a flamboyant, combat-experienced tanker who had served in the ETO with the 9th Armored Division, which made history by capturing the Ludendorff Railway Bridge over the Rhine River. Growdon, who had won a decoration for his role in that outstanding feat, arrived in Korea eager to fight. A war correspondent in Korea wrote: "Growdon is a tough, rough, hard-driving tank commander of the old George Patton type. . . . [He] likes nothing better than smashing his way through enemy strongpoints with lightning speed and ear-shattering fire."[45]

This drastic overhaul greatly strengthened the 24th Division. Its regimental commanders—Moore, Stephens, and Throckmorton—were judged to be first-rate. All nine battalion commanders were combat-experienced. As a result, the 24th Division was to become one of the most reliable outfits in Eighth Army.

\* \* \*

Following the staff discussions and the tour of Eighth Army, Joe Collins concluded that Johnnie Walker should not be relieved of command. As a "personality" Walker was less than inspiring, and he was certainly no military genius. He had made mistakes, but he was an aggressive "fighter," and considering the slim resources at hand, he had done a commendable job. On the whole the army was improving day by day. The new chief of staff, Lev Allen, would greatly strengthen the senior staff and provide Walker urgently needed administrative backup.

# III

Collins and Sherman returned to Tokyo from Korea on August 23 to confer with MacArthur about Inchon. By then they had been thoroughly briefed on the main features of the operation. These were:

• The 1st Marine Division, initially composed of two regiments—Eddie Craig's 1st Marine Brigade (Fifth Marines), which would be withdrawn from the Pusan Perimeter, and the newly activated 1st Marine Regiment ("First Marines"), mostly manned by called-up reservists—would spearhead the assault. The Army's Japan-based three-regiment 7th Division, brought to full strength by newly arriving battalion cadres and individual fillers and by the addition of 8,600 ROKs, would come ashore immediately behind the Marines. These five American infantry regiments would fan out from the Inchon lodgment, cross the Han River, recapture Seoul, and cut the main NKPA supply lines to the south. Another Marine regiment ("Seventh Marines") would reinforce the beachhead.

• Simultaneously, or close on the heels of the Inchon landing, Walker's Eighth Army would break out of the Pusan Perimeter in a power drive, overrun the NKPA, and dash 180 miles northward, Patton-like, to effect a rapid linkup with the Inchon forces. In theory this maneuver would stun and "trap" the NKPA between "giant pincers" and destroy it. Or, to put it another colorful way, the Inchon forces would be an "anvil" against which the Eighth Army "hammer" would pound the NKPA to pieces.

Joe Collins was not opposed to an amphibious landing per se, but he found fault with almost every aspect of Inchon. His main concerns:

• The withdrawal of the 1st Marine Brigade and its highly effective organic close air support from the Pusan Perimeter to land at Inchon would so weaken Walker's thin perimeter defenses that the NKPA might crack through and decisively rout Eighth Army before Inchon could be mounted.
• Eighth Army, weakened by the withdrawal of the Marines, might not be able to shift from its precarious defense to aggressive offense and break out of the Pusan Perimeter. Withdrawal of the Marines would leave Walker only four divisions, including the still-reorganizing 24th. The troops were exhausted from weeks of tough fighting; the rush to mount Inchon would allow no time to rest and reequip them before launching the offensive.
• Even if Eighth Army succeeded in breaking out of the perimeter, Collins had real doubt that it could "dash" 180 miles to Inchon. It was likely to meet NKPA roadblocks every mile of the way. In the retreat to the perimeter the Americans had blown all bridges. Walker had only minimal bridging equipment. To support the offensive, a major supply line would have to be improvised. Eighth Army did not have sufficient trucks to do so.
• If Eighth Army failed to make a speedy linkup, the Inchon forces could be dangerously exposed. Although Inchon itself was known to be lightly defended, the NKPA could quickly bring in troops from bases in North Korea, a mere 100 miles away. The weak and green Inchon forces (especially the 7th Division, composed of unbloodied fillers and 8,600 ROKs) and the newly activated First Marines, might be cut off and routed or destroyed.
• The emphasis on a speedy linkup would not allow Eighth Army time or resources for short envelopments to destroy the NKPA. It might slip away into the hills to North Korea and reorganize to fight again. The paramount objective of war—utter destruction of the enemy army—would not have been achieved.

Apart from these considerations there was the concern over Inchon itself as a site for an amphibious landing. The admirals and Marine Corps generals involved with the planning had concluded that Inchon was one of the worst possible places in the world to mount an amphibious assault. As one naval planner put it, "We drew up a list of every natural and geographic handicap—and Inchon had 'em all." The chief handicaps:[46]

- *Inaccessibility:* Inchon was located on the south bank at the mouth of the Han River behind a thick nest of offshore islands. There was only a single deepwater channel—Flying Fish—leading from the sea through the islands into Inchon Harbor. The channel was narrow, treacherous, and easily mined. The loss of a single ship in the channel from mines, accident, or air attack could block it, imperiling the entire operation.
- *Tides:* Because of Inchon's peculiar, formidable, and much-discussed tides, Inchon Harbor was a vast, sticky mud flat for most of the day. Deep-draft vessels such as LSTs could get in and out only on extreme high tides, which occurred twice a day (twelve hours apart) for several hours at certain times of the month (depending on the phase of the moon) during the year. The first wave of an amphibious assault could not unload its LSTs in time for the ships to get out; the vessels would be stranded on the mud and exposed until the next high tide. The second wave could not come in until that next high tide, when the surviving (if any) first-wave LSTs were going out. The first wave had thus to be self-sustaining for almost twelve full hours.
- *Wolmi:* Inside Inchon Harbor the small island of Wolmi, with a hill rising 350 feet, dominated the waterfront. It was known to be manned and fortified. Before the main assault could be launched, Wolmi had to be invaded and absolutely secured. Since this was to be done on the morning high tide, the main assault would have to wait for the evening high tide. Thus the element of surprise for the main assault would be lost.
- *Seawalls:* There were only a few small, scattered beaches in the harbor. Most of the waterfront consisted of piers and concrete seawalls, twelve to fourteen feet high. The assault troops would thus have to scale the seawalls with ladders, like troops in ancient times going up a castle wall.
- *Urban warfare:* The assault troops would land directly in the heart of a city with a population of 250,000. A determined enemy could force the troops into house-to-house fighting, the most difficult and hazardous form of infantry warfare. Conceivably the enemy would impress Inchon's civilian population to serve as human shields—as it had in the south—further complicating an already formidable task.
- *Han River:* Beyond Inchon lay the broad Han River, yet another natural barrier. In order to secure the Inchon beachhead, the invading troops would have to cross the Han almost immediately, in effect, stage a second amphibious landing immediately on the heels of the first. This would initially require landing craft (transported overland) and, later, bridging.

• *Weather:* The proposed Inchon D day, September 15, would fall within the typhoon season. The entire enterprise—at sea or already ashore—could be wrecked by the howling winds of a cyclonic storm.

As Collins saw it, there were better possibilities for employing the 70,000 men earmarked for Inchon. One was to feed them into the Pusan Perimeter, immediately and powerfully increasing Walker's strength (from 122,000 to 192,000 men) for a breakout and conventional short envelopments designed to destroy the NKPA. However, this option would require a frontal assault and, possibly, a long, tedious, and costly fight up the peninsula, with the NKPA enjoying the advantage of a constricting main supply line while Eighth Army's became ever longer and more complex. The other option was to land amphibiously behind the NKPA at a more hospitable site much closer to the Pusan Perimeter. A closer landing would reduce the risk of the amphibious forces' being cut off, by making Eighth Army's "dash" to link up shorter and less arduous. It would also position the amphibious forces in such a way that they could, if necessary, attack the NKPA forces at the perimeter from behind, thereby assisting—or assuring—a breakout of Eighth Army.

Collins preferred the latter course—a shorter and closer amphibious envelopment. He chose Kunsan, about 130 air miles south of Inchon, directly west across the peninsula from Taegu. Kunsan was a more hospitable site geographically and lightly defended, too far from North Korea for rapid deployment of a NKPA counterforce. If the NKPA elected to oppose the landing, it would have to draw troops from the perimeter, thus making Walker's breakout easier. Advancing north and east from Kunsan, the amphibious forces could cut the NKPA main supply line (the Seoul–Taegu highway) at Chonan and Taejon, which would be as effective as cutting it at Inchon-Seoul. If necessary, the amphibious forces could attack the NKPA in the rear at the perimeter. In sum, the Kunsan amphibious forces and Eighth Army would be truly mutually supporting.

In seeking alternatives to Inchon, the Navy and Marine planners were thinking along the same lines, although not so radically. They preferred a landing at Posung-Myon, about twenty miles south of Inchon. However, since a landing there would be too distant from Eighth Army to assist in its offensive, and the roads leading from it were poor, Collins was cool to that site. Nonetheless, he welcomed the Navy and Marine planners as allies in opposition to Inchon and hoped that he could persuade them to see the advantages of Kunsan.[47]

Forrest Sherman, the senior naval officer, would determine the official Navy–Marine Corps position. He was torn. From a strategic standpoint Sherman agreed with other JCS members that in the existing crisis Europe should have first priority, the Far East second. For that reason he had resisted sending ever-greater numbers of troops to the Far East, including Marines. On the other hand, he was not without service loyalty. Notwithstanding Sherman's impressive leadership, the Navy still did not enjoy the confidence of Harry Truman or the majority of the public. A successful amphibious landing in Korea, leading to a Korea-wide victory, would do much to restore the prestige of the Navy and Marine Corps and ensure those services a far stronger position in America's post-Korea military establishment.

There was another consideration. The Navy and Marines despised Omar Bradley as much as they did Louis Johnson. Bradley had voted against the Navy's supercarrier, urged a drastic cut in the Marine Corps, and publicly humiliated the Navy and Marines in his "Fancy Dan" speech which ended the "Admirals' Revolt." In that same speech Bradley had discussed the future of amphibious warfare. These remarks had been unfairly canted and truncated by Navy partisans to read: "I predict that large-scale amphibious operations . . . will never occur again." A successful amphibious operation in Korea would make Bradley look the fool and undermine his influence.[48]*

For all these reasons, and others, Forrest Sherman had arrived in Tokyo willing to support an amphibious operation, and so told his senior subordinates. However, after conferring with them on the details of Inchon, and after his trip to Korea with Joe Collins, Sherman concluded that Collins was right; that the landing should be made at Kunsan, not Inchon.[50]

# I V

As he prepared for his meeting with Collins and Sherman on Inchon, Douglas MacArthur was apparently consumed by frustration and turmoil, perhaps even rage. The war in Korea had been in progress nearly eight weeks. His forces had suffered one major defeat after another, incurring appalling casualties. These setbacks had diminished MacArthur's prestige.

In his eyes, Washington still did not appreciate the gravity of the Far East crisis. Truman had demeaned MacArthur's heroic effort in Korea as a "police action." The Pentagon had been niggardly in sending troops. It had denied him the two full armies (comprising eight divisions) he had deemed essential to win the war. Apparently it had even dragged its feet on sending an airborne RCT

---

*Bradley's remarks clearly related to a huge amphibious assault against Soviet-occupied territory defended by A-bombs. What he actually said was that he predicted that large-scale amphibious operations "such as Sicily and Normandy" would never occur again. He added: "Frankly, the atomic bomb properly delivered almost precludes such a possibility. I know that I, personally, hope that I shall never be called upon to participate in another amphibious operation like the one in Normandy." These remarks were not meant to apply to a relatively small-scale operation against the NKPA, which did not have atomic bombs or air superiority.[49]

and the Seventh Marines for Inchon. Visitors from Washington—Collins, Vandenberg, Harriman, Ridgway—kept harping on the need to build up American military power in Europe, where all was quiet, at the expense of the Far East, which was caught in the roar of real war.

His situation was eerily akin to that which he had faced in the spring of 1942. At that time MacArthur's forces in the Philippines were backed into another peninsular perimeter—Bataan—much like the Pusan Perimeter. He had begged Roosevelt for help—a relief force to land amphibiously at Lingayen Gulf on Luzon, to strike the Japanese in the rear, cutting their supply line, enabling him to break out of the Bataan perimeter. In outline, the Inchon plan was not unlike the old Lingayen Gulf plan. Roosevelt, like Truman, had repeatedly assured MacArthur that help was on the way. But it had failed to arrive, in part, MacArthur believed, because Washington gave Europe priority over the Far East, in part because the 1942 Navy did not have sufficient courage. The upshot had been a disgrace—the largest surrender of American forces in history. Was history repeating itself? Would Washington again let him down? Two actions MacArthur took at this time would seem to indicate that the frustration and rage he felt may well have dangerously distorted his judgment:

First, in response to a routine request from the Veterans of Foreign Wars for a "message" to be read at its annual convention, MacArthur, notwithstanding orders to the contrary, issued after the furor over his visit to Formosa, and his assurances to Harriman that he would be a good soldier and do nothing to provoke the Chinese Communists into entering the Korean War, decided to condemn publicly the Truman-Acheson Formosa policy. To an edited version of his June 1950 memorandum on Formosa, describing the dangers to America's Far East offshore defensive perimeter should Formosa be ignored or neglected and fall to the Communists, MacArthur appended this damning indictment of the Truman-Acheson policy of trying to woo Peking back into the American orbit:

Nothing could be more fallacious than the threadbare argument by those who advocate appeasement and defeatism in the Pacific that if we defend Formosa we alienate continental Asia. Those who speak thus do not understand the orient. They do not grasp that it is in the pattern of oriental psychology to respect and follow aggressive, resolute and dynamic leadership–to quickly turn from leadership characterized by timidity or vacillation, and they underestimate the oriental mentality.[51]

The "message" to the VFW was not only insubordinate and insulting to Truman but also arrogantly challenging to Peking. Up to then the Chinese Communists had not overtly assisted the NKPA. Peking was not likely to come to North Korea's aid merely as a response to MacArthur bombast. But the message, coming so soon after MacArthur's provocative visit to Formosa, would no doubt cause further deep concern in Peking.

Secondly, without consulting the Pentagon or specifically Frank Pace or Joe Collins, as custom and protocol required, MacArthur decided that an Army general should command the Inchon forces (which had been organized into an independent corps designated X) and gave this prestigious post to Ned Almond as additional and temporary duty. That is, Almond was to retain his title and power as MacArthur's chief of staff and command X Corps at Inchon as well.[52]

Learning about this highly unorthodox arrangement while he was in Tokyo, Joe Collins was flabbergasted and furious. An officer who was present when Collins got the news remembered that Collins "got half out of his seat and said, '*What?*' "[53] Apart from MacArthur's slight in not consulting him in advance and his longtime and intense personal dislike of Almond, there were several reasons for Collins's ire:

• Up to then Collins and those concerned with Inchon planning had assumed that since the majority of American forces at Inchon would be Marines, the corps would be directed by a senior Marine general, specifically Lemuel C. Shepherd, Jr., who commanded Fleet Marine Forces, Pacific, directly under Pacific Fleet commander Arthur Radford. Shepherd was an able, combat-experienced general (Guadalcanal; Cape Gloucester; Guam; Okinawa) who headed a large staff with extensive combat experience. Neither Almond nor the staff he was hurriedly throwing together for X Corps had any combat amphibious experience.[54]

• Collins may have believed that the appointment of Almond to command X Corps, which would operate at Inchon under MacArthur's direct control like a separate army, was a devious device, conceived by MacArthur or Almond to get Almond promoted to three stars. Collins had consistently opposed promoting Almond, but a successful Inchon landing could build such pressure to promote Almond that he could not reasonably continue in opposition.

• Collins did not approve of the independent status of X Corps, commanded by an officer who would also retain his post as MacArthur's chief of staff. Under that arrangement it seemed probable that X Corps would receive favored treatment and priority over Eighth Army in manpower and logistics. Moreover, owing to the enmity that existed between Almond and Walker, it was not likely that after the forces had linked up at Inchon, Almond would willingly consent to incorporate X Corps into Eighth Army in the conventional manner. This could lead to a dangerous division of American forces in Korea, commanded by two men who were not on speaking terms.

MacArthur's "message" to the VFW and his appointment of Almond to command X Corps—both done in the same week—outraged almost the whole of official Washington: the White House, State, and the Pentagon—especially Collins, who until then had been one of MacArthur's strongest supporters, and Sherman, who represented the Marines. The actions were to raise further searching questions about MacArthur's loyalty and his mental stability.

\* \* \*

Ned Almond had been present at the birth of the Inchon idea. Within GHQ he had been its most tireless advocate. As the hour for the climactic meeting about Inchon with Collins and Sherman drew near, he did all in his power to minimize opposition to Inchon and "sell" it as the best possible solution:

• When the admiral in overall charge of the Inchon amphibious landing, James H. Doyle, proposed to Almond that MacArthur's meeting with Collins and Sherman include a detailed briefing on the risks at Inchon, Almond attempted to cut him off at the knees. "The general is *not* interested in details," Almond declaimed loftily. However, Doyle, who was a lawyer skilled in argumentation, refused to be cowed by Almond's "most dictatorial manner." MacArthur "*must* be made aware of the details," Doyle declared, and eventually he won his case.[55]

• When Marine Generals Lemuel Shepherd and Oliver P. ("O. P.") Smith (University of California, 1916), fifty-six, who commanded the 1st Marine Division, arrived in Tokyo, Almond, aware of their opposition to Inchon, excluded them from the meeting. This was a profound insult, especially to Shepherd, a fellow VMI graduate (1917) and an old friend who outranked Almond by one star and who had been Almond's strongest ally in persuading the JCS to send Marines to Korea. Almond further alienated O. P. Smith by patronizingly calling him "son" and by "superciliously" dismissing the difficulties at Inchon as "mechanical." By date of commission, Smith was actually senior to Almond; by date of birth, a mere ten months younger. This high-handed and rude treatment of Shepherd and Smith was to lead to a needlessly difficult relationship between Almond and the Marines—especially between Almond and Smith, who was to be one of his chief subordinate commanders at Inchon and later.[56]

\* \* \*

The meeting on Inchon convened at 5:30 P.M. on August 23 in MacArthur's office in the Dai Ichi Building. In addition to MacArthur, Almond, Collins, Sherman, and Doyle, a dozen others crowded into the room: FEAF commander Stratemeyer; Pacific Fleet commander Arthur Radford; C.

Turner Joy, commander, Naval Forces, Far East; Seventh Fleet commander Arthur Struble; Almond's deputy, Doyle O. Hickey, who temporarily was to take over Almond's desk duties in Tokyo; the GHQ G-3, Edwin K. ("Pinky") Wright; and others.[57]

After Pinky Wright had sketched the "big picture," detailing the forces and scheme of maneuver, Doyle's team took over and described the difficulties of Inchon: ingress, tides, seawalls, Wolmi, etc. The tenor of the briefing, Collins wrote later, was "frankly pessimistic." Summing up, Doyle turned to MacArthur and said: "General, I have not been asked nor have I volunteered my opinion about this landing. If I were asked, however, the best I can say is that Inchon is not impossible."

MacArthur sat through this litany of negatives, silently puffing on his pipe. Then, suddenly and dramatically, he seized the floor and delivered a forty-five-minute soliloquy which no one present would ever forget. Collins and Sherman described it as spellbinding. Collins elaborated: "Even discounting the obvious dramatics, this was a masterly exposition of the argument for the daring risk he was determined to take by a landing at Inchon." Doyle declared: "If MacArthur had gone on the stage, you never would have heard of John Barrymore."

The thrust of MacArthur's argument was that Inchon would succeed precisely because of the difficulties it presented. That is, the problems were so obvious and so great that the NKPA would never expect an attack there and could not react in time to thwart it. He would therefore achieve a vital element of an amphibious landing: stunning surprise. He likened Inchon to British General James Wolfe's brash and successful river assault on the French under Montcalm at Quebec during the French and Indian War. (He did not mention that Wolfe was killed in that battle.)

Collins had been temporarily mesmerized, but he snapped back to reality and made a strong case for a landing at Kunsan, rather than Inchon. His critique was "seconded" by Sherman. In response, MacArthur disdainfully dismissed that alternative as "ineffective and indecisive." He went on: "It would be an attempted envelopment which would not envelop. It would not sever or destroy the enemy's supply lines or distribution center, and would therefore serve little purpose. It would be a 'short envelopment' and nothing in war is more futile. Better no flank movement than one such as this. The only result would be a hookup with Walker's troops on his left. It would be better to send the troops directly to Walker than by such an indirect and costly process."

As MacArthur continued his exposition, it became obvious that he was less concerned about tactical maneuvers than he was about delivering a knock-out psychological blow. A successful landing at Inchon would not only cut the NKPA supply lines but also almost immediately result in the liberation of

Seoul. As he saw it, this would be a devastating psychological setback not only to Pyongyang but also to Communist regimes throughout the Far East—and the world. Hence Inchon could not be looked at purely from the standpoint of military feasibility. There was that "oriental mind" to consider.

Although this was one aspect of Inchon they had not considered in any depth, neither Joe Collins nor Forrest Sherman was yet convinced that the liberation of Seoul was worth the risks. A similar line of reasoning—the psychological impact of the liberation of Rome—had led to the Allied landing at Anzio. That landing had turned into a bloody fiasco because Mark Clark's forces at the Rapido River had been so thinned-out to provide forces for Anzio that Clark could not crack north of the Rapido promptly enough to link up with the Anzio forces. However, neither Collins nor Sherman raised this obvious parallel.

Pressing his case to a climax, MacArthur chose emotional—even apocalyptic—language. The "only alternative" to Inchon he could see was a "continuation of the savage sacrifice" in the Pusan Perimeter, "with no hope of relief in sight." He rhetorically put that monkey on Washington's back: "Are you content to let our troops stay in that bloody perimeter like beef cattle in the slaughterhouse? Who will take the responsibility for such a tragedy? Certainly, I will not." He could hear the "ticking of the second hand of destiny. We must act now or we will die." The prestige of the Western world "hangs in the balance." The "test" was in the Far East, where communism had elected to launch its global conquest. "Here we fight Europe's war with arms, while there it is still confined to words," he proclaimed. "Lose the war to communism in Asia" and "the fate of Europe will be gravely jeopardized. Win it and Europe will probably be saved from war and stay free."

In conclusion, MacArthur conceded the many technical difficulties of Inchon. It was "a 5000 to 1 gamble." If it failed—if he could not cope with the defenses—he would withdraw the forces before they encountered a "bloody setback." He added: "The only loss then will be my professional reputation." But he did not think Inchon would fail. "Inchon will succeed," he said, "and it will save 100,000 lives. . . . We shall land at Inchon and I shall crush them."

Most of those present were so hypnotized that no one could immediately find appropriate words of response. Finally, Sherman rose and said lamely: "Thank you. A great voice in a great cause." But neither Sherman nor Collins was "sold" on Inchon. They still preferred Kunsan or Posung-Myon. On the following day, August 24, Sherman, Radford, Joy, and Doyle, with the two Marine generals Shepherd and Smith in tow, met again with MacArthur in an effort to change his mind. In reply, MacArthur delivered another long soliloquy stressing the psychological importance of liberating Seoul and refused to consider an alternate site. As they left, Sherman said: "I wish I could share that man's optimism." Collins, meanwhile, went to work on MacArthur's G-3, Pinky Wright, urging a landing at Kunsan, but he, too, met a stone wall.

In all these tedious discussions the emphasis had been placed on the landing, the Eighth Army breakout, and the linkup. There was no discussion of what would happen after the capture of Seoul. What would the next objective be? Would X Corps continue to operate more or less as an independent army, directed from Tokyo? Or would the two forces be merged? If they were merged, who would command, Walker or Almond? The failure to address these questions would come back to haunt all concerned.

## V

On August 25, while Collins and Sherman, still torn by doubt over Inchon, were flying back to Washington, MacArthur's "message" on Formosa to the VFW leaked. The conservative newsmagazine *U.S. News & World Report* and the Associated Press had obtained advance copies. *U.S. News* went to press with the full text; the AP distributed lengthy excerpts for publication on August 27.[58]

Learning of this—and the thrust of the message—Truman and Acheson were monumentally outraged. The following day, August 26, Truman, "lips white and compressed" in anger, met with Acheson, Louis Johnson, Harriman, the JCS, and advisers in the Oval Office. Dispensing with the "usual greetings," Truman set aside the business for which the meeting had been called to deal with MacArthur's "message." He asked Collins and Sherman, just off the plane from Tokyo, if they had any prior knowledge of it. They did not; it was a complete shock to them—as it was to all those present. Harriman, his earlier warning about MacArthur dramatically borne out, declared that the "release" of the message (already, in fact, released) would be a catastrophe. Acheson and Truman agreed emphatically.[59]

Finally, it was decided that the message must be "withdrawn" by MacArthur himself, even though that would be complicated and would probably call further attention to the issue and make matters worse. Without mincing words, Truman directed Johnson to telephone or cable MacArthur and order him to "withdraw" the message. In part because he was in complete sympathy with MacArthur's message (especially the implied criticism of Acheson), in part because he was still in secret league with Truman's right-wing critics, in part because he did not want to challenge MacArthur's great prestige, Johnson dragged his feet, suggesting alternatives. Finally, Truman telephoned Johnson and dictated to him the order to be sent to MacArthur: "The President of the United States directs that you withdraw your message for National Encampment of Veterans of Foreign Wars, because various features with respect to

Formosa are in conflict with the policy of the United States and its position in the United Nations."[60]

MacArthur later wrote that upon receiving this cable, he was "utterly astonished." He insisted that the VFW message was in complete harmony with administration views and that others had twisted its meaning. He cabled an appeal to Truman via Johnson to allow the message to stand as a "personal" view, but Truman was adamant that it be withdrawn—and it was. The furor, as expected, was ear-shattering. The China Lobby and right-wing critics seized on the incident as another club with which to beat Truman and Acheson for the "loss" of China and "bungling" in the Far East, the list of examples of which now included the Korean War.[61]

The incident was important less for the damage it did the United States than for the damage it did Louis Johnson and Douglas MacArthur. Truman at last decided that Johnson must go. At the same time he seriously considered taking steps to strip MacArthur of all military power and command. He would send Omar Bradley to command military forces in the Far East—and Korea—leaving MacArthur as a figurehead occupation chief in Japan, probably to remain there until the Japanese peace treaty was signed and the occupation terminated.[62]

Perhaps because Inchon was imminent or because he feared the political consequences, Truman changed his mind about stripping MacArthur of power but held to his decision to fire Johnson. That chore, Truman believed, would be less onerous because he had talked George Marshall, whom he revered, into returning to government to replace Johnson.

Yet the firing of Johnson proved to be extremely painful for Truman. He remembered: "He came and I opened the conversation by telling him he'd have to quit. He was unable to talk. I've never felt quite so uncomfortable. But he finally said he'd like a couple of days to think about it. I said all right." Late on the following day, after a cabinet meeting, Truman met again with Johnson. "He looked like he had been beaten," Truman wrote. "He followed me into my office after the Cabinet adjourned and begged me not to fire him. Then he handed me the . . . letter [of resignation] . . . unsigned. I said, 'Louis, you haven't signed this—sign it.' He wept and said he didn't think I'd make him do it."[63]

The sacking of Louis Johnson had a profoundly positive impact on the professional American Army officers in Korea. An artillery officer, James H. Dill, aboard a ship bound for Korea when the news of the sacking became public, remembered acidly:

The result was a reaction among the troops such as I never saw among American troops at any other time. Cheers broke out all over the ship. Soldiers slapped each other on the back and clapped. . . .

We hated Louis Johnson. We hated that man with the hatred of a blood feud. We damned him day and night. We damned anyone anywhere who would not damn him. . . .

He had cut the Army to the bone and then scraped the bone to the quick. . . . He had declared over and over that we had the most powerful defense establishment in the world and had nothing to fear from anyone. And we knew he lied. . . . We knew the truth. . . .

To us a simple proposition presented itself. We were apt to get killed—and had already had so many friends killed—because that man had cut our strength so much. . . . The last bitter joke on Louis Johnson was that the JCS had advised him he could call off his planned reduction in the armed forces since enough men had been killed to bring our strength down to his desired level.[64]

So history condemned Louis Johnson. But Dill's venom was misdirected. It was Harry S. Truman who had savaged the United States Army. Johnson was merely Truman's overeager and obnoxious bludgeon.

* * *

George Marshall was to bring enormous prestige to the office of secretary of defense, but he was no longer the robust man of the World War II and postwar years. To assist with the tough, tedious day-to-day management of the Pentagon, Marshall recruited Robert A. Lovett, a smart, hardworking public servant who administered with a firm but reasonable hand and disdained the limelight. Simultaneously with Marshall's arrival, President Truman, who was increasingly relying on Omar Bradley as his chief military adviser, promoted Bradley to five stars. The promotion not only gave Bradley added prestige and salary ($17,000 per year) but placed him on a level, in terms of rank, with MacArthur.[65]

* * *

The JCS, meanwhile, received a thorough briefing from Collins and Sherman on Inchon. It was far from optimistic; both men still foresaw possible disaster. Yet the JCS was reluctant to overrule MacArthur and cancel Inchon for several reasons. One was the "tradition," born in the Civil War and religiously adhered to in World War II, of giving the theater commander wide latitude in tactical operations. Another was the fear of incurring MacArthur's wrath.[66]

The JCS did, however, do its utmost to persuade MacArthur to choose an alternate site to Inchon. On August 28 it cabled him a tactful message, which was drafted by Sherman and approved by Truman, urging a landing at Kunsan:

After reviewing the information brought back by General Collins and Admiral Sherman we concur in making preparations and executing a turning movement by

amphibious forces on the west coast of Korea, either at Inchon in the event that
enemy forces in the vicinity of Inchon prove ineffective or at a favorable beach
south of Inchon if one can be located. We further concur in preparation, if desired
. . . for envelopment by amphibious forces in the vicinity of Kunsan. We understand that alternative plans are being prepared in order to best exploit the situation
as it develops. We desire such information as becomes available with respect to
conditions in the possible objective areas and timely information as to your intentions and plans for offensive operations.

Perhaps fearing that the JCS would ultimately order a cancellation of
Inchon, MacArthur embarked on an astounding course of deceit and deception designed to thwart such an order. He did not reply at all to the JCS August
28 cable. On August 30, Tokyo time, he issued operational orders for Inchon
to proceed in accordance with his plan. However, he deliberately delayed
sending copies of his operational order to the Pentagon. They would not arrive
in Washington until September 8, one week before the Inchon D day. The
dodge fooled no one; it served only to undermine further MacArthur's dwindling credibility within the JCS.[67]

*　*　*

All the while the Truman administration was engaged in secret discussions over the course to take in Korea after the NKPA had been crushed.
The key question was: Should the United States be content with its original
goal of restoring the status quo ante bellum, or should its ground forces cross
the 38th Parallel to ensure the utter destruction of the NKPA and thereafter
occupy North Korea with the goal of "unifying" the peninsula under a single,
popularly elected government?[68]

Truman, Acheson, the JCS, and others at the top level of the administration leaned toward crossing the 38th Parallel and "unifying" Korea. Not to
do so would be indecisive, inconclusive, and unsatisfactory and would leave
the administration open to further charges of being "soft on communism."
Moreover, the situation presented the administration with a unique opportunity to deliver communism—and Joe Stalin—a devastating blow. For the first
time in the cold war a satellite could be "liberated" from Moscow. The
liberation would certainly diminish Soviet influence in the Far East and might
diminish it worldwide. The American public, the media, and, ironically, Truman's greatest critics, Republicans or otherwise, shared this view.

However, there were important dissenters within the administration.
These included, among others, the foremost Kremlinologists at State, George
Kennan and Charles ("Chip") Bohlen; the head of State's Policy Planning
Staff, Paul H. Nitze; and the leading Soviet experts at the CIA. These experts
argued that crossing the 38th Parallel, no matter how the act was cloaked or
rationalized, amounted to an invasion of a Soviet satellite—the first such

invasion—and that Joe Stalin was not apt to stand idly by. Aggressive Moscow counterreaction was "likely": either direct Soviet intervention or a Moscow-directed Peking intervention. For these reasons they urged a halt at the 38th Parallel.

In the papers they presented, these Soviet experts drew attention to recent ominous shifts in the deployment of Chinese Communist military forces. There was an impressive buildup in progress in Manchuria. Intelligence reported that during August the number of "regular" (as opposed to "militia") Chinese troops in Manchuria had doubled—from 115,000 to 246,000. Moreover, there was every indication that the buildup was continuing. It was possible, the CIA paper suggested, that the Chinese troops might be ordered to aid the NKPA and would confront American forces at the 38th Parallel.

Even so, the momentum for crossing the 38th Parallel continued to build in Washington. "It would have taken a superhuman effort to say no," Harriman reflected later. "Psychologically, it was almost impossible not to go ahead and complete the job." While the precise details, orders, and caveats were being hammered out, Truman and Acheson launched diplomatic moves at the UN to gain support for this course. In a nationwide radio broadcast on September 1 Truman signaled American intentions: "We believe that Koreans have a right to be free, independent and united." The key word was "united."[69]

Nonetheless Truman was still very much concerned about possible Chinese Communist intervention in Korea. In the same speech he went out of his way to placate and court Peking. "We do not want the fighting in Korea to spread into a general war. . . . We hope in particular that the people of China will not be misled or forced into fighting against the United Nations and against the American people, who have always been and still are their friends." Since the speech came only a week after the furor over MacArthur's VFW message, he felt compelled to add: "We do not want Formosa or any part of Asia for ourselves."

There was no direct response from Peking. However, there were already indirect signs that Peking was edging toward more intimate association with Pyongyang. A Peking progaganda magazine, *World Culture,* wrote in August that the "barbarous action of American imperialism" in Korea not only menaced peace in Asia but also threatened the security of China in particular. "It is impossible to solve the Korean problem without the participation of its closest neighbor, China," the article went on. "North Korea's friends are our friends. North Korea's enemy is our enemy. North Korea's defense is our defense. North Korea's victory is our victory." At the UN, representatives of Peking, seeking recognition (and the "seat" held by the Chinese Nationalists) and abetted by the Soviets, increasingly intruded, covertly and overtly, into discussions relating to the Korean War.[70]

# 9

# MAGNIFICENT VICTORY

## I

MacArthur and Almond conducted all Inchon planning behind an elaborate wall of secrecy. Even so, the North Koreans probably knew in advance that an amphibious envelopment on the west coast of Korea was in the works. Reporters accredited to GHQ, Tokyo, and the Pentagon were briefed off the record well in advance and informed their home offices for planning purposes. In its July 24, 1950, issue *Time* magazine speculated that an Eighth Army breakout from the Pusan Perimeter "could be supported by Allied amphibious attacks behind the North Korean lines on either coast." In Tokyo the war correspondents freely discussed Inchon, ridiculing the security measures as "Operation Common Knowledge." Tokyo and Japanese seaports, where the ships were loading out for Inchon were no doubt infiltrated by communist spies. Two Soviet spies, Guy Burgess and H. A. R. ("Kim") Philby, then working in the British Embassy in Washington, had access to private discussions and secret documents relating to the Korean War.

The rumors or hard information received in Pyongyang presented the NKPA with vexing questions. Was the information true or a deception planted by the Americans? If true, exactly where would the amphibious force strike? Owing to the hazards entailed, Inchon seemed unlikely. The invasion could come at any place on the west coast from Chinnampo, near Pyongyang, to Kunsan. Or it might come on the east coast, at Wonsan or elsewhere. Having committed most of its forces to the Pusan Perimeter, the NKPA lacked resources to mount effective defenses at one possibility, let alone several.

The best NKPA defense to an amphibious envelopment in its rear—

indeed, the *only* feasible defense—was to make one last do-or-die attempt to crack the Pusan Perimeter and overrun Eighth Army. A decisive NKPA victory in the perimeter would almost certainly force a cancellation of the amphibious invasion.

In any case, the situation the NKPA faced at the Pusan Perimeter demanded a do-or-die offensive. The invasion of South Korea had been postulated on a quick, easy victory over the ROKs. Owing to the American intervention, the once fast-moving and victorious NKPA troops were now virtually stalemated in costly, indecisive, and discouraging positional warfare. The NKPA was losing the logistical and manpower battles. Inevitably it would lose the war.

And so it was decided. On about September 1 the NKPA would make one last, desperate effort to push the Americans into the sea. The offensive would, for the first time, be intricately coordinated. But because of the lack of time and ability to redeploy forces and other factors rapidly, the plan was flawed. Rather than mass at one place for a decisive breakthrough, the NKPA would again attack everywhere at once around the perimeter. Four-plus divisions would renew the drive to Pusan in the southwest sector toward Masan and the Naktong Bulge; three-plus divisions would renew the drive to Taegu in the northwest sector; four divisions would renew the drive on Pohang in the northeast sector.[1]

In preparation for this offensive the NKPA substantially reinforced the perimeter. It added fresh, trained combat units, principally the 7th Infantry Division, sent to reinforce the 6th Division in the southwest sector, and two new armored regiments, the 16th and 17th, equipped with about forty T-34 tanks each. In addition to regular forces, the NKPA rounded up about 35,000 boys and young men in North and South Korea and sent them south to help reman the divisions at the perimeter. These troops brought the NKPA tactical forces to a total strength of about 98,000 men.[2]

The new tanks and the 7th Division gave the NKPA added punch, but on the whole it was a desperately tired and ragtag army. The surviving old hands had been fighting continuously for two months. There was an acute shortage of everything: artillery; rifles; burp guns; ammo; food; gasoline; medicine. The 35,000 fillers—constituting about one-third of the army—were cannon fodder. They had no training whatsoever. Many had not even been issued individual weapons.

Of the three main NKPA drives, the strongest would again be that mounted in the southwest sector. It would be carried out by a total of five numbered divisions: the wrecked 4th (5,500 men); the recently mauled 6th (reinforced to 10,000 men); the newly arrived veteran but understrength 2d (6,000 men); the newly arrived green 7th (9,000 men); and the newly arrived green 9th. The last had dropped one of its regular regiments, the 87th, in the

Seoul-Inchon area but had created a new regiment with fillers, bringing it back to near full strength (9,350 men). These forces, supported by elements of the new 16th Armored Regiment, constituted nearly 40 percent of all NKPA troops at the perimeter: about 40,000 men.[3]

In planning the offensive in the southwest sector, the NKPA generals committed yet another tactical blunder. Rather than mass the four-plus divisions on a single line of advance for a power punch-through, they spread them out along a long front for a simultaneous frontal attack. The 2d and 9th (and surviving remnants of the 4th) would attack toward the Naktong Bulge; the 6th and 7th, toward Masan. By this arrangement the NKPA denied itself power in depth to exploit a breakthrough. To succeed, the offensive had to break through across the entire front simultaneously.

Fortunately for Walker and his troops, the Eighth Army code breakers had intercepted and decoded NKPA radio traffic describing some features—but not all—of the offensive. Believing the strongest NKPA effort would once more come in the southwest sector, Walker had time to redeploy to meet that threat. He pulled Michaelis's Wolfhounds and Paul Freeman's 23d Regiment out of the Bowling Alley and sent them to the southwest sector: the Wolfhounds back home to Bill Kean's 25th Division at Masan; the 23d back home to Dutch Keiser's 2d Division, which had displaced Church's reorganizing 24th Division in the Naktong Bulge area immediately north of the 25th. In addition, Walker postponed the transfer of Throckmorton's 5th Regiment, then deployed on the "south road" at Chingdong, to the 24th Division, which had moved into reserve near Taegu. Finally, he did his utmost to delay the departure of Eddie Craig's Marines, then near Masan preparing to embark for Inchon.

These redeployments gave Walker far more strength in the southwest sector than he had enjoyed theretofore. There were, in total, eight infantry regiments, most of which now had three battalions. On the extreme south flank near Masan, Bill Kean's 25th Division controlled four regiments (south to north): Throckmorton's 5th; Champeny's 24th; Michaelis's 27th; and Fisher's 35th. Continuing the line northward into the Naktong Bulge, Dutch Keiser's three 2d Division regiments were disposed (south to north): John Hill's 9th (less the 3/9); Freeman's 23d (less the 3/23); and the 38th. The Fifth Marines, near Masan, were in position to reinforce either the 25th or the 2d Division. All eight regiments were powerfully backed by tanks, artillery, and Marine and FEAF close air support.

The weakest sector was the Naktong Bulge, held by John Hill's 9th and Paul Freeman's 23d. Both regiments were shy one battalion. McMains's black 3/9 was still in the northeast sector near Pohang. Freeman's 3/23 had been temporarily attached to the 1st Cav. Moreover, Hill had incurred heavy casualties in his 1/9, and these losses had not yet been fully replaced. As a result of all this, there were only about 3,500 men in the four battalions defending the Naktong Bulge.

\* \* \*

The NKPA offensive began in earnest during the night of August 31. Most of the troops, responding to the do-or-die challenge, were fired up to an extraordinary degree. They attacked fanatically, showing little or no concern for losses.

These were trying days for Johnnie Walker—worse than the fall of Taejon and the retreat to the Naktong River in July. Every morning he faced frantic messages from his division commanders reporting enemy breakthroughs and urgently requesting immediate help. He had to weigh carefully the threat of one enemy breakthrough against the other before committing his reserves. At the same time he had to exert every effort to rally the spirits of his troops, many of whom were in Korea much against their will and not yet convinced that South Korea was worth saving.

To accomplish these daily tasks, Walker was almost always in the field. Every morning at dawn he flew over the entire front line in his small plane. After returning to Taegu, he met briefly with his staff, issued orders, then took off again at terrifying speed in his siren-equipped jeep, trailed by a small convoy of well-armed vehicles, one carrying a powerful radio by which he maintained continuous contact with Eighth Army headquarters and the division CPs. His jeep had a custom-built steel handhold which enabled him to stand as he rode along, displaying himself to his troops (and to the enemy). He kept a shotgun close at hand in the jeep to defend himself should his convoy be ambushed.[4]

His personal pilot, infantryman Eugene M. ("Mike") Lynch, twenty-three, an enlisted tanker in World War II who won a battlefield commission and learned to fly in the postwar years as a sideline, remembered: "He was not an impressive individual. He did not have physical 'command presence.' His chest had slipped; he was pudgy. He didn't talk much. All business. No chitchat. But he was a great man, a fighter. A *fundamental* fighter. When we flew the front every morning—to look at the enemy and our own troop deployments—we'd fly very, very low, sometimes only fifty feet up. He had no fear whatsoever of ground fire. It meant nothing to him. He was determined to find out for himself what was going on. After these flights he knew more than the Eighth Army staff knew. When he saw our troops bugging out, he'd get me to chop the throttle. We'd glide down over them, and he'd yell out the door: 'Stop where you are! You're not under attack. You've got a good defensive position. Hold it.' "

The exec of Ned Moore's 2/19, Kenneth Woods, recalled Walker's presence on the battlefield:

Our very conscientious supply officer, Bob [Robert E.] Nash, went to the rear by jeep to check on some rations and ammunition. He came to a major crossroads, which was congested from all four directions by heavy traffic, with no one directing traffic. No MPs. Nash jumped out of his jeep to investigate the problem. Reaching the intersection, he heard someone say in a loud, authoritative voice, "Captain, come here." Nash looked around to face the Eighth Army commander, General Walker, who asked: "What's going on here? What are these units?" Nash replied: "I just arrived, sir. I don't know." Walker said: "Are you in command here?" Nash said: "No, sir." With that the general threw up his arms and shouted: *"Then assume command!"* Several hours later, when he got back to our CP, Nash was still shaking.[6]

## II

The scale of the NKPA September 1 offensive was large; its main parts were complex. Clockwise around the perimeter were four major battles, all launched simultaneously.

### Southwest Sector

The NKPA 6th and 7th divisions (about 20,000 men), attacking out of Chinju toward Masan, moved line abreast along two familiar routes: the 6th on the "south road" and the 7th on the "north road." They were supported by tanks and motorized artillery.

The NKPA 6th Division, perhaps deliberately, aimed enormous power—two full regiments—directly at the black 24th Regiment. The result, in the account of the Army historian, was instant chaos and disaster.[7]

Ever since its minor victory at Yechon in July, morale in the 24th Regiment (under two successive white commanders, Horton White and the fifty-seven-year-old Art Champeny) had been going steadily downhill. Many black officers who were present would continue to insist that the fault was largely attributable to inept white leadership.

During the month of August the 24th Infantry had been continuously on the front line on Hill 625, which would be remembered as "Battle Mountain." The fighting there had been particularly vicious and arduous. The regiment had incurred a total of 500 battle casualties (75 dead, 425 wounded); many others were felled by the heat. A veteran of the fight remembered that Battle Mountain changed hands "nineteen times" in August. During the battle the 2/24 had three commanders: Horace Donaho, George R. Cole, and finally, Paul Roberts, the regimental exec, who assumed command temporarily.[8]

The Army historian's account of the 24th's August fighting on Battle Mountain is the most scathing indictment of an Army regiment (white or black) ever published. Black GIs are repeatedly depicted as fleeing cowards, white officers as heroic figures attempting to stem the stampedes, often at great personal risk. Many black officers who were on the scene insist that the historian's account (which fails to note the 24th's 500 battle casualties) is grossly inaccurate and racist, part of the Army's public "lynching" of the regiment, which, they assert, did no worse than some white regiments. Until an objective history of the 24th Infantry in Korea is produced the truth of this account cannot be assessed.[9]

When the NKPA 6th Division struck the 24th Infantry on September 1, the Army historian wrote, "most of the 2nd Battalion . . . fled its positions" and was soon "no longer an effective fighting force."[10] This opened a gap in the 25th Division front through which the two NKPA regiments poured, endangering the whole 25th Division and its supply base at Haman. But the commander of the 2/24's F Company, paratrooper Roger Walden, whom the historian did not interview, took issue with the official account:

My F Company held the right sector of the battalion and G Company held the left sector. When the North Koreans struck I was personally in the OP [outpost] position in my right platoon's area. My left platoon was adjacent to G Company, just off the road passing through the battalion sector. My third platoon was in reserve.

The North Koreans attacked down the road and (I assume) penetrated G Company, then continued on the road to overrun the battalion CP area. My F Company *did not flee*. It never evaporated or disappeared, nor did it panic. We stayed put and engaged the enemy all night long and suffered heavy casualties. My left platoon was badly mauled. . . . During the night we lost all communications with battalion headquarters.

Previous instructions had stated that [in event of a NKPA penetration] we were to move rearward to the next high ground. At daylight we did so—*on my order*. But the North Koreans were in our rear and now held that ground. Having only fifty to seventy troops with me and no communications with battalion, I figured an attack on the hill would have been disastrous. Believing it more important to move north and tell the 35th Infantry its left flank was now exposed, we did so—again *on my order*—giving them a complete report of the North Korean penetration. On my order we then marched several miles rearward to the 25th Division CP [near Haman] where we manned a perimeter while the 2/24 was reorganized. On about September 4 the reorganized battalion moved back into its original positions.[11]

In the meantime, the historian wrote, Art Champeny had ordered the 1/24, commanded by Gerald G. Miller, to counterattack and close the gap. The temporary 2/24 commander, Paul Roberts, and about forty of his men joined the attack. However, the historian wrote, "upon contact with the enemy, the 1st Battalion broke and fled to the rear."[12]

When word of the heavy NKPA penetration in the 24th Infantry sector reached Bill Kean he had a contingency plan ready. It called for Throckmorton's 5th Regiment to counterattack northward out of Chingdong, while Michaelis's 27th counterattacked westward out of Masan. Since the Wolfhounds were still technically in Eighth Army reserve, Kean had to request authority to commit them. Walker was cautious; he would release only one battalion, Gilbert Check's 1/27.[13]

When Check reached Champeny's CP near Masan, the scene, as described by the Army historian, was "chaotic":

Vehicles of all descriptions, loaded with soldiers, were moving down the road to the rear. Many soldiers on foot were on the road. Colonel Champney [*sic*] tried repeatedly but in vain to get these men to halt. The few enemy mortar shells falling occasionally in the vicinity did no damage except to cause the troops of the 24th Infantry and intermingled South Koreans to scatter and increase their speed to the rear. The road was so clogged with this frightened, demoralized human traffic that Colonel Check had to delay his counterattack. In the six hours he waited at this point, Check observed that none of the retreating troops of the 1st and 2nd battalions, 24th Infantry, could be assembled as units.[14]

The counterattack by Check, supported by Throckmorton, temporarily closed the hole in the 24th's line and inflicted heavy casualties on the NKPA. Champeny, Roberts, Miller, and Check rounded up the 1/24 and 2/24 and put them back in the line, but almost immediately, the Army historian wrote, the units gave way again. In the ensuing debacle Walker authorized Kean to commit George De Chow's 3/27 to assist Check. Utterly exasperated, Kean, writing that the 24th Infantry was "untrustworthy and incapable of carrying out missions expected of an infantry regiment," urged Walker to disband the outfit and reassign its troops as fillers in the white regiments. But Walker was not willing to commence formal integration in Eighth Army or lose yet another numbered regiment.[15]

On September 6 Art Champeny and some staffers visited the 24th's forward positions in Walden's F Company sector. Walden remembered: "Informed that they were going to check the front line, I told them to be careful, that when they topped the ridge they might receive sniper fire. Colonel Champeny made some demeaning comment about whether I was afraid or something of that nature. It kind of teed me off that he would make such a statement when I was trying to tell him something to protect him. A few minutes later he had been shot and evacuated."[16]

Champeny's wound was not serious, fortunately. After a month in the hospital he was discharged and ultimately assigned to KMAG. Later promoted to brigadier general, he was placed in charge of training ROK troops for combat. Still later, however, Champeny got into serious trouble in that job. His boss, the KMAG chief, Cornelius E. Ryan, recommended that Champeny be busted back to colonel and sent home, for what was officially deemed to be a "flagrant failure to render prompt and loyal support to the expressed policies and decisions of his superior officers." The Far East high command concurred, remarking that Champeny's characteristics" were "not compatible with those required in an officer holding a high rank in the united States Army." Champeny returned to the States, but he held on to his star, retiring at that rank in 1953.[17]

Who would replace Champeny as commander of the 24th Infantry? Was there anyone willing and able to take what was perceived to be a perilous, thankless, and possibly career-ruining chore?

One man stepped forward: John Corley. Bill Kean was pleased. Corley had taken a firm grip on the 3/24. Perhaps he could work his magical leadership on the entire 24th Infantry. Kean gave Corley a battlefield promotion to colonel and named him commander. Having turned thirty-six on August 4, Corley became the youngest regimental commander in Korea.[18]

His first task was to assess and reorganize the 24th's subordinate senior white commanders. Gerald Miller was not blamed for the bugout of the 1/24; he retained command. The able Paul Roberts, temporarily commanding the disorganized 2/24, returned to his job as regimental exec. To the regimental staff, Corley added his combat-experienced (ETO) West Point classmate (1938) and best man at his wedding, Joseph B. Missal. Both the 2/24 and the 3/24 had several temporary commanders during the next several weeks, until Corley settled on two men with World War II combat experience: George A. Clayton, thirty-three, for the 2/24, and Melvin R. Blair, thirty-four, for the 3/24. Blair seemed a fitting prospect to fill Corley's big shoes in the 3/24. He had won a DSC and a Purple Heart and other awards fighting with Merrill's Marauders in the Burma jungles in World War II.[19]

In an attempt to rebuild morale in the 24th Infantry, Corley adopted "Remember Yechon!" as the regimental rallying cry and issued a statement to his men: "In sixty days of continuous combat you have witnessed a roughness of battle which I have not seen in five campaigns in Africa, Sicily, Europe with the 1st Infantry Division. You have held ground against superior odds. You have lived up to the regimental motto, *Semper Paratus* [Always ready]. The first United States victory in Korea was your action at Yechon. It has been noted in Congress. The people back home cover in detail your efforts. . . . Other units have been unable to accomplish what depleted companies of the fighting 24th have done. I am proud of you."[20]

\* \* \*

Immediately to the north of the 24th Infantry sector, powerful elements of both the NKPA 6th and 7th divisions struck Hank Fisher's 35th Infantry, deployed along the much fought-over "north road." Fisher was ready. Like the 5th and 27th regiments, his 35th was combat-hardened. Recently it, too, had been brought to full strength by the addition of the other Okinawa battalion, the 1/29 (redesignated 3/35), now commanded by a World War II veteran, Robert L. Woolfolk III, thirty-five.[21]

Thousands of NKPA troops swarmed at Fisher's positions. In an awesome display of courage, tenacity, and battlefield skill, the 1/35 under Bernard Teeters, the 2/35 under John Wilkin, and Woolfolk's 3/35 held steady on their positions, inflicting an appalling slaughter on the NKPA. However, when an attached ROK element gave way, 3,000 of the enemy went around Fisher's flanks and isolated the 35th.[22]

When Kean heard that Fisher was surrounded and cut off, he urgently requested authority to commit the remaining battalion of the Wolfhounds. Maddeningly, Eighth Army headquarters refused. Believing Walker had not been apprised of the gravity of the situation, Kean ignored the refusal and, on his own authority, ordered Gordon Murch's 2/27 forward. Later, again on his own authority, Kean diverted George De Chow's 3/27 from Corley's 24th sector to assist in the rescue mission.[23]

Backed by tanks and unusually effective FEAF close air support, Murch and De Chow broke through the swarms of NKPA to Fisher's perimeter. They found him coolly manning his CP. "I never intended to withdraw," Hank Fisher said laconically; "there was no place to go." Thereafter, while he remained on his perimeter positions, Murch and De Chow, soon joined by Check's 1/27, savaged the NKPA in Fisher's rear, killing no fewer than 2,000.[24]

By these timely and aggressive actions, Kean's 25th Division not only repulsed but virtually destroyed the NKPA 6th and 7th divisions. Much of the credit was due Kean for overriding Eighth Army's obtuse orders to hold the Wolfhounds in reserve. Throckmorton and Fisher were credited for outstanding work in holding firm on the division flanks; in particular, Fisher won a DSC, and the 35th was awarded a Presidential Unit Citation. The publicity again went to Michaelis's Fire Brigade, first for closing the hole in the 24th Infantry, secondly for cracking through to Fisher's perimeter, thirdly for the savage slaughter inflicted on the NKPA in Fisher's rear. The publicity was not undeserved.

## The Naktong Bulge

Owing to the recent carnage inflicted on the NKPA 4th Division in the Naktong Bulge and an unusual and unfortunate breakdown in intelligence, Walker did not expect the strong NKPA attack in Dutch Keiser's 2d Division sector. Paul Freeman, who was not privy to the secrets of code breaking, later put it this way: "Eighth Army had superior intelligence. . . . They seemed to know where everything was coming. General Walker and his staff did a magnificent job of getting his few troops to the right place at the right time to stop some attack or other, and how he missed out on this one I can't understand. But we certainly did miss out on it."[25]

Lacking a battalion each, Hill's 9th and Freeman's 23d were thinly deployed, one battalion outposting the river, one behind in reserve. Moreover, the battalions were not solidly dug in. Dutch Keiser did not encourage the customary (and prudent) use of sandbags, barbed wire, and other measures to strengthen defensive positions on the dubious ground that it would rob the troops of their offensive spirit.

This need to act offensively—no doubt heartily approved by Walker—had led Keiser to dispatch the Manchus of John Hill's 9th Infantry on a strong but, as it turned out, ill-timed probing mission across the Naktong. To man this hush-hush mission (Operation Manchu), Hill called on his reserve company, some engineers, elements of his two heavy-weapons companies, and other forces, consisting of nearly 700 men. This redeployment further, and drastically, thinned out the 9th Infantry river line, rendering it highly vulnerable to enemy attack.[26]

Opposite Hill and Freeman, the NKPA had concentrated two divisions, the 2d and green 9th in the 4th Division sector. The 9th Division (9,350 men) in the southernmost zone, faced Hill's Manchus. The 2d (6,000 men), to the north of it, faced Freeman's 23d. These divisions and surviving elements of the 4th (about 5,500 men) comprised in total about 21,000 men. They were to cross the Naktong, drive through the bulge to Yongsan, then angle southeasterly toward Miryang, linking with the 6th and 7th divisions for the all-out assault on Pusan. They were backed by considerable artillery.

The NKPA 9th Division, reinforced by some 4th Division survivors, crossed the Naktong into John Hill's 9th Infantry sector. The attack utterly surprised Hill and his regimental staff and Keiser's aide-de-camp, West Pointer (1945) Thomas A. Lombardo, all of whom were at the river, launching Operation Manchu. Hill survived, but his S-3 and Lombardo were killed in the onslaught, as were many others. Caught flat-footed and ill-deployed for defense, the 9th Infantry was almost immediately overrun and disorganized, leaving the door to Yongsan wide open.[27]

Many men of the 9th Infantry caved in and surrendered. But others fought back heroically, at or beyond the river or before Yongsan. Four enlisted men of the 9th Infantry, all killed, won the Medal of Honor in these actions: Luther H. Story of the 1/9 and Loren R. Kaufman, Joseph R. Ouelette, and Travis E. Watkins of the 2/9. Two other enlisted men of the 2d Division units supporting the 9th Infantry also won the Medal of Honor: Ernest R. Kouma, who survived, and Charles W. Turner, who was killed. In the 2/9 West Pointer (1950) John M. Murphy, who was cadet first captain of the class, and later a congressman (1962–1980) from New York, won a DSC.[28]*

Simultaneously the weaker NKPA 2d Division, also reinforced by some 4th Division survivors, crossed the Naktong and struck Paul Freeman's 23d, in the sector directly north. Fortunately Freeman was not also engaged in a probing attack. But his river line was paper-thin, manned only by Claire Hutchin's 1/23. Overwhelmed by the force of this massive surprise attack, the 1/23 was scattered and disorganized, and many of the surviving elements were cut off and isolated. Freeman counterattacked with part of his reserve, James Edwards's 2/23, but despite the bravery of the 2/23 exec, Lloyd K. Jenson, who led the attack and won a DSC, the 2/23 could not link with the 1/23. In the chaos of this hand-to-hand battle Freeman's CP was overrun, and he was very nearly lost.[30]

To the north of Freeman's 23d Infantry sector stood Keiser's green three-battalion 38th Regiment, which had been in Korea a total of eleven days. The 38th was commanded by West Pointer (1925) George B. ("Pep") Peploe, fifty. Unlike Hill and Freeman, whom the Pentagon had foisted on Keiser at the last minute, Peploe was a "Keiser man" who had commanded the 38th since August 1949. However, like Hill and Freeman, Peploe was a "staff officer" who had never commanded troops in battle. In World War II he had been G-3 of a Stateside infantry division of the Armored Command at Fort Knox, and of XIII Corps, which fought in the ETO.[31]

Those who knew Peploe well admired his professional competence and coolness under fire, but they had mixed and contradictory recollections of him as a person. His 2/38 commander, West Pointer (1937) James H. Skeldon, thirty-six, judged him this way: "I considered Pep to be an extremely able C.O. who was courageous, peppery (hence his nickname, Pep), smart, aggressive, analytical, cynical, vindictive at times but amenable to reason." Another West Pointer who served under Peploe remembered: "He was a driver, not a leader. He would rip into you, but he wouldn't balance it out with praise. He'd try, but when it came to praise, he'd freeze up and people would wind up mad at him." Peploe's S-3, Warren D. Hodges, twenty-seven, thought Peploe was able and brave but could be "impetuous." Hodges told this story to illustrate the latter characteristic: "When we were first facing the North Koreans on the Naktong, some of the GIs, showing good initiative, fashioned rafts and swam the river in darkness to make probes in enemy positions. In the process they

---

*Murphy was wounded during this action but returned to his unit. About one-half of the West Pointers from the classes of 1949 and 1950 in the infantry branch were rushed to Korea to serve as platoon leaders or company commanders. Casualties in this group were very high. In the class of 1949: 27 killed; 52 wounded. In the class of 1950: 34 killed; 84 wounded. Casualties among junior officers from the classes of 1945–1948 were less severe, but still heavy compared to casualties among non-West Point officers: a total of 61 killed, 124 wounded.[29]

lost their helmets and shoes and other equipment. Since they had gulped some river water, they were advised to get typhoid boosters. Pep, unaware of all this, happened to come along when the men were in the aid station getting the shots. Seeing them without helmets and shoes, he laced into them something awful. Later, when he was briefed on the initiative they had shown, he gave all of them medals."[32]

The NKPA 10th Division, which had been trounced by the 7th Cavalry in the August fighting, was positioned opposite the 38th Regiment. It was under orders to attack easterly in coordination with the NKPA 2d Division, but for reasons not known, it failed to execute these orders. A few scattered 10th Division troops infiltrated Peploe's sector, but not in sufficient numbers to pose a serious threat. So spared, Peploe was able to "lend" Paul Freeman his 3/38, commanded by Everett S. Stewart.[33]

*  *  *

The heavy NKPA penetration into Keiser's 2d Division in effect cut it in half, with Freeman's 23d and Peploe's 38th on the northern side of the breach and Hill's shattered 9th on the southern side. Operating from his well-guarded CP, Keiser put his ADC, Sladen Bradley, in charge of the southern sector and his artillery commander, Loyal Haynes, in charge of the northern sector.[34]

Paul Freeman and Loyal Haynes clashed. Freeman remembered:

I scarcely knew Haynes. He was fifty-five at the time, not robust. . . . Finding himself nearly in the front lines of desperate hand-to-hand combat did not appeal to him—to say the least. My first problem with Haynes was his calling me to report to him at his CP some miles to the rear. Twice this happened when we were at the critical stage of repulsing strong enemy attacks. Not only did I have to leave my CP but literally had to fight my way through rear area infiltrators to get to his CP. I finally told him in a *respectful* way that I believed it improper to summon a commander to the rear during a firefight and suggested he send one of his staff forward to *my* CP if he didn't want to come himself. Moreover, he diverted a tank company, sent to reinforce my sector, to reinforce the protection of his own CP.[35]

The command relationship rapidly deteriorated to the point that Haynes made the drastic decision to relieve Freeman. Freeman continued: "The only time Haynes came to my position was when he came mincingly through the mud to tell me I was relieved and to report to the division CP. I was so shocked and furious that I got in my jeep and drove right through the enemy positions to get there. . . . I had no respect for him from then on."[36]

The division G-3, Maurice G. Holden, remembered the incident this way: "Haynes went up there and not long afterwards we got a coded message from him like 'Request permission to relieve Freeman of command Twenty-third

Infantry.' Keiser was an old friend of Freeman's, and he didn't really want to relieve him; but under the circumstances he had to follow the recommendation of the task force commander. He sent a message back to Haynes like 'Concur. Send Freeman to division headquarters.' So Freeman—relieved—turned over the Twenty-third to his exec [Ed Messinger] and came in, totally exhausted, and fell dead asleep. In the meantime, Keiser sent me up to see the Twenty-third—to find out what happened and if the relief was justified. The Twenty-third staff thought Haynes was terrible; he'd never even been near the front. He had no idea what was going on. Keiser was glad to hear that. We woke up Freeman, and Keiser sent him back to his command."[37]

Thereafter Freeman ignored Haynes and ran the battlefield the way he thought best. Making good use of Peploe's 3/38 and ably assisted by his combat-experienced senior officers (Ed Messinger, James Edwards, Butch Barberis, Lloyd Jenson among others), Freeman got the 23d reorganized and dug into strong defensive positions on the "north shoulder" of the NKPA breakthrough. The fighting that ensued was furious and bloody. The 1/23 and 2/23 suffered nearly 50 percent casualties, including the commanders of all six rifle companies. In return, the 23d claimed to have virtually wiped out the NKPA 2d Division, inflicting, according to Freeman, "more than 5,000 casualties." Later official records confirmed this claim.[38]

Meanwhile, to the south the division ADC, Sladen Bradley, and John Hill were desperately trying to piece together the badly shattered 9th Infantry. As Bradley remembered it, Hill became physically exhausted and suffered a mental shock at having his regiment so badly decimated. Bradley recommended to Keiser that Hill be temporarily relieved for a rest at the division CP, but Keiser balked at that. He had already decided to sack Hill and reinstate the 9th's former commander, Chin Sloane. Hill, Bradley remembered, made a rapid recovery and demonstrated remarkable leadership by gathering together the companies of his regiment as they were able to escape and organizing them into an effective fighting force, which fell back on Yongsan.

\* \* \*

When Johnnie Walker learned that the 2d Division had been cut in half, he rushed to Keiser's CP. There Walker issued another of his unfortunate "stand or die" edicts. "We shall not surrender another inch," he told Keiser (who dutifully relayed the message to his troops), "and we shall hold regardless of cost."[39]

After sizing up the situation, Walker came to a difficult and drastic decision: Once again he would have to call on Eddie Craig's Marines for help. The decision was drastic both because of the humiliation it would again cause the Army and because Craig's Marines were a vital element in the Inchon invasion plan. MacArthur had limited Walker's control of the Marines to September 4, with the tacit understanding they would not again be committed to combat in the perimeter. Walker had not only to commit them to combat but also to ask for an indefinite extension of his control. As he well knew, this request could cause a postponement, or even a cancellation, of Inchon.[40]

For Walker it was a case of immediate and urgent need. He became "extremely excited" and telephoned Ned Almond to deliver an ultimatum that shook GHQ, Tokyo: "If I lose the 5th Marine Regiment I will not be responsible for the safety of the front." After consulting with MacArthur, Almond called back to say that Walker could use the Marines in combat as was necessary; his control of them was extended beyond September 4.[41]

\* \* \*

As Walker had foreseen, the decision to recommit Craig's Marines in the perimeter led to extreme difficulties among Inchon planners in Tokyo. The Fifth Marines and the First Marines (made up of called-up reservists not yet annealed in combat) were to spearhead the assault. The more experienced Fifth Marines were scheduled for the most hazardous missions at Red Beach: the assault on Wolmi Island, the seawalls, and the city of Inchon itself. It would not be prudent or fair to order the First Marines, scheduled to land at the less hazardous Blue Beach, to carry out these Red Beach missions. Furthermore, the other regiment, the Seventh Marines, would not arrive in time to substitute in the assault.

Seeking a possible solution to the problem, Ned Almond suggested that Charles Beauchamp's 32d Regiment (of the 7th Division), which was scheduled to go ashore behind the Marines, be substituted for Craig's Fifth Marines. The commander of the 1st Marine Division, O. P. Smith, was flabbergasted. The 32d Infantry had had no amphibious training. It was composed of about 40 percent ROKs—raw recruits with no training who could not speak English. "It became apparent to me," Smith noted in his journal, "that there was a complete lack of understanding at GHQ concerning the manner in which amphibious forces are mounted out." He said later that he "bitterly protested" this idea.[42]

The Marine objections led to a *High Noon* meeting between Almond and the Navy-Marine contingent on September 3. Almond opened the meeting by categorically stating that Inchon would go, as planned, on September 15 and the 32d Infantry would substitute for the Fifth Marines. A "heated discussion" ensued. Admiral Turner Joy, who "carried the ball," Smith remembered, "really read off General Almond." When asked for his view on substituting the 32d Infantry in "Red Beach" missions originally assigned to the Fifth Marines, Smith absolutely refused to use the 32d in the assault. Rather than do that, he would substitute the First Marines at Red Beach and cancel Blue Beach, a modification in the plan that would be "very risky."[43]

As the meeting dragged on in acrimonious debate, Admiral Struble suddenly proposed a compromise: Pull the Fifth Marines out of the perimeter after brief use in the Naktong Bulge and send Walker another regiment of the 7th Division—the 17th—for a reserve. In Struble's proposal, the 17th would remain aboard ship off Pusan and not land except in case of dire emergency. If the situation in the perimeter developed in such a way that Walker could get by without it, the 17th would then be brought around to form the tail end of the Inchon force.[44]

This idea appealed to Almond. Later he enlarged upon it. He would not only give Walker the 17th Infantry as a floating reserve but also divert to him (to land in Pusan) the Puerto Rican 65th Regiment, vanguard of the Army's 3d Division, which was en route from the States to Japan and which could be in Pusan by September 20, substituting for the 17th Infantry. Although MacArthur had assured the JCS that the 3d Division would remain in Japan (substituting for the Inchon-bound 7th Division), he approved the plan without further recourse to the JCS and said to Almond: "Tell Walker he will have to give up the Fifth Marine Regiment."[45]

And so it was decided. Walker could employ Eddie Craig's Fifth Marines in the Naktong Bulge in support of the 2d Division with a twenty-four-hour extension, to midnight, September 5. After that it would outload at Pusan for Inchon. As a substitute, Walker would get the 17th Regiment in floating reserve to be relieved on September 20 by the 65th Regiment, which would land in Pusan. Walker could not have been pleased with this decision. The Puerto Rican 65th Regiment, ridiculed in the Army as the "Rum and Coke" Regiment, was perceived as no more reliable than the 24th Infantry. It was a poor substitute for the Fifth Marines. However, knowing that MacArthur had approved the compromise, Walker made no further comments.[46]

\* \* \*

The Fifth Marines reentered combat on September 3 in John Hill's 9th Infantry sector around Yongsan. It was the second time the Marines had come into the Naktong Bulge to rescue the Army. They knew the enemy and the terrain well. They counterattacked without delay, with Hill's ragtag 9th Infantry covering the right (or north) flank. By then, Sladen Bradley remembered, Hill had "regained his composure and had recuperated physically to a marked degree."[47]

The Marines, advancing methodically and well supported by tanks, artillery, and Marine close air, inflicted a terrible slaughter on the green NKPA 9th Division. The Marine historian wrote that the "picture of devastation" was "unequalled even by the earlier defeat of the NKPA 4th Division." There were "hundreds of enemy dead" strewn along the road, hillsides, and ridgelines. Moreover, as they drove toward the Naktong, the Marines provided the Army an unexpected dividend. They recaptured "a great quantity of United States Army equipment" abandoned earlier in the war: tanks, artillery, mortars, vehicles, small arms, ammo.[48]

In a mere two days—by September 5—the Marines wiped out the NKPA 9th Division. No exact accounting of its casualties was ever made. Perhaps as many as 5,000 NKPA troops fell. Whatever the number, the 9th Division was "not able to resume the offensive," the Army historian wrote. When the Marines withdrew at midnight—per MacArthur's decision—the remnants of Hill's 9th Infantry took over the ground regained by the Marines.[49]

As the Marines were withdrawing from this battle, Commander in Chief Harry Truman delivered them a grievous and gratuitous blow below the belt, which arose from his long and petty distrust of the Navy and its admirals. In response to a letter from a congressman proposing that the Marine Corps be enlarged, Truman wrote, in part: "For your information, the Marine Corps is the Navy's police force and as long as I am President that is what it will remain. They have a propaganda machine that is almost equal to Stalin's." The congressman released the letter to the press; Marines worldwide were naturally outraged. Although Truman publicly apologized to Marine Commandant Clifton B. Cates, most Marines remained bitter toward him.[50]

John Hill did not enjoy the fruits of this victory. Dutch Keiser sacked him, giving the 9th back to Chin Sloane. Hill was the fifth American regimental commander to be fired in Korea. Not much was said about the others, but Hill's case became controversial. Some believed the sacking was justified; others, including Sladen Bradley, believed it was unfair, that the 9th had been mauled principally because it was carrying out Keiser's ill-timed Operation Manchu. When Hill came up for promotion to brigadier general in 1953, Bradley (then a major general) and Matt Ridgway (then Army chief of staff) sided with Hill against Keiser, and Hill got his star. But it was a Pyrrhic victory: Owing to an Army rule, Hill was forced to retire.[51]*

*       *       *

The job of rebuilding the two shattered battalions of the 9th Infantry fell to its new commander, Chin Sloane. He retained John Londahl as commander of the 1/9 but replaced the 2/9 commander, Joe Walker, with the able, aggressive, and combat-experienced Butch Barberis from Freeman's 23d. To fill out the depleted ranks in the two battalions Sloane (almost alone among regimental commanders in Korea) willingly accepted black fillers. Barberis remembered the infusion of blacks into his 2/9: "I was very, very low on men—less than half strength—and raised hell to get more troops. The division G-one called and, knowing that I had previously commanded a battalion of black troops [in the 25th Infantry], said he had almost two hundred blacks

---

*The so-called thirty and five rule, put into effect in 1954 and designed to rid the Army of its "bulge" of senior officers left over from World War II. Under its terms, officers who had thirty years' service and had not been promoted within five years were compelled to retire. Hill's promotion came a little too late.

from labor units in Pusan that had served in my battalion who would transfer to the infantry if they could serve with me. I agreed. In fact, I was proud to have them. Keiser asked me if I realized what a can of worms I was opening up, to which I said, 'So what? They are good fighting men. I need men.' "[52]*

## Northwest Sector

Directly to the north of Keiser's 2d Division stood Hap Gay's 1st Cavalry Division, still holding the northwest sector. Gay's responsibility had been enlarged—and complicated—by Walker's decision to withdraw Michaelis's Wolfhounds and Freeman's 23d from the Bowling Alley. To fill that critical gap in the defense of Taegu, the 1st Cav had extended itself farther north and east and redeployed two of its regiments. Marcel Crombez's 5th Cav remained on its positions east of Waegwan, blocking the Taejon–Taegu road, but Cecil Nist's 7th Cav had leapfrogged from the 5th's left flank to its right flank, and Ray Palmer's 8th Cav had come around to the right of the 7th Cav to block the Bowling Alley. Into the void on the left (or south) flank of the division, caused by the repositioning of the 7th Cav, Walker had temporarily deployed Freeman's attached 3/23 at Yongpo, where the 2/7 had trounced the NKPA 10th Division, which was still opposite that place but was still mysteriously quiescent.[53]

The 1st Cav's front was very long by the usual military standards, but the division now had a little more manpower and artillery to cover its key roads and hills. In the last week of August three new American battalions arrived to bring the three regiments up to authorized strength. In addition to these, Gay could call on the two infantry battalions of the British 27th Infantry Brigade, which arrived from Hong Kong at about the same time and which Walker placed in reserve in hills on the division's south flank, behind the attached 3/23. Altogether Hap Gay had at his call twelve numbered infantry battalions, backed by five artillery battalions—the four normally serving the 1st Cav, plus the 9th FAB (155-mm howitzers) which had come independently to Korea and which had been supporting the ROK 1st Division.

Inasmuch as the six "veteran" infantry battalions of the 1st Cav had suffered very heavy casualties in the July and August fighting, Gay warmly welcomed the three new American battalions. These had been hurriedly slapped together in the States and rushed to Pusan. Two of the three had had

---

*Inasmuch as the full-strength 3/9 (still at Pohang) was entirely black, the infusion of black fillers into the 1/9 and 2/9 would give the 9th Regiment as a whole a very high percentage of black personnel.

no field training; however, all were well equipped and well officered, and each contained many combat-experienced NCOs. The units were:

- *The 3/5:* Commanded by West Pointer (1935) Edgar J. Treacy, thirty-six, this battalion had been the 3d Battalion of the 14th Infantry Regiment at Camp Carson, Colorado. Treacy, a combat intelligence expert in the ETO and Southwest Pacific, had not before led troops in combat; but his battalion was full-strength (900 men) and it had been trained in mountain climbing and cross-country skiing. Its men were thus in excellent physical condition.[54]
- *The 3/7:* Commanded by West Pointer (1938) James H. Lynch, thirty-six, the younger of two sons of a West Point general and former chief of infantry, the nearly full-strength battalion (800 men) had been formed from disparate remnants of the gutted 3d Division elements at Fort Benning. Lynch, who had not commanded troops in combat in World War II, had only had time for "about two weeks' " training before embarking, but aboard ship he had rigged telephones between staterooms and rehearsed his officers in command exercises, while the NCOs directed rifle practice topside.[55]
- *The 3/8:* Commanded by West Pointer (1933) Harold K. ("Johnny") Johnson, thirty-eight, this battalion had been formed from the 7th Infantry Regiment of the 3d Division at Fort Devon, Massachusetts. Comprised of 704 men who had not even trained at platoon level, the battalion was described by Johnson as a "thrown-together outfit," rated "zero" in combat effectiveness. But the battalion had a "crackerjack" exec, Johnson remembered, who was a "very good technician" and a "stiff disciplinarian" and who "loved soldiering"; some "cracking good lieutenants"; and "some good non-commissioned officers, longtime professionals."[56]

Of these three battalion commanders, Johnny Johnson was destined to go right to the top of the Army: four stars and chief of staff (1964–68) in the Vietnam War era. He was, in the words of a contemporary, "a very intelligent, very serious," restrained, and modest man, a "devoutly religious Catholic" who could "say a prayer without sounding phony" and who insisted that no one blaspheme in his presence. Early in World War II Johnson, commanding a battalion on Bataan, had been captured by the Japanese. His religious faith and strong inner courage had carried him through the Death March and three years' imprisonment in the Philippines, Japan, and Korea. He emerged from that experience a skeleton (100 pounds) who was barely able to walk and who believed his Army career was finished because of the Army prejudice against those who had surrendered on Bataan. But in the postwar years he had brought himself up-to-date, he had attended the Command and General Staff School, and by quietly but firmly asserting himself, he had got assigned to the 7th Infantry.

When Johnson's battalion was attached to the 8th Cav, its commander, Ray Palmer, in recognition of Johnson's ability and seniority, offered to promote him regimental exec. Johnson turned the job down. "I believed that somebody who knew the battalion had to stay with it until it had engaged in battle. I preferred being a battalion commander to being a regimental executive officer anyway."[57]

In contrast, Marcel Crombez resented the arrival of Edgar Treacy in the 5th Cav. During World War II Treacy, a handsome, bright Army "comer," had become a protege of XIV Corps commander Oscar W. Griswold and was promoted to full colonel—on a par with Crombez, who was ten years his senior. As such—the story went—Crombez and Treacy had crossed swords someplace. One account had it that Treacy had served on a board which had recommended Crombez's reduction in rank to lieutenant colonel after the war. Whether this was the case, or whether, as others in the 3/5 analyzed it, Crombez was "jealous" of Treacy's high Army connections and "command presence" and obvious bright future, there was an instant personality clash between Crombez and Treacy which would lead to extreme difficulties for the 3/5 and ultimately, some would charge, to Treacy's death. The S-3 of the 1/5, Jim Gibson, remembered: "The Third Battalion hated Crombez and vice versa."[58]

\* \* \*

The NKPA offensive in the northwest sector was mounted by the three NKPA divisions already in place: the 1st, 3d, and 13th. The 3d and 13th had been reinforced with fillers, the former to 7,000 men, the latter to 9,000 men. In total, the three divisions numbered about 22,000 men, of whom probably a third were green, untrained recruits, many of whom did not possess individual weapons. Many of these fillers had to be prodded into battle at pistol point.[59]

Knowing in advance this NKPA attack in the northwest sector was coming, Walker gave Gay orders to launch a "spoiling" attack to disrupt it. These orders were in keeping with Walker's personal belief in a strong offense as the best defense, a view that was not in conflict with Army doctrine. However, in view of the fact that the 1st Cav was only just finding itself, had never engaged in large-scale offensive operations, and was composed of many depleted or green, untried battalions and two regimental commanders (Cecil Nist, Ray Palmer) who were question marks, Walker's orders may have been premature and ill advised. The creation of a strong defensive posture with a substantial mobile reserve (such as Clainos's Clouters) to meet the NKPA attack might have been a better alternative.[60]

At first Gay—no shrinking violet—wanted to attack straight up the Bowling Alley with Ray Palmer's 8th Cav. The staff, however, persuaded him to attack from the division center with Cecil Nist's 7th Cav, which had recently got its 1/7 back from the Eighth Army reserve and one of the new battalions from the States. Although the 7th Cav had never fought as a unified three-battalion unit, Gay bowed to his staff recommendations. To support this attack, Gay put most of the division artillery behind the 7th Cav, thus dangerously thinning out other defenses. In addition, he called on FEAF to deliver a massive strike, employing bombs and napalm.[61]

Nist designated his two battle-tested battalions to spearhead the attack: the 1/7 under Pete Clainos and the 2/7, which, because of the temporary absence of Gil Huff, recovering from a wound, was commanded by Omar T. Hitchner. But Murphy's Law prevailed; everything that could go wrong did. The FEAF strike was a flop; the massive artillery salvos did little damage; the plan of attack was poor. The well-entrenched NKPA troops, supported by 82-mm and 120-mm mortars, decisively repulsed Clainos and Hitchner. A second ill-advised attack by James Lynch's new and untested 3/7, replacing the 1/7, did no better.[62]

This futile spoiling attack had the effect of poorly disposing the entire division to meet the NKPA offensive. When it struck, the 1st Cav reeled in disarray. Major elements in all three regiments were soon outflanked. In some units soldiers bugged out, abandoning weapons, vehicles, and ammo. The 7th Cav was the worst offender. Finding hundreds of NKPA soldiers on the hills in its rear, it had to fight its way back toward its point of departure. In so doing, it all but disintegrated. In this chaotic withdrawal through the hills, some 7th Cav companies became separated and had to fight alone. The temporary 2/7 commander, Omar Hitchner, was killed; pending Gil Huff's return, the battalion was completely reorganized by a new exec, thirty-four-year-old West Pointer (1942) John W. Callaway.[63]

When the 7th Cav fell apart in the division center Marcel Crombez's 5th Cav, on the left at Waegwan, was exposed. At that time Paul Clifford's 2/5 had just retaken Hill 303 again. When the NKPA 3d Division swarmed at Hill 303, Clifford prudently and wisely requested permission to withdraw, but Crombez refused, giving as his reason that Clifford had to hold Hill 303 until all elements of the 7th Cav had safely withdrawn. Clifford stayed put on Hill 303 as ordered, but in doing so he incurred very heavy casualties.[64]

On the division right the NKPA 13th Division hit hard at Ray Palmer's poorly deployed 8th Cav, astride the Bowling Alley. The enemy overran Gerald Robbins's thin 2/8, forcing it to withdraw hurriedly. Palmer brought up Johnny Johnson's 3/8, which managed to block long enough for the 2/8 to straggle through to the rear. This NKPA victory gave it not only the long-sought town of Tabu, but also the commanding high ground on Hill 902, where the ruins of an ancient walled city, Kasan, provided good long-range mortar positions overlooking Taegu—merely ten air miles to the south.[65]

Believing the main NKPA attack was aimed down the Bowling Alley, and that the NKPA hold on Hill 902 imperiled the 1st Cav—and Taegu—Johnnie Walker insisted that Hap Gay retake Hill 902 immediately. Gay delegated that tough task to Ray Palmer's 8th Cav, reinforcing it with D Company of William C. Holley's 8th Engineer Combat Battalion. Palmer chose E Company of Robbins's 2/8 for this vital mission, but its commander balked and had to be relieved of command. The new commander was almost immediately wounded; yet another new one finally led E Company up the hill behind the engineers.

Ray Palmer himself joined the troops in this hurried, ill-planned, uphill counterattack. Mounted in miserable wet, foggy weather against very strong enemy positions in the ruins atop Hill 902, it had not the slightest chance of success. Scores of men in D and E companies were lost, including Private First Class Melvin L. Brown, who, though mortally wounded, heroically stood at his post—to win a posthumous Medal of Honor. During this futile fight the engineers incurred 50 percent casualties, including D Company commander John T. Kennedy, who was wounded and evacuated.[66]

\* \* \*

These initial NKPA successes compelled Johnnie Walker to order a general withdrawal of the 1st Cav Division to positions in an arc about eight miles above Taegu on September 5. This maneuver—difficult under ideal circumstances—did not go well. Some troops panicked and bugged out, leaving weapons and equipment. Many were cut off and trapped. Casualties in all three infantry regiments were very heavy.[67]

Taegu was again in the grip of crisis, and evacuation seemed almost a certainty. As a precaution Walker ordered some American elements to withdraw to Pusan: most of the Eighth Army staff; the 1st Cav's ammo trains. The ROK Army headquarters followed the Eighth Army staff. But Walker and his "tactical staff" did not abandon the city. By then Walker had apparently made the decision to die defending Taegu, as Robert Martin had died defending Chonan and Bill Dean had died (it was believed) defending Taejon. Walker told one American division commander (probably Gay) defiantly: "You will not withdraw your division beyond terrain from which it can cover Taegu. If the enemy gets into Taegu, you will find me resisting him in the streets and I'll have some of my trusted people with me. And you had better be prepared to do the same. Now get back to your division and fight it." The Army historian wrote that Walker told another general "he did not want to see him back from the front again unless it was in a coffin."[68]

Dug into new positions before Taegu, the 1st Cav was compelled, in the words of one historian, "to fight for its very existence." It was a terrible ordeal. The weather was ghastly: steaming heat and heavy rains. The NKPA swarmed over the hills like goats, taking high ground, lobbing mortars and grenades. They had to be rooted out, hill by hill, in an endless succession of company and platoon attacks. Some hills changed hands four or five times or more. The casualties on both sides were appalling. Among the hundreds of evacuated American wounded were the 2/8 commander Gerald Robbins and his S-3, Richard Cohen, who was hit while temporarily serving as commander of the troubled E Company.[69]

In these desperate actions, the 3/8 commander, Johnny Johnson, emerged as a strong, cool, and intelligent commander. His 3/8 suffered appalling casualties—400 of 700 men—but Johnson himself survived unwounded—a miracle, some thought, in view of his continual presence in the very front lines. Hap Gay awarded Johnson a DSC and marked him down as a potential regimental commander, possibly a replacement for Ray Palmer, who had been further sickened and unnerved by the terrible losses in his regiment.[70]

The NKPA offensive at Taegu reached its high-water mark on September 11, when it seized Hill 314, a mere seven miles due north of Taegu. This 1,000-foot peak provided the NKPA positions from which it could observe almost all 1st Cav movements and from which it could—and did—shell Taegu with 120-mm mortars. Unless the NKPA was driven from that hill, the fall of Taegu seemed inevitable.

That NKPA victory and the dire threat it posed seemed to galvanize Johnnie Walker and his commanders. In response, Walker ordered a loosely coordinated but all-out "do or die" counterattack by the 1st Cav and ROK 1st divisions. The 1st Cav would recapture Hill 314; the ROK 1st Division would recapture Hill 902 and the ruins of Kasan.

The 7th Cav drew the task of capturing Hill 314. Cecil Nist delegated the mission to the strongest of his battalions, Jim Lynch's newly arrived but well bloodied 3/7, which then numbered 535 men. In a brilliantly planned and executed attack on September 12, Lynch and his men retook Hill 314. But the cost was frightful: In the first two hours Lynch incurred 229 casualties, leaving him but 300 men to hold the position against repeated NKPA counterattacks over the next week. However, these brave men held.[71]

The recapture of Hill 314 on September 12 would prove to be the turning point in the battle to save Taegu. The victory, which won the 3/7 a Presidential Unit Citation, inspired others. The shattered 2/8, now commanded by another newly arrived, combat-experienced commander, William Walton, thirty-eight, rallied and captured another key hill, 570. Johnny Johnson's 3/8 followed up by capturing Hill 401, during which one of his mortally wounded men, Sergeant First Class Earl R. Baxter, won the Medal of Honor. The ROK 1st Division boldly encircled the NKPA on lofty Hill 902, driving them out of the ruins of Kasan.[72]

Little by little the 1st Cav ground the NKPA 1st, 3d and 13th divisions to a pulp and "saved" Taegu. Before the fight was over, the ADC, Frank Allen, had to lead a task force composed of division headquarters clerks and cooks—

and the division band—forward to provide manpower reinforcements. No exact accounting of the 1st Cav's casualties was ever made for the Battle of Taegu, but they were frightful. The Army historian wrote that when it was over, the three battalions in Crombez's 5th Cav "were so low in strength at this time as to be scarcely combat effective." One typical company of Paul Clifford's 2/5 had only 69 survivors. Edgar Treacy's newly arrived 3/5 lost two-thirds of its strength (600 of 900 men) through casualties and transfers to fill Morgan Heasley's 1/5 and Clifford's 2/5. In the 1/7 Pete Clainos's C Company had but 50 men. Johnny Johnson declared that any company of his 3/8 that could muster half strength (about 100 men) was designated the assault "company" of the day.[73]

## Northeast Sector

The NKPA offensive on the northeast front, designed to recapture Pohang and drive on Taegu through the "back door," was to be carried out by the four NKPA divisions already in place: the 8th and 15th in the Taebaek Mountains; the 5th and 12th on the coast. These divisions, chewed to pieces in the August fighting, were reinforced by independent NKPA units or raw fillers to an average strength of about 6,500 men each (for a total of about 26,000 men). In keeping with the NKPA strategy of attacking everywhere at once, the four divisions were not concentrated but rather spread across a rugged front, forty miles wide.[74]

This sector was still defended by four ROK divisions: 3d, 6th, 8th, and Capital. Since early August these ROKs, supported by American warships and carriers operating in the Sea of Japan and advised by KMAG, had been fighting with increased élan and skill, inflicting heavy casualties on the NKPA. However, the ROKs were still an unstable quantity: valorous one moment; panicky the next. They could not be completely trusted.[75]

For that reason Walker had moved John Church's rebuilding 24th Division to Taegu, in position to backstop the ROKs. Inasmuch as Walker had deactivated the 34th Regiment and delayed the attachment of Throckmorton's 5th Regiment, Church had only two regiments: Ned Moore's 19th and Dick Stephens's 21st. However, these regiments had been brought up to full strength by the addition of Ayres's and Perez's battalions from the 34th and by fillers from the States. Should the ROK divisions fail, these two American regiments, comprising six infantry battalions, were available to reinforce them. In addition, D. M. McMains's black 3/9, plus support forces, was still in the area near Pohang.

Up to this time Walker had been commanding Eighth Army without the benefit of subordinate corps headquarters. In the occupation years the four divisions of Eighth Army had been organized into I and IX Corps (each commanding two divisions), but these corps headquarters had been abolished before the war for economy reasons. In his July shopping list MacArthur had requested that the Pentagon send him two corps headquarters; but other reinforcements had taken priority, and the first of these headquarters—I Corps—did not arrive in Korea until mid-August.[76]

The corps commander was a very senior two-star general, John B. Coulter, fifty-nine, who, like Walker, came to his post from command of the Fifth Army in Chicago. He had been chosen for this important job in Walker's army by MacArthur and Almond, without the usual and customary consultation with Walker. For that reason, and others, Walker received Coulter with less than overwhelming enthusiasm.[77]

Coulter's ties to MacArthur and Almond stretched back over many years. Like MacArthur, he was a graduate of the West Texas Military Academy (1911). In World War I he had served with MacArthur in France in the 42d ("Rainbow") Division. During World War II he commanded the 85th Infantry Division in Italy, fighting alongside Almond's 92d Division. In the postwar years he had been assistant commanding general of John Hodge's XXIV Corps in the Korean occupation and, until its deactivation in March 1950, commander of Eighth Army's I Corps in Japan.[78]

When the NKPA 5th and 12th divisions began the attack on Pohang, the ROK 3d and Capital divisions gave way and then suddenly collapsed. Owing to Coulter's extended occupation experience in Korea, Walker placed him in command of the ROK front and issued the ROKs a stern order to "stand in place and fight." With only his chief of staff, Andrew C. Tychsen, fifty-seven, in tow, Coulter hurriedly established an advanced CP at Kyongju, behind the crumbling ROK front at Pohang. Tychsen, who had served Coulter as G-3 during the Korean occupation, was named the "hatchet man," authorized by Coulter to use "whatever force" he needed to restore order in the panicky ROK high command. Knowing the ROKs well, Tychsen did not particularly relish the chore. "There we were, only General Coulter and myself, mind you," he remembered.[79]

Overrunning the more powerful ROK 3d and Capital divisions, the NKPA 5th and 12th divisions recaptured Pohang on September 3. In an effort to halt the bugout of the ROKs, Coulter sacked the "hysterical" 3d Division commander and other ROK generals. When this failed to do the trick, he had to call on Walker for American help. In response, Walker sent Dick Stephens's 21st Infantry and the newly created ROK 7th Division. As the NKPA drove on Kyongju, the ROKs urged Coulter to abandon his CP, but Coulter, apparently having decided to stand and fight to the death, refused to withdraw.[80]

By September 5 the situation on Coulter's front had reached a crisis. On his right the NKPA 5th and 12th divisions had driven south to the outskirts of Kyongju. On his left, farther west, the NKPA 8th and 15th divisions were pushing the ROK 6th and 8th divisions back on Yongchon, posing the possibility that Coulter's forces would be cut off, encircled, and destroyed. In response to yet another call for help, Walker committed Ned Moore's 19th Infantry and, hard on its heels, all available support units of the 24th Division, plus the black 3/9.[81]

Walker was to credit John Coulter for his personal courage at Kyongju and for restoring some order in the ROK high command, but he was not impressed with his battlefield tactics. Some of Coulter's orders, the Army historian wrote harshly, had resulted in a "useless dispersion" of the American reinforcements. Furthermore, Tychsen had antagonized the Eighth Army staff by his frequent and insistent cries for help. Upon commitment of all available 24th Division units, Walker ordered Coulter back to Taegu, as the historian put it, to "resume his planning duties" and placed John Church in charge of the northeast front.[82]

The arrival of the 19th and 21st Infantry and McMains's 3/9 prevented a cave-in on the northeast front. In the first few days the fighting was intense and the American losses were heavy. In a single engagement Ned Moore's 3/19 lost eight lieutenants killed. Eventually all American forces in this sector were grouped into a task force commanded by the 24th Division ADC, Gar Davidson. Under his able leadership the Americans gradually drove the NKPA back and stabilized the front. The reorganized ROK units, commanded by new generals, went back into the line with determination.[83]

### III

The fighting in the four main sectors went on day after endless day. As the battles violently surged back and forth, hills changed hands with maddening monotony. The early September heat was dreadful. No one dared sleep. Very few men got a decent meal; even drinking water was scarce. The American casualties were ghastly: By September 15 total Eighth Army casualties had climbed to 18,165: 4,599 killed or mortally wounded; 12,377 wounded; the rest missing. Truly it was a "savage sacrifice" of "beef cattle in the slaughterhouse." Worse, there were few or no replacements. Beginning on August 23, MacArthur had diverted 390 officers and 5,400 enlisted men to build up the 7th Division for Inchon.[84]

And yet Eighth Army hung on magnificently. The NKPA seriously threatened Masan and Pusan, the Naktong Bulge, and Taegu, but owing to its unwise decision to attack everywhere at once, it lacked sufficient power and depth to exploit any of its initial successes. Six NKPA divisions (1st, 2d, 6th, 7th, 9th, and 13th) were virtually wiped out.

The defense of the Pusan Perimeter was truly a great victory for Eighth

Army, but the extent of the victory was not immediately apparent, especially in distant Washington. Looking at battle maps during the first week of September, the JCS had rightly grown increasingly apprehensive and once again questioned the Inchon landing. In view of the precarious state (as it seemed) of Eighth Army, it appeared absurd to be pulling the Fifth Marines from the Pusan Perimeter to land at Inchon. Moreover, even if Walker held on without them, it seemed impossible that Eighth Army could rebound from the NKPA offensive in time to mount a successful breakout and link up with the Inchon forces.[85]

Accordingly, the JCS resumed a tactful campaign to persuade MacArthur to delay Inchon or switch the landing from Inchon to Kunsan, as Collins and Sherman had urged in Tokyo. Having had no response to its August 28 cable suggesting the switch to Kunsan and requesting the Pentagon be kept informed, on September 5 the JCS cabled MacArthur that it "desired to be informed of any modifications which may have been made in your plans for a mid-September amphibious operation." MacArthur's reply was terse: "General outline of the plan remains as described to you." In response, on September 7 the JCS made one final effort to bring MacArthur around to its point of view and remind him of the disastrous consequences that would ensue if Inchon miscarried or failed to produce a quick victory:

While we concur in launching a counter-offensive in Korea as early as is feasible, we have noted with considerable concern the recent trend of events there. In light of all factors including apparent commitment of practically all reserves available to Eighth Army, we desire your estimate as to feasibility and chance of success of projected operation if initiated on planned schedule. We are sure that you understand that all available trained Army units in the United States have been allocated to you except 82 Abn Div and that minimum of four months would elapse before first of partially trained National Guard divisions could reach Korea in event that junction of main Eighth Army Forces with Tenth Corps bridgehead should not quickly be effected with forces now available to Far East Command.[86]

This cable, MacArthur wrote in his memoirs, "chilled me to the marrow of my bones." He went on: "What could have given rise to such a query at such an hour? Had someone in authority in Washington lost his nerve? Could it be the President? Or Marshall who had just become Secretary of Defense? Or Bradley? Or was it merely an anticipatory alibi if the operation should run into trouble?"

MacArthur's reply was persuasive:

• The situation within the perimeter was "not critical," he assured the JCS. It was possible that "some contraction" might take place, but "defensive positions" (the Davidson Line) had been chosen for that contingency. "There is not the slightest possibility, however, of our forces being ejected from the Pusan bridgehead." The envelopment at Inchon would prevent further enemy manpower and logistical buildup at the perimeter and "instantly relieve" pressure on Walker.

• Contrary to all prior discussions, MacArthur did not now believe that success at Inchon was dependent on Walker's linkup offensive. "The prompt juncture of our two forces, while it would be dramatically symbolic of the complete collapse of the enemy, is not a vital part of the operation."

• Overall, there was "no question" in MacArthur's mind that Inchon was feasible and the chances of success were "excellent." It was the "only hope" of delivering a "decisive blow" to the NKPA, he asserted. "I and all of my commanders and staff officers," he concluded, "without exception, are enthusiastic for and confident of the success of the enveloping movement."[87]

By now it was clear to the JCS that nothing would persuade MacArthur to modify the Inchon plan. To continue further pressures on MacArthur or to order Inchon canceled would contravene the JCS "tradition" of giving the theater commander widest possible latitude in tactical operations. Moreover, anything other than complete approval was certain to invite MacArthur's fury and, quite possibly, a public attack on Washington for its loss of nerve. Therefore the JCS met with Truman on September 8 and hashed it out one last time. Truman, perhaps still influenced by the favorable reports on the Inchon landing from Averell Harriman and Matt Ridgway, following their visit to the Far East in early August, enthusiastically endorsed Inchon. He later wrote: "It was a daring strategic conception. I had the greatest confidence that it would succeed." Following this session, the JCS sent MacArthur a terse cable: "We approve your plan and president has been so informed."[88]

# PART FIVE

## The Liberation of South Korea

# 10

# SEOUL RECAPTURED

I

In Japan it seemed for a time that all the pessimism about Inchon was fully justified. In early September not one but two typhoons bore down on Japan and Korea, imperiling final preparations. The first, Jane, with winds of 110 mph, struck Kobe on September 3. It generated forty-foot waves which tore up the harbor, broke ships loose from their moorings, and delayed the loading of the First Marines for thirty-six hours. Hard on its heels, the second typhoon, Kezia, with winds of 125 mph, took a course for the Korea Strait, which the 260 ships earmarked for Inchon were to cross.[1]

Notwithstanding the dangerous threat posed by Typhoon Kezia, the Inchon forces put to sea in a complicated mosaic. The First Marines and the 7th Infantry Division embarked from Kobe and Yokohama, respectively, on September 11. The 17th Infantry Regiment of the 7th Division sailed independently for Pusan to become the Eighth Army floating reserve, until the arrival at Pusan of the Puerto Rican 65th Infantry from the States. The Fifth Marines, in effect relieved by the 17th Infantry, left Pusan on September 12 to join the converging Inchon forces at sea.[2]

These deployments stripped Japan bare of American ground forces. Should Moscow's or Peking's reaction to Inchon include an overt or covert threat to Japan, there was no way America could defend the place. The defense of Japan was MacArthur's "primary" responsibility in the Far East. In his single-minded pursuit of Inchon he gambled that neither Moscow nor Peking would take advantage of Japan's vulnerability. Inasmuch as Sovietologists in Washington were predicting a strong reaction in Moscow or Peking to Inchon, it was a dangerous gamble.

MacArthur had assured the JCS that he would accompany the Inchon forces, ostensibly to be close at hand should a disaster occur. His detractors would insist that the trip was completely unnecessary, that with the instantaneous communications available to him he could easily direct operations from Tokyo. They would argue that his decision to go to Inchon arose from his megalomania, a compulsion to be physically present—and photographed and quoted—during this dramatic military operation. Another reason may have been that he believed his presence at a victorious Inchon would also make the nervous Nellies in the JCS look a little silly.

Accompanied by Ned Almond, Lem Shepherd, senior GHQ staffers, and a battalion of favored reporters and photographers, MacArthur flew from Tokyo to Kyushu on the afternoon of September 12 and boarded Doyle's amphibious command ship, *Mount McKinley,* at Sasebo. Putting to sea during

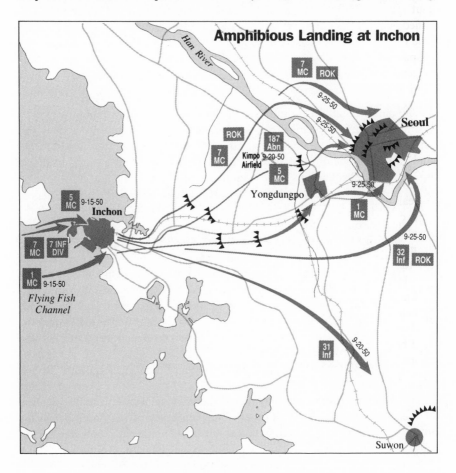

the early hours of September 13, *McKinley* plowed into the outer fringes of Typhoon Kezia, which Doyle characterized as "one of the worst storms" he had ever encountered. The typhoon battered the converging Inchon vessels, causing widespread fear and seasickness among the Marines and soldiers, but fortunately for all, it veered to the northeast without inflicting any substantial damage on the armada.[3]

\* \* \*

In advance of the amphibious forces, Navy, Marine, and FEAF aircraft and surface ships (including the demothballed battleship *Missouri*) mounted heavy raids on the east and west coasts of South Korea. Most of the raids—heavy attacks on Kunsan, for example—were designed as diversions to confuse the NKPA. Those at Inchon itself, however, were designed to knock out specific NKPA military defenses. Highest priority was assigned the fortified island of Wolmi, dominating Red Beach in the Inchon Harbor, where the Fifth Marines would land and scale the seawalls. Repeatedly bombed and napalmed, the island was virtually pulverized. The survivors of the 400-odd green, poorly trained NKPA troops emplaced on the island to man its 75-mm and 76-mm artillery pieces were traumatized.[4]

On the morning of September 13 the Inchon pessimists again appeared to be justified. A naval bombardment group, composed of four cruisers (two of them British) and six destroyers, brazenly nosing up the narrow, intricate Flying Fish Channel to bombard Wolmi and Inchon, discovered the worst possible obstacle: a recently planted NKPA minefield. For a brief moment the discovery caused grave concern, and the ships stopped. But investigation revealed that the field was quite small (perhaps no more than two dozen mines) and composed of obsolescent "contact mines" (as opposed to more sophisticated and lethal influence or "magnetic" mines). The sailors exploded the mines with small-arms fire and kept on up the channel. One destroyer dropped off to continue dealing with the mines.[5]

Here again, the Inchon forces were lucky. Later investigation revealed that unknown to GHQ, Tokyo, beginning on about August 1, the Russians had persuaded the NKPA to mine possible amphibious invasion points on the east and west coasts of North and South Korea. The mines for Flying Fish Channel had begun arriving in late August, but owing to a bureaucratic foul-up, the more sophisticated magnetic mines had arrived lacking some vital parts. The two small fields of contact mines had been emplaced in the channel as a stopgap measure pending arrival of the misplaced parts for the magnetic mines.[6]

The bombardment force—destroyers leading—continued up the channel to preselected locations, then stopped and anchored. From these positions the seven vessels blasted Wolmi with more than 1,000 rounds of five-, six-, and eight-inch shells. The ships drew sporadic but deadly counterfire from several artillery pieces on Wolmi, which hit three destroyers and killed one officer. This NKPA counterfire may have been ill advised; it revealed the positions of the guns and invited swift and telling retaliation from ships and aircraft.[7]

The bombardment force withdrew to sea, then returned the next day, September 14, for a similar raid. From these raids the NKPA deduced that despite its hazards, Inchon seemed to be the real target for the amphibious force. Accordingly the NKPA alerted ground forces to reinforce the 2,000-odd troops in and around Inchon; but owing to its all-out commitment to the Pusan Perimeter, there was not much to call upon, and much of what was available was poorly trained and equipped.

Aboard Doyle's command ship *McKinley,* farther back in the Yellow Sea, MacArthur was in a garrulous mood, pontificating to the press and senior officers on a wide range of subjects: George Marshall's choice to succeed Louis Johnson as secretary of defense was good. Although he did not have enough iron in his veins, Averell Harriman would probably replace Acheson as secretary of state. Eisenhower was a good man. If the Chinese intervened in Korea, "our airmen will turn the Yalu River into the bloodiest stream in all history." Marine General O. P. Smith, his mind preoccupied with the task his 1st Division faced at Inchon, found "the pomposity of his pronouncements a little wearing."[8]

Late on the eve of the invasion, September 14, a very restless MacArthur roused his most trusted sycophant, Courtney Whitney, from sleep. According to Whitney's memoir, a bizarre scene ensued. For about two hours MacArthur, pacing his cabin in bathrobe and slippers, delivered a "remarkable soliloquy" or "monologue" which "amounted to a kind of self-debate." Relating Inchon to his World War II experiences, MacArthur reviewed in minute detail all the pros and cons. Inchon was a "tremendous gamble"; it might go down in history as "one of the great United States military disasters." On the other hand, the alternative of continuing the slaughter in the Pusan Perimeter, where Walker was (as Whitney put it) "hopelessly outnumbered by the hordes of Communists," was unacceptable. Finally summing up, MacArthur concluded the decision for Inchon "was a sound one, the risks and hazards must be accepted."[9]

\* \* \*

On D day, September 15, the landing proceeded more or less as designed. The weather during most of the day was fair; the mines in the channel had been eliminated. There were no surprises from Moscow or Peking—no sudden, massive air attacks, for example—or from the NKPA. Notwithstanding the local hazards presented by the tides and the seawalls, Inchon was a piece of cake, one of the easiest landings in the history of modern warfare. The NKPA defenders were not surprised; they were simply over-whelmed by the power of the American forces.

At 6:33 A.M. following yet another devastating air and naval bombard-ment, O. P. Smith landed a battalion of Ray Murray's Fifth Marines on Wolmi. The green, inept NKPA troops put up slight to no resistance. Within thirty minutes the Marines, who could not be resupplied because of the ebbing tide but who were well covered by air all that day, controlled the northern half of the island. By noon they had killed or captured the 400-odd NKPA defend-ers and controlled the whole island. It proved to be well stocked with artillery pieces connected by an elaborate system of trenches and tunnels. Here again the Inchon forces were lucky. Had the NKPA manned these weapons with well-trained, disciplined troops, Inchon might have been a different story. In the afternoon the Marines zeroed in artillery and small arms to command the seawalls, where the rest of the Fifth Marines would land on the tide, almost in darkness. The price for Wolmi was cheap: no Marines killed; only seventeen wounded. MacArthur, no doubt vastly relieved, crowed: "The Navy and Marines have never shown [sic] more brightly than this morning."[10]

That afternoon at about five, amid yet more air and surface ship attacks, the main units of the Marine assault force headed for their Inchon objectives on the high tide. These forces were the other two battalions of Murray's Fifth Marines, bound for the seawalls to the left (or north) of Wolmi in "downtown" Inchon, and the three-battalion First Marines, commanded by Lewis B. ("Chesty") Puller, bound for Blue Beach, to the right (or south) of Wolmi, in a less well-defended nonurban area. By then the fair weather had gone; rain-squalls lashed the landing craft. These and the smoke and haze generated by the air and naval bombardment reduced visibility drastically.[11]

Despite strict orders from MacArthur to the contrary, the publicity-hungry Marines had smuggled several brave war correspondents into their landing craft. These included Marguerite Higgins and *Life* photographer Henry G. ("Hank") Walker, who had teamed with *Time* correspondent James Bell. Owing to the haze and darkness, Walker's photographs hardly justified the risks he ran, but wordsmiths Higgins and Bell filed vivid copy. To Bell the seawall they had to scale seemed "as high as the RCA Building." As they strained to see Red Beach from the boats, Higgins wrote, "a rocket hit a round oil tower and big, ugly smoke rings billowed up." The dockside buildings, she continued, "were brilliant with flames. . . . [I]t looked as though the whole city was burning. . . . The strange sunset, combined with the crimson haze of the flaming docks, was so spectacular that a movie audience would have consid-ered it overdone."[12]

To Hank Walker, a Marine combat photographer in World War II who had landed with the Marines at bloody Saipan, the experience of going at a seawall with scaling ladders was "eerie." He remembered that "the flimsy ladders stuck out of the front of the LCVPs [landing craft, vehicle, personnel] like the antennas of bugs." At the climactic moment the LCVP slammed into the seawall, engines wide open, holding it in place against the wall. "We went up the ladders, two men at a time," he remembered. "Then we dived over the top of the wall—as we had been told—into a ditch behind the wall." Fortunately the Marines on Wolmi had the seawalls covered; there was no enemy fire. "A single well-emplaced enemy machine gun," Walker recalled, "could have chewed the Marines to pieces and badly interfered with the Red Beach landing."[13]

The worst fire at Red Beach came from the rear. Trigger-happy men on seven of eight LSTs coming in behind the LCVPs panicked and cut loose a hail of bullets and cannon shells at Red Beach. This raking, mindless fire inflicted more casualties on the Marines (one dead, twenty-three wounded) than did the NKPA. "The Marines ashore were furious and rightly so," Hank Walker recalled. "They turned around and lobbed a few mortar rounds near the LSTs to scare the sailors away from their guns." Fortunately this counter friendly fire had the desired effect, and the fire from the LST soon ceased.[14]

The 3/5 on Wolmi, which had ably covered Red Beach, soon pushed across a causeway to link up in "downtown" Inchon with the rest of the Fifth Marines. Thereafter, under cover of darkness, the Fifth Marines fanned out through the city to preassigned objectives, against slight NKPA resistance. By late evening the Fifth Marines had captured most Inchon objectives and were making plans to move out the following day to the next objective: Kimpo Airfield, urgently required for basing Marine close air support aircraft.

At Blue Beach Chesty Puller's green First Marines did not do nearly so well. In fact, their landing was a near disaster. The first three waves of the two assault battalions landed as designed, but the twenty-two follow-up waves became lost in haze and smoke. As a consequence, the Marine historian wrote, "incredible confusion" reigned. Here again the Inchon forces were lucky: NKPA resistance at Blue Beach was "negligible." In time Puller was able to sort out much of the confusion and struck inland, although with considerably less manpower and armor than called for in the plan.[15]

Notwithstanding the mess at Blue Beach, by midnight September 15—the end of D day—the Marine landing at Inchon was deemed an overwhelming success. About 13,000 Marines with weapons and equipment were ashore. Total casualties were slight: 174, including 21 killed. Dozens of transports and LSTs were inside Inchon Harbor, unloading men and supplies that would go in on the following high tides. The NKPA was unable to muster sufficient force for a counterattack. The best it could do was to fall back to blocking positions on the Han River and at Seoul, as Johnnie Walker had earlier fallen back on the Naktong River and Taegu.[16]

MacArthur could not have been more pleased, but he was restrained in his initial report to the JCS. After a late-afternoon tour of the harbor in Admiral Struble's barge he cabled Washington: "Our losses are light. . . . The command distinguished itself. The whole operation is proceeding on schedule."[17]

*　*　*

On September 16 and 17 the Marines cleared Inchon, captured Kimpo Airfield, consolidated the beachhead, and prepared for the campaign to liberate Seoul. The X Corps plan was as follows: Ray Murray's Fifth Marines, "reinforced" by a regiment of ROK Marines (to add ROKs to the liberation forces) and the late-arriving Seventh Marines, would cross the Han River from Kimpo and come at Seoul from the west. Immediately on Murray's right Chesty Puller's First Marines would liberate Yongdungpo, a city on the south bank of the Han opposite Seoul, then go north across the river. In militarese, Murray's Fifth Marines would be the "maneuver" element; Puller's First Marines, the solid "holding" element, or "hub" around which Murray would pivot.[18]

Recovering from the shock of the landing, the NKPA began bringing up forces to thwart these plans. These included the full new (but green) 18th Infantry Division (10,000 men), which had been earmarked to join the NKPA at the Pusan Perimeter, plus four independent regiments (of about 2,500 men each), the 25th, 70th, 28th, and 87th. These organized combatant units comprised in total about 20,000 men. To those were soon added miscellaneous units (engineers, police, etc.), comprising perhaps 15,000 men, bringing the total NKPA troops in defense of Seoul to about 35,000 or 40,000 men.[19]

A substantial force of NKPA troops took positions in front of Chesty Puller's First Marines, advancing on Yongdungpo. The NKPA troops were reinforced by about a dozen T-34 tanks and a considerable number of artillery pieces and mortars. Although most of these troops were green, they had been given the vital military and psychological mission of "saving Seoul" and fought with unusual ferocity. Notwithstanding Chesty Puller's legendary combat savvy and valor (four Navy Crosses earned in previous combat), the First Marines, entering combat for the first time after a botched landing, made slow progress. The liberation of Yongdungpo became far more difficult—and costly—than had been anticipated.[20]

There was no rigid timetable for liberating Seoul. However, MacArthur wanted it done as quickly as possible to achieve maximum military and psychological impact. Prodding Ned Almond, MacArthur suggested it could be done within "five days" of the landing—by about September 20. In light of the ever-increasing NKPA resistance, Almond did not believe that this timetable was possible, but he did assure MacArthur that Seoul would be liberated within ten days—by September 25, the three-month anniversary of the NKPA invasion. Thereafter, O. P. Smith wrote, Almond became "so obsessed" with liberating Seoul by that date at whatever cost that he "lost touch with reality."[21]

Almond's obsession propelled him almost immediately into deep command conflict with Smith. The Marines believed that the liberation of Seoul should be governed by careful tactical maneuvers which ensured minimum casualties and exposure of the green First and Seventh Marines, not by a public relations "anniversary." Smith wrote that he soon had "little confidence" in the "tactical judgment" of X Corps or in the "realism of its planning." The X Corps view of Smith and the Marines was summed up by Almond's G-3, West Pointer (1936) Jack Chiles: "The Marines were exasperatingly deliberate at a time when rapid maneuver was imperative." Almond later said that Smith was "overly cautious" in executing orders and "always had excuses for not performing at the required time the task he was requested to do."[22]

While Almond and Smith were outwardly civil, they grew to "hate each other," Jack Chiles remembered. Chiles thought that "Smith resented being under an Army commander of any sort" and "came as close to getting insubordinate as he could be." Smith was still smarting from the patronizing way Almond had treated him and Shepherd earlier in Tokyo and the fact that he was actually senior to Almond by date of rank. Moreover, Chiles remembered, Almond was "very proud, very intolerant," and "also overbearing." He bypassed Smith on the battlefield and gave orders directly to Murray and Puller; not having a helicopter of his own, he usurped Smith's. "It was a very unfortunate personality conflict," Chiles concluded.[23]

* * *

The Army's 7th Infantry Division, which arrived at Inchon on September 16, began coming ashore on September 18. Its mission was to advance inland on the right of the Marines and face south to block any NKPA forces coming up from that direction for the defense of Seoul. The 7th Division would, in effect, protect the Marines' rear while they liberated Seoul. In addition, it would serve as the "anvil" against which the advancing Eighth Army "hammer" would pound the NKPA to pieces.[24]

The 7th Division was commanded by David G. Barr, fifty-five. Born in Nanafalie, Alabama, Barr was a student at Alabama Presbyterian College when America entered World War I. Commissioned in 1917, he got to France in September 1918 and won a Silver Star for heroism while serving in the 1st Division. In the peacetime years he became a tanker. In 1940, when Patton began organizing the Army's armored forces, he drafted Barr to be the supply officer of his I Armored Corps. However, Barr did not go with Patton to North Africa. Like Hap Gay, Bill Kean, and Dutch Keiser, Barr served out World War II in a series of senior staff jobs, culminating with the prestigious two-star position of chief of staff of Jacob L. Devers's Sixth Army Group in the ETO.[25]

In the postwar years Barr loyally remained a staff officer to Devers until early 1948, when Army Chief of Staff Eisenhower sent Barr to China to head the 1,000-man Army mission advising Chiang Kai-shek. Thereafter Barr succeeded Bill Dean as commander of the 7th Division, which Dean had transferred from occupation duty in Korea to occupation duty in Japan.

Barr's two-year tour with Chiang Kai-shek, 1948 and 1949, coincided with Chiang's defeat by Mao Tse-tung's Communist armies. During this tumultuous time Barr's reports to Washington, which helped shape administration policy toward Chiang, were consistently negative. He judged that Chiang's Nationalist Army had the "world's worst leadership." He recommended withholding further American military aid to Chiang and, finally, withdrawal of his own advisory group. In a final report, he summed up his views: "The Nationalist military collapse stemmed primarily from a weak and unstable government which was over-centralized, which had little or no popular support, and which had as a primary interest the protection of the privileged class."[26]

Dave Barr was a brainy staff officer, but not a strong battlefield commander. Shortly after he had arrived in China, the old China hand Albert Wedemeyer, who knew Barr well, described him to Secretary of Defense James Forrestal thus: "Polite and loyal, a good officer, but almost entirely lacking in force." This view was echoed by 7th Division staffers. The G-2, John W. ("Bill") Paddock, an able, tough-minded airborne artillery battalion commander in the ETO, wrote: "I admired and respected General Barr, although he was not what I would term a combat officer or troop commander type. . . . He was courtly, kind, friendly, very intelligent, capable and, I think, aware of his shortcomings [as a field commander]." Barr's aide-de-camp, Charles E. Davis, remembered: "He didn't look or act the part of a commanding general. He was rumpled and round, a super guy, but more like a father figure. He was not the best leader or field general."[27]

After Ned Almond, Dave Barr was the senior Army general at Inchon. He got on with Almond no better than did Marine General O. P. Smith. Barr was highly annoyed by Almond's driving intensity, dictatorial manner, and brashness and had such doubts about his battlefield competence that he had asked Almond to find someone else to command the 7th Division at Inchon. In turn, Almond and the X Corps staffers viewed Barr as a liability. One X Corps staffer said: "He was a fine man but he didn't have a clue as to how a division worked." Another wrote: "He was an inept, vacillating commander who exasperated General Almond continuously . . . [and] only their long friendship kept him from being relieved by General Almond." In retort, the

7th Division G-2, Bill Paddock, wrote: "Barr was a hellova [sic] better division commander than Almond was a corps commander."[28]

Like the other four Army division commanders in the Pusan Perimeter, Dave Barr had been assigned an ADC who had ably commanded troops in combat in World War II. He was West Pointer (1920) Henry I. ("Hammering Hank") Hodes, fifty-one. A gruff old cavalryman, Hodes during World War II had commanded the 112th Infantry Regiment of the 28th Infantry Division in very tough fighting from Omaha Beach to the Siegfried Line. Twice wounded, Hodes won a Silver Star for heroism before he ran out of gas in September 1944 and returned to the Pentagon, where he soon earned a star. At the time of Inchon his son, John T., a West Pointer (1949), was aide-de-camp to the 1st Cav ADC, Frank Allen. Barr's aide Charles Davis remembered: "Hank Hodes did the real generaling in the division."[29]

Ever since the beginning of the Korean War the 7th Division had been something of a madhouse. First, GHQ had stripped it of about 1,300 key noncoms and officers to beef up the 24th and 25th divisions. Next, upon the departure from Japan of the 24th, 25th, and 1st Cav divisions, GHQ had ordered it to redeploy into the areas vacated by those divisions, all over Japan. Then, upon its assignment to Inchon, the 7th had to build up its strength from about 8,700 to 18,000 men, with disparate cadres and fillers from Okinawa and the States, in about six weeks. Next, the division had to absorb 8,600 ROKs. Finally, the division had to attempt some training. "It was a hellova [sic] mess," Paddock commented, "a three-ring circus."[30]

Owing to MacArthur's decision to assign the 17th Infantry temporarily as Walker's floating reserve at Pusan, Barr initially had only two regiments at Inchon. These were the 31st and 32d, each with a strength of about 5,000 men, including nearly 2,000 ROKs of doubtful value. The ROKs, Barr wrote, could not "by the wildest stretch of the imagination" be considered "combat-worthy troops." They were "civilians," he went on, who had been picked from the streets and fields of South Korea without any prior warning and rushed to Japan, "stunned, confused, exhausted." There had been no time to train them.[31]

Of the two regiments, the 32d, commanded by young Charles Beauchamp (who had temporarily led the 34th Infantry in Korea) was considered superior. One reason was Beauchamp's combat experience in Korea; another was that by luck or design the 32d had been assigned exceptionally fine subordinate commanders. The 31st, originally activated in the Philippines in 1916, had never been stationed in the continental United States and was thus jokingly referred to by some as the "Foreign Legion" of the Army. Furthermore, it had been trapped in Bataan in World War II and ordered to surrender. Although it had received a Presidential Unit Citation for defense of the Philippines, in the eyes of some the 31st had been dishonored. For these and other reasons it had suffered. Although its own officers passionately defended the regiment, one of its enlisted members, Gerald A. Francois, remembered that it had become a "dumping ground" for "derelicts and problem kids." Dave Barr's aide, Charles Davis, remembered it this way: "The Thirty-first was lousy."[32]

\* \* \*

Beauchamp's green 32d Infantry landed first. Its rather substantial mission was twofold: first, to relieve Chesty Puller's First Marines, who were blocking south, freeing these Marines for use in the increasingly difficult task of liberating Yongdungpo; secondly, to drive south on the main highway, liberate Suwon and its good airfield, and establish a strong block (the "anvil") there.[33]

Going ashore, Beauchamp was surprised by the strength of the NKPA resistance. What was believed would be a routine relief turned into an arduous chore for his men. To reach Puller's rear positions, Beauchamp had to root NKPA troops from one hill after the next. In so doing, Beauchamp was very nearly killed when his jeep wandered into a minefield. Chesty Puller, a Marine historian wrote, was "caustic" in his comments over the 32d's delays, which he asserted significantly retarded his attack on Yongdungpo. O. P. Smith, with typical Marine pride, blamed the annoying delays on the fact that the "quality" of the 7th Division "was in no way comparable to that of the 1st Marine Division."[34]

The landing of the 32d Infantry and other units on September 18 brought MacArthur's total forces within the beachhead to about 25,000 men. Taking into consideration his vast superiority in tanks and artillery and the support of aircraft overhead and naval surface ships offshore, his total military power greatly exceeded that of the NKPA gathering to defend Seoul. Yet the Americans fell farther and farther behind on Almond's timetable, especially Puller's First Marines and Beauchamp's 32d Infantry, which were back to back and going—or trying to go—in opposite directions at the same time.[35]

The most encouraging note within the beachhead was struck by Ray Murray's battle-hardened Fifth Marines. More or less as planned, on September 20 they crossed the Han River west of Seoul, near Kimpo Airfield. They were transported in armored tracked landing craft called amtracs (LVTs, or landing vehicles, tracked), which had been earlier used at Inchon and driven overland. At first the Fifth Marines encountered slight resistance, but the NKPA soon divined the plan of the maneuver and erected a powerful defense in this sector, delaying Murray, thereby throwing Almond's timetable further askew.

Almond toured the battlefield every day in his jeep, going at breakneck speed, like Johnnie Walker. On September 17 and 20 MacArthur, heedless of the danger of enemy fire or ambush, came ashore to join him. On the second visit—principally to watch the Fifth Marines cross the Han—Almond drove MacArthur's jeep while the GHQ G-3, Pinky Wright, rode in the back seat, scared silly by Almond's reckless speeding, which led to a near collision with a truck. When they finally got back to Inchon in one piece, Wright asked Almond with a straight face if he had a driver's license.[36]

By September 21 the American buildup in the perimeter had swelled to 50,000 men, probably twice the number of surviving NKPA troops. The new American forces included the green 31st Infantry; the green Seventh Marines, which joined Ray Murray's Fifth Marines for the attack on Seoul from the west; and the ROK 17th Regiment, which, like the ROK Marine regiment, was to be placed in the forefront of the forces liberating Seoul for political and psychological reasons. The forces included five American infantry regiments (First, Fifth, and Seventh Marines; the 31st and 32d Infantry); two ROK infantry regiments; and seven battalions of artillery.[37]

Although Seoul was not yet liberated—far from it—that day MacArthur was satisfied that the situation was sufficiently well in hand that his presence was no longer required. He boarded his private plane at Kimpo Airfield and flew back to Tokyo. No doubt it was one of the most satisfying days of his long life. Despite all the naysaying from virtually every military expert who examined it and the caution and worry of the JCS, Inchon had worked more or less as he and Almond had thought it would.[38]

## II

Punch-drunk from the fury and slaughter of the NKPA offensive against the Pusan Perimeter, the Eighth Army staff, presided over by the cool and efficient Lev Allen, finalized plans for the counteroffensive or "breakout" from the perimeter. Originally MacArthur had set D day for September 15, to coincide exactly with the Inchon landing. However, believing the news of Inchon would panic or demoralize the NKPA forces at the Pusan Perimeter, Walker asked for and got a one-day delay, to September 16.[39]

Walker's plan for the breakout grew, quite naturally, from his cavalry background and experience in Patton's Third Army in the ETO. Armored task forces would crash out of the perimeter everywhere at once, on available roads, to be followed by infantry. The tanks would stun and awe and overrun the NKPA in a single, overpowering blow; the infantry would come along to mop up. It was reminiscent of old cavalry tactics in which (as the joke had it) "the soldiers went out and charged in all directions at the same time, with a pistol in each hand and a saber in the other." In proper militarese, it was known as "an attack to unlimited objectives."[40]

There would be three main lines of attack:

- In the Taegu sector Church's rebuilt 24th Division and Gay's 1st Cav Division would cross the Naktong River at Waegwan and attack northwest up the road to Taejon and beyond, the 24th Division in the lead, the 1st Cav behind. Advance elements of the 24th Division would link at Suwon with X Corps.

- In the southwest sector Kean's 25th and Keiser's 2d divisions would strike northwest across the peninsula on three more or less parallel roads toward Kunsan.

- In the north and northeast sectors the six available ROK divisions would attack north into the Taebaek Mountains and up the east coast road.

The westward attacks of the four American divisions would throw four "lines" across South Korea, dividing it into four distinct "tiers." The theory was that these lines would "trap" the NKPA in South Korea within the tiers. In this fashion Eighth Army would achieve its principal mission—destruction of enemy forces—and the secondary mission of "linking up" with X Corps.[41]

In retrospect, some professionals faulted the plan of attack to "unlimited objectives." It was, in effect, an all-out race to gain real estate. The critics would say that Walker did not have sufficient manpower to both man the four lines, or tiers across the peninsula, and accompany the armor. Since the armor had to be protected, it meant the lines or tiers would be "pencil-thin." Inevitably the NKPA would "leak" through the lines. A better plan, the experts argued, would have been the conventional infantry tactic of turning "palms in," or destroying the NKPA by a series of short or limited and methodical envelopments.[42]

To conduct this offensive, Walker grouped the four American divisions of Eighth Army into two corps formations with two divisions each. The 1st Cav and 24th divisions at Taegu were assigned to John Coulter's I Corps, already in Taegu; the 2d and 25th divisions, to IX Corps, newly arrived at Pusan. However, Walker did not believe Coulter was sufficiently aggressive to command I Corps for the breakout. Had Bill Dean "survived," Walker would have recommended him for that command. He confided to his deposed chief of staff Gene Landrum: "I wish I had Bill Dean here now. I would put him in command of I Corps and know that he would crack through the Red line, open a gap and push everything through that I could give him."[43]

So Walker chose the newly arrived IX Corps commander, West Pointer (1914) Frank W. ("Shrimp") Milburn, fifty-eight, who by date of rank was two years junior to Coulter. In his youth Milburn had been a famous West Point athlete (football, baseball) and coach. During World War II he had ably commanded XXI Corps in Patch's Seventh Army in the ETO. In the postwar years he had commanded the 1st Infantry Division in Germany. When Joe

Collins chose him to take a corps to Korea, he was serving as deputy commander of all American Army forces in Europe.[44]

Upon receiving the assignment for Korea, Milburn had drafted his wartime chief of staff, West Pointer (1925) Rinaldo Van Brunt, forty-eight, who remembered: "I was on maneuvers near Frankfurt, Germany, with my regiment, the Eighteenth Infantry of the First Division. Milburn telephoned and said he was going to Korea and wanted me to be his chief of staff again. I said sure. We flew to Chicago—Fifth Army headquarters—where we picked up a cadre of twenty-five or thirty officers. These included Percy W. Thompson, young John Eisenhower's father-in-law, who was G-two, the best G-two in the business. Then on to Tokyo to confer with MacArthur. I had served under MacArthur (and Eisenhower) in Manila in the late 1930s, but Milburn had never met him. We had a hard time getting by Ned Almond. He kept us sitting outside MacArthur's office that day from eight A.M. to late afternoon. Almond made us mad; we came to detest him. When we finally got in to see MacArthur, he remembered me, and we talked about the old days in the Philippines. Milburn was a wonderful soldier but a very quiet type. He'd never talk in meetings. MacArthur told us about the situation in Korea—the Pusan Perimeter and the plans for Inchon—then said, theatrically: 'You'll leave in the morning at eight, and I want you to attack by twelve!' "[45]

Milburn and Van Brunt flew on to Korea to meet Walker in Taegu. The trip had been a long ordeal for Milburn, who dreaded flying. He emerged from the plane with his long-haired dachshund, Ebbo, on a leash, to a warm reception from Johnnie Walker. Walker was apparently pleased to discover that Milburn shared his detestation of Ned Almond. "Walker was rough," Van Brunt recalled, "but he never got rough with us. Milburn and Walker got along well."[46]

When Walker switched Milburn and Coulter around, giving I Corps to Milburn and IX Corps to Coulter, he gutted IX Corps of communications gear and personnel to beef up I Corps. Thereafter Coulter's IX Corps became an "orphan," so desperately short of manpower that its overworked Gs, chief of staff Tychsen remembered, "soon began to collapse from sheer fatigue." Coulter was not pleased at this treatment and at being forced to take a back seat to his junior, Shrimp Milburn. That Coulter was a "MacArthur-Almond man," as opposed to Milburn, who was a "Collins-Walker man," may have influenced Walker's decision not a little.[47]

\* \* \*

Johnnie Walker launched the breakout offensive on September 16, one day behind the Inchon landing. Morale in Eighth Army had soared at the news of Inchon. Every GI immediately perceived its strategic significance. It was like a miracle. It would liberate them from the ghastly prison of the perimeter, crush the barbarous NKPA, and enable them to get out of Korea soon. And the sooner, the better.

Notwithstanding the 20,000 casualties he had sustained, by this time Walker commanded a formidable combat force. On September 16 there were 150,000 men serving in the army and corps headquarters and the four American and six ROK divisions, plus about 75,000 more in rear-area service units. Owing to the diversion of infantry and artillery fillers to the 7th Division, the American divisions were still greatly understrength (about 14,500 men, rather than 18,800), but each had about 2,000 ROKs to do menial work. The six ROK divisions were at nearly full strength, about 10,000 men each.[48]

Because Eighth Army continued to underestimate grossly the carnage inflicted on the NKPA, Walker believed he still confronted a strong enemy: thirteen NKPA divisions comprising about 100,000 men with 75 percent of their equipment. It was later determined that in fact, on September 16 the NKPA comprised only about 70,000 men with about 50 percent of their equipment. Of the surviving 70,000, only about 21,000 were combat-hardened veterans; the rest, raw fillers with little or no training. Moreover, the NKPA suffered from an acute shortage of everything, and morale was sinking.[49]

The big problem for Walker was that in too many areas around the perimeter the NKPA still held commanding terrain. The NKPA had converted many of these hilltops to minifortresses. Not untypical was a hill in Cecil Nist's 7th Cav sector. The regimental historian wrote that this hilltop was fortified by twelve 120-mm and 82-mm mortars, plus tanks and other flat trajectory weapons. The NKPA had "dug into solid rock" or "deep holes" with cover and connecting tunnels, and the gunners fired weapons by periscope, like submariners.[50]

In order to crack out of the perimeter, Walker's divisions had first to seize these minifortresses, then, in most of the American sector, to stage a difficult crossing of the Naktong River. Seizing these hilltops required utmost courage, military professionalism, physical stamina, and a willingness to endure yet more severe casualties. The task was made more difficult by an acute shortage of artillery ammunition, caused in part by the diversion of ammo to Inchon. The river crossings were made more difficult owing to a scandalous shortage of bridging equipment and bridge builders. In the whole of Eighth Army there were only two pontoon vehicular bridges available.[51]

For these and other reasons, the Eighth Army offensive did not at first go well. Clockwise around the perimeter there were four major breakout battles.

### Southwest Sector

At H hour on September 16 Bill Kean's 25th Division (15,000 men) was, as the Army historian put it, "in an embarrassing situation." Remnants of the battered NKPA 6th and 7th divisions were still on the attack toward Masan in the weak mountainous center of the division's line, held by John Corley's 24th Infantry. The division could not shift over to a general offensive until the 24th Infantry, still bracketed by Fisher's 35th Infantry and Michaelis's 27th Infantry, had got its front under control. This task was complicated by bad weather—perhaps an offshoot of the typhoon—which canceled FEAF close air support.[52]

To assist Corley, Kean directed that a battalion from Fisher's 35th and a company from Michaelis's 27th, plus other divisional elements, reinforce the 24th's sector. The task force was organized around Robert Woolfolk's 3/35. On September 17 and 18 these forces, linking with Corley's three battalions and supported by FEAF close air, attempted to drive the NKPA from the hilltop fortress. But Task Force Woolfolk failed and was dissolved after incurring heavy casualties. Meanwhile, the 27th and 35th regiments, weakened by the diversion of force to the 24th sector, were still not able to advance as planned.

However, the situation on Kean's front dramatically changed on the morning of the fourth day of the offensive, September 19. The remnants of the NKPA 6th and 7th divisions suddenly withdrew in good order, abandoning the hilltop enclaves and most roadblocks. What prompted the withdrawal was never determined. It may have been in response to an order from NKPA headquarters—perhaps a preliminary step to redeploying the divisions to the defense of Seoul—or it may have been a local tactical decision. It was not because the NKPA had collapsed, as hoped, on receiving the news of Inchon. The Army historian wrote that that news was withheld from NKPA troops for five days or more.

Capitalizing on the withdrawal, Bill Kean ordered Corley, Michaelis, and Fisher to attack with their regiments. Thus, after a delay of nearly four days, the 25th Division began a slow, careful movement westward in the general direction of long-sought Chinju. But it was not by any means the flashy breakthrough Walker had sought. If the NKPA decided to make a determined stand before Chinju, the 25th Division might well bog down again.

## Naktong Bulge

Dutch Keiser's 2d Division (15,000 men), still occupying the Naktong Bulge sector immediately to the north of Kean's 25th, was also in an awkward position for launching an offensive. Despite the earlier parting shot of the Fifth Marines, the NKPA still held a number of commanding hilltops on the east side of the Naktong, in the bulge, notably in Sloane's 9th Infantry sector. Before Keiser could mount a textbook crossing of the Naktong, the division had first to root out these NKPA troops and to secure completely the east bank of the river.

On September 16, when these ground operations began, they were also bedeviled by foul weather, which canceled FEAF air attacks. As foreseen, the toughest opposition occurred in Sloane's 9th Infantry sector, where remnants of the NKPA 4th and 9th divisions still held some hills. Badly shattered in earlier fighting, Londahl's 1/9 and Barberis's 2/9 were slowly rebuilding; but both battalions were still far understrength, and the men were exhausted from the heat and well over a full month of vicious combat.[53]

The 9th Infantry, however, had been significantly strengthened. Its black 3/9, commanded by D. M. McMains, had returned from assignments at Yonil Airfield and elsewhere in the northeast sector. These missions had served to introduce the 3/9 to combat gradually, and the battalion had done well and suffered only slight casualties. It was at full strength and included some outstanding black officers, such as platoon leaders Ellison C. Wynn and Julius W. Becton, Jr. Becton, twenty-four, who had served with the 93d Division at the tail end of World War II, ultimately (1978) rose to three stars.[54]

The 9th Infantry, supported by John Keith's 15th FAB, attacked with a will, but the going was very, very tough. Ably led, McMains's 3/9 fought well and aggressively. In the process it suffered harsh casualties. The (white) exec, William Frazier, was killed. Leading his platoon with awesome courage and determination, Julius Becton was wounded in three places. Frazier was replaced by a black officer, John C. Harlan. Becton (awarded a Silver Star Medal) was to return to the regiment.[55]

For all its will—and exertion—the 9th Infantry failed to crack through. The enemy was simply too numerous and too well dug in.

Farther north in the 2d Division sector the story was better—far better:

• Paul Freeman's 23d Infantry, spearheaded by the 3/23, only recently returned from loan to the 1st Cav and commanded by West Pointer (1935) Robert G. ("Gib") Sherrard, Jr., thirty-five, a veteran of ETO combat, cracked through "stubborn resistance" by remnants of the NKPA 2d Division and drove straight through to the Naktong River on the first day. In this dramatic advance, Freeman estimated, the 23d inflicted 1,200 casualties on the NKPA. However, further progress—an attempted bridgehead across the river—was not possible owing to the exposure caused by the slow progress of the 9th Infantry on Freeman's left flank. Furthermore, after Freeman had reached the river, Keiser detached James Edwards's 2/23 to assist the 9th.

• To the north of the 23d George Peploe's 38th Infantry, the bulk of which had not yet seen much heavy fighting and which was therefore still at nearly full strength, continued to have good luck. On September 16 and 17 the 2/38, commanded by James Skeldon, also drove straight through to the Naktong. On the following day, September 18, Keiser authorized Peploe to send Skeldon across the river and, if possible, establish a bridgehead. Skeldon crossed with ease in assault boats, achieving temporary fame of sorts by becoming the "first" unit of Eighth Army to cross the Naktong. On September

19 Peploe enlarged the bridgehead with the addition of Everett Stewart's 3/38. The 1/38, commanded by William P. Keleher, thirty-nine, remained east of the river, keeping a wary eye to the west, where the puzzling do-nothing NKPA 10th Division was deployed.[56]

Johnnie Walker made haste to further exploit Peploe's river crossing by directing that one of the two pontoon vehicular bridges he had available in Eighth Army go to the 38th's sector. As was his custom, Keiser sent a senior subordinate, ADC Sladen Bradley, to direct this vital operation. On Peploe's left Paul Freeman, intensely competitive, was frustrated. Had Sloane's 9th Infantry not bogged down, exposing his left flank and causing the temporary detachment of his 2/23 to reinforce it, Freeman might have had the honor—and glory—of crossing the Naktong first and thereby gained priority on the scarce bridging equipment. In his frustration Freeman began to feel hostile toward Peploe and Bradley and became determined to outdo them at the first chance.[57]

By the fourth day of the offensive, September 19, Keiser could feel some degree of satisfaction. Peploe had put two battalions across the Naktong and had a vehicular bridge under construction. With the help of James Edwards's 2/23, Sloane had cleared most of the hills in the bulge and was preparing to proceed onward to the river. Paul Freeman was at the river, champing at the bit. However, this was not nearly what Walker had hoped for. The 9th Infantry had not only slowed down two-thirds of the division but also retarded the progress of Fisher's 35th to the south. The element of surprise was gone. Nor was there any evidence of a NKPA "collapse" in this sector. To the contrary. It was believed that the NKPA was consolidating on the west bank of the Naktong River for a strong counterattack when the 9th and 23d regiments attempted to cross.

### Northwest Sector

The breakout plan for Shrimp Milburn's I Corps, composed of the 24th and 1st Cav divisions, was more complex than that of the 25th and 2d divisions. It would be a three-step operation:

First, John Church's 24th Division (15,000 men), greatly reinforced with the Patton tanks of Growdon's 6th Tank Battalion and massively supported by FEAF, would recapture Waegwan and seize a bridgehead on the west bank of the Naktong. To accomplish this, Johnny Throckmorton's 5th Infantry, assisted by Crombez's 5th Cav on his right, would attack Waegwan frontally from the east and cross the Naktong in assault boats. At the same time Dick Stephens's 21st and Ned Moore's 19th would cross the Naktong about five miles below Waegwan and go north on the west bank of the river, linking with Throckmorton in his bridgehead.

Secondly, engineers would immediately put two bridges across the Naktong at Waegwan. One would be a treadway bridge for foot soldiers; the other, a pontoon vehicular bridge, capable of supporting trucks, motorized artillery, and tanks. After the 24th's heavy equipment got across, Church would attack straight up the main highway to Taejon.

Thirdly, the battered 1st Cav Division (14,000 men), having helped Throckmorton take Waegwan and having contained or eliminated the enemy threat in the Bowling Alley, would pivot and follow the 24th Division across the Naktong. Its weak and exhausted battalions would be dropped off along the route of advance to maintain local security.[58]

\* \* \*

On September 16, Throckmorton's 5th Infantry, assisted by Crombez's 5th Cav on the right, got off on schedule. But it proved to be very difficult going. Remnants of the NKPA 3d Division were solidly dug in on the hilltops; both Throckmorton and Crombez were hampered by a shortage of men. The 5th Infantry had but 2,599 Americans (1,194 short); the three battalions averaged only about 585 men. Crombez, who had even fewer men, made no progress at all until Gay temporarily reinforced him with the 2/7. Both regiments suffered severe casualties. By the evening of September 18 the 2/7 was so badly shattered (down to 50 men per rifle company) that it had to be pulled into the Army reserve for yet another reorganization.[59]

The battles in this area, as in others, were focused on NKPA strongholds in the hilltops. For Edgar Treacy's newly committed 3/5, the mission was Hill 174. Day after day in the sapping heat the 3/5 assaulted the hill, taking ground, then yielding under terrific NKPA counterfire. The I Company commander, Norman Allen, remembered that Hill 174 had been taken—and lost—seven times before the 3/5 drew the task. His company and L Company made eleven separate or combined attacks up its steep, rocky sides. He lost nearly half his company, 80 men; L Company lost more than 100 men.[60]

Hill 174 was littered with old and new NKPA dead. One of Allen's men, Victor Fox, remembered the carnage:

Around our positions the enemy dead lay in terrible positions. . . . Most had been badly mangled by artillery fire . . . [and] the stench . . . became stifling. . . . In all the time I spent on Hill 174 there was never an opportunity to remove the corpses that surrounded us. The continual, deadly firefight made such venture an impossibility. . . .

While eating our C rations amid this human carnage [my buddy] Haltom and I had time to contemplate how the human body is put together from the brains to the feet. There were certainly enough dissected examples lying around for close up analysis.[61]

To the south of Throckmorton, the advance of Stephens's 21st to the Naktong crossing site did not go well either. The I Corps engineers had failed to sandbag a ford on the small but deep Kumho River east of the Naktong, and by nightfall on September 18 traffic was backed up five miles. As a result, Stephens's crossing of the Naktong in assault boats could not go as planned under cover of darkness. Because of this foul-up, Brad Smith's 1/21 crossed in daylight early on the morning of September 19 (merely twelve hours behind James Skeldon's 2/38). Smith met withering enemy fire, which caused 120 casualties. Later in the day the 3/21 crossed in assault boats to join Smith's 1/21; Ned Moore's 19th crossed in assault boats farther south.[62]

Meanwhile, in the Bowling Alley Ray Palmer's depleted and exhausted 8th Cav got nowhere in its efforts to clean out the NKPA. Remnants of the NKPA 1st and 13th divisions fought Palmer to a standstill. Since the 1st Cav could not pivot and follow the 24th Division across the Naktong to Taejon until the NKPA threat in the Bowling Alley was contained or eliminated, Palmer's failure to fight the 8th Cav more aggressively placed the whole I Corps breakout scheme in jeopardy. Walker, furious at Palmer, reinforced the 8th Cav with James Lynch's aggressive (but depleted) 3/7 and hurriedly improvised a plan to launch Pete Clainos's 1/7 on a daring cavalrylike sweep behind the NKPA forces facing Palmer.[63]

By the morning of the fourth day of the offensive, September 19, the situation in the I Corps sector appeared bleak indeed. Throckmorton's 5th Infantry and Crombez's 5th Cav seemed unable to advance on Waegwan. Stephens's 21st Infantry had got across the Naktong below Waegwan but was under heavy attack and was in danger of being cut off—or driven back across the river—if Throckmorton and Crombez failed to take Waegwan. Although Palmer's 8th Cav had been reinforced by all the available power of Nist's 7th Cav (the 1/7 and 3/7), Palmer appeared to be hopelessly bogged down.

## III

The apparent inability of Eighth Army to break out of the Pusan Perimeter was not viewed as a grave military crisis. Owing to the ease of the Inchon landing, the light casualties, and the growing power of the American forces there, short of overt Peking or Moscow intervention there was no danger that X Corps could be "cut off" and destroyed piecemeal. Nor was there any longer any danger that Eighth Army could be driven out of the Pusan Perimeter. However, the apparent inability of Eighth Army to break out did substantially threaten the grand design of Inchon, which was to stun, overwhelm and trap the NKPA in South Korea. Lacking the swift decisive advance of Eighth Army, the NKPA might fight on for months, inflicting more and more American casualties in a dreaded winter campaign for which neither Eighth Army nor X Corps was prepared. The "unification" of Korea would necessarily be postponed; the American public, still supporting Truman—and MacArthur—might rebel.

On the night of September 19 MacArthur—still aboard the *Mount McKinley* at Inchon—met with Almond, Struble, Shepherd, Doyle, Wright, and others to review the situation in the Pusan Perimeter. According to Shepherd's notes, MacArthur was deeply concerned and immensely annoyed with Johnnie Walker. It seemed that Joe Collins had been right after all. Eighth Army had been hemmed in the perimeter for so long and at such cost in manpower that it did not seem capable of a decisive offensive. The distance between Taegu and Inchon might well be too great to effect a linkup. Astonishingly MacArthur went on to tell the group—virtually a public meeting—that perhaps Walker ought to be replaced by a more forceful general.

As one solution to the situation MacArthur turned to the idea Joe Collins had earlier suggested and that he had ridiculed: an amphibious landing at Kunsan, closer to Eighth Army. All present agreed that a second amphibious landing was probably necessary. Struble and Shepherd again proposed Posung-Myon—closer to Inchon—but gave way to Doyle, who appeared to favor Kunsan. There followed a detailed discussion of shipping, beaches, hydrography, road nets, scheme of maneuver, and other matters. Concluding the meeting, MacArthur decreed that if Eighth Army showed no definite progress soon, an amphibious landing at Kunsan by three divisions (two American, one ROK) should take place on about October 15, and he directed Pinky Wright so to inform planners at GHQ, Tokyo.[64]

The news of this meeting must have landed like a bomb in Walker's headquarters. It signaled a complete lack of faith in Eighth Army and in his leadership. The GHQ pistol so long held at Walker's head finally seemed likely to go off. Moreover, Walker had grave misgivings about the proposed second landing plan. Since MacArthur had declared that the 1st Marine Division would remain at Seoul, the two American divisions contemplated for Kunsan would have to come from Eighth Army. If so, this would again drastically—perhaps fatally—weaken Eighth Army.

Walker's reaction to all this was strong and immediate. He told Almond's deputy in Tokyo, Doyle Hickey, that any plan to weaken Eighth Army in order to mount a Kunsan or any other amphibious landing was ill advised and inappropriate and would be opposed by Eighth Army. Bitterly referring to the priority given X Corps over Eighth Army, Walker went on: "We have been bastard children lately, and as far as our engineering equipment is concerned we are in pretty bad shape." By "engineering equipment" he meant bridging. He elaborated: "I don't want you to think that I am dragging my heels, but I have a river across my whole front and the two bridges I have don't make much."[65]

Thus the apparent inability of Eighth Army to break out of the Pusan

Perimeter planted in MacArthur's mind the idea for a second large amphibious landing in Korea. Excluding use of Eighth Army forces, the two American divisions available to carry it out were Dave Barr's 7th and the 3d, en route from the States to replace the 7th Division in the occupation and defense of Japan. He had assured the JCS that the 3d Division would not be employed in Korea. He had already partly broken that promise by directing the Puerto Rican 65th Regiment (attached to the 3d Division) to Pusan, to replace the 17th Regiment in Eighth Army reserve. He may have believed that in light of his success at Inchon, JCS authorization for further commitment of the 3d Division to Korea would not be withheld.

As the situation developed, the amphibious landing at Kunsan soon proved to be unnecessary, and it was canceled. However, the idea for a second large amphibious landing in Korea did not die. The wheels continued turning in MacArthur's mind, and GHQ, Tokyo, responded with a variety of plans. Omar Bradley believed the impetus came principally from MacArthur's vanity. "There was an aura of glamor about an amphibious landing," Bradley wrote. "A sudden bold and decisive strike in the enemy's rear made big headlines and generated editorials about 'military genius' at work. In the first act, MacArthur had overridden staff objections and pulled it off at Inchon, bringing down the curtain amid thunderous applause. A second-act curtain would generate even more headlines, editorials and applause."[66]

## I V

On the day MacArthur left Inchon, September 21, Ned Almond established X Corps headquarters ashore and assumed command of all ground operations. Until then he had functioned more as MacArthur's chief of staff than as military field commander. With MacArthur out of his hair, Almond could now devote his boundless energies to directing tactics that would ensure his goal of liberating Seoul by September 25, the three-month anniversary of the NKPA invasion.[67]

Keeping in step with their commander, O. P. Smith, the senior Marines viewed Almond and the X Corps staff with mounting contempt. They ridiculed Almond's "luxurious" field living quarters—a van rigged with a refrigerator, a hot-water shower, and a flush toilet. They made jokes about the X Corps mess, which was provided with fine china, linen, and silverware, even silver napkin rings, and which FEAF supplied daily with fresh fruit, vegetables, and meat. Almond's G-3, Jack Chiles, a more than willing beneficiary of these comforts, conceded: "General Almond lived first class."[68]

The criticism of the quality and experience of the X Corps staff did not, however, appear to be justified. Although X Corps had been hurriedly formed in Tokyo, MacArthur had given Almond carte blanche to draft almost any-body he wanted. The upshot was that X Corps contained an astonishing array of high-caliber officers, many of whom were to go far in the Army or the government. Two rose to four stars: the chief of staff, Clark L. ("Nick") Ruffner (VMI, 1924), and Almond's aide-de-camp, Alexander M. Haig, Jr. (West Point, 1947). Three rose to three stars: the deputy chief of staff, William J. ("Bill") McCaffrey (West Point, 1939); the G-2, William W. Quinn (West Point, 1933); and the engineer, Edward L. ("Ed") Rowny (West Point, 1941). The G-3, Chiles, would rise to two stars.[69]*

On paper the most influential of these men was the chief of staff, Nick Ruffner, forty-seven. In practice it was Ruffner's assistant, Bill McCaffrey, thirty-five, who had been chief of staff of Almond's 92d Division in Italy. Ruffner, a cavalryman, had not seen any combat in World War II. He had been chief of staff to his father-in-law, General Robert C. ("Nellie") Richardson, in charge of training Army forces in the Pacific, under Admiral Chester W. Nimitz in Honolulu (the so-called Pineapple Army). In Italy McCaffrey and Ed Rowny, who was G-3 of Almond's 92d Division, had been Almond's closest advisers and confidants. McCaffrey and Rowny had represented and spoken for Almond in all the Inchon planning. Both men were tough and aggressive; both had won Silver Stars for heroism in Italy.[70]

*　*　*

Reviewing the tactical situation, Almond was still dissatisfied with the speed of the Marine advance on Seoul. He decided that what was needed was an added wide envelopment on the right to attack Seoul from the southeast. He proposed to O. P. Smith that Chesty Puller's First Marines, then slogging into Yongdungpo, be assigned that mission, but Smith dug in his heels and said no. Smith did not want to separate the First and Fifth Marines or have them come into Seoul face-to-face from two different directions, incurring the risk of friendly fire. Moreover, Smith believed that the NKPA would defend Seoul street by street, regardless of an American flanking attack from the southeast, and that on the whole, it would be more prudent to conduct the American attack out of one solid, closely coordinated formation.[71]

Almond was furious. To refuse a corps commander's strongly presented suggestion was tantamount to insubordination. Had Smith been an Army general, Almond might well have sacked him. But Smith was a Marine, and the Marines were the heroes of Inchon. Sacking Smith would create a political

---

*Haig became White House chief of staff to President Richard M. Nixon and secretary of state to President Ronald Reagan. Rowny became Reagan's chief strategic arms negotiator, with the rank of ambassador. McCaffrey became a high official in the CIA.

storm reminiscent of that which had occurred on Saipan in World War II when Marine General Holland M. Smith sacked an Army general, Ralph Smith, commanding the lagging 27th Infantry Division, which was assigned to Holland Smith's corps. The storm would very likely destroy Almond.[72]

Apparently believing this flanking attack was necessary to liberate Seoul by September 25, Almond pursued the idea with single-minded zeal. He soon conceived a plan that would not be refused. Charles Beauchamp's 32d Infantry, reinforced by the ROK 17th Regiment (for psychological and political reasons), would make the maneuver. The commitment of Army troops to the Seoul battle might spur the Marines to greater aggressiveness. Not incidentally, it would give the Army, until then submerged by a Niagara of Marine Corps publicity, a more prominent role in the liberation of Seoul.[73]

This idea met opposition from some 7th Division planners. It had been expected that the 7th Division would carry out an important follow-up Inchon mission: to advance, with the full power of its three regiments, in a generally easterly direction and thereby throw another line across western South Korea. This line was designed to trap NKPA troops leaking northward from Eighth Army's tiers. It was to be the so-called anvil against which Eighth Army's hammer would pound the NKPA to pieces. The diversion of the 32d Infantry and supporting armor and artillery for the attack on Seoul would delay and probably preclude the formation of the anvil. But Almond overrode the opposition.

At the time of this decision Beauchamp already had his hands full. After relieving Puller's Fifth Marines in the southern sector, Almond had Dave Barr send an armored task force, built around the tanks of the 7th Division's 73d Tank Battalion, commanded by Calvin Hannum, south down the main highway to liberate Suwon and its fine airfield and to establish a strong block there to repel NKPA reinforcements coming up from the south. Beauchamp had provided the infantry for the task force.[74]

At Suwon Task Force Hannum ran head-on into elements of the NKPA 105th Armored Division coming north. During the confused night fighting the 7th Division's able G-3, Henry J. Hampton, Jr., who had come to Suwon to lend a hand, was killed. The division G-2, Bill Paddock, who was also at Suwon (and who replaced Hampton as division G-3), remembered that the task force captured Suwon but that the loss of Hampton in doing so was a heavy price to pay.[75]

Having been detailed to make the flanking attack on Seoul, Beauchamp hurriedly pulled all his forces out of the southern sector, including Suwon, and began regrouping. To replace Beauchamp's forces in the south, Almond chose the 31st Infantry, which had come ashore on September 19 and was then the sole X Corps reserve. In turn, the 31st would be replaced in reserve by the 17th Infantry, coming up from Pusan and scheduled to reach Inchon on September 24. The reserve would be further strengthened by the 187th Airborne RCT, which had finally reached Japan, and which would be airlifted to Kimpo Airfield on September 24 and 25.[76]

The 31st Infantry was commanded by West Pointer (1919) Richard P. Ovenshine, fifty. Ovenshine was descended from an old Army family; both his grandfather and father had retired as brigadier generals. A classmate of Al Gruenther, Al Wedemeyer, Bill Kean, and Sladen Bradley, Ovenshine was lagging far behind them. His combat experience was slight. During World War II he had been chief of staff to an old friend, George Griner, who commanded two infantry divisions in training before going to Saipan to replace Ralph Smith as commander of the troubled 27th Division. After the division had been retrained and remanned, it had been committed to the invasion of Okinawa, where Ovenshine commanded a regiment at the tail end of the campaign. In the postwar years he had served in the inspector general sections of Eighth Army and the Pentagon.[77]

No doubt the Almond-Smith dispute gave Ovenshine a sense of déjà vu, but of far greater immediate concern was the fact that Almond took a dislike to him as well. Ovenshine thought it was because he was too old and too conservative. He was not a charismatic leader. He did not display that brash "can do" spirit Almond looked for in his subordinate commanders. For his part, Ovenshine viewed Almond in much the same way that O. P. Smith and Dave Barr saw him. Ovenshine later damned Almond with this terse judgment: "I considered General Almond to be impulsive."[78]

In substituting the 31st Infantry for the 32d in the vast, hostile southern sector, Almond ran a serious risk. The defense in that sector was still weak and overextended, especially in the extreme tip at Suwon. A concentrated NKPA attack in this sector while the 31st and 32d were changing places, could have resulted in a serious setback, perhaps even endangering Inchon and Kimpo Airfield, the landing of the 17th Infantry and 187th Airborne RCT. The apparent inability of Eighth Army to break out of the Pusan Perimeter heightened the risk by indefinitely postponing the linkup.

When the Marines learned of Almond's decision to bring up the 32d for a "flanking" attack on Seoul, they were further infuriated with Almond. They did not believe the capture of Seoul by September 25 justified the serious risks being taken in the southern sector. If anything, the southern sector should be strengthened in order to destroy utterly the NKPA attacking—or fleeing— north. Moreover, there was the important matter of service pride. Until then the liberation of Seoul had been exclusively a Marine responsibility. Now the Army was horning in, taking away part of the battle and the glory.[79]

*　*　*

On September 24 the assault on Seoul moved toward a climax. That day Puller's First Marines, having taken Yongdungpo, crossed directly north over the Han River into the southwestern outskirts of Seoul. There, on the north bank of the Han, Puller linked with Murray's Fifth Marines, who were advancing from the west and were now backed up by the newly arriving Seventh Marines, commanded by Homer L. Litzenberg, Jr., forty-seven. Inasmuch as Murray was meeting do-or-die NKPA resistance and suffering heavy casualties, he was very glad that Smith had not allowed Almond to withdraw the First Marines and send them to the other side of the city in a flanking attack. The First Marines rendered decisive assistance to the hard-pressed Fifth Marines.

The same day Charles Beauchamp regrouped his 32d Infantry at the village of Sinsa, facing Seoul's southeast quarter, in preparation for crossing the Han River at dawn on September 25. The ROK 17th Regiment, which would cross behind the 32d, camped nearby. Adding insult to injury, Almond had ordered the Marines to provide these forces landing craft; not having anticipated a Han River crossing, Beauchamp had no assault boats. Dave Barr placed his ADC, Hank Hodes, in charge of the operation.[80]

At four on the following morning, September 25, Almond arrived at Beauchamp's CP to observe the crossing. There was no sign of the division commander, Dave Barr. When Barr showed up an hour or so later, Almond demanded testily: "Where have you been?" Highly annoyed but outwardly unruffled, Barr put Almond in his place: "Up on top of that bluff back there, where I can fight my division if I have to. I'm not going to stay down here and fight one battalion."[81]

Blessed by a heavy ground fog, the crossing began at six-thirty. The 2/32, commanded by West Pointer (1934) Charles M. Mount, thirty-four, led the assault. The 2/32 met no resistance and pushed ashore. Immediately behind came the 1/32, commanded by Don Carlos Faith, Jr., thirty-two, followed by the 3/32, commanded by Heinrich G. Schumann, forty. When the Americans were safely deployed in preselected positions, the ROK 17th Regiment crossed.[82]

By luck of the draw Beauchamp had three of the ablest battalion commanders in Korea. Of the three, the standout was the 1/32 commander, Don Faith. He was the son of a retired brigadier general who had helped Oveta Culp Hobby create the Women's Army Auxiliary Corps (WAACs). In World War II paratrooper Matt Ridgway had handpicked the younger Faith from the OCS at Fort Benning to be his aide-de-camp. As such Faith had become a paratrooper and served at Ridgway's side throughout the war, jumping with the 82d Airborne Division into Normandy. On the battlefield Faith was a clone of Ridgway: intense, fearless, relentlessly aggressive, and unforgiving of error or caution.[83]

Later in the morning Almond crossed the Han in an amtrac to see how Beauchamp was faring. The 32d, he decided, was not pushing hard or fast enough. He spoke "briefly but emphatically" to the 2/32 commander, Charles Mount, who required no further prompting. By nightfall the 32d Regiment had secured its objectives. Later that evening Almond attempted to shift the publicity spotlight from the Marines to the Army. He told the *New York Times'* reporter: "The 7th Division is doing a lot of good, very fast."[84]

Just how much military good this flanking attack actually did would forever remain moot. Almond, Barr, Beauchamp, and the X Corps staff were convinced that it was decisive in the liberation of Seoul. It gave the Americans high ground dominating the entire city, closed off two main roads to the east and southeast, drew NKPA strength away from Murray and Puller, and resulted in the capture of a high NKPA headquarters and a considerable amount of weapons and supplies. The Marines scoffed at these claims, arguing that the maneuver did not significantly influence the battle for Seoul.[85]

Projecting Beauchamp and the ROK 17th Regiment into the city on September 25 gave Almond sufficient military force there to justify in his mind a claim that Seoul had been recaptured "three months to the day" after the NKPA invasion. Almond hastened to release this boast to the press that night, September 25, pointedly stressing that "elements" of the 7th Division had participated. On the following day Almond and MacArthur made the liberation of Seoul official in communiqués.[86]

But it was not true. Most of Seoul was still in NKPA hands. These fanatical troops had to be rooted out, street by street, in a campaign that virtually destroyed Seoul. Most of this grim, dirty, and dangerous work was carried out by the First, Fifth, and Seventh Marines over a three-day period following release of the communiqués, September 26 to September 28. The Marine infantry was mightily supported by the thundering artillery pieces of the Eleventh Marines and Marine close air support. Hundreds, perhaps thousands of South Koreans died in the crossfire and chaos. A British war correspondent, Reginald Thompson, vividly described part of the scene:

It is an appalling inferno of din and destruction with the tearing noise of dive bombers blasting right ahead, and the livid flashes of the tank guns, the harsh, fierce crackle of blazing wooden buildings, telegraph and high-tension poles collapsing in utter chaos of wires. Great palls of smoke lie over us as massive buildings collapse in showers of sparks, puffing masses of smoke and rubble upon us in terrific heat. . . . Few people can have suffered so terrible a liberation. . . .[87]

Meanwhile, in the extreme southern sector of the beachhead at Suwon, where Ovenshine's 31st Infantry had replaced the 32d, a serious threat arose. Elements of the NKPA 105th Armored Division, comprising perhaps two dozen tanks and other motorized elements, and NKPA infantry, coming north to help eject the invaders, struck Ovenshine's thin positions during the night of September 24. In response, Almond hurried more 7th Division artillery and armor to Suwon to back up Ovenshine and sped up the unloading of the reserve 17th Infantry at Inchon. In addition, Almond ordered that a company from the 1st Battalion, 187th Airborne RCT, which had begun landing that day at Kimpo, make a forced march to Suwon to lend temporary help.[88]

With these considerable reinforcements Ovenshine soon got the situation at Suwon under control. Then, on Almond's orders, he organized a powerful armored force to attack and destroy the surviving elements of the NKPA 105th Armored Division. This force, built around Hannum's tanks and the 2/31, commanded by Robert R. Summers, an able, combat-experienced officer, thirty-nine, pushed south from Suwon on September 26 and caught the NKPA in a well-executed double envelopment near the place where Brad Smith's 1/21 had first met the NKPA on July 5. The 31st proudly claimed a stirring victory: fourteen enemy tanks destroyed or immobilized, several hundred NKPA troops killed, Osan liberated, the Suwon–Osan highway secure. But the price was high: Summers and the 31st's able S-3, Lester K. Olson, were seriously wounded and evacuated.[89]

Ovenshine himself did not professionally survive these operations. He was a fine, proper, "by-the-book" officer; but most 7th Division officers thought he was simply "too old," and in Ned Almond's eyes, he was not sufficiently aggressive. Almond gave Ovenshine a Silver Star and then sacked him. Nonetheless, like John Hill, Ovenshine got a star before he was forced to retire in 1954 under the thirty and five rule, thereby equaling the retirement rank of his grandfather and father.[90]

In his planning and command decisions at Inchon, Ned Almond demonstrated characteristics familiar to those who had served with him in combat in Italy. He was demanding, arrogant, and impatient. He had only slight regard for conventional doctrine governing the deployment of infantry divisions in a well-integrated mass. Rather, he had a marked tendency to fragment his forces, to create special task forces and to employ these or BCTs or RCTs in independent and risky actions without the usual reserves or firm flank support. He placed greater emphasis on the quick capture of real estate (Seoul) for psychological or publicity reasons than he did on the creation of a strong line (the anvil) to stop the leakage of the NKPA northward. He antagonized his division and regimental commanders by flying or driving around the "front" and giving orders directly to battalion (or even company) commanders. He was courageous, at times to the point of recklessness, and expected everybody else to be. But this attitude was interpreted by many subordinate commanders as a callous indifference to casualties and the welfare of the men.

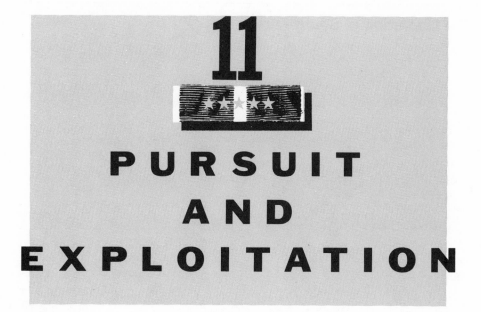

# PURSUIT AND EXPLOITATION

## I

In the Pusan Perimeter Johnnie Walker was an angry and frustrated general. Inchon, which had robbed him of so many resources, had galvanized the world. Commentators had proclaimed it "brilliant," a "masterstroke," a "work of genius," even a "miracle." Meanwhile, Walker was still mired in ghastly, positional warfare. If he did not break out soon, he faced the humiliating and demoralizing prospect of losing two of his four American divisions for the proposed second amphibious landing at Kunsan and perhaps even replacement by his sworn enemy Ned Almond.

Such was the picture in the perimeter until about September 19, the fifth day of fighting at Inchon. Then, suddenly, the NKPA divisions at the perimeter appeared to follow the precedent set by the NKPA 6th and 7th divisions in the southwest sector opposite Bill Kean's 25th Division. Either on orders of distant or local authority or without orders, all NKPA divisions seemed to be yielding and withdrawing.

Although documentary proof is lacking, it seems reasonable to suppose that the "news" of Inchon was an important, perhaps decisive factor in these NKPA withdrawals. But a great deal of credit must also go to Eighth Army. In the four days of frustrating "offensive" operations following the "jump-off" on September 16, it had inflicted further punishing damage on the NKPA. No exact accounting could be made, but it is not unlikely that the NKPA suffered as many as 5,000 casualties in these operations, reducing its strength in combat personnel from about 70,000 to about 65,000. Half—or more—of the survivors were raw, untrained fillers of dubious loyalty and value.[1]

295

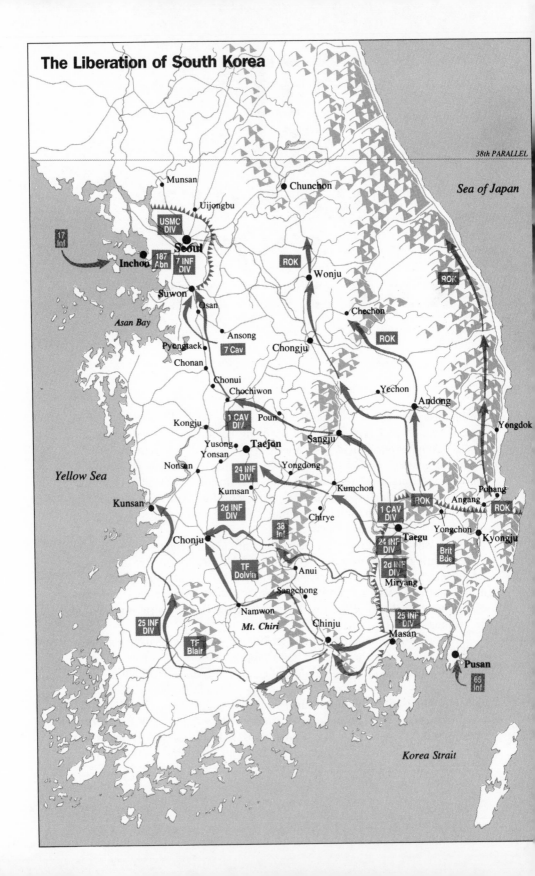

# The Liberation of South Korea

*38th PARALLEL*

*Sea of Japan*

*Yellow Sea*

*Asan Bay*

*Korea Strait*

*Mt. Chiri*

Munsan
Chunchon
Uijongbu
USMC DIV
17 Inf
187 Abn
7 INF DIV
Seoul
Inchon
Suwon
Osan
ROK
Wonju
Chechon
ROK
Pyongtaek
Ansong
7 Cav
Chongju
Chonan
Yechon
Andong
Chonui
Chochiwon
Yongdok
Kongju
1 CAV DIV
Poun
Sangju
Yusong
Taejon
Yonsan
Nonsan
Yongdong
24 INF DIV
Kumchon
Pohang
Kumsan
Kunsan
2d INF DIV
Chirye
1 CAV DIV
ROK
Angang
ROK
Chonju
38 Inf
Taegu
Yongchon
Kyongju
24 INF DIV
Brit Bde
TF Dolvin
Anui
2d INF DIV
Miryang
Sangchong
Namwon
Chinju
25 INF DIV
Masan
25 INF DIV
TF Blair
Pusan
65 Inf

Many in Eighth Army would claim in hindsight that by September 16 the NKPA at the Pusan Perimeter was in fact "beaten." This view was reinforced when the true strength and quality of the NKPA at the perimeter on September 16 later came to light. The proponents of the "beaten" theory argued in retrospect that Inchon was not even necessary to the defeat of the NKPA, that considering the overwhelming manpower and weapons superiority of Eighth Army (150,000 men versus 70,000; 500 tanks versus 50) it was simply unthinkable that Eighth Army, supported by FEAF close air, could not roll over the NKPA with one or two weeks of coordinated offensive operations.

But that was hindsight. On September 19 Eighth Army believed it faced a formidable and—considering the shortage of ammo and bridging—conceivably impossible task. No one could be certain what the NKPA withdrawals meant. It seemed too much to hope that these fanatical fighters would turn tail and run overnight. Perhaps they were merely regrouping into tighter, better manned and armed blocking positions.

In any case, Walker gave not a minute to these speculations. He was everywhere at once, it seemed, prodding, cajoling, demanding that his army take immediate advantage of the softening in the NKPA lines. Commencing that day, September 19, Eighth Army began to crack through. It was by no means a dramatic breakthrough caused by a "sudden collapse" of the NKPA. It was slow and hard slogging for several more days, then, finally, a thrilling, climactic chase. Clockwise around the perimeter there were four major battles.

## II

### Southwest Sector

Upon detecting the withdrawal of the NKPA 6th and 7th divisions on September 19, Bill Kean ordered his 24th, 27th, and 35th regiments to pursue westerly toward long-sought Chinju. Hank Fisher's 35th Regiment, advancing warily along the Masan–Chinju road, made fair progress. Michaelis's 27th and Corley's 24th, negotiating more difficult terrain south of Fisher, came on more slowly. By September 21 Bernard Teeters's 1/35 had reached the much-fought-over road fork at Muchon, but it was stopped cold by a strong NKPA blocking force six miles west of Chinju on the following day.[2]

All 25th Division operations were significantly restricted by a shortage of artillery ammunition and bridging. The 25th Division artillery commander, Bittman Barth, remembered that because of the ammo shortage, Kean had to impose severe daily firing limits (twenty-five rounds per 105 mm; forty rounds per 155 mm). There was also "a serious shortage" of mortar ammo, Barth wrote, "particularly" for the 4.2-inch mortars, which the infantry used for close-in support. Because Walker had given priority for bridging to the other American divisions, the 25th Division had none.[3]

Believing the NKPA might mount a do-or-die defense of Chinju, Kean drew up a complicated plan to seize the city. In some respects the plan resembled that of Task Force Kean, launched against Chinju in early August. As before, Fisher's 35th would continue pressing from the east on the Masan–Chinju road. An armored force, commanded by Charles J. Torman, would displace the 27th Wolfhounds on the "south road" and retrace the path of the Fifth Marines through Kosong and Sachon, then attack Chinju from the south, serving as a spearhead for Corley's 24th Infantry. The added element to the plan involved Michaelis's Wolfhounds. They would shift from the extreme left (or south) flank to the extreme right (or north) flank, swing up through Uiryong, cross the Nam River, and attack Chinju from the north.[4]

The plan went well, perhaps in part because on September 25—the day Almond prematurely announced the liberation of Seoul—NKPA headquarters ordered all NKPA divisions south of Waegwan to withdraw northward. Torman's task force, followed by Corley's 24th Infantry, blazed through Kosong and Sachon. By September 24 Torman was three miles south of Chinju. Meanwhile, Fisher, in an all-out drive east on the Masan–Chinju road spearheaded by John Wilkin's 2/35, broke the now-slight resistance east of Chinju. On September 25 Fisher overran Chinju (by then a ruin of rubble) and seized it with the help of tank fire from Task Force Torman. The same day Task Force Torman and Corley's 24th Infantry came into the town from the south. Going the longer way around, via Uiryong, Michaelis and his Wolfhounds were to reach Chinju without great difficulty on September 28.

The NKPA withdrawal from Chinju led Kean to believe the 6th and 7th divisions were in full flight. Accordingly, he made final plans for the all-out dash across the peninsula to Kunsan, 100 miles away. However, there was a massive obstacle in the way: 7,000-foot Mount Chiri, the tallest mountain in South Korea. Two roads ran around Chiri, one on the north side, one on the south, converging on the west side at Namwon. Kean's plan called for Fisher's 35th, led by an armored task force, to take the north road and Corley's 24th, led by Torman's task force (less Torman, severely wounded at Chinju), to take the south road, believed to be less strongly defended. After the 24th and 35th regiments met at Namwon—and the extent of enemy opposition had been ascertained—further orders would be forthcoming.[5]

John Corley's 24th Infantry set off first, on September 26. Corley gave the honor of leading the armored caravan to his former outfit, the 3/24, now commanded by Melvin Blair. Blair and elements of the 3/24 climbed on the rear decks of the tanks in high spirits. But the force encountered three blown bridges outside Chinju and had to stop for twenty-four hours while engineers improvised sandbag fords.

Fisher moved out the same day, September 26. Since his route to the north of Mount Chiri was believed to be the main avenue of retreat for the NKPA 6th and 7th divisions, his armored spearhead, built around two companies of Tom Dolvin's 89th Tank Battalion, was more powerful and better organized. Commanded by Dolvin (and called Task Force Dolvin), it included two companies of Teeters's 1/35 and a platoon of 4.2 mortars, some combat engineers, and other supporting elements. It was helped by a Mosquito spotter aircraft, which was to scout ahead and relay information on the NKPA to Dolvin and direct FEAF close air support to targets.

For tanker Dolvin, this was the first opportunity his outfit had really been given to show its stuff. Up to then it had been engaged in tedious, closely controlled defensive operations. He and his tankers were determined to show the infantry how to "hit the road" Patton-style, sowing fear in the ranks of a disorganized, retreating enemy and gaining great swaths of real estate. They would disprove the canard that Korea "was not good tank country."

Dolvin expected to encounter two principal obstacles: land mines on the roads and blown bridges. He would not waste time sweeping the roads of mines. He counted on his speed to deny the retreating NKPA time to plant many minefields. If his lead tanks did encounter mines, they might be disabled, but the crews would not be harmed. He now had plenty of tanks; they could be replaced while engineers cleared the mines. Nor, in most cases, would he waste time waiting for engineers to improvise sandbag fords across the rivers and streams. He would find a place where the tanks could ford, then tow the jeeps and trucks across, dry out the ignition systems, and keep going.

The result was one of the finest, most aggressive—and spectacular—advances of the war. After smashing into the loose rear guard of the retreating NKPA, Dolvin overtook and overran hundreds of NKPA troops. He encountered several hastily planted minefields and many blown bridges. The minefield damage was minor: three tanks disabled; no casualties. As planned, his tanks towed jeeps and trucks across many rivers and streams; but at three crossings the water was too deep, and he had to wait for engineers to create sandbag fords. Thanks to spotting by the Mosquito aircraft, on two occasions Dolvin was able to race ahead and grab bridges before the retreating NKPA could blow them. In one such instance, strafing FEAF fighters held the NKPA away from the bridge until Dolvin's infantry came on the scene.[6]

Meanwhile, Corley's 24th Infantry, led by Melvin Blair's 3/24, resumed its part of the charge on September 27. As believed, the road south of Mount Chiri proved to be lightly defended. Corley and Blair encountered only a few, scattered NKPA troops and no minefields or blown bridges. En route they liberated ninety-seven haggard, half-starved Americans from POW compounds abandoned by the NKPA. Late on the afternoon of September 28, a few hours ahead of Dolvin, Corley and Blair pulled into Namwon and secured the town.[7]

While the two task forces refueled in darkness, Bill Kean, consulting with

Walker, received authorization for the 24th and 35th regiments to proceed onward to Kunsan. Corley would again take the lightly defended (but longer) route: Namwon northwest to Chongup, north to Chonju, thence along the coast road to Iri and Kunsan. Dolvin would go directly northwest up the main highway from Namwon to Chonju, thence to Iri and Kunsan, again on the heels of the retreating NKPA.

The two task forces departed Namwon shortly after midnight. By then a heavy overcast had obscured the moon and the visibility was poor. Nonetheless, the task forces continued onward through the pitch-black at good speed and without stopping. At dawn on September 29 Dolvin pulled into Chonju, linking with advance elements of George Peploe's 38th Infantry, which had come due west from the Naktong (see below). After a pause to refuel Dolvin continued north to Iri. Corley and Blair, having come north on the coast road, linked with Dolvin's force in Iri. Later in the day Dolvin advanced to the south bank of the Kum River, where he stopped and bivouacked, having traveled 136 miles in three days and three nights. Corley's 1/24, commanded by Gerald Miller, proceeded on to Kunsan and took it without noteworthy difficulty.

Following in the path of these dramatic armored spearheads, the rest of the 25th Division combat elements hastened westward. Michaelis came last with his Wolfhounds, mopping up and dropping off his three battalions at strategic points along the Chinju–Chonju road, north of Mount Chiri. The 25th Division CP—virtually imprisoned at Masan since about August 1— moved to the Kunsan area in high spirits. What was particularly heartening was the performance of the 24th Infantry. Although Corley had encountered only slight resistance in his 220-mile roundabout dash to Kunsan, the 24th had carried out its part of the operation—and rescued ninety-seven American POWs—with remarkable aggressiveness and without a single foul-up. Kean recommended Dolvin, Corley, and Blair for DSCs. Later Johnnie Walker happily approved these awards.[8]

# III

## Naktong Bulge

By September 19 Dutch Keiser's 2d Division, having cleared most of the NKPA from the east bank of the Naktong River and established a pontoon bridge in George Peploe's 38th Infantry sector, was ready to cross the Naktong in full force. The plan was that Peploe's 38th Infantry, supported by the 38th FAB and commanded by Robert J. O'Donnell, and Paul Freeman's 23d Infantry, supported by the 37th FAB, now commanded by John B. Hector, would spearhead the division drive west. They would first mount a joint attack on the remnants of the NKPA 2d and 4th divisions near Hyopchon, then push westward to Kochang and Anui and from there make a seventy-mile motorized dash across the peninsula to Chonju. Sloane's 9th Infantry (less Butch Barberis's 2/9, in division reserve), supported by John Keith's 15th FAB, would push west along a road running south of Freeman's 23d, adjacent to Bill Kean's 25th Division sector. The three regimental task forces would have armored spearheads provided by the 2d Division's 72d Tank Battalion, and would be further reinforced by the very effective A/A vehicles and the 155-mm howitzers of the division's black 503d FAB, commanded by Joseph E. Buys.[9]

These operations were also restricted by a shortage of ammunition and bridging. Paul Freeman remembered: "In Korea we were always conserving ammunition. We were always on the brink of running out. Always scared to death that we were going to get caught with no ammunition. I believe it was rationed the whole time that I was there. Even small-arms ammunition . . . we never had enough." Since Peploe had been given priority on the bridging, Freeman and Sloane had to improvise means to cross the Naktong. Freeman built a sandbag ford. Sloane used World War II amphibious trucks (fitted, like boats, with propellers for locomotion in water) called DUWKs.[10]

By this time Freeman's three battalion commanders—Claire Hutchin (1st), James Edwards (2d), and Gib Sherrard (3d)—had considerable Korean combat experience; the outfits were tough and battlewise. Of the three, Freeman judged Sherrard's 3d to be the most aggressive and dependable. West Pointer Sherrard, thirty-eight, son of a retired Army officer (who by coincidence had commanded the 3/23 in the late 1920s), had served in the ETO as G-3, G-4, and chief of staff of the 42d ("Rainbow") Division. Freeman had known Sherrard's father; he later characterized the younger Sherrard as a "genius" at battlefield planning and exploitation.[11]

Because the 23d was short of trucks, Sherrard drew on his ETO battle experience and devised a plan to mechanize the 3/23 completely. The ammo and other gear would be stored on the artillery vehicles; the men would ride on the trucks and tank decks. So organized, the 3/23 would be used as a powerful spearhead to lead the regiment in a blazing dash across the peninsula to Chonju. In this way Freeman would not only get there before Peploe but also cut off a substantial number of retreating NKPA troops.

Freeman and Sloane began crossing the Naktong River on September 21, supported by a feint from forces of Peploe's 38th in its bridgehead. However, both Freeman and Sloane met unexpectedly heavy enemy resistance. Freeman brazened it out and finally got Sherrard's 3/23 across, followed by the other two battalions, but Sloane's 9th was decisively repulsed. The NKPA shot up nine of Sloane's ten DUWKs, leaving him with no handy means to get across. Thereafter the 9th Infantry was assigned to guarding the bridge in Peploe's sector and other missions, freeing all of Peploe's battalions for the big push west.

By September 23 it appeared to Keiser that the strong NKPA forces opposing Peploe and Freeman by the river were beginning to cave in. Accordingly he placed the ADC, Sladen Bradley, in charge of the 23d and 38th with orders to move westward. On the following day the two regiments converged on Hyopchon in a well-executed double envelopment, trapping (and killing) about 300 NKPA troops. The surviving NKPA fled to the hills in "utter disorder."[12]

These and subsequent operations of the 23d and 38th regiments were impaired by a bitter dispute which broke out in the senior command. As Freeman had resented Keiser's earlier delegation of tactical command to the division artillery chief Loyal Haynes, so he now resented the presence of Sladen Bradley. Freeman wanted above all to launch Sherrard's mechanized 3/23 on a power drive across the peninsula. In Freeman's eyes Bradley was holding him back in favor of Peploe, who, Freeman believed, was advancing too slowly and too cautiously, allowing too many NKPA troops to escape. Freeman recalled: "We made very rapid progress. We got to our objective way ahead of the other regiments and the other units in the division. Now is when some backbiting and jealousy began to occur. Having gotten to this objective, we could see the enemy fleeing in the Thirty-eighth zone to our north. We requested permission to enter that zone and cut them off—bring fire into their zone. Permission denied. General Bradley and Colonel Peploe were going ahead on foot very determinedly but very slowly, and they resented that we were offering to give them any assistance. I think this went back to World War Two, where people were ambitious and competitive and wanted to get objectives first. It was a race all the way."[13]

After securing Hyopchon, Bradley ordered Peploe and Freeman to advance west to Kochang and Anui. Peploe complied, sending his battalions forward on foot, but Freeman balked. Freeman had "mechanized" and intended to stay that way. He would move out after the engineers had provided him a crossing over a local river. Bradley became "quite impatient" over the delay. Nonetheless, Freeman, believing that he would soon overtake Peploe's footslogging troops, stuck to his guns.

Late that afternoon, September 25, the engineers finished the river crossing, and Freeman set off with a roar of engines. The delay meant that Freeman had to travel by night. Although he encountered several minefields and more blown bridges, by dawn on September 26 he had covered forty miles and caught up with Peploe's lead battalion, James Skeldon's 2/38, on the outskirts of Kochang. The men of the 38th, Freeman remembered, were "nearly exhausted from their foot effort." Having ridden all the way, Freeman's men were fresh and ready for battle. Freeman got Skeldon's permission to pass through his battalion and went "barreling up the road" to take Kochang.

Then an infuriating command snag developed. As Freeman remembered, "I received word to halt, pull my column over to the side of the road, and give priority to the Thirty-eighth Regiment. Well, I thought this was a great mistake, and the jealousy apparently of General [Sladen] Bradley and Colonel Peploe in wanting to heap some glory on themselves unfortunately ruined a great operation. General Bradley and I had a few words on the side of the road. It was embarrassing to everyone. We had our whole regimental combat team, including our artillery, ready to roll on. We could have gone as fast as our fuel would permit. The Thirty-eighth went through us, and they bogged down. . . ."[14]

The 3/23 commander, Gib Sherrard, remembered:

This order was, I believe, the most ridiculous order I ever received in my entire career and Paul Freeman said substantially the same thing. Here we were motorized with a powerful task force up front with a point out ahead consisting of tanks protected with infantry, advancing rapidly (5–10 m.p.h.) with practically no opposition, except scattered sniper fire. And to receive orders to permit another less organized outfit to overtake and pass us, thus stopping our advance for several hours was the height of stupidity. Needless to say, everyone in the 23rd Infantry was pissed off, to put it mildly, at such unreasonable and unwarranted orders.

Nor was that the end of it. Sherrard went on:

After I received the radio orders from Paul Freeman to pull over and was in the process of doing so as rapidly as I could pass the word by radio and messenger and staff officers, Sladen Bradley came up afoot and chastised me for not clearing the road more rapidly. Everyone in and on the nearby tanks, which I had already cleared from the road, could hear him ranting and raving. Everyone also knew that our division commander [Dutch Keiser] was afraid of his shadow and never came forward. . . . Keiser was incompetent and mentally sick. . . . He even kept out of sight in his own CP. And here was his assistant division commander running the show in a cavalier fashion. Never have I been so ashamed of our so-called leadership in the 2nd Division. Paul Freeman was a superb leader of men; we all felt he had been betrayed by the orders of Sladen Bradley. What a blow to morale—to everyone in that noble 23rd Infantry—by such an insolent, vainglorious upstart, showing favorites at a time when men's lives were at stake and teamwork was the order of the day.[15]

The "honor" of capturing Kochang and leading the division dash to the west went to Peploe. Freeman's force was fragmented for local mopping-up operations. Hutchin's 1/23 was sent north to Koryong; Edwards's 2/23 and Sherrard's 3/23 went on a few miles to Anui. Freeman remained with Sherrard.

The 3/23 pulled into Anui after dark on September 26. The rice paddies had been flooded, making reconnaissance difficult. Sherrard chose the school-yard for his CP. It looked suspiciously "clean" to Freeman—perhaps some kind of trap—but in view of the flooded rice paddies and the darkness, "there was nowhere else to go."

It was indeed a trap. Moments after they had settled in and set up a perimeter defense, preregistered NKPA 120-mm shells fell on the 3/23 CP. It was a horror. Six senior officers were killed outright: the exec, John C. Brinsmead; the S-2; the assistant S-3; the motor officer; the antiaircraft officer; and the artillery liaison officer. Twenty-six other officers and men were wounded; they included Sherrard, who barely survived evacuation back to a mobile hospital. The slightly wounded S-3, Charles F. Kane, thirty-eight, replaced Sherrard as battalion commander, but it would take the 3/23 some time to recover from the shock of this tragedy.[16]

Sherrard and Freeman would blame the tragedy on Sladen Bradley—for stopping the 23d earlier that day in favor of the 38th. Sherrard explained: "It is highly likely that due to our rate of advance, we would have overrun Anui in daylight and been much farther along in our pursuit, had Bradley not delayed us. Both Paul Freeman and I were reluctant to go into Anui upon our arrival at dusk. But we were overruled by Bradley and told to take the town that night and hold it."[17]

The upshot of this competition, controversy, and tragedy was a lasting and bitter feud between Freeman and Peploe, and Freeman and Bradley. Freeman remarked later that both Bradley and Peploe were "small people." He damned Bradley as "not too smart" and Peploe as "an ETO officer who never learned to fight Asiatics." According to Peploe's S-3, Warren Hodges, Peploe, in turn, remained hostile to Freeman. As Hodges remembered it, Peploe sacked his 3/38 commander, Everett Stewart (who had been "loaned" to Freeman in the earlier fighting), at least in part because Stewart made the mistake of express-ing admiration for Freeman's outfit to Peploe.[18]

While Freeman remained in the Anui-Kochang-Koryong area, mopping up, Bradley and Peploe completed plans to make a motorized dash on west-ward. By this time the NKPA withdrawal order of September 25 was three days old and the remnants of enemy forces in this sector had cleared out. Departing Kochang on the morning of September 28, Bradley and Peploe covered seventy-three miles in nine and a half hours, arriving in Chonju out of gas in the early afternoon. Finding the town lightly defended (300 NKPA troops), they quickly seized it. Later in the day Keiser sent fuel trucks forward to fill Peploe's vehicles and those of Task Force Dolvin, which pulled into Chonju at about 6:00 A.M. the following day. Like Dolvin, Peploe received a DSC for his role in the breakthrough; Freeman did not.[19]

Over the next several days the rest of the 2d Division came westward to Chonju behind Peploe—first Freeman, then, finally, Sloane's 9th Infantry, which was relieved of its duties at the Naktong River by the temporarily attached Puerto Rican 65th Regiment. Peploe sent his 3/38 probing north to the Kum River (on Dolvin's right) above Nonsan. Keiser established the division CP in Chonju.[20]

## I V

### Northwest Sector

On September 19 Shrimp Milburn's I Corps, composed of John Church's 24th and Hap Gay's 1st Cav divisions, became the happy beneficiary of two unrelated and wholly unexpected events:

First, the NKPA 3d Division, fiercely defending Waegwan against attacks by Throckmorton's 5th and Crombez's 5th Cav regiments, suddenly abandoned its hilltop positions and fled west in disarray across the Naktong River, leaving Waegwan wide open.[21]

Secondly, the ROK 1st Division, attacking immediately on the right of Ray Palmer's 8th Cav Regiment in the Bowling Alley, broke through a seam in the NKPA 1st Division and shot north about thirteen miles. This remarkable ROK achievement created a grave threat to the rear of the NKPA 1st and 13th divisions, facing Palmer's 8th Cav. As a consequence, the NKPA 1st Division withdrew from its strong hilltop fortifications, significantly weakening the NKPA position in the Bowling Alley.[22]

In the 24th Division sector Johnny Throckmorton, who had been attacking Waegwan frontally, took immediate advantage of the NKPA 3d Division withdrawal. He entered the town in the late afternoon, September 19, and on the following day his infantry cleaned out pockets of resistance along the east bank of the Naktong and proceeded to seize a bridgehead on the opposite shore.

That night, September 20, Throckmorton's troops began crossing the Naktong in assault boats. Thomas Roelofs's 1/5 led the crossing. After Roelofs had established a perimeter on the opposite bank, the 2/5 commanded by Albert N. Ward, Jr., thirty-six, came across in assault boats to reinforce it. On the next day, September 21, Ben Heckemeyer's 3/5 crossed into the bridgehead. Although Throckmorton braced for a strong NKPA attack, none came.[23]

The stage now belonged to Eighth Army's senior engineer, West Pointer (1922) Paschal N. ("Pat") Strong, forty-eight. Strong, a veteran of the ETO, was a well-educated man (Cornell College, 1925) of many talents. He had a flair for writing fiction. Beginning in the 1920s, he had had many short stories published in slick and pulp magazines and was the author of several boys' adventure books. When the creator of the hit radio program *Jack Armstrong, the All American Boy* died in 1940, Pat Strong became the chief conceptualist and writer for the show (with time out for ETO duty) until it was pushed off the air by television in the late 1940s.[24]

Pat Strong arrived at Waegwan immediately behind Throckmorton. His task was formidable: to build three bridges across the 700-foot-wide, 8-foot-deep Naktong River: first, a temporary treadway bridge for foot traffic; second, a more substantial floating or pontoon bridge for vehicles, including tanks and trucks; and third, a railroad bridge so that trains could bring forward the thousands of tons of supplies Eighth Army would require in the drive north.[25]

Of the three bridges, the most urgently needed was the floating vehicular bridge. Owing to the failure to provide Eighth Army bridging, Strong had only 1,000 feet of floating or pontoon bridging and 120 feet of steel Bailey bridge. Since Eighth Army would need this scanty supply of bridging to span other rivers on its advance northward, Strong could not install it permanently at Waegwan. His solution was complex: He would first put in the floating bridge, then build a parallel bridge, using the Bailey augmented with trestle bents and timbers. When the Bailey bridge was ready for use, the pontoon bridge would be removed and sent forward to span another river. Meanwhile, he would start building two "permanent" bridges, one highway and one railroad, made of timber and steel I beams. When the "permanent" highway bridge became operational, the Bailey bridge would be removed and sent forward to replace the pontoon bridge, which, in turn, could be sent farther forward yet.[26]

Strong's engineers began work on September 20. By 10:00 A.M. on September 22 the treadway and pontoon bridges were ready for use. The Bailey and railroad bridges took longer. One reason was the difficulty in finding timbers in South Korea, where there were few trees. Strong made do by "stealing" telephone poles from the Signal Corps and, where necessary, splicing them together. Despite many obstacles, the Bailey highway bridge was completed within one week; the timber-I beam railroad bridge within two weeks.[27]

While waiting for Strong to put the floating vehicular bridge in place, John Church assembled his infantry on the west bank and completed plans for the attack up the highway toward Taejon. Dick Stephens's 21st and Ned Moore's 19th regiments, which had crossed the Naktong in assault boats below Waegwan, came north on the west bank into Throckmorton's bridgehead. The two-battalion 27th British Infantry Brigade, temporarily attached to the 24th Division, replaced Moore's 19th, which had been blocking the Songju road. In turn, the oft-shattered 2d Battalion of the 7th Cav, grandly designated Eighth Army reserve, took over the British positions on the west bank of the Naktong.

\* \* \*

The fall of Waegwan and the remarkable breakthrough of the ROK 1st Division in the Bowling Alley sector convinced Hap Gay that the time had come to deliver the NKPA in the Bowling Alley a knockout blow. The principal feature of this blow would be the proposed cavalrylike armored sweep of Cecil Nist's 7th Cav behind enemy lines, designed to unhinge the NKPA defenses in front of Ray Palmer's 8th Cav. Pete Clainos's 1/7 would lead the sweep; James Lynch's 3/7 would reinforce it.

The sweep began on the morning of September 20, the 1/7 in the lead. Notwithstanding Clainos's personal bravery and aggressiveness (which at times seemed to border on recklessness), the 1/7 bogged down, drawing a blast of angry criticism from Hap Gay. Inasmuch as this daring sweep depended on speed for success, Gay ordered Cecil Nist to ignore and bypass enemy enclaves and "hightail" it for Tabu. But Nist was a cautious, methodical commander. He further angered Gay—and slowed down the sweep—by dismounting Lynch's 3/7 short of its designated jump-off point.[28]

By late afternoon Hap Gay was in a towering rage. Owing in large part to Nist's caution, the 7th Cav's sweep was failing. Then another calamity occurred: Pete Clainos's command jeep hit a mine; Clainos was wounded.

That evening Hap Gay reached the end of his patience and sacked Cecil Nist. His choice to replace Nist was highly unorthodox: the 77th FAB commander, Billy Harris, whose aggressive outfit had been supporting the 7th Cav for most of its tour in Korea.[29]

Harris remembered: "I got a radio call from [the artillery commander] Charlie Palmer to report to Gay. When I did, Gay said, 'Do you know the mission of the Seventh Cav?' I said yes. Gay went on: 'What's its next objective?' and so on. Then he gave me command of the regiment, saying, 'If you don't have the objective by tomorrow night, I'll have another regimental commander.' I went to the Seventh Cav CP. Nist had a bottle of bourbon in his footlocker. We had a drink. He was a wonderful guy, a good friend. But he was too old, and he never left his CP. He was brokenhearted."[30]

Although he was wounded, infantryman Pete Clainos, who was a West Point classmate of Harris's, was angry to find artilleryman Harris the new man in charge. "I should have gotten command of the regiment, not Billy Harris," he said later.[31]

Harris remembered the meeting that night: "Pete was wounded. I tried to evacuate him right then. Besides the wound, he had had too much combat. He needed R and R. He begged me to let him stay on until we had the objective. I did, but I assigned the regimental S-three, [William O.] Witherspoon, to back him up and prepare to relieve him temporarily as battalion commander."

The appointment of Billy Harris to command the 7th Cav wrought a change in the outfit. To replace Witherspoon as regimental S-3, Harris drafted the able, combat-experienced S-3 of Lynch's 3/7, James B. Webel, who remembered:

Billy Harris was the most outstanding regimental commander known to me in twenty-seven years of regular Army service. He was absolutely fearless. He was constantly in the front lines where he could influence the action yet take care to insure he always had communications to his key means of influencing the battle, i.e., his infantry, artillery and tank battalions, the tactical air force, engineers, division command post and adjacent unit command posts. . . . He had a fine sense of timing and the ability to mass the full resources of combat in attaining the mission of his regiment, whether attack, defense, delay, withdrawal, reconnaissance or rapid advance, or in breakouts. He had the uncommon good sense to delegate full command and authority to his subordinate commanders and staff without ever shirking his own full responsibility for the operation of the unit. He always went to bat for the unit and his men, often at risk to his own personal situation.[32]

On the following morning, September 21, Billy Harris—soon nicknamed Wild Bill—resumed the sweep of the 7th Cav, with Pete Clainos's 1/7 leading, Lynch's 3/7 coming behind. The outcome was electrifying. By noon the 7th Cav had reached Tabu. After clearing the town of enemy, Harris divided his forces. Lynch's 3/7 turned north to link with elements of the ROK 1st Division, which were angling south from positions in the rear of the NKPA 1st and 13th divisions. Clainos's 1/7 turned south to link with Palmer's 8th Cav. These deft and aggressive maneuvers—described by the 7th Cav historian as "one of the outstanding feats of the war"—corralled an estimated 2,000 NKPA troops between the 7th and 8th Cavs. During that night these fleeing NKPA troops attempted to crack through Lynch's 3/7 perimeter, but the 3/7 repulsed them, forcing them, as Lynch later wrote, to shift their escape route to the west.[33]

These maneuvers also netted an important NKPA prisoner. He was the chief of staff of the NKPA 13th Division, Colonel Lee Hak Ku, thirty, the highest-ranking NKPA prisoner to be taken in the war. For reasons never determined, Lee blabbed out vital intelligence for Gay, Milburn, and Walker. He revealed the astonishing fact that the NKPA 13th Division had a strength of but 1,500 men. Of this number, he said, only 500 were North Korean. The remainder were raw, disgruntled South Korean conscripts. He gave the location of these men and a list of the few heavy weapons remaining in their possession.[34]

This intelligence, together with the fine work of the ROK 1st Division and the 7th Cav under Billy Harris, led Walker to make a drastic change in Milburn's I Corps breakout plans. Rather than follow the 24th Division to Taejon on mopping-up and policing duties, Walker decided, the 1st Cav Div should attack northwest up the Bowling Alley. It would crack through the weak (virtually nonexistent) NKPA 13th Division, cross the Naktong at a ferry site near Sonsan, then drive northwest to Sangju and Poun, thence to Chonan and Osan, linking up with X Corps. Rather than proceed from Taejon to Osan, as the linkup force in accordance with the original plan, the 24th would halt at Taejon.

This hurried change in I Corps plans may have been ill advised. No doubt a primary factor in the change was the heavy pressure on Walker to effect an early linkup with X Corps. The 1st Cav route through Poun would be shorter and faster than the 24th's route through Taejon. But owing to the tactical success of Inchon, the "linkup" was now less important than "fixing" and capturing or destroying the NKPA within South Korea. The Taegu–Taejon highway offered Eighth Army the best opportunity to emplace a strong and final line for that purpose. Removing the 1st Cav from that line to go off in another direction, largely for symbolic (or public relations) purposes, would greatly reduce the capability of Eighth Army to bottle up the NKPA at or below the line.[35]

Although the 1st Cav was battered and weak, the change in mission was warmly welcomed. It elevated the division from the ignominious role of mop-up and local police force to the place of honor as Eighth Army's spearhead, *the* linkup to X Corps. This important new mission led Hap Gay to make a change in command of the 8th Cav. In recent days Ray Palmer had disappointed Walker, Milburn, and Gay. In the view of the higher command, Palmer did not have the ginger to lead the 8th Cav on the linkup offensive. Accordingly, Walker ordered him back to Japan for extended R and R.[36]

By this time the Pentagon had sent Walker four aggressive West Pointers to be "spare" regimental commanders. All had outstanding combat records in World War II. All had previously commanded battalions and regiments. One of these was Hallett D. ("Hal") Edson, forty, class of 1934. In World War II Edson had commanded a battalion in Shrimp Milburn's 83d Division during its Stateside training. Later he had served as a battalion and regimental commander in the 3d Infantry Division at Anzio and in the ETO. In all, Edson had spent 400 days in combat, winning two Silver Star medals for valor. He remembered: "Joe Collins had gone to Korea and come back saying the regimental commanders over there were too old and had no combat experience. He wanted new, experienced colonels sent there. . . . I was sent to Korea with three other prospective regimental commanders. When I got over there, Milburn's chief of staff, Rinaldo Van Brunt, called me in. . . . Van Brunt said Milburn wanted me to take command of the Eighth Cav from Ray Palmer, who was older [and] had had no previous combat experience. . . . I assumed command of the Eighth Cav on September twenty-third, for the breakout."[37]

The senior staff of the 8th Cav was not overjoyed by the arrival of this "outsider." One officer in particular was furious: Johnny Johnson, the able commander of the 3/8, who had won a DSC and by date of rank was senior to Edson and who may have felt that the "prejudice" against those who had surrendered to the Japanese on Bataan was still working against him. He recalled: "Ray Palmer was going back to Japan on R and R. . . . One story was that he was not going to return. . . . When Palmer took off, an individual showed up with a pair of dark glasses on and said: 'I'm the new regimental commander, Hal Edson.' . . . I knew him. . . . The ADC [Frank Allen] showed up later on during the day, and I said to him, 'What gives with the new regimental commander? I am senior to him by something like about eight months in date of rank, and I am a year ahead of him at the Military Academy. If I am not qualified to command this regiment, you should fire me as a battalion commander and get somebody else.' . . . He allowed as there was some merit in my argument."[38]

Frank Allen passed Johnson's beef on to Hap Gay. Gay admired Johnson, but there was nothing he could do about the situation at the moment. The corps commander, Shrimp Milburn, had, in effect, placed Edson in command of the 8th Cav. Edson would command the 8th Cav for the breakout.*

Walker's decision to send Gay's 1st Cav off on its own tangent complicated the proposed attack of Church's 24th Division up the highway from Waegwan to Taejon in one important aspect. The problem was the enigmatic NKPA 10th Division, which was headquartered at Songju, south of the highway. Although this division had made no aggressive move since early August, it was in position to attack due north into the rear of the advancing 24th Division, or northeast to Taegu.

Walker's initial solution to this knotty problem had been as follows: The two-battalion British Brigade, attached to the 24th Division, would cross the Naktong behind Moore's 19th Infantry. It would then attack southwest into Songju to contain or destroy the NKPA 10th Division and would send patrols from Songju north to the Waegwan–Taejon highway, linking with elements of the 1st Cav, following behind the 24th Division.

Minus the 1st Cav, this plan had to be modified. Church's 24th Division would now have to serve as support and backup for the British. Since no one could guess the extent of opposition the British might encounter at Songju, or how well the green British Brigade could cope with it, Church had to designate Moore's 19th Infantry as a standby force. This need significantly weakened Church's available power for the drive on Taejon.

---

*With the appointment of Edson to command the 8th Cav, all twelve regimental commanders in Eighth Army were now West Pointers. By academy class, the range was fifteen years: 1923 (Fisher) to 1938 (Corley). The average age was 43.3 years. The four oldest were Fisher (50), Crombez (50), Peploe (49), and Sloane (48). The four youngest were Corley (36), Throckmorton (37), Michaelis (38), and Billy Harris (39).[39]

The British Brigade, commanded by Brigadier General Basil A. Coad, attacked toward Songju on September 22. It was supported by American tanks, artillery, and FEAF aircraft. At first all went well; it appeared that NKPA opposition would be slight. Both the Middlesex and Argyll battalions made substantial gains into the hills. But on the next day, September 23, the NKPA snapped back with surprising fury. In the ensuing fight the hard-pressed British called in a FEAF napalm and bombing strike. Three F-51 Mustang fighters responded, but the pilots confused hills and forces and mistakenly attacked the Argylls, inflicting sixty British casualties.[40]

This tragic foul-up took much of the heart out of the British attack. Because of that—and the unexpected strength and fury of the NKPA—Church was compelled to send Moore's standby 19th Infantry to the rescue. Led by Morris Naudts's 1/19, the regiment split from the 24th Division and attacked due south to Songju that same night. In the early-morning hours of September 24 the 19th overran Songju and later linked with the British. Following orders from their headquarters, on September 25 the remnants of the NKPA 10th Division buried its artillery and retreated northwest through the hills toward Taejon. Walker withdrew the British Brigade from combat and put it in I Corps reserve.

Meanwhile, on September 23 Church launched his 24th Division attack up the Taejon highway. He could expect no backup, as originally planned, from the 1st Cav. He therefore had to proceed cautiously and methodically, mopping up as he went, leaving no NKPA enclaves to threaten his flanks or rear.[41]

There was no sign of an NKPA "collapse" in this sector. To the contrary, the attack, led by Dick Stephens's 21st Infantry, ran head-on into furious NKPA resistance east of Kumchon. The NKPA had positioned remnants of the NKPA 9th Division (withdrawing from the Naktong Bulge area) athwart the highway, reinforced by a dozen tanks, to block for other NKPA units withdrawing northward. Notwithstanding heavy pressure from Walker, Milburn, and Church, Stephens bogged down. In the tank battles four new Pattons of John Growdon's 6th Tank Battalion were lost.

Bringing fresh power to bear in the early morning on September 24, Church sent Throckmorton's 5th Regiment through the 21st to lead the attack. Six more of Growdon's Pattons were lost. As a consequence, later in the day Church recommitted Stephens's 21st on Throckmorton's right for a combined nighttime "pincers" attack on Kumchon. It was at this time that the NKPA ordered a general withdrawal. On the following day, September 25, Ben Heckemeyer's 3/5 pushed into Kumchon, now a deserted mass of rubble.

By this time all NKPA units remaining south of the Waegwan–Taejon highway were retreating northward on NKPA orders. Some came due north behind Church, briefly blocking the highway, then continued north. But the vast majority retreated northwestward into Taejon. Had Church had more power and backup from the 1st Cav coming behind him, he might have forced his way into Taejon, drawing another line and trapping thousands, perhaps tens of thousands of NKPA troops within the tier. But the 24th Division was far too weak for the task. Church could not advance until the NKPA had completed its withdrawal.

Pausing in Kumchon for a full day, Church brought up Ned Moore's 19th Infantry from Sangju to spearhead the division. On the next day, September 26, Moore jumped off. Owing to the NKPA withdrawals, he made good progress to Okchon. However, on the following day, September 27, Moore encountered a strong NKPA block about eight miles east of Taejon. This was a last NKPA effort to give its units time to clear Taejon.[42]

The block held Moore in place for a full twenty-four hours. During that time, the Army historian wrote, "thousands" of NKPA troops from seven different NKPA divisions (2d; 3d; 4th; 6th; 7th; 9th; 10th) cleared Taejon and retreated northward into the hills. After they had gone, elements of Ollie Kinney's 2/19—one of the last American units to abandon Taejon in July—led the advance into the empty, rubble-strewn city. Later, at 6:00 P.M. on September 28, a 24th Division artillery spotter plane landed at the Taejon Airfield. During the night the 5th and 21st regiments joined Moore to proclaim the city liberated.[43]

The recapture of Taejon was sweet revenge for the 24th Division, but the celebration was muted by the discovery of an unspeakable NKPA atrocity. During the final days of the NKPA occupancy North Korean "Security Police" had murdered an estimated 5,000 to 7,000 South Korean civilians and 40 American GIs and 17 ROK soldiers. The bodies were found wired together in shallow trenches. Six men—two American GIs, one ROK soldier, and three civilians—had survived the massacre by feigning death. They were found buried alive in shallow graves, still wired to the dead.[44]

\* \* \*

Meanwhile, at 8:00 A.M. on September 22, Hap Gay launched the 1st Cav Division on its linkup dash to Osan. The drive was spearheaded by Billy Harris's 7th Cav, followed by Hal Edson's 8th Cav and Crombez's 5th Cav.

Owing to the fact that the shattered 2/7 had been consigned to Eighth Army reserve, Harris had only two battalions: the 1/7, temporarily commanded by William Witherspoon while Clainos recovered from his battle wounds, and James Lynch's 3/7. Harris designated the 3/7, reinforced by two motorized batteries of the 77th FAB and seven tanks of Bill Rodgers's 70th Tank Battalion, to spearhead the attack. Because of all the sevens entailed, Lynch's force was officially designated Task Force 777, but in practice it was called Task Force Lynch.[45]

After Hap Gay, ADC Frank Allen, and Billy Harris had put their command jeeps in line, Lynch began rolling. With the seven tanks in the lead and a FEAF Mosquito Spotter overhead to direct close air support, Task Force Lynch barreled up the wreckage-strewn Bowling Alley toward the first objective: the Naktong ferry crossing at Sonsan, twenty-five miles north. Lynch's orders were to stop only if the force met "determined resistance." He encountered sporadic NKPA troops but nothing close to "determined resistance." The shattered NKPA 13th Division had melted into the hills.

When Lynch was about halfway to Sonsan, a liaison plane flew over and dropped a message from the 1st Cav G-3. It stated that the 1st Cav objective had been changed from the Sonsan ferry site to a Naktong crossing ten miles farther north, at the town of Naktong, where there was a ford and a good, direct road to Sangju. Since the message was not signed or "authenticated," Gay decided he had better return to Taegu and verify it with Shrimp Milburn or Walker. Lynch was not to proceed beyond the Sonsan ferry site until he heard from Gay.

Task Force Lynch reached Sonsan at 3:30 P.M. and waited. Finally, at 6:00 P.M., a message arrived from Gay: Proceed to Naktong. By sunset, 7:00 P.M., Lynch was rolling again. The force made good time, closing on Naktong at about 10:30, thirty-five miles deep in "enemy territory."

Here, for the first time, Lynch encountered substantial enemy: first the rear of a retreating "column"; then a strong force at the "underwater bridge." His armor and men attacked immediately and aggressively. As Lynch later wrote, "all hell broke loose." One of his tanks blew up a NKPA ammo truck, which set fire to five others. "Shells, grenades, and small-arms ammunition were bursting and popping and whizzing all over the place," Lynch went on. The burning trucks revealed a column of about 400 NKPA crossing the underwater bridge. Lynch's gunners turned on them, "and the resulting slaughter in the river was terrific." Perhaps 200 NKPA troops were caught in the crossfire and killed.

After this fight Lynch began the river crossing. It was no easy task in this dark, unfamiliar terrain, possibly defended by a strong enemy force. First his men pushed the six burning, exploding trucks off the road. Then they captured two tanks, fifty trucks (many with American Army markings), and ten artillery pieces which had been stranded and abandoned on the east bank. After that they found the underwater "bridge," an artificial ford, made of rice bags filled with sand, strong enough to support trucks and jeeps, but not tanks. By 7:30 A.M. on September 23, when all the men of Task Force Lynch were across the river and compressed into a tight, well-defended bridgehead, Lynch modestly reported this remarkable achievement to Billy Harris as "mission accomplished."

The 7th Cav then leapfrogged onward. That day, while Lynch's men rested inside the bridgehead and engineers constructed a raftlike ferry capable of floating tanks across the Naktong, Witherspoon's 1/7 forded the river (trucks towing jeeps) and passed through. The 1/7 advanced ten miles beyond the Naktong to Sangju, which was abandoned. That night Lynch got his tanks and trucks across the river and set off again. By 6 A.M. on September 24 his task force had joined the 1/7 in Sangju. There Lynch passed a scouting element through the 1/7. It barreled thirty miles up the road to Poun. The next day, September 25, Task Force Lynch consolidated in Poun.

Meanwhile, Gay brought the rest of the 1st Cav Division forward: Edson's 8th Cav, followed by Crombez's 5th Cav, then the supply trains and other impedimenta. These crossed the Naktong River at Naktong on an intricate schedule, by means of the raft ferry and the sandbagged underwater bridge. Thereafter the entire division assembled along the long stretch of road between Sangju and Poun, poised to race on to Chongju–Chonan–Osan. To screen the division's right flank, the ROK 1st Division came across the river into Sangju, sending elements due north toward Hamchang.[46]

These maneuvers had, in effect, begun another line across the Korean peninsula, forming yet another tier. The line was more or less parallel to John Church's line along the Waegwan–Taejon highway, twenty miles to the south. The new line was well placed to trap NKPA troops leaking northward through Church's thin line. A westward extension of the 1st Cav line to Chonan (above Taejon) could have created a new and formidable barrier for the fleeing NKPA to cross. Had Ned Almond not committed Charles Beauchamp's 32d Infantry to the battle of Seoul, this line could have been substantially reinforced at Chonan by the 32d Infantry (backed up by the 31st), brought south from Suwon.

It is possible that Shrimp Milburn or a staffer in I Corps recognized the potential of this added line. On the night of September 25 I Corps issued an order forbidding Gay to advance beyond Poun. Inasmuch as Gay was hell-bent on a flashy, symbolic linkup at Osan to the exclusion of all else, he found the order inexplicable. Bypassing Milburn, Gay protested the order directly to Walker. Walker, no less determined to make the linkup, rescinded the order. The upshot was that by the morning of September 26 Hap Gay had Walker's permission to proceed northwest to Osan with the entire 1st Cav Division, screened on the right flank by the ROK 1st Division. This decision, in effect, would all but empty American and ROK military power from the newly created line, leaving the center of the peninsula above Church's line completely accessible to the retreating NKPA.[47]

The plan for the 1st Cav advance as conceived by Gay and his staff was as follows. As before, the 7th Cav's Task Force Lynch would spearhead the division drive from Poun to Chongju, Chonan, Pyongtaek, Osan, a distance of 70 miles by air, 106 miles by road. Hal Edson's 8th Cav would follow the 7th Cav to Chongju, then turn north on secondary roads to Ansong. The 5th

Cav would follow the 7th Cav as far as Chonan and Chochiwon, where it would halt, face south, and protect the division's rear.[48]

Led by six tanks, Task Force Lynch rolled out of Poun at 11:30 A.M. on September 26. For most of the day it was a milk run. "We went for many miles without opposition," Lynch wrote, "and with cheering crowds of South Koreans greeting us along the way." At about 5:30 P.M., having traveled sixty-four miles nonstop, the six tanks ran out of gas. Owing to a logistical foul-up, the refueling trucks were somewhere near the rear of the long column. Not wishing to pause a minute longer than necessary, Lynch refilled three of the tanks with spare gas from his trucks at the front of the column, then the other three with gas captured from an NKPA truck convoy which by good luck blundered onto the scene.

At about that same time, unknown to Gay or Lynch, Johnnie Walker flew to the newly liberated airfield at Suwon held by the 31st Infantry. There Walker conferred with staffers of the 31st, informing them that the 1st Cav was on the way and that the 31st Infantry should be warned to expect it and to exercise great care not to fire on these friendly troops. Walker then flew back to Taegu.[49]

At Chongju, meanwhile, Hal Edson's 8th Cav split off and turned north on secondary roads. Johnny Johnson's 3/8, organized as an armored task force similar to Lynch's, led the regiment. Johnson remembered that it was a "mistake" to send these tanks over secondary roads "because the tanks broke down the first two bridges that we came to and mired themselves down." Edson and Johnson sent them back to Chongju to follow the better roads behind the 7th Cav. Thereafter Edson and Johnson proceeded into the night "at fair speed" in jeeps and trucks, with headlights burning, over terrain none of them had seen before.

After refueling his six tanks, Lynch continued, also boldly burning headlights. He wrote: "The moon had risen but a cloudy night obscured vision. Behind me were miles of vehicle lights winding their way through enemy-held territory—a weird sight to behold." At about 8:30 P.M. the leading elements reached the main Seoul–Taejon highway, a few miles below Chonan. Turning north, the column soon began to encounter NKPA troops. Lynch "shot up one truckload," but he bypassed most. He sped on, driving straight into Chonan, which was jammed with retreating NKPA units. The NKPA troops stared dumbly at Lynch's tanks, perhaps believing they were their own. Taking advantage of this apparent ignorance, one of Lynch's lead tankers made so bold as to ask one NKPA soldier for directions to Osan![50]

Beyond Chonan, three of Lynch's tanks, under command of Robert W. Baker, pulled ahead of the main column. They sped through Pyongtaek, then Osan. Three or four miles north of Osan, headlights still blazing, they suddenly encountered heavy antitank fire, which decapitated one of Baker's machine gunners. This intense, concentrated fire came from the 31st Infantry, which was then engaged in a battle with some NKPA tanks. The 31st had been alerted to expect the 1st Cav per Walker's instructions, but not so soon. Fortunately for Baker, the men of the 31st soon recognized the tanks as friendly and withheld fire. Pressing on, Baker penetrated into the 31st sector, logging his arrival—the unofficial linkup of Eighth Army and X Corps—at 10:26 P.M. on September 26. He had traveled 106.4 miles in eleven hours.[51]

Lagging behind Baker by about one hour, Lynch heard—and saw—fire ahead. This was the 31st Infantry, firing at both Baker and the NKPA tanks it was stalking. Not having any clear idea of what was going on, Lynch wisely ordered all headlights doused and proceeded cautiously. Moments later two NKPA tanks, which had apparently drawn up to the highway after Baker had passed, opened fire. Lynch quickly dismounted from his jeep and "hit the ditch."

Lynch had unknowingly driven into a formation of about ten NKPA tanks caught between his task force and the 31st Infantry, about four miles south of Osan. A wild nighttime melee ensued. Coached by Lynch, the 7th Cav and 3/7 battalion staffs, and others, deployed into the fields to give heroic battle with bazookas and whatever else they could bring to bear. The battalion S-2, John Hill, Jr. (son of the former 9th Infantry commander), got one tank with a bazooka team. The regimental S-3, James Webel, got another by climbing aboard and dumping a five-gallon can of gasoline into the engine hatch. Although the explosion blew Webel twenty feet through the air and broke two ribs, he recovered, grabbed a bazooka, and helped disable two more tanks. A sergeant, Willard H. Hopkins, mounted another tank and put it out of action by throwing grenades down the hatch. (Moments later, Hopkins was killed by fire from another tank.) In all, Lynch's men knocked out seven of the ten NKPA tanks, at a cost of two men killed and twenty-eight wounded.

Following this wild battle Lynch wisely decided to camp in this tank graveyard for the rest of the night. Then, after daylight, September 27, he proceeded cautiously through Osan and slightly beyond. At 8:26 A.M. Lynch's men met men of the 31st Infantry. With this merger the "linkup" of Eighth Army and X Corps became "official". On the right flank of the 7th Cav Hal Edson's 8th Cav arrived at its destination, Ansong, at noon that same day, September 27.[52]

The linkup operation of the 1st Cav Division—Wild Bill Harris's 7th Cav in particular—was electrifying and headline-making. It earned Harris, Lynch, and Webel (and, posthumously, Sergeant Hopkins) well-deserved DSCs; Task Force Lynch was awarded another Presidential Unit Citation.* Hap Gay

---

*The 3rd Battalion, 7th Cavalry Regiment, became the only battalion in Army history to win two Presidential Unit Citations within two weeks.

could be justly proud. His famous division had finally and fully regained the honor lost during the retreat to the Naktong and the defense of Taegu.

## V

### Northeast Sector

By September 16 the four ROK divisions (3d, 6th, 8th, Capital) deployed east of Milburn's I Corps were, the Army historian wrote, "near exhaustion." Fortunately for the ROKs, the four NKPA divisions (5th; 8th; 12th; 15th) facing them were in worse shape. They were at the far end of the NKPA supply line; the priority on manpower had gone to the NKPA divisions in the west.[53]

The ROK 6th Division, immediately to the right of the ROK 1st Division, began the offensive with a hard push at the NKPA 8th Division. Surprisingly the NKPA gave way and collapsed. The ROKs, gaining momentum, overran the division and massacred it, inflicting 4,000 verified casualties. The NKPA survivors fled north toward Yechon. Pursuing on foot, the ROK 6th Division made astonishing gains up the center of the peninsula. By September 25 it had reached Yechon and Hamchang (displacing the ROK 1st Division, which moved westward with the 1st Cav Division). The next day it set a course to Chungju, on the upper Han River.

Immediately to the right the ROK 8th Division made equally spectacular gains. Going on the attack, it easily overran and destroyed the remnants of the NKPA 15th Division. It then sped north, overrunning Uisong. By September 24 it had reached the outskirts of Andong, where it overtook the NKPA. It was delayed there fighting the NKPA and crossing the Naktong River (flowing east-west in this area), but by September 26 it had cleared the city and pushed twenty miles north to Yechon, linking with the ROK 6th Division. The next day, September 27, it raced to Tanyang, near the headwaters of the Han River.

On the east coast the ROK Capital and 3d divisions, organized into a corps, at first made small headway. The ROK Capital Division, attacking the NKPA 12th Division (depleted to 2,000 men), bogged down for several days. It could not get rolling until the NKPA 12th Division began a general withdrawal. Aggressively pursuing, the Capital Division overran Kigye on September 22 and then raced north, now making spectacular gains. By September 27 it had reached Chunyang, sixty air miles north of Kigye.

On the east coast road the ROK 3d Division, assisted by naval bombardment (including the battleship *Missouri*), attacked with a determined frontal assault on Pohang. But the NKPA 5th Division, stubbornly hanging on to the port, repulsed the ROKs in a bloody seesaw battle. Renewing the attack, the

ROK 3d Division finally cracked through on the morning of September 20. The ROKs recaptured Pohang, then pursued the fleeing NKPA 5th Division northward along the coast. On September 25, still well supported by naval and air bombardment, the ROKs reached Yongdok. What was left of the NKPA 5th Division fled westward into the mountains, leaving the coast road wide open. The ROK 3d Division sped north along the road, advancing farther and faster than any other ROK unit in Eighth Army, matching the 7th Cav's northward advance mile for mile until the 7th Cav's linkup with X Corps on September 27. Thereafter the ROK 3d Division continued northward, racing at high speed for the 38th Parallel.

Owing to the remarkable gains of the ROK divisions, the impression was created that the ROKs had finally become militarily mature and dependable. On September 25 Walker told the *New York Times* reporter: "Too little has been said in praise of the South Korean Army, which has performed so magnificently in helping us turn this war from the defensive to the offensive." The hoopla for the ROKs may have arisen partly from wishful thinking; the sooner the ROKs achieved real maturity, the sooner Eighth Army could get out of Korea. Whatever the case, the confidence in the ROKs proved to be dangerously—and tragically—premature.[54]

\* \* \*

So ended what in the mythology of the Korean War was to be called the Eighth Army breakout. It was not, in fact, a breakout but rather the pursuit and exploitation of an enemy force that was compelled to withdraw because Inchon made its position in South Korea untenable. Possibly Eighth Army could have achieved a true breakout without Inchon. It certainly could have achieved one had the Inchon forces been utilized to reinforce the Pusan Perimeter. It probably could have achieved one earlier had the Inchon forces landed at Kunsan.

Whatever the correct terminology, it was indisputedly a remarkable achievement. It freed Eighth Army from a demoralizing, costly, positional warfare and instilled it with pride. It "shattered" or "destroyed" or "routed" the NKPA as a viable entity in South Korea. It liberated all of South Korea below the Han River. It achieved a linkup with X Corps.

However, in one important respect the operation had to be marked down: It had failed to "trap" or "pound to pieces" the NKPA in South Korea. The trap lines Walker threw across the peninsula were too little, too late, especially the all-important, Waegwan-Taejon line, which was decisively weakened by Walker's last-minute decision to divert the 1st Cav to its celebrated but largely militarily meaningless linkup with X Corps. Nor was the Eighth Army hammer blow on the X Corps anvil ever realized. That colorful metaphor became, in reality, the 7th Cav and 31st Infantry trapping a dozen T-34 tanks near Osan in a successful but singularly uncoordinated operation from which most of the NKPA troops escaped.

It was impossible to determine how many NKPA troops escaped from Eighth Army in South Korea. The official Army historian guessed "25,000 to 30,000," but the total was probably much greater, perhaps as many as 40,000. Whatever the figure, it was a very serious loss, reminiscent of two major Allied blunders in World War II: allowing a comparable number of German troops to escape from Sicily to fight again; then through the Falaise gap in Normandy. Presumably the majority of the NKPA troops who managed to escape were mostly combat-wise veterans, not recent North or South Korean conscripts. The numbers were more than sufficient to provide cadres to rebuild the NKPA, should Moscow be inclined to support such a course.[55]

# VI

By September 29 the city of Seoul was sufficiently safe to permit its restoration as the seat of the Rhee government. As planned, MacArthur and Rhee flew into Kimpo Airfield to stage an appropriate ceremony in the bombed-out National Assembly Hall in Government House. From Kimpo they traveled in a motorcade of sedans to the center of the city, crossing the Han River on a temporary pontoon bridge, which had been grudgingly built by O. P. Smith's Marines. Seoul was a shambles; the Marines, Beauchamp's 32d Infantry, and the ROK 17th Regiment were still fighting NKPA troops in the northern suburbs. At MacArthur's invitation Johnnie Walker had joined the host of generals and admirals and civilian VIPs who had gathered in Seoul.[56]

The ceremony started promptly at noon. At the dais MacArthur delivered a brief, mesmerizing address, declaring the liberation of Seoul in God's name and the restoration of the Rhee government. As he spoke, the concussion of nearby artillery jarred loose heavy panels of window glass, which showered into the hall, encouraging the military to put their steel helmets back on and glance uneasily upward. Concluding his remarks, MacArthur invited those present to join him in the Lord's Prayer. Then he turned the dais over to a tearful, uncommonly grateful Syngman Rhee, who expressed his "undying gratitude" to the American military and launched into a formal peroration.

No one present mentioned the cost to America of Inchon and the liberation of South Korea. It was ghastly. Almond's X Corps had incurred 3,151 casualties (including 536 dead) at Inchon. Walker's Eighth Army had suffered another 10,000 casualties since September 16. The total American ground casualties in the Korean War now stood at about 27,500, including about 6,000 dead, about 19,000 wounded, and about 2,500 captured or missing.[57]

\*  \*  \*

When these formal proceedings were concluded, MacArthur called Johnnie Walker and Ned Almond aside for another ceremony. He awarded each general a medal. Rather than the Distinguished Service medals customary for men of their rank and station, he gave them Distinguished Service Crosses, the citations of which stressed their personal courage over their management talents. It was the first time either man had received a DSC. Some who had won DSCs on the battlefield would question if the awards were appropriate.[58]

After returning to Kimpo, MacArthur boarded his plane at one-thirty, having been on the ground but three and a half hours. He flew back to Tokyo to find his desk awash with heartwarming congratulatory messages from President Truman, Winston Churchill, George Marshall, Eisenhower, the JCS, and many others. Truman wrote: "No operation in military history can match either the delaying operation where you traded space for time in which to build up your forces, or the brilliant maneuver which has now resulted in the liberation of Seoul." The JCS said: "Your transition from defensive to offensive operations was magnificently planned, timed and executed. . . . We remain completely confident that the great task entrusted to you by the United Nations will be carried to a successful conclusion."[59]

Among these letters was a personal one from MacArthur's strongest Inchon supporter in the Pentagon, Matt Ridgway. Its flowery prose out-MacArthured MacArthur:

Under God's guidance, the full fruits of the indomitable courage and unshakable perseverance of our forces seem about to reach harvest. They will attest again to the incomparable brilliance of your unsurpassed leadership and judgment. They will demonstrate again the unfailing response of American forces to true leadership, regardless of odds. What a tribute, to be recorded in our military history to our dead and maimed![60]\*

In the narrowest sense Inchon had worked, no doubt of it, but that was only the beginning of the story. Many Allied amphibious landings in World War II had worked as well in the early stages only to bog down later with savage, inconclusive results, owing to command error or prompt and unexpected enemy reaction. Anzio was the classic case. In the broader sense the

---

\*MacArthur replied that he was "deeply grateful" for the support he had received from Ridgway and the "Defense echelons in Washington" and that "events in Korea are going far to vindicate the soundness of our military forces and the strength of American character." He hoped to wind up "military operations" within "a reasonably short period of time."

success of Inchon could not be gauged accurately until its primary objective—the destruction of the NKPA—had been achieved and the "likely" reactions from Moscow or Peking had been met and dealt with. In that broader sense Inchon militarily still hung very much in the balance. Its final success, or failure, would depend upon the shrewdness and perspicacity of MacArthur's follow-up decisions.

# PART SIX

# The Invasion of North Korea

# CROSSING THE 38TH PARALLEL

I

Initially America had entered the Korean War with the aim of evicting the NKPA from South Korea and restoring the status quo ante bellum. By the time of Inchon President Truman had made the decision to enlarge the war. American forces would cross the 38th Parallel, wipe out whatever was left of the NKPA, depose the Communist regime of Kim Il Sung, and unify Korea under a single, popularly elected government.

The decision to invade North Korea was unanimously supported by the senior members of the Truman administration: Dean Acheson; George Marshall, the new secretary of defense; Omar Bradley and the other members of the JCS; and, of course, MacArthur, his GHQ, and his senior field commanders, Johnnie Walker and Ned Almond. The decision was also approved by Dwight Eisenhower, still president of Columbia University.

Many factors influenced Truman's final decision:

• An overpowering urge to get rid of the "Korean problem" once and for all. If the Communist government of North Korea remained in power, there was every likelihood that it would rebuild the NKPA and attempt to invade South Korea again. Such an invasion could be deterred only by maintaining American troops in South Korea indefinitely—a costly, unpopular diversion of American military resources to a nonstrategic area. Moreover, Washington had to confront this reality: Syngman Rhee had not the slightest intention of stopping his ROK Army at the 38th Parallel. He was hell-bent to unify Korea by force. The ROK Army could be restrained only by American military force, an unthinkable course of action.

325

• The growing public demand for complete victory and revenge. Only five years after World War II Americans were conditioned to clear-cut and overwhelming victories, concluding with "unconditional surrender," followed by war crimes trials designed to punish aggressors legally. Americans were outraged by the Communist resort to "raw aggression," the atrocities inflicted on the South Koreans and American GIs, and shocked and grieved by the 27,500 American battle casualties.

• The unspoken but urgent need to liberate American (and ROK) prisoners of war from the NKPA. By the time of the decision the NKPA had captured an estimated 2,500 American soldiers and perhaps ten times that number of ROKs.

• The pressures of American politics. The Democrats faced a tough off-year election in November. The Republicans had made considerable headway in planting the idea that the Truman administration was "soft on communism" at home and abroad and, as a result, had "blundered" in the Far East. To stop at the 38th Parallel would bring further accusations of "appeasement" and "timidity," perhaps (in view of his VFW statement) even from MacArthur himself. A resounding, unequivocal victory in Korea would show the Truman administration to be decisive and tough.

• The hope that wresting North Korea from Moscow's yoke would not only profoundly diminish Soviet strategic designs and influence in the Far East but also eventually drive a wedge between Peking and Moscow. A unified, non-Communist Korea, it was suggested, might someday provide adjacent Manchuria with a market for trade, ultimately drawing China back into the American orbit.

• The hope that a smashing American victory in Korea would have a positive impact on Asians who had embraced or were flirting with communism in Indochina, Malaya, Indonesia, the Philippines, and elsewhere. MacArthur had told visitors at GHQ: "Victory is a strong magnet in the East."

• A belief that Moscow was not willing to run the risks of global war—including deployment of nuclear weapons—by directly supporting the NKPA on the battlefield.

• A belief that Peking was not willing to run the risks entailed in Korean intervention. The Mao government, then preparing to celebrate its first anniversary in office, was burdened by massive domestic political and economic problems. It did not appear likely that it could afford the time, money, and resources to challenge the powerful American forces in Korea. While its army was impressive in numbers (and battlefield experience), it was so lacking in artillery, tanks, and other mechanized weapons as to invite contempt by the American Army.

• A new confidence in MacArthur. In war, as elsewhere, nothing succeeds like success. As a result of Inchon, MacArthur's stock had climbed at the

White House. Truman was more disposed to give MacArthur's military views greater weight. MacArthur was insistent that North Korea be invaded and was personally convinced that neither Russia nor China would intervene in Korea.

• The influence of George Marshall. Although he was no longer the vigorous figure of World War II, Marshall was still revered by Truman, who had unreserved faith in his judgment. Marshall was not a zealous advocate of invading North Korea, but he shared MacArthur's belief that North Korea must be invaded.

• An unwillingness to engage in negotiations with Pyongyang, Peking, or Moscow, aimed at gaining a peaceful settlement of the war and unification of Korea. Negotiations with Communists smacked of appeasement and timidity. Furthermore, no senior members of the Truman administration believed that negotiations could result in a satisfactory outcome.

• A new Washington impulse, seldom (if ever) publicly expressed, to assume a power position worldwide and roll back communism. Acheson had planted the seeds of this new concept in NSC-68. Although NSC-68 had not yet been formally "implemented" by the government, as a result of Korea Washington was then embarked on the massive rearmament program recommended in NSC-68. America had intervened in Korea at first merely to "draw a line" on Soviet expansionism, the ultimate expression of the containment policy. The decision to cross the 38th Parallel into North Korea and engage in a "rollback" reflected the new aggressiveness recommended in NSC-68.[1]

The pros and cons of crossing the 38th Parallel, and recommended courses of action, were summed up by the National Security Council in a paper numbered NSC-81, produced on September 1. While this paper was a masterpiece of equivocation, the thrust was clear. Provided there was no indication of Soviet or Red Chinese intervention, America should persuade the United Nations to pass a resolution authorizing MacArthur's forces to cross the 38th Parallel to destroy the NKPA and to provide for the unification of Korea by free elections. Truman approved NSC-81 on September 11 and directed the State Department to initiate action at the UN to obtain the enabling resolution. On the day of the Inchon landing, September 15, the JCS cabled MacArthur the gist of NSC-81, so that he could begin planning for operations north of the 38th Parallel. But, the JCS stated, he was not to execute such plans without the specific "approval of the President."[2]

Although Washington was dead set to invade North Korea, Truman believed it was essential to have the moral sanction of the UN. He made every possible effort to give the impression that future American action in Korea would be responsive to the desires of the UN. For example, when a reporter asked him (at a September 21 press conference) if he had reached a decision with respect to military action in North Korea, Truman dissembled: "No, I have not. That is a matter for the United Nations to decide. . . . It will be worked out by the United Nations and I will abide by the decision that the United Nations makes."[3]

At the UN Washington encountered considerable difficulties. America's allies, Britain in particular, were not wild to rush through a resolution authorizing an invasion of North Korea. The British were chary because they believed an invasion of North Korea might provoke Peking into intervention, which could lead to the loss of the British colony of Hong Kong. Moreover, UN Secretary-General Trygve Lie secretly circulated the draft of a resolution calling for a halt at the 38th Parallel, and India introduced a similar resolution. As a consequence, in order to have any hope of passage, the language of the American resolution (offered by the British and seventy other nations) was ambiguous to an absurd degree. Authorization to cross the 38th Parallel to destroy the NKPA and overthrow the government of Kim Il Sung emerged as a recommendation that "all appropriate steps be taken to ensure conditions of stability throughout Korea".[4]

Curiously, the Soviet delegates to the UN displayed unusual cordiality and began sending strong signals that they were willing to talk negotiated settlement and Korea-wide free elections. Although George Kennan urged that the United States accept these overtures to talk, Washington listened skeptically, finally concluding the terms offered by the Soviets were too high, that the offer might be a diplomatic ploy to sabotage its own resolution or merely a desperate effort to "save the North Korean regime." In any event, Washington refused even to consider negotiations.[5]

## II

Militarily the invasion of North Korea was a more difficult problem than it seemed at first glance. There were two principal deterrents to conventional military operations:

• *Terrain:* North Korea is substantially more mountainous than South Korea. The rugged Taebaek range, running north-south, rises to formidable heights in the north, virtually dividing North Korea into two separate zones, east and west. There were few good east-west roads. Thus, UN forces could not easily advance northward along a conventional, cohesive, well-defined military front with lateral communications, centralized close air support, and a common supply line.

• *Logistics:* UN forces were being supplied through two seaports, Pusan and Inchon, both already taxed to the limit. Supplies coming through Pusan had to go north by road and railroad. This flow was significantly impeded by

# The UN Invasion of North Korea

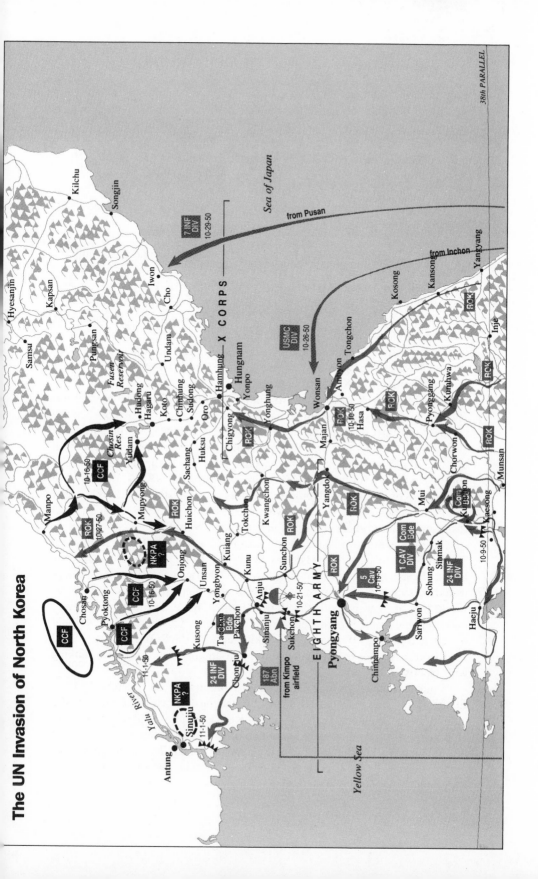

the lack of bridging. Owing to the peculiar tidal conditions at Inchon, which severely limited unloading, that port could not be counted upon to supply more than about two divisions on active operations. In order to mount large-scale military maneuvers in both sectors of North Korea, it was necessary early in the operation to seize two large seaports, one on the east coast, one on the west coast. The likeliest targets were Chinnampo, serving the North Korean capital of Pyongyang (as Inchon served Seoul) on the west coast, and, opposite it, Wonsan, a large, protected bay on the east coast.

After Johnnie Walker and his staff had viewed these and other military obstacles, their solution for the invasion of North Korea was as follows:[6]

First, integrate Ned Almond's X Corps into Eighth Army so that operations within North Korea could be coordinated and commanded from a central headquarters in close proximity to the battlefield. It was assumed that Almond would relinquish command of X Corps and return to Tokyo to resume his duties as MacArthur's chief of staff and that a new corps commander, compatible with and willing to take orders from Walker, would assume command of X Corps.

Secondly, attack northwestward from Seoul with X Corps (1st Marine and 7th Army divisions) almost immediately. The corps was then deployed in the northern outskirts of Seoul, ideally positioned to continue in hot pursuit of the fleeing NKPA, denying it time to regroup and man prewar defense lines north of the 38th Parallel. It would be adequately supplied through Inchon. Its objective would be to trap and destroy remnants of the NKPA, then to seize the North Korean capital, Pyongyang, and its seaport, Chinnampo. When that had been accomplished, X Corps would send troops eastward along a lateral road (and railroad) connecting Pyongyang and Wonsan.

Thirdly, simultaneously attack north by northeast from Seoul with Shrimp Milburn's I Corps (1st Cav, 24th and ROK 1st divisions, and the British Brigade) on a straight line through Chorwon for Wonsan. I Corps would be supplied initially through Pusan with help from FEAF airlifts. It would link at Wonsan with the ROK 3d and Capital divisions, which were making phenomenal progress up the east coast road. Thereafter I Corps would be supplied through Wonsan. After linking up with the ROKs, I Corps would send troops west over the Pyongyang–Wonsan road (and railroad), linking with troops of X Corps.

Fourthly, after the line Pyongyang–Wonsan had been established, all Eighth Army forces would advance simultaneously northward another fifty miles or so to the extreme narrow neck of Korea, on a line Chongju-Yongwan-Hamhung. This advance would gain two other seaports, Sinanju on the west coast, Hungnam on the east coast. The staff at GHQ, Tokyo, including Almond's deputy, Doyle Hickey; the G-3, Pinky Wright; and MacArthur's G-4,

George L. Eberle, generally approved of this plan or some slight variation of it. All assumed, as did Ned Almond, that X Corps would be absorbed by Eighth Army.[7]

But no one had consulted MacArthur. In the meantime, he had conceived his own plan. It was astonishing. X Corps, remaining an independent force under Almond's command and responsible directly to MacArthur, would be withdrawn from the battlefield, loaded aboard ships, and relanded amphibiously on the east coast of North Korea at Wonsan on or about October 20. From Wonsan X Corps would attack west across the peninsula and take Pyongyang, while Eighth Army, replacing X Corps at Seoul, would attack north across the 38th Parallel toward Pyongyang to create a double envelopment.

In drawing this plan, MacArthur was influenced by a number of factors:

• A belief that surviving NKPA forces manning prewar defensive lines would mount a fierce defense of their homeland in the Seoul–Pyongyang corridor (120 air miles). To overcome these defenses would require an all-out, prolonged frontal assault, the bloodiest and least desirable form of maneuver. A lightning attack west from Wonsan (90 air miles), coordinated with an Eighth Army attack north (pinning down NKPA forces in the Seoul–Pyongyang corridor), would outflank the NKPA defensive lines and the bulk of its manpower and armament.

• The failure of the Inchon anvil and the Eighth Army hammer to trap and destroy the bulk of NKPA in South Korea. Some 25,000 to 40,000 NKPA troops were fleeing north on foot through the mountains in the center of the peninsula. Yet another American line across Korea (Wonsan–Pyongyang) might still trap these forces, preventing them from gaining a redoubt in extreme North Korea or Manchuria. If these forces got clean away, MacArthur could not credibly claim that the NKPA had been "destroyed."

• An urge to reward Almond and his X Corps and leave Eighth Army in a secondary role. As MacArthur viewed matters, Almond and X Corps had performed brilliantly; Walker and Eighth Army, poorly. The capture of the enemy's capital, Pyongyang, would be a historic achievement, like the capture of Hitler's Berlin on a smaller scale. Almond and X Corps—notably the Marines—had earned the honor.[8]

• The command difficulty entailed in the absorption of X Corps by Eighth Army. Almond obviously could not serve under Walker, nor did Walker want him. One general or the other would have to go—Almond back to Tokyo or Walker (perhaps replaced by Almond as Eighth Army commander) into retirement. In either case it would appear to be an unfair "demotion" in the wake of a sensational "victory." The best temporary solution to the problem was to keep Walker and Almond separated and allow X Corps to operate in effect as an independent army for the time being.[9]

• A belief that the early capture of Wonsan by amphibious assault would reduce the logistical strain on Pusan and would save wear and tear on heavy machinery and weaponry entailed in an overland march on secondary or tertiary mountain roads.

While this plan appeared at superficial glance to make a great deal of sense, on close inspection it was seen to contain several major weaknesses:

• It would throw away a golden opportunity for "hot pursuit" up the Seoul–Pyongyang corridor. Standard Army doctrine for dealing with a retreating, disorganized enemy called for the fastest possible pursuit and exploitation. A continued X Corps attack up the corridor might catch the NKPA and crack straight through to Pyongyang before it could stoutly man its defensive lines. Substituting Eighth Army for X Corps on this front would take at least two weeks, giving the NKPA time to man the defensive lines. Moreover, Almond's X Corps was fresher and, including the Marines' organic close air support, far stronger than Milburn's I Corps, the only American force Eighth Army could immediately send in hot pursuit.

• It would create a logistical nightmare. Owing to the peculiar tidal conditions at Inchon, which severely limited loading and unloading time, it was not possible to outload both the Marines and 7th Division in time for an October 20 D day at Wonsan. Because of that, MacArthur had ruled that only the Marines would outload at Inchon, that the 7th Division would motor-march to Pusan and outload there. The outloading of the Marines at Inchon would tie up that port for at least ten days, during which no supplies could be brought in for Eighth Army. The motor-march of the 7th Division would siphon off desperately needed Eighth Army trucks, which, pending the rebuilding of the railroad, were the only means Walker had for bringing supplies north from Pusan. Their outloading at Pusan would tie up facilities in that port as well.

• It would present X Corps with a formidable military challenge. The proposed X Corps attack westward across the peninsula from Wonsan to Pyongyang cut directly across the "leak" or "drift" of NKPA troops fleeing from South Korea. Almost nothing was known about the strength and weaponry of these forces. They might be strong enough to block the mountainous Wonsan–Pyongyang road indefinitely. In any case, that line (125 miles by road) could not be made strong enough to "trap" fleeing NKPA troops and to capture Pyongyang simultaneously.

• Contrary to standard Army doctrine, it would divide the major elements of the American ground forces in Korea into two separate and noninteracting commands. Like two different armies, they would be directed by MacArthur or GHQ in Tokyo. Many believed MacArthur and GHQ were too distant from the battlefield to manage these disparate forces properly. Ironically, in World War II MacArthur had repeatedly protested to Washington against a similar division of Army ground forces in the Pacific (the "two roads to Tokyo" strategy) and the absence of unified military commands, particularly during the invasion of Leyte, when the naval support group was not under his control.[10]

\* \* \*

When MacArthur unveiled this plan, many senior generals and admirals in the Far East opposed it. These dissenters included 7th Division commander Dave Barr, who stood to gain great glory if it succeeded. Barr urged an alternate plan: that his 7th Division be mated with the 1st Cav (to form a new corps) for hot pursuit up the Seoul–Pyongyang corridor or, if that were not feasible, that X Corps "take the high road" overland to Wonsan, as Walker had proposed. Because he was geared for it, Marine division commander O. P. Smith preferred an amphibious landing to an overland march, provided it was mounted in the right place, but he had "quite a few reservations" about the cross-peninsular attack on Pyongyang. MacArthur's naval chief, Turner Joy, urged flatly that the plan be scrapped, in part because of his growing belief that Wonsan Harbor might be heavily mined.[11]

This time, however, MacArthur permitted no agonizing debates. When Joy called at the Dai Ichi Building in Tokyo to talk MacArthur out of the scheme, MacArthur refused to see him. When Barr and O. P. Smith met with Ned Almond to point out the flaws in the plan and suggest alternatives, Almond turned them aside. "The road directly from Seoul to Wonsan," Almond wrote later, was "on enemy grounds and subject to untold interruptions and guerilla activities," making it "most dangerous to move directly overland." Almond not only approved of Wonsan unreservedly but also attempted to push its D day forward from October 20 to October 15.[12]

\* \* \*

Before the murky UN resolution authorizing the invasion of North Korea was even introduced, Truman formally and officially approved that course. At his direction the JCS cabled MacArthur a directive authorizing the invasion on September 27. Incorporating some of the caveats and much of the language of NSC-81, the directive specified that:

• MacArthur's military objective was the "destruction of the North Korean Armed Forces." To attain this objective, he was "authorized to conduct military operations, including amphibious and airborne or ground operations north of the 38th Parallel in Korea, provided that at the time of such operations there had been no entry into North Korea by major Soviet or Chinese

Communist Forces, no announcements of intended entry, nor a threat to counter American military operations militarily in North Korea."

• Under no circumstances, however, would MacArthur's forces cross the Manchurian or USSR borders of Korea, and "as a matter of policy," no non-Korean ground forces would be used in the northeast provinces bordering the Soviet Union or in the area along the Manchurian border.

• When organized armed resistance by North Korean forces had been brought substantially to an end, MacArthur should direct ROK forces to take the lead in disarming the remaining North Korean units and enforcing the terms of surrender. Guerrilla activities should be dealt with primarily by the forces of the Republic of Korea with minimum participation by United Nations contingents.

At the suggestion of Dean Acheson a "political guidance" paragraph was added, stating in part: ROK forces would be expected to "cooperate" in UN military and occupation operations north of the 38th Parallel, "but political questions, such as the formal extension of sovereignty over North Korea, should await actions by the United Nations to complete the unification of the country."

The directive also specified what MacArthur should do if the Soviets or Red Chinese intervened with ground forces in Korea. In the event either nation announced in advance the intention of intervening in Korea and warned that their forces should not be attacked, he should refer the matter immediately to Washington. In the event the Soviets intervened with major forces overtly or covertly without prior warning south or north of the 38th Parallel, MacArthur would "assume the defensive, make no move to aggravate the situation and report to Washington." In the event the Chinese Communists intervened with major forces overtly or covertly without prior warning "south of the 38th Parallel," MacArthur would "continue the action as long as action by your forces offers a reasonable chance of successful resistance." In the event of an attempt to employ small Soviet or Chinese Communist units covertly south of the 38th Parallel, MacArthur should continue the action. (Oddly, instructions on what MacArthur was to do in event of overt or covert Chinese Communist intervention *north* of the 38th Parallel were not included.)

Mindful of MacArthur's propensity to stretch his authority and go his own way, the directive stated specifically that he should submit all plans for military operations and the occupation of North Korea to the JCS "for approval." Moreover, the JCS added, the directive was not "final"; it might require "modification in accordance with developments." The JCS advised: "In this connection, you will continue to make a special effort to determine whether there is a Chinese Communist or Soviet threat to the attainment of your objective." If such a threat developed, MacArthur was to report it to the chiefs "as a matter of urgency."[13]

Upon receipt of this directive, MacArthur responded immediately. He cabled that there was "no indication of present entry into North Korea by major Soviet or Chinese Communist Forces." He dutifully submitted an outline of his plans for the invasion. As in the case of the early plans he submitted for Inchon, it was stark—no more than a rough sketch.[14]

Upon receiving the plan for an amphibious landing at Wonsan, the chiefs were somewhat shocked. Omar Bradley fretted over the logistical complications. "To me it didn't make sense," he wrote later. "It was the worst possible solution. . . . The enemy himself could not have concocted a more diabolical scheme to delay our pursuit. . . ." Joe Collins worried about the "command arrangements," which left X Corps independent of Eighth Army. However, having been "proven wrong" in its objections to Inchon, the JCS was reluctant to register objections. As Matt Ridgway later put it, "No one was questioning the judgment of the man who had just worked a military miracle."[15]

At the highest civilian levels in the administration, however, MacArthur's plan was warmly endorsed. Although the UN resolution still had not been introduced, on September 29—the day MacArthur reestablished the Rhee government in Seoul—the JCS cabled MacArthur to say that his plan had been approved.[16]

The same day George Marshall sent MacArthur yet another cable which the secretary of defense soon regretted. Having received a press report that Walker planned to "halt" at the 38th Parallel for "regrouping," Marshall was disturbed. Owing to the delicacy of the situation in the UN, the Truman administration was attempting to downplay all official talk of crossing the parallel. Indeed, it seemed that if possible, Truman wanted to slip over the parallel unnoticed. In an attempt to get this point across, Marshall told MacArthur: "We want you to feel unhampered tactically and strategically to proceed north of the 38th Parallel. [Any] announcement [of] above referred to may precipitate embarrassment in the U.N. where evident desire is not to be confronted with necessity of a vote on passage of 38th Parallel, rather to find you have found it militarily necessary to do so." MacArthur responded that he knew nothing about the Walker announcement but would caution Walker to say nothing further. He went on: "Parallel 38 is not a factor in the military employment of our forces. . . . In exploiting the defeat of the enemy forces, our own troops may [soon] cross the parallel at any time in exploratory probing or exploiting local tactical conditions. . . . I regard all of Korea open for our military operations. . . ."[17]

In this exchange MacArthur seemed—wittingly or unwittingly—to have missed the main point. In a follow-up message he told the JCS he intended to make publicly known his views and plans on the invasion of North Korea. The

JCS hastened to clarify or emphasize the pith of Marshall's message. It informed MacArthur that any such public statement would be "unwise." Washington, the JCS cautioned, "desires to avoid having to make an issue of the 38 Parallel. . . ." He should therefore proceed to cross the parallel "without any further explanation or announcement and let actions determine the matter."[18]

MacArthur made no specific comment on this exchange. However, it is clear from his writings and those of his sycophant Courtney Whitney that he regarded the restraints placed upon him with disdain. MacArthur apparently believed that a ringing public declaration would have a greater psychological and military impact on the Oriental mind.

## III

As it happened, the invasion of North Korea actually began without regard to these elaborate directives and the diplomatic nuances. It was led by the ROK 3d Division, which was speeding up the east coast highway against slight to no opposition. Spurred by Syngman Rhee, the ROKs crossed the 38th Parallel on September 30 without pause and established a CP about eight miles north of the line. The ROK Capital Division, also advancing with astonishing speed, followed on the heels of the ROK 3d Division.[19]

This remarkable feat rendered academic all debate about crossing the parallel. Nonetheless, Washington and Tokyo proceeded with the diplomatic formalities. At the UN the British delegate introduced the vaguely worded resolution which, in effect, authorized crossing the parallel. In Tokyo MacArthur broadcast a Washington-approved surrender ultimatum to the NKPA.[20]

There was no response of any kind from Pyongyang. However, there was an immediate and ominous reaction from Peking. In a tough public pronouncement Premier Chou En-lai declared that the Chinese people "absolutely will not tolerate foreign aggression [in Korea] nor will they supinely tolerate seeing their neighbors being savagely invaded by imperialists." In private, Chou summoned the Indian ambassador to Peking, K. M. Panikkar, and told him that if UN forces, other than ROKs, crossed the 38th Parallel, China would send troops into North Korea to oppose them.[21]

Both these messages soon arrived in Washington. The specific threat of Chinese intervention, relayed by Panikkar, evoked urgent and prolonged discussion. Finally, however, the warning was discounted, for several reasons. Panikkar was believed to be pro-Communist and anti-American; therefore, he was not trusted to be impartial. The warning might be pure fiction. His message contradicted one from him several days earlier in which he had

The commander of the 38th Infantry, George B. Peploe, sitting on a bridge section at the Naktong River. Peploe's troops (among the few in the 2d Division with bridging) were the first to cross the Naktong in Eighth Army's "breakout" from the Pusan Perimeter.

Paul L. Freeman, commander of the 23d Infantry, who gained fame for his pivotal defense of Chipyong, later rose to four stars.

Trucks of the 38th Infantry crossing the Naktong River on an "underwater ford" constructed of sandbags.

The first of the floating or pontoon bridges over the Naktong at Waegwan provided a crossing for the 24th Infantry Division and became a key link in the logistics chain.

The forward progress of Eighth Army armor units was often slowed by enemy mines planted in the road. Preceding the tank columns with metal detectors, Army engineers find and remove mines.

Approaching Inchon for the great gamble, Douglas MacArthur *(center)* poses aboard the bridge of a naval vessel with his senior assistants *(left to right):* Courtney Whitney, the GHQ G-3; Edwin K. ("Pinky") Wright; and *(pointing)* the GHQ chief of staff and X Corps commander, Ned Almond.

Inchon conquered. The massive tidal swings (up to thirty-one feet) made unloading difficult. The four beached LSTs shown unloading are stranded by the broad mud flats astern.

Heading north and uphill. Army engineers, working with small logs and rocks, repair a typical Korean mountain road in dry weather.

Troops follow—always uphill it seemed—passing a command jeep. In rainy weather such unpaved roads turned muddy and became nearly impassable, even for foot soldiers.

Heavy artillery, such as these long-range 155-mm howitzers, was confined to main "highways."

Reaching high ground, these soldiers dig in with a light machine gun and scan enemy terrain with binoculars.

After landing in northeast Korea in early November, American infantry began to encounter frigid weather and snow in the mountains.

The tanklike full-tracked M-16 antiaircraft vehicles, which fired twin 40-mm cannons ("Twin Forties"), proved to be devastating antipersonnel weapons. Some men huddle near the engine exhaust to keep warm.

Others, crammed aboard "Easy Eight" Shermans, ride forward to battle wearing long overcoats, fur-lined parkas, and fur-lined caps with ear flaps. Proper winter clothing was in short supply everywhere.

Herbert B. Powell, commander of the 7th Infantry Division's 17th Infantry Regiment, posed here at the 7th Division command post, led a drive to the Yalu River in northeast Korea. He reached Hyesanjin on November 21, 1950.

Powell *(right)* was joined at the Yalu for picture taking by the senior Army commanders in northeast Korea *(left to right):* 7th Division artillery commander Homer W. Kiefer; 7th Division assistant commander Hank Hodes; X Corps commander Ned Almond; and 7th Division commander Dave Barr. The "publicity drive" to the Yalu was to have serious adverse consequences at the Chosin Reservoir.

The 3d Infantry Division, which came from the States, reinforced X Corps in northeast Korea. Its commander was paratrooper Robert H. ("Shorty") Soule *(left),* shown here with the commander of the 65th Puerto Rican Regiment, William W. Harris.

The commander of the 7th Infantry, John S. Guthrie *(right),* was soon promoted to chief of staff of Ned Almond's X Corps, the most difficult job of his Army career.

The famous retreat from Hagaru, at the Chosin Reservoir, to Hungnam. On this narrow, frigid road 15,000 Americans escaped encirclement by Chinese forces.

Grim wreckage litters the "gauntlet" below Kunu, where the Chinese Communists ambushed the American 2d Division.

When Eighth Army commander Johnnie Walker was killed in a jeep accident, he was replaced by paratrooper Matthew Bunker Ridgway. On the battlefield Ridgway wore a grenade on the right strap of a parachute chest harness and a first aid kit, which was often mistaken for another grenade, on the left strap. As part of his effort to re-energize Eighth Army, Ridgway relied on "public relations." Here he strikes a suitably dramatic pose for photographers.

Ridgway made numerous changes in the leadership of Eighth Army. He brought Bryant E. Moore *(right)* to Korea to replace John Coulter as commander of IX Corps. However, he kept Leven C. ("Lev") Allen *(left)* in the job of Eighth Army chief of staff.

When Moore suddenly died of a heart attack, Ridgway chose William M. Hoge to replace him as IX Corps commander.

Touring Eighth Army subordinate headquarters, Ridgway confers with 25th Division commander Bill Kean *(left)* and his assistant commander, Joseph Sladen Bradley *(right)*, whom Ridgway chose to replace Kean.

When Mike Michaelis moved up to replace Bradley as 25th Division ADC, the 1st Battalion commander, Gilbert J. Check, was named commander of the famous 27th Infantry Wolfhounds.

Bradley *(right)* later named tanker Tom Dolvin *(center)*, shown after receiving the Distinguished Service Cross from I Corps commander Frank W. (''Shrimp'') Milburn, to the post of 25th Division chief of staff.

declared flatly that China would not enter the Korean War. It seemed doubtful that if the Chinese had intended to enter the war, they would give advance warning. Moreover, the timing for intervention seemed illogical. American forces were now very powerful. Militarily the most favorable time for Chinese intervention had passed. The warning was most likely a form of "diplomatic blackmail" or bluff or "war of words" designed to scare the UN out of passing the resolution or to force the Americans to stop at the parallel.[22]

There was no reliable way to check on Peking's intentions. America had no high-level spies in Peking, nor was it able to intercept and decode Chinese radio communications. The GHQ intelligence officer, James H. Polk, remembered: "We were not reading Red Chinese radio traffic at all. One reason was that they employed the Mandarin dialect. We had no Mandarin linguists. Chiang Kai-shek's people were reading the traffic, but no one trusted what they produced because it was invariably biased or self-serving. I wanted to bring some of Chiang's people to Korea [to work under American code breakers], but the Pentagon refused permission."[23]

Even so, other American intelligence sources had produced a fairly accurate picture of Chinese Communist Forces (CCF) in Manchuria. The principal element was the Fourth Field Army, which was returning "home" after three years of combat in the Chinese civil war. The Fourth had fought with great distinction. It had, in fact, been the main CCF military unit in the defeat of Chiang Kai-shek. It was commanded by Red China's ablest military strategist and battlefield commander, Lin Piao, a veteran of the 1934 and 1935 "Long March."

The Fourth Field Army, comprised of about 450,000 men, was the largest and most battle-hardened indigenous army in Asia. Its principal subunits were called "army groups." Each group was composed of about four 30,000-man numbered "armies," made up of three 8,000-to-10,000-man infantry divisions, plus artillery and service units. Six of these armies, totaling about eighteen infantry divisions, several artillery divisions, plus service troops (about 210,000 men in all), were then deployed behind the Yalu River, the border between North Korea and Manchuria.

The CCF soldiers were highly motivated, well-disciplined troops, accustomed to fighting with minimum comforts and equipment. The old veterans had raised mobile "guerrilla warfare" to a fine art. They specialized in quick, surprise ambushes, followed by rapid withdrawals. They were adept at camouflage and concealment. They could march great distances on foot at night. They could make do for days on a small bag of rice. Mao Tse-tung had reduced CCF tactics to a set of principles: "Enemy advancing, we retreat; enemy entrenched, we harass; enemy exhausted, we attack; enemy retreating, we pursue."[24]

Although the CCF was rich in resourceful manpower, by modern warfare standards it was poor in many major categories. Having no air force, it was deprived of aerial reconnaissance and close air support. It had few tanks or other tracked vehicles and few modern antiaircraft batteries. It was weak in artillery. Its small arms (machine guns; mortars; rifles; pistols) had been amassed from many sources (America, Japan, Russia) and therefore employed a wide variety of ammo, which complicated logistics. Its radio communications were primitive.

\* \* \*

President Truman, deeply concerned over these mounting threats from Peking, requested that the CIA conduct a sweeping new assessment of Soviet and Red Chinese intentions. This assessment was conducted under the direction of the new CIA director, Walter Bedell Smith, Eisenhower's brilliant and tough-minded wartime chief of staff, recently returned from a three-year tour as ambassador to Moscow. It was less pessimistic than earlier CIA assessments:

• The Soviet Union was still dedicated to communizing the world and might resort to global war to achieve that end. The "peak" danger period would probably be in 1952, after Moscow had a larger atomic bomb stockpile and new bombers to deliver them.

• Soviet forces in the Far East, recently strengthened, had the capability of intervening "overwhelmingly" in North Korea. However, "it is believed that Soviet leaders will not consider that their prospective losses in Korea warrant direct military intervention and a consequent grave risk of war."

• The Chinese Communists, "lacking requisite air and naval support," were "capable of intervening effectively but not necessarily decisively" in Korea. "Despite statements by Chou En-lai, troop movements to Manchuria and propaganda charges of atrocities and border violations, there are no convincing indications of an actual Chinese Communist intention to resort to full-scale intervention in Korea." Moreover, "the most favorable time" for Chinese intervention in Korea had passed.[25]

# I V

On October 2 MacArthur issued formal orders to Eighth Army, X Corps, and ROK Army to begin the massive redeployments he had designed for the invasion of North Korea. Shrimp Milburn's I Corps (1st Cav, 24th, and 1st ROK divisions, plus the British Brigade) moved through Seoul to relieve X Corps (7th and 1st Marine divisions) and began formulating plans to attack across the 38th Parallel. Ned Almond's X Corps withdrew to the Inchon area, where the 1st Marine Division prepared to reembark. The 7th Division assembled near Suwon for the motor-march to Pusan. Northeast of Seoul the ROK 6th, 7th, and 8th divisions, designated ROK II Corps, prepared to attack directly northward from the vicinity of Uijongbu, on the right flank of Milburn's I Corps. On the east coast the ROK 3d and Capital divisions, designated ROK I Corps, prepared to continue driving north toward Wonsan. John Coulter's IX Corps (2d and 25th divisions, plus the Puerto Rican 65th Regiment) assumed responsibility for mopping up and policing all of South Korea below Seoul.[26]

\* \* \*

Shrimp Milburn's I Corps had every right to be resentful of the role it had been assigned for the invasion. Its American divisions (1st Cav; 24th) had been in continuous fighting for more than two months. They were tired, understrength, and strung out from Suwon to Taejon. Now they faced the new and very tough job of cracking through the NKPA defensive lines north of the 38th Parallel, which would probably be manned by troops fighting fanatically for their homeland. Moreover, because X Corps was itself headed for combat, it had taken everything it owned with it, leaving nothing for I Corps. Owing to this and to the higher priority accorded X Corps and the logistical jam-up at Inchon, I Corps suffered from an acute shortage of supplies. Almost everything had to come by truck from Pusan.

The resentment in I Corps generated an overwhelming desire to make MacArthur and Almond look like fools—that is, to mount such a determined and aggressive drive up the Seoul–Pyongyang corridor that I Corps would crack through to Pyongyang before X Corps could get there, perhaps even before X Corps could land at Wonsan.

MacArthur had given Walker a rather loose timetable for the I Corps attack: not earlier than October 15 and not later than October 30. Since each day the I Corps attack was postponed gave the NKPA another day to strengthen defenses, Walker and Milburn became determined to beat that timetable.[27]

Accordingly on October 5 Milburn began moving his I Corps forces northward. They would assemble for the invasion at Kaesong, immediately south of the 38th Parallel. Since Hap Gay's 1st Cav was already farthest north in the Suwon-Ansong area, it led the way. John Church's 24th Division decamped from policing duties in Taejon and followed. The ROK 1st Division on the corps's right flank joined the parade north. Last came the 27th British Brigade, which had been substantially strengthened (to a full regiment) by a recently arrived Australian battalion and renamed the 27th British Commonwealth Brigade.[28]

Marcel Crombez's 5th Cav spearheaded the 1st Cav division motor-march to Kaesong. His 3/5 Cav, commanded by Edgar Treacy, took the lead. The 5th Cav met no NKPA opposition. Indeed, it was cheered along by throngs of South Korean civilians lining the highway. It made good time until it reached the Imjin River near Munsan. There it ran into difficulty: The NKPA had blown the highway bridge.[29]

Inasmuch as 5th Cav had no bridging at hand, crossing the Imjin proved to be a formidable challenge. The river was broad (500 feet) at that point and swollen by the Yellow Sea tides. Some NKPA rearguard elements and snipers were still on the opposite shore. After plunging into the freezing cold water, the men floundered across at a ferry site, where the NKPA had constructed an underwater sandbag ford. On the opposite bank some of the men, encountering sporadic and weak enemy fire, panicked and bugged out—but not for long. The 3/5 soon regrouped and pushed on warily, followed by the entire 1st Cav Division.[30]

By the evening of October 8 all of I Corps had crossed the Imjin and assembled in the vicinity of Kaesong. Coincidentally at about the same time (October 7, New York time) the UN passed the resolution (by a vote of 47–5, with 5 abstentions) in effect authorizing the invasion of North Korea. On the following day (October 9 in Tokyo and Korea) MacArthur, as previously directed by Washington, broadcast a second surrender ultimatum to the NKPA, this time including the gist of the UN resolution. Almost simultaneously (at 9:00 A.M., October 9, Korean time) I Corps attacked in force across the 38th Parallel.[31]

Immediately there followed two bellicose public reactions from the Communists. In Pyongyang a defiant Kim Il Sung exhorted his troops to fight to the last man, assuring them that they did not "stand alone," that they had the "absolute support" of the Soviet Union and the Chinese people. In Peking the Ministry of Foreign Affairs issued a statement which came very close to a declaration of war. It proclaimed that "the American war of invasion in Korea has been a serious menace to the security of China from the very start and now that the American forces are attempting to cross the 38th Parallel on a large scale, the Chinese people cannot stand idly by. . . ."[32]

These statements were duly noted in Washington and Tokyo (and other Western capitals), but American intelligence experts continued to discount or disbelieve them. MacArthur's G-2, Charles Willoughby, reflected the prevailing view in this assessment: "Recent declarations by CCF leaders, threatening to enter North Korea if American forces were to cross the 38th Parallel, are probably in the category of diplomatic blackmail." The Americans continued to believe that the "most favorable time" for Chinese intervention had passed.[33]

These increasingly bellicose threats from Peking did, however, cause the JCS to take a closer look at MacArthur's directive. It was then discovered that while the document contained specific provisions for Chinese intervention south of the 38th Parallel, there was none to cover the possibility of Chinese intervention north of the parallel. Accordingly, the JCS amended the directive, substituting the word "anywhere" for "south of the 38th Parallel." Significantly the amendment also touched on the matter of retaliation directly against Chinese territory. Since the JCS believed Truman would order such retaliation in the event of Chinese intervention, it was not categorically ruled out. However, MacArthur was instructed to "obtain authorization from Washington" prior to launching such action.

\*  \*  \*

Shrimp Milburn's plan to crack the NKPA defenses north of the 38th Parallel called for a multipronged envelopment of the village of Kumchon, twenty air miles north of the parallel and well behind the known NKPA lines.[34] Assisted by FEAF close air support, Hap Gay's 1st Cav pushed off into North Korea. As expected, NKPA resistance was strong and, at times, fanatical. Hal Edson's 8th Cav, going north on the Seoul–Pyongyang highway, was soon checked by mines and withering antitank fire. In the early fighting the veteran 1/8 commander Robert Kane was severely wounded and evacuated. On Edson's right Crombez's 5th Cav made slight headway in the heavily defended hills. Coming up behind Crombez, the British Commonwealth Brigade took a wrong turn and got lost in a mountainous cul-de-sac. As a result, it could play no further role in the battle for Kumchon.[35]

In drawing plans for the Kumchon envelopment, Hap Gay did not really expect much help from Billy Harris's 7th Cav, which was to make a wide flanking attack to the left (or west). The reason was that the 7th Cav had first to cross the Yesong River. There was a big (2,400-foot) partially destroyed combination railroad-highway bridge still standing, but it was certain to be heavily defended and would probably be demolished before Harris could seize it. In that event the 7th Cav would have no way to cross until I Corps engineers could lay in a pontoon bridge.[36]

As Harris and his men viewed it, the seizure of the Yesong bridge would be a feat almost comparable to the Allied seizure of the Rhine River bridge at Remagen in World War II. It could outflank and unhinge the entire NKPA defensive line, opening all North Korea to rapid attack by the 1st Cav Division. Not incidentally, it also would put the 7th Cav in ideal position to lead the attack on Pyongyang. Harris was determined not to fail. The attack was planned in infinite detail. To support it, Harris even created his own 7th Cav "logistical system." He persuaded Army authorities at Inchon to send him a dozen landing craft loaded with gasoline and supplies. After the craft had been unloaded, Harris would use them to get his tanks across the river.[37]

The assault on the Yesong bridge commenced in the late afternoon of

October 9. The 1/7 led the attack, again commanded by Pete Clainos, returned from the hospital. Not unexpectedly it met heavy NKPA fire. In the furious fight which ensued, the 1/7 suffered seventy-eight casualties. But Clainos captured the bridge and got a foothold on the west bank. Later that same night the 2/7, commanded by Gil Huff, also returned from the hospital, crossed, and it, too, met heavy fire. In this action Huff was again wounded and replaced—this time permanently—by his exec, West Pointer John Callaway. With this appointment able West Pointers now held all the key command slots in the 7th Cav.[38]

In the meantime, Harris had reconstituted Task Force 777, composed of James Lynch's 3/7 and elements of the 77th FAB and the 70th Tank Battalion. On October 10 and 11 this force crossed the river. The jeeps and trucks went over the damaged bridge; the tanks and artillery crossed in the landing craft which had arrived from Inchon. Almost without pause Lynch sped north about twenty miles to Hanpo, a village on the Seoul–Pyongyang highway behind Kumchon. By noon on October 11 Lynch (soon reinforced by the 1/7 and 2/7) had taken Hanpo.[39]

It was another spectacular tactical achievement for the 7th Cav. The NKPA fled into the hills. Crombez's 5th and Edson's 8th Cav regiments were thus able to advance to Kumchon, where they arrived on October 14, linking with the 7th Cav. Moreover, the 7th Cav's bridgehead over the Yesong provided an assembly site (at Paekchon) for John Church's 24th Division attack on Chinnampo, via a parallel road leading northwest. In sum, the 7th Cav had set the stage for an all-out I Corps assault on Pyongyang and Chinnampo.[40]

Meanwhile, on the extreme right flank of I Corps the ROK 1st Division pulled off an equally spectacular maneuver. Crossing the Imjin River in the hills near Korangpo, it outflanked the NKPA defensive lines and drove through Sibyon to Miu, twenty miles due north of Kumchon. By October 15 it was merely sixty air miles southwest of Pyongyang.[41]

It had taken about two weeks for Milburn's I Corps to replace Almond's X Corps and crack through the NKPA defenses. Had the stronger, fresher, better-equipped X Corps continued the attack northward in this corridor, it unquestionably would have achieved the same results much sooner.

In these attacks toward Pyongyang the shortage of supplies in I Corps began to hurt. One private in Edgar Treacy's 3/5 remembered that the lack of food and cigarettes was "unbearable." A typical 3/5 meal in mid-October, he said, was "a slice of Spam and a half canteen of grapefruit juice once a day." Moreover, the weather was unusually cold. On some mornings frost covered the ground. The men were still wearing summer uniforms. At night they huddled together, doubling or tripling blankets to keep warm.[42]

*  *  *

Across the peninsula on the east coast, meanwhile, the ROK 3d and Capital divisions continued their dash north of the parallel. By October 9—the day the 1st Cav launched its attack on Kumchon—the ROKs reached the outskirts of Wonsan, 110 air miles north of the parallel. On the next day the ROKS entered Wonsan, overpowered the slim NKPA forces there, and secured the city and its airfield.[43]

By this time the American Navy had begun reconnoitering the shallow Wonsan Harbor for mines. What it found was astonishing: a vast field of perhaps 2,000 or 4,000 contact and magnetic mines, planted by the NKPA under the supervision of Soviet technicians. On the day the ROKs secured Wonsan, October 10, three large minesweepers arrived offshore to clear a channel. However, these vessels proved to be ill adapted for sweeping in shallow water, compelling the Navy to send to Japan for smaller wooden-hulled vessels. Meanwhile, as a desperate resort, the Navy dispatched thirty-nine carrier-based dive-bombers to drop 1,000-pound bombs into the fields, hoping to set off a chain reaction of exploding mines. This tactic had not worked against Axis mines in World War II; as feared, it did not work at Wonsan. In follow-up operations two of the smaller minesweepers, *Pirate* and *Pledge,* hit mines and sank, incurring ninety-two casualties.

It was soon apparent that the Navy faced a monumental challenge at Wonsan. Owing to the Truman-Johnson budget cuts and a lack of interest and foresight in the postwar years, the Navy was scandalously ill prepared in terms of gear and skilled manpower for minesweeping on so vast a scale. In effect (as one panicky admiral put it), the Navy had "lost control of the seas" at Wonsan. Despite emergency improvisations, it seemed unlikely that the Navy could clear Wonsan of mines by the X Corps D day, October 20.[44]

* * *

The arrival of the ROKs at Wonsan would rob the amphibious landing there of much of its drama, but it did not deter MacArthur from his grand scheme of sending X Corps across the peninsula from Wonsan to capture Pyongyang and create a line to trap the fleeing NKPA. However, the discovery of the vast array of minefields at Wonsan led MacArthur to propose substantial modifications to the plan.

Because of the minefields, the Wonsan landing would be scaled down. The Navy would clear a path to land only the 7th Division. Following the landing, the division would attack west across the peninsula toward Pyongyang, as originally envisioned. The Marine division would land fifty air miles farther north at Hungnam. It would then backtrack by land to Wonsan and join the 7th Division for the attack across the peninsula.[45]

When apprised of these new plans, MacArthur's naval chief, Turner Joy, vigorously objected to them for several reasons:

• Joy had discovered that Hungnam, too, was mined. To carry out the new plan, the Navy's weak, hard-pressed minesweeping force would have to clear not one but two harbors. Joy did not believe this could be done in time.

• The Marines were to combat-load in landing craft to make an assault. The 7th Division was to load in big ships, then use the same landing craft to come ashore at Wonsan behind the Marines. If the Marines went to Hungnam with the landing craft, there would be no easy way to unload the 7th Division at Wonsan.

• The X Corps forces would be dangerously split between Wonsan and Hungnam, deep in enemy territory, and could not be rejoined until the Marines backtracked to Wonsan. Even a modest NKPA attack between these forces could keep them divided, possibly throwing the whole operation into chaos.[46]

Although Johnnie Walker was not consulted, he could have added another strong objection. The best solution to his critical supply problem was to open quickly the port of Chinnampo, which served Pyongyang. Chinnampo was also mined. A prolonged diversion of the Navy's weak minesweeping capability to operations on the east coast would delay the clearing of Chinnampo, causing further hardship on Eighth Army.

In the ensuing discussions MacArthur was urged to abandon the east coast amphibious landing as a lost cause. But he refused, offering yet another modification to the plan, in which the landing sites of the Marines and 7th Division would be reversed, the Marines to go in at Wonsan (per the original plan), the 7th Division to land (after the mines had been cleared) at Hungnam, which had facilities to accommodate its big ships. When Turner Joy continued to argue that clearing two minefields was simply not feasible, MacArthur proposed yet another modification: that the 7th Division be landed about seventy-five miles northeast of Hungnam at Iwon, which had good beaches and was known to be free of mines.[47]

This last suggestion must have come as something of a shock to Turner Joy. A landing of the 7th Division at Iwon could not support the principal aim of Wonsan, which was to capture Pyongyang and throw a line across the peninsula. Iwon was too far away for that. A 7th Division landing at Iwon would serve only one purpose: occupation of the northeast provinces of Korea by American forces. Washington had directed that "as a matter of policy" only ROK forces should be used in the northeast provinces. Only one week earlier MacArthur had cabled Washington that he would comply with that policy. A 7th Division landing at Iwon would be a flagrant violation of the spirit of his directive.

For the moment, however, MacArthur did not press for a 7th Division landing at Iwon. After his talk with Turner Joy he appeared to concede that Joy was right, that Wonsan should proceed as originally designed: the Marines to land first, the 7th Division second. Both would attack west across the peninsula toward Pyongyang. Accordingly, on October 10 Joy issued orders to that effect. But as matters developed, these plans would be again modified. The 7th Division, in fact, landed at Iwon rather than Wonsan.

\* \* \*

The reembarkation of X Corps therefore continued. At Inchon the Marines, working in "feverish bursts" when the tides were favorable, loaded tens of thousands of tons of gear aboard ships. It was an awesomely complicated operation. When the gear was all stored, about 30,000 men (including X Corps staff, ROKs, etc.) boarded the ships to occupy extremely cramped quarters. Although the minesweeping at Wonsan was not completed—and that operation had grown even more complicated—most of the X Corps ships departed Inchon about October 16. The outloading of the Marines had tied up Inchon for ten full days, during which time few supplies for Eighth Army could be brought in. The commander of the Army's 3d Logistical Command at Inchon, West Pointer (1923) George C. Stewart, wrote that the operation "came as a devastating blow" to his outfit. "It reduced the flow of supplies [for Eighth Army] . . . to a trickle. It lowered morale of all who were trying so hard to perform our principal mission . . . [and] halted the advance of the Eighth Army. [The decision] seemed to me to be unreasonable and unwise."[48]

The 7th Division, assembling near Suwon, commenced its motor-march to Pusan on October 5. It utilized its own trucks, plus those of Eighth Army and some borrowed from the Marines. To avoid clogging the main Seoul–Pusan highway over which Eighth Army's supplies were coming north, the division (less its tanks, which would go by LST) was ordered to take a roundabout 350-mile "inland" route (Suwon–Chungju–Hamchang–Kumchon–Taegu). The 31st and 32d Infantry regiments reached Pusan on October 8; the last of the 17th Infantry and the artillery, on October 12. By October 16 the division and its gear had been packed aboard big transports, and ten LSTs with the tanks had arrived. Owing to the minesweeping delays at Wonsan, however, the ships remained in Pusan Harbor. The movement and reequipping of the 7th Division had drained desperately needed trucks from Eighth Army and drastically depleted its supply stocks.[49]

By the time X Corps was fully loaded aboard its ships, Shrimp Milburn's I Corps had cracked through the main NKPA defenses and taken Kumchon and was deploying for its assault on Pyongyang. Because of the unswept minefields at Wonsan, it seemed highly unlikely that X Corps could land there by the original D day, October 20. Even if by some lucky turn it managed to meet that deadline, it could probably not get across the peninsula to Pyongyang before about October 27. Unless I Corps met heroic NKPA resistance, it seemed likely that it would capture Pyongyang by October 20—before X Corps could even land at Wonsan.

Thus the primary reason for the X Corps landing at Wonsan—the capture of Pyongyang—was being overtaken by events. In all likelihood, only its secondary mission—throwing a line across the peninsula to trap fleeing NKPA troops—would remain by the time it landed. By any yardstick, this task was simply not worth the expenditure of effort and diversion of resources. Even if a line across the peninsula would achieve its aim of trapping fleeing NKPA (a doubtful assumption), the ROKs at Wonsan and I Corps at Pyongyang could establish it with considerably less effort.

In sum, X Corps was all dressed up—at huge effort and hardship on Eighth Army—with no rational place to go. By all logic, MacArthur should have canceled Wonsan. However, to have done so would have entailed an admission of error. MacArthur had not ever conceded professional error; with the eyes of the world focused on his operations in Korea, it was not a likely time to start.

These factors, and others, soon led MacArthur to conceive another mission for X Corps. That new mission proved to be even more ill advised than its original mission. As Joe Collins later wrote, MacArthur, having reached a peak of brilliance at Inchon, now seemed to be marching "like a Greek hero of old to an unkind and inexorable fate".[50]

## V

Since the success at Inchon, Truman's White House aides had been pressing him to travel to the Pacific for a face-to-face meeting with MacArthur, whom Truman had never met. The initial motivation for this idea had been "political." The aides thought it would be "good election-year stuff" to project a concerned Truman in a Pacific setting, conferring with his principal field commander. It would give the impression that Truman was doing all he could to support MacArthur.[51]

Neither Truman nor any of his senior cabinet members liked the idea. When he heard about it, Acheson was quick to condemn the scheme as "distasteful." He wanted no part of it and saw no good coming from it. Nor did George Marshall. Some senior officials even believed the meeting could be dangerous. Peking might interpret it as a conference called to plan an invasion of Red China.[52]

After the success of Inchon the White House aides prevailed, and Truman agreed to the meeting. Perhaps remembering Roosevelt's election-year meeting with MacArthur at Pearl Harbor in 1944, Truman suggested that it take place there, on about October 15. George Marshall, however, did not believe that

MacArthur should be so far removed from Korea on the eve of the American attack on Pyongyang and the amphibious landing at Wonsan. He proposed instead that the meeting take place at Wake Island. Truman agreed, and so it was arranged.

The two parties converged on Wake Island on October 15. Truman's group included Omar Bradley, representing the JCS; Frank Pace, standing in for Marshall; Dean Rusk and Philip Jessup, representing the State Department; Averell Harriman and other White House aides; and Arthur Radford, who joined the entourage in Hawaii. MacArthur's group included Ambassador John Muccio and several trusted aides. To ensure that the media focus would be on Truman, reporters and photographers from Washington were permitted at Wake; those from Tokyo, barred.[53]

Then, and later, journalists and some historians would inflate the "historic" importance of the Wake Island meeting. However, nothing "historic" occurred, other than the first meeting of Truman and MacArthur. The hurried and brief "discussions" and "exchanges of views" during the short official session were almost farcical, merely oral reviews of positions previously spelled out in far greater detail in cables or letters.

President Truman and MacArthur first met privately in a Quonset hut. There MacArthur apologized for the embarrassment his letter to the VFW on Formosa had caused and disclaimed any political ambitions. In further discussions of the Formosa problem, Truman later said, they reached "complete agreement," meaning apparently that MacArthur had unequivocally agreed to support Truman's policy. The president then asked the general's opinion about the likelihood of Chinese intervention in Korea. MacArthur assured Truman that "the victory was won in Korea" and that there was "little possibility of the Chinese coming in." Even if they did, MacArthur continued, he would defeat them, primarily with overwhelming air power. They went on to discuss a Japanese peace treaty, NATO, economic problems in the Philippines, and other matters.[54]

The official or formal meeting convened at 7:30 A.M. and lasted for about an hour and a half. Most of the discussion centered on Korean rehabilitation, economic and unification problems. However, during the course of the meeting MacArthur, either in response to questions or voluntarily, touched on several strictly military matters. He told Truman he had taken Wonsan and would land X Corps there. He added that X Corps "will take Pyongyang in one week." In addition, he was driving the 1st Cav Division "up the line to Pyongyang" and was thinking of making up an armored column to "take Pyongyang directly." He believed formal NKPA resistance in North Korea would "end by Thanksgiving." He twice stated that it was his "hope" to be able to withdraw Eighth Army to Japan by Christmas. Thereafter he would leave X Corps, recomposed of the 2d and 3d divisions, plus "U.N. detachments" from other nations, on occupation duty until Korea-wide elections were held, after which the security of Korea could be maintained by a ten-division ROK Army. The ROKs would also be "a tremendous deterrent to the Chinese Communists moving south," who were a "threat that cannot be laughed off." In response to a question from Bradley, who asked if one of the American divisions could soon be released for duty in Europe, MacArthur replied yes. He recommended the 2d Division, which he would "make available in January."

He declared that a suggestion by Prime Minister Jawaharlal Nehru of India to station Indian and Pakistani troops along the Chinese and Soviet borders as a "buffer" was "indefensible from a military point of view." He went on to say: "I am going to put South Korean troops up there. They will be the buffer. The other troops will be pulled back south of a line twenty miles north of Pyongyang to Hamhung. I want to take all non-Korean troops out of Korea as soon as possible."[55]

Although Truman had asked MacArthur during their private talk about the possibility of Chinese intervention in Korea, the president evidently felt he should bring it up again for the official record. He therefore posed the question "What are the chances for Chinese or Soviet intervention?"

MacArthur replied in two parts. As for the chances of Chinese intervention, he said:

Very little. Had they interfered in the first or second months it would have been decisive. We are no longer fearful of their intervention. We no longer stand hat in hand. The Chinese have 300,000 men in Manchuria. Of these probably not more than 100/125,000 are distributed along the Yalu River. Only 50,000 or 60,000 could be gotten across the Yalu River. They have no air force. Now that we have bases for our Air Force in Korea, if the Chinese tried to get down to Pyongyang, there would be the greatest slaughter.[56]

In the second part of his answer MacArthur dealt with the possibility of Soviet intervention:

With the Russians it is a little different. They have an Air Force in Siberia and a fairly good one. . . . They can put 1,000 planes in the air with some 200 to 300 more from the Fifth and Seventh Soviet Fleets. They are probably no match for our Air Force. The Russians have no ground troops available for North Korea. They would have difficulty in putting troops into the field. It would take six weeks to get a division across and six weeks brings the winter. The only other combination would be Russian air support of Chinese ground troops. Russian air is deployed in a semi-circle through Mukden and Harbin, but the coordination between the Russian air and the Chinese ground would be so flimsy that I believe Russian air would bomb the Chinese as often as they would bomb us. Ground support is a very difficult thing to do. I believe it just wouldn't work with Chinese Communist ground and Russian air.[57]

In the light of later events MacArthur's remarks about Chinese intervention would be used by Truman and his supporters to flail MacArthur. However, the views he expressed were nothing new or startling. They coincided precisely with the majority view in Washington as set forth in the most recent CIA assessment. MacArthur would quite rightly defend himself by asserting that it was the prime responsibility of Washington, not the field commander, to determine if Peking or Moscow would intervene in Korea.

As MacArthur's biographer D. Clayton James has recently observed, the most "astonishing fact" about the exchange on this crucial matter was that it went no further. "One question by Truman," James wrote, "a single response by MacArthur, and absolutely no follow-up questions, challenges, or further mention."[58]

The Wake Island conference terminated in an air of cordiality. A smiling Truman awarded MacArthur his fifth Distinguished Service Medal and gave him a box of candy. Then, and by letter, both men exchanged friendly comments about how useful the meeting had been. But it was all a façade. Privately Truman continued to vent his long-held contempt for MacArthur, referring to him in a personal letter written soon after the meeting as the "Right Hand Man of God." MacArthur wrote later (and paranoically) that the meeting convinced him that "a curious and sinister change" had overtaken Washington, that Truman's bold decision to "meet and defeat communism in Asia" was apparently being "chipped away" by the "constant pounding whispers of timidity and cynicism" from "selfish politicians of the United Nations."[59]

\* \* \*

As Truman and MacArthur flew back to their respective seats of power that day, October 15, major elements of Lin Piao's Fourth Field Army were crossing the Yalu River into North Korea. The Chinese moved mostly by night, on foot, and were not detected. In total, six armies of the CCF Thirteenth Army Group, comprising eighteen infantry divisions—about 180,000 men or more—were to come into North Korea during the next two weeks. In addition, Peking ordered the Ninth Army Group of the Third Field Army, then based in Shantung Province, to entrain through Manchuria for deployment in North Korea. This would add another three armies composed of twelve infantry divisions—about 120,000 men—to the CCF already committed to North Korea. In all, nine CCF armies composed of thirty divisions (about 300,000 men) were to deploy to North Korea.[60]

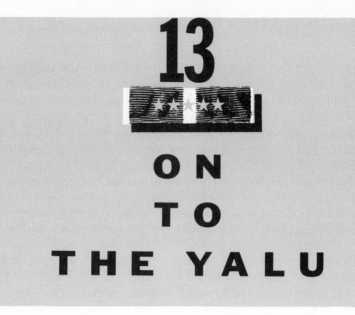

# 13

# ON
# TO
# THE YALU

I

When MacArthur returned to Tokyo from Wake Island, he had no inkling of the CCF armies gathering in North Korea. Eighth Army and X Corps operations were proceeding more or less according to his orders, but the situation in North Korea was not unfolding in the way he had envisioned.

Notwithstanding its shoestring supply system, Shrimp Milburn's I Corps had cracked through NKPA defenses in the Seoul–Pyongyang corridor and was ideally poised for an immediate all-out assault on Pyongyang. Intelligence sources had reported that the Communist government and NKPA troops were abandoning the capital and fleeing northward, taking American and ROK POWs. The ROK Capital Division, continuing the phenomenal ROK I Corps drive up the east coast road, had advanced another fifty air miles, to the outskirts of Hamhung. Intelligence sources reported that the NKPA were abandoning Hamhung and its fine seaport, Hungnam. Ned Almond's X Corps had boarded ships at Inchon and Pusan, but owing to the thousands of mines discovered at Wonsan, it was not likely that it could land there by D day, October 20.

It was now clear that MacArthur had made a grave miscalculation by insisting on the X Corps landing at Wonsan. Barring an unfortunate disaster, the primary X Corps mission—the capture of Pyongyang—was almost certain to be carried out by Milburn's I Corps before X Corps could land. Its secondary mission—throwing a line across the peninsula—would be too late to trap any large numbers of fleeing NKPA troops. Its tertiary mission—liberating the Wonsan–Hamhung sector of North Korea—had already been achieved by the ROK I Corps.

350

As a result of this miscalculation, MacArthur was botching his primary mission: complete destruction of the NKPA. Half the American divisions immediately available for hot pursuit (1st Marine, 7th Army divisions) at this critical time were sealed aboard ships with no place to land. The other half (1st Cav; 24th) was not strong enough or sufficiently supplied to overtake and encircle the fleeing NKPA forces. At best, the Americans could be counted upon only to occupy territory abandoned by the NKPA.

These factors, and others, led MacArthur to revise drastically his military strategy. As he now viewed the situation, contrary to Washington's expressed desires, it would be necessary for American forces to overrun the whole of North Korea—right up to the Chinese and Russian borders—in order to ensure complete destruction of the NKPA. As he saw it, this vital task could not be left up to the ROKs, as Washington preferred; too many NKPA troops had escaped. Despite their recent electrifying achievements, the ROKs were not strong enough or sufficiently reliable to do the job.

Perhaps fearing that Washington would veto his plans, MacArthur did not forthrightly convey his new views to the JCS. Rather, he again appeared to engage in a deliberate deception, apparently designed to conceal or at least to reduce the impact of his decision. At a glance the first step in this new strategy, promulgated on October 17, appeared to be well within the stipulation of his directive:

• Shrimp Milburn's I Corps would capture Pyongyang and continue hot pursuit north toward the Chongchon River at Sinanju.
• The 187th Airborne RCT would jump about twenty-five miles north of Pyongyang, near Sukchon–Sunchon, to intercept fleeing Communist government officials and NKPA troops and to rescue American and ROK POWs.
• Most of Dutch Keiser's 2d Division, which had moved north to Suwon, would follow I Corps to the Pyongyang area for occupation and policing.
• Ned Almond's X Corps would proceed to Wonsan, as originally planned. It would absorb the ROK I Corps (3d and Capital divisions), becoming, in effect, a separate army of two corps reporting directly to MacArthur. If Walker had taken Pyongyang by the time X Corps landed at Wonsan, then X Corps would advance not west but north.

These plans, however, contained a subsection which clearly foreshadowed MacArthur's intent to stretch the spirit of his directive and implement his new strategy. Without clearing it with Washington, he moved the line beyond which American troops were not to go northward about thirty miles. The new line would be Sonchon–Pyongwon–Songjin, about 40 miles south of the Manchurian border for most of its length and about 100 miles south of the Soviet border.[1]

By shifting this line, MacArthur had set the stage for deployment of

American troops much deeper into North Korea. He appeared to go a step farther two days later, on October 19. He directed that "all concerned" make a "maximum effort" to seize the new line rapidly and be "prepared for continued rapid advance to the border of North Korea."[2]

In a strict legal sense, these new orders were not in violation of MacArthur's general directive. However, MacArthur was under orders to submit all plans for the invasion of North Korea to Washington "for approval." He had earlier submitted the line Chongju–Yongwon–Hamhung, which the JCS had approved. By moving the line thirty miles north without JCS clearance, he had substantially stretched his orders.

Worse, MacArthur had issued these orders in the face of further warlike statements from Peking. While it is true that neither he nor Washington believed these statements, military prudence and common sense dictated that in view of the CCF military capabilities in Manchuria, all moves toward the Red Chinese border be conducted with utmost caution and due regard for a possible counterattack. By substantially advancing the American zone of operations closer to the border and splitting his American forces ever wider, MacArthur was pressing his legendary luck to foolish limits.

## II

Unaware of the extent of the minefield problem at Wonsan, Johnnie Walker still believed that X Corps might land there in time to beat Eighth Army to Pyongyang. Since Walker was still dead set to win this "race" and make MacArthur and Almond look like fools, he continued to demand superhuman efforts from Shrimp Milburn's weak and inadequately supplied I Corps. He went so far as to tell his old friend Hap Gay that if the 1st Cav did not capture Pyongyang by October 21, he would relieve Gay of command.[3]

Gay well appreciated the psychological gain to be had from the capture of Pyongyang. However, he believed that MacArthur and Walker were placing too much emphasis on that objective at the expense of destroying the NKPA. He expressed this view to Walker, but it seemed to make no impression.[4]

To make doubly sure Eighth Army would be first in Pyongyang, Walker and Shrimp Milburn conceived an elaborate envelopment employing six-plus infantry divisions. Gay's 1st Cav (with the British Commonwealth Brigade attached) and Church's 24th divisions would advance due north from Sariwon, on the Seoul–Pyongyang highway. The first of the American divisions to reach Sariwon would have the honor of leading the onward attack to Pyongyang. The ROK 1st Division would attack northwest from Mui. Finally, ROK II Corps (6th, 7th, 8th divisions), advancing on the right of I Corps, would turn left and attack west.[5]

Hap Gay's point was well taken. This massive concentration of force was likely to gain Pyongyang at the earliest possible date, but it did not adequately provide American forces for cutting off and trapping the fleeing NKPA. That formidable task was left solely to the airborne RCT, which was to jump north of Pyongyang in the Sukchon–Sunchon area. At best this was an "iffy" plan. The airborne RCT was green. It had never made a "combat jump." Its parachuted firepower was not great.[6]

Had there been closer personal and professional communications between Walker and Almond (or had X Corps been integrated into Eighth Army), Walker would have been fully aware of the formidable mine problem at Wonsan. He would therefore have known that there was small likelihood that Almond could land there and beat him to Pyongyang. Knowing that, he may have given less weight to capturing Pyongyang and greater weight to cutting off the NKPA north of Pyongyang. A wide, encircling American envelopment, east and north of Pyongyang culminating in the Sukchon–Sunchon area, where the airborne RCT was to jump, would have been one possible solution. The aircraft required to lift the paratroopers could have been employed to bring supplies forward for Eighth Army.

\* \* \*

Owing principally to the relentless pressure from Johnnie Walker, the attack of Milburn's I Corps toward Pyongyang, which began on October 16, was ill conceived and ill executed. Since every unit in the corps wanted to be first into Pyongyang, the competition was fierce. There was poor communications between units. Nobody had a clear picture of the campaign.[7]

For Hap Gay's 1st Cav Division, the first task was to take Sariwon before John Church's 24th Division could get there, thus earning the right to lead the onward attack of I Corps to Pyongyang. In this competition Gay held the advantage. Owing to the earlier fine performance of Billy Harris's 7th Cav, the 1st Cav was ideally positioned to continue up the main Seoul–Pyongyang highway to Sariwon.

Hap Gay's plan was as follows. Billy Harris's 7th Cav would lead the division to Sohung. Basil Coad's Commonwealth Brigade would pass through Harris's 7th Cav at Sohung for a direct attack on Sariwon. The 7th Cav and Crombez's 5th Cav would go north and west from Sohung over secondary roads, to cut the main highway north of Sariwon and trap NKPA troops. Hal Edson's 8th Cav would remain in division reserve.

The 7th Cav attack on Sohung, mounted hastily, did not go according to plan. James Lynch's 3/7 led the attack and reached Sohung by noon. However, Callaway's 2/7 somehow failed to get the word, or misinterpreted orders, and did not jump off on time to "leapfrog" the 3/7. Hap Gay was furious, blaming Harris. Pete Clainos's 1/7 bypassed the 2/7 and, upon reaching Sohung, swung north, as planned, following secondary roads and "cow paths." Because of the late start of the 2/7, Harris decided to hold the 3/7 and 2/7 at Sohung for the night, in keeping with a new 1st Cav Division policy, which forbade night movements. Accordingly, Harris established a tight perimeter at Sohung and "buttoned up" to await daylight.[8]

Behind the 7th Cav the main highway clogged in an epic traffic jam. Coad's Commonwealth Brigade, Crombez's 5th Cav, and even Ned Moore's 19th Infantry (attempting to use the best road) were intermingled, bumper to bumper, along with artillery, engineer, and other units. Owing to the 7th Cav roadblock at Sohung, no one could move forward. Learning of this, Hap Gay again became furious with Harris, this time for adhering to the letter of division policy to stop at night. Gay believed that the 1st Cav had achieved "a complete breakthrough" and that Harris should have kept going. He sent his ADC, Frank Allen, forward to order Harris to get moving, but infuriatingly, not even Allen could get past the stout 7th Cav perimeter guards.[9]

Marcel Crombez, caught in the traffic jam, was fit to be tied. Ever since leaving the Pusan Perimeter, his 5th Cav had played second fiddle to the 7th Cav. Now the 7th Cav was again in a commanding position and would lead the division into Pyongyang. Moreover, it appeared that it was deliberately blocking the highway to ensure that no other 1st Cav (or 24th Division) units could get around it and dash into Pyongyang to claim all the glory.[10]

Perhaps believing that he might, after all, "pass" the 7th Cav, Crombez made the decision to keep going through the night. He left the main highway (clogged by the Commonwealth Brigade) and took a secondary road which, in a roundabout way, led into Sohung from the south. Since his intent was to "pass" the 7th Cav and dash on to Pyongyang, Crombez did not inform Harris that he was coming.

The upshot was a near disaster. At about 3:00 A.M. on October 17 the lead elements of Morgan Heasley's 1/5, approaching Sohung from the south, rumbled into the 7th Cav perimeter. Unaware that the 5th Cav was coming at night (in violation of new division policy) or from the south (rather than from the east on the main highway), Harris's men thought it must be the NKPA and opened fire, per orders to "shoot first and ask questions later." Believing the 7th Cav to be NKPA, the 5th Cav returned the fire. In this "pitched battle" seven men of the 5th Cav were wounded before the error was discovered and a cease-fire could be imposed.[11]

When Hap Gay learned of this unfortunate collision, he again blamed Harris. Without taking the time to investigate all the factors involved, he immediately relieved Harris of command. Harris was replaced that day, October 17, by West Pointer (1932) James K. Woolnough, thirty-nine, another of the four well-qualified "spare" regimental commanders Joe Collins had sent out to Walker. Burning with anger, Harris went back to Seoul.[12]

Later, when all the facts in the incident had been brought to light, completely exonerating Harris, Gay denied that he had relieved Harris. He passed it off as merely "temporary." Harris was "worn out" and "over-anxious," Gay wrote, and needed a "few days" of R and R. However, this explanation did not square with 7th Cav regimental records or the recollections of Harris and Woolnough, and it defied plain common sense. Harris may have been tired and anxious, but it was no time to send him on R and R.

When Woolnough reported to the 7th Cav wearing an eyepatch, he reminded some staffers of a Hollywood pirate. Knowing that their revered former commander, Billy Harris, had been unfairly relieved, the staffers received Woolnough coldly. Upon investigation of the incident that had led to Harris's relief, Woolnough himself concluded that Hap Gay had "made a big mistake," and he felt somewhat awkward in his new command.[13]

Meanwhile, that morning, October 17, after daylight Coad's Commonwealth Brigade, outfitted with American tanks and vehicles, passed through Sohung and attacked west toward Sariwon. Up to that point the performance of the brigade, through no fault of its own, had been, in the American view, spotty. But the attack on Sariwon, led by the Argyll battalion, commanded by Leslie Nielson, was aggressive and almost flawless. With the 1st Cav ADC, Frank Allen, present and exhorting, the brigade overran Sariwon that same day, thereby ensuring the 1st Cav's right to lead I Corps into Pyongyang. Capping this triumph, the newly arrived, well-trained, aggressive Australian battalion, commanded by World War II veteran Charles H. Green, established a roadblock five miles north of town and bagged 2,000 fleeing, confused NKPA troops.[14]

The same day Woolnough's 7th Cav moved out of Sohung to interdict the main highway north of Sariwon. Led by Pete Clainos's 1/7, with Callaway's 2/7 on its heels, the regiment made good time against slight to no opposition. Late in the day, as Clainos approached the highway, he received a modification in his orders. One battalion was to go south to Sariwon to link with the Commonwealth Brigade; another north, to Hwangju. Clainos elected to take the 1/7 south; Callaway's 2/7 was to go to Hwangju.

Soon after he had turned south, Clainos came upon the advance elements of a strong NKPA "cavalry force" fleeing north. It consisted of about 2,500 NKPA soldiers, 37 of them horse-mounted. On instructions from Clainos, an interpreter went forward, established contact with the NKPA, and told them that the 1/7 was a "Russian outfit," come to defend Pyongyang. Thus deceived, the NKPA marched forward to be captured and disarmed by the 1/7.[15]

This proved to be one of the greatest single bags of NKPA prisoners in the war. Clainos was justly praised, but what he prized most were the thirty-seven horses. He used them first for shepherding the NKPA into Sariwon. Then he divided up the leather saddles for souvenirs, keeping one for himself.

He strapped his saddle to the hood of his jeep, thereby establishing a colorful custom that evoked the earlier illustrious history of the 7th Cavalry Regiment.[16]

These operations of the 1st Cav, in effect, hemmed in John Church's 24th Division south of the main highway. Having "lost the race" to Sariwon, its three regiments—Johnny Throckmorton's 5th; Ned Moore's 19th; Dick Stephens's 21st—fanned out over secondary roads, mopping up and policing and preparing to follow the 1st Cav into Pyongyang. Inasmuch as the NKPA troops in this sector had fled north, the striking power of the 24th Division was largely wasted. Had Walker given more weight to cutting off the NKPA, the 24th Division could have been utilized to make a flanking movement north of Pyongyang.[17]

* * *

Having intersected the main highway north of Sariwon near Hwangju, Woolnough's 7th Cav was still in the best position to lead the 1st Cav Division into Pyongyang. On the morning of October 18 Lynch's 3/7, which had been on the move all the previous night and was fatigued, led the attack. Supported by twenty tanks, the 3/7 advanced rapidly to Hukkyo, a mere ten miles south of the capital.[18]

For a while it seemed likely that the 7th Cav would crack right into Pyongyang that very day. Shrimp Milburn went forward to have a look and perhaps to join the lead column. But by then Lynch had been checked at Hukkyo by a strong NKPA roadblock. The 1/7 and 2/7 (also tired) were moving up, but Woolnough, believing Lynch would momentarily break through, had not yet committed them to battle. Watching from the sidelines, Shrimp Milburn became increasingly impatient.[19]

Later that day Hap Gay came forward to the block. By that time the 7th Cav's S-3, James Webel, believed Lynch was on the verge of breaking through. But Gay, angry that Lynch had been stopped all this time, ordered that the 1/7 and 2/7 be immediately committed on a deep, wide envelopment, to the left and right of the NKPA position. Milburn strolled over and said sarcastically: "I thought it was time someone took some action around here."[20]

This comment Gay found "astounding." Milburn had been there most of the day. Why hadn't he earlier ordered Woolnough to commit the other battalions? Reflecting on this, Gay, as he later wrote, became "so damn mad" he had to walk away from Milburn. Had Milburn done what was necessary in his absence, Gay reflected, "Pyongyang could have been taken on the 18th."[21]

By now Hap Gay was thoroughly exasperated with the 7th Cav. He therefore made the drastic decision (as the 7th Cav viewed it) to punish the regiment. He ordered Marcel Crombez to bring his 5th Cav forward to lead the division into Pyongyang. On second thought, Gay decided that the 5th Cav ought to share the honor. Accordingly, he ordered that elements of the Commonwealth Brigade and 7th Cav be attached to the 5th. Coad volunteered the Australian battalion; Woolnough provided Lynch's 3/7, which, by then, had finally broken through at Hukkyo, clearing a path for the 5th Cav. The 7th Cav historian wrote bitterly that "after leading the drive all the way from Seoul," the rest of the 7th Cav "remained in place and watched other elements of the 1st Cav Division drive into Pyongyang."[22]

\* \* \*

On the morning of October 19 the 5th Cav passed through the 7th Cav sector for the climactic drive on Pyongyang. Crombez was in a hurry: Word had been received that the ROK 1st Division, approaching the city from the southeast (on the 1st Cav's right flank), had broken through NKPA defenses. It would be humiliating if the ROKs got to Pyongyang first.

John Clifford's 2/5 Cav led the attack. It soon ran into yet another NKPA block, which included three tanks. After one of Clifford's 3.5-inch bazooka teams had courageously knocked out all three tanks, the battalion pushed on rapidly. At about 11:00 A.M. Clifford reached the southern outskirts of Pyongyang.[23]

There the 5th Cav confronted a formidable obstacle: the 500-yard-wide Taedong River. In prewar days the river was spanned by three bridges: two railroad and one vehicular. Approaching the riverbank, Clifford's men found both railroad bridges partially destroyed, the vehicular bridge intact. However, before Clifford could seize the vehicular bridge, the NKPA blew up its center span. Until assault boats could be brought forward, the 1st Cav Division could not cross into Pyongyang.[24]

Meanwhile, the same day, October 19, elements of the ROK 1st and 7th divisions were closing on Pyongyang. The ROK 1st Division had been helped along considerably by the Patton tanks of John Growdon's 6th Tank Battalion, temporarily detached from the 24th Division and attached to the ROKs. Finding fords or other means of crossing, lead elements of both ROK divisions entered the capital from the east and northeast. By nightfall the ROK 1st Division had captured the center of the city; the ROK 7th Division held Kim Il Sung University in the northern outskirts. Thus, with the help of Growdon's tanks, the ROKs "won" the race to Pyongyang after all.[25]

The 5th Cav spent a miserable, frustrating, cold night waiting for the assault boats. When they finally arrived the following morning, October 20, Treacy's 3/5 Cav, staging from an "island" in the middle of the river, led the assault to the north bank and into the city proper. By that time all but a few diehard NKPA troops had fled and resistance was light or nonexistent.[26]

For the men of the 5th Cav the capture of Pyongyang proved anticlimactic, even depressing. There was no real battle, as there had been in Seoul, and no victory parade. Most of the Communists—Russian and North Korean— had fled. The Russian Embassy was stripped bare, as were many of the factories. Bombed repeatedly by FEAF, Pyongyang was a rubble-strewn mess. The sections that had not been bombed were "dirty" and "shabby," reminding one GI of "Chicago's Skid Row district." They could find no American POWs. The single prize was a warehouse chock-full of canned food and whiskey, which the hungry GIs greedily devoured.[27]

The ROKs in Pyongyang were not gentle conquerors. One GI would never forget a scene he saw in a Pyongyang schoolyard:

Sitting on the ground were well over 1,000 North Korean POWs. They sat in rows of about fifty with their hands clasped on their heads. In front of this mob, South Korean officers sat at field tables. It looked like a kangaroo court was in session. ROK officers and NCOs walked between rows of prisoners. Occasionally, one of them would beat or kick a POW. To one side several North Koreans hung like rag dolls from stout posts driven into the ground. These men had been executed and left to hang in the sun.[28]

In the aftermath of the capture of Pyongyang Hap Gay made two important executive changes. First, he restored Billy Harris to command of the 7th Cav and sent the outfit to capture Pyongyang's seaport, Chinnampo. Having commanded the 7th Cav for four days, Woolnough was "happy" to see Harris restored to his job and returned to the Pentagon (and, ultimately, to a distinguished career and four-star rank). Secondly, as the result of his past occupation experience in South Korea, Marcel Crombez was temporarily relieved of command of the 5th Cav and named "mayor" of Pyongyang. This appointment enabled Gay to promote the 3/8 commander, Johnny Johnson (who was still unhappy serving under his junior, Hal Edson), to temporary commander of the 5th Cav. Crombez was not at all pleased with this arrangement, but Gay assured him it was temporary. By the time the division returned to Japan for its victory parade in Tokyo about a month later, Crombez would be restored to command of the 5th Cav.[29]

# III

MacArthur's original scheme for utilizing the airborne RCT called for a jump at Sukchon–Sunchon on October 21. But when the ROK 1st and 7th divisions entered Pyongyang on October 19 and found that the Kim Il Sung government and most of the NKPA had fled, he advanced the time of the jump to dawn, October 20.[30]

These orders were warmly received at the 187th Airborne CP. The outfit had arrived in the Far East a month earlier, too late for its original mission at Inchon. Ever since then it had been assigned to demeaning rear-area mopping-up and policing tasks around its base at Kimpo Airfield.

But the orders were not warmly received at Eighth Army. Johnnie Walker was not an airborne enthusiast. He resented the fact that MacArthur had retained the 187th under his direct control (as theater reserve) and had more or less wasted it for a full month. He could have made good use of this highly motivated infantry in the capture of Pyongyang. Now it appeared that the proposed Sukchon–Sunchon jump might be too late. Moreover, he believed that the 100-odd planes required to mount the airborne operation could be far better utilized in the emergency supply lift for Eighth Army.

Walker did not, however, make these views known to MacArthur. Nor did anyone else challenge MacArthur on the validity of the airborne operation. The paratroopers were at hand. Conceivably the operation might even work as MacArthur had designed it, resulting in the capture of a large segment of the Kim government and the rescue of hundreds of American and ROK POWs.

\* \* \*

The 187th had begun its brief history in World War II as a glider regiment of the 11th Airborne Division, which had been assigned to MacArthur's Southwest Pacific Theater. In the postwar years it was converted to a parachute outfit. Mated with the 674th FAB to form an airborne RCT, it had arrived in the Far East numbering about 4,000 men.[31]

Many able combat-experienced paratroopers had sought command of the 187th. The job finally went to an "older outsider," who had only recently (May 1950) joined the airborne forces and who had been a staff officer in World War II. He was West Pointer (1926) Frank S. Bowen, Jr., forty-five, son of a West Pointer who had retired as a colonel. Bowen's political strength derived from Robert Eichelberger, whom he had faithfully served from October 1940 to June 1947, first as aide, finally as G-3 of Eichelberger's Eighth Army, a temporary one-star job. As such Bowen had won a DSC and three Silver Star Medals for heroism—and had got to know MacArthur well. The appointment of this "outsider" to command the 187th was widely resented in the airborne establishment.[32]

The 187th was predominantly a "West Point" outfit. In addition to Bowen, the exec and the three battalion commanders were West Pointers. All three battalion commanders had commanded battalions in combat in World War II, two of them in the 11th Airborne itself. All were qualified by experience and ability to command the regiment; one battalion commander had, in fact, briefly commanded the outfit before the Korean War. Many of the company and platoon commanders were also West Pointers.[33]

The 187th staged for the jump at Kimpo Airfield along with the 100-odd troop carrier aircraft. So great was the congestion of aircraft that all other activities at Kimpo, including Eighth Army's emergency air supply lift, had to be diverted elsewhere or temporarily shut down. As a result, the airborne operation, like the outloading of the Marines at Inchon, put a big crimp in the flow of supplies to Eighth Army.[34]

In the early morning of October 20 the men of the 187th rose to eat and board aircraft. However, the prospects of a takeoff were not good; a heavy rain was falling both at Kimpo and in the Sukchon–Sunchon area. Bowen had to postpone the takeoff hour after agonizing hour. Finally, in late morning, the skies began to clear. At noon FEAF declared the weather suitable for airborne operations. One by one the heavily laden planes rose to circle overhead and form into tight V formations.[35]

The air armada, consisting of seventy-one new C-119 "Flying Boxcars" and forty old C-47 "Skytrains," flew east, then north over the Yellow Sea, escorted by flocks of FEAF fighters. Other FEAF fighters and fighter-bombers went ahead to clear the drop zone (DZ) of enemy flak guns and other threats. Before turning inland toward the DZs, the armada was joined by MacArthur's private aircraft. He had flown over from Tokyo to watch the jump, after which he was to land at Pyongyang to salute his victorious ground forces. His plane was jammed with staff and favored Tokyo reporters, who would record his presence at this dramatic moment in the Korean War.[36]

The airborne plan was as follows. Bowen, his command group, the 1st and 3d battalions, plus artillery and other units (in all, about 1,500 men), would drop on DZs adjacent to Sukchon. This force would take Sukchon and block the two highways and railway leading north from Pyongyang. The Commonwealth Brigade (attached to John Church's 24th Division) would attack north out of Pyongyang to link with the 187th on the second day, October 21. The 2/187, plus artillery and other units (about 1,300 men), would drop at Sunchon to block another highway and railway leading north from Pyongyang. An armored task force of Bill Rodgers's 70th Tank Battalion would attack north from Pyongyang and link with the 2/187 at Sunchon on the second day.[37]

This jump, led by Bowen himself, began at about 2:00 P.M. and continued for about twenty minutes. Fortunately NKPA resistance was slight. Only 1 paratrooper of the 2,800 was killed in the descent. Forty-five others, including the 2/187 exec, whose chute fouled, were injured in jump accidents. Three of the 674th FAB's twelve 105-mm howitzers (parachuted on wooden pallets) were lost, but tons of ammo, 90-mm antitank guns, 75-mm recoilless rifles, jeeps, three-quarter-ton trucks, trailers, etc. came to earth by parachute, mostly intact. Compared with most World War II airborne operations, the jump was outstanding—indisputably the best combat jump the Army had ever staged.[38]

The regiment formed up in its two separate areas and began ground operations within one hour. In Bowen's sector the 1st Battalion, commanded by West Pointer (1937) Arthur H. ("Harry") Wilson, thirty-eight, and the 3d Battalion, commanded by West Pointer (1940) Delbert E. Munson, thirty-two, took Sukchon and threw up road and railway blocks at preselected sites north of the town. At Sunchon the 2d Battalion, commanded by West Pointer (1939) William J. Boyle, thirty-three, secured its DZ and established blocks per plan.[39]

In launching his attack on Sunchon, Boyle unexpectedly met what he believed to be a powerful NKPA force. For about thirty minutes there was a furious firefight. Then it was discovered that the force holding Sunchon was not NKPA but, rather, ROK. The ROK 6th Division, bypassing Pyongyang to the east and making dramatic speed and meeting little or no resistance, had overrun Sunchon several hours before the jump. Neither Bowen nor Boyle had been told to expect the arrival of the ROK 6th Division in Sunchon that day. Fortunately, casualties resulting from this exchange of friendly fire were slight.[40]

The presence of the ROK 6th Division so far north of Pyongyang was an embarrassment to the paratroopers. It tended to rob the airborne operation of its dangerous aspect. Some would suggest that Walker had deliberately urged the ROKs onward to make the airborne operation look a little silly and undercut MacArthur. More likely it was simply happenstance. Prodded by Syngman Rhee, the ROK 6th Division was racing hell-bent for the North Korean border.

Later that afternoon, when MacArthur landed at Pyongyang, he held a press conference. He, in effect, portrayed the parachute jump as a brilliant tactical stroke, which would achieve the final task of complete destruction of the NKPA. He estimated that about 30,000 of the NKPA had been trapped between the 187th and the UN forces advancing north from Pyongyang. These NKPA troops would soon be killed or captured. He did not mention the presence of the ROK 6th Division at Sunchon.[41]

This boast, soon published worldwide, was wildly off the mark. By that afternoon all but one NKPA regiment, serving as a rear guard, had retreated well north of the Sukchon–Sunchon line, taking all the American and ROK POWs. So had all the principals in Kim Il Sung's government. Notwithstanding the courage and professionalism of the paratroopers, the main objective of the airborne operation could not be achieved. It was too little, too late. The territory it occupied could easily have been taken by the ROK 6th Division at far less effort and without crimping the Eighth Army emergency supply lift.

The paratroopers did, however, have one opportunity to show their stuff. On the second day on the ground, October 21, Bowen sent Delbert Munson's 3/187 south from Sukchon to meet the advancing Commonwealth Brigade. Just north of Yongyu Munson ran into the NKPA 239th Regiment, which was serving as rear guard. Caught between the oncoming British and the paratroopers, the NKPA (some 2,500 men) fought viciously on the night of October 21–22, attempting to break out to the north. During these attacks the paratroopers held their ground magnificently, even though Munson was severely wounded and at times the situation was chaotic. In so doing, the paratroopers virtually annihilated the NKPA regiment, killing about 800 and capturing about 680.[42]*

During this action the Commonwealth Brigade was bivouacked for the night south of Yongyu. On the following morning, October 22, it resumed the northward drive, attacking into the rear of what was left of the NKPA 239th Regiment, firmly blocked by the paratroopers. Led by Charles Green's Australian battalion and supported by American tanks, the brigade overran the surviving NKPA. In wild, brutal, hand-to-hand fighting the Australians killed 270 and captured 200 enemy before linking up with the 3/187.[43]

Meanwhile, to the east, early on the morning of October 21, Bill Rodgers's armored task force rolled into Boyle's 2/187 sector at Sunchon. By the time it got there Boyle and members of the ROK 6th Division had heard rumors that NKPA troops had massacred many American POWs close by. Learning of this, 1st Cav ADC Frank Allen, who had come forward in his jeep, led a search mission.

The rumors, unfortunately, proved to be true. The American POWs had been northbound on a NKPA train when the paratroopers jumped. When the train pulled into a tunnel to hide, the NKPA had murdered 66 POWs. Allen found their bodies as well as the bodies of 7 other American POWs who had apparently died of disease or starvation. He also found 23 American POWs who had survived the massacre, many of them badly wounded, two mortally. These 96 were all that could be found of the estimated 2,500 American POWs in NKPA custody.[44]

In the wake of this much publicized but largely ineffective combat jump, Bowen, who won a DSC, was promoted (as expected) to brigadier general but remained in overall command of the regimental combat team. The exec, West Pointer (1934) George H. Gerhart, thirty-eight, was named commander only of the regiment. Harry Wilson retained command of the 1/187. William Boyle, who had won a DSC during the Battle of the Bulge with the 517th Parachute Regiment but who clashed with Bowen, was transferred out, replaced by West Pointer (1937) John P. Connor, thirty-seven. Later Munson (awarded a Silver Star) recovered from his wounds and returned to command the 3/187.[45]†

The well-led airborne combat team would have made a fine addition to

---

*For this heroic action the battalion received a Presidential Unit Citation.
†Gerhart had fought in the ETO with the 89th Division. Wilson and Connor had commanded battalions in the 11th Airborne Division in combat in the Pacific; Munson had commanded a battalion of the 35th Infantry in combat in the Pacific.

Walker's scanty ground forces. However, the policy was to reserve highly trained and elite forces for "special missions." Accordingly, the 187th was soon withdrawn from the forward area and returned to theater reserve, serving mostly as glorified policemen in Pyongyang and elsewhere, always, however, on instant call.

*   *   *

It was now clear from various intelligence sources that the NKPA had withdrawn well to the north of the Chongchon River at Sinanju. Without pause Johnnie Walker's Eighth Army continued the pursuit beyond Bowen's sector. The Commonwealth Brigade, spearheading John Church's 24th Division, passed through the 187th's sector at Sukchon and drove north on the main highway to the Chongchon River at Sinanju, where it arrived on October 23. On the 24th's right flank the ROK 1st, 6th, and 8th divisions advanced in concert from Sunchon to Kunu, fifteen miles up the Chongchon River from Sinanju. Elements of the ROK 1st Division turned left (or west) to establish a link along the river line with the 24th Division at Sinanju, but the bulk of the division continued due north toward Unsan. The ROK 6th and 8th divisions turned right and prepared for a long drive northeast, deep into remote, trackless wastes of North Korea.[46]

*   *   *

In Tokyo MacArthur, still unaware of the CCF pouring into North Korea, set in motion the third—and final—step of his new plan to send American troops all the way to the borders of Red China. This final step may have been influenced in part by the failure of the airborne operation to trap the NKPA and Kim Il Sung's government. On October 24, in clear violation of the spirit, if not the letter, of his directive, MacArthur advised Walker and Almond that in view of the enemy's refusal to surrender, he was now lifting the restrictions previously imposed on the employment of American forces in North Korea. The stop line previously set forth was merely to be regarded as an "initial objective." They were now "authorized to use any and all ground forces . . . as necessary to secure all of North Korea." They were to "drive forward with all speed and with full utilization of all their forces."[47]

These new orders, drastically enlarging the American role, were not submitted to Washington for approval. However, within a matter of hours the JCS learned of them through back channels. In contrast with its previous mincing posture, this time the JCS reacted promptly and firmly. It cabled MacArthur to point out that the new orders were "not in consonance" with its previous instructions, which stated that "as a matter of policy no non-Korean ground forces would be used in the area along the Manchurian border or in the northeast province bordering the Soviet Union." The JCS went on to say, tactfully, that while it realized MacArthur "undoubtedly had sound reasons for the subject instructions," it "would like information of these reasons since the action contemplated was a matter of concern to them."

MacArthur cabled a sharp and terse reply. The instructions he issued to Eighth Army were, he said, a "matter of military necessity." The ROK forces, he explained, "were not strong enough to secure North Korea by themselves, and their commanders were often highly emotional and unreliable." Owing to those factors, any other course of action might produce "tactical hazards."[48]

He then went on to argue, legalistically, that he was not in violation of his directive, first, because his directive did not specifically prohibit use of American troops in northernmost Korea but merely recommended that course "as a matter of policy"; secondly, because his directive had stated it was not "final" and might require modification; thirdly, because George Marshall had cabled him to "feel unhampered tactically and strategically to proceed north of the 38th Parallel"; fourthly, because "this entire subject was covered in my conference at Wake Island."[49]

The JCS was absolutely flabbergasted by this reply. It was full of spurious argumentation and downright lies. As MacArthur knew perfectly well, Marshall's message to "feel unhampered" related specifically to crossing the 38th Parallel, not to the employment of American forces in extreme North Korea. No one in Washington could recall that the subject had been discussed at Wake Island. His orders were not final and were subject to modification—but by Washington, not by MacArthur.[50]

The JCS did not, however, countermand the orders. By that time MacArthur's forces were marching victoriously toward—and even beyond—the Chongchon River. It seemed that the war would be over in a matter of days. To have raised objections over a "matter of policy" which MacArthur regarded as a "military necessity" and which might result in "tactical hazards" would again lay the Joint Chiefs open to charges of being nervous Nellies or, more seriously, to needlessly exposing ROK and American GIs to military risks.

Nonetheless, the incident was profoundly disturbing to the JCS. It was all too reminiscent of MacArthur's trip to Formosa and his letter to the VFW. It destroyed the recent trust created at Wake Island. As Joe Collins later put it, "This was one indication, among many others . . . that General MacArthur was not in consonance with . . . basic policies. . . . [It] led us gradually to fear that just as he violated a policy in this case without consulting us, perhaps the thing might be done in some other instance of a more serious nature."[51]

## I V

The amphibious landing of Ned Almond's X Corps at Wonsan proceeded with its own inherent logic—or illogic. Owing to the minefields there, the operation fell farther and farther behind schedule, so much so that it began to take on a ludicrous aspect, much like the airborne operation.

The armada carrying the Marines arrived off Wonsan on October 19. Some progress had been made in clearing the mines, but not enough. Two more small minesweepers had hit sophisticated magnetic mines and blown up. It now appeared that the landing could not take place until about October 25. Exasperated, Ned Almond flew ashore in a helicopter and opened X Corps headquarters in Wonsan. By that time Eighth Army had taken Pyongyang. Accordingly, MacArthur made a drastic change in Almond's orders: When it got ashore, X Corps would attack not west but north.[52]

Over the next several days Almond and his staff roughed out a new plan. In outline it was as follows: The ROK Capital Division would continue the advance up the coast road toward the Russian border. The ROK 3d Division would go north from Hamhung to the Chosin Reservoir and beyond, to the Manchurian border. The Marines would land at Wonsan, then go north to Hungnam and Hamhung, thence into the interior of North Korea behind the ROK 3d Division to the Chosin Reservoir and beyond, to the Manchurian border. The 7th Division would land not at Wonsan, but much farther north at Iwon, as MacArthur had first suggested to Turner Joy on October 8. From Iwon the 7th Division (on the distant right flank of the Marines) would attack due north toward the Manchurian border. MacArthur's October 24 order, lifting restrictions on employment of American troops beyond the original stop line, cleared away the political obstacles to a 7th Division landing at Iwon and the advance of the Marines and 7th Division to the Manchurian border.[53]

While the minesweepers at Wonsan worked feverishly, but gingerly, the armada containing the Marines steamed back and forth off shore for seven full days, October 19 to October 25. During that time the 1st Marine Air Wing flew into Wonsan and launched air operations, and Bob Hope's USO show came to entertain the American forces. Stranded aboard ships the Marines, who ridiculed the voyage to nowhere as "Operation Yo-Yo" felt miserable and "humiliated." Adding to the mental misery, an epidemic of dysentery swept through the crowded transports. One ship reported 750 Marines on the sick list.[54]

The men of Dave Barr's 7th Division were likewise discomfited. Having crowded aboard ship at Pusan on October 19, they went nowhere. At first, unaware that their objective had been switched from Wonsan to Iwon, the GIs began to believe rumors which said that the war was over and the division would sail directly for Japan or even the States.[55]

Finally, the Marines began landing at Wonsan. The advance elements reached the beach on October 25. The main body (30,000 men), led by Chesty Puller's First Marines, came ashore on October 26—Puller to find that he had just been promoted to brigadier general and was to replace Eddie Craig as division ADC. O. P. Smith established his CP ashore on the 27th. It was, the official historian wrote, "as anti-climactic a landing as Marines ever made." Altogether the Marines had been out of action for three crucial weeks.[56]

At about the same time Dave Barr received orders to land his 7th Division at Iwon. Inasmuch as Iwon still lay in "enemy" territory, Barr could no longer land "administratively" as planned. At least one regiment would have to combat-load for a possible assault on a hostile beach. For that task Barr chose his 17th Regiment, which had not seen much action at Inchon. It debarked from the transports and reloaded into seven LSTs. While it was doing so, welcome word came that the ROK Capital Division had reached and overrun Iwon. It had found no NKPA—or mines offshore.[57]

The 17th Infantry was commanded by Herbert B. Powell, forty-seven. At that time Powell had the distinction of being the only non-West Pointer commanding an Army regiment in Korea. A former National Guard sergeant, upon graduation from the University of Oregon (1926), Powell had won a commission in the Regular Army by competitive examination. He had not heretofore commanded troops in combat. In World War II he had served in the ETO, first as chief of staff of the 75th Infantry Division, then in the First Army G-1 section, working under Bill Kean, whom he knew well from previous assignments.[58]

Directed by the Pentagon to command the 17th Infantry, which had just arrived in Japan from Korea, Powell had arrived in Japan in September 1949. In this capacity he had done well with very little, inheriting many freewheeling paratroopers from the 11th Airborne Division who had elected to remain in Japan when the division was sent back to the States. Among the junior officers on the 17th's roster was the oldest son of Al Gruenther, Richard L. ("Dick"), a West Pointer from the class of 1946.[59]

Powell's experience in the ETO had given him considerable insight into those tangible—and intangible—qualities necessary to be a good division commander in combat. While he admired Dave Barr's "distinguished career," he did not think Barr measured up. "He didn't have the drive," Powell said later; "he worried about everything and he couldn't hold up under stress."[60]

On October 29 the 17th Infantry landed unopposed on the beach at Iwon. During the following ten days the rest of the 7th Division, and other units, landed at Iwon: in all, 28,955 men, 5,924 vehicles, and 30,000 tons of cargo.[61]

When all was said and done, Ned Almond commanded a sizable force: two beefed-up American divisions and two full-strength ROK divisions, plus supporting elements. In all, X Corps then numbered about 83,000 men, of which about 50,000 were Americans. Moreover, there were to be substantial American reinforcements: Without clearing it with Washington, MacArthur had ordered the full 3d Division (originally sent to defend Japan) to join X Corps. This would add another 19,000 Americans, raising total X Corps manpower to about 102,000, nearly equal to the strength of Eighth Army forces operating north of the 38th Parallel.[62]

Almond immediately sent elements of his American forces racing at top speed for the Yalu River. Homer Litzenberg's Seventh Marines struck north from Hamhung behind elements of the ROK 3d Division, which were on the way to the Chosin Reservoir area. Herb Powell's 17th Regiment, leading the 7th Division, made plans to head north without delay from the Iwon beachhead on a line Pungsan to Kapsan then to Hyesanjin, on the Yalu River.[63]

To lead the 17th Regiment's dash north to the Yalu, Powell chose his 1/17, commanded by the able Francis P. Carberry, forty, who had won a high honor with the 3d Division in World War II. It would be directly supported by the 105 howitzers of Barney D. White's 49th FAB, Quad 50s of the 15th A/A Battalion, and, after they could be unloaded, some Pershings of Calvin Hannum's 73d Tank Battalion. Carberry's C Company, commanded by Dick Gruenther, who had been with the regiment since 1948, would spearhead the drive.[64]

In briefing his troops, Carberry laid out the objectives, stressing that the 1/17 was in a race to the Yalu with the Marines and that he expected the 1/17 "to be there first." Grabbing the first nine two-and-a-half-ton trucks on the beach, Gruenther's C Company (300 men, including attached ROKs) climbed aboard (about 35 men per truck) and raced to the first objective, the village of Cho. Behind came A Company, Carberry, the battalion staff, and other units.[65]

By late afternoon, October 31, Gruenther and his men had reached the outskirts of Pungsan, to be greeted by men of the Capital Division. But almost immediately the Americans ran into unexpected trouble. The well-armed and organized NKPA 71st Regiment, backed by mortars and artillery of the 23d Coast Guard Regiment, was defending Pungsan. The NKPA attacked that night, directing its main force at the ROKs. Gruenther remembered "a fierce hand-to-hand battle," during which Carberry ordered his A and C companies to assist the ROKs.

On the morning of November 1 Gruenther attacked, aiming for high ground. As customary, the NKPA flanked and headed for the American artillery. Gruenther remembered:

I glanced back and saw a sight which will live forever in my mind. Approximately one company of Commies with mortars had maneuvered to our flank and were staging an all-out attack on Battery B of the 49th FAB. . . . In order to ward off the intruders, the 105 howitzers were forced to level off and fire point blank into the attacking horde, which was less than 200 yards away. The result was devastating. As shells burst, I could see arms, legs, and mortar tubes flying through the air. A five-minute shelling stopped the attack and left a mass of twisted bodies and just a few fleeing Reds.

The 1/17's bitter fight with the NKPA at Pungsan dragged on for four full days. Gruenther recalled that by November 5 the NKPA had been "almost completely annihilated." The 1/17 then proceeded northward about seven miles on foot, to the banks of the Ungi River, where they halted, facing not only a difficult (and cold) river crossing but also yet another well-organized NKPA formation. Believing they could reach the Yalu in another five days, Dick Gruenther's troops were "somewhat discouraged" at the order to halt. But Almond, Barr, and Powell had concluded that the "dash" to the Yalu was going to be far more difficult than anticipated. The full 17th Infantry, supported by White's 49th FAB and tanks, would be committed to the river crossing. It would take time to bring forward all these elements over the treacherous mountain roads and trails.

## V

By the time X Corps commenced landing at Wonsan, elements of Johnnie Walker's Eighth Army had crossed the Chongchon River at Sinanju and Kunu and were fanning out over the mountain roads leading to the Yalu. It was not a meticulously planned campaign; rather, it was a wild "hot pursuit" of a routed enemy.

The strategic positions of Eighth Army and the NKPA were now exactly reversed from the positions of early September. The NKPA had withdrawn into a "perimeter" close to its source of supply; Eighth Army was hobbled by an overextended and inadequate supply line. Inchon was now being utilized to help supply Eighth Army, but owing to the tidal restrictions and other factors, it could provide only a fraction of the required tonnage. Because the railroad bridges over the Han, Imjin, and Taedong rivers were not yet in place, the bulk of Eighth Army supplies still had to come by rail/truck, truck, or emergency airlift from Pusan. What finally came out of the spout of the pipeline at the Chongchon River was a trickle.

As a result of the supply shortages and the mopping-up and policing obligations farther south, Walker could commit only four of Eighth Army's fifteen non-ROK regiments to the campaign beyond the Chongchon. These were Basil Coad's Commonwealth Brigade and the three regiments (5th; 19th; 21st) of John Church's 24th Division.[66]

Walker well realized that condensing the campaign to four non-ROK regiments was very risky. However, he was under the gun again. MacArthur's order of October 24 had specified that he should drive forward to the border "with all speed." To sit down and wait for the arrival of supplies sufficient to support another American division in the campaign would have appeared excessively conservative. The majority view was that the NKPA was beaten, Red China would not intervene, the advance to the Yalu would be a cakewalk. He therefore proceeded without pause.

As it developed (more or less spontaneously), the "plan" of the campaign was as follows. Coad's Commonwealth Brigade, leading Church's full (but understrength) 24th Division, would attack west from Sinanju through Chongju along the "coast road" to the Yalu River at Sinuiju. The other regiments of the 24th would go northwesterly on interior roads. The ROK 1st Division would attack due north from Kunu to Unsan, thence northward to the Yalu River. The ROK 6th and 8th divisions (designated ROK II Corps), staging from Kunu, would attack northeasterly toward Chosan and Kanggye, thence to the Yalu.[67]

The Commonwealth Brigade began its advance to the west of Sinanju on October 25. It was a bitterly cold day: frost in the morning, snow flurries later on. Soon—and unexpectedly—the brigade ran into very strong resistance from fresh and well-organized NKPA forces. Astonishingly these forces were supported by two dozen or more new T-34 tanks, self-propelled guns, and other heavy weapons. Led by Charles Green's Australian battalion, the brigade hastily regrouped for heavy combat and drew on Tom Dolvin's 89th Tank Battalion for added firepower. Finally, with the help of Dolvin and FEAF close air support, the brigade bulled into Chongju on October 29, only to suffer a vicious counterattack, during which the gallant Green was killed. He was succeeded by Ian B. Ferguson.[68]

By now the Commonwealth Brigade had been spearheading the 24th Division for eight days. Coad, complaining that his troops needed rest, requested relief. In response, John Church directed Dick Stephens's 21st Infantry to replace the brigade. After Stephens had relieved Coad in Chongju on October 30, he put Gines Perez's 2/21 in the lead. Mounting a bold and aggressive night attack, Stephens and Perez rolled over tank-led NKPA forces, deflected a 500-man NKPA counterattack, and by dawn, October 31, had broken into the clear beyond Chongju. For this action Stephens awarded Perez a well-deserved DSC and recommended him for command of the regiment in the event he was incapacitated.[69]

Brad Smith, still commanding the 1/21, had received orders to return to the States for other duty. Perhaps because the 1/21 had been first to meet the NKPA at Osan or because Smith was on the verge of leaving, Stephens gave Smith and the 1/21 the "honor" of leading the regiment onward to the Yalu

River. Passing Perez's 2/21 on the morning of November 1, Smith led the 1/21 westward. He had got as far as Chonggo—eighteen miles south of the Yalu— when he received baffling orders from Stephens to halt in place and button up. It proved to be a timely order. In the afternoon a tank-led NKPA force of about 500 men attacked the 1/21. Smith held his ground and repulsed this attack, but afterward the 1/21 was less than eager to race to the Yalu.[70]

On Stephens's right flank, Johnny Throckmorton's 5th and Ned Moore's 19th regiments were also headed for the Yalu via interior roads. Throckmorton followed a road that led northwesterly through Pakchon to Taechon, where it joined a railroad, thence northwest to Kusong and Sakchu, close by the Yalu. Nearing Taechon on October 29, Throckmorton was suddenly checked by a powerful NKPA force supported by tanks and self-propelled guns. With fine help from FEAF fighters, which destroyed nine tanks, Throckmorton overcame the block and took Taechon.[71]

The power of this NKPA block was puzzling—and disquieting. Even more so were two of the eighty-nine prisoners. They were not North Korean but Chinese, the first to be captured by American forces in Korea. Throckmorton remembered: "We had interrogaters who were part Chinese, who spoke Chinese. There was absolutely no question that these prisoners were Chinese. After we had questioned them, we sent them to the rear—back to the division G-2 people for further interrogation. But nobody back at division, or higher echelons, believed they were Chinese."[72]*

Throckmorton pushed on warily toward Kusong. The division ADC, Gar Davidson, joined him. Davidson remembered: "We kept going toward the Yalu. Throckmorton sent patrols out in all directions, but we couldn't really find out what was up there. Twice Shrimp Milburn came up to see us and look at our maps. He was worried but, finally, his order was to go."[74]

Approaching Kusong on October 31, Throckmorton was again checked. This time the block proved to be an immensely powerful NKPA force: perhaps 5,000 men, well supported by tanks, self-propelled guns, conventional artillery, and antitank guns. In the pitched battle which ensued, Throckmorton prevailed and took Kusong, killing about 350 NKPA troops and capturing all their weapons. But Throckmorton became increasingly concerned over the extent of his exposure.[75]

The next day, November 1, Throckmorton sent a recon patrol probing northward from Kusong. It had advanced about ten miles north of town— thirty air miles south of the Yalu—when Church sent word by liaison plane for the 5th to halt and hold in place. No reason was given. Throckmorton and

---

*Later investigation confirmed that the two men were indeed Chinese—two stragglers or deserters, perhaps trying to make their way back to Manchuria.[73]

Davidson were mystified but somewhat relieved. "By that time," Throckmorton recalled, "I could feel the hair raising on the back of my neck."[76]

\* \* \*

On the extreme right flank of Eighth Army, the ROK 1st and 6th divisions, staging out of Kunu, commenced driving north and northeasterly toward the Yalu on October 25. The ROKs spread out over a multiplicity of roads. Many of these roads led directly into the heart of the massive concealed CCF concentrations in extreme North Korea. The CCF was watching and waiting, ambushes laid.

The ROK 1st Division, supported by Pattons of John Growdon's 6th Tank Battalion and American artillery and A/A vehicles, heading due north from Kunu, drove through Yongbyon and Unsan. Just beyond Unsan the CCF suddenly and powerfully attacked the leading ROK elements. The ROK 1st Division had unwittingly driven into the middle of the three-division 30,000-man CCF Thirty-ninth Army.[77]

Ably assisted by the American Pattons, artillery, and A/A vehicles, the ROK 1st Division wobbled, fell back, then held its ground. Later in the day, when the ROKs captured some soldiers, they discovered they were Chinese. The prisoners boasted truthfully that there were some 20,000 CCF soldiers in the Unsan area. Investigating more closely, ROK 1st Division commander, Sun Yup Paik, who had served in the Japanese Manchurian Army in World War II and who knew the Chinese well, concluded that he had engaged a regular CCF division of about 10,000 men.[78]

To the right of the ROK 1st Division, the ROK 6th Division drove north and northeastward toward Onjong and Huichon. Its 7th Regiment zoomed all the way to Kojang. From there patrols were sent to the south bank of the Yalu. The men filled a bottle with "Yalu water" as a present for Syngman Rhee and afterward urinated in the river as a gesture of defiance. However, at Onjong the 2d Regiment ran headlong into the three-division 30,000-man CCF Fortieth Army. At Huichon, its other regiment, the 19th (reinforced by the 10th Regiment of the ROK 8th Division), ran headlong into the three-division 30,000-man CCF Thirty-eighth Army.[79]

Massively outnumbered, shocked, pathologically fearful of Chinese, and ill disposed for heavy combat, the 2d and 19th ROK regiments collapsed and bugged out. (Of the 6,000 ROKs in these two outfits, 3,500 filtered back to Kunu.) Cut off to the north, the 7th Regiment at first attempted to fight its way south, but finally, it, too, broke and fled. With that, the ROK 6th Division (and one regiment of the 8th) ceased to exist as combat elements, leaving Eighth Army's Chongchon River baseline at Kunu dangerously exposed.[80]

Fifty air miles to the east of the ROK 6th Division—in Almond's X Corps sector—the 26th Regiment of the ROK 3d Division, which was going north from Hamhung to the Chosin Reservoir, had also unexpectedly encountered Red Chinese. These ROKs had advanced into an area occupied by the three-division, 30,000-man CCF Forty-second Army. Unaware at first of the massive size of the Chinese force, the ROK regiment pressed onward. On October 28 and 29 the CCF, supported by a few NKPA tanks, attacked the regiment in full fury. Stunned, fearful, and demoralized, the ROKs broke and bugged out, finally taking defensive positions considerably south of the reservoir.[81]

Upon hearing of this debacle, on October 30 Ned Almond flew by helicopter to these ROK positions. There he discovered the ROKs had taken sixteen CCF POWs. Under interrogation the Chinese had revealed that they were members of the CCF 124th Division and that a sister division was close by. Upon returning to Wonsan, Almond directed a personal radio message to MacArthur, informing him that fully organized CCF units were present in northeast Korea, adding such details as he had gathered from the ROKs.[82]

# PART
# SEVEN

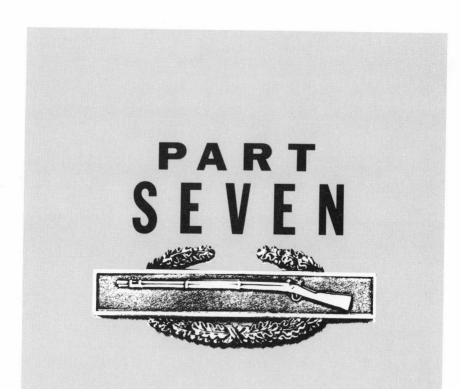

# Drastic
# Miscalculations

# 14

# THE CHINESE STRIKE

## I

By the last days of October the frontline commanders did not doubt that Eighth Army and X Corps had encountered powerful, organized elements of CCF armies across a wide spectrum of extreme North Korea. The ROK 1st Division, Throckmorton's 5th Infantry, and Almond's X Corps forces near the Chosin Reservoir had taken numerous CCF prisoners. Yet rear-area intelligence analysts continued to doubt the evidence.

The biggest doubter was MacArthur's G-2, Charles Willoughby. He took the position (as he told the Pentagon) that the "most auspicious time" for CCF military intervention had "long since passed." By that he meant that if the CCF were going to enter the war, it would have done so much earlier—perhaps in defense of Pyongyang—before the NKPA had been utterly shattered and had abandoned all viable defensive positions. It did not seem logical to Willoughby that the CCF would enter the war so late and in the teeth of a victorious Eighth Army on full offensive, supported by powerful air and naval forces.[1]

Furthermore, as viewed in Tokyo, CCF intervention entailed enormous military and political risks for the new Communist government in Peking. MacArthur and GHQ believed, as MacArthur had told Truman at Wake Island, that if the CCF intervened, American air power would inflict the "greatest slaughter" on the Red Chinese forces. If successful, the "slaughter" would be a costly setback for the Communists. It could lead to widespread internal dissatisfaction and unrest in China and a grave loss of face and a diminution of Communist prestige in the Far East.

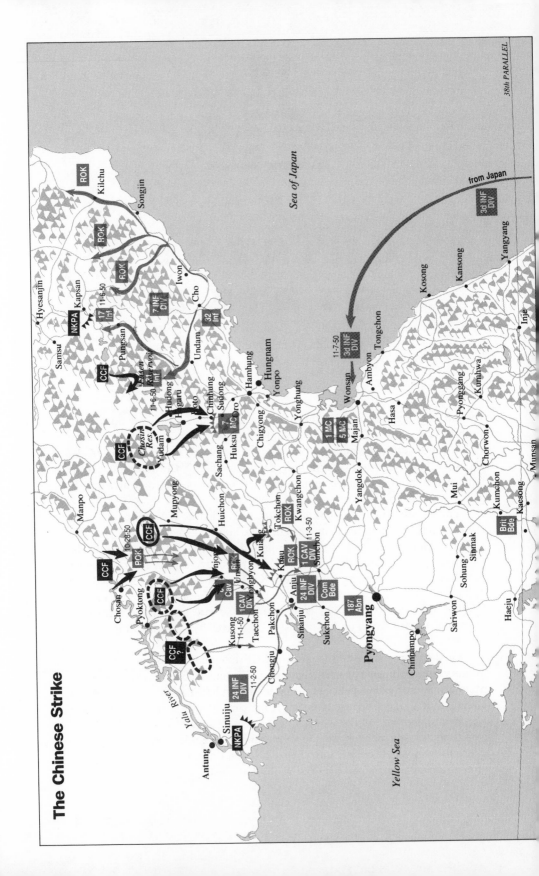

# The Chinese Strike

Yellow Sea

Sea of Japan

38th PARALLEL

from Japan

3d INF DIV

ROK — Kilchu
Songjin
ROK
ROK
Hyesanjin
Kapsan
NKPA
Samsu
17 Inf
11-6-50
7 INF DIV
Iwon
Cho
32 Inf
Pungsan
Undam
1-4 xm 11-6-50 31 Inf
CCF
Hudong
Hagaru
Chinhung
Sudong
Hamhung
Hungnam
Yonpo
Oro
Chigyong
Yonghung
Wonsan — 3d INF DIV 11-7-50
Ambyon
Tongchon
Kosong
Kansong
Yangyang
Inje
Manpo
Mupyong
Chosin Res
Yudam
7 DIV
Sachang
Huksu
Yangdok
Hasa
Pyonggang
Kumhwa
Chorwon
Munsan
1 MC 5 MC
Majan
Mui
Sohung
Sinmak
Kumchon
Kaesong
Haeju
Huichon
Tokchon
ROK
Kwangchon
10-28-50
CCF
CCF
ROK
Chosan
Pyoktong
Onjong
ROK Cav
Unsan
Tongnyong
Kunu
Kuju
ROK
1 CAV DIV
Tokchon 11-3-50
Sunchon
Com Bde
Brit Bde
CCF
Kusong
11-1-50
1 CAV DIV
Taechon
Pakchon
Anju
24 INF DIV
Sukchon
187 Abn
Yalu River
CCF ?
Chongju
Sinanju
Pyongyang
Chinnampo
Sariwon
Antung
Sinuiju
NKPA
24 INF DIV
11-2-50

Finally, there was the "MacArthur factor." Almond's G-3, Jack Chiles, an alumnus of GHQ who had observed Willoughby at close hand, remembered: "MacArthur did not *want* the Chinese to enter the war in Korea. Anything MacArthur wanted, Willoughby produced intelligence for. . . . In this case, Willoughby falsified the intelligence reports. . . . He should have gone to jail."[2]

In any event, as Tokyo saw it, there was no reason for concern. If the CCF intervened in North Korea, its movement would be detected by American air reconnaissance. There could be no overwhelming and decisive surprise such as that at Pearl Harbor. The "slaughter" would be mounted at once by FEAF and Navy and Marine aircraft. Even if the American air attack was hampered by bad weather and some elements of the CCF leaked through, Eighth Army and X Corps were more than capable of dealing with them. The CCF was large in numbers but possessed only a small quantity of primitive artillery and no tanks or close air support. It had scant battlefield communications and logistical backup. It had beaten Chiang Kai-shek's cowardly and ineptly led forces, but it had never fought a modern American Army.

\* \* \*

When Eighth Army and X Corps captured CCF prisoners, Willoughby at first disbelieved the evidence. Noting an Eighth Army G-2 report on October 27 announcing the capture of two CCF soldiers who candidly boasted that the CCF had massively intervened in North Korea, Willoughby wrote that their stories were "unconfirmed and thereby unaccepted." When on October 29 Ned Almond interviewed the sixteen CCF POWs captured by X Corps and alerted MacArthur by personal message, Willoughby flew to X Corps headquarters to interview them himself. Willoughby could not reasonably deny they were Chinese, but he cavalierly dismissed them as possibly "stragglers" or "volunteers" of no real significance.[3]

As MacArthur's G-2 Willoughby basked in the reflected glory and genius of his commander. Willoughby's views thus powerfully influenced those of the entire intelligence community in the Far East Command. A challenge to Willoughby's views was tantamount to a challenge to MacArthur's views. No one in the intelligence community was willing to undertake that challenge.[4]

Among the intelligence arms in the Far East powerfully influenced by Willoughby was Eighth Army's G-2 section. Despite the evidence to the contrary, Walker's senior intelligence officers also doubted a massive Chinese intervention in Korea.

The Eighth Army G-2 was a young, relatively inexperienced, and junior officer, Lieutenant Colonel James C. ("Clint") Tarkenton, thirty-four. Tarkenton had begun his military career in high school at the Oak Ridge (North Carolina) Military Institute, where he was a standout: corps commander and honor graduate. He entered West Point in 1937, but, his son remembered, "unable to maintain an adequate grade point average," he left the academy in his plebe year. Subsequently he attended North Carolina State College for one year and obtained a Reserve Army commission.

Called to active service in 1940, Tarkenton was assigned to intelligence duties. He rose to the rank of lieutenant colonel and the job of S-2 of the 13th Infantry Regiment of the 9th Division in the ETO. After the war he obtained a Regular Army commission and attended the Command and General Staff School (1948). In September 1949, after being graduated, he was assigned to the GHQ G-2 section, where Willoughby named him executive officer, Operations Branch, Theater Intelligence Division. Ten months later, when the Korean War broke out, Willoughby gave Tarkenton his "big break" by assigning him to Walker, whom Tarkenton had never met, for the senior post of Eighth Army G-2. Despite Tarkenton's youth and lack of high-level intelligence experience, Walker was impressed by him and relied upon him to an extraordinary degree. In the Pusan Perimeter Tarkenton had justified this confidence by producing very good intelligence on the NKPA.[5]

Curiously, Tarkenton's second-in-command was the more senior and experienced of the two. He was West Pointer (1936) Lieutenant Colonel Robert G. Fergusson, thirty-nine. During World War II Fergusson had been G-2 of the 7th Division in the Pacific, then G-2, Central Pacific Base Command and, finally, Deputy G-2, U.S. Army Pacific Command. In the postwar years he held the post of chief, G-2 Dissemination Branch, Department of the Army. That post provided him a loftier view of the world and considerable experience at the highest levels of the Washington intelligence community. Although senior to Tarkenton, Fergusson took this wartime assignment in good grace and later commended his youthful boss as "outstanding."[6]

\* \* \*

Clint Tarkenton's intelligence reports in the latter days of October mirrored the Willoughby view. On October 26 he issued an analysis in which he stated that there was "no indication of open intervention on the part of Chinese Communist Forces in Korea." Even after Eighth Army had interrogated ten Chinese prisoners, Tarkenton continued to doubt that any large-scale CCF intervention had occurred. On October 30 the State Department's chargé in Seoul, Everett Drumright, cabled Washington: "While information is still sketchy and confirmation lacking, Eighth Army intelligence now feels there may be two regiments of Chinese Communists engaged Eighth Army sector. . . . It not yet definitely established whether Chinese fighting as independent units or sandwiched among North Koreans." The following day, October 31, he told Washington: "Eighth Army intelligence considers there possibly 2,000 Chinese engaged in Eighth Army sector."[7]

Then a vexing problem arose. By November 1 G-2 interrogators had identified Chinese POWs from several different CCF armies, indicating a greater commitment of force than theretofore calculated. In order to make these facts fit the estimates, Tarkenton produced this interesting explanation: The armies identified had each provided one or more battalions from these divisions to form the regiments. Drumright thought that a reasonable explanation and cabled Washington:

On basis information obtained from Sino prisoners, which of course subject to confirmation, Eighth Army intelligence considers there now two Sino regiments, possibly a third, in Eighth Army sector of North Korea. Appears these units were formed by taking one battalion each of six divisions said to constitute Sino 39th and 40th armies, deployed along Manchurian-North Korean border. It further appears Sino Communist units engaged in Northwest Korea are not integrated with North Korean forces, but fighting as separate units. . . . . Eighth Army Intelligence is of view, with which Embassy inclined to concur, Sino Communists will avoid overt intervention.[8]

Within the Eighth Army staff there soon arose a sharp division of opinion over the extent of CCF intervention. The G-3, John Dabney, and his senior planner, William F. Train, who pored over the intelligence reports late into the night, concluded that the CCF was coming into North Korea in great numbers. However, Tarkenton believed it inconceivable that such a mass movement could occur without its being spotted by FEAF or other intelligence sources, and he continued to doubt. In retrospect Dabney wrote that Tarkenton's views were "unduly influenced" and "colored" by Willoughby's views. Train agreed, adding that Tarkenton may also have been overwhelmed by the paperwork, which included "10,000 intelligence items a month."[9]

In view of the uncertainty over the extent of CCF intervention, and the strong views of Walker's G-3s, it would have been prudent to hold Eighth Army at the Chongchon River until the intelligence picture had clarified. But Walker was under great pressure from MacArthur to press on. Nonetheless, on October 28 and thereafter Walker took some precautionary steps. Believing that he should not proceed without bringing forward substantial additional forces, he ordered that:

• Basil Coad's Commonwealth Brigade would come out of reserve and take position to protect the rear of the 24th Division on Eighth Army's left flank.

• Hap Gay's full 1st Cav Division would immediately depart Pyongyang and Chinnampo, go north at best speed, and reinforce the besieged ROK 1st Division at Unsan, for its attack to the Yalu in Eighth Army's center.

• The surviving elements of the ROK 6th and 8th divisions on Eighth
Army's right flank would be reinforced by the ROK 7th Division at Kunu.
In addition, Dutch Keiser's 2d Division would prepare to rush north to
reinforce the ROKs, should they continue to fail.[10]

## II

Inasmuch as Walker's intent was to continue the offensive with the least
possible delay, the most urgent task was to bring Hap Gay's 1st Cav forward.
It responded with remarkable speed. On October 28 Hal Edson's 8th Cav came
north, crossed the Chongchon and moved up behind the ROK 1st Division
at Unsan. The next day Johnny Johnson's 5th Cav crossed the Chongchon to
protect the 8th Cav's rear. Billy Harris's 7th Cav, policing farther south in
Chinnampo, began moving northward on October 31.[11]

Edson's 8th Cav arrived in the Unsan area in a cavalier frame of mind.
Still wearing summer uniforms, the outfit believed the assigned task would be
a simple power punch through a thin NKPA line, followed by a one- or
two-day dash to the Yalu, then a return to the home base in Japan by Thanksgiving Day.

By this time the I Corps G-2, Percy Thompson (John Eisenhower's father-
in-law), had no doubt that organized units of the CCF had entered North
Korea in force. When Edson and other senior 1st Cav officers rushed to the
combat zone, Thompson briefed them to be prepared to fight strong, well-
organized CCF units. But the 1st Cav officers—those in 8th Cav in particular—perhaps influenced by Eighth Army and Tokyo intelligence reports,
greeted this news, Thompson wrote later, "with disbelief and indifference."[12]

Powerfully supported by tanks and the 99th FAB, Edson's 8th Cav moved
into the rear of the ROK 1st Division (holding north of Unsan) on October
31. The 1/8, now commanded by thirty-two-year-old West Pointer (1941)
John Millikin, Jr. (son of one of Patton's corps commanders in the ETO), took
position north of Unsan. The 2/8, commanded by William Walton, set up to
the west of Unsan with only a thin, tenuous link to the 1/8. The 3/8, commanded by Robert J. Ormond (who had recently relieved Johnny Johnson),
took position southwest of Unsan. Edson placed his CP several miles south of
the "front," between Unsan and the 3/8 CP.[13]

Upon the arrival of the 8th Cav, Shrimp Milburn ordered most of the
ROK 1st Division to pull back. Its 11th Regiment was sent southeast to
reinforce the wobbling ROKs at Kunu. Its hard-hit 12th Regiment went into
reserve. But its 15th Regiment remained in place on Millikin's right flank,
northeast of Unsan, supported by American tank and artillery units.

After Johnny Johnson had established his 5th Cav CP south of the 8th

Cav, he jeeped forward to visit Edson's positions. He had heard rumors that large enemy forces were coming from the hills to the west to cut the road. He found no evidence of the enemy, but he was worried. "It was just dead," he said later. "Anytime you encounter that kind of atmosphere it arouses a feeling of apprehension. . . ." It made the back of his neck "prickle."[14]

In the 8th Cav sector Johnson made a point of visiting his former battalion, the 3/8. He did not like what he found. The 3/8 was casually disposed in a valley. He told his replacement, Robert Ormond: "You had better get out of this low ground and get yourself up on a slope where you can provide some protection for the position." Johnson thought Ormond would comply with this warning, but, as he said later, his advice was "ignored."[15]

On the morning of November 1 Edson and his men awoke to find the skies around Unsan dense with smoke. Forest fires were burning in the hills. Edson supposed the enemy had lit the fires to conceal its movements from FEAF. This hypothesis gained credibility later that morning, when rumors spread that large enemy forces (2,000 here, 3,000 there) were circling from the west to cut the road between the 8th Cav and the 5th Cav. Edson jeeped south to Johnson's CP to alert him to the rumors and the smoke, then returned.[16]

About midday Hap Gay arrived in the sector and established his CP at Yongsang, below Unsan. Hearing the rumors and other reports and seeing the smoke, Gay became uneasy over the disposition of his division. It was scattered all over the landscape. The 8th Cav, in particular, seemed vulnerable; it was a salient with scant flank protection. Gay asked Shrimp Milburn for permission to consolidate the 1st Cav. He wanted to pull the 8th Cav back, bring the 7th Cav forward, and get back Edgar Treacy's 3/5, which Milburn had split from the 5th Cav and sent to Kunu, to reinforce the ROKs.[17]

Milburn said no to all these proposals. Ever since breaking out of the Pusan Perimeter, I Corps had been on the attack. Pulling 8th Cav back would be a negative maneuver, which might further frighten and demoralize the ROKs, setting off yet another stampede. The big problem was not Unsan but Kunu, where the CCF was mounting a major attack. I Corps would remain on the offensive.[18]

Early that afternoon Johnson, concerned about Treacy's 3/5, jeeped to Kunu. While he was away, word reached the 5th Cav CP that the road to Unsan and 8th Cav positions had been cut by a strong but unidentified enemy force. Since the 5th Cav's primary responsibility was to keep the road open, in Johnson's absence his staff sent Morgan Heasley's 1/5 north to confirm the report and, if true, to break the block. Word soon came back to the 5th Cav CP that the report was true. Not only that, but the 1/5 needed help. Accordingly, the staff ordered Paul Clifford's 2/5 to join the northward attack. When Johnson returned to his CP, he went forward to direct these units personally.[19]

At about dusk the same day, November 1, the CCF fell on Unsan in full fury. It was later determined that two full CCF divisions (20,000 men) mounted the assault. It came simultaneously from the north, northwest, and west against the ROK 15th Regiment, Millikin's 1/8, and Walton's 2/8. Blowing bugles, horns, and whistles and firing signal flares, the Chinese infantry, supported solely by light mortars, swarmed skillfully—and bravely—over the hills. To the ROKs and Americans, the oncoming waves of massed manpower were astonishing, terrifying, and, to those Americans who believed the war was over, utterly demoralizing.

The majority of these Chinese troops were veterans of the victorious CCF campaigns against Chiang Kai-shek's Nationalist forces. They wore two-piece (blouse and pants) mustard-colored, quilted cotton outer garments over summer uniforms and cotton caps with fur-lined earflaps. A few had fur-lined boots, but most were shod in poor-quality canvas shoes with crepe soles. Each carried a four- or five-day supply of food (rice; corn; beans), which had been cooked to avoid telltale campfires. Each man had been issued about eighty rounds of small-arms ammo; some had grenades.[20]

Since the CCF had no close air support, no tanks, and very little artillery, it specialized in fighting under cover of darkness. The whistles, bugles, and horns were not only signaling devices (in place of radios) but also psychological tools, designed to frighten the enemy in the dark and cause him to shoot, thereby revealing the position of men and weapons. The fighting tactics were relatively simple: frontal assaults on the revealed positions, infiltration and ambush to cut the enemy's rear, and massed manpower attacks on the open flanks of his main elements. War correspondents were to describe the attacking waves of the CCF as a "human sea" or "swarm of locusts."

The UN forces at Unsan wobbled, then caved in under the massive weight of the CCF. Within about two hours the ROK 15th Regiment had utterly collapsed. With its fall the attached American tanks, artillery, and A/A elements began a hurried and disorderly night withdrawal through Unsan to the south. At the same time the CCF drove a wedge between the loosely deployed 1/8 and 2/8. Both battalions were forced back on Unsan. The commanders, Millikin and Walton, urgently called for help and ordered vehicles and supply trains to begin withdrawing. By 10:00 P.M. both units were out of ammo, more or less overrun, cut off from the rear, and desperate.[21]

At about the same time Shrimp Milburn met with Hap Gay and John Church's planners. It was now clear that I Corps was in precarious shape to deal with the CCF. The ROKs at Kunu were caving in; the 8th Cav was surrounded and cut off. To the west John Church's three regiments were badly exposed. Milburn reluctantly conceded that I Corps must go over to the defensive, more or less on the Chongchon River line, to hold a shallow salient, or bridgehead, north of the river at Sinanju, from which Eighth Army's offensive could be resumed eventually. In consultation with Walker, it was decided that:

• The three regiments of Church's 24th Division (5th; 19th; 21st) would withdraw to the Chongchon River at Sinanju, covered by the Commonwealth Brigade. Ned Moore's 19th would link with the Commonwealth Brigade to hold a bridgehead north of Sinanju; Stephens's 21st would go into reserve on the south bank of the river; Throckmorton's 5th would go to Kunu, to backstop the ROKs.

• The 8th Cav would withdraw from Unsan. Johnson's 5th Cav, reinforced by Pete Clainos's 1/7 (and later Treacy's 3/5), would mount an all-out attack north to open the road for the 8th Cav. Billy Harris and his 2/7 would come up to assist the 5th Cav. Lynch's 3/7 would go to Kunu to replace Treacy's 3/5. When Throckmorton's 5th Infantry reached Kunu, the 3/7 would join it.

• Dutch Keiser's 9th and 38th regiments, and later his 23d, would take position on Eighth Army's right flank, south of Kunu, to guard against a deep CCF envelopment that could cut off and strand Eighth Army at the Chongchon River.[22]

By about eleven the same night Hal Edson had received an order to withdraw the 8th Cav. Edson's plan was dictated by the situation. Ormond's 3/8, which had not yet been hit, would serve as rear guard. Millikin's 1/8 and Walton's 2/8 would withdraw in that order through Ormond's positions; then the 3/8 would follow the others out.

This plan really had no chance of succeeding. By that time the 1/8 and 2/8 had lost all semblance of organization, and the CCF was swarming everywhere. Bands of Americans, with a tank here, an A/A vehicle there, were retreating pell-mell in the dark, many engaged in hand-to-hand combat with the CCF. Edson tried desperately to hold open a key road fork, but a truck towing a 105 howitzer turned over and blocked the road, thereby ending all hope that the other artillery and vehicles could get out. The 99th FAB abandoned twelve of its 105-mm howitzers.

In the ensuing hours Edson, Millikin, Walton, and the survivors of the 1/8 and 2/8 took to the hills, fleeing in the darkness, leading bands of men. All three of these commanders got out, as did a majority of the men. The heaviest loss of manpower occurred in Millikin's 1/8, in which 265 men of about 800 were killed or captured.[23]

In the meantime, at about 3:00 A.M., on November 2, the CCF descended on Ormond's 3/8, blowing bugles and horns. In the wild melee and hand-to-hand fighting that ensued, Ormond was mortally wounded, and his exec, Veale F. Moriarty, took command of the battalion. Many men bugged out, but others heroically banded into tight perimeters to fight to the death in a replication of Custer's Last Stand.[24]

By daylight on November 2 it was clear to Hap Gay that the 8th Cav had suffered a disaster. No one knew what was left of it at Unsan, but whatever was left certainly must be rescued. Heroic measures were needed. As a result, all three battalions of Johnson's 5th Cav, plus Clainos's 1/7 and the 2/7, were thrown into the attack. But the rescue force lacked adequate artillery and close air support, and none of it could crack through. In the attempt that day Johnson incurred a ghastly 350 casualties—250 of them in Paul Clifford's 2/5.[25]

Later that afternoon Milburn, alarmed at the heavy casualties, ordered Gay to break off the rescue mission and withdraw the entire 1st Cav below the Chongchon. With heavy heart Gay complied, later writing that it was one of the most difficult orders he had ever had to issue. The 3/8 was left to its fate. Enclaves of brave men fought on for several more days, inflicting heavy casualties (500 or more) on the CCF. When it was all over, about 600 of the 3/8's 800 men were dead or captured.[26]

In the next several days the survivors of the shattered 8th Cav reassembled at a camp three miles south of Sinanju. Its total losses could not be immediately ascertained. On November 3 Edson reported the regiment at less than half strength, but in subsequent days many stragglers came in. Edson later calculated the net loss in the regiment as 800 men. Whatever the numbers, the unit was so badly mauled and demoralized that it could not be committed to combat without a complete reorganization.[27]

Hal Edson received a Silver Star for his efforts to save his regiment, but he did not retain command. Apparently believing the reorganization of the regiment should include a new leader, Hap Gay sacked Edson, with the idea of giving the regiment to Johnny Johnson after Crombez could be released as "mayor" of Pyongyang to reclaim command of the 5th Cav. In the interim Gay recalled the 8th Cav's former commander, Ray Palmer, to carry out the rebuilding job. Edson returned to the States and later rose to the rank of one-star general.[28]

The 5th Cav, badly roughed up in its effort to save the 8th Cav, was likewise withdrawn from the combat sector. It motor-marched about sixty miles to the rear, to bivouac and regroup at Sunchon, where Dutch Keiser's 2d Division was assembling and where it could be reoutfitted more easily. By then the full shock of the CCF intervention had sunk home. The situation reminded one company commander of the "grim" days in September at Taegu. "This is certainly no time for optimism," he wrote home on November 4. "The enemy is well trained and organized. . . . Anyone who says they ain't Chinks is crazy!"[29]

Billy Harris's 7th Cav had not yet met the CCF. The 7th Cav (minus

Lynch's 3/7, which was attached to Throckmorton's 5th Regiment at Kunu) deployed in the forward area, taking positions on the south bank of the Chongchon River between Anju and Kunu. It remained, in effect, an I Corps Fire Brigade, prepared to dash west to Sinanju or east to Kunu as required or to block a CCF river crossing directly into its sector.[30]

\* \* \*

On the extreme left (or west) flank of Eighth Army John Church began withdrawing his 5th, 19th, and 21st regiments on the morning of November 2. Fortunately for him and his men, a direct CCF attack on the 24th Division was not in the plan. However, the withdrawal was not lacking in danger. If the Commonwealth Brigade at Pakchon could not hold, the division would be cut off west of Sinanju.

By and large the withdrawal of the 24th Division was a model of orderliness. Approaching Pakchon, Stephens and Perez learned that the Commonwealth Brigade was under severe attack by elements of the CCF Thirty-ninth Army, which had taken Unsan, then swept southwest to Pakchon. Perez was worried; he did not hold the Tommy in high regard. But at Pakchon the brigade, ably supported by the 61st FAB (of the 1st Cav), now commanded by Joseph W. Knott, was outstanding. Despite severe losses, it and the 61st FAB stood like a rock, holding open a vital "door" through which the 5th, 19th, and 21st could reach Sinanju. After that Perez concluded that the British were poor on offense but terrific on defense. "They don't back up very easily," he said gratefully.[31]

Without pause the 24th Division took up its preassigned missions on the Chongchon River line. Ned Moore's 19th picked up some ammo and rations, then dug into positions on the right of the Commonwealth Brigade, north of the Chongchon River to hold a bridgehead from which Eighth Army's offensive would eventually be resumed. Stephens's 21st, in division reserve, took up positions on the south bank of the Chongchon, just west of Billy Harris's 7th Cav. Throckmorton's 5th went east to Kunu, to back up the ROKs, incorporating Lynch's 3/7.[32]

The battle to hold a bridgehead north of Sinanju proved to be very tough going. Morris Naudts's 1/19 got into position on November 4 and was almost immediately overwhelmed by the CCF. Its C Company ("a hard-luck outfit") was cut off and forced to surrender. In the chaos Johnnie Walker's son Sam, commanding A Company, kept his head. Assuming temporary command of B Company as well, after dark Sam Walker found a ford on the Chongchon and withdrew most of the men of A and B companies to safety, a "great achievement," for which he earned a Silver Star. Moore sent the 3/19, now commanded by Edward Logan (replacing Red Ayres, who became ill), to regain the position—and rescue the 1/19's equipment—but Logan was firmly repelled. Ollie Kinney's 2/19 held, but only barely. In savage hand-to-hand fighting two of Kinney's men fell heroically: a Wisconsin Indian, Mitchell Red Cloud, posthumously awarded a Medal of Honor; and Joseph W. Balboni, posthumously awarded a DSC.[33]

By November 5 the CCF had virtually overrun the 19th Infantry, forcing the Commonwealth Brigade to fall back to the north bank of the Chongchon. In a last-ditch effort to save the bridgehead, Church committed Stephens's 2/21 and 3/21 and, later in the day, Naudts's reorganized 1/19 into the 19th's sector. These three battalions, backed with armor and artillery, gave Moore's 2/19 and 3/19 sufficient time to restore their positions and straighten out lines.

Meanwhile, several miles to the right above Kunu, the CCF had pushed the ROK 7th Division back against the town. It was vital for Eighth Army to hold Kunu, a major road hub near the junction of the Chongchon and Kuryong rivers. Its loss would give the CCF not only this key river junction but also access to roads leading west and south, opening the possibility of an encirclement of Eighth Army forces at the Chongchon.

Jim Lynch's crack 3/7 was backstopping the ROK 7th Division, but by November 3 it was obvious that for all its skill and élan, the 3/7 was not enough. To assist it, Johnny Throckmorton's 5th Infantry was rushing east and Chin Sloane's 9th Infantry, at Sunchon, was rushing north. Throckmorton reached Kunu first, on November 4. Temporarily absorbing the 3/7, the 5th Infantry, in another superb performance, repulsed an all-out CCF assault and "saved" Kunu.[34]

Rushing up the road from Sunchon, Chin Sloane's 9th Infantry was led by Butch Barberis's 2/9. He vividly remembered that on that day, November 5, the 2/9 "began taking prisoners identifiable as members of the CCF." He interrogated them, sent them to the rear, and submitted written reports to the regimental S-2 and the division G-2. Barberis was startled to find these CCF troops so far south of Kunu and the Chongchon River. He concluded they were CCF infiltrators who were hiding in the many mine shafts in the nearby mountains on the division right flank. The reports apparently made no very great impression. The 2d Division did not aggressively patrol the right flank to determine the extent of CCF infiltration.[35]

By the morning of November 6 Eighth Army forces were fully redeployed on the defensive at the Chongchon from Sinanju to Kunu. They were braced for a renewed, all-out CCF attack, but bafflingly it never came. The CCF simply vanished. No one would ever know why. Some believed it was because the CCF had merely intended to give Eighth Army a bloody nose and push it back below the Chongchon. Others believed that in the five days of hard fighting the CCF had run out of food and ammo and needed to regroup and replenish before resuming the offensive.[36]

## I I I

To the extreme right of Eighth Army in northeast Korea Ned Almond's independent X Corps proceeded with its plans to occupy that sector from its beachheads at Wonsan and Iwon.

Almond was fully aware that the CCF had entered North Korea and was close to the Chosin Reservoir. He had interrogated sixteen CCF POWs, had directed a personal message to MacArthur calling attention to that fact, and had shown the POWs to Charles Willoughby. Yet he and his G-2, forty-three-year-old West Pointer (1933) William Quinn, who was perhaps also influenced by Willoughby, concluded that the CCF posed no real danger to X Corps.[37]

Almond therefore directed X Corps forces to "mop up" remnants of the NKPA in northeast Korea, to occupy the key seaports of Wonsan and Hungnam, seize the inland towns and roads, and—not least—reach the Yalu River before Johnnie Walker's Eighth Army. Since Almond did not anticipate any substantial enemy resistance, the X Corps forces were to be fragmented and operate over a huge, rugged "front." One of Almond's chief planners, Ellis W. Williamson, remembered the strategy this way: "We became 'land happy.' All units were racing to see who could cover the most mileage every day. The Yalu River became 'The' objective."[38]

Almond's initial orders:

• ROK I Corps (3d and Capital divisions) would continue racing northeasterly up the coast to Chongjin. Serving as X Corps right flank, the ROKs would also send elements from the coast road north and northwesterly to the Yalu.

• The Army's 7th Division, loosely occupying a thirty-mile front in the center of X Corps, would push north to the Yalu from Pungsan to Hyesanjin. It would anchor its right flank at Hysenjin (adjacent to ROK I Corps forces) and its left flank on the Fusen Reservoir (east of the Chosin Reservoir).

• The 1st Marine Division would guarantee the safety of Wonsan and Hungnam, then send the Seventh Marines from Sudong to the Chosin Reservoir area, then on to the Yalu River at Huchangganggu and Singalpajin, west (or to the left) of the 7th Division forces.

• The Army's green 3d Division, preparing to land at Wonsan at MacArthur's direction, would relieve the Marines at Wonsan and Hungnam and conduct such offensive operations as ordered by Almond.[39]

The terrain over which X Corps forces were to maneuver was formidable. The Taebaek Mountains rose to 7,000 to 8,000 feet through a large part of the sector. There were few inland roads. Those that existed were (in the American view) primitive "cow trails," running through the valleys and steep gorges, scarcely able to support a jeep and loaded trailer, let alone the standard two-and-a-half-ton military truck and artillery tractors and tanks. Throughout these high mountains it was already cold.[40]

Marine General O. P. Smith took a dim view of the plan. It would leave his various elements very widely dispersed and strung out from Wonsan to Chosin to the Yalu, serving in the role of regular infantry, as opposed to that of elite amphibious forces, which were accustomed to sticking close to a beachhead. He protested strongly to Almond, but Almond angrily dismissed the protests, believing, as he had at Inchon, that Smith was overly cautious and too conservative.[41]

Having received word of the massive CCF attack on the 8th Cav at Unsan, Smith had ordered Homer Litzenberg's Seventh Marines to proceed through the rugged terrain at Sudong with utmost caution. He had assumed, correctly, that the main CCF attack had been aimed at Eighth Army, but he also knew that elements of the CCF Forty-second Army were in the Chosin Reservoir area and had roughed up the ROK 26th Regiment. It was possible that all three divisions of the CCF Forty-second Army (30,000 men) might attack the Seventh Marines.

Fortunately for Litzenberg and the Seventh Marines, such an attack was not part of the CCF plan. However, shortly after midnight, November 3, the full CCF 124th Division, deployed at the Chosin Reservoir, swarmed into the Seventh Marines, blowing whistles and horns. In savage, hand-to-hand night fighting the CCF at first got the upper hand. But with the onset of daylight Marine artillery and close air support inflicted a punishing slaughter on the enemy: some 700 dead; untold numbers, perhaps thousands wounded.[42]

The fight with the 124th continued off and on over the next three days. The Seventh Marines, ably supported by Marine close air, punched northward, slowly and carefully, buttoning up tight at night. As the Marines progressed, they continued to chew up the 124th Division, inflicting several thousand more casualties. Then, suddenly, on November 7 the CCF mysteriously disappeared. The Marines concluded that the 124th had withdrawn because it was so badly mauled that it was "militarily noneffective." That may have been true (the Army historian estimated it had suffered 7,000 casualties), but since it was not replaced by either of its sister divisions, the complete disappearance of the 124th Division was probably part of the general CCF withdrawal all across North Korea.

Smith's caution and conservatism had paid off. Although the Seventh Marines had been considerably more exposed than the 8th Cav, it had prevailed in this first Marine encounter with the CCF. The Marines incurred a total of 314 casualties. Had Smith followed the spirit of Almond's orders and dashed willy-nilly to the Chosin Reservoir and beyond to the Yalu, the casualties would undoubtedly been far worse, perhaps worse than those in the 8th

Cav. The encounter, Smith remembered, gave Almond pause. However, Smith wrote with asperity, "This conservative attitude did not continue long."[43]

* * *

Almond could—and did—exercise more direct and forceful control over the Army's 7th Division, commanded by Dave Barr. After Inchon Almond had made no secret of his dissatisfaction with Barr and the division and had personally sacked the 31st regimental commander, Richard Ovenshine. Barr and his staff were therefore under heavy pressure to excel in northeast Korea. As a result, unlike the Marines, they were reluctant to protest, or even to question, any order issued by Almond or X Corps headquarters and obeyed all of them with a "can do" alacrity.

The 7th Division had disembarked at Iwon and launched operations in northeast Korea with the kind of aggressive spirit Almond demanded. Herb Powell's 17th Infantry had charged inland to take Pungsan and had advanced to the Ungi River, en route to Kapsan and the Yalu River at Hyesanjin. The 7th Division's other two regiments, the 31st and Charles Beauchamp's 32d, landed at Iwon behind the 17th on November 3 and 4 and prepared to push inland no less swiftly: the 31st on the left of the 17th in the division center; the 32d on the left of the 31st, on the division left flank, to be anchored on the Fusen Reservoir.[44]

The new commander of the 31st Infantry was West Pointer (1930) Allan D. ("Mac") MacLean, forty-three. A classmate of Beauchamp's and Ned Moore's, MacLean had been an aggressive tackle on the academy's football team. "He was a bull of the woods," Beauchamp remembered, "a great guy. Don't open the door; just walk through it. He possessed ceaseless energy, a dynamic personality, and an uncompromising will to get things done. . . . He never undertook a job with reserve."[45]

Like Beauchamp, MacLean had missed the fighting in World War II. He had served in the ETO as a staff officer, coordinating troop movements. He arrived in Japan in early 1949, directed by the Pentagon to command the 32d Regiment. A year later he turned the outfit over to Beauchamp, having won the highest accolades from Walker for a fine job of training under difficult circumstances. Following that, Walker drew MacLean into his G-3 section. Until taking over the 31st, MacLean had served as Walker's personal "eyes and ears" at the fronts. As such he had been a close—and fearless—observer of the war since July 1950. MacLean was more than willing to take the 31st; early in his career he had served with it in the Philippines.

Upon landing at Iwon, MacLean's 31st, supported by Raymond O. Embree's 57th FAB, moved northward on the left of Pungsan and established a headquarters. The "roads" in this area were nonexistent. The regiment, in effect, spread out, mostly on foot, into the mountains, "holding" or "advancing" in the division center. In this barren region an element of the 3/31, commanded by a combat-experienced West Pointer (1939), William R. Reilly, thirty-three, encountered a few CCF troops, the first Chinese the 7th Division had met. These CCF men fought desultorily or not at all, leading MacLean, Reilly, and other leaders in the 31st Infantry unwisely to regard all Chinese with contempt. After chasing them into the hills, MacLean and Reilly later surmised they were stragglers from the CCF 124th Division, which the Marines had shattered at Sundong, but (it was learned still later) they were actually members of a sister division, the 126th, who were apparently under orders to avoid combat. MacLean reported these CCF soldiers by radio, but as Herb Powell (who overheard the transmission) remembered, "GHQ, Tokyo, refused to believe that any substantial Chinese troops had entered the [7th Division] combat zone."[46]

Unloading last at Iwon, Charles Beauchamp's 32d Infantry, supported by Ulrich G. Gibbons's 48th FAB, prepared to go north to anchor the division's left flank at the Fusen Reservoir. By that time the roads were jammed. In order to reach his sector, Beauchamp had to go south on the coast highway to Hamhung, thence north to the reservoir. There he deployed Charles Mount's 2/32 on the left, Heinrich Schumann's 3/32 in the center, and Don Faith's 1/32 on the right, "abutting" MacLean's bleak 31st sector. Beauchamp encountered no CCF, but on a visit to MacLean's CP he learned of Reilly's earlier encounter with CCF troops and of a second, more recent encounter. However, Beauchamp remembered, he knew they were nearby. "I had the impression that MacLean was having difficulty convincing people they were CCF troops."[47]

These slight and inconsequential contacts with the CCF by the 7th Division forces did not develop into a battle such as the Seventh Marines had experienced nearby at Sudong. In fact, as elsewhere, the CCF seemed to melt away, leaving the men of the 7th Division puzzled—and contemptuous. Ned Almond, feisty and aggressive, laid plans to push on to the Yalu.

## IV

Lin Piao was to designate these initial attacks on Eighth Army and X Corps the "First Phase Offensive." His objectives have not been revealed. If his intent was to drive American forces from North Korea and reestablish the Kim Il Sung government in Pyongyang, the offensive must be judged a failure. If it was merely to give Eighth Army a bloody nose and halt its advance beyond the Chongchon River, as seems more likely, it must be judged a success.

Whatever the intent, Eighth Army had been hard hit. The CCF had utterly routed the ROK 6th Division and part of the ROK 8th Division, had forced the ROK 7th Division back on Kunu, had devastated the 8th Cav, had roughed up the 5th Cav, and had forced the 24th Division to break off its attack to the Yalu and retreat to the Chongchon, where the Commonwealth Brigade and the 19th Infantry were badly mauled. However, the blow was by no means decisive. Of the seven non-ROK regiments engaged, only one—the 8th Cav— had been put entirely out of action. American and British casualties probably did not exceed 2,500.

\* \* \*

Notwithstanding the mounting weight of the CCF attacks on Eighth Army, the G-2, Clint Tarkenton, and MacArthur's G-2, Charles Willoughby, had clung stubbornly to the view that the CCF had not intervened in North Korea in great numbers. However, following the 8th Cav disaster at Unsan, the powerful CCF attacks on the Commonwealth Brigade and 19th Infantry, and the division-size attack on the Seventh Marines at Sudong, both men began to increase their estimates of CCF strength. On November 3 Willoughby put the "minimum" at 16,500, with a possible "maximum" of 34,000.[48]

These figures were wildly off the mark. By that time the Ninth Army Group of the CCF Third Field Army from Shantung Province had begun arriving undetected in North Korea to augment Lin Piao's Thirteenth Army Group. The total CCF force in North Korea had grown to thirty infantry divisions, comprising 300,000 men, plus some artillery, cavalry, and support units. The CCF Thirteenth Army Group, comprising six armies of eighteen divisions (180,000 men) remained deployed before Eighth Army; the Ninth Army Group, comprising twelve infantry divisions (120,000 men), deployed before X Corps.[49]

Although MacArthur had repeatedly asserted (most recently at Wake Island) that the CCF would not intervene in Korea, and the CIA had concurred in this view, President Truman was troubled by the signs indicating otherwise. At his specific behest the JCS cabled MacArthur on November 3 to ask for an "interim appreciation" of the situation and its implications at the earliest possible date, "in light of what appears to be overt intervention in Korea by Chinese communist units."[50]

MacArthur replied the following day, November 4. Reflecting the Willoughby-Tarkenton view, the message was reassuring. He believed that while large-scale CCF intervention in Korea was a "distinct possibility," there were "many fundamental logistic reasons against it." He suggested a "final appraisal" should await "a more complete accumulation of military facts." He leaned to the belief that rather than open intervention, Peking would render covert assistance to the NKPA, providing "voluntary personnel" to retain a "nominal foothold in North Korea" and "salvage something from the wreckage."[51]

Confronted with this new and potentially perilous military situation, MacArthur threw caution to the wind. He demanded an immediate explanation from Walker about why Eighth Army had broken off the attack in the face of a few CCF "volunteers" and withdrawn on the defensive behind the Chongchon River. Implied in the question was that Walker should return to the offensive and complete the assigned task, regardless of the CCF troops he had encountered.

Perhaps believing his job was in jeopardy, Walker drafted a restrained reply, blaming the setback on logistical difficulties and the ROKs. In launching this final Eighth Army campaign, Walker wrote, he had taken a "calculated logistical risk." Supplies, reaching him "almost entirely by airlift," were barely sufficient to maintain one reinforced American and several ROK divisions. His forces had been ambushed by "fresh, well-organized and well-trained units, some of which were Chinese Communist forces." Owing to the "intense, psychological fear of the Chinese" and "complacency" and "overconfidence" at all levels, the ROKs had completely collapsed and disintegrated.[52]

Walker still had no exact picture of the extent of the CCF intervention. Consequently, in his heart of hearts he was now reluctant to press the offensive beyond the Chongchon River. He believed the "wise" thing to do was to hold Eighth Army where it was, keep X Corps south of Hamhung, and establish a combined Eighth Army–X Corps line across the narrow neck of the peninsula: Sinanju–Kunu–Yongwan–Hamhung. This was approximately the "line" MacArthur had originally drawn and cleared through the JCS.

However, Walker did not propose this more sensible alternative. He assured MacArthur that as soon as the ROK divisions on his right flank could be stabilized and redirected and adequate supplies and more American forces brought forward, Eighth Army would resume the offensive.

There has never been [Walker wrote] and there is now no intention for this Army to take up or remain on a passive perimeter or any other type of defense. Every effort is being made to retain an adequate bridgehead to facilitate the resumption of the attack as soon as conditions permit. . . . These plans will be put into execution at the earliest possible moment and are dependent only upon the security of the right flank, the marshalling of the attack troops and the restoration of vital supplies.[53]

MacArthur had told everyone from Truman on down that in the unlikely event of CCF intervention in North Korea, his air power would "slaughter" the Red Chinese. The mandatory pause of Eighth Army to bring up more supplies—estimated to be about ten days—afforded an opportunity to make good on this promise. So without consulting the JCS or even informing it officially, on November 5, MacArthur called in his FEAF chief, Stratemeyer, and gave him orders to launch this slaughter. It was to be a maximum air assault of at least two weeks' duration, designed to "isolate the battlefield" and destroy "every means of communications and every installation, factory, city, village" within it. Air crews would be "flown to exhaustion if necessary." Incendiary bombs, as well as conventional bombs, would be employed against cities and towns.[54]

In order to "isolate the battlefield" or stop the flow of CCF men and matériel, MacArthur ordered that FEAF was to bomb out the "Korean end" of the twelve bridges along the Yalu River, with a maximum effort directed at the three big bridges at Sinuiju. In so doing, MacArthur cautioned Stratemeyer, "there must be no violation of the border."[55]

Stratemeyer believed this order would be very difficult, if not impossible, to carry out. The Yalu was not a straight line; it followed a tortuous, twisting course. It would be very difficult for pilots to fly a course close enough to hit the bridges yet not violate the border, which ran down the middle of the river. The bridges at Sinuiju were protected by heavy concentrations of antiaircraft weaponry. Moreover, FEAF had recently discovered Russian-built fighter aircraft in the Sinuiju area, including some Russian-built swept-wing MIG-15 jets, which were believed to be superior to FEAF's F-80 jets. The combination of these enemy threats and the requirement to bomb south of the center of the river would not only expose FEAF air crews to great risk but also require flying and bombing accuracy beyond their capability.[56]

Even if the bridges could be knocked out, there was doubt that it would stop the flow of the CCF into North Korea. Such measures had not stopped the NKPA. They had demonstrated a remarkable talent for constructing substitute underwater sandbagged fords, which were difficult to detect from the air. Moreover, with the onset of the cold weather the Yalu would soon freeze over. Barring an unseasonable thaw, within about two weeks soldiers could walk across the river. In perhaps three or four weeks the ice would be strong enough to support trucks and artillery and perhaps even a temporary rail line.

* * *

MacArthur's instruction to Stratemeyer ordering the destruction of the Yalu bridges was a clear violation of his JCS directive to stay "well clear" of the Manchurian border. Aware of that, and perhaps desiring to protect his rear politically, three hours before the scheduled takeoff of the bombers, Stratemeyer passed word of the impending operation to Air Force Chief of Staff Hoyt Vandenberg.[57]

A monumental flap ensued in Washington. Dean Acheson and the JCS were appalled. MacArthur not only had clearly violated his directive for the second time but also, in the process, had jeopardized a major political maneuver in the UN. Washington was then urging the Security Council to consider a report that in effect condemned the CCF intervention in Korea. Bombs falling on the Sinuiju bridges—and very probably into Manchuria itself— would undermine Washington's position, alienate the fence sitters, and might well evoke a Soviet UN resolution condemning American aggression. It would also violate a pledge Washington had made to London not to take any action toward Manchuria without prior consultations.[58]

That day President Truman was en route to Independence, Missouri, to cast his vote in the off-year election. When Acheson reached him by telephone, Truman shared the secretary of state's deep concern. The mission should be carried out, the president ruled, "only if there was an immediate and serious threat to the security of our troops." MacArthur should be asked to justify more fully the reasons for it. After further hasty meetings in Washington the JCS, on November 6, cabled MacArthur to say that Washington was urgently reviewing the Korean situation and honoring its commitment to London not to take action in Manchuria without consultations. Meanwhile, he would, "until further orders, postpone all bombing of targets within five miles of Manchurian border" and, as a matter of urgency, supply Washington an "estimate of situation and reason for ordering bombing of Yalu River bridges."[59]

This was the first time in the Korean War that Washington had directly countermanded a MacArthur field order. His reaction, as he wrote in his memoir, was one of "astonishment" and "inexpressible shock." He later said to his acting chief of staff, Doyle Hickey: "For the first time in military history, a commander has been denied the use of his military power to safeguard the lives of his soldiers and safety of his army . . . [and] it clearly foreshadows a future tragic situation in the Far East. . . . It will cost the lives of thousands of American soldiers and place in jeopardy an entire army. . . ."[60]

These words were written long after the fact. It is difficult to credit that on November 6 MacArthur truly believed UN forces were in grave "jeopardy." The same day Willoughby and Tarkenton estimated the total strength of the CCF in all North Korea (facing both Eighth Army and X Corps) as merely 34,500. Total UN strength that day was more than 250,000.

If MacArthur felt "inexpressible shock," a more likely reason was the blow to his ego. The cancellation of the air strike at Sinuiju was an indication that Washington might assume a more direct role in directing operations. He apparently viewed this prospect as intolerable and became determined to thwart it.

As a first step, MacArthur appeared to threaten to resign. He wrote in his memoirs that he drafted a cable to Washington requesting "immediate relief." But when Doyle Hickey saw the dispatch, MacArthur continued, Hickey talked him out of sending it. "Hickey protested that the Army would not understand my leaving at such a critical moment, and might become demoralized and destroyed; that it was my duty to the country and to my own honor not to go in such a crisis." Perhaps so. But more likely this was merely MacArthur theatrics. He knew that Hickey would relay the threat through back channels to Washington. The possibility of MacArthur's resignation arriving on the day before the voters went to the polls in the off-year elections (November 7, Washington time) would no doubt powerfully influence Truman to let MacArthur have his way.[61]

As a second step, MacArthur resorted to apocalyptic rhetoric. Earlier, when he had violated his directive by ordering American troops into extreme North Korea, he had gotten away with it—forced a modification in policy—by arguing forcefully that any other course could subject his forces to "tactical hazards." He again resorted to that technique, this time with a dramatic escalation in the language, not by any means justified by the "facts" as he knew them on November 6:

Men and materiel in large force are pouring across all bridges over Yalu from Manchuria. This movement not only jeopardizes but threatens the ultimate destruction of the forces under my command. . . . The only way to stop this reinforcement . . . is the destruction of these bridges. . . . Every hour that this is postponed will be paid for dearly in American and other United Nations blood. . . . Under the gravest protest that I can make, I am suspending this strike and carrying out your instructions. . . .[62]

In a final white-hot paragraph, he insulted and challenged the authority of the JCS: "I cannot overemphasize the disastrous effect, both physical and psychological, that will result from the restrictions which you are imposing. I trust that the matter be immediately brought to the attention of the President as I believe your instructions may well result in a calamity of major proportions for which I cannot accept the responsibility without his personal and direct understanding of the situation."

This cable stood Washington on its ear. It was in stark contrast with MacArthur's reassuring cable of November 4, in which he had said there were "many fundamental logistic" reasons against large-scale CCF intervention. Reached at his Fort Myer quarters, Omar Bradley was stunned by the message and immediately telephoned its contents to President Truman in Independence.[63]

By this time President Truman and the Democratic party were in deep political trouble. McCarthyism was rampant. Right-wing Republicans had succeeded in planting the idea that the Truman administration was crawling with Communists, that its bungling Far East policy had "lost" China. Although the extent of CCF commitment to Korea was not yet clear, its presence had blurred the victory over the NKPA and raised many uneasy questions. Pleading that he was preoccupied with Korea, Truman had unwisely declined to campaign in behalf of Democrats standing for election or reelection. On election eve the political polls indicated that the Democrats might lose control of the Senate and suffer a substantial erosion of strength in the House.[64]

In response to Bradley's telephone call Truman backed down and authorized MacArthur to bomb the Sinuiju bridges. Although no direct evidence has come to light, it is inconceivable that the tight political situation Truman faced did not significantly influence the decision. Had he stuck by his guns, he ran the risk that the text of MacArthur's cable—and possibly news of MacArthur's resignation—might appear in the media on election day, with disastrous consequences for the Democrats in the voting booth.

\* \* \*

The success of Lin Piao's First Phase Offensive, while limited, must have been another blow to MacArthur's ego. MacArthur had been caught unawares and outgeneraled. On November 6, compelled as always to address the great unseen audience—and history—MacArthur issued in Tokyo a long communiqué, which was designed to recast the setback into a kind of victory. The Pentagon ridiculed this communiqué—and others to come—as MacArthur's "posterity papers," unnecessary and ill-advised bombast. But it was worse than that: It contained priceless intelligence for Lin Piao in that it revealed that MacArthur was still ignorant of the extent of CCF intervention in North Korea:

The Korean War was brought to a practical end with the closing of the trap on enemy elements north of Pyongyang and seizure of the east coastal area, resulting in raising the number of enemy prisoners-of-war in our hands to well over 135,000, which, with other losses mounting to over 200,000, brought enemy casualties to 335,000, representing a fair estimate of North Korean total military strength. The defeat of the North Koreans and destruction of their armies was [sic] thereby decisive.

In the face of this victory for United Nations armies, the Communists committed one of the most offensive acts of international lawlessness of historic record by moving, without any notice of belligerence, elements of alien Communist forces across the Yalu River into North Korea and massing a great concentration of possible reinforcing divisions with adequate supply behind the privileged sanctuary of the adjacent Manchurian border. A possible trap was thereby surreptitiously laid, calculated to encompass the destruction of the United Nations forces engaged in restoring order and the process of civil government in the North Korean border area. This potential danger was avoided with minimum losses only by the timely detection and skillful maneuvering of the United Nations commander responsible for that sector, who with great perspicacity and skill completely reversed the movement of his forces in order to achieve the greater integration of tactical power necessitated by the new situation and avert any possibility of a great military reversal.

The present situation therefore is this. While the North Korean forces with which we were initially engaged have been destroyed or rendered impotent for military action, a new and fresh army faces us, backed up by a possibility of large alien reserves and adequate supplies within easy reach of the enemy but beyond the limits of our present sphere of military action. Whether and to what extent these reserves will be moved forward remains to be seen and is a matter of gravest international significance. . . .[65]

# V

Truman's decision to allow MacArthur to bomb the Yalu bridges amounted to a drastic change in policy. The war in Korea would be carried right up to (and possibly by error across) the Manchurian border, regardless of the risks. Accordingly, Dean Acheson, George Marshall, and other aides met with Bradley and the JCS in the Pentagon, to draft new instructions to MacArthur and to review the radically changing situation in Korea.[66]

When the conferees met, they were still much puzzled over the size, shape, and meaning of the CCF intervention in Korea. One aspect of the situation seemed certain: The CCF intervention in Korea (whatever its ultimate form) clearly indicated that Moscow and Peking had accepted the increased risk of general or global war. To the conferees this seemed to mean (as a CIA analysis put it) that the "Kremlin is ready to face a showdown with the West at an early date" or that "circumstances have forced them [the Soviets and Chinese] to accept that risk." Global war could come at any hour, anyplace.[67]

Given that possibility, the conferees were still of the belief that Western Europe, not Korea, was the decisive battleground. In "drawing a line" and rescuing South Korea, America had already diverted enormously greater military resources to the Far East than had ever been anticipated. These commitments had significantly cut into America's physical support (as opposed to rhetorical support) of NATO, the "seed" money and forces that would encourage physical contributions by other NATO nations. An escalation of the conflict in Korea to a conflict with Red China, as Omar Bradley later trenchantly put it, would involve Washington "in the wrong war, at the wrong place, at the wrong time, and with the wrong enemy."[68]

Mindful of MacArthur's strong contrary views, skeptical of his estimate of the CCF threat to his forces, and distrustful of his motives and loyalty, the conferees drafted careful—and tactful—instructions to him to reflect Truman's change in policy:

The situation depicted in your message [of November 6] is considerably changed from that reported in last sentence your message [of November 4] which was our last report from you. We agree that the destruction of the Yalu bridges would contribute materially to the security of the forces under your command unless this action resulted in increased Chinese Communist effort and even Soviet contribution in response to what they might well construe as an attack on Manchuria. Such a result would not only endanger your forces but would [also] enlarge the area of conflict and U.S. involvement to a dangerous degree. However in view of first sentence your [message] you are authorized to go ahead with your planned bombing in Korea near the frontier including targets at Sinuiju and Korean end of Yalu bridges provided that at the time of receipt of this message you still find such action essential to safety of your forces. . . .

Because of necessity for maintaining optimum position with United Nations policy and directives and because it is vital in the national interest of the U.S. to localize the fighting in Korea it is important that extreme care be taken to avoid violation Manchurian territory and airspace and to report promptly hostile action from Manchuria.[69]

Although this message was laced with restrictions designed to assert Washington's authority and control, it was, in fact, a total capitulation to MacArthur. For the second time MacArthur had forced Washington to modify his directive to suit action he had initiated.

The conferees next turned to a general discussion of Korea. They felt instinctively that a disaster in Korea might be in the making. To minimize it, they believed MacArthur should be ordered to halt ground operations and (as Walker wanted) consolidate all UN forces at the narrow neck of Korea, along a line Sinanju–Hungnam. However, since they lacked precise information on the extent of CCF intervention and intentions, they did not formally recommend this course. Instead, they proposed a "crash" NSC review of the Korean situation, with the aim of arriving at a new and comprehensive strategy which could be discussed at a NSC meeting on November 9.[70]

On the following day, November 7, as the Democrats were taking a severe beating at the polls, MacArthur responded to the JCS request for fuller information. In contrast with his earlier message, this one was cool and brief. Intelligence received since his earlier message [November 4] had "confirmed" his estimate of probable Chinese motives and intentions. That is, while the CCF had "unquestionably" intervened in Korea with "organized units," it had not intervened in North Korea in force. However, the CCF posture in North Korea could be "augmented at will," MacArthur warned, possibly reaching a point "rendering our resumption of advance impossible" and perhaps even requiring UN forces to perform "a movement in retrograde" (retreat). He intended to try to resume the attack with Eighth Army "possibly within ten days," provided "the flow of enemy reinforcements can be checked" by the air offensive. Meanwhile, he considered bombing the Yalu bridges "essential" to prevent the CCF buildup. That action was so "plainly defensive," he said, that it was "hard to conceive that would cause an increase in the volume of local intervention or, of itself, provoke a general war." He assured the JCS that he would not violate the Manchurian or Soviet borders or destroy hydroelectric installations.[71]

That same day MacArthur appeared to challenge another aspect of American policy in Korea. "Hostile planes," he said in a separate cable, "are operating from bases west of the Yalu River against our forces in North Korea." These planes were increasing in number; they were hitting FEAF's planes, then skipping back across the Yalu. "The present restrictions imposed on my area of operations," MacArthur went on, "provide a complete sanctuary for hostile air immediately upon their crossing the Manchurian–North Korean border. The effect of this abnormal condition upon the morale and combat efficiency of both air and ground troops is major." Unless "corrective measures were promptly taken," MacArthur continued, "the air problem could assume serious proportions."[72]

The JCS agreed with MacArthur that the new, Soviet-furnished Chinese Air Force should not be allowed a "complete" or "privileged" sanctuary. Logically the Chinese air threat could be eliminated by authorizing MacArthur to bomb CCF air bases in Manchuria. However, this would be a significant "widening of the war," and it could lead to Chinese Air Force retaliation on American airfields in Korea (or carriers at sea) which had thus far also enjoyed a "sanctuary." Accordingly, the JCS recommendation was restrictive: that FEAF fighters be permitted "hot pursuit" for "six or eight" miles inside Manchuria, considered sufficient for purpose of shooting down the hit-and-run MIGs. Dean Acheson and George Marshall approved this recommendation and put it on the agenda for the November 9 NSC meeting.[73]

In the meantime, within the White House, State, Pentagon, and elsewhere there was powerful sentiment to halt MacArthur's forces at the narrow neck of Korea and attempt to settle the Korean problem by negotiations and diplomacy. Those who held this view argued that owing to the virtually unlimited manpower at its disposal, Peking was in a position to feed masses of soldiers into North Korea almost indefinitely, thwarting the unification of Korea by force of arms and tying down substantial American military resources in a nonstrategic area. Possibly Moscow was at the point of launching global war, and the CCF entry into North Korea had been conceived as a strategic diversion.[74]

There was another matter which could not be ignored. Casualties suffered by American forces in Korea were again mounting sharply. The total was near 30,000. Yet another offensive could incur as many as 10,000 more. For many months the citizenry had been remarkably complacent over these losses. But the defeat of the Democrats in the November 7 elections indicated a growing dissatisfaction. It was possible that the dissatisfaction could escalate into open rebellion. The Army could not successfully fight a war in Asia or anywhere else without popular support.[75]

On November 8, in preparation for the next day's NSC meeting on Korea, the JCS cabled MacArthur to obtain his very latest views. The JCS stated that in light of CCF intervention in Korea, MacArthur's mission "may have to be re-examined." The JCS signaled the growing sentiment for a negotiated settlement.[76]

MacArthur's reply arrived in Washington early on the morning of November 9. It was a withering blast that again stood Washington on its ear.

In my opinion it would be fatal to weaken the fundamental and basic policy of the United Nations to destroy all resisting armed forces in Korea and bring that country into a unified and free nation. I believe that with my air power . . . I can deny reinforcements coming across the Yalu in sufficient strength to prevent the destruction of those forces now arrayed against me in North Korea.

I plan to launch my attack for this purpose on or about November 15th with the mission of driving to the border and securing all of North Korea. Any program short of this would completely destroy the morale of my forces and the psychological consequences would be inestimable. It would condemn us to an indefinite retention of our military forces along difficult defense lines in North Korea and would unquestionably arouse such resentment among the South Koreans that their forces would collapse and might even turn against us. It would therefore necessitate immediately a large increment in foreign troops. That the Chinese Communists after having achieved complete success in establishing themselves in North Korea would abide by any delimitations upon further expansion southward would represent wishful thinking.[77]

Having heard that the British were urging a halt at the narrow neck of Korea—and possibly that Acheson, Marshall, and the JCS were leaning toward that course—MacArthur devoted three paragraphs to denouncing it in vitriolic language. He ridiculed the idea as a "British desire to appease the Chinese Communists" which found "its historic precedent in the action taken at Munich." If adopted by the UN, it would be a "tribute to aggression which encourages that very international lawlessness which it is the fundamental duty of the United Nations to curb."

The penultimate paragraph was no doubt aimed directly at Truman:

To give up any portion of North Korea to the aggression of the Chinese Communists would be the greatest defeat of the free world in recent times. Indeed to yield to so immoral a proposition would bankrupt our leadership and influence in Asia and render untenable our position both politically and militarily. We would follow closely in the footsteps of the British who by the appeasement of recognition [of Red China] lost all the respect of all the rest of Asia without gaining that of the Chinese segment. It would not curb deterioration of the present situation into the possibility of general war but would impose upon us the disadvantage of having inevitably to fight such a war if it occurs bereft of the support of countless Asiatics who now believe in us and are eager to fight with us.

He concluded by recommending that Washington press for a UN resolution condemning Chinese Communist aggression in Korea and demanding that the Chinese withdraw behind their border "on pain of military sanctions" by the UN if they failed to do so. "I recommend," he signed off, "with all the earnestness that I possess that there be no weakening at this crucial moment and that we press on to complete victory which I believe can be achieved if our determination and indomitable will do not desert us."

President Truman was in the depths of despair. The Republicans had won big in the off-year election, gaining five seats in the Senate and twenty-eight in the House. The Democrats retained a two-vote majority in the Senate, but three prominent and powerful Democrats in that body had been defeated. The many liberal measures Truman contemplated for the next two years had been placed in jeopardy. Aboard the presidential yacht *Williamsburg* on election night Truman, his biographer Robert Donovan wrote, was drunker (on bourbon) and "more dejected" than anyone had ever seen him.[78]

When the NSC met on the afternoon of November 9 to hammer out new policies and courses of action in Korea, President Truman was not present. He wrote in his memoirs that he was "unable" to attend. By that time those who were present—Acheson, Marshall, Bradley, others—had received MacArthur's cable as well as formal recommendations from the JCS. The two papers were distinctly at odds. MacArthur, in effect, recommended an all-out fight with the CCF; the JCS recommended that "every effort should be expended as a matter of urgency" to solve the problem by "political means."[79]

The JCS did not, however, recommend that MacArthur cancel his offensive and hold at the narrow neck of the peninsula. Such a course would cede ground gained by American blood to the enemy. It would appear vacillatory, defeatist, and weak. It might cause another ROK stampede. Inasmuch as MacArthur had opposed this course in the most strident language, it could conceivably lead to his resignation and an unprecedented public furor.

The chiefs recommended that "pending further clarification as to the military objectives of the Chinese Communists and the extent of their political commitments," MacArthur's mission (or directive) "should be kept under review, but should not be changed"—that is, that MacArthur be allowed to "continue the action" so long as there appeared to be "a reasonable chance of success." With little discussion the conferees adopted, word for word, the JCS position. All effort would be made, as a matter of urgency, to settle the Korean problem by political negotiations. Meanwhile, MacArthur would be free to continue military operations, including the Eighth Army offensive, as he saw fit. The important—and urgent—issue of hot pursuit was deferred—and later prohibited by Truman, mainly on the insistent recommendation of the British.[80]

This large concession to MacArthur proved to be one of the worst mistakes in American history—and indisputably the worst of Truman's presidency. In their memoirs Acheson and Bradley dealt with it candidly. "All the president's advisers in this matter," Acheson wrote, "civilian and military, knew that something was badly wrong, though what it was, how to find out, and what to do about it, they muffed. . . . None of us, myself prominently included, served him as he was entitled to be served." Bradley wrote: "We read, we sat, we deliberated and, unfortunately, we reached drastically wrong conclusions and decisions. . . . The JCS should have taken firmest control of the Korean War and dealt with MacArthur bluntly. . . . At the very least the chiefs should have canceled MacArthur's planned offensive. Instead we let ourselves be misled by MacArthur's wildly erroneous estimates of the situation and his eloquent rhetoric, as well as by too much wishful thinking of our own."[81]

The advice was bad, but the ultimate blame was Truman's. The war in Korea and MacArthur's challenges that week demanded his undivided—and utmost—attention. Badly rattled by the election, deeply depressed, and no doubt preoccupied with ways and means to stem McCarthyism and rescue his legislative programs from almost certain defeat, Truman evidently did not give Korea and MacArthur the time and thought these issues deserved. Strategic vision, decisive leadership, and a resolute decision to face up to CCF intervention and the "MacArthur problem" were not forthcoming from the White House during this crucial week.

In retrospect, President Truman told an interviewer: "What we should have done is stop at the neck of Korea. . . . That's what the British wanted. . . . We knew the Chinese had close to a million men on the border and all that. . . . But [MacArthur] was commander in the field. You pick your man, you've got to back him up. That's the only way a military organization can work. I got the best advice I could and the man on the spot said this was the thing to do. . . . So I agreed. That was my decision—no matter what hindsight shows."[82]

\* \* \*

Having gained full clearance from Washington to continue the war on his own terms, MacArthur drew plans and issued instructions for what he believed would be the final stages of operations. These would entail two major military efforts: FEAF's all-out air assault designed to "isolate the battlefield," followed by all-out ground attacks by Eighth Army and X Corps. Owing to the onset of cold weather, for which Eighth Army and X Corps were not prepared, these plans were to be carried out with utmost haste. The Eighth Army attack would be launched on November 15 and, by MacArthur's schedule, conclude at the Yalu River border about November 25.

The first FEAF priority was to knock out the Yalu bridges and stop the supposed flow of the CCF into North Korea. The most important of these bridges were the three at Sinuiju, where, it was believed, the bulk of the southbound CCF traffic crossed. The attack there, which Washington had canceled, then approved, was remounted on November 8. Some seventy B-29 bombers, heavily escorted by fighters, carried out the mission from an altitude of 18,000 feet against heavy antiaircraft fire and attacking MIG fighters. One MIG was shot down, the first of the war.

Ironically, this much debated, politically sensitive attack failed; not one bomb hit the bridges. Follow-up attacks the next day by carrier-based naval dive-bombers knocked out one span on the "Korean end" of the highway bridge, but repeated attacks in subsequent days by FEAF and Navy planes failed to knock out the other two bridges. On November 19, when the Yalu River at Sinuiju froze over, the surviving two bridges lost their importance, and subsequently, air attacks at Sinuiju were curtailed, then finally stopped.[83]

Elsewhere within the target zone, FEAF and carrier-based aircraft were hardly more effective. Upriver from Sinuiju three other Yalu bridges were knocked out, but the CCF replaced them with pontoon bridges. FEAF bombs leveled or burned out seventeen cities or towns, killing and maiming untold thousands of civilians. But these raids completely missed the CCF troops, all of whom were hiding in the hills or elsewhere. Air Force reconnaissance outfits—sadly neglected in the prewar budget squeezes and operating with poor equipment—utterly failed to detect the well-camouflaged CCF.[84]

Perhaps misled by overenthusiastic reports from Stratemeyer and his airmen, MacArthur believed this all-out air attack was achieving its aim. In Tokyo he bragged to visiting Ambassador Muccio that FEAF "was destroying all resources in the narrow stretch between our present positions and the border." He added: "Unfortunately, this area will be left a desert." Apparently he also believed the air attacks had stopped the flow of the CCF into North Korea. He told Muccio that he was "sure" that the CCF had sent "certainly no more than 30,000 soldiers across the border." As a result, MacArthur crowed, when Eighth Army went on the offensive, all of North Korea would be "cleared within ten days."[85]

*　*　*

Meanwhile, Johnnie Walker prepared for Eighth Army's final offensive. Chastened by his first encounter with the CCF, Walker was determined to conduct operations with greatest care and with all the manpower he could possibly muster, including even the most recently arrived UN forces in Korea. In all, he would employ seven-plus divisions, backed by an unprecedented array of artillery, tanks, and other supporting forces.

Walker's logistical situation was still not good. He needed 4,000 tons of supplies a day to mount the offensive; he was receiving only about half that amount. There were now four bridges over the Han River—one railway and three pontoon—but there was a bottleneck at the Imjin River, and a 3,000-foot railway bridge over the Taedong River in Pyongyang was not yet finished. The minesweeping at Chinnampo had begun on November 2, but it had been hampered by high tides, swift currents, storms, and cold weather. A shallow-draft LST successfully entered Chinnampo on November 10, but another ten days were to go by before the first deep-draft transport could enter the port. Owing to these delays, Walker still had to rely on the emergency airlift, which produced about 1,000 tons a day.[86]

Because of these logistical problems, Walker was compelled to postpone his offensive by a full eight days—from November 15 to Friday, November 24, the day after Thanksgiving. In explaining the delay to Washington, MacArthur put the blame on Walker. However, he had good news for the JCS. "The air attack of the last ten days," MacArthur boasted, "has been largely success-ful in isolating the battle area from added reinforcement and has greatly diminished the enemy flow of supplies."[87]

# 15

# "LAND HAPPY"

## I

While Johnnie Walker's Eighth Army, at the Chongchon River, prepared for its big offensive, Ned Almond's X Corps, operating independently in northeast Korea, continued its "land happy" campaign, spreading itself far and wide. Its strength was significantly enhanced by the arrival of the Army's 18,000-man 3d Infantry Division, composed of the 7th, 15th, and Puerto Rican 65th regiments, which disembarked at Wonsan between November 7 and 15.[1]

The 3d Division was commanded by a feisty, pint-size paratrooper, Robert H. Soule, fifty. Born in Laramie, Wyoming, Soule had attended the University of Wyoming for two years and obtained a reserve commission in 1918. Ordered to the Philippines, Soule had been assigned to the 31st Infantry Regiment, which was sent, along with the 27th Infantry, to Vladivostok as part of an Allied expeditionary force to help the Russian White Army fight the Bolshevik Red Army in Siberia. Thus Soule had earned the distinction of being one of the "first American Army officials to fight communists" and was one of the few who had a working knowledge of the Russian language.[2]

This indoctrination into the ideological turmoil of the Far East apparently fascinated Soule. In 1930 he returned to Asia for a three-year tour as a Chinese-language student in Peking. In 1933 he extended his tour in China to a total of six consecutive years by serving a three-year stint in the 15th Infantry. During those years he observed the civil war between the Nationalists and Communists from close up and became fluent in the Chinese language.

Early in World War II, when George Marshall decided to create additional paratrooper units, he chose the artillery commander of Ridgway's 82d Airborne Division, Joseph M. Swing, to command the 11th Airborne Division. Swing in turn handpicked Soule to be commander of the 188th Glider Regiment. Soule, who then underwent paratrooper training, became a dedicated "Swing man" during the 11th Airborne Division's long, arduous jungle fighting in the Southwest Pacific under MacArthur's command. After the 11th had helped recapture Manila, Swing (with MacArthur's concurrence) promoted Soule to one star and ADC of the division.[3]

In 1947, after the war, Soule returned to China with the military group advising Chiang Kai-shek. This tour gave Soule not only a ringside seat at Mao Tse-tung's great military victory but also an inside view of the Communist consolidation over the country in the next six months. As a result, probably no American government official was more up-to-date about Red China than Soule.

Soule was about five feet six inches and therefore nicknamed Shorty. One war correspondent, Stan Swinton, characterized him as a "human dynamo" who "jeeps over rutted beachhead roads at least five hours a day visiting his front line doughboys." His motto, Swinton reported, was "Get tough." His oft-repeated advice to his men was "Shoot back. As long as you're firing at them they're not going to shoot at you." One of his battalion commanders said: "Like all small people, he was very, very aggressive."[4]

Soule was very much Almond's kind of general, but there was a problem. Soule had a fondness for the bottle. One of his regimental commanders remembered: "Every night he got drunk. It only took two drinks for him to get loaded. I'd have relieved him." One of his battalion commanders agreed: "He was drinking too much. He'd go into his tent at night, pick up the phone, and issue crazy orders. Apparently his staff couldn't stop him."[5]

Fortunately the division had been assigned a capable ADC and chief of staff. The former was West Pointer (1924) Armistead D. Mead, forty-nine; the latter, West Pointer (1922) Oliver P. Newman, fifty-one. In World War II Mead had been the G-3 of Bill Simpson's Ninth Army in the ETO. Both Eisenhower and Bradley believed the Ninth Army staff to be the best in the ETO. Mead had won a DSM for his contribution. No less capable, Newman had been a regimental commander and chief of staff of the 41st Division in the Pacific. Both men were on their way to two stars. "We finessed Soule's drunken nighttime orders by dealing with Mead and Newman," a 3d Division regimental commander remembered.[6]

\* \* \*

The Puerto Rican 65th Infantry led the 3d Division ashore at Wonsan on November 5, hard on the heels of the Marines. The regiment had been established in 1899, when, in the wake of the Spanish-American War, Puerto

Rico became a United States territory. The senior commanders and about half of the junior commanders were "continentals," but the ranks were composed mostly of Puerto Rican nationals and other Latins, many of them of mixed blood, many of them blacks. Although the regiment was incorporated into the Regular Army, it had served over the years principally in the role of a "home" guard. In World War II it had been shipped to Italy to fight in Mark Clark's Fifth Army, but it was not trusted and was therefore never committed to combat. In the postwar years it had been cut back to two battalions, but upon assignment to Korea a third battalion from the 33d Infantry in Panama had been added.[7]

The commander of the 65th was West Pointer (1930), William W. Harris, forty-three. During World War II Harris had been a staff planner in the Mediterranean Theater and did not command troops in combat. After a post-war tour in the supply service, to his utter dismay, he was given command of the 65th in 1949. He wrote: "I was outraged at what I considered being sent to pasture for two years to command what the Pentagon brass referred to as a 'rum and Coca-Cola' outfit. . . . There was no question about it in my mind, the Pentagon was relegating me to obscurity."[8]

As it turned out, however, Harris came to admire the people and the spirit he found in this offbeat outfit, and he was soon its most ardent booster. He encouraged "Latin pride" by rescinding the standing orders of his predecessor that anyone speaking Spanish would be court-martialed, and he fought to overturn Army racial discrimination, which had barred Puerto Rican officers from the Infantry School and Command and General Staff College. He in-stituted tough discipline and field training. One result was that in an exercise, Portrex, conducted on Vieques Island in early 1950, the 65th "beat" the "invaders" of the 3d Division.[9]

When the 65th landed at Wonsan, Harris encountered strong skepticism and racial prejudice, notably from Ned Almond, who had seen his own all-black 92d Division fail in Italy and who knew that Puerto Rican troops in Italy had been denied combat and relegated to service, ceremonial, or other duties. As Harris remembered, Almond came up, looked the outfit over, then said he "didn't have much confidence in these colored troops." Harris conceded that he had some "colored" Puerto Ricans and Virgin Islanders in the regiment but protested that his troops were not "colored"; they were mostly "white." More-over, in the six weeks of mopping-up and occupation duty the 65th had seen in South Korea, his men had "fought like real troops."[10]

These arguments apparently made little impression on Almond. He con-tinued to display small confidence in the 65th and to think of it mostly as "colored" and therefore unreliable. He ordered the Puerto Ricans to be mated with the 3d Division's black 58th Armored FAB, commanded by West Pointer (1940), all-American football player, and team captain Harry A.

Stella. In addition, in its initial operations the 65th was supported by the 3d Division's black 999th FAB, commanded by West Pointer (1935) Kenneth F. Dawalt.[11]*

As it happened, the 3d Division's 64th Tank Battalion was also "black" (mostly white officers, black enlisted men). It traced its lineage back to the "first" black tank battalion of World War II, the 785th, which had gone overseas to Italy, assigned to Almond's 92d Division. In the postwar years it had been redesignated the 64th Heavy Tank Battalion and assigned to the 2d Armored Division. It was commanded by forty-year-old West Pointer (1933) William G. Bartlett, whose father and grandfather were West Pointers. Early in his career Bartlett had chosen the cavalry, but after mastering the French language, he had served in the OSS in World War II and had been assigned to Army intelligence duties after the war. He had not before commanded troops—or tanks—in combat.[12]

*　*　*

The commander of the Puerto Rican 65th, William Harris, found his introduction to the X Corps staff bizarre and unsettling. Invited to dinner in its posh mess, Harris was surprised to be greeted by the G-4, West Pointer (1930) Aubrey D. Smith, who was a classmate and one of Harris's closest friends. Smith was married to Dorothy Krueger, daughter of retired four-star General Walter Krueger, who had commanded MacArthur's Sixth Army throughout the war in the Southwest Pacific. Harris wrote that Aubrey Smith was "probably the most outspoken officer I ever knew" and that because of his status as son-in-law to Krueger, he had "few inhibitions around officers of very senior rank."[13]

Before dinner Smith privately revealed to Harris the dangerous mission Almond had conceived for the 65th Infantry. It was to go north to Yonghung, then "west" sixty or seventy miles across the peninsula to make contact with Eighth Army's right flank near Tokchon. The news made Harris's "hair stand on end" and put him in such a "state of trauma and fidgets" that he broke into a "cold sweat" and "couldn't sleep at night." Later, at dinner with Almond and his chief of staff, Nick Ruffner, and senior X Corps staffers who outlined the mission in greater detail, Harris "did manage to keep my cool," but Smith, as was his habit, spoke freely. "Bill," he said to Harris in front of Almond and Ruffner, "I wouldn't go where you are being sent unless the corps commander gave me written orders to do so and at least four infantry divisions. . . . Unless

---

*The 999th FAB was substituting for the 3d Division's 9th FAB, which earlier had been sent to Korea to support ROKs. Equipped with eighteen 155-mm self-propelled howitzers mounted on tank hulls, the 999th often was to be employed in northeast Korea as "corps artillery," augmenting the 92d and 96th FABs of X Corps, which were similarly equipped.

you are crazier than I think you are, if you go out there on those missions, they'll eat you alive."[14]*

Believing that he faced a suicidal mission, Harris nonetheless rushed the 65th to Yonghung, piecemeal and without adequate ammo, with Almond breathing down his neck and "heckling me." The outfit was typically fragmented by Almond, who, without notifying Harris, split off the 1/65 and 3/65 to relieve some of the Marines at Wonsan and continue operations against bypassed NKPA and guerrillas. The result was that the 2/65, commanded by forty-year-old Herman W. Dammer, who had commanded a battalion at Anzio, and Dawalt's 999th FAB were ambushed and overrun by an NKPA raid on the way to Yonghung. In this wild melee, Harris wrote, the 2/65 (and the 65th headquarters) were surrounded and cut off and had to be "saved" by a FEAF airdrop.[16]

When he had finally assembled his full regiment at Yonghung on November 13, Harris struck west into wild, mountainous country toward Kwangchon. Believing the whole venture "was crazy," Harris remembered that he advanced "gingerly at first—on tiptoe, so to speak."[17]

\* \* \*

The 15th Infantry, which came from Fort Benning, landed next at Wonsan on November 11. It was commanded by Dennis M. ("Dinty") Moore, who celebrated his fiftieth birthday on October 2, while the regiment was in temporary training in Japan. It was mated with the 39th FAB, commanded by West Pointer (1933) Robert B. Neely, forty-one.[18]

Dinty Moore, a veteran of World War I, entered West Point in 1920 with the class of 1924. In the early days of World War II, while serving as a G-2 in the Philippines, he was with the Americans who surrendered on Bataan, and he served three years in Japanese POW camps. That grim experience ground him down mentally and physically. He was "austere" and "imperious," totally lacking in charisma. A senior West Pointer remembered: "I think the time in POW camps affected his brain. He was also kind of pooped-out, physically, when he got to Korea." A junior reserve officer, new to the regiment, Henry P. Russe, remembered: "He was tall, lean, with a beaky nose, rheumy eyes, wrinkled face, and silver hair—*old.* "[19]

Moore was backed up by an able exec, Thomas R. Yancey, forty-two. A Missourian, Yancey was a graduate of Kemper Military School and Central Missouri State University (1930) and had a master's degree in history and political science from the University of Missouri (1937). Mobilized for World

---

*When Aubrey Smith was later rotated to Japan, his wife, Dorothy, apparently under the influence of drugs, murdered him. Tried by a military court, she was found guilty and sent to prison.[15]

War II in a Missouri National Guard unit, Yancey was later assigned to intelligence duties in Hawaii and, oddly, wound up as an assistant G-2 in the Marine Corps V Amphibious Corps. As such he had fought the war with the Marine Corps, participating in its landings in the Marshalls, the Marianas, and finally Iwo Jima and Okinawa. In the postwar years he had joined the Regular Army and had been serving continuously with infantry units. "He was a strong officer—really dominating—and with good credentials," one 15th Infantry battalion commander said. "Tom Yancey ran the regiment, rather than Dinty Moore."[20]

During its postwar service at Fort Benning the two battalions of the 15th Infantry (1/15 and 3/15) had provided manpower for the Infantry School student officers to conduct war games in the field. When the Korean War broke out, the 1/15 had been gutted to provide replacements for other Korea-bound units. Alerted for Korea, the 15th Infantry had fielded a third battalion (the 2/15) made up of men from the other units, called-up reservists, and draftees. The 1/15 was commanded by West Pointer (1933) Robert M. Blanchard, Jr., forty-one; the 2/15, by West Pointer (1936) Allen L. Peck, forty. Like his boss Dinty Moore, Peck had been captured on Bataan and served out the war as a prisoner of the Japanese. But Peck had survived in far better mental and physical shape than Moore.[21]

The 3/15 was "black." It was commanded by another Missourian and graduate of Kemper Military School, Milburn N. ("Mel") Huston, forty, who had graduated from the University of Missouri (1933) with a degree in journalism and an ROTC commission. In the 1930s, while on temporary active duty, Huston had commanded a company of blacks in the CCC. In World War II he first manned a war planning desk in the War Department, then joined Gee Gerow's V Corps, landing on Omaha Beach with 1st Division elements. Later he briefly served with the 38th Infantry of the 2d Division, then went to China for the final days of the war. In the postwar years he helped establish the CIA, witnessed the AEC A-bomb test Sandstone and attended the Armed Forces Staff College. He had assumed command of the 3/15 from Ned Almond's deputy chief of staff and confidant, Bill McCaffrey, in June 1950.[22]

Inasmuch as the blacks of the 3/15 had been serving at Fort Benning as demonstration troops for the students or in menial service chores and the battalion was drastically short of equipment and was black, there was serious doubt about sending it to Korea. Conceding the outfit was "in no way fit" for combat, Huston nonetheless argued that with a substantial "augmentation" of white officers, a full allotment of equipment, and hard training at Benning and in Japan, he thought he could get the battalion ready for combat in time. When Dinty Moore and his superiors finally approved, Huston inaugurated a tough calisthenics program, scrounged weapons, and, most important, he believed, received sixteen white officers, half of whom went to the battalion staff, the other half to command the heavy weapons (mortars, machine guns, recoilless rifles) of the skeletal M Company.[23]

In its shakedown at Benning and later in Japan Huston evaluated his white and black officers and switched them around. The upshot was that I Company, led by Harold A. Jenkins, was commanded entirely by black officers, including Harry E. Sutton, formerly of the elite "Triple Nickles" parachute battalion. K and L companies were commanded by whites (Eric L. Hahn and Richard F. Morgan), presiding over a mixture of black and white staffers and platoon leaders. The key jobs in M Company, led by John C. Seabury, were retained by whites. Huston's aim in placing all black officers in I Company, he remembered, was to promote "competition" between it and the white-led K and L companies.[24]

Under Mel Huston's spirited leadership the 3/15 finally arrived in Wonsan in "good" shape. In manpower it was strong: a total of 1,300 men, including 600 ROKs and 400 new enlisted black fillers picked up in Japan. Dinty Moore officially commended Huston for the fine job of building and training the battalion and getting the men in good physical condition and for expeditiously guiding it during its hurried and difficult journey from Fort Benning to Japan to Korea. For his part Huston was forgiving of Dinty Moore's "peculiar" leadership. He thought Moore was "gutsy" to return to Korea, where as a Japanese POW Moore "had done a lot of time being humiliated by the Japs in rice paddies and other demeaning labor."[25]

The incorporation of 600 ROKs into the black 3/15 gave rise to an unexpected problem. Bernard W. Abrams, a white West Pointer (1947) in M Company, remembered: "The Koreans went on strike during training, claiming that the black soldiers discriminated against them because they were yellow in complexion. This claim was based on the fact that the Koreans felt the food they were being given was not as good as the Americans' food." The "strike" was broken up, Abrams remembered, by the M Company first sergeant, who was "six feet, six inches tall and weighed 300 pounds and who carried a shepherd's staff." The first sergeant actually flailed the ROKs out of their tents with the staff, but the blacks of the 3/15 never developed much confidence in these ROKs, most of whom were illiterate and many of whom had been shanghaied off the streets of Seoul.[26]

The arrival of the 15th Infantry significantly increased the number of "colored" units under Ned Almond's command. In his view of the racial makeup, the Puerto Rican 65th Infantry was to all intents and purposes "black." The 58th FAB supporting it was black. The 64th Tank Battalion was black. The 999th FAB was black. In sum, there were seven "black" battalions in the 3d Division; four infantry, two artillery, and one tank. Most of the blacks remained strictly segregated—and, in Almond's view, not fully trustworthy.

* * *

Upon landing, Dinty Moore's 15th Infantry, mated with Neely's 39th FAB, was assigned to relieve Chesty Puller's First Marines in the Wonsan area and provide "mopping-up" protection for the port, assisted by several ROK battalions. Inasmuch as the mountains to the west and south of Wonsan were still crawling with bypassed NKPA troops, this mopping up proved to be an arduous and dangerous chore. The 3d Division historian wrote:

It became apparent that the Division was engaged in something considerably more extensive than had been anticipated. The strength of the NKPA remnants and guerrillas in the area seemingly had been underestimated. . . . Men in every [3d Division] unit learned the bitter taste of ambush, the sudden shock of receiving burp-gun fire from darkness or other concealment. They learned that there was not a moment during which they were completely safe from sneak attack, never a time when danger could not appear from any point of the compass.[27]

Dinty Moore sent Robert Blanchard's 1/15 due west to relieve a Marine battalion which had been fighting bypassed NKPA soldiers for more than two weeks. Assigned to the G-2 section of First Army in the ETO in World War II, Blanchard had not commanded troops in combat, but in the postwar years he had served a tour in Greece, advising Greek forces in their mountain war against the Communist guerrillas. Inasmuch as the 1/15 had been serving as "school troops" at Fort Benning, Blanchard remembered only half in jest: "I was more up-to-date on infantry tactics than the generals were." He continued:

Chesty Puller warned me of the problem—that we'd get shot up. We went west—delayed by a blown bridge which we rebuilt—then relieved the Marines. There were about 2,000 NKPA in the hills. They would attack us at night, then we'd attack them in the daylight. This went on for days and days. Dinty Moore came up during one of these attacks and huddled in a corner. I think he was sort of shell-shocked. Finally we got word that a CCF division was bearing down on us. This was followed by seven consecutive changes of orders from Dinty Moore: "Pull back half way." "Stay put." "Pull out, but leave one company." "Leave two companies." "Stay put," and so on, until finally, "Pull out."[28]

Allen Peck's 2/15 also relieved one of Puller's First Marine battalions. Almost immediately (November 15) Peck suffered a grievous loss in his E Company: an idolized platoon leader, West Pointer (1950) John C. Trent, who had been a star player on the academy's 1948 undefeated football team. A departing Marine officer, William B. Hopkins, wrote that Trent's body was being escorted to the rear by a weeping master sergeant with a thick southern accent, who blamed the fouled-up fight that killed Trent on the incompetence or panic or even perfidy of the ROKs attached to the 2/15. "I been in this man's Army mor'n half my life," Hopkins quoted the sergeant as saying, "and this is the most fucked-up unit I ever seen. We burnt out three machine-gun barrels last night, and nobody ain't seen . . . [no enemy]. . . . Trouble is we'll never know whether he [Trent] got kilt accidental or on purpose. Cain't nobody say there ain't some gooks among them ROKs."[29]

\* \* \*

Mel Huston's black 3/15, too, relieved a Marine unit to the west of Wonsan. On November 19, after settling into a strong perimeter, Huston's K Company boldly struck from the perimeter to attack an NKPA force which appeared to be assembling to attack the perimeter. In this action K Company soon found itself in difficulty. White platoon leader John W. Timmins, Jr. (Citadel, 1949), until recently aide to 3d Division ADC Armistead Mead, became "overly aggressive" and "exposed himself heroically" (as Huston put it) and was killed with several others. Timmins's heroism, however, enabled K Company to get out of trouble and back to the perimeter. Timmins, who won a posthumous Silver Star, was enshrined as the 3/15's "first hero" in Korea.[30]

Several days later Mel Huston was shocked to find himself "abruptly relieved of command." Although no explanation was given, the relief ("without prejudice") generated much controversy and speculation. Some thought it came about because the ADC, Mead, was angry and grieved at the loss of his former aide. Others thought it was because of a clash between the 15th's commander, Dinty Moore, and Huston. The 15th Infantry exec, Tom Yancey, remembered that the two officers "got into it." Whatever the reason, Huston left immediately, replaced by the young but highly decorated and charismatic exec of the 2/15, Edward L. Farrell, Jr., thirty. Perhaps "rescued" by Ned Almond's deputy chief of staff and confidant, Bill McCaffrey (who had preceded Huston as commander of the 3/15 at Benning), Huston was assigned to the G-2 section of X Corps, but he was to go on to a more important job in Korea and, ultimately, to a star.[31]

\* \* \*

The third and final regiment of the 3d Division, the 7th Infantry, which had come from Fort Devens, Massachusetts, by way of Japan, landed at Wonsan on November 17. It was commanded by West Pointer (1930) John S. Guthrie, forty-two.\* Its artillery support was the 10th FAB, commanded by West Pointer (1933) Walter A. ("Bing") Downing, Jr., forty-three.[32]

---

\*At that time, five of the six Army regimental commanders in X Corps were West Point graduates, Herb Powell of the 17th Infantry being the exception. Four of them (Beauchamp, Guthrie, Harris, and MacLean) were from the class of 1930. Excluding Powell (47) and Moore (50), their average age was 42.5 years.

Grandson of a Civil War general and son of a West Point (1901) colonel, Guthrie had been reared in the bosom of the Army establishment and had married the daughter of a West Point colonel. During World War II he had been stuck in troop training assignments until early 1944, when he was sent to North Africa to become G-3 of Sandy Patch's Seventh Army. Six months later that army had landed in southern France, per Guthrie's meticulously drawn (and highly successful) plan, which earned him a Distinguished Service Medal and a temporary star. Although he had commanded the 7th Infantry for about one year, Guthrie had not previously led troops in combat.[33]

The 7th Infantry, too, had been earlier and "relentlessly" gutted of men and units for Korea, including Johnny Johnson's battalion, which had wound up in Korea assigned to the 8th Cav. The 7th had been frantically rebuilt almost day by day with an infusion of men from the deactivated 30th Infantry at Benning, called-up reservists, and draftees. In Japan it had also received about 2,000 illiterate, untrained ROK fillers. Guthrie remembered: "We received some fine American NCOs and men from the Army Reserve, most of whom were World War II veterans, although when we moved to Korea we still had woefully few Americans to train and supervise the Koreans."[34]

After all the gutting, the 7th Infantry arrived in Korea with a fine exec but with three lackluster battalion commanders who were short on combat experience and soon had to be replaced. The exec was West Pointer (1933) James O. Boswell, forty, a "brilliant," well-educated (M.A., Harvard, 1941) officer, who was fully qualified to command the regiment. The 1/7 was commanded by Charles T. Heinrich, who Guthrie remembered was a "stubborn, Germanic" officer with slight combat experience, who "did things his own way, right or wrong." The 2/7 was led by West Pointer (1937) Robert Besson (whose older brother Frank, from the West Point class of 1932, was to rise to four stars). Besson had won a DSC early in World War II in the Philippines but had spent most of the war as a prisoner of the Japanese and was still "frail" from the experience. The 3/7 was commanded by forty-year-old West Pointer (1934) Thomas A. O'Neil, who had been a rear-area staff officer in World War II.[35]

All in all, Guthrie later judged, the 7th Infantry was about "50 percent" ready for combat. As in the 15th Infantry, one of its biggest problems was overcoming the language barrier and assimilating its large contingent of ROKs. "There *is* no language problem," Shorty Soule insisted to John Guthrie. "I will not *accept* a language problem."

Guthrie replied, "Yes, sir, General. There is no language problem. But we better tell that to the American GIs out there so they know."[36]

When the 7th Infantry got ashore, Ned Almond directed Shorty Soule to place its three battalions in reserve: two battalions for the 3d Division; one for X Corps. John Guthrie established his CP at Kowon, a village about midway

between Wonsan and Hamhung. At Kowon Bob Besson's 2/7 and Tom O'-
Neil's 3/7 relieved the 2/65, which rejoined its parent unit, then preparing for
its perilous solo attack west to "link" with Eighth Army. Charles Heinrich's
1/7 went to X Corps in Hamhung.[37]

* * *

There were many shortcomings in the 3d Division. It had been
slapped together hurriedly with disparate elements coming from a variety of
locations. Until arriving at Wonsan and absorbing the Puerto Rican 65th
Regiment, it had not functioned as a composite unit. Other than the 65th, its
regiments had had little realistic training. The 7th and 15th regiments had been
assigned thousands of ROKs in Japan, who were viewed as a mixed blessing.

Yet the 3d Division played a useful role at a critical time in X Corps
history. It relieved the 1st Marine Division of responsibility for ensuring the
safety of Wonsan and Hungnam and the coastline between those places. This
enabled O. P. Smith to reassign Chesty Puller's First Marines and Ray Murray's Fifth Marines, and other division elements, to reinforce Homer Litzenberg's Seventh Marines, which, on November 15, reached the village of
Hagaru at the Chosin Reservoir. Smith still viewed his mission with deepest
misgivings, but the addition of the First and Fifth Marines to the task at least
provided him forces to outpost the long, tortuous Hamhung–Hagaru road.

II

In Tokyo MacArthur's G-3, Pinky Wright, became increasingly concerned
over the operations of X Corps. As the Army historian put it, Wright and his
planners "did not like the look of the situation in northeast Korea and did not
completely endorse Almond's plan for operating there." Almond had fragmented X Corps across a huge front.[38]

Wright was not alone in his concern. Marine General O. P. Smith became
so worried over the fragmentation and dispersion of units in X Corps that he
took the extraordinary step of writing a personal letter to Marine Commandant Clifton Cates to complain. "I do not like the prospect of stringing out a
Marine division along a single mountain road for 120 air miles from Hamhung
to the border," Smith wrote. "There is a continual splitting up of units and
assignment of missions to small units which puts them out on a limb" with
"disregard for the integrity of units and the time and space factor. . . . Mani-
festly we should not push on without regard to the Eighth Army. We would
simply get farther out on a limb."[39]

Pinky Wright directed his planners to analyze the situation and recommend courses of action. One suggestion soon emerged: the possibility of direct-

ing X Corps to deemphasize its widespread drive to the Yalu River and attack in force due west in a consolidated formation from the Chosin Reservoir to Mupyong (forty air miles). If successful, this maneuver could cut an important Communist road and railroad running south from Manpojin (on the Yalu) along the Chongchon River valley to CCF/NKPA positions facing Walker's ROK II Corps near Kunu. It would also threaten the entire rear of the enemy facing Eighth Army.

The more Wright studied this idea, the more he became enamored of it. Yet he was reluctant to urge it because it was politically hazardous. The mission would tend to diminish X Corps's role to one of "supporting" Eighth Army. Moreover, if the maneuver led to a merger of Eighth Army and X Corps (as it must, inevitably), the thorny problem of the hostile Walker/ Almond relationship would arise again.

Nonetheless, Wright bit the bullet and began taking steps to get his idea approved. First, his staff produced a tactful analysis of X Corps operations which seemed to say that the wide dispersion of X Corps was not only risky but also not worth the effort. Next, Wright persuaded MacArthur that X Corps operations should be reoriented to do "everything possible to assist Eighth Army" and obtained MacArthur's authority to advise Almond "to be prepared" for a change in X Corps mission to provide for "coordinating with Eighth Army attack."

Almond reacted negatively. In a letter to Wright on November 14 he stated that while he could "fully appreciate" MacArthur's desire to have X Corps "assist Eighth Army in every possible way," he believed that it would be "inadvisable" for "X Corps forces to operate in any strength to the west." The lateral roads available to him, Almond said, would bring him across the peninsula to the rear of Eighth Army, which would be a "fruitless operation." He could better assist Eighth Army, he went on, by first going well to the north of the Chosin Reservoir, then going west "if desirable."[40]

Almond did not say so, but it is clear from other sources, and subsequent actions, that the goal of putting X Corps troops on the Yalu River was still paramount in his thinking. Eighth Army had failed to do so; X Corps would not. In pursuit of this goal he was supported by Dave Barr and most senior officers in the 7th Division. All wanted to "go to the Yalu" and show up both the 24th Division, which had failed to make it, and the Marines, who had so thoroughly dominated the publicity from X Corps that the existence of the 7th Division was scarcely known.

Sentiment in Tokyo continued to build for a radical change in X Corps mission. Pinky Wright was the prime mover. He may well have been supported by Turner Joy and Marine and Navy factions in the Pentagon, reflecting O. P. Smith's frank criticism of Almond's planning. Whatever the case, MacArthur, concurring with Wright's views, issued new orders to Almond on November 15. As the Army historian interpreted these orders, Almond was to "develop, as an alternate feature of his operation, plans for reorienting the attack to the west upon reaching the vicinity of Chongjin Town," north of the Chosin Reservoir. In a follow-up instruction, perhaps as a concession to Almond or the 7th Division, MacArthur directed that "minimum forces only" could advance to the Yalu.[41]

The new orders were not warmly received at X Corps; they were regarded as something of a slap in the face. Almond's grand "conquest" of northeast Korea and the "race" to the Yalu, in effect, were to be canceled in favor of a less glamorous operation in support of Eighth Army.

The upshot was that X Corps continued to drag its feet on mounting GHQ's proposed westward attack. Most of the serious, detailed planning was left to the Marines; the 7th Division was not only permitted but encouraged to continue its drive to the Yalu River through Pungsan–Kapsan, placing its center of gravity ever more distant from the Marines at the Chosin Reservoir. In these actions Almond did not explicitly disobey orders (his existing orders merely directed him to *plan* a westward attack), but indisputably he took liberties.

*   *   *

Herb Powell's 17th Infantry continued to spearhead the 7th Division's drive to the Yalu. After a long hold at the Ungi River above Pungsan, waiting for backup, Powell finally got a green light on November 13: The 17th was to proceed north to the Yalu on the following day at maximum speed.[42]

The first objective was to cross the Ungi River, no easy task. It was now almost unbelievably cold: thirty-two below zero near Pungsan on the nights of November 13 and 14. The division had no bridging. Engineers of the 7th Division's 13th Engineer Combat Battalion, wading into the waist-deep icy water, improvised a footbridge of empty oil drums and planks.[43]

On the morning of November 14 Powell's men began crossing this shaky bridge. The 2/17, commanded by Denzil L. Baker, thirty-eight, ran across first, followed by Francis Carberry's 1/17. It was planned that the 3/17, led by thirty-two-year-old Robert B. Pridgen, who had won a DSC in World War II, would wade across at a ford farther upstream, but the unit met unexpected and deadly NKPA fire. Trapped in the frigid water in midstream, one man was killed and seven were wounded before the crossing was canceled. Eighteen men who entered the water were incapacitated by severe frostbite.

On the east side of the river Powell ran into further stubborn and at times fanatical NKPA resistance. The NKPA checked Powell for two full days, launching many "suicide attacks," Dick Gruenther remembered. On November 16 Carberry's 1/17, led by Earl Meredith's B Company, at last broke through. But farther up the road the 1/17 was stopped by yet another strong

NKPA roadblock. On November 17, while helping break this block, Dick Gruenther was severely wounded in the chest and evacuated. Awarded a Silver Star, he did not return to the regiment.

Two days later, November 19, Powell, in a well-conducted drive, captured the town of Kapsan, thirty-one miles south of the Yalu. On the following day Ned Almond, Dave Barr, and the 7th Division ADC, Hank Hodes, flew in to visit Powell. All indications were that the road north to Hyesanjin (on the Yalu) was wide open. Almond ordered Powell to send a flying column (or armored task force) on to the river. Led by the armor and Carberry's 1/17, the 17th Infantry proceeded north from Kapsan against no opposition.

At this time Ned Almond issued a curious order to Dave Barr. Notwithstanding MacArthur's recent instruction that "minimum forces only" were to be employed in the advance to the Yalu, Almond decreed that Charles Beauchamp's full 32d Infantry would decamp from the 7th Division's extreme left sector at the Fusen Reservoir and proceed to Kapsan. The 32d would first provide backup for the 17th Infantry, then deploy northwest from Kapsan through Samsu to the Yalu, on Powell's left. This order had the effect of shifting the bulk (two of three regiments) of the 7th Division to the Kapsan area, far away from the Marine division, which was deploying at the Chosin Reservoir. The consequences were to be tragic.[44]

On the following day, November 21, Powell's 17th Infantry closed on Hyesanjin unopposed. The armored element, commanded by Carroll Cooper, was first into the town and to the Yalu. Fittingly (as Dick Gruenther wrote from a distance) C Company of Carberry's 1/17 was the first infantry to reach this long-sought goal. *Life* photographer Hank Walker and Army photographers recorded this climactic event. Almond, Barr, Hodes, and the 7th Division's artillery commander, West Pointer (1920) Homer W. Kiefer, fifty-two, flew up to pose for an official group photograph. Others performed the "hallowed ritual" of urinating in the Yalu.[45]

It was a moment of great triumph for the U.S. Army and the principals concerned. MacArthur was ecstatic. He sent a message to Almond: "Heartiest congratulations, Ned, and tell Dave Barr that the 7th Division hit the jackpot." Herb Powell, wounded in a subsequent skirmish with the NKPA, received a DSC.[46]

For the troops of the 17th Infantry it was not much of a triumph. The "liberation" of Hyesanjin was hardly comparable with the liberation of Paris or Rome—or even Pyongyang. The troops were tired, cold, and hungry. A combat engineer, Lenoise Bowman, remembered that the temperatures still hovered near thirty degrees below zero (F). The first night his squad found warmth in a Korean house and ate the "six or eight" chickens they found in a side room, but thereafter they slept and ate frozen C rations outside. He went on:

Our job was to work on a road running parallel to the Yalu River—make it passable for the infantry. We were not clothed for this kind of weather. . . . By the time you took three swings with a pick, your hands would be so cold that it felt as though they would fall off. Our feet were past feeling. . . . The Chinese were across the river, lobbing mortars at us while we worked. Since we were instructed not to return fire, we would just duck out of the way and continue working.[47]

Upon receiving orders to redeploy his 32d Infantry to Kapsan, Charles Beauchamp, many, many miles to the left, chose an easterly route over a mountain trail. But before he could begin moving, a heavy snowstorm closed the trail. He therefore was compelled to backtrack through Hamhung, thence north again to Kapsan. Since the 7th Division could provide transportation for only "one battalion at a time," this tedious movement took "several days," Beauchamp remembered. In fact, only Heinrich Schumann's 3/32 and Charles Mount's 2/32 got to Kapsan. Last in the slow backtracking line of march, Don Faith's 1/32 was finally diverted to another mission.[48]

Beauchamp's orders were to attack northwest of Powell's 17th Infantry positions, through Samsu to the Yalu at Singalpajin, originally a Marine Corps objective. The 17th Infantry would push west along the road that combat engineer Bowman and others were attempting to make passable and would link up. Beauchamp assigned his mission to Schumann's 3/32. Unwilling or unable to commit the full battalion to this task, Schumann created a thirty-four-man motorized task force, led by a twenty-two-year-old second lieutenant and platoon leader in K Company, Robert C. Kingston, a high school graduate who had enlisted in the Army as a private in late 1948 and had won an OCS commission a year later.[49]

This mission proved to be one of the most arduous of the war. The Siberian weather, lack of maps or aerial photos, rugged terrain, rockslides, and NKPA fire repeatedly retarded or blocked Kingston's force. The group took Samsu, a deserted village in the frozen wasteland, twenty-three miles south of the Yalu. But the weather or NKPA forced it back into Samsu three days in a row. Thereafter Schumann reinforced Kingston with I Company, artillery, tanks, engineers, and other support, but he wisely left young Kingston, an extraordinary and doggedly determined leader, in command. Finally, on November 28, Task Force Kingston reached Singalpajin, secured the village in a house-to-house fight with NKPA troops, and became the second—and last—American force to reach and urinate in the Yalu. The story of this remarkable feat was eclipsed by other events, but it put Kingston on the road to four stars.[50]

*   *   *

After Herb Powell's 17th Infantry had reached the Yalu and Charles Beauchamp's 32d Infantry had begun its arduous redeployment to Kapsan,

Ned Almond's G-3, Jack Chiles, produced a plan to implement Pinky Wright's proposed scheme for X Corps to attack westward from the Chosin Reservoir to link with Eighth Army. Approved by Almond on November 23, it directed that:

- The 1st Marine Division would attack west from the Chosin Reservoir at Yudam, to Mupyong, then go north to the Yalu.
- The 7th Division, having relieved the Fifth Marines, which had occupied the lower east side of the Chosin Reservoir, would attack on the right flank of the Marines (east of the reservoir), then advance to the Yalu.
- The 3d Division would continue to provide security for the Wonsan–Hamhung area, but it would also vigorously attack westward on the left flank of the Marines.[51]

At Almond's behest, Chiles flew to Tokyo to obtain approval of the plan. Wright and MacArthur made only slight technical changes. On November 24 MacArthur gave the plan his official go-ahead, leaving it to Almond to set the D day. Almond chose November 27.

As a result of Almond's prior orders to send Beauchamp's 32d Infantry to join Powell's 17th Infantry at Kapsan, the 7th Division was ill prepared to launch an attack from the Chosin Reservoir on November 27. Most of the 17th and 32d were then eighty air miles from the reservoir and probably twice that far by road. It would take days and days to redeploy the three 7th Division regiments and the artillery and armor over the miserable clogged roads and prepare for a major offensive in another direction.

One possibility was to let the Marines go ahead, with the 7th Division catching up in due course. But O. P. Smith, who was growing ever more cautious—and properly so—refused to move until his Fifth Marines had been relieved east of the Chosin and consolidated with the Seventh Marines. To conform to Smith's sensible desire, Almond ordered Dave Barr to rush his closest available forces to relieve the Fifth Marines east of the Chosin Reservoir.

This X Corps order was deeply resented by the 7th Division staff. The G-3, John Paddock, remembered: "We planned an orderly concentration and movement of the division to Chosin, by first concentrating the regiments and moving them one by one . . . [but] this plan was never carried out. Before we knew it, Almond ordered our closest battalions and smaller units to Chosin, individually, and as fast as they could get there."[52]

The 7th Division redeployment "plan" that ensued was as follows. Don Faith's 1/32, which had been delayed en route to Kapsan by the shortage of trucks and, because of the delay, was closest to Chosin, would lead the parade. William Reilly's 3/31, near Pungsan, would follow. Last would come the 2/31, which was also near Pungsan. The infantry would be supported by Ray Embree's 57th FAB (105 mms) and A Battery (155 mms) of the 7th Division's 31st FAB, commanded by George P. Welch, eight A/A vehicles, and the 31st Tank Company.[53]

The 7th Division ADC, Hank Hodes, was to go to Hagaru to supervise the forward deployment of the division elements. Tactical command, however, would rest with Mac MacLean, whose 31st Infantry was to provide the bulk of the troops. Because a "foreign" element (Faith's 1/32) was to be included, the conglomeration was designated Task Force MacLean rather than the 31st RCT.

These 7th Division movements were carried out but not without difficulty. The roads were jammed and precarious, and the weather was bitterly cold. Nonetheless, Faith's 1/32 reached Hagaru on November 25 and prepared to relieve Ray Murray's Fifth Marines. However, Reilly's 3/31 and the 2/31 and the artillery, A/A vehicles, tanks, and other equipment were repeatedly delayed en route, and Welch's 155s had to be deleted from the mission. The 2/31's E Company, banged up (or frozen) in earlier duty near Pungsan, was temporarily replaced by B Company of the 1/31.[54]

No one would ever forget the cold. The 7th Division artilleryman James Dill remembered a night drive near Pungsan:

Twice we stopped at MP checkpoints and warmed ourselves at their fires. The two-man posts were one of the most dangerous jobs of all. They were just two men, alone at night, usually with no other troops within miles. Those who did not build a fire were sometimes found frozen to death the next morning. Those who did build a fire were sometimes found shot to death the next morning beside the ashes of their fire.

Along the way the 3/4-ton truck behind me started honking. I stopped my jeep to run back and investigate. Two of the men had passed out from the cold, and the other men were huddled up against them, trying to revive them with their own body heat. I ordered everybody out and set the strongest to cutting down bushes with their bayonets. With the aid of gasoline from the spare cans we soon had two fires going between which we placed the men who had fainted. When they revived we loaded up and started off again. I believe they would have died if I had not stopped and built fires. The rest of us were not much better off. Somehow my driver kept going but toward the end he was actually moaning when he drove. I have never been particularly robust and I was close to collapse. . . . Division HQ, located in a valley, recorded 36 below that night. It must have been colder than 40 below in the mountain passes.[55]

Later a legend took root that MacArthur proceeded with final ground operations in North Korea in total disregard of the "gap" between Eighth Army and X Corps and that the CCF exploited this "gap" with telling effect. The legend was only partly true. Pinky Wright had recognized and persuaded MacArthur that there was a need for coordinating X Corps operations with Eighth Army, in effect, to close the "gap." The problem was that the warning came a little too late and was not welcomed by Almond. Had Almond reacted more promptly and vigorously to the warning—canceled Dave Barr's public relations drive to the Yalu and concentrated the full power of the 7th Division at the Chosin Reservoir with the Marines earlier—it might have been possible to launch the westward offensive a week sooner, on November 20. Given the (then unknown) CCF strength in that sector, the offensive no doubt would have failed. However, it might have substantially upset CCF plans for the Chosin area. In any case, prompt and enthusiastic preparations for the offensive would have substantially raised the American strength at the Chosin Reservoir, possibly changing the outcome of future events there. The real gap between the Marines and the 7th Division proved to be far more damaging than the legendary gap between Eighth Army and X Corps.

\* \* \*

While the 7th Division forces were shuffling around to regroup at the Chosin Reservoir, the 3d Division laid plans for its westward drive on the left flank of the 1st Marine Division. It would consist of two major thrusts:

• William Harris's full Puerto Rican 65th Infantry would press its erstwhile attack from Yonghung toward Kwangchon and beyond, toward Tokchon.
• John Guthrie's 7th Infantry would launch an attack from Chigyong toward Sachangi, over a road ten miles west of, and roughly parallel to, the Hamhung–Hagaru road.[56]

The 65th Infantry proceeded into the unknown mountains. In the early-morning hours of November 21 a strong CCF element (perhaps 300 or more soldiers) attacked the 1/65, commanded by West Pointer (1939) Howard B. ("Saint") St. Clair. Although his B Company got into a tight spot, St. Clair handled his unit "with almost parade-ground precision and unbelievable calm" and escaped with blessedly few casualties. Edward G. ("Jerry") Allen's 3/65, closing up to lend a hand, was likewise attacked but repelled the enemy without heavy losses. Meanwhile, Herman Dammer's 2/65 had to fight off other NKPA bands.[57]

In these actions the Puerto Ricans, experiencing subfreezing temperatures for the first time in their lives and still dressed in summer clothing, performed with astonishing valor and élan. As Harris put it, they "demonstrated to even the most skeptical of their critics that they were a force to be reckoned with."[58]

Guthrie's 7th Infantry could not immediately comply with the new plan.

Almond had shifted it from Kowon through Hamhung to Hongpyong, thirty-five miles northeast of Hamhung to serve as X Corps reserve. As a result, it had to backtrack through Hamhung to Chigyong over roads clogged with the reshuffling 7th Division units.[59]

* * *

The Marines, meanwhile, had begun moving west from Hagaru toward Yudam, where they would concentrate for the attack west. Litzenberg's Seventh Marines reached Yudam on November 25. Ray Murray's Fifth Marines, to be relieved on the east bank of the Chosin Reservoir by Task Force MacLean, prepared to follow. Chesty Puller's First Marines outposted the torturous Hamhung–Hagaru road (south to north): one battalion at Chinhung; one battalion at Koto; one battalion at Hagaru.[60]

As final preparation for the westward offensive was being made, no one in X Corps had the remotest idea of CCF strength in the Chosin Reservoir area. O. P. Smith, who identified two prisoners from a new CCF division, the 89th of the CCF Twentieth Army, on November 23, believed it could be considerable. However, Almond and the X Corps staff continued to believe the opposite. The Army historian wrote that Almond doubted that there were more than "one or two" CCF divisions on his Chosin front, comprising 10,000 to 20,000 CCF troops. The true figure was twelve CCF divisions comprising about 120,000 men.[61]

# III

Washington remained lost in a fog of uncertainty, groping for answers to grave and momentous questions. Had Moscow goaded Peking into intervention in Korea? If so, was it a first step in a Soviet plan to launch global war? Had Peking intervened on its own? If so, what were its ultimate intentions? Reams of articulate position papers issued from State and the Pentagon, but none had answers to those key questions.

All the while Washington continued its efforts to seek a "political" solution to the war. Believing that its best chance of bringing Peking into negotiations lay in dealing from a position of strength, Washington gave no further serious consideration to canceling MacArthur's offensive. The administration did deem it prudent, however, to reassure Peking publicly that America had no intention of going beyond the Yalu. At his press conference on November 15 President Truman made that point, stressing that Washington "never at any time entertained any intention to carry hostilities into China." He went on to say: "So far as the United States is concerned, I wish to state, unequivocally, that because of our deep devotion to the cause of world peace and our long-standing friendship for the people of China, we will take every honorable step to prevent any extension of the hostilities in the Far East."[62]

The principal diplomatic efforts were directed through the UN. That body already had before it a special report from MacArthur on the Chinese intervention. In addition, on November 10 Washington caused the introduction of a six-power resolution in the Security Council which called for the Chinese to withdraw from Korea but which also declared the Chinese border to be "inviolate" and urged that "no action be taken which might lead to the spread of the Korean conflict." In hope of establishing an unofficial diplomatic pipeline into Peking, Washington persuaded the UN to invite a Chinese Communist delegation to the UN to discuss the situation.[63]

All these overtures got nowhere. In response to Truman's public reassurances, Peking Radio declaimed: "America has lied and smashed her way across the world to Chinese territory and into it, has seized Chinese Taiwan [Formosa] and is threatening another neighbor, Vietnam." The *People's Daily* newspaper, referring to the recent fighting in Korea, trumpeted: "The imperialists have only begun to be battered and they will continue to carry out atrocities. Therefore we must continue to conduct firm counter-attacks against them. Forward! March on under enemy gunfire and bombs, to final victory." Other bellicose Peking media warned of the probability of an American nuclear attack on Chinese cities. The Peking delegation to the UN dawdled en route.[64]

In the midst of all this the British, gravely concerned over the situation in Korea, formally proposed to Washington a demilitarized buffer zone at the narrow neck of the Korean peninsula, along a line Chongju–Hamhung—in other words, a cancellation of MacArthur's upcoming Eighth Army offensive and a pullback of X Corps. Since the French and other allies supported the British proposal and there was also considerable sentiment for it in Washington, it prompted yet another high-level reappraisal of MacArthur's mission. A meeting took place in Marshall's office at the Pentagon on the afternoon of November 21. Present were all of Truman's senior advisers on the Korean War—Acheson, Harriman, Bradley, the JCS—but again not the president.[65]

Acheson dominated the discussions, restating Washington's broad objectives in Korea and noting the "anxiety" of America's allies. It was "desirable" to "find some kind of an agreement." He was "searching for something that would be useful, not harmful, to MacArthur." He believed the concept of a buffer zone had considerable merit and should be seriously explored. However, the details and timing of the British proposal were complicated, and he had "discouraged" the British from "pressing" the proposal at this time. He believed that MacArthur should go ahead with the Eighth Army offensive; then afterward, perhaps, a buffer zone could be established, possibly by a pullback of UN forces from the Yalu to some line. Marshall "expressed satisfaction" that Acheson favored going ahead with the offensive. He preferred to consider "political action" based on the premise that MacArthur would succeed and that "the time for making political proposals would be after MacArthur had had such a success." Marshall favored a buffer zone but agreed it was very complicated and had "some doubt" that it might ever be achieved.[66]

An intense discussion about the buffer zone ensued. Joe Collins, producing a map, suggested a line about ten to twenty-five miles south of the border "on the high ground" overlooking the Yalu. Having successfully reached the Yalu, MacArthur might withdraw to that line, which could form the southern end of a buffer zone. The other chiefs, Philip Jessup later noted, "seemed to agree" with Collins. Many questions were posed: Should MacArthur announce the buffer zone in advance? After the offensive had begun? After it had been completed?

This was the final meeting of Truman's advisers before MacArthur launched the Eighth Army offensive. In effect, the conferees agreed on the concept of a buffer zone but not on halting MacArthur. If there were to be a buffer zone, it would be located after the offensive, not before, as the British and other allies desired. Meanwhile, Acheson would continue other efforts at a "political" solution to the war.

Earlier MacArthur had denounced the British proposal for a buffer zone, which would have halted his offensive, in the most vitriolic terms ("appeasement," "Munich"). The conferees decided that they should now obtain his official views on establishing a buffer zone *after* the offensive. Dean Rusk drafted the query, which went out in Joe Collins's name on the evening of November 23:

Other members of the United Nations [Collins began] indicate growing concern over the possibility of bringing on a general conflict should a major clash develop with Chinese Communist forces as a result of your forces advancing squarely against the entire boundary between Korea and Manchuria-USSR. This might not only result in loss of support within the UN and leave US standing alone but would also involve increased risks of a military nature. Proposals in UN may suggest unwelcome restrictions on your advance to the north since some sentiment exists in UN for establishing a demilitarized zone between your forces and the frontier in the hope of thereby reducing Chinese Communist fear of UN military action against Manchuria and the corresponding sensitivity on the part of the USSR with respect to Vladivostok.

The "consensus of political and military opinion in Washington," Collins went on tactfully and obsequiously, was that there should be no change in MacArthur's mission but that there should be formulated a course of action that would "permit establishment of a unified Korea" and at the same time "reduce risk of more general involvement." Recent Washington discussions,

Collins wrote, had explored "what military measures (which you might in any event wish to take) might lend themselves to political action which would reduce tension with Peking and the Soviet Union and maintain a solid UN front." These discussions had suggested several measures, Collins continued, among them a pullback of Eighth Army "after advancing to or near the Yalu," to create a buffer zone "on terrain dominating the approaches from the valley of the Yalu," and a limit on X Corps advances on the east coast to Chongjin, this to be carried out principally by ROKs and other non-American units. Collins went on:

While it is recognized from the point of view of the Commander in the field this course of action may leave much to be desired, it is felt that there may be other considerations which must be accepted and that the above procedures would not seriously affect the accomplishment of your military mission. At the same time it might well provide an out for the Chinese Communists to withdraw into Manchuria without loss of face and might lessen the concern of the Russians as to the security of Vladivostok. This concern may be at the root of Russian pressure on the Chinese Communists to intervene in Korea.[67]

MacArthur's reply was predictable: resounding disagreement. The proposed buffer zone, he wrote, "would not only fail to achieve the desired result but would be provocative of the very consequences we seek to avert." The terrain (as Collins had outlined it in detail) was "not adaptable" for the purpose. Moreover, any "failure" to prosecute the military campaign all the way to the border "would be fraught with most disastrous consequences." The ROKs would regard it as a "betrayal." Peking would see it as "a weakness reflected from the appeasement of Communist aggression," and thus it would encourage "further international lawlessness and aggression." He went on:

Our forces are committed to seize the entire border area, and indeed, in the east, have already occupied a sector of the Yalu River with no noticeable political or military Soviet or Chinese reaction. . . . We have repeatedly and publicly made it unmistakably clear that we entertain no aggressive designs whatsoever against any part of Chinese or Soviet territory. . . . By resolutely . . . accomplishing our military mission as so often publicly delineated lies [the] best—indeed only—hope that Soviet and Chinese aggressive designs may be checked before those countries are committed to a course from which for political reasons they cannot withdraw.[68]

# PART EIGHT

# Disaster and Retreat

# 16

# THE SECOND CHINESE OFFENSIVE

I

By November 22 Johnnie Walker had fully deployed Eighth Army for its climactic offensive to the Yalu. In all, his combat forces numbered about 118,000 men, in eight infantry divisions and two brigades, organized into three corps on a seventy-mile-wide front. The grand plan was as follows:

• On the left flank Shrimp Milburn's I Corps, consisting of (west to east) John Church's 24th Division and the ROK 1st Division, would attack northwest and north respectively, more or less retracing their earlier paths. The Commonwealth Brigade (about 5,000 men) would serve as corps reserve.
• In the army's center John Coulter's IX Corps, consisting of (west to east) Bill Kean's 25th Division and Dutch Keiser's 2d Division, would attack north and northeast respectively. The newly arrived Turkish Brigade (about 5,000 men) would serve as corps reserve.
• On the army's right flank the ROK II Corps, consisting of the ROK 7th and 8th divisions, would attack northeasterly. The recently mangled ROK 6th Division (about 5,000 men) would serve as corps reserve.

In the preceding two weeks Hap Gay's 1st Cav Division, rebuilt and remanned after the Unsan debacle, had been employed almost continuously to gain footholds above the Chongchon River in the army's center. For that reason Walker believed the division had earned a rest, and he placed it in army reserve. However, its four artillery battalions were temporarily detached and added to IX Corps to support the 25th and 2d divisions.[1]*

Believing that the main enemy strength facing Eighth Army probably lay near Unsan and east of there, Walker had concentrated his main power for the Eighth Army offensive in Coulter's IX Corps in the center: Kean's 25th and Keiser's 2d divisions, backed by fifteen artillery battalions, including the four on loan from the 1st Cav and the 17th FAB, equipped with huge eight-inch howitzers.

The two divisions deployed in standard combat formation: two infantry regiments up; one back in reserve. In the 25th Division Hank Fisher's 35th Infantry was assigned the left sector; John Corley's black 24th Infantry, the right sector. As added punch Bill Kean deployed an armor-infantry task force commanded by Tom Dolvin between them, in the center of his line on the road paralleling the Kuryong River. Mike Michaelis's 27th Infantry was designated reserve. In the 2d Division Chin Sloane's 9th Infantry held the left sector, abutting the 24th Infantry; George Peploe's 38th Infantry held the right sector adjacent to ROK II Corps. Paul Freeman's 23d Infantry was designated division reserve.

There was one possible weakness in the center line. The 24th Infantry was tied in on the right flank with the 3/9. This placed all four of the black infantry battalions in Eighth Army line abreast. Although Corley and his exec, Paul Roberts, had improved morale and stiffened the 24th, it was still not fully trusted. A stampede in the 24th could have a "contagious" effect on its neighbor, the 3/9. D. M. McMains had led and fought the 3/9 well in its two prior battles, but hitherto it had been sandwiched between white battalions. Why Walker deployed the blacks in this formation is not known—possibly to keep them "segregated."

Walker's orders for the offensive were ultraconservative. The two divisions would advance roughly line abreast to preselected "phase lines," maintaining lateral communications between adjoining units. High ground would be taken. No enemy enclaves would be knowingly bypassed. Flanks would be tied in where the terrain permitted. Telephone landlines would be laid. All units would maintain close liaison with assigned artillery battalions.

That was the paper lineup. The reality was a nightmare. The terrain was ghastly: hill upon hill upon hill, most snow-covered and divided by narrow gorges and defiles. There were few roads, none in some sectors. The geography was confused by the confluence of the Kuryong and Chongchon rivers and minor tributaries, all of them partly frozen but their ice not yet strong enough

---

*Only two non-ROK infantry regiments were not employed: the 187th Airborne Combat Team, in Pyongyang, and the newly arrived 29th British Brigade, which was getting its baptism of fire in the hills near Kaesong, rooting out guerrillas and the bypassed NKPA.

to support vehicles. And it was very, very cold, actual temperatures well below freezing, often in the low teens. The windchill factor plunged the apparent (or felt) cold to well below zero. Few of the men had proper clothing for such inhospitable weather. Vehicles would not start; radios conked out; weapons—notably carbines—would not fire; mortar base plates cracked in recoil on the frozen ground. Under such conditions it was almost impossible to tie in flanks and lay wire, maintain liaison with artillery, and do the other things called for in the plan.

Nor were the GIs in IX Corps properly equipped for heavy combat. A tabulation in one infantry company was typical: All but 12 of 129 men had thrown away their steel helmets, preferring to wear warm pile caps. Only 2 men—new arrivals—had bayonets. About half the men had discarded entrenching tools for digging foxholes. All were acutely short of grenades and ammo: an average of less than one grenade per man; as few as sixteen to thirty rounds per rifle and carbine.[2]

\* \* \*

Walker still had no clear idea of the enemy he faced. On November 17 MacArthur had told Ambassador Muccio in Tokyo that "certainly no more than 30,000" CCF soldiers had crossed the Yalu. Four days later, on November 21, Walker's G-2, Clint Tarkenton, doubled that estimate to 60,000, of which, he believed, 27,000 were directly facing Eighth Army, the rest in rear areas or near the Chosin Reservoir. On November 24 MacArthur's G-2, Charles Willoughby, raised the number of CCF troops in Korea to "at least 40,000" and, adding a hedge, perhaps as many as 71,000.[3]

In addition, there was now a growing realization that the NKPA had also to be reckoned with. In his first "posterity paper," the public communiqué of November 6, MacArthur had made the preposterous assertion that the NKPA had been utterly wiped out, suffering 335,000 casualties. However, during November American and ROK forces in both Eighth Army and X Corps had encountered numerous organized NKPA units and guerrillas above and below the 38th Parallel. Accordingly, on November 24 Willoughby pronounced with incredible exactitude that the NKPA now numbered 82,799 men. Where this figure originated or whether or not it was accurate is not known. How many of this total were deployed before Eighth Army was not known either, perhaps 23,000.[4]

In sum, on thebasis of the estimates provided by Tarkenton and Willoughby, Walker believed the enemy deployed before Eighth Army numbered about 50,000, about half of which were CCF and about half NKPA. That assumption gave Walker a numerical superiority of slightly over two to one. In fact, it was closer to being the reverse. If the figure of 23,000 NKPA was nearly accurate, the total enemy force facing Eighth Army numbered about 203,000, nearly twice Eighth Army's strength.

*   *   *

On the eve of the Eighth Army offensive—Thursday, November 23—
the Americans enjoyed a traditional Thanksgiving Day dinner. They were
served shrimp cocktail, stuffed olives, sweet pickles, roast young tom turkey,
sage dressing, giblet gravy, cranberry sauce, candied sweet potatoes, mashed
potatoes, buttered corn, green peas, fresh baked bread and butter, pumpkin
and mince pies, fruitcake, candies, nuts, oranges, and apples. Some units also
got a ration of whiskey; others were provided hot showers and a change of
uniform.[5]

In his rear-area position in army reserve Hap Gay took advantage of the
holiday to hold regimental parades and award medals. It was a stirring moment in the 1st Cav. The regimental adjutants read off battle streamers. Makeshift bands played sentimental divisional and regimental songs: "She Wore a
Yellow Ribbon" and "GarryOwen."[6]

Feelings in the Eighth Army ranks were mixed. Most men believed that
this time the drive to the Yalu would easily succeed. But many, including a
number of senior commanders, were deeply worried. Among these were 23d
Infantry commander Paul Freeman and his 1/23 commander, Claire Hutchin.
In the move up from the south they had encountered some CCF units near
Sunchon. In view of that, Freeman thought the offensive was foolhardy, a
"mystery." He remembered: "The night before the attack . . . Colonel Hutchin
and I had dinner with our division commander General [Dutch] Keiser. We
expressed our dilemma or inability to understand what was going on. . . . The
fact that we had identified and were fighting Chinese units down at Sunchon
. . . apparently hadn't convinced anyone in Far East Headquarters. . . . We
never could understand it. . . . We could only conclude that General MacArthur held some very, very secret* information [indicating] that these Chinese
were not really going to resist, but allow us to push them back across the [Yalu]
river."[7]

On the following morning, November 24, MacArthur and party flew into
Sinanju to be present for the jump-off. He was met at the Sinanju Airfield by
Walker and Shrimp Milburn, who had his dachshund, Ebbo, in tow. MacArthur gave Ebbo a pat, then "toured" the I Corps and IX Corps fronts in a jeep
for about four hours. It was freezing cold: fifteen degrees.

One cause for deep concern was the ROK II Corps on the extreme right
flank of Eighth Army. The ROKs, MacArthur wrote in vast understatement,
were "not yet in good shape."[8]

That day ROK II Corps was deployed in orthodox formation for the

---

*E.g., code breaking.

attack: two divisions forward; one division in corps reserve. The ROK 7th Division held the left (or west) sector, abutting the American 2d Division; the ROK 8th Division, the right (or east) sector. The ROK 6th Division was in reserve. The KMAG adviser, West Pointer (1940) Robert C. Cameron, later wrote that the ROKs were only lightly armed. They had but a "fraction" of the normal supply of mortars and machine guns and only one "light" (75-mm "pack howitzer") artillery battalion per division, no corps artillery, no armor, and no American supporting units of any kind.

That these three ROK divisions were dreadfully weak was not fully recognized or appreciated until later, when Cameron submitted an official report. The 7th Division had been badly banged up in its effort to hold Kunu in early November. Since then its three regiments (3d, 5th, 8th), remanned with green fillers, had seen only "limited" combat. The 8th Division's 10th Regiment had also been shattered earlier by the CCF and was equally green. Its 16th and 21st regiments had just completed a tough fight with CCF troops merely to reach the "start line" for the Eighth Army offensive. It had gained Tokchon, where ROK II Corps located its headquarters, but the fighting had sapped the strength and supplies of the two regiments. The reserve 6th Division, earlier shattered by the CCF, had merely two understrength regiments (2d and 19th). The 19th had been sent south to fight off NKPA guerrillas that were harassing ROK II Corps supply lines, leaving only the depleted 2d Regiment in ROK II Corps reserve.[9]

The failure of Johnnie Walker to appreciate fully the grave weakness in ROK II Corps was a major blunder which would have dire consequences. It was also inexplicable. Merely two weeks earlier, in his letter to MacArthur, Walker had blamed the ROKs for the forced withdrawal of Eighth Army behind the Chongchon River. Since then, as Walker well knew, ROK II Corps had not been appreciably strengthened. To the contrary, it had been significantly weakened. It would have been prudent to reinforce ROK II Corps with American forces—for example, Hap Gay's 1st Cav, which could have been replaced in army reserve by the 187th Airborne Regiment and the 29th British Brigade.

On the whole, MacArthur wrote later, his tour of the front "worried me greatly." The entire Eighth Army line was "deplorably weak in numbers." Yet at Coulter's CP, his aide Courtney Whitney wrote, MacArthur, within the hearing of several war correspondents, said: "If this operation is successful, I hope I can get the boys home by Christmas." The war correspondents thereupon labeled the Eighth Army offensive the "Home by Christmas offensive."*

---

*Time* magazine reported that MacArthur made his "Home by Christmas" remarks at John Church's 24th Division CP. It quoted MacArthur as saying to Church: "I have already promised

After taking off from Sinanju, MacArthur impulsively directed his pilot to fly north to the Yalu River. He wanted to "interpret with my own long experience what was going on behind the enemy's lines." Although the plane was escorted by fighters (three propeller-driven F-51s alongside; jets above), the detour over enemy territory was extremely hazardous. Refusing to don a parachute, MacArthur stared out his window. His plane circled Sinuiju at 9,000 feet, then flew northeast up the Yalu River. MacArthur saw no sign of the CCF. Later he wrote: "All that spread before our eyes was an endless expanse of utterly barren countryside, jagged hills, yawning crevices, and the black waters of the Yalu locked in the silent death grip of snow and ice. It was a merciless wasteland."

Calmly smoking his pipe, MacArthur gave further routing instructions to his pilot: "Let's slip down and say 'hello' to Powell." He meant Herb Powell and the 17th Infantry withdrawing from Hyesanjin, on the northeastern Yalu. The pilot descended over Powell's position, waggled the plane's wings in salute, continued south, passing over the Chosin Reservoir, then headed for home. A wire service reporter on the plane wrote that all told, MacArthur had spent "one hour and ten minutes over enemy territory." For this daring foray Stratemeyer awarded MacArthur a Distinguished Flying Cross.[11]

Some senior commanders in Eighth Army deeply resented MacArthur's visit that day. His comings and goings from Tokyo were akin to a public appearance of the emperor and were well noted by the Japanese. Chinese Communist spies in Tokyo—or Sinanju—were almost certain to learn of the visit and report it to Peking or Lin Piao. So rare was a MacArthur appearance at the "front" itself that it was bound to presage a major UN military move—in this instance, a renewed offensive. Thus the tight security which had cloaked Walker's preparations almost certainly was breached.

But these security details were minor compared with what followed when MacArthur returned to Tokyo. He released another of his ill-advised communiqués that not only boasted that a major offensive was under way but revealed his general strategy. The three-week air offensive, he said, had isolated the battlefield and had "sharply curtailed" CCF manpower reinforcements and "markedly limited" the flow of supplies. After a series of "brilliant" maneuvers the "eastern sector" of his forces (X Corps) was now in a "commanding envelopment position" for "cutting in two the northern reaches of the enemy's geographical potential." The "western sector" (Eighth Army) of the "pincer"

---

wives and mothers that the boys of the 24th Division will be back by Christmas. Don't make me a liar. Get to the Yalu and I'll relieve you." A wire service reported MacArthur as saying: "Tell the boys when they reach the Yalu they are going home. I want to make good on my statement that they are going to eat Christmas dinner at home."[10]

moves forward "this morning" in a "general assault in an effort to complete the compression and close the vise." He added: "If successful this should for all practical purposes end the war. . . ."[12]

* * *

Seldom in any war had a commanding general so foolishly revealed his hand. This communiqué gave Lin Piao priceless information: first, that the commitment of the vast CCF units into North Korea was still largely undetected and that he still held the element of surprise; secondly, that the UN troop movements were not readjustments in the line, but that a major UN offensive was actually under way; thirdly, that an enveloping movement and linkup with Eighth Army by X Corps was an essential part of the plan, that X Corps movements would not be feints.

At the time MacArthur released this communiqué, Lin Piao was already well along with his own battle plans. He had regrouped and reinforced his armies, and his intent was a massive strike against Eighth Army and X Corps nearly simultaneously with all the forces at his command. The CCF attack plan was as follows:

• On the Eighth Army front Lin Piao's Thirteenth Army Group, consisting of eighteen divisions, plus NKPA units, would mount its primary assault from the northeast, directly at ROK II Corps. The attack would go on the evening of November 25, by the bright full moon. The CCF plan was to overrun the ROKs, cut deep into Eighth Army's right flank, then go westward to the Yellow Sea below Sinanju, thereby enveloping and trapping Eighth Army at the Chongchon River. Other CCF forces facing IX and I corps in the center and west of Eighth Army's line would fight mainly a holding or blocking action, designed to engage the bulk of Eighth Army in place during the envelopment. The destruction of Eighth Army would eliminate all UN forces from northwestern Korea.

• On the X Corps front the CCF Ninth Army Group, consisting of twelve divisions, would envelop and capture the 1st Marine Division at Yudam, Hagaru, and Koto and Task Force MacLean east of the Chosin Reservoir. Thereafter these CCF units would destroy the U.S. 3d Division, other units of the 7th Division and the ROK 3d and Capital divisions. These operations would not only prevent a linkup of X Corps and Eighth Army but also eliminate UN forces in northeastern Korea. The Ninth Army Group attack would go in the Chosin Reservoir area on November 27.

It is not known if Lin Piao made any changes in his plans upon learning the contents of MacArthur's communiqué. Probably not. His forces were already well disposed. However, knowing the opponent's plan in advance must have been comforting. He could be fairly certain that there would be no surprises, such as an unheralded amphibious assault in his rear.

One concern Lin Piao may have harbored was the possibility of an American atomic bomb attack on his massed ground forces. But he need not have worried. The JCS had explored the concept of using A-bombs tactically in Korea and had rejected the idea on several grounds: first, because America's allies—the British in particular—were adamantly opposed; secondly, because America still had too few A-bombs to squander in a nonstrategic area; thirdly, because even if a suitable mass of enemy could be located and promptly bombed, the rugged mountain terrain in Korea would severely limit the impact of the blast, perhaps with wholly indecisive results; fourthly, because possible indecisive results on the Korean battlefield might diminish the deterrent effect of the A-bomb in Western Europe.[13]

Some historians have asserted that in drawing his plan, Lin Piao took tactical advantage of the gap in the rugged terrain between Eighth Army and X Corps. But this was not true. He did not sneak CCF troop formations into the gap to attack Eighth Army directly from the east on its right flank. There was no need to mount such a difficult and possibly detectable maneuver. From his experience in the First Phase Offensive Lin Piao knew that the ROKs had a pathological fear of the CCF and that a massive assault directly against the ROK II Corps front would quickly buckle the right flank of Eighth Army, gaining his initial objective far more economically than an attack from the gap in the east.[14]

## II

The Eighth Army offensive got under way with a thunderous roar of artillery at 10:00 A.M. on November 24. For about thirty-six hours all went well. As the army advanced to contact with the enemy, there was little resistance. The various units reported gains ranging from two to eight miles.

On the extreme left flank Shrimp Milburn's I Corps had the easiest day. In John Church's 24th Division Dick Stephens's 21st Infantry led the assault, rolling forward about seven miles against no opposition. On Church's right the 11th and 12th ROK regiments of the ROK 1st Division made equally spectacular gains. By nightfall there was talk in I Corps of reaching the Yalu River in a day or two.

In the center John Coulter's powerful IX Corps likewise had an easy time. The five assault units in Bill Kean's 25th and Dutch Keiser's 2d divisions reported gains of two to three miles against light or no resistance.[15]

On the left flank of the 25th Division Hank Fisher's 35th Infantry, supported by Arthur Hogan's 64th FAB, moved out toward Unsan, more or less retracing the path of the ill-fated 8th Cav. With the slaughter of the 8th Cav fresh in mind, it was believed the 35th would have a very tough fight. But as one historian of the battle, S.L.A. Marshall, put it, "Nothing happened. The 35th met no Chinese." The enemy had apparently shifted east and west of Unsan. Fisher soon reached the high ground overlooking the town and laid plans for capturing it and recovering a dozen 8th Cav trucks and jeeps he saw parked unattended in a schoolyard. He was somewhat mystified at having encountered no Chinese, but pleased. He said later: "I was confident I could get to the Yalu in a breeze or, if need be, stand at Unsan until hell froze over." For a while the 35th "marked time in a tactical vacuum," largely ignorant of all that was happening on its flanks and at its rear.[16]

* * *

On Fisher's right, but out of touch, was Tom Dolvin's formidable armor-infantry task force. It was composed of tanks, mobile assault guns, recon vehicles, and nearly the equivalent of a battalion of infantry: one rifle company (B) from Fisher's 35th; one rifle company (E) from Michaelis's 27th; and a company of Rangers, newly arrived from the States. These highly trained, elite Rangers had been attached (one company per American division) for "special missions." Having no immediate use for their unique talents, Bill Kean had elected to employ them as conventional infantry. The task force was supported by the 77th and 90th FABs, the 77th on loan from the 1st Cav.[17]

Encountering slight to no resistance, Dolvin made about three miles the first day. Along the way he picked up twenty-nine American POWs from the 8th Cav, abandoned by the CCF. That night Dolvin dug in on the hillsides, leaving one infantry company (B) at his rear, to hold open an escape route should one be needed.[18]

To Dolvin's right John Corley's 24th Infantry, mated with Walter Preston's black 159th FAB, met no enemy at all. Performing smartly and in high spirits, Gerald Miller's 1/24, George Clayton's 2/24, and Melvin Blair's 3/24 charged ahead in very rugged terrain, gaining an average of about three and a half miles. In so doing, Miller's 1/24 lost lateral contact with Task Force Dolvin, but at the time the lapse was not deemed a serious cause for concern.[19]

Still farther right, in the 2d Division sector, Chin Sloane's 9th Infantry moved ahead to its objective, advancing about two miles. Ordinarily the 9th was supported by John Keith's 15th FAB; but Sloane and Keith had had a falling-out, and as a consequence, Dutch Keiser and his artillery commander, Loyal Haynes, had decided to swap John Hector's 37th FAB, which usually supported Paul Freeman's 23d Infantry, with the 15th. The upshot was that both the 9th and 23d went into battle with "unfamiliar" artillery. Freeman remembered: "You and your assigned artillery battalion established a close relationship. The artillery FOs [forward observers] actually live with the infantrymen, become buddies, and develop trust and teamwork. When Keiser decided to swap artillery battalions because Sloane and Keith didn't get along, I pleaded with him not to do it. It meant you'd have to swap all the FOs and so on. But Keiser went ahead and did it."[20]

The 9th's line of attack took it northeastward, straddling the Chongchon River. McMains's 3/9 held the extreme left sector, on the west side of the river, which in this area bends north-south. Most of Butch Barberis's 2/9, holding the regimental center, was also on the west bank of the river. The 1/9, with a new commander, Eugene Wolfe, and temporarily reinforced by Barberis's E Company, held the right flank, on the east side of the river. As for newcomer Wolfe, Barberis remembered: "He was a very nice old gentleman, too old for the job and totally unsuited because of age and physical condition."[21]

In the 2d Division's right sector George Peploe's 38th Infantry, supported by Robert O'Donnell's 38th FAB, moved out in conventional formation. James Skeldon's 2/38 attacked on the left; the 3/38, now commanded by Harold V. Maixner, thirty-three, attacked on the right. William Keleher's 1/38 was in reserve.[22]

Of the American regiments in Eighth Army, the 38th was in the most precarious position. Its left abutted the 9th Infantry, but its right rested on the dreadfully weak ROK II Corps. If the ROKs met trouble and bugged out, as they had in the early November CCF attacks, the 38th would be dangerously exposed on its right flank. A vast gap to the east could develop, extending all the way to the Marines at the Chosin Reservoir.

Like Freeman and Sloane, Peploe had encountered scattered CCF troops near Sunchon on his way north and found reason for concern. More recently rumors had reached him that "bands" of unidentified enemy (of various sizes) had been spotted in the mountain wastes east of ROK II Corps. Peploe worried that if not dealt with, these bands might circle to the east and seize Tokchon, directly to his south, thereby getting behind ROK II Corps and blocking Peploe's most direct line of withdrawal should that become necessary. For these reasons, and others, Peploe had made up his mind—exhortations from MacArthur and Walker notwithstanding—to advance to contact with the CCF with proper caution.

Communications with ROK II Corps on the army's extreme right were imperfect. However, the fragmentary reports reaching Walker that first day were heartening. In spite of the very rugged terrain in that area, the ROK 7th Division's 3d and 8th regiments reported gains of three miles; the ROK 8th Division's 10th and 21st regiments reported gains of about two miles.[23]

* * *

In Shrimp Milburn's I Corps the second day of the offensive, November 25, was very much like the first. John Church's 24th Division—still led by Dick Stephens's 21st Infantry—blazed ahead and recaptured Chongju. Although it encountered increasing enemy resistance, the ROK 1st Division also continued to make large gains.

In John Coulter's IX Corps some of the assault forces began to encounter heavy enemy resistance on the second day. The resistance was not unexpected. No one believed the CCF and NKPA would allow Eighth Army to make a cakewalk to the Yalu. It was believed that the enemy, however weak, would fight a series of delaying actions as it retreated northward under the weight of the Eighth Army attack.[24]

In Bill Kean's 25th Division the left and right assaulting forces (Fisher's 35th Infantry; Corley's 24th Infantry) met no enemy and advanced several more miles, but Task Force Dolvin, attacking in the center, ran into a hornet's nest. By noon Dolvin was engaged in a very heavy firefight. Believing that two battalions of the supporting artillery (77th and 90th FABs) might become exposed, Kean pulled Gordon Murch's 2/27 from reserve and sent it forward to backstop Dolvin. During the afternoon the fighting increased in intensity.[25]

In Dutch Keiser's 2d Division both assaulting regiments, Sloane's 9th and Peploe's 38th, encountered CCF troops.

For Chin Sloane the resistance occurred first in Eugene Wolfe's 1/9. At about 10:00 A.M. Wolfe's B Company, attacking a hill, was suddenly itself violently counterattacked. At first Wolfe was not overly concerned; he believed it to be merely a "local" reaction. But Sloane, smelling big trouble, telephoned Dutch Keiser's CP and said: "I think this is different; it may be the real thing. We had better watch it." Division saw it as Wolfe did: Sloane's warning was ignored.[26]

Taking personal control of this tough little fight, Sloane committed two more rifle companies (A and C) plus some A/A Quad 50s and armor to assist B. All that afternoon the 1/9 attempted earnestly but unsuccessfully to dislodge the CCF from the hill. Meanwhile, the other rifle company of the 1/9, E (lent from the 2/9), occupied a hill without difficulty. It was puzzling; the CCF seemed to be concentrated in force only on that single hill. Keiser remained unconcerned. His G-2, Ralph L. Foster, declared that the CCF could be expected to mount a "screening action" as it pulled back toward the Yalu.

Advancing on Sloane's right, Peploe received word from a FEAF aircraft that CCF units with heavy mortars lay in his path. Peploe halted and directed the 1/38 commander, William Keleher, to send a company forward to scout. Keleher gave the task to Jack W. Rodarm's A Company.[27]

Rodarm's outfit proceeded up a steep, twisting gravel road toward the reported CCF emplacement. About halfway to the goal the men ran into a CCF roadblock, which they disposed of without undue difficulty, but it took time. In late afternoon Peploe sent Keleher forward to prod Rodarm, who refused to be rushed. He had encountered several more CCF troops. His own men were all too thinly spread out along the mountain road, and they were tired. Rodarm insisted that A Company stop for the night. Sizing up the situation, Keleher gave approval for the halt. Rodarm, out on a limb several miles ahead of the main body of the 38th, pulled his men into a perimeter and buttoned up. Most of the men were too tired to dig foxholes in the frozen rocky ground. They huddled together to keep warm.

\* \* \*

By nightfall on November 25 the situation across the Eighth Army front still gave Walker no cause for concern. The ROK 1st Division, Task Force Dolvin, the 9th Infantry, and the 38th Infantry had met CCF troops; Dolvin and Sloane had engaged in some tough fighting. But the army as a whole had advanced an average of several miles on the second day of the offensive.

There was, however, one disquieting note. Incomplete and fragmentary reports from ROK II Corps indicated that its 7th and 8th divisions had encountered very heavy CCF resistance. These reports were noted at Walker's headquarters, but because of the imperfect communications, the reports could not be confirmed immediately. However, no special measures were taken to improve communications to find out exactly what was going on. Nor was anyone inclined to reinforce the ROKs. The possible danger to ROK II Corps was, in a word, ignored.[28]

### III

On the night of November 25 Eighth Army was almost casually disposed. The men had two successful days of combat under their belts; the task lying ahead did not appear to hold great danger. Few men took the precaution of digging foxholes in the frozen ground.

It was a very cold, clear night with a full moon. Thermometers in some sectors fell to fifteen degrees. The main concern of the Americans was how to keep warm. A few lucky men found refuge in Korean houses, but most were out in the open. Only a few had received winter clothing. Some unwisely built campfires.

At about 8:00 P.M. the Chinese Communists attacked in massive force. They swarmed over the hills, blowing bugles and horns, shaking rattles and other noisemakers, and shooting flares into the sky. They came on foot, firing rifles and burp guns, hurling grenades, and shouting and chanting shrilly. The total surprise of this awesome ground attack shocked and paralyzed most Americans and panicked not a few.

The main weight of the Chinese attack came at John Coulter's IX Corps

# The Second Chinese Offensive

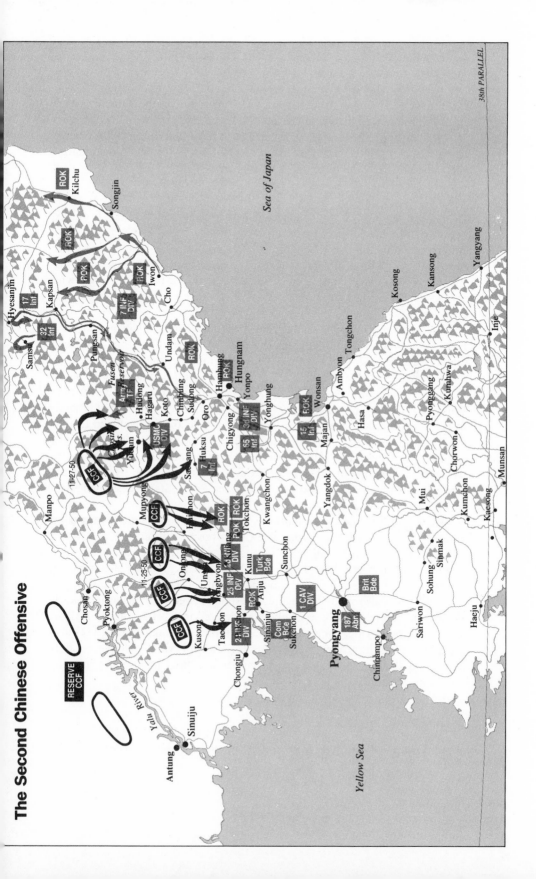

and the ROK II Corps. It was focused (left to right) on the American 25th and 2d divisions and the ROK 7th and 8th divisions. It missed Hank Fisher's 35th Regiment on the far left of IX Corps, but it hit (left to right) Task Force Dolvin, Corley's 24th Infantry, Sloane's 9th Infantry, Peploe's 38th Infantry, and the ROK 3d, 8th, 10th, and 21st regiments.[29]

\* \* \*

In Dolvin's sector hundreds, perhaps thousands of CCF troops swarmed into his hillside perimeter. The Rangers and E Company were swamped and nearly overwhelmed; the Rangers lost sixty-four of eighty-five men in the initial assault. E Company sustained comparable losses, but inspired by its gallant commander, Reginald B. ("Dusty") Desiderio, who shrugged off a battle wound, these Wolfhounds gave ground only slowly and unwillingly.

The next morning the CCF pressed the attack on Dolvin in full fury. Fearing that the enemy might crack through the center of his front, Bill Kean sent forward his able ADC, Vennard Wilson, to take tactical command of Task Force Dolvin, Gordon Murch's 2/27, and, if it could be found and brought into play, Gerald Miller's 1/24 in the adjacent sector to the right. By the time Wilson got forward to establish a CP, Dolvin's forces, engaged in bitter hand-to-hand fighting, had been pushed back half a mile and had suffered further heavy casualties. Wilson rose to the challenge with magnificent courage and command presence. The 25th Division artillery commander, Bittman Barth, wrote: "His handling of the fight probably saved the division. He was decorated once with the DSC and again with the Silver Star. He earned them several times over."

Task Force Wilson (né Dolvin) was very nearly overwhelmed by a second "human wave" assault that night. The CCF overran Wilson's CP and forced the command group to fall back in confusion. In the melee B Company, fighting valiantly, lost 177 of 203 men but held its ground. The surviving Wolfhounds of the shattered E Company, still operating independently of Murch's 2/27, also made a magnificent stand under their inspiring leader, Desiderio, who finally fell, mortally wounded, crying, "Hold on till daylight and we've got it made!"\* Farther back, the Wolfhounds of Murch's 2/27 also fought bravely. The artillerymen of Gus Terry's 8th FAB, in a desperate effort to stay on their position, leveled their 105s and fired point-blank into the oncoming masses.[30]

---

\*Desiderio was awarded the Medal of Honor posthumously; E Company won a Presidential Unit Citation.

\* \* \*

To the right of Task Force Dolvin some elements of Corley's 24th Infantry were poorly deployed when the Chinese struck. B Company of Miller's 1/24 had zoomed well ahead of the other units. Corley ordered Miller to pull back B Company and tie the 1/24 into Task Force Dolvin. Miller sent his C Company forward to assist B in the withdrawal. B Company got out, but C Company was surrounded and, as historian Marshall wrote, forced to "surrender in a body." As a result, the 1/24 was soon in "very bad shape."

To the right Melvin Blair's 3/24 was lucky. It had unwittingly advanced deep into the rear of the CCF assembly areas and had lost touch with Corley. The CCF, apparently unaware of its presence, swarmed around the 3/24 perimeter. Like Fisher's 35th Infantry, Blair's 3/24 was untouched. When Corley finally made contact with Blair, he ordered him to withdraw and consolidate with Miller's shattered 1/24, but the consolidation was never achieved.[31]

On the extreme right of the 24th Infantry's sector, held by George Clayton's 2/24, the CCF hit very hard. Under the weight of the attack the battalion came apart. Two of its four companies (F and H) were surrounded, and many men were captured. The F Company commander, Roger Walden, remembered that it was "an indescribable situation . . . really a mess," with troops intermingled and jumping on trucks bound for rear areas. But Clayton and two rifle companies (E and G) carried out their wounded and sideslipped to the right (or southeast) into the adjoining sector held by McMains's 3/9, and as Sloane wrote later, they fought "in an excellent manner" and did "fine work" in repulsing several CCF attacks.[32]

\* \* \*

When the Chinese struck, Chin Sloane's 9th Infantry was spread far and wide, its sector split by the Chongchon River. In no more than an hour most of the regiment was in complete chaos.

On the left flank, held by McMains's 3/9, two understrength rifle companies (K and L), which were poorly supplied, ill deployed, and imprudently out of physical and telephonic contact with all other units (including the 37th FAB), were immediately and decisively overwhelmed. After pouring through this gap in huge numbers, the CCF soon gained a crossing of the Chongchon River and cut the highway between the 9th's forward infantry line and the divisional artillery base at Kujang.[33]

In the center of the line—also on the west bank of the Chongchon River—Butch Barberis's 2/9 (minus E Company) was stoutly dug in on high ground. He heard and saw the din of battle nearby, but the 2/9 was not taken under attack. "They missed us practically entirely," he remembered. Later, when he reconstructed the action that night, he calculated somewhat ruefully that hundreds, perhaps thousands of CCF troops had stolen silently by or through his positions. They crossed the river to join those who had broken through the 3/9 sector.[34]

On the right flank Wolfe's 1/9 was hit simultaneously. The weight of the attack fell on A, B, and C companies. Aided by forces infiltrating across the river through the 2/9 and 3/9 sectors, the CCF overran the 1/9 CP. Wolfe—and most of his staff—retreated to Sloane's CP. Sloane sent Wolfe to the rear—never to return—and the assistant regimental S-3, James F. Hill, thirty-nine, replaced Wolfe as 1/9 commander.[35]

Of the 1/9 units engaged in this desperate fight, one would inspire awe and legend. That was B Company, commanded by William C. Wallace. Owing to the shortage of replacements and Chin Sloane's liberal attitude toward blacks, the 1/9, like the 2/9, had earlier absorbed a large number of black fillers. Of B Company's 129 men when the fight began, about half were black, including the big, strong company exec, Lieutenant Ellison C. Wynn.[36]

The historian Marshall recorded that the brave and stubborn B Company was the last unit in Eighth Army to "yield its forward ground." Wounded early in the action (and awarded a DSC), Wallace turned over command to his black exec, Wynn. In the fierce fighting, the understrength company was gradually whittled to thirty-four men holding a hilltop with little or no ammo. Among the survivors was a defiant black BAR man, Robert Noel, Jr., who won a Silver Star.

But Wynn was the most defiant of all. Marshall wrote that when Wynn ran out of ammo, he gathered up "an armful of rocks and canned C rations" and began hurling them at the CCF. "The enemy was so startled by the fury of his personal attack," Marshall continued, "that momentarily the fire slackened. One white enlisted man stood with him, swinging his empty rifle as a club, ready to brain anyone who tried to rush his lieutenant." Wynn was finally felled by a grenade that "blew the side of his face away," but he staggered to the rear under his own steam—later to recover and to receive a DSC.

The attached E Company (of the 2/9) likewise had a tough fight. It was brutally ejected from its hilltop, suffering about 30 percent casualties: fifty-two dead and wounded. But E Company was "Barberis trained"; it did not yield easily either. By dawn its survivors had doggedly recaptured its hill. Forced to contract his 1/9 "front," Sloane sent those men of E Company back across the Chongchon River to their home, the 2/9, which had spent a quiet night out of combat. With the return of E Company, Barberis now had all four of his undermanned companies together—the strongest surviving element of the 9th Infantry.[37]

\* \* \*

Earlier, on the afternoon of November 25, Paul Freeman had begun moving his reserve 23d Infantry up behind the 9th Infantry at the Chongchon River. His mission was to attack through the 9th Infantry on the next day, in effect, to displace the 9th, which would go into reserve. Freeman established his CP near a forward artillery position which was held by Joseph Buys's black 503d FAB, plus the 61st FAB of the 1st Cav Division, commanded by Joseph Knott. Claire Hutchin and most of his 1/23, which would spearhead the 23d's attack, bivouacked nearby.[38]

Freeman had only just settled in when the CCF struck the 9th Infantry. Pouring through the gaps in the 3/9 or sneaking by the 2/9, the CCF crossed the Chongchon River in darkness and hit the 61st FAB (but not the 503d FAB). The men of the 61st FAB ("strangers" from the 1st Cav Division), who had themselves only just arrived, were furious. They had detected the oncoming CCF and had requested permission from Loyal Haynes's 2d Division artillery headquarters to open fire, but the request had been stupidly and inexplicably denied. The men of the 61st FAB suffered the consequences. One, James Marks, remembered:

All up and down the river valley, all hell had broken loose. Tracers and explosions, left and right. Flares would explode, giving too much light, then flutter down and extinguish themselves in frozen corn stubble. The Chinese blew bugles and whistles and shouted American profanity. I thought their bugles were playing "Silent Night, Holy Night." Between shots and explosions I could hear the wounded crying for help. . . . Men sprinted in every direction. I grabbed our medic (who was killed later that night): "What'n hell's going on?" "Get out of here. We're overrun."[39]

Indeed so. The 61st was swamped by CCF troops, who forced the artillerymen to abandon their eighteen 105-mm howitzers and fight for their lives. In the melee and withdrawal A Battery commander Rex Gunnell was killed, replaced by his exec, West Pointer (1948) John P. Kean. Paul Freeman later remembered that the 61st stampeded and ran away, but its survivors hotly denied that. They claimed that they withdrew, fighting all the way, and that furthermore, on the following morning they went back and retrieved half of their abandoned howitzers under fire. (Nine 105-mm howitzers were not recovered.) "The 61st was not shattered at Kunu," Kean wrote. "We were hard hit when the Chinese attacked across the Chongchon River near midnight, and we were knocked out of action for about 10 hours. We recaptured our guns and equipment and we were operational in a new gun position near Kunu by ten A.M. the next morning, November 26."[40]

Freeman had camped for the night well prepared for trouble. Three companies of Hutchin's 1/23 (A; B; D) had taken positions behind the 61st FAB, facing the river, supported by tank and heavy mortar companies. When the oncoming CCF hit Freeman's positions, they met a hurricane of well-directed fire. The enemy fell by the score, regrouped, then reattacked in successive waves. But they could not crack the 1/23 perimeter. CCF casualties in this assault were frightful: 410 dead; 111 captured; untold numbers wounded. Orientalist Freeman personally interrogated many of the prisoners in Chinese. He found them "scared to death that they were really going to be clobbered by the Americans."[41]

The mission of this mass of Chinese was to destroy the artillery of the 61st and 503d FABs. About half of them had no weapons; they carried satchel charges to blow up the guns. They had not expected to encounter Freeman's infantry and armor. The latter had deflected their attack against the 503d FAB and distracted them from destroying the 61st's guns and vehicles. Except for driving the men of the 61st to the rear temporarily, these CCF troops had failed in their mission.[42]

But on the following morning, as the 1/9 was falling back on the 23d's sector in disarray, other CCF troops posed yet another threat to Freeman's positions. These came in large numbers from the north and east, driving off Hutchin's C Company to occupy a tall hill (Chinaman's Hat), which dominated Freeman's sector. In that action a wounded sergeant, John A. Pittman, threw himself on a CCF grenade and survived—to win the Medal of Honor. At Freeman's urgent request Dutch Keiser released James Edwards's 2/23 from reserve. It arrived in the afternoon with a company of tanks. Freeman threw four rifle companies (A; B; E; G), backed by massive firepower, at Chinaman's Hat, but he was still not able to recapture it.[43]

That night, as Freeman was shifting his forces around to tighten the perimeter, the CCF again attacked in massive numbers. The attack carried straight through to Freeman's CP, forcing him and his staff to abandon it so hurriedly there was not even time to grab secret code books. In the wild, close fighting that ensued, Freeman assembled a variegated "task force" and attempted to retake his CP (and get the code books), but this effort failed.

Chin Sloane ordered Butch Barberis to bring his 2/9 east across the river to reinforce Freeman's 23d sector. As Barberis prepared to respond to these orders, his 2/9 itself was suddenly and overwhelming attacked by other CCF troops. In a matter of twenty minutes Barberis's F and G companies were decimated by swarms of enemy; in G company alone, seventy-three men fell dead or wounded. His E Company, already shattered in the previous day's fighting, was reduced to a handful of men. Only his heavy-weapons company (H) escaped without grievous losses. Collecting what was left of the 2/9, Barberis led them east across the river to tie in with Hutchin's 1/23 for a Custer's Last Stand. But by the time Barberis got across the river, the CCF had mysteriously withdrawn from the battlefield and Freeman had reoccupied his CP and recovered the code books.[44]

The shift of the 2/9 east of the river had left McMains's 3/9 absolutely alone in left field, on the west bank of the Chongchon. He had lost his K and L companies, but his I and M companies were still in fair shape. Moreover, his strength had been substantially enhanced when E and G companies of Clayton's sideslipping 2/24 came into his sector. Although about half of Clayton's 350 men were wounded, frostbitten, shell-shocked, or otherwise incapacitated and had to be sent to the rear, McMains was able to salvage and rearm enough able-bodied men to form two understrength "provisional" rifle companies, in effect to replace his missing K and L companies. In this way the 3/9 now became the strongest surviving element of the 9th Infantry.[45]

From reports of the few K and L Company survivors trickling across the river, Chin Sloane believed that the 3/9 had been either wiped out or cut off. Late on the evening of November 26, when the crisis in Freeman's 23d sector had temporarily abated, Sloane ordered Barberis to take his 2/9 back across the Chongchon River to find McMains, whatever was left of the 3/9, and other stragglers. With the 2/9 reduced by this time to about one-third strength (about 259 men), Barberis plunged back into the icy waters of the Chongchon.[46]

By this time Barberis had devised a means of easing the misery of crossing the icy river. He remembered: "We had been allowed to buy a bottle of whiskey each for the first three grades [senior NCOs] and the officers. When it arrived, many of the NCOs had been wounded and evacuated or were missing, so we had a great surplus [of whiskey] which my S-four carried around in a supply truck. It proved to be a godsend. After we crossed the river, I'd have my men go into a well-heated Korean house and give them a finger of whiskey in their canteens. They sipped whiskey and warmed and dried their feet."[47]

\* \* \*

When the Chinese attacked Peploe's 38th Infantry, Jack Rodarm's A Company, which had been sent ahead to scout, was still bivouacked well forward of the regiment. The CCF hit A Company first, inflicting thirty-one casualties (five dead). Fortunately for Rodarm the CCF paused to loot A Company's abandoned gear: sleeping bags, rations, guns, and ammo. Granted this respite, the survivors filtered back through the hills to Skeldon's 2/38 positions and later reassembled in the rear. But nearly half the company was missing.[48]

By this time Skeldon's 2/38 itself was under severe CCF attack. Survivors remembered that the Chinese troops blew bugles and trilled "sweet music" on flutes. It was a "terrible moonlight serenade," like a "scene from a nightmare—a lunatic's delight." In the initial onslaught Skeldon's G Company was overwhelmed, losing 104 of 160 men. However, his F Company, holding a strong position on a hill and reinforced by reserves from E Company, deflected the waves of Chinese and, after a harrowing night fight, survived mostly intact. One of F Company's courageous machine gunners, Robert K. Imrie, killed at his post, won a posthumous DSC.[49]

On the right of Skeldon Harold Maixner's 3/38, the easternmost of the American battalions in Eighth Army, was also massively hit. The main blow fell on L Company, which was not only holding a position in the line but also providing security for the 3/38 CP. The CCF quickly overran L Company's position, forcing Maixner to withdraw his CP rearward. In this initial assault L Company was devastated, losing 110 of its 200 men. Maixner survived, but his battalion staff also sustained heavy casualties.

Oddly, Maixner's other two rifle companies, I and K, holding down the extreme right flank of the 2d Division, were untouched. They abutted the ROK 7th Division, the left flank of ROK II Corps. However, landline communications to I and K companies were lost during the night with the result that neither Maixner nor Peploe could learn anything about their status.[50]

By daylight Peploe was deeply concerned. During the night four of his nine rifle companies (A, G, F, and L) had been hard hit, and another (B), attempting to reinforce the line, sideswiped. Having received no word from I and K companies, he concluded that they had probably been lost. Moreover, at about that time the ROK 3d Regiment sideslipped into his sector, reporting that ROK II Corps on his right was collapsing.

* * *

Inasmuch as no measures had been taken to improve communications with ROK II Corps, its status was still not known to Walker. The KMAG adviser, Robert Cameron, later wrote that in the initial assault the CCF struck massively at the seam between the ROK 7th and 8th divisions "with the suddenness of a bolt of lightning." The abutting ROK 8th and 10th regiments (at the seam) were forced to give way flanks under the pressure. The CCF poured through the gap, raced to the rear of both divisions, and blocked the Tokchon road behind the 7th Division. When the seriousness of the penetration was realized, the corps reserve (ROK 2d Regiment) was committed to break the block and counterattack the CCF behind the ROK 7th Division, but the CCF adroitly repelled this effort. By the morning of November 26 ROK II Corps was in utter chaos.[51]

* * *

George Peploe believed that the CCF must have committed the bulk of its troops in North Korea to strike at the ROKs and his 38th Infantry. Because of the grave situation in ROK II Corps, he wisely concluded that he should break off the 38th's attack, incorporate the orphan ROK 3d Regiment, and regroup on the defensive, facing east. He recommended this course to

Dutch Keiser and also that measures be taken to reinforce Tokchon, to prevent an encirclement of the 38th and the ROKs, and to hold open an egress should they be forced to withdraw.

In keeping with his management style, Keiser was at his CP. He had not gone out to get the feel of the battlefield; he depended on ADC Sladen Bradley and others to serve as his "eyes and ears." Peploe's telephone call that morning reporting the plight of ROK II Corps was the first word Keiser received of serious trouble on the army's right flank. But the real gravity of the situation did not sink in. Believing CCF opposition could not, finally, amount to much, he dismissed Peploe's alert as "a local problem," possibly a CCF spoiling attack to screen its general withdrawal to the Yalu. However, he accepted Peploe's recommendation that the 38th shift from offense to defense and that Tokchon be reinforced.

That day, November 26, Peploe attempted to realign his regiment on the defensive, but not without great difficulty and further heavy losses. An armored patrol "found" his I and K companies, both miraculously intact and unscathed. Peploe decided to pull them back, face Maixner's 3/38 east, and back it with the ROK 3d Regiment and Keleher's 1/38, plus major elements of O'Donnell's 38th FAB. But these orders could not be executed. While pulling back, K Company was encircled by the CCF and wiped out. In an attempt to restore the 3/38 CP on position, the shattered L Company was enveloped from the rear and never heard from again. In that fight Maixner and his CP were again forced to flee rearward. The 38th FAB came under heavy attack, as did a battery of the 503d FAB, which was reinforcing the 38th. Artillerymen of both outfits beat back repeated CCF attacks, firing 105-mm howitzers into the CCF masses at point-blank range.[52]

By evening Peploe's situation was nothing less than dire. It was now obvious that ROK II Corps on his right had utterly collapsed. Although Peploe's shattered units and some ROKs of the 3d Regiment had fought credibly—and often heroically—Peploe had been unable to establish a firm east-facing blocking line. His possible route of withdrawal, south through Tokchon, was cut; The sole hope of survival for the 38th's regiments lay in a fighting withdrawal southwest down the Chongchon River into the congested heart of the 2d Division at Kujang and Kunu.

Peploe perceived early and clearly that the right flank of Eighth Army had been decisively and dangerously breached and turned. At higher headquarters Keiser, Coulter, and Walker obstinately continued to view the situation on the right flank of the army as a "local problem," which, while growing ever more serious, could still be rectified by proper tactical maneuvers and reinforcements. There was still no clear perception that the CCF had struck Eighth Army in such massive strength that it was in imminent danger of encirclement from CCF positions on the east flank formerly held by ROK II Corps.[53]

# IV

Throughout the day of November 26 Johnnie Walker was profoundly puzzled, perhaps even in mild shock. It seemed inconceivable that the CCF could have entered North Korea in great numbers undetected, yet the mounting evidence indicated otherwise. He did not, however, cancel his offensive; it was not in his nature. Besides, to have done so would no doubt have invited another thunderbolt from MacArthur. He merely informed GHQ, Tokyo, that something strange was afoot. The CCF, Walker told MacArthur in vast understatement, was "attacking in strength," but it was "too early" to tell if this action constituted local counterattacks or a major offensive.[54]

Exactly what had happened to ROK II Corps was still not known at Eighth Army headquarters by nightfall on November 26, twenty-four hours after the onset of the CCF offensive. The G-3, John Dabney, logged that the ROK 7th and 8th divisions had "collapsed" but that "practically nothing was known with respect to the location of ROK units" except for the 3d Regiment, which had drifted into Peploe's sector. Dabney conceded that Eighth Army headquarters did not know "whether the collapse of the entire ROK front was caused by enemy counterattack action alone, coupled with infiltration, or by a full scale offensive."[55]

The deteriorating situation on the army's right flank demanded urgent and all-out reinforcements. Walker's response on November 26 was tentative. First he ordered that Basil Coad's Commonwealth Brigade, the reserve for I Corps (where the front was still relatively quiet and stable), reinforce the right flank near Sunchon. Then he alerted Hap Gay's 1st Cav, in Eighth Army reserve, for possible movement to Sunchon, but he did not order the movement.

On the morning of November 27 it finally became clear to Walker that he confronted a major CCF offensive. He then took belated measures to shore up his collapsing right flank. He ordered that:

• John Coulter's IX Corps was to assume full responsibility for the entire ROK II Corps sector and guarantee the integrity of Eighth Army's right flank.

• Hap Gay's 1st Cav Division was to assemble at best speed at Sunchon, on the right of the Commonwealth Brigade. Gay was to turn the fleeing ROK II Corps around, backstop it, and be prepared to counterattack the CCF.

• John Church's 24th Division, as yet not under attack, was to prepare to withdraw south through Sinanju for probable redeployment to Sunchon.

• The Turkish Brigade,* bivouacked near Kunu in IX Corps reserve, was to attack east to Tokchon and recapture that place.

In sum, all available army and corps reserves—the 1st Cav Division, the Commonwealth and Turkish brigades—were to be employed to shore up the army's right flank under IX Corps control.[56]

Of these measures, the first that could be carried out was the attack of the Turks toward Tokchon. It proved to be a disappointing maneuver.

The Turks, commanded by Brigadier General Tahsin Yazici, had arrived in Korea like the Marines, in a blaze of publicity. With their colorful, flowing mustaches, swarthy complexions, and fierce demeanors, they gave war correspondents and others the impression they were very tough soldiers. The reality was that they were ill trained, ill led, and green to combat. Mike Michaelis remembered: "The Turks were commanded by an aged brigadier who had been a division commander at Gallipoli in 1916 fighting the British! He was highly respected, high up in the Turkish military establishment, and took a bust to brigadier to command the brigade. The average Turk soldier in the brigade came from the steppe country of Turkey, near Russia, had probably had only three or four years of school, was uprooted, moved to western Turkey, given a uniform, [a] rifle, and a little smattering of training, stuck on a ship, sailed ten thousand miles, then dumped off on a peninsula—'Korea, where's that?'— and told the enemy was up there someplace, go get him! The Turk soldier scratches his head and says, 'What's he done to me?' "[57]

There was another problem. Very few of the Turks spoke English, and no Americans spoke Turkish. Hence communications between IX Corps headquarters and the Turks were primitive.

On Coulter's order Yazici sent one of his battalions east toward Tokchon. After it was on the road, Coulter, acting on information that indicated large numbers of CCF troops were converging on Tokchon, instructed the Turks to halt on the road near Wawon and dig into defensive positions. The Army historian wrote that Yazici "misunderstood" these instructions. Believing Coulter had ordered him to return the battalion to its original point of departure, Yazici did so, leaving Eighth Army's right flank wide open. Later that day, returning to Wawon, the Turks made another mistake: They "captured" what they believed to be 125 CCF troops. The "CCF troops" turned out to be ROKs.[58]

It should have been clear from these episodes that there was going to be

---

*Officially the brigade was called the Turkish Army Command Force. Having been the first recipients of military aid under the 1947 Truman Doctrine, the Greeks and Turks felt obliged to repay Truman by committing military forces to Korea. A Greek battalion, which sailed after the Turks, was soon to land in Korea.

a problem with the Turks and that closer liaison and control were necessary. However, nothing was done. Like the war correspondents, Coulter apparently was mesmerized by the Turks and continued to regard them as superhuman fighters rather than the poorly led green troops that they were. Coulter's misplaced confidence in the Turks led to disastrous consequences.

\* \* \*

All that day, November 27, Dutch Keiser's 2d Division and Bill Kean's 25th Division remained under relentless CCF attack. During the day Walker authorized both divisions to make "fighting withdrawals." They were to converge gradually on the road hub of Kunu—the 25th from the north, the 2d from the northeast—where it was believed (or hoped) they could consolidate into strong, mutually supporting positions on or just below the Chongchon River.[59]

The first stop in the 2d Division's withdrawal was to be Kujang. The plan was that Paul Freeman's 23d Infantry would replace Chin Sloane's badly shattered 9th Infantry on the left; George Peploe's 38th (plus the attached ROK 3d Regiment) and Turks would remain on the right. The two infantry regiments would be supported by five battalions of artillery (including the attached 17th FAB with its eight-inch howitzers), tanks, A/A Quad 50s, combat engineers, and other units.

Before these shifts could be executed, the CCF again struck the 2d Division's forward outposts in awesome numbers. On the right George Peploe's mauled and withdrawing 38th Infantry was beset from all sides. The attached ROK 3d Regiment gave way and bugged out. On the left (or west) side of the Chongchon River, Sloane's 1/9, commanded by James Hill, also gave way and fell back in disarray. Barberis's 250-man 2/9 and McMains's 3/9 (reinforced by the two provisional companies of the 2/24) held for a while, but finally, the 3/9 also gave way. In this wild fighting many 3/9 officers and men were killed, wounded, or captured. Among the wounded was Julius Becton, exec of I Company, who earlier had been wounded on the Naktong River. Among the captured were McMains's black exec, John Harlan, and the black adjutant, Clifford Allen.[60]

\* \* \*

Bill Kean's plan was to pull back and regroup his 25th Division elements at Yongbyon, a walled city about nine miles above Kunu. The remnants of Vennard Wilson's shattered task force, in the division's center, were placed under command of Gordon Murch and loosely integrated into Murch's hard-hit 2/27, which had been brought forward to support the task force. Murch would hold at Ipsok, while Hank Fisher's as yet unscathed 35th Infantry, in the division's left sector, withdrew from the hills near Unsan and crossed Murch's rear to Yongbyon. At the same time the two surviving battalions of Corley's 24th Infantry (1/24 and 3/24), backstopped by Michaelis's 27th Infantry (less Murch's 2/27), would fall back on Yongbyon.[61]

Murch collected the remnants of Task Force Wilson and dug into positions at Ipsok soon after dark that night, November 27. Moments later the CCF hit him in force. Murch's Wolfhounds in F and G companies, assisted by Gus Terry's 9th FAB, put up a magnificent defense, delivering punishing fire on the swarming CCF. In this fight F Company was wiped out; G Company lost forty-nine men. Murch himself fought the enemy with small arms from his besieged CP.[62]

Fisher, meanwhile, was pulling back in the dark as fast as he could go. For the most part his withdrawal was as free of CCF contact as was his advance. At the end, while preparing to cross the Kuryong River behind Murch's 2/27, Fisher became heavily engaged with CCF troops, but his K Company held them off until most of the tanks, guns, and vehicles of Hogan's 64th FAB and the regimental trains got out safely. As Fisher was arriving at Yongbyon (having yet to experience an all-out CCF attack), Murch was withdrawing his mangled 2/27 and the remnants of Task Force Wilson.[63]

By the following morning, November 28, most of the 25th Division was assembled and holding new positions around Yongbyon. Some elements had suffered grievously: Task Force Wilson (né Dolvin), including Fisher's B Company; Corley's 1/24 and 2/24 (half of it now fighting with the 3/9); Murch's 2/27. But the rest of the division was in pretty good shape. The artillery and seven of its nine infantry battalions were still more or less intact. Between them, Fisher and Michaelis could count five infantry battalions that had yet to meet the CCF. The big problem was ammo; few of the 25th Division units had sufficient stocks for a sustained defense at Yongbyon or anywhere else. Owing to the traffic jams on the roads, caused by the shifting around of troops and panic among some of the truck drivers, only a trickle of ammo was getting forward.

*　*　*

The same morning, November 28, it became obvious that the 2d Division could not make a stand at Kujang and that it would probably be lucky to escape encirclement. Accordingly, Walker ordered a further withdrawal to Won, a few miles northeast of Kunu. Paul Freeman's 23d Infantry—still in good shape—was designated to fight a delaying action, then to hold strong positions at Won, so that Keiser could regroup the 9th and 38th infantry and other divisional elements at Kunu. Butch Barberis's 2/9—still on the west side of the Chongchon River—would assist Freeman in the delaying action.[64]

The withdrawal of the 2d Division down the single road to Won on November 28 resulted in an epic traffic jam. The CCF did not attempt to interdict or block the road but attacked the columns from the rear. Paul Freeman designated Claire Hutchin's 1/23 to serve as the rear guard. As such Hutchin had first to rescue his C Company, which had been overrun and forced to abandon its equipment. In an extraordinary display of heroism, which earned him a DSC, he gathered up the remnants of C Company and personally led them back up a hill to recover their gear. Thereafter he positioned himself with the hindmost unit of the 1/23 (A Company), leading it in fighting off repeated battalion-strength CCF attacks on the heels of the column.[65]

Meanwhile, Keiser kept Barberis and his depleted 2/9 on the west side of the Chongchon River until almost everyone on the east side except Hutchin's 1/23 had cleared Kujang. Finally, Barberis, who had been wounded, and his men were released and, for the third time in as many days, waded across the icy Chongchon. Barberis leapfrogged ahead of Hutchin toward Won to set up positions through which the 1/23 could safely withdraw. By then it was dark and the CCF was closing in from all sides. Hutchin, severely wounded in the face by mortar fragments, brought his valiant 1/23 through Barberis's positions, then deployed into new blocking positions at Won.[66]

At about that time Barberis and what remained of the 2/9 came under vicious CCF attack. The remaining fragment of E Company and its commander, Joseph Manto, were swallowed up; Manto was captured. Learning that Barberis was in serious trouble, Hutchin, who was now solidly on new positions just south of Won, suggested Barberis withdraw through him. Barberis did so, arriving at Kunu with but 147 men left of the 970 who had constituted the 2/9 a week earlier. A nightlong stream of walking stragglers from the 9th and 38th Infantry and the ROK 3d Regiment followed Barberis through the 1/23 block.[67]

In contrast with Bill Kean's 25th Division, Dutch Keiser's 2d Division was in very bad shape. Sloane's 9th and Peploe's 38th Infantry regiments had been devastated, Sloane's 9th virtually wiped out. Some ancillary units thrown in to support the infantry, such as the 2d Combat Engineer Group, had likewise been shattered, and the group's commander, West Pointer (1929) Frank H. Forney, killed. The 72d Tank Battalion and the 82d A/A Battalion had been riddled. Except for the 17th FAB (with its eight-inch guns), most of the artillery units had been hard hit. Only Freeman's 23d Infantry, with its attached but "unfamiliar" 15th FAB, could be described as combat-effective, but Hutchin's 1/23 had sustained crippling losses in the rifle companies.[68]

Meanwhile, John Coulter had deployed the Turkish Brigade to the right (or southeast) of Peploe's 38th. As originally intended they dug in at Wawon, filling in the yawning gap between Peploe and the Commonwealth Brigade, assembling in the south at Sunchon. It was vital to hold this gap; otherwise, the CCF could drive a wedge between the 2d Division and the Commonwealth Brigade, thereby cutting off the 2d Division at Kunu.

Soon after the Turks had dug in at Wawon, they were massively attacked by CCF. The Turks fixed bayonets and lunged bravely. For several hours they held Wawon. Later a heroic legend would circulate that they bayoneted 200 CCF troops to death. But the truth was that these overrated, poorly led green troops broke and bugged out, again leaving the entire right flank of Eighth Army exposed. The Turks took a "look at the situation," Paul Freeman remembered, "and they had no stomach for it, and they were running in all directions."[69]

\* \* \*

The chaotic situation on the army's right flank led Walker to take drastic action on November 28. He ordered Shrimp Milburn to withdraw John Church's 24th Division (still untouched) and the ROK 1st Division (under increasing CCF pressure) below the Chongchon River. Church's 24th was to swing around to Sunchon to reinforce the army's right flank; the ROK 1st would fall back on Sukchon.

In view of the mounting CCF pressure, this was a complex and risky maneuver. The detailed plan was as follows. Johnny Throckmorton's 5th Infantry would hold a bridgehead at Sinanju, while Ned Moore's 19th and Dick Stephens's 21st regiments withdrew and headed for Sunchon. Throckmorton would hold at Sinanju until the ROK 1st Division had also crossed the river, then would blow the bridges. The newly arrived 29th British Brigade would come up from Kaesong to relieve Throckmorton, who would then join the 24th Division at Sunchon.

The maneuver was well executed. Throckmorton established a strong position on the south bank of the Chongchon. All elements of the 24th and ROK 1st divisions crossed the river into Sinanju, bringing out all weapons, heavy equipment, and supplies. There was no panic, no stampede. Except for some casualties in Moore's 19th Infantry, both divisions emerged in good shape. "All the men were mounted on some type of vehicle," Throckmorton recalled. "Hundreds of vehicles with lights burning moving south through a snowstorm."[70]\*

The lead regiments of John Church's 24th Division, Ned Moore's 19th and Dick Stephens's 21st, hurried first south, then east to the vicinity of Sunchon. There they assembled close behind the 1st Cav Division, which had come up from its reserve positions in the south. Some confusion resulted. The 19th's S-3, Elliott Cutler, remembered that Hap Gay attempted to assume control of the 19th and 21st regiments, but both Ned Moore and Dick Stephens

---

\*Exhibiting a curious touch of "leadership," Johnnie Walker telephoned Throckmorton in the midst of this grave crisis to say he had just given him a battlefield promotion to full colonel. It was the third such promotion after Michaelis and Corley.

balked at that and, on appeal to the IX Corps staff, won their case. Throckmorton, meanwhile, blew the bridges at Sinanju, but on Walker's orders his 5th Infantry remained at Sinanju to hold open the Sinanju–Kunu road as a possible escape route for the forces at Kunu.[71]

## V

On the second day of the CCF offensive against Eighth Army, November 27, Ned Almond launched the X Corps offensive from the Chosin Reservoir. Conceived by GHQ, Tokyo, as a maneuver to "support" Eighth Army, the tactical goal was to strike west to the vicinity of Mupyong, northeast of Kunu in the CCF "rear," to cut the Chinese supply lines and, possibly, to envelop the CCF in front of Eighth Army from that flank. The final plan:

• O. P. Smith's 1st Marine Division would spearhead the offensive from Yudam on the west side of the Chosin Reservoir, employing the Fifth and Seventh Marines.
• The Army's 7th Division, led by Task Force MacLean, assembling on the east shore of the Chosin Reservoir on the right flank of the Marines, would go due north to Changjin, thence to the Yalu River.
• The Army's 3d Division, led by John Guthrie's 7th Infantry, assembling at Sachang (twenty-five miles south-southwest of Yudam), would attack westward on the left flank of the Marines.[72]

In view of the rugged, nearly impassable terrain, the bitter cold weather, the paucity of forces available, the logistical difficulties, and—not least—the growing weight of the CCF offensive against Eighth Army, the X Corps offensive on November 27 ranks as the most ill-advised and unfortunate operation of the Korean War. The X Corps staff members had never liked the idea, and had dragged their feet, perhaps hoping GHQ would change its mind. Almond's chief of staff, Nick Ruffner, later wrote: "It was an insane plan. You couldn't take a picnic lunch in peacetime and go over that terrain in November and December."[73]

The X Corps staff laid the blame on MacArthur and the GHQ staff—specifically, Pinky Wright—for the insanity. But Almond was not without fault. He was the senior man on the scene. Had he forcefully recommended cancellation of the offensive, MacArthur surely would have reconsidered. But Almond, like Walker, was reluctant to challenge MacArthur's legendary military genius. His deputy chief of staff and confidant, Bill McCaffrey, remembered: "General Almond was not about to protest an order from General MacArthur. After all, everyone said Inchon wouldn't work. . . ."[74]

The Marines, from O. P. Smith on down, were exceedingly reluctant to proceed with the offensive. Smith's CP, newly established at Hagaru, was sixty road miles from Hamhung; Yudam was another fourteen miles from Hagaru. There was still only a single tortuous road over which supplies for the Marines could be brought forward. Chesty Puller had outposted the road with his First Marines, placing one battalion at Chinhung, one battalion at Koto, and one battalion at Hagaru. But these battalions were about ten miles apart and in no way mutually supporting. Hence the road was vulnerable. The enemy could cut it almost at will.

Underlying all considerations at the Chosin Reservoir was the doubt that X Corps faced serious opposition. Charles Willoughby had planted that doubt. It was shared by Almond's G-2, Bill Quinn. Although by November 27 the Marines had captured Chinese identified as members of six different CCF divisions (the 58th, 60th, 89th, 124th, and 126th)* who freely boasted that the CCF was on the verge of an all-out offensive to annihilate the 1st Marine Division and X Corps, O. P. Smith's G-2 also shared the doubt. He apparently believed the Clint Tarkenton theory that these Chinese were "volunteers" from those divisions in Manchuria. He judged that opposition would be minimal and that as the Marines advanced from Yudam to Mupyong, the enemy would withdraw.[75]

\* \* \*

The underestimation of CCF strength and the rush to launch the X Corps offensive per schedule on November 27 had led to an ill-advised thinning out of American forces on the east side of the Chosin Reservoir. There the lead elements of Task Force MacLean, Don Faith's 1/32, had relieved the Fifth Marines on November 25 and 26, but without support from artillery, A/A vehicles, or tanks. Because of the delays in redeployment, the rest of Task Force MacLean had encountered, Faith's battalion, which occupied the forwardmost Fifth Marine positions, stood alone east of Chosin for a full day.[76]

The 7th Division ADC, "Hammering" Hank Hodes, arrived at Faith's CP about noon on November 26. Such was Faith's confidence—and underestimation of and contempt for the enemy—that he made an astounding proposal. If Hodes could borrow a tank platoon from the Marines, Faith was prepared

---

*The 124th, 125th, and 126th divisions, constituting the CCF Forty-second Army, which had originally deployed at Chosin, had been transferred west. They constituted a major portion of the CCF that shattered ROK II Corps on Eighth Army's right flank and the Turkish Brigade. The Marines thus had correctly identified only four of the twelve CCF divisions making up the CCF Ninth Army Group at Chosin. The complete enemy force was composed of three CCF armies, each reinforced by an extra division. These were: the Twentieth Army (58th, 59th, 60th, plus 89th); the Twenty-sixth Army (76th, 77th, 78th, plus 94th); and the Twenty-seventh Army (79th, 80th, 81st, plus 70th).

to attack north on the following day, November 27. That would, in effect, launch Task Force MacLean simultaneously with the attack of the Fifth and Seventh Marines from Yudam. Hodes may have been tempted to compete with the Marines—and perhaps bring credit to the Army—but he rightly viewed the scheme as overly risky and scotched it. The attack of Task Force MacLean would go a day after the Marines, on November 28, after all its elements had arrived.

Early on the morning of November 27 Ned Almond jeeped north sixty miles from his headquarters at Hamhung to Hagaru, then another fourteen miles northwest to Yudam, to watch the Marines launch the offensive. Along the way he passed various strung-out elements of Task Force MacLean: Bill Reilly's 3/31, Ray Embree's 57th FAB, MacLean's 31st Infantry headquarters group, the eight A/A vehicles of Company D, 15th A/A Battalion, commanded by James R. McClymont, and lastly, the twenty-two tanks of the 31st Tank Company.[77]

The weather at Yudam was miserable: zero degrees and a blinding snowstorm. Because of the intense cold, carbines and BARs locked, mortars cracked, canteens burst, blood plasma and rations froze solid. Ray Murray's Fifth Marines, which had arrived only the day before to join the Seventh Marines, mounted what one Marine historian described as an "unenthusiastic" attack. Almost immediately the men met unexpected and fierce CCF resistance. In sixteen brutal hours of struggle, the Fifth Marines suffered heavy casualties and gained merely 1,500 yards.[78]

While the Marines were undergoing this ordeal on November 27, the rest of Task Force MacLean arrived east of Chosin. MacLean and Embree got there first in command jeeps. MacLean went forward to see Faith and his officers, whom he knew well. (Earlier, in Japan, MacLean had briefly commanded the 32d Infantry.) MacLean confirmed to Faith that Task Force MacLean would attack north on the following day with whatever forces were on hand and that the 1/32 would spearhead the attack.

Among the first elements of Task Force MacLean to arrive that afternoon was the 31st's I and R Platoon. Late in the day MacLean sent it out to scout. It was never heard from again. Unknown to MacLean, it was ambushed in the hills by CCF troops, who killed or captured the entire platoon.

MacLean stacked his other forces in a line north to south, more or less in the order of arrival: Faith's 1/32; MacLean's forward or tactical CP; the 31st Heavy Mortar Company; Bill Reilly's 3/31; batteries A and B of Ray Embree's 57th FAB four miles south of the 1/32; Embree's CP and the eight A/A vehicles; and lastly, the 31st's headquarters or "rear" CP, located in a schoolhouse at Hudong, together with the 31st Tank Company. In all, Task Force MacLean then numbered about 3,200 men, including about 700 ROKs. Significantly absent were MacLean's 2/31, which was lagging badly in the redeployment, and, with it, C Battery of the 57th FAB. The 2/31 had not yet left the Pungsan area.[79]

After arranging these dispositions, MacLean returned to his rear CP at the Hudong schoolhouse to have dinner with Hank Hodes, who was camping there temporarily. MacLean laid out his plan of attack for the following day. Although the 2/31 had not arrived and neither man apparently knew where it was, Hodes registered no objections to MacLean's plans. Thereafter Mac-Lean jeeped forward to Faith's CP, where he found Faith issuing final orders for the attack at dawn.

The communications in Task Force MacLean were deplorable. The unit had no radio contact with 7th Division headquarters near Pungsan or with O. P. Smith's CP close by in Hagaru. Locally there had been no time to lay out all the landlines between the units. Radio contact between the units was imperfect or nonexistent. In effect, if not in fact, the disparate elements of Task Force MacLean were not connected, physically or otherwise.

\* \* \*

During that day, November 27, the massive CCF troops at the Chosin Reservoir prepared to launch an offensive that night. Their plan was to hit the widely dispersed X Corps forces at Chosin everywhere simultaneously, cut them off, and destroy them piecemeal. Three CCF divisions (59th, 79th, and 89th) would assault the Marines at Yudam and Hagaru and, farther south, John Guthrie's 7th Infantry at Sachang. One division (80th) would attack Task Force MacLean.

After dark, in zero-degree weather, the Chinese struck per plan. They attacked, blowing the familiar bugles and horns and shooting flares. They swarmed into American positions, firing burp guns and mortars, throwing grenades, and shouting shrilly.

West of the Chosin Reservoir at Yudam, the CCF 79th and 89th divisions hit the Fifth and Seventh Marines frontally. They overran outposts and swarmed into the Marine positions, causing chaos. Quickly recovering from the shock, the Marines fought back with skill and courage. They cut down the CCF troops by the hundreds, but by dawn the CCF had made substantial gains. The CCF 59th Division, per plan, cut the road between Yudam and Hagaru.[80]

Directly south of Yudam a battalion or similar-size task force of the CCF 89th Division struck John Guthrie's 1/7, commanded by Charles Heinrich. The CCF knocked out Heinrich's CP with mortar fire and penetrated the C Company perimeter. In furious hand-to-hand fighting the 1/7 finally repulsed the attack, restored the CP, and reestablished its perimeter.

To reinforce Heinrich, Guthrie hurried forward Robert Besson's 2/7. By that time the CCF had outflanked the 1/7, and Besson's G Company, leading the 2/7 attack, had to fight through the enemy to reach Heinrich's perimeter. Later in the day Guthrie arranged a FEAF airdrop to the 1/7 and sent forward a heavily armed convoy from the 2/7 to the perimeter to provide supplies and evacuate wounded. Thereafter the 1/7 (plus G Company) "sat tight" in a "battered" perimeter, blocking the CCF advance.

This little-known action of the 7th Infantry, making its debut in combat, assisted American forces at the Chosin Reservoir in two important ways: First, it presented a threat to the right flank of the CCF and drew off substantial numbers of those CCF troops attacking Yudam and Hagaru; secondly, it blocked the path of CCF troops attempting to circle deeper south to cut the Hamhung–Hagaru road.[81]

\* \* \*

East of the Chosin Reservoir, unknown to anyone in Task Force MacLean, troops of the CCF 80th Division encircled the Americans early that evening. At about 10:00 P.M. they simultaneously and suddenly attacked, blowing bugles and horns. Because of the absence of adequate communications, the various elements of Task Force MacLean could not help one another. Each fought separate and desperate actions.

The CCF hit Don Faith's 1/32 perimeter on the north side, where Faith had deployed his A and B companies, and initially made serious gains. The situation was further threatened by the bugout of the 300 ROKs in the 1/32. During this fighting many men of the 1/32 fell. They included three key officers: A Company commander Edward Scullion (killed); C Company commander Dale L. Seevers (wounded); and the assistant S-3, Robert F. Haynes (killed).

The battle in the 1/32 raged through the night. In the early hours of November 28 Faith and his men rallied, inflicting severe casualties on the CCF. At dawn Edward P. Stamford, a Marine forward air controller attached to the battalion, called in Marine Corps aircraft. Their strikes inflicted heavy casualties on the CCF at the 1/32 perimeter, but the CCF held its ground.

Mac MacLean had fought through the night side by side with Faith. At daylight he assessed the outcome. Although the 1/32 had suffered "heavy" casualties (about 100), MacLean judged that the 1/32 had come through in "pretty good shape." Although he apparently could not reach his other units by radio, he was still "reasonably optimistic." With the arrival of his 2/31 that day (as he supposed) and the tank company at Hudong, he could regain control of the situation.[82]

Several miles south of the 1/32 Bill Reilly's 3/31 and A and B batteries of the 57th FAB (twelve howitzers), arriving late on the afternoon of November 27, had hurriedly created a perimeter on low, poor defensive ground. When the CCF struck, the perimeter was only about six hours old. There had not been sufficient time to erect properly stout defenses. As a result, the CCF, attacking through I and K companies, overran most of the perimeter, including Reilly's CP and the 57th FAB's A Battery. The retreating Americans grouped at B Battery and from there began to fight back, doing so until dawn, when the CCF, apparently fearing air attacks, withdrew.

No one totaled the casualties in the 3/31 perimeter, but they, too, were heavy. Bill Reilly was hit in four places by grenades, mortar fragments, and bullets. Knocked unconscious and assumed to be dead, he survived. His S-4, the assistant S-3, and a FEAF air controller were killed. The 31st medical company, which had arrived late the night before, was wiped out while attempting to reach the perimeter.[83]

Still farther south, at about dawn, the CCF struck the perimeter where Ray Embree had established his CP. Initially the CCF made gains and almost overran the CP, but Embree had prudently retained his eight A/A vehicles. When these killing machines went into action, they cut down the CCF by the score. During this fighting Embree's exec, Max A. Morris, was killed, Embree was wounded in the legs, and one A/A vehicle was lost. Embree's S-3, Robert J. Tolly, who survived uninjured, assumed temporary command of the 57th FAB.

Perhaps wary of the twenty-two tanks parked nearby, the CCF did not attack the 31st rear CP at Hudong. When Hank Hodes arose on the morning of November 28, he could hear heavy gunfire to the north. But because of the absence of communications, he did not know that Task Force MacLean had been hard hit by an all-out CCF attack.[84]

Nonetheless, Hodes believed something was amiss. He therefore ordered the 31st Tank Company commander, West Pointer (1944) Robert E. Drake, to prepare to go forward to the 3/31 and 1/32 perimeters. Leaving one platoon to defend the 31st rear CP, Drake set off at 10:00 A.M. with his other sixteen tanks. Hodes and Drake rode in a jeep behind the lead tank.

As this tank column proceeded north from Hudong, it encountered difficult terrain. The ground was icy in some places, mushy in others. Some tanks skidded out of control; others mired. Then, suddenly and unexpectedly, CCF troops assaulted the column with American 3.5-inch bazookas. Other CCF troops climbed aboard the tanks and attempted to open the hatches.

A wild fight ensued. During the melee the Chinese got the upper hand. They knocked out two tanks with the bazookas; two other tanks became hopelessly mired and had to be abandoned. The surviving tankers raked one another's tanks with machine-gun fire, killing many enemy, but without American infantry or air support Drake could see no possibility of prevailing. He therefore called off the attack and retreated to Hudong with his surviving twelve tanks. Believing that Task Force MacLean might be in serious difficulty, Hodes borrowed one of Drake's tanks and rode in it to Hagaru to get help.

The failure of Drake's tank column to punch through killed the best hope of reinforcing Task Force MacLean that day. Later those who survived and who were perhaps unaware of the difficulties Drake had encountered would criticize Hodes for turning back and not remounting a second effort that day and for going on to Hagaru, from which he never returned.

During that morning the situation had improved within the 3/31 perimeter. After the CCF had withdrawn, Reilly's men and the artillerymen regained the six overrun howitzers of A Battery, the eighty-one-mm mortars of M Company, and the battalion CP. Although very badly wounded, Reilly was conscious, and he continued to command the 3/31. During the morning Tolly brought the 57th FAB headquarters (and the wounded Embree) and seven surviving A/A vehicles into the 3/31 perimeter. These measures, and others, greatly strengthened the perimeter.

\* \* \*

That morning—November 28—Almond and his aide, Alexander Haig, flew to Hagaru to confer with O. P. Smith. By this time both Ray Murray and Homer Litzenberg at Yudam had recommended to Smith that the offensive be canceled and that the Fifth and Seventh Marines go over to the defensive. Smith, concurring, ordered a general constriction within the Yudam perimeter, together with an attack by the Seventh Marines southeasterly, to regain and reopen the Yudam–Hagaru road. Smith briefed Almond on these and other plans. Almond probably was not pleased at this conservative line of action, but as at Inchon, he did not exercise total control of the Marines, and it would have been politically hazardous to raise strong objections to their plans. After he had departed, Smith issued orders officially canceling the Marine Corps offensive.[85]

From Hagaru Almond helicoptered to Don Faith's 1/32 perimeter to confer with MacLean and Faith. He arrived at about 1:00 P.M. Notwithstanding the setback at Yudam, Almond appeared to be in a feisty, aggressive mood. He unfolded a map on the hood of a jeep, and then (as reported by Army historian Martin Blumenson) he said, "The enemy who is delaying you for the moment is nothing more than remnants of Chinese divisions fleeing north. . . . We're still attacking and we're going all the way to the Yalu. Don't let a bunch of Chinese laundrymen stop you."[86]

In view of the dangerous situation at the Chosin Reservoir, Almond's exhortation seems asinine. One Army historian of the Korean War dismissed it as merely an effort to "raise morale." However, former Army historian Roy E. Appleman, in his recent book *East of Chosin,* insists that Almond, apparently unaware of the heavy losses in the nearby 3/31 and of the delays en route incurred by the 2/31, was serious. He instructed Faith to retake the high ground lost the night before and to prepare to attack north after the 2/31 arrived, with the whole of Task Force MacLean. According to Appleman's account, MacLean raised no objections.[87]

This meeting proved to be a pivotal moment in the history of the weak and exposed Task Force MacLean. Considering the dangerous situation at the Chosin Reservoir, prudence dictated that Almond order MacLean to withdraw into Hagaru. Why he did not—indeed, why he chose the opposite course to attack—would remain the subject of much speculation. And that MacLean would raise no objection to Almond's plan to attack rather than withdraw would also evoke speculation.

Before leaving the 1/32 perimeter, Almond, as was his custom on visits to the front, announced that he would present Faith and two other men of Faith's choice Silver Star medals. Apparently Faith believed this sort of arbitrary and random distribution of awards was a bad practice. He protested his own award; others were more deserving. Then he not so subtly conveyed his displeasure by simply choosing the two closest men at hand: a wounded platoon leader from C Company, Everett F. Smalley, and a headquarters mess sergeant, George A. Stanley, who happened to be walking by. According to the recollections of several 1/32 officers, after Almond had departed, Faith angrily ripped the medal from his jacket and threw it in the snow. Smalley removed his medal and put it in his pocket.[88]

Almond flew directly back to Hagaru, bypassing Bill Reilly's 3/31 perimeter and the 31st's rear CP. Had he stopped at those places, he might have gained a clearer picture of the situation in Task Force MacLean. As it was, he returned to X Corps headquarters in Hamhung believing what MacLean had told him: that, in effect, Task Force MacLean could take care of itself.

A serious command failure was thus in the making. MacLean was at fault for failing to have a clear picture of the situation in his own task force or for concealing it from Almond. But Almond was also at fault for failing to appreciate the enemy strength at the Chosin Reservoir and for failing to assess the situation in Task Force MacLean correctly, regardless of what he had heard from MacLean.

Shortly before midnight, November 28, the CCF 80th Division again attacked Task Force MacLean. The fighting inside both perimeters was savage and close, often hand to hand. In this second attack Don Faith's 1/32 was more hard pressed than was Bill Reilly's 3/31, which had been reinforced by the seven A/A vehicles.[89]

At about 2:00 A.M. MacLean, still isolated in Faith's 1/32 perimeter, arrived at a drastic decision. The 1/32 would withdraw in darkness into the 3/31's perimeter, taking the wounded and all weapons, the wounded in the kitchen trucks. This was to be merely a temporary withdrawal to consolidate forces. MacLean would mount the Almond-ordered attack the following day, after (as he supposed) his 2/31 had arrived. (It was then at Hamhung, trying to arrange onward transportation to Hagaru.) The men of the 1/32 were not abandoning the vehicles left behind in the perimeter. They would remove certain parts to make them inoperable, and the vehicles would be recovered and made usable on the attack north the next day.

## VI

By November 28 it must have been clear to Douglas MacArthur that he had blundered badly in Korea. The wine of victory had turned to vinegar. In a broad sense, Inchon had become another Anzio. He had been outsmarted and outgeneraled by a "bunch of Chinese laundrymen" who had no close air support, no tanks, and very little artillery, modern communications, or logistical infrastructure. His reckless, egotistical strategy after Inchon, undertaken in defiance of war warnings from Peking and a massive CCF buildup in Manchuria, had been an arrogant, blind march to disaster.

What must have been even more galling and humiliating was that MacArthur was on record with everyone from the president on down as unequivocally assuring that the CCF would not intervene in Korea in force, and if it did, he would "slaughter" it with his air power. His considerable intelligence-gathering apparatus had scandalously failed to detect or interpret the massive scope of the CCF intervention. His air power had abjectly failed to "slaughter" any appreciable number of CCF or even to knock out all the Yalu bridges.

He had made many mistakes in Korea, but the most egregious was his insistence that Johnnie Walker launch the "final offensive" on November 24. He had done so against cautionary advice from Washington and knowing full well that Walker, and probably many of his field commanders, believed it to be ill advised. He had rejected the reasonable British idea for a buffer zone (and other similar proposals) as "appeasement." The price for this arrogant blunder would be high: thousands more Americans killed, maimed, or captured on the battlefield; MacArthur himself shorn of his reputation for brilliance and infallibility.

That day—November 28, Tokyo time—MacArthur composed another top secret "posterity paper" for the Pentagon, releasing a virtually identical version in a public communiqué. This document contained the seeds of a theme, developed more fully later, in which he dishonestly (and absurdly) claimed that he had not blundered by rashly launching full-scale offensives to the Yalu but rather had merely conducted limited "assault movements" or a "reconnaissance in force" for the purpose of probing enemy strength.

The developments resulting from our assault movements [MacArthur wrote] have now assumed a clear definition. All hope of localization of the Korean conflict to enemy forces composed of North Korean troops with alien token elements can now be completely abandoned. The Chinese military forces are committed to North

Korea in great and ever increasing strength. No pretext of minor support under guise of volunteerism or other subterfuges now has the slightest validity. We face an entirely new war.

As MacArthur saw it that day, the CCF strength in North Korea had risen to 200,000 men. The enemy intention, he believed, was to gain a foothold in preparation for a "spring offensive." He continued:

It is quite evident that our present strength of force is not sufficient to meet this undeclared war by the Chinese with the inherent advantages which accrue thereby to them. The resulting situation presents an entire new picture which broadens the potentialities to world-embracing considerations beyond the sphere of decisions by the Theater Commander. This command has done everything possible within its capabilities but is now faced with conditions beyond its control and strength. . . . My strategic plan for the immediate future is to pass from the offensive to the defensive with such local adjustments as may be required by a constantly fluid situation.[90]

MacArthur's cable arrived at the Pentagon in the early-morning hours of November 28, Washington time. It was delivered to Omar Bradley at his Fort Myer quarters. Bradley telephoned President Truman at 6:15 A.M. to relay its contents and to say that the CCF had "come in with both feet." That morning, Bradley wrote, the newspapers were "screaming disaster." He described the situation to Truman as "serious" but doubted that it was "as much a catastrophe" as the newspapers made it out. What worried Bradley then was the CCF Air Force. The Soviets had recently increased it to 300 aircraft, including, ominously, 200 twin-engine bombers. If the CCF unleashed this air power against the retreating, bunched-up UN ground forces and the UN airfields in Korea, that would indeed be catastrophic. It would almost certainly compel American retaliation against CCF air bases in Manchuria, with who knew what possible consequences.[91]

Reports that morning from Korea and Tokyo painted an increasingly grim picture. The president was stunned, as indeed, were the whole of America and much of the world. The mood was reminiscent of the day the Nazis had invaded Poland, bringing on World War II, or the day the Japanese had attacked Pearl Harbor. At his morning staff meeting Truman said: "We've got a terrific situation on our hands." The latest message from MacArthur, he said, was "terrible." It was the "worst situation we have had yet."[92]

The "terrible" news from Korea had one positive effect. It jarred the administration from the torpor that had enveloped it in the three weeks since the election. Having surrendered control of the Korean War to MacArthur during that time, President Truman—and the JCS—began to take it back, beginning on November 28.

That afternoon Truman convened an extraordinary emergency session of the NSC, expanded to include numerous of his most trusted advisers, such as Averell Harriman and Secretary of the Treasury John W. Snyder. In all, twenty senior leaders of the administration were present. Acheson set the tone and spoke for all when he said, "We are much closer to the danger of general war" with the Soviet Union. Moscow—Joe Stalin—was still the master culprit. Peking would not have intervened in force in Korea unless he had desired or ordered it. "We must consider Korea not in isolation," Acheson said, "but in the world-wide problem of confronting the Soviet Union as an antagonist." Would World War III erupt tomorrow morning? Or had it already erupted?[93]

Whatever the case, the conferees unanimously agreed that under no circumstances should the United States get involved in a big war with China. Washington—and the UN—should denounce the CCF intervention in Korea in strong language and (as Acheson put it) "see what pressures we can put on the Chinese Communists to make life harder for them," meanwhile continuing to search all avenues for a means of negotiating a settlement. "We want to achieve a termination of this involvement," Acheson said. "We can't defeat the Chinese in Korea," he went on. "They can put in more than we can." George Marshall agreed, stating that America had to find a way to "get out" of Korea "with honor."

Could MacArthur "hold a line" while negotiations were pursued? Bradley thought so. Truman agreed that "we could hold the line." Where should this line be? Joe Collins, and others, thought MacArthur could hold "in the narrow neck"* unless "the X Corps is cut off." But not if Chinese Communist Air Force attacked American troops, Sherman cautioned. At least not without retaliatory air attacks into Manchuria.

Did MacArthur need a new directive, as he seemed to imply? Bradley said the JCS did not think so, although he might in another "48 to 72 hours." It was "desirable," he said, to "wait for clarification." Acheson agreed, but he said: "We should be sure he understands his directive. He seems to have thought he had to occupy the northeast part of Korea. Perhaps we should tell him that from the UN and US point of view he need not occupy that territory."

Other than that comment there was no criticism of MacArthur's battlefield strategy. However, the complete collapse of faith in him as a field commander was reflected indirectly by a lengthy discussion of a minor matter, first raised by the vice president, Alben W. ("The Veep") Barkley. Breaking into the discussion of strategy, Barkley wanted to know if MacArthur had

---

*Conferees and note takers at these meetings frequently confused the "narrow neck" of Korea (Sinanju–Hamhung) with the "narrow waist" (Pyongyang–Wonsan). In all probability Collins meant the "narrow waist."

actually said that he would "get the boys home by Christmas" (as reported by almost every newspaper in the country), or was it "a hoax"? Even if the offensive had succeeded, there was no way he could have gotten anybody "home by Christmas." Truman responded tartly that "MacArthur did indeed make the statement" but that the Veep "would have to draw his own conclusions as to why." Army Secretary Frank Pace said he understood that MacArthur had "officially denied the statement." Omar Bradley said it was certainly "no hoax." Coming to MacArthur's defense, he suggested that MacArthur may have said it to reassure the CCF that "we would get out after the attack."* Marshall said the statement was "an embarrassment which we must get around in some manner." Truman finally cut off the discussion, stating that "loads of questions will be asked about this" but that "we could not cause the Commanding General in the field to lose face before the enemy."

Returning to more serious matters, the conferees decided that the long-term challenge posed by Russia—Joe Stalin—had to be faced, finally and decisively. Marshall's deputy, Robert A. Lovett, put the matter squarely on the table. The administration had immediately and enthusiastically to embrace Acheson's cherished but long-dormant NSC-68, calling for a massive American military buildup. Acheson agreed: "We must press faster to build our strength."

There now occurred one of the more historic moments in the Truman administration. During most of the meeting the president had been reticent, inviting suggestions and comments as usual, adding few of his own—and no apparent leadership to the discussions. Averell Harriman then broke in with a startling change in the tone and content of the discussions. Calling attention to an article in the Russian newspaper *Pravda,* which had quoted anti-Truman newspapers in America to Truman's detriment, Harriman forthrightly "urged" that the president "strongly assert his leadership" not only in the United States but also in the UN and NATO.

Truman suddenly came alive. Tight-lipped and glowering, he vented his pent-up anger at his critics, especially the Hearst and McCormick newspaper chains, which had been relentlessly assailing the administration and promoting McCarthyism. It was a campaign of "vilification and character assassination," Truman declaimed, constituting the "best asset of the Soviet Union." Some people, he said, "would rather see the country go down than for the Adminis-

---

*Ironically, in his memoir MacArthur dishonestly blamed his gaffe on Bradley. Of his visit to the front, MacArthur wrote, "I told them of General Bradley's desire and hope to have two divisions home by Christmas. . . ." At Wake Island, the origin of this discussion, Bradley had expressed a desire to MacArthur to have "the 2nd Division or the 3rd Division" made "available to be sent over to Europe by January." MacArthur had replied he would recommend the 2d Division and would make it available "by January."[94]

tration to succeed." He would "meet" that "campaign of vilification and lies," Truman promised.

Having gotten that off his chest, Truman then made the most important decision of his administration. Setting aside his deeply held convictions about fiscal conservatism and his dreams of balancing the national budget and even reducing the national debt, he let go of the tight reins he had held on defense spending. He, in effect, gave his approval to the recommendations of NSC-68. "We are confronted by certain facts and conditions," he said simply but firmly, and must "meet them."[95]

Up to that day Truman, still hoping to fight the Korean War on the cheap, had merely authorized "creeping" manpower mobilizations and modest increases in defense spending. In September he had authorized the JCS to *plan* for the huge force levels and outlays for defense matériel proposed in NSC-68, but he had not yet asked Congress for money to begin that buildup. But three days after this meeting (December 1) he submitted to Congress a supplemental appropriations bill requesting an additional $16,844,247,000 for this purpose.[96]*

If Joe Stalin had goaded the CCF into war in Korea to rescue the NKPA, as was almost universally believed in 1950, then it was certainly the biggest strategic blunder of his postwar dictatorship. Until the CCF intervention NSC-68 had not been approved. It is conceivable that upon the wind-down of the Korean War Truman would have returned to conservative defense budgets, thereby diminishing Washington's ability to deal with worldwide Soviet aggression. The CCF intervention set America on a course of massive rearmament that was to continue almost unabatedly for decades to come.

\* \* \*

After getting off the cable to the NSC on November 28, MacArthur took an extraordinary and unprecedented step: He summoned both Walker and Almond to Tokyo for a war council. It was the first time the three men had met together since September 29 in Seoul, following the ceremony reestablishing the Rhee government. It was probably the first time that the antagonists Walker and Almond had ever exchanged detailed views on tactics and strategy of the war.

---

*Before the Korean War Truman had planned to pare the fiscal year (FY) 1951 defense budget to $12 billion or less. His two additional supplemental requests (of $11.6 and $16.8 billion), plus funds voted by Congress, brought the total FY 1951 defense budget to $43 billion. The costly long-range rearmament program growing out of NSC-68 called for a FY 1952 buildup to an Army of 1,353,000 men manning eighteen combat divisions, plus seventeen other combat regiments; a Navy of 397 combatant ships; a Marine Corps of two and one-third divisions; and an Air Force of ninety-five wings, manned by 971,000 men.[97]

Wearing battlefield dress, Walker and Almond flew separately to Tokyo. The meeting convened at MacArthur's home in the American Embassy at 9:50 P.M. It continued for three hours and forty minutes. Also present were MacArthur's acting chief of staff, Doyle Hickey; his G-3, Pinky Wright; his G-2, Charles Willoughby; and his amanuensis, Courtney Whitney. Willoughby later wrote that the atmosphere was "grim."[98]

As was customary, MacArthur dominated the proceedings with eloquent monologues. No full record of the meeting can be found, but it is clear from the scraps of notes that survive, and other sources, that while recognizing the gravity of the situation, MacArthur continued to misread CCF strength and intentions grossly. As he viewed it from his distant, lofty peak, the CCF was now unequivocally in North Korea but not yet in full, overwhelming strength. Peking had committed no more than 200,000 men, MacArthur concluded. The CCF strategy, MacArthur believed, was most likely to push Eighth Army and X Corps back in order that the CCF would have ample territory to continue its buildup "for a spring offensive," designed to eject the UN from all of Korea.

But owing to the "collapse" of ROK II Corps, the CCF had made sufficient gains to endanger Eighth Army seriously. MacArthur therefore authorized Walker to shift from offense to defense and to take all necessary steps, including, if warranted, limited withdrawals. With the 1st Cav, Commonwealth Brigade, and 24th Division at or assembling at Sunchon to reinforce the right flank and reorganize ROK II Corps, perhaps Walker could hold a line on the Chongchon River (Sinanju–Kujang), with a solid right flank extending south through Sunchon.

If the right flank could not be immediately reestablished and held, it might become necessary for Eighth Army to fall back farther yet. Walker was fairly confident that he could hold an arc-shaped enclave embracing Pyongyang and utilizing Chinampo at his rear as a supply port. Conceivably the CCF massing against this enclave could be destroyed—or at least decisively decimated—by a combination ground- and carrier-based UN air power. The problem was that the CCF might "leak" around to the east, bypassing Walker's enclave, and go on to Seoul and Inchon, compelling Walker to remain "enclaved" in a perimeter indefinitely or to evacuate Eighth Army through Chinnampo.

To prevent the "leakage," would it be possible to establish a line across the narrow waist of Korea, Pyongyang–Yangdok–Wonsan? That is, link Eighth Army and X Corps and strongly defend along the road MacArthur had originally chosen for X Corps to use for its assault on Pyongyang? The conferees agreed this would be extremely difficult, probably impossible. The line would be about 125 miles long. Each of the seven available American divisions would have to defend almost a 20-mile front. Besides that, the line would be difficult, if not impossible, to supply over icy or snow-drifted roads.

The discussion then turned to how X Corps could best "help" Eighth Army. As MacArthur viewed it, X Corps was already "helping" Eighth Army substantially by draining off an estimated six CCF divisions (actually twelve). The conferees agreed that X Corps should continue to maintain aggressive "contact" with these CCF forces, keeping them pinned down at the Chosin Reservoir and off Eighth Army's back. Other available elements of the 7th Division would reinforce the Marines and Task Force MacLean. If CCF pressure became intolerable, the X Corps forces at the Chosin Reservoir could gradually fall back on the Hamhung-Hungnam area, merge with the 3d and 7th divisions, and hold an enclave.

Pinky Wright, however, believed that X Corps might do yet more to "help" Eighth Army immediately. He proposed that the 3d Division attack in utmost force due west across the peninsula from Yonghung toward Tokchon, the route the 65th Infantry had earlier attempted to blaze. If this were done, the 3d Division could "help" the 1st Cav Division, perhaps even catching the CCF in a "pincer." At the least, the 3d Division attack would divert CCF from the 1st Cav's "front" and possibly make the task of reinforcing Eighth Army's right flank more feasible.[99]

Ned Almond objected to this proposal for several reasons. First, substantial elements of the 3d Division were absolutely required at Wonsan and Hamhung to ensure the safety of those areas, which were still under attack by NKPA guerrillas and some CCF units. The enemy pressure was still especially heavy at Wonsan, where Dinty Moore's 15th Infantry was deployed. Secondly, William Harris's 65th Infantry had met heavy CCF resistance on its westward advances to Kwangchon. Thirdly, John Guthrie's 7th Infantry was then under heavy CCF pressure at Sanchong. Fourthly, the available roads to the west were worse than terrible; many "roads" shown on the maps did not exist.

MacArthur, however, believed Wright's idea had merit. He overrode Almond's objections and ordered that the most powerful 3d Division forces that could be spared mount the strongest possible attack to the west. Almond finally agreed to this scheme, provided that he did not have to supply the 3d Division task force after it had crossed the mountains, that Walker would supply it from his thin resources.[100]

In sum, the grand strategy was as follows: Walker would restore his right flank and attempt to hold along the Chongchon River. If necessary, he would fall back and form an enclave embracing Pyongyang-Chinnampo. Almond would reinforce those X Corps elements at the Chosin Reservoir with available 7th Division units, maintaining aggressive "contact" with the CCF to every extent possible, and also send a powerful 3d Division force westward. As a last resort X Corps would fall back to an enclave embracing Hamhung–Hungnam.

\* \* \*

On the morning of November 29, Washington time, the JCS met again in urgent session. Forrest Sherman was gravely concerned about the exposed position of his Marines at the Chosin Reservoir. Breaking the long-standing tradition of leaving tactical operations strictly in the hands of the local commander, Sherman insisted that MacArthur be told to withdraw X Corps into a "consolidated defense line." The other chiefs were still reluctant to give MacArthur direct tactical orders, but there was sufficient loss of faith in him to justify pointed questions. After clearing the text with the president, at 2:30 P.M. that day (3:30 P.M., November 30, Tokyo time),[101] the JCS cabled MacArthur: "We approve your plan [to go on the defensive] . . . and any directive in conflict therewith is deferred. Strategic and tactical considerations are now paramount. What are your plans regarding the coordination of operations of the Eighth Army and X Corps and the positioning of X Corps the units of which appear to us to be exposed?[102]

Crossing this cable was yet another from MacArthur that day. Reversing an earlier view, he now strongly recommended that Washington accept a long-standing offer from Chiang Kai-shek to provide some 30,000 Nationalist soldiers to fight with the UN in Korea. These soldiers, which could arrive in Korea in "approximately fourteen days," MacArthur cabled, "represent the only source of potential trained reinforcements available for early commitment to the war in Korea." Since this request involved touchy political considerations, the JCS passed it to Marshall and Acheson. The JCS informed MacArthur that the proposal was "under consideration" but reminded him of its controversial aspects—for example, that the British Commonwealth nations considered it "wholly unacceptable."[103]

Since the JCS cable (or back channel talk) had seemed to suggest the desirability of a linkup of Eighth Army and X Corps to form a line across the narrow waist of Korea (Pyongyang–Wonsan) and that plan had been rejected at the MacArthur/Walker/Almond war council, MacArthur cabled the JCS:

Any concept of actual physical combination of the forces of Eighth Army and X Corps in a practically continuous line across the narrow neck of Korea is quite impracticable due to the length of that line, the numerical weakness of our forces and the logistical problems due to the mountainous divide which splits such a front from north to south.

The X Corps will contract its position, as enemy pressure develops, into the Hamhung-Wonsan sector. The Corps Commander has been enjoined against any possibility of piecemeal isolation and trapping of his forces. While geographically his elements seem to be well extended, the actual conditions of terrain make it extremely difficult for an enemy to take any material advantage thereof.[104]

In the same cable MacArthur repeated another absurd claim:

The X Corps geographically threatens the main supply lines of the enemy forces bearing upon the right flank of the Eighth Army. This threat is emphasized by thrusts from elements of the Corps all along its west flank as far north as Mupyong-ni and as far south as the roadnets west from the Wonsan sector. This threat is now being met by the enemy commitment of a reported 6 to 8 divisions [actually twelve] which otherwise would have been available for use against the Eighth Army. The enemy's penetration southward could not be safely accomplished until this threat of the X Corps is contained or nullified.[105]

Perhaps realizing belatedly that he had said nothing about the Eighth Army sector, two hours later MacArthur got off another cable. He stated that "despite all interdiction of our Air Command," the Chinese Communists "continue the buildup of their forces in North Korea" (actually, they were already there). Since there were "several hundred thousand" CCF troops in Manchuria and they could reach the front "in two night marches," the potential existed for "a continuous and rapid buildup." In contrast with his earlier view that the CCF was preparing for a "spring offensive," he now believed its objective was "the complete destruction of UN forces and the securing of all of Korea." And as a result of these developments, "it is quite evident that the Eighth Army will successively have to continue to displace to the rear."[106]

Whatever credibility MacArthur had left with the JCS was utterly destroyed by his message about X Corps. Bradley rightly regarded as preposterous MacArthur's statement suggesting that X Corps posed a threat to the CCF rear. He angrily annotated the message with question marks in the margins. Twenty years later Bradley still remembered that message as "insulting" and told an interviewer in reference to it that MacArthur "treated us as if we were children."[107]

Under the circumstances, the JCS continued to display remarkable restraint and tact, yet it moved another step closer to giving MacArthur direct tactical orders. In a single response to his two messages concerning X Corps and Eighth Army, the chiefs "expressed fear" that "a progressively widening gap" would develop as Eighth Army continued to withdraw in the west, leaving X Corps farther and farther behind, virtually stranded in its Hamhung-Hungnam enclave. It seemed important to the JCS that the elements of X Corps be "extricated from their exposed positions as soon as practicable" and that the forces on the two coasts "be sufficiently coordinated to prevent large enemy forces from passing between them or outflanking either of them."

After approving this message, George Marshall added a note, stressing the urgency for withdrawing X Corps. Marshall told MacArthur that "the entire region northeast of the waist of Korea should be ignored except for strategic and tactical considerations relating to the security of your command."[108]

# 17

# SHOCKING LOSSES

I

When Johnnie Walker returned from Tokyo to his Eighth Army CP on November 29, he issued formal orders for a general withdrawal. The aim was to create a solid enclave around Pyongyang. The first step would be to establish a line across the western sector of the peninsula, Sukchon–Sunchon.

Eighth Army's withdrawal was complicated by the lack of good roads. The best route was the main highway, Sinanju–Pyongyang, on the west coast. That highway was initially reserved for the Eighth Army and I Corps infrastructure and the 24th Division and ROK 1st Division. The 25th and 2d divisions (plus attached ROKs and Turks) would withdraw through Kunu, due south over a two-lane gravel road, Kunu to Sunchon. However, later that day, Walker, believing that the Kunu–Sunchon road would become severely overtaxed, ordered the 25th Division, which had been transferred to I Corps, to withdraw via Kunu, thence west along the south bank of the Chongchon River to Sinanju, thence south to Pyongyang. Throckmorton's 5th Infantry was to hold at Sinanju until these withdrawals had been completed.[1]

Owing to the terrain, roads, and available river crossings, it was still vital to hold Kunu. Walker's plan assigned that task to Keiser's 2d Division. It would hold Kunu until Kean's 25th Division had crossed the Chongchon River and proceeded west to Sinanju. After that the 2d would withdraw from Kunu and go south on the Sunchon road. Accordingly, the regiments of the 2d Division deployed on an arc northeast and east of Kunu, with the 9th and the 23d regiments on the left, the ROK 3d Regiment in the center, and the 38th Regiment and what could be found of the Turks on the right. The

473

division's four artillery battalions, plus the attached 17th FAB (with eight-inch howitzers), backed up the infantry from sites a mile or so west of Kunu.

\* \* \*

In I Corps the first task was to get the supply trains and other rear-area elements of the 25th Division across the Chongchon River at Kunu and westbound to Sinanju. It was not easy. The 25th Division artillery commander, Bittman Barth, wrote: "Our trains started moving back shortly after noon. The traffic was indescribable. A solid column of vehicles, extending for over ten miles, moved at a snail's pace. Refugees moving on foot that we passed early in the afternoon re-passed us hours later. In Kunu-ri our column merged with that of the 2nd Division. . . . It took our headquarters column eight hours to move twelve miles."[2]

During the 25th Division withdrawal most of its units—especially John Corley's hard-hit 24th Infantry—were subjected to extreme pressures. Communications were difficult or nonexistent. No one had any clear idea of who was in charge of what or exactly where American forces were deployed. The CCF was pressing so hard on the heels of the withdrawing American troops the division artillery could not be used to full effect for fear of hitting its own men.

During this withdrawal the CCF struck Melvin Blair's 3/24, which until then had been spared.[3] The truth of what ensued would be difficult to determine. At the time Blair claimed that the 3/24 bugged out. The blacks, however, denied this, blaming the disorder in the 3/24 on Blair's ineptitude and what appeared to them to be panic on his part.

Blair gave his version of events to the *Saturday Evening Post* war correspondent Harold H. Martin, who published them in the magazine in these damning words:

The battalion commander was a hurt and angry man as, down the icy road from Kunu-ri, he rode in his jeep, brooding on his troubles. Two nights before, he had been roused from sleep in his command post by the roar of enemy burp guns thrust through the windows. He had fled through the wintry dark in his drawers, his boots unlaced, and only by great good fortune had he managed to make his way unhurt through the encircling enemy who had put his security guard to flight without firing a shot. Finally at dawn he had reached safety with an element of a sister regiment, and from the high ground, where he had found refuge, he then had watched the three companies of his battalion cut to pieces. . . . As the Chinese came running, all three [rifle] companies broke at once. The men fled like rabbits across the great open field and the commander could see them fall, wounded, and see them drop from fatigue in the mud of the paddy, and he could see groups of them being surrounded and marched off by the Chinese, their hands above their heads. And he also saw a few brave men who knelt and fired into the onrushing Chinese, waving the running Americans on past to safety. And he saw these men overrun.
All these things were in the mind of Lt. Col. Melvin Russell Blair, commander

of the Third battalion . . . as, driving down the road, seeking the shattered remnants of his force, he suddenly heard the sound of singing. It was good singing, with a rhythm to it that pleased him—a bounce and a swing. So he stopped his jeep and called to the Negro soldiers huddled around a little fire in the snow, and asked what was the song they sang. A soldier came to the side of the jeep. "Sir," he said, "that is the official song of the Twenty-fourth Infantry Regiment. That is the Bugout Boogie."[4]

A black warrant officer in 3/24 headquarters, Thomas H. Pettigrew, Jr., who was to receive a battlefield promotion to second lieutenant, was present in Blair's CP when the CCF struck. Later, when he read the Blair-Martin version of events, he was incensed. Still later he wrote and published a small, passionless book, *The Kunu-ri Incident,* designed specifically to refute the Blair-Martin version, "which in many respects," Pettigrew wrote, "was contrary to the facts."[5]

As Pettigrew told it, when the CCF hit the 3/24 on the night of November 30, it was poorly deployed on a line on the northern outskirts of Kunu. Blair had established his CP in a large schoolhouse in Kunu itself. "The danger of this location," Pettigrew wrote, "was that the troops stood out like a sore thumb which made the command vulnerable to being attacked, surrounded and captured."

Everyone was asleep in the CP when the CCF hit. Pettigrew awoke, grabbed his weapon, and went outside. There, he wrote, he found Blair "hysterically and incoherently giving orders to defend the Command Post." Few of the 3/24 officers at hand responded. "Some were trying to escape on vehicles which congested the one entrance and exit to the school." Pettigrew saw the 3/24 exec, carrying his rifle at port arms, "walking cautiously and slowly" near the door to the CP, but did not see him again.

In Pettigrew's account, Blair and his 3/24 staff more or less panicked and collapsed at the schoolhouse CP. Receiving no firm leadership from the CP, the rifle companies scattered, incurring a total of 140 casualties, including 1 killed, 30 injured, and 109 captured. "The personnel of the 3d Battalion . . . would not have 'fled like rabbits' in the face of the onslaught," Pettigrew wrote, "had the leadership not failed them; the leadership in the battalion command post at Kunu-ri . . . [where] I saw and realized the tragedy of leaderless men."

As confusion and fear mounted at the 3/24 CP and the enemy closed in, Pettigrew wrote, Blair became even more hysterical. Giving the appearance that he had lost all self-control, Blair finally shouted, "Someone take me out of here!"

Pettigrew, who remained cool and clear-thinking, assumed a leadership role in the vacuum and led Blair, other staffers, and about sixty enlisted men out to safety. For this feat Pettigrew was later awarded a Bronze Star Medal.[6]

Pettigrew's version of events that night differed markedly from the Blair-

Martin version. Furthermore, Pettigrew wrote, he was "shocked" to read about the song "The Bugout Boogie." There was no such song in the battalion or regiment, he asserted. Blair's description of blacks gathered around a campfire jubilantly singing the song "was not only out of place but out of the question." The song's "words and psychological stereotyped meaning portraying the Negro as a coward, as a minstrel man and indifferent to a serious cause . . ." was pure racism.

After that disgraceful episode, Pettigrew wrote, Blair continued to behave erratically. The next day, when he refused to obey a deployment order from the 24th's exec, Paul Roberts, Corley came to Blair's CP to back up Roberts, insisting that Blair do as he was told. Pettigrew wrote:

The conversation centered about that subject for a short while. Then Lieutenant Colonel Blair started talking about his troops, telling Colonel Corley that he did not have enough men and that they did not have the will to fight, that they did not have enough weapons or equipment and that they should not be put back on the line. Colonel Corley, sounding a little perturbed and displeased by these remarks, told Lieutenant Colonel Blair that he didn't give a damn what condition the troops were in, that he had orders to defend a sector and that he was going to do it and that he wanted those troops in line and in place no later than 5 P.M.

After Corley and Roberts had departed, Blair set out to comply with orders and get his troops deployed, Pettigrew wrote, shouting hysterically, "The Colonel's going to relieve me, the Colonel's going to relieve me." Many things went wrong that afternoon, and later that day, Pettigrew wrote, Corley did, in fact, sack Blair, temporarily promoting the 3/24's S-3, Roscius C. Newell, to replace him. Blair left the regimental area with "tears streaming down his face" and went on to further duty in the 25th Division G-2 section. He retired from the Army in 1954 as a lieutenant colonel.[7]

The Blair-Martin account in the *Saturday Evening Post* angered other blacks as well. They asserted that it was not only grossly inaccurate and racist but also self-serving for Blair to justify or cover up his incompetence and hysteria, which they believed were the real reasons for his departure from command of the battalion.* The blacks would single out Blair as one example of the inept and erratic white leadership in the 24th Infantry.[9]

---

*The Martin article did not mention that Blair had left the battalion. It emphasized that Blair wore two DSCs, four Silver Stars, and a "handful of Bronze Stars with a V for Valor on them for gallantry in combat." The *Post* later published two articles by Melvin Blair himself, "I Send Your Son into Battle" and "A Christmas Story." Neither article related to the black problems; however, both tended to enhance the deposed Blair's image as a heroic soldier. Blair finally destroyed his image—and himself—in 1958, when he attempted a bizarre (and unsuccessful) armed robbery of the Bing Crosby Golf Tournament. At his trial, Blair pleaded guilty and was sentenced to five to twenty years for armed robbery. He was paroled after serving fourteen months.[8]

* * *

To the right of the 25th Division Dutch Keiser's 2d Division was still waging a desperate fight to hold Kunu and the road south from it to Sunchon. The collapse and bugout of the Turkish Brigade had seriously jeopardized the division, as had the terrible losses in Chin Sloane's 9th and George Peploe's 38th Infantry. Of the 2d Division forces, only Paul Freeman's 23d Regiment, fighting with John Keith's "unfamiliar" 15th FAB, could be classified as combat-capable.

At about noon on November 29 disquieting news arrived at Dutch Keiser's CP, located just south of Kunu and itself under sporadic mortar and sniper fire. A truck convoy traveling north from Sunchon to Kunu had been ambushed by CCF troops at two separate places about four miles apart. The warning was garbled or misunderstood. Keiser's staff got the impression that the CCF unit responsible for the ambush was slight (probably no more than one company) and thus no great threat. Believing the division Recon Company could deal with these minor annoyances, Keiser's staff sent it southbound to "clear" the road to Sunchon.[10]

The misinterpretation of the warning proved to be a terrible mistake. The CCF 113th Division had punched through the Turks' soft defenses on the southeast rim of the "arc," and two of its regiments were then digging in astride the Kunu–Sunchon road over which the 2d Division was to withdraw. Had Keiser and his staff fully grasped what had happened, they could have altered the 2d Division withdrawal plan to follow the 25th Division west through Sinanju. But grossly underestimating the threat, they stuck by the original plan, thereby consigning a large portion of the 2d Division to a ghastly ordeal.

The gravity of the threat became apparent as the afternoon wore on. The division Recon Company was abruptly and decisively checked not far south of Kunu. Upon learning of this, Keiser's staff reinforced it with a platoon of tanks from the 72d Tank Battalion and a (depleted) company (C) of infantry from Bill Keleher's 1/38. But this was insufficient force. The road remained blocked, and the division supply trains began backing up in a massive traffic jam.[11]

About then, Shrimp Milburn, who had heard of the block on the Sunchon road and instinctively grasped its significance, telephoned Keiser. "How are things going?" Milburn asked.

"Bad," Keiser replied. "We're getting hit in my CP."

Milburn replied, "Well, come out my way."

That was guarded talk, inviting Keiser to withdraw through I Corps sector at Sinanju. But Keiser was still reluctant to make a drastic change in plans. He had heard of the massive traffic jams on the Kunu–Sinanju road. His provost marshal, Henry C. Becker, wrongly reported that the CCF had cut that road as well. Moreover, even though John Coulter had (in Paul Freeman's words) "fled the battlefield," Keiser was still assigned to IX Corps, not I Corps. A change in withdrawal plan would have to be cleared through IX Corps and up the chain of command to Eighth Army. This could take precious hours Keiser could not spare. He declined the invitation.[12]

At least in part. Notwithstanding the traffic jams on the Sinanju road and Becker's report of a roadblock, Keiser's G-3, Maurice Holden, urged that the division's trains and many of the ambulances and vehicles carrying out the wounded go out by way of Sinanju. After Holden had more or less "cleared" this proposal with IX Corps, Keiser approved. Thereupon Holden withdrew the division's trains and many vehicles with wounded from the Sunchon road, turned them around, and sent them (and other service units) west on the Sinanju road. These hundreds of vehicles merged into the hundreds of vehicles of the withdrawing 25th Division supply trains and the thousands of refugees moving on foot. But Keiser insisted that the division's combat elements stick by the original plan and, if it came to it, conduct a "fighting withdrawal" down the Sunchon road.[13]

In the meantime, IX Corps was working on a plan to help Keiser clear the Sunchon road. The Commonwealth Brigade—still in IX Corps reserve— would attack north toward Kunu. Orders went out to Basil Coad that afternoon to move north early on the following morning. Coad chose the Middlesex Battalion to spearhead the attack, to be backed up by the Argylls and Australians.[14]

By that night, November 29, the combat elements of the 2d Division holding Kunu were very hard pressed. Sloane's 9th and Peploe's 38th regiments had been cut down to about 600 men apiece. All men were exhausted from lack of sleep, numbed by the intense cold, and hungry. Remarkably, Freeman's 23d Regiment remained combat-worthy. But it could not hold Kunu alone; the division must withdraw on the morrow.

Keiser called a war council to lay out the final withdrawal plan. It was as follows:

• Freeman's 23d Regiment, mated with Keith's 15th FAB, would provide the rear guard while other division elements evacuated over the Sunchon road. The 23d would hold until all 2d Division elements and the remaining elements of the 25th Division had cleared Kunu. Thereafter Freeman and Keith would decamp and follow the 2d Division down the Sunchon road.

• Sloane's 9th Infantry, less its 1/9, would spearhead the division attack down the Sunchon road, clearing out the first roadblock. Its shattered 1/9, now commanded by its exec, Homer C. Henckley (replacing James Hill, who had been wounded), would remain behind, to reinforce Freeman's 23d. Butch Barberis's 2/9 would attack on the right; McMains's 3/9, on the left.

• Peploe's 38th Infantry, mounted on tanks and trucks, would attack through the 9th. It would clear any roadblocks beyond the first block and meet the advancing British head to head. To avoid friendly fire in this linkup, neither Peploe nor the British would employ artillery. Tankers would not fire unless the target were absolutely identifiable as enemy.

• Behind Peploe would come the division headquarters and artillery, less the 15th FAB, which would remain mated with the 23d.[15]

*  *  *

All men in the 9th Infantry were hollow-eyed with exhaustion and cold and desperately hungry. None, however, was closer to the edge than the commander, Chin Sloane, who had not slept much in days and who felt deeply the responsibility for the savage losses in his command. Believing Sloane might not last much longer, Dutch Keiser decided to relieve him of command, choosing as his replacement the able West Point (1931) paratrooper Ed Messinger, then Paul Freeman's exec and recently promoted to full colonel. Messinger joined the 9th Infantry that same night, but by mutual agreement the relief of Sloane was postponed until the regiment reached safer ground.[16]

Later that night Sloane withdrew the 9th Infantry from the defensive arc northeast of Kunu and regrouped the 2/9 and 3/9 on the Sunchon road for the attack on the first block. All other units made preparations to follow. Unknown to Keiser, or anybody else, by this time the two CCF regiments had dug into positions in the high ground along a six-mile stretch overlooking the road.

*  *  *

During the early-morning hours of November 30 Sloane's 9th proceeded down the Sunchon road toward a prearranged assembly and jump-off point. Butch Barberis, whose 2/9 consisted of but one jeep, one truck, and 150 men, led the march. McMains, with 250 men and several tanks and trucks, followed. Sloane and the regimental CP brought up the rear. Unknown to Barberis, Keiser had added a provisional ROK battalion (composed of remnants of the ROK 3d Regiment) to the spearhead. It was to come up on the right of Barberis in the high ground overlooking the road.

At dawn, long before he reached his assembly area, Barberis saw unusual "movement" on his right in the high ground. He got on his radio and asked, "Who's on my right flank?" Division reassured him; it was the provisional ROK battalion. But Barberis was leery. He trained his field glasses on the ridges. By the "incipient sunlight" he saw two machine guns "looking right down my throat." He radioed Sloane: "I'm four thousand yards from my assembly area, and I see enemy positions. I think I've got my tit in a wringer." Barberis remembered: "The Chinese machine guns opened up, and all hell broke loose. Simultaneously we were attacked from the right flank. We

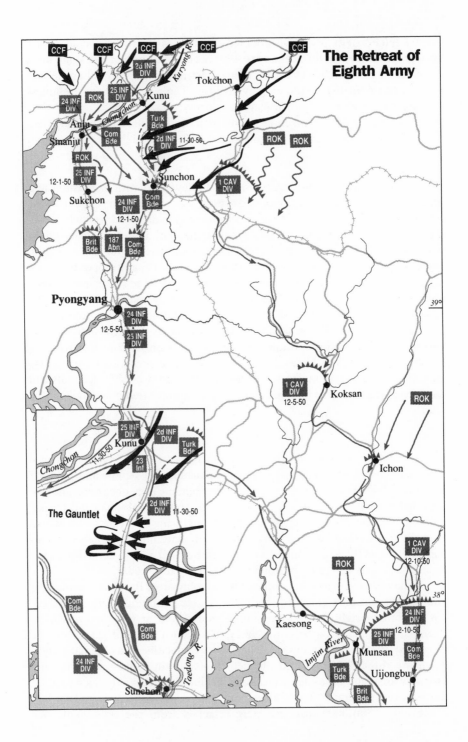

**The Retreat of Eighth Army**

CCF CCF CCF CCF CCF

2d INF DIV

Kuryong R.

Tokchon

25 INF DIV
ROK
24 INF DIV
Kunu
Anju
Chongchon
Turk Bde
Com Bde
2d INF DIV 11-30-50
ROK ROK
Sinanju

ROK
25 INF DIV 12-1-50
Sukchon
24 INF DIV Com Bde 12-1-50
Sunchon
1 CAV DIV

Brit Bde 187 Abn Com Bde

Pyongyang
24 INF DIV 12-5-50
25 INF DIV

39°

1 CAV DIV 12-5-50
Koksan

ROK

Ichon

1 CAV DIV 12-10-50

**The Gauntlet**

25 INF DIV 2d INF DIV
Kunu Turk Bde
Chongchon 11-30-50
23 Inf
2d INF DIV 11-30-50

Com Bde
Com Bde
24 INF DIV
Sunchon
Taedong R.

Kaesong
ROK
Imjim River
Munsan
Turk Bde
Brit Bde

38°

24 INF DIV 12-10-50
25 INF DIV
Com Bde
Uijongbu

repulsed those attacks, but it was impossible to move. I called Sloane up to report. He said to come back to his CP for a conference. I started back, and all hell broke loose again. A whole mass of Chinese attempted to overrun my position. I and two other officers were hit—one, [Marshall W.] Stark, my H Company commander, mortally. I found myself engaged with a number of Chinese; I took care of that situation.*[17]

It was now clear that the CCF was present in strength and the pitiful remnants of the 9th Infantry were in for a brutal fight. Sloane sent McMains's 3/9 forward on the left side of the road.[18] Shooting every yard of the way, McMains's black GIs gave a good account of themselves, but they did not get far. Nor did the provisional ROK battalion on the right. It mounted two attacks, then broke and ran. With his rapidly dwindling band Barberis continued the fight. He recalled: "The road was fast becoming clogged with the dead and disabled vehicles. I had twenty-two men left, of which nineteen were wounded that day. I split them into two groups, sending one to the high ground on the right of the road, one to the high ground on the left, with orders to do their best to keep Chinese fire off the road. This went on for hours. We were knocked off the hill several times by [FEAF] fighters, who thought we were the enemy. We would go back down to the road to strip the dead of ammo, then back into the hills again. One of these [Oriental-looking] 'bodies' moved and said, 'I'm a GI. If you don't believe it, look in my wallet.' It was one of my platoon leaders, a Chinese-American, Cheu-Mon Lee, from H Company, caked with blood and dirt. I put him on a truck and sent him back to the medics. He lived.† We stayed on those ridges fighting until after dark, trying to keep enemy fire off the road."[19]

\* \* \*

It was quite apparent that this CCF enclave was much more than the reported shallow roadblock manned by "one company." The repeated bold flank attacks and the backup in the high ground indicated battalion strength or greater. Keiser attached two companies of Turks to McMains's 3/9 to help deal with it. The CCF flank attacks were momentarily contained, but the enemy was not cleared from the high ground. Nor did anyone yet have a clear picture of how deep the block might be.

The intensity of the CCF resistance and the severe casualties in the 9th Infantry should have led to a reconsideration of the withdrawal plan. At the least Keiser should have immediately deployed Peploe's 38th Infantry with

---

*Barberis was officially credited with personally killing ten CCF and great gallantry under fire. He was recommended for a Medal of Honor, but the award was reduced to a Silver Star—his second.

†Lee won a DSC for heroic action the previous night.

tanks and A/A vehicles to reinforce the 9th and clear the CCF from the ridges. Had he done so, he could have developed a clearer picture of the enemy strength he faced and, possibly, the depth of the block.

But Keiser continued to misread his situation grossly. He persisted in the belief that the roadblock was shallow or "local," that with a concerted "push" and with FEAF help it could be overcome, that the road beyond the block was "clear." Moreover, he was under the impression that the Commonwealth Brigade had attacked north along the road that morning, that it was probably no more than three or four miles away, that it would soon close on the CCF roadblock from the south, helping eliminate it. For these reasons he stuck to the original plan.[20]

The Middlesex Battalion had indeed attacked north that morning, in accord with IX Corps orders. But the British, consistently excellent in defense, were cautious and slow on offense. Soon after the jump-off, the Middlesex Battalion ran into the CCF and bogged down about six miles south of Keiser's advance positions. But because of a failure to establish a direct communications link with the 2d Division, this vital information, which would have further clarified the depth of the CCF threat, did not reach Keiser.

Meanwhile, Peploe's 38th Infantry had mounted up. The plan was that the motorized column would "bang" through the block and keep going. The march order of the infantry was this: Skeldon's 2/38 (220 men) would ride on about a dozen Sherman tanks in the vanguard, prepared to dismount and deal with other roadblocks that might be encountered; Maixner's 3/38 (only 63 men) would come next in line, crowded into about a dozen jeeps; Keleher's 1/38 (about 275 men) would bring up the rear. Because of the shortage of vehicles, most men of the 1/38 would ride on the vehicles of the division artillery headquarters, which was in the column immediately behind the 38th Infantry. Maixner's men would provide infantry protection for the artillery.[21]

Sometime during the morning, however, this sensible march formation was drastically altered. Keiser or his staffers decided that rather than lead the column, the tanks (and the A/A vehicles as well) should be scattered along its entire length, to provide protection for the many nonarmored vehicles. Inasmuch as Skeldon's men were riding these tanks, this meant that the 2/38—the strongest surviving infantry element in the 38th Infantry—was scattered along the length of the column as well. So dispersed, the 2/38 was no longer capable of fighting as an integrated unit. This proved to be yet another mistake.[22]

At about noon Sloane, who had been fighting the CCF since dawn and had seen his 9th Infantry finally torn to pieces, concluded that the 38th's "bang through" was very likely to fail. He sought out the ADC, Sladen Bradley, and proposed in its place a "tank shuttle" whereby one or two tanks would "escort" a few nonarmored vehicles at a time through the block, or blocks, then return to repeat the process. But Bradley saw little merit in this scheme and refused to propose it to Keiser.[23]

Moments later Keiser issued Peploe verbal orders to "How Able" (or "haul ass"). Up to that time the 2d Division, although badly shattered, was still more or less a cohesive unit, with communications and a chain of command. But Keiser's order, as Sloane aptly put it, "changed the nature of the operation." Thenceforth the 2d Division lost its cohesiveness and integrity. The "march" down the Sunchon road was to turn into a mad, chaotic scramble and, finally, a desperate every-man-for-himself fight for survival.[24]

By common agreement it had been decided that one tank, carrying twenty infantrymen of Skeldon's G Company, would precede the column, serving in the role of a pathfinder or stalking-horse. It would test the ground and draw fire, forcing the CCF to reveal the positions of its machine guns and mortars, enabling those coming behind to deal better with them. It was a deadly, dangerous assignment, but the men on the pathfinder tank had one advantage: surprise. They hoped to dash through the block before the CCF could hit them.[25]

It proved to be a hair-raising ride. In the first mile the pathfinder tank was riddled by at least five well-emplaced machine guns. A little farther on it was forced to stop and clear a CCF road barrier consisting of three abandoned and disabled vehicles—debris from the convoy. During that hurried operation CCF machine guns raked the pathfinder tank, forcing the infantry to dismount temporarily, then to remount. Still farther on, five miles beyond its starting point, the tank came upon what soon became legendary in the 2d Division as the Pass. This was a quarter-mile-long cut in a hill, with steep fifty-foot banks on both sides. Without pause the pathfinder tank sped through the cut, surprising CCF troops at mess, and broke into the clear terrain beyond it. After cracking through a second road barrier of disabled vehicles, it reached the British lines. Almost by a miracle, not a single man had been hit or left behind.

This mad dash provided valuable intelligence. It revealed that the CCF firmly held a six-mile stretch of the Sunchon road, that it had the road covered with about forty machine guns and about ten mortars and countless riflemen, that the Pass was the perfect place for an ambush, that the British were nowhere near as close as had been supposed. But this vital information was not relayed to Keiser because the tank's radio could not reach him; and the British still had no direct communication link with 2d Division.

In any case it was too late to take advantage of the intelligence. Peploe's column was already on the move, already in deep, deep trouble. It had begun moving behind the pathfinder, but when the pathfinder stopped to clear the first road barrier, the column, too, had stopped. This proved to be another mistake. As historian Marshall put it, "With the enemy gauntlet firmly established, the column's one chance for successful survival was that it could barrel on through, losing a vehicle now and then, but never giving the enemy a broadside standing target which would enable him to perfect his adjustment on the road. One wait killed that possibility, and all of the other waits, and hurts, misery and death which followed came partly of it."[26]

George Peploe ran the gauntlet in his command jeep. His assistant S-3, William E. Manning, remembered: "Peploe was born in England and had acquired that British reserve and cool. He was always calm and collected, always in charge, and did not abide fools. I thought nothing could shake him—until that day. Under the heavy fire on the road his driver froze. He simply refused to go another yard. He was plugging up the road. I was nearby and saw what was going on. I put the driver in the rear seat with Peploe's South Korean bodyguard, got behind the wheel, and off we went. I took the left lane, passing the vehicles clogging the road. The jeep got hit, but nobody in it. We stopped once to pick up a wounded man, then barreled on. George Peploe was shaken that day. He was not alone."[27]

When the column halted, the CCF, having been alerted by the dash of the pathfinder tank, raked it with a hurricane of machine-gun fire. This forced the infantry off the tank into ditches. Some nonarmored vehicles blew up or were put out of action, blocking the road. After this initial pause the lead tanks started moving again, pushing the disabled vehicles off the road and leaving the infantry stranded in ditches. Behind these tanks, other nonarmored vehicles blew up or were disabled, again blocking the road, forcing the following tanks to stop temporarily. Scattered far and wide and pinned down in ditches, the infantry could not organize for concerted attacks on the CCF. Everywhere there was soon chaos and terror and noise and death.

In the column were two West Pointers who were sons of generals: Alan W. Jones, Jr. (1943), and Lucian K. Truscott III (1945). Jones's two-star father, Alan senior, had been commander of the 106th Division, which had been shattered by the Wehrmacht in the opening hours of the Battle of the Bulge. In subsequent days the senior Jones had been relieved of command; his son, serving in the same division, had been captured and finished out the war in a German POW camp. Truscott's father began the war as commander of the 3d Division in Sicily, rose to command a corps, then to replace Mark Clark as commander of the Fifth Army in Italy, and finally, after the war, to replace George Patton in the Third Army, retiring with four stars.

Young Jones preceded young Truscott in the column. About halfway through the gauntlet, machine-gun fire raked his jeep, destroying it and wounding him and his driver. Unable to walk, Jones crawled into a ditch, certain that for the second time in his life he would become a POW, until he heard Truscott's familiar voice. Braving CCF machine-gun fire, Truscott dismounted, rescued Jones, and made a place for him in the jeep. Both finally got out. Hospitalized, Jones did not return to the division; Truscott remained to become a 9th Infantry company commander.[28]*

Behind Truscott came his West Point (1945) classmate, Rolfe L. Hillman, Jr., who commanded the 9th Infantry Heavy Mortar Company. Hillman, too, lost his jeep and was cast adrift on the road. He remembered:

When we got the order to load up, line up, and "run it," I remember a great relief. With driver Hayes Hewitt and company clerk MacDaniels, we made an easy run up the winding road on the right ridge, but then our world changed. Within sight of the cut at top, everything stopped in a hail of small arms fire and from all the vehicles I could see men scrambling out to find some protection and return fire. The next part of the passage is a black and white blur of moving and stopping, shoving vehicles and getting people on our trailer. It was after maybe a half a mile beyond and below the pass when our jeep was rammed from the rear and crashed into whatever vehicle was ahead. We scrambled out between the jeep and the steep bank on the left, but right away we were jolted by what seemed to be concussion grenades, with dirt and rock chips flying.

Those still on the road were going over the bank to the right and our group also made that leap. I landed almost on top of Lieutenant John N. Ford, a black officer in our 3rd Battalion. He had a long open gash over the top of his head; I put my first aid packet on him and told him to keep ahead of us. He did that very well, because we later heard he was in a hospital in Japan by the next day. From that over-the-cliff point, MacDaniels and I spent some long period of time crawling down a ravine in a ditch that protected us from spattering small arms fire. I gave Mac my West Point ring and asked him to get it to my wife if necessary. Why did I think he would make it and I wouldn't?[29]

John Ford, who won a Silver Star, was one of the very few men of McMains's 3/9 to survive the gauntlet. The (white) commander of the 3/9's I Company, Harris M. Pope (who also won a Silver Star), was another. Pope remembered: "Our losses were devastating. The next day we could find only thirty-seven men of our battalion. Some more straggled in later, but not many." McMains himself survived—to win a DSC. "When I found McMains and reported we had only thirty-seven men, he threw his arms around me and broke down. I don't think he ever recovered from the terrible shock of those losses."[30]

The remnants of the column pushed onward: tanks; trucks; jeeps; trailers; ambulances; vans; mobile kitchens. Those men who survived and could move jumped on any passing vehicle or ran or walked. Some men played dead. Some surrendered. A few officers and NCOs attempted to collect bands of men and

---

*Truscott's son, Lucian K. IV, was to enter West Point (1969), then resign to write a best-selling antiwar novel, *Dress Gray.*

fight back. But strangers thrown together in such dire circumstances do not fight well.

The six miles of road held by the CCF were a classic gauntlet. The Americans could not turn back. To leave the road was suicidal. They could only attempt to go forward, enduring CCF fire. Hundreds died on the road; hundreds more were wounded. A surgeon, Paul A. Maxson, who was escorting and attending the 38th Infantry wounded, remembered: "We stopped numerous times because the vehicles ahead of us had become engaged and we had no choice. But when this happened, we searched the ditches alongside for our wounded, and, as we found them, we stacked them in the trailers of the jeeps until they were three or four deep."[31]

Had the Commonwealth Brigade pressed the northward attack more aggressively, it might have taken the Pass from the south. But this was not the "finest hour" for the British. Had Skeldon's 2/38 remained in the van of the column as originally intended, it might have taken the Pass from the north. But the 2/38 was hopelessly scattered. As a result, those who survived the gauntlet had to face the fury of the Pass at its end.[32]

By the time the two leading tanks of the column reached the Pass the CCF had machine guns and mortars well emplaced and the troops were on full alert. The CCF attacked these tanks savagely with machine-gun fire and a captured 2.36-inch bazooka, then swarmed out and climbed on the tanks with grenades. Some American infantry coming behind the tanks shot many of these attackers off the tanks. Among them was Skeldon, who had given up his command jeep to some wounded and was walking. Already wounded in action the day before, Skeldon seemed utterly fearless. He faced down an advancing CCF skirmish line of forty to fifty soldiers, who were "pumping lead" from rifles and tommy guns at him, then turned and calmly "picked off" a single rifleman in a foxhole.[33]

At that moment, almost providentially, FEAF fighters arrived over the Pass. They attacked the swarms of CCF with well-aimed rockets and napalm. This attack probably saved Skeldon's life and gave the tankers a moment's respite to maneuver and train their guns on the Chinese. The combined firepower of the aircraft and tanks temporarily drove the Chinese off, giving the lead elements of the column an opportunity to run the Pass. Skeldon, who received a DSC for his valor, got out without further physical wounds.[34]

\* \* \*

One of the FEAF rockets exploded close to a group of Americans that included a junior tank officer, Tom W. Turner, who was knocked cold by the blast. He told historian Marshall a bizarre tale.

When he came to, Turner saw that the long column of vehicles was stalled. After running back to the first vehicle in line, he found it empty. Its riders were in the ditch, shooting at the CCF. Turner ordered these men back into the truck and sent it onward. Two trucks followed the first, but no more. The men from the fourth and succeeding trucks were also in ditches, taking cover and returning fire. Continuing north along the road, Turner also routed these men from the ditches and back into their trucks and directed an oncoming tank to knock out a CCF machine gun until, astonishingly, he had got the whole column moving again toward the Pass.

Believing the column would continue nonstop through the Pass, Turner jumped on the running board of a passing truck. But a CCF round hit Turner's handhold and knocked him off. He fell hard and rolled into a ditch, unconscious for the second time. When he came to again, he found himself a prisoner of a small group of CCF. One polite Chinese soldier instructed him—in perfect English—to walk south, toward the Pass, and collect the "walking wounded." Complying with these instructions, Turner rounded up three wounded Americans and continued toward the Pass. He soon became aware that his CCF captors had inexplicably disappeared and he was once again a free man.

By this time the truck column had stopped again, bumper to bumper, jammed up short of the Pass. The problem this time was a well-emplaced CCF machine gun. Turner decided to rush the gun. He rounded up a scratch force of ROK stragglers and charged—only to find himself all alone. The ROKs were hanging back. Thinking "What the hell!," Turner ran on alone, screaming, "Banzai! Banzai!" Inspired by this bravery, the ROKs jumped up and followed. The combined manpower overwhelmed the CCF and silenced the gun—one of the very few put out of action at the Pass by American infantry.

This small success inspired Turner to keep moving into the Pass itself. Running through the hail of fire directed on the stalled truck column, Turner entered the cut, keeping close to the right embankment, only to find his way blocked by a mass of about 200 soldiers immobilized and hugging the dirt. Investigating, Turner found that these soldiers were being held up by two riflemen who were barely inching along, half carrying, half dragging a wounded buddy. Running forward, pistol drawn, Turner ordered the men to get out of the way and let the others pass. One of the soldiers put his rifle on Turner and said: "You son-of-a-bitch, I'm helping a wounded man. You get out of my way or I'll shoot you."

Turner, in turn, leveled his pistol on the man and replied coolly: "I gave you an order. Move that man as I said or I'll shoot *you.*" In the face of this threat, the men pulled aside to let the others pass, Turner exhorting them onward: "Doubletime! Doubletime!" Turner himself hung back to help the three men he had ordered aside. All got through the pass to British lines— Turner later to receive a Silver Star Medal.[35]

\* \* \*

Behind this group came Harold Maixner and his 3/38 "battalion," which had run the gauntlet, losing five of the eleven jeeps and about nine of the sixty-three men. Along the way Maixner had commandeered a Sherman tank, which was serving as "escort" for his little convoy. When it reached the Pass, the CCF, now recovered from the FEAF strike, rained devastating fire on the column. Historian Marshall wrote:

Three of the men riding with Maixner were hit. He stayed at the wheel and kept pounding forward until suddenly the . . . tank stopped. . . . Ahead of the tank, a jeep had been hit by fire and knocked out just as it came abreast an already immobilized 2 1/2 ton truck, thus blocking the road. The tank started forward toward the jeep, with the object of running it down and crushing it. At that moment Maixner saw a human foot projecting from under the jeep's trailer. Maixner yelled at the top of his voice. By some miracle the tank driver heard him and braked. But it was a split second too late. The tank track had squashed the foot flat. Its owner, a colored soldier, already hit by a bullet through the abdomen, had crawled under the trailer to escape the fire. He lay there screaming, "Kill me, I can't stand the pain."

Having no room in his jeep for the wounded soldier, Maixner directed that he be dragged to a "safer" place under the two-and-a-half-ton truck. Then the column proceeded onward through a hail of CCF fire. The tank crashed over the jeep; Maixner's jeeps went around it. Soon the column broke into open terrain and thereafter reached the British lines. Of the sixty-three men on the 3/38 roster that morning, only forty-five got out. The 3/38 was the last "major element" to make it through the Pass. Thereafter the Pass became clogged by disabled vehicles and rendered impassable.[36]

## II

Dutch Keiser usually kept close to his CP, but not this afternoon. Ailing with a severe chest cold that bordered on pneumonia, he turned over his command van to the wounded and rode in a jeep, running the gauntlet like everybody else. At about 3:30 P.M. he arrived at the Pass. What he found was appalling. The Pass was clogged shut—a junkyard of vehicles. Nothing was moving. Masses of men had collected; they were like zombies. Marshall wrote:

The dead lay in the ditches and sprawled across the roadway. Most of the living—even those still unwounded—were in such a state of shock that they responded to nothing, saw nothing, and seemingly heard nothing. The Chinese fire beat like hail among the rocks and next to the vehicles where they stood or reclined. But they neither cried out nor sought better cover. Their facial expressions remained set, appearing almost masklike because of the heavy coating of dust and the distortion from the dropping of the jaw. . . .

Heedless of the CCF fire, Keiser walked among the men, barking questions designed to shock them into action: "Who's in command here? Who are you? Can any of you do anything?" But he got no answers from anyone. He then turned and walked south through the entire length of the Pass. Scores of his dead and the wounded men littered the cut, lying in the open road or huddled in the cover of wrecked vehicles or pressed against the embankments. Only one man—an unidentified 9th Infantry sergeant—was shooting back. Most of the living were tending to their wounded buddies. Sick physically, sick at heart, drained physically and emotionally, Keiser turned around and made his way back through the cut. Near the north end he stumbled and kicked what he believed to be a corpse. The "corpse" suddenly came alive, sat bolt upright, and cursed Keiser's clumsiness: "You damned son-of-a-bitch." Keiser could only manage to say: "My friend, I'm sorry."[37]

Keiser, his ADC, Sladen Bradley, and other senior officers improvised a division CP on the north side of the cut. This mass of brass devoted its full attention and energy to mobilizing sufficient scratch forces to unclog the Pass. For a while Generals Keiser and Bradley acted the roles of platoon leaders, exhorting desultory infantry to the high ground to eliminate the machine guns. But none of this did any good; the CCF held and continued to kill and maim.[38]

The solution, finally, proved to be absurdly simple. When two light tanks from the division Recon Company arrived on the scene, one of Peploe's captains—unfortunately never identified—volunteered to lead them into the Pass and employ them as bulldozers to clear a path through the junkyard. Keiser himself approved this plan; Bradley joined the captain to direct the operation. They began working about sunset, as FEAF fighters were making their final runs of the day at the CCF. With this parting help from the airmen Bradley, the unidentified captain, and the tankers bulldozed a lane through the debris.[39]

\* \* \*

Last in the long battered column came the division artillery, with Keleher's scattered 1/38 deployed on its forwardmost trucks and tractors.

The first artillery battalion in line, the attached 17th, commanded by Elmer H. Harrelson, began moving through Sloane's 9th Infantry sector about 2:00 P.M. All its many vehicles were crowded with a miscellany of hitchhikers. About two miles down the road the column ran into CCF machine-gun fire, aimed from both flanks. The column halted; most of the artillerymen and hitchhikers dismounted to find cover and return fire. Soon the men remounted the vehicles, and the column proceeded onward, stopped again and again by wrecked vehicles in the road or CCF machine guns. These assaults destroyed twenty-two vehicles and eleven trailers, but on the whole, the 17th FAB ran most of the gauntlet without heavy manpower losses and without losing any of its valuable eight-inch howitzers. It reached the Pass about sunset.

At that time the cut was still blocked, and darkness was approaching. The division artillery commander, Loyal Haynes, summoned Harrelson, Keleher, and other senior officers to his command vehicle for a conference. Haynes had in mind for the night a scheme to draw all the artillery into a laager (or circular perimeter), which could be defended by Keleher's 1/38 infantrymen and other stragglers. But before this plan could be explored in detail, word came that the Pass had been opened. Haynes, his staff, the 17th FAB, and Keleher's hitch-hiking 1/38 rolled on into the pitch-dark night.[40]

Beyond the Pass there were new problems. Keleher remembered:

For the next five hundred yards the road was temporarily impassable because of the numerous burning vehicles and the pile-up of dead men, coupled with the rush of the wounded from the ditches, struggling to get aboard anything that rolled. When we checked to make a turn-out, away from a blazing wreck, either there would be bodies in our way, or we would be almost borne down by wounded men who literally threw themselves upon us.

At one point I got out of the quarter-ton to remove a body from the road. Then I saw that the man was still moving. . . . I squeezed him into our trailer. But as I put him aboard, other wounded men piled on the trailer in such numbers that the jeep couldn't pull ahead. It was necessary to beat them off. . . . I had to get out and wrestle off a dozen wounded who were trying to board us. There wasn't space for even one of them and I couldn't give them my place because I had to keep my battalion moving.[41]

Beyond the pass, and closer to the British lines, Harrelson and Keleher discovered that the CCF (or the Americans) had blown a concrete bridge in the road. This forced the column to detour and cross the stream by way of a makeshift ford. It proved to be a difficult challenge for Harrelson's big tractors and guns, made more difficult when two British-manned Sherman tanks came on the scene from the south with headlights burning. The lights illuminated the ford—and drew heavy CCF machine-gun fire. On this detour one eight-inch howitzer toppled over into a forty-foot gorge, irretrievably lost. Remark-ably, the eleven other big guns reached British lines safely.

Keleher and Harrelson were lucky; their outfits incurred modest casualties compared with others that day. The 1/38 lost about a quarter of its strength, sixty-eight men. The 17th FAB lost only eight men wounded.

\* \* \*

It was a far different story for the artillery battalions coming behind the 17th: the 37th, 503d, and 38th. Starting later in the afternoon, they, too, were repeatedly blocked, stopped, and riddled. All were still on the road well north of the pass when darkness fell. Under cover of night the CCF attacked these columns with swarms of infantry, blowing whistles and bugles. Supported by some hitchhiking infantry of the 9th and 38th infantry, the artillerymen fought back. Some even fired artillery pieces point-blank at the CCF, but they were soon overwhelmed. The commander of the 37th, John B. Hector, fought his way out (to receive a Silver Star Medal), but he lost ten of his eighteen 105-mm howitzers, fifty-three vehicles and thirty-nine trailers. When the CCF swarmed into the black 503d (which had already lost a third of its strength in fighting at Kunu), its new commander, West Pointer (1939) Geoffrey Lavell, lost his composure and "wandered off" into the night. (He died in a CCF POW camp about fourteen months later.) Despite a desperate effort by the black artillerymen, only one of the 503d's eighteen 155-mm howitzers survived. Last in line, the 38th FAB was hit even harder. Its commander, Robert O'Donnell, wounded five times by a CCF machine gun while trying to organize a defense, somehow survived and was carried out (to receive a Silver Star Medal), but his outfit broke and ran, leaving behind all its eighteen 105-mm howitzers and all its vehicles. Total artillery losses: forty-six pieces.[42]

Ironically, some of the last rounds fired by the 503d FAB caused severe damage not to the CCF but to the 2d Division. These rounds, fired in confusion, whistled through the darkness and fell into a column of thirty-four vehicles stalled near the Pass farther south. The vehicles were transporting a contingent of division MPs who, until then, had run the gauntlet without losing a single vehicle or man. Six of the 503d's rounds landed squarely on five vehicles, destroying them, wounding twenty-one men, and dismounting perhaps four times that number.[43]

The physical and psychological beating the men of the 2d Division endured on the gauntlet that day was ghastly. The surviving commanders estimated that about 3,000 casualties had been incurred. The survivor Rolfe Hillman wrote: "You don't forget Kunu-ri. The author of a World War I novel wrote a passage that surely pertains—no two men have exactly the same reaction to such an experience, and no one man comes through it unchanged. If you made it out of the Kunu-ri you have to wonder, then and now, if you did what you were supposed to do and could do."[44]

# III

That terrible day Paul Freeman's 23d Infantry, mated with John Keith's 15th FAB, plus some tanks of the 72d Battalion, had been holding Kunu while the last combat elements of the 25th Division withdrew over the Chongchon River and headed west for Sinanju. In this task Freeman was helped considerably by FEAF, which flew an astonishing 287 close air support missions over Kunu that day, attacking the advancing CCF troops with bombs and napalm and strafing them with machine guns. The airmen claimed to have killed 1,000 CCF men in these attacks.[45]

All that day, as he fought the CCF, Freeman had been keeping one eye on the Sunchon road, down which he, too, would withdraw. As the afternoon wore on, he heard sporadic, but alarming, reports over the division communications net describing the slaughter taking place. In the late afternoon Freeman reached a sensible, but controversial, decision. He felt it would be more prudent if the 23d Infantry and 15th FAB withdrew behind the 25th Division through Sinanju than over the bloody Sunchon road, which, to Freeman, seemed a "suicidal" route.[46]

Such a drastic change in plans, of course, required Keiser's personal approval. But when Freeman called up the division CP to request it, Keiser was not there. At the time Keiser was probably at the Pass, trying to unclog the road. In Keiser's absence, the chief of staff, Gerry Epley, did not feel he could give the authorization, and in fact (as he said later), he was very much opposed to it. Epley believed that if Freeman were to withdraw by way of Sinanju, it would uncover the hindmost 2d Division elements on the Sunchon road (mainly the artillery battalions), making them vulnerable to CCF attack from the rear. ADC Bradley, who happened by (or came on the radio), agreed with Freeman and urged Epley to grant Freeman's request, but Epley would not do so without Keiser's "blessing."[47]

Freeman persisted in his efforts to reach Keiser. Finally, he did so—in a manner of speaking—by means of a relay through Sloane's CP. Sloane, who could talk to both men, passed the messages back and forth. But apparently this crude means of communicating resulted in a mixup. Freeman believed he got clear, unequivocal permission from Keiser to go out via Sinanju, and that was also Sloane's impression.* But Keiser later denied that he had given it; to the contrary, he had proposed that Freeman organize an armored task force to attack the Pass from the west. Later, when Epley asked Keiser if he had given Freeman permission to withdraw through Sinanju, Keiser's reply, Epley wrote, "was an emphatic No!"[48]

Believing he now had the required authorization from Keiser, Freeman began making plans for a change in the direction of his withdrawal. The supposed authorization, Freeman said later, was reinforced by two further authorities. First, Sladen Bradley got through to Freeman by radio, Freeman recalled, and gave "an order that I should put my plan into effect." Secondly,

---

*As well as that of Freeman's former exec, Ed Messinger, who was at Sloane's CP to relieve Sloane, and Sloane's exec, Joseph O. Gerot.

a IX Corps liaison aircraft flew over and dropped a "message" which directed Freeman to withdraw through Sinanju. It apparently was not signed. Many years later, Freeman said, he discovered that the man who dropped the message was his "friend" West Pointer (1926) Thomas E. de Shazo, commander of the IX Corps artillery.[49]

By the time Freeman had his plans firmed up it was nearly sunset. He and Keith had decided not to take Keith's 105-mm howitzers; one might topple over on a hairpin turn and block the road. Instead, they would gather all the 105 ammo, fire a final massive salvo at the CCF, then utilize Keith's trucks and trailers to carry out both the withdrawing infantry and artillerymen. Everyone who could be spared, even the cooks and clerks, would handle ammo for the big final shoot.

It was almost dark when the shoot commenced. It was an awesome display of heavy firepower: 3,206 rounds fired in the space of twenty minutes. According to Keith's FOs, it stopped a massive CCF attack in its tracks. When all the ammo was expended, the gun barrels were so hot the paint peeled. They had probably been ruined by the heat, but to make certain they remained useless, Keith's men removed the firing locks and sights, then blew the guns with thermite grenades. The destruction of these howitzers raised the 2d Division artillery losses that day to sixty-two pieces.[50]

While the artillery salvo was in progress, the men of the 23d Infantry and 15th FAB began boarding vehicles. The withdrawal order was: James Edwards's 2/23; Claire Hutchin's 1/23, followed by Charles Kane's 3/23, which served as rear guard. Although Homer Henckley was invited to withdraw the pitiful remnants of his 1/9 with the column, he refused. The 9th's heavy-weapons platoon commander, William Ellis, remembered:

Hinkley [sic] had been an OSS member in China during World War II and was on the Chinese Communist "black list" to be killed as a spy if captured. In fact, an officer from Eighth Army was on the way down to the 9th Infantry headquarters to get Hinkley removed from the battle zone. Hinkley was too brave for his own good. He took [what was left of] the 1st Battalion down with him. My best friend, the S-3 of the 1/9, John F. Ellis (no kin), whom I had served with in World War II, was killed along with Hinkley and most of the officers and men of the 1/9 that night.[51]

The column proceeded west in haste, merging into the stream of traffic of the 25th Division. Almost immediately thereafter the column stalled for an hour and a half, blocked by a massive traffic jam. During the stop some CCF troops worked in close and attacked the rearmost trucks with four or five machine guns. Several trucks were shot up and lost, but the men scrambled aboard other vehicles. Finally, the column began to move again and proceeded a full three miles—and out of immediate danger—before it once again stopped.

In this halting fashion the 23d Infantry and 15th FAB (less its guns) got away, spared the horrible ordeal on the Sunchon road.[52]

But the controversy over Freeman's decision lingered for decades. Many, such as Gerry Epley, believed that the decision was wrong: that it uncovered the 2d Division artillery on the Sunchon road; that as a result, all the artillery was savaged; that Freeman should have been given a "reprimand." Had Freeman attacked the Pass from the west (as Keiser apparently had in mind), arriving about sunset, much of the afterdark slaughter might have been prevented. However, most survivors doubted that the proposed attack—or any other attack—would have been successful; that given the circumstances, Freeman took exactly the right course. In the aftermath of the disaster Keiser refused to discuss the matter or to criticize Freeman and, outwardly at least, seemed "content that the regiment had been saved."[53]

# IV

The men of the 2d Division who ran the gauntlet from Kunu to Sunchon on November 30 barely escaped a further disaster—and possibly total annihilation—at Sunchon. They were spared by courageous but little-known actions of Hap Gay's 1st Cav Division, which Johnnie Walker had ordered to shore up Eighth Army's right flank.

The 1st Cav began deploying over the roads to the east of Sunchon on November 29. Johnny Johnson's 5th Cav and Billy Harris's 7th Cav led the deployment. Ray Palmer's 8th Cav, rebuilt since the November 2 Unsan disaster but not yet tested in combat, remained in reserve. The division's loaned-out artillery had been returned. It included Joseph Knott's 61st FAB, overrun with the 2d Division elements at Kujang, now back in full combat status, mated, as usual, with the 5th Cav.[54]

During this advance the 5th and 7th Cav operations were greatly impeded by a sea of Koreans clogging the roads. Thousands of ROK soldiers from the shattered 6th, 7th, and 8th divisions were bugging out, southbound. In addition, there were thousands of Korean civilian refugees fleeing the CCF. It was believed that the CCF (like the NKPA in the earlier days of the war) had mingled with the refugees in order to infiltrate through 1st Cav roadblocks. Norman Allen, commanding I Company in the 3/5, remembered one night in particular when "a million refugees" pressed against his roadblock. To keep them back, he had his men fire tracer bullets over their heads. Soon, however, his block was hit by CCF mortar fire, apparently coming from positions among the refugees. A platoon leader radioed that he had been overrun by CCF mixed in with refugees. The men wanted to fire on the refugees. Allen went on:

I asked who the refugees were—men, women, what? They replied "Mostly women and children, but there are men dressed in white, right behind them, who look to us to be of military age." I paused. The pause went on. The road block came on [the radio] again—urgent, desperate, requesting permission to fire.

By this time the other company C.O. had called in artillery, high bursts . . . fired [more] to discourage than to kill. I instructed the road block to fire full tracers along the final protective line, then fall back onto the high ground. If an enemy unit was among those refugees, well, then they simply would be in our rear in the morning. I could not order firing on those thousands upon thousands of pitiful refugees.[55]

The CCF Forty-second Army, which earlier in November had been in the Chosin Reservoir area, had overrun ROK II Corps. The CCF army's three divisions—the 124th (badly shattered by the Marines at Sudong), 125th, and 126th—came through Tokchon, then headed south on November 29 with the apparent aim of swinging west through Sunchon and cutting off the 2d Division. Northeast of Sunchon the 5th and 7th Cav met the 125th Division head-on.

Johnny Johnson's 5th Cav was first to engage the enemy. It was a shocking confrontation. John Clifford's 2/5, leading the regiment, was engulfed by a sea of bugle-blowing CCF troops, and his CP was overrun. His situation was soon so perilous that Johnson had to send his I and R platoon, then Edgar Treacy's 3/5 to the rescue. The I and R Platoon was overrun and lost. Norman Allen of the 3/5, who was part of the rescue effort, remembered: "The 2nd Battalion came out in pieces; it had lost most of its vehicles and heavy weapons along with 202 men and thirteen officers . . . [and] it became really nasty. Men continued to come back in threes and fours, sometimes a dozen—lost, wounded, and confused, officers and men alike."[56]

Billy Harris's 7th Cav met the CCF due east of Sunchon, near Singchang, on the night of November 29–30. It was another shock. Harris was tightly buttoned up, with Pete Clainos's 1/7 on the right of the road, John Callaway's 2/7 on the left, James Lynch's 3/7 in reserve. The CCF 125th Division swarmed at the 1/7 and 2/7 about 9:00 P.M. The fighting was close and fierce and soon hand to hand. Both the 1/7 and 2/7 CPs were overrun and forced back.[57]

In this developing crisis Billy Harris committed his reserve, Lynch's steady 3/7. Lynch came up with tanks and A/A vehicles blazing. So reinforced, the 1/7 and 2/7 managed to regroup and mount counterattacks, supported by the faithful howitzers of the 77th FAB, now commanded by Ross Lillard. A terrible slaughter ensued. By dawn the 7th Cav's perimeter had been restored. Harris's men counted 350 CCF bodies inside the perimeter and estimated that another 1,250 lay immediately outside. The 7th Cav suffered 156 casualties, including 38 dead and 107 wounded.

These blocking moves by the 1st Cav temporarily thwarted the CCF Forty-second Army's drive on Sunchon. They enabled the 2d Division's gauntlet survivors to complete their withdrawal through Sunchon on December 1. As the 7th Cav's historian wrote with justifiable pride, Johnnie Walker commended the 1st Cav, describing its actions as "a major factor in preventing the encirclement of United Nations Forces."[58]

The withdrawal of the 2d Division through Sunchon left the 1st Cav exposed. On December 1 it fell back on Sunchon in a heavy snowstorm. It was freezing cold; the men of the 1st Cav still wore summer uniforms. There was still an acute shortage of rations. Notwithstanding its fine showing, morale plummeted and tempers were short. It was disheartening and demoralizing to be retreating again, ceding territory to the CCF which had been purchased at such high cost in American blood.[59]

In Sunchon Billy Harris's 7th Cav was substantially reinforced to create a powerful RCT. To it were added the Commonwealth Brigade's Argyll Battalion and the 3/8, giving Harris five infantry battalions. His mission was to serve as a rear guard, blocking CCF attacks from the north or east. Bafflingly, the RCT found little to fight. The CCF did not press on Sunchon from either direction. Having been in full-scale combat for a week, the CCF had apparently expended its ammo and rations and had to regroup and resupply its divisions before it could continue its offensive.[60]

In the aftermath of this tough fighting, Billy Harris became deeply worried about the health of his able 3/7 commander, James Lynch. "He was blacking out, and he couldn't rest," Harris remembered. "Both the regimental surgeon and chaplain came to me and suggested he needed relief. He had done a wonderful job, and I hated to lose him; but there was really no choice." Reluctantly Harris called his old friend, the I Corps chief of staff, Rinaldo Van Brunt, and asked him to request Lynch through channels. Having won two DSCs—and the unprecedented two Presidential Unit Citations in the Pusan Perimeter for the 3/7 within two weeks—Lynch left the 7th Cav and joined the I Corps G-3 section. He was to rise to one-star general before retirement.[61]

\* \* \*

The surviving elements of the 2d Division continued south through Sunchon to Pyongyang, thence to Munsan, below the Imjin River. The head count there on December 1 was shocking. In two weeks of fighting the division had been wrecked almost as badly as Bill Dean's 24th Division in the early days of the war. It had incurred about 33 percent casualties (4,940), the vast majority in the last few days of November. It then numbered but 10,000 men, 8,662 short of its authorized battle strength. The three infantry regiments, the artillery, and the engineer battalions had suffered most: Ed Messinger's 9th,

1,267 casualties; George Peploe's 38th, 1,075; Paul Freeman's 23d, 485; the division artillery, 1,461; and the two engineer battalions, 561.[62]*

Several senior officers in the 2d Division were fired and evacuated, some ostensibly for "medical reasons." Chief among these were Dutch Keiser, Sladen Bradley, and Chin Sloane, all of whom left the division within a few days, never to return.

The Army historian Marshall, a reserve colonel, was on temporary active duty in Korea to prepare classified Army studies on tactics and weapons. He had decided to focus closely on the 2d Division and was therefore present at division headquarters on the day the command shakeup occurred. In his memoir, *Bringing up the Rear,* Marshall wrote that there occurred "one of the strangest scenes in my military life."

While Marshall was having breakfast with the division chief of staff, Gerry Epley, and the new 9th Infantry commander, Ed Messinger, Sladen Bradley, the ADC, came in and said, as Marshall remembered it, "Gentlemen, I have just learned that General Keiser is being relieved as commander of the division. I want that command. I deserve it. Now, each of you must know something to do that will help me. What have you to suggest?" All present were thunderstruck at Bradley's raw display of ambition; none expressed any concrete suggestions. "Bradley was himself bounced out that afternoon," Marshall wrote. Apparently genuinely ill, Bradley went to a hospital in Japan, but he was to return to a high command position in Eighth Army.

Later in the day, Marshall remembered, Dutch Keiser called him to his command van. Keiser wanted to tell Marshall what had happened to him that day "for the record." Keiser said that early that morning he had received a message from Eighth Army headquarters "advising him that he was ill with pneumonia and must report to a hospital in Tokyo." Believing that he was to be the "goat for MacArthur's blunder," Keiser decided he would "not take it lying down." He went to Eighth Army's main headquarters in Seoul for a confrontation with the chief of staff, Lev Allen. Marshall wrote that the following terse dialogue took place in Allen's office:

"What the hell are you doing here? You're ill with pneumonia."
"You can see for yourself I don't have pneumonia, so cut the bunk."
"But are you going to comply with the order?"
"Yes, because it is an order, but I don't want you to kid around with me." Then Dutch turned toward the exit.

---

*Of the authorized regimental strength of 3,800 men, on December 1 Messinger had but 1,406 men; Peploe but 1,762, and Freeman 2,244. Of the authorized strength of 3,695 men, division artillery had but 1,970.

Allen called after him: "By the way, General Walker says he will take care of you with a job around his headquarters."

Dutch turned back to say, "You tell General Walker to shove his job up his ass."[63]

Later, at Johnnie Walker's request, Marshall, who was also an Army booster, held a press conference which was designed to exonerate Keiser and the soldiers of the 2d Division of any blame for the disaster which had befallen the division. Marshall went out of his way to praise the performance of black soldiers in the "integrated companies of the 9th Infantry Regiment." They "had fought as well as any such units ever in national history," he said. His remarks were published widely in American newspapers, but they drew a sharp rebuke from MacArthur's acting chief of staff, Doyle Hickey. He summoned Marshall to Tokyo and told him that senior Army officers could not publicly "raise issues that have to do with separation or integration. That is forbidden." The Army did not "recognize that there was any such thing as a Negro soldier or a white soldier." Nonetheless, upon returning to the States, Marshall became an outspoken advocate of integration in the Army. His views carried much weight in the professional Army officer corps.[64]

\* \* \*

Dutch Keiser's replacement as commanding general of the 2d Division was a "Collins man," fifty-four-year-old Robert B. McClure. Born in Georgia, McClure had entered the United States Naval Academy in 1916 but washed out, Collins wrote, owing to "some breach of regulations or academic deficiency." Thereafter McClure had enlisted in the Army, obtained a commission (1917), fought in the AEF with the 26th ("Yankee") Division, and been decorated for gallantry.[65]

After the usual slow peacetime climb up the career ladder, McClure had entered the Army War College in 1938. One of the senior instructors there was Joe Collins, who took a shine to McClure. When Collins was named commander of the 25th Infantry Division in Hawaii early in the war, he found McClure serving as the division G-4 and promoted him to command the 35th Infantry Regiment, which McClure ably led under Collins in tough fighting on the islands of Guadalcanal, New Georgia, and Vella Lavella. Upon the departure of the division ADC, John Hodge, Collins promoted McClure to replace him, with the temporary rank of brigadier general. Soon thereafter both Collins and McClure left the division. Promoted to two stars, McClure was given command of the ETO-bound 84th Infantry Division, then in training. But after six months the orders were changed, and McClure returned to the Southwest Pacific to command the Americal Division, which was rooting out Japanese on Bougainville.

Earlier in his career McClure had served a double tour (1927–1933) with the 15th Infantry in Tientsin, China. There he became fluent in Chinese and overlapped for two years with a fellow officer in the 15th, Albert Wedemeyer. In late 1944, when President Roosevelt and George Marshall sent Wedemeyer to China to replace Vinegar Joe Stilwell as chief of staff to Chiang Kai-shek and commander of American forces in China, Wedemeyer requested McClure as his chief of staff. Soon after that Wedemeyer found a new chief of staff and sent Bob McClure into the field to become the senior American combat commander. As such McClure not only commanded American ground forces in China but also was chief trainer and supplier for dozens of Chinese Nationalist divisions. Wedemeyer judged that McClure performed that role in "a superior manner," and was a "competent and aggressive combat leader," and he recommended him for promotion to three stars for the coming all-out campaign against the Japanese in China.[66]*

When McClure took over the 2d Division, he made no immediate changes in the senior commanders. Ed Messinger remained in command of the 9th Infantry. Paul Freeman remained in command of the 23d Infantry, promoting his S-3, West Pointer (1940) Frank Meszar, to succeed Messinger as exec. George Peploe retained command of the 38th Infantry. However, Peploe's exec, West Pointer (1932) John G. Coughlin, who was also promoted to full colonel, replaced Maurice Holden as the division G-3. The not inconsiderable task of finding commanders and personnel to rebuild the division's four shattered artillery battalions was left up to the artillery commander, Loyal Haynes, who was still going strong.[67]†

McClure proved to be an even more controversial division commander than Dutch Keiser. One reason was that McClure, like the 3d Division commander Shorty Soule, had an overfondness for the bottle. The historian Marshall was back at 2d Division headquarters, helping to build morale, when McClure arrived. McClure, too, called Marshall to his van for an extraordinary private chat. Marshall remembered in his memoir:

Not drunk, he was well on his way. He said right out that the new orders were a terrible shock to his nervous system, that he had never expected to lead troops in battle again, and that for the first time he was not up to it. He went on. "I can

---

*The plan was that upon termination of hostilities in the ETO Generals Patton, Simpson, and Truscott would come to China to help the Chinese defeat the Japanese. Wedemeyer would be overall commander; Simpson would be his deputy. Patton would command the northern sector armies; Truscott, the center sector; and McClure, the southern sector.

†The addition of McClure to the roster of the six Army division commanders in Korea reduced the average age to 54.3 years. John Church, at 58, was still the oldest. All had been commissioned in 1917 or 1918. Only one (Bill Kean) was a West Point graduate, and he had attended the academy for only two years. Only one (Hap Gay) had attended college for four full years and been graduated. Four (Gay, Kean, Church, and Barr) were "ETO generals," but Barr had served postwar in China. Two (McClure and Soule) were "Far East generals." The appointment of Messinger brought the average age of regimental commanders in the 2d Division to 45.3 years.

only brace myself by hitting the bottle. I'll be doing a lot of drinking, so you go ahead. Program whatever you wish. When something calls for my appearance, give me fair warning and I'll get in shape, but don't expect too much."

He stayed in his van day after day and did not get out to the troops. Every night I arranged for a special group of outstanding leaders to dine with him at the general's mess. Sometimes it would be sergeants who had starred in the battle in the North, on other nights captains or battalion commanders. There would be a reception and cocktails, with the feed following. A few hours before the formation I would go to McClure and tell him it was time for a brace. He would shower and take a few pills. Usually when he appeared he would be shining, with no sign of wooziness.

Fortunately eight of the nine combat-tested battalion commanders in the 2d Division had survived: Barberis and McMains in the 9th; Hutchins, Edwards, and Kane in the 23d; Keleher, Skeldon, and Maixner in the 38th. On the night they came for dinner, Marshall wrote, McClure "was something less than his best." McClure gave Jim Skeldon a bear hug, Marshall remembered, and said, "You old son of a bitch, they tell me you're quite a fighter." As Marshall remembered the scene, Skeldon's reaction was less than convivial. "Jim shook him off, straightened, and glared. 'Sir, when you call me that you better have a smile on your face.' McClure smiled."[68]

One of McClure's first orders to his division proved to be highly controversial. Each man in the division, he decreed, would grow a beard. There would be a prize for the best beard. McClure even distributed a mimeographed drawing "to illustrate the desired results." The reasons for this order are obscure. One officer remembered that since most Asians did not have facial hair, it was designed to "facilitate identification of division personnel in the dark." Another thought it might also have been conceived as a division morale builder, to "make the men look tougher." Whatever the reasons, the order evoked scorn and ridicule. The chief of staff, Gerry Epley, remembered: "McClure was not too bright. The beard contest was stupid."[69]

The general who replaced Sladen Bradley as ADC was George Stewart, chief of the 3d Logistical Command at Inchon. Since at the time it seemed possible that the CCF might overrun Seoul and Inchon, Eighth Army had ordered Stewart to evacuate his command from Inchon and move it to Pusan. Stewart's son, West Pointer (1945) George, Jr., was then in Frank Bowen's 187th Airborne RCT. "The thought of retiring to a safe location while my son was still fighting didn't set well with me," Stewart remembered. He continued:

I went to the Army chief of staff [Lev Allen] and requested a new assignment. He told me to obey the order I had received. As I was leaving headquarters I ran into General Robert McClure, whom I had known before. . . . I asked if he would like a good Assistant Division Commander. He replied that he might. A day or so later

I was summoned by the Army chief of staff who told me I could go with McClure [but only] on a temporary basis, that General Sladen Bradley would return to the division as ADC as soon as he was released from the hospital. But he went elsewhere and I remained ADC of the Second until rotated home some nine months later.

Before leaving the 3d Logistical Command for his new job, Stewart dealt with one final and difficult logistical task. During the X Corps capture of Seoul and Eighth Army advance to the Chongchon River, NKPA POWs had been sent rearward to be confined in an old walled prison on the outskirts of Inchon. The number had grown to 40,000. Responsibility for caring for these POWs— a huge task—had been delegated to Stewart's 3d Logistical Command. Having been ordered to move his command to Pusan, Stewart was faced with the problem of what to do with these 40,000 POWs. Leave them to be "liberated" by the CCF or move them still farther rearward to Pusan?

Believing that if the Americans left those NKPA POWs behind, they might be murdered by South Koreans before the CCF arrived, thereby encouraging an "indefensible war crime that would have been a disgrace to our country," Stewart, on his own initiative, decided to move them by rail, truck, and ship to Pusan. "God bless the Navy," Stewart remembered. It provided sufficient LSTs to carry the majority of the POWs to Pusan. From there the POWs were moved to Koje, an island off Pusan, where all the NKPA and CCF POWs were consolidated and confined.[70]

The thousands of replacements for the 2d Division came from a variety of sources. One of Paul Freeman's was twenty-year-old Charles A. Strong, son of the Eighth Army engineer Pat Strong. Earlier, in 1948, at age eighteen, in order to avoid the two-year draft, Charles had enlisted in the Army for a special one-year Stateside tour, serving with the 23d Infantry. When he learned of the CCF entry into the war and the heavy losses in the 2d Division, he reenlisted in Japan and was sent directly to his old outfit.[71]

# V

By December 2 the withdrawal of Eighth Army from the Chongchon River had been carried out. Three ROK divisions (6th; 7th; 8th) had disintegrated. The American 2d Division had been wrecked; the Turkish Brigade had lost a fifth of its men (about 1,000) and was utterly disorganized. Bill Kean's 25th Division had suffered heavy losses in Corley's 24th and Michaelis's 27th regiments and Dolvin's 89th Tank Battalion. Hap Gay's 1st Cav Division had incurred heavy losses in Johnson's 5th Cav and not a few in Harris's 7th Cav. Of the major Eighth Army units which had been at the Chongchon on November 27, only John Church's 24th Division and the Commonwealth Brigade had escaped severe losses.

Eighth Army fell back to create an enclave around Pyongyang. The 25th Division held a blocking position below Sukchon. The 1st Cav and the Commonwealth Brigade held a blocking position below Sunchon. The 24th Division deployed to a blocking position south of Sunchon and east of Pyongyang. The Eighth Army reserve, the newly arrived 29th British Brigade and the 187th Airborne RCT, moved north through Pyongyang to serve as additional blocking forces in the Sukchon area. For the moment, at least, the CCF was not pursuing.[72]

Earlier, when Walker proposed holding a Pyongyang enclave, he had done so in the belief that he would have four American and four ROK divisions at his command. But now these eight divisions had been cut to three American divisions (1st Cav; 24th; 25th) and one ROK division (1st), plus the three reserve regiments (Commonwealth and British brigades; 187th). Two of the three American divisions had been roughly handled. The men of the shattered ROK 6th, 7th, and 8th divisions were being rounded up and reorganized; but they had abandoned most of their equipment, and Walker had none to give them. Clearly Walker did not have adequate manpower to defend a Pyongyang enclave.

There was another problem. The Americans of Eighth Army had been dealt another stunning psychological blow. The easy Home by Christmas offensive had turned into a bloody nightmare. In MacArthur's phrase, they were fully engaged in "an entirely new war." It seemed hopeless. Morale in Eighth Army was plunging out of control. There was real doubt in Walker's mind that his men had the spirit for a defense of Pyongyang in the face of a concerted CCF attack. The entire army might panic and run.

For these reasons, and others, Walker made the controversial decision to abandon Pyongyang and all of North Korea. He would make a hurried and deep withdrawal below the 38th Parallel to the Imjin River. There the geography was more favorable for a defense by his limited forces, and he could be closer to his main supply base at Pusan. If Eighth Army could not hold at the Imjin, he would withdraw it farther south, to the Han River, the Kum River, or even all the way back to the Naktong River.

The decision was controversial because Walker was not then under attack by the CCF. All contact with the enemy had been lost. Walker did not know whether or not the CCF intended to pursue. If it did not, if the enemy offensive had been launched merely to drive Eighth Army off the Chongchon River to establish a buffer zone, or for other reasons, then Walker would be guilty of handing over Pyongyang and all North Korea to the CCF without a fight. Moreover, yet another withdrawal was bound to demoralize the American and ROK forces further.[73]

Walker communicated his decision to GHQ, Tokyo, with the usual request for MacArthur's personal approval. He got no immediate reply. Nonetheless, he summoned his staff to a mass meeting at the Eighth Army main headquarters in Seoul to announce his decision. The engineer Pat Strong, who was present, remembered Walker's statement in these words: "I have not been able to get MacArthur's headquarters to advise me of their intentions. In the absence of instructions, I shall assume that the tactical integrity of this Army, on which the entire defense of Japan depends, is my paramount objective. Accordingly, I will give up any amount of real estate if necessary to prevent this army from being endangered."[74]

Eighth Army, Walker ordered, would withdraw to the Imjin River, fighting a delaying action. To avoid overtaxing the roads, no effort would be made to salvage the considerable stocks of supplies (ammo; gasoline; rations; winter clothing) which had been accumulated in Pyongyang. These were to be destroyed by engineer demolition teams. To impede the pursuit of the CCF, all railroad and highway bridges and culverts would be blown behind the retreating troops. Eighth Army would leave a "scorched earth."

For engineer Strong, the order to blow all the bridges was "heartbreaking." As he recalled, "For three weeks, in punishing weather that reached below zero at night, a battalion of engineers had worked around the clock to complete the three thousand feet of pile trestle railroad bridge [over the Taedong River at Pyongyang] needed to push the railroad toward the Yalu. . . . Every man of the engineers was working himself to exhaustion to get the bridge completed. On the day when the last steel beam was put in place the dismayed battalion commander was told to blow the bridge."[75]

For the cold, hungry, and miserably equipped American GIs retreating through Pyongyang, the destruction of the Eighth Army supply stocks there was infuriating. A GI in Stephens's 21st Infantry remembered scornfully that "the engineers burned a rations dump about the size of a football field." When a 5th Cav sergeant came upon engineers burning winter clothing, he leveled his carbine on the officer in charge and held him at bay until he had salvaged a truckload of this priceless gear for the men of the 5th Cav.[76]

The 44th Ordnance Depot Company had set up a repair facility on a large drill field at the military academy in Pyongyang. An Army historian wrote that the outfit had amassed (for repair) "30 to 40 tanks, 500 vehicles, an 8-inch howitzer, and three or four 105 mm howitzers . . . [and] 2,000 boxes of truck engines, transmissions, differentials and transfer cases." When the evacuation order was received, the repair company did not even have enough operable transportation to move its own equipment, let alone the weapons and matériel it had collected for repair. "The gates of the collecting point were thrown open," the historian wrote, "and cannibalization [was] invited. Demolition crews later destroyed what was left."[77]

In all this no one was more frustrated than Captain Willard Baker, commanding the 57th Ordnance Recovery Company of Milburn's I Corps. The job of his outfit was to salvage disabled tanks and howitzers from the battlefield. Based in Pyongyang, Baker received urgent word that nine Pattons of John Growdon's withdrawing 6th Tank Battalion "were limping down the Sukchon and Sunchon roads" and urgently needed tow tractors.[78]

Baker sent out recovery teams to rescue the valuable Pattons. Bucking a massive tide of withdrawing vehicles and men, the teams found the nine limping Pattons and got them into the Pyongyang railyards for loading on flatcars. There a problem developed: The officer in charge had given loading priority to the Air Force, which, the Army historian wrote bitterly, was evacuating "some vehicles, but a lot of items like mess tables, Korean chairs, and office equipment." The Air Force officer in charge refused to yield the loading ramp or any rail cars for the Pattons.

As it happened, a ROK train pulled in from the south with six flatcars, loaded with new Pattons and Pershings for the 6th and 70th tank battalions. Baker unloaded these new tanks (which could evacuate by road on their own) and began loading the nine disabled Pattons, plus five other disabled Pershings that had been towed into the yard. When it was discovered that two of the newly arrived tanks would not start, these were added to the other tanks for rail evacuation. In all, Baker's men laboriously loaded sixteen disabled Pattons and Pershings on the flatcars, notified I Corps they were ready for evacuation, and then evacuated themselves.

Thereafter something went wrong, and the tanks never got out of Pyongyang. Since they would be valuable booty for the CCF, Eighth Army asked the Air Force to go back and destroy them. By coincidence, *Life* photographer Hank Walker was in an Air Force plane, flying low, taking pictures of the evacuation of burning Pyongyang, when the formation of Air Force bombers arrived overhead. "We looked out and saw dozens of bombs falling by our plane," Walker remembered. "The aim was good." The salvos of bombs hit and destroyed all sixteen tanks on the flatcars. Walker confirmed the destruction with photographs that sickened him and, when published in *Life,* many other Americans.[79]

# VI

After the summit meeting with MacArthur and Walker, Ned Almond remained in Tokyo until about noon on the following day, November 29. During his absence the situation in X Corps worsened dramatically.[80]

In the Marine sectors at Hagaru and Yudam, the CCF pressed its attack with renewed fury. The Marines fought back in the bitter cold with heroic stubbornness, but they incurred heavy casualties at both places. Proceeding with his plans to withdraw the Marines from Yudam, O. P. Smith ordered Ray Murray's Fifth Marines to hold at Yudam in a constricted perimeter while Homer Litzenberg's Seventh Marines attacked rearward to open the road from Yudam to Hagaru.

The situation made it vital that Smith hold Hagaru. Inasmuch as there was merely one Marine infantry battalion at that place, Smith requested that Chesty Puller, who had established his First Marines CP at Koto (eleven miles south of Hagaru), send all possible reinforcements. At the time Puller, himself under heavy CCF attack, was hard pressed to provide a single man. However, fresh UN forces providentially arrived in Koto.

This new force was the 41st Commando Battalion of the British Royal Marines. Commanded by Douglas S. Drysdale, these 250 Royal Marines had come up to join the American Marines. They had only recently arrived in Korea and had not yet seen any combat. Puller beefed up the outfit with thirty tanks and the Army's B Company of the 1/31,* commanded by Charles L. Peckham, which was en route to join Task Force MacLean east of the Chosin Reservoir, some newly arrived Marine replacements, and other units. As finally organized, Task Force Drysdale comprised about 900 men.

Led by Peckham's B Company, this pickup force set off from Koto early on the morning of November 29, enjoined to get to Hagaru *"at all costs."* By that time, as Puller and Drysdale knew, the CCF had cut the Koto–Hagaru road in numerous places and had dug in on high ground overlooking the road. When the column reached a place which was to be named Hell Fire Valley, the CCF opened fire. Fighting back from exposed positions on the road, often heroically, the American and British forces tried but failed to crack through to Hagaru. In so doing, they incurred severe casualties. About half the Royal Marines were killed or wounded or missing. Among the wounded was Drysdale. About 300 of the 900 men, including B Company commander Charles Peckham, were captured. Only about 300 men (including the wounded Drysdale) managed to press on to Hagaru. The other survivors were forced back to Koto.[81]

\* \* \*

Early the same morning, November 29, east of the Chosin Reservoir, Mac MacLean proceeded with his plan to withdraw Don Faith's 1/32 into Bill Reilly's 3/31 perimeter, thereby consolidating the dispersed infantry of Task Force MacLean.[82]

---

*B Company was substituting in the 2/31 for E Company, which was left behind at Pungsan. For reasons forgotten, B Company had got far ahead of the 2/31.

Having loaded the 100-odd wounded into trucks and disabled the other vehicles, Faith and the 1/32 began moving toward the rear at about 5:00 A.M. It was still dark, and it was snowing hard. As a result, the difficult maneuver did not go smoothly at first. Fortunately, however, the column was not attacked or pursued by the CCF. The Chinese apparently paused to plunder the equipment and supplies that had been left behind.

On its way south the column gathered up the 31st Heavy Mortar Company, which had established itself in a laager about midway between the 1/32 and 3/31 perimeters. Commanded by a combat-experienced World War II paratrooper, George R. Cody, the company had fired its big (4.2-inch) mortars in support of both the 1/32 and the 3/31. Oddly—and fortunately—the CCF had not attacked the company on either night. It was virtually intact but very low on ammo.

At about dawn the lead elements of the column reached high ground overlooking the 3/31 perimeter. Faith's men were shocked by what they saw: The perimeter was under heavy CCF attack. Through the fog and smoke of battle it seemed to one of Faith's men that the 3/31's perimeter was "a scene of total devastation."[83]

It soon became apparent to MacLean and Faith that the 1/32 would have to fight its way into the 3/31 perimeter. Since neither man had any communications with the men inside it, this would be a difficult and hazardous task, made more difficult by a CCF roadblock of logs at the foot of a bridge on the road just outside the perimeter. Both the bridge and the block were under heavy CCF fire.

Confronting this daunting situation, Faith led his men well. He deployed a flanking force into the higher ground east of the bridge and personally led another force in a frontal attack on the block. Reaching the block first, Faith and his party drove off the CCF, took the bridge, and tore away the block. In this small victory Faith may have been assisted by artillery or A/A fire from the 3/31 perimeter. Such was the fog and confusion of battle that no one would remember with certainty.

During this pause Mac MacLean came forward in his command jeep. Through the haze and smoke he spotted a column of troops advancing on the 3/31 perimeter from the south. Believing these troops to be his long-overdue 2/31, MacLean was "overjoyed" for a moment. But joy soon turned to dismay as the men inside the besieged 3/31 perimeter began firing on that column.

MacLean was wrong. The column approaching from the south was a formation of CCF troops. That morning his 2/31 (less B Company) was still far away—in Hamhung, climbing aboard a train which would take the men north on the Hamhung–Hagaru road to the last railroad stop at Majon.

Having misidentified the troops approaching from the south, MacLean impulsively leaped from his jeep. Shouting, "Those are my boys," he raced out on the frozen reservoir toward the 3/31 perimeter, apparently intending to do all he could to stop the friendly fire on his supposed 2/31. He did not get far. Almost immediately CCF troops hiding near the bridge cut down MacLean with a hurricane of small-arms fire. Watching in horror, Faith's men saw MacLean fall and get up about four times. Then a CCF soldier ran onto the ice and dragged the wounded MacLean into the brush.[84]

There was no time, then, to attempt to rescue MacLean. Faith had to devote his full energies to getting his column inside the 3/31's perimeter. Inasmuch as the bridge was still under heavy CCF fire, he directed his men to cross the frozen stream on the ice—away from the bridge. Then he ordered the trucks to dash across the bridge, one at a time. Although the CCF fire at the bridge was hot and close, most of the 1/32, including the 100-odd wounded men in the trucks, finally reached the 3/31 perimeter during that morning.

Inside the perimeter Faith and his men found a ghastly mess. Hundreds of Chinese and American frozen bodies lay intermingled on the ground amid the wreckage of battle. Bill Reilly was still alive, propped on a stretcher in his CP, cheerfully directing the survivors of his riddled staff. His outfit had incurred an estimated 300 casualties; his L Company no longer existed.

In MacLean's absence Faith assumed command of the consolidated forces. He reorganized the group, appointing his exec, Crosby P. Miller, to command the 1/32, and Reilly's exec, Harvey H. Storms, to command the 3/31. Robert Tolly, substituting for the wounded Ray Embree, remained in temporary command of the artillery and A/A vehicles. In response to Faith's orders the new infantry commanders divided up the infantry to reconstitute six rifle companies and deployed them into a tight, strong perimeter, with overlapping fields of fire, backed up by the artillery and A/A vehicles. The Marine air controller, Edward Stamford, radioed for close air support and an airdrop of supplies, the latter to include urgently needed 40-mm and .50-caliber rounds for the A/A vehicles.

That done, Faith sent out search parties to look for MacLean. They had no luck. By then the CCF had sent MacLean to the rear. He was officially declared "missing," but much later it was learned (from another American POW) that he had died of his wounds on his fourth day of captivity and that his fellow POWs had buried him on the roadside. After Robert Martin, who briefly commanded the 34th Infantry in the early fighting at Chonan, MacLean was the second—and last—regimental commander to die in Korea.

* * *

The same morning, November 29, Robert Drake, the 31st Tank Company commander, who was still at the 31st regimental rear CP in Hudong, decided to make a second try to break north to the 3/31 perimeter. This time he recruited about fifty soldiers, mostly clerks, from the 31st Headquarters

Company and arranged for an air strike to support the tanks. Although Faith's perimeter was merely four miles to the north, there were still no communications between it and Hudong. Therefore, Drake had no way to advise Faith that he was coming or to ask him for infantry and artillery support.

Drake set off at about 8:00 A.M. with twelve tanks. The terrain was still icy or mushy, and again the tanks skidded and mired. The CCF, well dug in on high ground (Hill 1221) dominating the road, attacked again, riddling Drake's "infantry." The air strike arrived, but since Drake had no controller to direct the pilots, they mistakenly attacked the Americans. After four hours of hard fighting, during which he lost about half his "infantry," Drake again conceded defeat and withdrew into Hudong.[85]

All that day Faith and his men remained buttoned up inside the perimeter out of touch. His last orders, personally delivered by Ned Almond the afternoon before, called for an attack north when the 2/31 arrived. Faith must have known by then that these orders could not be carried out. The 1/32 and 3/31 were shattered. He had about 400 wounded to care for and very little ammo. Logic and prudence dictated not an attack but, rather, a withdrawal of the consolidated force to Hudong or Hagaru. Yet Faith could not order a withdrawal without orders from higher authority. An unauthorized withdrawal might be seen as a cowardly act which could lead to his relief. He therefore prepared for a Custer's Last Stand.

That day Faith received some help from aircraft. In response to requests from Edward Stamford, the Marines mounted numerous close air support missions and FEAF sent two C-119s to air-drop supplies. The strikes helped, but the airdrop was only partly successful: One-third of the bundles fell into the perimeter, one-third into no-man's-land, and one-third into CCF positions. The drop included some 4.2-inch mortar rounds but, disappointingly, no rounds for the Twin 40 A/A vehicles, which had exhausted nearly all their ammo. A Marine helicopter—apparently arranged by Hank Hodes—arrived to evacuate the severely wounded. It made only two trips. On the first it took out the two senior wounded officers, Bill Reilly and Ray Embree; on the second, two other men (not identified in the accounts).

* * *

When Ned Almond arrived back from Tokyo late that afternoon, November 29, he went immediately to his war room in Hamhung. At that time the forces of X Corps were in a chaotic mess:

• West of the Chosin Reservoir the Fifth and Seventh Marines were cut off at Yudam, the Seventh attacking rearward to open the Yudam–Hagaru road.

• South of Yudam, at Sachang, the 7th Infantry of the 3d Division was also way out on a limb, locked in battle with the CCF.

• At the foot of the Chosin Reservoir Hagaru itself was under heavy attack, defended by one Marine infantry battalion. Attempting to reinforce Hagaru, Task Force Drysdale had been massacred.

• South of Hagaru, at Koto, Chesty Puller's First Marines CP, defended by one battalion of Marines and some Army engineers, was also under heavy siege.

• East of the Chosin Reservoir Task Force MacLean was apparently dangerously exposed, but owing to the absence of communications, nothing definite had been heard.

• On the coast, at Yonghong, the Puerto Rican 65th and the 15th regiments of the 3d Division were regrouping to attack "west," in accordance with the GHQ plan to send 3d Division forces to assist Eighth Army.

• Far to the northeast the 17th and 32d Infantry regiments of the 7th Division, having reached the Yalu River, were withdrawing from the Pungsan area, en route to the Chosin Reservoir in accordance with earlier orders.

It was during that night that the JCS cabled MacArthur stating that X Corps appeared to be "exposed" and asking about his plans. Since Almond was still MacArthur's chief of staff and had excellent communications with Tokyo, no doubt the text of this JCS message reached Almond that night. Although tactfully composed, the cable clearly expressed deep concern. In a sense, it amounted to a rebuke, not only to MacArthur but also to Almond.

Exactly what Almond told MacArthur or GHQ that night in response to the cable is not known. The inference from MacArthur's reply to the JCS on the next day, November 30, is that Almond remained absurdly optimistic. "While geographically his [Almond's] elements seem to be well extended," MacArthur told the chiefs reassuringly, "the actual conditions of terrain make it extremely difficult for an enemy to take any material advantage thereof." Nonetheless, MacArthur went on, Almond had been "enjoined against any possibility of piecemeal isolation and trapping of his forces." As enemy pressure developed, "the X Corps will contract its positions into the Hamhung–Wonsan sector."[86]

For several days the harassed and overburdened X Corps staff, in response to Almond's directives, had been issuing a Niagara of orders to its far-flung units. These orders came down to the divisions, and then to the regiments, in a steady stream. The recipients remembered them as a series of conflicting "march and countermarch" orders that were consistently overtaken by events and that seemed to make little sense and gave the impression that X Corps had lost all control of the situation. The messages spewing out of X Corps from November 30 on intensified that impression.[87]

Notwithstanding his reassuring response to the JCS cable, MacArthur, in effect, directed Almond to break off the X Corps offensive and go over to the defensive and consolidate X Corps's far-flung forces. That morning, in compliance with MacArthur's expressed desires, Almond canceled the 3d Division attack "west" and the redeployment of the 7th Division to the Chosin Reservoir. The 65th and the 15th regiments of the 3d Division would go instead to Hamhung to safeguard that vital sector; the 7th Infantry would hold in place at Sachang until the Fifth and Seventh Marines reached Hagaru and would continue to block CCF attacks east toward the Hamhung–Hagaru road. The 17th and 32d regiments of the 7th Division would halt in Hamhung.

Later that day, November 30, Almond flew to Hagaru to confer with O. P. Smith, Hank Hodes, and the 7th Division commander, Dave Barr, who had flown up earlier to find out what had happened to Task Force MacLean and the badly lagging 2/31. By that time the full impact of the possible disaster confronting the X Corps forces at the Chosin Reservoir had finally sunk home. At the Hagaru meeting, the historian Roy Appleman wrote, Almond was "an entirely different man from the one who had visited his troops there two days earlier." He showed "genuine alarm" and "stressed the need for speedy action."

It was now clear that all X Corps forces in the Chosin Reservoir area must be withdrawn as rapidly as possible toward Hamhung. The plan arrived at was as follows. O. P. Smith would be delegated command of all forces near the Chosin Reservoir, including Task Force MacLean. He would first withdraw the Fifth and Seventh Marines and Task Force MacLean into Hagaru. Chesty Puller's thin forces at Koto would be reinforced by the Army's 2/31, which that morning had reached Funchilin Pass, about three miles south of Koto. The consolidated forces at Hagaru would be supplied with ammo, food, and medicine by C-47 aircraft, which would land on the enlarged airstrip at Hagaru. The Hagaru forces would first evacuate all wounded on the returning C-47s, then fight south to Koto and beyond. Combat forces of the Army's 3d Division would come up the Hagaru–Hamhung road as far north as Chinhung, to assist the Hagaru forces by holding open the road and providing trucks.[88]

While he was in Hagaru for this commanders' meeting, Dave Barr flew into Don Faith's perimeter by helicopter. By that time Barr was apparently again high on Almond's hit list, probably because Almond viewed the slow redeployment of the 7th Division—especially the 2/31*—as one cause of the debacle at the Chosin Reservoir. Barr, in turn, may have been angry at Mac-

---

*Later the 7th Division staffers would argue that one long delay in the movement of the 2/31 was actually the fault of the X Corps staff. When the 2/31 left Hamhung for Majon by train early on the morning of November 29, its trucks went by road. The X Corps staff had said it would provide other trucks at Majon, but the promised trucks were diverted to the north, carrying urgently needed ammo. Later that day, when the 2/31's own trucks arrived at Majon, the X Corps staff obtusely refused it permission to use the trucks to go on to Hagaru. As a result of this inexplicable (but documented) foul-up, the 2/31 had been forced to bivouac that night in Majon, in effect losing a full—and crucial—twenty-four hours in its movement forward.[89]

Lean for the poor deployment of his task force east of Chosin. Whatever the case, when Barr deplaned in the perimeter, one officer remembered (according to Appleman), he "discouraged our enthusiastic welcome with a brusque and unsympathetic response and stalked off to locate Colonel Faith."

Barr brought nothing but bad news to Faith. The situation had changed radically since Almond's visit two days earlier. All X Corps forces were to withdraw. Faith's task force was now under Marine command and control. There was no Marine force at Hagaru that could be spared to help Faith and his men, nor were there any Army forces. In view of the disaster which had befallen Task Force Drysdale the day before and the precarious situation at Koto, the 2/31 would stop in Koto to reinforce Chesty Puller. The Marines would provide Faith air support, but he and his men would have to fight their way back to Hagaru.[90]

Under ordinary circumstances, this would have been no great challenge for Task Force Faith. Faith had withdrawn the 1/32 four miles to the 3/31 perimeter without great difficulty. The 31st CP at Hudong and Drake's tanks were merely four more miles to the south. But the problem was the wounded. By then Faith was burdened with about 500 of them. He would have to take them out in the trucks. This would make the withdrawal very dangerous.

The task was made even more dangerous later that afternoon by an inexplicable development at the 31st rear CP at Hudong. At about 4:00 P.M. the senior officer present, the 31st Infantry's S-3, Berry K. Anderson, evidently acting on an order from Hank Hodes or someone else in Hagaru, directed the CP—and Drake's tanks—to decamp and withdraw into Hagaru. The men at Hudong welcomed the order. Anderson's assistant S-3, George A. Rasula, remembered that they responded with unseemly haste and that the "withdrawal" resembled a headlong flight.[91]

The evacuation of Hudong was total. In all, the rearward move to Hagaru included about 325 men from the 31st headquarters staff and company, the 57th FAB headquarters battery (which had been stranded there), and Drake's tankers, who left behind two disabled tanks. The evacuees were not attacked, and they reached Hagaru about dark and joined other Army forces in the defense of Hagaru.* Recovering the tank Hank Hodes had borrowed,

---

*The disparate Army forces in Hagaru included Company D of the 10th Combat Engineer Battalion of Shorty Soule's 3d Division, commanded by Philip A. Kilbes. Composed of eighty-one Americans and ninety ROKs, it had been sent there to build a X Corps CP for Ned Almond but had been thrown into the line to defend the town. During a massive CCF attack on the night of November 28 the ROKs broke, but the green American engineers held, suffering 50 percent casualties. When daylight came, they counted 400 CCF dead lying in front of their positions. One survivor of this heroic action, West Pointer (1947) Norman R. Rosen, wrote bitterly: "Months passed before the Marines gave us recognition for even having been in their perimeter." Kulbes and Rosen were belatedly decorated with Silver Star medals.[92]

Drake's force (sixteen tanks) stoutly defended the important East Hill sector.

The CCF 80th Division troops occupied Hudong that night. Unknown to Faith, his stepping-stone to the rear was gone. His task force was now absolutely cut off and completely surrounded. Just why Hank Hodes or some other officer ordered the evacuation of Hudong would never be established. Roy Appleman concluded that the order probably came down to Hodes from Dave Barr, who had apparently written off Task Force Faith and, Appleman wrote, "could not see any good coming from losing more men in behalf of those already lost."[93]

*　*　*

Late that same afternoon the lagging 2/31, which was about three miles south of Koto, met CCF troops and bogged down in disarray. One reason for the disarray was the 2/31 commander, the very senior West Pointer (1931) Richard F. Reidy, forty-three. As a troop commander Reidy was a disappointment. A senior 2/31 staffer remembered: "He was not an effective leader. . . . Chunky, about five feet, [he] had been a boxer at the academy and, I presume, later. He had cauliflower ears, a battered nose and was suffering from high blood pressure and a badly infected foot." Dave Barr's former aide Charles Davis, then serving in Reidy's G Company, remembered bitterly that "Reidy was a disaster, a very poor battalion commander and a consummate asshole who drank too much."[94]

When Almond learned that the 2/31 had bogged down short of Koto, he called his chief of staff, Nick Ruffner, and told him to send a X Corps staffer forward to get it moving. That assignment went to a X Corps assistant G-3, West Pointer (1944) Joseph I. Gurfein, an outspoken, combat-experienced paratrooper, who had obtained a master's degree from Harvard in the postwar years.[95]

Gurfein raced north to the 2/31 in a jeep. When he got there about 5:00 P.M., he found that Reidy was "frozen and paralyzed." In accordance with Almond's and Ruffner's instructions, Gurfein issued Reidy orders to get going and make an all-out attack to Koto. Having only two rifle companies, F and G, which had to attack in darkness, in bitter cold, and through a heavy snowfall, the battalion did not do well. It faltered. Then, when a booby trap on a bridge exploded (wounding one man), it broke. Gurfein remembered:

Within ten seconds a near rout had started, with the tail and lead companies turning to the rear and starting to overrun the battalion command group. . . . Not an NCO nor junior officer raised his voice to stop the rout. The battalion commander, pushed aside by his troops, stood there silently. I had to personally step in and stop the men, order them to halt, and then turn them around. By this time the battalion commander was moving back with the column. To the best of my knowledge he did nothing to stop the rout, or to control the men.

In effect Gurfein took command of the 2/31 and directed its march north. Just short of Koto it was again hit by the CCF, and another debacle ensued. Gurfein recalled he "had to personally come back on the road, collect the men, and move them off in orderly fashion." One company abandoned its vehicles and went ahead on foot. Finally the 2/31 straggled into Koto to reinforce that place, under command of Chesty Puller.*[96]

After Reidy had deployed these forces in positions designated by Chesty Puller, Ned Almond flew into Koto by helicopter. Almond impulsively dug in his pocket and awarded Reidy a DSC for getting the 2/31 into Koto. Joe Gurfein, who believed that he, not Reidy, deserved the lion's share of the credit, was furious. Later, when Gurfein told the true story (as he saw it), he said, "They gave me a Silver Star."[98]

# VII

The same evening, November 30, Task Force Faith prepared to face the fourth night of the CCF offensive east of Chosin. It was bitterly cold—zero or lower. The men were exhausted and frozen. They were depressed that they had been shifted to control of the Marine Corps command and that the Marines had decreed that they and the wounded would have to fend for themselves. Moreover, because of the fouled-up airdrop that day, they were still critically short of 40-mm and .50-caliber ammo for the A/A vehicles.

The CCF 80th Division launched its fourth attack on the task force at about 8:00 P.M. The assault came at several points on the perimeter and steadily mounted in intensity all during the night. It reached such fury that the 1/32 S-3, West Pointer (1943) Wesley J. Curtis, believed the CCF had orders to take the perimeter "at any cost." Fighting back doggedly, the Americans held most of the ground and, in so doing, inflicted heavy casualties on the enemy. The A/A vehicles, artillery, 4.2-inch and 81-mm mortars were deadly effective that night. They killed or wounded hundreds of the CCF and forced hundreds more to flee in shock or fear. The Americans incurred another 100-odd casualties during the night, bringing the total wounded in the task force to about 600.[99]

By dawn on December 1 Don Faith had concluded that the task force could not survive another major attack. There was not sufficient ammo of any

---

*The 2/31 linked with other Army units at Koto, including the survivors of B Company of the 1/31; about 150 engineers of the 13th and 185th Engineer Combat battalions, who were building an airstrip; and other "strays" who had been cut off on their way to Hagaru or to reinforce Task Force MacLean. In all, "Army forces" at Koto numbered about 1,500 men, counting substantial numbers of ROK fillers in Army units.[97]

kind; his hundreds of wounded desperately required greater care than he could give them. Although he had not received orders (by airdrop or other means) from Marine headquarters to withdraw, Faith summoned his staff and commanders and told them to prepare to move out at about noon. The Marine air controller, Edward Stamford, was to radio for close air support. When it arrived, the task force would begin the move south, taking all the wounded in about thirty two-and-a-half-ton trucks. The twelve 105-mm howitzers and the 4.2-inch and 81-mm mortars and other heavy weapons and equipment were to be destroyed.[100]

The four-mile route south to Hudong, where Faith expected to find support from the 31st headquarters contingent and Drake's tank company, would not be an easy run. Midway between the perimeter and Hudong stood the formidable Hill 1221 (about 3,600 feet), where the CCF had blocked Drake's tankers on November 28 and 29. The road circled east at the base of Hill 1221, made a hairpin turn to the west, then ran southwest. Unknown to Faith, CCF troops were massively entrenched on Hill 1221, holding good positions prepared earlier by Ray Murray's Fifth Marines. They also had blown two bridges and erected two roadblocks.

In retrospect some would question why Faith chose that difficult land route rather than go out onto the frozen reservoir to Hudong or even directly to Hagaru. The answer was that he and his staff did not believe the ice was thick enough to support the weight of the trucks in which the wounded were to be transported, and they thought the CCF might fire mortar rounds to break up the ice. The ice field provided no natural cover. If it gave way—or if the CCF broke it up—the task force could be trapped in the open. But some members of the Force, including artilleryman Thomas Gregory, later said the men could have walked out on the ice carrying the wounded on stretchers.[101]

*　*　*

Later that morning Faith and his officers formed up the column. They placed the 1/32 rifle companies (A, B, and C) at the head and the three reconstituted rifle companies of the 3/31 (I, K, and L) and the 57th FAB artillerymen at the rear. Because of the acute ammo shortage the column would include only four A/A vehicles: a Twin 40 at the head and tail and two Quad 50s in the middle. The 600 wounded were crowded into the thirty trucks.

While these preparations were being made, a barrage of CCF mortar rounds fell into the perimeter. It wounded five more key officers: the 31st Regiment's S-1, Hugh W. Robbins; the 1/32's D Company commander, Erwin B. Bigger; one of Bigger's platoon leaders, James G. Campbell; the 1/32's S-4; and one other. These new wounded were treated and then squeezed into the already overcrowded trucks.

The Marines provided the requested air support. A total of about twenty aircraft, arriving in flights of four or six, were to remain over the task force until dark. The aircraft were directed by Edward Stamford, whose radio jeep remained close by Don Faith's jeep near the head of the column. So disposed, Stamford was to play a major role in the afternoon's events.

The first flight of Marine aircraft arrived one hour later than called for, at about 1:00 P.M. When it appeared, the column struck off, the 1/32 rifle companies leading, the single Twin 40 vehicle in support. The riflemen encountered CCF fire almost immediately. In response Stamford directed the aircraft to attack.

By mistake the lead plane dropped its napalm short. It crashed down near the A/A vehicle at the head of the column. Its billowing, searing flames engulfed about a dozen Americans. These included two 1/32 platoon leaders, George E. Foster (West Point, 1950) and Henry M. Moore, both badly burned, Foster fatally. Private First Class James Ransome, Jr., remembered that the napalm "hit and exploded in the middle" of his squad. He continued: "I don't know how in the world the flames missed me. In my lifetime, I'll never know. Men all around me were burned. They lay rolling in the snow. Men I knew, marched and fought with begged me to shoot them. . . . I couldn't. . . . It was terrible. Where the napalm had burned the skin to a crisp, it would be peeled back from the face, arms, legs . . . like fried potato chips."[102]

The friendly air attack was a dreadful psychological blow to Task Force Faith. The wounded Hugh Robbins remembered that it was "one of the most horrible sights and incidents I ever hope to witness." To avoid being mistakenly hit in a second attack, the men bolted in all directions. Don Faith did his utmost to corral and rally his men, but it was not easy. "Up to this point," an Army historian wrote, "units had maintained organizational structure, but suddenly they began to fall apart. Intermingling in panic, they disintegrated into leaderless groups of men."[103]

Soon a degree of order was restored. Faith then assigned one of his most dependable platoon leaders, James O. Mortrude, twenty-eight, of C Company (who had won a DSC at Inchon), to take the point. Joined by the acting 1/32 commander, Crosby Miller, and C Company commander, Dale Seever, hobbling from his earlier wound, Mortrude bravely led his men toward the CCF positions and cracked through. At last the long column began to move, but without the Twin 40 A/A vehicle at the tail. The vehicle would not start and had to be abandoned, leaving the riflemen of the 3/31 and the artillerymen serving as rear guard without heavy firepower.

As the column snaked forward in fits and starts, the CCF raked the men and trucks with relentless—and seemingly endless—fire from the flanks. Many of the wounded in the trucks, including the C Company platoon leader, whom Almond had decorated, Everett Smalley, were killed. The fire also caused casualties and fear among the troops who were providing the rear guard. Upon learning this, Faith assigned the combat-experienced Hugh R. May to help keep the rear intact.

Two hours into the march, at about 3:00 P.M., the column confronted a formidable and entirely unexpected obstacle: a blown bridge at the north base of Hill 1221. The full-track A/A vehicle bypassed the bridge, crunching through tough grass and reeds in the creek bed. The trucks, however, bogged down in the grass and could not follow. It thus became necessary for the A/A vehicle to winch all thirty trucks one by one across the stream bed, a tedious task which also denied the men on the point the firepower of the A/A vehicle.

This obstacle imposed an agonizing and perhaps fatal delay on the column. It took a full two hours to winch all thirty trucks around the blown bridge. By the time the last truck got back on the road it would be dark. During those two hours hundreds of CCF soldiers came down off Hill 1221 and converged on the stalled column, raking the men and trucks—and the wounded inside the trucks—with heavy rifle and machine-gun fire. Scores of wounded inside the trucks were killed. Others crawled out of the trucks and hobbled toward the reservoir or surrendered to the Chinese.

Scouting ahead toward the hairpin curve, the C Company platoon leader, James Mortrude, found another major obstacle: a CCF roadblock, well covered by the CCF on Hill 1221. Within minutes of confronting this block and the CCF fire the 1/32 suffered further ruinous casualties among its senior commanders and staffers: Mortrude, wounded; his replacement, West Pointer (1949) Herbert E. Marshburn, killed; the B Company commander, killed; the C Company commander, Dale Seever, killed; the acting 1/32 commander, Crosby Miller, severely wounded; the 1/32 acting exec, Wesley Curtis, wounded.[104]

The column was then in desperate straits. The men were stalled at the front by the roadblock and crippled at the rear by the blown bridge. The CCF on Hill 1221 dominated the entire length of the column. Nightfall was coming on, the dark terminated the air cover. There was only one hope for breaking through: muster enough manpower for an all-out assault on Hill 1221.

In this crisis Don Faith was still a tower of strength, moving up and down the column in his jeep in the growing darkness, exhorting the men. Many wounded joined the assault on the hill, preferring to die there rather than in the trucks. One was the severely wounded D Company commander, Erwin Bigger, who crawled out of a truck, flailed his two canes at the men, and said: "If you are going to die, do it while in the attack. Let's get moving and secure this hill." The wounded officers Hugh Robbins, James Mortrude, and Henry Moore also rallied, but not all the men shared Bigger's views. Too many cowered in ditches, refusing to move, or ran away toward the reservoir. The ROKs were the worst malingerers. When Faith found two ROKs hiding under a truck chassis, Appleman wrote, he shot them with his .45 pistol.

The "attack" on Hill 1221 was more a desperate charge than a military maneuver. In the 1/32 "sector," up the hill went Bigger, hobbling on his canes, Robbins, Moore, and others, straight into the CCF fire. Many more 1/32 men were killed; they included Henry Moore, napalmed earlier. Harvey Storms, acting commander of the 3/31, joined the assault, assisted by his stouthearted M Company commander, Earle H. Jordan, Jr., who had been wounded earlier in the perimeter. In the assault Storms was wounded and fell, but Jordan kept moving uphill, followed by two brave platoon leaders, both wounded in earlier fighting, and by some men of the rear guard. One 3/31 platoon leader, Robert Schmitt, was killed in the charge; the other was wounded a second time. Many more men of the 3/31 were killed or wounded.

Astonishingly, this ragtag group from the 1/32 and 3/31 managed to seize most of Hill 1221. However, many of those who charged up Hill 1221 simply kept going—over the top and down the other side to the reservoir, where they continued on foot, singly or in small groups, directly to Hagaru. Many men of the 3/31 and the artillerymen followed in their footsteps, leaving the rear of the stalled column even more vulnerable.

Meanwhile, at the head of the column Don Faith had organized an assault on the roadblock at the hairpin turn. He was ably assisted by the 1/32's S-1, Robert E. Jones. Faith, personally leading a scratch force of about 100 men, charged from the left; Jones, leading about 200 men, attacked from the right. In a wholly unplanned but valuable assist the M Company commander, Earle Jordan, and one of his surviving platoon leaders, who had been wounded again, plus about ten men, charged down from Hill 1221 toward the roadblock, yelling and shouting. These three converging forces dispersed the CCF and seized the block.

At that moment a lone CCF soldier, hiding in the brush, threw a grenade. Its fragments hit Don Faith above the heart. Mortally wounded, Faith staggered, then fell. West Pointer (1946) Fields E. Shelton, commander of the 31st Infantry Heavy Mortar Company, also wounded by the same grenade, attempted to help Faith to his jeep, but Shelton had no strength. He wrapped the dying Faith in a blanket, laid him on the roadside, and went off looking for help. Later some men moved Faith to the hood of his jeep, and still later others placed him in the cab of the first truck in the convoy.[105]

The capture and demolition of the roadblock at the hairpin curve enabled the riddled and shrinking column to resume its perilous journey. By then about five of the trucks had been disabled. The men transferred the wounded from these trucks to others and pushed the disabled trucks over the hillside. The remaining twenty-five-odd trucks, jammed tight with wounded, ground on slowly. They made the hairpin turn, then turned southwest toward Hudong.

After Faith was wounded, there was no longer even a semblance of a command structure. As the 1/32's S-1, Robert Jones, put it, "When Faith was hit, the task force ceased to exist." A sergeant, Chester Bair, who had been Faith's driver in Japan, agreed: "The chain of command disappeared. It was every man for himself." The 1/32's acting exec, West Pointer Wesley Curtis, although wounded, was the senior surviving officer able to function. But Curtis believed the task force command structure was beyond repair, that no single man, not even a Patton or a MacArthur, could have "reversed the situation." Jones concurred: "If I had decided to shoot anyone in order to get their [*sic*] attention—it wouldn't have worked—those people were too far along from injuries, freezing cold, shock, fear and confusion to care."[106]

Nonetheless, for a while several men attempted to lead. Jones was one. He was joined by the rearguard shepherd Hugh May. Jones instructed May to round up twenty or thirty men and take the point. May and his men found—and knocked out—a CCF machine gun but then came upon a second, wholly unexpected, formidable, and disheartening obstacle: another roadblock, made of two of Drake's tanks, several vehicles of the ambushed 31st Medical Company, and logs. Jones and May detailed a dozen-odd men to dismantle the block, then went on, leading a group of about 200, many of them wounded. They walked south to the reservoir, collecting little bands of survivors, including one group led by the 31st's S-1, Hugh Robbins. Eventually Jones, May, Robbins, and most of this group reached Hagaru.

The Marine controller, Edward Stamford, likewise provided leadership for a time. He arrived at the second roadblock with the badly wounded acting 1/32 commander, Crosby Miller, lying on the hood of his jeep. Stamford jumped out and pulled away the logs, then drove to the rear to get the truck column moving. Again it was necessary to push several disabled trucks over the hillside. The wounded from these trucks crowded into the surviving trucks or wandered away or lay down in ditches, too weak to move. Scores died there or were captured.

After returning to the head of the column in his jeep, Stamford led the way, detouring around the debris of the second roadblock. The fifteen or so remaining trucks inched southwest in pitch-darkness another quarter of a mile and, at about 7:00 P.M., arrived at the village of Twiggae. The disastrous six-hour journey around Hill 1221 was over; Hudong, a mere mile and a half away, seemed within reach.

At Twiggae, however, the column encountered yet another obstacle: the second blown bridge. Scouting in the dark, Stamford found a parallel railroad bridge, which he believed the trucks could cross if the drivers exercised great care. He went back to the front truck in line and asked the dying Don Faith if he wanted the column to stop for the night or continue on to Hagaru. Faith managed a very weak "yes," meaning "go on to Hagaru." Thereafter Stamford guided the trucks across the railroad bridge. The ties of the tracks made it a rough, jolting, and excruciatingly painful ride for the wounded. Many more left the trucks and hid in the Korean houses in Twiggae or wandered out onto the ice.

The area between Twiggae and Hudong was alive with CCF troops, who kept the truck column under continuous fire. Many more able-bodied and wounded Americans deserted the column to hide or walk to the reservoir. Scores of these made it across the ice to Hagaru, but scores more died or were captured.

As the column approached Hudong, Stamford was still leading it in his jeep, with the wounded Crosby Miller lying on the hood. Suddenly Stamford was surrounded, captured, disarmed, and led away. A little later he eluded his captors and made his way south to Hagaru. Miller rolled off the jeep hood into a ditch and later found refuge in a Korean hut. Some CCF soldiers discovered him but, upon seeing his many wounds, apparently left him to die. Eventually Miller, too, got away and made his way to Hagaru.

The CCF had erected yet another roadblock a few hundred yards north of Hudong. The truck column coming behind Stamford's jeep arrived at the block and stopped. This was the end of Task Force Faith. The CCF brought heavy fire to bear on the trucks and lobbed phosporus grenades into the masses of wounded. One of the wounded, D Company platoon leader James Campbell, escaped from his truck and watched in horror. He remembered that the third truck in line rammed the stopped second truck and sent it crashing down into a deep gully. The Army historian wrote: "Wounded men inside were spilled and crushed. The frantic screams of these men seemed to Lieutenant Campbell like the world gone mad." Campbell eventually joined a group of survivors and walked on to Hagaru.[107]

In this final assault on the stalled column the CCF killed scores, perhaps hundreds of Americans. Most of these were the wounded in the trucks or the walking wounded who were too badly hurt or too exhausted to mount an effective defense or to escape to the ice. They included Don Faith; the acting 3/31 commander, Harvey Storms; the 31st Heavy Weapons Company commander, George Cody; the 3/31's I Company commander, Albert Marr; the 57th FAB's A Battery commander, Harold A. Hodge; and a valorous sergeant of the 1/32, Charles Garrigus, who was awarded a DSC posthumously.

\* \* \*

All during the night of December 1–2 the survivors of Task Force Faith straggled into the Marine lines at Hagaru. Many came into a sector held by the Marine 1st Motor Transport Battalion, commanded by Olin L. Beall, fifty-two. The survivors were a pitiful lot: wounded, injured, frostbitten, many in shock or worse from the horror they had witnessed and endured. Perhaps 600 reached the Marine lines at Hagaru that night. The most seriously wounded were treated and evacuated the next morning or the day after from the Hagaru airstrip.[108]

After daylight on December 2 the Marine Beall launched a rescue mission. Driving north over the ice toward Hudong in his jeep, accompanied by two Marine helpers, Beall found six dazed, frostbitten survivors and brought them back. On the next trip Beall and his men towed a sled behind the jeep and picked up seven more frostbitten survivors. Later in the day other Marines joined in the rescue mission with jeeps and sleds. By nightfall the Marines had rescued 319 American and ROK survivors of Task Force Faith.

During these missions Beall and other Marines came close to Hudong. At first CCF snipers shot at them and the Marines shot back. But as the day wore on and the rescue operation mounted in size and scope, the Chinese allowed it to proceed virtually unhindered. Moreover, that day and later some CCF soldiers released many wounded Americans, among them the acting 57th FAB commander, Robert Tolly.

The Army forces at Hagaru also mounted rescue missions. One was led by Hodges S. ("Sam") Escue, an assistant S-3 of the 31st Infantry, who had come up to Hagaru with Task Force Drysdale. He first went up to Hudong over the ice in a jeep and brought back, he remembered, "fourteen to nineteen" survivors. Next, escorting two Marine two-and-a-half-ton trucks, he went by land to Sasu, a village below Hudong. Under the eyes of CCF soldiers in the high ground "just one hundred and fifty yards away," Escue and his men filled both trucks with wounded survivors. He remembered that he was "astonished" that the CCF permitted this mission.[109]

On December 3, having rescued a total of 323 survivors of Task Force MacLean-Faith, Olin Beall returned to the Hudong area to scout for more. With Marine aircraft providing cover, Beall boldly went ashore at Hudong and explored the burned-out truck convoy. He found about 300 dead bodies still in the trucks, but not a living person. It was a ghastly sight that he would never forget.[110]

\* \* \*

Because of the rapid air evacuation of Army personnel from Hagaru and other factors, it would be difficult to arrive at an accurate figure of the total American casualties sustained by Task Force MacLean-Faith. The best guess was that of the original 2,500 Americans east of Chosin, about 1,000 were killed, left to die of wounds, or captured and placed in CCF or NKPA POW camps. After the air evacuation had ended, there remained at Hagaru about 500 7th Division soldiers, including about 385 survivors of the task force fit for duty, most of them from the 31st headquarters group and Drake's tank company, which had evacuated from Hudong.[111]

In the larger disaster unfolding all across Korea the grim story of Task

Force MacLean-Faith went virtually unnoticed. Within Army circles, however, the story was well known, as was the heroism of MacLean and Faith and many others in the task force. MacLean, Robert Jones, Earle Jordan, and several other officers were awarded DSCs. Don Faith received the Medal of Honor posthumously. He was the only battalion commander in the Korean War to be so honored.[112]

To many professional Marine and Army officers the destruction of Task Force MacLean-Faith became a tragic monument to Ned Almond's brashness, tactical incompetence, and callous disregard for the welfare of his men. They argued that the force had been too little, too late for its assigned mission. When the CCF attacked the Marines and Task Force MacLean on November 27, they believed Almond should have withdrawn the task force to Hagaru immediately. Instead, Almond had ridiculed the CCF as a "bunch of Chinese laundrymen" and "remnants of Chinese divisions fleeing north" and had mindlessly ordered Task Force MacLean to remain in place, then to attack.

Yet MacLean and Faith and their men did not suffer and die to no purpose. Their dogged heroism had virtually destroyed the CCF 80th Division and had blocked or delayed the CCF drive down the east side of the Chosin Reservoir to Hagaru for about five days. These Army blocks and delays bought vital time, enabling the Fifth and Seventh Marines to withdraw into Hagaru. But the same Army blocks and delays could have been mounted at Hagaru, with far fewer casualties and to greater effect.

These battles near the Chosin Reservoir dealt the 7th Division a severe blow. Five senior combat commanders—MacLean, Faith, Reilly, Miller, Storms—as well as a dozen company and platoon commanders were lost. The 31st Infantry was as thoroughly gutted and disorganized as the 8th Cav had been a month earlier at Unsan. Charles Beauchamp's 32d Infantry emerged in better shape, but minus his entire 1/32. Ray Embree and two-thirds of his 57th FAB firing batteries were gone. Of the infantry regiments in the 7th Division, only Herb Powell's 17th, far removed from the Chosin Reservoir, remained as a fully effective RCT.

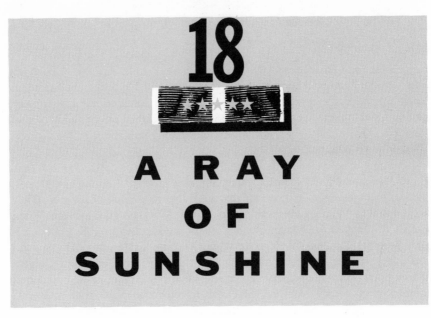

# 18

# A RAY
# OF
# SUNSHINE

I

The massive, overt CCF intervention in Korea shocked and frightened the Western world. Free men turned to Washington for reassurance—a Churchillian declaration of faith and solidarity. It was not forthcoming from the White House. Instead, in one of the worst blunders of his presidency Harry Truman intensified the anxiety by publicly implying that if necessary, America would launch a nuclear war.

This implication was made at a press conference on November 30. It grew out of an exchange between the president and reporters over future courses of action in Korea. When the president routinely stated that "we will take whatever steps are necessary to meet the military situation just as we always have," a headline-hunting reporter followed up: "Will that include the atomic bomb?" The exchange then took this irresponsible course:

*The President:* That includes every weapon we have.
*Q:* Mr. President, you said "Every weapon we have." Does that mean that there is active consideration of the use of the atomic bomb?
*The President:* There has always been active consideration of its use. I don't want to see it used. It is a terrible weapon and it should not be used on innocent men, women and children, who have nothing whatever to do with this military aggression—that happens when it's used.

The loyal White House press corps, realizing that Truman had misspoken or overstated the case, offered him a chance to back off or "clarify" his position, but Truman blundered on, restating that the use of the A-bomb

522

"always has been" under active consideration because "It's one of our weapons." When another reporter tried to ask if he meant use against civilian or military targets, Truman interrupted to introduce a new—and highly misleading—aspect: that not he but the Pentagon would make that decision. He said: "It is a matter that the military people will have to decide. I am not a military authority that passes on these things."

Another reporter, attempting to clarify the issue further, asked Truman if what he had said meant "We would not use the atomic bomb except on a United Nations authorization." This led Truman into another misstatement: "No, it does not mean that at all. The action against Communist China depends on the action of the United Nations. The military commander in the field will have charge of the use of weapons, as he always has."

Reporters bolted for their telephones to convey the gist of this exchange to the world: that America was "actively" considering use of the atomic bomb in Korea; that not Truman but the Pentagon would decide whether the targets would be civilian or military; that MacArthur himself had "charge" of the "use" of atomic bombs in the Far East. Later in the day the White House issued a clarification—"Only the President can authorize use of the atomic bomb, and no such authorization has been given"—but the damage had been done. The eight-column banner headline in the *Green Bay Press Gazette* that afternoon was typical: US TO USE A-BOMB IF NEEDED—TRUMAN.[1]

This inflammatory "story" landed in London like a real atomic bomb. The Labour government of Prime Minister Clement Attlee was then under heavy attack by the Conservatives for its escalating participation in the Korean War. No one in Britain—Labourite or Tory—wanted to get into war with Red China. The vision of MacArthur with a free hand to decide whether or not to use the A-bomb against Red China was appalling. It spurred Attlee to hurry to Washington for an urgent conference.

\* \* \*

Adding to the fear and anxiety, MacArthur chose this moment to "go public" with more "posterity papers." Designed to exonerate him of blame for the reversals in Korea, the underlying themes were familiar: that the Truman administration had made a strategic blunder by focusing its military and economic resources in Western Europe, where there was no war, at the expense of the Far East, where there was a war. Then, having committed itself to a shooting war in Korea, the administration had compounded the blunder by trying to fight it on the cheap, by adopting a mincing or appeasing attitude toward Peking, and by refusing Chinese Nationalist troops. These blunders, in turn, had led to punitive restrictions on American fighting men, such as permitting Peking a "privileged sanctuary" where CCF manpower could assemble freely and from which CCF aircraft could operate.

MacArthur's public statements made more black headlines worldwide. In response to a query from Hugh Baillie, president of the United Press, MacArthur accused European leaders and newsmen (and, by implication, Washington) of a "somewhat selfish though most short-sighted" preoccupation with NATO and the safety of Western Europe at the expense of the Far East. "Any breach of freedom in the East," MacArthur cabled Baillie in familiar rhetoric, "carries with it a sinister threat to freedom in the West. If the fight is not waged . . . here, it will indeed be fought, and possibly lost, on the battlefields of Europe." In answer to a series of questions from the editors of the *U.S. News & World Report,* MacArthur wrote that the limitations imposed on him by the denial of "unlimited pursuit" and "unlimited attack" on Red China was "an enormous handicap, without precedent in military history." In response to a query from Arthur Krock, Washington bureau chief and columnist for *The New York Times,* asking if he had been told to halt his forces at the 38th Parallel, MacArthur replied that he had received "no suggestions from any authoritative source that in the execution of its mission the command should stop at the 38th Parallel or Pyongyang, or at any line short of the international boundary." Similar self-serving, canted statements were issued to G. Ward Price of the *London Daily Mail;* Barry Faris, managing editor of the International News Service; and others.[2]

The long interview in *U.S. News & World Report,* edited by conservative David Lawrence, infuriated Truman and Acheson. Lawrence customarily reprinted such interviews and distributed them to fellow conservatives in Congress and elsewhere. In providing Lawrence this "exclusive" headline-making material, Truman believed, MacArthur was not only writing "posterity papers" but was also guilty of supplying powerful ammunition to administration critics, as Louis Johnson had done. It was blatant disloyalty. Venting his displeasure on his desk calendar, Truman wrote: "General Mac, as usual, has been shooting off his mouth."[3]

For the second time Truman gave serious consideration to sacking MacArthur. "I should have relieved General MacArthur then and there," he wrote in his memoirs. But he did not. Moreover, he publicly defended MacArthur's conduct of the war. In his memoirs he explained his reasoning: "I did not wish to have it appear as if he were relieved because the offensive failed." On the desk calendar he wrote: "I must defend him and save his face even if he has tried on various and numerous occasions to cut mine off. . . . I must stand by my subordinates."[4]

There were probably other, more complex and subtle reasons that restrained Truman from firing MacArthur. Among them:

• It was bound to create an immense public uproar. MacArthur was a mythic public figure. The conservatives and the China Lobbyists, who lionized him, would flail Truman and Acheson for the sacking and no doubt demand a congressional investigation, perhaps even an impeachment proceeding against the president. Gripped in world crisis, the administration could ill afford those distractions.

• It could further undermine public support for the war. The November elections and ongoing opinion polls indicated a drastic turn against the war—down from 66 percent approval in July to 39 percent in December. Firing MacArthur was almost certain to provoke a "great debate" in which MacArthur would drive home his charge that the administration had shortchanged and hamstrung his command, inevitably turning more Americans against the war.[5]

• It could lose votes in the 1952 presidential elections. Informed rumor had it that Robert ("Mr. Republican") Taft, emerging as the Republican front-runner, was considering MacArthur as a running mate. Although MacArthur's political strength was an unknown factor, a Taft-MacArthur ticket might be a formidable challenge to Truman and the Democrats. If Truman fired MacArthur, the general might welcome an invitation from Taft to run against Truman.

• It would prematurely remove a convenient "fall guy." If, as seemed possible, the CCF threw the Americans out of Korea, someone would have to take the blame. If there was no MacArthur in the Far East, the blame was likely to fall on Washington or on Truman himself.

Yet Truman felt that something had to be done to restrain MacArthur from "shooting off his mouth." The solution was an extraordinary set of presidential directives, ordering that all government officials "reduce" the number of "public speeches pertaining to foreign or military policy" and, in any case, obtain prior clearance from the State Department or White House before issuing them. Moreover, State and Defense officials overseas were to "exercise extreme caution" in public statements and "refrain from direct communications" with newspapers, magazines, and other media in the United States. Ostensibly meant to apply to everyone in the government, the directive was aimed specifically at MacArthur.[6]

\*  \*  \*

Behind the scenes Truman, Acheson, Marshall, and the JCS met often and urgently during the first several days of December. In all these sessions the atmosphere was grim. CIA Director Walter Bedell Smith was convinced that war with the Soviet Union was virtually at hand. He believed Moscow's strategy was to "bog" America down in Asia and "bleed us to death," leaving the Soviet Union free to dominate Western Europe. That could not be allowed to happen. America had to avoid a big war with Red China at all costs. All the conferees held this view.[7]

As for Korea itself, the Washington strategy was still to seek some way to negotiate a cease-fire. This aim was complicated by several factors, foremost among them, the extreme difficulty American military forces faced in trying to find a line which they could hold. Without an unbreachable line, Peking was not apt to negotiate. Even if Peking consented to negotiations, the "price" it might ask could be very high—perhaps too high. It might demand that America get out of Korea altogether. It might couple that with a demand for a seat in the United Nations—formal recognition to the exclusion of Nationalist China. It might also demand that Washington abandon Formosa. Finally, it might demand a role in the Japanese peace treaty negotiations, with the aim of denying the United States military base rights in Japan and other security provisions essential to maintaining America's strategic offshore perimeter.[8]

The conferees discussed options. One was a possible immediate, voluntary, and total withdrawal of American forces from Korea. This course had one major advantage: it would put an end to the "bleeding" and enable the Pentagon to redeploy American military resources in support of its primary strategic imperatives, the defense of Western Europe and Japan. However, the disadvantages outweighed these considerations. In abandoning Korea, Washington would appear cowardly and lose credibility as a bulwark against communism. Besides, abandoning the South Koreans would be inhumane and morally reprehensible. On the basis of the NKPA atrocities uncovered so far, the ROKs would certainly face a bloodbath, perhaps one of epic proportions.

The consensus arrived at was that America should hang on in Korea for as long as possible and attempt to establish an unbreachable line, which would encourage or even force Peking to negotiate. Much of the discussion, therefore, finally focused on where this line might be established. Acheson and his assistant secretary, Dean Rusk, urged that X Corps be merged with Eighth Army to form a line across the narrow waist or, failing that, the 38th Parallel. But MacArthur had by now persuaded the JCS that a line across the narrow waist was not, as Joe Collins put it, "a practical proposition." Nor was one at the 38th Parallel, where defensive positions were simply unfeasible. It seemed more likely the line should be two strong, independent enclaves—one around Seoul-Inchon, the other around Hamhung-Hungnam—or, in a worst case scenario, a single enclave at Pusan—a reincarnation of the Pusan Perimeter.

In these discussions, what worried the JCS most was the possibility that if such enclaves were established, the CCF might, for the first time, commit its new Soviet-supplied Air Force against American ground forces and installations. If so, there was a good likelihood that the CCF could inflict devastating casualties on the closely bunched troops inside the enclave, forcing a complete evacuation, or a Dunkirk. To prevent a bloody slaughter during the evacuation, Americans would almost certainly have to strike back at CCF airfields in Manchuria. That undertaking could well "draw" the Soviet Air Force (or even submarines) into the war in support of the CCF. In that scenario the "only chance," as Collins put it, was "the use—or the threat of the use—of the A-bomb." Use of the A-bomb in that context could well invite Soviet nuclear retaliation on America itself, bringing on global nuclear war.

The conferees finally agreed that should this scenario become reality—should the CCF Air Force attack American ground forces, airfields, or military installations—America had no choice but to strike back, not only in Manchuria but elsewhere in China, regardless of the ultimate consequences.

Ordinarily the JCS would have sent MacArthur standby orders to that effect for contingency planning purposes. But such was the distrust of him in Washington that these orders were prepared and approved by the president but deliberately withheld from MacArthur. As Bradley put it to the conferees, "We should not now decide to give authority to the Theater Commander."[9]

\* \* \*

Complicating all these discussions were the increasingly pessimistic—and somewhat panicky—telecoms and cables and back channel discussions from GHQ, Tokyo, and MacArthur. These reached a dramatic climax on December 3, when MacArthur cabled Washington to say, in effect, that unless some drastic new measures were taken, Eighth Army and X Corps would be destroyed and all Korea would be lost.

He wrote that he doubted that Washington had a "full comprehension" of the "basic changes" that had been "wrought" by the "undisguised entrance" of the CCF "into the combat." His command now faced about twenty-six "fresh" and "splendidly trained" CCF divisions, plus 50,000 "remnants" of the NKPA and another 20,000 CCF troops immediately behind them. Repeating a familiar refrain he said that the situation was "an entirely new war against an entirely new power of great military strength and under entirely new conditions." He reiterated that his directives were "completely outmoded."[10]

It was "clearly evident," MacArthur wrote, that "unless ground reinforcements of greatest magnitude are promptly supplied," this command "will be either forced into successive withdrawals with diminished power of resistance after each such move, or will be forced to take up beachhead bastion positions, which, while insuring a degree of prolonged resistance, would afford little hope of anything beyond defense." Although the command had previously "exhibited good morale and marked efficiency, it has been in almost unending combat for five months and is mentally fatigued and physically battered." The combat effectiveness of the ROKs was "negligible"; the foreign contingents supplied him so far were too small to exercise any significant influence.

Tactically, he reiterated, there was no "practicability" or "benefit" in attempting to unite Eighth Army and X Corps to hold a line across the "waist of Korea." Such a line would have "no depth" and "little strength" and would invite "penetration" and "piecemeal destruction." Accordingly, X Corps would withdraw into the Hamhung area "as rapidly as possible," and Eighth Army, which "cannot hold the Pyongyang area," would "unquestionably be forced to withdraw to the Seoul area."

This defeatist cable, and similar defeatist remarks in the telecons and back channel talks with GHQ officials, deeply alarmed Washington. It appeared to many that MacArthur had suddenly lost the will to fight, to organize for one last effort to make a "really effective" stand. Should this be the case, it would cancel out Washington's strategy of holding unbreachable enclaves and encouraging or forcing Peking to negotiate.[11]

By now the loss of confidence in MacArthur was complete. Truman, Acheson, and Marshall decided to send Joe Collins to the Far East to make an independent evaluation of the situation. Collins left Washington on December 3. Acheson urged that Collins "stay in Tokyo" indefinitely to continue evaluating the situation. Dean Rusk, deeply concerned over the "extremely dejected" attitude of the Far East command, proposed to Acheson that the president appoint Collins "field commander" in Korea and restrict MacArthur to "full time" duty in Tokyo, working on the Japanese peace treaty and other routine matters.[12]

The same day, December 3, the senior conferees, in response to MacArthur's cable, gathered at the Pentagon for yet another review. Matt Ridgway briefed the group on the military situation and the evolving enclave strategy. After a prolonged rehash of the dangers and options the conferees decided that any political decisions should be postponed until the president and Prime Minister Attlee had conferred and turned their attention to the military situation in Korea. Did MacArthur have a clear grasp of the enclave strategy? Should he be told specifically what to do? Yes, said Forrest Sherman. He urged that MacArthur be told that the "safety of his forces was paramount" and that he be "ordered" to "get his troops into the beachhead at once. . . ." Bradley produced a long and detailed draft order to that effect, but Marshall, adhering to the principle of giving the theater commander latitude and tactical freedom, thought it was too specific. A tedious discussion ensued over what or what not MacArthur should be told.[13]

To Matt Ridgway all this talk and hairsplitting in this grave crisis were exasperating. As he wrote later, he regarded MacArthur's "insistence on retaining control from Tokyo, 700 miles from the battle areas, as unwarranted and unsound" and "largely responsible for the heavy casualties and near disaster which followed." Moreover, he was "convinced" that many military decisions MacArthur had made were "wrong": the retaining of direct command of X Corps after its junction with Eighth Army at Seoul; the withdrawal of X Corps through Inchon, "preventing the urgently needed resupply of Eighth Army" and "precluding the prompt dispatch of forces overland to the

Wonsan area"; the "reckless" dispersion of all ground forces in Korea; the advance of Eighth Army after taking POWs from "major units" of the CCF; the assignment of zones of advance to Eighth Army and X Corps which separated them by "hundreds of miles of extremely rough terrain, practically devoid of roads essential to the supply of our large units, with few and inaccurate maps, and with no possibility of the two commands being mutually supporting"; and, finally, the ordering of all American units to "advance with all possible speed to the Yalu."[14]

For these reasons Ridgway believed that the command customs and niceties that had governed the JCS's relationship with MacArthur should be abandoned. MacArthur should be given specific instructions about what to do. He later wrote in his account of the Korean War that "no one" apparently "was willing to issue a flat order" to MacArthur "to correct a state of affairs that was going rapidly from bad to worse." Ridgway continued:

Yet the responsibility clearly resided right there in the room and my own conscience finally overcame my discretion. Having secured permission to speak I blurted out—perhaps too bluntly but with deep feeling—that I felt we had already spent too damn much time on debate and that immediate action was needed. We owed it, I insisted, to the men in the field and to the God to whom we must answer for those men's lives to stop talking and to act. My only answer from the twenty men who sat around the wide table, and the twenty others who sat around the walls in the rear, was complete silence. . . .

The meeting broke up with no decision taken. The secretaries of State and Defense left the room and the Joint Chiefs lingered to talk among themselves for a few moments. I approached Hoyt Vandenberg, whom I had known since he was a cadet and I an instructor at West Point. With Van I had no need for double-talk.

"Why," I asked him, "don't the Joint Chiefs send orders to MacArthur and *tell* him what to do?" Van shook his head. "What good would that do? He wouldn't obey the orders. What *can* we do?"

At this I exploded. "You can relieve any commander who won't obey the orders, can't you?" I exclaimed. The look on Van's face was one I shall never forget. His lips parted and he looked at me with an expression both puzzled and amazed. He walked away without saying a word. . . .[15]

What finally emerged from these discussions was not a new directive for MacArthur, but rather another tactful message that was designed to prod him into adopting the enclave strategy at once. Approved by President Truman and sent on to MacArthur that day, December 3, it stated: "We consider that the preservation of your forces is now the primary consideration. Consolidation of forces into beachheads is concurred in."[16]

The conferees also agreed that in view of the probability of war with the Soviet Union, American forces worldwide should be placed on full alert. Accordingly, the JCS drafted and sent all theater commanders a somber "war warning": "The JCS consider that the current situation in Korea has greatly increased the possibility of general war. Commanders addressed take such action as is feasible to increase readiness without creating atmosphere of alarm."[17]

## II

Joe Collins arrived in Tokyo on December 4. He conferred briefly with MacArthur and his staffers in the Dai Ichi Building. Then he flew on to Seoul to meet with Johnnie Walker and the Eighth Army staff, Shrimp Milburn, Bill Kean, and others.[18]

It was a humiliating and desperate time for Eighth Army, which was in the midst of a full-scale withdrawal. Walker had given the order to demolish supplies, blow bridges, abandon Pyongyang, and fall back to the Imjin River, a retrograde movement of about 120 miles. The main Eighth Army headquarters was in process of moving back from Seoul to Taegu. Some war correspondents at the front believed the withdrawal was an uncontrolled bugout, one of the worst disgraces in Army history.[19]

After Collins had conferred with Walker and his staff, it became apparent to him that the earlier idea of holding two "enclaves" (one at Seoul-Inchon, one at Hamhung-Hungnam) was simply not feasible. The main reason was that Walker did not have sufficient manpower to hold Seoul-Inchon against a concerted CCF attack employing eighteen divisions (180,000 or more men). If Walker failed to hold, a terrible disaster might result. Owing to the restrictive tides and geography at Inchon and the ice buildup, it would be virtually impossible to evacuate Eighth Army safely.[20]

Rather than two enclaves, Walker preferred one, the old Pusan Perimeter. He believed that if Almond's X Corps were evacuated and moved to the Pusan Perimeter and placed under Eighth Army control, Eighth Army could hold in Korea "indefinitely." To effect this linkup, Walker would build up the Imjin River line (B), place all available ROK forces in the central peninsula, and then fight a series of delaying actions at the Imjin, Han, and Kum rivers designed to hold the CCF long enough for X Corps to evacuate northeast Korea and move to the Pusan Perimeter.[21]

Walker's plan was, in effect, a repetition of his strategy for defeating the NKPA the previous summer on a larger scale. Each mile of withdrawal would shorten his supply lines and lengthen those of the enemy. The Americans now had stronger and more battlewise air and naval forces to attack the ever-lengthening enemy supply lines. As Walker constricted and consolidated his forces into the Pusan Perimeter, he would again enjoy more advantageous "interior lines of communication" over which to shift his resources. Moreover, the engineers had greatly improved the port facilities in Pusan and the roads and railroads to bring supplies forward to the battle lines. Once Eighth Army had stabilized in the Pusan Perimeter with the added power of X Corps, there was every good chance that it could grind the CCF to pieces as it had the NKPA.

Joe Collins was heartened by this talk. It stood in stark contrast with MacArthur's recent panicky estimate to the JCS in which he had said that unless he received "ground reinforcement of greatest magnitude," UN forces would be forced to fight "to final destruction." If the Walker plan were successful, it would mean the war could probably be contained within Korea without bombing or blockading China or using the A-bomb or taking other drastic measures which would increase the risk of Soviet intervention. Moreover, America could stay in Korea without committing more divisions or acceding to MacArthur's demand that the offer of Chinese Nationalist troops be accepted. The UN could systematically grind down the CCF until Peking was forced to negotiate an acceptable settlement.

The strategy would not be inexpensive. It would require tens of thousands of American replacements, plus an endless stream of weapons, ammo, rations, and other impedimenta. The already high American battle casualties in Korea would climb even higher. Much of America's ground power would have to remain in Korea for an indefinite period, delaying the buildup of NATO.

\* \* \*

From Seoul Collins flew to Hamhung to confer with Ned Almond and others. It was a humiliating time for X Corps as well. Task Force MacLean-Faith had been destroyed. Forced out of Yudam, the Fifth and Seventh Marines were consolidating at Hagaru, but they still faced the long, perilous withdrawal from there to Koto to Hamhung. The rest of Dave Barr's 7th Division had withdrawn hurriedly from Pungsan to Hamhung. Shorty Soule's 3d Division had abandoned Wonsan. It was to support the Marine withdrawal, then join the 7th Division in the defense of Hamhung–Hungnam.

Yet Almond, too, was optimistic. He believed the withdrawal from Hagaru could be achieved without another major calamity. Notwithstanding the severe losses already sustained by the Marines and the 7th Division, he believed that with air and naval support his five infantry divisions (three American; two ROK) could hold an enclave at Hamhung–Hungnam "throughout the winter."[22]

Collins flew back to Tokyo on December 6 for further conferences with MacArthur and the GHQ staff. There he found that MacArthur's G-3, Pinky Wright, concurred in the consolidation of Eighth Army and X Corps in a Pusan Perimeter. Collins, who now unequivocally favored this plan, wrote that MacArthur "was reluctant to place Almond under Walker's command," but after "thinking it over," he gave his approval.[23]

Before Collins left Tokyo on December 7, MacArthur notified Walker and Almond as follows:

Current planning calls for a withdrawal in successive positions, if necessary, to the Pusan area. Eighth Army will hold the Seoul area for the maximum time possible short of entailing such envelopments as would prevent its withdrawal to the south. Planning further envisions the early withdrawal of X Corps from the Hungnam area and junction with Eighth Army as practicable. At such time, X Corps will pass command to the Eighth Army.[24]

One of the curious features of this new strategy was that MacArthur now accepted the concept of a continuous line across Korea. It would be manned (more or less as it was in July) by Eighth Army on the left and ROK divisions on the right. As spelled out in detail by GHQ on December 8, the initial transpeninsular line (B) would run from about Kaesong in the west to Samchok on the east coast, or roughly the same distance as the line at the narrow waist (Pyongyang–Wonsan) which MacArthur had so vigorously rejected as unfeasible in his cable to the JCS a mere five days earlier.[25]

MacArthur's sudden turnabout on this issue remains unexplained. One reason, perhaps stressed by Collins, may have been the realization that there were more ROK forces available then than theretofore. The ROKs had recently fielded a brand-new three-division corps, designated III. If ROK II Corps could be quickly reorganized and reequipped, and ROK I Corps could be lifted by ship from Hungnam to reinforce the ROK line on the east coast at Samchok, nine ROK divisions (comprising about 90,000 men) could be employed on the line in the mountainous terrain eastward of Eighth Army.

The JCS soon learned of this new strategy. It came as welcome news. It indicated a renewed determination to fight and seemed to offer a possible chance of success. The JCS cabled MacArthur on December 8 to express concurrence, stressing, however, that the evacuation of X Corps should take place "as early as practicable." On the following day, December 9, MacArthur officially ordered Almond to withdraw X Corps through Hungnam and reland it in South Korea, the Americans at or close to Pusan; the ROK I Corps at Samchock.[26]

Collins had a final, almost formal exchange of views with MacArthur on the situation. MacArthur's outlook had not changed one whit. He believed that if the CCF attacked below the 38th Parallel and the "limitations" (i.e., privileged sanctuary, no bombing or blockading of China) on his forces remained in effect, and he did not immediately receive about 200,000 reinforcements (50,000 to 60,000 Chinese Nationalists; about 70,000 additional troops from the U.K. and France; some 75,000 American replacements), then the UN military position in Korea was untenable, and the UN would have to "pull out of Korea." If, on the other hand, the CCF attacked below the 38th Parallel and MacArthur received the manpower and reinforcements and was permitted to bomb and blockade Red China, he believed the UN forces could hold "the best possible position in Korea" and should do so "as far north as possible." Under such circumstances, he might also propose that "other Chinese Nationalist" forces be "introduced into South China, possibly through Hong Kong" to open a second front. In the remote event that the CCF did not attack below the 38th Parallel, MacArthur said, the UN "should accept" an armistice with safeguards which would prevent another NKPA invasion of South Korea.[27]

What was clear from this talk was that MacArthur and Walker were poles apart in their views of the situation. Walker believed he could hold in Korea without major reinforcements or new rules; MacArthur believed the opposite or else was using the crisis to advance his case for widening the war with Red China. On the basis of his battlefield tour of Korea, Collins was solidly in Walker's corner. He wrote: "While I did not presume to argue the point with General MacArthur, I did not feel that, even with the limitations to be placed upon the United Nations command, the Chinese could force its withdrawal from Korea."[28]

*　*　*

Collins arrived back in Washington on December 8, at the tail end of the Truman-Attlee talks. He reported to the JCS and later that day briefed Truman, Attlee, and other members of both delegations at the White House. He told the conferees that while the military situation "remained serious," it was "no longer critical." Walker probably could not hold Seoul-Inchon against an all-out CCF attack, but when the new plan was executed and X Corps joined Eighth Army in South Korea, Walker could probably hold a fairly sizable Pusan Perimeter indefinitely. The Collins report, Omar Bradley wrote, "was like a ray of sunshine"; Washington "now had options to discuss other than catastrophe."[29]

By that time the Truman-Attlee talks had been in progress for four days. Attlee had come principally to dissuade any use of the atomic bomb in Korea without "formal agreement" with the U.K., to discourage other measures leading to general war with Red China, and to urge that Washington accept a negotiated cease-fire in Korea even if Peking's price included a seat in the UN and withdrawal of UN forces from Korea, Formosa, and Indochina. Truman agreed that he would not use the atomic bomb in Korea without "consulting" London, but he declined to enter into a written protocol.

He likewise agreed not to take any measures that would "widen the war" beyond Korea and to continue all efforts to seek a cease-fire—but not at the expense of granting Peking a seat in the UN or deserting Formosa and Indochina. The cease-fire would be pursued without linkage to other issues. If

Peking refused to consider a cease-fire and continued the attack, America would fight in Korea "to a finish," with or without help from other UN nations.

These talks, like most such talks, wound up on an inconclusive note. Little of substance had been settled. However, they were probably useful in one respect: They had compelled Truman and his advisers to face rigid choices and set formal policies theretofore only expressed as hopes or desirable courses of action. Of these, the most important was that Washington had abandoned all hope of unifying Korea by force. It would vigorously and publicly pursue a negotiated settlement. It was willing to settle on a "line" on or near the 38th Parallel, restoring the status quo ante bellum. Joe Collins's upbeat report—that Walker could hold a Pusan Perimeter indefinitely—made that policy appear attainable.[30]

## III

At Hagaru, as he prepared for the withdrawal, O. P. Smith remained unflappable. He was surrounded by CCF troops, but with the consolidation of Ray Murray's Fifth Marines and Homer Litzenberg's Seventh Marines at Hagaru the CCF had not been able to break through that perimeter. Moreover, Chesty Puller at Koto, reinforced by the Army's 2/31, was also holding stoutly that stepping-stone. The airlift to Hagaru was another blessing. It had brought in 500 Marine replacements and tons of ammunition and supplies. The outgoing aircraft had evacuated a total of about 4,300 wounded, thereby relieving Smith of that great burden.[31]

Ned Almond flew in and out of Hagaru almost daily. The Marines continued to view him and his ideas and plans with utmost contempt. One big, dramatic idea proposed by FEAF and seconded by Almond was that the Marines destroy all equipment and evacuate Hagaru by air. Although the idea was appealing on paper, it was unrealistic, and Smith rightly rejected it. As the Marines evacuated Hagaru by air, the perimeter would shrink finally to merely the airstrip. The CCF could bring the strip under mortar fire and destroy the strip and aircraft, thereby stranding possibly thousands of Marines, who would then not be strong enough to fight out to Koto.[32]

Smith left this damning portrait of Almond at Hagaru:

After Litzenberg and Murray had fought their way out [of Yudam to Hagaru] he came up and gave us all DSCs and [he] was weeping. I don't know what he was weeping about, whether from the cold or emotion, or what. . . . I didn't know anything about this in advance. He came up to me and asked me if I'd line up Murray and Litzenberg and myself and [Olin] Beall [who had rescued 323 members of Task Force MacLean-Faith]. He had [only] one DSC with him. We sug-

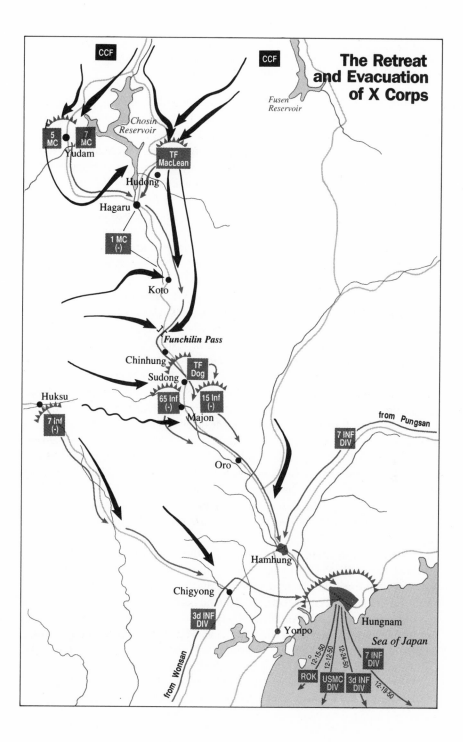

**The Retreat and Evacuation of X Corps**

CCF

CCF

*Fusen Reservoir*

*Chosin Reservoir*

5 MC
7 MC
Yudam

TF MacLean

Hudong

Hagaru

1 MC (-)

Koto

Funchilin Pass

Chinhung

TF Dog

Sudong

Huksu

65 Inf (-)
15 Inf (-)
Majon

7 Inf (-)

from Pungsan

7 INF DIV

Oro

Hamhung

Chigyong

3d INF DIV

Yonpo

Hungnam

*Sea of Japan*

7 INF DIV

from Wonsan

12-15-50
12-12-50
12-24-50
12-18-50

ROK
USMC DIV
3d INF DIV

gested he give the cross to Beall, who was the junior [in rank]. Let him have the cross, we'd get ours sometime later. I never did get a citation for that cross. I suppose I would have had to write my own.[33]

Smith had 10,000 men under his direct command at Hagaru. Among them were about 800 Army personnel—survivors of Task Force MacLean-Faith, the engineers of the 10th Battalion, and other stragglers and strays. The senior Army officer present, the 31st's S-3, Berry Anderson, organized the Army personnel into a "provisional 31st Regiment," with himself as commander and the 31st's S-2, Carl G. Witte, as exec. Anderson created two infantry "battalions" from the Army men available. One (the "3/31"), composed of a few 3/31 survivors, artillerymen of the 57th FAB, and others, was commanded by Witte. The other (the "1/32"), composed of a few 1/32 survivors and others, was commanded by the senior 1/32 survivor, the battalion S-1, Robert Jones. Attached to Litzenberg's Seventh Marines, the Army forces were designated by the Marines as the "31/7."[34]

The plan for the breakout was as follows. Murray's Fifth Marines would launch an attack on East Hill, known to be infested with CCF troops, who could threaten the rear. Litzenberg's Seventh Marines, reinforced by Berry Anderson's provisional "31st Infantry" (or the "31/7"), would be attached to and assist the Seventh Marines in the attack toward Koto. When Litzenberg and Anderson had broken through the CCF blocks, all Hagaru forces would follow, destroying the town. Murray's withdrawing Fifth Marines, reinforced by Marine tanks and Drake's 31st Tank Company, would serve as rear guard.[35]

The Hagaru forces first were to withdraw eleven road miles to Koto. This section of the road was strongly held by the CCF troops that had earlier ambushed Task Force Drysdale. Smith was prepared for a bloody gauntlet and would fight every yard of the way. At Koto Puller had 4,200 men, including about 1,500 Army troops, the majority of them in Richard Reidy's 2/31. They would defend Koto while the incoming Hagaru forces rested and warmed up. Then the combined forces (nearly 15,500 men) would go onward in a single vast column.

South of Koto there was a problem in the road. The CCF had blown a bridge at Funchilin Pass, leaving a twenty-four-foot gap in the road. The plan was that FEAF would air-drop eight treadway bridge sections into the Koto perimeter. The Army engineers at Koto, who had two bridge-laying (or Brockway) trucks, would bring the bridge sections forward from Koto, and, with help of Marine engineers, lay them in place. Marine and Army infantry from Koto and the 1st Battalion, First Marines at Chinhung would converge at the site to hold the CCF away.[36]

Shorty Soule's 3d Division would support the withdrawal in an important way. It would send a powerful task force (Dog) north up the road to Chinhung.

Task Force Dog would hold the entire length of the road from Chinhung to Hamhung (forty-three miles) as well as relieve the Marine 1st Battalion at Chinhung, so that these Marines could go forward to the bridge-laying site. When the task force got into place on the road, John Guthrie's 7th Infantry, which had withdrawn easterly from Sachang to Huksu, where it had fought a tough and costly defensive battle, would pull back to Hamhung.[37]

\* \* \*

By December 6, when Smith was ready to evacuate Hagaru, numerous war correspondents, including Marguerite Higgins and *Life* photographer David Douglas Duncan, had flown into Hagaru. They were to make the Marine withdrawal the most famous episode of the Korean War.

Smith, ordinarily low-key and uncolorful, contributed to the publicity with a battle cry that would become legendary. During a press conference to brief correspondents on the plan a British war correspondent dared suggest that the operation might be a "retreat." Smith said no, that was incorrect. There could be no "retreat" when there was no "rear." He went on, "We're not retreating. We are just advancing in a different direction."[38]\*

\* \* \*

The dual attacks of the Fifth and Seventh Marines began at about 7:00 A.M. on December 6. Fog and other factors impeded close air support. Nonetheless, Murray's Fifth Marines mounted a spirited attack on East Hill. That battle raged all day and through most of the night—in all, about twenty-two hours. After dark the CCF counterattacked the Fifth Marines in massive numbers. But Murray was prepared, and his men killed an estimated 1,000 CCF troops. Having thus contained the CCF attack on the rear of the Marine column, Murray's men proceeded to demolish Hagaru.[39]

Meanwhile, Litzenberg's Seventh Marines attacked south down the main road to Koto. Owing to the morning fog, close air support was initially limited and not much help. There was no artillery support; it was turned the other way, defending the rear. One of Litzenberg's battalions attacked straight down both sides of the road, meeting strong CCF fire, which checked it for about four hours.[40]

During this check Litzenberg ordered Berry Anderson to commit Witte's "3/31" Army forces to screen the left (east) flank of the Marine battalion. George Rasula, commanding I Company (which had three platoons com-

---

\*The retort entered Marine Corps legend slightly toughened: "Retreat, hell! We're not retreating; we're just attacking in a different direction." This version was an echo of a famous World War I Marine battle cry at Belleau Wood: "Retreat, hell! We just got here."

manded by 57th FAB officers), led the screen. He met a rude reception. In this tough action, four of his men were wounded. Astonishingly, however, 115 Red Chinese jumped up and surrendered to Rasula's men. Burdened with CCF prisoners, Rasula's I Company was replaced by K Company, commanded by Robert J. Kitz (a survivor of Task Force MacLean-Faith) and L Company, commanded by Robert M. Boyer. Before Rasula could catch up, Boyer and one of his platoon leaders, Roland Skilton, were killed.[41]

For the tired, freezing Marines and Army infantry, the going was extremely tough. The CCF attacked again and again from positions in the hills, lobbing mortars and grenades. Determined to hold casualties to a minimum and to avert a catastrophic encirclement, Litzenberg proceeded with caution. By nightfall his infantry had advanced only two and a half miles. In the fighting the "3/31" commander, Carl Witte, was wounded by a grenade.[42]

Marine commander Smith, who had flown on to Koto that day, ordered Litzenberg to keep the Seventh Marines moving south during the night. The men slogged on wearily, repelling repeated CCF attacks. In a clear dawn, December 7—Pearl Harbor Day—Marine and Navy close air support appeared overhead to assist. During that morning the lead elements of the Seventh Marines arrived in Koto. By 5:00 P.M. all 2,200 men of the Seventh Marines and the Army's "3/31" and "1/32" had come into the village, having covered nine and a half miles in thirty-six hours.[43]

The rest of the Hagaru forces followed in a long snaking line. By noon on December 7 all 10,000 men were strung out along the route, interspersed among artillery, trains, and vehicles of all types, the tanks, including Drake's 31st Tank Company, last. It was bitterly cold. The men were exhausted, walking like zombies. The CCF attacked the column repeatedly, like raiding Indians in the Old West. The Americans fought back. Many men fell by the wayside, wounded or too weary to go on. Medics picked up these men and put them on trucks. The road and ditches were littered with burned-out vehicles and dead CCF bodies, frozen stiff.[44]

*  *  *

To the south Shorty Soule's Task Force Dog assembled for the long march north to Chinhung. Commanded by 3d Division ADC Armistead Mead, it consisted of five of the division's nine infantry battalions, powerfully supported by tanks and 3rd Division and X Corps artillery. The force contained many blacks: those in William Harris's Puerto Rican 65th Infantry, which was temporarily reinforced by Ed Farrell's black 3/15 and backed up by Walter Preston's black 159th FAB; William Bartlett's black 64th Tank Battalion; and Kenneth Dawalt's black 999th FAB.[45]

In the early hours of December 7 Mead's forces started moving north. The Puerto Rican 65th Infantry led the way. Herman Dammer's 2/65 went forward to Majon and Jerry Allen's 3/65 to Oro, while Saint St. Clair's 1/65 and Ed Farrell's 3/15 established a baseline near Oro. Attacking through these 65th Infantry positions, Tom O'Neil's 3/7, supported by the self-propelled 155s of Dawalt's 999th FAB and the 92nd FAB, commanded by Leon F. Lavoie, continued north to Chinhung.[46]

Until this time Tom O'Neil's 3/7 had been in X Corps reserve near Hamhung. The outfit was green to combat, as was O'Neil. He was well aware of the difficulties Reidy's 2/31 had encountered on the road one week earlier. Like Marine General O. P. Smith, O'Neil was leery of blasting ahead at top speed. This resulted in a conflict with the task force commander, Armistead Mead, who, O'Neil remembered, was "red-haired, impatient and short-fused." The road north was "infested with CCF and littered with wrecked trucks," O'Neil said. "I knew the CCF had earlier ambushed Marines and Army troops and other forces trying to go north. I put a bulldozer at the front of the column to clear the debris from the road. . . . Every mile of the way he [Mead] was nit-picking me, even in front of Soule. He insisted we go faster."[47]

Despite O'Neil's caution, Task Force Dog made good time. It arrived about 2:30 P.M. on December 7 at Majon. There Mead's forces relieved most of Dammer's 2/65. Leaving one company (G) behind to help outpost the village, Dammer withdrew south toward the 65th's base line at Oro, to link with the 3/65. Pushing onward, Task Force Dog passed through Sudong and reached Chinhung in the late afternoon that same day, whereupon the 1st Battalion of the First Marines, supported by Army artillery, moved north several miles toward the bridge-laying site at Funchilin Pass.

The northward movements of Task Force Dog enabled John Guthrie to withdraw his 7th Infantry from Huksu to Hamhung. In its unpublicized operations at Sachang and Huksu the men of Robert Besson's 2/7 and Charles Heinrich's 3/7 had performed ably but had incurred heavy casualties from CCF fire and frostbite. A "good part" of Besson's F and G companies had been lost. Ironically, during the withdrawal a Navy plane mistakenly attacked Besson's jeep, and while diving for cover, Besson shattered his ankle so badly he had to be evacuated. His exec, West Pointer (1939) Samuel G. Kail, a paratrooper, moved up to command the 2/7.[48]

\* \* \*

The Hagaru forces spent the night of December 7–8 in Koto, where they were fed and protected by Chesty Puller's 4,200-man garrison, which still included the 1,500 Army troops. The X Corps assistant G-3, Joe Gurfein, who had come up to goad Reidy's 2/31 into Koto, was no longer present. He had flown out of Koto on December 5, by which time, he remembered, Reidy was fully functional as the 2/31 commander. However, Gurfein's damning report on Reidy to X Corps resulted in Reidy's relief from command in due course.[49]

After a fitful night in cold Koto the Seventh Marines and Anderson's "31st Infantry" led the attack south on the morning of December 8. The immediate objective was Funchilin Pass, where the bridge which FEAF had air-dropped into Koto would be emplaced. Again Anderson assigned Rasula's I Company to spearhead the Army's forces. The attack was conducted in a swirling snowstorm, the worst Rasula could remember: "We couldn't see twenty-five yards." Using the poor visibility to advantage, the Marines and Army infantry took all objectives and then buttoned up for another numbingly cold (ten to twenty below, Rasula guessed) night on the road. The Army's Brockway trucks transporting the bridge sections turned around and went back to Koto, where the rest of the Hagaru forces were collecting.[50]

The next day, December 9, was blessedly clear and bright. Marine and Navy close air support appeared at Funchilin Pass at first light to bomb, napalm, and strafe CCF positions. These well-coordinated air attacks assisted not only the Seventh Marines and the "31st Infantry" but also the Marine battalion advancing north on Funchilin Pass from Chinhung, supported by the artillery of Armistead Mead's Task Force Dog. After the CCF had been cleared out or driven off, the engineers came forward with the bridge sections and got to work under CCF fire, assisted by CCF POWs who did the hard labor. By about 3:30 P.M. the bridge was in place. There followed a moment of great anxiety: The first tractor derailed because the treadways were too close together. However, a skillful driver backed the vehicle off, and the sections were properly opened out. Just before dark the first jeep in line safely crossed by flashlight.[51]*

With the way south open, the senior Marine officers at Koto issued a new march order for the column. For the second time the Army's Robert Drake was ordered to position his Sherman tanks at the tail end of the line to serve as rear guard. But this time Drake balked. Chesty Puller's Marine contingent at Koto included some heavy (50-ton) Pershing tanks. Drake feared that if the Pershings went first they might cave in the bridge at Funchilin Pass and leave his tanks and tankers stranded on the north side. He argued that it would be more logical for his lighter Shermans to precede the Pershings in line. However, the senior Marines refused to see it Drake's way. The Pershings would go first, they insisted, and Drake's Shermans last. "But I got around that," Drake remembered. "I just broke into the line and went first. The Pershings came last. They got across the bridge okay, but they lost about five tanks to Chinese fire."[52]

---

*Because the progress of the Marine withdrawal was being reported almost hour by hour to a fascinated world, the "Bridge at Koto-ri" became momentarily famous. Some overdramatized media accounts gave the impression that the bridge had been air-dropped in one piece, that day, precisely into the gap.

That night and all the next day, December 10, the column, swollen to 15,000 men by the addition of the Koto garrison, crossed the bridge in a steady stream. The Seventh Marines, with the attached "31st Infantry," remained in the vanguard. These combat forces were followed by the division trains and artillery, Ray Murray's Fifth Marines, and Chesty Puller's First Marines. Among the last troops to leave Koto before it was demolished were Reidy's 2/31 and the Army engineers. One of the 2/31 senior staffers, Richard F. Mitchell, remembered proudly that the 2/31 came out in good order, "shaved, with their weapons and packs."[53]

*Life* photographer David Douglas Duncan was busy that day taking candid photographs of the men in the column. His remarkably vivid and stark photographs, published in *Life* and a book, *This Is War,* immortalized the withdrawal. Duncan, a former Marine, tended to focus his cameras on the Marines, almost entirely ignoring the 2,300 Army men in the column. To the Army personnel, who were proud of the role they had played at Chosin, Hagaru, and Koto, this was utterly infuriating. Ironically, in 1985 the United States Postal Service unwittingly chose one of Duncan's few photos of Army personnel (a medical platoon of the 2/31) to commemorate a stamp honoring Korean veterans.[54]

During the final leg of the trek—the several miles from the bridge to Chinhung—the withdrawing forces came under the protection of the Marine battalion and then the infantry, artillery, and tanks of the 3d Division's Task Force Dog. "It sure was a wonderful sight to see friendly troops on the ridges," George Rasula remembered. "And even better when we passed through the 3rd Division perimeter." The main infantry element of Dog, Tom O'Neil's 3/7, with the attached G Company of the 2/65, repelled a strong CCF attack at the road during the afternoon and night of December 10, sustaining heavy casualties. Farther south, at Sudong and Majon, the withdrawing forces were protected by the 65th Infantry's 2/65 and 3/65. At Majon, where the withdrawing forces boarded trains and trucks (40 of the 110 trucks were provided by the 3d Division's 52d Truck Battalion), the men of the 65th gave them what food they could spare. A 2/31 medic, John J. Zitzelberger, remembered sharing a gallon jar of ketchup and pickles. "God, it was good!" he said.[55]

The exec of the 65th, West Pointer (1936) George W. ("Chick") Childs, who had commanded a battalion in combat in the ETO, was the tactical commander of the 65th's forward units. Under his able leadership the Puerto Ricans continued to perform well. Many were decorated for heroism. One sergeant, Felix G. Nieves, won not only a Silver Star Medal but a special commendation from Shorty Soule. The 65th could not, however, absolutely guarantee every yard of the way. About midnight on December 10, near Sudong, the CCF cut the road, halting the truck column. In the ensuing battle the CCF inflicted about twenty Marine casualties and destroyed nine trucks.

The CCF block was broken by a pickup force of Marines led by two senior Army lieutenant colonels: the 52d Truck Battalion commander, Waldon C. Winston, and a X Corps artillery officer, John U. D. Page (Princeton University, 1926), forty-six. Newly arrived in Korea, Page had gone up to Koto on November 29 to lay some communications lines and had been trapped there. He was killed in the action that night and was posthumously awarded the Medal of Honor for his heroism.[56]*

The Marines and Army forces continued south by train and truck, protected by the Puerto Rican 65th Infantry and Ed Farrell's attached all-black 3/15. The Marines came out expecting to defend a sector of a Hamhung-Hungnam "enclave," but by that time the new plan to evacuate X Corps and redeploy it in Eighth Army was in effect. Accordingly, the Marines marched straight down to the docks, and from December 11 to 14 they boarded twenty-eight ships. On December 15 the Marines sailed from northeast Korea to Pusan amid a blizzard of heroic publicity. In total, they had suffered about 10,500 casualties since landing at Wonsan: 4,418 in battle and 6,174 nonbattle. (Most of the latter subsequently returned to duty.) The entire division was accorded a rare honor: a Presidential Unit Citation, an award usually reserved to commend smaller units for outstanding performance under fire.[57]†

* * *

While the Marines were outloading at Hungnam, Ned Almond deployed the Army's 3d and 7th divisions into an arc-shaped perimeter to defend Hamhung-Hungnam and the airfield at Yonpo. Shorty Soule's 3d Division occupied the left sector; Dave Barr's 7th Division, the right. Clockwise, the defending infantry regiments were: John Guthrie's 7th; William Harris's 65th; Charles Beauchamp's 32d (less its annihilated 1/32); and Herb Powell's 17th. Dinty Moore's 15th and the 31st Infantry (less its annihilated 3/31) initially occupied reserve positions inside the arc. The infantry was backed by the artillery, A/A vehicles, and tanks of both divisions, the X Corps artillery, plus an array of cruisers and destroyers standing off the beach, and Marine, Navy, and FEAF aircraft.[59]

The objective was to carry out an orderly evacuation of all military personnel, equipment, and supplies and certain Korean refugees. ROK I Corps (3d

---

*In total, seventy-eight Army personnel won the Medal of Honor in Korea. Eighteen were awarded to officers; sixty to enlisted men. Of the officers, the 24th Division commander, Bill Dean, was the most senior; Page was next senior; Don Faith third.

†About fifty Marines had worn new, experimental bulletproof vests, evolved from Air Corps flak jackets of World War II. In one documented case, this body armor, made of thin but strong plates of fiberglass, had repelled a CCF bullet. In due course all frontline American infantry in Korea were issued body armor.[58]

and Capital divisions) would embark first, for Samchok, to anchor the east end of Eighth Army's transpeninsular line. Dave Barr's 7th Division would outload next and go to Pusan for refitting, thence into the Eighth Army main line. Shorty Soule's 3d Division would be last to leave, holding a constricted perimeter near the Hungnam docks. It would demolish Hamhung, the Yonpo Airfield, rail facilities and rolling stock, bridges, tunnels, supplies, and all military equipment that could not be taken out, and then, finally, Hungnam. Nothing of value to the CCF would be left behind.

Fortunately for the defenders, the twelve CCF divisions (comprising some 120,000 soldiers) deployed in northeast Korea were by then in terrible shape. A Marine Corps study, based on captured CCF documents and prisoners and other sources, estimated that the Marine ground and air forces alone had inflicted 37,500 CCF casualties. There was no comparable Army study, but it is likely that the Army's 3d and 7th divisions inflicted at least another 5,000 casualties on the enemy, bringing total CCF battle casualties to about 42,500. The intense cold likewise took a heavy toll. More than 90 percent of the CCF Twenty-sixth Army "suffered from frostbite." The CCF Twenty-seventh Army reported 10,000 cases of incapacitating frostbite. If the figures in the CCF Twentieth Army were comparable, the CCF could have incurred upwards of 30,000 nonbattle casualties. In all, CCF battle and nonbattle casualties could have been as high as 72,500, or 60 percent.[60]*

Whether it was the result of these personnel losses or adherence to CCF doctrine to avoid attacks on heavily fortified enclaves, the CCF did not vigorously attack the defenders of the Hamhung-Hungnam perimeter. This was a tactical error. Even with its drastically reduced forces (45,000 men?), had the CCF mounted major assaults on X Corps, it probably could have inflicted a severe blow. A rain of CCF mortar shells falling into closely bunched troops and supply dumps inside the tight perimeter or on the docks and ships could have caused chaos, perhaps even a small-scale Dunkirk.[62]

There were, however, numerous and notable CCF attacks mounted against the perimeter, especially in Guthrie's 7th Infantry sector. Charles Heinrich's 1/7 and Sam Kail's 2/7 were hit several times during darkness by bugle-blowing CCF troops. Robert Blanchard's 1/15 and Jerry Allen's 3/65 were also subjected to heavy night attacks. Charles Beauchamp remembered that his 3/32, commanded by Heinrich Schumann, sustained a "severe attack" one night, but it was contained and thrown back with "the help of division artillery fire and some splendid fire support from a naval vessel off shore." In

---

*The figures may be inflated, but no doubt the Marine Corps historian is correct in stating that the losses sustained by the CCF in northeast Korea in November and December 1950 "amounted to a disaster." The CCF Twentieth, Twenty-sixth, and Twenty-seventh armies (comprising the Ninth Army Group) were not again identified in battle until the spring of 1951.[61]

these actions three of the 7th Infantry officers won DSCs: John T. Powers (of the 1/7) and James K. Ladd and Charles L. Butler (of the 2/7).[63]

In the Hungnam perimeter Ed Farrell's black 3/15 performed stoutly. A *Time* magazine war correspondent reported that when the Chinese flung a regrouped NKPA force at the 3/15, its black-led I Company fought valiantly for eleven hours nonstop. One of its platoon leaders, paratrooper Harry Sutton, won mention in *Time* (and later a Silver Star) for heroism during this tough fight, which ended, finally, in a decisive victory for the 3/15. That victory did much to inspire the battalion.[64]

As the Army troops gradually withdrew into the Hungnam perimeter, the Navy gave unstinting and powerful support. Twenty-two Navy and Marine Corps air squadrons (comprising about 400 aircraft), flying off carriers or from Korean airfields, blasted the CCF attempting to approach the perimeter. Two cruisers *(St. Paul* and *Rochester)* and seven destroyers fired 3,000 rounds of eight-inch and 18,600 rounds of five-inch shells at specific targets or at random. At Ned Almond's request, the battleship *Missouri* came in and lobbed 162 rounds of awesome sixteen-inch shells at the CCF.[65]

Little by little the 3d and 7th divisions fell back toward the Hungnam waterfront. On December 16 the Army forces demolished and abandoned Hamhung. They withdrew to Line A, above Hungnam, in good order, carefully coordinating movements and fire. The CCF did not pursue. The 65th Infantry commander William Harris was puzzled that the CCF "hadn't really hit us."[66]

ROK I Corps was the next major military force to withdraw from Hungnam after the Marines. Consisting of 25,000 men and about 700 vehicles, it embarked on December 17. The weather that day was ghastly: forty-knot winds; a mixture of rain and snow. Four landing craft broke loose and drifted into unswept minefields; an incoming cargo ship hit a mine but was subsequently salvaged. The ROKs, safely outloaded in ten ships of all types, were relanded that day and the next, December 18, on a beach near Samchok.[67]

The 7th Division began outloading on December 18. Everything—ammo, gasoline, even inoperable vehicles and machinery—was taken out. During the next two days the infantry regiments gradually fell back to a final line (F) and, upon relief by units of the 3d Division, on December 20 began boarding ships at the docks. The infantry completed embarkation that day and sailed for Pusan the following day, December 21.[68]

While demolition teams blew up nearly everything in sight, the three regiments of the 3d Division, backed by six artillery and three A/A battalions, dug in behind Line F. The division historian recorded that Army artillery units fired 46,244 rounds over a five-day period, December 19 to 24. The trains began loading on December 22. At noon on Christmas Eve the infantry regiments began loading on seven LSTs.[69]

The evacuation at Hungnam was in every way remarkable. In all, the Navy took out 105,000 troops, 17,500 vehicles, 350,000 measurement tons of cargo, and 91,000 Korean refugees, jammed into every available square foot on the ships. (Sadly, a like number had to be left behind.) Remaining on the beach were 400 tons of frozen dynamite, considered too dangerous to move, 500 huge (1,000-pound) aerial bombs, and about 200 drums of gasoline. These were blown up in a final, awesome fireworks display which left Hungnam and its waterfront in smoking ruins.[70]*

The 3d Division, en route by ship to Pusan, celebrated Christmas Day with a turkey dinner served by the Navy. Although the division's role in assisting the withdrawal from Hagaru and Koto was scarcely noted then or ever, the men knew they had done well and took great pride in their performance in northeast Korea. Almond was especially pleased by the performance of Shorty Soule. In contrast with the 7th Division commander Dave Barr, Soule was an aggressive "frontline" commander in the hyperactive Almond mold, usually on hand for the toughest and most hazardous battalion actions. For his performance in northeast Korea, Almond awarded Soule a DSC.[72]

# IV

Johnnie Walker's Eighth Army abandoned northeast Korea and withdrew below the 38th Parallel during the week of December 6 to 13. The CCF did not pursue and attack aggressively below the parallel. No one knew whether this was a political decision, whether the CCF was logistically incapable of rapid pursuit, or whether the CCF had forsworn a frontal attack in favor of a deep, encircling attack from the east, duplicating its earlier offensive at the Chongchon River.

At the Imjin River Walker commenced shaping the defensive position known as Line B. It was manned by (west to east) Bill Kean's 25th Division, with the Turkish Brigade attached; the ROK 1st Division; the ROK 6th Division; and John Church's 24th Division. East of the 24th, the line was held by five more ROK divisions (2d; 5th; 7th; 8th; 9th). The line was extended by ROK I Corps (3d and Capital divisions), which moved by ship from Hungnam to Samchok, on the east coast. The 1st Cav and rebuilding 2d divisions, the Commonwealth and British brigades, and the 187th Airborne RCT went into Eighth Army reserve.[73]

Bill Kean's 25th Division occupied the key position astride the main

---

*Earlier the Navy had evacuated 3,834 troops, 1,146 vehicles, 10,000 measurement tons of cargo, and 7,000 Korean refugees from Wonsan. In addition, 3,600 troops and 196 vehicles were evacuated by air from Yonpo.[71]

Pyongyang–Seoul highway near Munsan. The regrouped Turks held the division's extreme left flank, John Corley's 24th Infantry the center, the 35th Infantry the right flank, abutting the ROK 1st Division, while Michaelis's 27th remained in division reserve. The men dug foxholes and slit trenches in the frozen ground, strung barbed wire, planted thousands of mines, and set out drums of gasoline, rigged with thermite grenades which could be set off by remote control. To illuminate the battlefields against CCF night attacks, they brought up searchlights. Behind this line Bittman Barth's artillerymen registered their howitzers on the most likely routes of CCF attack. The line reminded old-timers of World War I battlefields in France.[74]

During the withdrawal the 35th Infantry's stern but able commander, Hank Fisher, had become ill with a severe cold, bordering on pneumonia, and had to be medically evacuated. He returned to the States and retired in 1953, still a colonel.[75]

The man chosen to replace Fisher was a forty-two-year-old firebrand, Gerald C. ("Gerry") Kelleher, a fighter in the mold of the 24th Infantry's John Corley. In fact, Kelleher and Corley had much in common. Both were devout Catholics; they had served in World War II side by side in Africa and Sicily as battalion commanders in the 26th Infantry of the 1st Division. Like Corley, Kelleher had won a DSC, several Silver Star Medals, and many other decorations. After Sicily, where he was hospitalized, Kelleher returned to the States to join the newly activated 104th Division. He went back into combat as a battalion commander with the 104th in the ETO and earned several more decorations and a battlefield promotion to full colonel. After the war he returned to the 1st Division, which was on occupation duty in Germany, and rose to command the 18th Infantry Regiment.[76]

In that job Kelleher soon made a favorable impression on Shrimp Milburn, who was commanding the 1st Division, and on Milburn's chief of staff, Rinaldo Van Brunt. Soon after Milburn had arrived in Korea, Kelleher wrote him to ask for a combat command; Milburn was delighted and arranged the transfer. Van Brunt remembered: "Kelleher was a wonderful soldier, a fighting fool, . . . He . . . ruled with an iron hand [and] soon had the best regiment in the business."[77]

Kelleher's appointment lifted eyebrows in the West Point-dominated Eighth Army. He was not a West Pointer, not even a college graduate. He had attended Rensselaer Polytechnic Institute for two years, intending to become a civil engineer, but had dropped out. He had enlisted in the Army Reserve in 1932 as a private and had won a reserve commission in July 1933. He was the only non-West Pointer then commanding a regiment in Eighth Army.*

---

*The appointment of Kelleher for Fisher reduced the average age of regimental commanders in the 25th Division to 38.6 years.

Adjacent to the 35th Infantry, John Corley's black 24th Infantry, badly roughed up at the Chongchon River, was simultaneously manning the line and absorbing hundreds of green fillers. Gerald Miller's 1/24, which had lost its entire C Company, was "in very poor shape," reported Corley, who was on the lookout for a new commander. George Clayton's 2/24 was also in poor shape. Its E and G companies, which had temporarily linked with McMains's 3/9 at Kunu November 26 to 29, had fought well but suffered heavy casualties. Moreover, Corley reported the regiment had incurred 639 "nonbattle" casualties, most of these caused by carelessness, which had resulted in frostbite and trench foot.[78]

\* \* \*

During this time on Line B the 25th Division suffered a serious loss in the senior command. Its able ADC, Vennard Wilson, was severely injured (broken back) when his liaison aircraft ground-looped and crashed while taking off on a tricky stretch of road. The injury confined Wilson to hospitals for four months and ended his prospects for higher command. He retired from the Army in 1953.[79]

Inasmuch as Bill Kean was wearing down and might soon have to be replaced, it was likely that Wilson's replacement as ADC would move up to command of the division. Johnnie Walker believed that honor (and promotion to two stars) should go to the 2d Division ADC, Sladen Bradley, who was hospitalized in Japan. Bradley hastened back to take the job, but he did not fully recover his health. Mike Michaelis remembered: "Frankly, I did not think Bradley was the right man for the division. He had a very nervous stomach. He'd get violently ill. He'd break out in a sweat. He wasn't a very prepossessing person to be around at that time." Tank commander Tom Dolvin remembered: "He had hepatitis. When visitors from higher headquarters showed up, we'd hide him in a command van and say he was at the front."[80]

\* \* \*

The right side of Line B at the Imjin River above Uijongbu was held by John Church's 24th Division. It had fought longer than any other division in Korea, and fortunately it had suffered least in the Chinese offensive. It was, therefore, fully manned and combat-ready.

There were, however, serious weaknesses in the ranks of the senior commanders. The frail and worn-out Church suffered cruelly in the bitter cold, which seemed greatly to exacerbate his arthritis, and to kill the pain, he was drinking heavily. The ADC, Gar Davidson, in effect commanded the division. The 19th Infantry commander, Ned Moore, who had been fighting without rest since July, was also worn-out and ill with hepatitis. His 2/19 commander, Ollie Kinney, promoted to exec, ran the regiment. The 21st commander, Dick

Stephens, forty-eight, was also running out of steam. Moreover, on more than one occasion Stephens crossed swords with Gar Davidson, causing a red-faced Davidson to mutter within the hearing of junior officers, "That guy is riding for a fall." Of the three regimental commanders, only the 5th Infantry's young Johnny Throckmorton (proudly wearing his new eagles) was still in prime mental and physical condition.[81]*

Farther south near Seoul, Hap Gay's 1st Cav Division, assigned to Eighth Army reserve, had only a moment's respite. Deeply concerned about the stability of the ROKs on the Army's right flank, Johnnie Walker sent major elements of the division northeast on roads leading to Chunchon and Hongchon on December 16, to serve as a backstop.[82]

The shifting around of regimental commanders in the 1st Cav finally came to a halt during the respite. On December 15 Marcel Crombez, erstwhile "mayor" of Pyongyang, returned to reclaim command of the 5th Cav, displacing Johnny Johnson, who returned to command the 8th Cav, displacing Ray Palmer, who returned to the States. Palmer soon retired from the Army in the rank of colonel.[83]†

The return of crusty old Crombez to the 5th Cav did not help morale, especially in the Edgar Treacy's 3/5, where Crombez was heartily disliked. The 3/5 company commander, Norman Allen, remembered:

Colonel Crombez tried to raise the men's morale by going about kicking the snow and saying loudly enough for men around him to hear: "See here, just kick the snow away and you'll find green grass. I've been in Korea before. Spring is almost here. Just any day now." This to GIs who had been living every day for the last six or seven weeks in foxholes in subzero weather. I walked through the company area and told the men: "Don't believe that bullshit about spring being just around the corner. This is the dead of winter. It's gonna get a lot worse before it gets better."[84]

Morale in the 7th Cav had improved substantially, especially in the regimental CP. One reason was that Billy Harris now wore brand-new bird colonel insignia.‡ Another reason was that the 7th Cav was substantially reinforced on December 19. On that day the Greek Battalion became, in effect, a permanent "fourth battalion."[86]

---

*The average age of regimental commanders in the 24th Division was forty-three years.

†The average age of regimental commanders in the 1st Cav was now 42.3 years. Crombez, who celebrated his fiftieth birthday on October 3, was then the oldest regimental command in Eighth Army—older by a month than George Peploe.

‡The entire West Point class of 1933 had been promoted, en bloc, to full colonel, including Harris and 8th Cav commander Johnny Johnson, and, awkwardly, Harris's 1/7 commander, Pete Clainos. Inasmuch as the more junior regimental commanders Mike Michaelis, John Throckmorton, and John Corley had already won battlefield promotions to full colonel, all Army regimental commanders in Korea were now "bird colonels."[85]

Pete Clainos, who had trained a Greek battalion in World War II, became the "godfather" of the Greeks. He remembered: "General Gay asked me, 'You speak Greek, don't you?' I lied and said no, then admitted that I did. He said, 'The Greek Battalion's yours.' I met these Greeks to break them in. I stood up on a rock and gave them a little pep talk—indoctrination—in Greek. The effect was almost magical. They received me like a king."[87]

Originally the Greeks, like the Turks, had intended to send a full brigade to Korea. But in October, when it appeared that the war was nearly over, the Greek government cut the contingent back to a battalion combat team comprised of about 1,000 men. It was a "regular" battalion of the Greek Army, which had been fighting Communist guerrillas at home since 1945. The officers, however, were handpicked, and in contrast with the Turks, a large percentage of them spoke English. The battalion commander was thirty-eight-year-old Dionyssios G. Arbouzis, who had been in combat, off and on, since 1940, fighting Italians, Germans, and Communist guerrillas. In 1974, as a four-star general, he was to become commander in chief of the Greek armed forces.[88]

The 7th Cav warmly embraced the Greeks in both body and spirit. The Greeks would remain permanently attached, giving the 7th Cav substantial added manpower and firepower. "It was a superior outfit," Clainos remembered. "The Greeks were good fighters. . . . The officers were exceptional leaders."[89]

\* \* \*

As the days of mid-December passed, Eighth Army remained uneasily rooted on Line B at the Imjin River, buying time for X Corps to come around to Pusan. The illusion of a strong, cohesive front with normal artillery and logistical support gave the men a feeling of greater security. Fed by rail and truck from Pusan—now much closer—most units replaced lost weapons and vehicles, replenished ammo stocks, and received winter clothing, warming tents, and other amenities. Mobile kitchens moved up to provide three hot meals a day. American replacements, including a substantial infusion of Reserve World War II veterans, arriving by air and ship (about 23,000 came in December) fleshed out the understrength units.[90]

Yet every man, from the Army commander down to the lowliest private, was under great mental strain. The G-2, Clint Tarkenton, believed there were 115,000 CCF troops "within one day's march." It was doubtful that Eighth Army could hold at Line B against an all-out CCF frontal assault. If one came, the Army would be forced back on Seoul and the Han River. Or if, as Walker believed more likely, the CCF mounted another flanking attack at the ROKs (as it had twice before) and the ROKs collapsed (as fully expected), Eighth Army's right flank might again be exposed dangerously, forcing another hurried and messy withdrawal.[91]

\* \* \*

While Eighth Army was dug in at the Imjin River line, Washington was suddenly confronted by a new and different crisis. In mid-December Moscow began a series of radio broadcasts directly threatening Japan. In view of the tense world situation—the belief in Washington that global war could be imminent—these broadcasts were taken very seriously in Tokyo and Washington. Inasmuch as MacArthur had committed the 3d Division to Korea without JCS authorization, no provision had been made to replace it. Japan was utterly defenseless; the Japanese people were deeply apprehensive.[92]

MacArthur's solution to this developing crisis had a familiar ring: Send more American troops. On December 18 he cabled the JCS to suggest that the four National Guard divisions called up in September and still undergoing basic training be sent at once to Japan. The troops could complete their training in Japan and, at the same time, provide a reassuring American military "presence."[93]

The Moscow broadcasts, together with MacArthur's proposed solution and the battlefront crisis in Korea, triggered yet another urgent and sweeping review of Far East policy within the highest levels of the Truman administration. The root question was: Should Washington send the four National Guard divisions to protect Japan or should Eighth Army be voluntarily withdrawn from Korea to perform that mission?

The chiefs were unanimous in their view that no more American divisions should be sent to the Far East. But they were divided over a voluntary withdrawal of Eighth Army from Korea. Air Force Chief of Staff Vandenberg and Chief of Naval Operations Sherman recommended an immediate voluntary withdrawal. Ham Haislip (substituting for Collins) and Omar Bradley, no doubt impressed by the optimistic report Collins had given after his trip to Korea, opposed a voluntary withdrawal, especially since there was no indication, as yet, that the CCF would attack below the 38th Parallel. Bradley even thought that MacArthur "might well be able to spare one or two divisions from Korea" for Japan.[94]

In response to the MacArthur cable, the JCS replied on December 19 that pending further review (and the return of Joe Collins from a NATO meeting in Europe), it could give MacArthur no definite answer. However, the JCS added, it seemed "unlikely" that any National Guard division would be sent to the Far East. Adopting the Bradley view, the chiefs suggested that "part" of X Corps (e.g., the 3d or 7th Division) "might be landed in Japan without prejudice to its future disposition."[95]

The policy review continued over the next several days. Secretary of State Acheson vigorously opposed voluntary withdrawal from Korea, stating that the "reverses did not warrant withdrawal." President Truman agreed, saying,

"We should not pull out of Korea and leave our friends there to be murdered." Gradually the conferees reached these general conclusions: that neither the National Guard divisions nor Chinese Nationalist troops should be sent to MacArthur and that Eighth Army should not be withdrawn from Korea voluntarily. Eighth Army, reinforced by the full X Corps, should continue to fight and fall back toward Pusan, as necessary, to avoid crippling casualties or destruction. It would evacuate only if forced to. Meanwhile, Washington would continue to pursue a negotiated settlement with Peking, through the UN and elsewhere, which would enable America, in George Marshall's phrase, to "withdraw from Korea with honor." Alternate ideas for the defense of Japan (such as secretly arming the Japanese) would be explored.[96]

* * *

The CCF intentions in Korea remained a mystery. On December 15 Ambassador Muccio in Seoul cabled Acheson: "Past three days have seen no contact between Eighth Army units and CCF. . . . Eighth Army intelligence is without firm evidence CCF have moved south of Pyongyang in any significant numbers." On December 18 he cabled: "Eighth Army and ROK forces remain out of contact with CCF. . . . Eighth Army still without firm evidence CCF have penetrated south of Pyongyang in any appreciable numbers. . . ."[97]

There was, however, one worrisome sector on the line. North of Chunchon, in the mountainous center of the peninsula, the ROK 8th Division had begun to feel some pressure. It was being mounted by "elements" of NKPA II Corps, occupying old NKPA defensive positions at the 38th Parallel. There were "indications," Muccio reported on December 15, that this sector was "being steadily reinforced by re-equipped NKPA forces coming from the north." On December 18 he reported that the "buildup of NKPA forces north of Chunchon appears to be proceeding" and that NKPA prisoners had stated that their mission was to "hold" in the vicinity of the 38th Parallel, "pending arrival of CCF." The G-2, Tarkenton, estimated there were 65,000 NKPA troops above Chonchon.[98]

The mystery came to an end on December 20. On that day the NKPA hit the ROK 8th Division a hard blow. This attack was "contained" but it was thought to be a screening action to cover movement of the CCF. Muccio cabled Acheson that Eighth Army had developed intelligence "indicating movement of CCF southeast from Pyongyang area and south from Koksan area toward [38th] Parallel areas opposite Uijongbu and Chunchon corridors leading to Seoul."[99]

As tracked by Eighth Army G-2 Clint Tarkenton, the CCF activity indicated that it was on the move in mass toward the 38th Parallel. The weight of movement seemed to be southeasterly from Pyongyang. This led Tarkenton to believe that the CCF was preparing to repeat its Chongchon River strategy.

It would mount a holding attack against the American forces at the Imjin River, meanwhile striking the ROK forces on Eighth Army's right flank with its major strength. The attack, Tarkenton believed, would come on Christmas Day. If the ROKs again collapsed, the CCF could sweep behind the American forces into Seoul.

In a repetition of his own strategy at the Chongchon River, in response to this intelligence, Johnnie Walker called on Bob McClure's 2d Division to backstop the ROKs on Eighth Army's right flank. The division was then at Suwon, having enjoyed about two weeks out of the line. Although it had drawn equipment and replacements and had been beefed up with newly arrived foreign contingents, the division was nowhere near combat-ready. Nonetheless, McClure sent two of his three infantry regiments to the center of the peninsula to replace the 1st Cav units and backstop the ROKs: George Peploe's 38th (plus a Dutch battalion) and Paul Freeman's 23d (plus a French battalion).[100]

Walker knew very well that these forces could not stop a major CCF offensive. His purpose in deploying the 2d Division northeasterly was to give the ROKs moral support and prevent a disastrous ROK bugout. Meanwhile, he continued drawing plans for a deep withdrawal to a line at the Kum River.

On December 22 Walker called the engineer Pat Strong to Eighth Army's tactical CP in Seoul. He gave Strong orders to prepare for a "scorched earth" policy. He would blow up "every bridge and culvert" on the railways and highways, "every foot of railroad line," and a huge "tidal lock" at Inchon. Strong was aghast. He viewed these orders as utterly defeatist, "the scorched earth policy of an army that would never return." He did not have sufficient resources to rebuild these structures should Eighth Army regain the offensive. For that reason he "pleaded" with Walker to restrict demolition to "key bridges" and merely a single span in other bridges and, since the U.S. Navy controlled the seas and would deny the CCF use of Inchon, to spare the tidal lock, which would take "months" to rebuild. But Walker refused to change the order.[101]

During all of his many months in Korea Johnnie Walker, who had celebrated his sixty-first birthday on December 3, had been ceaselessly on the go, visiting divisional CPs and frontline units by liaison plane and jeep. The sight of him standing in his jeep, wearing his shiny steel helmet with the three stars on the front and holding the special grab bar, chest puffed out, had become commonplace, as had the remarks about his reckless speeding, the speculation that one day he would be killed in a car wreck, like his mentor George Patton.

And it came to pass that way. It happened on the morning of December 23, as the CCF pressure against the ROK 8th and 9th divisions near Chunchon was building toward a full-scale offensive. Walker had a busy itinerary that cold, misty day. First he called at Bill Kean's 24th Division CP to confer with

Kean and the ADC, Gar Davidson, and to see his son, Sam, in Ned Moore's 19th Infantry, who had received a Silver Star Medal the day before. From there he set off for the Commonwealth Brigade CP, to present the outfit a ROK Presidential Citation. "Ten minutes after leaving us he was dead," Davidson remembered.[102]

Walker's jeep, siren screaming, had been speeding up the icy northbound lane of a highway which was jammed bumper to bumper in the southbound lane with vehicles. A weapons carrier from the ROK 6th Division suddenly pulled out of the jammed-up southbound lane, directly into the path of Walker's jeep. Walker's driver, Master Sergeant George Belton, could not avoid a collision. Walker; his aide, Lieutenant Colonel Layton C. Tynor; his bodyguard, Sergeant Francis S. Reenan; and Belton were thrown into a ditch. All four badly injured men were taken immediately to the nearby 8055th MASH unit. Walker was dead on arrival; the others survived and were eventually evacuated to hospitals in Japan.[103]*

Young Sam Walker was designated to escort his father's body back to the States. He did not return to the 19th Infantry. Posthumously promoted to four stars, Johnnie Walker was buried in Arlington National Cemetery. Sam, who later commanded a brigade in Vietnam and won further decorations, likewise rose to four stars, and upon retirement in 1978, he was appointed superintendent of VMI.[105]

\* \* \*

As was customary, Walker had designated his temporary successor in the event of his incapacitation or death. The line of temporary succession revealed Walker's assessment of his generals. By protocol, the Eighth Army job should have gone to IX Corps commander John Coulter, who was two years senior to I Corps commander Shrimp Milburn. But Coulter had fallen from favor after the disaster to the 2d Division at Kunu, and as Walker had specified, the temporary command went to Milburn. Similarly Walker had designated Milburn's temporary successor. By seniority, the job should have gone to either 24th Division commander John Church or 1st Cav commander Hap Gay (both commissioned in 1917). But the junior man, 25th Division commander Bill Kean (1918), got the job because Walker considered him the ablest. The 25th's artillery commander, Bittman Barth, who was senior to the ADC, Gar Davidson, by nine years, temporarily assumed command of the 25th Division.[106]

---

*The four ROKs in the weapons carrier were civilian employees of the vehicle maintenance unit of the 2d Regiment of the ROK 6th Division. All were arrested. The driver, Kyong Nei Pak, was tried by civilian "authorities" and sentenced to three years' imprisonment. The other three ROK "passengers" were released.[104]

The news of Walker's death had reached MacArthur within minutes. He, in turn, had immediately telephoned Joe Collins in Washington. As had been previously agreed between MacArthur and Collins, should anything happen to Walker, Matt Ridgway was to succeed him as Eighth Army commander. MacArthur, Collins wrote, "requested that Ridgway be sent at once." Collins telephoned President Truman, Defense Secretary George Marshall, and Army Secretary Frank Pace, all of whom concurred in the Ridgway appointment.[107]

Finally, Collins telephoned Ridgway. He and his wife, Penny, were having dinner with Army friends. Not having been previously notified that he had been selected to succeed Walker, Ridgway, who was "sipping an after-dinner highball," was stunned. After hanging up, he momentarily rejoined the group in the living room. Then, without revealing the substance of the call or his inner turmoil, he bade his hosts good night and returned with Penny to his Fort Myer quarters. Astonishingly he did not tell Penny the news that night. "She could get some sleep," Ridgway wrote, "even if I couldn't."[108]

*　*　*

Walker's death occurred at a turning point in the Korean War: the CCF invasion of South Korea and the X Corps withdrawal from North Korea and consolidation into Eighth Army. Henceforth the war was to assume a more conventional shape, with opposing forces massed along a single conventional front.

To this point the war had not been well fought. Most of the large mistakes had been MacArthur's: grossly underestimating the professionalism of the NKPA; the inhumane, piecemeal commitment of the untrained Eighth Army; the shift of X Corps after Inchon from hot pursuit to a meaningless amphibious landing at Wonsan; scandalously underestimating CCF strength and intentions; the foolish "race" to the Yalu in both the Eighth Army and X Corps sectors. As a result, some 60,000 American soldiers and Marines and probably five times that number of ROK soldiers were dead, wounded, or missing.

Walker's generalship in Korea was to draw mixed reviews. He was not physically or mentally imposing. He did not have "command presence" or a clever mind or a glib tongue. He was not a warm person. He rarely smiled; he had no sense of humor. He was a "fighter," but except for his closest advisers, he was not well liked. On the whole, the nickname the press gave him in Korea—Bulldog Walker—seemed a fitting one, except in one regard: He would not challenge his superior, MacArthur. In that relationship he groveled, lest he lose his job.

Walker made many mistakes, especially in the early days of the war. The first was to underestimate vastly and even to ridicule his enemy. That led to a second mistake: the decision to commit the green 24th Division, battalion by battalion, well forward of the Kum River. The piecemeal destruction of these battalions left him without sufficient forces to defend a Kum River line. The ensuing decision to defend Taejon in the hope the 1st Cav Division could reach there in time was another mistake. The defense of Taejon was clearly beyond his capability, and it led him unwisely to commit the green 1st Cav piecemeal into combat as well. Tightly hemmed into the Pusan Perimeter, he capitalized on his valuable intelligence and his interior lines of communications, shifting scanty reserves to meet known NKPA attacks adroitly and sometimes masterfully. But it was the mistakes by NKPA generals and squad-level American courage rather than superior American generalship that "won" the Battle of the Pusan Perimeter.

Within the Pusan Perimeter Walker was overly forgiving of too many old, inexperienced, or incompetent staffers and division and regimental commanders for far too long. Korea was a "young man's war." The mountainous terrain and brutal weather demanded young officers in superb physical as well as mental condition, such as Mike Michaelis, John Corley, and Johnny Throckmorton. The Pentagon should have promptly realized the need and filled it, but when it failed to do so (as Ridgway noted in his August visit), Walker should have raised Cain until he got the competent leaders he required. He did not do so apparently out of concern that he would offend the Pentagon or MacArthur or old friends. This reluctance cost many lives.

Walker's pursuit of the NKPA from the Pusan Perimeter was not well conceived. He placed the major emphasis on glamorous, headline-making armored "attacks to unlimited objectives" or, in the vernacular, gaining "real estate," rather than on destruction of enemy forces. The lines and tiers thrown across South Korea to "trap" the NKPA were absurdly inadequate; the hard-core NKPA forces slipped away to fight again. A better plan would have been to employ the traditional infantry tactic of turning palms in, or well-executed short envelopments to encircle and destroy or capture opposing enemy units.

Following the liberation of Seoul, Walker's plan for X Corps to pursue the NKPA from Seoul to Pyongyang and beyond, and for I Corps to pursue NKPA overland to Wonsan, was sound. Had his plan been adopted, rather than MacArthur's, it is possible or even probable that the numerous hard-core NKPA troops that escaped into North Korea could have been trapped and destroyed, and the American and ROK POWs in their possession liberated. Walker must share some of the blame for the disarray that ensued. Had he strongly challenged MacArthur, he might have overturned the decision and saved many lives.

Walker must also share some of the blame for launching Eighth Army's Home by Christmas offensive from the Chongchon River. All his battlefield instincts and experience warned him that the offensive was not right. His army was pitifully undersupplied. His men had no ammo or warm clothing or food. ROK II Corps on his right flank was not armed or competent to anchor that important sector. His field commanders had already met substantial CCF troops in early November, and his G-3 section (Dabney, Train) believed the CCF had come into Korea in full strength. Yet in response to intense pressure from MacArthur, Walker proceeded northward, grudgingly accepting the gross underestimate of CCF strength of the GHQ G-2 (Willoughby) and his own G-2 (Tarkenton). In his favor he was sufficiently cautious and tentative to enable his army to shift quickly to the defensive, but he was much too slow to recognize the dangerous CCF threat to his right flank when ROK II Corps collapsed. The disaster which befell the 2d Division as a result was largely Walker's fault. His decision to withdraw Eighth Army from Pyongyang—and destroy its supplies—was probably premature and deserved the criticism it provoked. However, Walker's insistence to Joe Collins that X Corps be brought around from Hungnam and incorporated into Eighth Army set the stage for Eighth Army's ultimate victory over the CCF.

# PART NINE

# Ridgway to Korea

# 19

# A "DEFEATED" ARMY?

## I

Matthew Bunker Ridgway was an impressive figure. In his younger years he was so handsome, physically trim, and impeccably attired that he could well have been a soldier conceived in Hollywood. Now, in his mature years, he had the classical countenance of a Mediterranean aristocrat: piercing, deep, and wide-set hazel eyes, sharply chiseled and well-proportioned cheekbones and chin, a thin Roman nose, and remarkably unblemished swarthy skin.

He was a fine physical specimen. He stood five feet ten inches and weighed 175 pounds. He had not been a varsity athlete in his youth, but he had closely associated with athletes at school and thereafter. He had acquired the athlete's pride in keeping physically fit, and he did so by riding horseback, running, swimming, hunting, chopping wood, and playing handball and tennis. He ate, drank, and smoked (mostly cigars) in moderation. His body was taut, he had great stamina, and he was strong. His posture was ramrod straight. Even while sitting down, he did not slouch or cross his legs.[1]

The most striking feature about Ridgway was the aura of force or determination he radiated. Even his closest associates found this aura difficult to describe. One recalled: "The force that emanated from him was awesome. It reminded me of Superman. You had the impression he could knock over a building with a single blow, or stare a hole through a wall, if he wanted to. It was a powerful *presence.*"[2]

In breeding, speech, and taste Ridgway was almost Edwardian, reflecting a polished Eastern upper-middle-class background. His forebears, mostly Episcopalians, had been well-to-do New Yorkers, a family of professionals. His paternal grandfather, James Ridgway, had been a surrogate judge in Brooklyn. His father, Thomas Ridgway, was a West Point graduate (1883), an artillery specialist who had retired as a full colonel after World War I. His mother, Ruth Starbuck Bunker, of Garden City, Long Island, was a concert-class pianist and a collector of objets d'art. In a social setting, Ridgway was well mannered, warm, charming, and tactful.[3]

He had never seriously considered any career other than the military. After a comfortable childhood on Army posts and some prep school cramming, he had made a beeline for West Point, determined to be a general. He was graduated on April 20, 1917, two weeks after the United States had declared war on Germany, and was eager to test his mettle in the trenches of France. But he was denied that opportunity. By the luck of the draw, he was ordered back to West Point as an instructor in Romance languages, and no amount of string pulling in the War Department could overturn the decision.

It was a bitter, bitter pill. He had missed the Great War and felt humiliated and professionally ruined, his life's goal beyond reach. But that pill may well have been a powerful stimulant. During the ensuing peacetime years Ridgway attacked the rungs of the Army's ladder with relentless zeal. Within the small peacetime officer corps, he was soon noted and marked as a "comer." As the years rolled by, he was selected for all the right graduate schools: two one-year tours at the Infantry School; a two-year (1933–1935) stint at the Command and General Staff School; and, finally, a year (1936–1937) at the Army War College.[4]

Ridgway was uncommonly bright and a quick study. Encouraged by his parents from childhood, he became an obsessive reader. As a cadet he had devoured every military biography and memoir he could lay his hands on. He had memorized great martially stirring swaths of Kipling and delighted in quoting him and other poets. Although he was not an intellectual, Ridgway had a facility with words that enabled him to draft complicated war plans and analytical staff papers and speeches with comparative ease. Having been assigned to teach Spanish during his World War I tour at West Point, he mastered the language and, during the twenties and thirties, had been one of only a half dozen officers in the Regular Army fluent in Spanish. This accomplishment had led to several special high-level politicomilitary assignments in Latin America, which had broadened his horizons and further enhanced his career.[5]

Along this climb up the ladder Ridgway had formed devout religious convictions and a personal philosophy. The latter he described as "dichotomous." On the one hand, he believed that most individuals and societies were motivated by greed, acquisitiveness, a thirst for power and brutality. For that reason, he believed it was imperative that the United States maintain an

Gerald C. Kelleher *(left)*, talking with 25th Division artillery commander Bittman Barth, was named commander of the 35th Infantry. Kelleher, a disciplinarian and a "fighting fool," ran a fine regiment.

Inasmuch as Bradley and the commander of the black 24th Infantry John Corley did not get along, Henry C. Britt replaced Corley.

Blackshear M. ("Babe") Bryan, Jr. *(left),* was named to replace John Church as commander of the 24th Division. He vowed to command the division from the front lines. Here he does so, lying prone, un-general-like, on a straw mat, with staffers, observing enemy from a ridgeline in his sector.

Ridgway insisted that all weapons of every unit be employed to the maximum. The 75-mm recoilless rifle, whether mounted on the ground (as shown above) or on a jeep, proved to be useful in blasting out enemy bunkers.

Ridgway requested—and received—ten extra artillery battalions, including one equipped with these powerful self-propelled 155-mm "Long Tom" howitzers.

Encouraging results: a lone Chinese Communist (center, wearing white blouse) surrenders to an American patrol.

At Almond's insistence, Ridgway *(left)* sacked the 7th Division commander Dave Barr, who was replaced by big, aggressive Claude B. (''Buddy'') Ferenbaugh, another general who commanded from the front lines.

Ferenbaugh's new assistant division commander was Robert F. Sink, a dapper paratrooper, famous within the Army for his courage. Like Mike Michaelis, Sink had commanded a regiment of the 101st Airborne Division in Normandy, Holland, and the Battle of the Bulge.

Ferenbaugh named Almond's G-2, William W. (''Buffalo Bill'') Quinn *(below),* to command the 17th Infantry, replacing Herb Powell, who was promoted to 7th Division chief of staff.

Almond's G-3, John H. ("Jack") Chiles, replaced Paul Freeman, wounded at Chipyong, as commander of the 23d Infantry.

Messinger's new exec, Olinto M. Barsanti, another officer from the X Corps staff, helped Messinger put ginger in the 9th Infantry.

Paul Freeman's exec in the 23d Infantry, Edwin J. Messinger *(right)*, posed here with Nick Ruffner, replaced Chin Sloane as commander of the 9th Infantry.

The French battalion was normally attached to the 23d Infantry. Its aged and colorful commander Ralph Monclar (a nom de guerre) poses in a jeep with Ridgway *(right)*.

When 38th Infantry commander George Peploe was promoted to IX Corps chief of staff, he was replaced by his able but reserved exec John G. Coughlin *(far right)*, shown here reviewing his troops with a visiting senator.

Spring rains seriously impeded Eighth Army's offensive operations against the Chinese Communists. In this typical scene a tank and a two-and-a-half-ton truck join forces to tow a mired truck out of the mud.

In the spring fighting, the rejuvenated Eighth Army drove the Chinese Communists back across the 38th Parallel.

Attacking through open rice paddies, American infantry with fixed bayonets charge an enemy position.

In late April 1951, the Chinese Communists counterattacked, forcing Eighth Army to retreat to Seoul. The exhausted, retreating soldiers of the 35th Infantry hitch rides to the rear on Sherman tanks.

Returning to the offensive in May, American infantry stormed a Communist hillside position.

They took the Communist position, but the cost was high and the task exhausting, as reflected in the vacant stares of these GIs.

Under relentless Eighth Army pressure, the Chinese soldiers, perhaps weary of war, began to surrender in increasing numbers. The GI at left holds a ''burp'' gun, stripped from one of the Chinese.

American soldiers inspect a captured Russian-built T-34 tank (facetiously named ''Ninochka'' and bearing 32d Infantry Regiment markings). Much feared in the early days of the war, Communist tanks were ultimately neutralized by American tanks, antitank weapons, and the Air Force.

A collection of captured Communist artillery includes weapons of many nations, some of them antiquated. Nonetheless, these weapons assisted in inflicting severe casualties on UN forces in the first year of the war.

In late June 1951, in response to overtures from Washington, the Communists agreed to enter into armistice talks. The Communist negotiation team was led by North Korean General Nam Il *(center)*.

The UN negotiating team was led by Vice Admiral C. Turner Joy *(center)*.

The negotiating teams initially met in this teahouse in Kaesong. Later the site was switched to Panmunjon. The negotiations proved to be intensely frustrating and dragged on for two years, until July 1953, when an armistice agreement was signed.

During the two years of negotiations, the fighting continued on a limited scale: trench warfare, as in World War I *(below),* or more aggressive struggles for hilltops and ridgelines. The main battle line, however, changed only slightly.

unassailable military posture. On the other hand, he believed that there was some "high, although inscrutable," guiding purpose behind this miserable state of affairs and that every individual had an "inescapable duty" to do whatever lay in his or her power to achieve "a better world order" through nonmilitary endeavors.[6]

\* \* \*

Fundamentally Ridgway was a soldier. He much preferred life in the field to a desk or a classroom. From his earliest years he was a dedicated outdoorsman. He loved to camp out, sleep on the ground, hike endless miles, hunt birds and big game, fly-cast in remote mountain streams, blaze trails through impenetrable jungles on foot or horseback. But opportunities to savor life in the field had come all too infrequently. Owing to his talent for paper-work, his fluency in Spanish, and the shortage of peacetime field units, he had drawn mostly staff jobs. Before World War II he had spent only two years in the field directly in command of troops—five different companies and a battalion—and never for very long at a stretch.

On those rare peacetime occasions when he commanded troops, Ridgway had excelled. In this, his true element, he demonstrated a pronounced talent for getting men to pull together and take pride in their work. One reason was that he was no tent hog grinding out orders. He was out front all day, exhorting, cajoling, teaching. His working motto, delivered in a deep, commanding voice tinged with a New York accent, was: "Haven't got time? Well, get up earlier . . . stay up later at night." He had little patience with human failings and was notoriously outspoken and short-fused. His dedication, zeal, and intensity led his sweating GIs to joke: "There's a right way, a wrong way and a Ridgway."[7]

He had developed leadership tricks, at least one of which inspired awe: an uncanny memory for names. By graduation from West Point Ridgway, who was the corps adjutant, could give, on sight, the first and last names of all 700 cadets. He continued this feat throughout his career in the belief that "calling people by their names had a powerful effect." Many a private, corporal, or sergeant who had not seen Ridgway for years had been stunned when he approached them and said, "Hello, Smith! Haven't seen you since . . ." A legend arose that by 1950 Ridgway knew the names of "four or five thousand" men, half of them enlisted, and could "recall them without hesitation."[8]

There was yet another aspect about Ridgway that did not go unremarked. Women found him irresistibly attractive. Whether it was deserved or not, he had a reputation as something of a Don Juan. That reputation had attached to him during his days at West Point, where he was known to some as the "Black Knight of the Hudson." He had married a New Yorker on graduation, beneath the traditional arch of swords. But that marriage, which produced two daughters, had ended after thirteen years in divorce, a rare and drastic step in the peacetime Army, as elsewhere in American society in the 1930s. He then married another New Yorker (and Army widow) with a young daughter, whom he adopted. Both his divorce and the remarriage evoked gossip.[9]

The second marriage also had ended in divorce. His third marriage—in December 1947—had been no less controversial. Then twenty-nine years old, Penny Ridgway, a very pretty, vivacious brunette, was about twenty years younger than the wives of Ridgway's contemporaries. She had not had to endure the long peacetime climb up the career and social ladder; she had come from "civilian" life straight into the highest levels of the Army. Moreover, Penny was a divorcée. She had been married to a former enlisted man, an Air Force sergeant in World War II. For these reasons Mrs. Ridgway was not welcome in Army-wife circles.[10]

Apart from the critics of his erratic affairs of the heart, a few of Ridgway's fellow officers were put off by his single-mindedness, his zeal, his tendency to evoke the flag and a divine being, to call attention to his accomplishments needlessly, or to use big and flowery words and phrases when simple ones would do. To them Ridgway came across as a stuffed shirt and a drudge who took life—and himself—far too seriously. They were resentful that he seemed unable to relax, or get drunk, or put his feet up, or tell a joke.[11]

Despite some surface indications to the contrary, Ridgway was at root a modest and at times a self-deprecating man. In private conversation he was apt to paraphrase an old poem: "When you are beginning to think you're so important, make a fist and stick your arm into a bucket of water up to your wrist. When you take it out, the hole you left is the measure of how much you'll be missed."[12]

\* \* \*

During the long peacetime climb up the career ladder Ridgway had the good fortune to serve under George Marshall on four occasions. In these tours Marshall had noted well Ridgway's professionalism and loyalty and had come to regard him somewhat like an adopted son. When Roosevelt appointed Marshall Army chief of staff in 1939, Marshall called Ridgway to the War Department to serve in his War Plans Division, first as a detail officer, then as chief of the Latin American section. Shortly after World War II began, Marshall promoted Ridgway to brigadier general and assigned him to be assistant commander of Omar Bradley's newly activated 82d Infantry Division, then in training. When Bradley was promoted to duty elsewhere, Marshall named Ridgway to replace Bradley as commander of the division.[13]

Marshall had been fascinated and intrigued by the operations of the German airborne forces, especially their envelopment of the island of Crete. He believed that with America's nearly unlimited aircraft production potential, the American Army could utilize airborne forces to great advantage, both in the ETO and the Pacific. He even conceived a visionary plan to make the invasion of German-occupied France (Operation Overlord) primarily an airborne operation. Accordingly, in the summer and fall of 1942 Marshall ordered the creation of five American airborne divisions, complete with artillery, engineers, medics, and other ancillary units.

This was a massive undertaking about which the American Army knew very little. To see that it was done right and with proper dispatch, Marshall chose Ridgway to pioneer the experiment. Ridgway's 82d Infantry Division was converted to "airborne," then split up to create a second, the 101st Airborne Division. Four airborne divisions eventually went to the Mediterranean and ETO; one, to the Pacific.

Ridgway led the introduction of American airborne forces into combat with the invasion of Sicily in July 1943. Owing principally to the ineptitude or lack of training of the troop carrier pilots, the Sicily operation was a fiasco. However, in subsequent airborne operations (Salerno, Normandy, Holland, and Germany) and in ground operations during the Battle of the Bulge, Ridgway's paratroopers performed so brilliantly and heroically that they became the stuff of legend. Despite his age and a trick back, Ridgway himself made five parachute jumps (including the D day jump into Normandy), thus qualifying as a bona fide paratrooper. After Normandy he was promoted to command the newly formed XVIII Airborne Corps (of three American airborne divisions), and James Gavin took command of the 82d.

As a division and corps commander Ridgway was an inspiration on the battlefield. He commanded his troops from the front lines, in battalion CPs, where the action of the day was likely to be hottest. His point was not to showboat but to be on hand to help the men in the tightest situations by his authority to summon support forces instantly if required. This style of leadership often exposed him to heavy enemy fire; his close calls at the front also became legendary. Wounded once by German grenade fragments, he had refused hospitalization and thus still carried the fragment in his shoulder.[14]

Ridgway emerged from World War II as a three-star general with a chestful of medals (DSC, etc.) and an enviable reputation. His successor as commander of the 82d Division, Jim Gavin, thought Ridgway was "undoubtedly the best combat corps commander in the American Army in World War II," even better than Joe Collins. Although Eisenhower was never fully won over to the concept of airborne warfare, he judged that Ridgway personally was "one of the finest soldiers this war has produced." He elaborated: "He has never undertaken a job that he has not performed in a soldierly and even brilliant way."[15]

## II

On the morning of December 23, Washington time, Ridgway finally broke the news to his wife over coffee in their Fort Myer quarters. It would be a painful separation. In three years of marriage they had scarcely been apart a single day.[16]

Ridgway had hoped to spend Christmas Eve with his wife and their adored son, Matty, twenty months old. But when he arrived at the Pentagon that morning to wind up his affairs, Frank Pace, Joe Collins, and Ham Haislip thought Ridgway should leave for Japan at once. Ridgway agreed, and while he attended to urgent, last-minute office matters, Ham Haislip telephoned Mrs. Ridgway to give her the bad news.

Among the cables on Ridgway's desk that morning were two from MacArthur, one addressed to Collins, one to Ridgway. To Collins MacArthur wrote: "Thanks and deepest appreciation, Joe, to you and the Secretary [Pace] for letting me have Ridgway." To Ridgway MacArthur wrote: "I look forward with keenest anticipation to your joining this command. Your welcome by all ranks will be of the heartiest. To me personally it will mark the resumption of a comradeship which I have cherished through long years of military service."[17]

Ridgway dictated two cables to his secretary, one to Johnnie Walker's widow, one to MacArthur. To Mrs. Walker he wrote: "May knowledge of the deep respect and affection of lifelong comrades for your splendid soldier somewhat soften the shock of his passing." To MacArthur he wrote: "Consider highest honor share service with the gallant command under your inspired leadership."[18]

Like other senior Army generals, Ridgway had acquired a coterie. It was composed mostly of his World War II airborne staffers, plus several officers who had come aboard in the postwar years during Ridgway's tours at the United Nations and in Panama, the latter as the commander in chief, Caribbean. One of the coterie—his wartime aide Don Faith—had been killed in Korea; another, his loyal wartime chief of staff, West Pointer (1924) Ralph P. ("Doc") Eaton, fifty-one, badly injured in a D day glider crash in Normandy, was not physically up to another war.[19]

When Ridgway's appointment was announced that day, others in the coterie telephoned, wired, or came by his office to volunteer their services. Believing that they should spend Christmas with their families or continue in their assignments or schools, Ridgway did not immediately order them to Korea. However, in due course most members of the coterie followed him there.

Two members of his coterie were then serving in the General Staff Secretariat. They were West Pointers Frank W. ("Bill") Moorman (1934) and John

R. ("Bo") Beishline (1931). Moorman, one of Ridgway's closest confidants, had fought side by side with him throughout World War II, winding up as G-4 of XVIII Airborne Corps. In the postwar years he had served with Ridgway at the UN. Beishline, a scholarly field artilleryman and personnel expert (G-1 of the Ninth Army in the ETO), who held a doctorate in philosophy from Ohio State University (1949), was a new member of the coterie. Moorman followed Ridgway to Korea fairly soon; Beishline, then serving as a liaison officer between the Army Department and the White House, remained in Washington to provide what Ridgway euphemistically was to describe as a "safe line of communications back home." That is, he was to be Ridgway's high-level spy in the Pentagon.[20]

* * *

Later that day Ridgway returned to his Fort Myer quarters to pack and pose for press photographers. Into his luggage he crammed various uniforms and battle regalia, including his .45 pistol, M-1 rifle, six unused pairs of wool socks that Jim Gavin had given him during the Battle of the Bulge, and the parachute harness he had worn in combat in the ETO.[21]

The Air Force provided a posh four-engine Constellation to fly Ridgway to Japan. At ten o'clock that night, December 23, it was airborne. The plane made refueling stops in Tacoma, Washington, and Adak, Alaska. In Tacoma Ridgway sent off messages accepting the services of two members of his coterie, to report to him after New Year's. In Adak he got a haircut from a Navy barber.[22]

The officers he invited to join him in Korea were two West Pointers, Walter F. ("Walt") Winton, Jr. (1940), and Blackshear M. ("Babe") Bryan, Jr. (1922). Winton was a paratrooper, a wartime cohort and confidant, who had risen from battalion commander to G-2 of the 82d Airborne Division and who had served on Ridgway's staff at the UN and in Panama. Bryan, a famous military academy football star (when Ridgway was graduate manager of athletics) and later an assistant coach, was a senior brigadier general. During World War II he had been a Pentagon policy planner and, in the immediate postwar years, provost marshal general. In 1948 he had become Ridgway's chief of staff in the Caribbean Command and was still holding down that job. In Korea Winton was to serve as Ridgway's senior aide; Bryan, fifty, was qualified for command of a division.[23]

* * *

Ridgway landed in Tokyo at 11:30 P.M. on December 25. MacArthur's acting chief of staff—and Ridgway's good friend—Doyle Hickey, and other senior GHQ staffers met the plane and escorted Ridgway to MacArthur's guest quarters at the American Embassy. Before going to sleep, Ridgway drafted a message for Hickey to transmit to Eighth Army, eulogizing Johnnie Walker.[24]

The next morning, December 26, at nine, Ridgway met with MacArthur and Hickey in MacArthur's office in the Dai Ichi Building. Notwithstanding MacArthur's cable to Ridgway alluding to a "comradeship which I have cherished through long years of military service," their prior personal contact had actually been limited.

It had begun one day at West Point in September 1921, when Ridgway was an instructor in Romance languages. MacArthur, then superintendent of the academy, was a sports fanatic who was determined to restore West Point to a position of preeminence in the athletic world, but things had not gone his way. Learning that Ridgway had been an outstanding manager of the West Point football team in his undergraduate days and retained a deep interest in athletics, MacArthur decided to appoint him graduate manager of athletics.[25]

Ridgway had worked closely with MacArthur in that job for about nine months—to June 1922, when MacArthur left West Point for other duty.* Thereafter he had seen MacArthur on only three occasions, each a brief encounter: a courtesy call in Washington in the early 1930s; a five- or ten-minute chat in Manila in 1945, when Ridgway's XVIII Airborne Corps had been assigned to MacArthur's proposed invasion of Japan, and the previous August, in company with Averell Harriman.[26]

MacArthur's greeting was "congenial," Ridgway remembered.[27] He immediately launched into a one-hour-and-twenty-minute monologue that Ridgway judged to be "masterly." Ridgway later wrote:

To confer with him was an experience that could happen to few others. . . . I found my whole attention focused on the dramatic figure of Douglas MacArthur. Of course I had known MacArthur since my days as a West Point instructor but, like nearly everyone who ever dealt with him, I was again deeply impressed by the force of his personality. . . . He was a great actor . . . with an actor's instinct for the dramatic—in tone and gesture. Yet so lucid and so penetrating were his explanations and his analyses that it was his mind rather than his manner or his bodily presence that dominated his listeners.[28]

The thrust of MacArthur's remarks was familiar. Communism had elected to launch war against the West in the Far East. That challenge had to be met unreservedly with all the power at Washington's command. "There isn't any question that MacArthur wanted to go to war, full war with Commu-

---

*Ridgway remained in the post of athletic manager until the summer of 1924. He was so good at it that he received several offers to manage professional sports teams. He seriously considered these offers and nearly resigned his commission to accept one.

nist China," Ridgway remembered. "And he could not be convinced by all the contrary arguments. . . . He reluctantly acted in accordance with the policy, but he never did accept it. He wanted to go to war with China."[29]

Above all else at that dark time MacArthur believed it was asinine for Washington to have declined Chiang Kai-shek's repeated offers of assistance. MacArthur had a new idea: Washington should support a Chinese Nationalist "invasion" of the Chinese mainland. "China is wide open in the south," MacArthur told Ridgway. "A Nationalist offensive in that area, initiated at the earliest possible date, would, even if only moderately successful, relieve the pressure in Korea" by forcing the CCF to withdraw troops from Korea to defend its homeland from the Nationalists.[30]

MacArthur found a sympathetic listener in Ridgway. Ever since the NKPA had crossed the 38th Parallel into South Korea, Ridgway had been urging mobilization for World War III. The idea of a Chinese Nationalist invasion of southern China struck him as brilliant. The next time he had a free moment he wired Joe Collins, without MacArthur's knowledge: "Logic for this recommendation is convincing to me and I feel I would be negligent were I not to state my full concurrence at once."[31]

Turning to the tactical situation in Korea, MacArthur was of the opinion that while there was as yet no unequivocal evidence that the CCF would cross the 38th Parallel in full force and invade South Korea, he believed it would, and soon, probably launching the attack on New Year's Eve. "We are now operating in a mission vacuum," MacArthur said, "while diplomacy attempts to feel its way. A military success of any substantial kind would strengthen our diplomacy." His orders to Eighth Army remained unchanged: Defend in successive positions (Lines B, C, D, etc., per his order of December 8) as required. For psychological reasons Ridgway should make every possible effort to hold Seoul, but should the ROKs again give way, Eighth Army should "drop back" to avoid being isolated at Seoul in a "citadel situation."[32]

Concluding his remarks, MacArthur expressed utmost faith in Ridgway: "Form your own opinions and use your own judgment. I will support you. You will make mistakes, as, of course, we all do, but even if you do, I will assume responsibility. You have my complete confidence."[33]

Finally, Ridgway got a word in. He had three key questions:

- In the unlikely event Russia entered the war, what did MacArthur want to do with Eighth Army? Answer: Withdraw it to Japan.
- Should the CCF make further deep penetrations, was there a possibility that the ROKs would defect? Answer: Not now, but possibly in due course.
- If he found the combat situation "to my liking," would MacArthur have any objections to "my attacking"? Answer: "The Eighth Army is yours, Matt. Do what you think best."[34]

To Ridgway the last pronouncement was electrifying. It represented a radical change in MacArthur's modus operandi. Theretofore MacArthur and GHQ had directed every major tactical phase of the ground combat in Korea. Henceforth that task would be delegated to Ridgway. "That is the sort of order that puts heart in a soldier," Ridgway later wrote. "Now the full responsibilities were mine." But he knew he had to be "very careful," he said later. He was on "dangerous ground," he added. "I knew his temperament," Ridgway remembered. "I knew there would be no hesitancy in relieving me if I did something he disliked."[35]

One command matter was left undiscussed and dangling: Ned Almond's favored—and confusing—status as both chief of staff to MacArthur and commander of X Corps. MacArthur had given Almond a choice of returning to Tokyo or remaining as commander of X Corps within Eighth Army. Almond had elected to remain with X Corps. But MacArthur had not officially severed Almond's position with GHQ. On paper Almond was still GHQ chief of staff; Doyle Hickey was still "acting" chief of staff.[36]

\* \* \*

After his session with MacArthur, Ridgway met with Hickey, Pinky Wright, and other senior GHQ staffers, including MacArthur's naval and air chiefs, Turner Joy and George Stratemeyer. Having devoted about twelve hours a day for the past six months mostly to Korea, Ridgway had the fullest possible grasp of the problems he would face. Nonetheless, he tactfully endured a stylized "GHQ briefing" and dutifully asked questions. Some of the information was of value, but the meeting was useful to Ridgway primarily as an occasion to take the measure of the men who would be providing him support and to project forcefully his own positive command presence.[37]

The Air Force Constellation that had brought Ridgway from Washington was to take him on to Korea at noon that day. Airborne once again, Ridgway had a brief glimpse of Mount Fuji before the plane flew into foul weather. Then he settled back and ate a solitary lunch.[38]

Ridgway was indeed on "dangerous ground." As he knew, the political situation was difficult. Truman and MacArthur held diametrically opposing views about what to do in Korea, Truman being in favor of a "limited war" and a negotiated settlement restoring the status quo ante bellum, MacArthur being opposed to negotiations and favoring unlimited war against Red China. Ridgway was in sympathy with MacArthur's views, but his duty—and oath of office—demanded that he carry out the wishes of his civilian authority: Commander in Chief Truman.

He had received no direct orders from Truman or the JCS. Yet he knew full well what Washington expected of him: to restore Eighth Army's confidence and self-esteem, to prevent a Dunkirk and stay in Korea, and then to punish the CCF to the point that Peking would be forced to the negotiating table. Ironically, if he were successful, he would greatly undermine MacArthur's position and his own deeply held views about how to deal with the threats posed by world communism. He would, in effect, become an instrument of what many might call "appeasement."

His task, in any case, was to command an army in the field. His own high standards demanded that he do it well, regardless of the ultimate political outcome. As the plane droned westward, pitching in the storm, he fixed his mind on the immediate task ahead. He made long lists of details to check on and drafted a message to be read, upon his assumption of command of Eighth Army, to every officer and to as many enlisted men as practicable: "I have with little advance notice, assumed heavy responsibilities before in battle, but never with greater opportunities for service to our loved ones and our nation in beating back a world menace which free peoples cannot tolerate. It is an honored privilege to share this service with you and with our comrades of the Navy and Air Force. You will have my utmost. I shall expect yours."[39]

At 4:15 P.M. on December 26, Korea time, Ridgway's Constellation landed at Taegu. Going down the deplaning ramp, he felt the stab of bitter cold. "It struck to the bone," he wrote.

The Eighth Army chief of staff, Lev Allen, was at the airfield to greet Ridgway. He was a lifelong friend and a "great" soldier. At Ridgway's request Allen had not turned out the usual VIP honor guard. He shook hands, smiled, and led Ridgway to a jeep. The two men drove through the "reek and clamor" of Taegu to Eighth Army's rear, or main, headquarters. There Ridgway found "many an old friend" and talked late into the night.[40]

The combat situation remained unclear. One reason was that Eighth Army had broken contact with the CCF on about December 5 and had not regained it. The "intelligence situation was deplorable," Ridgway said later. No one yet had a good idea of how many CCF troops had been committed to Korea or if the CCF had crossed the 38th Parallel in full force to invade South Korea. On the Eighth Army situation maps, Ridgway remembered, the CCF was depicted merely by a large red "goose egg" with "174,000" scrawled on its center. The true figure was closer to 300,000.[41]

By that time Eighth Army, including Ned Almond's X Corps, then reorganizing and reequipping south of Taegu, was, on paper, a formidable force of 350,000 men. The three American corps were comprised of seven American divisions plus the 187th Airborne RCT. The ROK Army had fielded three corps (I, II, and the new III), consisting of nine divisions. Contributions from other UN nations were the Commonwealth Brigade; the British Brigade; the Turkish Brigade; individual infantry battalions from Canada, Belgium, France, Greece, the Netherlands, the Philippines, and Thailand; and a FAB from New Zealand. In all, Ridgway commanded 163 infantry battalions, the equivalent (in battalions) of eighteen infantry divisions. Eighth Army was thus about twice the size of the great and famous armies in the ETO commanded by Hodges, Patton, Simpson, and Patch and no doubt the largest field army ever commanded by an American general.[42]

The weakness—the great weakness—was that about half the fighting strength of Eighth Army (81 of the 163 battalions) was composed of ROKs. At the beginning of the war the ROK officer corps had been weak and corrupt. In the fighting since, many of the most courageous and competent ROK officers had been killed, incapacitated by wounds, or captured. Too many of the ROK officers remaining were cowards and shirkers or young and inexperienced. Ridgway remembered that the "experience level" of the average ROK division commander was about equivalent to a "young U.S. Army captain."[43]

As one of his key questions to MacArthur had indicated, Ridgway's great concern was that if the going got tougher and Eighth Army was forced to retreat farther, as seemed possible, the ROK Army might defect to the CCF, as many Chinese Nationalists had in 1949. "I served in China as a young captain,"* Ridgway said later, "and knew the Orientals. Some would turn over for 'silver bullets,' as they called them, or for any other reason. Just quit." Accordingly Ridgway judged that his most urgent and immediate task would be to put backbone into the ROK Army, beginning with a personal visit to Syngman Rhee on the following day.[44]

# III

At dawn on December 27 Ridgway, wearing his ETO parachute harness with a grenade taped to one chest strap and a first-aid kit to the other,† was airborne in the Eighth Army command plane. It was an old four-engine B-17 Flying Fortress bomber, on permanent loan from FEAF, now christened *Hi Penny!* Ridgway sat in the bombardier's seat, where he could get a good view of the snowy, frigid terrain. At Ridgway's instructions the pilot flew a roundabout course at 3,000-foot altitude, while Ridgway traced the path of the plane on an Army map. He wrote:

The sight of this terrain was of little comfort to a soldier commanding a mechanized army. The granite peaks rose to 6,000 feet, the ridges were knife-edged, the

---

*With the 15th Infantry, in Tientsin for ten months in 1925 and 1926, as commander of the Headquarters Company.

†The first-aid kit was often mistaken for another hand grenade. The widespread belief that Ridgway wore grenades on both chest harnesses led the GIs to nickname him Old Iron Tits.

slopes steep, and the narrow valleys twisted and turned like snakes. The roads were trails, and the lower hills were covered with scrub oaks and stunted pines, fine cover for a single soldier who knew how to conceal himself. It was guerrilla country, an ideal battleground for the walking Chinese riflemen, but a miserable place for our road-bound troops who moved on wheels.[45]

On this flight, if not before, Ridgway made the decision that Eighth Army should shift from a static defense to a limited offensive-defensive posture. Only by doing so—making contact with the CCF—could Ridgway obtain an accurate picture of its power and deployment. The shift in posture would by no means be a major "offensive." He would begin with aggressive platoon- or company-size patrols and build to battalion size or larger. In the process he would commence killing the CCF.

The *Hi Penny!* landed at Kimpo Airfield at 9:45 A.M. Shrimp Milburn, until then temporarily commanding Eighth Army, met the plane with his dachshund, Ebbo, in tow. He then escorted Ridgway to the Eighth Army advance headquarters in Seoul. There Ridgway began an evaluation of Eighth Army and its senior commanders.[46]

He remembered: "I must say, in all frankness, that the spirit of the Eighth Army as I found it on my arrival there gave me deep concern. There was a definite air of nervousness, of gloomy foreboding, of uncertainty, a spirit of apprehension as to what the future held. There was much 'looking over the shoulder,' as the soldiers say. . . ."[47]

The situation was really much worse than that. Eighth Army was under orders from GHQ that should the CCF attack, it would "defend in successive positions" (Lines B, C, D, etc.), but not many soldiers were willing to do so with any vigor or conviction. Most men were mentally poised for another deep withdrawal and probably evacuation through Pusan—a Dunkirk. As the 8th Cav's commander, Johnny Johnson, said later, "It was a . . . defeated army . . . a disintegrating army. It was an army not in retreat [but] in flight. It was something bordering on disgrace."[48]

The defeatist attitude in Eighth Army, Ridgway believed, stemmed in large part from what he perceived as poor leadership at the corps and divisional levels. There was a "lack of aggressiveness" at those levels, Ridgway later wrote Collins, so much so that he "could not execute my future plans with present leaders." For that reason, "above all else," he wrote, "we had to learn to be ruthless with our general officers." Ridgway believed he had to have "young, vigorous division commanders of greatest potential value for war service." In short, there needed to be a complete housecleaning in the Eighth Army high command.[49]

A "ruthless" cleanout of Eighth Army generals presented several large problems. First, it would unfairly inflict professional ruin and great personal pain on many generals with fine World War II records who had given their utmost under very trying—or worse—conditions during the first six months of the Korean War. Secondly, it might provoke an uproar in the media, possibly leading to an embarrassing congressional investigation by Truman's critics. Thirdly, there could be a counterproductive backlash within the units whose leaders were sacked.

Yet Ridgway was convinced the housecleaning must be carried out. His solution to minimize controversy was to do everything possible to disguise the sackings by various artifices. He would do it gradually over several weeks. The generals fired would be routinely "rotated" or "promoted." All would receive medals and public acclaim.

In meetings that day with his three corps commanders—Milburn, Coulter, and Almond—Ridgway started the housecleaning. The discredited IX Corps commander, John Coulter, and his lackluster chief of staff, Andrew Tychsen, would be among the first to go; IX Corps would get a whole new team. Coulter (awarded a DSM) would be "promoted" to three stars, be named "deputy commander" of Eighth Army, and serve as senior liaison officer to the ROK Army and Syngman Rhee, whom Coulter knew well from his postwar occupation tour in South Korea. Tychsen (awarded a DSM) would return to Japan for other duty, then retirement.[50]

Neither Milburn nor Almond fully met Ridgway's very high professional standards. Milburn, he remembered, was a wonderful man, beloved by his troops, but he lacked the "spark of initiative." Almond was the opposite: recklessly bold, "one of the few commanders I've had I didn't have to push," but a man who was "apt to be pretty rough on other people's sensibilities . . . cutting and intolerant." Notwithstanding these serious shortcomings, Ridgway decided to keep both men on the job. Milburn was an old and devoted friend; Ridgway "would not have relieved him for the world." Almond was still MacArthur's close confidant and chief of staff; to have relieved him would have been tantamount to slapping MacArthur in the face. Ridgway would build the necessary fire under Milburn by camping on his doorstep (i.e., using I Corps as his own personal advanced CP); meanwhile, he would keep a close eye on Almond, "unless maybe in his boldness he would have jeopardized his command or executed a very risky operation. . . ."[51]

Theretofore Ned Almond had operated entirely independently of Eighth Army and had taken full advantage of his other "hat" as MacArthur's chief of staff. Acting in the latter capacity from Korea by telex and telephone, Almond had assured that X Corps got priority and favored treatment. "It was a ridiculous situation," Almond's deputy chief of staff and confidant, Bill McCaffrey, conceded. "We used to send requisitions for mittens and that kind of stuff directly to GHQ, Tokyo. We got prompt service. GHQ knew that if they disapproved a request, someday they might have to face Almond back in Tokyo."[52]

Ridgway did not have the authority formally to terminate Almond's status as MacArthur's chief of staff, but he made it clear to Almond that he and X Corps would no longer enjoy a favored status in Eighth Army. McCaffrey went on: "I didn't sit in on this critical first meeting of Ridgway and Almond. But Ridgway was smart enough and sure enough of himself and his position that he wouldn't permit that ridiculous situation to go on. He was going to operate Eighth Army as a unified army. Almond came out of that meeting a very sober guy. My opinion is that Ridgway told him how things were going to go in Eighth Army from now on. Almond got the point, and that's how it went. There wasn't any question as to who was the army commander. Ridgway straightened out that ridiculous situation that first day. Almond was a fighter, and Ridgway respected a fighter. Almond had all kinds of courage and drive and energy. What he needed was a good army commander to point him in the right direction. Ridgway was that fellow."

To this point no provisions had been made for possible replacement corps commanders who might be lost in combat. Believing several generals ought to be placed on standby for that purpose, Ridgway suggested four names, all close and good friends: Joe Swing, then commandant of the Army War College; Bryant E. Moore, superintendent of West Point; Edward H. ("Ted") Brooks, the Department of the Army's G-1; and John W. ("Iron Mike") O'Daniel, serving as an inspector in the Army's training command.[53]

These four men had one achievement in common: All had been (like Ridgway) outstandingly aggressive and smart commanders of famous divisions in World War II. Three were "ETO generals": Moore, who commanded the 8th Infantry Division (for a time, assigned to Ridgway's XVIII Airborne Corps); Brooks, who commanded the 2d ("Hell on Wheels") Armored Division (and later VI Corps); and O'Daniel, who commanded the 3d Infantry Division after Lucian Truscott. (Joe Swing had commanded the 11th Airborne Division in the Pacific.) Two of the four were West Pointers: Swing (1915) and Moore (1917).[54]*

Joe Swing and Bryant Moore headed Ridgway's list. Ridgway made the mistake of asking Swing off the record and out of channels if he would consider coming to Eighth Army. Swing was so eager to go that he imprudently telephoned the Pentagon to discuss his replacement at the War College. When Army Vice Chief of Staff Ham Haislip, who had not been consulted, heard what was going on, he slapped Ridgway on the wrist for getting out of channels

---

*Significantly Ridgway's list did not include his World War II protégé Jim Gavin, who had volunteered to come to Korea under Ridgway. During the war the Ridgway coterie had formed the opinion that Gavin was not sufficiently grateful for the unstinting support and promotions Ridgway had given him and that he was an egocentric publicity hound, intent on displacing Ridgway as "Mr. Paratrooper." Gavin went to Europe to command VII Corps in the embryonic NATO standing force.[55]

and cut Swing from the list. Haislip then approved Ridgway's request for Moore and O'Daniel (but not Brooks). Moore would replace Coulter; O'Daniel would come to Korea in due course to replace Shrimp Milburn, after Milburn had completed one full year's duty in Korea.[56]

Contrary to World War II custom, the corps commanders in Eighth Army did not at that time have deputy commanders. Since Ridgway expected his corps commanders to follow his example and get out of their CPs and up to the frontline regimental or battalion CPs—wherever the action was hottest—he believed deputy corps commanders would be necessary to run the corps headquarters or to substitute at the front for the commanders. Accordingly, he asked Collins and Haislip to send him three men to fill those slots. He got three West Pointers, two of them with extensive combat experience.*

\* \* \*

Ridgway had spared his devoted friend Shrimp Milburn, but he evidently believed the I Corps staff required shock therapy to restore the "spark of initiative." After sitting through a briefing by I Corps G-3 John R. Jeter, who described the plans for "defending in successive positions" (Lines B, C, D, etc.) as proscribed by GHQ and the Eighth Army, Ridgway—the story goes—said, "But what are your attack plans?"

Flustered, Jeter, who had no "attack" plans, replied, "Sir, we are withdrawing." In response—the story goes—Ridgway snapped, "Colonel, you are relieved."[58]

That story spread like wildfire through Eighth Army. In the telling, the name of Eighth Army G-3 John Dabney was often and incorrectly substituted for that of John Jeter. Nor was the story about Jeter strictly correct: Ridgway did not relieve Jeter on the spot; he went through channels, with Shrimp Milburn serving as the executioner. But the thrust was true: Jeter had no attack plans, meaning he was "defeatist." Therefore, Jeter was sacked.[59]

The incident caused an uproar and considerable resentment within the I Corps staff. Jeter, forty-six, who came from an old South Carolina military family (he and two brothers, graduates of the Citadel, had made the Army a career; Jeter's son was preparing to enter West Point) and who had commanded three different regiments in hard ETO combat from Normandy to Germany, was very popular. In presenting the withdrawal lines to Ridgway,

---

*Thomas L. Harrold (1925), forty-eight, a tanker in the 9th Armored Division in the ETO (Bulge; Remagen Bridge), went to I Corps; William L. Mitchell (1920), fifty-three, went to IX Corps; and Laurence K. Ladue (1924), forty-seven, G-3 of Mark Clark's Fifth Army and chief of staff of IV Corps in Italy (where Almond had fought his 92d Division), went to X Corps. Mitchell (then in GHQ, Tokyo) and Ladue (then a JCS planner) had been temporary brigadier generals in World War II but reverted to colonels in the postwar years. On their arrival in Korea, Ridgway recommended both for repromotion to brigadier; Harrold, then commander of the Armored Center and School, was already a brigadier general.[57]

the corps staff believed, Jeter was merely complying with instructions from GHQ, Eighth Army, and his boss, Shrimp Milburn. Furthermore, many were dismayed at the way Milburn had rolled over and played dead.[60]

\* \* \*

In company with Ambassador Muccio, Ridgway proceeded with the most urgent business of that first day: a call on President Syngman Rhee. By that time Ridgway had concluded that the best way to prevent a wholesale defection in the ROK Army was to assure the Rhee government that no matter how rough the going got, Eighth Army would not suddenly pull out of Korea and leave the ROKs to cope with the Chinese alone. If the CCF were victorious and forced the UN from South Korea, Ridgway would take the ROK government, the ROK Army, and all dependents with him.[61]

Later Ridgway gave that assurance to the ROK government in writing: "First, there is here but one ultimate objective—freedom for your people. To attain that objective, there is only one force—our combined Allied Army. Second, there is but one single common destiny for this combined Allied Army. It will fight together and stay together whatever the future holds."[62]

In his first meeting with Rhee, however, Ridgway was less eloquent. He remembered:

[Rhee] greeted me rather impassively but I extended my hand at once and said, right from the heart, for I had no time to sort over ceremonial phrases: "I'm glad to see you, Mr. President, glad to be here, and I mean to stay." That was the one word the old gentleman seemed to have been awaiting. His face broke into a smile as warm as the Eastern Sun, his eyes grew moist and he took my extended hand in both of his. He led me then to meet his charming wife and we shared a cup of cordial tea, while I endeavored as best I could to impress him with our determination not to be driven from the peninsula, and to go on the offensive again as soon as we could marshal our forces.[63]

Ridgway did not on this occasion criticize the ROK officer corps or attempt to impress upon Rhee the urgent need for a complete command housecleaning. That would come later, in forceful language, unsuitable for the delicate ears of an Oriental first lady. He did, however, raise the possibility of further limited withdrawals and asked Rhee to provide 30,000 Korean laborers to help build defensive positions. Ridgway remembered: "He said, 'You'll have them tomorrow.' I said: 'Well, I don't think I can provide the tools—but turn them out anyway.' The next morning 30,000 men began digging defensive positions."[64]

\* \* \*

By late afternoon that first day Ridgway had acquired a sense of the battlefield. He "felt in his bones," he recalled, that the CCF was poised for a major offensive and that it would come within a few days, probably on New Year's Eve. His plan was to do everything possible to absorb and repel that blow and, when, as customary, the CCF ran out of food and ammo and broke contact, to launch limited counterattacks.[65]

He expected that the CCF would mount its major effort in the western sector with the aim of recapturing Seoul. That attack, like the NKPA attack the previous June, would most likely be two-pronged: down the main Pyong-yang–Seoul highway through Munsan and down the Uijongbu Corridor. To absorb and stop the attack and prevent the capture of Seoul, Milburn's I Corps and Coulter's IX Corps would resist to the greatest extent possible at Line B on the Imjin River—but without taking "heavy" casualties—then be prepared to fall back, on Ridgway's orders, to a Seoul "bridgehead," in the defensive positions which the Korean laborers were preparing. To prevent CCF artillery fire from falling into Seoul and on the Han River bridges, the defensive perimeter would be large, extending northward as far as Uijongbu.[66]

Perhaps because he was the son of an artilleryman, infantryman Ridgway had an unusual appreciation for the power and efficiency of artillery. He arrived in Korea convinced that properly placed and coordinated artillery fire could do much to offset the CCF advantage in manpower. He was thus dismayed to discover that Eighth Army was operating with an acute shortage of artillery. At army level there was but one artillery battalion (the 17th FAB with its eight-inch howitzers). At corps level there were only three battalions (the 92d, 96th, and 999th FABs with self-propelled or tractor-pulled 155s), and the 999th was attached to the 3d Division. On paper the seven American divisions had the normal complement of four artillery battalions, but five of these battalions had been mauled at Kunu and the Chosin Reservoir recently, and were filled with green replacements.[67]*

No one then in Eighth Army could be blamed for this appalling situation. It was due in part to Truman's postwar military economy program; in part to the earlier decisions to fight in Korea with limited forces; in part to the repeated, disgraceful loss of artillery to the enemy; in part to the near impossi-bility of rapidly organizing, manning, and training American artillery units

---

*The total loss of artillery pieces in Korea to that time had been scandalous. In the ROK Army: 95 pieces, of which 90 were M-3 105-mm howitzers and the other 5, 75-mm "pack" howitzers. The American Army forces had lost 143 standard pieces, of which 115 were 105-mm howitzers, 27 were 155-mm howitzers, and one was an eight-inch howitzer. (Of these, 36 pieces had been lost by the 24th Division in July 1950; 11 pieces by the 25th Division in August 1950; 21 pieces by the 1st Cav Division at Unsan and the Chongchon River in November 1950; 62 pieces by the 2d Division, plus the eight-inch howitzer in November 1950; 12 pieces by the 7th Division in Task Force MacLean-Faith in December 1950.) Total ROK Army and American Army losses: 238 pieces, enough to equip thirteen regular artillery battalions with the normal complement of eighteen howitzers.

from scratch. However, Ridgway summoned the senior artillery commanders in Eighth Army* and told them in no uncertain terms that he wanted immediate and dramatic improvement in the employment of the available artillery. And as part of the divisional housecleaning he recommended the replacement of several division artillery commanders.

Earlier, in his capacity as Army "general manager," Ridgway had ordered ten recently activated National Guard and Army Reserve artillery battalions to prepare for duty in the Far East. The plan had been that these green battalions would first go to Japan for further intensive training and to lend a "military presence." Believing he must have as many of these ten battalions as soon as possible, Ridgway cabled Joe Collins requesting that their destination be changed from Japan to South Korea and that "all necessary action" be taken to "speed" and "advance" the arrival date.[69]†

Lacking adequate artillery, Ridgway called on FEAF and the Navy to support Eighth Army's defense of Seoul with "maximum" close air support. The response from FEAF was disappointing. The FEAF airmen really had little heart for close air support missions. They still were not good at it; they insisted they could better support the Eighth Army ground forces by "interdiction" raids on CCF supply facilities and lines of communication deeper in enemy territory.‡ Moreover, at this time FEAF morale was also near rock bottom. Its leaders in Korea were preoccupied with plans to abandon the Kimpo and Suwon airfield complexes and withdraw to Taegu, Pusan, and Japan.[71]

The Navy was more helpful. It provided a carrier task force *(Sicily, Badoeng Strait)* with two Marine Corps close air support squadrons, plus several cruisers and destroyers, then a squadron of new Marine Corps jets (under FEAF control) based near Pusan. These aircraft and ships not only provided close air support and naval bombardment directly to Eighth Army but also patrolled the Yellow Sea to thwart a possible CCF amphibious encircling attack utilizing junks or other small craft.[72]

---

* These were the Eighth Army artillery commander, West Pointer (1919) John J. Burns, fifty-two; James F. Brittingham, fifty-six, of I Corps; West Pointer (1926) Thomas E. de Shazo, fifty-one, of IX Corps; and West Pointer (1926) William P. Ennis, Jr., forty-six, of X Corps.[68]

† As a result, five standard 155-mm artillery battalions (the 196th, 204th, 936th, 937th, and 955th) were to arrive in Korea in January. The other five, consisting of one battalion with eight-inch howitzers (the 780th) and four with self-propelled 105-mm howitzers (the 176th, 213th, 987th, and 300th) were to arrive later.

‡ The 8th Cav's Johnny Johnson damned FEAF close air support with these words: "If you want it, you can't get it. If you can get it, it can't find you. If it can find you, it can't identify the target. If it can identify the target, it can't hit it. But if it does hit the target, it doesn't do a great deal of damage anyway."[70]

* * *

Having laid out these plans for the defense of a Seoul bridgehead, Ridgway next focused his attention on the dangerous situation in the center of the transpeninsular line, held by the ROKs. By that time the enemy mounting pressure in that sector had been identified as the NKPA I, II, and V corps, consisting, it was estimated, of about 65,000 troops. The ROK 8th Division had held off the initial assaults, but the NKPA had sideslipped east into the zone held by the newly fielded, poorly trained and led ROK 9th Division, had pushed it back about seven miles, and were then closing on Hongchon.[73]

Earlier Johnnie Walker had ordered Bob McClure's hastily reorganizing 2d Division to backstop the ROKs in this sector. Paul Freeman's 23d Infantry (with the French Battalion) and George Peploe's 38th (with the Dutch Battalion) had deployed toward Wonju, and Ed Messinger's 9th Infantry was on the way. This was deemed to be sufficient backup to delay seriously or even to stop the NKPA, but what if the NKPA were merely a screening force for a major CCF attack down the center of the peninsula aimed at outflanking Eighth Army at Seoul (in effect, repeating the CCF strategy at the Chongchon River)?

Believing this to be more a probability than a possibility, Ridgway ordered Almond to move the X Corps headquarters to Wonju at once to take charge of and reinforce the central sector. Wonju, a road hub, was the key to the "central front," Ridgway believed, "second only to Seoul" in tactical importance. Almond would take command of McClure's 2d Division and rush Dave Barr's 7th Division forward to help. As further backup on the right flank, Ridgway shifted the 1st Cav Division to the northeast and east of Seoul under Coulter's IX Corps control, to backstop the adjacent ROK.[74]

In response, the same night, December 27, Almond flew directly to the Eighth Army rear headquarters in Taegu, to get things rolling. He found the staff "all pessimistic," once again talking about moving the Eighth Army headquarters from Taegu to Pusan and a possible Dunkirk. Almond astonished one and all with the news that X Corps (barely one week out of Hungnam) was going forward to meet the enemy. He remembered that he said to the staffers: "General Ridgway told me he planned to fight cohesively and to kill as many CCF as possible. That's what I'm going to do, and tomorrow I shall be back at my own headquarters, moving my divisions to our sector in the central part of the front."[75]

These orders committed to action the six Army divisions in Korea, but not the 1st Marine Division, which was remanning and reequipping in Masan, more or less expecting to serve as rear guard when Eighth Army withdrew through all its defensive lines and evacuated South Korea at Pusan. Inasmuch as Ridgway had no intention of evacuating South Korea, he wanted the Marines committed into the Eighth Army line at once. Accordingly, he summoned O. P. Smith to a meeting at Almond's headquarters at Kyongju.[76]

Ridgway was much impressed by the Marine general. He remembered: "Smith was top flight, a splendid commander. Good tactical judgment and a gentleman. He was very calm and had extreme consideration for his troops. If it hadn't been for his moral courage and doing some of the things he did, which were not in full accord with the instructions he had received [from Almond] he'd have lost a great part of that division."[77]

The Marines were likewise impressed with Ridgway. They had arrived at Kyongju with a set of Eighth Army withdrawal plans. Ridgway told them to "throw those maps away." Smith recalled: "He gave us a talk expressing his complete confidence regarding the outcome in Korea. He had no orders regarding evacuation and hoped to be able to defend on some line and launch limited counterattacks. He stressed the necessity for reconnaissance and maintaining contact. . . . He wanted less looking backwards. . . ." Smith's G-3, Alpha L. Bowser, Jr., who accompanied Smith to the conference, remembered that Ridgway "brought a new fresh attitude, a new fresh breath of life to the whole Eighth Army."[78]

Ridgway was worried about the extreme east flank of the transpeninsular line, held only by the ROK 3d and Capital divisions. It was possible that the CCF that had forced X Corps from Hamhung and Wonsan might be driving south. If it overran the ROKs, it could take Yongdok and Pohang, threaten Taegu via the "back door," and possibly push all the way down the east coast to Pusan. Ridgway thought the Marine division, under command of Almond's X Corps, should move forward to Pohang to backstop the ROKs. From that position the Marines could also backstop X Corps at Wonju, should the NKPA break through and angle south through Andong to the coast.[79]

Although Smith and Bowser were impressed by this aggressive talk, neither was overjoyed by the proposed mission. The Marine division, recently fleshed out with 1,650 replacements, was still short about 4,000 men in the infantry and artillery regiments. The new men required unit training. The division was short of weapons (seventeen 105- and 155-mm howitzers, 2,000 carbines, etc.), armor (23 tanks), transport (232 trucks), radios (285), and even sleeping bags (3,500). Unless the division was absolutely needed, Smith believed it should be allowed at least another two weeks to shake down and reequip.[80]

There was another problem. By that time Smith had so little confidence in Ned Almond and his staff that he was determined that the Marine division would never again serve under X Corps. Somehow, without saying so directly to Ridgway, Smith conveyed his feelings about Almond, and although it greatly complicated his planning, Ridgway sympathized and assured Smith that (as Bowser remembered it) "as long as he, General Ridgway, commanded the Eighth Army, the 1st Marine Division would never again be placed under command of the X Corps."[81]

The upshot was that Ridgway made the decision to leave the Marine division in Masan, in Eighth Army reserve, for the time being. It would be prepared to move—in emergency, on his orders only—to reinforce the central or eastern fronts, as the situation might require. Meanwhile, Ridgway began formulating longer-range plans to bring the Marine division forward on the western front, under command of IX Corps.

I V

Having laid out his plan to meet the expected CCF offensive, Ridgway believed that in the several days remaining before it burst upon him, he should devote his entire energies to putting backbone into Eighth Army. "Before Eighth Army could return to the offensive," he wrote, "it needed to have its fighting spirit restored, to have pride in itself, to feel confidence in its leadership, and have faith in its mission." He would inspect every major tactical unit on the front, excepting the ROK divisions on the extreme right flank. He would show himself to his men, talk aggressively, and, at the same time, take the measure of the senior commanders.[82]

Two smart young officers, who knew Eighth Army, its commanders, and the terrain well, assisted Ridgway in laying out the tour. One was a combat-experienced paratrooper from the Eighth Army G-3 section, Paul F. Smith, thirty-five, who had come to Korea with Johnnie Walker. The other was Johnnie Walker's personal pilot, Mike Lynch, whom Ridgway had retained. Smith and Lynch constituted the initial cadre of Ridgway's personal or tactical staff, which would remain small—and independent of the large "defeatist" Eighth Army staff in Taegu.[83]

Ridgway began his tour in I Corps, which was holding the left flank of Eighth Army at the Imjin River near Musan. The Turkish Brigade manned the extreme left, Bill Kean's 25th Division the center, and the ROK 1st Division the extreme right. The British Brigade was in reserve.

Ridgway conducted this first leg of the inspection in an open jeep so that the men could see the Old Man "up there, in snow and the sleet and the mud, sharing the same cold, miserable existence they had to endure." Since he as yet had no overcoat, long underwear, or other cold-weather gear and the jeep had no heater, he "damn near froze." He was not pleased by the men he encountered on the road. They had "lost confidence." Ridgway could "read it in their eyes, in their walk."[84]

He remembered:

The first MP I came upon as my jeep toured the forward zones, immediately impressed on me the sharp contrast between this army and those I had known in other actions in Europe. He was correct in posture and in gesture—correct in every way except in spirit. That extra snap to the salute, that quick aggressive tone and gesture, that confident grin that had seemed to me the marks of the battle-seasoned American GI, all were missing. The men I met along the road, those I stopped to talk to and solicit gripes from—they too all conveyed to me a conviction that this was a bewildered army, not sure of itself or its leaders, not sure what they were doing there, wondering when they would hear the whistle of that homebound transport. . . . Even their gripes had to be dragged out of them and information was provided glumly, without the alertness of men whose spirits are high.[85]

Before the start of his tour Ridgway had decided that he must sack a host of frontline generals: four of the six division commanders, several of the ADCs and artillery commanders. Among the division commanders, the two exceptions were Bob McClure, who had only recently replaced the luckless Dutch Keiser in the 2d Division, and Shorty Soule, whose appointment to command the 3d Division Joe Swing and Ridgway had influenced and to whom Almond had awarded a DSC for his performance at Wonsan and Hungnam. To disguise and mute this housecleaning, Ridgway announced a "rotation policy": division commanders and other generals who had completed six months' continuous duty in Korea would go home. They were to receive glowing fitness reports, medals, and seemingly important new assignments in the States in which they could impart their combat experience in Korea to troops in training.[86]

Under this proposed policy the four division commanders were to be relieved more or less in this sequence: Church (first to arrive in Korea), Kean (second to arrive), Gay (third to arrive), and Barr (last to arrive). However, Ned Almond upset that schedule. Insisting that Dave Barr was not competent to command the 7th Division, Almond demanded that Barr be among the first to be sacked, even though Barr had been in Korea fewer than four months. Accordingly, Ridgway revised the order of relief to make Barr the first and Kean the last.

As he traveled from one division CP to the next, Ridgway carried out the delicate job of informing the senior commanders of the new "rotation policy." No matter how tactfully and softly he delivered the word, it came as a tough blow. Many of these men were old and close friends, notably the 25th Division commander, Bill Kean, whom Ridgway visited first.

Ridgway was probably glad for an excuse to delay replacing Kean. He ran a good division. Its 27th and 35th regiments had never suffered a major setback. The division staff was sharp; the highly decorated, able regimental commanders were topflight. Although he was not in good health, the new ADC (from the 2d Division), Sladen Bradley, impressed Ridgway favorably. He was a "fighter," a possible replacement for Kean (as Walker had planned) when the time came.

The three regimental commanders in the 25th Division were well known to Ridgway from earlier battlefields. Mike Michaelis (27th Infantry) had been a regimental commander and chief of staff of the 101st Airborne division in Ridgway's XVIII Airborne Corps. John Corley (24th Infantry) and Gerry Kelleher (35th Infantry) had commanded battalions in the 1st Infantry Division, which had fought in Sicily with Ridgway's 82d Airborne Division. Corley was still commanding a battalion in the 1st Division when it was assigned, temporarily, to Ridgway's XVIII Airborne Corps to mount a counteroffensive after the Bulge. Much pleased to find these three strong regimental commanders in place, Ridgway decided to make no immediate changes, but it occurred to him that notwithstanding his youth (thirty-eight), Michaelis might be an ideal ADC for the division.*

The big problem in the 25th Division—the same old problem—was the black 24th Regiment. Notwithstanding Corley's splendidly aggressive leadership, and that of his exec, Paul Roberts, Bill Kean still did not have confidence in the outfit, and he was concerned about Corley, who was believed to have ulcers and appeared to be driving himself toward an early grave. Kean recommended to Ridgway, as he had earlier to Walker, that the 24th be deactivated and replaced by a "conventional" regiment and that its men be integrated into other combat units. Ridgway favored this suggestion and asked that later, when the situation had stabilized, Kean send him a report officially proposing these radical and politically sensitive recommendations.[87]

\* \* \*

When he visited the 24th Division CP, Ridgway reaffirmed his decision to replace the frail, sickly fifty-eight-year-old John Church as quickly as possible. In the understated words of the ADC, Gar Davidson, "Church was quite the opposite of a Ridgway man." Ridgway decided that his protégé Babe Bryan, en route to Korea from his job as chief of staff of the Caribbean Command, was the man to replace Church.[88]

Nor was Ridgway satisfied to see his devoted old friend Gar Davidson holding down the ADC job. He thought that Davidson's well-known engineering talents, desperately needed by Eighth Army, were going to waste in an infantry assignment. He therefore temporarily detached Davidson and reassigned him to oversee construction of the Eighth Army defensive lines (C, D, E, etc.). He was to give particular emphasis to the "final" line above Pusan, which would become the second, but far stronger and more famous, "Davidson Line."[89]

Inasmuch as Babe Bryan had not before led troops in combat, Ridgway would give him an experienced ADC as backup. Ridgway chose Bryan's West

---

*In World War II, Ridgway had turned a number of heads when he promoted Jim Gavin, then but age thirty-six, to brigadier general and ADC of the 82d Airborne Division.

Point (1922) classmate, Numa A. Watson, fifty-one, who was then attached to X Corps as a spare brigadier general. Watson was a "fighter," who had commanded the 13th Infantry Regiment in Bryant Moore's 8th Infantry Division in the ETO when the division was attached to Ridgway's XVIII Airborne Corps during the Ruhr Pocket campaign. Under Watson's able—and very aggressive—leadership, the 13th Infantry had spearheaded the XVIII Airborne Corps drive to the Ruhr River, earning Ridgway's deepest gratitude—and, in the postwar years, a star for Watson.[90]

The regimental commands in the 24th Division raised some problems as well. Young Johnny Throckmorton (5th Infantry) was outstanding, on a par with or superior to Michaelis, Corley, and Kelleher. But Ridgway decided that it was time to replace Ned Moore (19th Infantry) and Dick Stephens (21st Infantry). Both had been in almost continuous hard combat since the previous July, Stephens longer than any other regimental commander in Korea. Both were mentally and physically exhausted, and Moore was ill with hepatitis. Ridgway approved their recommendations that deserving senior battalion commanders within the regiments (both non–West Pointers) be promoted to full colonel and replace them: Ollie Kinney in the 19th; Gines Perez in the 21st. Stephens and Moore were to go on to other assignments, and later both rose to the rank of major general.[91]*

At the 1st Cav Division Ridgway likewise reaffirmed his decision that Hap Gay should be relieved of command. Originally Ridgway had planned for Babe Bryan to relieve Gay, but since the command crisis at the 24th Division was the more urgent, he postponed the relief of Gay to follow that of Barr and Church. Happily he found a suitable replacement for Gay within the 1st Cav staff: the tough-minded artillery chief, Charlie Palmer, who could gradually take over from Gay without a public clamor.

Charlie Palmer was a "Ridgway man" in every sense of the phrase. Ridgway had known Palmer since his early days at West Point. As Ted Brooks's chief of staff in the 2d Armored Division, Palmer had fought close by Ridgway in Normandy. Inasmuch as the 1st Cav ADC, Frank Allen, was seven years senior to Palmer and not, in Ridgway's opinion, a qualified candidate for divisional command, Ridgway decided to send him home as well. He would be replaced by West Pointer (1923) Elwyn D. Post, fifty-one, then commanding an administrative district in Japan.[92]

At the regimental command level in the 1st Cav, Ridgway found Marcel Crombez (5th Cav), Billy Harris (7th Cav), and Johnny Johnson (8th Cav). Although Crombez at fifty was too old and too senior for regimental command (older by two years and merely one year junior by date of rank to Charlie

---

* In 1955 Stephens was assigned to be chief of the Army's military history division and, as such, significantly influenced the Army's official history of the first six months of the Korean War.

Palmer) and not popular with his men, Ridgway liked his tough fighting stance and left him in command. He questioned having artilleryman Harris in command of the 7th Cav, but artilleryman Palmer assured Ridgway that Harris was outstanding—the most aggressive regimental commander in the division. Notwithstanding Johnny Johnson's able leadership, the 8th Cav, decimated at Unsan and skittish ever since, remained a problem. Ridgway decided he would promote Johnson to G-3 of I Corps (replacing John Jeter) and give the 8th Cav to the relentlessly aggressive 1/7 commander, Peter Clainos. That would also solve the awkward rank problem in the 7th Cav which had arisen when classmates Clainos and Harris were simultaneously promoted to full colonel.[93]

\* \* \*

Last on Ridgway's list of visits was the 7th Division, fresh from its mauling in northeast Korea. Responding to Ned Almond's request that Dave Barr be sacked immediately, Ridgway did so, replacing him with West Pointer Claude B. ("Buddy") Ferenbaugh, originally scheduled to replace Bill Kean in the 25th Division. Ferenbaugh, fifty-one, was a restless "giant." Like Bill Kean, he had been commissioned with the bobtailed class of November 1918, then returned to West Point as an officer to be graduated in 1919. A War College graduate (1940), Ferenbaugh had been G-3 of Fredendall's II Corps in the North Africa landings in November 1942. Thereafter he returned to the Pentagon as a war planner, where he served until January 1944, when—on Eisenhower's strong personal recommendation—he was assigned troop duty for the Normandy invasion: ADC of the 83d Infantry Division, which Shrimp Milburn and his chief of staff, Van Brunt, had trained before going to XXI Corps.[94]

After a slow start in Normandy the 83d, commanded by Robert C. Macon, had become one of the finest and most mobile infantry divisions in the ETO, and Ferenbaugh had been a tireless, tough, and aggressive "fighter." Milburn was naturally pleased to see that the division he had organized and trained had performed so well and gave Ferenbaugh a large share of the credit. In the postwar years Army Chiefs of Staff Eisenhower, Bradley, and Collins had brought Ferenbaugh along with important and prestigious jobs: commanding general of the Military District of Washington, D.C.; chief of staff of the 1948 atomic bomb tests, Sandstone; and (in October 1950) command of the 5th Armored Division. His selection by Collins for duty in Korea was, of course, roundly approved by both Milburn and Ridgway.[95]\*

Awarded a DSM, Dave Barr returned to the States to become comman-

---

\*These changes or planned changes would reduce the average of the six Army division commanders in Korea to 50.5 years, with Bob McClure at 54 the oldest.

ding general of the Armored School at Fort Knox. By coincidence, his former aide, Charles Davis, who was at Koto in the 2/31 and who had been medically evacuated (for frostbitten feet), flew back in the same plane with Barr. Believing that Barr should never have commanded a division in combat, Davis felt pity for him. The two men spoke in hushed tones about the terrible loss of officers and men of the 7th Division at Chosin and about Ned Almond's utter incompetence as a corps commander. Davis remembered that several months after returning to the States, Barr suffered a heart attack that forced his retirement from the Army, after which he lived for many more years, selling real estate in Washington, D.C.[96]

No doubt prodded by Ned Almond, Ferenbaugh carried out a drastic housecleaning of the 7th Division staff. Out went the ADC, Hank Hodes, who had clashed repeatedly and violently with Almond on tactics and other matters. Aware that Hodes had virtually commanded the 7th Division for Dave Barr and that he was a "fighter," Ridgway promoted Hodes to two stars and brought him to Eighth Army as a deputy to Lev Allen, thereby putting Hodes on the road to four stars. Ferenbaugh also relieved the 7th Division chief of staff, Louis T. Heath, and the G-2, Irwin A. Edwards (a smart young paratrooper who had won a DSC in the ETO), and "demoted" the G-3, Bill Paddock, to G-2. Herb Powell, commanding the 17th Infantry, who was an old associate of Ferenbaugh's, was named the new chief of staff. Another old associate of Ferenbaugh's, Mel Huston, who had brought the black 3/15 to Wonsan only to be sacked and who had been transferred to the X Corps G-2 section, was named G-3.[97]*

* * *

Ridgway had decided that in due course four of the six division artillery commanders should be replaced, plus, of course, Charlie Palmer in the 1st Cav. Those to be "rotated" were: Loyal Haynes (2d), Homer Kiefer (7th), Hank Meyer (24th), and Bittman Barth (25th). Only West Pointer (1916) Roland P. Shugg, fifty-seven, in Soule's 3d Division, would be retained. West Pointer (1918) John H. Hinds, fifty-two, came to Korea to replace Charlie Palmer in the 1st Cav, but owing to the shortage of qualified senior artillery commanders who were willing to come to Korea and to other factors, including intransigence and politics in the field artillery branch, the replacements of the other artillery commanders would proceed more slowly or be postponed indefinitely.[98]

---

*Heath went to the 1st Cav Division as chief of staff, replacing Ernest Holmes, who had been injured in a jeep accident. Paratrooper Irwin Edwards went to Ridgway's personal or tactical staff.

\* \* \*

In his meetings with the senior commanders in Eighth Army, Ridgway laid down some specific—and elementary—oral instructions. Among them:[99]

• All division commanders were to get out of their CPs and spend much more time on the front lines at battalion level (or lower) in order to "get to know" their subordinate commanders and the terrain and situation intimately. It was a commander's business to know "what lay in front of him, what kind of vegetation was there for cover, how the roads and streams ran, whether a tank could operate there or not." Corps and division staff officers would do likewise and henceforth prepare more precise firsthand and "honest" reports with "hard facts" and devoid of "hearsay or speculation." When a message arrived at a CP requiring action, the staff officer was not to "smoke a cigarette and think it over or maybe take a walk," but to "reach for the telephone" or his "hat and coat" and immediately "get going on the action called for."

• Selected units would commence strong and aggressive reconnaissance and patrol actions to reestablish contact with the CCF and keep it with "a bulldog grip." When the opportunity arose, units would attack for the purpose of disrupting CCF assemblies for attacks. Units would "get off the road," "take high ground," and "button up securely at night." If the CCF succeeded in making nighttime penetrations, commanders were "promptly and definitely [to] eliminate" them with armor and infantry teams after daylight, leaving no enclaves of enemy in the rear.

• All commanders would immediately start intensive training in night fighting and marches. Men reared in rural areas should be designated to teach those from urban areas how to navigate over terrain without light. All men would be taught that when they fired rifles at night, their aiming sights were of "little use" because they caused the riflemen to fire "three to five feet over the target."

• All engaged units would make greater use of available firepower. Infantry units were not using more than one-third of their available firepower. "It was back on the column on the road or somewhere—but unused." Ridgway did not want "to hear any commander asking for help until he could show me he was using every weapon he had—every rifle, every machine gun, every howitzer, A/A gun and tank."

• All commanders would make unusual and immediate efforts to provide the men in their units with the following: cold-weather clothing; at least two hot meals a day, three if practicable; small potbelly stoves and warming tents; writing paper. When sufficient fur caps were available, the cold, drafty steel helmets were to be stored until springtime.

- Where feasible, commanders would follow Ridgway's example and visit the wounded and nonbattle casualties in hospitals in an effort to instill a desire in the men to return to their original units. "A man already trained is worth several times a raw replacement." Commanders should enlist doctors and nurses in this drive.
- Commanders should decrease the "seemingly wholesale issue" of medals. That practice, rampant throughout Eighth Army, demeaned and trivialized the decorations. Where appropriate, there should be a greater emphasis on awarding the Medal of Honor to the living rather than the dead.
- Commanders would employ "foreign units" to provide "better utilization" of their specific talents. For example, use the British on defense rather than offense; the Turks on offense rather than defense.
- No one, under any circumstances, was to abandon "precious equipment." Any equipment, Ridgway stressed, had to "come from nine thousand miles away." It was expensive. He warned that any man who "lost or threw away or needlessly damaged any piece of equipment or property was going to be court martialed."

At the conclusion of this tour Ridgway returned to the Eighth Army advance CP in Seoul to prepare himself mentally for the CCF offensive, which he still expected on New Year's Eve. He could not be certain that this initial "exhortation" had made the intended dramatic impact. His guide, Paul Smith, however, believed it had. "The spirit generated during each of these meetings," Smith wrote, "was so evident and so strong it was palpable." From Tokyo came a personal message from MacArthur: "Cannot tell you how delighted I am at the energy and effectiveness with which you have taken hold."[100]

## V

Still believing that the world was poised on the brink of disaster—that global war could erupt at any hour—Washington planners sought new policies to meet this probability and at the same time to deal with the "entirely new war" in Korea.

The planners steadfastly clung to the view that the defense of Western Europe should receive first priority. President Truman therefore recalled Dwight Eisenhower to active duty on December 19 to become supreme allied commander in Europe (SACEUR). Eisenhower's first mission was, in effect, to coax the NATO nations toward full military mobilization. The grandiose war plan was to defend against a Soviet invasion at the Rhine River with a NATO ground force of forty divisions. The United States would contribute four additional divisions to Europe (for a total of six) to add muscle to the

NATO army and encourage other nations to follow its example. American air and naval forces would be increased proportionately.[101]

As in World War II, the Far East would receive secondary priority. America would, in essence, conduct a strategic defense of the "offshore" perimeter, until Western Europe was absolutely secure. It would hold Japan, Okinawa, and the Philippines, with first priority going to Japan and second to Okinawa, which had become the key Far East base for the bombers of the Strategic Air Command. As part of this Far East strategy, America would continue to "neutralize" Formosa—i.e., prevent a Red Chinese takeover, which would pose an air threat to Okinawa and the Philippines.

Viewed from this lofty strategic prospective, the war in Korea remained a terrible inconvenience or worse. It had diverted massive American military resources from the key strategic areas of Western Europe and Japan. It had sucked in seven American divisions, plus ancillary forces, and hundreds of American aircraft and ships. It had cost nearly 60,000 American casualties and uncounted billions of dollars.

From a strategic point of view, the American military commitment to Korea made no sense whatsoever. Yet America could not in all conscience simply pull out. It had made a moral commitment to the South Koreans, the United Nations, and the free world. An American "failure" in Korea could psychologically undermine the forces of anticommunism worldwide.

The Washington objective thus remained to find a military "solution" to Korea which would not require a significantly greater commitment of military resources to that "nonstrategic" area or a loss of honor or prestige. Viewed thus, the only solution seemed to be to "fight on" to the utmost with the forces already in Korea and to inflict such punishment on the CCF that Peking would be compelled to agree to a cease-fire or truce or armistice guaranteeing the freedom of South Korea.

The big question was: Could Eighth Army hold on and then inflict sufficient punishment on the CCF to force Peking to negotiate? On the basis of his visit to Korea on December 6, Joe Collins still thought it could—ultimately. Omar Bradley had adopted that view. But MacArthur still insisted that Eighth Army could not do the job without massive manpower reinforcements.

The great military risk was that Eighth Army might fail to absorb and repel the massive CCF offensive that seemed imminent. If it failed, an enormous debacle could ensue, a bloody Dunkirk in which Eighth Army might be utterly destroyed. The loss of life—and American prestige—could be catastrophic. The destruction of Eighth Army would leave Japan, Okinawa, and Formosa completely defenseless, wide open to conquest by either the Soviet Union or the CCF.

In the last days of December, given these factors and MacArthur's diametrically opposing views about what should be done, Washington deemed that

MacArthur should be given a new "directive." After many more tedious meetings to analyze the reams of position papers, the directive was drafted, approved by President Truman, and cabled to MacArthur on December 29.[102]

It began with Washington's gloomy overview of the strategic situation and a partial response to MacArthur's requests for massive ground reinforcements:

It appears from all estimates available that the Chinese Communists possess the capability of forcing UN forces out of Korea if they chose to exercise it. The execution of this capability might be prevented by making the effort so costly to the enemy that they would abandon it, or by committing substantial additional U.S. forces to that theater thus seriously jeopardizing other commitments including the safety of Japan. It is not practicable to obtain significant additional forces for Korea from other members of the UN. We believe that Korea is not the place to fight a major war. Further, we believe that we should not commit our remaining available ground forces to action against the CCF in Korea in the face of the increased threat of general war. However, a successful resistance to Chinese-North Korean aggression at some position in Korea and a deflation of the military and political prestige of the Chinese Communists would be of great importance to our national interests, if this could be accomplished without incurring serious losses.

The second portion of the message contained new—and specific—tactical instructions to MacArthur regarding Eighth Army. Above all else, Washington decreed, Eighth Army should not risk a catastrophic Dunkirk. For the first time, the possible evacuation of Eighth Army from Korea was seriously considered:

You are now directed to defend in successive positions [Lines B, C, D, etc., as outlined in MacArthur's December 8 instructions to Eighth Army] . . . inflicting such damage to hostile forces in Korea as is possible, subject to the primary consideration of the safety of your troops. Every effort should be continued to mobilize the maximum Korean contribution to sustained resistance, including both conventional and unconventional means.

Since developments may force our withdrawal from Korea, it is important, particularly in view of the continued threat to Japan, to determine, in advance, our last reasonable opportunity for an orderly evacuation. It seems to us that if you are forced back to positions in the vicinity of the Kum River [Line D] and a line generally eastward therefrom, and if thereafter the Chinese Communists mass large forces against your positions with an evident capability of forcing us out of Korea, it would then be necessary, under these conditions, to direct you to commence a withdrawal to Japan.

The message included a request to MacArthur to submit his views "as to the above-outlined conditions which should determine a decision to initiate evacuation, particularly in light of your continuing primary mission of defense of Japan for which only troops of the Eighth Army are available." The JCS concluded: "Following the receipt of your views you will be given a definite directive as to the conditions under which you should initiate evacuation."

MacArthur was dismayed by this cable. The talk of possible evacuation, he wrote, indicated Washington had lost the "will to win" and had sunk "almost into defeatism." Washington, he declared, was planning for not "counter-attack" but "rather the best way to run." His senior aide and confidant Courtney Whitney observed: "I have seen MacArthur in moments of great sorrow and distress; but I cannot recall when I have seen heartache etched so vividly on his countenance and in his every attitude as at this time. . . ."[103]

During the late-evening hours of December 30 MacArthur composed a reply to the JCS, as requested. In effect, his cable was a sober and eloquent plea to save South Korea by launching an immediate and all-out war with Red China. He proposed the following measures:[104]

- A blockade of the coast of China by UN naval forces.
- Destruction of China's industrial capacity to wage war by UN air and naval forces.
- Utilization of Chiang Kai-shek's "garrison" on Formosa both to reinforce Eighth Army and to conduct a "diversionary action" against "vulnerable areas of the Chinese mainland."

MacArthur did not believe these measures would widen the war in Korea. Red China was so fully committed to Korea that "nothing we can do would further aggravate the situation so far as China is concerned." He casually dismissed the possibility that these actions might provoke Soviet intervention or global war as "a matter of speculation," explaining that "I have always felt that a Soviet decision to precipitate a general war would depend solely upon its own estimate of relative strengths and capabilities with little regard for other factors."

If these measures against Red China were not taken, MacArthur implied, then the evacuation of Eighth Army from Korea would seem to be virtually inevitable. That course would have the "most adverse effect upon the peoples of Asia, not excepting the Japanese." Moreover, the entire "ROK potential" would no doubt "disintegrate or become of negligible value." The "loss of Korea" would "render the defense of Japan more vulnerable" and free the bulk of the CCF for "action elsewhere—quite probably in areas of far greater importance than Korea itself." Hence a "material reinforcement" of the offshore defensive perimeter "would be mandatory."

If his recommendation for all-out war against Red China was rejected, and the military restrictions imposed on him were to remain in effect, then the JCS "tactical estimate" of the situation in Korea seemed to be "sound." He continued: "The tactical plan of a successively contracting defense line south to the Pusan beachhead is believed to be the only possible way in which an evacuation could be accomplished. In the execution of this plan it would be necessary for you to make an anticipatory decision for evacuation until such time as we may be forced to that beachhead line."

This cable absolutely infuriated Washington. Boiled down to essentials, it seemed to say that unless Washington launched all-out war with Red China, Eighth Army would be forced to evacuate Korea, with disastrous consequences throughout the Far East. It left no room for the possibility that Eighth Army might absorb and repel the CCF offensive, mount a successful counterattack, and ultimately so punish the CCF that Peking would agree to negotiations. Omar Bradley wrote:

MacArthur's reaction arose, I feel certain, at least in part from the fact that his legendary pride had been hurt. The Red Chinese had made a fool of the infallible "military genius." . . . The only possible means left to MacArthur to regain his lost pride and military reputation was now to inflict an overwhelming defeat on those Red Chinese generals who had made a fool of him. In order to do this he was now perfectly willing to propel us into all-out war with Red China and, possibly, with the Soviet Union, igniting World War III and a nuclear holocaust.[105]

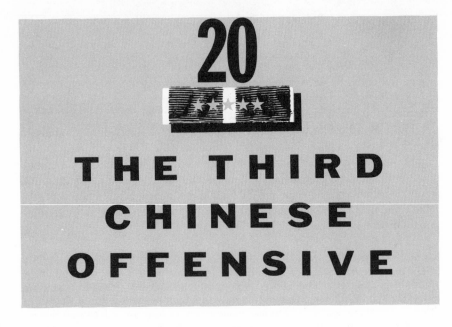

# 20

# THE THIRD CHINESE OFFENSIVE

## I

On New Year's Eve the CCF crossed the 38th Parallel and invaded South Korea. As Ridgway expected, the main weight of the invasion came on the western front, down the two roads leading to Seoul, where Shrimp Milburn's I Corps and John Coulter's IX Corps were dug in on Line B. But the enemy pressure, including that mounted by the NKPA, on the central front and eastward was also formidable.[1]

This time the CCF attack was preceded by massive artillery and large-caliber mortar barrages. After it came tens of thousands of infantry on foot, blowing the familiar bugles and horns and shooting off flares. As before, they rushed the UN forces with burp guns and grenades, shouting shrilly in the night.

On the western front the CCF avoided or bypassed the strong defensive positions of the American 24th and 25th divisions. The Chinese troops hurled themselves at the seam between the ROK 1st and 6th divisions, which was also the dividing line between I and IX corps. In reaction the ROK 12th Regiment of the ROK 1st Division broke and fled. Its 11th and 15th regiments were unable or unwilling to plug the gap, and they, too, soon failed. Caught in this chaotic bugout, the American 9th FAB, which was supporting the ROKs, lost four of its 155-mm howitzers and tractors.

Immediately to the right the ROK 6th Division held its ground for several hours. Soon, however, panic began to spread in its ranks, and all three of its regiments bugged out. This headlong flight enabled some CCF troops to make a small but alarming penetration between the American 19th and 21st regi-

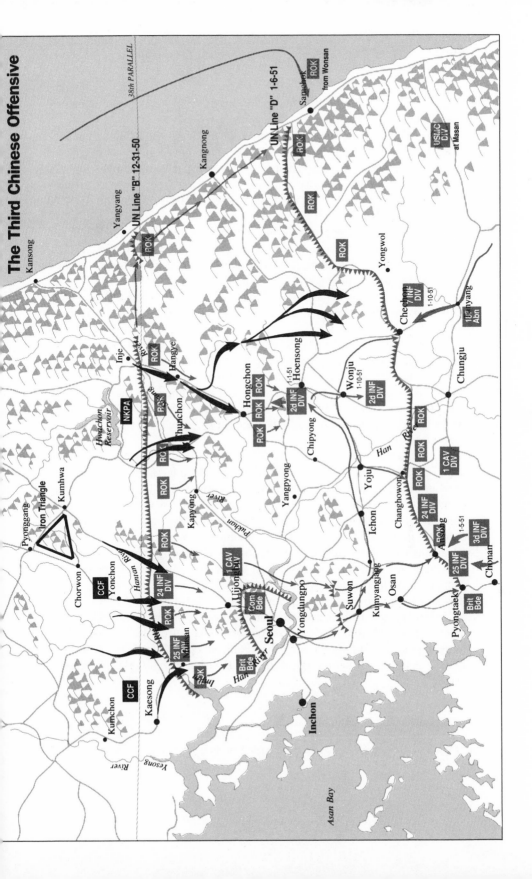

# The Third Chinese Offensive

ments of John Church's 24th Division, forcing the 3/19 quickly to withdraw one company.

To the immediate right of the American IX Corps the ROK 2d Division of ROK III Corps also wavered, then broke. Two of its regiments bugged out, but its third, the 17th, held valiantly. In so doing, it was chewed to pieces, losing six of its twelve infantry companies. The twenty-one pieces of artillery (twelve 105-mm and nine 75-mm "pack" howitzers) supporting the ROK 2d Division were abandoned.[2]*

Farther east, on the central front, the CCF, supported by NKPA II and V corps on the left flank, attacked simultaneously. ROK II Corps (3d, 5th, 7th, and 8th divisions), defending the sector above Wonju near Hongchon, also panicked and bolted, falling back on positions newly created by Bob McClure's 2d Division, hurriedly deploying to Wonju. To the right of ROK II Corps the ROK 9th Division, already under heavy NKPA pressure, apparently disappeared.

Camping at Eighth Army headquarters in Seoul, Ridgway was up most of the night, analyzing fragmentary reports and plotting the enemy attacks on terrain maps. He early perceived the grave threat posed by the collapse of the ROK 2d Division of ROK III Corps. It was soon apparent that in order to avoid the encirclement of I and IX corps in the Seoul area, another deep Eighth Army withdrawal would probably be necessary—perhaps all the way back to Line D, below Suwon.[3]

In its earlier retreat from the Chongchon River, Eighth Army had broken—and lost—contact with the CCF. It had yielded large swaths of territory without inflicting any significant casualties on the CCF. This time, Ridgway decided, the story would be different. Eighth Army would maintain close contact with the enemy and position its withdrawing forces so that it could carry out punishing local counterattacks, inflicting maximum casualties on the advancing CCF. It would not "run" but rather would withdraw cohesively and systematically, in a series of stops, first to the Seoul bridgehead, then to the south bank of the Han (Line C) and, finally, to Line D. At each of these "stops" it would fight vigorously and aggressively.

After laying out these general plans and getting off an upbeat New Year's greeting to MacArthur, Ridgway set off for the battlefront by jeep to lend his forceful presence and, if necessary, direct tactical operations. He soon encountered a dismaying situation: the ROK 6th Division in full flight. He remembered:

---

*The loss of twenty-five more howitzers that night brought the total loss of ROK and American artillery pieces to 263.

I'd never had such an experience before, and I pray to God I never witness such a spectacle again. They were coming down the road in trucks, the men standing, packed so close together in those big carriers another small boy could not have found space among them. They had abandoned their heavy artillery, their machine guns—all their crew-served weapons. Only a few had kept their rifles. Their only thought was to get away, to put miles between them and the fearful enemy that was at their heels.

I jumped from my jeep and stood in the middle of the road, waving them to a halt. I might as well have tried to stop the flow of the Han. I spoke no Korean, and had no interpreter with me. I could find no officer who spoke English. The only solution was to let them run and set up road blocks far enough back where they could be stopped. . . . I went back immediately to order these straggler posts set up. . . .[4]

Among these fleeing trucks on the road Ridgway encountered six vehicles transporting American soldiers of the 24th Division. Again he jumped out of his jeep. He stopped the convoy, ordered MPs to hold it in place, and later directed John Church to order the convoy to deliver the men back to their units. It is not likely that the order was ever carried out. Having twice escaped CCF encirclement at the Chongchon River by adroit withdrawals, Church was absorbed in preparing for a third.[5]

To fill the gap in the IX Corps line created by the bugout of the ROK 6th Division, Ridgway ordered the corps reserve—Coad's veteran Commonwealth Brigade—forward. Led by the aggressive Australian Battalion, the brigade moved north to Uijongbu on the double. By that time, however, Line B was merely a theoretical position. Ned Moore's 19th Infantry, on the right of the ROK 6th Division, had been exposed by its collapse and forced into what Ridgway described as an "untidy retreat," which "thoroughly dispirited" its men. Advancing into this confused zone, the Australians were almost immediately cut off by a CCF flank attack and forced to turn about and fight to the rear.[6]

Ridgway remained at the front all that day, flying over it in a light plane, dividing his time between the 24th and 25th divisions. He soon saw that his presence was of little avail. Most American units were poised for a bugout or already bugging out, and nothing Ridgway could say or do could prevent it. Indeed, considering the massive weight of the CCF attack and the collapse of the ROK 1st, 6th, and 2d divisions, he would be lucky to extricate the American 24th and 25th divisions without a disaster.[7]

Ridgway therefore issued orders for a general withdrawal to the Seoul bridgehead. On the left the Turks and the 25th Division, screened by the regrouping ROK 1st Division, began falling back on Seoul from Munsan. On the right, where the situation was more chaotic, the Commonwealth Brigade and the 24th Division began falling back on Uijongbu. Within the 24th Division only Throckmorton's 5th Infantry, serving as division rear guard, maintained close and aggressive contact with the CCF, but it was not able to inflict the desired punishment on the enemy.[8]

Nor did Bill Kean's 25th Division do any damage to the CCF. The enemy continued to avoid the division's strong defensive positions at the Imjin River. However, when the CCF hit the ROK 1st Division on the right flank of the 25th Division, presenting Kean an opportunity for counterattack, he remained rooted in place. Then later, on Ridgway's command, Kean withdrew the division in "orderly fashion." Sergeant W. B. ("Woody") Woodruff, a new squad leader in Gerry Kelleher's 35th Infantry, positioned on the immediate left of the ROK 1st Division, remembered that time with a note of scorn:

Around midnight the CCF struck the [1st] ROK division to our right, at a distance of several miles. The sound of firing, including artillery, was audible for hours, and the sky to that flank was filled with arcing tracers. The New Year thus came in accompanied by a tremendous fireworks display. At daylight the noise subsided and our front remained quiet. . . . At mid-afternoon our front was still quiet and up drove the mess truck burdened with the traditional Army holiday meal—turkey and all the trimmings.

A chow line promptly formed. Maybe ten men had been served, three or four were seated on the ground, taking the first bite, and the rest of us were in the line, mess kits at the ready. Suddenly a column of trucks approached at high speed, led by an officer in a jeep. The latter hit the ground shouting orders to close the chow line and mount trucks, on the double. . . .

Thus began what I characterized in my own mind as the "runaway." . . . Trucks would haul us an hour or so, then drop us off to return for some other unit, then pick us up for another ride. . . . Before dawn on January 2, we dismounted for the second or third time, but this time we were directed to dig in; here an effort would be made to hold. . . .[9]

By the morning of January 2 both I and IX corps had contracted into the Seoul bridgehead. The perimeter was manned by ten full infantry regiments. Clockwise in the I Corps sector, these were: the Turkish Brigade, Corley's 24th Infantry, Kelleher's 35th, Tom Brodie's British Brigade, several battalions of the ROK 1st Division, and Michaelis's 27th in reserve. Clockwise in the IX Corps sector, these were: Moore's 19th Infantry, Stephens's 21st, Throckmorton's 5th, with Coad's Commonwealth Brigade and Billy Harris's 7th Cav (plus the Greeks) in reserve.[10]

The UN infantry—some 50,000 men—was supported by several hundred tanks and an impressive array of artillery. The latter included the 17th FAB (with its eight-inch howitzers), the twelve organic artillery battalions of the 1st Cav, 24th, and 25th divisions, and the Turkish and British artillery units. In total, these batteries mounted about 250 howitzers of 105-mm caliber or larger. To reinforce them, Ridgway ordered that the thirty-six self-propelled or tractor-drawn 155-mm howitzers serving as X Corps artillery (the 92d and 96th FABs) proceed north to Seoul.[11]

In addition, he called on offshore naval guns and close air support. On direct orders from GHQ, FEAF postponed its withdrawal plans, joined the Marine carrier-based fighters, and flew an astounding 564 missions on January 1 (a bright, cold, clear day) and 531 missions on January 2 (another clear day) of which, FEAF claimed, 60 percent "secured close support targets." The two Marine squadrons flew about 150 close air support missions on January 1 and a like number the following day. The combined air effort on New Year's Day—700 plus sorties—was the "largest" close air support assault of the Korean War.[12]

With all this power at his disposal Ridgway, at Seoul, was in a good position to inflict a punishing blow on the advancing CCF. However, the collapse of ROKs, especially the ROK 2d Division, thwarted those aspirations. The CCF was through the gap, gaining a position to outflank Seoul from the northeast.

Ridgway was under explicit instructions from MacArthur not to risk the destruction of Eighth Army in a "citadel situation" at Seoul. Accordingly, he issued orders for I and IX corps to prepare to abandon Seoul on the following day, January 3. Eighth Army would withdraw to defensive Line C on the south bank of the Han River. There it would make another stand, prepared to inflict maximum punishment on the CCF.[13]

Inasmuch as the forces withdrawing from Seoul would be vulnerable to enemy attacks during the river crossing, Ridgway took steps to ensure that the south bank (Line C) would be secure. He withdrew the Turkish Brigade to Kimpo Airfield to anchor the left flank. He placed the reorganizing elements of the ROK 1st and 6th divisions in the center, near the bridges. He positioned Hap Gay's 1st Cav Division (less Billy Harris's 7th Regiment in Seoul) on the right flank, facing northeast and east, where the greatest flanking threat in a Han crossing was likely to develop. As a further precaution he ordered Frank Bowen's 187th Airborne RCT (at Suwon Airfield) to be prepared to attack northeast or east (toward Ichon and Wonju) on thirty minutes' notice.[14]

Somewhat impulsively Shrimp Milburn issued instructions to Bill Kean's 25th Division and Tom Brodie's British Brigade to hold Seoul "at all costs." For Brodie and his men it was to be their first real fight. Brodie rose to the occasion with a stirring exhortation echoing Milburn's instructions. His troops were to "knock hell out of" the CCF "with everything you've got." They were to give ground only on his specific order.

When Ridgway learned of these orders, he immediately countermanded them and dressed down Milburn. Only he, Ridgway, could issue a drastic order such as "Hold at all costs." Ridgway would issue no such order. Besides the waste of precious manpower, a stand-or-die order was "bad" for Eighth Army morale. No unit was to be sacrificed, least of all the green British Brigade. Should the British incur heavy losses in their first engagement, that could have a serious negative impact in England, where support for a war against China was not strong.[15]

Vastly complicating all these military preparations was the growing flood of South Korean refugees, who were fleeing the CCF. They were already clogging the roads and bridges by the tens of thousands. The abandonment of Seoul was certain to add tens of thousands, perhaps hundreds of thousands more. Since their presence was already interfering with military movements, Ridgway ordered Eighth Army engineer Pat Strong to expedite their evacuation southward, using the military trains returning to Pusan. Strong remembered:

The horrors of that civilian march southward are indescribable. . . . Unlike the flight of six months ago, the ground was frozen, the nights bitingly cold, the trails nearly impassable over the mountains. Every train we could divert from military needs were used for the civilians. And they swarmed [aboard] until the flat cars, the box cars, the gondolas were alive with near frozen bits of humanity. . . . Jammed on top of the cars, many were crushed in the mountain tunnels. Others froze to death, or half-freezing, lost their holds and fell off. . . . Untold thousands died of pneumonia in the refugee camps in the wintry hills.[16]

The refugee problem was merely one of many confronting Strong. His largest and most worrisome one at that time was the integrity of the Han River bridges. He was deeply concerned—"far more worried than I dare let Ridgway know"—that they might give way and collapse before Eighth Army could withdraw from Seoul. He explained:

The river crossing consisted of our one low level railroad and three floating [pontoon] bridges. All of Eighth Army, both [I and IX] corps, were funneling into Seoul and its environs. It would take days for the troops and their vehicles to cross over these three floating bridges, even with the best of planning and traffic control. . . . My worry was that there would be no bridges. The Han River was full of pack ice. . . . The great flows of pack ice surged back and forth against our fragile bridges. Unless we could hold these bridges, Eighth Army, as a tactical unit, was finished. . . . It would be a catastrophe that would dwarf the disaster below the Yalu.[17]

Assisted by I and IX corps engineers Emerson C. Itschner and William N. Thomas, Jr., respectively, Strong declared war on the ice. It was a "nightmare," he remembered:

Everything was tried—artillery, bangalore torpedoes, ice booms, explosives, extra cables and the ubiquitous DUKWs. . . . Explosives blew up the larger ice packs into smaller segments before they hit the bridges. Ice booms retarded them. The DUKWs churned back and forth on either side of the bridges, breaking the segments into smaller portions that could be forced under or between the pontoons.

Extra cables, stretched like a heavy spider web from either bank, kept the floating roadways in place. . . . The ice packs still swept back and forth, snapping cables, tearing out an occasional section of bridging. . . .[18]

Having arrived in Korea determined to go over to the offensive and "kill Chinese," Ridgway was "bitterly disappointed" at being forced to abandon Line B and the Seoul beachhead so precipitously. The main cause, of course, had been the craven collapse of the ROKs. That day, January 2, believing the time had come to address the ROK Army problem forthrightly, Ridgway called on Rhee in company with Ambassador Muccio and bluntly demanded a housecleaning.[19] Ridgway remembered: "I told President Rhee, 'We aren't going to get anywhere with your army until you get some leadership. . . .' I told him that until they got rid of their incompetents and demonstrated to me that they had an officer corps I would not give them equipment or increase their strength."[20]

Thinking that Rhee's presence at the front might quiet fears and instill heart in the ROK divisions, Ridgway invited him to address his troops. When Rhee readily agreed they flew in unheated liaison aircraft to Wonju, on the central front, where the situation was grave. Not one of the five ROK divisions in the sector was putting up a defense. The ROKs were frightened, dispirited, and frozen to the bone. Rhee confronted them, wearing his long white kimono and low shoes. He addressed them "with fiery eloquence." Later he reassured Ridgway: "Do not be discouraged. They will fight again."[21]

That day Ned Almond was moving his X Corps CP forward to Wonju. Pending his arrival, all American operations in the sector were under control of the new 2d Division commander, Bob McClure. Ridgway learned—to his satisfaction—that McClure was *attacking* northward into the teeth of the onrushing enemy. Paul Freeman's 23d RCT (with the French Battalion) was in the lead, north of Hoengsong, locked in fierce battle. George Peploe's 38th RCT (with the Dutch Battalion) had reached Hoengsong to backstop Freeman.[22]

Ridgway flew up to see Freeman. He was pleased to find Freeman on the attack. Freeman was glad to see Ridgway: "Things were in a hell of a mess. He gave us a very inspiring talk. We thought that the [Eighth] Army was really in strong hands and strong leadership. Ridgway was my number one combat hero."[23]

Fighting conditions in the mountains of the central front were ghastly, not unlike those at the Chosin Reservoir. It was very, very cold. At night the temperature fell to twenty-five degrees below zero. Howling blizzards swept through the mountain passes. The vital Hongchon–Hoengsong–Wonju "highway," down which the enemy was advancing, was scarcely more than a narrow third-class mountain road. Snow and ice-covered, it was treacherous, nearly impassable for artillery tractors and other heavy gear. Communist guerrillas, assisting the enemy attack, roved the mountains, throwing up roadblocks.[24]

Ridgway met with Freeman; his new exec, Frank Meszar; and his three veteran battalion commanders—Hutchin, Edwards, and Kane. He impressed upon them the absolute need to block the NKPA advance on Wonju. Wonju was a vital road hub. A road from Wonju led due east to Suwon. If the NKPA took that road, it could cut off Eighth Army at Suwon. Holding Wonju could prove to be the key to holding South Korea.[25]

Before leaving the Wonju area, Ridgway gave Almond authority to sack the cowardly and inept ROK generals who were responsible for the debacle in that sector. Later that night Almond opened X Corps headquarters at Wonju and took direct command of McClure's 2d Division and ROK II Corps, to which the remnants of the five ROK divisions in that area were assigned. On the following day advance men of Ferenbaugh's 7th Division began arriving at Wonju to scout likely defense positions.[26]

Returning to Seoul, Ridgway prepared upbeat messages to MacArthur and Joe Collins, perhaps designed to soften the blow of losing Seoul. To MacArthur: "The Eighth Army will continue its present mission of inflicting maximum punishment and delaying in successive positions maintaining its major forces intact."[27] To Collins: "Everything is going fine. We shall be in for some difficult days but I am completely confident of the ability of the Eighth Army to accomplish every mission assigned."[28]

## II

On the morning of January 3 Ridgway issued orders for the Eighth Army withdrawal from Seoul. He insisted that the maneuver be absolutely orderly, controlled, and deliberate. To Milburn and Coulter he commanded: "This retrograde movement will be executed with all necessary lateral coordination; with maximum losses inflicted on the enemy and with maximum delay consistent with the maintenance intact of major units. . . . Rigid control of units and of traffic will be exercised during withdrawal. . . . No usable equipment will be left behind."[29]

Inasmuch as strict control of traffic at the Han River bridges was vital to ensure an orderly withdrawal, Ridgway decided to place a single, tough, impressive general in direct charge. He chose Charlie Palmer from the 1st Cav. Ridgway delegated to Palmer "full authority" to "use" his (Ridgway's) name to impose "whatever measures were needed to keep Eighth Army traffic flowing." Refugees would be permitted to use the bridges only until 3:00 P.M. If they failed to obey that order, Ridgway directed, the MPs were authorized to fire warning shots over their heads. If this failed to stop the tide, Ridgway said, "MPs were, as a last resort, to use their weapons directly against the offenders."[30]

\* \* \*

By midafternoon that day the massive military withdrawal was well under way. First came the division trains, followed by the artillery, then the tanks and other heavy equipment, and, lastly, the infantry, some afoot, most in trucks. At the bridges Charlie Palmer—and a host of MPs—directed traffic. The army and corps engineers fought off the menacing ice by various devices; the churning DUKWs proved to be the best.[31]

In Milburn's I Corps the order of evacuation was as follows: Corley's 24th Infantry, the several battalions of the ROK 1st Division, Brodie's British Brigade, Kelleher's 35th Infantry, and Michaelis's 27th Infantry, which was to serve as rear guard.[32]

A very serious snag upset the I Corps plan. Brodie's brigade, which had yet to engage in a "serious" fight in Korea, had been hard hit by the CCF earlier in the day. Two of the infantry battalions (Gloucesters and Fusiliers) had escaped encirclement, but the other, the Royal Ulster Rifles, was cut off. To rescue it, Brodie counterattacked with a tank-infantry team which soon found itself locked in "desperate hand-to-hand fighting." In this fight the British suffered heavily (300 casualties, including the Ulsters' commander, C. A. H. B. Blake, killed) but finally managed to extricate the battalion.[33]

This incident, which marred an otherwise near-perfect withdrawal, infuriated Ridgway. Its effect was to delay the withdrawal of the British Brigade considerably, inadvertently placing it more or less in the rear guard of I Corps. Inasmuch as Ridgway had given Milburn explicit orders that the green British Brigade was not to serve as rear guard, at first he believed Milburn had violated his orders. When the circumstances of the matter had been ascertained and the brigade had finally withdrawn through the officially designated rear guard— Michaelis's 27th Infantry—Ridgway cooled down.[34]\*

In Coulter's IX Corps the order of withdrawal was: Ned Moore's 19th Infantry, Stephens's 21st Infantry, and Throckmorton's 5th Infantry, Billy Harris's 7th Cav, and, lastly, Coad's Commonwealth Brigade. These withdrawals proceeded without noteworthy incident and with only slight contact (by the Australian Battalion) with the CCF.[35]

In the late afternoon, after the bridges had been closed to the Korean refugees, Ridgway went down to observe Charlie Palmer at work and to be

---

\*Only to boil over again later when told that some thirty British and four or five tanks were still cornered in Seoul. Advising Milburn their loss would be a "blot" on I Corps, the 25th Division, and the U.S. Army, Ridgway personally organized a rescue force of three helicopters and assigned them to Milburn.

at hand should he require three-star assistance. By that time the masses of artillery, tanks, and trucks were crossing the bridges in a seemingly endless bumper-to-bumper stream. Ridgway watched apprehensively as the pontoons rose and fell under the weight of heavy American and British tanks, "praying, as I know all of us were praying, that the bridges would hold." But what made an even greater impact on him was the plight of the refugees. He remembered:

Off to the right and left of the bridges was being enacted one of the great human tragedies of our time . . . a sight to be remembered as long as those of us who witnessed it shall live. . . . In a zero wind that seared the face like a blow torch, hundreds of thousands of Koreans were running, stumbling, falling, as they fled across the ice. Women with tiny babies in their arms, men bearing their old, sick, crippled fathers and mothers on their backs, others bent under great bundles of household gear flowed down the northern bank and across the ice toward the frozen plain on the southern shore. Some pushed little two-wheeled carts piled high with goods and little children. Others prodded burdened oxen. . . . There was no weeping, no crying. Without a sound, except the dry whisper of their slippers on the snow, and the deep pant of their hard-drawn breath, they moved in utter silence.[36]

The withdrawal continued all through the night of January 3–4. During it Ridgway returned to his "bleak room" in Seoul and packed his briefcase and bag, less one item: an old pajama bottom, split in the seat. In a gesture meant to be defiantly obscene, he tacked the garment to the wall below this sign:

TO THE COMMANDING GENERAL CCF:
WITH THE COMPLIMENTS OF THE
COMMANDING GENERAL EIGHTH ARMY.[37]

\* \* \*

On the morning of January 4 the last UN unit in Seoul—the Australian Battalion of the Commonwealth Brigade—crossed over two bridges and passed through defensive Line C. Engineer Strong had planned to salvage the three pontoon bridges for future use, but by that time they were frozen solidly in the ice. On Ridgway's order he and the corps engineers, Itschner and Thomas, blew up all three plus every single span of the railroad bridge. At about the same time Strong's men "unhappily" demolished the big tidal basin lock at Inchon, while others blew up aviation supplies at Kimpo Airfield. In all, 1,600,000 gallons of gasoline, 9,300 tons of engineer material, and 12 railroad cars of ammo were destroyed.[38]

Having decreed these necessary military demolitions, Ridgway then issued a new directive which rescinded Johnnie Walker's existing scorched earth policy. Henceforth, Ridgway declared, demolitions would be limited to those that would "combine maximum hurt to the enemy with minimum harm to the civilian population." Power and water plants which "primarily serve civilian centers" were to be spared. Bridges would be blown, but with an eye to "substantial delay to the enemy without imposing undue hardship on the population" when they had to be rebuilt. There would be no more "destruction for destruction's sake."[39]*

*   *   *

Ridgway intended to hold defensive Line C on the south bank of the Han River long enough to deal the CCF a punishing blow. For that purpose he added the 25th Division to the line. On January 4 the composition of the line, left to right, was: the Turkish Brigade, ROK 1st Division, 25th Division, ROK 6th Division, and 1st Cav Division. Released from frontline duty, the British and the Commonwealth brigades and the 24th Division continued south to the Suwon area.[41]

The CCF swarmed into Seoul, raised a Red Chinese flag over the National Assembly Hall, and celebrated. However, it did not immediately attempt to cross the Han River in hot pursuit. Hence the men on Line C had little or no opportunity to inflict direct and harsh punishment on the enemy. A curious, uneasy lull set in, leading Ridgway to surmise that having captured Seoul principally for psychological reasons, the CCF would not pursue Eighth Army on the "open plain" of the Seoul–Pyongtaek "corridor," which was good UN tank and close air support country. Rather, it would shift the weight of the attack easterly.

An intelligence report that day appeared to bear out that surmise. CCF forces were positively identified above Yoju, a village about midway between Suwon and Wonju. This report, and others, seemed to indicate a major CCF effort to drive a wedge between Ridgway's I and IX corps and the X Corps forces at Wonju. If successful, this drive could result in a disastrous envelopment of both forces.[42]

To prevent this possibility, Ridgway was forced to abandon Line C almost immediately. He issued the following orders on January 4:

• The I and IX corps would withdraw from Line C at 8:00 P.M. and fall back toward Line D, with a temporary stop on an "intermediate line" at

---

*The policy did not apply to North Korea. At Ridgway's specific request, FEAF conducted two massive B-29 bomber raids on Pyongyang on January 3 (sixty-three planes) and January 5 (sixty planes) with the goal of burning the city to the ground with incendiary bombs. Pyongyang Radio reported the "entire city burned like a furnace for two days," but a postraid FEAF study concluded that owing to the fire-retarding snow on the roofs, "only 35 percent" of the city was destroyed.[40]

Suwon to enable logisticians to evacuate sixteen trainloads of supplies which were parked there.

• The X Corps would shift from offense to defense and contract its forwardmost elements (namely, Freeman's 23d and Peploe's 38th RCTs) into the Wonju area. The 7th Division would expedite its advance to the Wonju area.

• The 187th Airborne RCT would deploy east from Suwon toward Ichon and Yoju to block a possible CCF flanking movement toward Suwon.

• Shorty Soule's 3d Division in Eighth Army reserve would come forward immediately to reinforce Milburn's I Corps.[43]

*　*　*

I and IX corps paused on the intermediate line at Suwon for about twenty-four hours. During that time the logisticians worked at a feverish pace to move the sixteen trainloads of supplies south of Line D. Meanwhile, on the right Frank Bowen's 187th Airborne RCT occupied Ichon (and sent patrols east to Yoju), and farther right yet Almond's X Corps forces contracted into Wonju. These maneuvers produced a tidy, but very thin, east-west Eighth Army front fifty air miles wide, stretching from Suwon to Wonju.[44]

After the supply trains at Suwon had been routed south, on the afternoon of January 6 Ridgway gave the order for I and IX corps to fall back to Line D. The maneuver was accomplished without incident. During that night and the following day the western sector of Line D was occupied (from left to right) by the following forces of the two corps: Tom Brodie's British Brigade; Dinty Moore's 15th Infantry Regiment (of the arriving 3d Division); four regiments of the ROK 1st and 6th divisions; Coad's Commonwealth Brigade; Church's 24th Division, with Throckmorton's 5th and Ned Moore's 19th regiments on the line. Kean's 25th Division was placed in I Corps reserve; Gay's 1st Cav, in IX Corps reserve.[45]

*　*　*

Ridgway was not a happy general. The CCF-NKPA New Year's offensive had forced the bulk of Eighth Army to withdraw about sixty air miles (Munsan to Pyongtaek) in seven days. What was even more galling was that Eighth Army had not inflicted any substantial damage on the CCF. In effect, Ridgway had been forced to yield Seoul as Walker had yielded Pyongyang, without a fight. The only "comfort" Ridgway could find in this dismal situation was the knowledge that "a great part" of Eighth Army "had been saved." ROKs had suffered heavy casualties and complete disorganization, but the non-ROK elements had escaped intact and, except for the Royal Ulsters, with slight to negligible casualties.[46]

Ridgway called in his senior commanders and gave them a royal chewing out. It was "difficult to believe," he said, that UN forces could not defeat the CCF. The UN forces had every advantage except "sheer numbers": air power; sea power; "enormous" armor, artillery, communications. The UN forces had to adopt tactics suitable to the peculiar type of enemy and terrain. They had to block roads, button up tight at night, mount daylight counterattacks in concert with close air support, exploit superior UN ground firepower.[47]

He further vented his displeasure in a personal letter to Joe Collins. He wrote: "There continues to be a lack of aggressiveness among some corps and division commanders. Again and again," he complained, he had "personally instructed" both corps commanders (Milburn and Coulter) to conduct their withdrawals so as to leave strong forces positioned to permit powerful counterattacks. His instructions "were not complied with" or had "failed of execution," Ridgway went on. Moreover, there was a "marked absence" of the "vaunted American resourcefulness." Americans in Korea were still clinging to creature comforts: going by truck; sticking to roads. "The finest of our past infantry leaders must shudder in their graves if their all-seeing gaze now takes in the battlefield performance of some of their descendants."[48]

\* \* \*

Inasmuch as Eighth Army had again lost contact with the CCF in the western sector, Ridgway ordered Milburn and Coulter to commence immediate and aggressive patrolling north of Line D. Milburn chose elements of the reserve 25th Division to provide the first probe, Michaelis's 27th Infantry, well supported by tanks.

Ridgway visited Michaelis's CP to deliver a pep talk. Michaelis remembered: "Ridgway was such a breath of fresh air. Spit and fire. I'll never forget. He came to my CP in a jeep, grenades hung on his shoulder harness, brisk-walking, beetle-eyed, looking right at you. He said, 'Michaelis, what are tanks for?' I said, 'To kill.' He said, 'Take your tanks north.' I said, 'Fine, sir. It's easy to take them there. It's getting back that's going to be most difficult. They always cut the road behind you.' He said, 'Who said anything about coming back? If you can stay up there twenty-four hours, I'll send the [25th] Division up. If the division can stay up there twenty-four hours, I'll send the [I] corps up.' That was the magic that was Ridgway."[49]

The "tanks" of Michaelis Force would be provided by Tom Dolvin's 89th Tank Battalion. Ridgway visited Dolvin's CP, where he made another strong impression. Dolvin remembered: "My S-three started briefing him, but he interrupted and said: 'Throw away your defensive plans. I'm not interested. We're not going back anymore; we're going to advance.' Of all the men I've known personally or served under, I admire Ridgway the most. He turned Eighth Army around *personally.*"[50]

Michaelis Force thus became the first real "offensive" strike to be mounted by Matt Ridgway. In its final form the force was quite strong: the full 27th Infantry, most of Dolvin's 89th Tank Battalion, Gus Terry's 89th FAB, augmented by a battery of James Sanden's 90th FAB, and a company of engineers. Ridgway's order to Michaelis was to patrol north as far as Osan and "search out the enemy and inflict maximum punishment on him." Brodie's British Brigade would provide patrol backup and a communications link.[51]

Michaelis moved out through Brodie's sector on the night of January 7 and 8, proceeding with proper caution. At daylight he reached Sojong, a village about halfway to Osan.[52] The 25th Division artillery commander, Bittman Barth, jeeped forward to Michaelis's lead battalion, the 3/27, now commanded by a highly decorated (DSC, etc.) World War II veteran, Richard W. Keyes, thirty-nine. Barth remembered: "Masses of refugees, many leading bullock carts, literally packed the road for about three miles behind Keyes's battalion. It was physically impossible for the remainder of the task force to get forward through this milling mass of humanity. . . . It took three hours to divert the traffic onto the tracks so that the force could go forward."[53]

Michaelis was concerned that the CCF might be using the masses of refugees to screen troop movements or even concealing forces within the refugee columns. But this was not the case. His patrols revealed that the CCF had sent a regiment or so to occupy Suwon, but otherwise the Chinese were not pursuing. When this became evident, Michaelis sent patrols all the way to Osan.[54]

Although Michaelis Force found no enemy to punish, its aggressive deployment forward of Line D served several useful purposes. Foremost, it was an important morale builder. For the first time since November 25 Eighth Army was not withdrawing but, rather, "attacking," as Ridgway had vowed to do. Secondly, it played a valuable intelligence role: the discovery that the CCF were not pursuing in that sector. Thirdly, it probably led the CCF to retain combat forces in Seoul or Suwon to counteract the offensive threat it posed, thus diminishing the CCF troops available to conduct operations elsewhere.

* * *

By this time Shorty Soule's full 3d Division had come forward to Line D. It occupied positions to the immediate right of Bill Kean's 25th Division. William Harris's Puerto Rican 65th Infantry held the left sector, abutting the 25th Division; Dinty Moore's 15th Infantry the right sector, abutting the ROK 1st Division. The 7th Infantry remained in reserve near Chonan.[55]

The senior commanders of the 3d Division were glad to get out of Almond's X Corps and into Milburn's I Corps. They did not like Almond personally. They resented his practice of commanding from the front lines and issuing orders directly to the battalion or, in many instances, company commanders. Many also found his blatant bigotry offensive. By comparison,

Shrimp Milburn and his chief of staff, Rinaldo Van Brunt, were "wonderful people" to work for.[56]

7th Infantry commander John Guthrie was therefore dismayed when, without warning, he received orders relieving him of command and directing him to return to X Corps. He was to replace Nick Ruffner as Almond's chief of staff. The job was certain to restore permanently the temporary star Guthrie had held in World War II as chief of staff of Sandy Patch's Seventh Army. But it could also lead to an ulcer. Guthrie remembered: "I was shocked by my orders. I'd never known or served with Almond before Korea. He was a terrific soldier and fighter, but from what I'd seen in northeast Korea he was also a wild man, and he offended nearly everybody. Usually an army or corps commander is the nice guy, and his chief of staff is the son of a bitch and hatchet man. When I reported to Almond, I saw the roles would have to be reversed. My job became one of being the nice guy, a go-between, who trailed behind Almond to smooth ruffled feathers, to put his complicated orders in simple words. I also had to try to keep Almond throttled back. It was the hardest job I ever had."

Upon Guthrie's departure, Shorty Soule promoted Guthrie's exec, Jim Boswell, forty, recently promoted to colonel with his West Point class (1933), to command the 7th Infantry. "I hated to lose the regiment," Guthrie remembered, "but if I had to, Jim Boswell was the best possible choice to command it."[57]

Boswell came from an old Army family. His father, a West Point washout (class of 1902), had subsequently obtained a commission and served in the Philippines as aide to General John J. Pershing. After graduating from the Military Academy, Boswell had had an unusual career. He served with troops for several years, but when "an opportunity arose" to learn the Russian language, he seized it and spent two years at Columbia and Harvard universities, earning an M.A. (1941) from the latter. This rare specialty led to an arduous but fascinating wartime assignment in Russia with the American military mission, then, finally, in 1944, to the Army's "Russian desk" in the Pentagon.[58]

Disdaining a limited or "overspecialized" career, Boswell sought troop duty, got it, and finally wound up in Normandy as G-2 of Gene Landrum's shaky 90th Division. Boswell survived the various command purges and remained with the division to the end of the war, after which he commanded its 358th Infantry in Czechoslovakia. In the postwar years he returned to the Army's Russian desk, helped establish the fledgling CIA's Russian desk, and finally wound up in the 7th Infantry as it was embarking for Korea.

Upon assuming command of the regiment, Boswell commenced a shake-up. He "cleaned out" most of the regimental staff (the "Guthrie Mafiosi") and appointed two new battalion commanders. Ernest M. Layman, Jr., replaced Tom O'Neil in command of the 3/7; O'Neil became regimental exec. Frederick

C. Weyand, thirty-four, replaced Charles Heinrich as commander of the 1/7.[59]

Weyand, who came from the 3d Division G-3 section, was a remarkable leader who was obviously destined for high command. A Californian, he was a graduate of the University of California at Berkeley (1939) and had come into the Army in 1940 with an ROTC commission. During World War II and afterward (1943–1949) he was an intelligence specialist. One of his contemporaries described Weyand as "homespun yet debonair . . . deceptively shrewd and, when cast in the role, a superb diplomat." He eventually earned four stars and served two tours in Vietnam. During the second (1970–1973) he replaced Creighton W. Abrams as the senior American commander. Abrams returned to the Pentagon to replace his Vietnam predecessor, William C. Westmoreland, as Army chief of staff. In 1974, when Abrams died of cancer, Weyand succeeded him as Army chief of staff.[60]*

Ridgway was pleased to get the 3d Division to reinforce Milburn's I Corps. Shorty Soule came well recommended by Joe Swing and appeared to be competent and aggressive, a "fighter." However, there were some worries:

- The regimental commanders in the 3d Division were a question mark. The 7th's Jim Boswell was considered by his peers to be "brilliant," but he was untested as a combat troop leader. The 15th's dour Dinty Moore, fifty (the same age as Shorty Soule), was too old and unsuited for combat. Soule wanted to relieve him, but Moore was a veteran of Bataan and Japanese POW camps and, as such, was viewed as a "MacArthur man," hence more or less untouchable. The 65th's William Harris was a dedicated advocate (and publicist) for his Puerto Ricans, but at least one of his batallion commanders had strong reservations about Harris as a battlefield leader.[61]
- The 3d Division had a disproportionate share of blacks and black units. These included the blacks in the Puerto Rican 65th Infantry; Harry Stella's 58th FAB, supporting the Puerto Ricans; Kenneth Dawalt's attached 999th Armored FAB; Ed Farrell's 3/15; William Bartlett's 64th Tank Battalion; and other units. Some of these blacks, notably Farrell's 3/15 in the Hungnam evacuation, had performed quite well. But on the basis of his experience with the 24th Infantry, Bill Kean had persuaded Ridgway that black units could become unreliable at any moment and were thus not to be fully trusted.

\* \* \*

Shorty Soule and many others in the 3d Division tended to view the other units in Eighth Army with a degree of scorn. It was a "bugout" and

---

*In August 1950, Johnny Johnson had brought a provisional battalion of the 7th Infantry from Fort Devens, which became the 3d Battalion, 8th Cav. Thus it would be remarked that the "7th Infantry produced two battalion commanders in Korea who went on to become Army chief of staff."

"defeatist" army which had twice fled the CCF without putting up much of a fight. Soule and his 3d Division, which had emerged from northeast Korea with only slight damage, would show Eighth Army how to fight. In response to Ridgway's demands, it would aggressively attack, make contact with the CCF, and blunt the enemy advance. Perhaps the 3d Division could "save" the situation all by itself.[62]

As it happened, Dinty Moore's 15th Infantry arrived at Line D first. Full of vinegar (or perhaps stronger spirits), Shorty Soule ordered Moore to attack at once—that very night. Moore, in turn, chose Bob Blanchard's 1/15 to spearhead the attack, backed by the 39th FAB, commanded by Blanchard's West Point classmate (1933) Bob Neely, A/A weapons, tanks, and other supporting forces. Having only just arrived and having no information on the enemy positions or terrain or an integrated plan of battle, Bob Blanchard rightly thought Soule and his staff were overeager. He remembered:

We went off into this strange terrain, all alone, in the dead of night to stop the Red Tide. We went ahead in darkness, with both flanks wide open. After a while I decided this was simply too crazy and stopped [in defiance of orders] and buttoned up into a tight defensive perimeter. Fortunately nothing happened; we didn't get hit.
Then the division staff changed its mind. . . . They held us in this perimeter for several days—like a magnet—hoping to draw the CCF in to hit us. I thought that was worse than the first "plan" and when Soule flew in to visit, I told him so. We should be advancing, with proper infantry tactics, to meet the enemy in daylight. That got me in a heap of trouble: that night I got orders to get the battalion moving again and not to stop until I found the enemy.[63]

The next day Blanchard's 1/15 charged north on trucks and other vehicles deep into the unknown terrain. It raced ahead twenty-two miles, leaving Neely's 39th FAB far behind. That afternoon, however, it ran headlong into strong CCF positions near Ansong. The CCF attacked from strong defensive positions with heavy mortar barrages. In the midst of the attack the 3d Division ADC, Armistead Mead, flew up in a helicopter to help scout out the CCF. When he landed, he reported scads of enemy just ahead. In addition, he informed Blanchard that he had just been promoted to full colonel (with the class of 1933), as had artilleryman Neely. Both were overranked for their assignments. They would be replaced, Blanchard by Julius W. Levy, thirty-five. Now eligible to command a regiment, Blanchard would go to division headquarters as an "assistant division commander" on standby to replace Dinty Moore, when Soule could find a way to dump him.

Beset on all sides by aggressive CCF, Blanchard again drew his 1/15 into a tight perimeter for the night, this time without artillery. Rightly believing he was dangerously exposed (twenty-two miles ahead of the division), Blanchard radioed for permission to pull back. Headquarters responded: "Stay out there." The 1/15 survived the night, but when daylight came and Blanchard found himself virtually surrounded by the CCF, he insisted by radio that he be authorized to pull back. Headquarters responded: "You can come halfway back, but don't come any further." Blanchard got the 1/15 out and pulled back halfway. He had lost some men, but he felt lucky that the 1/15 had not been annihilated. Neely, too, barely escaped alive. The spotter plane in which he was riding accidentally crashed, but luckily it fell inside Blanchard's perimeter.

Blanchard was thoroughly upset and embarrassed by this inept debut of the 3d Division in Eighth Army. Soule's decision to attack with the 1/15 had demonstrated aggressiveness, but Blanchard believed it had been a foolhardy and haphazard stunt, unworthy of professional Army officers. The fragmentation and exposure of small units were reminiscent of Ned Almond's reckless tactics in northeast Korea. Shorty Soule would not defeat the CCF by such hip-shooting, middle-of-the-night orders. Victory would require meticulous staff planning, proper employment of mass, fire, and maneuver, and other standard Army doctrine.

# III

By January 6 the situation at Wonju had developed into a crisis. Following on the heels of the 23d and 38th regiments, which had contracted into Wonju, the NKPA, assisted by guerrillas operating in the rear of UN lines, made strong advances. At the same time CCF units (of undetermined but probably weak strength) probed south on the NKPA right (or west) flank toward Yoju.[64]

The NKPA forces committed to the Wonju offensive were not the quality of the CCF regulars. Most had received only slight training and had not been in combat before. Apparently the ROKs had initially mistaken the NKPA for the CCF—or believed the NKPA troops were screening for the CCF—and this had led to the ROK bugout. Emboldened by this "first victory" and perhaps the knowledge that 300,000 (or more) CCF stood behind them, the NKPA, notwithstanding the hideous cold and terrain, had reinvaded South Korea in a spirited and aggressive mood.

Although the American 2d Division was not up to full strength in all its components and the replacements had only brief unit training, in Almond's view the division should have been fighting with greater vigor. It had the advantage of being on defense; it was supported by artillery and close air support. It was galling and humiliating that a mostly green NKPA force, numbering not even twice the strength of the 2d Division, was doing so well.

One of the problems, as Almond saw it, was the 2d Division's new commander, Bob McClure. Shortly after incorporating the 2d Division into X Corps, Almond began criticizing McClure with the sort of harsh language he had earlier used about O. P. Smith and Dave Barr. In a report to Ridgway Almond wrote that he had found a "lack of supervision" at divisional level; the division artillery commander, Loyal Haynes, "was too far to the rear." At the regimental level commanders were not taking advantage of terrain and firepower; there was a "lot of aimless wandering around" by the French and Dutch battalions. There was an "alarming shortage" of mortar ammo, which no one had reported to X Corps headquarters. There was no mention of McClure's fondness for the bottle or his silly "beard contest," but it is not likely that they went unnoticed.[65]

Nor were the ROKs much help. Almond had deployed the five reorganizing divisions in the rugged mountains to the right (or east) of Wonju. The ROK mission was to block roads and prevent an encirclement of Wonju from the northeast or southeast. But the loose ROK "front" remained chaotic. The NKPA—still powerfully supported by guerrillas—again overran the ROKs, leaving McClure's 2d Division at Wonju holding an exposed salient.[66]

All tasks facing McClure were urgent, but none seemed more so than blocking the NKPA encirclement from the northeast. He therefore ordered Ed Messinger's 9th Infantry, supported by John Keith's 15th FAB, to deploy over and hold the Wonju–Chechon road. Subsequently he reinforced the 9th with Hutchin's 1/23. This left only Freeman's 23d (less the 1/23, but including the French Battalion) and Peploe's 38th (plus the Dutch Battalion), supported by the 37th and 38th FABs, to hold Wonju.[67]*

Ridgway had declared that Wonju was "second only to Seoul" in tactical importance. Therefore, Almond issued orders that it was to be held until he personally authorized withdrawal. But McClure thought this order was asinine.[68] Paul Freeman remembered: "The ROK divisions that were in our vicinity fled and left us exposed. General McClure, recognizing this situation and remembering what had happened to the division in the north [at Kunu] and recognizing that there was a defile through which our main supply route passed, had recommended all through the day that we be permitted to fall back to cover the defile and to cover Wonju by [artillery] fire. He was unable to reach General Almond. He finally made this decision on his own. In a blinding snowstorm we were ordered [by McClure] to pull out of Wonju, to move back to a position north of this defile—probably some twelve miles—and to establish minefields, booby traps, and so on."[69]

That night Almond came forward and discovered that McClure had

---

*The black 503d FAB, overrun in the Kunu gauntlet, was still reorganizing and remanning in the rear, awaiting the arrival of 155-mm howitzers.

withdrawn the 2d Division from Wonju more or less without a fight. Furious, he considered this action—regardless of the hazardous circumstances—a "direct disobedience of my orders, which were in compliance with Ridgway's orders." He probably made up his mind that night to relieve McClure of command, and he ordered him to retake Wonju at once.[70]

By this time the 23d (less the 1/23) and 38th regiments were dug into strong defensive positions south of Wonju. McClure ordered Freeman to send James Edwards's 2/23 back into Wonju to clear the town and the airfield. Freeman recalled: "The snow was very deep. All of the mines and booby traps [we planted] had been covered so that they couldn't be removed. . . . These were very very hard conditions for our troops. We didn't have real winter clothing. The temperature, after this wet snow, had fallen to about thirty degrees below zero, where it remained for three days and nights. . . . The division was in a very confused posture. . . . Our artillery was all mixed up. The artillery position was way back to the rear, as was the artillery commander [Haynes]. And we didn't have the teamwork that we would normally have had."[71]

Advancing on Wonju, Edwards's 2/23 ran into "very heavy fire." Trying to fight house to house, he was soon flanked by swarms of NKPA. As a result, Edwards radioed Freeman that the situation was impossible. He must be either "reinforced or withdrawn." McClure, observing the attack from Freeman's CP and still believing any attempt to hold Wonju was futile, gave the order: "Withdraw."[72]

During the evening hours Almond again brought heavy pressure on McClure to retake Wonju. McClure, in turn, ordered Freeman to reattack Wonju on the following morning, January 9, with *two* battalions, one of them from Peploe's 38th Infantry. In compliance, Peploe provided James Skeldon's 2/38, which joined Edwards's 2/23 "side by side." The combined force, however, could make no real headway against the NKPA, and the mission, the division historian wrote, "met with failure."[73]

\* \* \*

In the meantime, the reinforced 9th Infantry was defending the Wonju–Chechon road against hard and repeated NKPA attacks. The commander, paratrooper Ed Messinger, had virtually rebuilt the 9th Infantry from scratch in the previous month. Butch Barberis still commanded the 2/9, and D. M. McMains the black 3/9. Owing to the acute shortage of qualified battalion commanders, the 1/9—actually wiped out at Kunu—was now back in command of John Londahl, who had originally brought it from the States but who had been replaced earlier.[74]

In comparison with the 9th's two previous regimental commanders (John Hill and Chin Sloane), Ed Messinger proved to be outstanding. Barberis remembered that Messinger was "a very fine leader and combat commander—a joy to work for in that he had confidence in his subordinates and gave them their orders and left them alone."[75] The new regimental S-3, Thomas W. Mellen, agreed:

It took me a little while to realize and appreciate the wonderful qualities of this officer. He had just taken command of a regiment that had been savaged at Kunu-ri, was demoralized and still in shock when I joined it. The regiment had lost hundreds killed, wounded and missing and most of its equipment. . . . Officers stared at the floor and spoke in whispers. I was the only officer in the regiment who had not been through the Kunu-ri ordeal; I'd been in combat before but this was real spooky. Colonel Messinger brought the 9th Infantry back to life with a firm, but kind—even gentle—and understanding form of leadership. A smile, small joke, pat on the back, a nudge here and there. Other commanders may have done it differently but he was eminently successful. Weeks later I realized that the 9th Infantry was not unlike a family, into which I had been accepted, and that Colonel Messinger was the patriarch as well as the commander.[76]

All three battalions of the 9th Infantry were virtually brand-new, filled with warmly welcomed, called-up white reserve officers and NCOs, green draftees, and blacks from deactivated service units and elsewhere. Continuing his private "integration" policy, Butch Barberis's 2/9 was now one-third black (230 of 688 men). Barberis had even placed a black captain, Forrest A. Walker, in command of his E Company.[77]

The once-proud, reliable black 3/9 was wobbly and was to remain so. One reason was McMains, according to the S-3, Harris Pope. Pope believed McMains had not recovered from the shock of his terrible losses at Kunu and the "gauntlet." Another reason was an acute, even drastic shortage of officers of any kind but especially those with combat experience. McMains had a new (white) exec, Harlan C. Stine, thirty-two, to replace his (black) exec, John Harlan, captured at Kunu, but very few other officers. This was because there were very few black officers in the Regular Army, and there had been no large pool of black officers in the reserves to call up. Julius Becton, returning to the 3/9 and recovered from his second battle wound, deserved a less hazardous battalion staff job, but owing to the shortage of officers, he went right back into the line as a company commander.[78]

Deployed along the Wonju–Chechon road, the 9th Infantry, facing northeast, fought a miniwar of its own. It repeatedly repulsed NKPA attacks aimed at seizing Chechon, from which the NKPA could angle west to encircle the 23d and 38th at Wonju. The old hands—and many newly arrived called-up reservists—conducted themselves with courage and professionalism. As a result, the NKPA failed to crack through this vital front, which was soon to be reinforced by the arriving units of Ferenbaugh's 7th Infantry Division.

\* \* \*

Ned Almond camped virtually full-time on the Wonju front. He continued to find fault with McClure's handling of the 2d Division. In another report to Ridgway he stated that having "traversed the front line portion" of a rifle company in each of six deployed battalions, he found many things amiss. "Foxholes and fields of fire were not well sited and most were poorly constructed," he wrote. "Evidence was noted of men who had never fired their crew-served weapons. One outfit could not hit within 300 yards of the target 700 yards away. . . . I saw many glaring examples of lack of supervision and troop control." Commanders were not providing hot meals; socks were in critical short supply. And so on.[79]

The upshot was that Almond decided to sack Bob McClure. Ridgway concurred with Almond's recommendation and wrote MacArthur to say that he "had full confidence in the judgment" of Almond in this matter and that McClure's relief was "thoroughly justified." He further advised MacArthur that it was "not desirable" to reassign McClure to other duty in Eighth Army.[80]

Almond's relief of McClure caused intense controversy. Paul Freeman, who had defended Dutch Keiser, also defended McClure. He "liked" McClure and thought he was a "good tactician and good soldier." He thought the real cause of the relief was "bad blood" between Almond and McClure dating from some earlier incident or set of circumstances. McClure was a "Collins man"; Almond resented Collins for denying his third star. His relief of McClure, others speculated, could have been revenge.\*

The proposed relief of division commanders in Korea for inept performance had thus far been well disguised: Keiser had been "hospitalized with pneumonia"; Barr, Church, Gay, and Kean were to be routinely "rotated." But the abrupt relief of McClure could not be disguised; he had commanded the 2d Division for only one month. His relief thus made "news." Ham Haislip feared that if the relief, coming on the heels of the Barr and Church announcement, were not "handled skillfully," a congressional investigation might result. But none did.[82]

Collins did everything possible to soften the terrible personal blow to his

---

\*The former 2d Division G-3, Maurice Holden, was struck by the ironical circumstances surrounding the relief of Keiser and McClure. "They were not working for the right bosses at the right time," he said. "If the command sequence had been the reverse, McClure-Keiser, rather than Keiser-McClure, all would have been rosy. McClure was a Collins-Walker man—Walker's drinking buddy. If McClure had commanded at Kunu-ri, Walker would not have relieved him. Keiser was an Almond man; they'd served together in Italy. If Keiser had commanded at Wonju, Almond would not have relieved him."[81]

friend McClure. He named him to command the 6th Infantry Division at Fort Ord. But McClure was professionally ruined and retired in 1954. Thereafter his relief would be repeatedly cited by historians as an example (usually the only example) of how Ridgway rid Eighth Army of incompetent generals.[83]

To replace McClure, Almond recommended his loyal X Corps chief of staff (and fellow VMI graduate), Nick Ruffner, forty-eight. Collins may have resented the relief of McClure, but he could not quarrel with the replacement. Collins was deeply indebted to Ruffner's father-in-law, Nellie Richardson, whom Ruffner had served as chief of staff of the "Pineapple Army" in Hawaii. Richardson (and probably Ruffner) had helped Collins get his first big "break" in World War II: command of the 25th Infantry Division.[84]

The appointment of Ruffner placed the 2d Division in the hands of two generals, Ruffner and the new ADC, George Stewart, who were "strangers" to the division and who had never led troops in combat. "But that was no problem," the X Corps G-3, Jack Chiles, remembered. "Tactically Almond ran the division, the regiments, and the battalions. All Ruffner had to do was simply obey Almond's orders." Soon, however, both Ruffner and Stewart learned to stand on their own feet and earned the respect of the men, Ruffner by rescinding McClure's order requiring all the men to grow beards. Although Freeman resented the circumstances under which McClure had been sacked, he later conceded that Ruffner was "a hell of a good division commander." The division chief of staff, Gerry Epley, agreed: "Ruffner did a good job. He would spend all day up front, come back, and brief the staff. Then the staff would brief him. . . . But that's the way to run a division. The commander should be down with the troops all day; you have to see for yourself."[85]

\* \* \*

The 7th Infantry Division, now under command of Buddy Ferenbaugh, began arriving in the X Corps sector on January 9. Herb Powell's 17th Infantry led the difficult motor-march through the ice- and snow-covered mountain roads; Charles Beauchamp's 32d Infantry followed. The 31st Infantry, still recovering from its mauling at Chosin, remained in division reserve. The 31st was now commanded by a low-key "sharp gentleman," West Pointer (1932) John A. Gavin, forty. A Stateside staff officer for most of World War II, Gavin had brought the 3/65 from Panama.[86]

The 7th Division now had a new ADC, replacing Hank Hodes. He was West Pointer (1927) Robert F. Sink, forty-five. A pioneer paratrooper like Mike Michaelis, Sink had commanded a parachute regiment (the 506th) of Maxwell D. Taylor's 101st Airborne Division in Normandy, Holland, and the Bulge. Taylor had wanted to promote Sink to brigadier general during the war, but various circumstances had prevented that. In the postwar years Sink had served at West Point as commander of the "school troops." After a year at the National War College (1948) he was assigned to the Far East. His appointment as ADC of the 7th Division brought his long-overdue star.[87]

Bob Sink was universally admired. Paratrooper Bill Paddock, "demoted" from 7th Division G-3 to G-2, remembered: "Sink was a real soldier, combat commander and Number One general officer." Sink, however, had a serious flaw. Another senior officer in the 7th Division recalled: "He was a great character, an absolutely phenomenal regimental commander in World War Two. In Korea he was the bravest man I ever saw. But he was a terrible alcoholic. Ferenbaugh told him that if he took *one* drink in Korea, he'd fire him. I don't think he did—in Korea. But he would go on these terrific benders in Japan. It was tragic. Alcohol eventually ruined his career."[88]

After Herb Powell got the 17th into the battle line, he took over his new duties as Ferenbaugh's chief of staff. He was replaced as commander of the 17th Infantry by the X Corps G-2, Bill Quinn—another from the West Point class of 1933. As G-2 of Sandy Patch's Seventh Army, Quinn had won internal fame (and a DSM) for correctly predicting a strong German attack (Nordwind) on New Year's Eve, 1944, in the Colmar Pocket. In the postwar years he helped transform the wartime OSS into the CIA, attended the National War College (1948), then reported to the Far East Command and, eventually, to X Corps. That he had failed to assess accurately CCF strength or intentions at the Chosin Reservoir was not held against him.[89]*

Quinn had never before commanded troops in combat, but he was determined to make the 17th Infantry the "best" and most "famous" in Korea. He chose Mike Michaelis, "who had a flair for command and publicity," as his role model. He christened the 17th Infantry the "Buffaloes" (as opposed to "Wolfhounds") and called himself Buffalo Bill Quinn. At key points on the regimental front his men posted signs: DANGER, BUFFALO CROSSING! A regimental press agent mailed off reams of handouts for hometown newspapers and courted war correspondents. Astonishingly the publicity campaign worked as designed; almost overnight the Buffaloes became famous. Hundreds of GIs requested a transfer to the outfit; some, Quinn boasted, even went AWOL to join.[91]

When all these changes had been completed, the 7th Division reentered combat on the Chechon front with virtually a brand-new command team: Buddy Ferenbaugh and Bob Sink at the top, well supported by the brainy, diplomatic chief of staff, Herb Powell, and the new G-3, Mel Huston, plus regimental commanders Buffalo Bill Quinn (17th) and John Gavin (31st). Of

---

* To the contrary. Quinn would be the first of many colonels on the X Corps staff to be "rewarded" by Almond with command of a regiment, thus giving them a leg up for selection to general. This practice became so pronounced that the 2d Division chief of staff, Epley, concluded that Almond deliberately "fired people to get his staff people into command."[90]

the senior 7th Division command team in northeast Korea, only Charles Beauchamp (32d) remained. Counting his prior temporary duty in command of the 34th Infantry, Beauchamp, in terms of combat service, was now the "senior" regimental commander in Korea.*

Both Powell and Huston, who had served under Ferenbaugh earlier, gave him rave reviews for his generalship in Korea. "After its far-flung, 'hit or miss' operations in northeast Korea, followed by a depressing withdrawal by sea to South Korea," Huston remembered, "the officers and men of the division were in dire need of aggressive, common-sense leadership and a boost in morale. Buddy was especially good, just the right injection. Well built and athletic, he impressed all with his bulk—a pat on the back with his huge hand and a deep chuckle to put one at ease—and there was never any question as to who was in command." Powell recalled: "He had great concern for protecting the soldier as much as possible and used the firepower of his artillery in heavy concentrations for that purpose, even to the consternation of his artillery commanders at times when they wanted to fall back on the artillery doctrine of firing only on located targets in order to conserve precious ammunition."[92]

Ferenbaugh's deep concern for his men, Powell recollected, extended to the blacks in the 7th Division and to those black units supporting the division. Ferenbaugh believed strongly in integration, and he treated all blacks with dignity and compassion. That led to "lengthy arguments" with his boss, Almond, Powell went on. Powell remembered that Almond specifically "ordered that a 155 mm howitzer battalion and smaller units of black troops be bivouacked behind the lines and left there."[93]

\* \* \*

By January 9 it was clear to Ridgway and Almond that the Communists had elected to make a very strong drive through Wonju. To deal with it, Ridgway's strategy was conventional doctrine: Hold, defensively, on the Wonju front, and mount counterattacks on the western front—initially with a reinforced Michaelis Force, then gradually building to a full-scale offensive.

The most urgent problem was holding the Wonju front. Almond's X Corps was still composed of only two American divisions, Ruffner's 2d and Ferenbaugh's 7th, still slowly moving forward, and several utterly disorganized and undependable ROK "divisions." The CCF had not yet appeared on the Wonju front in strength. But NKPA II and V corps were still fighting with a high degree of spirit and boldness, and it seemed a good probability that the CCF would reinforce the NKPA to exploit its successes.

---

*The average age of the three West Point regimental commanders in the 7th Division was forty-one years.

Still believing that Wonju was the "key" to holding the central front, Ridgway directed Almond to deploy the bulk of the 2d Division's strength—the 23d and 38th regiments—directly south of the town to block the roads leading to Chungju and Chechon. Meanwhile, to the right rear (or southeast), the reinforced 9th Infantry would continue to hold the lower portion of the Wonju–Chechon road. The arriving 7th Division would take up blocking positions on a west-east line from Chechon to Yongwol. To add strength to that sector, the 187th Airborne RCT would come over to Tanyang, a road hub behind (or south of) the 7th Division. In sum, Ridgway committed seven of Eighth Army's nineteen American regiments—about 30,000 infantrymen—to defend the central front.[94]

For the defense of the Wonju sector, Almond and Ruffner created a "horseshoe-shaped" enclave on high ground south of Wonju, with the closed end facing north toward the oncoming NKPA. The perimeter of the horseshoe was manned by six infantry battalions (including the French and Dutch), surrounding the 37th and 38th FABs. The French and Dutch battalions, new to combat, were split into four elements comprised of two companies and interspersed among the Americans. Claire Hutchin's 1/23 remained with the 9th Infantry; the 3/38, also detached, guarded a lower section of the Wonju–Chungju road.[95]

In sub-zero weather the NKPA surged out of Wonju in strength to attack the horseshoe on January 10. An epic battle—one of the most important of the Korean War—ensued. The 2d Division found itself and began to redeem the honor it had lost at Kunu. The division historian found it difficult to convey the fierceness and terror of the battle:

Friendly artillery and air pounded the masses of advancing Communists, inflicting staggering casualties while the bitter weather exacted an increasingly heavy toll on attackers and defenders alike. Finally after savage fighting during which the 1st and 2nd French companies repulsed four successive attempts by the enemy to envelop their position, the enemy turned back, his attack broken, friendly lines remaining intact. All the next day the two forces poured murderous barrages of fire at one another while friendly units were shuffled through knee-deep snow to locate maximum strength at the most critical points. The 2/23 with the 3rd French company attached, moved forward from the 2nd Division defenses and struggled to wrest important positions from the enemy on the southern outskirts of Wonju from which he had been laying down bases of fire on friendly positions. Hill 247, a low lying enemy-infested mass, was taken by the French only after they fixed bayonets and cut their way to the top where they held in spite of savage counterattacks and sub-zero winds which cut through winter clothing.[96]

This important, little-publicized battle raged for several more days. The historian wrote that the 2d Division continued to inflict "staggering" casualties on the NKPA. Meanwhile, the reinforced 9th Infantry held the Wonju–

Chechon road and the 7th Division moved forward to block the Chechon–Yongwol road. The six American regiments of the 2d and 7th divisions, plus some miscellaneous ROK units scattered through the mountains, brought the NKPA offensive to a standstill.

This was an action to gladden Ridgway's heart: "maximum punishment" on the enemy; "maximum delay" imposed. However, intelligence soon confirmed Ridgway's belief that the CCF would reinforce the Wonju front; the CCF was on the move. The horseshoe "salient" had held against the NKPA; but it was virtually impossible to resupply it over the treacherous roads, and the Wonju Airfield had been lost. In preparation for what seemed a certain, early confrontation with the CCF in that sector, Ridgway ordered Almond to withdraw the salient and align the X Corps central front east-west, with Line D in the western front, tying in on the left with IX Corps. The result was a thin but tidy X Corps line above Chungju running through Mokkye–Chechon–Yongwal, manned by Ruffner's 2d Division on the left and Ferenbaugh's 7th Division on the right. The 187th Airborne RCT (which had not seen significant action) remained in X Corps reserve at Tanyang.[97]

* * *

During these desperate army actions on the central front it became increasingly difficult for Ridgway to accept the nonactive role of the 1st Marine Division, still in reserve at Masan. Accordingly, on January 8 he summoned O. P. Smith to Taegu for a conference. Notwithstanding his prior assurances that the Marines would never again be assigned to Almond, Ridgway, facing a crisis, was compelled to change his mind. He requested that Smith send one RCT forward to Andong to help the 187th Airborne RCT backstop X Corps. The Marine historian wrote that Ridgway said he realized "that no commander liked to have his division split up, and he assured Smith that as soon as the X Corps zone became stabilized the RCT would be sent back to him."[98]

After the conference was over and Smith had returned to Masan, Ridgway had second thoughts and reverted to his previous position. He telexed Smith to say that he would not assign the Marines to Almond after all. They would remain under Ridgway's (or Eighth Army's) direct control. Nor would he split off an RCT. The full Marine division would deploy "without delay" on a line, Andong–Yondok. This deployment, in effect, would throw an American line behind the scattered ROK divisions holding the eastern end of Line D. It would also position the Marines much closer to the Wonju front should X Corps fail to hold and require emergency assistance.[99]

On the following day, January 9, Ridgway flew to Masan to visit the Marines. En route he directed his pilot, Mike Lynch, to fly low over the Naktong River, from Taegu to Masan, so he could study the terrain. Thinking ahead to a possible disaster, he later directed that the Eighth Army staff prepare studies on "tank trafficability" on the flat plains west and southwest of Taegu and a "fordability chart" of the entire Naktong, so that if the American divisions were forced to fall back to the Naktong again, the men could "mine every known ford."[100]

At the Marine division CP Ridgway spoke to the entire senior staff. By this time Ridgway had got his upbeat "talk" down pat. "Upon arrival here I had hope for offensive action," he began, "but due to the numerical superiority of the enemy, and after conferring on the ground with my corps and division commanders, I gave up the idea." Accordingly, present UN action, he went on, must be planned around "powerful local counterattacks" designed to "inflict maximum loss to the enemy" and "achieve maximum delay consistent with maintenance intact of all major units." He had "fullest confidence" that "when delay merges into defense," Eighth Army could stay in South Korea indefinitely. UN forces had "all advantages" except "numerical superiority." The Marines should look for every opportunity "to initiate greater offensive action and bleed Red China white."

In order to do so, American soldiers had to be more resourceful and tenacious. All units from squads up had to get off the roads and master the terrain. They had to patrol vigorously, get accurate combat intelligence, bring coordinated firepower to bear, and exercise stringent supply discipline because "our supply warehouses and shelves are bare." The "loss or wanton destruction of equipment is a punishable offense." In conclusion, he declared: "This may be the [first] crisis of World War III. The issues that are really at stake are the power and prestige of our great nation."[101]

On this visit Ridgway established a fine working relationship with the Marines, based on mutual confidence and respect. The "talk" had an electrifying impact. For his part Ridgway was pleased to find the Marines, in contrast with many Army divisions, ready and eager to fight.[102]

That day the Marines began packing for the move north by truck and ship. As ordered, they would man a line, Andong–Yondok, to prevent enemy penetrations and, at the same time, patrol aggressively north of the line to hunt down guerrillas. They would operate directly under Ridgway's control.

## IV

From afar the situation in Korea still seemed dismal. The CCF had temporarily stopped at the Han River; but Seoul and Wonju had been lost, and Eighth Army had withdrawn to Line D. In Tokyo and Washington, a renewed CCF offensive and forced evacuation seemed inevitable. "We were at our lowest point," George Marshall said.[103]

Still unresolved were two major questions:

• Exactly when should Eighth Army irrevocably begin the immensely complex and dangerous process of "evacuation"?

• Who would actually give the final order to evacuate—Tokyo or Washington?

Neither question had a simple answer. Washington still clung to the fading hope that evacuation might not be necessary, that Eighth Army could "fight on." To order an evacuation before the CCF had actually forced it would be damaging to American prestige. Yet to "fight on" until "forced" to evacuate would entail the great risk of a disastrous Dunkirk.

MacArthur was not much help. His answers to specific military queries from the JCS about when to begin evacuation had been fuzzy and confusing and had elicited renewed demands for all-out war with Red China. It appeared to the chiefs that he was attempting to avoid all responsibility for providing sensible guidelines and advice on evacuation and that above all, he was averse to taking responsibility for actually giving the order. The "onus" for directing the evacuation of Korea would fall on Washington, not on Tokyo.

\* \* \*

In the directive cabled to MacArthur on December 29, the JCS had said "it seems to us" that if Eighth Army were "forced back to positions in the vicinity of the Kum River and a line generally eastward therefrom" and if the CCF massed forces with "an evident capability" of "forcing us out of Korea," it would then be necessary for the chiefs to "direct" a withdrawal of Eighth Army to Japan. In response, MacArthur had said that "tactical estimates" seemed to be "sound," but he had intentionally or unintentionally clouded the issue by specifying a "Pusan beachhead" line, rather than a "Kum River" line, and had said that there was no need for an "anticipatory decision" until the "beachhead line" had been reached.[104]

Since there was a considerable difference between a Kum River line and a line at a Pusan beachhead, on January 3 the JCS asked MacArthur for a "clarification." Did he mean a line at the Kum River? Naktong River? The new Davidson Line above Pusan? Or what? MacArthur again seized upon this purely technical military query to intimate that his prior suggestions for all-out war with Red China being barred, Korea could not be held. Unless there were "some possibility of policy change or other external eventuality favorable to the strengthening of our effort in Korea," MacArthur cabled, a JCS directive to begin withdrawal could be issued "at any time." However, he said—again confusingly—"if a reasonable possibility does exist for favorable developments," then it would be well for the JCS to withhold the evacuation order until Eighth Army was pushed back to the old Naktong River line.[105]

Ridgway had withdrawn Eighth Army to Line D, a mere thirty miles north of the Kum River line. Since he was provided copies of the exchanges between MacArthur and the JCS, he was well aware that he might receive an order at any hour to begin evacuation. Although it went much against his grain—and public posture—he was thus compelled to order the staff to expedite evacuation planning. The Eighth Army G-3 planner, Bill Train, was placed in charge of a "small, supersecret" group to draw the plans.[106]

On January 6 Ridgway directly addressed MacArthur on the subject. He wrote that whether Washington assigned him "a mission of indefinite defense of a beachhead" or "a direct evacuation," Eighth Army "will respond to the utmost." However, Ridgway tactfully pointed out, the measure of success "will vary directly with the advance notice received and the resultant opportunity to initiate many actions." He urged an immediate decision, one way or the other, stating: "To defer this decision until our troops are on or within the final perimeter may entail heavy losses." Following an early decision, Ridgway believed that with "proper planning" an evacuation of "both units and equipment can be accomplished so as to return to you the bulk of these forces in condition to discharge any future missions."[107]

The possibility remained that notwithstanding a near-perfect plan for withdrawal into the Pusan beachhead, something might go drastically wrong, exposing the UN forces to possible annihilation. Should that dire situation occur, Ridgway suggested, it might be wise to assemble stocks of "chemicals" (i.e., poison gas) in Pusan to use against the enemy as a last resort—that is, to prevent the utter destruction of Eighth Army.[108]

An evacuation of Eighth Army raised other vexing questions. What about the ROK Army, government, and police? They numbered about 300,000 men—800,000 to 1 million including dependents. What about the 140,000 CCF and NKPA POWs held by Eighth Army? What about the hundreds of thousands of refugees? Ridgway believed it would be unthinkable to abandon the ROK army, government, and police, to have them face "savage retaliation." It would gravely damage American prestige. As a practical matter it might be extremely dangerous. The ROKs might defect and attack the withdrawing Americans or, in a rage, engage in widespread sabotage. Similarly, it would be unthinkable to leave behind the 140,000 POWs. It was believed that many of them were deserters and defectors who would almost certainly be executed by the CCF. Moreover, CCF and NKPA POWs would be required to barter for the release of American and ROK POWs.[109]

MacArthur responded the next day, January 7. He shared Ridgway's "impatience" but found it "impossible to expedite a decision" from Washington about evacuation. He went on: "There seems to be confusion" in Washington and the UN about what to do. As for the ROK Army and government, MacArthur said, "If we are directed to evacuate I have assumed it would apply to all UN forces, which would, of course, include the South Korean Army, and, if possible, their dependents." Regarding the 140,000 POWs, MacArthur had already urged Washington to authorize "their immediate transfer to the United States." He had received no reply to this suggestion, and if none came over the weekend, he would send a "follow-up message in order to expedite this decision." Regarding employment of "chemicals" on the CCF, MacArthur said: "I do not believe there is any chance of that. The United States inhibitions on such use are complete and drastic. Moreover, our allies wouldn't like it."[110]

\* \* \*

The frustrating and dismal situation confronting Washington provoked a reappraisal of the existing "soft" policies toward Red China designed to limit the war. In these debates, naval chief Forrest Sherman, who played a leading role, assumed a hawkish stance. In a significant enlargement of long-standing Far East strategic objectives, Sherman urged that "all appropriate means" be taken to prevent the "further spread by force of Communism on the mainland of Asia." Washington should support the establishment in China of a government "friendly to the United States"; support the South Koreans "as much and as long as practicable," keeping alive "an exile ROK government if forced to evacuate; and block Communist aggression in Indochina, Thailand, and Malaya.[111]

With regard to the crisis at hand, Sherman urged four immediate courses of action which had previously been recommended by MacArthur:

- A naval blockade of Red China, preferably with UN "concurrence." If UN concurrence was "not obtainable," then, he stated, "the time has come for unilateral action by the United States."
- Removal of all "restrictions" imposed on Chiang Kai-shek's forces on Formosa.
- Provide "logistical support" for anti-Communist guerrillas operating on the Chinese mainland.
- Authorize intermittent aerial reconnaissance of Manchuria and the Red China coast.[112]

Sherman believed that Eighth Army should "occupy advantageous defensive positions" in South Korea "as long as practicable" and "inflict maximum damage" on the CCF and NKPA with forces already available. If Eighth Army could hold in Korea, then two of the four recently mobilized "partly trained" National Guard divisions "might be sent to Japan to provide security there." If Eighth Army could not hold and was forced to evacuate, and if the CCF attacked it (by air) while en route to Japan, or if the CCF attacked "any of our forces outside of Korea," then America should retaliate with air and naval attacks on Red China.

In the belief that evacuation of Eighth Army from Korea was almost a certainty, the JCS drafted a contingency paper in which it "tentatively agreed" with Sherman's broad strategic objectives for the Far East and three of his four major action proposals. The exception was the naval blockade of Red China. Rather than impose it immediately, the JCS recommended that Washington "prepare" to impose it and "place it in effect" as soon as "our position in Korea is stabilized or when we have evacuated Korea, and depending upon circumstances then obtaining."[113]

MacArthur argued later that the views expressed in this JCS contingency paper coincided with his own and that therefore, he and the chiefs were "in agreement" on actions to be taken against Red China. This was not altogether true. The JCS had agreed with MacArthur's (and Ridgway's) suggestion to remove the restrictions on Chiang Kai-shek's forces—a major turnabout in policy—but it had not approved an immediate naval blockade of Red China or, no less important, massive Air Force attacks on Red China's industry and warmaking capacity.[114]*

The JCS forwarded this paper (dated January 12) to George Marshall. Without approving or disapproving, Marshall sent it along for "information" to the NSC. There it was filed, along with papers from State and other departments and agencies, for presidential review.[116]

\* \* \*

In the meantime, the JCS continued exchanging messages with MacArthur. These exchanges were governed by the policies in force but included Sherman's tentative proposal to send additional American troops to Japan. On January 9, directly addressing MacArthur's December 30 proposal for all-out war with Red China, the JCS cabled him that "the retaliatory measures you suggest have been and continue to be given careful consideration." However, the chiefs cautioned, based on "over-all considerations" the following "must be accepted":

• There was "little possibility" that policy changes or other eventualities would justify an increase in UN ground forces in Korea. There was no possibility of "favorable action" on MacArthur's proposal to use Nationalist forces in Korea in light of the "improbability of their decisive effort on the Korean outcome and their probable greater usefulness elsewhere."

---

* Air Force Chief Hoyt Vandenberg, opposing this course, argued that his "shoestring Air Force" (then sixty-eight groups) was the "sole" deterrent to global war. To employ it in Red China, where there were few worthwhile strategic targets, would be to "peck at the periphery" futilely and might invite such heavy attrition in aircraft that America would be "left naked for several years to come."[115]

- If UN positions in Korea could be "stabilized" with existing forces, then two "partly-trained" National Guard divisions "could be deployed to Japan." In the event UN positions in Korea could not be stabilized, then "part of" the evacuated Eighth Army would serve for the defense of Japan. Meanwhile, the secret "program for arming of Japanese Security Forces" would be "expedited."

- Efforts were being undertaken to "intensify" the "economic" blockade of Red China. However, a military blockade, if undertaken, "must await either stabilization of our position in Korea or our evacuation from Korea." A military blockade would require "UN concurrence" and "negotiations with the British" in view of the extensive British trade with China through Hong Kong.

- Naval and air attacks on objectives in Communist China "probably can be authorized" only if the CCF troops "attack United States forces outside of Korea" and a "decision must await that eventuality."

In conclusion, the JCS returned to the matter of evacuating Eighth Army. Recognizing the futility and impracticality of defining or specifying defensive lines, the chiefs correctly delegated the responsibility for the final decision to the theater commander. They ordered MacArthur: "Defend in successive positions . . . [Line D, E, F, etc.] inflicting maximum damage to hostile forces in Korea, subject to primary consideration of the safety of your troops and your basic mission of protecting Japan. Should it become evident in your judgment that evacuation is essential to avoid severe losses of men and material you will at that time withdraw from Korea to Japan."[117]

This categorical rejection of MacArthur's proposal for all-out war with Red China was predictably greeted in Tokyo as "dismal news." Nor did MacArthur like being told that the decision to evacuate or not had been delegated to him. His aide Courtney Whitney described this delegation of responsibility as a "booby trap," designed to put the "onus for evacuation" on MacArthur's shoulders. However, Whitney wrote paranoically, MacArthur "refused so easily to be taken in." He "shot a query right back asking for clarification."[118]

In actuality it was more than a simple query. It was yet another forceful and eloquently stated case for all-out war with Red China. As MacArthur saw it, that was the only possible way to avoid either a bloody annihilation of Eighth Army or humiliating evacuation. Again he did not concede the possibility that Eighth Army might "hang on" and fight:

In view of the self-evident fact that my command as presently constituted is of insufficient strength to hold a position in Korea and simultaneously [to] protect Japan against external assault, strategic dispositions taken in the present situation must be based on over-riding political policy establishing the relativity of American interests in the Far East.

There is no doubt but that a beachhead line can be held by our existing forces for a limited time in Korea but this could not be accomplished without losses. Whether such losses were regarded as "severe" or not would to a certain extent depend on the connotation one gives the term. . . . The troops are tired from a long and difficult campaign, embittered by the shameful propaganda which has falsely condemned their courage and fighting qualities in misunderstood retrograde maneuvers, and their morale will become a serious threat to their battle efficiency unless the political basis upon which they are asked to trade life for time is clearly delineated, fully understood, and so impelling that the hazards of battle are cheerfully accepted.

Considering the "limitations and conditions" imposed on his command and the rejection of his proposal for all-out war with Red China, the concentration of the CCF in Manchuria and Korea "eventually will render the military position of the command in Korea untenable." In view of these restrictions and conditions and "in the absence of overriding political considerations," MacArthur believed Eighth Army "should be withdrawn from the peninsula just as rapidly as it is tactically feasible to do so." If, on the other hand, the "primary political interest of the United States" lay in "holding a position in Korea," thus "pinning down a large segment" of the CCF, the "military course is implicit in political policy," and "we should be prepared to accept whatever casualties result and any attendant hazard to Japan's security."

Finally, MacArthur, shifting the "onus" for the decision to evacuate back to Washington, said that "the issue boils down to the question of whether or not the United States intends to evacuate Korea." That involved a "decision" of "highest national and international importance," far above MacArthur's competence. "My query therefore amounts to this: Is it the present objective of the United States political policy to maintain a military position in Korea indefinitely, for a limited time, or to minimize losses by evacuation as soon as it can be accomplished?" He concluded: "Under the extraordinary limitations and conditions imposed upon the command in Korea its military position is untenable, but it can hold for any length of time up to its complete destruction, if overriding political considerations so dictate. Request your clarification."[119]

This cable, the JCS historian wrote, "produced profound dismay" in Washington. The president was "deeply disturbed" to be told that the course of action advocated by his administration was, in effect, "not feasible," that Eighth Army would be "driven off the peninsula, or at the very least, suffer terrible losses." George Marshall, Dean Acheson remembered, was alarmed by MacArthur's lugubrious comments on the morale in Eighth Army and remarked that "when a general complains of the morale of his troops, the time has come to look into his own." Acheson, also "deeply disturbed," concluded that, as he wrote, "nothing further was needed to convince me that the general was incurably recalcitrant and basically disloyal to the purposes of his Commander in Chief." Omar Bradley described the cable as "childish quibbling" over the meaning of "severe losses" and "yet another long, involved argument for widening the war." Forrest Sherman reflected that "the normal relationships which are desirable between one echelon of command and another had been seriously impaired."[120]

\* \* \*

Further confusing Washington were the upbeat letters, cables, and back channel communications from Matt Ridgway. He had written Joe Collins that everything was "going fine" and that he was "completely confident" of the ability of Eighth Army to "accomplish every mission assigned." Unaware of MacArthur's cable to the JCS, Ridgway wrote Ham Haislip on January 11:

All goes well here. There are several major problems, solutions to which lie behind the days ahead. Yet we discern their outline. We think we see inside. We believe we shall lick them all.
    The power is here. The strength and the means we have—short perhaps of Soviet military intervention. My one over-riding problem, dominating all others, is to achieve the spiritual awakening of the latent capabilities of this command. If God permits me to do that, we shall achieve more, far more, than our people think possible—and perhaps inflict a bloody defeat on the Chinese which even China will long remember, wanton as she is in the sacrifice of lives.[121]

MacArthur's latest diatribe provoked another series of top-level meetings, culminating in a White House gathering on January 12. By that time the JCS had prepared a response to MacArthur's cable, and most of the discussion focused on that document, which amounted to a third directive for MacArthur within two weeks. There was also considerable discussion of what to do about the ROK Army and government and the 140,000 POWs should evacuation become necessary. President Truman repeated what he had told Attlee—that he would not abandon the ROK Army and government "to be murdered"—and gave his approval to evacuate them and the 140,000 POWs with Eighth Army.[122]

Eighth Army would withdraw to Japan, but where to put the ROKs and the POWs? One suggestion was that the ROKs be relocated on Cheju, a very large island in the Korea Strait, about fifty miles off the southwest coast of Korea. There they could be safeguarded by American air and naval power (based in Japan), setting up a sanctuary not unlike that enjoyed by the Chinese Nationalists on Formosa. Safely ensconced on the island, the ROK Army could be properly equipped and thoroughly trained, with an eye to returning someday to the Korean "mainland," perhaps in concert with a Nationalist Chinese attack on the mainland of China.[123]*

\* \* \*

  The loss of faith in MacArthur was now total and absolute. He had rejected any possibility short of all-out war with Red China that Eighth Army could "hang on" and fight. In light of Ridgway's upbeat reports, MacArthur's remarks about the poor morale in Eighth Army could not be trusted. He had not technically been insubordinate—he had a right and responsibility to submit his views—but as Acheson aptly observed, he was deemed to be "basically disloyal."

  Truman had every justification in the world for sacking MacArthur, but again he held back, guided by the reasoning that had earlier restrained him from taking this drastic step. Instead, there began a gradual process of isolating and bypassing MacArthur, leaving him as a figurehead in Tokyo but ignoring his advice and information. Thenceforth the Pentagon, indeed, the entire administration regarded Matt Ridgway as the man to consult in the Far East.

  The process of bypassing MacArthur began that very day. George Marshall obtained Truman's approval to send yet another JCS mission to Korea to make an on-the-spot appraisal of the situation. Joe Collins and Hoyt Vandenberg, plus contingents of legmen, would constitute the mission. Traveling separately, CIA Director Walter Bedell Smith and the Army's G-2, Alex Bolling, would also visit the Far East for the purpose of strengthening America's Far East intelligence-gathering operations, which had failed so abysmally in recent weeks.[124]

  In the meanwhile, in response to MacArthur's latest cable, the JCS issued new instructions, which had been "cleared" at the White House meeting:

Based on [sic] all the factors known to us, including particularly those presented in your recent messages, we are forced to the conclusion that it is infeasible under existing conditions, including sustained major effort by Communist China, to hold for a protracted period a position in Korea.

However, it would be to our national interest, and also to the interest of the UN, to gain some further time for essential diplomatic and military consultations with UN countries participating in Korea effort before you issue firm instructions of evacuation of troops from Korea.

It is important also to United States prestige worldwide, to [the] future of UN and NATO organizations and to efforts to organize anti-Communist resistance in Asia that Korea not be evacuated unless actually forced by military considerations, and that maximum practicable punishment be inflicted on Communist aggressors.

---

*The CCF and NKPA POWs would be interned on another island, Koje (near Pusan), during the evacuation, after which they would be abandoned to their fate.

It is not possible in Washington to evaluate present state of combat efficiency and morale of UN forces. However, we are concerned about effect on troops, particularly ROK forces, if it should become known to them that a decision to initiate troop evacuation were made at this stage in operations. Instructions to evacuate are almost certain to become known soon after issue . . . [and] this might well result in partial collapse of ROK troops, thus seriously jeopardizing the ability of Eighth Army to reach a relatively secure beachhead about Pusan and hold it during period required for actual evacuation.

Recalling that MacArthur had earlier said that an "anticipatory decision to evacuate" need not be made until the "old Pusan line" (the Naktong River) had been reached, the JCS requested that he "reconsider" this question in light of the above considerations and submit new recommendations, if necessary. Meanwhile, the directive of January 9—to hold out if possible, otherwise to withdraw Eighth Army to Japan—remained in force.[125]

Acheson had proposed that Collins and Vandenberg carry to MacArthur a document providing him "political guidance" on the latest administration decisions. But Bradley believed this inappropriate; Collins and Vandenberg should stick strictly to "military matters."[126] The upshot was that President Truman wrote a "personal letter" to MacArthur. Its basic theme was similar to that of the latest JCS directive: Hang on in Korea for as long as possible.

Truman wrote that his message was not to be construed "in any sense" as a "directive," merely as background to keep MacArthur abreast of the "basic national and international purposes" which lay behind recent decisions. However, like the JCS, the president laid heavy stress (three times in the first three paragraphs) on the need to mount the utmost "resistance" in South Korea, listing ten obvious political and psychological reasons why it was important to American interests.

Considering the "limited forces" available to MacArthur, such "resistance" might not be "militarily possible," Truman conceded. In the worst case, Eighth Army might be compelled to evacuate. If so, Truman wrote, it would be important to make it "clear to the world" that evacuation was "forced upon us by military necessity." But that would not be the end of it: "Resistance" might be "continued" from "offshore islands, particularly Cheju-do," if MacArthur thought that course "practicable and advisable." Moreover, Truman wrote, "we shall not accept the result [of evacuation] politically or militarily until the aggression has been rectified."[127]

Neither Truman nor anyone else in the administration ever elaborated on that last bellicose sentence. Very likely it reflected the shift to a tough policy toward Red China taking place in the JCS and elsewhere. If forced to evacuate (as then seemed almost inevitable), Washington would not simply "write off" Korea as a bad experience. The CCF aggression would be *rectified*. Peking would be made to pay, probably by some—or all—of the courses of action recommended by Forrest Sherman and those already "tentatively approved" in the January 12 JCS contingency paper.

By the time Truman's letter reached MacArthur, he had no doubt heard through back channels of Forrest Sherman's tough anti-Peking proposals and the "tentative approval" by the JCS of the January 12 contingency paper, which included Sherman's proposal to remove restrictions on Chiang Kai-shek. That, plus Truman's warlike vow to *rectify* Peking's aggression—even fighting from Cheju if MacArthur thought it advisable—may well have led MacArthur to believe that he had won the policy battle after all, that his programs for all-out war with Red China now had a very good probability of being approved—provided, of course, that Eighth Army was forced to evacuate.

# PART
# TEN

# Counterattacks

# 21

# "EIGHTH ARMY IN GOOD SHAPE"

## I

Chinese Communist military aims in South Korea were still not clear. The CCF had captured Seoul on January 4, but there was still no solid indication that it intended to advance below the Han River. After the initial CCF attacks the only major enemy thrust had come at Wonju on the central front, and that had been carried out not by the CCF but by NKPA II and V corps.

The long pause was baffling. It seemed excessive for the usual CCF regrouping and replenishing. One theory was that the delay was linked to Peking's diplomatic maneuverings in the UN. Supported by the Soviets, the Peking delegation had so far blocked American efforts to condemn Red China as aggressors in Korea and appeared to be gaining some support in its quest for a seat in the UN and other considerations. Another theory was that owing to Peking's failure to live up to a promise to provide Lin Piao armor, artillery, and air support, the CCF New Year's offensive had actually been "a dismal failure," and Lin, rankled and bitter, was reluctant to press the attack.[1]

On January 14, however, there were some signs that the CCF pause might be coming to an end. The Eighth Army G-2, Clint Tarkenton, reported that sources had found evidence of a CCF "buildup" in the area between Osan and Suwon: one or two regiments, possibly more. It could be the real thing, or it could be a feint to cover a shifting of CCF troops to the central front. Whatever the CCF purpose, Ridgway seized upon the news as "the most lucrative opportunity for destruction of enemy forces we have had since enemy attack began."[2]

At that time Michaelis Force was still forward of Line D, gingerly patrolling and probing below Osan. So far it had not inflicted any damage on the enemy. It was, however, ideally positioned to be heavily reinforced for an aggressive attack on the CCF "buildup." Accordingly, Ridgway issued orders to Shrimp Milburn to make a "strong armored attack." I Corps was to "inflict maximum destruction on the enemy" and then "withdraw to present positions, leaving covering forces to maintain contact." John Coulter's IX Corps, on the right of I Corps, would provide flank protection. To ensure that this first major Eighth Army attack—code-named Wolfhound—proceeded with utmost vigor and skill, Ridgway flew to Shrimp Milburn's I Corps CP. He carefully reviewed all the plans, visited the assigned units to give pep talks, and, in private, attempted to ignite the "spark of initiative" he had found wanting in Milburn. The "existing situation," he told him, "offers you an opportunity to be a brilliant instead of just a good corps commander."[3]

This visit led to a decision on Ridgway's part to "camp" at I Corps temporarily. He wanted to be forward with troops—away from Eighth Army's rear headquarters in Taegu. The I Corps headquarters had the staff, communications, and other necessary support facilities, including a good mess. Ridgway set up a "mobile sleeping and office abode" in a two-and-a-half-ton truck. His personal staff, which now included his confidant Walt Winton and Joseph W. Dale, slept in a small tent beside the truck. Ridgway later conceded that it could not have been a "source of joy or comfort" for Milburn to have "the Army commander underfoot at all times," but Milburn was "patient and generous."[4]

Perhaps so. But as a whole, the I Corps staff, already upset by Ridgway's sacking of G-3 John Jeeter, found Ridgway's presence vastly discomfiting. He was "The Man Who Came to Dinner" or "an honor they didn't deserve." Chief of Staff Rinaldo Van Brunt lamented. "Oh God! He came to *every* briefing *every* morning. . . . The whole staff was always on pins and needles. My God! One morning a poor junior officer accidentally spilled coffee all over him! . . . He'd go out all day with the troops. Then, when he came back at night, I had to brief him again—on *everything,* even minor things, like which way the water drained in our sector."[5]

\* \* \*

Operation Wolfhound would be mounted by a powerful force, heavily supported by armor. The "spearhead" would be composed of Michaelis's 27th Infantry, Dolvin's 89th Tank Battalion, Gus Terry's 8th FAB, and James Sanden's 90th FAB. Two battalions of the 3d Division, Herman Dammer's 2/65 and Julius Levy's 1/15, backed by armor and by howitzers of Walter Downing's 10th and Robert Neely's 39th FAB would attack on the immediate right. Still farther right two ROK battalions would attack north to protect the right flank of the 2/65 and 1/15. In all, Wolfhound comprised seven infantry battalions (about 6,000 men), about 150 tanks, and the equivalent of about three artillery battalions.[6]

John Corley's 24th Infantry would play a supporting role. Two of its battalions, the 2/24 and 3/24, would deploy forward of Line D on the Pyong-taek–Osan highway (replacing the British) to protect the rear of the Michaelis-Dolvin spearhead and hold the highway against attacks by CCF or guerrilla infiltrators. Its still-reorganizing and weak 1/24 would patrol the highway south of Line D between Chonan and Taejon. Corley reported that participation in these offensive operations greatly improved morale and that partly as a result, nonbattle casualties had fallen off drastically.

Yet Ridgway was leery of committing the 24th Infantry. As he said later, the outfit was "a cause of constant concern." It was then undergoing yet another game of musical chairs in the ranks of the white battalion commanders. The 1/24 commander, Gerald Miller, who was evacuated, had been replaced by Corley's S-3, West Pointer Joseph Missal. He served briefly before being replaced by the exec of the 2/24, Martin L. Davis. He would also soon be replaced by yet another officer—the fourth 1/24 commander within about one month. Following the departure of Melvin Blair, the 3/24 had been commanded temporarily by the 3/24's S-3, Roscius Newell. Recently the able 3/24 exec, William D. Mouchet, had been promoted to "permanent" command.[7]*

The Wolfhound forces jumped off on schedule at dawn, January 15. Michaelis sent Gilbert Check's 1/27 wide on the left flank toward Paranjang, on the coast of Asan Bay. It met no opposition and made good progress, outflanking Osan. But Gordon Murch's 2/27 and Richard Keyes's 3/27, attacking up the main highway, progressed "with some difficulty." The ROK refugees had cleared off the highway, but Michaelis and Dolvin had to deal with the blown-out bridges that Eighth Army had left in its withdrawal. The battalions finally reached Osan, but just north of there (where Brad Smith's 1/21 had first met the NKPA in July), they ran into heavy CCF fire and were again delayed.[8]

On the right the attack of the 3d Division forces indicated that Shorty Soule had not yet demanded meticulous planning from his units. Julius Levy's 1/15 shot due north from Ansong toward its objective, Kumyangjang, making good time. However, owing to "inadequate reconnaissance," Herman Dammer's 2/65 found its planned route (on Michaelis's immediate right) "impassable." Dammer was therefore forced to double back and follow the 1/15 up the road toward Kumyangjang as far as Songjol. There Dammer turned left (or

---

* The turnover of battalion commanders in the 24th Infantry greatly exceeded that in its sister regiments, the 27th and 35th.

west) into Osan, which the Wolfhounds had already cleared, and bivouacked for the night.[9]

Racing on toward Kumyangjang, outpacing the Wolfhounds, Levy's 1/15 made remarkable time. At about dusk it reached the village, caught the "enemy unaware," killed about fifty, and captured that place, which at least temporarily "cut" the Suwon–Yoju–Wonju highway. Levy—now to the north of the Wolfhounds—turned left (or west) on the highway and headed directly for Suwon in pitch-darkness. He soon ran into heavy CCF mortar fire and buttoned up. The two ROK battalions, advancing on the right of the 1/15, came into the Kumyangjang area behind the 1/15 that same night without having met any opposition.[10]

On the morning of January 16, Michaelis's Wolfhounds converged on Suwon. Check's 1/27, coming up on the left flank, advanced from Paranjang against no opposition. However, while closing the pincers on Suwon, Check's 1/27 and Murch's 2/27 ran into heavy CCF machine-gun fire about a half mile south of the city. At the same time a CCF force attempted to charge in from the flanks and cut the road behind the 2/27. Dammer's 2/65 was no help. That morning it had taken a cow path leading northeast out of Osan and had bogged down in ice and snow.[11]

It was soon apparent to Ridgway and Milburn that the CCF was assembling at Suwon and Kumyangjang in considerable strength. The aim seemed to be a counterattack southwestward to cut the Suwon–Osan highway behind Michaelis and Dolvin. If so, the only force standing between the CCF and the highway was Dammer's 2/65. Since it could be bypassed or overrun, there was danger that Michaelis and Dolvin could be cut off and trapped at Suwon.

Weighing the risks and dangers, Ridgway and Milburn issued orders for Wolfhound to break off the attack and withdraw. All forces involved in the attack pulled back to a line running west-east just below Osan. There the forces more or less tied in flanks, forming a five-battalion front, left to right: Check's 1/27, Murch's 2/27, Keyes's 3/27, Dammer's 2/65, and Levy's 1/15. The two ROK battalions extended the line eastward into the mountains. The tanks and artillery backed up the line.[12]

Ridgway hoped to lure the CCF into this line for a slaughter. But curiously, the CCF did not pursue. This led to a belief that the Chinese generals had evidently made a firm decision not to fight in the "open" western sector, where the UN armor could operate efficiently and FEAF aircraft could find enemy targets. The CCF would probably continue to shift forces easterly—into the mountainous terrain in the Yoju–Wonju sector, where they could find concealment and where UN tanks, motorized artillery, and other vehicles could operate only with great difficulty.

Operation Wolfhound thus failed to achieve its principal mission of inflicting maximum damage on the CCF. In truth, it scarcely touched the CCF. But its intangible benefits were remarkable. Four regiments (27th; 24th; 65th; 15th) of two divisions (25th; 3d) had been involved. All men from generals to privates looked—and proceeded—north rather than south. A little ground north of Line D had been regained. No unit had been trapped or overrun by CCF "hordes." The reluctance of the CCF seriously to engage—or pursue— was well noted. Wolfhound thus gave Eighth Army a profound psychological uplift.

\* \* \*

This tentative employment of armor in the attack persuaded Ridgway that the widely held view that Korea was not good tank country was complete nonsense. The rugged terrain and primitive road nets prohibited mass employment of armor on a wide front as had been done in Europe in World War II, but it was manifest that even attacking on a "one-tank" front, armor could be highly useful. As the I Corps armor officer, West Pointer (1935) Thomas D. Gillis, put it in a report: "We have yet to find a situation in which armor, to some degree, could not be profitably employed. The tank has repeatedly exploited the situation in spite of the terrain."[13]

On January 14 Eighth Army had 670 tanks in its inventory. Of these 625 were American (light Chaffees, medium Shermans, heavy Pershings and Pattons) and 45 were British (medium Churchills and heavy Centurions). Most of the American tanks (about 400) were assigned to the six numbered tank battalions; the British tanks, to the British Brigade. The six American battalions were usually "attached" to the six Army divisions, although occasionally they were detached for special missions.\*

Although the total number of tanks in Eighth Army's inventory was impressive on paper, in reality it was less so. Nearly half the inventory was a question mark. Of the total, 64 were the light, thin-skinned Chaffees (with a 75-mm gun), useful only for reconnaissance, while 147 were the heavy Pershings (90-mm gun), which the Army tankers had unanimously condemned as "a lousy tank" and "a complete flop"; the Pershings were being withdrawn from the inventory and replaced as rapidly as possible. Of the total, 97 were new heavy Pattons (90-mm gun). Some tankers swore by the Patton, but others asserted that it was too big and clumsy, burned too much fuel, and required too much maintenance.

The remaining half of the American tanks in Eighth Army's inventory (317) were World War II–vintage medium Shermans (76-mm gun). Despite

---

\*The 6th Tank Battalion usually operated with the 24th Division; the black 64th with the 3d Division; the 70th with the 1st Cav; the 72d with the 2d; the 73d with the 7th; and the 89th with the 25th Division.

its older technology and smaller gun, many tankers, including World War II combat veterans Tom Dolvin and Bill Rodgers (recently promoted from command of the 70th Tank Battalion to be Eighth Army armor officer), much preferred a version of the Sherman known as the M4A3E8 (the "Easy Eight") to the Pattons. It was sturdy and reliable, was highly maneuverable, and had moderate fuel consumption and a "wide track" which gave "good flotation" in the rice paddies. Both Dolvin and Rodgers had been offered Pattons for their battalions, but both had declined them in favor of Easy Eights.

So viewed, Eighth Army's tank inventory was less than satisfactory for major and extended armored operations. Accordingly Ridgway took immediate steps to get more tanks. Knowing that he would meet resistance in Washington to a request for more numbered tank battalions, he resorted to a complicated bureaucratic ploy. The 2d and 3d divisions had arrived directly from the States with an "organic" tank company with most regiments, in addition to the attached 72d and 64th tank battalions. The four divisions which had come from Japan (1st Cav, 7th, 24th, and 25th) had not been authorized organic tank companies* and were, in a sense, being shortchanged. Ridgway therefore requested that the latter four divisions be officially authorized organic tank companies, a request that would increase his tank inventory by about 250 tanks to a total of nearly 1,000. The ploy failed. The Department of the Army rejected the request on the grounds that there were already "a large number" of tanks in Korea and the terrain was too "rugged."

The upshot was that Ridgway remained restricted in armor to the six tank battalions plus the regimental tank companies in the 2d, 3d, and 7th divisions. After the Pershings had been purged from the inventory, three of the tank battalions (6th, 64th, 73d) were equipped with Pattons; the other three (70th, 72d, 89th), with Shermans, most of which were Easy Eights. Those regimental tank companies equipped with Pershings likewise traded them for Easy Eights. After all these changes had been accomplished, the number of reliable American tanks (including Pattons) available for major armor operations was about 600.

In keeping with his philosophy of maximizing all available firepower of Eighth Army to kill Chinese, Ridgway directed his commanders to launch intensive training and to draw plans for more effective use of the available armor. These plans were *not* to include dramatic Patton-like armored attacks to "unlimited objectives," but rather limited operations, designed specifically to support the infantry with tank firepower.

---

* As part of the favored treatment of X Corps for Inchon MacArthur had allowed Ned Almond to beef up the 7th Division with three organic tank companies (17th, 31st, 32d) equipped with Easy Eight Shermans reclaimed from Pacific battlefields and refurbished by Japanese. However, these tank companies had not yet been officially authorized by the Department of the Army.

## I I

The JCS mission to ascertain the "facts" in Korea, comprised of Joe Collins and Hoyt Vandenberg, arrived in Tokyo on January 15. It was Collins's fourth visit to Tokyo in six months and Vandenberg's second. Both men were properly respectful of MacArthur, but they were now considerably less awed in his presence and more inclined to challenge and parry.[14]

Their initial meeting with MacArthur at the Dai Ichi Building began on a bizarre note. MacArthur came into the room, carrying a copy of Truman's January 13 letter. He sat down and read the entire letter aloud, then tossed it on the table, stabbed at it with his finger, and pronounced dramatically: "That, gentlemen, finally settles the question of whether or not we evacuate Korea. There will be no evacuation."[15]

Collins took the floor immediately to challenge MacArthur. He pointed out that Truman's letter—as the president explicitly wrote in its opening paragraph—did not constitute a new "directive" to "remain in Korea indefinitely." The JCS directive of January 12—to hold in Korea for as long as possible without endangering Eighth Army or the security of Japan—was still in force. However, despite "fervent protests" from Collins, MacArthur held to his conclusion. Truman's suggestion that UN forces might fight on from the island of Cheju if MacArthur approved and that CCF aggression in Korea could not be accepted and would be "rectified" had apparently convinced MacArthur that the president was swinging to his view, even if the JCS was not. He stressed again that a withdrawal from Korea would have profound repercussions throughout Asia and would "unquestionably result in the loss of Hong Kong, Indochina and all the rest of Southeast Asia."

Having interpreted his mission as one of keeping Eighth Army in Korea "indefinitely," MacArthur then went on to discuss the security of Japan. With "some emotion," as Collins put it, he declared he could not keep Eighth Army in Korea and also "assume responsibility" for Japan. Although there was then no clear-cut indication of a Soviet threat, and Soviet propaganda had diminished, there were sufficient Soviet military forces in Sakhalin and Vladivostok to mount an attack on Japan. MacArthur thus urged again that the four National Guard divisions which had been mobilized for the defense of Japan be sent "at once."

Collins responded with a correction. The four National Guard divisions had been called up not for the defense of Japan but, rather, to help fill the Army's depleted General Reserve. However, Collins continued, there was a possibility that, as Forrest Sherman had suggested, two of the four divisions *might* be sent to Japan.

Returning the discussion to possible evacuation, Collins introduced the problem of the ROKs and POWs. He informed MacArthur of Truman's desire that the ROK government, police, and Army—and possibly the dependents—be evacuated and of Washington's disinclination to transfer the POWs to the United States, as MacArthur had earlier suggested. The Washington thinking was that the POWs should be moved to the island of Koje during the evacuation, then abandoned there. MacArthur "expressed satisfaction" with the decision about the ROKs (and dependents) but not with the decision to abandon the POWs. He believed that would be a "sign of weakness."[16]

Finally—and in hindsight perhaps inadvisably—Collins produced the JCS contingency planning paper of January 12 and read it to MacArthur. Collins stressed that the proposals were "tentative" and subject to presidential approval. Although the JCS had unconditionally accepted only one of MacArthur's major recommendations for immediate action—lifting the restrictions on Chiang Kai-shek—MacArthur was pleased and "indicated his concurrence" with the paper. Apparently he interpreted this paper as another indication that Washington was swinging around to his views.[17]

* * *

Collins and Vandenberg flew on to Korea the same day, January 15, arriving in Taegu about noon. Ridgway met them at the airport with an appropriate honor guard and a relentlessly positive outlook. After the airport formalities had been concluded, Ridgway escorted them to a press conference which had been arranged in advance for several very specific purposes.[18]

Until Ridgway arrived, there had been no official press censorship in Korea. Reporters were asked voluntarily to censor their own stories, taking care not to give away information that would be valuable to the enemy or jeopardize American lives. By and large the reporters had faithfully discharged this responsibility. However, newspapers and newsmagazines had fallen into the custom of routinely publishing maps showing the disposition of major U.S. forces (corps and divisions) and even prospective UN defensive lines (B, C, D, etc.).[19]

During Eighth Army's December retreat from the Chongchon to the Imjin River, some of the press coverage had been harshly critical—unfairly so, the Army believed.[20] About the time Ridgway arrived in Korea, MacArthur ordered press censorship, and Ridgway concurred. One reason was to stop the flow of overblown or inaccurate "panic" stories which came back to the GIs in Korea via mail, radio, or other means, intensifying the morale problem in Eighth Army. Another reason was that Ridgway did not believe the CCF should be handed the UN "order of battle" on a platter. During his withdrawal from Seoul and the Han River, he had imposed a drastic, total "news blackout" so long as UN units were not in "full contact with the enemy."[21]

The responsible senior war correspondents abided by these rules; indeed, many actually welcomed press censorship. However, a difficulty soon arose.

Reflecting the early January mood of Eighth Army, most war correspondents assumed that evacuation was inevitable and began filing stories to that effect. But these stories were blocked by Ridgway's press censors on the grounds that they dealt with "tactical movements" or gave aid and comfort to the enemy. The correspondents vigorously protested this censorship of what could turn out to be the biggest story of the Korean War as "political" rather than "tactical."

Fuel was added to this fire by one of the senior war correspondents, Don Whitehead of the Associated Press. On January 13, back in the States and free of censorship restraints, Whitehead wrote and circulated from New York the big story that all correspondents in Korea were trying to file. "American troops and their UN allies," Whitehead stated, were "headed toward a mass evacuation," and the "evacuation was inevitable." Upon learning of this published story, the correspondents in Korea were, of course, furious and demanded release of their own stories.[22]

Still, Ridgway refused, for two reasons. First, he did not believe evacuation was "inevitable" and did not intend to evacuate unless ordered. Stories such as Whitehead's had a serious negative impact on the morale of his forces, defeating his efforts to instill a renewed fighting spirit which, if successful, would greatly forestall any evacuation. Secondly, he believed that such stories might have a similar negative impact on the ROK Army, leading to wholesale defections, which could imperil Eighth Army and perhaps even force an unwarranted evacuation.

The press conference Ridgway had set up upon arrival of Collins and Vandenberg thus had several purposes: first, to placate the irate correspondents by granting "access" to the "top brass" for a free exchange; secondly, to counter the negativism of the Whitehead story and discourage similar stories from correspondents; thirdly, to reassure the ROKs in order to prevent wholesale defections. Both Collins and Ridgway went "on the record" with "positive" (but carefully qualified) statements.[23]

*　*　*

After the conference the two chiefs parted company, Collins to inspect the ground forces, Vandenberg to inspect the air forces. Ridgway was to serve as Collins's personal guide throughout his stay.

Joe Collins and Matt Ridgway were close acquaintances but not intimate friends. Ever since their days as classmates at West Point, they had been professional rivals. During World War II Ridgway had lost some ground when he accepted the airborne command assignment, which was new and different, specialized, and not universally accepted. Assigned to command conventional forces, Collins had become Eisenhower's and Bradley's most dependable workhorse corps commander. One result was that Collins now wore four stars,

Ridgway, but three. Collins was Army chief of staff; Ridgway, merely the most likely contender to replace him. Ridgway did not really like Collins, and he was not pleased at the outcome of the professional rivalry so far.[24]

During the war the two generals had fought once, side by side, as equals. That was during the Battle of the Bulge, when Ridgway's XVIII Airborne Corps and Collins's VII Corps were rushed to the critical north side of the German penetration. Although the battle for Bastogne got the publicity, the lesser-known "north side" battle was the more critical. During it both men had performed magnificently, working in harmony, conferring daily, interchanging forces and men. Meeting Ridgway on a battlefield in Korea, Collins was reminded of those grim, but ultimately successful, days. He recalled with admiration what an indomitable rock and great battlefield commander Ridgway had been then. In Korea Collins could "feel in Eighth Army" the "improved spirit Ridgway had already imparted to his men."[25]

Operation Wolfhound had been launched that morning. In order not to distract Milburn at this vital time, Ridgway escorted Collins to the less active sectors of the front. They called first at Ned Almond's X Corps CP on the "central" front. There Collins had good news for Almond. In response to the long-standing requests of MacArthur—and more recent requests from Ridgway—Collins had approved the promotion of Almond from two to three stars, along with his fellow corps commanders Coulter and Milburn. White House and Senate approval were assured within a month.[26]*

The situation on the X Corps front was puzzling and worrisome. The NKPA forces that had taken Wonju (at considerable cost to themselves) appeared to be withdrawing. That day a patrol from Peploe's 38th Infantry had found the town almost deserted. On the basis of past experiences, Almond and his staff believed the break in contact and withdrawal could very likely signal preparation for a massive counterattack, possibly reinforced by those CCF troops that were believed to be shifting east to the central front. Whatever the case, Almond had issued orders to Ruffner's 2d Division to advance and retake Wonju but to be prepared to fall back again if a massive enemy attack developed.[27]

Another worrisome factor was the extent of NKPA infiltration into the X Corps sector. Almond believed that possibly a full NKPA division had slipped through ROK forces on the mountainous right flank to join with NKPA guerrillas "behind the lines." These NKPA regulars and guerrillas were throwing up roadblocks and striking at key X Corps strongpoints to such an extent that almost no area of the corps's "rear" could be considered "safe." X Corps had been compelled to divert dozens of units of all sizes to patrol the

---

*The promotions became effective on February 13, 1951.

key points and supply lines, sapping the corps's striking power. Until the "rear" had been "cleaned up," the corps was not in a position to launch a strong offensive attack. But Almond (justifying his relief of Barr and McClure) predicted better times ahead for the 2d Division under Nick Ruffner and the 7th Division under Buddy Ferenbaugh.[28]

Ridgway and Collins moved on to IX Corps. There Collins gave Coulter the good news about his promotion to three stars. It came as a mixed blessing. By then Coulter knew he was being "kicked upstairs," soon to be replaced by Bryant Moore; his own chief of staff, Andrew Tychsen, was to be sent home, along with IX Corps's two division commanders, John Church (24th Division) and Hap Gay (1st Cav). IX Corps had never been a happy outfit; it was certainly not one now.[29]

The bright spot at IX Corps was the G-3, West Pointer (1932) William B. Kunzig, forty. Kunzig had served in the crack G-3 section of First Army in the ETO under its chief of staff, Bill Kean. In compliance with Ridgway's directives, Kunzig was now churning out aggressive attack plans for IX Corps. Elements of Dick Stephens's 21st Infantry Regiment had patrolled well forward of Line D, near Yoju, on the upper reaches of the frozen Han River, where the temperature at night fell to twenty-five below zero. Men of Gines Perez's 2/21 had "walked across" the Han—a memorably aggressive event—but had found "no enemy." Subsequently, on corps orders, the 21st had withdrawn to Line D, but Stephens had left the 1/21 as a reconnaissance force in Yoju. Meanwhile, Throckmorton's 5th Infantry and Coad's Commonwealth Brigade were alternating patrols to Ichon. Neither had encountered noteworthy enemy forces.[30]

The absence of enemy contact in front of IX Corps was likewise puzzling. It had led Kunzig to propose a powerful reconnaissance in force similar to Operation Wolfhound to regain the Suwon–Yoju–Wonju highway running west-east across IX Corps's front, to be followed by strong armored patrols beyond the highway until contact was made with the enemy. Without hesitation Ridgway approved this plan, suggesting that after I Corps had regrouped from Wolfhound, it mount a diversionary armored attack toward Suwon to support the IX Corps attack.

*   *   *

That night Ridgway hosted a dinner for Collins and his party at Eighth Army headquarters in Taegu. Afterward, in privacy, Ridgway and Collins discussed the "rotation" scheme for the Eighth Army generals—Barr, Church, Gay, Kean—with Collins stressing the need to downplay the turnover to the greatest extent possible. In keeping with this policy, the actual change of command ceremonies would be "stretched out." In order to minimize any chance of a public blot, Kean, the best of the commanders, would be last to leave by several weeks.[31]*

They also discussed the high-level Army shifts in the Pentagon. Collins had lost two of his chief assistants at about the same time: Ridgway to Korea; Al Gruenther to NATO, as chief of staff to Eisenhower. Ridgway's slot (operations) had been filled by John E. ("Ed") Hull, fifty-four, a graduate of Miami University of Ohio (1917). Hull had been a high-level Pentagon strategist and planner during World War II. Gruenther's slot (plans) had been filled by Charles L. Bolté (Armour Institute of Technology, 1917), fifty-five, a longtime cohort of Collins's, who had fought with the AEF in World War I. Since 1948 Bolté had been a high-level Pentagon planner, noted for his warmth, wit, and diplomacy. Bolté had two West Point sons. The older, David E. (1949), had been badly wounded in September 1950 while serving with the 8th Cav near Taegu. The younger, Phillip L. (1950), was then a platoon leader in the 7th Cav.[32]

The appointment of Hull and Bolté to three-star jobs would in no way change the "plan of succession" Collins had devised. They would go no higher. When Ham Haislip retired, as planned, six months hence (July 1951), Collins would bring Ridgway back to the Pentagon to replace Haislip as vice chief of staff. Two years after that (July 1953), when Collins retired, Ridgway would move up to replace Collins. Meanwhile, Collins would recommend Ridgway for immediate promotion to four stars. Neither man was aware of Bradley's proposed plan to retire Collins one year earlier, in July 1952, and name Ridgway chief of staff of the Army.[33]

*　*　*

On the following day, January 16, Collins and Vandenberg continued the inspection. Vandenberg boldly—and foolishly—flew deep over enemy lines in the central sector. "It had snowed three days before," he remembered. "There was no sign of any life, any footprints, any wheelprints, or any movement." After returning to the rear area, Vandenberg boarded a helicopter and flew twelve miles forward of Line D, landed, and, in what the Army historian described as one of the more "remarkable" sidelights of the war, "joined a ground patrol" for a firsthand view of the situation. The historian thought that this exposure spoke well of Vandenberg's courage but reflected "some doubt on his judgment." Had he been captured, America would have been humiliated beyond words and the CCF might have gained a priceless intelligence source.[34]

By coincidence, that day Gene Landrum was finally rotated home. Setting the standard for all departing senior officers in Eighth Army, Ridgway gave

---

*The formal dates of departure agreed to: Barr and Church, January 26; Gay, February 5; Kean, February 25.

Landrum a proper "farewell ceremony" in Taegu and a second DSM. Perhaps touched by all this, when Collins returned to the Pentagon, he (who had recently refused Walker's request to give Landrum one star) arranged that Landrum would get his World War II rank of two stars restored upon retirement.[35]

That day the Operation Wolfhound forces, having tweaked the noses of the CCF at Suwon, pulled back to the line running west-east below Osan. After the Landrum ceremony Ridgway and Collins flew up to Milburn's CP. There Collins gave Milburn the news of his promotion to three stars and sat through an upbeat assessment of Wolfhound. Afterward Collins and Ridgway visited the CPs of Bill Kean's 25th Division, Shorty Soule's 3d Division, the Turkish Brigade, Tom Brodie's British Brigade, and William Harris's Puerto Rican 65th Regiment. Collins talked with generals, colonels, sergeants, and privates.[36]

Everywhere in Eighth Army Collins found a new, positive outlook. Milburn's staff was already formulating aggressive plans for another reconnaissance in force. The GIs Collins encountered were cold—the weather was still frightful—but well fed and cocky. Some had even become contemptuous of the CCF. They ridiculed press reports of Chinese "hordes" with humor: "How many hordes in a platoon?" "I was attacked by two hordes and killed both of them."[37]

The next morning, January 17, Collins continued his frontline tour, meeting with Syngman Rhee and visiting ROK III Corps and the ROK 5th Division. At Taegu he linked up with the Vandenberg party, and all embarked for Tokyo to consult again with MacArthur. Ridgway remained in Taegu to meet the incoming intelligence chiefs Bedell Smith and Alex Bolling, who had Charles Willoughby in tow.[38]

On the flight to Tokyo Collins and Vandenberg compared notes. Both men were gratified by what they had seen and heard. MacArthur had been dead wrong. Eighth Army was not "tired" and "embittered" and seriously threatened by low morale. To the contrary, owing to Matt Ridgway's strong and intelligent leadership, it was making a strong comeback.

Having analyzed Line D in detail, Collins had reached some conclusions. The left, or west sector, where UN armor and close air support could operate most effectively, was "very strong," practically impregnable. As a result, there was "no indication that the enemy wanted to fight it out there." The extreme right of the line, on the Sea of Japan, defended by the ROK Capital Division, would also probably hold. In that rugged area, where the Taebaek mountain range abutted the sea, there was only one major road, the coastal highway. Carrier-based aircraft and naval gunfire were blocking the enemy on the road. As a result, Collins did not think the eastern sector "would be a major source of trouble."[39]

The most vulnerable sector of the line was the center, in the Wonju area, defended by Almond's X Corps. In view of the heavy extent of infiltration in the sector, the difficult terrain, the unreliability of the ROKs, and the thinness of the American forces (2d and 7th divisions; 187th Airborne RCT; the Marine division then moving up to Andong), it seemed likely that if the CCF launched an offensive, it would come in that area, and it could very well succeed.

However, Ridgway was fully alert to that possibility and was "doing his best" to prevent a CCF success. The weight of a CCF offensive might force further withdrawals in the center, but Ridgway had worked out a new plan for the defense: holding "specific" strongpoints rather than a "line." If CCF forces achieved a breakthrough at one of these "points," he would attempt to consolidate UN forces on it and throw back the CCF. Ridgway was confident that he could hold off the CCF (and evacuation) for at least "three months."[40]

Upon landing in Tokyo, Collins immediately cabled Omar Bradley an optimistic report. In part it read:

Eighth Army in good shape and improving daily under Ridgway's leadership. Morale very satisfactory considering conditions. ROK forces lack confidence and instinctively fear Chinese but are still capable of resistance against NKPA troops. No signs of disaffection or collapse though this could change quickly in event of serious reverses.

Barring unforeseen developments, Ridgway confident he can obtain two to three months delay before having to initiate evacuation. Does not want to do this before Army is back in old beachhead [i.e., Pusan Perimeter].

Chinese have not made any move so far to push south from Han River. When counterattacked they have usually fled. They are having supply difficulties and there are many indications of low morale.

Ridgway taking steps to check NKPA infiltration on front of X Corps.

On the whole Eighth Army now in position and prepared to punish severely any mass attack.[41]

Bradley remembered that this "flash" report came as a "tremendous relief to all" in Washington. It was a "turning point," he wrote. "For the first time we began to think that the Chinese could not throw us out of Korea, even with the self-imposed limitations under which we were fighting." As "the word spread through the upper levels of government that day you could almost hear the sighs of relief." Meeting the same day to consider the proposals in the JCS January 12 contingency paper and proposals from other departments and agencies, the NSC rejected all ideas for widening the war with China and sent all papers back "for further study."[42]

Conferring again with MacArthur on January 18, both Collins and Vandenberg expressed fullest confidence in Ridgway and Eighth Army. Taking the floor—indeed, dominating the meeting—Collins read the cable he had sent to Bradley. Although it flatly contradicted MacArthur's lugubrious assessment of Eighth Army on January 9, MacArthur did not contest it. He must also have realized that this rosy assessment would dash all hope that Washington would approve his measures to widen the war with Red China. However, he did not reiterate these proposals or otherwise allude to them.[43]

In fact, quixotically, MacArthur now insisted that "UN forces could hold a beachhead in Korea indefinitely." He believed that with UN "domination of the sea and air, Chinese forces would never be able to bring up adequate supplies, over their lengthening lines of communications, to enable them to drive UN forces from Korea."[44]

Having returned to Washington, Collins and Vandenberg briefed President Truman, the cabinet, and the JCS on their findings. After repeating the substance of a written report signed by both men, Collins stressed that the "concern" in Washington over Eighth Army morale was "unjustified." There was "considerable fight in Eighth Army." Morale was improving rather than worsening. He sang Ridgway's praises. Ridgway had taken over "with great confidence and energy" and was "doing a magnificent job." Ridgway was "seen at the front by his men in difficult times," Collins went on, and this, too, had contributed to the improvement in morale. Indeed, there had been a "dramatic change" in Eighth Army, and "Ridgway alone was responsible."[45]

## III

After Joe Collins had left Korea, both X and IX corps launched aggressive actions to make contact with the enemy on their respective fronts.

On January 19, when news reached Ned Almond that most of the NKPA had withdrawn from Wonju, he ordered the 2d Division to reoccupy it. Ruffner delegated the task to Ed Messinger's 9th Infantry, which had been relieved of defensive fighting on the Wonju–Chechon road by units of Ferenbaugh's arriving 7th Infantry Division. Once again the 2d Division headed north.[46]

Messinger chose Butch Barberis's 2/9 to lead the return to Wonju. The 2/9 was built into a task force, reinforced by E Company of Peploe's 38th Infantry, a tank company, an A/A battery, and a battery of the 15th FAB. That day the new division ADC, George Stewart, showed his mettle. When the column cautiously stopped short of a railway tunnel believed to be concealing enemy, Stewart boldly strode alone to the mouth of the tunnel and fired six shots down its length. There was no enemy; the column proceeded.[47]

As it turned out, the NKPA had not completely abandoned Wonju, and Barberis soon found himself engaged in heavy fighting, during which Ridgway unexpectedly arrived. Barberis remembered: "We attacked Wonju with two companies abreast. We encountered very heavy NKPA opposition on the right. The airfield was south of town, and I had to attack across it. General

Ridgway arrived overhead and wanted to land. Because we had NKPA small-arms fire on the airfield, I refused him permission to land. Thank God I did, because not fifteen minutes after I waved him off, one of our own flights of fighters came over and strafed, bombed, and napalmed us by mistake. Luckily they missed us. We took Wonju after a classic fixed-bayonets, hand-grenade assault on protective positions that the gooks had up on a hill. That attack was led with great skill and courage by my E Company commander, Forrest Walker, who was black. When Ridgway finally landed, I proudly told him Captain Walker had commanded that assault, and by God, he was a damned good officer. Ridgway was very happy about it and ordered that Walker be awarded a Silver Star Medal. However, when General Almond found out about this he not only stopped the award, he also ordered Walker to be relieved of command of E Company. This was because Almond was a devout antiblack bigot. Walker had been in Almond's Ninety-second Division in Italy, and he had known Walker then."[48]*

After Barberis had retaken Wonju, Ed Messinger brought the rest of the 9th Infantry into the town. From that place Barberis's 2/9 and John Londahl's 1/9 patrolled north, northeast, and northwest. One armored patrol went as far north as Hoengsong, encountering a force of "3,000" NKPA. The patrol attacked aggressively and scattered these troops, then entered the town. Finding no further enemy, it withdrew to its base at Wonju to bivouac in unbelievable cold. Barberis remembered that one night the temperature fell to forty-five degrees below zero.[50]

* * *

On the day following the recapture of Wonju, January 20, MacArthur flew to Taegu. He had a perfunctory talk with Ridgway, then met with war correspondents, a session which seemed to be the primary purpose of his visit.

"There has been a lot of loose talk about the Chinese driving us into the sea," MacArthur said, "just as in the early days there was a lot of nonsense about the North Koreans driving us into the sea. This command intends to maintain a military position in Korea just as long as the statesmen of the UN decide we should do so. . . ."[51]

After one hour and twenty-five minutes on the ground MacArthur was gone. His brief visit left Ridgway and Eighth Army staffers somewhat speechless. Why had he come? What purpose had his bombast and posturing served? His aide Courtney Whitney wrote that MacArthur had gone over to stop "any further talk of evacuation" and personally to give Ridgway the "go-ahead" for

---

*Recalling this controversial incident, the 9th Infantry's S-3, Tom Mellen, wrote that "this admired and experienced black captain was back in the [black] 3/9 by nightfall."[49]

the "counteroffensive." But the "talk of evacuation," of which MacArthur had been a leading mouthpiece, had all but died out; Ridgway's "counteroffensive" was already well under way in all three corps. The real answer seemed to be that MacArthur wanted to associate himself publicly with Ridgway's successful turnaround of Eighth Army.

*  *  *

The negative reaction to this stagy and embarrassing MacArthur visit and no doubt other deeply felt emotions led Ridgway to compose a personal message to his troops that night. Issued the following day, January 21, it became his most famous utterance. Ridgway directed that it be "conveyed to every individual assigned or attached to Eighth Army." In its opening, he posed two questions: "Why are we here?" and "What are we fighting for?"

The answer to the first question [he wrote] is simple and conclusive. We are here because of the decisions of the properly constituted authorities of our respective governments. As the Commander in Chief, United Nations Command, General of the Army Douglas MacArthur has said: "This command intends to maintain a military position in Korea just as long as the statesmen of the United Nations decide we should do so." The answer is simple because further comment is unnecessary. It is conclusive because the loyalty we give, and expect, precludes any slightest questioning of these orders.

The second question is of much greater significance, and every member of this command is entitled to a full and reasoned answer. Mine follows.

To me the issues are clear. It is not a question of this or that Korean town or village. Real estate is, here, incidental. It is not restricted to the issue of freedom for our South Korean Allies, whose fidelity and valor under the severest stress of battle we recognize; though that freedom is a symbol of the wider issues, and included among them. The real issues are whether the power of Western civilization, as God has permitted it to flower in our own beloved lands, shall defy and defeat Communism; whether the rule of men who shoot their prisoners, enslave their citizens, and deride the dignity of man shall displace the rule of those to whom the individual and his individual rights are sacred; whether we are to survive with God's hand to guide and lead us, or to perish in the dead existence of a Godless world.

If these be true, and to me they are, beyond any possibility of challenge, then this has long ceased to be a fight for freedom for our Korean Allies alone and for their national survival. It has become, and continues to be, a fight for our own freedom, for our own survival, in an honorable, independent national existence.

The sacrifices we have made, and those we shall yet support, are not offered vicariously for others, but in our own direct defense.

In the final analysis, the issue now joined right here in Korea is whether Communism or individual freedom shall prevail; whether the flight of fear-driven people we have witnessed here shall be checked, or shall at some future time, however distant, engulf our own loved ones in all its misery and despair.

These are the things for which we fight. Never have members of any military command had a greater challenge than we, or a finer opportunity to show ourselves and our people at their best—and thus do honor to the profession of arms, and to those brave men who bred us.[52]

If by now Ridgway had not won the hearts and minds of his soldiers, he did so with this intelligent, eloquent, and moving declaration. Compared with the purple bombast from MacArthur and the melodramatic and absurd "stand-or-die" rhetoric from Johnnie Walker, it was a masterpiece.[53]

\* \* \*

In IX Corps the G-3, Bill Kunzig, completed plans for the powerful "reconnaissance in force," similar to the I Corps Operation Wolfhound. Perhaps deliberately Kunzig (or Ridgway) chose the most skittish regiment in the corps, Johnny Johnson's 8th Cav, to spearhead the attack. Ever since its mauling at Unsan the 8th Cav had not yet refound itself. Johnson, who had received orders to relieve John Jeter as I Corps G-3, was gratified that his regiment had received this important assignment.[54]

The operation, officially code-named Task Force Johnson, grew in size, to include almost the whole of the 70th Tank Battalion, now commanded by Henry Zeien. It was to attack north near Ichon and continue north beyond the Suwon–Wonju highway until it engaged the enemy. It would be supported on the right flank by a battalion of Throckmorton's 5th Infantry (Albert Ward's 2/5) and on the left flank by two battalions of Jim Boswell's 7th Infantry (Fred Weyand's 1/7 and Sam Kail's 2/7), which were brought up from 3d Division reserve and were supported by Harry Stella's 58th FAB. The 7th Infantry would retrace the path of Levy's 1/15 and capture Kumyangjang. As a feint Gerry Kelleher's 35th Infantry, supported by Tom Dolvin's tankers, would launch an attack on the far left, up the west coast road, through Paranjang toward Suwon.[55]

Johnson chose the 3/8, which he had brought from Fort Devens, to lead the 8th Cav attack. He explained why: "After Unsan, my old Third Battalion of the Eighth Cav had been reconstructed with replacements, the majority of whom were World War Two enlisted reservists. When Korea broke, they had been called to active service, given limited orientation (in some cases only eight days), limited and old equipment. No training was provided. . . . They were vocally dissident and highly skeptical about promises; perhaps 'cynical' might be a better word than 'skeptical.' Understandably their attitude left a great deal to be desired. As a result, [since Unsan] the Eighth Cav had only been used in a gingerly sort of way—not placed in a position of any great sensitivity. Believing that it was necessary for the Third Battalion to get a 'success under its belt,' I chose it for the lead battalion in the attack. As a confidence builder I moved my regimental CP well out in front of the line of departure for the attack. . . ."[56]

Task Force Johnson jumped off at dawn on January 22. Led by the 3/8, the 8th Cav struck north and reached the Suwon–Wonju road about midway between Kumyangjang and Ichon. On the right Ward's 2/5 advanced toward Ichon, where it found an Australian patrol from Coad's Commonwealth Brigade engaged with the enemy. Relieving the patrol, Ward moved elements into Ichon, from which he mounted patrols northeast and northwest. On the left Weyand's 1/7 and Kail's 2/7 (reinforced by ROKs) regained Kumyangjang. There Weyand's 1/7 sent patrols east toward Ichon, and Kail's 2/7 sent patrols to the west, toward Suwon. Weyand encountered no enemy; Kail ran into the CCF and, with the help of FEAF close air support, inflicted "heavy casualties."[57]

In its "feint" on the extreme left flank of the line Gerry Kelleher's 35th Infantry, replacing the Wolfhounds, achieved substantial gains. On its left front it advanced through Paranjang and approached Suwon. On its right front it recaptured Osan and the ground slightly beyond. Encountering only slight CCF resistance on both roads, Kelleher—on Milburn's order—stopped, dug in and threw up very strong roadblocks. The 35th Infantry now held a west-east line above Osan, with Corley's 24th Infantry immediately to the south and behind it, Brodie's British Brigade on Line D.[58]

On the basis of his World War II experience and his firm grip on the 35th Infantry, much had been expected of Gerry Kelleher. In this, his first opportunity to show his stuff, he did not disappoint. The 35th's "feint" actually achieved much more than was expected of it, and Ridgway was immensely pleased, as were the men of the 35th.

Like Operation Wolfhound, Task Force Johnson, intended primarily for reconnaissance, was terminated within about twenty-four hours, and the IX Corps elements withdrew. Its main force—the 8th Cav—had maneuvered well, but none of the units had encountered sizable enemy at Kumyangjang or Ichon or anywhere else. Therefore, Task Force Johnson had inflicted no significant damage on the enemy. However, as the Eighth Army historian wrote, it had served one important purpose: It had "proved that the enemy did not occupy in strength any positions close to the front lines of the US I and IX corps."[59]

It had served another important purpose as well. In total, four more American regiments (5th, 7th, 8th Cav, and 35th) of four American divisions (3d, 1st Cav, 24th, 25th) in I and IX corps had engaged in aggressive northward attacks. The operation had given the men new confidence in themselves and their units and the supporting tanks and artillery. They had met no CCF "hordes"; no American unit had been overrun; none had bugged out. Inasmuch as the CCF appeared to be reluctant to fight, morale in these regiments soared.

\* \* \*

On the basis of the information developed by Operation Wolfhound and Task Force Johnson and satisfied that his American divisions and regiments now had the confidence and skill to carry out a large operation, on January 23 Ridgway issued orders for I and IX corps to launch a general offensive on January 25.

In ordering this offensive, Ridgway took a "calculated risk." Various intelligence sources had revealed that the Russians had powerfully reinforced the embryonic CCF Air Force in recent weeks. By January 1951 it was estimated that the CCF air arm had grown to 650 first-line aircraft, including scores of new Soviet fighter-bombers and MIG-15 jet fighters. It was not known whether these aircraft were piloted by Chinese or Russians. If the latter, it could signal Soviet intervention in Korea, disguised as "volunteer" forces like the early CCF intervention, and it could lead to overt Soviet intervention. Whatever the case, the U.S. Air Force historian wrote, Washington and Tokyo (and Taegu) viewed the enemy air buildup with "a feeling approaching dismay."[60]

There was good reason for "dismay." With the retreat of Eighth Army to Line D, FEAF had lost its huge air complexes at Kimpo and Suwon and, in anticipation of Eighth Army evacuation, had withdrawn major air elements from the Taegu and Pusan areas and elsewhere. All F-86s, the only American jet fighter indisputably superior to the MIG-15, had been shifted from South Korea to Japan. Hence for the first time in the Korean War the enemy had achieved theoretical "air supremacy" over the peninsula. Owing to the withdrawal of American F-86s, the CCF Air Force was—or soon could be—in position to launch powerful fighter-bombers, escorted by MIGs, against Eighth Army.

To do so would, of course, incur the risk that America would almost certainly retaliate massively by air and naval forces against CCF air bases in the Manchurian "sanctuary" and possibly against Chinese mainland cities as well. America might even attack the CCF air bases with A-bombs. Nonetheless, there were signs that Peking might be willing to run that risk. As Ridgway was preparing for his offensive, MIG-15s appeared in ever-increasing numbers over North Korea, "reaching further southward," the Air Force historian wrote, "and revealing unusual aggressiveness." Moreover, intelligence reported the CCF was constructing a network of "advance" air bases in North Korea. In response, the Fifth Air Force commander in Korea, Earle E. ("Pat") Partridge, brought a small detachment of F-86s back to Taegu, but they proved not to have sufficient range to fly deep into North Korea, engage the MIGs (in what was dubbed "MIG Alley"), then return to Taegu. Until Ridgway recaptured Suwon and Kimpo airfields and could assure them safe for operation of F-86s, the CCF Air Force would retain theoretical "air supremacy" over Korea.[61]

The air situation had, in turn, led to a substantial reduction in FEAF's close air support and interdiction capabilities. All jets theretofore employed for that purpose (F-80s, F-84s) were also withdrawn to Japan. Some F-80s were "staged" from Japan into Taegu for refueling to carry out close air support missions, but this improvisation proved clumsy. This left FEAF only prop planes (F-51s; B-25 and B-26 medium bombers) to carry out close air and interdiction missions in support of Eighth Army.

Concern over the growing CCF air threat led Ridgway to issue orders for Eighth Army to be alive to the possibility of a CCF air attack. All units, including rear-area units, would adopt dispersion and camouflage measures, dig slit trenches alongside CPs, and formulate communications procedures to warn of and react to enemy air attack. Paratrooper Ridgway even cautioned Eighth Army not to disregard the possibility of a CCF paratrooper attack on frontline or rear-area positions.[62]

Ridgway also had to worry that should the Soviets intervene overtly with air power in Korea, they might employ A-bombs against suitable targets, such as the massive American supply base in Pusan. He calculated that "one [Russian] A-bomb could have taken out four-fifths of Eighth Army ammunition stockpiles in Pusan," leaving Eighth Army virtually helpless to defend itself in a forced evacuation and thus facing annihilation, thereby leaving Japan utterly defenseless as well.[63]

A Soviet A-bomb attack on Pusan would almost certainly lead to general war and probably to American A-bomb retaliation against Soviet Far East military targets. For emergency planning purposes (code-named Shakedown), SAC B-29 bombers on Okinawa were initially allotted a total of twenty A-bombs to drop on Soviet military targets in Vladivostok, Port Arthur, Darien, Sakhalin Island, and elsewhere. The nuclear warheads, however, were retained on American soil in the Marshall Islands (Guam, Saipan, Tinian) or in the United States.[64]

Like Johnnie Walker, Ridgway "war gamed" how, in the event of general war, some American A-bombs in the Far East might be diverted to tactical use to assist in the preservation and evacuation of Eighth Army from Korea. But like Walker, Ridgway concluded that such a course would not be feasible. Eighth Army might possibly locate a "remunerative" CCF target worthy of an A-bomb, but by the time MacArthur or Ridgway got permission from President Truman to use the A-bomb and the warheads were flown from the Marshall Islands to Okinawa and the bombers were loaded and got to Korea, more likely than not the CCF target would have dispersed. In sum, the red tape entailed in the tactical employment of A-bombs would defeat timely employment.[65]

## IV

Ridgway's plan for the I and IX corps offensive—code-named Thunderbolt— was to attack north, line abreast, about twenty miles. On the left I Corps would advance to the south bank of the Han River at Yongdungpo, opposite Seoul, and recapture Inchon and Kimpo Airfield. On the right IX Corps would also advance to the Han River, with the right flank anchored on Yangpyong (north of Ichon), a road and rail hub through which it was believed the Chinese were moving troops to the Wonju sector. Both corps were to ferret out enemy dispositions, disrupt hostile concentrations, and inflict maximum destruction on enemy personnel and matériel. No forces would attempt to cross the Han west of Yangpyong.[66]

As Ridgway conceived it, the offensive would begin with a gradual commitment of force, utilizing one American division in each corps, plus a ROK regiment if desirable. Then, if no massive enemy counterattacks developed, the remaining American division in each corps would be committed. All assault units would advance slowly, by rigidly controlled "phase lines." No enemy was to be bypassed. Reserve forces would protect the "rear areas" and root out any remaining guerrillas.

To facilitate Eighth Army operations, the Navy conceived two amphibious landing "deceptions," one for the west coast at Inchon, one for the east coast at Kansong and Kosong, north of ROK forces. The cruiser *St. Paul* (mounting nine eight-inch guns), escorted by destroyers, would steam up Flying Fish Channel and shell Inchon, simulating the onset of an amphibious assault. The more elaborate east coast deception would employ the battleship *Missouri* leading a force of transports, LSTs, and other vessels, to simulate an amphibious assault well north of the 38th Parallel.[67]

In addition, paratrooper Ridgway added an airborne operation, grandiosely code-named Downpour. Its purpose was to drop troops above Suwon at Anyang and "trap" high-ranking CCF generals and staffs escaping in front of Thunderbolt forces. He asked Frank Bowen to provide a battalion of the 187th Airborne RCT for this purpose, but it was still at Tanyang, rooting out guerrillas in the X Corps rear areas and could not readily be spared. In place of a 187th battalion, Ridgway was compelled to call on the smaller 4th Ranger Company, which was attached to I Corps for special missions. He placed that unit on standby, to be utilized only on his specific say-so.[68]

Shrimp Milburn chose Bill Kean's 25th Division to spearhead Thunderbolt in the I Corps sector. Gerry Kelleher's gung ho 35th Infantry, already holding positions above Osan, would attack on the division's left. Since Michaelis's Wolfhounds had only recently conducted an attack, it did not seem fair to put the 27th in the spearhead; but that left only Corley's 24th, and Kean did not have confidence in that outfit; he still wanted to deactivate it. The solution was somewhat unusual. The Turkish Brigade would, in effect, substitute for the 24th Infantry and attack in the division's right sector. The 24th would continue to patrol the roads and supply dumps behind the attacking elements. The Wolfhounds would remain in division reserve. Shorty Soule's 3d Division would hold in place on the right of the 25th Division.[69]

As a final precaution, on the day preceding the attack, January 24, Ridgway declared he would make a personal reconnaissance of the terrain lying between I and IX corps and the Han River. Fifth Air Force commander Pat Partridge volunteered to serve as pilot, and he chose a single-engine T-6 prop trainer for this dangerous mission. Ridgway remembered:

For two hours we flew over that lonely, empty land, skimming the ridge tops, ducking into valleys, circling over the dead villages. Over all this snowy land, which covered our entire battlefront, we saw no sign of life or movement. No smoke came from the chimneys, and nothing moved either on or off the roads, neither vehicles, men nor animals. . . . I flew back to my headquarters pondering what I had seen. The information I had gathered was negative. But I was satisfied in my own mind . . . that I would not be sending Eighth Army into a trap in which it could be destroyed.[70]

Milburn's I Corps attacked in five columns, advancing "shoulder-to-shoulder" or "hand-in-hand" to designated phase lines. On the extreme left the 25th Division Recon Company (reinforced by the 3d Division Recon Company) went up the west coast road, skirting Asan Bay to Omokchon, approaching Suwon from the southwest, on alert for a surprise CCF amphibious assault. To its right Kelleher's 35th attacked in two columns, one battalion going north from Paranjang toward Suwon, two battalions going directly up the Osan–Suwon road. On the right of the 35th the Turkish Brigade, in two columns, attacked northeast toward Kumyangjang. Corley's 24th Infantry moved up behind the 35th Infantry to protect the Paranjang road; Michaelis's 27th Infantry, in division reserve, advanced to Osan.[71]

The I Corps assault forces were backed by FEAF close air support and by massive artillery and naval gunfire from ships standing offshore. The 25th Division artillery commander, Bittman Barth, remembered that he directly controlled 108 guns of the 64th, 90th, and 159th FABs, the 45th British Artillery Regiment, and the Turkish Artillery Regiment. In addition, he could call on the nine eight-inch guns of the cruiser *St. Paul* and about thirty other four- or five-inch naval guns of the British light cruiser *Ceylon* and American destroyers.[72]

All these movements were conducted slowly and cautiously. No unit advanced beyond a phase line until all others had reached it. That first night the 35th Infantry and the tankers in effect surrounded Suwon, fully expecting a strong CCF counterattack. But the CCF had apparently withdrawn, leaving only a rear guard to harass. The historian of Dolvin's 89th Tank Battalion wrote:

They waited through the evening, then suddenly, the infiltration started. A Chinese patrol came [out] through the wall of the city at 0200 hours [2:00 A.M.] on the 26th of January. They came up so close and quietly that a pistol and machinegun fire fight at point blank range developed. . . . The tanks moved back to where they could fire and Chinese ran down behind the tanks with satchel charges, attempting to throw them on the tanks as they ran. Small fire fights broke out all over town. [A] lieutenant came out of the CP in time to see two Chinese with rifles approaching. He captured them waving a pistol at them. Why they did not fire still remains a mystery, but one did try to pull a grenade when he was brought into the CP. The guard at the CP hit him over the head with a rifle butt, and so it was that the battalion captured its first Chinese. The entire action at Suwon was characterized by this same sort of small-scale infighting . . . so well liked by guerrilla troops.[73]

Sergeant Woody Woodruff remembered the 3/35 moving forward on foot against virtually no opposition:

The weather was extremely cold and the hills were high and steep, one right after the other. We made enemy contact almost daily. Sometimes during daylight we would run up against a rear guard detachment; more often their patrols would harass us at night. . . . None that I saw had firearms. . . . They did use snipers, some of them all too accurate; and there was usually one "burp" gun per CCF squad. Most or all of the rest of the squad, however, might have nothing but hand grenades. The enemy did not really make much of an effort to hold . . . and did not succeed in delaying our advance more than a couple of hours. I never understood why they would leave such a small and poorly armed force. . . .[74]

On the second day of the offensive, January 26, MacArthur's seventy-first birthday, Kelleher's infantry and Dolvin's tanks "captured" Suwon. Ridgway got off a flowery and flattering birthday greeting to MacArthur,* then flew to Suwon to have a look at the town (a mass of rubble) and its airfield, an important prize which would enable FEAF prop planes providing close air support and cargo planes to move closer to the front. Immensely impressed with Kelleher's aggressive and skillful performance in command of the 35th, Ridgway decided to recommend him (as well as Michaelis) for battlefield promotions to brigadier general.[75]

The Turkish Brigade, attacking on the right of Kelleher's 35th Infantry, also achieved renown that day. After Barth's 64th and 90th FABs and the Turkish Artillery Brigade (and some FEAF prop planes) had pulverized a hill northeast of Suwon, the Turks assaulted the CCF positions with fixed bayonets

---

*Earlier Ridgway had sent MacArthur a captured Chinese scroll. Doyle Hickey telephoned Ridgway to say that when MacArthur opened the present, tears came to his eyes and he remarked that it was the most touching remembrance of his birthday he had received in seventy-one years.

and overran them. Word of this bold feat quickly spread throughout Eighth Army. It was reported that the Turks killed "400 enemy," most by bayonet. Later careful investigation revealed that only about 154 CCF troops had actually been killed on the hill—the "preponderant number" by Barth's artillery prior to the assault.[76]

Although Ridgway well knew the facts of the Turkish "bayonet charge" had been greatly exaggerated, he was impressed by the awe the story inspired. As a morale builder he therefore issued orders for all Eighth Army troops to fix bayonets. An Army historian explained:

The command greatly needed something to symbolize the birth of a new spirit. Restoration of the bayonet, and a dramatizing of that action, was at one with the simple message given to the troops: "The job is to kill Chinese." Once men could be persuaded that those in other units were deliberately seeking the hand-to-hand contest with the enemy, they would begin to feel themselves equal to the overall task. There can be no question about the efficacy of this magic in the particular situation: IT WORKED![77]

The successes of the 35th Infantry and the Turkish Brigade that day led Ridgway to cable MacArthur (not immodestly): "May I suggest for such use as you think it might merit, my firm conviction that recently-reported press statements that members of the JCS had announced 'The Eighth Army has plenty of fight left and if attacked will severely punish the enemy' are great understatements. This command, I am convinced, will do far more."[78]

\* \* \*

Bryant Moore's IX Corps attacked in concert with I Corps on the morning of January 25. The attack was spearheaded by the 1st Cav Division. Although Hap Gay was still present in Korea, his replacement, Charlie Palmer, conducted these operations.[79]

Palmer, nicknamed Charlie Dog for his initials, was a rough, tough, demanding commander and strict disciplinarian. His first orders to his men were explicit and detailed. All bayonets were to be "well sharpened." Any man found without a steel helmet would be punished. All outer garments (overcoats, jackets) were to be buttoned up at all times. No "foreign weapons" were to be utilized. All men on guard were to be "alert at all times" or suffer dire consequences.[80]

Palmer chose Billy Harris's 7th Cav and Johnny Johnson's 8th Cav to lead the division, keeping Marcel Crombez's 5th Cav in reserve. The 7th Cav would attack on the right through Ichon. The 8th Cav would attack on the left, more or less retracing its earlier path. The 7th Cav would be reinforced by a battalion of the 24th Division, which would temporarily hold in place on the right of the 1st Cav between Ichon and Yoju.[81]

The 1st Cav did well initially. Attacking through positions held by the

ROK 6th Division, Johnson's (it was hoped) rejuvenated 8th Cav made good time and by early afternoon had reached the Suwon–Wonju highway, where it repulsed a minor CCF attack. Billy Harris's 7th Cav, reinforced on the right flank by Albert Ward's 2/5 (of Throckmorton's 5th Infantry), reached Ichon on the same Suwon–Wonju road in good time. Both regiments then drew into tight perimeters and buttoned up for the night.[82]

Then matters took a bad turn. By the morning of January 26 Johnson's 8th Cav had drawn a full regiment of the CCF on its positions and was engaged in desperate close-in fighting. The 2/8 was surrounded, and for a while it appeared that the 8th Cav might give way. Accordingly, Charlie Palmer ordered Harris to maneuver the 7th Cav off its axis of advance to assist the 8th Cav. The three organic battalions of the 7th Cav pivoted west, the 2/7 coming up behind the 2/8. Pete Clainos's 1/7 and the 3/7 launched an encircling attack to the north and northwest in an attempt to get behind and unhinge the CCF.[83]

This action led to the belief that in spite of Johnny Johnson's efforts, the 8th Cav was not yet fully reliable. Palmer thus ordered Crombez's 5th Cav from reserve to replace the 8th Cav in the division's left sector. Supported by armor and artillery, Crombez attacked with a bang, but the 5th Cav, too, ran into fierce CCF resistance in the hills. The division historian wrote that at one hill (312) the men of the 1/5 found themselves engaged in a "desperate hand-to-hand struggle" during which the battle "hung in the balance." It was won, finally, by the outstanding courage of men like platoon leader Robert M. McGovern, who, mortally wounded, killed seven of the CCF and broke up a machine-gun nest. He was awarded the Medal of Honor posthumously.[84]

The 8th Cav remained in reserve near Kumyangjang. During this time Johnson left the regiment to replace John Jeter as I Corps G-3. Palmer finally "solved" the awkward command problem in the 7th Cav—Clainos in the 1/7, a full colonel, serving under his classmate Billy Harris—by appointing Clainos to command the 8th Cav. Perhaps still believing he deserved command of the more illustrious 7th Cav, Clainos was not happy with his new assignment.[85]

## V

By the end of the second day of Thunderbolt, January 27, Ridgway believed I and IX corps had sufficient confidence in themselves and momentum to justify committing his remaining two American divisions, the 3d (in I Corps) and the 24th (in IX Corps). They would attack on the following day. This was another calculated risk: It would leave only the British Brigade (in I Corps) and the Commonwealth Brigade (in IX Corps) in reserve. He cleared this plan—appropriately named Exploitation—with GHQ by telephone.[86]

The next day, January 28, at 11:30 A.M. MacArthur flew into Suwon Airfield. Although it was a great inconvenience, Ridgway met MacArthur's plane. MacArthur had made his first visit to the Korean War the previous June at Suwon. Now that he had "returned," he apparently believed a ringing declaration of some kind was in order. As he deplaned, a British war correspondent heard him say to Ridgway: "This is exactly where I came in seven months ago to start this crusade. The stake we fight for now, however, is more than Korea—it is a free Asia."

These remarks, which were published in the *London Telegraph,* evoked deep concern in the British government. It seemed to the British that "a free Asia" possibly implied that MacArthur "had in mind" all-out war with Red China and the utilization of Chiang Kai-shek's forces to attempt an invasion of the Chinese mainland. A British representative in Washington immediately instituted inquiries at State, but he was assured by Deputy Assistant Secretary for Far Eastern Affairs Livingston T. Merchant that there was no plan to invade the Chinese mainland, that MacArthur's remarks at Suwon "should be regarded as a mere form of words." The representative was glad to hear that, adding, however, that "broad statements with political overtones" from MacArthur seemed "somewhat improper."[87]

From the airfield Ridgway escorted MacArthur to Milburn's CP for a conference. It was attended by all the senior commanders in I Corps: Shrimp Milburn, Bill Kean, Shorty Soule, Tom Brodie, and the Turkish commander, Tahsin Yazici. Afterward MacArthur jeeped to Gerry Kelleher's 35th Infantry CP to congratulate him and his staff. One hour and forty-five minutes after his arrival MacArthur left for Tokyo.[88]

Ridgway was not pleased by this visit. It served no purpose other than to provide another "photo opportunity" for MacArthur's Tokyo press corps to show him in the "front lines" with Eighth Army's "victorious troops." Inasmuch as the visit coincided with a full-scale offensive—the commitment of the 3d and 24th divisions—Ridgway worried (as Walker's staffers had earlier worried at the Chongchon River) that the visit would signal the CCF that large-scale offensive operations were afoot.

*   *   *

In the I Corps sector Shorty Soule's 3d Division was "mentally" ready for action. One sure sign of that, the historian wrote, "was the increased attention" given to a weapon which had fallen into disuse: the bayonet. All through the division men were seen honing the blades and making "tentative thrusts and exploratory lunges."[89]

The 3d Division moved due north into the zone near Kumyangjang, which the Turks had occupied. William Harris's Puerto Rican 65th Regiment attacked on the left; Dinty Moore's 15th Infantry on the right; Jim Boswell's 7th

Infantry remained in reserve. At first it appeared that the attack would be a cakewalk to the Han. Both regiments advanced to phase lines against "light, scattered resistance," formed perimeters, and buttoned up for the night.[90]

The 65th and 15th regiments were likewise backed by a heavy, well-coordinated concentration of artillery: the 65th by the black 58th FAB; the 15th by the 39th FAB. In addition, the black 999th and the 92d and 96th FABs (all mounting self-propelled or tractor-drawn 155-mm howitzers) were brought into play. In total, the 3d Division artillery commander Roland Shugg could call upon about ninety guns.[91]*

During the dark, cold early-morning hours of January 29, the character of Exploitation suddenly and radically changed. Both I and IX corps encountered strong CCF units. The CCF counterattacked the 65th Infantry, hitting St. Clair's 1/65 and Dammer's 2/65 especially hard. The Puerto Ricans held the perimeter through the night, but it was not easy. After daylight the CCF, as customary, withdrew. Documents recovered from dead CCF soldiers indicated the 65th had run head-on into a regiment of the veteran CCF Fiftieth Army (148th, 149th, 150th divisions).[92]

Further patrolling that day, January 29, by the men of the 65th and 15th regiments established beyond doubt that powerful elements of the CCF Fiftieth Army were firmly dug in ahead of the 3d Division. The CCF had tunneled into strong hill positions in both regimental sectors. There was no alternative but to blast them out. The CCF stubbornly "clung" to these "well-constructed emplacements," the division historian wrote, "despite concentrations of friendly artillery and infernos created on the hills by supporting aircraft attacking with machine guns, rockets and napalm."[93]

Confronting two CCF-held hills, the 65th commander William Harris remembered:

There is no shortcut to the capture of a piece of enemy dominated terrain, especially when it is high ground and defended by a determined and well-fortified enemy. Nor are there any movie-like tactics acceptable to the military tactician that can be used to take that high ground. In the final analysis it comes down to who has the more firepower and which of the two antagonists is the more determined to win. . . . [I]t took us the better part of three days and nights before we captured those two hills. . . . On the morning of that third day both Saint and Dammer led their troops on an assault. . . . In closing with the enemy, the men of our two battalions fixed bayonets and charged straight at the enemy positions.[94]

---

*The four assault regiments of I Corps were thus backed up by a total of about 200 guns, plus the guns of the naval vessels standing offshore. This was by far the heaviest concentration of American artillery thus far in the Korean War.

It was equally tough going in the IX Corps sector. Charlie Palmer's 1st Cav Division had developed intelligence indicating that IX Corps had run head-on into the veteran CCF Thirty-eighth Army (112th, 113th, 114th divisions). Like the CCF Fiftieth Army, the Thirty-eighth held strong fortifications on key hills. Some CCF POWs had asserted the Thirty-eighth Army was under orders to hold its positions "at all costs." The Eighth Army historian reported that the CCF in this area had "plentiful amounts of ammunition, rations and adequate winter clothing," and apparently there was "no shortage" of proper field equipment.[95]

Both the 5th Cav (on the left) and 7th Cav (on the right) met increasingly strong CCF resistance north of the Suwon–Wonju highway. On the night of January 28–29 the 7th Cav's advance was rudely checked by a powerful CCF group, which compelled the 1/7 to give ground. The following night another CCF unit (later estimated to be a 3,000-man regiment) struck the attached Greek Battalion, which had encamped on top of Hill 381. The regimental historian wrote:

Fierce and bitter fighting raged throughout the night as three times the enemy reached the crest of Hill 381 only to be driven off by the ferocious counter-attacks of the brave Greek company holding the top of the hill. The fighting on this hill—hand to hand with grenades, rifle butts and bayonets—saw many personal examples of heroism as the tenacious Greek soldiers entered their first major action as part of the United Nations Forces. The hilltop on which they fought was vital to the security of the regiment and its seizure by the enemy would have allowed him to cut off and surround the 1st Battalion. . . . Those who ran out of ammunition fought with their bare hands to retain this important hill. . . . Arbouzis, the commander, estimated the enemy lost 800 killed, and the blood which covered the hillside was mute evidence of the terrific struggle. . . .[96]

Despite these very powerful CCF counterattacks, Ridgway proceeded with his decision to commit the 24th Division to the IX Corps offensive on January 28. It would attack on the right flank of the 1st Cav, in a narrow and tight triangular area above Ichon and Yoju, where the Han River curved sharply southeast.[97]

Although John Church was also still present in Korea, the 24th Division was now commanded by Ridgway's protégé Babe Bryan, who like Palmer was an artilleryman. In every respect Bryan was a stark contrast with Church. A onetime West Point football star and later (1925 and 1934) assistant football coach, Bryan was (like Buddy Ferenbaugh) a "giant" of a man, who weighed 250 pounds. He had a fine, quick mind and an excellent grasp of detail, and he issued orders in clear, unmistakable terms. He viewed his assignment as the "acme" of his career. Emulating Ridgway's command style, he believed his presence on the front lines was "essential," not only for morale purposes but also for (as he put it) "evaluating the strategy of a foxhole war."[98]

With the departure of Ned Moore in the 19th Infantry and Dick Stephens in the 21st Infantry, Bryan now had two new regimental commanders, neither of them West Pointers: Ollie Kinney, thirty-seven, and Gines Perez, forty-two. Both had rushed out from the States to Korea in late July to be battalion commanders. Both had done well in that capacity. Owing to Moore's illness, Kinney had been commanding the 19th Infantry in all but title since early December and by title since January 16.*

The staff of the 21st Infantry was pleased with the appointment of Gines Perez to command the regiment. The exec, Fritz Mudgett—still going strong—remembered:

Dick Stephens loved the limelight. He was at his best with the news media. He shared his martinis with reporters and photographers. Not Gines. He was not "colorful." If there were any of the 21st commanders one could classify as an intellectual, Perez would be my nomination. . . . In his quiet but forceful manner he became an outstanding tactical commander. . . . He worked well with his unit commanders and staff. Once a direction (orders) were given, he allowed sufficient leeway for the commanders and staffs to solve the problems involved without over-supervision. He got the job done without a lot of hassle.

He would be tough when the occasion warranted. This was made clear to everyone by the example of a few reliefs of officers who did not measure up to his standards. On occasion he would take his "chewings" from Division (primarily the ADC, Numa Watson) but this was not usually passed on to the unit commanders and staff. If the occasion warranted, he would "pass it on" in an acceptable manner. This, I believe, was one of his primary strengths.[99]

Like Stephens, Ned Moore had trained and proselytized on behalf of his replacement, Ollie Kinney. Born in California, son of a carpenter, Kinney was a graduate of the University of California at Berkeley (1936). In 1940, having obtained an ROTC commission, he went on full-time active duty, assigned to the 30th Infantry of the 3d Division. He fought in Sicily and Italy, rising to command a battalion (1/30) and winning two Silver Star Medals and other awards. Wounded at Anzio and ill with pneumonia and encephalitis, he was hospitalized in the States, and after the war he returned to civilian life. In 1947 he applied for and won a Regular Army commission (under the Thompson Act) and returned to active duty. Upon graduation from the Command and General Staff School in June 1950, he was ordered to Korea.[100]

When Bryan paid his first official visit to the 19th Infantry, he was not favorably impressed. The 19th's S-3, Elliott Cutler, remembered that Bryan,

---

*With these appointments, the average age of regimental commanders in the 24th Division was 38.6 years.

in particular, criticized the regiment's "supply discipline." Cutler wrote: "His specific words were, 'How could a fine old regiment like the 19th possibly be short 2,000 helmets?' " There were good and sufficient reasons for the shortage, but after this visit it seemed to the staff that Ollie Kinney's days were definitely numbered.[101]

Owing to the sharp southeasterly bend of the Han River, which confined the 24th Division to a tight triangular area, the regimental maneuvers were complicated. On the left, or west, adjacent to the 7th Cav, Johnny Throckmorton's 5th Infantry had a long way to go due north to reach the Han. In the center Kinney's 19th Infantry, also attacking due north, had less distance to cover. On the division's right Perez's 21st Infantry, anchored at Yoju (on the Han), would more or less hold in place.

Ridgway was present and watchful during the 24th Division attack. Meeting him for the first time, Kinney was amazed at Ridgway's attention to detail and ability to get helpful things done: "He flew into my sector in a light plane, looking for Babe Bryan. He stepped out of the plane wearing his grenade, a very impressive-looking guy. He shook hands and asked if I needed anything. As it happened, at that time we had an ammo delivery problem. Our ammo dump was ninety miles to the south of us. I told him that I had to send my own trucks back to get ammo and I never knew if I'd ever see those trucks again. The very next day we had full ammo trucks right behind us. Ridgway set up a very efficient system where we'd send our empty trucks to the ammo dump and swap them for full trucks, which were there, ready and waiting. I never had to worry about that problem again."[102]

The 24th Division soon ran head-on into strong CCF defensive positions in the hills. On February 1 Ridgway joined Albert Ward's 2/5, which was spearheading the 5th Infantry assault. Climbing the hill on foot with Ward and his men, Ridgway was so impressed with the operation that he commended Throckmorton and Ward in a telex to all American and ROK corps and division commanders:

The U.S. Fifth Infantry Regiment, Col. Throckmorton commanding, attacked in daylight across a mile wide open plain and took a series of ridges up to 150 feet above the valley which completely dominated the ground this regiment had to cross.

Chinese Communist forces had organized and defended these ridges tenaciously with individual foxholes and underground shelters, one of which with a connecting galley was large enough for the crew of the 120 mm mortar in which this weapon was emplaced.

In late afternoon I personally visited the 2nd Battalion, Lieutenant Colonel Ward commanding, and went over the ground taken by E and F Companies. This operation achieved the true measure of tactical success—key terrain, a vital mountain pass—seized with heavy losses inflicted and only light losses sustained.

The reason was due to the proper appreciation and use of terrain and high leadership whereby high class infantry with supporting air and artillery worked its way along the ridges until all dominating ground was taken. This operation furnishes a fine example of how it ought to be done.[103]

The Thunderbolt offensive of I and IX corps was supported in a limited way by Almond's X Corps, which manned a line running roughly east-west from Yoju to Wonju. Nick Ruffner's 2d Division was on the left (loosely linked with Babe Bryan's 24th Division); Buddy Ferenbaugh's 7th Division, moving up from Chechon, held the right. In the 2d Division sector Paul Freeman's 23d Infantry was on the left; George Peploe's 38th in the center, and Ed Messinger's 9th Infantry on the right in Wonju.[104]

Eighth Army intelligence had indicated a possible shifting of the CCF from the western to the central front. If it was true, more likely than not the CCF was assembling at, or passing through, the village of Chipyong, a rail and road hub about fifteen miles above Yoju. The Seoul–Yangpyong–Wonju railroad ran through Chipyong, as did the Seoul–Yangpyong–Hongchon road. It was the "gateway" to the central front.

Ridgway ordered that a strong X Corps patrol probe Chipyong, to serve as a "feint" to Thunderbolt and to develop information on the CCF. Ned Almond assigned that dangerous mission to Paul Freeman's 23d Infantry, which was in the best position to carry it out. Freeman's patrols would attempt to link with patrols of Gines Perez's adjacent 21st Infantry, which would strike from Yoju.

The two patrols met on the north side of the Han River on January 29. The combined 21st and 23d Infantry force (four officers, fifty-four men in jeeps) proceeded north to within a few miles of Chipyong without encountering hostile forces. At the village of Sinchon, where there were two end-to-end railway tunnels (Twin Tunnels), the men dismounted to probe on foot, while a liaison aircraft circled overhead.[105]

At about noon CCF troops, well entrenched in the hills, ambushed the patrol. Some Americans were immediately killed or captured, but the bulk of the men climbed another hill and dug in to make a heroic last stand. Learning from the liaison aircraft pilot that the men were cut off and trapped, Freeman quickly organized a strong rescue force (F Company of James Edwards's 2/23), which reached the area about dusk. In a well-conducted action F Company, commanded by Stanley C. Tyrrell, routed the CCF and rescued the survivors of the patrol, including thirty wounded.

Although this patrol had come to grief, in doing so it had developed vital intelligence. It confirmed that the CCF had indeed occupied Chipyong, perhaps as part of a general shift of forces to the east. It was believed that the CCF at Chipyong might be the tough, combat-wise Forty-second Army (124th, 125th, 126th divisions), which had spearheaded the CCF attack on the Marines at Chosin in early November, then shifted west to spearhead the attack on ROK II Corps at the Chongchon River, culminating in the savage assault on the American 2d Division at Kunu and the "gauntlet."

Upon learning of this, Ridgway ordered Almond's X Corps to develop further information and to throw up a strong block at the Twin Tunnels, to prevent a possible CCF attack southeast down the Han River valley. Paul Freeman's 23d drew this challenging assignment. Freeman would mount the attack with two of his four battalions: Charles Kane's 3/12 and the French Battalion. The 1/23, now commanded by thirty-one-year-old George H. Russell (replacing Claire Hutchin, who having won two DSCs was promoted to 2d Division G-3), and Edwards's 2/23 would remain on the Yoju–Wonju road, prepared to reinforce the other battalions if required.[106]

The lead infantry elements (about 1,500 men), supported by A/A weapons, five tanks, and John Hector's 37th FAB, began the advance on the morning of January 31. The French were on the left; Kane's 3/23 was on the right. It was "tiresome climbing and ridge-running," Freeman wrote, "a painful task" of scaling "slippery, snow-covered hills." There was no sign of the CCF. "The temptation to barge ahead was tremendous," Freeman went on, but "our troops had learned—learned months ago—that the enemy seldom appeared in daylight . . . when he would be at the mercy of our artillery and air." Therefore, the force proceeded warily and on full alert for what was certain to be "a violent reaction."[107]

The force reached the Twin Tunnels area in late afternoon and buttoned up for the night. The 2d Division ADC, George Stewart, who had accompanied the forces, remembered that Ned Almond was displeased that the force had not gone farther. "General Almond arrived [by helicopter] and told me he wanted a village two or three miles to the north to be taken before we stopped. I explained it was near dark and that the security of the unit required preparations for the night. He reluctantly agreed—but ordered me to personally see that the village was fired upon."

Believing that these orders were "probably wrong" but that if he refused to carry them out Almond would relieve him, as he had McClure, Stewart complied. He got in a tank and went north to the village. He found no CCF—nor anyone else—yet, as ordered, he fired several bursts of machine-gun and cannon fire, taking care to aim high lest he kill civilians inside the houses. He then returned to Freeman's perimeter and radioed Almond that he had "personally" fired upon the village.[108]

Freeman was furious at this action. If there were CCF troops near Chipyong, the firing on the village was certain to alert them and probably invite an attack. He was correct. Two hours before dawn on February 1, the CCF 125th Division (of the Forty-second Army) swarmed into the perimeter, blowing bugles, whistles, and shepherd's horns. Freeman's men lighted the battlefield with flares, then responded with an awesome barrage of artillery—A/A, tank, mortar, machine-gun, and small-arms fire. "The impact stunned the attackers," Freeman wrote, "and made them change their bold assault tactics. There was a lull as the enemy pulled back to reorganize."[109]

After regrouping, the CCF attacked again at 6:00 A.M., focusing on the dominant Hill 453, held by the French Battalion. The French were commanded by an amazing Foreign Legionnaire who called himself Ralph Monclar (a nom de guerre). Then fifty-nine years old, Monclar was scarred and crippled as a result of seven (or more) battle wounds in World War I and elsewhere. In the postwar years he had risen to the three-star rank of *général de corps d'armée* but had reverted to the rank of lieutenant colonel in order to have the honor of leading the French in Korea. Wearing a black beret and steel-rimmed spectacles and limping among his men with a cane, Monclar appeared casual and absolutely fearless. His troops, who came from French garrisons in Africa, Madagascar, Indochina, and elsewhere, emulated Monclar's style.[110]

It was not easy, but those tough French troops held Hill 453. Freeman wrote:

Despite his casualties, wave after wave of fanatical Chinese continued to surge on during the next three hours to attempt to seize the dominating ground. The gallant French 1st Company was finally engaged in hand-to-hand fighting and suffered heavy casualties. . . . With their position becoming almost untenable, the desperate French counter-attacked with the bayonet. The Chinese—with victory almost in their grasp—a victory which had they attained would have jeopardized our entire position—pulled back.[111]

The CCF continued attacking Freeman's perimeter all that morning, taking advantage of a heavy cloud cover which had grounded close air support. ADC Stewart remembered:

Around mid-morning the situation had become critical and we were running out of ammunition. . . . About every thirty minutes, General Ruffner would call me on the radio and ask how things were going. I told him of our increasing difficulties, and when he indicated a slight skepticism, I informed him that at the moment I was standing in a pool of blood from the wounded radio operator who had just been shot. I also held the microphone out the door so he could hear the firing.[112]

When it finally sank in that the Freeman force was in serious trouble, Ruffner ordered reinforcements to the rescue: George Russell's 1/23 and James Edwards's 2/23. Ed Messinger's 9th Infantry (in process of being relieved at Wonju by the 38th Infantry) moved west on the Yoju–Wonju road to replace the 1/23 and 2/23 and to reinforce the 23d at Twin Tunnels if required.[113]

At about noon the CCF renewed and intensified the attack on the French, driving the 3d Company from its positions on a key ridge. From these heights the CCF directed "murderous machinegun fire" into the 23d's perimeter, even hitting Freeman's CP. Freeman remembered that this was the most "desperate fight" he waged in Korea. He responded by focusing all available artillery, A/A, tank, and mortar fire on the CCF for ten full minutes. The French, with bayonets fixed and "screaming like mad men," Freeman wrote, "started on the run up the hill." Once again the enemy, "with victory just within his grasp, turned and ran." When the French regained the ridge, they found "hundreds of dead enemy piled up."[114]*

The CCF kept pressing, in wave after wave. By 3:00 P.M. they had pushed the French 2d Company from its high ground and inflicted heavy casualties on Kane's 3/23. Very low on ammo and believing both his battalions were on the point of caving in, Freeman drew plans for an "inner perimeter," where the 23d would make a "last stand." The ADC, George Stewart, did not believe Freeman Force could last more than another "twenty minutes." However, "just like a Hollywood battle," Freeman reported, the sun broke through and a flight of four Marine close air support aircraft appeared overhead. These planes, Stewart wrote, saved Freeman Force from "certain annihilation." Freeman agreed. He wrote:

They didn't waste one round! First, 500-pound bombs ("daisy cutters") right into the middle of the closely-packed Chinese who went up in pieces. Next, back to work with rockets ("gook-goosers"), then with the .50 calibers against the now disintegrating enemy. What beautiful air support! The next flight coming in before the first flight had barely started, was laid on the Chinese in front of the French. This mass of Commies on the bare ridge went down like prairie grass in a wind storm. . . . Flight after flight came in [twenty-five altogether] and what was left of the enemy began to "bug out."[115]

While the aircraft were still working over the retreating enemy, Freeman ordered a counterattack to cut them off. His infantry, artillery, tanks, and A/A vehicles savaged the remnants of the fleeing CCF. By nightfall, Freeman wrote, the CCF 125th Division "could be eliminated as an effective unit." His men counted 1,200 to 1,300 dead Chinese on the battlefield; the S-2 estimated that another 2,300 had been wounded. Freeman had incurred 225 casualties, almost all of them in the French and 3/23 battalions.[116]

The Battle of Twin Tunnels, begun merely as a probing attack and feint, had developed into an important Eighth Army victory. For the first time in

_____

*Freeman believed the tracked A/A weapons—the Twin 40s and Quad 50s—were the best possible weapons for countering CCF massed attacks.

the war an American Army force had not only repulsed but virtually annihilated a full CCF divisional attack. On the heels of the victory Ridgway flew into the perimeter with Assistant Secretary of the Army Earl D. Johnson in tow. Ridgway was absolutely elated. He gave Freeman a well-earned DSC, pronounced Monclar a "magnificent soldier," and awarded both the French and Kane's 2/23 a Presidential Unit Citation.[117]

# 22

# THE FOURTH
# CHINESE
# OFFENSIVE

I

By early February the limited offensive actions of Eighth Army's I, IX, and X corps had reestablished full—and violent—contact with the CCF. The CCF Fiftieth Army held the sector below Seoul facing Shrimp Milburn's I Corps. The CCF Thirty-eighth Army held the more mountainous sector opposite Bryant Moore's IX Corps. The CCF Forty-second Army had appeared at Chipyong, in the northwest corner of Ned Almond's X Corps sector.

The intentions of the Chinese were still not clear. The other seven CCF armies previously identified in Korea had not been located. The Fiftieth, Thirty-eighth, and Forty-second could be creating a permanent defensive line, or they might merely be screening movements of the other CCF armies for a massed attack. If the latter, where was that attack likely to take place? And when?

Ridgway continued to believe that the CCF intended to destroy Eighth Army or force it from Korea in a bloody Dunkirk. He could not be certain where the major offensive would come, but he leaned to the view that it probably would come on the central front, manned by Ned Almond's X Corps.[1]

One factor influencing this view was an unusual—and unexpected—fluke of nature. South Korea was experiencing an unseasonable warming trend. In some sectors of the Eighth Army front rainstorms had replaced snowstorms. The ice on the Han River was rapidly breaking up; the river waters were beginning to flow stronger and wider. The Han was once more becoming a natural "barrier" to military operations: difficult to cross; ideal for defense.[2]

Ridgway believed that I and IX corps could defend stoutly behind a thawing Han River as far east as Yangpyong (and Chipyong). But east of there, in the adjoining X Corps sector, the river flowed sharply southeast to Yoju, then nearly due south. The CCF could therefore attack X Corps without crossing the Han. Moreover, the thaw would make it extremely difficult for Almond to shift forces—heavy equipment, tanks, and artillery—over the primitive roads in his sector to meet a CCF offensive. The terrain in the X Corps sector definitely favored the lightly armed CCF traveling mostly on foot.

On the basis of these factors, and others, Ridgway concluded that a major shift of CCF forces to the east was probable. If that shift indeed were to occur, it would leave only the CCF Fiftieth and Thirty-eighth armies with their backs against the flooding Han River, confronting I and IX corps. Hence the odds were good that I and IX corps could root out those two armies and reach the south bank of the Han without a major CCF counterattack in these sectors. Ridgway therefore ordered I and IX corps to continue on the offensive: Thunderbolt-Exploitation.[3]

Inasmuch as X Corps had not yet developed full confrontation with the CCF and it was believed to be the likeliest sector for a major CCF offensive, Ridgway ordered Almond to launch a simultaneous X Corps offensive. Called Roundup, the operation was designed to make contact with the enemy (CCF or NKPA); ascertain his dispositions and, if possible, his intentions; and, if the opportunity presented itself, disrupt any assemblies for offensive operations.[4]

Ridgway's overall aim was to bring Eighth Army forward to the Han River and there establish a line running roughly east along the Han to Yangpyong, where the river turned sharply southeast. Leaving the Han, the line would extend east from Yangpyong to Hoengsong, thence east across the rugged Taebaek range to the Sea of Japan. The line would be very strong—almost impregnable—on the left in I and IX corps sectors, weaker in the X Corps sector at Hoengsong, weaker still in the nearly impassable Taebaek Mountains, but strong on the extreme right, the coastal road along the Sea of Japan.[5]

Ridgway had no illusions that the weak X Corps could hold the Hoengsong line against a massed CCF attack. In the event of such an attack, he foresaw that the corps would, if necessary, fall back on prepared defenses at Wonju and hold there for as long as possible. Then, if necessary, X Corps could fall back farther southeast to Chechon. The IX Corps would hold behind the Han, facing the right flank of the CCF salient southeasterly from Yangpyong to Yoju to Chungju. At the appropriate time both IX and X corps could attack the flanks of the CCF salient and destroy it.

Ridgway did not at that time intend to advance beyond the Han River–Hoengsong line. From a strictly military viewpoint, retaking Seoul was "unsound," he believed. There was really no "good defensible position" north of

the Han. Taking Seoul would place "an unfordable river" in the rear of Eighth
Army. The area east of Yangpyong was "exceedingly rugged" and "deficient
in roads." Any attempt to advance beyond Hoengsong would be extremely
difficult and not worth the effort. Ridgway's apparent aim was to sit behind
the Han River–Hoengsong line and slaughter the CCF as it attempted to
breach it.[6]

\* \* \*

Ridgway distilled his thinking in a letter to MacArthur on February
3. It was coolly received in Tokyo. MacArthur had no intention of making a
voluntary stop at a Han River line to await CCF reaction. According to his
aide Courtney Whitney, he was already working on plans to reinvade North
Korea and destroy all Communist military forces. Whitney described these
fantastic ideas in his memoirs:

As at Inchon he would go for their supply lines. First by constant and ubiquitous
thrusts at widely scattered points but only for limited objectives, he would gradually regain the Seoul line for a base of future operations. Then he would clear the
enemy rear, all across the top of North Korea, by massive air attacks. And then
he would employ an ingenious weapon: if he could not attack the massed enemy
reinforcements across the Yalu, and if he could not even destroy the bridges over
which they came, he would keep them back by making the south bank of the Yalu
impassable. He would sow across all the major lines of supply and communication
a defensive field of radioactive wastes, the by-product of atomic manufacture.
Then, reinforced by Chiang Kai-shek's Formosan troops if he was permitted them,
with simultaneous amphibious and airborne landings at the upper end of both
coasts of North Korea, he would close the gigantic trap. It would be Inchon all
over again, except on a far larger scale.[7]

MacArthur's response to Ridgway's letter was immediate and tactful. He
congratulated Ridgway for his performance during the "last two weeks." In
concept and execution it had been "splendid and worthy of the highest tradi-
tions of a great captain." He was in "complete accord" with Ridgway's overall
objective of ferreting out the enemy and inflicting maximum destruction.
However, he emphatically did not agree with Ridgway's plan to stop at a Han
River line and eastward. The river "would seem to be merely incidental in the
accomplishment of your purpose and need not be a definitive objective one way
or the other," MacArthur wrote. If Ridgway developed the CCF main line of
resistance south of the river, "you would not attempt to push further." If, on
the other hand, Ridgway reached the Han without serious resistance, "you
would continue your probing further northward until you developed his line
or the fact that he did not have such a line." Militarily the occupation of Seoul
was of no consequence, but it "would, of course, present certain diplomatic and
psychological advantages which would be valuable."[8]

Fundamentally, then, MacArthur and Ridgway held sharply differing views on strategy. Real estate meant little or nothing to Ridgway except when it provided him a better (and safer) position from which to kill Chinese. Real estate meant a great deal more to MacArthur. Ridgway had opted for "positional" warfare; MacArthur, for the far more dramatic "maneuver" warfare.

The difference in their views reflected the difference in views between Washington and Tokyo. As Ridgway knew well, Washington was not likely to authorize a second deep invasion of North Korea. Hence "positional" warfare at or below the 38th Parallel was virtually mandated; "maneuver" warfare of the type MacArthur envisioned was simply beyond consideration. Ridgway did not, however, appeal or challenge MacArthur's instructions. He dutifully "agreed" with MacArthur's "criticisms" and "incorporated these suggestions" into his planning, even to the extent of drawing plans for a combined I Corps and IX Corps envelopment of Seoul. Such plans meant little; they could change radically, depending upon CCF actions.[9]

## II

On Eighth Army's left (or west) flank the I and IX corps offensive Thunderbolt-Exploitation proceeded slowly and cautiously.

In Shrimp Milburn's I Corps sector the attack was mounted by (left to right) the 25th and 3d divisions. Bill Kean's 25th Division, deployed along the Seoul–Suwon Corridor, was powerfully reinforced by two full tank battalions: Tom Dolvin's 89th, which had long been temporarily attached to the division, and the 3d Division's black 64th, commanded by William Bartlett.[10]

As it crept northward, I Corps encountered unexpectedly hard resistance. The CCF Fiftieth Army had created a formidable network of defenses in the hills. Central to these was a horseshoe-shaped enclave near Anyang, with Hill 431 at the closed end of the horseshoe, facing south. Hill 431 was a heavily fortified CCF bastion which had to be taken before Dolvin's and Bartlett's tanks could operate to full advantage.

Milburn assigned the mission of capturing the Hill 431 horseshoe to Bill Kean's 25th Division. Kean delegated the task to two regiments: the Turks and Gerry Kelleher's 35th Infantry, both powerfully supported by artillery. The Turks and the 35th Infantry opened the assault on February 2. Over the next several days both outfits gained footholds in the lower hills, but the CCF "reacted violently" with strong counterattacks, which repeatedly forced the Turks off the hill. The division artillery commander, Bittman Barth, wrote that it "was easy for the enemy to block" the UN attacks: "The slopes were so steep that at some points the attackers had to move in single file along narrow ledges." They were thus vulnerable to enemy grenades and sniper fire.[11]

Ridgway and Milburn were on hand "almost daily," Barth remembered.

"By being present 'on the spot' they were able to evaluate the fast-changing situation and make decisions that could be executed immediately, saving much time. General Ridgway, a robust six footer, possessed a dynamic, forceful type of personality that would have made him stand out in any gathering."[12]

But Ridgway's presence could not move mountains—or at least not Hill 431. On February 3 he ordered Milburn to break off the frontal attack, "bypass" the south-facing closed end of the horseshoe, and hit it from the flanks. On February 4 and 5 the Turks and the 35th Infantry, supported by massive artillery, executed these orders and got "behind" the CCF. This maneuver unhinged the CCF defenders on Hill 431, forcing many of them to fall back toward the north-facing "open end" of the horseshoe.

For the infantry it was very rough going. Sergeant Woodruff in James H. Lee's 3/35 described those times in a letter to his wife:

Recently we spent 48 hours on a rocky, snow-covered peak. It took all afternoon and part of the night to climb, using hands and feet, one step at a time, with all our heavy weapons and ammunition. Practically all the chow we had during this time was the C-Ration powdered coffee we had in our pockets. We [only] had native [ROK] bearers enough to bring one overcoat for two men. That was all our cover and shelter. It was windy and the temperature was doggone close to zero. For water we had snow we melted with handfuls of twigs—all the firewood available. We came off that mountain, got a bite of what had been warm chow, and went right up another. Got dug in, mortars "zeroed in," etc. about midnight, along with our other defensive arrangements, shivered through a few hours [of] "sleep" and moved out so suddenly next morning half the outfit got no chow. We attacked and cleared five ridges that day, one after another, got too far out in front of our flank units, ran into substantial opposition, had to back up some, dig in again, got some chow that night at one A.M. During each of these nights from half to all the outfit was required to be awake and on guard.[13]

On February 5, judging that the CCF were weakening, Ridgway issued orders to Milburn for the armored task forces of Dolvin and Bartlett to begin major offensive armor-infantry operations (Punch). Dolvin would attack (on the right) ahead of the 35th Infantry; Bartlett would attack (on the left) ahead of the Turks. The 24th Infantry and the ROK 15th Regiment would support the left and right flanks of the 25th Division. In sum, the four infantry regiments would attack line abreast, the center two regiments spearheaded by armor.[14]

The armored task forces were identically composed. Each tank battalion was reinforced by a battalion of Michaelis's reserve 27th Infantry. Gilbert Check's 1/27 joined Dolvin's task force; Gordon Murch's 2/27 joined Bartlett's. Each tank (and infantry) battalion was broken down into three armor-infantry combat teams (A, B, and C) comprised of one tank company and one infantry company, plus a control section.[15]

The two task forces received identical orders. They were to proceed with utmost caution. On the right Dolvin would go north on the Suwon–Seoul highway, leading the 35th Infantry. Bartlett would follow a parallel secondary road on the left, leading the Turks. The primary task was not to gain real estate but to blast out CCF defensive positions. The teams would work with nearly parade-ground precision, coordinating armor, infantry, artillery, and close air support. No CCF positions would be "bypassed." At the end of the day, to avoid being overrun by nighttime CCF counterattacks, each armored task force would withdraw to positions *behind* the UN phase line held by the oncoming infantry.[16]

Task Force Dolvin's initial objective was the town of Anyang, where the CCF had dug in on two hills, 300 and 178. Skillfully maneuvering his teams by radio and liaison aircraft and coordinating these maneuvers with artillery fire and FEAF close air support, Dolvin carried out a classic attack, worthy of study at Army schools. After "tremendous expenditures" of ammo, his teams captured Hills 300 and 178.[17]

At 5:00 P.M., having seized its objectives, Task Force Dolvin was ordered to withdraw into positions in the rear of Kelleher's 35th Infantry, which had been moving slowly and cautiously toward Anyang behind the armor. The task force teams did not relish giving up these hard-won objectives, but they welcomed the security of the 35th Infantry positions. As Dolvin put it, the safe nighttime refuge "enabled the task force to rest during the night without the necessity of keeping the entire personnel awake in expectation of a counterattack," and as a result, "the task force was better able to meet the demands placed on it in the next day's operations."[18]

William Bartlett, promoted to full colonel with the West Point class of 1933, had the worst possible luck. After going to corps headquarters to get his final orders for launching his black tankers, he slipped on the ice, broke his ankle, and was immediately hospitalized and evacuated. "He was alone at corps headquarters," Tom Dolvin remembered, "and his own command headquarters didn't get the word of his injury for some little time." The 64th Tank Battalion thus sat in place, futilely awaiting Bartlett to deliver its final orders. As a result, the 64th, temporarily commanded by the exec, Joseph G. Fowler, got off to a very late start.[19]

Further trouble arose later in the day. Fowler's three teams, leading the Turks, encountered many antitank mines on his routes. The tankers were thus forced to halt repeatedly while engineers cleared the mines. The upshot was that Fowler lagged far behind Dolvin. Adhering to Ridgway's strict orders to advance shoulder to shoulder, Kean ordered Dolvin to wait for the left flank to catch up by repeating the first day's mission. Accordingly, on the second day Dolvin "recaptured" Hills 300 and 178, then, as before, withdrew behind the 35th Infantry for the night.[20]

On the third day, February 7, Dolvin again received orders to repeat his mission. Once more his armor moved north of Anyang to assault Hills 300 and 178. However, during the night the CCF had reinforced Hill 300. Dolvin brought tremendous tank, artillery, and A/A fire to bear—the Quad 50s fired 61,000 rounds that day—but he was not able to recapture all of Hill 300. At about 4:00 P.M. the task force was once again ordered to withdraw to positions behind the 35th Infantry, which had come into Anyang. By this time Task Force Fowler had caught up, and all division assault forces were line abreast through Anyang.[21]

That night the men of Task Force Fowler had an amazing tale to tell. Lewis W. Millett, a former forward observer for the 8th FAB, who had replaced Medal of Honor winner Reginald Desiderio in command of Gordon Murch's crack E Company, had led the entire company in a bayonet charge on a strong CCF hill position, manned by an estimated 200 troops. The Army historian S. L. A. Marshall later described this action as the "greatest bayonet attack by U.S. soldiers since Cold Harbor in the Civil War." Millett had displayed astonishing courage, bayoneting to death several of the 47 CCF men killed in the attack. Subsequently Millett was awarded the Medal of Honor for personal valor, thus becoming the second E Company commander in succession—and the third man in the 27th Infantry—to be so honored.[22]

\* \* \*

On the right flank of Bill Kean's 25th Division Shorty Soule's 3d Division kept pace with the slow northward advance. Each of its three regiments had formed armor-infantry teams built around the organic tank company of each regiment. Named for the tank company commanders (Tony, Myers, Fisher), the 3d Division task forces, reinforced with artillery and A/A weaponry, operated in a cautious manner, like the teams of Task Forces Dolvin and Fowler.[23]

The onward 3d Division offensive was still spearheaded by Harris's Puerto Rican 65th Infantry on the left and Dinty Moore's 15th Infantry on the right. Jim Boswell's 7th Infantry remained in reserve. Task Force Myers worked with the 65th; Task Force Fisher, with the 15th. The regiments were supported by their usual artillery battalions (58th; 39th) and the newly attached 9th FAB (155s) commanded by John R. Magnusson, plus I Corps artillery.*

The attacks of the 15th Infantry launched Ed Farrell's black 3/15 into its first battalion-size offensive actions since its arrival in Korea. The outfit had acquitted itself well in a defensive role during the evacuation of Hagaru and

---

*Upon the reassignment of the 9th FAB to the 3d Division, Kenneth Dawalt's temporarily attached black 999th, with its self-propelled 155s, was transferred to I Corps artillery, joining Leon Lavoie's 92d FAB, both supporting the 3d Division.[24]

Hungnam, and now it was primed and eager for more combat. A white platoon leader in K Company, West Pointer (1950) George L. Ball, Jr., remembered: "Farrell nicknamed the battalion 'Farrell's Fearless' and required that all hands physically sharpen their bayonets in preparation for the march north. The troops responded enthusiastically, especially to honing bayonets." Ball and his white academy classmate platoon leader John D. Howard, Jr., believed the 3/15 was, in Howard's words, "a top fighting machine."[25]

On February 3 the 3/15 plowed head-on into a strong CCF hilltop position. In the ensuing fight the men more than lived up to the battalion nickname. In so doing, they suffered heavy losses. The charismatic Ed Farrell was shot in the hand, but he kept going. Four other officers, including the black commander of I Company, Harold A. Jenkins, and white platoon leader George Ball, were wounded. Two platoon leaders were killed, one white, one black. The latter was paratrooper Harry Sutton, who had won a Silver Star at Hungnam. Fifteen enlisted men were killed; many were wounded. After this bloody engagement the white K Company commander, Eric L. Hahn, wrote Farrell's predecessor, Mel Huston: "Your former battalion has and still is following your doctrine and is getting quite a reputation in its efforts against the enemy. . . . These men are fighters and have proven themselves as such in every encounter we have entered. . . . Their morale and spirit is [sic] very high."[26]

In these actions the 3/15 had fought as well as the 3/9 before its utter destruction at Kunu. Neither of these black infantry battalions had stirred controversy or drawn public condemnation, as had the 24th Infantry. Those professionals who had argued in the postwar years that black units should be restricted to battalion size or smaller believed their views had been borne out. But the 3/15 West Pointers George Ball and John Howard believed the success of the 3/15 was due less to its size than to the fine quality of the (white) leadership, from Ed Farrell on down. Howard put it this way: "A segregated unit is too open to unjust criticism that their [sic] lack of success was somehow racial. . . . Units that are well trained, equipped, and led will perform well. . . . I feel that [beginning in World War I] poor leadership was the major source of any black unit failures, just as good leadership succeeded."[27]

The wounded Ed Farrell was reluctant to give up his command, but the medics insisted that he be evacuated. His exec, Clyde H. Baden, succeeded him, changing the battalion nickname to Baden's Battlers. Baden had difficult shoes to fill, and there was some doubt at first that he could. John Howard remembered that Baden was "not as colorful or aggressive as Farrell." Bernard Abrams, the white officer in M Company who replaced the assistant S-3, wrote that when the 3/15 won a hill, Baden "never came up to see all the dead Chinese and Americans. . . . When we returned to reserve, he or his staff would be checking everything from boots to fingernails." But gradually Baden won the confidence of his men. "He allowed his unit commanders much room to develop their own training programs," Howard wrote, "and this developed a lot of self-confidence." Abrams concluded: "I found out Baden was an outstanding company commander in World War II. One war climbing hills is enough for one soldier." In retrospect, Abrams judged that Baden was "a very brave officer" who was "cool" and "calculating" and "outstanding."[28]

Following this fight, Shorty Soule pulled Dinty Moore's 15th Infantry into reserve, replaced by Jim Boswell's 7th Infantry. By this time Boswell had taken firm hold of his new command and fought it well. Under his direction the 7th Infantry, supported by the 10th FAB, now commanded by Lewis B. O'Hara, became the workhorse regiment of the 3d Division, standing above the others in aggressiveness and dependability. One reason was the new 1/7 commander, Fred Weyand, who proved to be a superlative, smart, and courageous officer.[29]

To the left of the 7th Infantry William Harris's Puerto Rican 65th Infantry, supported by Harry Stella's black 58th FAB, also encountered tough going. Inasmuch as Ridgway himself had made the decision to send the Puerto Rican regiment to Korea over considerable dissent, he took special interest in its progress and visited often.

On the first of these many visits Harris set a careful stage. He selected the "two tallest Puerto Rican soldiers I could find," tied several "dummy grenades" to their field jackets, gave each of them a knife, daubed their faces with soot to make them look even more menacing, and posted them as guards at the CP. Ridgway no doubt viewed this headquarters stunt with a jaundiced eye, but he was favorably impressed by the Puerto Ricans in the ranks. After the inspection he wrote Harris: "What I saw and heard of your regiment reflects great credit on you, the regiment, and the people of Puerto Rico, who can be proud of their valiant sons."[30]

*   *   *

To the right, in Bryant Moore's IX Corps, both the 1st Cav and the 24th divisions experienced extreme difficulty. As the two divisions inched north on phase lines toward the Han River, the men of the CCF Thirty-eighth Army also clung tenaciously to hilltop redoubts. Every mile of advance entailed vicious fighting, some of it hand to hand. The few "roads" were icy or muddy, restricting the movement of armor, artillery, and other heavy equipment.[31]

The 1st Cav attack was still being spearheaded by Crombez's 5th Cav and Billy Harris's 7th Cav. On February 5 the enemy pressure in the 5th Cav sector slackened somewhat, but the 7th Cav had to fight hard for every yard. On the night of February 5–6 the crack 3/7, now commanded by Charles H. Hallden, was engulfed by a powerful CCF force, which nearly overran L Company.

Individual heroism, especially that of platoon leader Pierre C. Chrissis, prevented a disaster. The 7th Cav historian wrote:

In this action Lieutenant Chrissis fought the Chinese with his carbine until he ran out of ammunition, and then with his bare hands until he was mortally wounded by an enemy who shot him in the side as he battled on to high ground. One of his men came forward under fire and moved him to a position of safety; however, these efforts were to no avail and this officer died. Inspired by the heroic example of Chrissis, the men fought on, counterattacked, forced the enemy back and recaptured their position.[32]*

To the right of the 7th Cav, Babe Bryan's 24th Division continued squeezing northward into its tight triangular area above Ichon–Yoju, slowly pushing the CCF back against the bending Han River. On February 6 strong elements of the CCF Thirty-eighth Army suddenly attacked in the seam between Ollie Kinney's 19th Infantry and Gines Perez's 21st Infantry. The Eighth Army historian recorded that both regiments suffered "heavy casualties." Among them was Master Sergeant Stanley T. Adams in the 19th Infantry, who, although severely wounded, continued fighting with great valor and won a Medal of Honor. A second CCF attack the following day "penetrated" the 21st Infantry lines. Perez and his men repulsed the attack and cleaned CCF troops from the rear areas, but the penetration caused sufficient alarm to bring Ridgway to the scene.[33]

At that time the 24th Division was fully committed and had no division reserve. Concerned that another CCF attack at the 19th or 21st Infantry might cause serious setbacks, Ridgway directed Babe Bryan to pull most of Throckmorton's 5th Infantry from the battlefield. Thomas Roelofs's 1/5 temporarily reinforced the 21st Infantry, but the rest of the 5th Infantry got a much needed rest, which, as matters developed, extended to a full ten days. The ROK 19th Regiment (of the 6th Division) filled the gap left in the line by the 5th Infantry.[34]

A day later Ollie Kinney's 19th Infantry, attempting to resume the advance, was rudely thrown back. The S-3, Elliott Cutler, remembered that fight:

The division was under the usual orders to attack at dawn each day. We were facing a formidable ridge. I had a hunch the enemy might not be occupying the last nose on the right near the river . . . and recommended to Colonel Kinney that we try to [envelop]. He approved and before dawn we moved two battalions over to the right flank. The hunch proved correct and the leading battalion, the 3/19, rushed to the top of the ridge without opposition, cutting off the enemy on the fingers to the south. Just as all looked rosy we were struck by a counterattack

---

*Chrissis was posthumously awarded a DSC.

coming from the direction of the river, and our following battalion, the 1/19, could not hold the lower part of the ridge previously traversed by the 3/19. The 3/19 was thus cut off and had to fight its way back to our lines by coming down one of the ridge fingers leading toward us. I still don't know where that [CCF] reserve came from. . . .[35]

Soon after these actions Ollie Kinney, who had officially commanded the 19th Infantry for not quite a full month, was relieved and named G-2 of the division. The cause of his abrupt transfer was the subject of much speculation. Some believed that the IX Corps commander, Bryant Moore, most recently the superintendent of West Point, was prejudiced against Thompson Act officers and preferred to have young West Pointers (excepting the brainy Gines Perez) in command of the regiments. Some believed it was because of Babe Bryan's displeasure at the 19th's lax supply discipline and other administrative matters. Awarded a Silver Star (his third) for service in Korea, Kinney retired as a colonel in 1961.[36]

Kinney's replacement, West Pointer (1936) Peter W. Garland, thirty-eight, came from the Eighth Army G-3 section. Son of a distinguished judge and church elder in Gastonia, North Carolina, Garland had had a strict upbringing. The result was a polite, courteous "southern gentleman," who "never raised his voice either in anger or excitement." His West Point peers captured him perfectly in a yearbook portrait: "Pete's character is not immediately apparent to the casual observer; a quiet and unassuming demeanor quite modestly marks his many praiseworthy qualities. . . . It is not his desire to blast his personality upon everyone with whom he comes in contact; rather it is his apparent wish to live naturally and let only his intimate friends know him."[37]

Garland had spent most of the fourteen years since graduation from the academy with troops. During World War II he was S-3, exec, and (in the final two weeks) commander of the 385th Regiment of the 76th Division in the ETO. Arriving in France in early 1945, the 76th Division had joined Patton's Third Army counterattack after the Bulge and continued fighting into southern Germany, where in April, at the Mulde River, it met Russian infantry advancing to the west. Garland was in the forefront of the American forces linking with the Russians.[38]

Garland demanded military neatness and order and expected his men to give much. Kenneth Woods, in the 2/19, remembered:

After assuming command of the 19th Infantry, he visited the 2nd Battalion and gave a short pep talk to the officers present. At the close of the talk he stated: "I will expect this regiment to be second to none."

He was a typical spit and polish West Point grad who went strictly by the book and believed strongly in the rules of military courtesy and discipline. He expected junior officers to stand at attention when talking to him, particularly outside the battalion area. He was very conscientious in maintaining high standards for everyone's performance of duty. . . . He was dedicated to his profession.[39]

By this time O. P. Smith's 1st Marine Division (with an attached ROK Marine regiment) was fully deployed southeast of X Corps on a line Andong–Yondok. Still under Ridgway's direct control, the Marines were hunting down the NKPA 10th Division, which had earlier slipped through the ROKs in the mountains to join with guerrillas. On February 5 Smith reported to Ridgway that the Marines had "dispersed" the NKPA 10th Division to such an extent that it was no longer "capable of a major effort." He was confident that ROKs could take over the Marine sector, thereby releasing the Marine division for "another mission."[40]

This was good news for Ridgway. He very much wanted the powerful Marine division on the central front to lend strength to those operations and to help block a possible major CCF counteroffensive. However, since he had assured Smith that the Marines would not again serve under Ned Almond, Ridgway proposed this solution: The Marines would come up on the immediate left of X Corps and replace the 24th Division in IX Corps. Having fought without respite since July, the 24th Division would at last have time to rest and reequip properly.[41]

## III

In the western sector Shrimp Milburn's I Corps forces continued the methodical, cautious advance. By the morning of February 8 Ridgway and Milburn sensed a definite weakening in the CCF defenses. There were some indications that the CCF Fiftieth Army was pulling out. Later in the day this proved to be true. The NKPA I Corps—theretofore based in Seoul—replaced the CCF Fiftieth and began throwing up a new defensive line north of Anyang.[42]

Milburn and Bill Kean were eager to crash north on a nonstop power drive to the Han. However, Ridgway still insisted that I Corps continue its advance in a careful fashion. After Kelleher's 35th Infantry had occupied Hills 300 and 178 above Anyang, and the Turks had drawn abreast on the left, Task Forces Dolvin and Fowler proceeded northward as before, methodically and slowly. Although both task forces were held up repeatedly by mines, they succeeded in disrupting NKPA defensive preparations that day. Despite these gains and the certainty that the CCF Fiftieth Army had pulled out, Ridgway insisted— for the fourth day in succession—that the armored teams withdraw behind the infantry for the night.[43]

On the morning of February 9 it appeared to Bill Kean that the NKPA

I Corps was in "full flight." Apparently it had come south from Seoul merely to screen the withdrawal of the CCF Fiftieth Army and was now itself withdrawing hurriedly. Accordingly, Ridgway relaxed some restrictions on I Corps in order that the armored teams of the 25th and 3d divisions could pursue more aggressively and "trap" the NKPA below the Han. But owing to the many antitank mines encountered that day, neither Task Force Dolvin nor Task Force Fowler was able to move ahead fast enough to trap any NKPA soldiers. Even so, in the early afternoon, Dolvin's task force reached some high ground from which the men could see Seoul. They halted and fired "several rounds" into the city, then, per orders, withdrew for the fifth time to spend the night behind the advancing infantry.[44]

By the following day, February 10, Ridgway and Milburn were satisfied that neither the CCF nor the NKPA held any surprises. The enemy was unquestionably fleeing north of the Han. Accordingly Ridgway finally lifted all restrictions and allowed the armor to "cut loose" and pursue the enemy northwest through Kimpo Airfield and beyond to the western extremities of the Kimpo peninsula.

For this purpose Task Forces Dolvin and Fowler were "consolidated" and placed under a single commander. The force, supported by Harry Stella's black 58th FAB, assembled hurriedly. Dolvin's tankers, mated with Gilbert Check's 1/27, and designated "Speedy Force," drew the most important and glamorous assignment: the recapture of Kimpo Airfield.[45]

Speedy Force lived up to its name. By 3:30 P.M., having rolled out at noon, it had reached Kimpo. There Dolvin's and Check's men contemptuously hauled down the NKPA flag and proudly raised the Stars and Stripes. One hour later Dolvin declared the airfield "secure" and continued northwest into the Kimpo peninsula, only to find that, as he later reported, "The enemy had apparently withdrawn his forces to the north of the Han River."[46]

The infantry, meanwhile, came northward. On the extreme left flank of the 25th Division John Corley's 24th Infantry, preceded by a Ranger company, sent patrols into Inchon to link with a ROK regiment landed there as part of the amphibious deception. In the center the Turks and Kelleher's 35th Infantry, line abreast, advanced into the outskirts of Yongdungpo.[47]

On the right of the 25th Division Shorty Soule's 3d Division, still spearheaded by William Harris's 65th and Jim Boswell's 7th Infantry, continued to keep abreast. On February 10 the Puerto Rican 65th, which had had a long two weeks of tough fighting, became the first unit of I Corps to reach the south bank of the Han. That day it was relieved by Dinty Moore's 15th Infantry. The 65th pulled back into division reserve with a "festive air," establishing itself on the high ground near Shorty Soule's 3d Division CP.[48]

\* \* \*

The I Corps drive to the Han River was a notable, even electrifying achievement for Eighth Army and Matt Ridgway. For the first time since the CCF had intervened in the Korean War, it had been forced back decisively—in this instance, yielding real estate (Suwon and Kimpo airfields; Inchon) which would significantly enhance Eighth Army's fighting strength. No less important, Eighth Army had proved to itself that by closely integrating and managing the infantry, artillery, and armor at its disposal, it could more than offset the CCF advantage in manpower.

The I Corps victory also gave Eighth Army a powerful psychological boost. The new confidence was reflected in an order of the day proudly issued by Shrimp Milburn:

I Corps stands firmly on the south bank of the Han River.
A simple statement of an accomplished fact, made possible through an equally simple truth: The power of confident, fighting men and their commanders when given the opportunity to come to grips with a tangible enemy.
A month ago today this Corps seized the initiative from the forces of the Communist Chinese with a series of quick armor-infantry thrusts. Caught off balance by the rapidity of these moves the enemy could only fall back to successive defense lines. We pressed him relentlessly, fighting him yard for yard and hand to hand in treacherous terrain, throwing off his nightly counter-attacks. In the open valleys the superiority of our troops, training and firepower overwhelmed him. As the full fury of our offensive mounted, he threw in everything he had, and it was not enough to stop us. We drove on through to the final objective. . . . This sweeping tactical success will rank high in the recording of military achievements. All forces of this Corps have done their part and done it well.[49]

## IV

The Joint Chiefs of Staff were enormously pleased and gratified by the successes of I Corps. Omar Bradley dropped Ridgway a personal note, stating: "We are all very proud of the way you and your Eighth Army are performing these days. There certainly has been a change in spirit. I hope you can continue to keep them off balance until they are willing to talk some kind of permanent peace arrangements. We are all certainly pulling for you here."[50]

Indeed, the dramatic turnaround of the Eighth Army had generated yet another round of policy discussions in Washington. In view of this "now different and far happier" situation, the JCS had withdrawn its earlier recommendations to employ Chinese Nationalist troops in Korea or on the mainland of China and had tabled discussions of a blockade of China and other drastic measures. Most policy discussions now focused on whether or not Eighth Army should be allowed to recross the 38th Parallel and reinvade North

Korea, should the opportunity to do so arise. Although some Washington hawks advocated a reinvasion and relentless pursuit and punishment of the CCF and NKPA, the consensus in the Pentagon and State Department (as well as London and Paris) was to halt at the 38th Parallel and continue the search for a negotiated settlement.[51]

Dean Acheson, among others, believed that Washington should issue yet another directive to MacArthur, spelling out the decision to halt at the 38th Parallel.[52] As was customary, the Pentagon sought MacArthur's view. The form of the query was a curious departure from customary practice, perhaps deliberately intended to signal MacArthur that his views carried less weight. The cable requesting his opinion came not from the JCS, but from the Army's recently appointed G-3, Maxwell D. Taylor.[53]

Although MacArthur was already developing his fantastical plans for a reinvasion of North Korea by air, sea, and otherwise, he did not elect to unveil them in his response to Taylor's cable. His reply was routine and low-key, more or less a rehash of his exchange with Ridgway earlier in the month. He did, however, take advantage of Taylor's query to criticize Washington— twice—for permitting the enemy a "privileged sanctuary" in Manchuria:

It is my purpose to continue ground advances until I develop the enemy's main line of resistance or the fact that there is no such line south of the 38th Parallel. These advances serve to keep him off-balance so that his ground forces cannot get set for a blow. . . . If it should develop that no major enemy strength is disposed south of the 38th Parallel, report will be made to the JCS and instructions requested before proceeding further. It can be accepted as a basic fact that, unless authority is given to strike enemy bases in Manchuria, our ground forces as presently constituted cannot with safety attempt major operations in Korea. It is evident that the enemy has lost his chance for achieving a decisive military decision in Korea, but he retains the potential, as long as his base of operations in Manchuria is immune to attack, to employ a force which will enable him to resume the offensive and force retrograde movement upon us. We intend to hold the line of the Han up to the point of a major and decisive engagement. It is impossible to predict where, once we withdraw from this line, the situation will again stabilize, but stabilization will be certain. The capability of the enemy is inversely and geometrically proportionate to his distance from the Yalu. . . .[54]

After sending off this cable, MacArthur flew to Suwon on February 13. The purpose of this visit to Korea, his third since January 20, was not clear; perhaps it was to associate himself publicly with the I Corps victory and the recapture of Kimpo Airfield. Ridgway met the plane (which bore a fruitcake to him from Mrs. MacArthur) and accompanied the motorcade to Kimpo.[55]

There may have been another purpose for the visit. At the time Thurgood Marshall, special counsel for the National Association for the Advancement of Colored People (and future Supreme Court associate justice), was in Korea, conducting an investigation into charges that racial discrimination in Eighth Army had influenced the unusually large number of court-martial cases against blacks and the severity of the punishments handed down.* Perhaps to project the impression that he was not discriminating, MacArthur spent considerable time that day with John Corley's 24th Infantry at Kimpo, during which he inspected George Clayton's 2/24 and had lunch at Corley's CP.[56]

In the course of this visit John Corley astonished MacArthur (not to say Ridgway and Bill Kean) by this jesting assertion: "I have more Silver Star medals than you do." It was true: Corley had been awarded a total of eight (a record for that time); MacArthur, seven.[57]

The story of Corley's brazen one-upmanship with MacArthur spread like wildfire through the Eighth Army officer corps. It was soon followed by a rumor that because of it, Corley had been relieved of command. But the rumor was not true. Corley was leaving the 24th Infantry, but not because of the incident. Mike Michaelis, who regarded John Corley as a "great soldier" and "battlefield leader," explained: "Corley and Sladen Bradley did *not* get along. Bradley was getting ready to take over the division from Bill Kean, so Corley got out."[58]

Upon his return to Tokyo that evening MacArthur apparently felt compelled to make still another lofty public comment. His remarks may have been intended to lay groundwork and gain support for his as yet unveiled and fantastical schemes to reinvade North Korea. Whatever the purpose, he bluntly challenged Washington's (and Ridgway's) strategy and again alluded to the CCF's "privileged sanctuary" in Manchuria.

"The concept advanced by some," MacArthur said, "that we should establish a line across Korea and enter into positional warfare is wholly unrealistic and illusionary." Owing to the rough terrain and numerical superiority of the enemy, such tactics "would insure destruction of our forces piecemeal." He airily went on to discuss the extremely delicate and politically sensitive matter of crossing the 38th Parallel. "Before we can seriously consider major operations north of that geographic line," he stated, "we must materially reduce the existing superiority of our Chinese Communist enemy engaging with impunity in undeclared war against us, with the unprecedented military advantage of sanctuary protection. . . ."

MacArthur's remarks were, of course, widely published in the United States and abroad. Inasmuch as they were a direct violation of Truman's December directive that all government officials were to refrain from making

---

*Thirty-nine soldiers of the 24th Infantry had been convicted of serious breaches of discipline, including running away from the enemy. One black soldier, Marshall reported, had been tried, convicted, and sentenced to life imprisonment in forty-two minutes. Marshall's highly critical report resulted in reversed convictions or reduced sentences for most of the thirty-nine blacks.

uncleared public statements on foreign and military policy, they constituted insubordination. The insubordination was noted in the White House, State Department, and Pentagon; however, no one felt inclined to reprimand MacArthur.[59]

## V

On the central front, above Wonju, Ned Almond initiated the X Corps offensive, Roundup, on February 5, coinciding with the attacks of Task Forces Dolvin and Fowler in I Corps.

The attack was spearheaded by two ROK divisions: the 8th on the left and the 5th on the right. Each ROK division was backed by an unusually strong American "support force." Nick Ruffner's 2d Division, backing the ROK 8th Division, provided John Keith's 15th FAB, a five-gun battery of 155-mm howitzers from Cecil B. White's 503d FAB, A/A vehicles, and the 1st Battalion of the 38th Infantry. Buddy Ferenbaugh's 7th Division, backing the ROK 5th Division, provided Barney White's 49th FAB, a battery of six 155 mm howitzers from George Welch's 31st FAB, A/A vehicles, the 2d Battalion of Buffalo Bill Quinn's 17th Infantry, plus the 7th Division Recon Company.[60]

If, as suspected, the CCF was shifting to the central sector for a major attack, of the two ROK divisions, the 8th, attacking northwesterly, would be the more exposed. However, it was in part protected on the extreme left by Paul Freeman's 23d Infantry at Chipyong, which had been reinforced by John Hector's full 37th FAB, a 155-mm battery from the 503d FAB, the 1st Ranger Company, and a company of engineers.[61]

At first Roundup went well. The ROKs, backed by the American support forces, deployed smartly. Encouraged by Ned Almond, they began laying very ambitious plans for an encirclement of Hongchon, considerably to the north of Hoengsong and Freeman's 23d Infantry at Chipyong. In contrast with the tightfisted operations in I Corps, the American support forces under Almond's direct control became ever more widely scattered, evoking memories of Almond's operations in northeast Korea.

Meanwhile, in response to an order from Ridgway, the Eighth Army G-2 section had made an all-out effort to pinpoint the unlocated CCF armies and guess their intentions. This important study, based mostly on intensive POW interrogations and aerial reconnaissance, was conducted by the deputy G-2, Bob Fergusson, acting for the G-2, Clint Tarkington, who was ill. It confirmed the belief that the CCF was shifting east for an offensive. Fergusson predicted that on February 15 Lin Piao would launch a major offensive toward Wonju, employing four CCF armies (Thirty-ninth, Fortieth, Forty-second, and Sixty-sixth), probably to be reinforced by three other armies (Twentieth, Twenty-

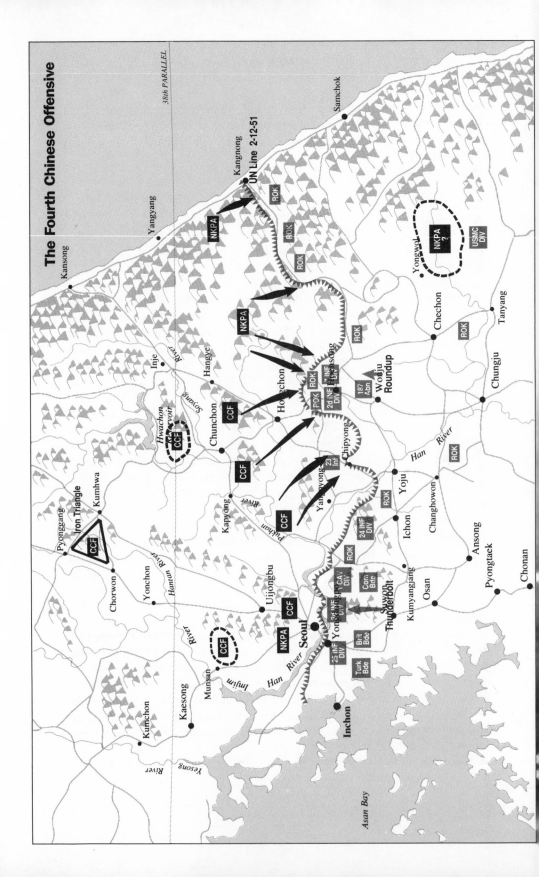

# The Fourth Chinese Offensive

sixth and Twenty-seventh) of Ninth Army Group, comprising twelve divisions), coming down from the Hamhung area, where they had been ever since the evacuation of X Corps.[62]

The complete details of Fergusson's report were presented to Ned Almond. Since X Corps would apparently be the CCF's prime target, the report should have induced caution, perhaps even a withdrawal to the well-prepared American defensive positions in Wonju. However, for reasons never explained, Almond pressed onward with Roundup. Perhaps he disbelieved the report or perhaps he believed that the capture of Hongchon might fatally disrupt the CCF assembly. Or as some observers speculated, perhaps he continued the offensive in order to "lure" the CCF into an offensive which he believed might be contained at Wonju and annihilated by attacks on the flanks.[63]

The Communist offensive actually started sooner than predicted. It began with a spirited NKPA II and V corps attack on the east flank of the ROK 5th Division. In response, Almond became increasingly aggressive. He shifted the ROK 5th Division into blocking positions on the right and brought the ROK 3d Division forward to replace the 5th. The American 7th Division support forces shifted to back up the ROK 3d Division. The X Corps artillery—the 96th FAB with self-propelled 155s and the 674th Airborne FAB with 105s— were ordered to back up the ROK 5th Division.[64]

The 38th Infantry was to play an important role in these forthcoming operations. It, too, now had a new commander. George Peploe, fifty, was promoted out of the 2d Division to replace Andrew Tychsen as chief of staff to Bryant Moore's IX Corps, a one-star job. Peploe's replacement was his former exec, West Pointer (1932) John Coughlin, who had been promoted to full colonel and G-3 of the 2d Division after Kunu.[65]*

John Coughlin was a professional soldier who was "methodical and damned good," according to a senior 38th staffer. He was also extremely closed-mouthed and "hard to know." Neither he nor his wife had socialized at Fort Lewis. A friend remembered that Coughlin and his older brother, Robert Lee, both born in Arizona, had been orphans, reared by a New York City schoolteacher who encouraged them to go to West Point. Robert, who entered with the class of 1935, had washed out but had subsequently obtained a Reserve commission and won a Silver Star Medal in World War II. He was then a full colonel in a Stateside training job. John, who had been a heavyweight boxer at the academy, had fought during World War II in the CBI Theater, where he had won a host of medals: DSC, two Silver Stars, four Legions of Merit, and a Bronze Star.[66]

---

* Peploe's departure reduced the "older" regimental commanders in Eighth Army to two: the 15th Infantry's Dinty Moore and the 5th Cav's Marcel Crombez, both fifty. The average age of the other sixteen regimental commanders was now 40.5 years.

Peploe had been a strict and tough commander, but the S-3, Warren Hodges, remembered, "Coughlin was even tougher—tough and aloof." He was also brave and cool under fire. Hodges's assistant, William Manning, remembered that when the going got tough, Coughlin told him, "Never take counsel of your fears."[67]

Ned Almond and the X Corps staff fragmented the 38th Infantry. Bill Keleher's 1/38 had been ordered well forward to support the ROK 8th Division. When the ROK 3d Division came up to replace the ROK 5th, Almond ordered Coughlin to send two of his three remaining battalions forward: the Dutch Battalion to Hoengsong and Harold Maixner's 3/38 farther forward yet to a road crossing four miles north of Hoengsong. These deployments scattered the four battalions of the 38th Infantry into four locations, north to south along the Hongchon–Wonju road. The battalions were not tied in or in communication with one another; it was not altogether clear whether these disparate units fell under command of Coughlin or Ruffner or Almond.[68]

On February 11, while Almond was absorbed in a complicated plan for a double encirclement of Hongchon by his ROK forces, the CCF struck. Three full CCF divisions hit the ROK 8th Division frontally in broad daylight. In the ensuing chaos, the division was virtually annihilated. A X Corps after-action analysis reported that all three of the division's regiments were almost immediately surrounded. It lost 323 officers and 7,142 men, almost all its equipment, and fourteen 105-mm and 75-mm "pack" howitzers. About 250 of its officers and 3,000 enlisted men escaped, but the division ceased to exist as a fighting unit.[69]

The sudden and total destruction of the ROK 8th Division seriously imperiled the forces from Nick Ruffner's 2d Division that were directly supporting it under X Corps control. These forces were, principally, John Keith's 15th FAB (plus the battery of five 155s from Cecil White's 503d), a battery of A/A vehicles, Bill Keleher's 1/38, and two small armor-infantry teams from the 38th and 9th Infantry, each composed of one platoon of tanks and one company of infantry. It also endangered the other two battalions of the 38th indirectly supporting the ROK 8th: Harold Maixner's 3/38, dug in four miles north of Hoengsong, and the Dutch Battalion in Hoengsong.[70]

When the 8th ROK Division ceased to exist, the CCF swarmed through the dark behind the American support forces and threw up roadblocks on the Hoengsong–Hongchon highway, thereby "trapping" Keith's reinforced 15th FAB and Keleher's 1/38 well north of Maixner's 3/38. Keith radioed the 2d Division artillery commander, Loyal Haynes, requesting permission to withdraw immediately. Such was the uncertainty about who was in command that Haynes refused to grant that permission on his own, telling Keith to hold until he cleared the withdrawal with Nick Ruffner and X Corps. Finally, one and a half hours after Keith's request, the X Corps artillery officer, William P.

Ennis, having cleared through Bill McCaffrey and Ned Almond himself, authorized the withdrawal. By that time—3:00 A.M. on February 12—it was too late. The CCF troops had created a gauntlet, in effect, not unlike that which the 38th Infantry had run below Kunu.

It was another ghastly ordeal. Keleher's 1/38 infantry led the way south, desperately trying to blast a path for the twenty-three towed howitzers and the scores of supply trucks and other vehicles. In this effort Keleher's B and C companies and the truck drivers were cut to ribbons. The men of the 503d's A Battery abandoned four of the unit's five 155s; the commander was captured. Later the 503d artillerymen abandoned the fifth gun, blocking the road. Keith's 15th FAB abandoned one 105-mm gun, but the other seventeen got out.

Shortly after dawn on February 12 the battered column reached Maixner's 3/38 perimeter above Hoengsong. But as it turned out, there was little comfort to be found there. Swarms of the CCF were attacking the 3/38 and had blocked the road south to Hoengsong. A small armor-infantry team from Hoengsong had been turned back by the CCF; half the infantry had been lost. Keith, Keleher, and Maixner circled the wagons in Maixner's perimeter, Keith's artillery firing point-blank into the ranks of the attacking CCF. Nick Ruffner refused Coughlin permission to send his reserve 2/38 forward from Wonju to help.

Inasmuch as Eighth Army was under orders from Ridgway to protect artillery at all costs, at 11:00 A.M. X Corps headquarters ordered Keith to continue a fighting withdrawal to Hoengsong, where the Dutch Battalion (and reinforcements from Wonju) were preparing a strong defensive perimeter. Maixner's 3/38 would hold until the artillery and trains cleared out.

Having already sustained 289 casualties, Keleher's 1/38 again led the way south. However, about a half mile below the 3/38 perimeter, Keleher encountered a wall of CCF which immobilized the 1/38 for four full hours. With darkness again approaching, X Corps ordered Maixner's 3/38 (which was running out of ammo) to withdraw from its perimeter and join the 1/38 and fight south. Meanwhile, X Corps sent forward from Hoengsong an armor-infantry team, built around G Company of the 187th Airborne RCT (which had come up from reserve to Wonju). It broke through the CCF and reached the combined 1/38 and 3/38 at 7:00 P.M.

Although it was dark and the CCF still held most of the road, there was hope that the combined force could shepherd Keith's artillery into Hoengsong. At 8:00 P.M. these hopes were dashed when a lead truck towing a 105 howitzer jackknifed and blocked the road. Seizing upon this calamity, the CCF concentrated such heavy fire on the disabled vehicles that no one could clear them away. The commanders on the scene concluded there was no alternative but to abandon the artillery and trucks north of the block and run for Hoengsong.

In all, 19 howitzers (fourteen 105 mm and five 155 mm) and about 120 trucks (many carrying wounded) were lost.

Much now depended on the Dutch Battalion in Hoengsong, commanded by Marinus P. A. den Ouden. The 2d Division ADC, George Stewart, remembered: "The Dutch Battalion lived up to the description 'stubborn Dutch.' If they approved of a defensive position assigned them, they would fight and seldom withdraw. If they did not like their orders—to attack or defend—they would just not obey. When they did fight, and that was many times, they were superb."[71]

The Dutch elected to fight. Their stand, which earned a Presidential Unit Citation, was awesomely stubborn and courageous. It enabled the battered survivors of Keleher's 1/38 and Maixner's 3/38—and the remaining four of Keith's twenty-three howitzers—to withdraw through Hoengsong and south to Wonju. Badly shot up, the Dutch Battalion withdrew behind them, without den Ouden and four of his officers, who were killed when the CCF, posing as ROKs seeking ammo, infiltrated the Dutch CP and opened fire at point-blank range.[72]

When all the 2d Division support forces finally reached Wonju, the casualties to them and to the Dutch Battalion were reckoned to be a disastrous 1,769. Among these, in addition to den Ouden, were John Keith, first listed as missing but later declared dead. Keleher's 1/38, Maixner's 3/38, and Keith's 15th FAB had incurred the majority of the casualties. Both infantry battalions, the 2d Division historian wrote, were "shattered." But Keleher and Maixner survived this second gauntlet.[73]*

\* \* \*

To the east of this disaster, the ROK 3d and 5th divisions were also smashed. A full CCF division hit the ROK 3d; NKPA II and V corps hit the ROK 5th, which had moved to the right to block and make room for the attacking ROK 3d.[75]

The collapse of the ROK 3d Division imperiled the American support forces provided by the 7th Division. At first these forces attempted to go west to withdraw with the 2d Division support forces on the Hoengsong–Hongchon road. Finding the road solidly blocked by the CCF, the 7th Division support forces turned southeast and blazed a new road out with bulldozers.[76] This arduous task was impeded first by the fleeing ROKs, then by the CCF. Combat engineer Lenoise Bowman, attached to Denzil Baker's 2/17, remembered:

---

*On March 9, 1951, the 2d Division revised the casualty figures downward to 1,537: 99 killed; 490 wounded; 948 missing.[74]

The battle drew ever nearer and the bugles, etc., got louder. . . . At first we were not that concerned because as "support troops" we were sure we would be withdrawn before we were in great danger. . . . [Nonetheless,] two buddies and I set up a machine gun and all the ammo and grenades we could find, vowing to take as many CCF with us as we could. About daylight the ROKs began falling back on us. My buddies and I started mowing down the ROKs, hoping to slow them down and keep them between us and the CCF, thereby buying more time. . . . Then came word to withdraw. With bulldozers clearing the way and our tanks leading, late in the evening we got into Hoengsong.

There was heavy fighting in Hoengsong. We climbed into a truck and with the tanks leading, drove right into the middle of the heaviest fighting. All hell really broke loose. Tracers were flying in all directions so fast and thick that it was like a storm. The CCF were climbing on our truck and fighting us hand to hand. I felt bullets thudding into my field pack, then a sharp pain in my left hand. A bullet had torn my rifle apart. My buddies left and right got hit; our medic, Robert Trout, was hit in the top of the head, scattering his brains all over. I picked up a .30 caliber machine gun, which I was going to set up on the ground outside the truck. When I stood up tracers were flying thick all around me. I cannot imagine how I wasn't cut to ribbons. . . . Then we were formed up and marched out of town. I don't know our casualty rate, but those of us who got out made it with just what we were wearing.[77]

Barney White's decision to bulldoze a road to the southeast and avoid the Hoengsong–Hongchon road proved to be wise. The 7th Division support forces escaped with relatively light casualties (12 killed, 125 wounded, and 43 missing) and slight loss of equipment: one 155-mm howitzer of George Welch's 31st FAB, a Quad 50 A/A vehicle, and thirty-five other vehicles. After passing through the fight (Dutch versus the CCF) in Hoengsong, White's 49th FAB withdrew to Wonju in relatively good order. Baker's 2/17 remained in Hoengsong to assist the Dutch Battalion, then withdrew with it to Wonju. The X Corps artillery forces (96th and 674th FABs) providing support to the ROK 5th Division reached Wonju without loss of any equipment.[78]

In the initial CCF assault the ROK 3d and 5th divisions lost about 3,000 men each. Both gave way disgracefully and bugged out. They were finally halted temporarily on a road running east from Wonju. An investigation of the ROK 5th Division revealed that although it had saved its artillery, "about half of its crew-served weapons were gone." The loss of weapons in the ROK 3d Division was not as severe. However, X Corps declared both divisions to be "disorganized" and virtually worthless as combat forces.[79]

\* \* \*

When Ridgway first learned of the CCF onslaught in the central front (four days sooner than Fergusson had predicted), he coolly issued a series of orders designed to contain and destroy it. The major steps:[80]

• John Coughlin's 38th Infantry and Frank Bowen's 187th Airborne RCT and Baker's 2/17, plus all the artillery that could be brought to bear, would make the strongest possible stand at Wonju to blunt the CCF. But Wonju was not to be held "at all costs." If it could not be held, the Wonju forces would withdraw southeast to Chechon, joining with Ferenbaugh's 7th Division. These combined forces would be in position to attack the left flank of the CCF salient.

• Paul Freeman's 23d Infantry at Chipyong would stay put. The Commonwealth Brigade at Yoju, in IX Corps reserve, would move due north to Chipyong to reinforce Freeman. The ROK 6th Division would replace the Commonwealth Brigade at Yoju. Ed Messinger's 9th Infantry, deployed on the Yoju–Wonju road, would also advance forces toward Chipyong. Should Wonju fall, Messinger's 9th Infantry would move east to Yoju.

• The 1st Marine Division, then in process of decamping from Andong to relieve the 24th Division in IX Corps, in accordance with an earlier plan, would instead halt at Chungju. That would place the Marines directly in the path of the CCF salient below Wonju in prepared and strong defensive positions on high ground.

• The 1st Cav Division, then attacking toward the Han River line on the IX Corps left flank, would withdraw as soon as possible to Changhowon, between the IX Corps forces concentrating at Yoju and the Marines at Chungju. This would possibly place the 1st Cav in a position to join the 24th Division for an attack on the right flank of the CCF salient.

• Bill Kean's 25th Division at Yongdungpo and Kimpo (in I Corps) would shift to the right of the 3d Division to replace the withdrawing 1st Cav Division.

This last step gave rise to another possibility that would be in conformity with MacArthur's instructions to Ridgway not to become fixated on a Han River "line." Leaving sufficient force at Yongdungpo and Kimpo to repel an unlikely CCF Fiftieth Army or NKPA I Corps attack south across the Han from Seoul, I Corps (3d and 25th divisions) might cross the Han well east of Seoul (in the old 1st Cav sector), attack the "rear" of the CCF moving to the central front, and cut the CCF supply lines from Seoul. As envisioned, the 3d and 25th divisions would cross the Han simultaneously. The 3d Division would face west (toward Seoul) to block the NKPA or CCF troops. Thus protected on the left flank, the 25th Division would attack north and northeasterly, with the 24th Division on its right flank.

Of all these steps, the most complex was the shift of Kean's 25th Division to the right of the 3d Division to replace the 1st Cav Division. It was decided to leave the Turkish Brigade and Kelleher's 35th Infantry in the Yongdungpo–Kimpo area with the ROK 1st Division. Tom Brodie's British Brigade (in I

Corps reserve), which would replace the Turkish Brigade in the 25th Division, moved up at once, relieving Marcel Crombez's 5th Cav in the left sector of the 1st Cav Division. John Corley's 24th Infantry prepared to relieve Pete Clainos's 8th Cav in the 1st Cav center; Mike Michaelis's 27th Infantry prepared to relieve Billy Harris's 7th Cav on the right.[81]

The assignment of the 25th Division to this new and taxing mission afforded Ridgway a fitting opportunity to make the long-delayed senior command changes. He stuck to the original plan of promoting the ailing but able ADC, Sladen Bradley, to replace Bill Kean. Upon his return to the States (with a DSM and glowing fitness report), Kean was named to command III Corps and then the Fifth (paper) Army in Chicago, a position that enabled Joe Collins to promote Kean to three stars before he retired.[82]

Ridgway also carried through with his idea of promoting young (thirty-eight-year-old) Mike Michaelis to brigadier general, replacing Bradley as 25th Division ADC. But no one told Michaelis. He received orders to return to the States via Japan. Upon his strong recommendation, the 1/27 commander, Gilbert Check, was promoted to full colonel and given command of the 27th Infantry.[83] Michaelis remembered: "I went back to Yokohama, was debriefed at GHQ in Tokyo, and got all set to return to the States, not knowing what my next assignment would be. On about my fourth day in Japan MacArthur's G-three, Pinky Wright, called and invited me to lunch with him at the Imperial Hotel. When my car pulled up at the front door, he came over, stuck out his hand, and said, 'Congratulations.' In response I said, 'I'm delighted to be going home.' He said, 'Do you mean to tell me you don't *know?* You're not going home. You're a brigadier general on the way back to Korea.' I said, 'The hell I am! I'm a colonel on the way back to the United States.' I went back to Korea."[84]

# V I

By the morning of February 13 all surviving X Corps forces north of Wonju had withdrawn into defensive positions near the town. These included John Coughlin's battered 38th Infantry (with the attached Dutch Battalion), Frank Bowen's fresh, eager 187th Airborne RCT, the ROK 18th Regiment (of the ROK 3d Division), and Denzil Baker's 2/17 (of the 7th Division support forces). In total, there were eleven infantry battalions (seven American, one Dutch, and three ROK), comprising about 8,000 men.[85]

The infantry was backed by a substantial collection of artillery. This included the 38th FAB (normally attached to Coughlin's 38th Infantry); the 674th Airborne FAB (normally attached to Bowen's 187th Airborne); the 7th Division's 49th FAB, plus a battery of the 31st FAB (all part of the 7th

Division support force); the 96th FAB; survivors of the 15th FAB (amounting to about one firing battery of six howitzers); and one battery of the 503d FAB. In total, this was the equivalent of five FABs, mounting about 100 howitzers, of which about 30 were 155s. In addition, the 2d Division's 72d Tank Battalion (in reserve at Wonju) could add its 76-mm guns.

Ned Almond placed all forces at Wonju, including the artillery, under command of the 2d Division ADC, George Stewart. Word of this assignment reached Stewart via the new X Corps chief of staff, John Guthrie. Stewart remembered that it was accompanied by a lot of unneeded advice, most of which proved to be worthless. Stewart remembered Guthrie's saying: "General Almond directs that you take command of all the troops in the vicinity of Wonju [and] defend and hold that important road junction at all costs. The General believes that the Chinese will attack on your right, BUT THE DECISION IS YOURS. The General believes you should place the one intact battalion of the 38th [Infantry] on the line, BUT THE DECISION IS YOURS."[86]

After Stewart, the next most senior infantry officer at Wonju was John Coughlin. Stewart and Coughlin got on well. Although Coughlin had commanded the 38th for only about two weeks, Stewart had unreserved confidence in him: "John was the coolest man under fire that I ever saw. He seemed absolutely oblivious to danger. On one occasion, I told him I was getting tired of trying to be as cool as he when fire was coming in. He only smiled."[87]

The CCF mounted the onward attack on the Wonju garrison during the early hours of February 14. Two full CCF divisions (197th and 198th) of the Sixty-sixth Army spearheaded the assault, attacking due south from Hoeng-song along the Som River, reinforced by elements of the CCF 119th and 120th divisions of the Fortieth Army, attacking from the northwest. The 38th and the 187th Airborne regiments, holding good defensive positions in high ground north of Wonju, met the attack head-on. By dawn all the American and Dutch infantry was furiously engaged in close, bitter fighting.[88]

Early in his career Stewart had served a tour at the Artillery School and had a great appreciation of the impact of artillery. During the previous evening he had browbeat the 2d Division artillery commander, Loyal Haynes, who was in command of the disparate artillery units, to "prepare data to enable them to fire promptly at specific areas on call." The data included overlays with numbers to identify the specific areas.[89]

This preparation now paid enormous dividends. The CCF, boldly attacking in full daylight in march formation, met the most concentrated, well-directed artillery barrage of the war to date. The 2d Division historian wrote:

Every available artillery piece in the 2nd Division and supporting corps artillery was laid upon the marching mass of men. Thunderous barrages roared across the hills as tons of shrapnel poured into the plodding troops. Thousands of shells wreaked havoc never before seen on any army as the pilots reported the river running red with the blood of the massacred troops. Still they came marching into the rain of death, heedless of the carnage around them. . . . Hour after hour the unbelievable slaughter mounted as dog-tired, exhausted artillerymen slammed an endless stream of shells into the exposed masses of Chinese who continued to press forward. . . .[90]

Stewart echoed the historian in his memoir. But a problem developed. Haynes, Stewart remembered, "called to say he would have to stop firing because his ammunition was running low." Stewart pleaded: "Keep firing until the last shell has been used." Haynes complied but soon called again to say that his guns "were so overheated he would have to stop firing." Stewart retorted: "Keep firing until the gun barrels melt."[91]

At about noon the CCF began to falter. The division historian continued the ghastly tale:

The staggering losses began to tell. The once-full ranks were now thin, blasted, shocked remnants without leaders, without hope. Slowly, as though dazed, the remains of the ranks broke. Now only unorganized bands of useless bodies, they tried to escape north out of reach of the murderous guns. The cracking rain of steel followed them northward and [close] air [support] took up where the artillery could not reach. The attack was broken, the threat to Wonju was no longer critical.[92]

The "Wonju shoot" of February 14 proved to be a decisive victory. Some 5,000 CCF troops lay dead on the battlefield; probably three times that number had been wounded. The four CCF assault divisions had been shattered. But owing to the shock waves created by the loss of the 1,700 Americans and the artillery in the ROK 8th and American 2d and 7th division support forces (in all, thirty-four howitzers), a further bugout of the ROK 3d and 5th divisions (finally halted above Chechon), and a second, fanatical (but futile) CCF attack on Wonju during the night of February 14–15, the importance of the victory at Wonju was not immediately apparent. Stewart, Coughlin, and the men they commanded never received the great credit they deserved.

On the contrary, when Ridgway visited the X Corps CP, his mind was fixed on the losses of artillery and men.* Furious at this disaster, Ridgway blistered Almond unmercifully. "I never heard such a chewing out," the G-3, Jack Chiles, remembered.[94] Inasmuch as he had vowed to court-martial those responsible for loss of artillery, Ridgway ordered an official investigation. George Stewart, expecting praise for the "Wonju shoot," was instead ordered

---

*The Army historian reckoned the casualties in X Corps from February 11 to February 13 to total 11,800, of which 9,800 were ROKs, 1,900 were American, and 100 were Dutch.[93]

to conduct the investigation, a perilous assignment politically since the main fault was obviously Almond's loose control and dispersion of forces. Stewart remembered:

I was amazed, angry, dumbfounded. I was being ordered to investigate the actions of my corps commander. I protested to no avail. I was told my orders came from the highest quarters. . . .

I assembled all the orders we had received taking units from our control. I took testimony from officers who had been in the thick of things; but I absolutely refused to place these brave and exhausted men under oath. I concluded the report with a statement to the effect that the cause of the disaster was the immediate and precipitous flight of the [8th] Korean Division and the failure of Korean commanders to advise or alert our units of their departure.[95]

The official report thus absolved Almond and all other Americans of blame, so there could be no court-martials. Even so, Ridgway continued to blame Almond. The Roundup offensive, Ridgway later recalled, showed "good initiative, good originality, boldness and all that." But he cited Roundup as one example of how Almond was apt to undertake "a very risky operation" that might "jeopardize his command." In this instance, Ridgway remembered, the various elements of the 2d Division "were not mutually supporting each other," and for that reason, "they got caught."*[96]

The Army unwisely concealed this disaster from war correspondents. The decision to do so was made by Ridgway's newly arrived public relations officer, James T. Quirk, a reservist who had served in a similar capacity in the ETO for Bradley and Patton and who was "on loan" from Walter Annenberg's *Philadelphia Inquirer.* Three weeks later, when the story leaked out and caused an uproar, Quirk wrote in regret: "In my original anxiety to protect the reputation of the 2nd Division, I made the mistake of giving out no information. . . . Sooner or later we have to admit our losses as well as tell of our successes. We waited too long. If the necessity should arise again, I hope that I shall be able to handle it more intelligently."[98]

# VII

On the left of Wonju, at Chipyong, Paul Freeman received the news of the withdrawal of X Corps into Wonju with distinct unease. The retrograde movement had opened up a huge gap on his right flank, leaving his force badly exposed and in danger of being encircled and destroyed. Aerial reconnaissance

---

*Almond issued a X Corps afteraction analysis which, in effect, blamed the missing artillery commander John Keith for most of the debacle.[97]

had reported the CCF closing in from three sides: north, east, and west. At noon on February 13, when Ned Almond flew into the perimeter by helicopter to discuss the situation, Freeman recommended that his forces withdraw south to the Yoju area no later than the following morning. Almond—and Nick Ruffner—agreed with this recommendation, and Almond relayed it to Ridgway.[99]

Freeman's desire to withdraw from Chipyong was intensified by several gloomy radio reports he received that afternoon. Ridgway had ordered two outfits to reinforce Freeman: Coad's full Commonwealth Brigade from Yoju and the 2d Division Recon Company (supported by the 3/9) on the Yoju–Wonju road. Both reinforcing columns had run into swarms of CCF. The Commonwealth Brigade had bogged down; the Recon Company and the 3/9 were engaged in a desperate fight. These reports clearly indicated that Freeman was already cut off at Chipyong.

After analyzing these reports, Freeman recommended to Ruffner and Almond that he withdraw at once—that very afternoon. But Ridgway rejected all recommendations for withdrawal. He had adopted the view that Chipyong was the vital "left shoulder" of the CCF penetration and that it must be held. He would further reinforce Freeman by directing Marcel Crombez's 5th Cav, only just relieved on the 1st Division front by Tom Brodie's British Brigade, to stage for Chipyong, through Yoju, on a road paralleling that taken by the Commonwealth Brigade.

By this time Freeman had been encamped on full alert at Chipyong for about ten days. During that time he and his staff had had ample time to prepare the perimeter for defense. They had done a good job. Lacking manpower to outpost all the many hills surrounding the village, they had withdrawn into a rectangular perimeter about one mile by two miles situated on relatively low terrain. The infantry of Freeman's three American and one French battalions and the 1st Ranger Company were well dug in around the entire perimeter, backed by fourteen tanks, ten A/A vehicles, and well-situated heavy mortars. The eighteen 105-mm howitzers of John Hector's 37th FAB, augmented by six 155s from B Battery of Cecil White's 503d FAB, were sited near the center of the rectangle. Freeman had stockpiled an enormous hoard of ammo—more than the 23d Infantry had ever had in Korea at any one time. The artillery was zeroed in on likely routes of a CCF attack.

That night, February 13, Freeman called his unit commanders into conference to give them the bad news. They were probably being surrounded by the CCF, he said, but "we'll stay here and fight it out." Help was on the way—Coad's Commonwealth Brigade and Crombez's 5th Cav—but almost surely the CCF would attack before they could arrive.

In fact, at that moment massive Chinese forces were closing in on Chipyong. Freeman believed, and later wrote, that the force was comprised of five divisions, two (116th and 117th) from the Thirty-ninth Army and three (124th, 125th, 126th) from the Forty-second Army. However, the Army historian, writing thirty-five years later, believed the Chinese force was considerably less. He wrote that it was composed of "no more than six regiments," one each from the 115th, 116th, 119th, and 120th divisions and two from the 126th Division. In sum: about 18,000 troops.[100]

Within the rectangular perimeter, Freeman's infantry forces were deployed as follows, clockwise: George Russell's 1/23 at twelve o'clock (north); Charles Kane's 3/23 at three o'clock (east); James Edwards's 2/23 at six o'clock (south); and Ralph Monclar's French Battalion at nine o'clock (west). Two rifle companies were placed in regimental reserve: Russell's B Company and the 1st Ranger Company.

Having encircled Chipyong, the CCF attacked that night, February 13. First came the sound of whistles, bugles, and horns, and then—surprisingly— came salvos of heavy (80- and 120-mm) mortars and artillery, probably Russian-made 76-mm "pack" howitzers. One lucky mortar or artillery round hit an A/A vehicle, which burst into flames; another round started a fire near Russell's 1/23 CP. The glow of these fires enabled the CCF to adjust artillery and mortar fire "with increasing accuracy." As a result, rounds began to fall on or near the more "vulnerable" inner installations: Freeman's CP, the artillery and mortar emplacements, supply dumps, and aid stations. Freeman remembered: "We hadn't received such a concentration of heavy weapons fire since the Naktong."[101]

During these preliminaries Freeman's infantry withheld small-arms fire and waited for the CCF to strike. The troops came on at about midnight, simultaneously attacking all around the perimeter but in greatest force on the north and south, held by Russell's 1/23 and Edwards's 2/23. The CCF assault waves "bungled" into trip flares, antipersonnel mines ("Jumping Johnnies"), and one-shot fougasses—half-filled gasoline drums fitted with remotely activated grenades. They then met an earth-shattering, perfectly coordinated artillery and heavy-mortar barrage. All this, Freeman wrote, forced the "terrified enemy" to "recoil."

But not for long. The regrouped enemy struck again at about 1:00 A.M. on February 14. "Not a small arms was fired until he hit the barbed wire in front of the main positions," Freeman remembered. Then, with the battlefield brilliantly illuminated by flares from the 503d's 155 battery, the well-emplaced machine guns, BARs, and A/A vehicles and tanks cut loose. The slaughter was absolutely terrific: The CCF fell dead or wounded by the hundreds. Once again the Chinese were compelled to pull back to regroup.

Soon the entire perimeter was again under heavy attack by company- and battalion-size CCF units. Freeman's four battalions remained rock-steady, raining grenades and firing small arms. Monclar's French were magnificent, cool, and brave. The Army historian wrote that when the CCF charged with fixed bayonets, blowing whistles and bugles, the French defiantly cranked a hand siren and then countercharged with fixed bayonets and grenades. "When the two forces were within twenty yards of each other," the historian went on, "the Chinese suddenly turned and ran in the opposite direction. It was all over within a minute."[102]

At dawn on February 14 the CCF withdrew into positions in the surrounding hills. Taking stock, Paul Freeman counted his blessings. "We had had a rough night but had not really been in grave danger at any point. No reserves had been committed and we had not suffered too many casualties." But it was now clear that Freeman Force was surrounded and cut off. The great hoard of ammo had been seriously diminished; Freeman could not evacuate his 200 wounded.[103]

Shortly after dawn the CCF lobbed a 120-mm mortar round into the center of the perimeter. It fell near the 23d's CP. At the moment of impact Freeman was sitting on the ground in the tent he shared with his exec, Frank Meszar; his S-2, Harold W. Shoemaker, was standing in the doorway. Mortar fragments instantly killed Shoemaker; the blast knocked Meszar down. Another thumb-size fragment "shattered a full bottle of Old Granddad" bourbon (the last in the perimeter), then slammed into Freeman's left calf, causing a "jagged, painful wound." A medic believed the legbone was cracked, but after the wound had been treated and bandaged, Freeman continued with his duties, albeit with a limp.[104]

News of Freeman's wound, probably exaggerated with the telling, soon reached Nick Ruffner and Ned Almond. Without consulting Ruffner, Almond ordered his G-3, Jack Chiles, to prepare to fly into Chipyong and relieve Freeman and evacuate him. West Pointer (1936) Chiles, thirty-eight, a classmate of Mike Michaelis's and Pete Garland's, was fully qualified for the job. Near the end of World War II he had been exec and commander of this very same regiment in the ETO, winning a Silver Star Medal and a Purple Heart for wounds. However, many believed that Almond acted too hastily, that it was another instance of placing a X Corps staff "teacher's pet" in a job that would lead to a promotion, that at the least, Almond might have consulted Ruffner.[105]

When Freeman got word of what was afoot, he angrily protested by radio. The 2d Division ADC, George Stewart, remembered:

Freeman refused to relinquish command or to be evacuated. The Corps Commander [Almond] insisted that his order be obeyed. Nothing that Ruffner said changed Freeman's refusal to leave his regiment. Ruffner turned the matter over to me.

I had a long talk with Freeman by radio. Paul said he was being relieved from command while his regiment was in combat, and that was the worst disgrace an officer could suffer; he said he was not going to come out. I finally convinced him that no one questioned his performance and that he would undoubtedly be decorated and promoted. He finally agreed to be evacuated.[106]

Chiles flew into the besieged perimeter later in the day. He remembered that enemy mortar fire was falling on the airstrip and that because of it, the pilot would not wait for Freeman. However, it is not likely that Freeman would have flown out that night. Notwithstanding his conversation with Stewart, he was not going to relinquish command until reinforcements had arrived and the 23d was out of danger. "I told Chiles to find a shelter and stay out of the way until my departure," Freeman remembered.[107]

The reinforcements designated for Chipyong—Coad's Commonwealth Brigade and Crombez's 5th Cav—would not arrive that day. The Commonwealth Brigade had been stopped by the CCF and could not move. The 5th Cav was hurriedly gathering at Yoju, but the assembly was very complicated. In addition to his full 5th Cav, Crombez commanded twenty-three tanks (a mixture of Pattons of John Growdon's 6th and Easy Eights of Henry Zeien's 70th tank battalions), the 61st FAB (commanded by John C. Breedlove), and another FAB with self-propelled 155s. All but the artillery had to be moved across the Han River on improvised bridges, then reassembled and deployed for attack.[108]

Keeping track of Crombez's progress by radio, Freeman soon realized that his force would have to stand alone a second night at Chipyong. He therefore requested that FEAF mount close air support and air-drop missions to replenish his ammo. That day, February 14, FEAF fighters were heavily supporting the Wonju shoot. As a result, only three close air strikes were mounted at Chipyong. However, twenty-four FEAF C-119 Flying Boxcars came from Japan to parachute supply bundles. This was a "Godsend," Freeman wrote, "but unfortunately no heavy mortar ammunition or illuminating shells were included and the rifle cartridges were not packed in clips—serious handicaps for night fighting."

The garrison, meanwhile, girded for what was certain to be another ghastly night. "Good hot meals were served," Freeman wrote, "ammunition was distributed, weapons cleaned and readied, wires spliced, armored vehicles serviced, trip flares and mines reset." The more "vulnerable" inner perimeter installations were reinforced with railroad ties and bags of rice. Finally, Freeman went on, "the garrison, with fine spirit, determination and confidence, waited for the next move."

It came after darkness. "This time the Chinese had a plan," Freeman remembered. For a full hour they blasted the perimeter with artillery and heavy-mortar fire. Then they attacked all around the perimeter, throwing the greatest force at Edwards's 2/23 on the south. The weight of the attack fell on Thomas Heath's G Company, which, in spite of a heroic hand-to-hand defense, finally gave way at 3:15 A.M. and pulled back. The retrograde movement uncovered the 503d's six-gun 155 battery, which had to be abandoned. Heath tried to enlist the 503d's black gunners as infantrymen, but the experiment was not a success.

Edwards appealed to Freeman for reserves to mount a counterattack to restore his position. Freeman fully realized the gravity of the situation, but owing to a very strong CCF attack in Charles Kane's 3/23 sector, he was reluctant to commit his full reserve. He sent a platoon of the 1st Ranger Company, which, together with a platoon from F Company, attempted the counterattack, but it bogged down and failed.

The loss of the 155s curtailed Freeman's capability of lighting the battlefield. Fortunately, however, FEAF had directed to the area a Firefly, a C-47 outfitted to drop large parachute-borne flares with about a fifteen-minute life. These "wonderful" aircraft, Freeman remembered, "changed night into day." The Firefly—and others replacing it—remained overhead. They "helped save our skins," Freeman wrote, "as much as any other gadget of the grim business of night fighting."[109]

By daylight on February 15 Freeman Force was in desperate shape. The CCF was still attacking furiously all around the perimeter and continued in broad daylight. Freeman was critically low on ammo—down to 90 81-mm rounds and 140 4.2-inch rounds—and the situation in Edwards's sector was especially grave. Finally, and reluctantly, Freeman committed his last infantry reserve, B Company, to the 2/23 sector. Going into battle hurriedly and piecemeal, it was unable to restore the 2/23 positions.

# VIII

While the 23d Infantry was holding valiantly at Chipyong, Ridgway's bold and complicated plan for Shrimp Milburn's I Corps (3d and 25th divisions) to cross the Han River and attack into the rear of the CCF was still unfolding. However, unexpected enemy reaction and resistance threw the plan farther and farther behind schedule.

The first setback occurred in Shorty Soule's 3d Division, which was under orders to cross the Han to the left of the 25th Division, face west toward Seoul, and block any NKPA or CCF attacks from that direction.

The men of the 3d Division, deployed below the south bank of the Han River, were pleased with themselves. For the first time since reaching Korea the division had participated in a fully organized divisional attack, and it had been eminently successful. But they were in for a rude shock.

On the night of February 13–14 the 8th Division of the NKPA I Corps unexpectedly launched its 1st Regiment south across the Han River into the 3d Division sector. Its mission, aptly described by the 3d Division historian as "fantastic," was to strike all the way south of Kumyangjang, "to cut and disrupt communications." Most likely it was designed as a feinting attack in support of the CCF main offensive on Wonju and Chipyong.[110]

Whatever its purpose, the NKPA regiment attacked and infiltrated through Dinty Moore's newly committed 15th Infantry. By plan or coincidence, the NKPA then headed directly toward Soule's 3d Division CP. Fortunately for Soule, William Harris's 65th Infantry, recently withdrawn from the front for a rest, had deployed nearby on high ground.

Jarred awake by the noise of a tremendous firefight, Harris experienced "absolute disbelief at what was happening." But the entire 65th Infantry responded magnificently. Also coming awake from a dead sleep, Saint St. Clair's 1/65, Herman Dammer's 2/65, and Jerry Allen's 3/65 swarmed down from the hills to encircle and annihilate most of the NKPA 1st Regiment. "And, man, did those Puerto Ricans have a ball," Harris wrote. The NKPA "didn't know what hit 'em." When the fight was over, the 65th Infantry was officially credited with killing 573 NKPA men and capturing 268. A full-scale division mop-up during daylight hours on February 14 killed another 100 NKPA and bagged an additional 70 prisoners.[111]

Although the NKPA attack failed to inflict any substantial casualties on the 3d Division, it completely disrupted Shorty Soule's preparations to cross the Han River. It also raised serious questions about the advisability of leaving only the Turks, Kelleher's 35th Infantry, and the 1st ROK Division to occupy the south bank of the Han opposite Seoul. Conceivably a concerted NKPA I Corps attack into that sector could play havoc—and possibly cut off the 3d Division north of the Han.

The affair produced a bitter aftertaste. In official commendations for this action Milburn and Soule credited the entire 3d Division for its "alertness and steadfast courage and determination." The 65th Infantry, which had done almost all of the killing and capturing, was furious at not having been singled out for special praise. William Harris later wrote acidly: "Somebody forgot to tell somebody what had happened. . . . The 65th was just about the only unit of the division which had participated in the fight. . . ." Instead of commending the rest of the 3d Division, Harris went on, "someone should have been chewed out for letting one entire NKPA regiment of over one thousand men get through the front lines."[112]

\* \* \*

On the right of the 3d Division there were also setbacks in Sladen Bradley's 25th Division, which had come around to replace the 1st Cav Division. Tom Brodie's British Brigade had promptly relieved Crombez's 5th Cav, but Corley's 24th and Check's 27th were delayed in relieving the 8th and 7th Cav regiments.[113]

The delays were caused by the CCF Thirty-eighth Army, holding a salient in the rugged terrain south of the Han. After a spectacular drive north Billy Harris's 7th Cav had bogged down against a CCF bastion (Hill 578) overlooking Mugam, about twelve miles short of the river, which was the division objective.* Ridgway had decreed that Hill 578 would be taken before the 27th Infantry relieved the 7th Cav.

Harris and his men had butted heads against Hill 578 for several days before they had realized that a massive, all-out attack would be required to root out the CCF. That massive assault was finally laid on for the morning of February 14. However, during the night of February 13–14 the CCF Thirty-eighth Army significantly upset these plans by launching an unexpected and powerful attack on Pete Clainos's 8th Cav, which was to make a diversionary attack toward Mugam on the left of the 7th Cav. As a result of the CCF attack, the 8th Cav was so busy repulsing the CCF and cleaning out CCF infiltrators that Charlie Palmer had to cancel its diversionary role.[115]

The 7th Cav launched a greatly modified and scaled-down attack at 7:00 A.M. on February 14. It was preceded by a heavy artillery barrage from the guns of the 77th FAB and others, but owing to the diversion of all close support aircraft to the Wonju shoot that day, the air missions planned for the 7th Cav were canceled. In their place the artillery barrage was extended, but Harris and his men deplored the absence of "napalm preparation."

Harris committed all four of his battalions (including the Greeks) at Hill 578 in a simultaneous attack. The infantry was directly supported by platoon-size armored task forces from the 70th Tank Battalion. The ensuing fight was one of the most difficult the 7th Cav had seen since Pusan Perimeter days. The enemy were dug in all over the hill with mortars and machine guns. They contested every inch of ground and, despite the massive firepower of the 7th Cav, did not yield for a full twenty-four hours. Supervising the attack from Harris's CP, Palmer later rightly commended the 7th Cav for a "magnificent" job. But the division had fallen several days behind schedule.

\* \* \*

Because of these setbacks and delays, by the morning of February 15 it was obvious that the possible I Corps attack across the Han into the rear

---

*During the 7th Cav advance Phillip L. Bolté, a platoon leader in the 3/7, was wounded and evacuated. Thus the Army's three-star chief of plans, Charles Bolté, earned the dubious distinction of having both of his West Point sons wounded in Korea. Both David and Phillip recovered to fight in Vietnam, where Phillip, who eventually retired as a brigadier general, was wounded a second time.[114]

of the CCF could not be mounted in time or with sufficient force to be certain of success. Ridgway was therefore compelled to cancel that idea and formulate a new plan.[116] Its chief features were these:

• Upon completing the relief of the 1st Cav, Sladen Bradley's 25th Division would advance to the Han River (Line Boston) but no farther. It would stop on the south bank, line abreast with Shorty Soule's 3d Division on the left. For the time being the Turkish Brigade, Kelleher's 35th Infantry, and the ROK 1st Division would remain on the south bank of the Han (left of the 3d Division) opposite Seoul.

• Bryant Moore's IX Corps would assume the I Corps mission of attacking into the rear of the CCF salient. Charlie Palmer's full 1st Cav Division would shift to the right of Babe Bryan's 24th Division and attack north and northwest through Yoju, behind the 5th Cav, after first relieving the besieged 23d Infantry at Chipyong. The 24th Division, pivoting around northeasterly on Yoju, would cross the Han and come up on the left of the 1st Cav for a combined attack east toward Hoengsong.[117]

At dawn on February 15 Crombez's 5th Cav, having crossed the Han at Yoju and assembled in the pitch-darkness, proceeded warily toward Chipyong. However, a mile south of the village of Koksu Crombez ran into a solid wall of CCF. Supported by his two full FABs, Crombez deployed his infantry battalions and girded for a tough fight. Earlier the 5th Cav (under Johnny Johnson) had failed to crack through to save the cutoff 8th Cav at Unsan; this time the 5th Cav could not and would not fail.[118]

Six miles to the north of Crombez in the Chipyong perimeter, the 23d Infantry's situation remained perilous. All efforts to dislodge the CCF penetrations in James Edwards's 2/23 sector on the south side had failed. From commanding positions in the low-lying hills, the CCF, boldly fighting in daylight, rained mortar and machine-gun fire into the perimeter. Encouraged by the prospect of a "rescue" by the 5th Cav, Edwards's men hung on gamely, blocking further CCF gains and planning an ambitious counterattack when the 5th Cav grew closer.

The defenders of Chipyong were probably saved from destruction that day not by Task Force Crombez but by airmen. The close air support which had been diverted to the Wonju shoot the day before now shifted to Chipyong. FEAF, Marine, and Navy fighters converged over the besieged perimeter, mounting a total of 131 well-conducted sorties. The aerial assault forced the CCF to take cover in all sectors of the perimeter except the south. There the CCF attacking the 2/23 remained in the open, firing machine guns and rifles at the planes, apparently "determined to die to the last man."[119]

While the fighters were at work, another aerial armada (thirty C-119s) arrived from Japan to parachute ammunition. Most bundles drifted down into the perimeter, but many went astray and landed in CCF-held terrain. The recovery parties that rushed out to collect the bundles inside the perimeter and distribute the ammo suffered "many casualties" from CCF mortars. Nonetheless, brave men jumped up to replace the wounded. This infusion of ammo and the close air support gave the men the means—and heart—to fight with renewed vigor.[120]

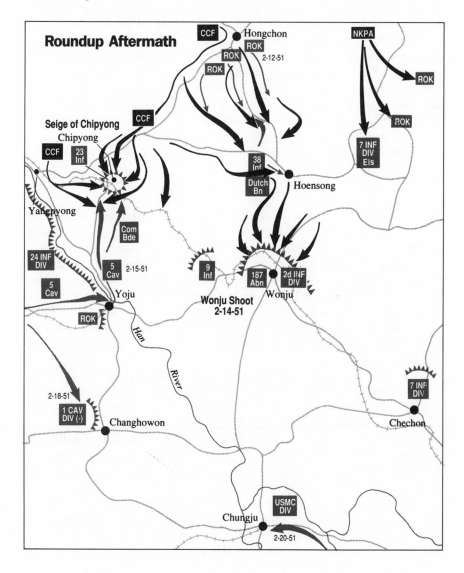

It was soon obvious to Marcel Crombez, to the south of Edwards, that no effort short of a full-scale regimental attack would crack the CCF wall blocking Crombez's task force below Koksu. Holding Edgar Treacy's 3/5 in reserve, he ordered Morgan Heasley's 1/5 up the right side of the road and Paul Clifford's 2/5 up the left. The two artillery battalions emplaced south of the Han supported these attacks. The aircraft mounting close air support missions at Chipyong helped Crombez as well.[121]

Shortly after eleven o'clock that morning, feeling confident that Crombez would break through within a matter of a few hours, Paul Freeman finally consented to be evacuated. He turned over his command to Jack Chiles, boarded a helicopter, and flew to a MASH unit at Chungju, where Ridgway met and congratulated and consoled him. Freeman gained the impression from Ridgway that after brief R and R in the States he would return to Korea, like Mike Michaelis, promoted to brigadier general. But in the States Joe Collins sidetracked Freeman into public relations (making speeches; technical adviser for a documentary film on Korea). As a result, Freeman did not return to Korea, but with boosts from Ridgway he went on to a distinguished Army career and four stars.[122]

* * *

Following his meeting with Freeman, Ridgway flew over the 5th Cav front. From the air Crombez appeared to be making good progress. Ridgway radioed Bryant Moore, Charlie Palmer, and Crombez encouragement.[123]

By that time, however, Crombez had concluded that his infantry could not break through to Chipyong before nightfall, if then. Under great pressure from Bryant Moore and Charlie Palmer, he had decided that he would hold the bulk of his infantry in place temporarily and attempt to send an armored column into Chipyong. He so notified Jack Chiles, regretting that he could not immediately bring up supply trucks or ambulances. "Come on," Chiles responded, "trains or no trains."[124]

The armored column had to proceed up a single narrow road. The CCF was certain to make an all-out attempt to block the road with mines or to disable the lead tanks with satchel charges and grenades and perhaps captured American bazookas. The close-in CCF attacks on the tanks might have been held at bay by 105- and 155-mm fire from Crombez's two artillery battalions (possibly coordinated with fire from the 37th FAB inside the 23d's perimeter); but there was no time to register and coordinate artillery fire, and besides, Crombez was afraid it might hit the tanks.

His solution to the problem was that infantrymen would ride atop the tanks. They would man their own weapons as well as the machine guns on the tanks. If the CCF fire became really intense, the tankers would stop and the infantry would dismount to silence it. He chose L Company (160 men) of

Edgar Treacy's 3/5, commanded by West Pointer (1946) John C. Barrett, Jr., for the mission.[125]

Inasmuch as the CCF fire on the road was already intense, Treacy and Barrett were naturally upset by Crombez's decision. They protested that the order violated Army doctrine and that casualties could be ruinous. Crombez assured the two officers that he would stop the tanks as required to silence the enemy fire. However, Treacy heatedly argued that the infantry mission was near suicidal and should not be undertaken. If Crombez insisted, he, Treacy, would not order his men onto the tanks unless he was permitted to join them. Crombez categorically denied Treacy that permission.[126]

The mile-long armored column assembled hurriedly on the road south of Koksu. In all, there were twenty-three tanks. John Growdon's Pattons (with the larger 90-mm gun) were placed at the head of the column; the Easy Eights at the rear. Wearing a dashing yellow scarf, Marcel Crombez climbed into the fifth Patton in line and (it was later pointedly noted) tightly closed the hatch. Barrett and his 159 men climbed atop nineteen tanks in the middle of the line—Barrett on the sixth tank from the front.

Treacy watched this assembly with mounting anger and frustration. He believed that Crombez's choice of the 3/5 for this mission was another instance of "punishing" the outfit. Unable to stand aside while his men embarked on this suicidal ride, Treacy disobeyed Crombez's specific order and climbed aboard the tank Barrett was riding.[127]

The column moved out at 3:45 P.M. All went well until it reached Koksu. There the CCF, on the hills overlooking the road, attacked with mortars and machine guns. Crombez halted the column; the infantry dismounted and sought cover. Directing the fire of his tank at the CCF, Crombez radioed exuberantly: "We're killing hundreds of them!" However, suddenly and without any warning to the dismounted infantry, Crombez ordered the tanks to proceed. Most of the infantry was able to get back aboard the tanks in a mad scramble, but about thirty men, including some wounded, were left behind. Treacy and Barrett were furious at Crombez. Barrett shouted to the men left behind, "Stay by the road! We'll come back for you." Treacy told Barrett that when it was all over, he intended to bring formal charges against Crombez.[128]

A mile north of Koksu heavy enemy fire forced the column to halt a second time. The infantry again dismounted. After firing the tank's guns at the enemy for several minutes, Crombez again rolled the tanks without notifying the infantry. This time about sixty men, including Treacy and Barrett, were left stranded. Barrett managed to climb aboard a moving tank, but Treacy was wounded and (it was learned later) captured by the CCF, along with a number of Barrett's able-bodied and wounded men. Again Barrett called out to the stranded men to stay close to the road, that he would return to collect them.[129]

The tanks smashed on nonstop, main guns and machine guns blazing. The CCF, in turn, raked the tanks with continuous fire, wounding many of the remaining sixty-odd infantrymen on the tanks. Several times the tankers inquired of Crombez if they should halt and attempt to silence the CCF fire, but Crombez, an Army historian wrote, "speaking in a calm and cool voice over the radio network, each time directed the column to continue forward."[130]

On the outskirts of Chipyong, where the road passed through a deep cut, the CCF made an "all-out" attempt to halt the relief column. They attacked the tanks with mortars, American bazookas, bangalore torpedoes, satchel charges, grenades, and small arms. They hit the fourth Patton in line, killing the 6th Tank Battalion's D Company commander, Johnnie M. Hiers, and all others inside except the driver, who, although severely burned, heroically kept going until the tank cleared the cut, thus leaving a clear path for the remaining twenty-two tanks, all of which ran this murderous gauntlet without loss.

The tank column approached the south end of the 23d Infantry perimeter at what Crombez described as the "most psychological moment." It was 4:45 P.M., and Edwards's 2/23 was mounting its counterattack in the G Company sector. Crombez's arrival contributed to the success of the counterattack. Four of Chiles's tanks which were supporting the 2/23 counterattack pulled aside to permit Task Force Crombez to enter the perimeter at 5:00 P.M. The defenders at Chipyong "cheered" its arrival. The CCF melted away, and the garrison, which had sustained 353 casualties (52 killed, 259 wounded, and 42 missing), was saved.[131]

Inside the perimeter Barrett made a head count: Only 23 of his L Company's 160 men could be found, and 13 of them were wounded, one fatally. He confronted Crombez and requested that the tanks return right then to pick up the men along the road, including (as he supposed) Treacy. Crombez refused to return, Barrett remembered. "He said, 'No, I'm not going back. There's too much enemy fire.'" Fortunately many of Barrett's men made it back to friendly lines unaided, but in all, the ride had cost Barrett about 50 percent casualties: 12 dead, 40 wounded, 19 missing.[132]

Barrett learned later (from American POWs) that Treacy survived his wounds but became ill and died about three months later in a CCF POW camp. One reason for the illness, Barrett was told, was that Treacy gave his food to other ailing POWs. "I put him in for the Medal of Honor," Barrett remembered, "but Crombez killed it." Not only that, but Crombez made a note in the official regimental and division records (with no extenuating remarks) that Treacy had "disobeyed" orders, thereby sullying Treacy's reputation.[133]

In the wake of this tank ride the hostility toward Crombez in the 3/5, if not in the entire 5th Cav, was open and bitter. Crombez sent his able S-3, Charles Parziale, to replace Treacy as commander of the 3/5 and to calm the troops, but the open criticism of Crombez continued. As a result, Barrett remembered, Crombez "transferred all of the Third Battalion officers out of the regiment."[134]

In later years Army tactical analysts roundly criticized Crombez for attacking into enemy-held territory with infantry riding atop the tanks. But at the time Matt Ridgway, vastly relieved that the 23d had not been lost, declared that Crombez had made the "best local decision of the war." He awarded Crombez a DSC and stated that Task Force Crombez "epitomized" the new offensive spirit of Eighth Army. Despite the contrary view and open grumbling in the 5th Cav, and Crombez's age, Ridgway permitted him to remain in command of the 5th Cav for many more months. Although Crombez's career went nowhere after Korea, Ridgway's support assured Crombez of a star before his retirement.[135]

\* \* \*

The relief of Chipyong was merely the first and most important job for the 1st Cav Division. Its principal mission was to assemble fully to the right flank of the 24th Division for the proposed IX Corps attack into the flank of the CCF salient. While the 5th Cav was evacuating the dead and wounded from Chipyong on February 16, the 7th and 8th Cavs, which had only just been relieved at Mugam by the 24th and 27th Infantry regiments, were alerted for movement to Yoju to join the 5th Cav for the onward attack.

That day Pete Clainos, a brave, intense, dedicated officer who was exhausted from six months of unrelieved combat, left the 8th Cav after commanding it for fewer than three weeks. He went to Pusan to assist Gar Davidson in building the Davidson Line. His West Point classmate Bob Blanchard, former commander of the 1/15, who had been serving on the 3d Division staff, replaced him.[136]

Blanchard was not overjoyed at getting command of the still-troubled 8th Cav either. He did not want to leave the 3d Division; he had been led to believe he was the obvious candidate to replace the old and tired Dinty Moore in command of the 15th Infantry. Nor was Blanchard confident that the 8th Cav was in shape to participate in a bold attack on the CCF flank. He remembered:

The Eighth Cav was a challenge. They still had not recovered from Unsan. They were always looking over their shoulders. I had to overcome this. I had to retrain the regiment, send them on patrols so they could get used to being shot at, even show them how to properly organize a field kitchen and cook. To complicate matters, Eighth Army directed that the Thailand unit be attached to the Eighth Cav. It came with a full regimental headquarters but only one infantry battalion. What do you do with another regimental headquarters—and a foreign one at that? Worse, the Thais had had only very rudimentary military training. The battalion arrived rated 'combat-ineffective.' I had to more or less train them from scratch."[137]

Nor was Billy Harris's 7th Cav in shape for another heavy fight. Its men were exhausted from three long weeks of very tough action, culminating in the bitter battle on Hill 578. Moreover, an outbreak of typhus was discovered in the 1/7, which had to be placed in quarantine. Since there was danger the typhus might become epidemic, the 7th Cav had to be temporarily relieved of further combat missions. It was placed in IX Corps reserve (with the 8th Cav) at Changhowon.[138]

For these reasons, and others, the newly conceived plan for IX Corps to attack into the flanks of the CCF salient was also canceled. Babe Bryan's 24th Division remained in place on the Han, in its tight triangle northwest of Yoju; the disparate IX and X corps elements (23d Infantry; 5th Cav; Commonwealth Brigade; ROK 6th Division; 9th Infantry), on its right, formed a rough L-shaped "front," Chipyong–Yoju–Munmang loosely linked with the 38th Infantry and 187th Airborne regiments and massed artillery at Wonju. There was no X Corps front to the east of Wonju, merely a huge gap, stretching southeast to Chechon, where Ferenbaugh's 7th Division was digging in and attempting to reorganize the ROK 3d and 5th divisions.[139]

The acting Eighth Army G-2, Bob Fergusson, had predicted that the twelve divisions of the three CCF armies (Twentieth, Twenty-sixth; Twenty-seventh) in the Hamhung area would probably reinforce the CCF offensive on the X Corps front. For that reason Ridgway kept his guard up and remained mentally braced for more heavy fighting and possibly the loss of Wonju. But these three armies did not materialize. Nor did the four mangled CCF armies (Thirty-ninth; Fortieth, Forty-second; Sixty-sixth) committed to the central front display any further signs of aggressive intent.

# I X

In the center of Eighth Army's front Sladen Bradley's 25th Division, having displaced Charlie Palmer's 1st Cav, was under orders to advance to the Han River (Line Boston) and hold. Inasmuch as the 7th Cav had taken Hill 578 at Mugam, it was believed that the division task would be a cakewalk. But such was not the case. The CCF Thirty-eighth Army clung fanatically to its salient south of the Han.[140]

Shrimp Milburn directed Bradley to attack with three infantry regiments abreast: Tom Brodie's British Brigade on the left, John Corley's 24th Infantry in the center, and Gilbert Check's 27th Infantry on the right. To lend additional power to the drive, Johnny Throckmorton's 5th Infantry (of the 24th Division), coming up from reserve, was attached to the 25th Division on the right of Check. Bradley and Babe Bryan, working out of a consolidated CP, more or less jointly directed the attack, closely coordinating Throckmorton's maneuvers with those of Check.[141]

The four regiments attacked, line abreast, on the morning of February 16. The attack was massively backed by closely coordinated artillery of both the 24th and 25th divisions. The 25th Division artillery commander, Bittman Barth, remembered that in the initial assault, Check's 27th Infantry was supported by eleven batteries of artillery. On the second day Check's support was increased to thirteen artillery batteries (seventy-eight guns). One artillery barrage of 2,000 rounds killed "over five hundred" CCF in Check's sector, Barth wrote. The carnage in Throckmorton's sector was as great, or greater.[142]

The next day, February 17, Ridgway toured the battlefronts. He spent the morning with Bradley and Bryan, observing the closely coordinated attacks of the 25th Division and 5th Infantry. Notwithstanding the massive artillery barrages, there was no sign that the CCF Thirty-eighth Army was ready to yield. In the afternoon he flew into the now-quiet Chipyong to visit Marcel Crombez and the 5th Cav and Jack Chiles and the 23d Infantry. Chiles escorted Ridgway to George Russell's 1/23 sector, where the napalming of the CCF on February 15 had been exceptionally effective. "The ground was littered with hundreds of burned Chinese," Chiles recalled. "We called them 'Chink fricassee.' Ridgway never forgot that."[143]

Early the following morning, Sunday, February 18, Ridgway received an astonishing report from IX Corps commander Bryant Moore. Throckmorton's 5th Infantry, advancing on the right (or east) of Mugam, reported the CCF had pulled out of the terrain south of the Han. Throckmorton had found 600 enemy dead in foxholes (more victims of the massed artillery supporting the attack), abandoned weapons and even cooking equipment. There was "no opposition."[144]

Ridgway flashed this word to I and X corps commanders Milburn and Almond. He dutifully cautioned them to be on their guard, that "it might be a ruse," but in his heart he knew it probably was not. Later that morning he received a report indicating a mass CCF and NKPA withdrawal from X Corps's central front. By early afternoon all signs positively pointed to a CCF and NKPA withdrawal across the whole of South Korea.[145]

Intelligence sources soon confirmed that the enemy withdrawal was real—and total. Defeated for the first time, Lin Piao had ordered all his shattered armies to pull back to the old NKPA defensive positions just north of the 38th Parallel, where he intended to regroup and reman his divisions for yet another offensive at a later date. It may well have been Lin Piao's last combat order. "Incapacitated either by wounds or illness," the Air Force historian wrote, he was relieved of command by Chinese General Peng Teh-huai.[146]

* * *

The CCF-NKPA withdrawal marked another magnificent victory for Eighth Army—one of the greatest victories in the history of the United States Army. The better part of fourteen CCF divisions—nearly half the CCF forces committed to Korea the previous October and November—had been wrecked.

Owing to the drama inherent in "cutoff" units and the Hollywood-like rescue mission of Crombez's 5th Cav, many writers were to credit Paul Freeman and his 23d Infantry for conducting the decisive battle of the victory. But Freeman's valiant and inspiring stand at Chipyong, which had shattered major elements of four CCF divisions, was only one important tile in the mosaic of victory. Shrimp Milburn's I Corps drive to the Han had not only mauled the three divisions of the CCF Fiftieth Army and a substantial part of NKPA I Corps but also gained airfields at Suwon and Kimpo and the port of Inchon. The determined, but unheralded, stand of John Coughlin's 38th Infantry and Frank Bowen's 187th Airborne and the artillery during the Wonju shoot had shattered four CCF divisions and decisively checked the enemy offensive on the central front. Billy Harris's 7th Cav, Gilbert Check's 27th, and Johnny Throckmorton's 5th regiments, and the artillery of the 1st Cav, 24th, and 25th divisions, had virtually destroyed the three divisions of the CCF Thirty-eighth Army near Mugam.

Behind these independent and widespread battles constituting the mosaic of this great victory stood its architect, Matthew Bunker Ridgway. Omar Bradley, who did not lightly bestow praise, characterized Ridgway's generalship as a "magnificent job." Indeed so. In a mere fifty-four days Ridgway had totally turned Eighth Army around. He had cleaned out the incompetent leaders, infused his men with that vital self-confidence required for success in battle, and refreshed them by lecture or example on the fundamentals of tactics and firepower. In his autobiography Bradley elaborated: "It is not often in wartime that a single battlefield commander can make a decisive difference. But in Korea, Ridgway would prove to be the exception. His brilliant, driving, uncompromising leadership would turn the tide of battle like no other general's in our military history."[147]

# PART
# ELEVEN

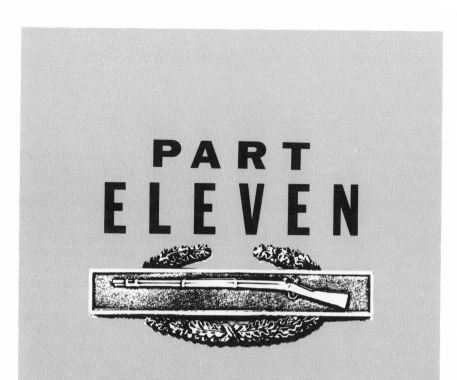

# Return
# to the
# 38th Parallel

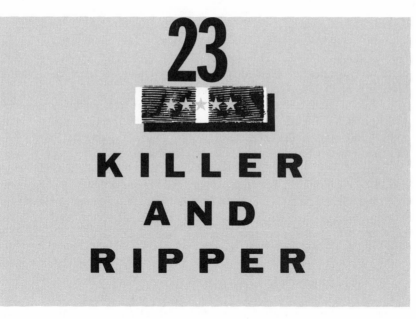

# 23

# KILLER
# AND
# RIPPER

## I

On Sunday evening, February 18, after intelligence sources had confirmed the CCF withdrawal, Ridgway summoned his personal staff to an urgent meeting at his advanced Eighth Army headquarters.[1] The personal staff had grown into a frontline listening post, planning group, and tactical command center. Its smart young members, serving as Ridgway's "eyes and ears," visited the combat elements daily, with or without Ridgway, taking the Army's pulse. They assisted Ridgway with tactical planning, serving as both critics and creators, and then relayed his formal orders to the Eighth Army staff in Taegu and to the corps and division commanders. They also served as internal and external public relations men, "interpreting" Ridgway to those in Eighth Army who did not know him—or of his exemplary World War II record—and to the media.

Chief among the newcomers to the personal staff,* indeed, Ridgway's alter ego was a handsome, brilliant West Pointer (1937), A. Day Surles, thirty-five. Son of a two-star West Point general, Surles in World War II had been Ridgway's G-3 in the XVIII Airborne Corps in the ETO and his confidant. Upon arriving in Korea, Surles dominated the personal staff and served as the

*Others: intelligence specialists Irwin A. Edwards (ex-7th Division) and Joseph E. Pizzi; artillery specialist Benjamin D. Capshaw; logistician Bill Moorman; airborne planner Emory S. ("Hank") Adams. Moorman and Adams were assigned on paper to Eighth Army headquarters but held a close relationship to the personal staff, as did Eighth Army G-2 Clint Tarkenton, one of the few of the old Eighth Army staff whom Ridgway drew into his inner circle.[2]

chief war planner, in effect displacing John Dabney's large G-3 planning apparatus at Eighth Army headquarters in Taegu.

After the staff had gathered in the operations tent, Ridgway stunned it with this news: Eighth Army would counterattack the CCF on the central front within sixty hours. The fresh, powerful (25,000-man) 1st Marine Division, arriving at Chungju and assigned to Bryant Moore's IX Corps, would be the centerpiece. All forces in Moore's IX and Ned Almond's X Corps except the 187th Airborne RCT would support the Marine attack. Its purpose was to restore Eighth Army's line extending east from Yangpyong to Hoengsong, to trap and kill all enemy that had penetrated that sector, and to disrupt possible CCF plans for another offensive. Named Operation Killer by Ridgway,[3] the main features of the plan were:

• The Marines would attack northeast from Wonju. To the left (or west) of the Marines, the other IX Corps forces—Coad's Commonwealth Brigade, Palmer's 1st Cav Division, and Bryan's 24th Division—would attack, line abreast, north from Yoju and Chipyong.

• To the right (or east) of the Marines the X Corps forces—the reorganized ROK 3d and 5th divisions; Ruffner's 2d and Ferenbaugh's 7th divisions—would assemble near Chechon and attack, line abreast, north toward Pangnim. Bowen's 187th Airborne RCT would return to Eighth Army reserve to prepare for an airborne operation in support of Killer, yet to be devised.

• In the west Milburn's I Corps—ROK 1st, American 3d and 25th divisions—would hold at the Han River on Line Boston. The corps would support Killer by feinting large-scale Han River crossings in several areas and by sending strong patrols across the river. It would prepare plans for a real Han River crossing possibly to follow on the heels of Killer. That crossing would be designed to outflank Seoul to the east, thereby avoiding a bloody frontal attack over the Han into the city.[4]

The scope of the proposed attack was breathtaking: eight infantry divisions (five American, three ROK) of IX and X corps, comprising more than 100,000 men. These divisions would be backed by about twenty-two FABs (with nearly 400 howitzers), five tank battalions, and FEAF, which had recently absorbed the full Korea-based 1st Marine Air Wing.[5]

Logistically Killer would be the toughest challenge of the Korean War. The unseasonable warming trend had brought torrents of rain. The rain was prematurely melting the snow in the hills; the Han and other rivers were already flooding from the rapid meltoff. Pontoon bridges over the Han at Yoju, Chungju, and elsewhere had washed out. Eighth Army engineer Pat Strong remembered that problem: "The debris would sweep down from above, cables would snap, and a chain reaction would begin. The upstream bridge would go first, and crash into the one a few miles below. The resulting wreckage would speed downstream to the next bridge, and so on." He went on: "We learned the hard way. At first we tried to hold the bridges. There is only one thing to do to a floating bridge in a flood: get it out of the water, or swing it to one side and lash it with everything you've got."[6]

The primitive, mostly unpaved road network on the central front presented another formidable challenge. Where roads did exist they were now virtually impassable quagmires; in some places the mud was a foot deep or more. To make them usable, Strong and his engineers would have to rebuild them with proper drainage culverts and bridges, gravel, crushed stone, or steel matting. Or they would have to build entirely new roads.

Engineer Strong was now far better staffed and equipped for these vital, difficult tasks than before. His command had grown to three American engineer combat groups (eleven battalions) and three American construction groups (nine battalions), plus about 100,000 male and female Korean laborers. The engineers were being supplied matériel from Pusan (bridging, etc.) at the rate of about 2,000 tons a day. Strong remembered that his men were "putting in place an average of about one thousand tons of bridge material a day" and that "a small engineer outfit could blaze and blast and bulldoze a rough road through mountains at the rate of a mile a day."[7]

Even so, Strong's combat engineers could not precede the infantry. It would have to slog ahead mostly on foot, rooting out the enemy. The armor and artillery would advance behind the infantry over the routes prepared by Strong's men and Korean laborers. Since even small CCF rear guards, dug in on hilltops, would have a considerable tactical advantage, it was bound to be very tough going—far tougher than any campaign yet.

Ridgway's stunning proposal evoked a lengthy discussion. There were large problems other than those confronting the engineers. There was an ammunition shortage, for example. Eighth Army never seemed to have enough ammo. The recent hard fighting had severely drained ammunition reserves in Korea and Japan. Some means would have to be devised to restock the depots in Korea rapidly. Another worry—a continuing cause of deep concern—was the growing CCF Air Force. It had not yet attacked UN ground forces in South Korea, but an all-out Eighth Army offensive which would require massing troops and vehicles closely could persuade Peking the time was ripe for an air assault, regardless of the consequences.

Notwithstanding the considerable list of negatives and the grave risks entailed, Ridgway's personal staff endorsed his plans. One major consideration which motivated the group was the need to maintain the "offensive spirit" of Eighth Army. In the recent fighting the army had generated not only immense self-confidence but also "momentum." If it halted and rested on its laurels, it would lose that momentum, and it would not be easy to regain it.

By coincidence that same day Ridgway had received a planning document from the Eighth Army's G-3, John Dabney. Obviously the product of considerable thought and discussion, it laid out the staff's views on how the war should be fought over the next several months. Astonishingly Dabney recommended that Eighth Army abandon all offensive operations and "defend in place" until the spring, when a renewed, all-out CCF offensive could be expected. In anticipation of that CCF offensive, Eighth Army should "voluntarily withdraw" into the Pusan Perimeter.[8]

To Ridgway this document was final confirmation—if any more was needed—of the "defeatist" attitude of the Eighth Army staff. It was so at variance with Ridgway's thinking and recent exhortations and orders as to be downright remarkable and perhaps even disloyal. For that reason Ridgway was to keep a copy of the paper close at hand for the rest of his life, a prized memento of the war and a constant reminder of the leadership difficulties he had faced in Korea.

The document, of course, hanged John Dabney. Although the real Eighth Army planning was carried out by Ridgway's tactical staff, Dabney's plan was so blatantly defeatist and negative—and widely circulated—that it could not be dismissed lightly or simply ignored. Like the G-3, John Jeter, in I Corps, John Dabney was to be sacked as an example—and the sooner, the better.

\* \* \*

On the following day, February 19, Ridgway flew to Bryant Moore's IX Corps CP at Yoju. There he outlined Killer to Moore; to the X Corps chief of staff, John Guthrie; and to O. P. Smith and Chesty Puller, who had replaced Edward Craig as ADC of the 1st Marine Division. When Ridgway announced that the Marines had to attack within forty-eight hours out of Wonju—on the morning of February 21—the Marine generals were somewhat taken aback. The division had not yet fully assembled at Chungju; a more reasonable date would be February 24. But Ridgway insisted that the Marines hold to his plan.[9]

What concerned O. P. Smith even more that day was the absorption of the 1st Marine Air Wing into FEAF. He had appealed this decision to Fifth Air Force commander Pat Partridge, to no avail. "Close air support frankly doesn't pay dividends," Partridge had told Smith, expressing a preference for "interdiction" missions. Smith asked Ridgway if merely "one squadron" of the wing could be assigned exclusively to the Marine division. Ridgway replied: "Smith, I'm sorry, but I don't command Fifth Air Force." For the first time in Korea the Marines would undertake a major mission without full control of their air wing.[10]

\* \* \*

MacArthur flew into Suwon the following day, February 20, and once again Ridgway had to take time out for escort duty. The MacArthur party switched to a smaller plane and flew to Wonju, where MacArthur conferred with Ned Almond, Nick Ruffner, Buddy Ferenbaugh, and others. After a visit with frontline units, the party stopped at Ralph Monclar's French Battalion CP, where MacArthur conferred honors and medals for the outstanding performance of the French at Chipyong.[11]

Back at Wonju MacArthur held the inevitable press conference, starting with these remarks:

I am entirely satisfied with the situation at the front where the enemy has suffered a tactical reverse of immeasurable proportions. His losses have been among the bloodiest of modern times. As these are from Communist China's best troops, it will be difficult to adequately replace them. The enemy is finding it an entirely different problem fighting 350 miles from his base than when he had this "sanctuary" in his immediate rear, with our air and naval forces practically zeroed out. . . . Our strategic plan—notwithstanding the enemy's great numerical superiority—is indeed working well and I have just directed a resumption of the initiative by our forces.

All ranks of this international force are covering themselves with distinction and I again wish to especially commend the outstanding teamwork of the three services under the skillful direction of their able field commanders, General Ridgway, Admiral Struble and General Partridge. Our successes are in great part due to the smooth synchronization of the power of the three arms. This, indeed, is the most vital factor in modern war.

By this time there was considerable public speculation over whether or not the revitalized Eighth Army might someday recross the 38th Parallel and reinvade North Korea. Believing the speculation to be militarily harmful, Washington had not yet announced any hard-and-fast decisions. In an attempt to discourage the premature speculation and deflect reporters' questions about the issue, President Truman had unwisely stated publicly that crossing the 38th Parallel was a military matter to be resolved by the commander in chief of the Far East. Although there was nothing to be gained by a public reminder of this issue from the battlefield, MacArthur went on to raise it in this imperious fashion:

The question of the recrossing of the 38th Parallel continues to arouse public discussion. While President Truman has indicated that the crossing of that parallel is a military matter to be resolved in accordance with my best judgment as Theater Commander, I want to make it quite clear that if and when the issue actually arises I shall not arbitrarily exercise that authority if cogent political reasons against crossing are then advanced and there is any possibility that a limitation is to be placed thereon.

These remarks contained thinly veiled criticisms of the Truman administration. MacArthur had again mentioned the enemy's "sanctuary," which had "practically zeroed out" American air and naval forces. Addressing the issue of recrossing the 38th Parallel, he had alluded to possible military "limitations" on his forces. In view of the speculation and controversy, to raise the issue of crossing the 38th Parallel in any form, but especially with a reference to political factors, was the second violation within eight days of Truman's December directive to clear such statements in advance.

In one particular sense, however, Matt Ridgway was dismayed and angered by MacArthur's remarks. That was MacArthur's assertion that he had "just ordered a resumption of the initiative." Ridgway later wrote:

There was no undue emphasis on the personal pronoun, but the implication was clear: He had just flown in from Tokyo, had surveyed the situation, and had then ordered the Eighth Army to attack. There had, of course, been no order at all concerning any part of the operation from . . . [MacArthur] or from the GHQ staff in Tokyo. . . . [N]either he nor his staff had had any part in the conception or in the planning of Operation KILLER.

It is not so much that my own vanity took an unexpected roughing up by this announcement as that I was given a rather unwelcome reminder of a MacArthur that I had known but almost forgotten. . . . To keep his public image always glowing.[12]

That night—the eve of Killer—Ridgway reviewed Clint Tarkenton's latest intelligence reports on CCF strength and deployment. It was a worrisome document, indicating that recently CCF strength in North Korea had probably increased from nine armies to sixteen, from about thirty divisions to forty-eight. It was believed that four new armies had arrived in the Pyongyang area and three new armies had joined the three in the Hamhung-Hungnam area. Any or all of these seven new armies, plus the three in the Hamhung-Hungnam area, were in position to replace the six battered CCF armies retreating before Eighth Army and launch a new offensive. In sum, CCF strength in North Korea could total sixteen armies (about 384,000 men), of which ten (about 240,000 men) were fresh and ready for combat.[13]

In addition, there was the NKPA. It continued to demonstrate a remarkable ability to reorganize and refield even its most severely battered elements in a relatively short time.

The combined CCF-NKPA ground strength in North Korea totaled about 500,000 men. Excluding the retreating and battered six CCF armies and some wrecked elements of the NKPA I, II, and V corps, the probability was that the enemy could throw a total of about 350,000 men into a new offensive.[14]

Owing to a recent dramatic increase in the size of the ROK Army (to 250,000 men), Eighth Army forces nearly equaled those of the combined CCF-NKPA: 500,000 men. Of this total, about 350,000 were assigned to frontline combatant units. Thus Eighth Army could nearly match the probable strength of a new CCF offensive man for man. Eighth Army's non-ROK ground forces (231,000)* nearly equaled the probable CCF offensive strength (240,000) in such an attack. The ROK strength (120,000) slightly exceeded frontline NKPA strength (110,000).[15]

Viewed in this light, the reported arrival of seven new CCF armies in North Korea was not cause for dismay. However, there were two major risks. First, the survivors of the retreating six CCF armies (perhaps 100,000 men) might be hurriedly reorganized and thrown into a new offensive, increasing CCF battle strength to 340,000 men. Secondly, the ROKs might again collapse and bug out, depleting Eighth Army's strength by about 120,000 men. If either or both occurred, Eighth Army could again find itself in grave difficulty.

Before retiring, Ridgway sent a message to corps commanders Milburn, Moore, and Almond. "You will confine the reading of this memo to yourself and your chief of staff," he wrote. "At the same time, you are enjoined to insure that all your principal commanders understand its spirit, which is entirely consistent with the present splendid offensive spirit of your command under your fine leadership."

Ridgway's main purpose was to call attention to "reported" seven new CCF armies in North Korea and the three already in the Hamhung-Hungnam area, a total of ten CCF armies. Ridgway did not know their "intentions," but he cautioned that they could "appear on the battle line in twenty-four hours."

Beyond that, Ridgway took this occasion to "reiterate the basis on which I want all operations conducted" during Killer. These were: Inflict maximum destruction on enemy personnel and matériel at minimum to our own; maintain all units intact (use terrain to facilitate attainment of this objective); maintain maximum coordination within and between corps; guard constantly against getting sucked in and destroyed piecemeal, "whether by ruse or the temptation [of] your own aggressiveness to pursue beyond our capability of providing powerful support or of timely disengagement and local withdrawal."[16]

## II

Operation Killer began as Ridgway had planned on the morning of February 21. From the outset it was bedeviled by rain and mud, washed-out bridges and roads.[17]

Having displaced the 2d Division at Wonju, the 1st Marine Division attacked north toward Hoengsong. The First Marines, now commanded by Francis M. ("Frank") McAlister (USNA, 1927), forty-five, manned the divi-

_____

*Army: 185,000; Marines: 25,000; other: 21,000.

sion's left sector; Ray Murray's Fifth Marines, the right sector. Homer Litzenberg's Seventh Marines were held in reserve. Carl A. Youngdale's Eleventh Marines (Artillery) and the tank battalion supported the infantry attack.[18]

Ridgway and Bryant Moore flew into the IX Corps sector and jeeped forward to observe McAlister's First Marines in action. After dismounting from his jeep, Ridgway climbed a snow-covered embankment for a better view. There he noticed that a Marine corporal carrying a heavy radio was stumbling along with an untied shoelace. Ridgway glissaded down the embankment on his rear, landed at the corporal's feet, then knelt and tied the shoe.

War correspondents who were accompanying the Marines seized on this "color" to humanize Ridgway. Some would report the act as a "theatrical gesture," Pattonesque battlefield showmanship. Not so, Ridgway wrote later: "It was purely an impulse to help a fighting soldier, a man in trouble." Whatever the case, the episode enhanced Ridgway's already high standing with the Marines.[19]

The Marines slogged north, meeting little or no resistance, except mud. The weather and the terrain were dreadful, a senior commander recalled, "a mixture of thawing snow, rain, mud and slush." Vehicles following the Marines with ammo, rations, and other supplies bogged down in muddy quagmires grandly labeled "roads."[20]

* * *

To the right of the Marines Ned Almond's X Corps, composed of Ruffner's 2d and Ferenbaugh's 7th divisions, and the several slapped-together ROK divisions attacked one day behind the Marines.

Almond now had a new G-3, replacing Jack Chiles. He was a smart West Pointer (1939), Frank T. Mildren, a thirty-seven-year-old officer who had long ties with the 2d Division. Upon being graduated from the academy, he had joined the 38th Infantry and remained with it for six years, through all its combat in the ETO. He had commanded the 1/38 at Omaha Beach and beyond and risen to regimental exec.[21]

Even though Mildren had been Chiles's assistant for a number of weeks, he was not certain he could handle the job. The pressure and Almond's demand for perfection, he remembered, very nearly did him in: "I would stay up until one or two o'clock in the morning preparing plans. Then I had to be present at six-thirty the same morning, when Almond reviewed them. Everything had to be perfect. If he found one mistake, he'd send the whole damned thing back for correction.

"Almond loved to draw arrows on maps," said Mildren. "One time I brought him a map depicting a ROK operation, but I only had two arrows: one for the main effort; one for a secondary effort. Almond got up and drew in a lot more arrows—seven or eight. I thought he was wrong; it was too great a dispersion of the available forces. So I went back to my office and took off most of the arrows. Later Almond demanded to know, 'Where are my arrows?' Instead of telling him forthrightly that he was overdispersing the forces, I said, 'If you'd presented that solution at Leavenworth [at the Command and General Staff School], they'd have given you a fuzzy U [unsatisfactory].' "

Mildren continued: "God, the air turned blue. In the midst of this tirade the chief of staff, John Guthrie, tried to sneak out—had his hand on the doorknob. Almond told him, 'You stay here!' Guthrie sat down. I said, 'General Almond, you don't need a G-three.' He said, 'You're right, I don't.' So I left and the next morning I let my assistant give the briefing. Almond demanded, 'Where's the G-three? The G-three is supposed to give the briefing.' So I got up and gave the briefing, and he never said a word about it.

"After two or three weeks," recalled Mildren, "I was churning inside and only getting three hours' sleep or not any at all. I felt sick. I wrote my wife that it was the first job in the Army that I thought I couldn't handle. Almond just didn't understand how to deal with people."

\* \* \*

The 2d Division attacked on the immediate right of the Marines. Ed Messinger's 9th Infantry manned the division's left sector; Jack Chiles's 23d Infantry, the right sector. John Coughlin's 38th Infantry was assigned to division reserve.

The men of the 2d Division were not happy at having been displaced at Wonju by the Marines. The Wonju–Hoengsong road had been "their" territory ever since mid-December. They had lost many good men in the sector and believed the "honor" of recapturing Hoengsong belonged to them. Unaware of Ridgway's promise to Smith that the Marines would never again be assigned to fight in Almond's X Corps, the 2d Division soldiers believed that Almond had some ulterior motive for pushing them out of the sector.[22]

The 2d Division was really not in good shape for another tough campaign. Coughlin's 1/38 and 3/38 had been wrecked at Hoengsong, leaving James Skeldon's 2/38 the only fully combat-ready battalion in the 38th Infantry. Jack Chiles's 23d Infantry, especially James Edwards's 2/23, had suffered harshly at Twin Tunnels and Chipyong. Edwards himself had been relieved of command (without prejudice) by Chiles, who judged Edwards to be "on the verge of complete exhaustion." Owing to the high casualties the French and Dutch battalions had sustained, Ridgway personally ordered that they go into division reserve, thus paring the 23d and 38th of further strength. The savaged 15th FAB, now commanded by West Pointer (1939) Carl H. Wohlfeil, was still reorganizing.[23]

Of the three regiments in the 2d Division, Ed Messinger's 9th had survived the CCF offensive at Wonju in best shape. It had been called upon to man defensive positions on the Yoju–Wonsan road and to reinforce the efforts of the division Recon Company to reach Paul Freeman's redoubt on February 13 and 14. Only its black 3/9, backing the Recon Company, had been hard hit in these actions.

In truth, the 3/9 had fallen on hard times. In early February its able commander, D. M. McMains, had been wounded near Wonju. While McMains was in the hospital, the doctors had learned of his earlier automobile wreck injuries and plastic surgery and had forbidden him to return to combat in Korea. Moreover, in the February 14 action below Chipyong the new (white) exec, Harlan Stine (who won a Silver Star), had also been wounded and evacuated.[24]

McMains and Stine had only recently been replaced. The new commander was James F. Nabors, the former regimental S-2 of the 38th Infantry and a courageous soldier (he was to win a total of four Silver Star medals in Korea). The exec, Stine, was replaced by the battalion S-3, Harris Pope, a "giant" (six feet five inches, 225 pounds) who had won a Silver Star at Kunu. Pope was the 3/9's fourth exec in six months. The first had been killed; the second had been captured; the third had been wounded. Pope wondered what his fate would be.[25]

There were other problems. The 3/9 still suffered from a drastic shortage of infantry officers in all categories and from an influx of disgruntled and green fillers. A "negative attitude had set in," Pope remembered. "There was a feeling that the battalion had been deliberately sacrificed at Kunu-ri to save others. Now the men just wouldn't fight."[26]

Almond and the X Corps staff harshly condemned the 9th Infantry as "unsatisfactory." In a report which reached Ridgway, Almond's deputy commander, Laurence Ladue, blamed its poor performance on the fact that the regiment was "40 percent colored." The figure included not only the 3/9 but also the blacks in Butch Barberis's 2/9 and John Londahl's 1/9.[27]

Owing to the general dissatisfaction with the 9th Infantry, Almond had ordered another of the X Corps "teacher's pets" assigned to the outfit. He was Olinto M. Barsanti (University of Nevada, 1940), thirty-three. Barsanti replaced the 9th's exec, Joe Gerot.[28]

Barsanti was another "fighting fool" in the mold of John Corley and Gerry Kelleher. His college roommate, Frank McCullough, remembered: "He was a tough mining family's kid from a tough town—Tonopah—and I fancied myself as a tough farm boy from a tough town—Fernley. Which is to say that we both drank and fought a lot, sometimes with each other, sometimes with anyone else who happened to be handy. . . ."[29]

Barsanti's ties to the 2d Division were nearly as long as those of the new X Corps G-3, Frank Mildren. After receiving an ROTC commission in 1940, Barsanti had also been assigned to the 38th Infantry. He remained with the 38th throughout World War II, during which he commanded all three of its battalions—the 3/38 at Omaha Beach alongside Mildren's 1/38. During the ETO fighting Barsanti had earned two Silver Star medals and had been wounded five times. The 23d Infantry exec, Frank Meszar, remembered: "The joke was: Don't ever stand near Barsanti."[30]

Barsanti had come to Korea early with John Church's advance command, from which he migrated to X Corps.[31] His impact on the 9th Infantry was immediate and strong. The 1/9's S-3, Tom Mellen, remembered fondly: "The 'Bar' (if you were of equal or senior rank) was something else. First and foremost a fighter. A vital, intense Italian, his style of leadership was right out of the Fort Benning 'Follow Me' school. Coal black eyes that I swear shot sparks when he got mad. And mad he got. In fact, he had a monumental temper; he also had a heart as big as a squad tent. A consummate ass-chewer, he could not stay mad at anyone very long."[32]

*  *  *

The 2d Division launched its attack north from Chechon on February 22. The division historian wrote:

The sector assigned to the 2nd Division presented enormous problems. The terrain was studded with mountains; it contained no reliable supply route and the few trails that did exist had been reduced to muddy quagmires by recent rains and thaw. Mud a foot deep in many places completely stopped vehicular movement. Bridges washed out and rushing streams made crossing difficult. . . . The initial advance was slow, not so much due to [enemy] resistance as to terrain.[33]

The first big obstacle was the flooding Chechon River. Normally an inconsequential stream, it was now four feet deep, freezing cold and rushing. Tanks could ford the river, but the jeeps and trucks could not. The crossing delayed most of the 2d Division—and Buddy Ferenbaugh's 7th Division on the right—for nearly two full days.

No doubt eager to make a good mark in his first operation as the 23d's commander, Jack Chiles ferried his 1/23 and 3/23 across the river by tank and kept moving. The 23d was soon far ahead of all elements in the 2d and 7th divisions.[34]

During the Chechon River crossing the 9th Infantry suffered another serious loss: Butch Barberis. A tank detonated a land mine and a bogie wheel blew off and hit Barberis in the head. "We thought he had been killed," William Ellis remembered. "Fortunately," Tom Mellen recalled, "General Ruffner's helicopter was close by. It was used to evacuate Barberis." Severely wounded in the head and eye, Barberis spent more than a year in Army hospitals, recovering. He was replaced as commander of the 2/9 by his long-time exec, Peter F. Bermingham.[35]

\* \* \*

The first objective of the Marine Corps division was a line of hills on the south side of Hoengsong about eight miles north of Wonju. The Marines reached these hills on February 24, having met only slight enemy resistance. However, when McAlister sent a patrol into Hoengsong itself (a pile of rubble), it encountered mortar and machine-gun fire. When an aircraft reported the CCF in position to ambush the patrol, McAlister withdrew it. All signs indicated that enemy rear guards would fight hard to hold Hoengsong.[36]

To the right the 2d and 7th divisions also advanced slowly, keeping more or less abreast of the Marines. On February 24 patrols of Chiles's 23d Infantry reached the Hoengsong–Pangnim road, running east from Hoengsong. But Nick Ruffner was reluctant to go farther. The 2d Division historian wrote:

The Division became increasingly concerned with the almost insurmountable logistical problems which hampered its activities. The combined factors of weather, terrain and lack of supply routes finally prompted a request to X Corps for relief. The appeal asked for (1) native bearers to establish a carrier supply network, (2) sufficient air drops to keep the forward elements supplied, or (3) a halt in the advance of the Division until the necessary road network could be built.[37]

Ned Almond received this "appeal" coolly. His reply: "The attack was to continue."

To the right of the 2d Division Buddy Ferenbaugh's 7th Division made no better progress. Almond's deputy, Laurence Ladue, told Ridgway on February 23 that John Gavin's 31st Infantry (savaged at the Chosin Reservoir and still skittish) had been "slow to the point of timidity" and had to be pushed hard. As a result of X Corps pushing, patrols of the 7th Division reached Pangnim on February 24.[38]

\* \* \*

To the left of the Marines Charlie Palmer's 1st Cav and Babe Bryan's 24th divisions were likewise bogged down in rain and mud and made scant progress. In the 1st Cav, Billy Harris's 7th Cav, still in reserve, had been temporarily replaced by Coad's Commonwealth Brigade. The brigade had recently been significantly strengthened to four battalions by the arrival of a Canadian battalion.\* However, the brigade was so slow off the mark that

---

\*2d Battalion, Princess Patricia's Canadian Light Infantry. The Commonwealth Brigade now consisted of an Australian battalion, English battalion, Scottish battalion, Canadian battalion, and New Zealand artillery battalion.

Ridgway was compelled to order Bryant Moore to "build a fire" under it. Moore lit a match, but on February 24 the leading battalions (Australian and Canadian) were stopped cold by CCF rear guards dug into the east of Chipyong. All 1st Cav and Commonwealth Brigade operations were delayed, then halted by muddy roads and by the washout of a big Han River bridge at Yoju. It had broken loose on February 22 and remained out of commission until February 25.[39]

\* \* \*

The IX Corps commander, Bryant Moore, was a hard driver. Like Ridgway, he spent most of his day with the frontline units. He showed promise of becoming the most reliable and aggressive of the corps commanders.[40]

At 10:30 A.M. on February 24, while coming in to land at Yoju, Bryant's helicopter hit a cable spanning the Han River. The helicopter spun out of control and crashed into the icy water. GIs fished Moore and the pilot from the river. Shocked and cold, Moore stumbled into Hank Meyer's 24th Division artillery CP. There he dried out, got a fresh uniform, and made some phone calls. At 11:00 A.M., while "sitting in a chair," Moore died of a heart attack.[41]

That morning Ridgway was en route to Eighth Army main headquarters in Taegu. When the *Hi Penny!* landed there at 12:30 P.M., Ridgway received the shocking news. He immediately telephoned Doyle Hickey in GHQ, Tokyo, to relay the news and for the second time to raise the possibility of bringing out Joe Swing to command IX Corps. MacArthur concurred, but again Joe Collins refused to release Swing from his job as commandant of the Army War College. Upon learning this, Ridgway requested—and got—an old and close friend (and an able, well-known general), West Pointer (1916) William M. Hoge, fifty-seven, then commanding U.S. forces in Trieste.[42]

Bill Hoge was one of three sons of an educator, all of whom went to West Point. Hoge was a football star (halfback) with Eisenhower and Bradley and a standout student. Graduating high in his class, he chose the Engineers and served with the AEF in France, winning a DSC. Early in World War II he won considerable fame as the chief engineer in the construction of the 1,000-mile Alaska-Canada (Alcan) Highway. Later he landed on D day at Omaha Beach, commanding a brigade of combat engineers. By December 1944, wearing one star, Hoge commanded an armored strike force of the 9th Armored Division, which distinguished itself first in the Battle of the Bulge, then later by its legendary capture of the Ludendorff railroad bridge over the Rhine River at Remagen. He finished the war wearing two stars and commanding the 4th Armored Division in Patton's Third Army.[43]

Denied Joe Swing, Ridgway was delighted to get Bill Hoge to replace Moore in IX Corps. At Omaha Beach, St.-Vith, and Remagen, Hoge had displayed remarkable intelligence, coolness under fire, tenacity, and aggressiveness. In Ridgway's view, Hoge was "a man in whom I had absolute implicit confidence, in his personal courage, in his professional competence and in his stability of character."[44]

Pending Hoge's arrival, Ridgway needed a temporary IX Corps commander. The most senior officer in IX Corps was Marine General O. P. Smith. Although Ridgway well knew that even a temporary promotion of Smith to command Army forces would raise eyebrows within the Department of the Army, he gave him the job. The temporary appointment served to express his high regard for the Marines as fighting men and for O. P. Smith in particular.[45]

Predictably the appointment touched off a flap. Some war correspondents failed to note in their dispatches that Smith's job was "temporary." Seeing these stories in the Washington papers, Ham Haislip fired a rocket at Ridgway on back channels, stating it was "advisable here you issue immediate press release indicating temporary nature of command." Even though Ridgway had already done that, he dutifully reemphasized to the correspondents that Smith was temporary and even talked the *Time* and *Newsweek* reporters out of filing stories on Smith's "promotion." Finally, at Haislip's urging "to take pressure off," Ridgway released the news of Hoge's appointment (undercutting Smith) much sooner than he had planned.[46]

Ridgway called at the IX Corps CP on the following day to give Smith a warm welcome and to reiterate that the assignment was temporary. While there, he instructed the IX Corps chief of staff, George Peploe, that he and other staffers were to "take maximum advantage of this opportunity to bring the Army and Marines closer together." Smith, Ridgway went on, should be "taken into their hearts . . . and, by definite action, made to feel he is there."[47]

## III

Operation Killer did not live up to its name. Poor weather, logistical difficulties, and Bryant Moore's death had undermined it. Very few enemy had been killed. Killer did, however, yield two important benefits:

• It restored and greatly strengthened the UN line east from Yangpyong through Hoengsong to Pangnim which the CCF offensive had breached. Moreover, the commitment of the powerful Marine division to this difficult sector opened up the possibility of more aggressive action than Ridgway had earlier contemplated.

• It gave engineer Strong and his troops valuable experience in coping with miserable Korean weather. The February rain had been a fluke. When the normal rainy season began later, the engineers would be far better prepared to deal with it.

In a report to MacArthur on the indifferent results of Killer, Ridgway stressed the second benefit:

The recent unseasonable rains and thawing conditions, which began in the combat area on 21 January, have served to highlight anticipated difficulties to be encountered from the weather for the next several months. . . . I view the condition experienced during the past few days as an act of providence which will prove of inestimable value in determining the points upon which to concentrate my engineer effort, in anticipation of further adverse weather conditions as the rainy season approaches. The highest priority will be given to critical lines of communication through the Sobaek Mountain Range [in the central sector]. I plan to exploit, to the maximum, indigenous personnel as well as animal transport, to assist combat elements in over-coming the neutralizing effect of weather on terrain and consequently on motor transport. Most of the difficulties resulting from the recent rains have now been overcome and lines of communication restored.[48]

On February 25 Ridgway began a reappraisal and refinement of his strategy. Still mindful of MacArthur's earlier injunction not to become fixated on the Han River or other arbitrary lines and to keep pushing until he encountered the CCF main line of resistance, Ridgway decided to throw the entire Eighth Army into a general, peninsula-wide offensive, which he named Operation Ripper. If successful, it would take Eighth Army to the 38th Parallel.[49]

Planning for Ripper moved the sensitive issue of recrossing the 38th Parallel to the fore. The issue was then being hotly debated in Washington, London, and elsewhere. In some respects it was the most difficult political issue yet posed in the Korean War.

The reasons *for* recrossing the parallel were:

• Washington and the UN had made a moral commitment to create "a unified, independent and democratic Korea." Although the CCF intervention had knocked that high-minded goal off its pedestal, after all the bloodshed, to settle for less than a total ground "victory" would be a display of craven weakness and morally irresponsible. Moreover, the CCF should be made to pay for its aggression.

• Washington's efforts to induce Peking to negotiate had got nowhere. Continued pursuit and punishment of the CCF across the parallel might persuade Peking to negotiate. To stop arbitrarily and sit at the parallel would terminate pressure on and punishment of the CCF, and it would leave Eighth Army deployed in poor defensive positions, vulnerable to a counterattack.

The reasons *against* recrossing the parallel were:

• Notwithstanding its bellicose pronouncements to the contrary, Peking might well be on the verge of agreeing to negotiate and might settle for the status quo ante bellum. The precipitous CCF withdrawal above the 38th Parallel reinforced this view. If Eighth Army were to cross the 38th Parallel into North Korea, Peking would "lose face" and might decide not to negotiate.

• In any case, a total ground "victory" in Korea was probably not attainable. Peking had virtually unlimited manpower. It had shown no hesitation in committing manpower to Korea and would probably continue to commit resources indefinitely. If CCF manpower were not sufficient, Moscow might overtly intervene in the war. The recent Soviet buildup of the CCF Air Force and an unusual and bellicose "interview" with Stalin in *Pravda* ("The war in Korea can only end in a defeat of the interventionists") reinforced that speculation.

• Washington's allies, especially the Attlee government, were adamantly opposed to crossing the 38th parallel. All allies feared that crossing the parallel would lead to "widening the war" with Peking and possibly to Soviet intervention and World War III.

• The war was an expensive drain on American and allied resources. A continued commitment of UN manpower and matériel to "nonstrategic" Korea would seriously retard the buildup of NATO in "strategic" Western Europe.

• The war had become distinctly unpopular and a political liability. American casualties already exceeded 60,000. Crossing the 38th Parallel could increase opposition to the war, perhaps even leading to open rebellion and eventual political catastrophe.

Dean Acheson, who had championed crossing the 38th Parallel to pursue the NKPA, now strongly opposed crossing it again. His views were set forth on February 23, in a major State Department policy paper that argued that neither Washington nor the UN had incurred a legal obligation to unify Korea by military force. (The October 7, 1951, UN resolution was "persuasive but not mandatory.") Forwarding this paper to George Marshall and the JCS for comment, the secretary of state suggested that it serve as a basis for discussions with President Truman and, furthermore, that MacArthur be sent "more precise instructions" regarding the 38th Parallel.[50]

The JCS took a dim view of this paper, declaring that "from the military point of view" it was "an unsound approach." The chiefs argued that State was attempting to predetermine military operations (a halt at the parallel) on the basis of "interim political factors" rather than formulate new long-term political objectives in Korea to which military operations could be tailored. Furthermore, to announce a halt at the 38th Parallel would give the enemy valuable information. The halt itself could place Eighth Army in grave jeopardy militarily.[51]

In fact, two members of the JCS had in mind a substantial Eighth Army penetration into North Korea. Forrest Sherman "personally favored" retaking the North Korean capital, Pyongyang, because that would put Washington in position to "talk better" in negotiations with Peking. Joe Collins more or less agreed. The Chinese Communists had been "dumb enough to fight us with their best troops," he proclaimed, and had taken a "terrible beating. They have filled up their hospitals," Collins went on, "and it will be very hard for them to replace their losses." If the UN retook Pyongyang, it should also retake Wonsan and establish a line Wonsan–Pyongyang "following the most desirable terrain." A Wonsan–Pyongyang line "was a good defensive position," Collins went on, "a difficult one for the Chinese to break through."[52]*

Matt Ridgway agreed with the chiefs. To him the 38th Parallel was a "mystic line" which was "neither defensible nor strategically important." He was "still not satisfied" with the destruction Eighth Army had inflicted on the CCF. He was concerned about the continuing Communist buildup and wanted to pursue the CCF north of the 38th Parallel, not only to inflict further destruction but also to disrupt any assembling for an offensive.[53]

Ridgway's plan for crossing the 38th Parallel was considerably more conservative than the Sherman-Collins plan. He would advance Eighth Army into North Korea no more than about twenty miles and that only in the center of the Eighth Army front. When he recaptured Seoul, he would advance the army's left flank (I Corps) to the Imjin River at Munsan (the old Line B) and hold on the 38th Parallel, with the army's left flank on the Yellow Sea. He would bulge the army center (IX and X corps) north above the parallel to Chorwon and the Hwachon Reservoir. The right (ROK III and ROK I corps) would extend east from the reservoir, anchoring the army's right flank on the Sea of Japan.[54]

Ridgway's proposed "line" was a radical departure from previously proposed "lines." In the west it was a "diagonal," going up the Imjin River valley to Chorwon, whence it turned due east. Ridgway believed the bulge at Chorwon and the Hwachon Reservoir was essential. The towns of Chorwon, Kumhwa, and Pyonggang, linked by rail and roads, formed a "triangle" which was known to be the main assembly area for the CCF. Eighth Army command of the triangle would decisively thwart CCF preparations for offensive actions. Command of the Hwachon Reservoir was necessary to prevent flooding of the Pukhan River and the consequent damage to Eighth Army's supply lines.[55]

When informed of Ridgway's proposed plan, the JCS swung behind it. In

---

*Hoyt Vandenberg disagreed, stating that FEAF could "not operate effectively" against "shortened Chinese lines of communications" and the Wonsan–Pyongyang line would present "twice as much difficulty."

a presentation to Marshall and Acheson, Joe Collins pointed out its advantages but erroneously described it as "roughly diagonal, running from the Imjin River to Wonsan." Marshall rightly questioned the advisability of pushing the right flank as far north as Wonsan and doubted that the ROKs could do it and hold. Upon investigation, Collins discovered Ridgway intended to put the right flank not at Wonsan, but much farther south at Yangyang, east of the Hwachon Reservoir.[56]

After all this had been cleared up and thoroughly discussed, Marshall endorsed the JCS position. In a formal response to Acheson's February 23 policy paper, he wrote on March 1 that it was essential that Eighth Army have "freedom of action and freedom of maneuver" and that, in any case, to announce a halt at the 38th Parallel would subject Eighth Army to "risk." He agreed with the chiefs that Acheson's paper should not go to the president and that a sweeping NSC-level review of political policy in Korea was necessary. Pending the outcome of that review, MacArthur did not require "more precise instructions" since he had already promised not to cross the 38th Parallel without first clearing it with Washington.[57]

Inasmuch as President Truman left for vacation in Key West, the sweeping NSC policy review was postponed. Meanwhile, as it had the previous September and October, the administration sought (with resounding lack of success) to discourage "talk" about crossing the 38th Parallel. When publicly queried about the issue, Truman again dissembled and evaded, repeating that it was a "tactical" decision "to be handled by the field commander."[58]

*  *  *

Ridgway, meanwhile, continued planning for Ripper. Improving weather and logistics influenced the plans. The temperature was returning to normal for February: cold. The rains had stopped. Meteorologists predicted continued cold, probably a refreezing of roads, diminishing snow meltoff, hence a lowering of water levels and velocities in the rivers. The bridges at Chungju and Yoju (and elsewhere) were under control and back in operation. The railroad from Andong to Wonju (supplying X Corps) would soon be in full operation.[59]

The main thrust of Ripper would be two parallel and simultaneous maneuvers:

• In I Corps Sladen Bradley's 25th Division would cross the Han River east of Seoul at the juncture of the Han and the north- and south-flowing Pukhan River, then go directly north into high ground, outflanking Seoul and Uijongbu. This axis of advance would (as Ridgway expressed it) point a dagger at the CCF "heart-line" or the "brain" of the CCF commander, forcing him to choose between attacking Eighth Army at "tremendous disadvantage to himself" (since Eighth Army would hold high ground protected on the right flank by the Pukhan River) and abandoning Seoul.[60]

• In IX Corps the 1st Marine Division would attack due north from Hoengsong to Hongchon to Chunchon near the 38th Parallel. The 1st Cav and 2d divisions would continue to provide left- and right-flank protection for the Marines. To the right (or east) of the 2d Division the 7th Division and various ROK divisions would keep abreast.[61]

Ridgway unveiled Ripper to his three corps commanders in Changhowon at 5:00 P.M. on February 26. By that time his key staffers—Day Surles, Paul Smith, and others—had further refined the plans and set D day for March 10. The primary purpose of Ripper, Ridgway stated, was to inflict maximum punishment on the enemy and disrupt any plans for a new offensive. A secondary purpose would be to retake Seoul. As before, the Eighth Army advance would be methodical and tightly controlled by phase lines. There would be no "extravagant pursuits."[62]

There was one aspect of the offensive that O. P. Smith regarded as tricky. Directly north of Babe Bryan's 24th Division sector lay the Chungpyong Reservoir. Since it blocked the 24th Division's route of advance, the planners had decided that most vehicles of the 24th would go around it to the west, through Bradley's 25th Division sector, thence northeast on the Seoul–Chunchon road. It would be a complicated maneuver; the chances of a snafu of some kind were good.[63]

The Chungpyong Reservoir was linked to another, even larger reservoir, the Hwachon, created by a huge (250-foot-high) Japanese-built dam on the upper Pukhan River above the 38th Parallel. The Hwachon Reservoir posed a greater problem. If the CCF demolished the Hwachon Dam, the pent-up water would burst forth, flooding the lower reservoir and then the Pukhan and Han rivers, making them impassable. Engineer Strong calculated the water would rise fifteen feet at the junction of the Pukhan and Han (where the 25th Division was to cross) and seven feet at Seoul, for a period of forty-eight hours, then gradually recede to normal levels. During the flood phase the 25th Division would be vulnerable—virtually isolated north of the Han and west of the Pukhan.[64]

The danger posed by the Hwachon Reservoir was a constant worry. Ridgway well remembered that in the ETO the Germans had stalled a massive American First and Ninth army attack (to which Ridgway's XVIII Airborne Corps had been committed) for two full weeks by partly demolishing dams and flooding the Roer River. As Ridgway saw it, the solution was to destroy the Hwachon Dam. Although FEAF had failed to do so in January with two six-ton guided bombs, Ridgway had requested another attempt. But the request had not been approved; Pat Partridge considered the dam virtually impervious to conventional explosives.[65]

Owing to the logistical problems that had impeded Killer, Ridgway would not launch Ripper until "all units" had a "basic load" of ammo plus a five-day surplus. The Eighth Army G-4, Albert K. Stebbins, had estimated that the buildup would be completed by March 4. To be on the safe side, Ridgway had set D day for March 10. However, corps commanders should be prepared to attack sooner if the stockpiling of supplies exceeded the estimates.[66]

Ripper would also feature an elaborate deception. The ROK 1st Division would make a "demonstration" at the Han River northwest of Kimpo Airfield, "to create the illusion that a crossing of the Han River" was in progress. Since this "demonstration" could conceivably draw CCF upon it from the Pyong-yang area, Ridgway had asked the Navy to simulate an amphibious invasion of Chinnampo to hold the CCF at Pyongyang. In order to give the "sluggish" CCF more time to react to the deception, the Navy would commence fake minesweeping operations in the Taedong River estuary (near Chinnampo) on February 28 and send a fake "amphibious" force there to coincide with the launching of Ripper.[67]

\* \* \*

The logistical buildup for Ripper progressed faster than anticipated. Meeting again with the corps commanders on March 1 in Changhowon, Ridgway moved its D day forward from March 10 to March 6. The phase lines were designated: Albany, Buffalo, Cairo, and, finally, Idaho, above Chunchon but below the 38th Parallel. That night Eighth Army issued formal orders for the offensive. The corps and division commanders would issue orders in compliance on March 2 and 3 (Ridgway's fifty-sixth birthday). To the great relief of Shrimp Milburn and the I Corps staff, Ridgway announced that he would establish his permanent tactical (or advance) headquarters at Yoju, which was centrally located behind Eighth Army's long front.[68]

As it turned out, a hitch that developed in the artillery ammo buildup compelled Ridgway to postpone Ripper. The corps artillery commanders* were not satisfied with the stockpile. In a meeting in Taegu on March 5 with Ridgway, Eighth Army artillery commander John J. Burns, G-4 Stebbins, and others, the corps commanders insisted on a stockpile sufficient to fire sixty-five

---

*James F. Brittingham in I Corps, but two new men in the other corps. In IX Corps West Pointer (1925) William N. Gillmore, forty-seven, arrived from the States to replace Tom de Shazo, who relieved Loyal Haynes as commander of the 2d Division artillery. In X Corps West Pointer (1930) James K. Wilson, Jr., forty-two, relieved William Ennis. Although neither Haynes nor Ennis had been officially reprimanded, both had been the responsible artillery commanders in Roundup on February 12 and 13, when the thirty-four pieces of artillery had been lost.[69]

rounds per day per howitzer. Characterizing that demand as "excessive," Ridgway agreed with Stebbins's more "reasonable" ration of thirty rounds per day for 155s and forty rounds per day for 105s. More ammo was arriving at Inchon; when it reached the front, Ridgway would consider less severe rationing. Meanwhile, he requested cooperation and harmony.[70]

The same day Bill Hoge arrived to take command of IX Corps, relieving O. P. Smith, who was amused by the Army's frantic rush to fill his shoes. To Smith, who had taken his temporary assignment with good grace, Ridgway wrote that he was "personally gratified" for Smith's "instant response to the situation." Ridgway went on to say: "Your personal qualities and high leadership have won their rightful place in the affection, as well as the respect, of the command and staff of the IX Corps."[71]

# IV

Of the proposed maneuvers entailed in Ripper, the most complex and possibly perilous was the Han River crossing by Sladen Bradley's 25th Division at Mugam. There the fast-flowing Han River was 700 feet wide and too deep for anything except possibly tanks to ford. Patrolling on the north side of the river by Rangers and conventional infantry had led to the conclusion that the CCF was present in large numbers, backed by substantial artillery, mortars, and machine guns. Unless it were conducted with great care and professionalism, the crossing could result in the slaughter of hundreds of American troops, and that could be a decisive setback for the rejuvenated Eighth Army.[72]

Since complete "surprise" could make the difference between success and failure, plans for the crossing were produced in utmost secrecy. These were:

• Gilbert Check's 27th and Gerry Kelleher's 35th Infantry would comprise the asault regiments. The 27th would cross to the left (or west) of the Pukhan River; the 35th, to the right (or east) of the Pukhan.

• The 24th Infantry and the Turkish Brigade (replacing Tom Brodie's British Brigade, which went into I Corps reserve) would play important subsidiary roles. The 24th Infantry would put one battalion across the Han, to the left of the 27th Infantry, to block the road from Seoul. The Turks would feint to the right of the 35th Infantry, simulating an assault crossing, to draw the CCF away from the 27th and 35th sectors.[73]

The assault battalions would cross the river in boats and push inland. When they were deep enough into the bridgehead to keep enemy fire off the river, two battalions of engineers would build bridges and ferries. First would be footbridges for the 24th, 27th, and 35th regiments; second, pontoon bridges for the 27th and 35th regiments; and finally, three "heavy" and two "light" ferries, the former capable of transporting tanks, the latter a two-and-a-half-ton truck with trailer or three jeeps.[74]

The crossings would be massively supported by Bittman Barth's artillery and other firepower. In all, Barth would control 148 guns. Notwithstanding the ammo shortage, these would fire a twenty-minute barrage of 5,000 rounds before the assault troops commenced crossing, then would continue heavy fire thereafter at selected, presighted targets. In addition, Shermans of Tom Dolvin's 89th Tank Battalion (with 76-mm guns) and Pattons of the 64th Tank Battalion (with 90-mm guns), now commanded by Wilson M. Hawkins, and A/A weapons and 4.2-inch mortars would lend heavy support.[75]

John Corley, who had commanded the 24th Infantry since September 6, would not be present for this most challenging of the outfit's assignments. After Sladen Bradley had assumed command of the 25th Division, Corley had left for Japan, officially classified as a "nonbattle casualty"—exhausted, believed to be suffering from ulcers, and known to have a bad back that was so agonizing he had to wear a steel-reinforced corset. Corley went on to one star and retired in 1966; his able exec, Paul Roberts, temporarily commanded the regiment until a replacement for Corley could be found.[76]

This was not easy. Regular Army officers avoided the assignment. The job finally went to a senior West Pointer (1932), Henry C. Britt, forty-one, who had commanded a battalion in the 365th Infantry Regiment in Ned Almond's all-black 92d Division in Italy. More recently Britt had been serving in Shrimp Milburn's I Corps G-2 section. Britt was a close friend of the 25th Division's new ADC, Mike Michaelis (he had been the best man when Michaelis was married).[77]

\* \* \*

MacArthur sent word from Tokyo that he would come to Korea for the launching of Ripper. This time, however, Ridgway put his foot down—gingerly. He engaged in a "long session of carefully choosing my words" and telexed MacArthur this extraordinary message:

Look forward with deepest pride and pleasure to your visits. Each brings so much of inspiration. Hope each may be conducted in full accord with your desires. As you know Operation Ripper has been postponed one day and at this moment I am almost certain I will be compelled to further postpone for two or even three days additional.

Not knowing reasons for your selection of date of visit, believe you would want to consider possibility of enemy deduction. He knows, as does all the world, of your fearless personal gallantry. He no doubt is fully aware that your intrepidity and tactical acumen reveal to you in advance where each crisis of battle will occur and take you there in person for that phase of action. It may well follow that the pattern of your many visits will clearly point to him the conclusion that some major tactical action, almost certainly an attack, in the circumstances, is pending. If he acted on such deduction our casualties might increase substantially.

If this reasoning seems valid to you, would not your visit on D plus one or even later annul the value of his deductions, while still probably permitting you the opportunity of witnessing more tactical action than is likely to occur on D. You know, sir, your wishes are my only guide but I thought it possible this view may not have had your consideration. Faithfully.[78]

MacArthur's reaction is not known. In any event, he altered his plans only slightly. He had come over on the eve of Killer to pronounce that he had ordered a "resumption of the initiative." This time he would arrive on the morning Ripper began, as he had on the day Johnnie Walker launched his Home by Christmas offensive from the Chongchon River. If the CCF had found a correlation between Eighth Army attacks and MacArthur's visits to Korea, the postponement would help, but only marginally.

D day for Ripper was finally set for March 7. Aware that MacArthur would arrive early at Suwon that same day, Ridgway took steps to ensure that another "I-have-ordered-a-resumption-of-the-initiative" statement would fall on indifferent ears. A full twenty-four hours before MacArthur was due to arrive, Ridgway held an unprecedented background press conference with war correspondents to outline the details of Ripper. During this session Ridgway, hoping to offset stories in American newspapers that he was becoming "independent" of MacArthur, tactfully—or shrewdly—praised MacArthur for the "freedom of action" and "loyalty" MacArthur had given and shown him.[79]

\* \* \*

Ripper began at 5:45 A.M. on March 7 in the 25th Division sector, with an awesome and deafening display of army firepower. In the space of twenty minutes the 148 artillery pieces fired 5,000 rounds at suspected CCF positions on the north bank of the Han. The tanks, A/A guns, 4.2-inch mortars, and heavy machine guns, which had been secretly brought to the riverbank under the cover of fog, joined the barrage. Bittman Barth estimated that the combined firepower killed "over a thousand" CCF and stunned hundreds more senseless.[80]\*

Ridgway had earlier flown in to observe the attack. He joined Sladen Bradley and the ADC, Mike Michaelis, who were directing operations from a CP near the river.[82]

The artillery slacked off at 6:15 A.M. and shifted fire deeper into the bridgehead. The men of the three assault battalions climbed into boats. These battalions were George Clayton's 2/24 on the left (west), Richard Keyes's 3/27 in the center, and James Lee's 3/35 on the right (east). All assault units

---

\*The participation of four Pattons of the 64th Tank Battalion in the barrage drew a sharp rebuke from the I Corps armor officer, Thomas Gillis. Noting that the "life cycle" of a Patton's 90-mm gun was only about 1,600 rounds, he criticized the tankers for firing about 900 rounds combined in four hours. As a result, two Pattons had burned out their guns, which had to be replaced in Pusan; the other two had shortened the gun "life cycles" considerably.[81]

achieved complete surprise. Casualties in the boats were extremely light, except in the 3/35, which lost two boats to a CCF gun concealed in a tunnel. That gun was soon silenced.[83]

Sergeant Woodruff in L Company of Lee's 3/35 was in the assault force. He remembered:

The artillery preparation was indescribable. At Fort Sill, years before in basic training, I had seen firepower demonstrations involving multi-battalion concentrations; but nothing prepared me for this. The earth shook and a deafening roar went on and on. Toward the end a faint light fell on the snow-covered mountain across the Han. Across the entire visible expanse of these mountains shells burst in absolute profusion, each burst first flaring orange, then turning to black smoke, against the whiteness of the snow. I watched, near hypnotized. Then it ended, as suddenly as it had begun.[84]

Woodruff and his squad grabbed the first returning boat and went across in the "second wave," hurrying to get to the far shore before dawn. The strong current swept the boat downstream into the K Company sector. When it got ashore, the squad had to walk two and a half hours to find the L Company zone. Moving inland, the company met few CCF troops, but a sniper killed or wounded a dozen L Company men within a two-hour period.

Tom Dolvin's A Company, commanded by Herbert A. Brannon, was supporting the 35th Infantry. Believing these tanks might conceivably find a fording place, Dolvin had directed Brannon to scout for a path. Brannon had found one, and at about 8:00 A.M. he sent the first tank across, trailing a retrieving cable should it founder. When this tank made it safely to the north bank, Brannon sent the rest of the company across. One tank flooded out, but by 10:00 A.M. all the others had joined Lee's 3/35 in the beachhead. Lee was very glad to have this timely armor support; he believed it substantially contributed to the success of his assault.[85]

*   *   *

The plan was that once the assault waves had crossed in the boats, engineers would build footbridges in the 24th, 27th, and 35th Infantry sectors, then later, pontoon bridges and ferries. But the footbridge construction in the 24th and 35th Infantry sectors went awry. In the 35th sector unexpectedly heavy river currents frustrated the engineers. In the 24th sector a lucky enemy bullet hit and snapped the main bridge cable. David Carlisle, that day acting commander of the black 77th EEC, supporting the 24th Infantry, remembered the crisis:

Dumbfounded, officers and some NCOs standing in a tight knot at the water's edge watch sections of the newly-assembled, just-launched footbridge start to swing downstream. Suddenly—literally out of nowhere—an engineer soldier begins running toward the near end of the footbridge carrying another roll of anchor cable. He jumps onto the bridge and starts running across, paying out the cable behind him as he goes. He is almost to the middle of the river when enemy small arms fire begins to seek him out. But he runs on, unhit. At the far end of the bridge, which is now swinging downstream alarmingly, he vaults into shallow water some 20 yards from shore. Enemy fire splashes into the water around him but he wades ashore. He moves 5, 10 yards up the bank. There he flops to the ground. He lies exhausted, still clutching the coil of cable, which now arrests the bridge's movement downstream. Back on the near shore other engineer soldiers run onto the bridge and begin attaching guy wires from sections of the footbridge to the replacement anchor cable.[86]

Clayton's E and F companies had crossed first in the assault boats. When the footbridge was firmly anchored, G and K companies crossed. Meanwhile, Carlisle's 77th engineers, using more assault boats for floats, began building a light ferry (or raft) for transporting the two-and-a-half-ton trucks. An enemy mortar round hit the raft and blew it to pieces. After clearing away the debris, the engineers constructed another raft. At 3:00 P.M. the first truck crossed the river.

On the far shore Clayton's full 2/24 headed for high ground. Although the near loss of the footbridge had delayed the battalion's river crossing, Clayton made up for lost time. Meeting slight enemy resistance, the 2/24 reached assigned objectives before dark. Later that day the rest of William Mouchet's 3/24 crossed to support the 2/24.[87]

*   *   *

Upriver the crossing of the full 27th and 35th regiments proceeded fairly smoothly, notwithstanding the absence of a footbridge in the 35th's sector. The 1/27, commanded by Check's replacement, Charles R. Kearney, followed the 3/27, which received a Presidential Unit Citation. The 2/27, commanded by Richard J. Byrne (replacing Gordon Murch), came last. The 2/35, led by Hiram M. Merritt, followed Lee's 3/35 into the beachhead by boat. The 1/35, commanded by Lloyd G. Huggins, crossed last. Engineers of the 65th Combat Battalion, commanded by West Pointer (1943) McGlachlin Hatch, supported the 27th and 35th. Those in the 35th sector continued to experience difficulty. Owing to the heavy currents, it took a full twenty-four hours (rather than ten) to install the pontoon bridge and the footbridge. As a result, Gerry Kelleher had to rely completely on rafts and two DUWKs for water transport.[88]

*   *   *

Much pleased at the success of the river crossing, Ridgway departed by lightplane for Suwon to greet MacArthur, who was arriving that morning. After taking off, Ridgway directed his "intrepid and indefatigable" pilot, Mike

Lynch, to fly into the beachhead and land for a brief visit. Ridgway remembered: "I stepped out and walked among the men who were leading the attack. This never failed to provide me with a deep inner satisfaction and I believe it always had a heartening effect too upon the troops, who were always glad to see the 'Old Man' up with them when the going was rough."[89]

Ridgway found that all was going well in the beachhead. However, a setback occurred that first night. The CCF counterattacked E and F companies of Clayton's 2/24 and drove them off the high ground and back 1,500 yards before they held. On orders from Sladen Bradley, the following morning Henry Britt (who had assumed command of the regiment from Paul Roberts) brought the 1/24, now commanded by Roscius Newell, across the river to reinforce the 2/24 and 3/24. That day, March 8, the 24th regained the lost high ground (incurring 135 casualties in the process) and remained thereafter facing Seoul to provide the 25th Division flank protection.[90]

On the first day north of the Han the 25th Division captured 317 CCF prisoners, the largest "bag" so far in the Korean War. The Chinese had been dazed and frightened by the overwhelming American firepower, but interrogators noted something else as well. The prisoners were (in Barth's words) "thoroughly beaten and demoralized." This discovery led to speculation that the CCF morale had decisively cracked. That, in turn, raised morale in Eighth Army to even greater heights.[91]

* * *

Far to the right at Hoengsong, in Bill Hoge's IX Corps sector, the 1st Marine Division also began its attack on March 7. It was flanked by Charlie Palmer's 1st Cav on the left and Nick Ruffner's 2nd Division on the right. Going north toward Hongchon (Line Albany), five miles distant, the Marines met little or no resistance. The 1st Cav and 2d divisions likewise encountered few enemy, but the advance of the 2d Division was again impeded by rugged terrain and logistical difficulties.[92]

As the Marines advanced north of Hoengsong, they entered the area where the 2d Division forces in support of the ROK 8th Division had been cut off and savaged on February 12 and 13. The battlefield was still littered with hundreds of American dead, but a few live Americans were rescued from hiding places. Among the dead was the body of the brave Dutch Battalion commander Marinus den Ouden, who was buried with honors. The Marines tagged the area "Massacre Valley." One Marine erected a sign:

MASSACRE VALLEY
SCENE OF HARRY S. TRUMAN'S POLICE ACTION
NICE GOING HARRY[93]

War correspondents with the Marines, realizing the Army had "covered up" a big fiasco, began filing critical Massacre Valley stories. On the basis of its correspondent's file, *Time* wrote:

Forty half-burned trucks and jeeps and the blown-out barrels of six 155 millimeter field pieces were scattered along the road. In the vehicles and under them lay the burned and decomposed bodies of U.S. and South Korean soldiers. Other bodies, stripped of their uniforms, sprawled by the roadside. This was the sight met by advancing U.S. Marines two miles northwest of Hoengsong. It was part of the most horribly concentrated display of American dead since the Korean War began.[94]

\* \* \*

MacArthur arrived at Suwon, as planned, at 10:45 A.M. on March 7. Ridgway met the plane. After descending the ramp, MacArthur gave Ridgway a box of candy. In a private aside Ridgway told MacArthur he had held a press conference the previous day, during which he had confided the details of Ripper. He also told MacArthur that to help offset stories that he was growing "independent" of him, he had expressed to the correspondents his appreciation for MacArthur's backing and loyalty. That (Ridgway noted in his diary) "seemed to please" MacArthur, who added: "Don't let them give you the slightest concern."[95]

Ridgway served as MacArthur's escort for most of that critical day. Having boarded smaller aircraft at 11:00 A.M., they flew to Bill Hoge's IX Corps CP at Yoju. After a briefing, MacArthur, Ridgway, and Hoge flew on to Charlie Palmer's 1st Cav CP and spent about two hours touring the division, which was attacking on the left of the Marine division near Yondu, toward Line Albany.[96]

The party visited all three regimental CPs, stopping first at Billy Harris's 7th Cav (including the Greek Battalion), next at Bob Blanchard's 8th Cav (including the Thai Battalion). Harris and Blanchard were leading the division attack, supported by armor of the 70th Tank Battalion, now commanded by Jack R. Metzdorf. The last stop was at Marcel Crombez's 5th Cav, which was in division reserve.[97]

It was not evident to the visiting VIPs, but the unhappy 5th Cav was then recovering from a traumatic command shake-up. Beginning with its now famous—or infamous—tank charge to Chipyong to rescue the 23d Infantry, the outfit had undergone four changes in battalion commanders and numerous changes in company commanders in the ensuing three weeks.[98]

• In the 3/5 Charles Parziale had replaced the missing Edgar Treacy on February 16. At Crombez's direction Parziale was transferring out the senior officers (John Barrett, Norman Allen, et al.) who were openly critical of the callous loss of men in the Chipyong rescue.

• In the 2/5 the steady West Pointer Paul Clifford, who had won three Silver Star medals (and a Purple Heart), was promoted to 1st Cav Division G-1. He was replaced by his able exec, Claude E. Allen, who had come to Korea with the battalion. On March 2, while the regiment was preparing to move back into reserve, Allen was killed by a CCF mortar round. He was replaced as 2/5 commander by thirty-three-year-old Richard L. Irby (VMI, 1939), who later rose to three stars and, after retirement, became superintendent of VMI.

• The 1/5 commander, Morgan Heasley, was sacked and replaced by Charles T. Heinrich.

The last change—Heinrich for Heasley—would be long remembered because of the black humor associated with it. West Pointer Harry Buckley recalled it this way: "Heasley had been drinking steadily for months. Jim Gibson, promoted to exec, was really running the battalion. When Heasley was on a bender, he could be very, very mean. You wouldn't want to shake him awake in the morning. We got orders to pull to the rear in reserve, to be relieved by the British. At that time Heasley was sleeping one off in his tent. Gibson started moving the battalion out, but he told Heasley's driver not to wake him up—to let Heasley sleep—and, when he woke up, bring him to the rear. The Brits moved into the area and found this lone tent with Heasley asleep inside. The brigadier was astonished and said, 'I say, old chap, what sort of army is this that you pull out and leave your battalion commander behind?' "[99]

The story—or similar versions—spread all through the 1st Cav Division. Charlie Palmer was no doubt aware of Heasley's drinking problem and had tolerated it, as Crombez had, for reasons not known. But the story reflected adversely on Palmer and Crombez, and for that reason Palmer was forced to relieve Heasley.

\*    \*    \*

At 3:00 P.M., after his tour of the 1st Cav Division, MacArthur returned to Suwon. There he held his customary press conference. The correspondents immediately sensed that this one would be something out of the ordinary. Standing by a potbellied stove in a tent, lighted by a bare bulb hanging from its ceiling, MacArthur read a written communiqué:[100]

Progress of the campaign continues to be satisfactory, with all three services— army, navy, air—performing well their completely coordinated tactical missions. Designed to meet abnormal military inhibitions, our strategic plan, involving constant movement to keep the enemy off-balance with a correspondent limitation upon his initiative, remains unaltered.

Our selection of the battle area, furthermore, has forced him into the military disadvantage of fighting far from his base and permitted greater employment of our air and sea arms against which he has little defense. There has been a resultant continuing and exhausting attrition upon both his manpower and supplies. There should be no illusions in this matter, however. In such a campaign of maneuver, as our battle lines shift north, the supply position of the enemy will progressively improve, just as inversely the effectiveness of our air potential will progressively diminish, thus in turn causing his numerical ground superiority to become of increasing battlefield significance.

Assuming no diminution of the enemy's flow of ground forces and matériel to the Korean battle area, a continuation of the existing limitations upon our freedom of counter-offensive action, and no major additions to our organizational strength, the battle lines cannot fail in time to reach a point of theoretical military stalemate. Thereafter our further advance would militarily benefit the enemy more than it would ourselves.

The exact place of stabilization is of necessity a fluctuating variable dependent upon the shifting relative strengths of forces committed and will constantly move up or down. Even now there are indications that the enemy is attempting to build up from China a new and massive offensive for the Spring. These are the salient factors which must continue to delimit strategical thinking and planning as the campaign proceeds.

This does not alter the fact, however, that the heavy toll we have taken of the enemy's military power since its commitment to war in Korea cannot fail to weaken his hold upon the Chinese nation and people and materially dampen his ardor for engaging in another aggressive adventure in Asia.

Even under our existing conditions of restraint it should be clearly evident to the Communist foe now committed against us that they cannot hope to impose their will on Korea by military force. They have failed twice—once through North Korean forces, and now through the military might of the Army of Communist China. Theirs was the aggression in both cases. Theirs has been the double failure. That they should continue this savage slaughter despite an almost hopeless chance of ultimate military success is a measure of their wanton disregard of international decencies and restraints and displays a complete contempt for the sanctity of human life. . . .

Vital decisions have yet to be made—decisions far beyond the scope of the authority vested in me as the military commander, decisions which are neither solely political nor solely military, but which must provide on the highest international levels an answer to the obscurities which now becloud the unsolved problems raised by Red China's undeclared war in Korea.[101]

Indeed, the statement *was* extraordinary. It was laced with subtle phrases criticizing the Truman administration: "abnormal military inhibitions"; "existing limitations upon our freedom of counter-offensive action"; "no major additions to our organized strength"; "our existing conditions of restraint"; "vital decisions have yet to be made"; "obscurities which now becloud the unsolved problems." It also ridiculed—and challenged—Peking at a time when the administration was still doing its utmost to coax Peking to the negotiating table. Beyond that it was an indiscreet and wholly unnecessary public review of military strategy. In that sense it provided Peking and the Chinese generals with a priceless look inside MacArthur's mind.

Seeking headlines, the media seized upon two phrases: "savage slaughter" and "theoretical military stalemate." In journalese, MacArthur's discourse would be boiled down and known as his "Die for Tie" statement. Thus truncated and interpreted, the statement had an unsettling and, in some quarters, a demoralizing impact on Eighth Army. "Stalemate" connoted defeat, not victory.

Beyond any doubt, MacArthur's broadside was clearly a calculated and premeditated flouting of Truman's December directive to clear such policy statements in Washington—the third violation within a period of about three weeks. To MacArthur watchers, a pattern seemed to be emerging. Mac-Arthur would fly to Korea, visit the battlefront, then issue a communiqué containing criticism of the administration's war policies. But again, no one in Washington felt inclined to rebut or reprimand him. Officially MacArthur was ignored.

## V

Operation Ripper proceeded. Eighth Army attacked across a fifty-mile front. Six corps (three American, three ROK), comprising eleven divisions (six American, five ROK), numbering about 150,000 men, were committed. The regiments inched along, uphill and down, line abreast ("shoulder to shoulder") leaving no pockets of enemy bypassed and no "gaps" for a CCF flanking move. Each regiment was supported by armor-infantry task forces and by division and corps artillery. Enemy resistance was light; nonetheless, the army progressed no more than a mile or two a day.[102]

In the early stages Ridgway kept a close eye on Sladen Bradley's 25th Division operations designed to outflank Seoul. The division moved slowly north into high ground of the Pukhan Valley, expanding its Han River beachhead. Its attached Turkish Brigade, which had adroitly feinted right on D day, crossed into the bridgehead and occupied ground on the right of Gilbert Check's 27th Infantry. On the left of Check, facing Seoul, Henry Britt's 24th Infantry performed in an outstanding manner, seizing all objectives on time or ahead of time. On the right (east) bank of the Pukhan River, Gerry Kelleher's 35th Infantry was relieved by elements of Babe Bryan's 24th Division, which had also, but less dramatically, crossed the Han on March 7.[103]

By March 10 it appeared that Ridgway's gambit had succeeded. Seoul was solidly outflanked; the NKPA I Corps had declined to attack the 25th Division in high ground. Enemy evacuation of the capital within a few days was now inevitable. With great pride Sladen Bradley reported to Shrimp Milburn that "the bridgehead is secure" and continued inching north on the west bank of the Pukhan River.[104]

The same day Ridgway opened his new advanced CP at Yoju. He described his new digs to George Marshall: "We are on a 25-foot bluff, facing north across the Han, with an incomparable view, rimmed in by mountains, which, as Spring now rapidly approaches, will yield more and more of the beauty of God's outdoors. . . ."[105] Having so established himself, Ridgway ordered Eighth Army main headquarters to decamp from Taegu and move forward eighty air miles to Chongju. This move, which placed the headquarters merely twenty-five miles south of Yoju, was both psychological and practical: to emphasize to the world that Eighth Army's movement north was permanent, to place senior staff officers closer to the reality of the battlefield, and to shorten Ridgway's commuting time between the headquarters.[106] Coincidental with this move Ridgway sacked the G-3, John Dabney, for whom he had developed a personal as well as professional dislike. In keeping with the policy of protecting the professional reputations of the senior officers in Korea, Ridgway endorsed a rave efficiency report for Dabney (prepared by Lev Allen) and gave him a DSM. Dabney returned to the States and subsequently rose to three stars before his retirement.[107]

Dabney was replaced by West Pointer (1922) Gilman C. ("Gim") Mudgett, fifty, older brother of the 21st Infantry exec, Fritz Mudgett. Gim Mudgett was a distinguished cavalryman and protégé of Lev Allen's. In World War II, after helping Don Faith's father (and Oveta Culp Hobby) establish the WAACs, Mudgett briefly commanded and trained an armored regiment but did not take it into combat. In England before D day, he was drafted into Omar Bradley's G-3 section, then into Bernard Montgomery's tactical headquarters as a senior American planner and liaison officer to Bradley. When Bradley activated his Twelfth Army Group, his chief of staff, Lev Allen, brought Mudgett back to serve as G-3 in Bradley's tactical headquarters. In these jobs Mudgett and Ridgway renewed an old acquaintanceship, and after the war Mudgett had served briefly with Ridgway in Panama, before becoming an instructor at the Command and General Staff School.[108]

Mudgett arrived to find the Eighth Army G-3 section still dominated by artillerymen. He left the artilleryman exec, William Bullock, in place, but he increased the infantry's voice by promoting Bill Train to chief of plans. Thereafter the G-3 section played a more prominent role in Eighth Army planning. However, Ridgway's primary war planner, Day Surles, remained independently in Yoju with Ridgway's personal staff.[109]

\*  \*  \*

From his CP in Yoju Ridgway could reach any part of Eighth Army's front by liaison plane in fifteen minutes or less. As the misnamed Ripper proceeded at its deliberate and methodical snail's pace, Ridgway spent most of every day at the front lines. War correspondent Gertrude Samuels wrote: "You could meet the general time after time in Korea. . . . He has been without rival as the most ubiquitous personality in the theater. He seemed to live on the air strips—he was constantly coming and going in his helicopter or light plane, to the front lines, to see field commanders, to find out how it went with the line men."[110]

On March 12 Ridgway spent the morning with the Marine division, which was closing in on its objective, Hongchon. After touring the frontline units on foot and having lunch with O. P. Smith, Ridgway jeeped and flew over the recovered Massacre Valley near Hoengsong, where the 2d Division support forces had been savaged.[111]

For five days Ridgway had stewed and fumed over MacArthur's unsettling and negative "Die for Tie" statement at Suwon. The tour of Massacre Valley may have intensified his frustration. Whatever the case, later that day Ridgway held a press conference at which he declared—in direct contradiction to MacArthur and with no prompting from Washington—that if Eighth Army reached the 38th Parallel, it would be a "tremendous victory." He went on:

We didn't set out to conquer China. We set out to stop Communism. We have demonstrated the superiority on the battlefield of our men. If China fails to throw us into the sea, that is a defeat for her of incalculable proportions. If China fails to drive us from Korea, she will have failed monumentally. . . .

The things for which we are fighting here are of such overwhelming importance I can't conceive of any member of our fighting forces feeling that there lies ahead any field of indefinite or indeterminate action.[112]

Dean Acheson himself could not have put it better. Possibly in rebuttal, or probably as part of his calculated campaign against the Truman administration, MacArthur let fly with yet another broadside. In response to a query from the United Press president Hugh Baillie, who had asked how many troops would be required to hold the 38th Parallel "inviolate," MacArthur again ridiculed positional warfare on a line:

As I have on several occasions pointed out, the conditions under which we are conducting military operations in Korea do not favor engaging in positional warfare on any line across the peninsula. Specifically with reference to the 38th Parallel, there are no natural defense features anywhere near its immediate proximity. The terrain is such that to establish a conventional defense system in reasonable depth would require such a sizable force that if we had it, and could logistically maintain it, we would be able to drive the Chinese Communists back across the Yalu, hold that river as our future main line of defense, and proceed to the accomplishment of our mission in the unification of Korea. Under the realities existing, however, we can and will, unless the situation is radically altered, continue our campaign of maneuver as the best means to neutralize the military disadvantage under which we fight and keep the enemy engaged where it best serves our own military purposes. Such a point of engagement will of necessity be a fluctuating variable, dependent upon the shifting relative strengths of the forces committed and will constantly move up or down. The problem requires much more fundamental decisions than are within my authority or responsibility to make as the military commander—decisions which must not ignore the heavy cost in Allied blood which a protracted and decisive campaign would entail.[113]

This broadside prompted not only headlines but also renewed and heated discussion. On the day it was released, White House reporters confronted Truman at a press conference for comment. Although MacArthur's statement was clearly another instance of insubordination—a fourth clear violation of Truman's December directive in as many weeks—the president remained remarkably calm and noncommittal. He continued to dodge, reiterating that any decision to cross the 38th Parallel was in the hands of the field commander.

\* \* \*

Ripper continued.

By March 14 the Marines had reached Line Albany and captured Hongchon. Enemy resistance had been "light," the Marine historian recorded. The Marines had "occupied rather than seized ground." Everywhere along the Eighth Army front the CCF and NKPA withdrawals appeared to be continuing.[114]

On the right of the Marines, progress in Almond's X Corps was less dramatic. The corps consisted of Ruffner's 2d Division, adjacent to the Marines, the rebuilt ROK 5th Division in the center, and Ferenbaugh's 7th Division on the right. In this sector the terrain was almost indescribably rugged. The "roads" were merely mountain trails. Jeeps, trucks, and tractors bogged down in deep mud. Most supplies had to be brought forward on A frames by Korean porters.[115]

By this time Buddy Ferenbaugh and his ADC, Bob Sink, had a firm grip on the 7th Division. Both men led bravely at the very front lines. The new staff worried that one or the other—or both—would be killed or captured. Almost inevitably Ferenbaugh had a very close call.

A tanker in the 32d Tank Company, Chester Bair, a survivor of Task Force MacLean at the Chosin Reservoir, remembered that day. His platoon of tanks were roadbound, waiting for the infantry to clear considerable enemy from the high ground overlooking the "road" before proceeding. Ferenbaugh came up in his command jeep with its two-star flag flying and impatiently "demanded to know why the tanks were blocking the road" and ordered them out of the way. "We tried to explain the situation," Bair wrote, "but he wasn't listening."

Ferenbaugh got around the tanks and went up the road. Moments later enemy machine guns raked his command jeep and another following with MP bodyguards. The heavy fire killed Ferenbaugh's driver and the MPs in the second jeep. Ferenbaugh and his aide dived into a ditch, then crawled up the side of a hill until they found cover. There they remained under enemy fire for hours while the division attempted a rescue. Bair remembered:

We contacted the infantry and requested permission to go forward and rescue the general. Permission denied. The infantry wanted this glory—they needed Brownie points. They sent a platoon of Rangers. The Rangers got shot up and had to fall back. Then the infantry sent a full line company. They took heavy casualties and had to return to the perimeter. While all this was going on, we kept telling the infantry we could rescue him with our tanks. By now it was late afternoon and if they didn't rescue the general before dark, the enemy would probably take him POW. Finally the infantry sent us in.

The tank platoon went forward into intense enemy machine-gun fire, Bair's tank leading. When the tanks reached the wrecked jeeps, they spotted Ferenbaugh and his aide on the hill, "waving a flag." The tank platoon leader, a lieutenant, bravely left his tank and ran through a hail of enemy fire to Ferenbaugh's position, while Bair and others provided a fusillade of covering fire. Ferenbaugh and his aide wanted to wait until dark to come out, but the lieutenant insisted they leave at once because the tanks would be too vulnerable to enemy attack after dark. Bair went on:

So they all got up and ran like hell down to my tank. When they got close I dropped down through the escape hatch and motioned them to crawl in. We all got inside and returned to friendly lines. The general and his aide thanked us and had us all stand in front of the tank for pictures. The general's aide got a Silver Star for his bravery; but our lieutenant only got his picture sent to his hometown newspaper. His girlfriend's name was Alice; the name of our tank was "Grace." So the lieutenant got a "Dear John" from Alice.[116]

Notwithstanding this kind of frontline leadership, the division's 31st Infantry remained a weak sister. One large problem in the regiment was its commander, West Pointer John Gavin. In the words of his senior subordinates, Gavin was "a fine man," "very proper" and "studious," but also "a real cold fish" who "acted as though he really didn't wish to get himself dirty with combat." For Ned Almond, the situation must have been exasperating. He had sacked the 31st's original commander, Richard Ovenshine; the second, Allan MacLean, had been killed at Chosin. Now its third commander within five months had failed to inspire the regiment.[117]

Believing the 31st required very special attention, Almond sacked Gavin on March 12. To replace him, Almond chose one of the brightest stars in X

Corps, his deputy chief of staff and protégé, Bill McCaffrey. West Pointer (1938) McCaffrey thus became the youngest officer and the first in his class to command a regiment in Korea. His assignment was ridiculed in some quarters as another case of Almond firing someone to give one of his "teacher's pets" a job,* but within the 31st Regiment McCaffrey was warmly welcomed. One of its veteran officers, Richard Mitchell, remembered that his new commander was "quite a contrast to Gavin." McCaffrey was "always enthusiastic, very outgoing with an impish grin and a twinkle in his eye, and one hell of a combat commander."[118]

McCaffrey took over with a firm but intelligent hand. He found that two of the three battalion commanders were very good: William R. Lynch (2/31) and Donald C. Rubottom (3/31). They had been appointed to command in the wake of the regiment's arduous withdrawal from Chosin and Koto and had rebuilt and retrained their outfits. However, the 1/31 commander, McCaffrey remembered, was "one of the greatest frauds I've ever known." After McCaffrey had replaced him with a new and able commander, the regiment began to pull together as a team. "All the raw material was there," a senior officer 31st commander remembered. "It just needed to be shaped and properly led." McCaffrey recalled modestly: "I had good lungs and stout legs."[119]

At about this same time the 32d Regiment also got a new commander, but for a different reason. Its commander, Charles Beauchamp, who had rushed to Korea in July to command the 34th Infantry temporarily at Taejon, had been in combat almost continuously for nine months and was overdue for relief. He left to join Pinky Wright's G-3 section in Tokyo and subsequently rose to two stars. He was replaced by his exec, West Pointer Charles Mount, who had commanded the 2/32 at Inchon and later. Mount was a classmate of McCaffrey's but, at thirty-five, a year younger. Mount thus superseded McCaffrey as the youngest officer in Korea to command a regiment.[120]

# VI

In all the debate about crossing the 38th Parallel, no one had bothered to consult Syngman Rhee. In fact, his views were already well known: Total victory; total unification of Korea by force.

Rhee was encamped in Pusan with the ROK government. Infuriated by Ridgway's March 12 declaration that an Eighth Army advance to the 38th

---

*To date, the X Corps parade to command included, among others, Nick Ruffner for Bob McClure; Jack Chiles for Paul Freeman; Bill Quinn for Herb Powell; Olinto Barsanti for Joe Gerot, to understudy Ed Messinger. The parade was to continue.

Parallel would be a "tremendous" victory for the UN, Rhee felt betrayed and drafted a communiqué demanding a return to the Yalu.

Ambassador John Muccio attempted to stop the communiqué and admonished the Rhee government. Muccio cabled Acheson:

I emphatically pointed out . . . that it was time for all Koreans to stop getting agitated every time anyone mentioned the 38th Parallel and that this would be a good time for all of them to re-read the United Nations resolutions passed since June 25. In this connection I mentioned that the all-important issue and the United Nations commitment is to stop aggression. The United Nations policy is still aimed at a united, independent and democratic Korea, but there is no commitment anywhere that I know of requiring the United Nations or United States to bring in any amount of force that may be needed to unify Korea.[121]

Rhee was also furious about two other matters. First, Eighth Army was advancing all across Korea except against Seoul. Why was the capital being bypassed and left in the hands of the enemy? Secondly, Eighth Army had barred most ROK farmers from returning to liberated areas to plant the rice crop. Did not Ridgway realize that the rice crop would be essential not only to feed South Korea but to bolster the ROK economy by exports?

Muccio believed a personal call on Rhee by Ridgway might do much to placate the Korean government. Accordingly, on March 15, Ridgway flew to Pusan, consulted with Muccio, then called on Rhee.[122] Muccio remembered that Rhee "brought up the matter of the 38th Parallel, speaking in a rambling fashion of vague plans to telegraph President Truman and General MacArthur concerning the necessity of bombing Manchuria." Muccio attempted to calm Rhee, but he got nowhere. "It is doubtful," Muccio cabled Acheson, "that any words or logic could swing the President from his insistence that Korea must be unified at whatever risk or cost." That view, Muccio cautioned in conclusion, "could logically lead to violent charges of betrayal in the event of any compromise of the Korean conflict."[123]

Ridgway addressed the matter of bypassing Seoul and restricting the return of the farmers to the rice paddies. He pointed out to Rhee that "I was not ready to work on Seoul; that we were playing a dangerous game, with a numerically vastly superior enemy in terrain which stretched our logistics capabilities to the limit; and that therefore, the tide of battle might go back and forth repeatedly. For these reasons I hoped that only a minimum number of farmers essential to plant the coming crop be permitted to return to the northern areas.[124]

Ridgway, fresh from his tour of Massacre Valley, took this occasion to denounce the performance of the ROK Army. He told Rhee: "This was war we were in and not peacetime maneuvers or training. Therefore I expected that senior [ROK] commanders whose troops disintegrated under attack, and above all, those whose troops abandoned equipment, would be sternly and summarily dealt with."[125]

As it happened, the very same day, March 15, the ROK 1st Division, holding static defensive positions across the Han from Seoul, received word from a line crosser that the NKPA had withdrawn well north to Uijongbu, leaving the capital deserted. The ROKs sent a patrol across the Han and discovered the report to be true. Seoul, now a devastated, disease-infested pile of rubble, was unoccupied by the enemy. Having reached the National Assembly Hall, the patrol hauled down the NKPA flag and raised the ROK flag, then spent the night. For the fourth time in the war Seoul had changed hands—this time with no ceremony.[126]

Ridgway was enormously pleased. The key feature of Ripper—the flanking move on Seoul—to force the enemy either to attack I Corps in high ground under adverse conditions or to abandon the city had worked as designed. Seventeen years later he wrote: "I consider the surprise crossing of the Han River by I Corps . . . in the face of numerically superior stronger Chinese Communist forces during Operation RIPPER, was the most successful single action fought by troops under my command during either World War II in Europe or in Korea."[127]

\* \* \*

Ridgway's cool and intelligent management of Eighth Army in Operations Killer and Ripper transformed him almost overnight into a world celebrity. War correspondents in Korea found Ridgway, in contrast with Johnnie Walker, friendly, cordial, and approachable. They described him with copy that fairly gushed with praise. *Time* magazine featured Ridgway on the cover of the March 5 issue. The accompanying story was a glowing tribute, with more praise from Omar Bradley. This was Ridgway's second appearance on *Time*'s cover. The first time had been April 2, 1945, to highlight a review of airborne operations in the ETO.[128]

Accolades from notables poured in. George Marshall, whom Ridgway respected over all other men in American history, wrote to say: "I think you are doing a magnificent job amidst many hardships." From his NATO headquarters Eisenhower cabled Ridgway via MacArthur to say he thought Ridgway was performing "brilliantly" and that "every success you have makes our job easier." Omar Bradley wrote again, commenting on the "masterly fashion" Ridgway was handling Eighth Army. Dean Rusk, no doubt reflecting the general view at State, said: "Your spectacular success in getting the situation turned right around and in getting tails up has had a tremendous effect right round the globe. . . . If we succeed, there will be hundreds of millions of people eternally grateful to you and your men who are packing the load."[129]

There was, in fact, only one criticism. Some seniors in the State Department objected to the code name Killer. One high-level State planner memoed Rusk: "The term 'Operation KILLER' has had a most unfortunate effect. This slogan has stuck in the public mind as representing the objectives, nature, and meaning of the whole action in Korea. I fear that to many people Korea now means only killing, a process of killing Americans, Chinese and Koreans." Collins passed the comments to Ridgway with the recommendation that Ridgway adopt more benign code names. Ridgway "did not understand why it was objectionable to acknowledge the fact that war was concerned with killing the enemy." He was "by nature opposed to any effort to 'sell' war to people as an only mildly unpleasant business that requires very little in the way of blood."[130]

Nonetheless, Ridgway acquiesced. Code name Killer and its extension, Ripper, were deleted from further operational orders. The onward Eighth Army advance was rechristened Operation Courageous.

# 24

# COURAGEOUS, TOMAHAWK, AND RUGGED

## I

The enemy withdrawal from Seoul opened a path northward to the Imjin River, where Ridgway intended to anchor Eighth Army's left flank. To exploit this withdrawal, Ridgway enlarged the I Corps role in Courageous. On March 15 he ordered that:

* Shorty Soule's 3d Division, still encamped on the south bank of the Han opposite Seoul, would immediately cross the river, skirt Seoul to the east, and occupy the eastern sector of Line Lincoln, north of the city athwart the Seoul–Uijongbu road. It would tie in with the 25th Division on the right.
* The ROK 1st Division, likewise encamped on the south bank of the Han, would simultaneously cross the river west of Seoul and proceed to Line Lincoln, athwart the Seoul–Munsan road. It would tie in with the 3d Division.
* Tom Brodie's British Brigade, in I Corps Reserve, would move forward to Yongdungpo to maintain local security and reinforce Line Lincoln if required.[1]

The 3d Division had long been planning for a Han River crossing. William Harris's Puerto Rican 65th Regiment, supported by Harry Stella's black 58th FAB, had been designated to make the assault. Harris, in turn, had chosen Herman Dammer's 2/65 to spearhead the crossing. Believing that the crossing "could have been murder," Dammer's men had been rehearsing the operation in rear areas for about two weeks.[2]

When Harris got the word that the enemy had pulled out of Seoul and the

753

crossing would be a "Sunday stroll," he was vastly relieved. "It was almost unbelievable," he wrote. "The Chinese must have known that they could have cut us to ribbons—they couldn't help but know—yet here they were pulling back. . . . Why they did what they did, we will probably never know."[3]

Supported by the 10th Engineer Combat Battalion, commanded by Leslie M. Gross, and by Stella's 58th FAB, A/A weapons, and tanks, Dammer's 2/65 crossed the Han in boats and DUKWs, unopposed, on March 16. The assault boats were utilized to build rafts to ferry across trucks and tanks. Subsequently Gross's engineers built a pontoon bridge, unofficially named for Al Jolson, then, finally, Carney Bridge, after an engineer, Robert W. Carney, who had been killed in earlier action.[4]

The 2/65 pushed warily north, skirting east around Seoul to Line Lincoln, on the Uijongbu road. The Puerto Ricans encountered no enemy resistance but found numerous booby traps and land mines. They were followed by Saint St. Clair's 1/65, which crossed the Han on March 17, and Jerry Allen's 3/65, which crossed on the 18th. The full 65th Regiment occupied Line Lincoln, tying in with the 1st ROK Division, which had crossed the Han west of Seoul, according to plan, and the 25th Division, which had come up on the right.[5]

Moving into Seoul to pick up the pieces, UN service forces found a sorry mess. Of the city's original 1.5 million population, only about 200,000 remained. Most citizens had fled south; the NKPA had brutally murdered hundreds. The survivors had no water, electricity, or food. Typhus and other diseases were rampant. *Time* magazine concluded: "The fourth fall of Seoul was a sad business, something like the capture of a tomb."[6]

Peking Radio pronounced the CCF-NKPA withdrawal from Seoul to be "temporary"; the CCF would return. Ridgway did not doubt that the capital would be a prime CCF objective in the near future. When the CCF offensive came, Ridgway would again make every effort to hold a "Seoul perimeter." Accordingly he ordered Gar Davidson and Pat Strong to make Line Lincoln (sometimes called Line Golden), north of the city, as nearly impregnable as possible.[7]

Although Strong had his hands full—rebuilding bridges, restoring Inchon's demolished port facilities, bringing the railroads forward, building roads—he gave Line Lincoln highest priority. Pursuing these many tasks around Seoul, he was astonished—and pleased—to find that the CCF and NKPA had left undisturbed matériel that Eighth Army had earlier abandoned. Attributing this to a "reluctance to destroy military property," Strong added later: "At Seoul, where we had abandoned and partially destroyed a floating bridge because it was frozen hard into the ice, we found the component parts of the bridge neatly stacked on the bank of the river, awaiting our return."[8]

\* \* \*

On the central front the Marine division closed slowly and cautiously on Hongchon, flanked by Palmer's 1st Cav on the left and Ruffner's 2d Division on the right. Believing Hongchon to be a CCF-NKPA assembly point and therefore infested with enemy, Ridgway ordered the new IX Corps commander, Bill Hoge, to do everything possible to trap and kill, rather than simply to push back, the enemy. He urged Hoge to abandon the "stereotyped" line abreast (or "shoulder to shoulder") advance and capture Hongchon by "maneuver" of regiments or battalions, "within and between division zones."[9]

Division, regimental, and battalion planners churned out reams of maneuver plans, but all for naught. On March 15 and 16 the enemy rear guard abruptly withdrew from Hongchon to retreat north toward Chunchon. Homer Litzenberg's Seventh Marines occupied the deserted town. On the left the 1st Cav moved forward to the Hongchon River and, after rooting enemy from nearby hills, crossed and struck for Chunchon. On the right the 2d Division pulled abreast of the Marines at Pungam.[10]

The 2d Division had had a rough few days. The terrain was so rugged the lead regiments had had to advance in single file. After Chiles's 23d Infantry had gone into reserve on March 13, John Coughlin's 38th spearheaded the attack; Ed Messinger's 9th followed in its footsteps. On March 14 and 15 Coughlin's 38th had been checked by a large NKPA force, which blocked a pass. After punching through the block with tremendous artillery barrages and A/A fire, the 38th had counted 345 enemy dead (and estimated another 800 NKPA dead or wounded) and had captured 139 POWs. In return, Coughlin had incurred a stiff 168 casualties: 12 killed and 156 wounded.[11]

\* \* \*

On March 17 MacArthur flew to Korea to visit the Marine division. Ridgway again met his plane in Suwon. It was MacArthur's sixth trip to Korea since Ridgway had assumed command of Eighth Army.

The party transferred to a C-47 and flew from Suwon to Wonju. During the half hour flight Ridgway raised a subject the two men had not discussed before in detail: possible Soviet military intervention in Korea.

Rumors about Soviet intervention had intensified since Stalin's bellicose "interview" in *Pravda*. The FBI had received an anonymous but authoritative-sounding letter which stated that the writer had information to the effect that the Soviet Union would enter the war in Korea in April with full-scale army, navy, and air attacks and might also invade Japan and Alaska. Some CCF POWs told similar stories: Soviet aircraft and ground units, fully equipped with artillery, would enter the war in Korea. Chiang Kai-shek's intelligence section on Formosa reported that "two mechanized Soviet divisions" were already in Korea and that other Soviet ground forces were poised at the Tumen River on the Soviet-Korean border. The British attaché in Moscow had cabled that a "reliable source" had informed him that Soviet "volunteers" were being recruited for service in Korea.

Allied intelligence agencies in Washington, London, Tokyo, and elsewhere had analyzed these reports minutely. The conclusion was that "there is no military indication of a Soviet intention to enter the Korean conflict." However, the Pentagon had warned GHQ in Tokyo: "It must be emphasized that the USSR military forces in the Far East are considered to be currently organized, equipped and disposed in such manner to permit initiation of action without warning."[12]

Ridgway had no means of independently evaluating the rumors. However, he had begun preliminary work on plans in case they proved to be true. Should Soviet ground forces intervene in support of the CCF and NKPA ground forces in the coming favorable weather, Eighth Army would withdraw immediately to the Davidson Line at Pusan, in preparation for evacuation from Korea. The plan would include a "single code word," which, when flashed, would initiate the withdrawal "without the slightest delay."[13]

The plans were very closely held. One reason was Ridgway's continuing fear of wholesale ROK defections. In an emergency evacuation of the type envisioned, there probably would not be time to evacuate the ROKs. Should that happen, Ridgway (as he wrote) would not "blame them" for defecting. As an added precaution, Ridgway ordered that no intent to evacuate would be announced until Eighth Army had withdrawn below Wonju; "otherwise ROK defections might leave us with both flanks exposed at a point where we could be enveloped and severely damaged."[14]

Ridgway revealed these plans to MacArthur. MacArthur, Ridgway noted, "stated his full concurrence."[15]

At Wonju Bill Hoge and O. P. Smith met the party with a caravan of jeeps. Smith, who had been informed that MacArthur would spend "three hours" with the Marines, told MacArthur that the division was so spread out—from Wonju to Hongchon and beyond—that a complete tour could not be accomplished within three hours. MacArthur replied that he had plenty of time and that he was particularly desirous of seeing an "assault battalion" at work on the front.[16]

The tour turned into a long (nearly five-hour) grueling ride over terrible roads, during which MacArthur never once left the jeep. On the return trip to Wonju, MacArthur was full of five-star gossip. Omar Bradley might leave the active list* when his two-year term as JCS chairman expired in August. Eisenhower might also be leaving NATO toward the end of the year and go on the inactive list.[17]

---

*By law, five-star generals could not retire in the conventional sense but served at the pleasure of the president. When not serving the president, they reverted to the inactive list.

Another rumor directly affected Ridgway. If, as expected, Eisenhower left NATO, MacArthur said, Joe Collins might replace him as supreme commander. "If that happens," MacArthur grandly pronounced, "I want to put you in as chief of staff." No doubt astonished, Ridgway answered something to the effect that "Washington service" had "no appeal" to him and "let the matter drop."[18] There was, in fact, some truth to that rumor. The proposed appointment of Collins to NATO was part of Bradley's scheme to limit Collins's tour as chief of staff so that Ridgway could replace him.[19]

Finally, at 4:00 P.M., the party arrived back at the Wonju airstrip. Since MacArthur had never left the jeep and it would have been a violation of protocol, or at least awkward, for Ridgway or Smith to have done so, both men were nearly desperate to urinate. Smith remembered:

If you've ever ridden for four or five hours in a rough-riding jeep, you've got to go to the head. Well, nobody ever suggested stopping. . . . The general marched majestically off to his plane and all the rest of us just disappeared! General Ridgway came to me and said, "Smith, why in hell didn't you suggest that we stop and take a leak?" I said, "Well, you're the senior, and I think it was up to you to suggest that." Maybe the Old Man had a rubber bag, or something.[20]

The next important objective on the central front was Chunchon, another road hub and CCF assembly point, eight miles below the 38th Parallel. There Ridgway hoped IX Corps would finally trap and kill some CCF or NKPA forces by maneuver. Chunchon lay in the path of the 1st Cav Division, now spearheaded by Marcel Crombez's 5th Cav on the right and Bob Blanchard's 8th Cav on the left. Charlie Palmer directed Blanchard and Crombez to seize Chunchon with armor-infantry teams deployed in an intricate double envelopment.[21]

To this plan paratrooper Ridgway added a new element on March 19: a drop of the 187th Airborne Combat Team slightly north of Chunchon to block the escape of the CCF and NKPA. The paratroopers would jump on the morning of March 22, as the 5th and 8th Cav closed the armored pincers. The plans were drawn by Ridgway's paratrooper protégé in the Eighth Army G-3 section, Hank Adams, who christened the operation Hawk.[22]

Frank Bowen welcomed the assignment. His elite force had been in Korea for six months. It had conducted only one airborne operation, and that had been a disappointment. The outfit was eager and ready, but again the logisticians frowned. Hawk would remove about 135 aircraft from supply-hauling duties for nearly a week. That would deny Eighth Army at least 2,000 tons of high-priority cargo. The G-4s protested in vain; the 187th wanted to show its stuff.[23]

The 5th and 8th Cav regiments, heavily supported by tanks, closed on Chunchon. Both regiments ran into pockets of enemy fire, but an artillery spotter plane, flying over the city at fifty feet, reported it deserted.[24] Charlie Palmer ordered patrols into Chunchon; Ridgway went to look for himself:

Mike Lynch and I flew over the city just as the patrols were entering. . . . We found a street that seemed long and straight enough for a landing strip. The only problem was provided by some still-hanging telephone lines on high poles at the end of the street. After two or three passes Mike decided he could come in under the wires without trouble and set the plane down safely.

We had spotted a jeep patrol as we were circling and I set out immediately on foot in search of it. It turned out to be a 1st Cavalry Division Engineer patrol which, when I approached, was checking a major bridge to disarm any demolition charge the enemy might have placed. They were surprised to find the bridge undamaged and unwired. But when they looked around to discover the Army Commander peeking over their shoulders they were really astonished, hardly knowing how to react.[25]

This extraordinary reconnaissance revealed to Ridgway that Hawk would be unprofitable because the enemy had withdrawn too deeply, and he therefore canceled the operation. By this time, however, the huge fleet of troop carrier planes had arrived in Taegu. To have returned them to Japan unused would have been acutely embarrassing and would have drawn criticism. Accordingly Ridgway incorporated the 187th Airborne Combat Team into a plan he was working on to advance Shrimp Milburn's I Corps from Line Lincoln to the Imjin River at Munsan. Hank Adams and Frank Bowen hurriedly shifted targets and renamed the drop Tomahawk. It would be carried out on the morning of March 23.[26]

## II

In Tokyo on March 20 MacArthur confronted two important documents. The first was a letter from an old, old friend, Congressman Joseph W. Martin, Jr., of Massachusetts, who was minority leader in the House of Representatives. Martin was an "Asia first" zealot and a harsh critic of the Truman administration. In particular, he deplored the Truman decision to reject the use of the Chinese Nationalist forces on Formosa.[27] Martin wrote MacArthur:

In the current discussions of foreign policy and overall strategy many of us have been distressed that, although the European aspects have been heavily emphasized, we have been without the views of yourself as Commander in Chief of the Far Eastern Command.

I think it is imperative to the security of our Nation and for the safety of the world that policies of the United States embrace the broadest possible strategy and that in our earnest desire to protect Europe we not weaken our position in Asia.

Martin enclosed a copy of a speech he had delivered on February 12, stressing that point and further—much further—suggesting that "the forces of Generalissimo Chiang Kai-shek on Formosa might be employed in the opening of a second Asiatic front to relieve the pressure on our forces in Korea." He requested MacArthur's views "on a confidential basis or otherwise." He concluded: "Your admirers are legion, and the respect you command is enormous. May success be yours in the gigantic undertaking which you direct."[28]

The second document was a "Top Secret-Priority" message from the JCS. It indicated that State had won the debate over whether or not to cross the 38th Parallel:

State planning Presidential announcement shortly that, with clearing of bulk of South Korea of aggressors, United Nations now prepared to discuss conditions of settlement in Korea. Strong UN feeling persists that further diplomatic effort towards settlement should be made before any advance with major forces north of 38th Parallel. Time will be required to develop diplomatic reactions and permit new negotiations that may develop. Recognizing that parallel has no military significance, State has asked JCS what authority you should have to permit sufficient freedom of action for next few weeks to provide security for UN forces and maintain contact with enemy. Your recommendation is desired.[29]

The JCS cable must have enraged MacArthur. It was a clear signal that he had finally and decisively lost the Korean War policy battle. There was no longer the slightest hope that Washington would adopt his plan for a complete military subjugation of North Korea and for expanding the war to Red China itself: the naval blockade; the bombing of the defense industry; an invasion of the mainland by Chiang Kai-shek. He later said (paranoically) that this JCS cable, moreover, revealed to him a sinister and disgraceful Washington conspiracy to turn Formosa over to Peking and to seat Red China in the UN.[30]

It was likely that on that day, March 20, MacArthur made the decision to launch an all-out public attack on the Truman administration. His four earlier broadsides evidently had not made the desired impact; they had been overshadowed by the electrifying successes of Eighth Army. In the opinion of his biographer D. Clayton James, MacArthur's objective was "nothing less" than to cause a "major redirection of American foreign and military policies, particularly toward placing a much higher priority on what he believed to be national self-interests at stake in East Asia."[31]

MacArthur had to know that this public campaign would almost certainly result in his relief from command. To attack the administration strongly and publicly would be not only a flagrant act of disloyalty but also yet another direct violation of Truman's December directive, constituting legal justification for dismissal. His decision to set himself up for almost certain dismissal was later described by some historians as an unconscious act of self-destruction. More likely it was a deliberate, coolly calculated act of martyrdom, designed to dramatize and personalize his attack on the administration.[32]

MacArthur's all-out attack on the Truman administration would be twofold:

• An unrestricted response to Joe Martin's letter, which was certain to be released by Martin and which might serve to polarize and strengthen anti-Truman sentiment in Congress.
• A communiqué directed at Peking which would upstage—and sabotage—Truman's proposed "announcement" of a new peace initiative.

That day MacArthur wrote Joe Martin:

I am most grateful for your note . . . forwarding me a copy of your address. . . . The latter I have read with much interest, and find that with the passage of years you have certainly lost none of your old-time punch. My views and recommendations with respect to the situation created by Red China's entry into the war against us in Korea have been submitted to Washington in most complete detail. Generally, these views are well known and clearly understood, as they follow the conventional pattern of meeting force with maximum counterforce, as we have never failed to do in the past. Your view with respect to the utilization of the Chinese forces on Formosa is in conflict with neither logic nor this tradition.

It seems strangely difficult for some to realize that here in Asia is where the Communist conspirators have elected to make their play for global conquest and that we have joined the issue they raised on the battlefield; that here we fight Europe's war with arms while the diplomats there still fight it with words; that if we lose the war to Communism in Asia the fall of Europe is inevitable, win it and Europe most probably would avoid war and yet preserve freedom. As you pointed out, we must win. There is no substitute for victory.

With renewed thanks and expressions of most cordial regard, I am faithfully yours.[33]

In response to the JCS cable requesting his "recommendations" to the proposed presidential "announcement," MacArthur directed one more curt slap:

Recommend that no further military restrictions be imposed upon the United Nations Command in Korea. The inhibitions which already exist should not be increased. The military disadvantages arising from restrictions upon the scope of our Air and Naval operations coupled with the disparity between the size of our command and the enemy ground potential renders it completely impracticable to attempt to clear North Korea or to make any appreciable effort to that end.[34]

Washington sent MacArthur no further guidance or directives about crossing the 38th Parallel. On March 21 (March 22, Tokyo time) Dean Acheson stated in a press conference that MacArthur required "no new authority" to cross the 38th Parallel.[35] President Truman had said publicly that the decision was up to the commander in the field. Even so, MacArthur was at first uncharacteristically cautious. On March 22 he telexed Ridgway a "flash" message:

Do not cross 38th Parallel in force without previous authority from me. If Press forces you to discuss question, evade direct reply, by saying matter is for my decision. I expect new directive from Washington shortly.

My present intention is to continue current type of action north of parallel but not to proceed further than your logistics would adequately support a major operation. At that time to pass from present tactics which you have so ably conducted to ranger type of probing by battalions or companies from divisional fronts operating for ten day periods with self-contained supplies supplemented by various guerrilla-type activities. If you have any suggestions let me have them. I will try to come over on Saturday [March 24] to talk with you.[36]

Ridgway responded immediately: "Shall issue all necessary instructions to insure compliance, interpreting the phrase 'in force' as permitting up to and including one reinforced infantry battalion per corps, should opportunity offer for useful employment of such force. Shall handle Press in accordance with your wishes."[37]

By this time Ridgway had solidified his thinking about how far Eighth Army should advance beyond the 38th Parallel to ensure its safety and disrupt the expected CCF offensive. He contemplated far more than MacArthur's battalion-size probes and guerrilla raids. For the first time he revealed his plan to MacArthur: Eighth Army would advance to a "general line" (named Kansas) running northeast at the Imjin River to Chorwon (the Iron Triangle), thence easterly on the south shore of the Hwachon Reservoir to the Sea of Japan at Yangyang. Ridgway went on to say:

Operations incident to reaching such a line would still have as their objective not the seizure of terrain but the maximum destruction of hostile persons and matériel at minimum cost to our forces and maintenance intact of all major units.

. . . In event you find it inconvenient to visit here within next few days would like to send two of my senior officers to you so that the foregoing concepts may be amplified in more and clearer detail.[38]

## III

Ridgway revised and refined his plans to bring I Corps forward from Line Lincoln at Seoul to the Imjin River at Munsan. The corps would attack with a big glamorous bang on March 23, employing all the available weapons at Ridgway's command: airborne troops; massed armor; motorized artillery; regular infantry. It was hoped that the advance to the Imjin would "trap" the 60,000 men of the NKPA I Corps, which had occupied Seoul and had withdrawn northward to Munsan.* The final plan:

• The 187th Airborne Combat Team would jump at Munsan (Operation Tomahawk) to capture it and establish a block to trap the NKPA I Corps.
• Two powerful armored task forces would strike north Patton-style, from Line Lincoln, one up the road to Munsan, one up the road to Uijongbu. The task force to Munsan would "link up" with the paratroopers to help trap the NKPA I Corps.
• The ROK 1st Division and Shorty Soule's 3d Division would follow the armored task forces, the ROK 1st to Munsan, Soule's 3d to Uijongbu and beyond.[39]

If successful, these I Corps maneuvers would bring Eighth Army forward to a west-east line running from Munsan to Chunchon, about eight miles south of the 38th Parallel. Even though this line left Eighth Army weak and vulnerable in the center, Ridgway would not go beyond the line without specific authorization from MacArthur. To ensure compliance with this restriction, Ridgway telexed Milburn, Hoge, and Almond: "Employment of major forces across the 38th Parallel will not be made without express authority from me. You may employ forces not to exceed one reinforced infantry battalion per corps."[40]

The two armored task forces which would spearhead the I Corps ground attack assembled on Line Lincoln. The force assigned to Munsan and the paratrooper linkup was John Growdon's 6th Tank Battalion (Pattons), which had been operating in support of the 24th Division in IX Corps. It was supported by all-black self-propelled armored artillery units: two 105-mm batteries of Harry Stella's 58th FAB (normally in support of the 65th Infantry) and one 155-mm battery of Kenneth Dawalt's 999th FAB (then in support of the ROK 1st Division). Jim Boswell's 7th Infantry provided Growdon a

---

*It was believed the NKPA I Corps consisted of about four combat divisions: the 7th (mechanized), the 8th, the 19th, and 27th, plus corps support forces and numerous police and occupation personnel.

battalion of infantry—the 2/7, commanded by Lawson McGruder—for protection. The force assigned to Uijongbu was Wilson Hawkins's black 64th Tank Battalion. It was reinforced by two tank platoons, one each from the 15th and the 65th Infantry Regiments, but it had no direct infantry support.[41]

The paratroopers assembled at the Taegu Airfield. For a while Ridgway seriously considered jumping with them, repeating his Normandy adventure. But he concluded (as he said later) that would be a "damned fool thing to do." If he broke an ankle or cracked a knee (or threw out his trick back), he would probably have to relinquish command of Eighth Army to someone else, "the last thing in the world I wanted to do." Instead of jumping, he decided to have Mike Lynch fly him into the DZ in a lightplane during the operation.[42]

\* \* \*

On the morning of March 23 an aide woke Ridgway early to bring him an urgent and astonishing message from MacArthur. He had rescinded his twenty-four-hour-old instructions and authorized Ridgway to cross the 38th Parallel in force and attack northward to Ridgway's proposed new "general line" (Kansas). MacArthur cabled: "Am in complete accord with the plan you have outlined to advance to the phase line indicated in your message. Make no announcements to this effect and allow the actual events to constitute sole press information. Further action beyond your suggested phase line will be determined by you in accordance with my previous message. Will see you at Seoul airfield Saturday."[43]

Washington had still sent no further instructions to MacArthur about crossing the 38th Parallel. Although both Truman and Acheson had stated publicly that the decision to cross the parallel was up to the commander in the field, these statements were not official directives. The last official message from the JCS on the subject had implied that MacArthur should not cross with "major forces," pending diplomatic talks with allies. MacArthur himself had stated in his February 11 cable that he would request instructions from the JCS before crossing the 38th Parallel.\* But he did not adhere to this promise; he made the decision on his own. No JCS authorization to cross the 38th Parallel was ever issued.[44]

Later that morning, March 23, Bowen's paratroopers, reinforced by two Ranger companies (2d and 4th), boarded the 135 aircraft at Taegu: 80 C-119s; 55 C-46s. The weather was "perfect." At seven-thirty the planes began taking off in clouds of dust. The air crews were relieved to get away. Their planes had been parked at Taegu wingtip to wingtip for two long days, presenting a rich

---

\* "If it should develop that no major enemy strength is disposed south of the 38th Parallel, report will be made to the JCS and instructions requested before proceeding further."

target to the CCF Air Force or guerrillas. Besides that, the dust had begun to gum up engines.[45]

The planners had selected two DZs for the drop, one to the north of Munsan, one to the south. The bulk of the combat team would jump on the north DZ: Bowen and staff, Delbert Munson's 3/187 (in the lead), John Connor's 2/187, the two Ranger companies, and Harry F. Lambert's 674th FAB. Harry Wilson's 1/187 would jump on the south DZ to provide a linkup base for the I Corps armored task force.[46]

FEAF flooded the air between Seoul and Munsan with supporting aircraft. These aircraft bombed and strafed the Seoul–Munsan road, suspected enemy emplacements or assembly areas, and the DZs. Sixteen F-51 Mustangs escorted the formation of troop carrier planes, which flew over the Yellow Sea to come at Munsan directly from the west.[47]

Shortly after takeoff the lead aircraft in the serial carrying Harry Wilson's 1/187 developed mechanical problems and was forced to abort and return to Taegu. The deputy flight leader moved up to the lead position. As luck would have it, Wilson was riding in the aborted plane. On the ground in Taegu, he demanded that a replacement plane be provided at once. It was, but Wilson, his exec, and some other staffers fell far behind the schedule.[48]

At about 9:00 A.M. the lead serial, Munson's 3/187 and the 4th Ranger Company, jumped on the north DZ. Moments behind came the second and third serials with Connor's 2/187, the 2d Ranger Company, Bowen and the regimental staff, engineers, medics, and others, including the Eighth Army assistant G-3, Hank Adams, who had planned the operation. The jumpers drew some light, sporadic NKPA machine-gun fire in the air and some mortar fire on the DZ, but fortunately no one was hit in the air.[49]

Then a serious hitch developed. The deputy flight commander, leading the following serials with Wilson's 1/187 (less Wilson), elected to skip a landmark and head directly for the south DZ. Owing to a "navigational error," he became confused and dropped the 1/187 on the north rather than south DZ. Munson remembered: "All those unscheduled people dropped right on top of us. It was like a Chinese fire drill. But what was more serious was that we didn't have a force on the south DZ, which was the linkup point for the armored task force."[50]

More planes arrived with the "heavy drop" on pallets: the 105-mm howitzers, jeeps, ammo trailers, etc. Last into the sector came a lone substitute aircraft with Harry Wilson and his staffers. When it arrived over the south DZ, Wilson was understandably puzzled. "There was nobody there. We thought they must have picked up their chutes and moved on. So we jumped anyway."[51]

On landing, Wilson and the twenty-nine other parachutists from the plane were immediately greeted by heavy NKPA machine-gun fire from the nearby hills. Had the NKPA been more aggressive or had there been CCF nearby,

Wilson and his thin party could have been wiped out. But the NKPA remained in the hills, and the paratroopers found cover. They were "rescued" later in the day by B Company of the 1/187, which Bowen sent south.[52]

Bedeviled by this fiasco, Operation Tomahawk proceeded shakily. In total, 3,447 paratroopers jumped. Of these, 84 broke ankles or legs or were bruised (half soon returned to duty), 18 were wounded, and 1 was killed on the ground. In addition, FEAF dropped a total of 220 tons of howitzers, ammo, food, and other gear. Owing to the wild misdrop of the 1/187, airborne veterans rated the operation "poor." In addition, they judged that the troop assembly and the departure from the DZ were sloppy and slow and that the cargo drop was too widely scattered.[53]

Circling overhead in his lightplane, Ridgway watched Munson's 3/187 jump. Then, at about 10:00 A.M., he asked Mike Lynch to land. Mike Lynch remembered: "We were right in the middle of everything. The next battalion jumped almost on top of us. I had to land to get out of the way! I said, 'Hold on! We're going in.' I made a bouncy landing on a piece of raised straight road—like a dike—about a hundred yards long. Ridgway went to find Bowen; I turned the plane around by its tail. Then a group of about fifteen or twenty gooks began to rake the 'landing strip' with machine guns. I had to dive over the embankment. I led a charge of paratroopers to get those gooks. The paratroopers got them."[54]

Ridgway found Bowen and the regimental staff. The exec, George Gerhart, was astonished to see him. "At first I thought he had jumped with us." Ridgway chewed Bowen out for the sloppiness of the operation and for "other things" he did not like about the regiment, then left, promising to discuss the latter at "some other time."[55]

While the paratroopers were still jumping, the two armored task forces, Growdon and Hawkins, rolled forward from Line Lincoln toward Munsan and Uijongbu respectively. Growdon told his men: "We're going direct to Munsan. No delays. No sucker skirmishes." But as luck would have it, there were agonizing delays caused principally by numerous enemy mines—the "most extensively mined area yet encountered in Korea." Growdon lost four Pattons, two jeeps, and a scout car to mines and two Pattons to NKPA artillery. Having traveled about fifteen miles in twelve hours, Task Force Growdon dramatically "linked up" with the paratroopers at 6:30 P.M. Meeting fewer obstacles and mines and having far fewer miles to travel, Task Force Hawkins reached Uijongbu in about two hours.[56]

As expected, the publicity attending these operations was enormous and favorable. War correspondents and photographers with the paratroopers and Growdon's tankers filed reams of copy and film. In eight-column banner headlines *Pacific Stars and Stripes* proclaimed: REDS' KOREA CONQUEST AIMS BLASTED; TASK FORCE LINKS UP WITH PARATROOPERS. *Life* magazine published a seven-page picture story, entitled "Airborne and Armor Link Up in Korea," in which the operation was minutely described and Frank Bowen and John Growdon were lionized. Milburn, Hoge, and Babe Bryan officially commended Growdon for "a first-class performance" but, curiously, gave him no medal.[57]

Notwithstanding the publicity and commendations, Tomahawk was judged a mixed success. It achieved its principal purpose of bringing I Corps forward to the Imjin River, but it failed to realize its secondary mission of trapping the NKPA I Corps. "It appeared the enemy was forewarned of a possible airborne assault," the 187th's historian wrote. The main enemy force had withdrawn north of the Imjin River, leaving only an understrength "second-rate" regiment of the NKPA 19th Division as a rear guard.[58]

* * *

The 3d Division's onward attack to Uijongbu behind Task Force Hawkins was spearheaded by William Harris's 65th and by Dinty Moore's 15th regiments. North of Uijongbu, both regiments encountered strong, well-organized CCF resistance. Despite a heroically aggressive assault by Julius Levy's 1/15, which earned five of Levy's men DSCs, the 3d Division bogged down. This check led to yet another plan to "trap" the enemy: the 187th Airborne Combat Team would attack east, directly across the 3d Division front, hitting the CCF on its exposed right flank.[59]

# I V

MacArthur arrived in Korea at 11:00 A.M. on Saturday, March 24, as planned. Ridgway and Shrimp Milburn met the plane at Kimpo Airfield, which was again in full operation. The party set off in jeeps north through Seoul to spend several hours with Shorty Soule's 3d Division, deployed in combat at Uijongbu.[60]

In preparation for the visit the 65th Infantry commander, William Harris, alerted Dionisio Ojeda, who commanded the attached Filipino Battalion.[61]* "The empathy between General MacArthur and the Filipinos was well known," Harris wrote. He went on: "About noon in came the caravan with General MacArthur in the lead jeep. Following along behind, like a string of elephants with each holding the tail of the one in front, came a column of twenty or thirty other jeeps. Each was loaded to capacity with assorted air

---

*The Philippine 10th Battalion Combat Team had been assigned to the Puerto Rican 65th Regiment in the mistaken belief that the Filipinos spoke Spanish. The Filipinos spoke Tagalog. A Filipino artillery battery was attached to the 39th FAB.[62]

force and army generals, admirals and other ranks. It was quite a show just to see the procession wheel into my headquarters.[63]

Harris had put out strict instructions to his unit commanders that all troops were to remain on their positions during the visit. While conducting a "routine briefing," Harris looked up, and, he wrote, "incredible as it may seem, we were almost completely surrounded by, at the very least, five thousand of our soldiers." Virtually the entire Puerto Rican regiment and Filipino battalion had left their positions to catch a glimpse of the famous general.

Harris was certain he would be sacked: "I almost swallowed my tongue. I gasped for breath and I came very close to passing out, like a Plebe at parade. Imagine the situation!" But MacArthur "didn't bat an eye." He sat silently through the remainder of the briefing and thanked Harris. Then, as the jeep was pulling away, MacArthur startled and mystified Harris with this unusual farewell: "Felicitations upon you."[64]

After visiting Jim Boswell's 7th Infantry CP, MacArthur left Kimpo Airfield at 2:40 P.M.[65] By then his office in Tokyo had released an extraordinary communiqué, apparently timed to coincide with the visit to Korea, which would generate photographs of the general "at the front" or in reliberated Seoul.

This communiqué was the second step (after the Joe Martin letter) in MacArthur's all-out public attack on the Truman administration. It was designed to preempt the proposed Truman "announcement" of a peace initiative, which State had completed and was then in process of "clearing" with the other nations which had troops in Korea. MacArthur proclaimed:

Operations continue according to schedule and plan. We have now substantially cleared South Korea of organized Communist Forces. It is becoming increasingly evident that the heavy destruction along the enemy's lines of supply, caused by our round-the-clock massive air and naval bombardment, has left his troops in the forward battle area deficient in requirements to sustain his operations. This weakness is being brilliantly exploited by our ground forces. . . . Of even greater significance than our tactical success has been the clear revelation that this new enemy, Red China, of such exaggerated and vaunted military power, lacks the industrial capacity to provide adequately many critical items essential to the conduct of modern war.

He lacks manufacturing bases and those raw materials needed to produce, maintain and operate even moderate air and naval power, and he cannot provide the essentials for successful ground operations, such as tanks, heavy artillery, and other refinements science has introduced into the conduct of military campaigns.

Formerly his great numerical potential might well have filled this gap, but with the development of existing methods of mass destruction, numbers alone do not offset vulnerability inherent in such deficiencies. Control of the sea and air, which in turn means control over supplies, communications and transportation, are no less essential and decisive now than in the past.

When this control exists as in our case and is coupled with the inferiority of ground fire power, as in the enemy's case, the resulting disparity is such that it cannot be overcome by bravery, however fanatical, or the most gross indifference to human loss.

These military weaknesses have been clearly and definitely revealed since Red China entered upon its undeclared war in Korea. Even under inhibitions which now restrict activities of the United Nations forces and the corresponding military advantages which accrue to Red China, it has been shown its complete inability to accomplish by force of arms the conquest of Korea.

The enemy therefore must by now be painfully aware that a decision of the United Nations to depart from its tolerant effort to contain the war to the area of Korea through expansion of our military operations to his coastal areas and interior bases would doom Red China to the risk of imminent military collapse.

These basic facts being established, there should be no insuperable difficulty arriving at decisions on the Korea problem if the issues are resolved on their own merits without being burdened by extraneous matters not directly related to Korea, such as Formosa and China's seat in the United Nations.

The Korean Nation and people which have been so cruelly ravaged must not be sacrificed. That is the paramount concern. Apart from the military area of the problem where the issues are resolved in the course of combat the fundamental questions continue to be political in nature and must find their answer in the diplomatic sphere.

Within the area of my authority as military commander, however, it should be needless to say, I stand ready at any time to confer in the field with the Commander-in-Chief of the enemy forces in an earnest effort to find any military means whereby the realization of the political objectives of the United Nations in Korea, to which no nation may justly take exceptions, might be accomplished without further bloodshed.[66]

This communiqué was MacArthur's fifth violation of Truman's December directive and by far the most flagrant and challenging. The text reached Washington by radio and wire services at about 10:00 P.M. on March 23, Washington Time. Deputy Secretary of Defense Robert Lovett, Dean Rusk, and two others from State met with Acheson at his home at 11:00 P.M. and discussed it for about two hours. All were shocked and angry. Acheson believed the communiqué to be "a major act of sabotage of a Government operation" and "insubordination of the grossest sort." Lovett, Acheson remembered, "usually imperturbable and given to ironic humor under pressure, was angrier than I had ever seen him." Lovett proclaimed that MacArthur "must be removed and removed at once." Acheson "shared his sense of outrage."[67]

Truman, too, was furious. His daughter, Margaret, quoted his reaction: "I couldn't send a message to the Chinese after that. He prevented a cease-fire proposition right there. I was ready to kick him into the North China Sea at that time. I was never so put out in my life. It's the lousiest trick a commander-in-chief can have done to him by an underling. MacArthur thought he was proconsul for the government of the United States and could do anything he damn pleased."[68]

On the following day, March 24, Washington time, Acheson, Lovett, and Rusk met with the full JCS. The conferees decided that as Joe Collins put it, "the idea of having the president make his announcement should be dropped, losing, according to Secretary Marshall, 'whatever chance there may have been at that time to negotiate a settlement of the Korean conflict.' " It was also proposed that MacArthur should be officially and specifically enjoined from making further uncleared statements on foreign policy, that Dean Rusk should brief the ambassadors of those nations with troops in Korea that MacArthur's communiqué was "unauthorized and unexpected," and that State should release a communiqué to the effect that the "political issues" raised by MacArthur were being dealt with by the UN and Washington.[69]

Later that day Truman summoned Acheson, Lovett, Rusk, and Collins to the White House. "Although perfectly calm," Acheson wrote, the president "appeared to be in a state of mind that combined disbelief with controlled fury." He had irrevocably decided to sack MacArthur—"I could no longer tolerate his insubordination," Truman wrote later—but he was determined to go slowly, and he gave no hint of his intentions at that meeting. The president agreed to the measures proposed by his advisers: He would drop his plans for a peace initiative, Rusk would brief the appropriate ambassadors, and the JCS would specifically direct MacArthur to refrain from further statements on foreign policy.[70]

Many would express astonishment that Truman did not immediately fire MacArthur. But there were numerous reasons for going slowly, among them the need to gain unqualified concurrence of George Marshall, Omar Bradley, and the JCS. A single dissenting "vote" in the senior military establishment could have been politically troublesome, if not disastrous. Moreover, even if Marshall and the JCS did approve MacArthur's relief, under the law MacArthur *could* request a legal hearing or a board of inquiry. An "acquittal" from such a board or hearing could have been equally troublesome or disastrous. Therefore, it would be prudent to prove "insubordination" (in a legal sense) beyond a shadow of doubt, and time was required to review the record.

There was another problem. Stripped of its rhetorical threats and insults, MacArthur's communiqué was, at root, an invitation to the commander in chief of the CCF to "confer . . . in an earnest effort" to arrive at a cease-fire. There was a possibility—albeit faint—that Peking might accept the invitation. Should Truman instantly sack MacArthur for issuing this invitation, it could send a wrong signal to Peking: that despite its recent overtures to Peking, Washington did not sincerely seek negotiations.

For these and other reasons, the official reaction to MacArthur's communiqué from Washington greatly belied Truman's true feelings. It was a mild reprimand, sent that day on Truman's orders by Bradley:

The President has directed that your attention be called to his order as transmitted . . . 6 December 1950. In view of the information given you 20 March 1951 any further statements by you must be coordinated as prescribed in the order of 6 December.

The President has also directed that in the event Communist military leaders request an armistice in the field, you immediately report that fact to the JCS for instructions.[71]

Meanwhile, it was business as usual at GHQ, Tokyo. MacArthur still had responsibility for Formosa. On March 25, Easter Sunday, MacArthur relayed to the JCS for consideration a request from his naval chief to send a carrier task force to the long-neglected Formosa Strait in early April. Good weather was returning to that area, raising anew the possibility of a Red Chinese invasion of Formosa. The naval mission would serve as a deterrent, provide photo reconnaissance, and "boost the morale" of the Chinese Nationalists. Since the mission would be of "short duration," MacArthur did not believe the CCF and NKPA would be able to take advantage of the decrease in air power over Korea to augment their troops, and he therefore endorsed the idea.

The JCS gave its approval the following day, judging the mission to be "desirable." The chiefs recognized that "as sea conditions in the Formosa Strait improve it will be necessary to increase general readiness" in that area to carry out the president's Formosa policies. Subsequently, in reaction to British nervousness, the JCS sharply restricted the area for photographic reconnaissance to exclude Hong Kong and Hainan Island.[72]

## V

Ridgway proceeded with detailed planning to cross the 38th Parallel and place Eighth Army in the more secure defensive positions he had selected. As the plan was finally worked out, the onward attack of Eighth Army would entail two methodical steps:

• A continuation of Eighth Army's advance (renamed Operation Rugged) to Line Kansas, running diagonally along the Imjin River from Munsan northeast to the Hantan River, thence east above the 38th Parallel to the south shore of the Hwachon Reservoir, thence eastward to Yangyang on the east coast. Rugged would begin on April 5.

• A further attack (Operation Dauntless) from Line Kansas by I Corps to establish the bulge toward the Iron Triangle at Chorwon. Dauntless would proceed in two cautious phases, the first to Line Utah, the second to Line Wyoming. Dauntless would start on April 11.[73]

In drawing these plans Ridgway made four assumptions:
- The enemy was certain to launch a massive "spring offensive" at any time, with a minimum of nine CCF armies (270,000 men) and probably more, plus NKPA forces.
- More likely than not, the CCF would throw air power into the offensive. Intelligence had estimated the CCF had 800 aircraft located on ninety airfields in North Korea, Manchuria, and the Shantung peninsula of China.
- South Korea would soon experience cloudy weather and heavy rainfall, which could severely impair close air and logistical support of Eighth Army. The CCF would probably take advantage of heavy rains for its "spring offensive."
- Overt Soviet intervention was a distinct possibility.[74]

When the CCF launched its spring offensive, Ridgway specified, Eighth Army would not attempt to hold Line Wyoming, Utah, or Kansas in the face of certain destruction. It would "roll to the rear" (Operation Audacious) to a series of prepared lines (Delta, Lincoln or Golden, Nevada) near Seoul and the Han River. These withdrawals were to be conducted under Eighth Army's standing orders to inflict "maximum loss on the enemy and achieve maximum delay, consistent with thorough coordination with and between corps and the maintenance intact of all major units." For political and psychological reasons, every possible effort would be made to hold Seoul, but holding real estate per se was not an overriding objective.[75]

* * *

During the last days of March Eighth Army consolidated positions below or near the 38th Parallel in preparation for Operation Rugged, the advance to Line Kansas. In the sector between Munsan and Chunchon, through which (left to right) the American 3d, 25th, 24th, and 1st Cav divisions were attempting to move north, enemy rearguard resistance was moderately strong and, in some places, heavy.

On the west end of the line Bowen's 187th Airborne Combat Team (initially supported by some Pattons of Task Force Growdon), attempting to cut east across the 3d Division's front to help it "trap" the enemy, ran into severe difficulties.

Owing to the poor conditions of the roads, a shortage of fuel for the tanks, and the lack of an established supply line, the 187th was almost entirely dependent on airdrops. In fifty-six resupply missions between March 24 and 27, FEAF provided 264 tons of ammo and food. These special support missions further diverted numerous aircraft from regular cargo runs with a consequent drop in regular tonnage delivered to Eighth Army. While most of the drops were well executed and welcomed, the 187th's exec, George Gerhart, complained in a critique that "many articles requested were *not* dropped and articles we didn't need *were* dropped."[76]

Bowen's men had several tough battles. The regimental historian wrote that on one hill (228) the "enemy resistance was extremely heavy." The CCF "had constructed an elaborate system of entrenchments and extremely deep bunkers. In some cases the holes were as much as fifteen feet deep . . . [and] the enemy seemed to possess an almost unlimited supply of grenades."[77]

The 3d Division, attacking north from Uijongbu to link with the 187th, continued to face tough resistance. When William Harris's 65th and Dinty Moore's 15th regiments bogged down, Shorty Soule threw Wilson Hawkins's 64th Tank Battalion back into the fight. But the tanks encountered mines and mud and could not get through. When, finally, the infantry punched through to make a loose linkup with the 187th, Jim Boswell's 7th Infantry came forward to relieve Moore's 15th.[78]

The 3d Division and 187th loosely closed the jaws of the pincers on the enemy on March 28. But the difficult maneuvers of the 187th failed to trap any substantial numbers; the CCF slipped north across the Imjin River. Having incurred heavy casualties, the 187th returned to Taegu in army reserve. On March 31 an armored task force of the 64th Tank Battalion, according to the 3d Division historian, "became the first U.S. unit to cross the 38th Parallel."[79]

* * *

Sladen Bradley's 25th Division still occupied the sector to the right of the 3d Division. Ever since it had crossed the Han River on March 7, it had been moving slowly but steadily northward on a three-regiment front. Its immediate objective was the town of Chongsong, at the 38th Parallel, near the confluence of the Imjin and Hantan rivers.[80]

The 24th Infantry, holding the division's left sector adjacent to the 3d Division, had performed unusually well. Following the Han River crossing, "morale soared," the new commander, Henry Britt, reported. The success of that crossing had given the 24th new self-respect and pride. On the ensuing attack north the 24th had often pulled ahead of Gilbert Check's 27th Infantry in the center and of the Turkish Brigade, which had replaced Gerry Kelleher's 35th Infantry on the division's right flank.[81]

Notwithstanding this success, Ridgway worried constantly about the 24th Infantry. Before his departure Bill Kean had complied with Ridgway's suggestion to propose officially the desegregation of the 24th Infantry and other black units and the "integration of white and negro troops." A week after the Han River crossing, on March 14, Ridgway had directed Lev Allen to provide him "a summary embodying the conclusions and recommendations of General Kean's report," so that he could review the issue with MacArthur "as soon as possible," bearing in mind that MacArthur would have to "sound out" Washington. He also directed Allen to explore the possibility of "stopping any further negro replacements for Ed Messinger's 9th Infantry," which X Corps deputy commander Laurence Ladue had faulted for being "40% colored."[82]

As the 25th Division drew abreast of Uijongbu, Babe Bryan's 24th Division on the right was compelled by terrain features to angle west, thus pinching out the Turkish Brigade, which went into reserve. About the same time Gerry Kelleher's 35th Infantry came out of reserve and replaced the 27th Infantry. On March 27 the 24th and the 35th regiments continued the 25th Division attack on an increasingly narrow front.[83]

The next day, March 28, the 24th Infantry, beginning its twenty-first day of continuous combat, ran into a brick wall. As Bittman Barth put it, the regiment "reached a strongly held enemy position where they were counterattacked and driven back." Sladen Bradley committed Check's 27th Infantry into the 24th's zone the following day. The two regiments "massed on narrow fronts," overpowered the CCF rear guard, and "the strong position was quickly taken." On March 30 the 27th relieved the 24th in the left sector.[84]

The same day Gerry Kelleher's 35th Infantry drew the task of capturing Chongsong on the 38th Parallel. It was not easy. "Bradley and I watched the attack from a hill just south of the town," Barth remembered. "The Reds occupied deep bunkers covered with heavy logs and had to be dug out laboriously by the attacking infantry. Artillery was relatively ineffective against this type of defense, but Kelleher's men did a good job with grenades and explosive charges. The town was heavily mined, causing the loss of several vehicles and a number of men," but "the fight . . . broke the last determined Red resistance." On the following day, March 31, an armor-infantry team, built around elements of Tom Dolvin's 89th Tank Battalion, cautiously crossed the 38th Parallel.[85]

* * *

On the right of the 25th Division Babe Bryan's 24th Division kept pace. It, too, drove north on a three-regiment front: Johnny Throckmorton's 5th on the left, Pete Garland's 19th in the center, and Gines Perez's 21st on the right. The Commonwealth Brigade remained in division reserve until March 27, when it moved up to relieve the 19th in the center of the line. It now had a new commander replacing Basil Coad: B. A. Burke, who had been Tom Brodie's deputy commander in the British Brigade.[86]

Throckmorton's 5th Infantry continued to perform with sharp professionalism. On March 31 it sent across the 38th Parallel an armor-infantry patrol, which killed thirty-five CCF in the process. This was one of Throckmorton's last actions. In response to a request from Joe Collins for a combat-experienced colonel to serve as his senior aide, Ridgway offered the job to Throckmorton.

"He gave me an option," Throckmorton recalled. "I didn't have to take it. But there was not much real fighting going on, so I decided to leave."[87]

Command of the 5th Infantry—a plum—would go to paratrooper and West Pointer (1937) Harry Wilson, commander of the 1/187. Wilson. thirty-eight, was the first man in his West Point class to command a regiment in Korea and, after Bill McCaffrey and Charles Mount in the 7th Division, one of the youngest.[88]

Babe Bryan, meanwhile, focused his attention on future operations. The 24th Division would be transferred to Shrimp Milburn's I Corps for what was, in effect, a three-step attack to the Iron Triangle: Operation Rugged (to Line Kansas), to commence on April 5; and Operation Dauntless (first to Line Utah, then to Line Wyoming), to commence on April 11.

\* \* \*

On the central front near Chunchon, Operation Rugged specified an advance from Chunchon to Line Kansas, which ran along the south shore of the Hwachon Reservoir. The line lay only twelve miles north of Chunchon, but it would not be easy to reach. The terrain was inhospitable, and there were few roads. Moreover, there was a formidable obstacle north of Chunchon: the Soyang River, which was swollen by rain and snowmelt. It would have to be bridged.[89]

There was another complication. When I and IX corps launched Operation Dauntless (the attacks to lines Utah and Wyoming near the Iron Triangle) on April 11, the offensive was almost certain to provoke a CCF counterattack—perhaps the expected, all-out spring offensive. When the counterattack occurred and Eighth Army withdrew (per Audacious), Ridgway wanted reserves to strike the flanks of the CCF salient. The 1st Cav would provide that reserve in the western sector; most of the 2d Division would provide that reserve for the central sector.[90]

Accordingly the plans for Operations Rugged and Dauntless in this sector grew increasingly complex and required considerable reshuffling of forces over the few available roads. The plan:

• In IX Corps the ROK 6th and the 1st Cav divisions (less the 5th Cav but reinforced by the Seventh Marines) would lead the attack per Rugged north from Chunchon to Line Kansas. Upon reaching the line, the full 1st Marine Division would relieve the 1st Cav, which would go into reserve in Eighth Army's western sector for Dauntless. During Dauntless the Marines would hold on Line Kansas.[91]

• In the X Corps sector only one reinforced regiment (the 23d) of the 2d Division would attack north to Line Kansas per Rugged. During Dauntless it would hold. The 9th and 38th regiments would remain in reserve during

Rugged and Dauntless, prepared to attack the flanks of a major CCF offensive. In the corps's right (or east) sector the American 7th Division would swap places with the ROK 5th Division, moving west to adjoin the 23d Regiment for Rugged. Two 7th Division regiments (17th and 32d) would attack to Line Kansas on the right of the 23d Regiment. Still farther right, the ROK 5th 3d divisions would attempt to keep abreast. During Dauntless all these units would hold on Line Kansas.[92]

The redisposition of Buddy Ferenbaugh's 7th Division westward imposed an enormous burden. It was still operating in ghastly terrain and weather. The artilleryman James Dill noted in his diary: "Rain and sleet, mud deep . . . quite a problem. . . . Hard march through one half to one foot of snow . . . mostly straight up and down . . . roads terrible. . . . Only jeeps can pass. One [105-mm] howitzer was taken apart and sent over the next pass in sections by jeep [and] assembled on the other side. Ammo sent up by jeep."[93]

On Eighth Army's extreme right flank, abutting the Sea of Japan, the ROK Capital Division, in a replay of its operations the previous October, sped north on the coast highway. Its advance was assisted considerably by naval bombardment and close air support from American and British vessels operating along the east coast.

On March 27 patrols of the Capital Division on the coast road crossed the 38th Parallel and took Yangyang. These ROKs thus became the "first" UN troops to recross the 38th Parallel. On the following day Ridgway flew to Kangnung—on the coast, south of Yangyang—to visit the Capital Division CP. He returned by way of Yangyang, flying along the 38th Parallel near Inje and Chunchon, following the winding Soyang River.[94]

\* \* \*

These operations in preparation for Rugged had brought most of Eighth Army's twelve frontline divisions to or close to the 38th Parallel by April 1. They concluded the offensive phases of Killer-Ripper-Courageous. In three months of careful and cautious operations the army had advanced seventy air miles. All South Korea had been cleared of CCF and NKPA troops. Militarily Eighth Army had for the second time achieved the status quo ante bellum.

Ridgway judged Killer-Ripper-Courageous to be merely a "qualified success." South Korea had been cleared of enemy for the second time; but again all too few had been killed or captured in the process, and too many had escaped. "The enemy's ability to withdraw faster than the UN could pursue him," the Eighth Army historian wrote, "had prevented the Army from destroying him in force." The goal of inflicting such punishment on the CCF that Peking would be compelled to negotiate had not been realized.[95]

Meanwhile, the enemy buildup in North Korea continued at an alarming rate. On March 31 MacArthur informed Washington that the grand total had reached 475,000 troops (with another 478,000 in reserve in Manchuria). The enemy in North Korea consisted of 274,000 CCF (about twenty-seven 10,000-man divisions) and 198,000 NKPA, the latter including 14,000 guerrillas.[96]*

The buildup of the CCF Air Force was also a source of deep concern, especially the increase in its twin-engine prop bombers. In a State Department briefing Dean Rusk said:

We are vulnerable to heavy air attacks, especially since our troops have gotten used to fighting without fear of enemy air opposition. Our ports are generally unprotected except for friendly aircraft. If in the opening phase of an enemy attack there should be a heavy air offensive, the enemy could do us considerable damage. . . . While we may be out of range of MIGs based in Manchuria, heavy two-engine bombers from bases north of the Yalu could endanger our troops, our ships at sea, as well as our bases in Japan.[98]

There was not the slightest doubt anywhere that the buildup presaged a new, all-out CCF-NKPA offensive. Peking and Pyongyang radios threatened it almost daily, repeating that the "imperialist aggressors" would be thrown back into the sea. MacArthur informed Washington that the offensive could begin "anytime after April 1."[99]

The rumors about Soviet intervention in Korea also continued to generate gravest concern, prompting the JCS to produce a paper to deal with that contingency. The chiefs conceded that they did not have a clue to Moscow's strategic goals. If its "immediate objectives" lay in the Far East, then it would be to Moscow's advantage for UN forces to leave Korea. If, on the other hand, its "immediate objectives" lay in Western Europe, it would be to Moscow's advantage for the maximum number of UN forces to remain in Korea. In any event, the chiefs recommended that:

• If the USSR precipitated a general war, UN forces should be withdrawn from Korea as rapidly as possible and deployed to serve elsewhere.

• If the USSR committed units of Soviet "volunteers" sufficient to be critical to the safety of UN forces, UN forces should be withdrawn and the United States "should then mobilize in readiness for general war."

---

*The Pentagon agreed with these figures, breaking them down thusly:

|                  |         |                                |
| ---------------- | ------- | ------------------------------ |
| NKPA in action   | 28,000  |                                |
| NKPA in the rear | 159,000 | *(occupation duty or training)* |
| NKPA guerrillas  | 14,000  |                                |
| CCF in action    | 122,000 |                                |
| CCF in the rear  | 152,000 |                                |
|                  | 475,000[97] |                            |

The chiefs employed this paper as a vehicle to urge again that the president and the NSC establish long-term political objectives for Korea. "The Korean problem cannot be resolved in a manner satisfactory to the United States by military action alone," they wrote. Perhaps in frustration, they concluded with a series of short-term recommendations that went beyond strictly military considerations. Assuming no covert or overt Soviet intervention in Korea and no general war, the chiefs stated:

- U.S. forces in Korea must pursue their current course of action there until a political objective for that country appeared attainable without jeopardizing U.S. positions with respect to the USSR, Formosa, and seating the Chinese Communists in the UN.
- Preparations should be made immediately for action by naval and air forces against the mainland of China. "As a matter of urgency," action should be taken to ascertain the "degree and nature of the support" which could be expected from Allies "if while continuing our present military course of action in Korea, operations against the mainland of China are initiated."
- Dependable ROK units should be generated as rapidly as possible and in sufficient strength to take over "the major part of the burden" from other UN forces.[100]

President Truman remained strangely noncommittal and provided scant or no leadership or reassurances.[101]

# VI

Perhaps out of concern that Washington might overrule MacArthur and veto an Eighth Army crossing of the 38th Parallel to Line Kansas, Ridgway precipitously advanced the date of Rugged from April 5 to April 3. This order caused consternation at X Corps, which, owing to logistical difficulties and poor roads, was lagging in the reshuffling of its forces. In response to its objections Ridgway criticized the corps for being "too slow" and demanded it "cut 48 hours" out of preparations.[102]

Curiously, Ned Almond chose this critical time to return to Japan for what he described as a "small vacation," April 2 to April 9. He explained later that he did so in order to see his family and MacArthur. Perhaps Almond realized—or had been told—that MacArthur had launched an all-out public attack on the Truman administration and was likely to be relieved of command. Whatever the case, Almond (with Ridgway's approval) appointed his protégé 2d Division commander Nick Ruffner to command X Corps temporarily. The 2d Division ADC, George Stewart, temporarily replaced Ruffner.[103]

As Ridgway viewed Rugged, by far the most important aspect of the plan was Shrimp Milburn's I Corps attack toward the Iron Triangle. Milburn assured Ridgway the corps would be ready to go on the advanced date, April 3. Ridgway thus decided to launch Rugged on that day, whether X Corps was ready or not.

Believing the attack of I Corps toward the Iron Triangle could invite a CCF counterattack in the west down the Kaesong–Munsan–Seoul road, Ridgway took steps to reinforce greatly the Imjin River line at Munsan. He attached Tom Brodie's British Brigade (reinforced by the Belgian Battalion) to Shorty Soule's 3d Division and brought it forward to the Imjin. He positioned Dinty Moore's 15th Infantry behind these forces on the Munsan–Seoul road. He placed William Harris's Puerto Rican 65th Infantry behind the 15th at Seoul itself.[104]

These necessary defensive dispositions diverted important 3d Division forces from the I Corps attack. The deficit was made up, however, by Babe Bryan's 24th Division, which was attached to I Corps, less the Commonwealth Brigade, which remained on the IX Corps front adjacent to the ROK 6th Division. Counting the 7th Infantry of the 3d Division and the Turkish Brigade in the 25th Division, Milburn would have a total of eight infantry regiments for the attack.

Milburn commenced the Rugged offensive on the morning of April 3. It was spearheaded by five American infantry regiments, deployed shoulder to shoulder. West to east there were: Jim Boswell's 7th; Gilbert Check's 27th; Gerry Kelleher's 35th; Johnny Throckmorton's 5th; and Gines Perez's 21st. The infantry was supported by three tank battalions (6th; 64th; 89th), massive artillery barrages, and FEAF close air. The artillery included a newly arrived Arkansas National Guard outfit, the 937th FAB, commanded by Thomas E. Douglas. It was equipped with self-propelled 155-mm Long Toms, with a greater range (fifteen miles) than regular 155s.[105]

Milburn's forces proceeded north with utmost care. All units maintained close lateral communications and were on alert for a CCF counterattack. No enemy was bypassed. Advancing two miles on the first day, the lead elements crossed the 38th Parallel.

Notwithstanding the terrain and logistical difficulties and the delays in X Corps redispositions, Bill Hoge's IX Corps also met the new Rugged deadline and jumped off on April 3. West to east the Commonwealth Brigade, the ROK 6th Division, and the 1st Cav Division moved cautiously north. Of these advances, the most dramatic and significant were those of the 1st Cav, directly above Chunchon. Having already established a beachhead on the north bank of the Soyang River, Billy Harris's 7th Cav (plus the Greeks) and Bob Blanchard's 8th Cav (plus the Thais) crossed in force and proceeded north toward the 38th Parallel (eight miles) and the Hwachon Reservoir (twelve miles). Homer Litzenberg's Seventh Marines, temporarily attached to the 1st Cav

Division, followed the 7th and 8th Cavs into the beachhead. Forces of the 7th Cav were first to cross the parallel.[106]

\* \* \*

The same day, April 3, MacArthur flew to Korea for his eighth visit in 1951. Again his trip coincided with the launching of an Eighth Army offensive. MacArthur would skip over the west and central fronts, where American forces of I and IX Corps were on the move per Rugged, and fly to the town of Kangnung, on the east coast, where the ROK I Corps had its CP. This visit, his last to Korea, would thus be limited to a review of ROK forces: the Capital Division, which had crossed the 38th Parallel first to Yangyang on the east coast, and the ROK 9th Division, which had come up behind it, north of the 38th Parallel. This was the one place in Korea where MacArthur could safely go north of the parallel. Perhaps that was his aim.[107]

Ridgway met the plane at 11:30 A.M. and had a private chat with MacArthur. Ridgway was still deeply concerned about the unverified rumors of Soviet intervention in Korea. He had reached the point in his thinking where he believed the matter should receive MacArthur's "personal consideration." No directives for Eighth Army had yet been issued to cover this contingency. Repeating an earlier conversation with MacArthur, Ridgway said he "earnestly hoped" that Washington would not order the evacuation of Eighth Army until it had withdrawn well south, lest ROK defections place the army in dire jeopardy.[108]

Turning to less apocalyptic matters, Ridgway expressed the hope that he could get a third star for Eighth Army's chief of staff Lev Allen. Ridgway's idea was to send the honorary deputy Eighth Army commander John Coulter home and give Allen the job. MacArthur concurred but expressed doubt that the move would get Allen a third star, giving as his reason, Ridgway later wrote, "his repeated [earlier] efforts to have his own chief of staff [Ned Almond] promoted to three-star rank, which Collins never agreed to."\* However, MacArthur told Ridgway to "go ahead and submit it anyway."[109]

\* \* \*

The MacArthur jeep convoy rolled north from Kangnung and crossed the 38th Parallel into the ROK 9th Division sector. The KMAG adviser to that division was a World War II paratrooper veteran, Adam A. Komosa, who had served under Ridgway in Sicily and Italy. Komosa remembered, somewhat cynically, that the 9th Division's sector had been purposefully created to be a "safe . . . parade ground" of the UN front line in Korea.[110]

---

\*Almond had gained his third star as a corps commander in the field.

When the procession pulled up and stopped at Komosa's formation, Komosa remembered, MacArthur was "slumped in the front seat—a solemn dejected person . . . a beaten man." MacArthur extended his hand to Komosa and said, "How are you? . . . Any enemy contact to your front, colonel?" Komosa replied: "None but partisan activity, sir." Since MacArthur seemed more than willing to have a look at that activity, the jeep convoy suddenly took off "like a bat out of hell" and proceeded north.[111]

After climbing into his own open jeep with a situation map, Komosa pursued the speeding convoy. Along the way the wind tore the overlays off the maps and scattered them all over the landscape. Thus when the procession reached what was believed to be the "front," Komosa was not able to tell MacArthur exactly where he was or where the enemy was. "At that moment I would have liked to have dug a hole and crawled in after it," Komosa remembered. But MacArthur "appeared satisfied" anyway—he was as far forward in North Korea as any senior American officer had been recently—and soon the convoy returned to Kangnung. MacArthur departed at 4:25 P.M., having been on the ground nearly five hours.[112]

A day after his return to Tokyo, on April 5, when all the forces assigned to Rugged had crossed the 38th Parallel, MacArthur finally and officially informed the JCS. Eighth Army would advance to Line Kansas, he amplified, to be followed by Operation Dauntless, the two-step twenty-mile I Corps "bulge" to Lines Utah and Wyoming aimed at the Iron Triangle. After Line Wyoming had been reached, Eighth Army would dig in, limiting further advances to patrols no larger than battalion size. The existing logistical limitations, combined with the terrain, weather conditions, and intelligence of enemy dispositions, had convinced MacArthur that a further advance in force beyond Wyoming "was not feasible."[113]

On the day after that, April 6, MacArthur sent off what was to be his last important communication with Washington. It was a recommendation to George Marshall for a slew of promotions: Ridgway, George Stratemeyer, and Turner Joy to four stars; Lev Allen, Bill Hoge, and Doyle Hickey to three stars; and Pinky Wright to two stars. Ridgway had urged (or later concurred in) the promotion of Allen, Hoge, Hickey, and Wright, and they were subsequently approved. However, the Pentagon rejected the promotions to four stars of Stratemeyer and Joy.[114]

# PART
# TWELVE

# Van Fleet
# to Korea

# 25

# MᴀᴄARTHUR
# SACKED

## I

President Truman had made the decision to sack MacArthur on March 24, following MacArthur's communiqué, which was deemed to have sabotaged Truman's intended "announcement" of a new peace initiative. He had told no one of his intent; he took his own good time, perhaps waiting for MacArthur to commit one more blatant, earthshaking, and clear-cut act of insubordination.

This occurred on Thursday, April 5. That day, while delivering an attack on administration policies in the House, Truman's archcritic Minority Leader Joe Martin read the text of MacArthur's March 20 letter, in which MacArthur stated there was "no substitute for victory" and by implication concurred with Martin's proposal for employing Chiang Kai-shek's Nationalist forces in an invasion of the China mainland. As MacArthur no doubt had intended, the letter made instant headlines worldwide and created furors in Washington, London, Paris, and elsewhere.[1]

Learning of Joe Martin's speech from an aide, Truman telephoned George Marshall. Marshall's deputy, Bob Lovett, remembered that Marshall was "revolted" that MacArthur would publicly attack the administration through the "leader of the opposition." On his desk calendar Truman jotted calmly: "The situation with regard to the Far Eastern General has become a political one. MacArthur has made himself a center of controversy, publicly and privately. He has always been a controversial figure." He added this catty non-sequitur: "He has had two wives—one a social light [sic] he married at 42, the

783

other a Tennessee girl he married in his middle fifties after No. 1 had divorced him."[2]*

The next day, Friday, April 6, following the regular morning cabinet meeting, Truman summoned Marshall, Acheson, Bradley, and Harriman to the Oval Office. Still giving no hint of his own position, he asked the four men what should be done. Marshall advised caution; he was especially worried about the adverse effect a relief of MacArthur might have on the huge military appropriations bill then before Congress. Although Acheson emphatically favored firing MacArthur, he, too, advised caution. "If you relieve MacArthur," Acheson said, "you will have the biggest fight of your administration." Bradley also advised caution. He was not certain in his own mind that "MacArthur had committed a clear-cut case of military insubordination as defined in Army Regulations." Harriman reminded Truman that it was a problem he had faced the previous August and put off, but he did not say (as Truman wrote) that Truman "should have fired MacArthur two years ago."[3]

The upshot of this meeting was to defer any decision. Truman asked the advisers to "meet again" later that same day "and go over all phases of the situation." He requested that Marshall review the key messages between MacArthur and Washington over the last two years, with an eye for insubordination. Bradley would sound out the JCS members, a task that was complicated by the absence of Joe Collins, who was on an inspection trip in the South and was not scheduled to return until Saturday night.[4]

After the meeting Truman vented some spleen in his diary:

MacArthur shoots another political bomb through Joe Martin, leader of the Republican minority in the House. This looks like the last straw. Rank insubordination.

Last summer he sent a long statement to the Vets of Foreign Wars—not through the high command back home, but directly! He sent copies to newspapers and magazines particularly hostile to me. I was furnished a copy from the press room of the White House, which had been *accidentally* sent there.

I ordered the release suppressed and then sent him a very carefully prepared directive dated December 5, 1950, setting out Far Eastern policy† after I'd flown 14,404 [miles] to Wake Island to see him and reach an understanding face to face. He told me the war was over, that we could transfer a regular division to Germany Jan. 1st. He was positive Red China would not come in. He expected to support our Far Eastern policy.

I call in Gen. Marshall, Dean Acheson, Mr. Harriman and Gen. Bradley before cabinet to discuss situation. I've come to the conclusion that our Big

---

*MacArthur, age forty-two, married wealthy socialite divorcée Louise Cromwell in 1922. They were divorced in 1929. In 1937, age fifty-seven, he married Jean Marie Faircloth.

†Truman apparently confused his brief directive of December 5, requiring that public statements on foreign and military policy be cleared, with his long personal letter to MacArthur of January 13, 1951.

General in the Far East must be recalled. I don't express any opinion or make known my decision. . . .[5]

As Truman had requested, Marshall, Acheson, Harriman, and Bradley met later that Friday in Marshall's office. Bradley wrote: "Marshall did not want to fire MacArthur outright. He suggested we first call him home for consultations. Acheson was opposed to this idea, as were Harriman and I." Acheson believed that to bring MacArthur home "in the full panoply of his command" would be the "road to disaster." He foresaw an alliance between Truman's right-wing critics and MacArthur that might be ruinous to Truman and impair his freedom of decision. Marshall withdrew his suggestion. The conferees decided to postpone any decision until Bradley could consult with Collins and other JCS members and until all had had the full weekend to think over the matter.[6]

The next day, Saturday, April 7, Marshall, Acheson, Harriman, and Bradley met again with Truman at 8:50 A.M. The conferees learned then that MacArthur had committed yet another public indiscretion. This one appeared in the right-wing magazine *Freeman*. The editor had written MacArthur, citing a news report that the ROK Army was releasing young ROK draftees because the United States would not give them equipment. The editor asked MacArthur why the United States had refused to arm these ROKs. MacArthur's published reply was that the question "involves basic political decisions beyond my authority." In sum, it was Washington's fault. However, MacArthur himself had advised against arming any more ROKs on January 6, 1951, owing to the abysmal performance of existing units.[7]

Truman wrote that Marshall reported that he had examined the file of MacArthur-JCS messages for the past two years and that Marshall said, "MacArthur should have been fired two years ago." But Bradley later asserted that Truman's memory was in error. The advisers merely asked Truman to postpone any decision or actions until they all had had an opportunity to "cogitate" over the weekend and Bradley had had time to consult the full JCS. Truman agreed.[8]

After the meeting Marshall and Bradley returned to Marshall's office for a private chat. For each it was an agonizing time. Both intended to go on the inactive list soon—Bradley in August, Marshall in September. Ever since Marshall's appointment as secretary of defense, right-wing administration critics had savagely abused him; the firing of MacArthur was certain to bring on another round of abuse. Bradley had so far been spared these attacks, but if MacArthur was fired, he too, was certain to draw vicious criticism. Neither man wished to end his long and distinguished career under this kind of fire.

There was a larger point that worried both. If the JCS were to endorse Truman's decision to fire MacArthur and if the firing were construed as mainly "political," it would be perceived as "politicizing" the JCS. This, in turn, could lead to a drastic erosion in the standing of the JCS as objective military advisers to any and all presidents, whatever the political party. Conceivably this could ultimately result in a practice of changing the membership of the JCS with every change of administration. Bradley (and probably Marshall) viewed that prospect as "calamitous."[9]

Still not certain that firing MacArthur was the wisest course, for these and other reasons, Marshall and Bradley sought alternatives. One was to send a frank letter to MacArthur, Bradley remembered, "telling him to shut up." They jointly tried to draft such a letter, but Bradley wrote, "this grew too complicated" and they "tore it up," and Bradley "went home to think."[10]

The following day, Sunday, April 8, Bradley convened the full JCS from 2:00 to 4:00 P.M. He revealed that Truman was considering the relief of MacArthur and that Marshall wanted the JCS view "from a strictly military viewpoint." Bradley wrote: "We discussed every conceivable aspect. We even considered proposing that MacArthur be left in his Tokyo post with no direct control over Ridgway and the Eighth Army. But owing to the close interrelation of the defense of Japan and the war in Korea, this idea was rejected." In the end Collins, Vandenberg, and Sherman "agreed unanimously" that MacArthur should be relieved.[11]

Because of legal complexities that might arise, the chiefs avoided any direct reference to military insubordination. MacArthur had been repeatedly and flagrantly "insubordinate" in his violation of Truman's December directive. He had repeatedly attempted to mislead or con or "sell" his contrary views to the JCS and "stretched" his formal directives, but except for sending American troops (rather than ROKs) close to the Manchurian border the previous November, he had not specifically violated any JCS military directive. Moreover, that violation was somewhat murky and certainly shaky legal grounds for dismissal.

Instead, the chiefs gave these reasons for concluding that MacArthur should be dismissed:

• By his public statements and by his official communications to us, he had indicated that he was not in sympathy with the decision to try to limit the conflict to Korea. This would make it difficult for him to carry out Joint Chiefs of Staff directives. Since we had decided to try to confine the conflict to Korea and avoid a third World War, it was necessary to have a commander more responsive to control from Washington.

• General MacArthur had failed to comply with the Presidential directive to clear statements on policy before making such statements public. He had also taken independent action in proposing to negotiate directly with the enemy field commander for an armistice and had made that statement public, despite the fact that he knew the President had such a proposal under consideration from a governmental level.

• The Joint Chiefs of Staff have felt, and feel now, that the military must be controlled by civilian authority in this country. (The Congress itself was very careful to emphasize this point in the National Security Act of 1947 and its Amendment in 1949.) They have always adhered to this principle and they felt that General MacArthur's actions were continuing to jeopardize the civilian control over the military authorities.[12]

Following this meeting the JCS reconvened in Marshall's office. The five senior military men present were, as Collins put it, "a sad and sober group." After they had taken seats, Marshall polled them individually for their views. Each agreed that if Truman decided to sack MacArthur, he concurred. Marshall made no comment other than to ask Bradley to convey the views of the JCS to the president.[13]

After the cabinet meeting on Monday, April 9, Truman met again with Marshall, Acheson, Harriman, and Bradley. Acheson and Harriman were "very emphatic" that MacArthur should be dismissed. Marshall reluctantly voted for dismissal. Bradley conveyed the unanimous views of the chiefs. Although by law Bradley had no "vote" in the JCS, he made it clear that he concurred with the decision "by not expressing disagreement."[14]

Then, for the first time, the president declared his decision: MacArthur would be relieved. He instructed Bradley to prepare the necessary documents. Upon the recommendation of Marshall and Bradley, Truman approved Ridgway to be MacArthur's successor as commander in chief in the Far East and commander of UN forces in Korea. It was also agreed that James Van Fleet would succeed Ridgway as commanding General of the Eighth Army in Korea.

There was one last item. Owing to the mounting fear of Soviet intervention in Korea or an air attack on Eighth Army by CCF twin-engine bombers, the JCS had earlier recommended to Truman that in order to mount an instantaneous and effective response to such an attack, MacArthur should be sent prior, specific authorization to retaliate on CCF air bases on the Chinese mainland. The proposed authorization was: "If and when the enemy launches from outside Korea a major air attack against our forces in the Korean area you are authorized with the US forces assigned to the Far East Command to attack enemy air bases and aircraft in Manchuria and the Shantung Peninsula in the immediate vicinity of Weihaiwei."

After it had been cleared through State and Defense, Truman had approved this directive on April 6 or 7. Such was the distrust of MacArthur that it was now decided that notwithstanding the possible risk to Far East military forces, the authorization should not be sent to him. He might twist its meaning to "prove" the JCS was in sympathy with his policies of attacking the Chinese mainland. Or, he might stretch its rather strict provisions to launch an unprovoked air attack on the Chinese mainland or, as Bradley put it, "make a premature decision in carrying it out."[15]

The plans for notifying MacArthur of his dismissal were drawn in strictest secrecy. Mindful of MacArthur's long and distinguished service to the country, Truman insisted the act be carried out with utmost courtesy and dignity. George Marshall finally decided that the most courteous and dignified way to do it would be to have the secretary of the Army, Frank Pace, who was coincidentally en route to Tokyo and Korea on an inspection tour, personally call on MacArthur in Tokyo and deliver the papers. To avoid a premature leak through the Army radio network, the instructions and official documents would go encoded to Pace over State Department channels to Ambassador Muccio in Pusan. Pace would pick them up there and then proceed to Tokyo.[16]

\* \* \*

Unaware that he had been chosen to carry out this historic chore, Frank Pace arrived with his party in Tokyo at 9:00 A.M. on April 9. As customary, Pace was to confer with MacArthur before going on to Korea. MacArthur met the plane with an honor guard and ceremonies appropriate for the secretary of the Army. Pace had attended the Truman-MacArthur conference on Wake Island the previous October, but he had not formally met MacArthur there or anywhere else. At 2:00 P.M. that day at his embassy residence, MacArthur hosted in Pace's honor a large formal lunch, which was attended by all the senior brass at GHQ. Later in the day MacArthur and Pace met in MacArthur's Dai Ichi office for several hours to discuss "the Army and the war."[17]

One of the ironies of this meeting was that MacArthur, but not Pace, probably knew that Truman was gearing up to relieve him at any hour. There had been a leak to MacArthur from Washington. The day before, April 8, Ned Almond, winding up his "little vacation" in Tokyo, had seen MacArthur (for the second time that trip) at 5:45 P.M. Almond remembered: "I went to tell General MacArthur good-bye. He looked rather disconsolate and said to me: 'I may not see you anymore, so good-bye, Ned.' I said: 'I don't understand what you mean.' He said: 'I have become politically involved and may be relieved by the president.' I said: 'Well, General MacArthur, I consider that absurd. I don't believe the president has the intention of taking such drastic action. . . .' "[18]

After his evening conference with MacArthur in the Dai Ichi Building, Pace turned in for the night. Meanwhile, in order to make certain that Pace got to Pusan and remained there until the instructions and official documents relieving MacArthur arrived, George Marshall sent a cable in care of GHQ which Pace found utterly baffling. As Pace remembered it, it said: "This is explicit, repeat, explicit. You will proceed to Korea and remain there until you hear from me." Already scheduled to leave for Korea at 2:00 P.M. on the following day, April 10, Pace left his schedule unchanged.[19]

No doubt MacArthur saw the cable from Marshall to Pace. Its urgency and extraordinary instructions for Pace to "remain" in Korea may have mystified Pace, but it was a signal to MacArthur that something out of the ordinary was afoot, probably that the ax was actually falling. Hence the official act of relief would come as no real surprise.

## I I

During those fateful days in the first week of April Operation Rugged, the Eighth Army advance to Line Kansas, proceeded with great care and caution.

In the I Corps sector on the extreme left flank of Eighth Army, the ROK 1st Division and Tom Brodie's British Brigade held in place on Line Kansas at the Imjin River, backed by Dinty Moore's 15th Infantry. Both outfits patrolled vigorously north of the Imjin, probing enemy defenses. To the right of the British Jim Boswell's 7th Infantry halted near the juncture of the Han and Hantan rivers on Line Kansas to await the arrival of William Harris's 65th Infantry, which would relieve the 7th for the onward push (Operation Dauntless) to the Iron Triangle on April 11.[20]

At Ridgway's direction Shorty Soule mounted a strong armored probing attack beyond the Hantan River on April 7. The operation was conducted by Wilson Hawkins's 64th Tank Battalion and by infantry from F Company of Boswell's 2/7. The force encountered an estimated battalion of CCF occupying deep, well-fortified bunkers in the old NKPA defensive positions north of the 38th Parallel. Crashing into these defenses, the force shot up the area, dispersed the CCF, and captured forty-eight prisoners. Hawkins reported "enemy annihilated or captured and only three friendly casualties, none of them serious."[21]

Farther right, Sladen Bradley's 25th Division moved up to Line Kansas, which ran along the south bank of the Hantan River. Bradley had decided that the Turkish Brigade and Henry Britt's 24th Infantry would mount the crossing of the Hantan and lead the division in Dauntless. On April 6 the Turks relieved Gilbert Check's 27th Infantry on the left (adjacent to the 7th Infantry) and Britt's 24th Infantry relieved Gerry Kelleher's 35th Infantry on the right. The 27th and 35th regiments went into reserve, both sending detachments back to Line Lincoln to prepare designated positions to which the division would withdraw (according to plan Audacious) when the CCF spring offensive came.[22]

Bittman Barth was eager to try out the long-range 155-mm Long Toms of Tom Douglas's newly arrived 937th (Arkansas) FAB, assigned to I Corps. On April 8 Barth moved one battery (six guns) to forward positions immediately behind the infantry. At dark these guns fired off a fast 102 rounds at

Chorwon, which lay just inside the extreme range of the guns. Barth was satisfied that the guns had hit the target, sowing confusion and fear among the CCF in this "rear area." He was also much impressed by the gunners; the 937th FAB was "an excellent unit" that "had its feet on the ground from the start."[23]

To the right of the 25th Division, Babe Bryan's 24th Division came abreast on Line Kansas. For Dauntless, Bryan decided to replace Throckmorton's 5th Infantry (on the left, abutting the 24th Infantry) with Pete Garland's 19th Infantry. It and Gines Perez's 21st Infantry would spearhead the attack. The 5th would go into reserve, at which time its newly designated commander, Harry Wilson, would take over from Throckmorton.[24]

To the right of I Corps in Bill Hoge's IX Corps sector on the central front, the ROK 6th Division and Burke's Commonwealth Brigade advanced toward Line Kansas against slight resistance. However, above Chunchon, the 1st Cav Division ran into intense enemy opposition. On April 8 both Billy Harris's 7th Cav and Bob Blanchard's 8th Cav, operating in difficult terrain, were checked, and later in the day the 8th Cav was driven back. Fearing a possible all-out enemy counterattack, Charlie Palmer requested that Hoge give him Marcel Crombez's 5th Cav from reserve. Hoge agreed, and Crombez brought the regiment forward to Chunchon.[25]

\* \* \*

The next day, April 9, the CCF opened the sluice gates on the dam at the Hwachon Reservoir and flooded the Pukhan River. A "wall" of water four feet high rushed downstream. It washed out one IX Corps bridge and compelled the engineers to swing another back against the bank. The flooding of the Pukhan, which ran north-south between the sectors of the Commonwealth Brigade and that of the 1st Cav, "divided" IX Corps forces and posed additional logistical problems in the IX Corps rear.[26]

Ridgway was at his CP in Yoju when the news of the flooding reached him. He was not surprised; he had been expecting it to happen for weeks. His real concern was that it might presage the all-out CCF offensive.[27]

Mike Lynch flew Ridgway directly to the dam for an inspection. They circled low, heedless of CCF small-arms fire, watching the outflow of water. It did not appear to be as serious as the initial panicky reports had indicated. Back at Chunchon, Ridgway conferred with Bill Hoge and Charlie Palmer. Then he flew over the dam a second time in a helicopter. He confirmed that the flooding was not calamitous. It appeared that the CCF had not opened the sluice gates all the way or that the water pressure behind the dam was less than had been calculated.[28]

Nonetheless, the Hwachon Dam remained, if not a serious threat, a distinct annoyance. Believing it would be imprudent to leave it in CCF hands,

Ridgway ordered Hoge and Palmer immediately to send an Army "combat team" forward to capture it. Moreover, he directed that when O. P. Smith's 1st Marine Division relieved the 1st Cav Division on Line Kansas during Dauntless, the Marines would move to a line north of the dam (and reservoir), which the Marines dubbed Quantico.[29]

Billy Harris's 7th Cav drew the dangerous but glamorous assignment of "capturing" the Hwachon Dam. Harris organized a special combat team built around John Callaway's 2/7. It would not be an easy mission. "The regiment's rapid advance over the rugged terrain during the preceding few days," the 7th Cav historian wrote, "had placed them in an area where it was impossible for vehicles larger than a one-quarter ton jeep to travel due to poor roads." The division's three battalions of 105-mm howitzers could not reach the dam area; the one battalion of 155s could just barely do so, providing only limited support. Even so, this "special mission" held great appeal for Billy Harris and his dashing cavalrymen.[30]

The team jumped off on the morning of April 10. It met a "stubborn defense" in rugged terrain, mounted by an estimated two companies of CCF. Callaway bashed through these defenses, and by nightfall the 2/7 had drawn to within a half mile of the dam. But it could get no farther; the enemy was well dug in, apparently determined to hold the dam at any cost.

Billy Harris conceived a novel solution to this tactical impasse. He would mount an "amphibious operation" north across the reservoir, designed to outflank the CCF. After Palmer had approved this scheme, "emergency calls" went out for motor-powered assault boats and FEAF was asked to air-drop life rafts. Nine assault boats (four with outboard motors) precariously loaded on jeeps, finally got to the south shore of the reservoir, along with infantry reinforcements: the 4th Ranger Company, commanded by Dorsey B. Anderson, and I Company of the 3/7.[31]

In the early hours of April 11 the 7th Cav gave the mission its legendary utmost. The "amphibious force" climbed into the boats and rafts and headed across the reservoir. Simultaneously Callaway's 2/7 mounted a renewed attack and the 1/7 feinted west across the Pukhan River. All these efforts came to naught. The CCF intercepted the two infantry companies in the "amphibious operation," inflicting "severe casualties." The 2/7 attack was checked; the 1/7 feint was blocked by floodwaters in the Pukhan. Furious over this botched operation, Bill Hoge ordered Palmer to withdraw the 7th Cav, which went into Eighth Army reserve with the rest of the 1st Cav Division for Dauntless.[32]

This dashing but wholly unsuccessful mission proved to be Billy Harris's swan song. Having been in continuous action for nine months, he left the 7th Cav and returned to the States to enter the fall class of the Army War College. Later he was promoted to brigadier general and rose to two stars before his retirement in 1966, for a physical disability.[33]

Ridgway himself chose Harris's replacement: West Pointer (1932) Dan Gilmer, forty-one. Gilmer proved to be a disaster, among the worst regimental commanders to serve in Korea, indisputably the "worst personnel mistake of Ridgway's career."[34]

Gilmer had not previously commanded troops in combat. In World War II he had been a senior staff officer and planner for Eisenhower (secretary of the General Staff) in North Africa and in England prior to Normandy and later a Pentagon planner. After the war he had served as Ridgway's chief of staff on the UN committee and, as such, became a close confidant and friend—Ridgway's best man at his wedding to Penny Ridgway. He was serving on Joe Swing's staff at the Army War College when Ridgway called him to service in Korea.[35]

Gilmer was an intense, indefatigable, and brilliant staff officer and a perfectionist. After he left the SHAEF staff to return to the Pentagon, Eisenhower wrote to thank him for his "magnificent work," for which "I owe you a lasting debt of appreciation." However, Eisenhower went out of his way to warn Gilmer of a personal deficiency: "Your only fault, as I see it, has been such a complete devotion to the concept of mechanical efficiency, that you have sometimes forgotten that all organizations are made up of human beings and that a sympathetic understanding of their personalities and abilities—and indeed their weaknesses—is essential to continuing smoothness in operations." If Gilmer could correct that fault, Eisenhower went on, he "must be considered one of the most valuable and efficient officers of your time and service in the Army."[36]

While serving as Ridgway's devoted and tireless chief of staff and friend at the UN in 1947, Gilmer received rave fitness reports and was recommended for repromotion to full colonel "as soon as possible." When this recommendation reached Army Chief of Staff Eisenhower's desk, he forwarded it to the director of Army personnel with this comment: "Colonel Gilmer served in important capacities under me during the war and I endorse everything General Ridgway has to say about his unusual capabilities. The only defect then noticeable was an impatience with others less gifted or less devoted to duty than himself, an impatience that sometimes expressed itself in irritation. This, I am informed, has been wholly corrected. . . ."[37]

The defect had not been corrected. In fact, it had intensified. Prior to formally turning over the 7th Cav command, Billy Harris sensed big trouble. He warned Charlie Palmer that a terrible mistake had been made and insisted that someone other than Gilmer be found to relieve him. But Palmer could do nothing. Dan Gilmer was "Ridgway's boy," in Korea at Ridgway's specific request. Gilmer needed to "get his ticket punched," so he would be better qualified for promotion to brigadier general and beyond. The upshot was to be utter disaster for the crack 7th Cav.[38]

\* \* \*

To the right of Chunchon, in the X Corps sector, implementation of Rugged had been delayed by the reshuffling of American forces. Jack Chiles's 23d Infantry relieved the Fifth Marines, which then moved westward to join the Marine division which was preparing to relieve the 1st Cav. In the 2d Division sector only the 23d Infantry would attack to Kansas. The 9th and 38th would remain in reserve during both Rugged and Dauntless. Buddy Ferenbaugh's 7th Division moved west to displace the ROK 5th Division, which moved east. Bill Quinn's 17th and Charles Mount's 32d regiments would lead the 7th Division attack to Line Kansas.[39]

The Fifth Marines had already secured a beachhead on the north bank of the Soyang River for Chiles's 23rd Infantry. On April 5 Chiles moved the 23d into the beachhead and the next day launched his attack north toward the eastern end of the Hwachon Reservoir. Three 2d Division artillery battalions (15th, 37th, and 503d) supported the 23d. Leading the regiment's attack, the French Battalion reached Line Kansas on April 8, near the southern shore of the reservoir, but it was checked by a strong NKPA bastion on Hill 796. To capture this dominating terrain, Chiles conceived a double envelopment (Operation Swing), launched on April 10. It "worked to perfection," and the 23d consolidated on Line Kansas to sit out Dauntless.[40]

To the right Ferenbaugh's 7th Division, delayed in swapping places with the ROK 5th Division, got off to a slow start. Led by Bill Quinn's 17th on the left and Charles Mount's 32d on the right, it inched ahead in rugged terrain (meeting some NKPA opposition) toward the Soyang River, which in this area ran east-west along the 38th Parallel. On April 9, not without difficulties, the 17th and 32d crossed the river. Thereafter the regiments continued north toward the division's final objective for Rugged: Inje, a road hub several miles north of the 38th Parallel on Line Kansas. Both regiments continued to meet NKPA opposition; McCaffrey's 31st remained in division reserve below the Soyang. The 7th Division was the last in Eighth Army to reach Line Kansas.[41]

\* \* \*

During the Eighth Army advances to Line Kansas, numerous CCF and NKPA prisoners had been taken. From them and other intelligence sources, the Eighth Army G-2 section was able to construct a fairly good picture of the CCF deployment in North Korea. It had lately increased significantly. The sobering lineup: nine CCF armies (about twenty-seven divisions of 270,000 men) definitely identified; ten CCF armies (about thirty divisions of 300,000 men) probably in immediate reserve—in total, possibly nineteen CCF armies comprising fifty-seven divisions (570,000 men).[42]

The CCF prisoners talked freely, as usual. They boasted that their spring offensive would commence on April 22. Four months earlier this kind of specific information from CCF soldiers had been accepted skeptically or disregarded. However, Eighth Army interrogators now believed that CCF troops were amazingly well informed on strategic plans and rated the information as accurate. Ridgway adjusted plans accordingly.[43]

## III

Frank Pace and his party arrived in Taegu at 5:00 P.M. on April 10. Ridgway met the plane with appropriate honor guard and ceremonies. It was Pace's first visit to the battlefield; the Eighth Army staff had arranged a busy VIP tour.[44]

During the briefing in Taegu, Ridgway brimmed with optimism. All major elements of Eighth Army except the American 7th Division had completed Operation Rugged with negligible casualties and were on Line Kansas. Shrimp Milburn's I Corps was to start Operation Dauntless (the attack toward the Iron Triangle) on the following morning, April 11. This attack was very likely to provoke a CCF counterattack—perhaps the spring offensive. If so, Eighth Army was fully prepared: All units would withdraw in orderly fashion to prepared defensive positions per plan Audacious; the 1st Cav and 2d Division would attack the flanks of the CCF salient. With any luck at all, Eighth Army would inflict a devastating blow on the CCF, perhaps sufficient to impel Peking to the negotiating table.

Pace was vastly impressed. He judged Ridgway to be "a dynamic man with great personal leadership." Ridgway was "maybe one of the finest" commanders in the Army. Privately he told Ridgway: "You have not only worked a miracle" but worked a "spiritual miracle" as well.[45]

\* \* \*

As Pace was turning in for the night in Taegu, President Truman was arriving in the Oval Office on the morning of Tuesday, April 10, Washington time. He was in a jaunty mood. All decisions pertaining to the relief of MacArthur had been made. The instructions and documents would go encoded to Pace via Ambassador Muccio in Pusan later in the day. Pace would pick them up, return to Tokyo, and do the deed at 10:00 A.M., Thursday, April 12, Tokyo time.[46]

With thirty-six hours yet to go, Truman was careless and indiscreet at the morning staff briefing. "So you won't need to read about it in the papers," he confided, "I fired MacArthur yesterday from all his jobs." When they recovered from the shock, the staffers raised questions about how he would explain the action to the public. "I can show," Truman replied confidently, "just how the so-and-so double-crossed us. I'm sure MacArthur wanted to be fired." He went on: "He's going to be regarded as a worse double-crosser than McClellan.* He did just what McClellan did—got in touch with minority leaders in the Senate. He worked with the minority to undercut the administration when there was a war on. . . . Everybody seems to think I don't have courage enough to do it. We'll let 'em think so, then we'll announce it."[47]

That afternoon Truman signed the relieving documents and turned them over to Acheson for encoded radio transmission to Pusan. By then the White House was buzzing. The senior staffers were closeted with Omar Bradley, preparing a press release and other "background documents." Any hope of keeping the news secret for another day had been thrown to the winds by the president himself. There was bound to be a leak.

And so it happened.

At about 5:00 P.M. on that April 10 Lloyd Norman, Pentagon correspondent for the *Chicago Tribune,* queried Bradley's Pentagon office for comment on a rumor of MacArthur's relief. Bradley's Army aide and speech writer, Chester V. Clifton, who took the call, telephoned Bradley at the White House. Meanwhile, Norman's boss, Walter Trohan, had lodged a similar query with Truman's press secretary, Joseph H. Short. Since the *Chicago Tribune* was stridently anti-Truman, Bradley, Short, and other White House staffers assumed (probably incorrectly) that MacArthur or GHQ was the source of the leak and that MacArthur would achieve a public relations coup by resigning with a blast at Truman before the relief could be consummated, thereby placing the administration on the defensive.

A tremendous internal crisis ensued. George Marshall was at the movies with his wife, but Acheson and Harriman and others joined Bradley at the White House to decide what to do: Stick to the original plan or release the news to undercut a possible MacArthur resignation. Ironically, MacArthur's archfoes Dean Acheson and Dean Rusk advised hewing to the original plan. Harriman, Joe Short, and White House senior aide Roger W. Tubby argued the opposite—and won. At about 10:00 P.M. a delegation (Bradley, Harriman, Short, Rusk) called on Truman, who was still living in Blair House, to persuade the president to act at once. A half hour later Truman authorized an official White House release of the documents. Joe Short called an extraordinary press conference for 1:00 A.M. on April 11, Washington time, which was about 2:00 P.M., April 11, Tokyo and Korea time.[48]

Meanwhile, the instructions to Pace and the relieving documents had been sent earlier that afternoon through State Department channels to Pusan. However, a "power failure" or "mechanical difficulty" delayed the receipt and

---

*West Pointer (1846) General George B. McClellan, commander of the Union's Army of the Potomac in the Civil War, connived with Democrats against President Lincoln, resigned his command, and ran against Lincoln for the presidency in 1864.

decoding of these documents, and they did not reach Pace that night as intended. Still unaware of the dramatic and somewhat frantic events unfolding in Washington, he slept through the night of April 10 in Taegu.[49]

In order to get official word to MacArthur before the 1:00 A.M. White House news conference, at midnight Omar Bradley got off a "personal" message to MacArthur over official Army channels:[50]

I have been directed to relay the following message to you from President Truman:

I deeply regret that it becomes my duty as President and Commander in Chief of the United States military forces to replace you as Supreme Commander, Allied Powers; Commander in Chief, United Nations Command; Commander in Chief, Far East; and Commanding General, U.S. Army, Far East. You will turn over your commands effective at once to Lieutenant General Matthew B. Ridgway. You are authorized to have issued such orders as are necessary to complete desired travel to such place as you may select. My reasons for your replacement will be made concurrently with the delivery to you of the foregoing order, and are contained in the next following message.
(Signed: Harry S. Truman)

The "next following" message stated:

With deep regret I have concluded that General of the Army Douglas MacArthur is unable to give his wholehearted support to the policies of the United States government and of the United Nations in matters pertaining to his official duties. In view of the specific responsibilities imposed upon me by the Constitution of the United States and the added responsibility which has been entrusted to me by the United Nations, I have decided that I must make a change of command in the Far East. I have, therefore, relieved General MacArthur of his command and have designated Lieutenant General Matthew B. Ridgway as his successor.

Full and vigorous debate on matters of national policy is a vital element in the constitutional system of our free democracy. It is fundamental, however, that military commanders must be governed by the policies and directives issued to them in the manner provided by our laws and Constitution. In time of crisis, this consideration is particularly compelling.

General MacArthur's place in history as one of our greatest commanders is fully established. The Nation owes him a debt of gratitude for the distinguished and exceptional service which he has rendered his country in posts of great responsibility. For that reason I repeat my regret at the necessity for the action I feel compelled to take in his case.
(Signed: Harry S. Truman)[51]

After returning to his Fort Myer quarters from the movies, George Marshall learned of the new plans. It was therefore necessary for him to cancel his instructions to Pace to return to Tokyo and relieve MacArthur formally. Accordingly, Marshall cabled Pace to "disregard" his earlier cable (which Pace had not yet received) and went on to say: "You will advise General

Matthew B. Ridgway that he is now the Supreme Commander in the Pacific; General MacArthur relieved. You will proceed to Tokyo where you will assist General Ridgway in assuming . . . his command."[52]

Joe Short convened the White House press conference at 1:00 A.M. In addition to the two official relieving documents Bradley had cabled to MacArthur an hour before, Short released seven "background documents," which were intended to prove MacArthur's insubordination to the president. These included Truman's December directive requiring prior clearance of public statements on military or foreign policy; the March 20 JCS message to MacArthur informing him of Truman's impending peace initiative or "announcement"; MacArthur's March 24 surrender ultimatum to the Chinese; the JCS March 24 message to MacArthur calling his attention to the December directive; MacArthur's March 20 letter to Joe Martin; a JCS January 5 message to MacArthur requesting his advice about arming more ROKs; MacArthur's January 6 message to the JCS recommending against that course. As MacArthur biographer James aptly wrote, the last two documents were "petty," designed merely to prove that MacArthur's response to the *Freeman* magazine query about arming ROKs had been dishonest.[53]

The radio bulletins ensuing from the press conference reached Tokyo before Bradley's official cable. MacArthur's aide Sidney L. Huff heard it on a public broadcast. MacArthur was then hosting a lunch at the embassy for Senator Warren G. Magnuson and others. Huff told MacArthur's wife, Jean, who entered the dining room and whispered the news to her husband. MacArthur apparently took it calmly, saying only, "Jeanie, we're going home at last." The lunch continued at an unhurried pace. Before leaving the embassy to return to the Dai Ichi Building, MacArthur received the official messages from Bradley.[54]

And so the deed was done.

MacArthur and his supporters would endlessly decry the discourteous and cold manner in which MacArthur was relieved. ("He heard it on the radio!") They had a point; the affair was indisputably botched. But it had not been a spiteful or vindictive act. The outcome ultimately worked in MacArthur's favor. His supporters could use the incident to build sympathy for their hero and to flail Truman further.

## I V

At dawn on April 11 Shrimp Milburn's I Corps began Operation Dauntless: the attack to Line Utah and the Iron Triangle. The corps consisted of the ROK 1st Division and Shorty Soule's 3d, Sladen Bradley's 25th, and Babe Bryan's 24th divisions. The ROK 1st and most of the 3d Division, including Brodie's

British Brigade, held in place on the left at the Imjin River line. William Harris's 65th Infantry, which had replaced the 7th Infantry on the 3d Division's right flank, joined the 25th and 24th divisions to lead the corps assault.[55]

The corps attacked with five infantry regiments (20,000 men) line abreast. The leading elements of the three left regiments were an interesting ethnic composition: St. Clair's Puerto Rican 1/65, the attached Filipino Battalion, the Turkish Brigade, and the black 24th Infantry. The right two regiments were conventional: Pete Garland's 19th and Gines Perez's 21st. Four regiments were designated reserve: Jim Boswell's 7th, Gilbert Check's 27th, Gerry Kelleher's 35th, and Johnny Throckmorton's 5th.[56]

The Turks and blacks had first to cross an inhospitable stretch of the Hantan River. "The river ran between steep banks with very few crossing sites," Bittman Barth remembered. "Patrols found the north bank heavily defended." The 25th Division had no pontoon bridge equipment; the engineers would have to build the more difficult trestle bridges.[57]

In Henry Britt's 24th Infantry sector, elaborate preparations had been made for an assault crossing. However, just prior to the attack, the regimental S-2, Major Richard W. ("Cuffy") Williams, the highest-ranking black in the outfit, made an important discovery at the riverbank: The Hantan had receded. It could be forded in certain places. Since the infantry would be much less vulnerable to enemy fire on foot as opposed to crowding into assault boats, Williams canceled the boats.[58]

Even so, the river crossing was not easy. The 1/24 led. The battalion had yet another new commander, the fourth since January: Joseph ("The Baron") Baranowski. George Clayton's 2/24 followed. Bill Mouchet's 3/24 crossed downriver of 1/24 and 2/24. All three battalions came under heavy CCF fire. Nonetheless, the 1/24 and 2/24 reached the north bank in what was considered a successful crossing.[59]

It was a different story for Mouchet's 3/24. After fording the river, the men faced a sheer cliff, which had to be scaled hand over hand. Firing from the heights on the flanks and from directly overhead, the CCF inflicted heavy casualties on the exposed cliff climbers. Commander Mouchet radioed Britt for permission to break off the attack temporarily until the opposing CCF fire could be silenced. Britt refused. Mouchet then asked to be relieved of command. Britt refused that request as well.[60]

David Carlisle, exec of the 77th Engineer Combat Company, supporting the 24th's crossing, overheard the radio exchange between Mouchet and Britt. Carlisle had a very high regard for Mouchet, who had replaced Melvin Blair and rebuilt the 3/24 after the CCF Chongchon River offensive. To Carlisle, Britt's obstinacy and insensitivity to Mouchet's losses were unconscionable, yet another example of inept white leadership imposed on the 24th Infantry.[61]

The upshot was a complete breakdown in the 3/24. The CCF fire drove it back across the Hantan. There it had to reorganize for a second attempt on the following day. Mouchet did not long remain in command. Carlisle felt that his departure was another great loss to the regiment.

The other Hantan River crossings by I Corps units were less traumatic. By noon most assault forces were well on the way north, meeting only sporadic "rearguard" CCF resistance. It was soon apparent that the CCF was not prepared for a determined defensive stand or for counterattacks. All CCF forces appeared to be withdrawing into the Iron Triangle.[62]

*   *   *

The same morning, still unaware of the MacArthur relief, Ridgway flew Frank Pace and his party from Taegu to Seoul in the *Hi Penny!* They paid the customary VIP visit to some wounded in an evacuation hospital near Seoul, then shifted to smaller aircraft to visit several I Corps combat units: Shorty Soule's, Sladen Bradley's and Babe Bryan's divisional CPs; Jim Boswell's 7th Infantry CP (in reserve); Pete Garland's 19th Infantry CP (leading the attack); Throckmorton's 5th Infantry CP (in reserve); and Tom Douglas's 937th (Arkansas) FAB (supporting the attack with 155-mm Long Toms).[63]

Pace, a native of Arkansas, was warmly received by the national guardsmen of the 937th FAB. They provided an Arkansas flag for his jeep and invited him to pull the lanyard and fire a projectile. Ridgway was mystified when a reporter, who by then had heard the news of the MacArthur relief asked, as Ridgway remembered, "whether I was not due congratulations." Ridgway later wrote: "I just stared back at the correspondent and told him quite honestly that I did not know what he was talking about."[64]

Following the visit to Pete Garland's 19th Infantry CP at about 3:00 P.M., the several small aircraft carrying the Pace party headed for Throckmorton's 5th Infantry CP. On the way the planes flew over CCF frontline positions. Minutes after the landing at Throckmorton's CP a violent hailstorm raked the area. Had it occurred about twenty minutes earlier, Pace thought, it might have forced the light aircraft down in CCF territory. "I would have been the first [Army] secretary captured by the Chinese," he joked.[65]

Throckmorton, who was in process of turning over command of the regiment to Harry Wilson, informed Pace that Eighth Army Chief of Staff Lev Allen was trying to reach him by phone. Pace got through to Allen at about 4:45 P.M. Allen read him the text of the cable from George Marshall telling Pace to "disregard" his earlier cable (which Pace had still not received) and to inform Ridgway that MacArthur was relieved, that Ridgway was now supreme commander, and that Pace should go with Ridgway to Tokyo to help with the turnover.

Utterly astounded, Pace said: "Read that to me once more, Lev—I don't want to relieve General MacArthur on one reading." Pace described what happened next: "So he read it once more, and I took General Ridgway out in the hail. General Ridgway used to wear those live grenades, and I thought if that hailstone hits one of those live grenades, they're going to need a new supreme commander *and* a new [Army] secretary. . . . I said, 'General Ridgway, it's my duty to advise you that you're now the supreme commander of the Pacific; General MacArthur [is] relieved.' He said, 'I can't believe it, Mr. Secretary.' I said, 'I can't either, so I'll repeat it. You're now the supreme commander of the . . . Pacific. . . . General MacArthur [is] relieved.' "[66]

Pace did not think they should embark immediately for Tokyo "because General MacArthur's got a great many things to do." He suggested that Ridgway wait until the next day, then call MacArthur and find out if it would be "convenient" for them to come. Meanwhile, Pace rightly thought it would be wise to track down the unreceived cable from Marshall.[67]

They terminated the inspection trip and flew to Ridgway's CP at Yoju. At about 10:00 P.M., twenty-four hours overdue, they received the earlier cable from Marshall, instructing Pace to go to Tokyo to relieve MacArthur. Spared this ordeal, Pace later joked about it. What would he have done if the cable had arrived on time? "No problem," he said. "Presidential order. I'd commandeer the first plane and fly to Tokyo. Being after hours, I would have gone immediately to General MacArthur's quarters. I'd have taken the order, rung the doorbell, and shoved it under the door and run like hell."[68]

Ridgway, too, was astounded by the day's events and by his sudden promotion (certain to bring four stars immediately) and the awesome new responsibilities he had inherited. One urgent problem he faced—or so he thought—was finding a successor for command of Eighth Army. Several possibilities occurred to him, first among them Joe Swing. Two other possible candidates had come to the Far East with Pace: Ed Hull, who had taken over Ridgway's job in Washington as deputy chief of staff for operations, and Ted Brooks, chief of army personnel, who had stayed behind in Tokyo. That night Ridgway asked Hull if he would "consider" the job; Hull replied: "Of course."[69]

The Eighth Army command problem was urgent because of the tactical situation. In one sense the current offensive, Dauntless, was a prudent move to gain proper defensive positions for Eighth Army. In another sense, however, it was deliberate goading of the CCF to provoke it into fighting. If the goading were successful, a big counterattack or the CCF spring offensive itself could come at any time. It would be well if the new Eighth Army commander had his feet on the ground for a few days before that occurred.

Before turning in for the night, Ridgway sent a personal cable on a back channel to the man in Washington who counted most with him, his idol and benefactor George Marshall: "Earnestly hope that great responsibilities entrusted to me may be discharged in manner to meet your approbation. Faithfully, Ridgway."[70]

\* \* \*

The next day, April 12, Pace, Ridgway, and others embarked on the voyage to Tokyo. They flew in the *Hi Penny!,* to Pusan, where they transferred to Pace's faster and more comfortable Constellation and briefly saw Ambassador Muccio. They departed Pusan at 2:00 P.M. and arrived in Tokyo at 4:30 P.M. Doyle Hickey met the plane and escorted Ridgway (but not Pace) to the embassy library to confer with MacArthur. Hickey was invited to sit in on the MacArthur-Ridgway conference, which lasted one hour, from 5:00 to 6:00 P.M.[71]

For Ridgway, the conference was a moment in his life never to be forgotten. In a memo written that night he stated that MacArthur's "indomitable spirit seemed undiminished" and that "he was as keen of mind as ever." Later, in his autobiography, Ridgway enlarged upon his recollections:

He received me at once, with the greatest courtesy. I had a natural human curiosity to see how he had been affected by his peremptory removal from his high post. He was entirely himself—composed, quiet, temperate, friendly, and helpful to the man who was to succeed him. He made some allusions to the fact that he had been summarily relieved, but there was no trace of bitterness or anger in his tone. I thought it was a fine tribute to the resilience of this great man that he could accept so calmly, with no outward sign of shock, what must have been a devastating blow to a professional soldier standing at the peak of a great career.[72]

Discussing his dismissal, MacArthur attributed it to Truman's mental instability. Ridgway recorded the gist of MacArthur's remarks: "He stated that he had been told by an eminent medical man, who had gotten it from [Brigadier] General [Wallace H.] Graham, the President's physician, that the President was suffering from malignant hypertension; that this affliction was characterized by bewilderment and confusion of thought . . . and that according to the medical man, he wouldn't live six months."[73]\*

Reflecting on these comments years later, Ridgway said: "Here is an indication of a man so monumentally egotistical that he could conceive of no possible reason why Truman would relieve him except [that] there was something wrong mentally. Isn't that something? Really amazing!"[75]

MacArthur went on to say that he would settle down in New York City. Not having seen it since the 1930s, he "had always had a hankering to get back there." He had already received several generous financial offers. Ridgway

---

\*This thirdhand diagnosis was not accurate. On the whole, Truman's mental and physical health was good, but he frequently drove himself or worked to exhaustion. Early in life he had been bedeviled by severe headaches. These recurred in 1950 and may have continued into 1951. But there was no clinical evidence of hypertension (unusually high blood pressure). Truman was to live for twenty-one more years—to age eighty-eight.[74]

listed them in his memo: $150,000 "for some unstated purpose"; another for $300,000 "to write fifty lectures" and "raise hell"; another for $1 million for some purpose "he did not enlarge upon."[76]

An exchange of loyalties and flattery ensued. MacArthur told Ridgway that his performance in Korea had been "brilliant" and that "if it had been up to him to pick his successor," he would have chosen Ridgway. It was still MacArthur's hope that Ridgway would be named Army chief of staff soon. In return, Ridgway told MacArthur that "he knew that for more than thirty years he had had my personal devotion and he could count on that remaining completely unchanged." Ridgway added a comment in his memo: "He seemed touched."[77]

\* \* \*

Following the conference with MacArthur, Ridgway met again with Frank Pace and Ed Hull. Thereupon he learned from a cable from George Marshall that Washington had already decided the matter of Ridgway's replacement as commander of Eighth Army: James Van Fleet. The news was upsetting. It was customary to consult the theater commander in such matters. Van Fleet was two years senior to Ridgway (and Joe Collins) by date of rank. His appointment could be construed as a step backward in the Army's policy of grooming "younger" men for positions of high responsibility. Moreover, Ridgway did not think Van Fleet was all that bright or capable, and he did not like him personally. "They were not hot buddies," Ridgway's confidant Day Surles said later.[78]

There was another problem. The cable from George Marshall was unintentionally ambiguous. Marshall had said that Van Fleet was being sent to Ridgway "for such duties as you may direct." Did this mean that Ridgway had veto power over Van Fleet's appointment? At Ridgway's request, Pace queried Marshall for a clarification. Marshall replied through the JCS:

We regret that time did not permit consulting you prior to announcement of appointment of Van Fleet. His appointment as your successor to command Eighth Army was approved personally by the President. In [Marshall's] message to you the last seven words "for such duties as you may direct" were added to cover our thought that you would probably desire to designate Van Fleet as your Deputy Commander, retaining direct command in the field yourself, until such time as you thought it advisable to turn over top command of Eighth Army, presumably after the threatening hostile offensive.[79]

Perhaps aware of Ridgway's reservations about Van Fleet, the JCS apparently felt the need to "sell" him to Ridgway. The message concluded: "Aside from the matter of Van Fleet's outstanding military qualifications, there is a special situation to be considered, which involves many reactions, both national and international, relating to Van Fleet's previous experience against Communist forces in mountainous Greece and his relations there in dealing with civil authorities. Already his name has been received with great favor especially in view of his service in Greece."[80]

This "clarification" was no less upsetting. In naming Ridgway to replace MacArthur, Washington had given Ridgway vast new responsibilities. He now commanded not only army forces in the Far East but also air and naval forces. His primary responsibility was the defense of Japan and the rest of the offshore perimeter. Rumors of direct Soviet intervention in Korea—and possibly elsewhere in Asia—were still rife. That very day FEAF, again attempting to knock out the Sinuiju bridges with B-29s, had met eighty MIGs, and the largest "air battle" of the war had ensued.* Far East naval forces (Task Force 77) were en route to the Formosa Strait for the JCS-approved "demonstration" designed to discourage a CCF invasion of the island. The "demonstration" might provoke a strong CCF—or even Soviet—military reaction.[81]

These important air and naval operations, and other matters, required Ridgway's closest supervision. It would be imprudent for him to continue in direct command of Eighth Army (with Van Fleet as "deputy") for any significant time. Yet Eighth Army also required closest supervision. It was engaged in the most perilous enterprise yet. An early CCF counteroffensive was virtually a certainty.

Confronting this Hobson's choice, Ridgway decided to return to Korea that very night. Van Fleet would arrive in Korea within two days. By that time Milburn's I Corps should have attained Line Utah, the first-phase objective of Dauntless. If so, Ridgway would turn over command of the Army to Van Fleet and return to Tokyo. Thereafter he would keep a tight tether on Van Fleet; virtually "commuting" to Korea. Meanwhile, of necessity, he would give the air and naval forces "freest rein."[82]

Concluding his meeting with Pace and Hull, Ridgway raised anew his concern about Soviet intervention in Korea. As a possible means of discouraging it, he proposed that Washington announce immediately that it would view such intervention as "an act of war." Pace and Hull agreed that the suggestion "makes sense" and assured Ridgway it would be proposed as a course of action at the highest levels.[83]

There was a final personal matter which Ridgway handled in a handwritten query to Pace. Ridgway very much wanted to move his wife and son to Tokyo. Yet it would be foolish to do so if the Collins plan to name Ridgway to replace Ham Haislip as Army vice chief of staff in July, "regardless of events

---

* Three of the forty-eight B-29s were lost; seven, damaged. The seventy-five escorting fighters shot down three MIGs. The bridges remained intact.

in the Far East," were still operative. Ridgway would be "grateful" for guidance.[84]

At 7:30 P.M. Ridgway left Tokyo for Taegu in Pace's Constellation. Four hours later the pilot commenced his landing at Taegu. Unfamiliar with the setup he chose the wrong airfield: a newly built strip for light aircraft, rather than the main field. Barely missing a mountain, the pilot landed the Constellation with a great "lurch" and crash. He finally got the plane under control and braked to a stop in mud and gravel. It was a very close call and, for Ridgway, a harrowing way to end a long and tedious day.[85]

* * *

The next day, April 13, Ridgway found that Dauntless was progressing slowly but satisfactorily. Milburn's I Corps had not received any surprises. On the whole, although there were isolated pockets of enemy resistance, the opposition was classed as slight. Except in Mouchet's 3/24, UN casualties remained light or negligible.[86]

With Ted Brooks in tow, Ridgway toured some sections of the battlefield. He made stops at the CPs of I Corps, Shorty Soule's 3d Division, the ROK 1st Division, and Charlie Palmer's 1st Cav. Having been replaced on Line Kansas above Chunchon by the 1st Marine Division, the 1st Cav was in secret Eighth Army reserve, northeast of Seoul, prepared to counterattack a CCF salient. Ridgway congratulated Palmer on the division's camouflage and dispersion.[87]

Returning to Yoju, Ridgway met with Milburn, Hoge, Almond, Lev Allen, Pat Partridge, and others at 5:00 P.M. He informed these senior generals that Van Fleet would be arriving the following day, at which time Ridgway would turn over command of Eighth Army. Echoing the JCS line, he expressed complete confidence in Van Fleet, stressing his outstanding service in Greece. He made it clear that he, Ridgway, intended to keep Eighth Army—and Van Fleet—on a tight leash. Under no circumstances would there be any advance beyond phase two of Dauntless, Line Wyoming. All commanders would be alive for a possible massive CCF counterattack at any hour and be prepared to execute a withdrawal, per plan Audacious, on Army command.[88]

# V

James Alward Van Fleet, fifty-nine, was reared in the redneck orange grove country of central Florida. After being graduated from a private school (Summerlin Institute), he entered West Point in 1911, along with his classmates Eisenhower, Bradley, Joe Swing, and George Stratemeyer. He was a loner. His peers described him thusly in the yearbook, *Howitzer:* "Van is a brusque, outspoken individual and not much of a mixer. He finds pleasure in the society of magazines and books, and is a frequenter of the gym. Perhaps this reticent attitude has kept some of us from knowing him as well as we should. . . ."[89]

In the fall of his first class year (1914) Van Fleet did, however, make one strong and lasting impression. He turned out for the varsity football squad and put on such a "remarkable exhibition" that he made the first team as a running back, alternating with Bill Hoge and others. He "improved so rapidly and did such consistent work" that by the time of the Army-Navy game he was a first-string starter and played the entire game. That year the squad had a "perfect" season (9–0), including, climactically, a 20–0 rout of Navy. Van Fleet earned a football letter and everlasting fame for this remarkable, late-blooming athletic achievement.[90]

After graduation Van Fleet married a hometown girl, Hazel Moore, then went to France with the AEF. Promoted to major and command of the 17th Machine Gun Battalion of the 6th Infantry Division, he won a Silver Star Medal and was wounded the last week of the war. After he returned to the States, he and Hazel began a family, and he spent six consecutive years as military instructor and football coach in colleges in Kansas, South Dakota, and Florida. The Van Fleets had three children: two daughters, Helen Elizabeth and Dempsie, both of whom married West Pointers from the class of 1938, and a son, James A, Jr., who was graduated with the West Point class of 1948 and chose the Air Force.[91]

In the late 1920s Van Fleet's career took a bizarre nosedive. It began with what Joe Collins euphemistically wrote was a "strange mixup" at the Infantry School at Fort Benning, where Van Fleet spent a three-year tour as both student and instructor. At the time George Marshall was assistant commandant in charge of the academic department and was creating a "minor revolution" in the way infantry tactics were taught throughout the Army. Among his teaching assistants were Joseph Stilwell, Omar Bradley, Bedell Smith, and Joe Collins. As Collins (and later Bradley) told it, when Van Fleet joined the staff, Marshall, who had a notoriously poor memory for names, confused teetotaler Van Fleet with an alcoholic on the staff with a remarkably similar name. Thereafter, as Marshall rose to prominence in the Army in the 1930s, Van Fleet's career stood still. He was not selected for Command and General Staff School or the Army War College. Steadfastly confusing Van Fleet with the alcoholic, Marshall several times rejected recommendations that Van Fleet be promoted to brigadier general.[92]

As a result of this outrageous "mixup," Van Fleet was still a colonel on D day in Normandy. He commanded the splendidly trained 8th Infantry of the 4th Division in Joe Collins's VII Corps, which led the attack on Utah Beach and which on D plus one, linked up with Ridgway's 82d Airborne Division, then encircled behind the beachhead. Although Ridgway and his

ADC, Jim Gavin, were critical of many aspects of the 8th Infantry linkup, Collins and Bradley were immensely impressed with Van Fleet. Bradley wrote that "Van Fleet was another Ridgway, an absolutely superb soldier and leader," who "was earning about three Distinguished Service Crosses a day." Bradley and Collins cleared away the "mixup" about Van Fleet's identity and promoted him to brigadier general. Thereafter Van Fleet rose meteorically from regimental commander to assistant division commander (2d Division) to division commander (4th and 90th divisions) and two stars. In early March 1945, when Bill Hoge's 9th Armored Division in III Corps captured the Remagen bridge, Bradley named Van Fleet (who had won a second DSC) to replace the sluggish corps commander John Millikin and exploit the bridge-head.[93]

Van Fleet proved to be a superlative corps commander. After Bradley had crossed the Rhine, his First and Ninth armies encircled the German forces in the Ruhr. In this operation Ridgway's XVIII Airborne and Van Fleet's III Corps fought side by side and bagged more than 200,000 German prisoners. In the final weeks of the war Van Fleet's III Corps (reinforced to six divisions) was shifted to Third Army and, side by side with Johnnie Walker's XX Corps, spearheaded Third Army's drive into Austria. In a May 1945 letter to Marshall recommending Van Fleet for a third star, Eisenhower wrote: "He is extraordinarily courageous, a driver, and a leader. I have heard Patton and others describe him as 'the greatest fighting soldier this war has produced.' " Marshall, however, was not persuaded; the promotion to three stars was not approved. Moreover, to Eisenhower's dismay, Marshall did not include Van Fleet on a postwar list for permanent brigadier general.[94]

When Eisenhower replaced Marshall as chief of staff, he took steps to correct these career slights. He promoted Van Fleet to permanent brigadier general and, in early 1948, when Marshall, then secretary of state, asked Eisenhower to recommend an "impressive personality" to head the military mission to Greece, Eisenhower (with incoming Chief of Staff Omar Bradley's enthusiastic endorsement) recommended Van Fleet. He was, Eisenhower wrote Marshall, "the only officer we had in the war who fought his way all the way from regimental to corps commander. He is definitely *not* the intellectual type, but is direct and forceful and has a fighting record that would make anyone respect him." Acting on this recommendation, Marshall chose Van Fleet for the job, which carried the rank of three stars.[95]

Ravaged during World War II by Italian and German invasions, Greece was a fertile ground for communism in the postwar years. With support from Moscow, Communist insurgents had begun a civil war to gain control of the country. Granted hegemony over Greece in the postwar division of spheres of influence, the British soon decided the situation was hopeless—and too expensive—and pulled out. The 1947 Truman Doctrine, which included $300 million in aid to Greece, was designed to fill the vacuum left by the British. Greece was an early "test" of the Truman administration's containment doctrine and, as such, ranked high on the administration's foreign policy goals.[96]

When Van Fleet arrived in Greece in late February 1948, he found the military situation less than encouraging. The 140,000-man Greek Army (seven divisions) "lacked offensive spirit" and was shot through with "incompetent" older officers. Half its maneuver battalions were on static or semistatic guard duty. Van Fleet persuaded the Greeks to sack the incompetent officers, field home guard battalions to replace the maneuver battalions, and launch two major offensive actions (Dawn and Crown), employing first three, then six divisions. With these steps (and helped by another $150 million in aid from Washington), Van Fleet started what proved to be a remarkable turnaround in the Greek Army.[97]

Prodded and guided by Van Fleet and enriched by yet another $130 million from Washington, the Greek Army began energetic offensive operations in 1949 (Rocket and Torch). These military operations were fortuitously assisted by Yugoslav Marshal Josip Tito's political split with Moscow, which resulted in the closing of the Yugoslovia-Greek border, through which the Communist insurgents had been supplied. By August 1949 the Greek Army had routed the insurgents and driven them from Greece. It was a "landmark victory" for the Truman Doctrine and a great personal triumph for Van Fleet, who was lionized in Athens and elsewhere. Van Fleet returned to command the Second (paper) Army, virtually assured of a fourth star on retirement. He looked forward to spending his golden years in Florida's orange grove country and renewing ties with the University of Florida, where he had been head football coach in his early career.[98]

Truman and others tended to view Greece and Korea as similar situations. Both were peninsulas. Both were mountainous. Communist aggressors in both peninsulas were supplied from Communist states on the northern borders. The ultimate long-term "solution" to the Korean problem, like that of Greece, was the creation of a reliable indigenous army. Van Fleet had been almost miraculously successful in Greece. Even though he had never set foot in the Far East, perhaps he could repeat the near miracle in Korea. This thinking in part had led Marshall, Bradley, and Truman to choose Van Fleet to command Eighth Army. It would also provide Truman, Bradley, and Collins an opportunity to give Van Fleet a well-deserved fourth star before retirement, to redress the career humiliations he had endured for thirteen years, owing to Marshall's poor memory for names.

\* \* \*

Van Fleet arrived in Taegu at 12:30 P.M. on April 14. Ridgway met the plane. There followed a formal change of command ceremony and a press conference and press party. The war correspondents were favorably impressed by Van Fleet. *Time* magazine described him as "a rugged combat soldier and crack commander" who was "big-boned and muscular (6 ft. 1 in., 190 lbs.), blue-eyed, with greying, close-cropped hair." *Newsweek* described him as a teetotaler and nonsmoker, a "bluff" and "slow-speaking" commander who composed "verse" and who liked to hunt deer with a .45 pistol.[99]

Following these public ceremonies Ridgway met privately with Van Fleet and Lev Allen. Ridgway made it clear to both that he would keep a tight rein on Eighth Army. "To the extent you feel the situation warrants," he told Van Fleet, "please inform me prior to advancing in force beyond [Line] Utah." Furthermore, "no operations in force" would be conducted "beyond the Wyoming Line without prior approval" from Ridgway.[100]

At 7:00 P.M. Ridgway boarded Pace's Constellation, which had been rescued and shifted from the light aircraft strip, and flew back to Tokyo to prepare for MacArthur's departure. Ridgway's party included four confidants who would serve him in Tokyo: Bill Moorman, Day Surles, Walt Winton, and Hank Adams.[101]

Upon landing in Tokyo, Ridgway proceeded to the Imperial Hotel, where a suite had been reserved for him. There he met again with Pace. Although Pace could not at this point predict future high-level Army assignments, in response to Ridgway's query Pace suggested that Mrs. Ridgway and Matty Ridgway come out to Tokyo. However, they should not plan to occupy MacArthur's quarters in the embassy on a long-term basis. John Foster Dulles was en route to Tokyo as Truman's special envoy, to press for an early Japanese peace treaty, which, owing to earlier JCS opposition, had never been concluded. If it was successful, an American ambassador would soon be arriving to occupy the embassy. Ridgway should chose another residence suitable for his high station. Pace would find money to refurbish the residence and provide Ridgway a "special" living allowance.[102]

\* \* \*

Washington was nervous about the reaction of the Japanese people to the MacArthur firing. During the nearly six years of the occupation MacArthur had virtually displaced Emperor Hirohito as the titular political and spiritual leader of the Japanese. To offset the uncertainty and possible adverse reaction to his departure, Washington took certain steps to encourage the Japanese to assume responsibility for their own affairs and destiny. Toward that end Truman publicly stressed that the John Foster Dulles mission to arrange an early peace treaty had his fullest support. Meanwhile, Ridgway should probably issue a statement designed to fill the leadership void temporarily. The JCS suggested:

In such a statement you should feel free if you so desire to inform the Japanese people that you intend to continue the Occupation policies so ably conducted by

General MacArthur. You might make reference to the President's statement of yesterday regarding a Japanese Peace Treaty and assure the Japanese that you are wholly in sympathy with their desire for the early consummation of a Treaty along the lines already initiated by Ambassador Dulles and General MacArthur and that you will do all in your power to assist in accomplishing the objectives outlined in the President's statement. You might care also to express confidence in the continued desire and ability of the Japanese people to establish a new Japan which will be accepted as an equal and respected member of the family of nations.

A final suggestion is that any statement you might issue should be couched in generous but firm tones, so as to leave no doubt in the minds of the Japanese or any other interested parties, that as SCAP [supreme commander, allied powers], you are endowed with all the powers and authority previously vested in General MacArthur.[103]

The MacArthurs, meanwhile, were packing to leave. In an unprecedented gesture Emperor Hirohito came by. It was the first time in history that a Japanese monarch had called upon a foreigner who held no "official" status. On Sunday, April 15, the MacArthurs' last day in Japan, GHQ staffers and wives flocked to the embassy for teary farewells. Keeping a low profile, Ridgway attended church services, then spent the rest of the day and evening at the Imperial Hotel, reading and digesting documents relating to his awesome and far-flung command.[104]

Beginning at dawn the next day throngs of Japanese lined the road from Tokyo to Haneda Airport, one-half million, perhaps 1 million people. As the MacArthur motorcade passed, the Japanese waved and bowed, and many wept. At 7:00 A.M. the motorcade reached the airport, where Ridgway and Hickey had turned out a special honor guard and Army band. While MacArthur and his wife trooped the line, howitzers boomed a nineteen-gun salute and FEAF jets and bombers flew thunderously overhead. The band broke into "Auld Lang Syne." The women wept openly; the generals strained mightily to hold back tears. Not all succeeded. MacArthur and Ridgway shook hands, and then the MacArthurs boarded the plane and were gone. Returning to the Dai Ichi Building, Ridgway officially terminated Ned Almond's status as GHQ chief of staff and named the "acting" officer, Doyle Hickey, to succeed him. Sensitive to "public relations," he drafted the former ADC of the 1st Cav, Frank Allen, then commanding the Yokohama military district, to handle these matters for GHQ.[105]

# V I

The MacArthurs flew to Hawaii, where they arrived on the evening of April 16. Admiral Radford met the plane with full military ceremony. On the following day Honolulu officials arranged a twenty-mile parade through the city and Pearl Harbor to the vast World War II cemetery at the Punchbowl. About 100,000 cheering Hawaiians lined the streets, a foretaste of the massive adulation which the general was to witness in the coming days.[106]

After flying onward the same day, April 17, the MacArthurs arrived in San Francisco at 8:30 P.M. Al Wedemeyer, commanding the Sixth (paper) Army, met the plane. It was the first time in fourteen years that the MacArthurs had been in the States; their thirteen-year-old son, Arthur, had never been there. While en route to a downtown hotel in the dark, the MacArthurs' motorcade was engulfed by crowds of onlookers who caused such massive traffic jams that the trip took two hours. Police estimated the crowd along the route at 500,000.[107]

The following day, April 18, San Francisco officials staged a downtown ticker-tape parade. It culminated at City Hall, where MacArthur made a brief speech of thanks. In response to an earlier query from a reporter, he said: "I do not intend to run for any political office. . . . The only politics I have is contained in a single phrase known to all of you—'God Bless America.' " Few took that disclaimer at face value.[108]

MacArthur had been invited to address a joint session of Congress on April 19. He arrived in Washington shortly after midnight. George Marshall, the JCS, Truman's Army aide Harry Vaughan, and Congressman Joe Martin met the plane. While Marshall and MacArthur were shaking hands, a surging crowd of about 12,000 men, women, and children broke through police barriers. After police had restored order and rescued everyone, the MacArthur motorcade set off for a downtown hotel. More cheering crowds lined the dark streets.[109]

MacArthur arrived at the Capitol at noon on April 19, wearing a trim Eisenhower jacket devoid of ribbons. At 12:31 officials escorted him into the House to thunderous applause. No member of the Truman cabinet or the JCS was present. MacArthur spoke for thirty-seven minutes, during which he was interrupted at least fifty times by applause. The speech was televised live and broadcast on radio. An estimated 20 million viewers (including Omar Bradley) saw it on television.[110]

No one who witnessed or heard this speech was ever likely to forget it. It was quintessential MacArthur, "One of the most impressive and divisive oratorical performances of recent American times," as his biographer James aptly put it. "He spoke in an unhurried, yet incredibly forceful manner," James wrote, "his voice sounding deeply resonant and his phrases and sentences blending eloquence and sincerity, emotionalism and sweeping generalizations, in a way that moved even many listeners who found his logic and his proposals faulty or downright dangerous."[111]

The content of the speech was familiar. The Communist challenge was global and interlinked. It had to be met equally in Asia as well as Western

Europe. He could "think of no greater expression of defeatism" than to say American strength was "inadequate" to protect both fronts. "You cannot appease or otherwise surrender to Communism in Asia without simultaneously undermining our efforts to halt its advance in Europe."[112]

In Asia, China, unified by communism, was displaying "the same lust for the expansion of power which has animated every would-be conqueror since the beginning of time." Those who for varying reasons "would appease Red China" were "blind to history's clear lesson, for history teaches with unmistakable emphasis that appeasement but begets new and bloodier war."

The intervention of Red China in Korea had "created a new war and an entirely new situation," requiring "new decisions in the diplomatic sphere to permit the realistic adjustment of military strategy." He had "constantly called for the new political decisions essential to a solution," but these decisions had "not been forthcoming." As a result, the best that could be hoped for in Korea was "an indecisive campaign with its terrible and constant attrition. . . ."

Nothing was "more revolting" to him "than war." But "once war is forced upon us, there is no other alternative than to apply every available means to bring it to a swift end. War's very object is victory, not prolonged indecision. In war there can be no substitute for victory."

To "bring hostilities to an end" and save "countless American and Allied lives" would require, in MacArthur's view:

• Neutralization of the "sanctuary protection" given the enemy north of the Yalu in Manchuria.
• Intensification of the economic blockade against China.
• Imposition of a naval blockade against the China coast.
• Removal of restrictions on air reconnaissance of China's coastal areas and of Manchuria.
• Removal of restrictions on Chiang Kai-shek's forces on Formosa and logistical support "to contribute to their effective operation against the Chinese mainland."*

MacArthur then indulged in a bit of deceit. He said that while he had been "severely criticized in lay circles, principally abroad," for advancing the last four of these views, they were "fully shared" by "practically every military leader concerned with the Korean campaign, including our own Joint Chiefs of Staff."

During the very dark days of the New Year the JCS had prepared the

---

*Noticeably absent from this familiar litany was MacArthur's earlier recommendation to the JCS for all-out air attacks on Red China's warmaking potential.

January 12 contingency paper advocating some of these drastic steps. Subsequently the chiefs had tentatively endorsed MacArthur's (and Ridgway's) proposal for Chiang Kai-shek to launch a diversionary attack on the China mainland. But these contingency plans had been drawn or tentatively approved for a disaster in which Eighth Army was forced into a Dunkirk. Ridgway's turnaround of Eighth Army had obviated the need for such actions. Short of another disaster—a possible CCF air attack on Eighth Army or Soviet intervention—none of the chiefs now believed any of these measures would be required. Moreover, British military leaders, who were deeply "concerned with the Korean campaign," had never agreed to these proposed courses of action, even in the face of disaster and certainly did not "fully share" them then.

In conclusion, MacArthur spoke the deeply moving words that brought tears and were most remembered and quoted:

I am closing my fifty-two years of military service. When I joined the Army, even before the turn of the century, it was the fulfillment of all my boyish hopes and dreams. The world has turned over many times since I took the oath on the Plain at West Point, and the hopes and dreams have long since vanished, but I still remember the refrain of one of the most popular barrack ballads of that day which proclaimed most proudly that old soldiers never die; they just fade away.

And, like the old soldier of that ballad, I now close my military career and just fade away, an old soldier who tried to do his duty as God gave him the light to see that duty. Goodbye.

President Truman and Dean Acheson were contemptuous of the speech. The president saltily characterized it as "nothing but a bunch of bull shit." Acheson dismissed it as "demagogic" and "more than somewhat bathetic." The president—and perhaps Acheson—believed that "once all the hullabaloo died down, people would see what he was."[113]

They were sadly mistaken. The MacArthur address to Congress was probably the most important political event of the Korean War.

By that time the American people were sick of the war in Korea. What had seemingly begun as a fairly simple military task had turned into a nightmare. Nearly 70,000 American casualties had been incurred. It was galling that the war apparently could not be "won," that after nearly a year of fighting friends and enemies were again back on a line at the 38th Parallel. There were no mass protests or marches, no campus riots, no burning of draft cards, but there was deep and widespread dissatisfaction.

In the emotional binge following the speech a Gallup Poll showed surprising public support for MacArthur's policies. Of those polled, 54 percent favored MacArthur's proposal to bomb CCF bases in Manchuria, blockade the China coast, and help the Chinese Nationalists invade the mainland. A mere 34 percent opposed these measures. However, those polled expressed very strong opposition to MacArthur's implied call for all-out war with Red China. Only 30 percent favored that drastic course.[114]

MacArthur's speech was thus immensely satisfying to the majority. It released pent-up frustrations and served to confirm that there were alternatives—not necessarily MacArthur's, but perhaps others overlooked by the administration. It hardened opposition to the war, diminished Truman politically, and strengthened and emboldened the Republican party.[115]

It did something else as well. The "hullabaloo" over MacArthur scared the daylights out of the centrist and liberal Republicans. A right-wing Taft-MacArthur ticket in 1952 now seemed a very strong possibility. Believing such a ticket would be disastrous at the voting booths, centrist and liberal Republican leaders started talking up Eisenhower, who was still on active duty at NATO, as a possible candidate to oppose Taft.[116]

* * *

After another parade in Washington, the MacArthurs flew to New York City to take up permanent residence in an apartment in the Towers of the Waldorf-Astoria Hotel. The next day, April 20, New York gave MacArthur an awesome four-hour ticker-tape parade—bigger than that staged for Charles Lindbergh in 1927. Police estimated that 7.5 million people turned out along the route. They came not necessarily to express sympathy for MacArthur's war policy but merely to see and welcome a legendary giant of World War II.[117]

# VII

In Korea James Van Fleet took command of Eighth Army with a sure, steady hand. He was no stranger to the senior commanders; he had overlapped at West Point and in the ETO with Shrimp Milburn and Bill Hoge. He respected their abilities and combat experience in Korea. He did not know Ned Almond as well, but they had service in common: Both had commanded machine-gun battalions in the AEF, both had been wounded and decorated for valor there, and both had served in the Army of Occupation in Germany.

Van Fleet was much impressed by Eighth Army. He remembered:

If you have lived with troops, as I had in World War I, World War II and in Greece, you can very quickly get the feel of an army. You can actually just take a fairly fast jeep ride through its installations, stop for a word or two here and there, and at the end of the day have a pretty accurate idea of how well it will do in combat.

Everywhere I went to inspect the Eighth Army my spirits rose. I would shout "Hi, soldier!" and back would come a grin, a salute and a "Hi, General!" The whole atmosphere was alert, well disciplined, friendly, confident. Once a corporal asked me in all seriousness, "What's holding us back, General? Why don't we get it over with?" In place after place I talked to young second lieutenants with grim, set fighting jaws—and I knew our army was ready. . . .

[It] had reached a peak which it never quite achieved either before or since. It was a truly magnificent outfit.[118]

Ridgway and the Eighth Army staff had thoroughly briefed Van Fleet on the CCF and the impending offensive. He wrote later:

The Chinese Reds were ready for the biggest attack of all. They were supremely confident. There was no secret at all about their intentions. In fact they were bragging openly on the radio that they were going to drive us back and recapture Seoul. This tactic of calling your shots in a war to frighten the enemy is as old as Julius Caesar, but it has an eerie kind of effectiveness in the Orient. Because "face" is so important, you know that no boast is an idle one. . . . The atmosphere in Taegu was tense.[119]

On April 16 a strange, almost scary quiet descended over the whole of Eighth Army's front. The Eighth Army historian wrote that the enemy continued to withdraw, the Army advance was "practically unopposed," and "the enemy continued to employ weak forces in his normal elastic type of defense. During the previous week a general decrease in intensity as well as in quality of resistance had been noted." This did not, however, "lessen the caution of UN forces in their advance . . . that the enemy was going to attack was a foregone conclusion."[120]

By April 19 all lead regiments of I Corps committed to the attack to the Iron Triangle were on Line Utah. These were (left to right): Harris's 65th Infantry, the Turkish Brigade, Britt's 24th Infantry, Check's 27th Infantry, Garland's 19th Infantry, and Perez's 21st Infantry. Upon reaching Line Utah, Babe Bryan decided that the 21st would go into reserve, replaced by the 5th. Throckmorton turned over to Harry Wilson and departed Korea to become senior aide and "coat holder" to Joe Collins. He went on to a splendid Army career and four stars.[121]

Before launching the onward attack to Line Wyoming, Van Fleet ordered a forty-eight-hour halt. This was designed to give all attacking elements time to consolidate their rear echelons on Line Utah and to bring up supplies. The general advance would resume on the morning of April 21. At that time, also, the 1st Marine Division would attack north from Line Kansas to Line Quantico above the Hwachon Dam.[122]

* * *

In Tokyo Ridgway was busy broadening his horizons and absorbing heavy new responsibilities. He "established a rapport" with Japanese Prime Minister Shigeru Yoshida. He met with John Foster Dulles to discuss the background and problems of the Japanese peace treaty. He initiated an "intense study" of GHQ's primary responsibility—the defense of Japan against a possible Soviet invasion—and the existing plans to meet it.[123]

The last investigation convinced Ridgway that he did not have clear-cut authority from the JCS to withdraw Eighth Army to protect Japan from a Soviet attack. He therefore cabled the JCS on April 17 requesting that "in event of Soviet attack against the Far East Command" he be permitted: "A) to initiate withdrawal at my discretion of UN forces from Korea and B) to utilize redeployed UN forces in defense of the Far East Command." The chiefs responded on April 19 that they agreed in principle and that he should plan accordingly. However, they would not give Ridgway the blanket authority he requested. He would commence actual withdrawals "only upon instructions furnished you" after the JCS had evaluated "information from you as to the conditions obtaining." Meanwhile, at Collins's suggestion, the JCS began a review of all outstanding directives to Ridgway with an eye to eliminating those that were no longer applicable to the existing situation and codifying the others.[124]

Ridgway was also deeply concerned about the impact of MacArthur's relief on the Far East Command. MacArthur was not universally loved, but many senior commanders shared his views on the war and resented what was perceived as the shabby and cruel way he had been dismissed. In a sense the dismissal could be interpreted as a reflection on their own performances. There was a possibility, albeit remote, that some of the senior commanders, out of misguided loyalty to MacArthur, might initiate actions resulting in a widening of the war.

These concerns and others led Ridgway to compose his first preliminary "directive" to his senior air, naval, and ground commanders. It was surely the most extraordinary document of the Korean War. Entitled "Prevention of World War III" and issued at about the time MacArthur was addressing the joint session of Congress, Ridgway advised the commanders that more detailed instructions would be issued soon, but meanwhile:

The grave and ever present danger of an extension of current hostilities in Korea places a heavy responsibility upon all echelons of this command, but particularly upon those capable of offensive action.
This responsibility in essence can be discharged to the satisfaction and in the interest of the American People, in fact of the free world, *only* if every commander

is fully alive to the possible consequences of his acts, if every commander has imbued his command with a like sense of responsibility for its acts; has set up, and by frequent tests, has satisfied himself of the effectiveness of his machinery for insuring his control of the offensive reactions of his command to enemy action; and, in final analysis, is himself determined that no act of his command shall bring about an extension of the present conflict, except when such act is taken in full accordance with the spirit and letter of the instructions which will issue.

International tensions within and bearing upon this theater have created acute danger of World War III. It is the intense determination of our people, and of all the free peoples of the world, to prevent this catastrophe, if that can be done without appeasement or sacrifice of principle.

In the day to day, in fact the hour-to-hour performance of his duties, I shall insist that every responsible commander, regardless of rank, bear constantly in mind that the discharge of his responsibilities in this respect is a sacred duty.

In accordance with the spirit of the foregoing, it is my intention to reserve to myself to a large extent responsibility for decisions which, by committing elements of this command to retaliatory or other forms of offensive action, might extend the area of current hostilities, and so heighten the danger of precipitating a world conflict.

In the course of implementing this intention it may well be that restrictions and restraints imposed will be viewed as unreasonable. To the extent that commanders at all levels appreciate the spirit of this communication, that feeling will be minimized, and attainment of the basic purpose made measurably easier.

I shall accept, in full, responsibility for such restrictions and restraints, expecting the full and willing cooperation of all concerned in insuring that my reasons, as set forth herein, are as fully explained to the members of their commands, as circumstances justify.[125]

Ridgway sent copies of this preliminary directive to the JCS, where it was received like a breath of fresh air. Bradley wrote later: "It was a great relief to finally have a man in Tokyo who was in agreement with the Administration views on containing the war."[126]

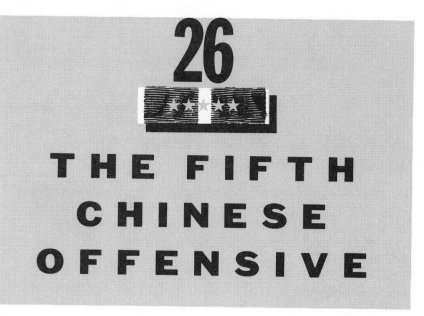

# THE FIFTH CHINESE OFFENSIVE

## I

Ridgway had assured Van Fleet that he would "stay out of his hair," but he evidently found it difficult to let go of Eighth Army at this critical time. Notwithstanding his earlier efforts to dissuade MacArthur from visiting Korea at the beginning of major offensive operations, Ridgway returned to Korea on the morning of April 21.[1] His visit coincided with the launching of step two of Operation Dauntless, the main objectives of which were two:

• The advance of Shrimp Milburn's I Corps, on Eighth Army's left, from Line Utah to Line Wyoming at the Iron Triangle.
• The advance of Bill Hoge's IX Corps in Eighth Army's center from Line Kansas to Line Quantico, above the Hwachon Reservoir.

Van Fleet, in command of Eighth Army for one week, had made a fine first impression. Everybody liked him. Eighth Army engineer Pat Strong remembered: "Van Fleet was, above everything else, a fighting field soldier. . . . [H]is broad face had a natural friendliness that instantly set his subordinates at ease. He was a man more at home in the out-of-doors with a gun and dog than at a plush desk. I never recall his voice raised in anger." Bittman Barth, who had served under Van Fleet in the ETO, recalled: "I was certainly glad to see him. . . . The years had not changed General Van Fleet. He was still the same big, kindly, soft-spoken man I had known before. His quiet self-assurance transmitted to us a feeling of confidence. . . . He looked younger and even more vigorous than when I first served under him in 1944."[2]

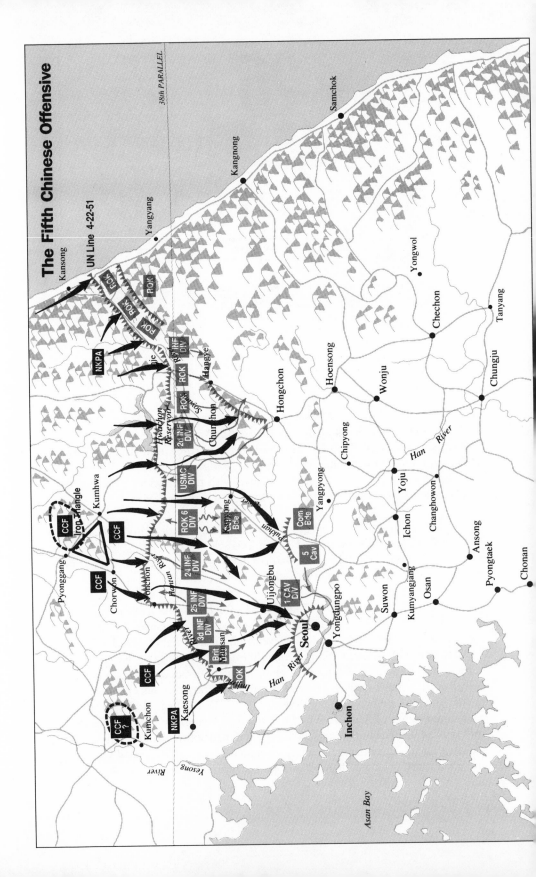

By this time Van Fleet had a good "feel" for the situation. He expected that the second step of Dauntless would provoke a major CCF counterattack. He was fully prepared. When it came, Eighth Army would, if necessary, fall back in orderly fashion, in accordance with Ridgway's plan Audacious. He generally agreed with Ridgway that for the time being real estate was not important; the main task was to kill Communists. However, his thinking differed sharply from Ridgway's in one respect: He believed it was vital politically and psychologically to prevent the recapture of Seoul. Giving up Seoul, Van Fleet said, would "ruin the spirit of the nation." He would do everything possible to hold on Line Lincoln (or Golden) and deny the CCF that prize, even though he would run the risk of fighting with the unfordable Han River at his back.[3]

Van Fleet likewise agreed with Ridgway that "at this time" there should be no advance into North Korea beyond Lines Wyoming and Quantico. However, Van Fleet believed that "later in the summer," depending on enemy moves, the weather, and other factors, it might be advantageous to advance Eighth Army's right flank as far north as Wonsan. This could be done by one or more amphibious operations. The Wonsan area was lightly held; the CCF would have difficulty maintaining a force to counter a UN thrust there. It would keep the enemy off-balance and possibly draw CCF strength away from Eighth Army's main front.[4]

Ridgway was not pleased to hear this talk. "It had the makings of the same damn situation that MacArthur had blundered into when he separated the X Corps. I thought he'd get heavy casualties out of it with little return. I would have none of it."[5]

There was a larger point. The Truman administration policy, to which Ridgway subscribed, was to hold Eighth Army roughly along the 38th Parallel and seek a negotiated settlement. Another dramatic amphibious advance deep into North Korea could diminish the chances for settlement by causing the Red Chinese to "lose face" or by again posing a theoretical threat to their border. Was it possible that Van Fleet did not understand these nuances? Was he in fundamental disagreement with administration policy? He had achieved "total victory" in Greece—killed or expelled the Communist insurgents. Had he decided he could do the same in Korea?[6]

This meeting led Ridgway to issue Van Fleet a written directive on the following day, April 22. Stipulating that "acquisition of terrain in itself is of little or no value" and that "at any time" Van Fleet could "be directed by competent authority to initiate a withdrawal to a defensive position and there be directed to defend indefinitely," Ridgway declared:

Your mission is to repel aggression against so much of the territory (and the people therein) of the Republic of Korea as you now occupy and, in collaboration with the Government of the Republic of Korea, to establish and maintain order in that territory. . . . You will direct the efforts of your forces toward inflicting maximum personnel casualties and matériel losses on hostile forces in Korea, consistent with the maintenance intact of all your major units and the safety of your troops.

In the pursuit of this mission Van Fleet was authorized "to conduct military operations, including amphibious and airborne landings, as well as ground operations in Korea north of the 38th Parallel," subject to two limitations:

- Any advances beyond Line Wyoming would be on Ridgway's orders only.
- Under no circumstances would any of Van Fleet's forces "of whatever strength" cross the Manchurian or USSR borders of Korea or would "any of your non-Korean forces even operate in North Korean territory contiguous to those borders."[7]

That morning the right flank of Shrimp Milburn's I Corps attacked toward Line Wyoming with six infantry regiments line abreast. Left to right they were William Harris's Puerto Rican 65th of the 3d Division; the Turkish Brigade, Henry Britt's 24th Infantry, and Gilbert Check's 27th Infantry of the 25th Division; Pete Garland's 19th and Harry Wilson's 5th of the 24th Division. Jim Boswell's 7th, Gerry Kelleher's 35th, and Gines Perez's 21st served as reserve regiments for these divisions; the 15th Infantry of the 3d division was assigned to I Corps reserve at Seoul.[8]

The attack was slow and methodical, tightly controlled by phase lines. Enemy resistance was light or nonexistent. Most regiments advanced a mile or a mile and a half. However, Britt's 24th Infantry, which encountered a "stubborn" pocket of opposition, advanced only a quarter of a mile.[9]

By this time the rumors and speculation that the CCF would throw its 800-plane Air Force at Eighth Army in conjunction with a counteroffensive was accepted as gospel. For that reason, on April 17 FEAF had commenced an all-out air assault on the new CCF airfields in North Korea. The attacks were mounted daily by about a dozen B-29s, plus scores of B-26s and fighter-bombers. The B-29s were escorted by F-86 jets based at Suwon and elsewhere. The jets usually met large formations of Manchuria-based MIG-15s in MIG Alley.

By April 21 the airmen were claiming the attacks on the airfields had achieved complete success. All runways had been cratered; control facilities had been knocked out; many CCF aircraft had been destroyed on the ground or driven back into Manchuria. However, Van Fleet and his ground commanders were skeptical. Experience had shown that Korean laborers could fill bomb craters rapidly—virtually overnight—and that meant CCF aircraft could redeploy to North Korea in a matter of a few hours.[10]

Hence ground commanders in I Corps, fully expecting CCF air attacks, kept wary eyes on the sky. But aerial observation was limited. The CCF had lighted immense brush fires, probably to conceal troop movements or concentrations. The battlefield was thus clouded over with billowing smoke and haze.[11]

* * *

To the right, in the central sector, Bill Hoge's IX Corps attacked north from Line Kansas with two divisions: the ROK 6th on the left and the 1st Marine Division on the right. Burke's Commonwealth Brigade, withdrawn to Kapyong, was in IX Corps reserve. The ROKs were supported by the New Zealand artillery battalion but by no non-Korean armor, A/A or infantry units. The ROKs and Marines were backed by IX Corps artillery, which included the veteran 92d, and the newly arrived 213th and 987th Armored FABs.[12]

The ROK 6th Division, commanded by Chang Do Yung, who was only twenty-eight years old, had been fighting fairly well for two months. It was fully manned by 10,000 Koreans. However, as Van Fleet later put it, the division had "limited firepower": rifles and light machine guns and a few 60- and 81-mm mortars, but no heavy machine guns and no 4.2-inch mortars. It had but one organic field artillery battalion, the ROK 27th, equipped with 105-mm howitzers.[13]

The division was composed of the normal three infantry regiments. The 19th and 2d regiments led the attack, left to right, line abreast; the 7th Regiment constituted the reserve. The terrain was very rough and mountainous. Because there were few roads in this sector, the divisional artillery battalion could not move forward easily and was thus "practically useless," as Van Fleet later put it. The New Zealand artillery battalion, closely backing up the division, was likewise hindered in its forward movement.[14]

On the right of the ROK 6th Division the Marine Corps sector was manned by the Seventh Marines on the left, the Fifth Marines in the center, and an attached ROK Marine Corps regiment on the right. Both American Marine regiments now had new commanders: in the Seventh, he was Herman Nickerson, Jr.; in the Fifth, Richard M. Hayward. Frank McAlister's First Marines were in reserve.[15]

The Marines—and ROK Marines—had an easy day. They advanced two and a half to four miles against "negligible resistance." The U.S. Marine historian wrote: "An ominous quiet hung over the front as green wood smoke limited visibility to a few hundred yards." Assigned to capture the Hwachon

Dam, ROK Marine patrols crossed the Pukhan River and entered the town of Hwachon, which was virtually deserted. American Marine engineers came forward to put a floating bridge across the Pukhan so a ROK Marine battalion could cross the following day and capture the dam. American Marines would then jam the sluice gates open, so that the enemy could not again flood the Pukhan River.[16]

During that day the ROK 2d Regiment, in the right sector of the ROK 6th Division, and the Seventh Marines, operating in difficult terrain along the snaking Pukhan River, lost lateral contact. By the end of the day there was a gap about a mile or more wide between the two forces. Upon learning of the gap, Bill Hoge ordered the ROK 6th Division commander to close it at once. For reasons not known, these orders were not carried out, and the gap remained.[17]

*　*　*

On the following day, Sunday, April 22, the assault regiments in I and IX Corps advanced slowly and carefully. The weather was clear and crisp but smoke still hung in the air. The most noteworthy achievement was that of the ROK Marine regiment. One of its battalions crossed the Pukhan River and captured the Hwachon Dam and occupied the town of Hwachon. As planned, American Marine engineers came forward to jam the sluice gates open. Upon inspection, the engineers concluded that task would be more formidable than anticipated.[18]

Late that afternoon the Turks in I Corps captured a garrulous Chinese officer and several enlisted men. The officer professed to be an artilleryman leading a party to make a survey for his battery, which had moved to forward positions. He told the Turks that the CCF would launch a major offensive that very night. The Turks passed the information to higher headquarters. A similar report came in from Babe Bryan. Based on the interrogation of a CCF soldier captured by his 24th Division at 7:00 P.M., Bryan warned Shrimp Milburn that the CCF offensive would begin in about two hours (9:00 P.M.). He added, "I think this is what we have been waiting for." The 3d Division historian wrote: "That evening command posts on the line received the message, in effect 'Watch out! Tonight's the night!' "[19]

## II

At about 10:00 P.M. April 22 the CCF struck Eighth Army with immense manpower across a forty-mile front. The Chinese committed nine armies (twenty-seven divisions, comprising about 250,000 men) to the attack. As before, the CCF came swarming out of the night by the light of a full but this time smoke-hazed moon, blowing bugles and horns and shooting flares. It was the start of the biggest battle of the Korean War.[20]

Van Fleet had assumed that the great mass of CCF would attack due south down the highways from Munsan and Uijongbu toward Seoul. He was mostly right: six CCF armies (eighteen divisions) struck directly at Shrimp Milburn's I Corps above Seoul; but the CCF also sent elements of three armies down the center of the peninsula at Bill Hoge's IX Corps. It was not clear at first whether the latter was merely a blocking force or whether it was a convergence force designed to encircle I Corps from the east.

\* \* \*

On the left (or west) I Corps sector near Munsan the CCF attack was mounted by two fresh armies (Sixty-third, Sixty-fourth) of six divisions. The aim of these armies was to capture Seoul in a powerful lightning stroke and present it to Mao Tse-tung on May Day, the Communist international holiday. The Sixty-third Army (about 30,000 men) spearheaded this important mission.

The left sector of I Corps was still held by the ROK 1st Division and Tom Brodie's British Brigade, the latter reinforced by the Belgian Battalion. Although they had engaged in aggressive patrolling north of the Imjin River, these UN troops, numbering about 15,000 men, were on static defense. They were backed by the 45th Royal Artillery battalion and the 9th and 58th FABs of the 3d Division. The American 15th Infantry and Calvin Hannum's 73d Tank Battalion, in I Corps reserve, were on standby to reinforce this sector if required.

The main weight of the CCF Sixty-third Army's three divisions fell on the British Brigade. It was deployed as follows: the Gloucester Battalion on the left, the Royal Northumberland Fusiliers Battalion in the center, the Belgian Battalion on the right, and the Royal Ulster Rifles Battalion in reserve. The Gloucesters and Fusiliers were on the south bank of the shallow, fordable Imjin; the Belgians held an enclave on the north bank at the junction of the Imjin and Hantan rivers. The brigade "front" spanned about nine miles. Contrary to Ridgway's orders, the units were not "intact"; only key points were held and there was scant lateral contact between companies. As one British historian aptly put it, "Under these conditions it was clearly impossible to prevent penetration by a strong, well-organized, and skillfully executed attack carried out by night."

The adjutant of the Gloucesters, Anthony Farrar-Hockley, remembered the onslaught:

The attackers enter; hundreds of Chinese soldiers clad in khaki suits; plain, cheap cotton caps; rubber-soled canvas shoes upon their feet; their shoulders, chests and backs criss-crossed with cotton bandoliers of ammunition: upon their hips, gre-

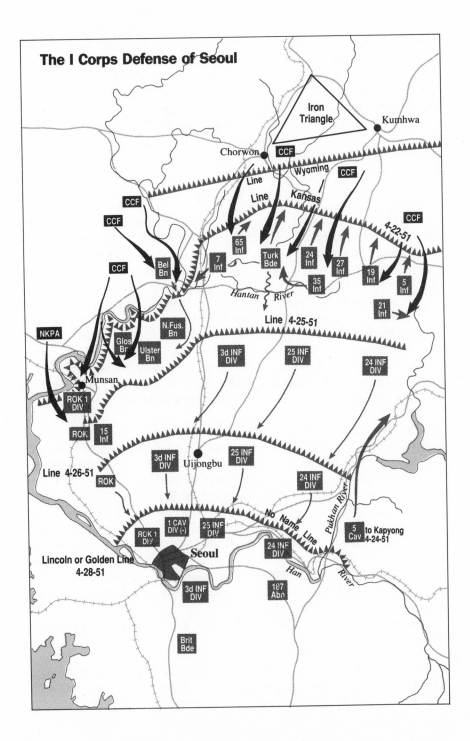

The I Corps Defense of Seoul

nades. . . . Those in the forefront of the battle wear steel helmets that are reminiscent of the Japanese. Their weapons—rifles, carbines, "burp guns," and Tommy guns that we supplied to Chiang Kai-shek—are ready in their hands. Behind, on mule or pony limbers, are their guns and ammunition. Between the two lines, on sweating backs, or slung between two men upon stout bamboo poles, their mortars and machine guns travel forward. No Oxford carriers, no jeeps or trailers, no gun prime-movers here; but if they lack these aids to war, they do not lack what we do most: men. The hundreds grow to thousands on the river bank as, padding through the night, they close with us: eight hundred Gloucesters astride the road to Seoul—the road the Chinese mean to clear at any cost.[21]

The British reputation for being slow on offense but unshakable on defense was demonstrated again. Notwithstanding the massive enemy manpower, the British Brigade held most of its ground during the initial onslaught and killed or wounded thousands of CCF. Fragmented, encircled, and cut off, British companies or smaller units fought with magnificent courage and sacrifice.

In the initial CCF onslaught the Belgian Battalion, commanded by B.E.M. Crahay, was cut off and surrounded north of the Imjin River. Learning of this, Brodie asked Shorty Soule for a rescue mission. In response Soule ordered Jim Boswell's reserve 7th Infantry to send armor and an infantry battalion to extricate the Belgians. Boswell chose Fred Weyand's crack 1/7. Reinforced by Patton tanks of Wilson Hawkin's 64th battalion, Weyand launched his urgent assignment, but it proved to be dangerous and difficult.[22]

By dawn on April 23 the British were under very heavy siege. Elements of the Gloucesters and Fusiliers, isolated from the Belgians, contracted into tighter hilltop perimeters or withdrew to more tenable positions. The Ulsters hurried forward from reserve to reinforce the three other embattled battalions. British casualties were heavy; CCF casualties were staggering.

\* \* \*

The I Corps sector to the immediate right of the British Brigade was held by William Harris's Puerto Rican 65th Infantry, reinforced by the attached Filipino Battalion, and farther right by the Turkish Brigade. In all, the Puerto Ricans, Filipinos, and Turks numbered about 10,000 men. The CCF attacked this sector with two full armies (Twelfth, Fifteenth) composed of six divisions (about 50,000 men). Chaos ensued.

The Turks, who were good on offense but poor on defense, also lived up to their reputation. Unfortunately—and inexplicably—the Turkish commander, Tahsin Yazici, was on R and R in Japan. Bittman Barth remembered that the Turks were "shattered":

The attack came at dark all along the Turkish front. Accurate enemy artillery fire of considerable volume was placed on our front line positions as far back as the artillery area. By 9 P.M. the Turkish 5th, 7th and 9th companies were surrounded and the 1st Company, in reserve about 3,000 yards behind the line, was fighting to escape envelopment. . . . By eleven o'clock the officer in temporary command of the Brigade reported that all companies were surrounded except two and requested authority to displace his headquarters south of the [Hantan] River. This was granted.[23]

The surviving Turks fled below the Hantan. Fortunately Barth was able to withdraw the Turkish artillery, his own 64th FAB, and I Corps's 936th FAB to safer positions south of the river. To fill the gap left by the Turks, Sladen Bradley ordered Gerry Kelleher's reserve 35th Infantry forward on the double.

The CCF simultaneously struck the Puerto Ricans and Filipinos. The 65th commander, William Harris, remembered:

They really hit us. . . . As I reconstructed the Chinese attack later, it seemed to me that the main thrust had been at the 65th and our boundary [on the left] with the British. I believe that the enemy attack bounced off us, spilled over on both sides of us and then concentrated on the British and the Turks. . . . On our left flank we had that reliable, unflappable British Brigade and they really caught hell. [On our right] the Turkish Brigade had fallen back some ten or twelve miles. . . . As long as the Turks were on the offensive and the Chinese were running, the Turks were pretty good. But when the going was tough, they were hard to find.[24]

All four battalions of the 65th Infantry came under severe attack. St. Clair's 1/65 and Jerry Allen's 3/65 held and inflicted yet more slaughter on the CCF. But the Filipino Battalion and the 2/65, now commanded by Laurence A. Johnson, which absorbed the brunt of the attack, were forced back. In an effort to retain an integrated front, the 1/65 and 3/65 were compelled to give ground as well. Harris recalled: "In the dark such a move becomes extremely difficult. In fact, about four that morning my CP came under terrific artillery fire and we were forced to move in the dark too. It was as though the enemy had laid hands on our defensive plans. . . ."[25]

Upon learning that the Puerto Ricans were falling back, Shorty Soule ordered Jim Boswell's reserve 7th Infantry (less Fred Weyand's 1/7, which was extricating the Belgians) to plug the gap in the line. Boswell came up smartly and temporarily incorporated Jerry Allen's 3/65 into the 7th Infantry. The hard-hit Filipinos and the 1/65 and 2/65 reassembled in some disarray below the Hantan River.[26]

The net effect of these maneuvers was a substantial change in the I Corps order of battle to the right of the British Brigade: Jim Boswell's 7th Infantry in place of the Puerto Ricans and Filipinos; Gerry Kelleher's 35th Infantry in place of the Turks. These regiments were backed by a powerful array of artillery situated on the south bank of the Hantan: the 10th, 39th, and 58th FABs of the 3d Division, the 64th FAB and Turkish artillery battalion of the 25th Division, plus the 176th, the 936th, and the 937th FABs of I Corps.[27]

The artillery had been pre-sighted on probable lines of CCF attack, and the gunners had stockpiled great quantities of ammo. By now most of the artillerymen were battle-hardened, highly trained, and well disciplined. In this crisis they stood stoutly at their posts and rained thousands of shells on the advancing CCF, killing or wounding thousands of the enemy. One proud gunner told a *Time* war correspondent: "The gullies in front of us are already full of Chinese dead, and we intend to keep adding to the pile."[28]

\* \* \*

The I Corps sector farther right was held by Henry Britt's 24th Infantry and Gilbert Check's 27th Infantry, about 8,000 men. Two CCF armies (Twenty-seventh, Sixtieth) of six divisions (about 50,000 men) attacked in this area.

Fortunately for Britt and his men the initial CCF attack bypassed the 24th Infantry. However, the collapse of the Turks on the left of the 24th Infantry exposed that flank. As a result, Sladen Bradley ordered the 24th to withdraw most of its element to the Hantan River but to maintain lateral contact with the 27th Infantry on the right. By dawn on April 23 the 2/24 and 3/24 had crossed to the south bank of the river; the Baron Baranowski's 1/24 held north of it, tied in diagonally with the 27th Infantry.[29]

The CCF hit the left sector of the 27th Infantry very hard with artillery, infantry, and—astonishingly—a few T-34 tanks. In another remarkable performance, the Wolfhounds held in close, hand-to-hand fighting, killing or wounding hundreds of the enemy. The CCF backed off in the dark, then hit the right sector of the regiment about dawn. By this time Bittman Barth had directed the firepower of eight artillery batteries (forty-eight howitzers) of the 8th, 90th, and 176th FABs into the 27th's sector. He remembered:

It was a machine gunner's and artilleryman's dream. The Reds came swarming across the rice paddies in front of the waiting doughboys in mass formation. Eight batteries of artillery, all the machine guns available, and several tanks poured in rapid fire. After about thirty minutes the Reds had had enough. The remnants retreated, carrying what wounded they could and leaving nearly a thousand dead and wounded behind. The Wolfhounds were not bothered any more that day.[30]

The five artillery battalions of the 25th Division, supplemented by the big howitzers of I Corps, maintained continuous fire on the CCF. Barth's exec, William Dick, later calculated that during the first twenty-four hours of the CCF offensive the four 25th artillery battalions alone fired 21,000 rounds of

105s and 2,500 rounds of 155s. This rain of steel continued to exact a terrible toll on the CCF.[31]

## III

To the right of Milburn's I Corps the CCF simultaneously launched the strong thrust down the center of the peninsula at Bill Hoge's IX Corps. Elements of three CCF armies (Twentieth, Thirty-ninth, Fortieth) comprising nine divisions of about 90,000 men were committed.[32]

Hoge's IX Corps was thinly disposed. The fully manned but poorly equipped and supported ROK 6th Division was on the left flank; the 1st Marine Division was on the right flank. Operating in rugged terrain in the Kapyong River valley, the ROK 6th Division had lost lateral contact with the Marines on its right and had only a tenuous link with I Corps on its left. As a consequence these 10,000 ROKs stood virtually alone.

The CCF threw two divisions (about 18,000 men) against the ROK 6th Division. The upshot was another disgraceful ROK bugout. The two forwardmost regiments, the 2d and 19th, "fled in disorder without offering the slightest resistance." The 19th fell back about six miles; the 2d, about twelve miles. The division's 7th Regiment, ordered from reserve to backstop the 19th, "failed to attack as ordered and fled to the rear in confusion." The ROKs in all three regiments abandoned arms, weapons (including thirteen howitzers of the ROK 27th FAB), and equipment "in great quantities."[33]

These ROKs were, of course, roundly condemned. Van Fleet remembered: "Everywhere—in the nearby battle lines and at headquarters all the way back to Seoul—our soldiers were damning the South Koreans. At the first sign of trouble they had collapsed; they had threatened our whole army with extinction. They were just no good and it was useless for us to be getting shot at 5,000 miles from home in our futile effort to help them."[34]

Later, in a report to Ridgway, Bill Hoge officially expressed that condemnation: "The rout and dissolution of the [ROK 6th Division] regiments was [sic] entirely uncalled for and disgraceful in all aspects. . . . The fact that all units in the division from squads to regiments withdrew in disorganized confusion without offering resistance, and that weapons and equipment were abandoned to the enemy, indicated a lack of leadership and control of all grades of officers and noncommissioned officers."[35]

The collapse of the ROK 6th Division gravely endangered non-ROK forces in its immediate vicinity. The closest was the New Zealand artillery battalion, which was directly supporting the division. "With some difficulty," a British historian wrote in understatement, "the 16th New Zealand Field . . . disengaged." It about-faced and proceeded south to Kapyong, where its parent organization, the Commonwealth Brigade, was in IX Corps reserve. It arrived there safely and without losing any of its guns.[36]

Two of the three IX Corps artillery battalions, the 987th and 92d, positioned to the right rear of the ROK 6th Division, were likewise imperiled. When the ROKs collapsed, both units began withdrawing to safer positions. One failed; the other succeeded.

The failure occurred in the green 987th FAB, which had been reinforced by the green 2d Rocket Field Artillery Battery (equipped with 105mm howitzers in place of nonavailable rockets). While attempting to backtrack, the weight of the 987th's vehicles collapsed the road. Inasmuch as there was no time to build a bypass or to find another road, all the equipment behind the collapse had to be abandoned. This included fifteen self-propelled 105-mm howitzers, sixty vehicles, and "critical command and fire direction equipment." However, most of the artillerymen escaped.[37]

The other IX Corps artillery battalion, the 92d, succeeded. Commanded by Leon Lavoie, this outfit was by now battlewise. It had landed at Inchon and Wonsan with X Corps and had helped extricate the Marines from the Chosin Reservoir. The 92d FAB normally consisted of eighteen 155-mm self-propelled howitzers. For this mission, however, it had swapped its six-gun B Battery for A Battery of the 17th FAB—four valuable eight-inch howitzers. Lavoie was determined not to lose any of his own guns; to lose one of the eight-inchers on loan was simply unthinkable. Rather than risk a hurried retreat over narrow, uncertain roads, Lavoie boldly elected to stand his ground and fight.

When the ROKs collapsed, he found a suitable site astride a road on Line Kansas near Chinchon and circled the wagons, placing the eight-inch howitzers in the center of the perimeter. Soon the road was jammed with fleeing ROKs, who washed southbound around the perimeter. The Army historian wrote that Lavoie and his men "tried desperately to collect stragglers and stop the withdrawal"; but "the momentum was too great," and most of the ROKs "continued determinedly on," leaving Lavoie and his artillerymen to face the oncoming CCF.*[38]

\* \* \*

The collapse of the ROK 6th Division left a gaping ten-mile hole in Eighth Army's central front, which stretched from Babe Bryan's 24th Division (on the extreme right flank of I Corps) to O. P. Smith's 1st Marine Division.

---

*Many men of the 987th FAB and 2d Rocket Battery and another American outfit, Company C, 2d Chemical Mortar Battalion (which had lost thirteen 4.2-inch mortars in the retreat), found refuge in Lavoie's perimeter.

Both American divisions were compelled to refuse (i.e., bend back) their exposed flanks and face the enemy penetration.

After smashing through the ROK 6th Division the CCF 60th Division sideslipped west to join its sister division, the 59th (of the Twentieth Army) in an attack on Babe Bryan's 24th Division. At that time Babe Bryan had deployed Pete Garland's 19th Infantry on the left, Harry Wilson's 5th Infantry on the right, and Gines Perez's 21st Infantry in reserve. By daylight on April 23, the Eighth Army historian wrote, the 59th Division had pushed three miles deep into some areas of the 24th Division sector. As a result of this, and the threat posed by the 60th Division on his right, Bryan was compelled to withdraw the 5th and 19th regiments and to commit Perez's 21st Infantry (with the 8th Ranger Company attached) from reserve to face into the "void" on the division's right flank. These maneuvers temporarily stabilized the division and saved it from being overrun, but Bryan and his men remained perilously exposed.[39]

\* \* \*

To the right of the gaping hole three CCF divisions (115th and 116th of the Thirty-ninth Army; 120th of the Fortieth Army) threatened the left flank of the 1st Marine Division. At the time the Seventh Marines (on the left) and the Fifth Marines (in the center) were on Line Quantico at the town of Hwachon, west of the Hwachon Reservoir, and the ROK marine regiment (on the right) was holding the dam.[40]

The Marine commander, O. P. Smith, ordered all Marines at Hwachon to withdraw to the original Line Kansas near Chinchon. The Seventh Marines began the withdrawal facing north and west—into the void. Its rearward course brought it toward Lavoie's 92d FAB perimeter, providing Lavoie some added infantry protection, while he, in turn, gave the Seventh Marines added artillery fire. Meanwhile, Smith committed his reserve First Marines to bolster the left flank. These infantry closing on Lavoie's perimeter from the south, also attempted without notable success to stop the fleeing ROKs.[41]

Remarkably, in all this confusion, Lavoie's 92d FAB remained steadfastly in place. It became, in effect, a gathering point on the exposed left flank of the Marine division toward which the Seventh Marines moved south and the First Marines moved north. Inside its tight perimeter Lavoie's seasoned artillerymen prepared to fight as frontline infantry until the Marines could converge and form a more or less integrated west-facing front. Fortunately the CCF did not attack the perimeter on April 23.

\* \* \*

The collapse of the ROK 6th Division posed grave tactical problems, and it was to have a far-reaching impact on the course of the battle.

First and foremost, it posed the probability that Shrimp Milburn's I Corps, on the Imjin and Hantan rivers, might be outflanked on the right. That meant I Corps had to abandon Line Kansas and withdraw toward Line Lincoln, just above Seoul, faster than planned. The hurried withdrawal under fire would be a difficult and dangerous maneuver; it was certain to embolden the six CCF armies attacking massively and directly toward Seoul.[42]

Secondly, it posed immediate and immense tactical difficulties for the 24th Division and the 1st Marine Division on the flanks of the CCF penetration. Both had to defend against swarming CCF attacks from two or more directions simultaneously. Neither was strong enough to carry out such a task. It seemed likely that both divisions would be compelled to withdraw farther, opening the ten-mile lateral gap in the line even wider.

Thirdly, it posed the danger of losing the Seoul–Chunchon highway and railway at Kapyong. The road and railway constituted the main line of communication behind IX Corps. Without them IX Corps units could not move laterally; all IX Corps elements could be isolated in mountainous terrain. More important, in enemy hands the road and railway would offer a direct route for a CCF attack southwest toward Seoul, which, if successful, could encircle I Corps.

The grave situation in the IX Corps sector presented Bill Hoge with numerous urgent challenges, but none more so than that of denying the onrushing CCF the town of Kapyong. Provided the 24th and 1st Marine divisions could hold the flanks of the salient, that miserable, bombed-out pile of rubble would obviously be the key real estate in the battle. He who held Kapyong would hold the central sector.

Fortunately the IX Corps reserve, Burke's Commonwealth Brigade, was at Kapyong. The brigade, however, was then in process of a major reorganization. In keeping with a British rotation plan, a new commander and staff had arrived to replace Burke and his staff. In addition, a newly arrived battalion of the King's Own Scottish Borderers was in process of relieving the Argyll and Sutherland Highlanders battalion, which was to return to Hong Kong. Hoge delayed the brigade command change but permitted the switch of battalions to proceed, designating the green Borderers as brigade reserve.[43]

Caught in this awkward and perilous situation, Hoge first attempted to stem the flight of the ROK 6th Division and send it back into battle. Toward this end he also ordered the New Zealand artillery battalion forward, this time protected by the Middlesex battalion. But nothing could stop the frantic ROK bugout. Engulfed in panicky hordes of ROKs and finding the situation "precarious," the New Zealanders (and Middlesex battalion) were again compelled to withdraw to Kapyong.[44]

Hoge restructured his defense. He ordered Burke to deploy two infantry battalions above Kapyong in the hills near the juncture of the Pukhan and

Kapyong rivers. The Canadian Battalion (Princess Pats) occupied the left sector; the seasoned Australian Battalion the right sector. Both battalions were reinforced by A Company of the 2d Division's 72d Tank Battalion, commanded by Kenneth W. Koch, and by two companies (A, B) of the 74th Engineer Combat Battalion.[45]

Hoge attempted to gather the survivors of the ROK 6th Division again, to reinforce Burke, but when this effort also failed, he was compelled to ask Van Fleet for infantry reinforcements. Nearest to hand was Charlie Palmer's 1st Cav Division, in Eighth Army reserve northeast of Seoul, then on standby to launch a counterattack in accordance with plan Audacious. In view of his determination to inflict maximum punishment on the CCF and to hold Seoul, Van Fleet was reluctant to part with any of this scant reserve; nonetheless, he ordered Marcel Crombez's 5th Cav and its 61st FAB to Kapyong. To reinforce the New Zealand artillery Hoge brought up the newly arrived 213th FAB, equipped with 155-mm self-propelled howitzers.[46]

* * *

The far right flank of Eighth Army was held by Ned Almond's X Corps: Nick Ruffner's 2d Division, Buddy Ferenbaugh's 7th Division, and several ROK divisions (3d, 5th, and 7th), extending the front eastward into the rugged Taebaek Mountains. The 23d Infantry (including both the French and Dutch battalions) of the 2d Division was well forward on the south shore of the Hwachon Reservoir; the 9th and 38th were in X Corps reserve near Hongchon. The three regiments of the 7th Division (17th; 31st; 32d) occupied a sector along or above the Soyang River, to the right of the 23d, in rugged terrain between Yanggu and Inje.[47]

Simultaneously with the CCF offensive, the NKPA III and V corps, composed of an undetermined number of divisions (perhaps three or four), attacked south into the ROK sector below Inje. This attack caught the ROK 5th and 7th divisions in the process of swapping places, the ROK 5th moving west to abut the American 7th Division, the ROK 7th replacing the ROK 5th on the line near Inje. One regiment of the ROK 7th Division was "surrounded" and "dispersed." Fleeing south, it became intermingled with a regiment of the ROK 5th Division, causing both regiments "to move south in a disorganized manner."[48] As a result, this sector of Eighth Army's front was chaotic for about twenty-four hours. During that time Charles Mount's 32d Regiment, abutting those confused ROK forces, repulsed a heavy NKPA attack, and Bill McCaffrey's 31st Infantry came up behind the ROK 5th Division to ensure that it would not again buckle and flee.[49]

These NKPA troops apparently had little heart for fighting. They held firmly to Inje but did not again mount an all-out attack southward. Emplaced behind the Soyang River and on key high ground dominating the roads and valleys, the ROK 5th, 7th, and 3d divisions remained steadfast on Line Kansas.[50]

Although the NKPA had not mounted a serious attack on Jack Chiles's 23d Infantry (near Yanggu), the rapid withdrawal of the Marines from Hwachon (on the left) and the ROKs from Inje (on the right) left the regiment exposed. By sunset on April 23, it was, in fact, the northernmost American force in Eighth Army. Ned Almond ordered Ruffner to withdraw the unit and tie in on the left with the 1st Marine Division, which was redeploying along Line Kansas.[51]

## IV

By dawn on April 24 the CCF offensive had mounted to full fury. Savage battles raged across the Eighth Army front from Munsan to Chunchon. All UN forces had pulled back to Line Kansas.

Receiving continuous reports from Korea by radio and telephone, Ridgway grew deeply concerned. Before turning Eighth Army over to Van Fleet, he had crafted a plan (Audacious) to deal with this expected CCF offensive. Under that plan Eighth Army was to make a quick but orderly withdrawal to prepared positions, with all units intact. It would, in effect, draw the CCF onward into a trap to be sprung by a powerful flanking attack by the 1st Cav Division, which had been secretly positioned northeast of Seoul.

Owing to serious errors on the part of Van Fleet and his corps commanders, it was clear that Audacious could not be executed as designed. These errors were principally two:

• Permitting the ROK 6th Division to proceed virtually alone and ill supported in the center of the army line. Its disgraceful collapse had opened a huge gap, exposing the right flank of I Corps and causing numerous other unforeseen and serious complications.

• Allowing the British Brigade to become fragmented and boxed in at the Imjin River. Because of that, I Corps could not proceed with a timely withdrawal, in accordance with Plan Audacious. The corps had to hold at Line Kansas, enduring punishing CCF frontal attacks until the British could be extricated, with ever-increasing risk of encirclement from the right.

Because of these errors, it appeared from a distance that not only would Eighth Army fail to inflict the planned heavy blow on the CCF, but also it might be in danger of a serious defeat. Ridgway left immediately for Korea.[52]

Van Fleet faced two urgent and interrelated problems that morning. One was to extricate the British Brigade so that I Corps could proceed with its planned withdrawal without incurring further heavy losses. The other was to make certain the onrushing CCF troops were blocked at Kapyong, where the ROK 6th Division had collapsed, so that they could not encircle I Corps before it could withdraw.

Of the two problems, the more urgent was that of extricating the British Brigade. In a remarkable operation Fred Weyand's crack 1/7 and the Ulsters got the Belgian Battalion out and back across the Imjin River, but the rescue of the cut-off Gloucesters did not go well.[53]

One reason was that early on April 24 the fresh CCF Sixty-third Army of three divisions (about 25,000 men) crossed the Imjin and struck the ROK 1st Division, which was holding the sector on the left of the Gloucesters. Remarkably, these ROKs did not buckle and flee. However, the massive weight of the CCF attack forced the ROK 12th Regiment back about three miles. The retrograde movement partly exposed the Gloucesters' left flank, further complicating its defense and the withdrawal.[54]

In response to this new threat Shrimp Milburn ordered heavy armor in I Corps reserve forward to reinforce the ROKs and to put them back on their position. One company (twenty-two Pattons) of Calvin Hannum's 73d Tank Battalion rolled up behind the ROK 15th Regiment to join in a counterattack. The ROKs and tankers smashed through, killing about 500 CCF troops and temporarily regained the position. However, the tankers would fault Milburn's tactics. In retrospect they argued that had Milburn committed a ROK regiment and the full 73d Tank Battalion (seventy Pattons) rather than merely one company, the tankers and ROK infantry could have thrown back the CCF troops decisively and opened a corridor in the western sector through which the Gloucesters could have withdrawn.[55]

To further reinforce the ROK 1st Division, Milburn committed his sole I Corps infantry reserve, the American 15th Infantry. Its lackluster and dour commander, Dinty Moore, fifty, a "MacArthur man," had been relieved—four days after MacArthur's departure from Tokyo.* Moore's able exec, Tom Yancey, had moved up to replace him. Yancey marched north with his three battalions: Julius Levy's 1/15, Allen Peck's 2/15, and Clyde Baden's black 3/15. Although "Baden's Battlers" had suffered heavily in earlier fighting, the 3/15 was still performing well. The white platoon leader John Howard remembered with pride that a visiting inspection team had rated Levy's 1/15 "best," Baden's 3/15 "second," and Peck's 2/15 "a more distant last." That assessment jibed with Howard's views, but the loser, West Pointer Allen Peck, disagreed emphatically, recalling that the 3/15 was "poor" and "no more reliable than the ROKs."[56]

---

*After duty in Japan and the States, Moore retired in 1954 as a colonel.

Milburn did not, however, commit Yancey's 15th Infantry into combat. He held it in reserve about six miles behind the ROK 1st Division. In view of the heavy CCF pressure all across his front (and the collapse of the Puerto Ricans and Turks), he was chary of letting go his only corps infantry reserve. Again his tactical judgment would be faulted. His critics would assert that had the 15th Infantry joined Hannum's full 73d Tank Battalion for a combined attack through the ROK 12th Regiment, there is little doubt that it could have opened a safe withdrawal corridor for the Gloucesters.

Milburn's decision to hold back American reserves on the left was to result in criticism of the ROK 1st Division for "exposing" the left flank of the Gloucesters. But, in truth, these ROKs, under attack by three CCF divisions, continued to perform well. The I Corps G-3, Johnny Johnson, remembered:

There was a good bit of derogation by the British of the protection afforded by the ROK First Division after that fight. I must say that my own sympathies and professional judgments were with the ROKs, who executed each day a very difficult operation to keep the British left flank covered to the maximum extent possible. . . . They launched a limited objective counterattack . . . to dislodge any close-in enemy units. . . . While there was some criticism of the ROK First Division, I considered the criticism to be unfair.[57]

Inasmuch as the British Brigade was under administrative control of Shorty Soule's 3d Division, Milburn delegated to Soule the responsibility for organizing. This turned out to be another mistake on Milburn's part.

That day—April 24—Shorty Soule was confronted with a battle situation which may have been beyond his capability and control. His 3d Division sector was under massive attack by three CCF armies (Twelfth, Fifteenth, Sixty-third), comprising nine divisions of about 90,000 men. His front was held, left to right, only by Tom Brodie's British Brigade and Jim Boswell's 7th Infantry, a total of about 8,000 men. Since Yancey's 15th Infantry was serving as I Corps reserve, Soule's only reserve consisted of the Puerto Rican 65th Infantry (with the attached Filipino Battalion) and the Belgian Battalion, but the Belgians were exhausted from their difficult fighting withdrawal and could not be employed.[58]

Another factor influenced Soule's decision making that day: the traditional British military understatement. The Gloucester commander, James P. Carne, like most British commanders who found themselves under siege, was inclined to downplay his situation. Carne had conveyed the impression to Tom Brodie that the Gloucesters were in pretty fair shape and there was no great emergency. Brodie, in turn, had passed that impression to Soule. Soule was to be faulted for failing to take into account the British stiff upper lip.[59]

As a result of his acute shortage of reserves and British understatement, Soule's plan that day to rescue the Gloucesters was absurdly inadequate. He ordered William Harris to provide the recently battered, uncertain Filipino Battalion to attack to the Gloucester positions, supported by four light Chaffee tanks. After the Filipinos broke through and set up an escape corridor, they would be reinforced by eight heavy Centurion tanks of the King's Royal Irish Hussars.

The Filipinos collected themselves and set off that morning, but they had no chance of success. When the point was nearing the Gloucester's rearmost positions, the CCF attacked, knocking out a Chaffee tank, which blocked the road and stalled the column. Learning of this, Brodie ordered the Centurions to about-face and withdraw before they were overrun. By mistake (or desire) the Filipinos interpreted Brodie's withdrawal order to apply to them as well. Unknown to Soule, who was at Jim Boswell's 7th Infantry CP, the entire force pulled back, having achieved nothing.

Believing the Filipinos were still in place but should be reinforced, Soule enlarged his rescue plan later in the day. He directed William Harris to organize a powerful force of Puerto Ricans to attack through the (supposed) Filipino position. The Harris Force would consist of his 1/65 and 2/65, Wilson Hawkins's 64th Tank Battalion, the 10th FAB, and other units. It was to carry out its mission early on the morning of April 25.[60]

\* \* \*

Upon arrival in Korea that day Matt Ridgway met with Van Fleet, Shrimp Milburn, and Shorty Soule. Ridgway was deeply concerned about all the reverses in Eighth Army, especially so about the perilous situation of the British Brigade. As before, he fretted over the negative political impact in England should the British Brigade suffer major losses.

Soule briefed Ridgway and Van Fleet on his enlarged rescue plan employing the Puerto Ricans and the black tankers of the 64th Tank Battalion. Unaware that the Filipinos and Centurion tanks had withdrawn, Soule described the plan to attack through those units. The senior generals pointedly asked why Soule was waiting until the following morning to launch the rescue mission. Soule replied that the Puerto Ricans were not ready yet and besides that, Tom Brodie had assured him that the Gloucesters could hold out until the following day.[61]

Ridgway had every right to be angry. Whatever lingering hopes he might have had for realizing the full potential of Audacious had slipped away. Owing to the heavy losses already incurred in the British Brigade and the certain further losses to occur, the brigade would not be available for sustained combat for some time. It would have to be withdrawn and remanned. That would leave a gap in the left I Corps front, which would have to be filled by the remaining two regiments (7th Cav; 8th Cav) of the reserve 1st Cav Division. The commitment of the 5th Cav to Kapyong and the commitment of 7th and 8th Cav to

I Corps would leave no forces for the punishing counterattack envisioned in Audacious.[62]

Later that day Tom Brodie obtained from James Carne a more accurate picture of the Gloucesters situation. It was, in a word, desperate. Dropping all pretenses and understatements, Brodie requested permission from Soule to withdraw the Gloucesters that night. Whether or not Soule was finally aware that the Filipinos and the Centurion tanks had withdrawn is not known. In any case, he obtusely denied Brodie permission to withdraw the Gloucesters. They were to hold until dawn, at which time Harris Force was to break through.[63]

*  *  *

Van Fleet's other grave crisis on April 24—blocking the CCF at Kapyong—had a better outcome.

That morning Kapyong was still held only by Burke's Commonwealth Brigade. Two battalions were forward: the Canadians (Princess Pats), commanded by J. R. Stone, on the left and the Australians, commanded by Ian Ferguson, on the right. Both were still supported by Kenneth Koch's A Company of the 2d Division's 72d Tank Battalion. The Middlesex and newly arrived King's Own Borderers battalions were in reserve. The 213 FAB had arrived to reinforce the New Zealand artillery. Marcel Crombez's 5th Cav, backed by the 61st FAB and A Company of Jack Metzdorf's 70th Tank Battalion, was on the way.[64]

Just before dawn, bypassing the Canadians, the CCF 118th Division fell on the Australians in a hard rain. Swarms of enemy infiltrated through the outer and inner defense lines and threatened the battalion CP. Reacting quickly, Burke reinforced the Australians with a Middlesex infantry company. Although the CCF blocked this force, the tough Australians, fighting courageously, routed the enemy and by dawn had restored the main lines of their defensive positions.[65]

Perhaps waiting for reinforcements to come up, the CCF eased off during the morning. At about noon, however, they again fell on the Australians. "This was the most determined attack we had experienced up to then," one officer wrote. "The enemy fairly ran headlong into our forward lines. . . ." The power of the attack was so great the Australians were forced to yield ground. During the withdrawal a flight of FEAF aircraft accidentally napalmed one rearguard Australian company, "causing casualties and destroying vital weapons and ammunition." The CCF took advantage of this "unexpected support" and stepped up the fury of the attack, pushing the Australians rearward to the Middlesex backup positions, where, finally, the enemy was solidly blocked. During this retrograde movement, the Army historian wrote, the two companies (A, B) of the American 74th Engineer Combat Battalion panicked and fled; the 213th FAB lost one howitzer.[66]

After dark the CCF turned against Stone's Canadian battalion, which until then had been ignored. Hundreds simultaneously swarmed into the battalion positions from all points of the compass, firing mortars and machine guns and throwing grenades. Fortunately and prudently the Canadians were stoutly dug in with interlocking fields of fire. Fighting doggedly and smartly in defense, like their British cousins, the Canadians refused to budge and, with the help of the New Zealand and American artillery from the rear, killed CCF by the score. The vicious fight raged throughout the entire night, but at dawn the riddled CCF began withdrawing.[67]

During the fight Koch's American tankers performed magnificently. They bravely supported the Australian infantry with direct fire, brought ammo forward, and evacuated wounded, killing CCF going and coming. Three American tankers, including platoon leader Peter DiMartino, were killed; twelve were wounded. Company commander Koch and another of his platoon leaders, West Pointer (1950) W. Donald Miller, won DSCs for extraordinary heroism.[68]

Crombez and his powerful 5th Cav task force arrived on the scene to

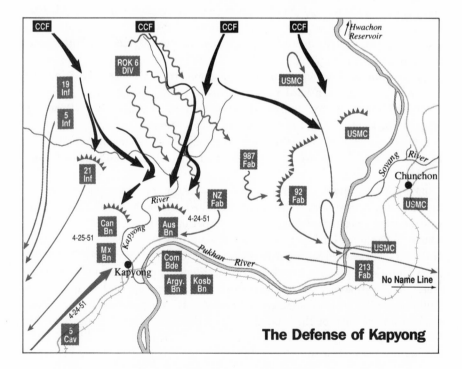

The Defense of Kapyong

reinforce the Commonwealth Brigade, but it saw only minor action. The remarkable stand of the Australians and Canadians—and the American tankers and the New Zealand artillerymen and the Middlesex battalion—had bloodied and apparently disheartened the CCF 118th Division, and it did not press the attack. The Australians and New Zealanders (known collectively as Anzacs) were pleased: April 25 was Anzac Day, a national holiday (commemorating the commitment of the Anzacs in the Battle of Gallipoli in World War I), and they were able to celebrate with Australian beer and stronger spirits. They did not stint. Bill Hoge thought the Australians and New Zealanders were "wonderful fighters," but while they celebrated, he was very glad he had the 5th Cav at hand.[69]

The holding action of the Commonwealth Brigade at Kapyong had been decisive. It plugged the hole left by the ROK 6th Division and blocked the CCF long enough for the 24th Division to withdraw. In gratitude Van Fleet awarded the Australian and Canadian battalions and Company A, 72d Tank Battalion, a Presidential Unit Citation.[70]

*   *   *

Farther right that same day—April 24—the three CCF divisions (115th; 116th; 120th) which had struck toward the 1st Marine Division near Chunchon went into action. Facing this enemy were the several battalions of the First and Seventh Marines, converging from the north and south on Leon Lavoie's exposed 92d FAB. Lavoie had wisely evacuated the four eight-inch howitzers, but he still had twelve self-propelled 155s inside his perimeter. Having had thirty-six hours' grace, his battle-hardened veterans had turned that perimeter into a fortress, but the artillerymen were tense and fearful. The CCF swarmed at the 92d FAB perimeter at about 5:20 A.M. that day, while Lavoie and his men were eating breakfast.[71]

What ensued was one of the most astonishing and valorous Army actions of the Korean War. Acting in the role of infantry, Lavoie's men manned rifles, carbines, and machine guns and promptly delivered an awesome stream of fire into the oncoming enemy. All the while Lavoie, heedless of heavy CCF machine-gun and rifle fire, walked among his men to reassure and encourage them and to request that they aim carefully and make every round count.

As the battle raged, Lavoie coolly directed John F. Gerrity, commander of A Battery, to prepare his 155s for direct (or point-blank) fire on the enemy. On Lavoie's instructions Gerrity aimed his six howitzers at two CCF machine-gun positions a mere 1,000 yards away and opened fire. "Lavoie saw fragments of Chinese soldiers thrown twenty feet or higher into the air," the Army historian wrote. With this success and others, the historian continued, Lavoie "noticed a great change in his troops. Over their initial scare, they now appeared to be enjoying themselves." The earlier fear "had been replaced by a cocky sort of confidence."[72]

Marine commanders nearby, hearing the noise of battle, sent several tanks to assist Lavoie. When these arrived, blasting away, Lavoie's men jumped from cover like veteran infantry and rooted out CCF who had penetrated the perimeter. In all, Lavoie's men killed 179 CCF in the immediate perimeter area, perhaps scores more beyond in the hills. The 92d FAB lost 4 dead and 11 wounded. "Artillery," Lavoie later wrote laconically, "if it makes up its mind, will set itself up so that it can defend itself from enemy infantry action."[73]

Shortly after this fight Bill Hoge issued orders for the 92d FAB—and the Marine infantry battalions—to withdraw southeasterly to less exposed positions. The 92d FAB pulled out without the loss of a single gun or vehicle or piece of equipment. The Army historian aptly wrote that on April 24 the 92d FAB had "acquitted itself with great honor," that it had exhibited "good leadership" at "all echelons."[74]

*   *   *

During this arduous day, April 24, Ridgway and Van Fleet discussed courses of action. The key offensive feature of Plan Audacious, the surprise counterattack of the 1st Cav Division, was of necessity discarded. It was decided that on the following day, April 25, after the Gloucesters had been extricated, Eighth Army would begin a methodical withdrawal from Line Kansas, making local counterattacks as appropriate, killing as many CCF as possible by infantry, artillery, and what FEAF close air support could be obtained.[75]

Van Fleet had arrived at some convictions about the CCF objectives and had a plan to deal with them. He believed the overriding and immediate CCF goal was to recapture Seoul by May 1. All else was secondary or tertiary. He therefore believed that the CCF might commit yet more armies in the western sector and that elements of the three CCF armies advancing in the center might turn southwest on a "convergence" attack to assist in the capture of Seoul. In sum, all nine (or more) CCF armies committed to the offensive might aim for the capital, leaving the central and eastern sectors of the front only moderately threatened.

Although Van Fleet still shared Ridgway's view that real estate per se was of little value in this war, he also still strongly differed over the matter of Seoul itself. He believed that for psychological or symbolic reasons, Peking had made the decision to recapture the capital at any cost. To deny Peking that objective, even at heavy cost in UN casualties, would, in effect, constitute a major UN victory. In the process, Van Fleet believed, he could inflict devastating casualties on the CCF. He therefore urged that Eighth Army be authorized to make an all-out stand for Seoul. Rather than withdraw below the Han (in accordance with Ridgway's Plan Audacious), Van Fleet would defend north of the Han.

An important consideration in Van Fleet's decision to defend Seoul was the now well-known inability of the CCF logistically to sustain a powerful offensive for more than five or six days. He believed that if I Corps could delay the CCF for several days during its withdrawal from Line Kansas to Line Lincoln, by the time the CCF reached Seoul they would have very nearly exhausted their ammo and rations. If FEAF aircraft could successfully interdict the tenuous CCF resupply lines—admittedly a big if—the CCF could not be replenished for a strong attack on Seoul. It would "run out of steam."[76]

Van Fleet's master plan for Eighth Army was as follows. On the left Milburn's I Corps would slowly fall back on Seoul and hold at Line Lincoln (or Golden). To the right Bill Hoge's IX Corps, with Babe Bryan's 24th Division returned to it, would hold a line above the Han running due east from Seoul to the Pukhan River, thence northeast, manned by (left to right) the 24th Division and the ROK 2d Division and the (reconstituted) ROK 6th Division, backstopped by the Commonwealth Brigade and the 5th Cav. Farther right the Marine division, which was to be reintegrated into Ned Almond's X Corps, would join the American 2d and 7th divisions to form a defense line at Hongchon. On the extreme right the ROK divisions would continue to block the fainthearted NKPA along the Soyang River.[77]

Van Fleet's plan for holding Seoul was not unlike Ridgway's plan of early January, which had failed. However, Van Fleet enjoyed several advantages. Eighth Army was now far better supplied and battle-hardened and its morale was still high. Line Lincoln had been vastly improved. The weather was far better, warming to the point that not even field jackets were required. Most important, Van Fleet had strong right flank protection (IX and X corps) with which to block the three CCF armies in the central sector, thus greatly reducing the chances that I Corps could be encircled and cut off in Seoul or that the enemy could strike straight for Pusan.

In addition to that Van Fleet had considerably more artillery firepower. About nine new artillery battalions had joined Eighth Army since January. Van Fleet intended to exploit the artillery to the maximum. He would park the howitzers and guns "wheel to wheel" and "expend steel and fire, not men." He wanted "so many artillery holes that a man can step from one to the other." He would increase the "basic daily load" of ammo expenditure to five times the normal rate: from about 40 to 200 rounds a day per gun and even more in emergencies. The CCF would beat itself to death in futile, bloody charges against impregnable UN lines.[78]

After carefully weighing the pros and cons, Ridgway approved these plans. Eighth Army would defend north of the Han. It would go all out to deny Seoul to the CCF. In the process it would inflict devastating losses on the enemy, enough perhaps to persuade Peking to give up these man-wasting offensives and negotiate a cease-fire.

The plan raised one delicate senior command problem. As envisioned, O. P. Smith's 1st Marine Division was to be reassigned to Ned Almond's X Corps, to help form the eastern enclave at Hongchon. This would violate Ridgway's promise to Smith that he would not ever again serve under Almond. However, the generals found a solution. Smith, due for rotation, was soon to turn over his command to Gerald C. ("Gerry") Thomas, fifty-seven, who was already in Korea. Van Fleet could simply speed up the relief, putting Thomas in command before the division was assigned to X Corps.

This change was carried out that very afternoon, April 24, much to Smith's chagrin. When Thomas arrived unexpectedly early at Smith's CP, Thomas remembered that Smith said tartly: "I can't turn over to you. We're fighting up on our front, and we have a fifteen-mile gap on our left where the Sixth ROK Division has retreated." Thomas retorted: "The table of organization only calls for one major general in a division. Either you turn over to me or I'm going to leave."[79]

Perhaps informed of the reason for the abrupt change in command, Smith turned over the division to Thomas that afternoon in a "simple ceremony." He returned to the States to command first the Marine Corps base at Camp Pendleton, California, then, promoted to three stars, the Fleet Marine force, Atlantic. He retired in 1955 and would be forever extolled for his brilliant management of the Marine division during its arduous retreat from the Chosin Reservoir.[80]

Ned Almond was delighted to have the Marine division returned to X Corps—but with a new commander. He later wrote that "it was a relief to all of us at X Corps headquarters" when O. P. Smith departed from Korea.[81]

\* \* \*

After returning to Tokyo that night, Ridgway issued a public statement, a copy of which he sent to the JCS. It could be read as a justification of his hurried trip to the battlefield, a public condemnation of Van Fleet, Milburn, Hoge, and Soule for the fate of the Gloucesters and ROK 6th Division, and praise for Van Fleet—all in the same breath.

It is a basic responsibility of command to anticipate when and where the potentially decisive phases of battle will occur; to be there in advance of their occurrence if practicable; and in any event to be there during the development, in order to obtain from commanders and from conditions on the spot at the time of action, an accurate sensing of the situation, as the best basis for command decisions.

I went to Korea for that reason. I had several hours on the ground with General Van Fleet at his forward command post, and then with him and some of his commanders at their forward command posts. It appears to me at this time that this attack is another major effort by our Communist enemy to drive United Nations forces from Korea, or destroy them, regardless of the further destruction of his own troops, and the continued criminal devastation of Korea. It appears also that this will be the heaviest offensive effort yet made, though it has not yet attained its maximum strength.

The conduct of operations is in the competent hands of General Van Fleet, and I have complete confidence that Eighth Army under his leadership—with unfailing support of our Navy and Air Force—will fully accomplish all assigned missions, and with high credit.

The battle is joined. It may well prove decisive.[82]

## V

In Korea that night, April 24–25, Shrimp Milburn's main task was to hold I Corps on Line Kansas until dawn so that Harris Force could crack through and extricate the Gloucester Battalion.

This task proved to be very difficult. The six CCF armies assaulting I Corps committed most of their reserve divisions into the battle that night and the NKPA I Corps joined the CCF Sixty-fourth Army attacking the ROK 1st Division. Under cover of darkness these fresh enemy troops moved forward, greatly increasing the weight of the attack. Furious fights raged across the western and central sectors of the I Corps front:[83]

• On the extreme left of the corps front the ROK 1st Division, reinforced intermittently by Hannum's 73d Tank Battalion, continued to fight skillfully and valiantly. Its fine performance in this battle would earn the youthful commander, Paik Sun Yup, a promotion to ROK I Corps commander and put him on a road that would lead one day to the post of chief of staff of the ROK Army.

But the attack of the fresh NKPA I Corps at the ROK 1st Division that night pushed the ROKs back a full mile. Doubtful that the ROKs could continue to hold under this added enemy pressure, Milburn ordered Soule to strip the Gloucester rescue mission (Harris Force) of its 1/65, 2/65, and the Filipino Battalion, and to send these units to backstop the ROKs. In addition, Milburn ordered Hannum's full 73d Tank Battalion to come up behind the ROKs.[84]

• In the corps center Shorty Soule's 3d division, already stripped of its 15th Infantry and now most of its 65th Infantry, hung on by its fingernails. On its left front the fragmented British Brigade had committed all four battalions, including the Belgians.

The magnificent Gloucesters, trapped and surrounded on what would be enshrined as "Gloucester Hill," were still holding on. At dawn, as the CCF massed for another attack, the Gloucesters' commander, James Carne, was still cool and, the British historian wrote, showing "powers of leadership" seldom surpassed in the history of the Royal Army. Mocking the CCF bugles, his own bugler stood up in his slit trench, disdaining cover, and defiantly blew every call in the book except "Retreat." Remarkably the Gloucesters, fighting back to back, repulsed seven CCF attacks within a period of four hours.[85]

On the 3d Division right front Jim Boswell's 7th Infantry, astride the Uijongbu–Seoul road, suffered a serious reverse during the night. A massive CCF force surrounded the 2/7 and cut it off. During this crisis the 1/7 and 3/7 held, but the men of the 2/7 were compelled to break up into small bands and get out the best way they could.[86]

• On the corps right, held by Sladen Bradley's 25th Division, the action was also violent and chaotic. The division front was held, left to right, by Kelleher's 35th and Britt's 24th regiments, with the Turks and Check's 27th Regiment in backup roles.

A massive CCF attack hit both forward regiments during the night, first the 24th Infantry, then the 35th Infantry. Under this heavy pressure the 24th Infantry reeled, and Baranowski's 1/24 "scattered." At midnight, Bittman Barth wrote, Bradley ordered the 24th Infantry "to withdraw and reorganize in an area fifteen miles to the south." Barth went on:

Up until eleven o'clock the front of the 35th Infantry had been quiet. Then a series of flares touched off a coordinated attack all over the area. . . .

The attack against the Command Post of the 35th Infantry was very violent. Small arms and mortar fire pinned down the personnel until finally Kelleher led his men out using tanks and A/A 50 caliber guns to blast a path through to safety. . . . All three battalions of the 35th were cut off but that fine regiment fought its way clear by battalion, coming out in good order and with surprisingly few casualties. . . .[87]

In L Company of James Lee's 3/35, Woody Woodruff remembered the withdrawal of his battalion:

Shortly commenced a nightmare that continued almost until daylight. In our column were infantry on foot, tanks, and attached half-tracks mounting Quad-fifties from the A/A battalion. Units got mixed up and mingled. Vehicles with dead engines, some as a result of enemy action, blocked the narrow trail. At one point a column of vehicles from Battalion trains had been ambushed and set afire; flames lit up a night otherwise pitch dark, and ruined what little night vision we had. Among those vehicles were some ambulances; it was reported that some patients aboard had been machine gunned as they lay on their stretchers.[88]

By daylight Bradley had got his forces in some kind of order, but the division clearly could not hold any longer on Line Kansas. Gilbert Check's 27th Infantry moved up to the rear guard positions and maintained contact while the rest of the division proceeded south.

\* \* \*

At 5:00 A.M. April 25, Shrimp Milburn issued formal orders for I Corps to abandon Line Kansas and to withdraw to an intermediate line (Delta) about ten miles south of Kansas. However, this order contained an important stipulation: The ROK 1st Division and Shorty Soule's 3d Division were to first extricate the Gloucesters, even if it meant a combined "counterattack." The stipulation was absurd; it was already too late. Shrimp Milburn and Shorty Soule had badly bungled the rescue of the Gloucesters.[89]

Nonetheless, the Americans gathered at Brodie's CP that morning at 8:00 to do what they could to implement the stipulation. Present were Shorty Soule's surrogate, the 3d Division ADC Armistead Mead, and the 65th Infantry commander, William Harris, who remembered:

What I saw and heard scared hell out of me. Their CP tent was actually being hit by rifle bullets, and the entire area was being bombarded with heavy mortars. I didn't really know whether I should stay or take off. . . . Seeing me enter, the Brigadier came over to welcome me and then offered me tea. . . . All the time we were sitting there the bullets were whizzing through the top of the tent and the mortars were exploding around the outside—if one of them had registered on that tent it would have been just too bad for us.[90]

As Harris remembered it, Brodie was angry at Shorty Soule. Brodie had been warning Soule for "thirty-six hours or so" that unless he authorized the Gloucesters to withdraw, they would be cut off. Now they were cut off. "The Brigadier was furious," Harris wrote, "and I didn't blame him." However, I Corps G-3 Johnny Johnson disputed that recollection. The British, Johnson remembered, were "too proud to call for help. . . . They suffered significant casualties before they would acknowledge that they were even in trouble."[91]

The commanders' conference was acrimonious. By then Shorty Soule had stripped Harris Force of most of its infantry to backstop the ROKs, leaving only the 3/65, which had been hit and disorganized during the night. The modified rescue plan that morning was that Harris Force, reduced to armor (Hawkins's 64th Tank Battalion; the 65th Tank Company) and artillery (10th FAB) would attack from the east, while Hannum's 73d Tank Battalion, supported by ROKs, attacked from the west. But without infantry to support the tankers, Harris Force could not succeed; its attack would be near suicidal.[92]

All present realized the proposed counterattack was an exercise in futility. Shortly after the conference broke up Tom Brodie radioed James Carne to fight his way out. Meanwhile, Brodie issued orders for the rest of the besieged brigade to withdraw.[93]

William Harris was still under orders to mount the modified rescue mission and he attempted to comply, even though he viewed it as a lost cause. "There was little we could do to help under the circumstances," he wrote later in his memoir; it was all "too little too late." No doubt reluctant to send the American tankers on a hopeless mission, Harris at first refused to commit more than one light tank platoon which, as it happened, was short one tank. The 64th Tank Company commander, Claude Smith, protested, the Army historian wrote, insisting that all his tanks be committed, but Harris was adamant.[94]

Finally reduced to four light tanks, Harris Force set off. In the confusion, the forward observer of the 10th FAB was left behind. With no way of directing the supporting artillery fire, this pitifully weak armored force never had a chance. The tankers fired off all their ammo, then withdrew without having achieved anything. Later Harris sent out a second tank platoon, but a British officer intervened and recalled it.[95]*

* * *

The British Brigade began withdrawing at about 9:00 A.M. It was a difficult maneuver. By then the CCF had swarmed into the hills behind the brigade's scattered units and had set up ambushes and gauntlets. On his own authority Brodie sent British armor forward to help extricate the Fusiliers, the Ulsters, and the Belgians. The British historian, Bryan Perrett, described the desperate fighting which ensued:

There can be little doubt that had it not been for the Centurion tanks of C Squadron, King's Royal Irish Hussars, commanded by Major [P.] Henry Huth, the brigade would have sustained far more serious casualties than it did. During this episode, one of the bloodiest of the entire battle, tank commanders fought at a distinct disadvantage; poor visibility and bad going meant that they could only operate with maximum efficiency if their hatches were open, yet the enemy's use of mortars and his willingness to come to close quarters demanded that they remained closed down.

After fighting their way through a serious ambush on the way forward the Hussars provided covering fire while first the Fusiliers and then one company of the Ulster Rifles broke contact. It then became apparent that the Chinese were tightening their grip on the track to the rear, and all but one of the remaining Ulster Rifles companies struck across the hills on a parallel route. With the tanks acting as rear guard the Belgians and the last Ulster Rifles company conducted a fighting withdrawal through the valley. The Chinese were now swarming all over the hills and, displaying insane courage, repeatedly tried to smother the Centurions with their human-wave tactics. Great swathes [sic] were cut through their ranks by the 20-pounders and the co-axial machine guns [on the tanks] but still they clambered aboard and attempted to pry open the hatches, to be shot off time and again by the fire of other tanks; one commander swept his vehicle clean of the enemy by driving straight through a house. . . . Several of the Centurions which reached safety were piled high with dead and wounded, their sides run-

---

*Fearing that a formal investigation into the "major catastrophe" of the Gloucesters would ensue and that he might become the "fall guy," Harris directed his exec to gather legalistic testimony from the men of the Puerto Rican 65th Infantry. "We were found to be not at fault in any way," Harris wrote.

ning scarlet with blood; there was blood on the tracks, too, but none of it was British or Belgian.

On Gloucester Hill, Carne gave his four company commanders permission to fight their units out independently. Three companies (A, B, C) went south, but all the men were either killed or captured. Carne (subsequently awarded the Victoria Cross and a DSC) was among those taken, and he was to survive captivity. Company D, commanded by Maurice G. ("Mike") Harvey, went north into the hills, then to the west, then south. While these survivors were approaching UN lines, American tankers mistook them for Chinese and opened fire, killing or wounding several more before the error was discovered and the fire halted.

These tankers were from C Company of Calvin Hannum's 73d Tank Battalion, who were trying to attack from the west with ROK infantry support. Earlier that morning 15 of the Pattons had tried, without success, to break through to Gloucester Hill. The tankers and infantrymen of the ROK 12th Regiment rescued Mike Harvey, 4 other officers, and 38 enlisted men of company D. These 43 men and another handful who got out were the sole survivors of the original 800 Gloucesters.[96]

Tom Brodie withdrew his remaining forces straight through to the south bank of the Han River at Yongdungpo. The brigade became the I Corps emergency reserve, enabling Milburn to release Tom Yancey's 15th Infantry to the 3d Division. An early muster showed the brigade had suffered 25 percent casualties—nearly 1,000 in total. However, in return, the brigade had shattered the CCF Sixty-third Army so badly—an estimated 11,000 casualties—that it had to be withdrawn from combat, and other CCF troops came forward to carry the attack onward to Seoul in this sector.[97]

In all, the British Brigade had held for sixty crucial hours. Not only had this hold severely gutted the CCF Sixty-third Army, but also it had significantly slowed the momentum of the enemy offensive. Van Fleet awarded the Gloucesters a Presidential Unit Citation, stating that their action on Gloucester Hill was the "most outstanding example of unit bravery in modern warfare."[98]

The loss of the Gloucester Battalion had been a terrible blunder, but it did not result in the official investigation that William Harris feared. However, it drew stinging private rebukes from Ridgway and Van Fleet. Ridgway put most of the blame on Shrimp Milburn and Shorty Soule for not going forward in the battle zone personally to assess the situation. Neither general, he wrote, had "by direct personal presence" at the "critical spot" been "fully aware" of the developing danger. Ridgway also partly blamed Brodie for failing to take into account that Carne would understate his situation and (by implication) Ridgway also blamed Carne for doing so. Brodie conceded "50 percent responsibility" for the loss of the Gloucesters because he failed to make it clear early enough that the unit was in trouble, but he laid the other 50 percent blame on Soule. Van Fleet put most of the blame on Shorty Soule for his "tardiness" in assessing the precarious position of the Gloucesters and for failing to make "timely decisions" that might have saved it.[99]

\* \* \*

The withdrawal of the British Brigade that morning and the shift of the Puerto Ricans and Filipinos westerly behind the ROK 1st Division left Jim Boswell's 7th Infantry as the sole force in the 3d Division capable of providing a rear guard.[100]

The 7th was still positioned astride the Uijongbu–Seoul highway, holding the high ground. It had lost its 2/7, but the 1/7 and 3/7 were still holding and fighting bravely, repelling repeated CCF attacks. Although Boswell and the men of the 1/7 and 3/7 were hollow-eyed from fatigue, they still had not broken contact, and they had slaughtered countless enemy.[101]

When Shorty Soule passed word to Boswell to withdraw, Boswell had a plan ready. Ernest M. Layman's 3/7, on the left, would pull out first, through Fred Weyand's 1/7. Then Weyand would decamp and follow.

While this tricky operation was unfolding, the CCF hit the 7th Infantry again with a massive frontal assault. Yet another furious close-in battle ensued. Adhering to the plan, Layman withdrew under heavy enemy fire, while Weyand's men provided cover. In this action Weyand's A Company, commanded by Harley F. Mooney, and B Company, commanded by Ray W. Blandin, Jr., staged one of the most gallant fights of the war. An A Company corporal, John Essebagger, Jr., mortally wounded, won the Medal of Honor for his "one-man" stand and for charging the CCF, "firing his weapon and hurling grenades." Another mortally wounded corporal in B Company, Clair Goodblood, also won the Medal of Honor for heroically remaining at his post and killing 100 of the enemy before he died. The weapons platoon leader, Lieutenant John N. Middleman, won a DSC.[102]

Because of the extraordinary courage of these men and others in the 1/7, both battalions completed the withdrawal without disaster. The 7th Infantry consolidated farther south and continued to provide rearguard protection for the withdrawing 3d Division elements. For extricating the Belgians on April 23 and 24 and for the "magnificent" rearguard action on April 25, Fred Weyand's 1/7 (plus attached units) was awarded the Presidential Unit Citation, which credited the battalion with killing "over 3,000 enemy troops" and wounding "an estimated 5,500."\*[103]

---

\*Later the same day two other soldiers in the 7th Infantry won the Medal of Honor: Private First Class Charles L. Gilliland, who was killed, and Corporal Hiroshi H. Miyamura, who survived.[104]

The stout holding action of the 7th Infantry enabled the 3d Division artillery to stay in forward positions longer and continue its devastating barrage on the CCF. Although the artillerymen ran repeated risks of surprise encirclement, they remained coolheaded and displaced rearward methodically and only on order. One typical 3d Division artillery outfit, the 10th FAB, reported that by 6:00 P.M. on April 25 it had occupied its "seventh position" in the rearward march and had fired an unprecedented total of 12,910 rounds in the first seventy-two hours of the CCF offensive.[105]

\* \* \*

To the right of the 3d Division Sladen Bradley's reorganized 25th Division fell back in lockstep. Gerry Kelleher's 35th Infantry on the left and Gilbert Check's 27th Infantry on the right alternated as rear guard; Henry Britt's 24th Infantry and the reorganized Turkish Brigade proceeded toward Line Lincoln. Finally the 35th and 27th "broke contact" with the CCF in order to proceed to a new, intermediate defense line (Elgin). Bittman Barth, manning an outpost, remembered the moment:

Gerry Kelleher, the commander of the 35th, stopped at our . . . headquarters on his way back. Seeing him gave me quite a lift. . . . Vigorous, alert, and thoroughly competent professionally, he never lost his head and was an inspiration to those around him. His courage in action coupled with all his other fine qualities made him a combat leader *par excellence.* . . .

We were highly elated. The division had come out almost intact without the loss of a single artillery gun. . . .[106]

\* \* \*

All this time Babe Bryan's 24th Division, holding down the distant right flank of I Corps and facing the huge gap created by the collapse of the ROK 6th Division, had had a very difficult time. Bryan had withdrawn (left to right) his 19th and 5th regiments several miles to regroup and consolidate and had committed Gines Perez's 21st Infantry (plus the 8th Ranger Company) to face the void on the right flank. But these maneuvers had not been easy in the rugged terrain where his division was deployed, and CCF pressure had increased in fury hour by hour.

The Eighth Army withdrawal plan called for the 1st Cav Division (less the 5th Cav at Kapyong) to go west and fill the gap on the left end of Line Lincoln created by the withdrawal of the British Brigade. Babe Bryan's 24th Division was gradually to fall back and replace the 1st Cav Division east of the city on an extension of Line Lincoln called No Name Line. The Commonwealth Brigade* and 5th Cav would remain at Kapyong, denying the CCF the Seoul–Chunchon road, while the 24th Division withdrew.[108]

On the morning of April 25th Babe Bryan began the withdrawal of the 24th Division in concert with the 3d and 25th divisions. His plan called for the 5th Infantry (with the 8th Ranger company attached), which Harry Wilson had commanded for merely two weeks, to serve as rear guard, covering the withdrawal of Pete Garland's 19th and Gines Perez's 21st regiments. The 5th Infantry (or RCT) still included the 555th FAB, commanded by Clarence Stuart. To reinforce Wilson, Babe Bryan attached Company D (twenty-two Pattons) of John Growdon's 6th Tank Battalion.[109]

During that day the 19th and 21st regiments broke contact with the CCF and withdrew in orderly fashion to a prearranged line. The 5th Infantry was to follow immediately, but Wilson was delayed when the CCF surrounded and trapped the 8th Ranger Company. To help extricate the Rangers, Wilson sent a tank platoon (five Pattons) forward. They cracked through the CCF but only managed to rescue sixty-five of the Rangers, most of whom were wounded. The delay meant that Wilson had to withdraw his force in darkness, an undesirable but necessary maneuver.

The plan was that the 5th Infantry would pull back to and through Pete Garland's 19th Infantry positions. The order of march was as follows: the 3/5, the 555th FAB, the 1/5, the 2/5, and lastly, the Pattons of Company D. Unknown to Wilson, by that time the CCF had got behind the Americans and dominated the high ground along the withdrawal route and had set up another gauntlet.

As the column was proceeding rearward in darkness the CCF opened fire. Stuart's 555th FAB, near the center of the column, was hardest hit. He and his artillerymen manned the 105mm howitzers and returned fire at point blank range. The oncoming 1/5 attempted three times to crack through to the artillerymen but each attack failed. Pete Garland sent forward Company A of Growdon's 6th Tank Battalion plus an infantry company, but this rescue force was also repelled.

What resulted was another terrible slaughter. Stuart and his artillerymen were finally forced to abandon 13 of the 18 105-mm howitzers and 60 vehicles. About 100 artillerymen were lost or missing. The Pattons of Company D at the rear of the column found an "alternate" route, and most escaped, but all

---

*As planned, G. Taylor and staff relieved Burke and staff en bloc, whereupon the designation of the outfit was changed from 27th to 28th Commonwealth Brigade. The Middlesex battalion, soon to be relieved by yet another newly arriving British battalion, prepared to return to Hong Kong. The Canadian battalion prepared to join two other arriving Canadian battalions to form an all-Canadian brigade, which was ultimately to become a part of a proposed British Commonwealth Division.[107]

were under enemy fire the whole time. In all, 7 tanks were lost, 5 Pattons of Company D and 2 from the 5th Infantry Tank Company. Total casualties to the 5th RCT that night according to Bittman Barth were about 800.[110]*

\* \* \*

To the right of the gap in Eighth Army's front near Chunchon in the 1st Marine Division sector, the pressure exerted by the three CCF divisions in operation there was less severe and the battles less ferocious. Now commanded by Gerry Thomas and attached to Ned Almond's X Corps, the Marines had withdrawn southeasterly to a less exposed line above Chunchon. However the division had incurred about 300 casualties during the two-day realignment. Among them was the commander of the First Marines, Frank McAlister, slightly wounded by a mortar fragment.[111]

By this time Van Fleet had issued new plans for the deployment of X Corps forces in this eastern sector. The three American divisions would man a new line (also No Name) running diagonally above Hongchon. The Marines would occupy the southwest sector of the line. The 2d Division would occupy positions on the right, or northeast, of the Marines. The 7th Division would hold farther northeast to the right of the 2d.[112]

These realignments put the Marine division into yet another "retreat." The Marines did not like giving up ground; as the saying went, no Marine ever willingly retreated. But this time the withdrawal was conceded to be a "retrograde" movement.[113]

Perhaps because the CCF in this sector were feinting or blocking, the offensive toward Chunchon was desultory. For that the division commanders Gerry Thomas, Nick Ruffner, and Buddy Ferenbaugh, realigning on the No Name Line, were grateful. They enjoyed a respite that was to pay dividends in the not too distant future.[114]

The withdrawal of the Marines had returned the Hwachon Reservoir to enemy control. The new worry was that the CCF would shut the sluice gates tight and dry up the Pukhan River, thereby facilitating its own advances by eliminating the need for bridging. Hence, for this entirely different reason, the Eighth Army staff believed it was important to mount yet another aerial assault on the Hwachon Dam.[115]

This time the staff turned to the Navy. The sailors responded by sending six dive-bombers from the carrier *Princeton,* each fitted with a 2,000-pound bomb. This attack punched one hole in the dam itself but unfortunately missed the sluice gates. In a second attack on the following day eight dive-bombers

---

*It was the second time that the 555th had been ambushed. Earlier, in the Task Force Kean operations on August 12, 1950, under command of John Daly, it had lost many men and six 105s.

were fitted with torpedoes. This was a "historic" first: No naval aircraft had ever attempted to torpedo a dam. Six of the torpedoes ran true. They knocked out the center sluice gate and severely damaged the lower half of another. This was sufficient damage to deny the CCF control of the reservoir waters, thereby removing that worry for the rest of the war.[116]

# VI

By the morning of April 26 the withdrawal of I Corps was proceeding more satisfactorily. It had paused on an east-west line (Delta) above Uijongbu. The divisional and corps artillery battalions continued to hold forward positions, blasting away at the CCF with an unprecedented expenditure of ammo. The carnage was ghastly. *Time* magazine quoted one officer: "They attack, and we shoot them down. Then we pull back, and they have to do it all over again. . . . They're spending people the way we spend ammunition."[117]

Later that day the weather, which had been good, suddenly turned abysmal. Heavy rains fell in the I Corps sector. Between the showers a dense fog covered the low-lying hills and valleys. Owing to the weather, FEAF's jets, which had withdrawn to southern Korea could not continue providing effective close air support. However, the slower, ground-hugging F-51 Mustangs of the 35th Group, based around Seoul, mounted about 100 sorties a day, flying below the clouds, bombing, napalming, and strafing formations of CCF. Milburn judged these close support missions to be highly effective; they killed or wounded or dazed hundreds more CCF.[118]

The FEAF commanders, meanwhile, remained on full alert for the expected all-out CCF Air Force attack on Eighth Army. Fortunately it did not materialize. No one ever found out exactly why. Perhaps it was because FEAF F-86s, based in Korea, had reattained "mastery of the air" in MIG Alley. Or perhaps it was because FEAF bombers and fighter-bombers had "destroyed" the network of new CCF airfields in North Korea.[119]

While I Corps was paused at the Uijongbu line on April 26, the Americans in the 3d Division detected a distinct slackening in the force of the CCF attacks. The 3d Division historian wrote:

While fighting in the Division zone continued, it was obvious that the steam roller charges of the Communists were weakening. Their assault units had been decimated by the terrific fire of the defenders and their supporting artillery and aircraft. . . . The price paid by the Reds for a few miles of ground was appalling. Many of their companies and battalions had disintegrated into disorganized fragments wandering aimlessly over the blood-soaked hills. . . . The Red commander had placed full dependence upon the weight of massed infantry to break and destroy the lines of the UN defenders. In the bright light of a full moon, he tried to smother the UN guns with bodies of his peasant soldiers. That they attempted bravely to do so is undeniable; their courage was worthy of a better cause.[120]

The slackening was not evident, however, in the left sector of the I Corps front. That night—April 26—the CCF Sixty-fourth Army and the NKPA I Corps troops fell on the ROK 1st Division and the supporting Puerto Rican 65th Infantry (and Filipinos) in massive force. Having regrouped all its disparate elements, the 65th Infantry (and the Filipinos) repulsed the enemy and held during the night, but the ROKs, exhausted from four full days of relentless enemy attacks, finally buckled in disorder.[121]

\* \* \*

During the next twenty-four hours I Corps slowly withdrew closer to Seoul. At noon on April 28 it began occupying Line Lincoln (or Golden). After weeks of engineering work, the line was very strong. It was comprised of a series of deep, interconnected trenches and sandbagged bunkers bristling with machine guns, 57- and 75-mm recoilless rifles, and flamethrowers. It was protected on the north side by half a dozen lines of coiled barbed wire. Beyond and inside the barbed wire were dense fields of antipersonnel mines, booby traps, and "thousands" of gasoline drums (fougasses) filled with napalm and white phosphorus to be exploded by trip wire or remotely activated thermite grenades. Powerful searchlights, located on nearby hilltops and beamed at the low-hanging clouds, lighted the battle zone.

The artillery was placed rearward from Line Lincoln. Closest to the line in direct support of the infantry were the twelve battalions of 105-mms of the four American divisions, plus the Turkish, British, and ROK FABs (and one battery of Filipino artillery). Farther back were the four 155-mm FABs of the American divisions with a total of about 72 howitzers. Farther back yet (some south of the Han River) were the five battalions of corps artillery with another 90 howitzers. All the FABs still had large stocks of ammo, and more ammo was coming forward by truck from Inchon and by train from Pusan.

That night—April 28—the enemy made two attempts to crack Line Lincoln (or Golden). The first was mounted by the NKPA 8th Division against the ROK 1st Division sector. Supported by Patton tanks of Hannum's B Company, 73d Tank Battalion, the ROKs yielded a hill, but then counterattacked, killing 1,241 NKPA troops. The second was a CCF attack at Gerry Kelleher's 35th Infantry sector. After Kelleher's men had decisively repulsed the attack, he reported they had inflicted "an estimated 1,000 dead and wounded" casualties on the CCF.[122]

\* \* \*

Dug in behind this powerful line on April 29, Van Fleet and his commanders remained tense. In six days of combat Clint Tarkenton's G-2 section had identified men from nineteen CCF divisions of twelve different armies "in actual combat or immediately available as reserves." Twelve CCF armies usually totaled thirty-six divisions. That meant the CCF could have another seventeen divisions "available as immediate reserve for the armies in contact." In addition, G-2 believed, there were two more CCF armies (six divisions) "immediately available." In sum, in addition to the forces that had survived the first six days of combat, the CCF could throw as many as twenty-three fresh divisions (230,000 men) at Line Lincoln.[123]

At 5:00 P.M. on April 29, Van Fleet issued a communiqué, summing up the weeklong battle and putting it in perspective. The CCF offensive, probably designed to capture Seoul by May 1, had not been a "surprise" to Eighth Army, he asserted. "Some factors could not be anticipated"; they included the collapse of the ROK 6th Division, which had required "unexpected employment of friendly reserve units." However, in the face of enemy "human-sea tactics" Eighth Army's soldiers had fought with "consummate skill and vigor" and had inflicted an estimated 70,000 enemy casualties.

He did not doubt that the CCF was regrouping for another assault at Seoul. He virtually dared the enemy to come on: "The present lull is a natural consequence for his reorganization, resupply, and forward displacement. . . . Morale of all UN forces is high. With fair weather for combat, the front line units and air welcome the opportunity to destroy the Communist Army north of the Han."[124]

The CCF did not rise to the bait. The Maoist military doctrine was to hit and withdraw; to hit again and withdraw; and, above all, to eschew frontal assaults on impregnable enemy positions. Consequently, there were no further suicidal CCF attacks on Line Lincoln. The CCF troops withdrew beyond UN artillery range into the hills around Uijongbu to lick severe wounds and plan other strategies.*

* * *

The eight days of combat between April 22 and 30, 1951, known as the CCF Spring Offensive, proved to be the biggest single battle of the Korean War. During it Eighth Army had suffered some reverses. It had been forced

---

*The Army historian concluded after an exhaustive search of existing records that the often published story that 6,000 CCF troops were slaughtered by FEAF and ROK Marines while attempting an encircling attack of Line Lincoln over the lower Han River could not be substantiated. The story may have sprung from a feeble attempt by NKPA troops to cross the lower Han, which was decisively repulsed, the historian wrote, by the fire of two Army FABs and the cruiser *Toledo*.[125]

off its positions on the 38th Parallel, had ceded about thirty-five miles of real estate, had sustained about 7,000 casualties. It had lost the Gloucester Battalion and another forty howitzers.* No one was proud of this withdrawal, which at times had been messy; nor did UN soldiers clearly understand that it had been fully planned. Morale had slumped. GIs began ridiculing the conflict as a "yo-yo war" without end.

Yet in reality the battle was another magnificent victory for Eighth Army. Although not always perfectly executed—war seldom is perfect—the withdrawal had repulsed and savaged the CCF's greatest offensive, inflicting 70,000 casualties, and had denied the enemy his primary objective, Seoul. Beyond that the battle must have caused grave concern in Peking. It demonstrated that in order to throw Eighth Army out of Korea—if it could be done at all—the CCF would require a massive new, possibly prohibitive commitment of manpower. Even so, Peking gave no hint that it was interested in negotiations. It was, in fact, planning yet another massive offensive.

---

*Raising the total loss of major artillery pieces by U.S. Army and ROK Army forces in the war to 303.

# PART
# THIRTEEN

# Red China
# Checked

# 27

# THE SIXTH CHINESE OFFENSIVE

## I

On the last day of April Van Fleet met with his three American corps commanders at Yoju to review the situation. Eighth Army had delivered the CCF a savage blow, but Van Fleet was naturally worried about the surviving enemy elements and the massive CCF reserves, which had not yet been committed to battle. Although the enemy usually required some weeks to prepare for a major new offensive, Van Fleet had concluded that this time they would mount a "second phase" or "second impulse" offensive in a matter of a few days. As before he believed that the enemy objective would be the capture of Seoul.[1]

By this time the Eighth Army G-2, Clint Tarkenton, had detected and reported a shift of several CCF armies easterly toward the center of the peninsula. This report led Van Fleet to believe that in this second all-out attempt to capture Seoul the CCF would mount not only a heavy frontal attack on Line Lincoln, but also a very powerful multi-army flanking attack down the Pukhan Valley, through Kapyong, thence southwest, in an attempt to encircle UN forces in Seoul with a shallow envelopment.

This line of thinking led Van Fleet to conclude that Eighth Army's center was much too weak. It was then held only by Babe Bryan's 24th Division on the No Name Line astride the Pukhan River above the junction of the Pukhan and Han and, east of there, by the ROK 2d and reconstituted ROK 6th divisions. Accordingly, Van Fleet had produced a plan to reinforce the center significantly: Frank Bowen's 187th Airborne Combat Team would be deployed with a corps FAB behind the 24th Division on the south bank of the Han River, and Buddy Ferenbaugh's 7th Division would be shifted from the

859

Army's extreme eastern flank to the center, to backstop the ROK 2d and 6th divisions.[2]

Van Fleet concluded the meeting with an exhortation:

We have successfully defended against about one-half of the enemy offensive strength so far. He has, in addition to the other half of his forces, salvaged probably 50 percent of his original attack force. He has used, so far, no armor, no air, and little artillery.

May is the month in which to defeat him. We can do it better in this area than in any other. If he is not given a bad set-back here, he can infiltrate forever. To stop him then, in that type of operation, we would have to meet the enemy man for man, which we can't do. If we don't beat him now we will have more and more unfavorable weather for some months—less air, less mobility [and] the enemy will have better concealment. *Now is the time to destroy him.* I would like to make this our maximum effort—and do it north of the Han.

All operations would be conducted with due caution and professionalism. Van Fleet continued: "I want no needless sacrificing of units. I don't want to lose a company—certainly not a battalion. Keep units intact. Small units must be kept within supporting distance. I want to emphasize again: don't let units get cut off . . . [like] the Gloucester battalion. Don't use any forces that way."[3]

Based on the intelligence reports available to him, the CCF proclivity for strong flanking attacks in prior offensives, and intuition, Van Fleet's decision to beef up Eighth Army's center appeared to be prudent and logical. But the analysis failed to take into account the Maoist military doctrine of eschewing ruinous attacks on heavily fortified enemy strongholds and to do the unexpected. As a result of Van Fleet's fixation on Seoul and Tarkenton's incomplete analysis, yet another serious Eighth Army intelligence failure was in the making.

* * *

The sudden shift of the American 7th Division from X to IX Corps proved to be a traumatic experience, physically and mentally. The division had been in X Corps ever since its arrival in Korea. Its officers had developed close contacts and operating procedures with the corps's officers. It had occupied Eighth Army's far right flank for four months. It had developed intricate supply lines over inhospitable terrain. All that was abandoned in a matter of a few hours. The shift, carried out expeditiously, was completed by May 1.[4]

The integration of the 7th Division into IX Corps did not go smoothly. Engineer Bill Hoge and infantryman Buddy Ferenbaugh clashed. The 7th Division G-3, Mel Huston, remembered:

General Ferenbaugh's greatest irritants were the visits by General Hoge, commanding general of IX Corps. These invariably saw the two generals poring over the war room maps, arguing their convictions of [the] proper tactics the doughboy [should use] in taking and holding a Korean hill position. Neither seemed to win these tactical expositions. As Buddy later confided, "Well, Mel, when I let a goddamn Engineer tell *me* how to fight an infantry battle, it'll be a sad day for the doughs of this fine division."[5]

In Tokyo Ridgway was putting in long days acquainting himself with his immense new duties and responsibilities. Two matters concerned him most: a likely CCF air attack on Eighth Army in conjunction with a renewed CCF offensive and a far less likely, although possible, Soviet attack on Eighth Army or on Japan itself. Believing he lacked sufficient authority to deal promptly with any of these prospects, Ridgway set in motion a paper exchange with the JCS to clarify and enhance his authority.

He dealt first, and urgently, with the possibility of a CCF air attack on Eighth Army. Earlier President Truman and the JCS had approved a directive giving the Far East commander standby authority to respond immediately (and without his further consulting Washington) to such an attack by mounting retaliatory attacks against CCF air bases in "Manchuria and the Shantung Peninsula in the immediate vicinity of Weihaiwei." But this directive had been deliberately withheld from MacArthur. On April 27 Ridgway requested that he be granted that standby authority, deleting references to "Weihaiwei" inasmuch as "information available here" indicated no CCF air buildup in Weihaiwei. He added another important request: that he be granted authority at once to begin surreptitious air reconnaissance of Manchuria and the Shantung peninsula in order to pinpoint the CCF air buildup and take photographs of the likely target areas.[6]

The JCS granted Ridgway both requests on the following day:

You are hereby authorized to use U.S. Forces assigned to the Far East to conduct air reconnaissance of enemy air bases in Manchuria and the Shantung Peninsula. Such reconnaissance should, if practicable, be made at high altitude and as surreptitiously as possible.

In the event of a major enemy air attack from outside Korea against UN forces in the Korean area . . . you are hereby authorized at your discretion, without further reference to the JCS or higher authority, to attack enemy air bases in Manchuria and the Shantung Peninsula. This authority here granted will not be delegated, except to your successor in command should you become a casualty. However, authority to attack should only be used in the event that in your judgment, time and circumstances do not permit reference to the JCS.[7]

The second matter—a possible Soviet attack on Japan—was, of course, far more complex to deal with. Two National Guard divisions (40th and 45th) had recently arrived in Japan, but they were not fully trained or equipped and would probably be overwhelmed by a determined Soviet amphibious assault. The JCS and GHQ had secretly created an organization of four partly equipped Japanese infantry divisions from the Japanese police reserve and planned to create six more such divisions. But this secret buildup of the Japanese reserve police force would take time and would require the unlikely approval of the antiwar Japanese government and population.[8]

The only realistic way to meet a Soviet invasion of Japan was quickly to withdraw Eighth Army from Korea to Japan. Prompted by Ridgway's earlier request (April 17) for authority to do so (which had been temporarily denied), the JCS, at Joe Collins's suggestion, had reviewed, codified, and revised all outstanding directives to GHQ. Upon the approval of President Truman, a new directive was sent to Ridgway on May 1.[9]

Notwithstanding the conscientious work of the Army G-3, Max Taylor, Ridgway found dismaying inconsistencies or weaknesses in his new directive. He objected in particular to two sections:

• On the one hand, the JCS reiterated that Ridgway's primary mission was the defense of Japan and the offshore perimeter. On the other hand, it continued to deny him authority to withdraw Eighth Army from Korea for that purpose at his own discretion. This issue was further complicated by the fact that there would probably be no time or facilities to withdraw ROKs, and in any case, ROKs could not be called upon to defend the Japanese homeland. Owing to Ridgway's continuing belief that a forced withdrawal of Eighth Army from Korea could precipitate mass defection among the ROKs, perhaps fatally endangering Eighth Army, Ridgway believed strongly that he should absolutely control all the decisions—and publicity—attending a forced withdrawal.

• On the one hand, the JCS specified that Ridgway's secondary mission was "to assist the ROKs in repelling aggression and to restore peace and security in the area" and to "destroy the armed forces of North Korea and Communist China operating within the geographic boundaries of Korea and waters adjacent thereto." On the other hand, Eighth Army was to make no general advance beyond the old Line Kansas to Wyoming without prior approval. Ridgway rightly viewed these statements as antithetical.

In order to clear up the mission ambiguities or conflicts and other points of disagreement once and for all, Ridgway initiated a tedious lawyerlike exchange with the JCS that continued for several more weeks. In addition, he sent a GHQ staff officer, West Pointer (1938) Roy C. Heflebower, Jr., to Washington to confer directly with Collins and Taylor. In due course these cables and discussions produced an entirely new directive with some major changes. Pending its receipt, Ridgway no doubt better understood the frustrations MacArthur had experienced over the GHQ "mission." However, Ridgway and the JCS continued to see eye to eye on the larger issues.[10]

* * *

On May 3 Ridgway flew to Korea to confer with Van Fleet and the corps and division commanders. He found them geared up for a massive CCF second phase or second impulse offensive at Seoul but, contrary to Van Fleet's presumption, it had not materialized. Nor, bafflingly, were there any indications that an all-out attack on Seoul was imminent. Once again the CCF seemed to have disappeared off the face of the earth.[11]

In order to reestablish contact with the enemy, Eighth Army had drawn up a plan for large-scale probing tactics similar to those employed by Ridgway in early January with Operation Wolfhound and Task Force Johnson. Each American division would deploy a strong battalion combat team well forward of the division positions. These forward deployments were called "patrol bases" or "outpost lines of resistance" (OPLRs). They would serve as self-contained bastions from which small infantry or infantry-armor patrols could probe even deeper into enemy territory in order to ferret out his dispositions and disrupt his assemblies for offensive action.[12]

In addition to these plans for the American divisions, Van Fleet had conceived an ambitious operation for the ROKs, who now held the right flank of Eighth Army on Line Kansas below Inje, opposite the desultory NKPA II, III, and V corps. The ROKs would attack north with the object of recapturing Inje and bringing the extreme right flank (anchored on the Sea of Japan) north to the coastal town of Kansong. This ROK-only offensive would regain the Kansong–Hongchon road. By developing Kansong into a port of supply, the ROKs could be logistically supported through Kansong, rather than over the tortuous, crowded roads and trails from Hongchon. To support this ROK-only operation, Van Fleet would have the ROK 1st Division, on the extreme left flank of Eighth Army, make a limited (two-day) attack north from Line Lincoln into the sector believed to be occupied by the NKPA I Corps. These ROK operations would begin on May 7.[13]

There was another reason for this plan. The recent utter collapse of the ROK 6th Division and the partial collapse of the ROK 5th and 7th divisions had given the ROK Army another black eye. Van Fleet believed that it desperately needed a success to restore its confidence, and that the operation (to be mounted only against the NKPA) could be a restorative step. Inasmuch as the CCF appeared to be concentrating for another attack at Seoul, it was not likely to appear in the extreme eastern sector to support the NKPA.

All in all, this plan seemed to make sense. In effect it would extend the eastern No Name Line northeastward in a tidy fashion, from Hongchon to Kansong. The logisticians were more than pleased at the prospect of developing Kansong to support the ROKs. However, there was risk: The transfer of Buddy Ferenbaugh's 7th Division to the center sector of the long Eighth Army line had left the ROKs in the east unsupported by American forces. If the NKPA counterattacked the ROKs with unusual vigor or if the CCF came over to help the NKPA, and the ROKs again collapsed, Nick Ruffner's 2d Division would be seriously exposed on its right flank.

Beyond that Van Fleet had conceived larger plans for Eighth Army. If his predicted CCF offensive at Seoul did not materialize soon, he proposed that Eighth Army go over to a "limited objective" offensive. His idea was to advance Eighth Army to an intermediate line (Topeka) running due east from Munsan; then, if no serious reverses were encountered, to return the entire army to Line Kansas. The offensive, named Detonate, would begin on or about May 12.[14]

Ridgway approved all these military maneuvers, then directed the discussion to a worrisome politico-military matter. Recently Syngman Rhee had touched off yet another controversy by publicly demanding that Washington supply sufficient arms to equip ten more ROK divisions. By coincidence Eighth Army had just completed a study which concluded that since the beginning of the war, bugging-out ROKs had abandoned to the enemy sufficient equipment to equip ten full divisions. In light of that study—and the recent experience with the ROK 6th Division—Ridgway and Van Fleet were in complete agreement that Rhee's latest request should be emphatically denied. Giving the ROKs more equipment, Van Fleet said, would be "a criminal waste." What the ROKs needed was not more equipment but a drastic overhaul of the corrupt and incompetent ROK officer corps.[15]

Ridgway and Van Fleet met with Rhee on May 4. Ambassador Muccio and the ROK Army chief of staff, Chung Il Kwon, were present. "I do not think there was room for a trace of ambiguity in the straight-from-the-shoulder talk we delivered to the old warrior that afternoon," Ridgway wrote.[16] The thrust of their remarks that day was contained in a letter from Van Fleet to Chung Il Kwon, a copy of which Muccio gave to Rhee and sent to Dean Acheson:

The primary problem in the Republic of Korea is to secure competent leadership in their army. They do not have it, from the Minister of Defense on down, as is clearly evidenced by repeated battle failures of major units. This is the chief and basic responsibility of the President of the Republic in the military field. Until we get competent leadership, there is little reason to expect any better performance of ROK troops, or any higher degree of confidence than presently exists among their UN comrades.

Until competent leadership is secured and it demonstrates its worth, there should be no further talk of the US furnishing arms and equipment for additional forces.[17]

This candor appeared to make an impression on Rhee. Muccio later cabled Acheson: "The President agreed to take stronger measures in enforcing discipline in the ROK Army, particularly at the higher levels, to address a statement of encouragement to the troops, to spend more time visiting the troops at the front, and to insure that ROK Chief of Staff rather than various politicians be able to deal responsibly with UN Forces on military matters."[18]*

Ridgway returned to Tokyo that night and got off two cables to the JCS. Summarizing his visit with the Eighth Army leadership, he said he "found these commanders with spirit of high confidence and self-assurance in their ability to handle the situation tactically and satisfied with their logistics capabilities to support their planned tactical operations." He explained the OPLR concept, the forthcoming ROK offensive, and the succeeding Eighth Army offensive, Detonate, concluding: "Eighth Army has in mind, with my approval, that if enemy does not soon attack, for which Eighth Army is fully prepared, it will itself initiate coordinated general offensive action." The second cable contained the gist of his and Van Fleet's meeting with Rhee "concerning the grave lack of leadership in ROK Army repeatedly evidenced in battle and most recently during current enemy offensive."[20]

## II

In compliance with Van Fleet's new directive, the American divisions of Eighth Army established OPLRs or patrol bases forward of Lines Lincoln and No Name on May 4. The forces assigned to these roles were not wildly happy. They were dangerously exposed, with no flank protection. A CCF surprise attack could cut them off from the rear.[21]

In the 1st Cav Division Charlie Palmer, holding on Line Lincoln astride the Uijongbu road, sent the 7th Cav, newly commanded by Dan Gilmer, to man the division's OPLR. Gilmer went up the road to Uijongbu, assisted by Hawkins's 64th Tank Battalion from I Corps reserve.

On this, his first combat mission, Dan Gilmer came across as a less than

---

*The ROK 6th Division commander, Chang Do Yung, and two of his three regimental commanders were reprimanded and docked about two months' pay but retained command. Six other ROK officers in the division, including a regimental commander, were court-martialed and sentenced to from two to fifteen years' hard labor. Yung felt so disgraced that he and his fellow officers organized a secret society, Yellow Tigers, whose members swore never again to yield a foot of ground or permit their troops to do so. According to Van Fleet, that step put the ROK 6th Division on the road to becoming one of the best ROK divisions in Korea.[19]

heroic character and an officer who showed little concern for the welfare of his men. "He was a brilliant staff officer," a contemporary remembered, "but as a commander, he didn't have it." His men accused him of sandbagging his own CP first, protecting it with "about fifty miles of barbed wire." They said he issued thoughtless orders, such as "Captain, I want you to take that hill within fifteen minutes," and often countermanded or nullified such orders with conflicting orders. He equipped his command jeep with a .50 caliber machine-gun ringmount and drove around standing up inside it, a practice the men thought was the "silliest thing you ever saw" and which led to a derisive nickname, "Ringmount Gilmer."[22]

Sladen Bradley was hard-pressed to find forces in his 25th Division with which to mount a patrol base. Owing to the earlier failure of a company in Henry Britt's 24th Infantry, Bradley had committed Gilbert Check's 27th Infantry to reinforce the 24th on Line Lincoln alongside Kelleher's 35th. This left only the Turks in division reserve. Bradley did not have sufficient confidence in the blacks to send elements of the 24th Infantry out to create the patrol base. If he sent either the 27th or 35th, he would be forced to put the Turks on the line, leaving him no reserve at all.[23] The problem was solved by pulling Jim Boswell's crack 7th Infantry (of the 3d Division) from corps reserve. Mated with the all-black 58th FAB, now commanded by Burrel C. Hassett, the 7th Infantry was assigned to the 25th Division and manned its OPLR.[24]

Coincidentally with these maneuvers, the most famous regimental commander of the Korean War, Mike Michaelis, left the scene. Earlier Eisenhower had cabled from NATO that he had a "critical need" for an American brigadier general of "outstanding qualifications and with Korean battle experience" and hoped he might get his former "personal aide and friend" Mike Michaelis. Inasmuch as Michaelis had served in Korea for ten months, Ridgway willingly released him. Replaced by Bill Hoge's deputy IX Corps commander, William Mitchell, Michaelis on May 6 went to NATO and onward to four stars.[25]

The OPLRs across Eighth Army's long front began active daylight patrolling on May 5 and 6. Armor-infantry teams fanned out from the perimeters into the hills. Many encountered pockets of CCF. Some rescued UN prisoners who were hiding out. The 7th Cav, which reoccupied deserted Uijongbu, captured ten long-haired "Manchurian ponies," which the CCF had been using to transport supplies over rugged terrain. Pleased to have "horses once again," the 7th Cav employed them for the same purpose, finding that these ponies could do the work of eighty Korean porters in half the time.[26]

Owing to the ability of the CCF to conceal its movements and a reluctance on the part of the Americans to probe too far, the OPLRs failed to develop much hard information on the whereabouts of the CCF. However, the absence of counterattacks on the OPLRs reinforced Van Fleet's new view that the CCF was not, as he had earlier believed, preparing for a second massive attack on

Seoul within a matter of days. He therefore issued orders for the OPLRs to remain in place and warned Eighth Army to prepare for a general offensive (Detonate) to begin on about May 12.[27]

* * *

The earlier planned all-ROK offensive in the eastern sector began on May 7. It was led on the left, in the American X Corps sector, by the ROK 5th and 7th divisions. Farther right ROK III and I Corps forces attacked in unison. Naval forces (the cruiser *Helena* and four destroyers) in the Sea of Japan supported the ROK attack by bombarding Kansong and simulating an amphibious landing there. FEAF provided heavy close air support.[28]

The ROK attack was only partly successful. On the left the ROK 5th and 7th divisions (of X Corps) did well, crossing the Kansong–Hongchon road to Line Missouri on May 10. On the right ROK I Corps (Capital and 11th divisions) did equally well, racing up the coast road to Kansong, supported by naval gunfire. In the middle, however, ROK III Corps (ROK 3d and 9th divisions) advanced slowly against spotty NKPA resistance in more rugged terrain and failed to keep pace. As a result, the ROKs did not secure the entire length of the Kansong–Hongchon road.[29]

Partly as a feint, partly to build confidence, partly to conduct reconnaissance, two regiments of the ROK 1st Division (11th and 15th) attacked north from Line Lincoln on Eighth Army's extreme left flank in concert with the ROKs in the east. They were supported by American artillery and Hannum's Pattons of the 73d Tank Battalion. The ROKs found NKPA resistance uneven or nonexistent and pushed north several miles for two successive days, until advanced patrols reached Munsan. On May 9 the ROKs returned to Line Lincoln. The apparent absence of enemy in front of the ROK 1st Division further reinforced Van Fleet's decision to proceed with the general Eighth Army offensive, Detonate, on May 12.[30]

* * *

Ridgway had inherited many unresolved problems. Ranking high among these was the large, complex, and touchy issue of black soldiers in the Eighth Army. Ridgway had embraced Bill Kean's view that the 24th Infantry should be deactivated and that the 3/9 and 3/15, the 64th Tank Battalion, the all-black FABs, the 77th ECC, and other black units should be desegregated. The black personnel of the 24th would be integrated into other units; white personnel would be brought into the 3/9 and 3/15 and other black units. He had intended to make a recommendation to MacArthur to that effect in mid-March, but the sacking of MacArthur had intervened.[31]

On May 12, one month after relieving MacArthur, Ridgway drafted a cable to Washington containing those recommendations. He later wrote: "It was my conviction . . . that only in this way could we assure the sort of *esprit* a fighting army needs, where each soldier stands proudly on his own feet, knowing himself to be as good as the next fellow and better than the enemy. Besides it had always seemed to me both un-American and un-Christian for free citizens to be taught to downgrade themselves in this way, as if they were unfit to associate with their fellows or to accept leadership themselves."[32]

Ridgway's historic cable went off to Washington on May 14. Because they had proved to be "ineffective" in combat, he asked for authority to abolish all-black units in the Far East Command. He would begin with the 24th Infantry, which he would replace with another regiment (the 14th Infantry in Japan) after reassigning most of its men to white units in Korea. He would then integrate other black combat units (the 3/9 and 3/15 etc.) and, finally, service units. He would limit blacks in desegregated units in his command to about 12 percent and future black replacements to the Far East to about 10 percent of the total. In order to have sufficient units through which to spread the many blacks at no more than 12 percent, he also would have to desegregate the 40th and 45th National Guard divisions in Japan.[33]

Ridgway's proposal did not come as a surprise to the Pentagon high command. Two recent Army studies of blacks in Korea had recommended desegregation. The Army's G-1, Tony McAuliffe, favored it, as did the G-3, Max Taylor. Joe Collins and Frank Pace also favored desegregation, although Pace stressed caution because "once a step was taken it was very much harder to retract." In the top levels of the Army only Ham Haislip strongly opposed desegregation, but he was soon to retire. On a higher level within the Department of Defense, the assistant secretary for manpower and personnel, Anna M. Rosenberg, and George Marshall both favored integration.[34]

The word soon spread via the grapevine to Eighth Army. Van Fleet and many other senior generals favored desegregation. But others, notably Ned Almond, did not. Almond opposed integration in the Army then and for the rest of his life.

Although the majority of Pentagon leaders approved Ridgway's proposal, Pace's advice on caution was followed. The wheels turned slowly. Weeks passed before the desegregation policy was officially established and announced. More weeks passed before desegregation became a fact of life in Eighth Army.[35]

## III

During the first two weeks of May the CCF military buildup continued at a frenetic pace. Its details were not known, but occasionally FEAF reconnaissance aircraft got an important glimpse. For example, FEAF reported sighting an unprecedented 3,700 vehicles behind enemy lines, 2,300 of them headed south. Other intelligence sources reported new, uncommitted CCF armies massing in the Iron Triangle and CCF troops moving forward and digging in under cover of darkness.[36]

These fragmentary reports were difficult to assess, but as they mounted in number the Eighth Army G-2, Clint Tarkenton, became increasingly concerned. By May 9 he had reached the conclusion that the CCF activity was "strongly suggestive" of the "pattern of events" which occurred during the "three or four" days prior to a major CCF offensive. The next day, May 10, he reported to Van Fleet that an all-out CCF offensive at Seoul seemed imminent. The continuing easterly shift of major CCF units convinced Tarkenton that the weight of the offensive would strike at the seam between I and IX Corps, near the confluence of the Pukhan and Han rivers, where Babe Bryan's 24th Division (of IX Corps) was deployed.[37]

These reports and Tarkenton's analysis persuaded Van Fleet on May 11 to cancel the proposed Eighth Army offensive, Detonate. Reporting this decision to Ridgway, Van Fleet guessed that the CCF would attack in the next "72 to 96 hours." He believed that three CCF armies (nine divisions), plus the NKPA I Corps (three or four divisions), would probably strike toward Seoul from the north and that possibly three CCF armies (nine divisions) would strike toward Seoul from the northeast on a flanking attack down the Pukhan Valley. In a secondary attack, supporting the main effort against Seoul, two CCF armies (six divisions) and the NKPA II, III, and V corps (perhaps four or five divisions) would probably strike at Chunchon and the ROKs on the eastern flank.[38]*

In preparation for the supposed massive (twenty-odd divisions) enemy attack on Seoul, Van Fleet ordered Shorty Soule's full 3d Division into Eighth Army reserve to serve as the new Fire Brigade. In the expected battle each of its three RCTs would be prepared to support an American corps: Tom Yancey's 15th Infantry to help Almond's X Corps; William Harris's 65th Puerto Ricans, Hoge's IX Corps; Jim Boswell's 7th Infantry (in Seoul), Milburn's I Corps.[39]

Facing the prospect of a supposed attack by some twenty-odd CCF and NKPA divisions, the men on the right flank of Line Lincoln at Seoul grew tense. Bittman Barth in the 25th Division remembered:

None of us at division headquarters were happy over the situation. We might have to fight an all-out defense with our backs to the wide, unfordable Han River. There was only one bridge behind us (although two other bridges spanned the river farther to the west at Seoul). A flash flood or surprise attack might deprive us of

---

*In this analysis the CCF Sixty-third, Sixty-fourth, and Sixty-fifth Armies would attack Seoul down the Uijongbu corridor; the Twelfth, Fifteenth, and Sixtieth Armies would attack down the Pukhan Valley; the Twentieth and Twenty-Seventh Armies would attack through Chunchon to Wonju.

the use of our vital bridge. Even the normal supply of traffic "bottle-necked" while crossing this 800-foot span at reduced speed. Serious fighting—especially if any withdrawal became necessary—might result in a disastrous traffic jam. Accordingly, all vehicles not absolutely needed for daily use or the maintenance of signal communications, were moved south of the river [as were] the 159th, 90th, and Turkish Field Artillery Battalions.[40]

Indeed, the situation in the 25th Division was somewhat precarious. The Turks had replaced Boswell's 7th Infantry on the OPLR, but lacking artillery, the OPLR was pulled back to within two miles of Line Lincoln, so it could be supported by the FABs of the 24th, 27th, and 35th regiments. The assignment of the Turks to the OPLR left the 25th Division with no reserve. The weak link between the 25th Division and the 24th Division (on the right) was plugged by the Filipino Battalion (detached from the 65th Infantry), but this brought only small comfort because the Filipinos had yet to prove they could fight.[41]

Nor was the situation in Babe Bryan's 24th Division on the No Name Line any less precarious. Bill Hoge had directed Bryan to place his 5th, 19th, and 21st regiments in strong blocking positions astride the Pukhan River, just north of the junction of the Pukhan and Han rivers. In Van Fleet's estimates, the Pukhan Valley was almost certain to be a CCF main line of attack. Unless the 24th Division vastly improved its defensive positions, it stood a very good chance of being overrun and forced back across the Han River. Frank Bowen's 187th Airborne Combat Team had been assigned to back up the 24th Division, but it was on the south bank of the Han, and would have to cross it and attack "head on" into the oncoming enemy. If the enemy got below the Han, it would be in position to go east or west, threatening the rear of the entire Army.[42]

Believing the 24th Division front to be the "most sensitive" area along Eighth Army's front, Van Fleet inspected it on May 14. He was not pleased by what he found. The Eighth Army historian wrote with unusual candor that Van Fleet chewed out Bill Hoge and Babe Bryan,

stating that he wanted more mines and that the [barbed] wire was only one-third enough. The Army Commander wanted wherever possible three bands of double apron wire fifty yards apart, with mines strewn between the bands. Inasmuch as the enemy frequently attacked down ridge lines, [Van Fleet] stressed that all approaches be secured with protective wire, covered by fire. [Van Fleet] exhorted General Hoge to build up his defensive positions, stating: "This is the best place to kill [the enemy]. It is better to do it here and now—this month and the next. I want lots of wire and mines expended—not human lives. This IX Corps position falls short of my desires. I want work speeded up."[43]

The Army and corps G-2s, using every resource at hand (possibly including some communications intelligence), continued to track the redeployment of the five CCF armies (of fifteen divisions, comprising about 150,000 men) eastward to the Hwachon Reservoir area above Chunchon. They confirmed without a doubt that the redeployment had taken place and guessed that the enemy would attack on or about May 16. As Van Fleet later put it publicly: "An imminent major enemy attack was anticipated and quite accurately timed."[44]

The enemy capabilities and timing had been accurately assessed, but Van Fleet's fixation on Seoul and Clint Tarkenton's shallow analysis continued to color and skew the assessment of enemy intentions. In fact, the Chinese had concocted a bold and ambitious new plan that included no direct attack on Seoul. The aim this time was to attack and annihilate X Corps on its No Name Line. That done, the CCF Armies would swoop south to Wonju, thence west below the Han River to Suwon and/or directly south to Pusan. In military parlance the Chinese had devised a "deep envelopment" of Eighth Army rather than the expected "shallow envelopment" down the Pukhan Valley.

By that time the four divisions of Ned Almond's X Corps were dug in stoutly on No Name Line. From southwest to northeast these were: Gerry Thomas's 1st Marine Division (near Hongchon), Nick Ruffner's 2d Division (near Hangye), and the ROK 5th and 7th divisions deployed diagonally northeast from the 2d Division toward Inje. The line lay south of the twisting Soyang River and parallel to the Kansong–Hongchon road. The forces occupied fortified positions in the hills, which averaged about 2,000 feet in height.[45]

The sector to the right (or east) of this No Name Line to the coastline was held by ROKs. On the immediate right was ROK III Corps, composed of the ROK 3d and 9th divisions. These divisions, traversing rugged terrain, had not caught up with the ROK 5th and 7th divisions. They were still advancing slowly north toward the Kansong–Hongchon road, under orders to extend the No Name Line northeast from Inje to the coast at Kansong. To the right (or east) of ROK III Corps, ROK I Corps (Capital and 11th divisions) had reached Kansong, which was twenty-five miles north of the 38th Parallel.

By a curious coincidence, Ruffner's 2d Division found itself in the same position it had occupied along the Chongchon River during Eighth Army's November 24 Home by Christmas offensive—that is, it anchored the American forces of Eighth Army on the extreme right. Facing northwest at Hangye on the No Name Line, the 2d Division was disposed as follows: Ed Messinger's 9th Infantry (abutting the Marines) held the left sector; John Coughlin's 38th Infantry (plus the Dutch Battalion) held the center; an armor-infantry task force (Zebra) held the right sector on the Kansong–Hongchon road, where the division joined the ROK 5th Division. Jack Chiles's 23d Regiment was in X Corps reserve. The infantry was backed by an awesome array of artillery: the four organic divisional artillery battalions (72 howitzers) plus the self-propelled howitzers of X Corps artillery.

Ed Messinger's 9th Infantry had had a busy and tough ten days. Initially assigned on May 4 to man an OPLR in front of Coughlin's 38th Infantry positions, its 1/9 and 2/9 (both with new commanders) had patrolled aggressively toward Chunchon. During these operations the 1/9, commanded by Gaylord M. Bishop, and the 2/9, commanded by James F. Perry, both had encountered very large, organized formations of CCF. During one of these fights Perry's G Company led by West Pointer (1945) William D. Clark, son of Mark Clark, was overrun, and Clark was wounded. He recovered and later returned to the regiment.[46]

By May 14 the 9th Infantry had pulled back close to No Name Line. In the 9th's regimental sector Perry's 2/9 held the left and James Nabors's black 3/9 the right. Bishop's 1/9, replacing the Dutch Battalion, took up positions behind the other two battalions on the No Name Line itself. A regimental report, remarking on the abundance of artillery, noted that during the 9th's ten days of operations on the OPLR, Carl Wohlfeil's 15th FAB had fired 11,127 rounds of 105 mm in direct support of the regiment, while division's black 503d FAB and the 96th and 196th FABs of X Corps had fired 3,239 rounds of general support.[47]

To the right of the 9th Infantry, John Coughlin's 38th Infantry (holding the center of the division sector) was disposed across a four-mile front as follows: The 3/38, commanded by Wallace M. Hanes, occupied the left sector of No Name Line. The 1/38, headed by George W. Kimbrell, occupied key high terrain (Hill 1051) in the right sector, backed up by the Dutch Battalion. The 2/38, commanded by Wallace W. Wilkins, held outpost positions or a patrol base about 3,500 yards northwest of the 1/38.[48]

Coughlin wrote:

All positions, including the patrol base, were dug in, wired and mined. Those on [No Name Line] were, of course, much stronger than the patrol base. The [No Name] positions had overhead cover that would withstand VT [variable time fuze] artillery fire [from friendly artillery]. Each front line company occupied the commanding terrain, each had an artillery FO in the best OP [observation post] and heavy weapons and mortar company FOs were well placed. Alternate means of communications had been emphasized. Much of the wire was underground and alternate lines [were] laid. Units were tied in by telephone wire both laterally and in depth, and a radio relay station was established as a precaution.[49]

Wallace Hanes, commanding the 3/38, had created a virtual fortress of sandbagged bunkers atop the key terrain in his area, Hill 800 (Bunker Hill). After an inspection of the No Name Line, Van Fleet declared the 3/38's positions to be the "most formidable" in the X Corps sector. Following his own inspection of his positions by helicopter, Hanes said to Nick Ruffner: "There's only one thing that worries me now, General. I'm afraid those bastards won't hit us. If they've seen what I've seen today, and if they are smart, they won't even give us a nibble."[50]

To the right of Coughlin, the 2d Division sector was occupied by the armor-infantry team Task Force Zebra. Originally it had been composed of two companies of the 72d Tank Battalion, the division Recon Company, the 1st Ranger Company, the French Battalion, plus one company each from the 9th and 38th regiments. On May 14, however, Ned Almond and Nick Ruffner drastically reorganized and weakened the Zebra force. The French Battalion and the two companies from the 9th and 38th were pulled out. The French went into division reserve close behind Zebra; the two companies, back to their parent organizations. These units were replaced by Lloyd K. Jenson's 2/23 (from X Corps reserve) and by a battalion of ROKs from the adjacent ROK 5th Division.[51]

Ned Almond and his staff had well noted the concentration of CCF in the Chunchon area. The new X Corps G-2, West Pointer (1933) James Polk, who had come from Willoughby's GHQ G-2 section, believed that the CCF were massing to hit not Seoul but X Corps. Recalling that canny prediction years later the I Corps G-3, Frank Mildren, said: "Jimmy Polk had line crossers; he had communications intelligence. He had found this huge concentration of Chinese. He said they would hit Tenth Corps—No Name Line. He was right. But nobody at Eighth Army believed him. They thought the Chinese were going to go to Seoul."[52]

Polk had been consistently accurate in his prior intelligence predictions. Although Almond had not always agreed with them or tailored his operations to fit, this time he listened. "Almond is the bravest man I've ever run into in my life," Mildren recalled. "He got in his plane and flew all around the enemy concentration area, to try to figure out what they were up to. Unfortunately, the custom was that the G-3 went on these flights. He flew very low over the ridges and valleys, looking down. He could see Chinamen down there, but not too many of them. They were clever; they kept their armies back and under cover."[53]

The massive concentration of CCF in the Chunchon area became an open secret in X Corps. The 2d Division historian wrote that late on the afternoon of May 14, "Air observers . . . reported masses of enemy troops moving southeastward along a trail . . . headed for the 2d Division positions." The division's presighted 38th and 503d FABs, joined by the X Corps 196th FAB, fired thousands of shells at these CCF. "As every indication pointed to an imminent mass attack, the Division readied itself to meet the onslaught," the historian went on. "Tanks from the regimental tank companies and 72nd Tank Battalion were located so they could be employed in indirect fire missions as well as direct."[54]

By this time the CCF generals had refined plans for annihilating X Corps.

Three CCF armies (Twelfth; Twentieth; Twenty-seventh) of nine divisions, deployed undetected well to the east of the Hwachon Reservoir near Inje would attack the ROK 5th and 7th divisions. They were to crack through the ROKs and Task Force Zebra, go southwest down the Kansong–Hongchon road *behind* (or east of) No Name Line, while the other two CCF armies (Fifteenth; Sixtieth) attacked the 2d Division frontally from the north and northwest. East of the CCF Armies the NKPA II, III, and V corps would hit the ROK 3d and 9th divisions simultaneously. After overrunning the ROKs and 2d Division the five CCF armies would merge to attack and destroy the 1st Marine Division holding the southern end of No Name Line, then press on to Wonju and beyond.

In retrospect, the CCF plan seemed desperate and foolhardy, and even suicidal to the Americans. That was because the CCF had chosen to launch a major offensive so distant from its main supply lines and bases in some of the most difficult terrain on the peninsula. But this analysis failed to take into account that the CCF was not so heavily dependent on supply lines and bases as were the roadbound Americans; that it counted on capturing and employing captured UN weapons and ammo; and that it operated best in rugged terrain where American vehicular mobility was restricted. Moreover, from the CCF point of view, the shift of Buddy Ferenbaugh's 7th Division to IX Corps had significantly weakened the upper UN line in the eastern sector. It was manned mostly by ROKs and the American 2d Division, which the CCF had already twice savaged—at Kunu in November and at Hoengsong in February. Once these forces had been overrun, only the 1st Marine Division would stand between the CCF and victory.

## IV

The Communist offensive burst upon Almond's X Corps and the ROKs to the east early in the evening of May 16. About fifteen CCF and five NKPA divisions—some 175,000 men—swarmed at the UN lines, blowing the familiar bugles and horns and firing flares. The weather was poor, overcast and rainy.[55]

Although the CCF offensive came as no great surprise, what was a surprise, if not a shock, was that its main weight was so far east. Geared up for an all-out defense of Seoul on his left flank, Van Fleet now confronted an all-out assault in his much weaker right flank. Moreover, X Corps, facing northwest, did not expect a CCF attack "behind" it from the northeast.

When the offensive began, the ROKs to the right (east) of the American 2d Division were disposed to the coast as follows: 5th; 7th; 9th; 3d; Capital. Most of the ROKs were terrified. Most, but not all, ROK regiments of the 5th, 7th, 9th, and 3d divisions collapsed or disintegrated within a few hours. In the

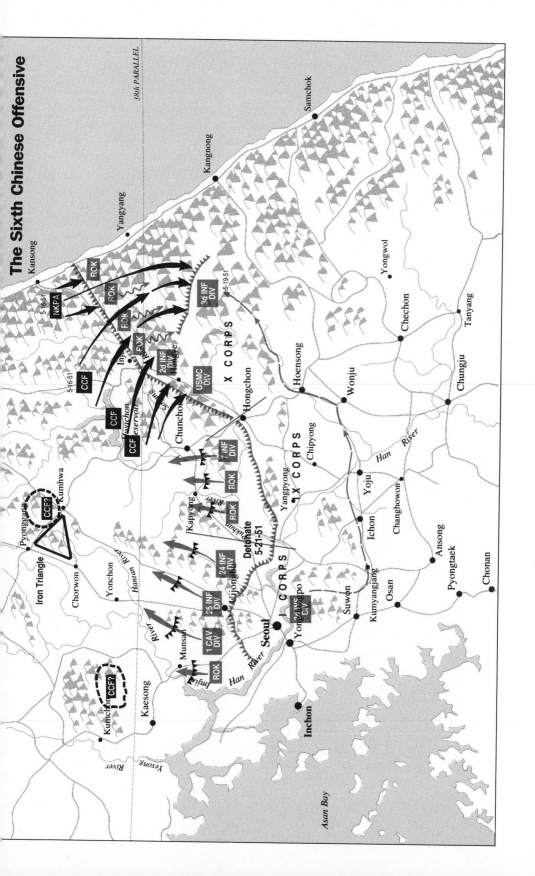

# The Sixth Chinese Offensive

Kansong

5-16-51 NKFA

ROK

ROK

ROK

38th PARALLEL

Yangyang

Kangnong

Samchok

5-16-51 CCF

ROK

Inje

3d INF DIV 5-19-51

CCF

2d INF DIV

CCF

Hwachon Reservoir

Soyang River

USMC DIV

Chunchon

Hongchon

X CORPS

Hoensong

Yongwol

Chechon

CCF2

Kumhwa

7 INF DIV

ROK

Kapyong

ROK

Pukhan River

Chipyong

Wonju

Han River

Yojn

Tanyang

Chungju

Pyonggang

Iron Triangle

Chorwon

Yonchon

Hantan River

24 INF DIV

Yangpyong

IX CORPS

Ichon

Changhowon

Ansong

Uijongbu

Detohate 5-21-51

Kumyangjang

Osan

Pyongtaek

Chonan

Munsan

25 INF DIV

1 CAV DIV

Seoul

Han River

I CORPS

Yongdungpo

Suwon

Kumchon CCF?

Kaesong

ROK

Injui

Han River

Inchon

Yesong River

Asan Bay

panic and ensuing chaos the ROKs abandoned most artillery and crew-served weapons and even rifles and fled far to the rear. The Americans advising the ROKs were left stranded. Adam Komosa and John J. Peattie, with the ROK 9th Division, escaped into the mountains and, after two days of evasion, reached safety. But two dozen or more less fortunate KMAG advisers were killed or captured.[56]

The ROK bugout, involving about 40,000 men, was the largest and most disgraceful of the Korean War. It left a huge gap on the X Corps right flank, exposing the entire rear of the eastern No Name Line. It directly and immediately imperiled the American 2d Division, which was left a lone salient, facing CCF troops to the north, west, and east, a situation eerily akin to that which the division had faced at Kunu.

In hindsight Van Fleet's decision to withdraw Buddy Ferenbaugh's 7th Division from X Corps's right flank appeared to be unwise. Had he not done so, it would have provided a steadying influence for the ROK 5th and 7th divisions. Had those divisions held, however shakily, the course of the battle might have been far different. As it turned out, Ferenbaugh's 7th Division, redeployed to IX Corps to backstop the ROK 2d and 6th divisions, was clearly in the wrong place at the wrong time.

\* \* \*

Masses of CCF troops of the Fifteenth and Sixtieth armies (six divisions of about 60,000 men) simultaneously struck the forward elements of Nick Ruffner's 2d Division. Those units which were hardest hit initially were Lloyd Jenson's 2/23, serving as the core infantry of Task Force Zebra in the division's right (or northeast) sector; George Kimbrell's 1/38 on No Name Line; and Wallace Wilkins's 2/38 manning an OPLR in the division's center. Task Force Zebra included the ROK 3/36 of the ROK 5th Division, which collapsed. But Jenson and his men managed to corral some ROKs and keep them on the line.[57]

Fortunately, the 2d Division and X Corps artillery was fully prepared. The artillerymen had mapped likely CCF attack routes well in advance. The artillery battalions were imaginatively placed so that several or more could fire on the likely routes simultaneously. The FOs had manned OPs on good terrain and had excellent communications links with the firing batteries. A huge quantity of ammo was available. Much credit for this careful preparation would go to the new 2d Division artillery commander, Tom de Shazo, replacing the unpopular and unadmired Loyal Haynes.[58]

The CCF attack on the 2d Division triggered awesome artillery response. On May 16 the howitzers of X Corps fired 17,000 rounds. On May 17 it was twice that: 38,000 rounds (250 rounds per gun). The barrage of artillery through night and day, rain or shine, killed and wounded or stunned the closely bunched CCF by the thousands and, ultimately, disorganized the attack.[59]

Of the 2d Division units, Task Force Zebra, on the extreme right, was weakest and most exposed. Nick Ruffner immediately reinforced it with the reserve French Battalion, deploying it with the 72d Tank Battalion behind Lloyd Jenson's 2/23, between Hangye and the "front." The next morning, May 17, Ruffner got Jack Chiles's 23d Infantry (less George Russell's 1/23) from X Corps reserve. Chiles rushed all the way forward with his staff and the 3/23, now commanded by Beverly T. Richardson, and assumed command of all forces in that sector. As a precaution, Chiles brought Russell's 1/23 (still in X Corps reserve) north of Hangye.[60]

Chiles was not pleased with the deployment. His 2/23 and 3/23 were badly exposed in positions well forward of the French Battalion, the 72d Battalion tanks, and Russell's 1/23. "I urgently requested General Ruffner to permit me to withdraw my 2nd and 3rd battalions under cover of darkness," Chiles remembered. "My right flank was wide open, there were gaps of two miles each between the French and the 2nd Battalion and the French and the 1st Battalion." The permission to withdraw was refused because, Chiles recalled, Ned Almond "did not believe the situation was precarious."[61]

Nonetheless, Chiles ordered Jenson (2/23) and Richardson (3/23) to send all "non-essential" vehicles to the rear. By "mistake" the kitchen trucks joined the column, which was led by the 3/23 exec, James E. Stacy, in a jeep. Unknown to Chiles, by then the CCF had cut the road to the rear. All these vehicles except one were disabled or destroyed and had to be abandoned on the road. The exception was Stacy's jeep. "It should have been sent to the Smithsonian Institution," Chiles remembered. "All five tires were flat. The hood had been blown off. The gas tank was riddled with holes, and otherwise the vehicle was like Swiss cheese. Stacy was unscratched—a true miracle."[62]

During the night of May 17–18 Chiles and his men stubbornly and valiantly held their ground. Chiles was hit in the leg by a CCF mortar fragment, but like his predecessor at Chipyong, Paul Freeman, he remained at his CP, limping around. The French, who had fought so magnificently at Chipyong under Ralph Monclar, now had a new commander who, Chiles recollected, was less than heroic: "TF [Task Force] Zebra [elements] were very jittery, especially the French, whose new commander's pessimism was reflected in his unit. When he showed up at my CP at midnight pleading to withdraw, I should have relieved him. Since I wasn't positive that I had the authority to do so and also wasn't sure of the effect [of his relief] on his unit, I dressed him down and ordered him back to his battalion."[63]

\* \* \*

To the left of the 23d John Coughlin's 38th also came under very heavy siege. Kimbrell's 1/38 and Wilkins's 2/38, the latter exposed in the OPLR, caught the brunt of the attack. The rifle companies of the 1/38 were immediately split and isolated on Hill 1051. In the 2/38, E Company was overrun and shattered. Believing the situation in the 2/38 to be "critical," Coughlin prudently requested authority to pull the battalion off the OPLR and back to No Name Line. After pointedly warning Ed Messinger's 9th Infantry (on the left) that the maneuver was "planned"—apparently to prevent a possible bugout—Ruffner gave Coughlin the go-ahead. The 2/38 withdrew to the hills on No Name Line to "consolidate" with the 1/38 and the Dutch Battalion, coming from reserve.[64]

In the 38th's left—and southernmost—sector, Wallace Hanes's 3/38, bunkered in its fortress atop Hill 800, escaped attack on the night of May 16–17. The men waited tensely in their positions, with a grandstand view of the blazing night action to the north. At dawn Hanes directed the men to improve their positions. They strung additional lines of barbed wire and planted more fougasses. With the withdrawal of the 2/38 from its OPLR, the 3/38 was now in the direct path of the oncoming CCF.[65]

On the left of the 38th the 9th Infantry was also spared that first night. Owing to the critical situation in the 2d Division center, Ruffner directed that the 9th reinforce the 38th. Perry's 2/9 and Nabors's 3/9 were ordered to withdraw from the OPLR, through No Name Line, then go northwest to blocking positions behind the 1/38. The Marines would move northeast to take over the 9th's sector; pending their arrival, Gaylord Bishop's 1/9 would hold on No Name Line.[66]

By daylight on May 17 Kimbrell's 1/38 was in desperate trouble: chewed up; surrounded; cut off. To help rescue its isolated units, John Coughlin directed the Dutch Battalion, commanded by W. D. H. Eekhout, to mount a counterattack on Hill 1051. The Dutch were slow to organize and respond to this dangerous mission.[67]

Nick Ruffner flew in a helicopter to watch the Dutch attack on Hill 1051. While the helicopter hovered over the battlefield, its engine quit. The craft fell out of the sky and crashed on a rocky crag. Although the helicopter was demolished, Ruffner and the pilot survived with merely a few bruises. After being rescued by infantry, Ruffner returned to his CP to learn that the Dutch attack was not going well. In subsequent action the Dutch Battalion suffered a disaster. The commander, his exec, most of the staff, and two company commanders were killed, wounded, or missing.[68]

* * *

Van Fleet arrived at Ned Almond's CP on the morning of May 17 to assess the situation. It was not good. Although the X Corps and 2d Division artillery was responding magnificently, the 2d Division was utterly exposed on the right flank and in danger of being overwhelmed. Most elements of the ROK 5th and 7th divisions had vanished to the rear right. Farther right the ROK 9th and 3d divisions (of ROK III Corps) were out of touch and presumed to be fleeing rearward. Although not hit, the ROK Capital Division at Kansong was prudently pulling back along the coast road.[69]

Ned Almond remembered: "The Second Division had received a severe blow and was suffering from it. . . . This operation convinced me that the full strength of the CCF offensive . . . was designed to demolish the Second Division if possible, but at least to flow around it and through the ROK corps areas on our right and to move straight south, to endanger our base of supply and the base of Eighth Army at Pusan. This was a startling development, and I felt it very strongly. . . . Van Fleet and I conferred about the general situation. General Van Fleet said, 'We are in a bad situation, and I understand it,' and asked me further, 'General Almond, what is your opinion?' I said, 'My opinion is worse than that. My fear is that I'm going to lose my base of supplies and, as a matter of fact, you are going to lose yours for Eighth Army, unless something drastic is done and I'm reinforced on this [right] flank. The Chinese are flowing like water around my right flank. The Second Division is holding . . . but the ROK divisions on my right, the Fifth and Seventh, are being disintegrated by this huge attack of the enemy, and this will continue on and be extended to the coast shortly, against the other ROK corps on the [extreme] right flank. I think we are in a very serious situation.' "[70]

Van Fleet asked for recommendations. Almond requested urgent American reinforcements from Eighth Army reserve: not only Tom Yancey's 15th Infantry, which had been designated to support X Corps in an emergency, but also the entire 3d Division and more artillery. At first Van Fleet demurred. He was still fixated on Seoul. The 3d Division was his only reserve for I and IX Corps. What if the CCF attacked Seoul as well? But Almond pressed; unless it was decisively checked, the CCF attack on X Corps might be a "fatal blow."[71]

Finally Van Fleet began to yield. "When would you want them and where?" he asked.

"The leading elements should arrive tonight if possible, in the vicinity of Wonju," Almond replied.

"What will you do with them?" Van Fleet asked.

"I will arrange them by RCT deployed in general areas about fifteen miles apart. These I will use as islands so that the advancing Chinese armies will have to bypass or eliminate them. In that effort to eliminate obstructing forces, widely separated, it would distract their main effort. . . ."[72]

And so it was decided. Van Fleet would release 3d Division elements to X Corps. The leading forces—the 15th Infantry and its 9th FAB—would leave at once from Ichon for Hoengsong. The remainder of the 3d Division would hold in army reserve positions for one or two days. If no CCF attack on Seoul developed, Van Fleet would release the entire 3d Division to X Corps. He would also send extra artillery, the 937th FAB (155-mm self-propelled Long Tom guns) less one battery, which would be made up by substituting one battery of eight-inch howitzers of the 17th FAB.[73]

In a parting comment Almond complained about an ammunition "bottleneck" at Wonju. Van Fleet had authorized Almond's 105-mm howitzers to fire 250 rounds per gun per day. In order to maintain that rate Almond required twenty truckloads of artillery ammo per hour; he was getting only twelve truckloads per hour. Van Fleet promised to break the bottleneck, and later in the day he directed his G-4, Albert Stebbins, to do so "by daybreak" the following morning.[74]

* * *

Although Van Fleet had been deceived by the CCF, he was determined that Eighth Army would do its utmost to capitalize on the situation. Following the staff briefing at his CP in Yoju on the morning of May 18, he proclaimed:

We want maximum casualties on the enemy [and] minimum on our own troops. Terrain in itself doesn't mean much, but certain localities with significance must be held, that is, Seoul.

If we back off the main line of resistance held by I and IX corps and the 1st Marine and Second Infantry Division, we will have to meet the enemy later, on poorer and less prepared terrain and in worse weather. We want to hit him here and now.

This "roll with the punch" conception is out and I have made this point clear to the corps commanders. We move back only to prevent loss of a major unit, that is, a battalion. Units will withdraw only on orders from higher headquarters. Regiment, division, and corps commanders must be alert to critical situations on battalion level and be quick to take needed action. Only an outpost line may be withdrawn at discretion of its unit commander. We must fight on this line and put a terrific toll on the enemy; here is our opportunity.[75]

Notwithstanding that exhortation, it was clear that same morning, May 18, that Nick Ruffner's 2d Division could no longer hold the No Name Line above Hangye. Accordingly, Ned Almond authorized it to withdraw to Hangye, where it would defend a new line running east-west. The chewed-up 38th Infantry would withdraw to division reserve, temporarily replaced on the division's left sector by the 9th Infantry. The Marines would bend their front to the right to tie in with the 9th Infantry. The 23d would withdraw due south to Hangye, to hold the right sector. Surviving elements of the ROK 5th and 7th divisions would extend the line farther right. When it arrived, 15th Infantry would backstop these ROKs.[76]

While these realignments were in progress the infantry had plenty of support. That day the X Corps and 2d Division artillery fired off 41,357 rounds. FEAF was "magnificent," Almond reported, mounting a total of 165 close support missions. The airmen bombed, napalmed, and strafed the massed CCF during that day and into the night. The nighttime flights were directed to CCF targets by a highly effective radar-navigation system.[77]

Even so, the withdrawing 23d and 38th regiments had a very difficult day. Both were face-to-face with enormous numbers of attacking CCF. As Chiles accurately put it, "There is no more difficult infantry operation" than a daylight withdrawal in the face of a greatly superior number of enemy attacking from the front and both flanks. Moreover, Chiles's withdrawal was further imperiled by the CCF behind the 23d above Hangye, blocking the road. In effect, the 23d Infantry, which had avoided the 2d Division gauntlet below Kunu, had to run a gauntlet of its own, fighting its way to the rear.[78]

Hobbling around on a wounded leg, Chiles prepared carefully for the withdrawal. An armor-infantry team would lead the attack to break the roadblock. Then Lloyd Jenson's 2/23 would attack south on the west side of the road; Beverly Richardson's 3/23 would cover the 2/23's withdrawal, then attack south on the east side of the road.[79]

This plan did not go well. The armor-infantry task force killed an estimated 300 CCF, but it could not break the roadblock. Jenson's 2/23, coming down on the west side of the road under terrific CCF flanking fire, stacked up behind the blocked armor-infantry team. Seeing the jam-up, Chiles ordered Jenson to pull his men back to the start line, reorganize, and then go down the west side of the road through the 3/23 sector.

Meanwhile, Chiles had to face the problem of extricating the jeeps and trucks and trailers of the 2/23 and 3/23 battalions. The plan he developed was that these vehicles (each restricted to only one driver) would "run" the roadblock with a tank escort. But the plan came to grief. The two lead tanks crushed a bridge, making it impassable, then hit mines, blocking the road completely. The vehicles in the column behind the tanks were thus immobilized. Some vehicles farther back in the column attempted to skirt the bridge and the roadblock and go cross-country. But most vehicles (117 jeeps and trucks; 76 trailers) of the 2/23 and 3/23 were destroyed.

The infantry continued with its revised withdrawal plan. Crossing east into Richardson's 3/23 sector, Jenson's 2/23 led the attack south on the east side of the road through intense CCF fire. Richardson's 3/23 fought a skillful rearguard action, decamping behind the 2/23. Both battalions continued to take heavy CCF fire from both flanks and the rear. The enemy pressure, Chiles wrote, was "continuous" and "vicious" and "often fanatical." Remarkably, most of the infantry held intact, withdrawing to successive positions without panic, one unit covering for the other. Throughout these difficult maneuvers the two tank companies (B and C) of Elbridge W. Brubaker's 72d Tank

Battalion provided steady and effective firepower: a total of 2,950 rounds of 76-mm, 215,000 rounds of .50-caliber, and 405,000 rounds of .30-caliber ammo.

In this fashion, the 23d Infantry escaped disaster and consolidated with the French Battalion and the 1/23 at Hangye. An early roll call revealed that 886 men were missing, but numerous stragglers came in during the night, reducing the figure dramatically. Nonetheless, the final casualty figure for the 23d for May 17 and 18 was high: 597. Astonishingly—and fortunately—only 21 had been killed. Some 417 were declared "missing" and presumed to be captured.

\* \* \*

To the left of the 23d the 9th Infantry assisted the 38th Infantry in its withdrawal, which took place under cover of darkness that night. Following a ten-minute barrage by seven FABs, the brave but exhausted survivors of the 1/38 and 2/38 and the Dutch Battalion withdrew through the 2/9. Total casualties in the 38th were shocking: well above 1,000 killed, wounded, and missing.[80]

This withdrawal did not, however, include Wallace Hanes's 3/38, entrenched in its fortress atop Hill 800. Spared attack so far, it would remain in its positions one more night in order to give the Marines time to "bend" No Name Line behind it. The withdrawal of the 1/38 and 2/38 opened a clear route to the 3/38, and during that night (May 18 to 19) the CCF took advantage of it, launching a powerful attack on Hanes, which penetrated I and K companies. The 3/38 rallied and counterattacked, even calling friendly artillery (10,000 rounds from the 38th FAB) down on its own besieged bunkers. The artillery slaughtered the CCF, and by dawn Hanes and his proud and defiant men were again undisputed kings of the mountain.[81]

## V

Matt Ridgway, wearing a brand-new set of four stars, arrived in Korea late on the morning of May 19. He changed from his C-54 (named *GHQ*) to a C-47 in Seoul and flew straight to Hoengsong, where he conferred with Van Fleet, Almond, and Ruffner.[82] By this time the shape of the battle was clear:

• Contrary to Van Fleet's oft-repeated predictions, there was no indication whatsoever that the CCF intended to attack Seoul. Shrimp Milburn's I Corps front was still eerily empty of enemy. Nor was there any indication of an all-out CCF attack on Seoul through the Pukhan Valley in Bill Hoge's IX Corps sector. The Americans and ROKs (fighting valiantly) in that sector had repulsed some regimental-size probes, but these were obviously feints or holding attacks.

• Beyond any doubt the main weight of the CCF attack had been thrown at Ned Almond's X Corps. Five CCF armies had been identified in the X Corps sector. Owing to the disgraceful ROK collapse on the right, the enemy penetration was serious. The 2d Division had been very hard hit. But thanks to the extraordinary courage of its men and the remarkable artillery support (50,000 rounds that day), and unusually effective close air support, the division appeared capable of holding on the new east–west line at Hangye. The Marines, not yet under serious attack, were poised for backup. Shorty Soule's 3d Division was arriving in the X Corps sector to provide further support.[83]

Boarding a liaison aircraft, Ridgway flew low over the new 2d Division front for an inspection. At that time Jack Chiles's 23d Infantry held the vital center on the Kansong–Honchon road at Hangye; Ed Messinger's 9th Infantry was shifting from the 23d's left to its more vulnerable right; John Coughlin's 38th Infantry, in reserve, was remanning and reequipping. The 1st Marine Division was bending right to tie in with the 2d Division. The First Marines, to be replaced by the Fifth Marines, had sideslipped right to replace the 9th Infantry; the Seventh Marines had withdrawn from the OPLR to replace the Fifth Marines.

Advance elements of the 3d Division, which had crossed half of Korea in darkness, arrived ready to fight. As planned, Almond was deploying these to the right of the 2d Division, into the sector formerly held by the ROK 5th and 7th divisions. The first of the 3d Division units to arrive, Tom Yancey's 15th Infantry, was to strike for Pungam. However, owing to the miserable roads and other factors, the second unit, Wilson Hawkins's 64th Tank Battalion, was held at Wonju.[84]

Returning to Almond's CP, Ridgway, Van Fleet, and Almond discussed future courses of action. The CCF had been on the attack in the X Corps sector for sixty hours. In the initial surge it had gained about ten miles against the 2d Division and twice that or more in the ROK sectors. It had paid a ghastly price for the gains in the 2d Division sector: perhaps 20,000 casualties or more, according to Ruffner. There was a discernible easing in the thrust of the CCF attack; it had not yet closed on the Hangye line. With the commitment of Shorty Soule's 3d Division on the right flank of X Corps, there was now every reason to believe the CCF penetration could be contained. In Almond's opinion the "crisis" was passing.[85]

In fact, Almond believed a golden opportunity to inflict a decisive defeat on the CCF was presenting itself. If X Corps could rebound quickly and counterattack northeasterly up the Kansong road to Inje and beyond, it might be possible to cut off the tens of thousands of CCF and NKPA in the ROK sector on the right. In a somewhat farfetched analogy Almond said the situation reminded him of the time in World War I when French Marshal Ferdinand Foch shoved the French XX Corps into taxicabs and raced out and cut off and destroyed a threatened German attack on Paris.[86]

In order to launch a X Corps counterattack, Almond said he required fresh shock troops. He could think of no better outfit than Frank Bowen's 187th Airborne Combat Team, which was in IX Corps reserve, going to waste in that "quiet" sector. Almond would assemble it behind X Corps, provide it with vehicles, tanks, and artillery, then, when the CCF had gone a little deeper, strike.

Would Van Fleet release the 187th for this purpose? It was a tough question. Ridgway had forbidden the employment of the 187th in a ground role except in an extreme emergency. One reason was that the very presence of the 187th near an airfield posed a theoretical threat to the CCF rear and presumably forced it to divert thousands of troops to antiairborne guard duty.* Another reason was that Ridgway did not want to expend these expensive, elite troops in ordinary ground warfare. Moreover, the conventional units which had to provide trucks, tanks, and artillery to the paratroopers would resent lending their equipment to a force that would get all the credit—and publicity—for the victory.

There was another consideration. The CCF still had sufficient manpower (and was obviously good enough at concealment) to mount a surprise attack on Seoul. Van Fleet had significantly weakened Seoul's defenses by releasing the reserve 3d Division and the extra artillery to Almond. A surprise attack on Seoul was certain to include a flanking attack down the Pukhan Valley at Babe Bryan's thinly held and "sensitive" 24th Division sector, which the 187th was backing up. If Van Fleet gave Almond the 187th and the 24th Division gave way and fell behind the Han, it would be necessary to abandon Seoul, thereby handing the CCF a great victory after all.

Yet Van Fleet recognized the potential for a smashing victory on the X Corps front. He took Ridgway aside—out of Almond's "earshot"—for a five-minute discussion. The upshot was a decision in Almond's favor. "We will give you the 187th tonight," Van Fleet said. "It will go to Hoengsong." The reorganized Commonwealth Brigade would replace the 187th as IX Corps reserve. Almond replied: "Thank you very much."[87]

By that time Ridgway and Van Fleet were thinking in grander terms. Both believed the CCF attack on X Corps could be contained, and they doubted that

---

*This was a holdover concept from the ETO, where Hitler had maintained numerous unused airborne divisions all through the war, requiring the Allies to divert thousands of troops in defense of vulnerable rear areas. It is doubtful, however, that the CCF was much influenced by this theoretical threat.

Seoul would be attacked. There was every good possibility that Almond's plan to cut off the CCF in the east could work. If so, notwithstanding the CCF armies facing I and IX Corps or believed to be in reserve, the overall situation appeared to offer an opportunity for a massive, all-out Eighth Army counterattack by all three American corps. If successful, the counterattack might regain the old Line Kansas and possibly later the Iron Triangle. At least it could disrupt any further CCF offensive preparations and, not incidentally, dramatically lift American morale by retaking the real estate recently ceded to the CCF.

The gist of the Ridgway-Van Fleet plan was as follows. Almond's X Corps would hold and contain the CCF for several more days and prepare for a counterattack on May 23 by all forces, to be spearheaded by the fresh 187th RCT. Meanwhile, Bill Hoge's IX Corps would go over to the offensive on May 20. It would drive due north to the left of Chunchon, to the town of Hwachon, through which the CCF armies in the east were being supplied and through which the CCF might withdraw when X Corps counterattacked. If IX Corps succeeded in blocking at Hwachon, most of the retreating CCF in the east could be trapped. Shrimp Milburn's I Corps would attack simultaneously to protect the IX's left flank from a CCF counterattack from the west.[88]

When the rough outline of this plan had been drawn, Ridgway decided to remain in Korea another full day to observe the launching of the counterattack by I and IX corps and to visit all major units. That night he cabled the JCS a full situation report and an outline of Eighth Army's proposed counterattack. He concluded: "Morale excellent. Confidence high."[89]

Meanwhile, Van Fleet's staff issued detailed orders for the Eighth Army offensive, which retained the former offensive code name, Detonate. From left to right across the Eighth Army front:

• Shrimp Milburn's I Corps, playing a supporting role, would cautiously attack north toward the old Line Kansas at the Imjin and Hantan rivers. The ROK 1st, Palmer's 1st Cav, and Bradley's 25th divisions would participate. The corps's principal mission would be to prevent a CCF counterattack into the left flank of IX Corps. Milburn would employ armored spearheads (with and without infantry) to break up CCF defensive enclaves.

• Bill Hoge's IX Corps, carrying the principal responsibility, would attack vigorously northward to the left of Chunchon to Hwachon. Babe Bryan's 24th Division and Buddy Ferenbaugh's 7th Division (bracketing the ROK 2d and 6th divisions) would carry out the attack, converging above Kapyong. The Commonwealth Brigade would reinforce the 24th Division. The ROK Marine Regiment, on X Corps's extreme left flank, would attack in lockstep to the right of—and in lateral contact with—Ferenbaugh's 7th

Division. The 187th Airborne Combat Team would remain in IX Corps reserve during the launching of the IX Corps offensive, then go to X Corps on Van Fleet's specific order.

• Ned Almond's X Corps would hold on the Hangye line during the initial stages of the IX Corps offensive, then attack two or three days later.

The X Corps offensive would be ambitious. In the left sector the Marine division, abutting Ferenbaugh's 7th Division, would attack to the center and right of the south shore of the Hwachon Reservoir, retaking Yanggu. The 2d Division, spearheaded by the newly attached 187th RCT, would attack to the right of the Hwachon Reservoir, toward Inje, then continue northeasterly to Kansong in order to trap withdrawing CCF and NKPA troops. The American 3d Division would attack on the right of the 2d. The surviving elements of the ROK 5th, 7th, 9th, and 3d divisions would support the X Corps offensive. The incompetent and disgraced ROK III Corps would be abolished. X Corps would absorb the remaining elements of the ROK 9th Division; ROK I Corps (on the coast) would absorb the remaining elements of the ROK 3d Division. Shorty Soule's 3d Division would oversee the reorganization and backstop the redeployment of the ROK 5th, 7th, and 9th division elements on the X Corps right flank. The green ROK 8th division would come up from ROK Army reserve to reinforce this sector.[90]

\* \* \*

By late afternoon of May 19 CCF pressure on the new X Corps line at Hangye remained light or nonexistent. Almond took advantage of the lull to complete the realignment of the line. The Fifth Marines, coming from the division's left to right sectors, replaced the First Marines and tied in on the right with the 23d Infantry. Wallace Hanes's proud 3/38, still staunchly holding its fortress on Hill 800, was finally ordered to pull back through the Fifth Marines to join the 38th in reserve. Owing to the possible connotations that the Marines had "saved" the battalion, the decision to withdraw was not happily received by Hanes and his men. They came out "proud and cocky and confident."[91]

\* \* \*

The weakest link in the new line through Hangye lay in the extreme right (east) flank near Pungam. Surviving elements of the ROK 3d Regiment (of the ROK 7th Division) still tenuously held a mountain pass below Pungam, but otherwise the sector was undefended. If the ROK 3d Regiment gave way, the CCF would gain a road leading to the rear of the 2d Division. Thus Pungam Pass became vital terrain to hold.

It was to this area that Almond had directed Tom Yancey's 15th Infantry (organized as an RCT). After attaching the 15th to the 2d Division, Almond had ordered Yancey to hurry to Pungam Pass, on the right of the 9th Infantry.[92] Almond remembered: "I informed Colonel Yancey that he should at once move to the area near . . . Pungam-ni and that it should not be a leisurely movement. On arrival there one battalion would be pushed through the pass to the north side and protect it against invasion. I also directed him to have tank support for that battalion."[93]

Almond was no stranger to Tom Yancey. The 15th Infantry had earlier served in X Corps in northeast Korea. Yancey well knew Almond's legendary impatience and his tendency to throw units willy-nilly into battle. If followed to the letter, Almond's orders to Yancey meant that the 15th Infantry would move up into utterly unfamiliar terrain, which might, or might not, be held by the ROK 3d Regiment, in pitch-darkness. Believing such a movement to be foolhardy—or worse—Yancey decided he would send some of his tanks ahead, then, after daylight, move his infantry forward.[94]

Almond was keeping a close eye on the vital Pungam Pass and Tom Yancey. He remembered: "The next morning, to be sure my instructions had been complied with, I took a small plane and flew to Pungam-ni and landed. My aide [Alexander] Haig followed [in another plane]. We did not know whether we were in protected territory or not, so we left our engines running. We found six tanks on the north side of the pass at Pungam-ni, but no infantry."[95]

Observing what appeared to be a formation of CCF about 700 yards away, Almond said to Haig: "That looks like enemy. . . . Why aren't the tanks firing? . . . Crawl up on that tank and have it open fire!"

Haig grabbed a rock and pounded on the tank until the hatch flew open. "See the enemy?" Haig exclaimed to the tanker. "Why don't you fire? Open fire!" The tankers complied, dispersing the CCF.

When this crisis passed, Almond was smoldering. He told the tankers to hold the pass while he got Yancey's infantry forward. He flew to the rear and chewed out Yancey, later recalling this incident as one example of "unnecessary danger that sometimes develops in combat when troops fail to carry out the orders of the commander." Having discovered this "error," Almond was "happy" that he had "corrected it," in time to furnish an "island of defense" such as he had described to Van Fleet and Ridgway.[96]

The deployment of the 15th Infantry on the immediate right of the 9th Infantry had, by sheerest coincidence, placed two of the five black infantry battalions (3/9 and 3/15) of Eighth Army in the same vital sector of X Corps. This was worrisome to Almond—and not without reason. Earlier the 3/9 had broken in the face of a surprise CCF night attack, the 9th's S-3, Tom Mellen, remembered.[97]

After Tom Yancey had deployed the 15th Infantry at Pungam Pass, Almond came up to express his displeasure and distrust of Clyde Baden's black

3/15. "He didn't think the colored troops made good soldiers," Yancey remembered. "They were not up to quote proper standards unquote. He did not want to integrate Eighth Army. I disagreed. It was my view, based on experience with the Third Battalion, that it was better to integrate than segregate. Blacks as individuals were good soldiers. All they needed was good leadership and motivation. Almond didn't agree."[98]

As it happened, the 3/15 drew the mission of leading the 15th Infantry attack to seize the village of Pungam and the high ground to the north of it. In an infantry operation so nearly perfect it led the West Point platoon leader, John Howard, to produce a written study of it, "Baden's Battlers" threw back the CCF and seized its objectives in a two-day fight, May 19 and 20. Howard concluded his report: "The enemy . . . was decisively beaten, leaving his dead strewn about the position. . . . Some 142 enemy dead were counted in the L Company area alone. The [3/15's] counter-offensive had been a signal success."[99]

Other elements of Soule's 3d Division moved into blocking positions to the right rear of Yancey's 15th Infantry. Next to arrive was Jim Boswell's 7th Infantry. Assembling at Hoengsong, the 7th moved smartly east to Soksa, where X Corps MPs and others were regrouping various elements of the ROK 3d and 9th divisions. The last of the 3d Division elements to arrive was William Harris's Puerto Rican 65th Regiment, which initially backstopped the 7th Infantry in the Soksa sector. The 3d Division historian wrote that the enemy was "shocked in a rude fashion by the sudden appearance of 3d Division troops in the area."[100]

## V I

By May 20, Almond reported, the "tide began to turn" in the X Corps sector. The various fronts "stabilized" and "defenses held firm." The reinforced X Corps artillery helped ensure the stability by firing off 49,704 rounds that day. FEAF also assisted with 154 close support missions, bombing, napalming, and strafing CCF positions.[101]

That day Milburn's I Corps and Hoge's IX Corps counterattacked in compliance with Van Fleet's Plan Detonate. The main objective was to move IX Corps rapidly forward to Hwachon, to stop CCF reinforcements to Almond's front, and, conversely, to block a CCF withdrawal through that sector when X Corps counterattacked. Milburn's I Corps would protect IX Corps's left flank.

The IX Corps attack, mounted in a driving rain over rugged terrain, was slow and wobbly. A terse entry in the diary of the 7th Division artilleryman James Dill told the story: "Terrible mountain to climb." The next day was similar: "Began advance. Much walking and mountain climbing. . . . Rain most of the day." Van Fleet was not happy. "It is imperative," he told Bill Hoge in a memo, "that greater progress be made in the 7th and 24th [division] sectors, so that the seizure of the Army and corps objectives be made early enough to deny the enemy the use of the road net in those areas—thus hindering his resupply and evacuation." Hoge, in turn, conveyed Van Fleet's displeasure to Babe Bryan and Buddy Ferenbaugh "in very strong terms."[102] On the left of IX Corps Shrimp Milburn's I Corps jumped off cautiously, supporting IX Corps's left flank.

Ridgway remained in Korea that day, May 20, touring the battlefronts. By the end of this two-day visit he had called at every corps and divisional CP in Eighth Army and quite a few regimental CPs besides. His last stop was on the east coast at Kangnung, where the ROK Army chief of staff, Chung Il Kwon, was encamped with the ROK I Corps headquarters. Reviewing the cowardly bugout of the ROK 3d, 5th, 7th, and 9th divisions, Ridgway explained the need for the deactivation of ROK III Corps (and the reassignment of its divisions) and demanded that Chung make "a particular effort to see that ROK units behaved like soldiers on the battlefield." He came away from this meeting concerned that Chung himself might not be capable of carrying out the job.[103]

That night, as he was preparing to return to Japan, Ridgway received word that FEAF commander George Stratemeyer had suffered a severe heart attack on a golf course in Tokyo. Fifth Air Force commander Pat Partridge temporarily relieved Stratemeyer, but Hoyt Vandenberg had another important assignment for Partridge. As a result, both Stratemeyer and Partridge soon returned to the States—Stratemeyer to convalescence and retirement with three stars, Partridge to head the Air Force's Air Research and Development Command, from which he rose to four stars. Otto P. ("Opie") Weyland (Texas A&M, 1923), forty-nine, until recently Stratemeyer's deputy, was sent back to Japan to replace Stratemeyer. West Pointer (1928) Frank F. Everest, forty-six, replaced Partridge as commander of the Fifth Air Force. In World War II Weyland had commanded the tactical air forces in support of Patton's Third Army; Everest had commanded a bomber group in the South Pacific and later a high-level air staff planning group in the Pentagon. Ridgway knew both men well from prior service; he had worked closely with Weyland in the postwar years on Latin American matters.[104]

Upon reaching Tokyo Ridgway cabled the JCS:

Having visited all US corps, all US divisions and ROK 1st Division, I wish to cite all these units to you for superior spirit and conduct in battle. I particularly cite the US Army's 2nd Infantry Division, Major General C. L. Ruffner, Commanding, which has received the principal blow of the hostile main effort. It has inflicted losses, which, conservatively estimated, exceed, I believe, 20 times its own.* It would be an inspiration to our people to know of the professional competence, the gallantry, and the fighting spirit of General Van Fleet's Eighth Army and its supporting Air Force and Naval forces.

The ROK 2 and 6th divisions have performed very credibly against moderate and in some cases, strong enemy attacks. Although full details are still lacking, it is clear that the ROK 3rd, 5th, 7th and 9th divisions have performed discreditably, with loss of large amounts of equipment. ROK I Corps has done well though it has had little contact. We are continuing our efforts to correct this lamentable situation.[106]

By May 22 the I and IX corps offensive Detonate was picking up steam. The weather remained poor: rainy and raw. Both corps advanced slowly and methodically. Both met stubborn enclaves of CCF holding key hilltops and road junctions, which had to be blasted and rooted out.

Operating in the more favorable terrain above Seoul, Shrimp Milburn's I Corps retraced familiar routes. On the left the ROK 1st Division went up the road to Munsan and halted on old positions at the Imjin River. In the center Charlie Palmer's 1st Cav Division marked time at its Uijongbu OPLR, then proceeded slowly northward from that place, spearheaded by Marcel Crombez's 5th Cav. On the corps's right flank Sladen Bradley's 25th Division, utilizing Tom Dolvin's 89th Tank Battalion to good advantage, attacked toward old ground at Chongsong. The Turks and Henry Britt's 24th Infantry advanced several miles, but Kelleher's 35th Infantry ran into very strong CCF resistance.[107]

During an attack on a hill Woody Woodruff in the 3/35 was wounded. He remembered that during the day the 3/35 had captured a "number" of CCF troops:

These seemed to be sick, at least most of them, which was curious. The CCF had often been known to make a major effort to recover all its wounded, and even its dead, from the battlefield. It seemed out of character that they would abandon sick men. Possibly the tank advance had taken them by surprise, before the sick men could be moved. I wondered if it were possible they had been left behind for humanitarian reasons, on some theory we could give them better medical care. This was unlikely; however, on any given occasion, a Chinese small unit commander was capable of acting out of any motive, logical or illogical, but in either event unrelated to accepted Communist doctrine.[108]

---

*The 2nd Division publicly claimed to have inflicted 37,750 casualties on the enemy by May 21, while understating its own losses at 900. The X Corps claims of enemy casualties were accepted uncritically by the Pentagon. At a military briefing of ambassadors of those nations with military forces in Korea, the Pentagon officially put enemy losses for the period May 17 to May 20 at 67,800, of which, the Pentagon briefer stated, 36,000 were killed and 31,800 were wounded.[105]

The surrender of these CCF soldiers was no isolated event. All across Eighth Army's front, CCF troops (both sick and well) were giving up in unprecedented numbers. The surrender of the able-bodied Chinese intensified speculation that the spirit in their armies had decisively cracked. The surrender of the ill led to speculation that the CCF was victim of rampant malnutrition and disease.

Attacking in the rugged terrain in the Pukhan Valley, Bill Hoge's IX Corps continued to advance sluggishly toward Hwachon. Babe Bryan's 24th Division, reinforced by Taylor's Commonwealth Brigade, attacked in the left sector; Buddy Ferenbaugh's 7th Division attacked in the right sector, linked with the aggressive ROK Marine Regiment of X Corps. Chang Do Yung's ROK 6th Division and the ROK 2d Division, advancing with the American divisions, continued to perform well.[109]

\* \* \*

Having stabilized the X Corps front, Ned Almond spent that day, May 22, reorganizing and redeploying his forces for his counterattack on the following day. The entire corps would attack simultaneously. Two special task forces in the American 2d and 3d divisions would strike northeasterly to set "traps" for the CCF and NKPA.

• In the 3d Division sector Task Force Able, commanded by Almond's deputy, Laurence Ladue, and composed of Tom Yancey's 15th RCT, the ROK 3d Regiment, and other forces, would strike northeast from Pungam to Habae-jae and beyond, toward Yangyang on the coast. This would throw a line across the old ROK III Corps sector, which would hold the enemy while Boswell's 7th regiment attacked northward to close the trap.

• In the 2d Division sector Task Force Baker, composed of Frank Bowen's 187th Airborne Combat Team, heavily reinforced with armor and corps artillery, would attack northeast from Hangye to Inje and beyond to Kansong on the coast. This would throw a second line across the upper region of the old ROK III sector, which would hold the enemy while the full 2d Division (9th, 23d, 38th regiments) attacked northward to close the trap.[110]

At 8:00 A.M. on the following day, May 23, X Corps launched the counterattack.

On the corps's left flank Gerry Thomas's powerful 1st Marine Division, abutting Ferenbaugh's 7th Division, attacked north toward the east shore of the Hwachon Reservoir at Yanggu. Nick Ruffner's 2d Division held the X Corps center sector. All three regiments were deployed, left to right, on the Hangye line: 23d; 9th; 38th, which had come up from corps reserve. Bowen's Task Force Baker attacked northeast up the Hangye–Inje road through

Chiles's 23d Infantry, which held in place. Messinger's 9th Infantry and Coughlin's 38th Infantry attacked in lockstep with Task Force Baker.[111]

On the corps's right flank Shorty Soule's 3d Division and various ROK elements attacked simultaneously. On the division left Ladue's Task Force Able (Yancey's 15th Infantry) struck northeast from Pungam toward Habaejae. In the center Jim Boswell's 7th Infantry attacked north.[112] Perhaps because Almond still distrusted the Puerto Ricans, William Harris's 65th Regiment was relegated to division reserve, where it attempted to reorganize ROK units. Harris remembered that difficult chore:

To say that the situation [in this sector] was confused is an understatement, for the North Korean, South Korean and Chinese troops were intermingled in one big scrap. And I am afraid that none of us could tell the difference between any of them. As a result, the usual orders, which were now Standard Operating Procedure, prevailed. They were if you don't know or cannot recognize the soldiers confronting you, take them prisoner—or kill them if they resist. Simple and direct orders. . . .

For several days we tried to restore order out of the confusion. Then I received word that the ROK commander of the 7th Division was "upset" because the 65th had disarmed and placed under guard at least three-fourths of his division. I immediately sent him my apologies and informed him that if he could identify to me which were his troops, I would have them released at once. This took some doing because I was not about to release anyone just because he happened to be wearing a ROK uniform. But it all worked out. After several days he had his troops back under control and no serious diplomatic error had been committed.[113]

Considering the miserable weather and the rugged terrain, the first day of the X Corps counteroffensive was by any reasonable standards a success. The Marines had the easiest day. They advanced two to three miles against "negligible resistance." Bowen's Task Force Baker, meeting "light resistance," gained three and a half miles. Farther east, in the 2d Division sector, the going was tougher. Nonetheless, the 9th advanced about three miles. In the even more rugged 3d Division sector Task Force Able gained a mile, and the 7th Infantry three miles.[114]

Van Fleet kept a close eye on operations in the eastern sector. He telexed Ridgway on May 23:

Have visited units along the front of ROK I Corps, X Corps and right of IX Corps. Eighth Army's counteroffensive now becoming effective, regaining much ground formerly occupied by 2nd Division and liberated over one hundred wounded of 38th Infantry Regiment. I am pressing corps commanders to be on objective soonest, stressing urgent necessity of liberating US personnel and capturing enemy personnel and equipment before it can be withdrawn.

Follow up plan for X Corps includes drive past Inje to coast, thereby cutting off NKPA and CCF units. I have deactivated ROK III Corps. . . . Enemy break-through in former zone of ROK III Corps serious but not critical. Am confident our counteroffensive is best method to deal with it.[115]

Relaying this cheery report to the JCS, Ridgway added a postscript: "Yesterday informed Van Fleet that within my current letter of instructions to him I consider reoccupation of the Kansas Line a highly important objective and that thereafter in the light of the situation then obtaining, consideration should be given to further successive advances to the Utah and Wyoming lines with appropriate advances on the east flank."[116]

*  *  *

Almond awoke on the morning of May 24 to shocking news. During the night his deputy commander, Laurence Ladue, who had been driving himself hard both physically and mentally, had died in his sleep of a heart attack. It was a serious loss which Almond felt keenly. Ladue, one of the most promising young (forty-seven years old) officers in the Army, had become a trusted associate. Almond had recommended (and Van Fleet had approved) that Ladue be promoted to brigadier general.*[117]

This loss may have adversely influenced Almond's mood and actions that day. Whatever the reason, Almond appeared to be more impatient, short-tempered, and inconsiderate than usual. The 187th Airborne Combat Team was one outfit which found that out the hard way.

Of the X Corps offensive operations, that of the 187th (Task Force Baker) was by far the most promising. If it could promptly get its line established from Inje to Kansong, it could trap thousands, perhaps tens of thousands of enemy. In the process it might also rescue scores of captured 2d Division men held by the enemy. That the 187th had twice been assigned similarly important "trapping" and POW rescue missions (in the October 1950 and March 1951 parachute drops) and had failed in both had apparently been forgotten or discounted. Like the Rangers, the paratroopers had a special aura and were credited with superpowers not always justified by the record.[118]

By the morning of May 24 Almond had detected that in response to the X Corps counteroffensive, the CCF and NKPA were beginning to withdraw. If the withdrawal picked up momentum, it was not only possible but likely that the enemy would escape before the 187th could get its Inje–Kansong line in place. He therefore concluded that the 187th (Task Force Baker) must attack all out for Inje at once.

Almond arrived in the 187th area by helicopter at about 9:40 A.M. At the

---

*Ladue was promoted to brigadier and awarded the Distinguished Service Medal posthumously.

time the 187th was attacking as conventional infantry, supported by one company (B) of Elbridge Brubaker's 72d Tank Battalion, commanded by William E. Ross. Two other of Brubaker's tank companies, plus a company of tanks from Wilson Hawkins's 64th Tank Company, were scheduled to join the 187th in due course (to complete Task Force Baker), but they were hours away, Brubaker's tanks supporting X Corps elements in the eastern sector, Hawkins's tanks still on hold in Wonju.

Almond stood the 187th staff on its ear. Owing to the enemy withdrawal, he said, it was imperative that the 187th get moving at utmost speed for Inje. The staff was first to form a battalion combat team (an infantry battalion, plus no fewer than two tank companies and support units), dash to the Soyang River, and grab a bridgehead. The team was to leave by noon. The staff was to send the rest of the 187th to the bridgehead as fast as possible by truck.

The 187th staff properly regarded this assignment as suicidal. The Soyang River was fifteen miles north of the 187th CP and the X Corps front line. The staff had heard nothing of an enemy withdrawal. All intelligence indicated the territory was still held by three or four—or more—CCF divisions. One battalion of infantry—even paratroopers!—plus two tank companies (twenty-four tanks) attempting to make that dash was certain to be annihilated before the rest of the 187th could get more tanks and follow. Probably the full 187th with a whole battalion of tanks would be annihilated.

Bowen did not argue with Almond. To do so would almost certainly have resulted in his relief. He ordered the 1/187 commander, West Pointer George Gerhart, a full colonel (and former exec or deputy commander of the rank-heavy 187th), to organize the task force around his battalion while he, Bowen, got the rest of the regiment organized to follow. Meanwhile, having heard the news, Brubaker flew in with his S-3, James H. Spann, and ordered his other two tank companies and B Company of the 64th Tank Battalion to close as rapidly as possible on the 187th's position.

It was soon apparent that Almond's orders could not be followed to the letter. First, it would be impossible to get one more tank company to the 187th area by noon. It would take at least three or four hours for Brubaker's two tank companies to get there; perhaps slightly less for Hawkins's tanks from Wonju. Secondly, there was no way Gerhart could entruck his 1/187 and the necessary supplies and equipment and get them all on the road by noon.

The upshot was an improvised plan designed to adhere as closely as possible to Almond's orders and at the same time to minimize the danger to all concerned. First, a point, consisting of Ross's 3d Platoon (four tanks), a recon squad in three jeeps, and an engineer platoon in two trucks, would take off as close as possible to noon to probe the road for mines. Secondly, the other two tank platoons of Ross's B Company (eight tanks), plus the twelve tanks of B Company, 64th Tank Battalion (on the way), would form up with the main 1/187 truck convoy. The last would depart as rapidly as possible and catch up with the point, which would go slowly. The rest of the 187th would follow later in the day, after the other tank companies of the 72d Battalion had arrived.

Even so, Gerhart could not make Almond's deadline. The point, placed in command of Brubaker's assistant exec, Charles A. Newman, riding in a tank, did not set off until 1:00 P.M.—an hour late. The column was composed of two tanks, a jeep, two tanks, a jeep, two trucks, a jeep. It proceeded cautiously—very cautiously—three miles down the road, then stopped at a forwardmost friendly outpost before plunging into the dangerous unknown.

Out of the sky came Ned Almond in a helicopter. He was boiling mad. Furiously shaking his swagger stick in Newman's face, he demanded to know what was going on. Where were the other tanks? Where was the battalion combat team? Why had Newman stopped? Newman attempted to explain that they were the point, that they had stopped to probe for mines and establish communications.

"I don't care about communications," Almond declaimed. "You get those tanks on the road and keep going until you hit a mine. I want you to keep going at twenty miles an hour."[119]

Almond climbed back into the helicopter and flew to the 187th CP. There he encountered Brubaker's S-3, James Spann. Raging, Almond demanded to know to what outfit Spann belonged, why all the tanks weren't moving, and the name of the commander of the 72d. When Spann answered these questions and attempted to explain the new plan, Almond cut him off. Almond wanted all available tanks on the road immediately. "You tell Brubaker to get that tank column moving whether the tanks have infantry or not."[120]

Word of this confrontation reached Gerhart almost instantly. He immediately ordered Ross to disengage his other two platoons of tanks from the 1/187 main column (still forming up) and send them forward to catch up with the point. Gerhart would follow in due course with the 1/187, the twelve tanks of the 64th Tank Battalion, and the support forces. Not without considerable difficulty Ross got his tanks out of line, formed up, and on the road. The 187th's dash to grab a Soyang River bridgehead had thus diminished to twelve tanks, the recon squad, and the engineer platoon.

The point group, commanded by Charles Newman, continued ahead at twenty miles per hour into enemy territory, per Almond's order. As it drew ever closer to the Soyang River, it encountered increasing numbers of CCF. Two. Ten. Two dozen. One hundred. Two hundred. The recon squad, the engineers, and the tankers courageously blasted away at these clusters of enemy with 76-mm guns and .30 and .50-caliber machine guns, killing and wounding some, dispersing others. Astonishingly, seventy-one CCF surrendered, creating a policing problem. Meanwhile, Newman, feeling ever more naked, repeatedly radioed Ross to get the other two platoons of tanks forward on the double.

When the point was about a mile and a half south of the Soyang River, a FEAF Mosquito aircraft dropped a chilling message. There was a formation of about 4,000 CCF one mile ahead. Two flights of FEAF jets were on the way to make an air strike, but . . . The tank platoon commander, Douglas L. Gardiner, handing the message to Newman, asked, "What are we going to do now?"

Newman replied without hesitation: "We're going to attack the Chinks. If we turn back, we'll run into General Almond!"[121]

The FEAF jets arrived as promised and delivered a close and effective attack. While the CCF was still reeling from the bombs, napalm, and strafing, Newman deployed his thin force in a skirmish line and attacked. Firing into the stunned and frightened masses of CCF with all available weapons, Newman and his men advanced steadily toward the Soyang River. At 4:30 P.M. his force reached the south bank and established and held a perimeter. Ross and the other eight tanks of B Company, having also encountered clusters of CCF, arrived two hours later. Still later Gerhart and the 1/187 and the twelve tanks came up to reinforce the perimeter.

In this unorthodox, even crazy, fashion, the 187th Airborne Combat Team secured a Soyang River bridgehead on May 24. But it remained a dangerous and tentative foothold. After the full 187th had come into the perimeter on the following day, the CCF cut and blocked the main road behind it at Koritwi-Gol. This block delayed for a full day, May 25, the Seventh Marines (on the left) and the 23d Infantry (on the right), which were moving up to occupy the bridgehead. The block was not fully overcome until Ruffner side-slipped the 9th Infantry leftward into Koritwi-Gol that same day. The delay enabled tens of thousands of CCF and NKPA to escape the trap. Almond blamed most of the delay on the Seventh Marines. "It appears that the delay of the [Marine] regiment in moving rapidly and aggressively forward," he wrote, "seriously impaired the progress and end result of the planned exploitation along the Hongchon–Inje axis."[122]

The X Corps offensive continued. To the right of this fighting, Coughlin's 38th Infantry and some ROKs attacked north toward Inje. Farther right Shorty Soule's 3d Division made limited gains in rugged terrain. On May 25 Tom Yancey's 15th Infantry (formerly Task Force Able, now reintegrated into the division) took Habae-jae. On its right Jim Boswell's 7th Infantry (organized as Task Force Charlie) continued north to Wongdang. Both regiments were fighting NKPA rear guards of the withdrawing enemy, in effect pushing them north into the trap which the 187th would set. By May 25, the division historian wrote, "Their withdrawal deteriorated from an organized retrograde movement to a frantic attempt by broken-up elements to get away over any available route." Still farther right William Harris's Puerto Rican 65th Infantry, which had seen little fighting, linked with the reconstituted ROK 9th Division in the mountain vastness at Hajinbu. The green ROK 8th Division came into the 3d Division sector to occupy rear areas.[123]

# VII

The performance of the Army elements of X Corps during the week May 16 to May 23 had been one of the most remarkable episodes of the Korean War—another magnificent victory. Nick Ruffner's 2d Division had withstood a savage pounding by most of two CCF armies (six divisions) and, with scarcely a pause, had launched a vigorous counterattack.* Shorty Soule's 3d Division had decamped from I Corps, raced halfway across the peninsula in a day or so, and had joined the counterattack with no pause at all. In addition, the 3d Division had played a key role in reorganizing and refielding the ROK 5th and 9th divisions for the X Corps counterattack. The X Corps artillery had staged the greatest artillery "shoot" of the war, firing about 300,000 rounds during that week.[125]

By May 26, however, it was clear that Ned Almond's plan to cut off and trap substantial numbers of CCF and NKPA was not going to work. The enemy had withdrawn too quickly. The 187th Airborne Combat Team (Task Force Baker), attacking out of the Soyang River bridgehead, encountered powerful enemy blocks at Inje, designed to hold open the enemy escape route. The tankers and infantrymen of the 2d Division supporting the 187th at Inje were severely depleted and exhausted from ten hard days of fighting. The Seventh Marines had failed to provide any substantial support.[126]

When it became apparent to Van Fleet that the enemy was eluding the trap, he was bitterly disappointed. The setback led him to resurrect the idea he had earlier mentioned to Ridgway as a possibility: an amphibious landing of the Marine division on the east coast above the retreating enemy forces. Van Fleet chose the lightly held seaport of Tongchon (sixty air miles north of the 38th Parallel) for the landing site. A good road ran southwest from Tongchon to Kumhwa. Van Fleet's plan envisioned that the Marines would land unopposed at Tongchon and attack southwest down the road to Kumhwa, to link there with Bill Hoge's IX Corps, attacking northeast from Hwachon. This would throw a diagonal line across the rear of the CCF and NKPA retreating from the eastern sector and trap them.

---

*Van Fleet awarded the entire 2d Division a Presidential Unit Citation for its heroic defensive stand from May 16 to May 22. Ruffner, Chiles, Coughlin, and Messinger received DSCs—Messinger's second DSC for service in Korea.[124]

Van Fleet met with Almond and Gerry Thomas to discuss this plan on May 28. Both generals heartily concurred. For Almond and the Marines it would be a repetition of the dramatic Inchon and Wonsan landings and a role for which the Marines were specifically designed and trained. It was a military capability which Americans possessed and the CCF did not. Van Fleet set D day for June 6, the seventh anniversary of the Normandy landings, where he had begun his belated rise to fame.[127]

When he learned of these plans, Ridgway was thunderstruck. Having earlier and emphatically discouraged Van Fleet's musings about an amphibious landing at Wonsan, Ridgway found it difficult to believe that Van Fleet had proposed a landing at Tongchon, a mere thirty miles south of Wonsan.[128] He left for Korea that same afternoon, May 28.[129] That night Ridgway and Van Fleet exhaustively reviewed Eighth Army's situation and plans. These were:

• Shrimp Milburn's I Corps (ROK 1st; Charlie Palmer's 1st Cav and Sladen Bradley's 25th divisions) were back on the old Line Kansas at the Imjin and Hantan rivers. The ROK 1st Division would (as before) hold at Munsan. Tom Brodie's British Brigade was moving up to occupy the ground it had so stoutly defended during the CCF April 22 offensive. It would be joined by the Commonwealth Brigade and the newly arrived Canadian Brigade to create the Commonwealth Division, which would hold at the Imjin River.

The I Corps would again mount an offensive (Piledriver) to Lines Utah and Wyoming, with the object of seizing the Iron Triangle. This offensive would be conducted by three American divisions: Palmer's 1st Cav on the left, Shorty Soule's 3d Division (returning to I Corps) in the center, and Sladen Bradley's 25th on the right.[130]

• Bill Hoge's IX Corps (Babe Bryan's 24th Division, Buddy Ferenbaugh's 7th division, and the ROK 2d and 6th divisions) had finally picked up steam. On May 25 the 24th and 7th divisions had merged at Sinpo (on the old Line Kansas). On the following day Gines Perez's 21st and Harry Wilson's 5th Infantry had trapped and captured 2,900 of the CCF. On the IX Corps's right flank Buffalo Bill Quinn's 17th Infantry had recaptured Hwachon. The 7th Division's advance to Hwachon had blocked the retreat of the CCF and NKPA westward along the southern shore of the Hwachon Reservoir. About 6,000 of the CCF had surrendered in that area.[131]

Under Van Fleet's proposed plan to land the Marine division at Tongchon on June 6, IX Corps was to continue attacking north to Kumhwa to link with the Marines. The northeastward attack of Bradley's 25th Division (in I Corps) toward Kumhwa, would cross the front of Babe Bryan's 24th Division. When that occurred, the 24th would go into IX Corps reserve. Thereafter Buddy Ferenbaugh's 7th and the ROK 2d and 6th divisions would carry the IX Corps attack to Kumhwa.

• Ned Almond's X Corps (Thomas's 1st Marine Division, Ruffner's 2d Division, Bowen's 187th Airborne Combat Team, the reconstituted ROK 5th and 7th divisions, and the green ROK 8th Division) had also reached the old Line Kansas, or very nearly so. The Fifth and Seventh Marines had taken Yanggu; the ROK Marine regiment, performing brilliantly, had come up to the left of these units to the south shore of the Hwachon Reservoir and had assisted in the capture of the 6,000 POWs. The 187th, engaged in heavy fighting at Inje, supported by the 9th, 23d, and 38th regiments, was preparing to spearhead the 2d Division on a fifty-two-mile dash from Inje to Kansong. Shorty Soule's 3rd Division, having assisted in launching the X Corps counteroffensive and reorganizing ROK elements, was decamping to rejoin I Corps.[132]

Van Fleet's proposed amphibious landing at Tongchon had not been worked out in detail. The general idea was that the 1st Marine Division would be withdrawn from combat within the next forty-eight hours, replaced by elements of the ROK 5th, 7th, or 8th divisions, backed by 2d Division and X Corps artillery and armor units. The Marines would embark from a nearby port (Kangnung or Kansong) by June 5.

Ridgway was well satisfied with the plans for the I and IX corps attack to the Iron Triangle (Piledriver). In his view, that strategic sector remained the prime objective. But he was not satisfied with the plans for X Corps, which raised both political and military problems. The proposed Marine landing deep in North Korea (well beyond the JCS-approved Kansas-Utah-Wyoming lines) would require a tedious prior clearance from Washington, London, and other capitals. Militarily that landing together with the 187th's dash to Kansong, would dangerously thin out and fragment the X Corps front, possibly inviting a CCF counteroffensive. Besides that, the 187th was not performing well in its ground role and was taking heavy casualties (286 so far), and the 2d Division supporting it had sacrificed enough and had earned a respite.

Ridgway therefore directed that X Corps would go over to the defensive. Van Fleet and Almond would:

• Cancel the proposed Marine landing at Tongchon. The Marines would remain on the right of the Hwachon Reservoir, advancing about ten miles north to good defensive positions around an ancient volcanic crater, which the Marines called the "Punchbowl." The reconstituted ROK 5th and 7th divisions would flank the Marines.[133]

• Cancel the proposed dash of the 187th from Inje to Kansong. The ROK I Corps could advance to Kansong. The paratroopers would withdraw to Eighth Army reserve at Wonju.[134]

• Withdraw the 2d Division from combat. It would go into X Corps reserve at Hongchon for a long rest and remanning. The ROK 8th Division and ROK I Corps (Capital, 3d, and 11th divisions) now commanded by Paik Sun Yup would assume responsibility for manning the twenty miles of Line Kansas to the right of the Punchbowl to the coast.[135]

Van Fleet, Ned Almond, and Gerry Thomas carried out these orders like good soldiers. But all were disappointed. Van Fleet and Almond, in fact, were hopping mad. Almond claimed that since May 16 X Corps alone had inflicted 90,609 casualties on the CCF and NKPA at a cost of 8,769 UN casualties, of which "only 4,000" were Americans.* Both Van Fleet and Almond later asserted (in published documents or congressional testimony or oral histories) that they unequivocally believed that the CCF had been decisively smashed in its April and May attacks and that had Eighth Army pursued in late May with all its power, it could have overtaken and wiped out the CCF in North Korea. "We had the Chinese whipped," Van Fleet told one historian. "They were definitely gone. They were in awful shape." Almond told an interviewer that "Van Fleet and I were of the opinion that we should pursue the enemy and complete the operation."[137]

\* \* \*

Ridgway remained in Korea for about forty hours—until noon on May 30.[138] He again toured all American corps CPs and most divisional CPs—this time in heavy rains. Upon completion of the tour he cabled the JCS a long situation report. He wrote:

The enemy has suffered a severe major defeat. Estimates of enemy killed in action submitted by field commanders come to total so high that I cannot accept it.† Nevertheless, there has been inflicted a major personnel loss far exceeding in my opinion the loss suffered by the enemy in the April 22 offensive [70,000 casualties]. . . . A majority of his casualties have been in the infantry so that the loss in combat

---

*Van Fleet increased the enemy casualty figure to 105,000 in his official report. Of these, he stated, 17,000 enemy were dead by actual body count, and about 10,000 had surrendered. The remaining 78,000 were presumably dead or wounded or otherwise incapacitated. The 2d Division historian wrote that the 2d Division alone had "killed more than 65,000 enemy soldiers, the cream of the Armies of Red China." He evidently based his figures on reports from the individual regiments and other units, such as that of the 23d Infantry, which claimed inflicting "over 13,000 casualties" on the enemy, and that of the 9th Infantry, which claimed "total enemy casualties . . . to be 16,505, of which 2,200 were 'counted.' " Other than the 27,000 counted dead and POWs reported by Van Fleet, there was little evidence to support any of these claims.[136]
†*Time* magazine wrote: "General Ridgway . . . asked for an end to such guesses [of enemy casualties], ordering that claims henceforth be limited to counted enemy dead and prisoners."[139]

effectiveness of his major tactical units is much greater than the mere reduction in numbers of effectives would indicate. . . .

Ridgway noted the unusually large bag of POWs and the large stocks of enemy weapons which were falling into UN hands. "All three US corps commanders," he wrote, "have reported a noticeable deterioration in the fighting spirit of CCF forces." In "many cases," he went on, CCF POWs reported that their units were so desperately short of rations that the men had to "eat grass and roots." The withdrawing CCF had abandoned unprecedented numbers of ammo dumps, mortars, machine guns, automatic hand weapons, and rifles, plainly indicating that "disorganization now exists among both CCF and NKPA forces."

Ridgway went on to review the enemy order of battle. He stated that there had been thirteen CCF armies "in the general battle area." Now only seven were estimated to be "capable of further strong offensive action."* Hence UN forces had mauled six CCF armies, comprising eighteen divisions, in the April and May offensives. There were rumors of a new CCF Army group, possibly located between the Imjin and Yesong rivers, but the Eighth Army G-2 had not confirmed either its presence or location. Five NKPA corps (I, II, III, V, VI) had been identified "in the general battle area." However, all NKPA corps were "believed to be at greatly reduced strength and severely short of equipment and ammunition."

Ridgway declared that the surviving seven CCF armies were capable of three possible actions: first, to continue delaying Eighth Army's advance; secondly, to defend "strongly" at Line Kansas-Utah-Wyoming; thirdly, to launch an offensive with five armies at either Seoul or Chunchon. The "most likely" action was the second: a strong stand at the Kansas-Utah-Wyoming Line.

Meanwhile, Ridgway continued, Eighth Army had gone over to the offensive (Piledriver), for the purpose of "inflicting maximum casualties on a defeated and retiring enemy." The army was "near full strength."† The morale was "excellent" and the confidence "high." Its main weight had been placed in I Corps, which was attacking toward Chorwon-Kumhwa or the Iron Trian-

---

*These were, the Twentieth; Twenty-sixth; Twenty-seventh; Thirty-eighth; Thirty-ninth; Fortieth; and Forty-second.
†UN forces in Korea totaled 546,714 men, 258,445 of whom were ROKs. American ground forces consisted of 237,915 men, 25,769 of whom were Marines. The total UN figure included: FEAF, 14,953; 1st Marine Air Wing, 3,599; Commonwealth forces (British, Canadians, Australians, New Zealanders), 16,680; the Turkish Brigade, 5,746; the combined French, Dutch, Belgian, Greek, Filipino, and Thailand battalions, 5,027; a newly arrived Ethiopian Battalion, 931; Indian, Swedish, Danish, and other medical personnel, 3,169.[140]

gle. Assuming no CCF surprises, Ridgway said, he expected Eighth Army to reach that area within two weeks. He would submit further reports and recommendations as the situation developed.

He concluded:

In view of the foregoing and without any pretense of precise prediction, it is my sensing that: 1) even assuming the as yet undetermined presence of a CCF Army Group between the Imjin and Yesong rivers, the Eighth Army can have brought against it within the next two months a force no larger than those forces which it has soundly defeated twice within the past two months, and on the occasion just past, with such decisiveness as to approach disaster. 2) Assuming that there is no force the size of a CCF Army Group in the area between the Imjin and Yesong rivers, the combined hostile forces now accepted as present in Korea will not again have the capability of making as strong offensive efforts as those launched, beginning 22 April and 16 May.

I therefore believe that for the next 60 days the United States Government should be able to count with reasonable assurance upon a military situation in Korea offering optimum advantages in support of its diplomatic negotiations.[141]

# 28

# STALEMATE

## I

The fine achievements of Eighth Army in May 1951 were duly noted in the American media. But they were eclipsed by the astonishing and continuing hoopla generated by MacArthur's return to the United States.[1]

This hoopla reached a feverish pitch during the first weeks of May. Urged on by right-wing Republicans, Asia Firsters, the China Lobby, and others, the Senate voted to conduct "an inquiry into the military situation in the Far East and the facts surrounding the relief" of MacArthur. The inquiry, which became known as the "MacArthur hearings," was carried out by an absurdly large (twenty-six-man) and unwieldy Senate committee composed of the members of both the Senate Foreign Relations and Armed Services committees. It was chaired by a courtly, conservative Democrat, Richard B. Russell, who was head of the Armed Services Committee.[2]

The inquiry served several purposes. For MacArthur it was a legalistic vehicle for carrying forward his all-out challenge to the Truman administration's Asian policy and conduct of the Korean War. For MacArthur's right-wing supporters it was a forum for politically flailing the administration. For the administration it was not only a platform for defending its Asian policies and relief of MacArthur but also a means of educating the public on the complex issues entailed in Far East geopolitics. It was an extraordinary opportunity for all concerned to submit "posterity papers" and self-serving testimony. The end product would be a priceless boon to historians of the era.

The proceedings resembled a trial or court-martial. MacArthur appeared first and testified for three full days. He leveled his familiar charges at the administration: that it had neglected Asia, where there was a war, in favor of Europe, where there was no war; that it had not adequately met force with force in Korea; that UN military forces available had been hamstrung by political limitations which gave the enemy "privileged sanctuaries"; that there was "no substitute for victory"; that the war should be carried to Red China by the bombing of Manchurian bases, imposition of economic and naval blockades on the China mainland, and support of Chiang Kai-shek in an invasion of the mainland. And so on.[3]

The administration responded with a parade of "rebuttal witnesses," who testified for several weeks. Dean Acheson was on the "stand" for eight days; George Marshall, for seven; Omar Bradley, for six; the service chiefs—Collins, Vandenberg, and Sherman—for two days each. They responded to MacArthur's policy challenges point by point and justified his being relieved. As for the main point at issue—whether or not to widen the war to Red China— Bradley scored many points with his terse, famous statement: "Frankly, in the opinion of the Joint Chiefs of Staff, this strategy would involve us in the wrong war, at the wrong place, at the wrong time, and with the wrong enemy."[4]

The MacArthur hearings were ostensibly closed to the public. However, each night the committee released to the media a transcript of the day's proceedings. It was censored of real military secrets, but the voluminous political argumentation remained intact. The substance of this argumentation dominated the media during the month of May, but public interest finally waned. Except for an occasional startling revelation, by mid-June the "story" had moved to the back pages.[5]

Inasmuch as there was no jury to reach a verdict, there was no declared winner or loser. MacArthur made an impressive case, but the administration rebuttal was no less so. It is doubtful that many minds were changed by the argumentation presented by either side. Perhaps unintentionally the hearings turned out to be largely a cathartic, emotionally purging both sides and gradually defusing the issues.

In truth, the great majority of Americans were thoroughly sick of this no-win yo-yo war. Omar Bradley revealed its terrible cost during testimony on May 24: 69,276 American battle casualties and 72,679 nonbattle casualties (trench foot, frostbite, etc.). The battle casualties included 13,349 who were missing in action, presumed to be dead or captive. Would the American public continue to tolerate these grievous losses merely to regain a few miles of miserable real estate in behalf of a corrupt South Korean regime that had repeatedly run from the enemy? Bradley seriously doubted that it would. The public appeared ready to accept the idea of an unwon or "limited war."[6]*

---

*Gallup Polls during this period indicated that only about 30 to 35 percent looked with favor on the war in Korea.[7]

## II

Following the entry of the CCF into North Korea, the Truman administration had unofficially pursued a policy aimed at achieving a negotiated settlement. While the CCF was "winning" and Eighth Army was "losing," a negotiated settlement seemed unattainable, and attempts to arrange it futile. However, the rejuvenation of Eighth Army and its return to the 38th Parallel in early April had raised hopes that Peking would be less intractable.

Although the goal of a negotiated settlement had guided all administration military and political decisions regarding Korea for months, that goal had never been formally adopted. On April 5 the JCS, declaring that "the Korean problem cannot be resolved . . . by military action alone," had recommended "as a matter of urgency" a general review of Asian policy and a specific review of Korean policy. Perhaps stimulated in part by the public challenge from MacArthur, the NSC responded to the JCS recommendation by producing a revision of its December 1949 Asian policy (NSC-48). Numbered NSC-48/5, the paper was approved by President Truman on May 17.[8]

The broad goals of the administration in the Far East remained unchanged. Washington would promote "stable and self-sustaining non-communist governments friendly to the United States." It would eliminate the "preponderant power and influence of the USSR in Asia" or diminish it to such a degree that Moscow would "not be capable of threatening from that area the security of the United States or its friends, or the peace, national independence and stability of the Asiatic nations." It would declare "power relationships" which would "make it impossible" for any nation or alliance to threaten the security of the United States in Asia. Insofar as practicable it would deny to the Communist world and secure for the United States and free world the "material resources" of Asia.

In order to realize these goals, the administration would attempt to "detach China" as an effective ally of the USSR and bring it into the American orbit; assist Japan in becoming a self-reliant nation friendly to the United States; help the countries of South and Southeast Asia (Indochina, Philippines, Indonesia, etc.) to develop the will and ability to resist communism; and, finally, maintain the security of the offshore defensive perimeter Japan–Ryukyus–Philippines–Australia and New Zealand.

With respect to Communist China, the paper recommended numerous specific courses of action. While recognizing the Nationalists as the legal government of China, Washington should continue strong efforts to deflate Red China's military strength and prestige by inflicting heavy losses on the CCF in Korea; support anti-Communist elements within and without China "by all available means" with a view to reorienting or overthrowing the Peking regime; "stimulate differences between" Peking and Moscow and "create cleavages" within the Peking regime; continue U.S. economic restrictions against Red China and persuade other nations to do likewise; oppose a Red China seat in the UN.

Should Red China attack UN or U.S. forces outside Korea, or should UN forces be compelled to evacuate from Korea, the United States should respond with MacArthur-like measures. The military should prepare plans for:

- Imposition of a blockade of the China coast by naval and air forces.
- Military actions against selected targets held by Communist China outside Korea.
- Participation, defensively or offensively, of the Chinese Nationalist forces and the necessary operational assistance to make them effective.

With respect to Korea, NSC-48/5 declared a radical change in the original American goals in the Korean War. Washington would no longer attempt to clear all North Korea of enemy, in effect unifying Korea by military force. The unification of Korea would be pursued only by political means. Militarily Washington would settle for the status quo ante bellum.

The specific "courses of action" Washington should follow in Korea were stated as:

- Seek an acceptable political settlement in Korea that does not jeopardize the U.S. position with respect to the USSR, to Formosa, or to seating Communist China in the UN.
- In the absence of such a settlement, and recognizing that currently there is no other acceptable alternative, continue the current military course of action in Korea, without commitment to unify Korea by military force, but designed to (1) inflict maximum losses on the enemy, (2) prevent the overrunning of South Korea by military aggression, (3) limit Communist capabilities for aggression elsewhere in Asia.
- Continue efforts to influence Allies to increase support and contributions to the UN operations in Korea.
- Develop dependable South Korean military units as rapidly as possible and in sufficient strength eventually to assume the major part of the burden of the UN forces there.
- Working through the UN where feasible, continue to strengthen the ROK government economically and rehabilitate areas liberated from Communist control.

Although the rumors of Soviet intervention in Korea had diminished, that possibility was not ignored. The paper recommended:

• If the USSR commits units of Soviet "volunteers" sufficient to jeopardize the safety of UN forces in Korea, immediate consideration should be given to withdrawing UN forces from Korea and placing the United States in the best possible position of readiness for general war.

• If the USSR precipitates a general war, UN forces should be withdrawn from Korea as rapidly as possible and U.S. forces should be deployed for service elsewhere.

Noticeably absent from this paper was a specific recommendation for (or against) crossing the 38th Parallel. It specified only that the political solution to the war should produce a South Korean military and administrative area "in no case below the 38th Parallel." Hence the question of how far *north* Eighth Army should go was again left unresolved.

The JCS continued to debate this question during the last two weeks of May following Eighth Army's defeat of the CCF's sixth offensive and the resumption of its own offensive, Piledriver. Recognizing that the 38th Parallel itself offered Ridgway poor defensive positions, the JCS had authorized a return to the old Kansas and Wyoming lines above the parallel. However, the JCS was not unaware that Van Fleet believed the CCF had been "whipped" and was "in awful shape" and that he had urged a deep penetration into North Korea, including an amphibious landing at Tongchon.

The issue was thoroughly reviewed at an important meeting of State and White House officials and the military on May 29. The White House was represented by Averell Harriman; State, by Acheson's deputy undersecretary, H. Freeman Matthews, Dean Rusk, and Paul H. Nitze. The military included Omar Bradley, Forrest Sherman, Ham Haislip (sitting in for Joe Collins), the Air Force's vice chief of staff, Nathan F. Twining (sitting in for Hoyt Vandenberg), and Thomas D. White, Max Taylor, and other senior military planners.[9]

Bradley said the issue of where Eighth Army should stop had to be settled once and for all because the JCS, having consolidated and brought up-to-date all the outstanding directives to Ridgway, wished to issue a new directive. It should specify a line beyond which Ridgway should not advance Eighth Army without prior JCS approval. "Is his mission to be the Yalu or the 38th Parallel or something in between?" Bradley asked.

The views expressed varied widely. Bradley and Haislip, taking issue with Van Fleet's assessment of the enemy, urged that Eighth Army halt more or less along Lines Kansas and Wyoming. Haislip saw no signs of "a Chinese collapse." They had pulled back merely to get "out of the way of our weapons." He elaborated: "Only on the east central front [of the American X Corps] have they been hurt. On the west they are sitting tight." I and

IX corps were "up against solid resistance in regimental strength and greater." Haislip concluded: "No line north of the present one" was "any better than any other." Bradley concurred. There had been "no wholesale surrenders" of CCF, and "the opposition would be stiff from here on." The "present position" of Eighth Army, he concluded, "was as good as we're going to get for some time."

Forrest Sherman disagreed. Apparently believing the Navy and the Marines could pull off another dramatic and decisive Inchon-like operation at Tongchon (as proposed by Van Fleet), he sided with Van Fleet's assessment of the enemy. There were "plenty of indications that the Chinese had taken punishment." Sherman urged (as he had earlier) a stop line much "further north," perhaps as far north as Pyongyang–Wonsan (the Korean waist). By holding such a line, he argued, "one could then dictate terms in exchange for drawing back to the 38th Parallel"; otherwise "one would have nothing to give up in exchange for what we are demanding."

For the nonce the views of Bradley and Haislip prevailed. It was decided that the previously designated stop line, Kansas–Wyoming, would remain in force in Eighth Army's western sector. In the eastern sector the stop line would pass "approximately through the Hwachon Reservoir area." But the chiefs were not inflexibly wedded to these "lines"; their views would alter in the coming weeks.[10]

\* \* \*

The JCS cabled the new directive to Ridgway on May 31. It rescinded all previous directives and resolved the conflicts and ambiguities of which Ridgway had complained. Its language and courses of action mirrored those of the new Asian policy paper, NSC-48/5. Generally, the JCS imposed tighter reins on Ridgway, for example, denying his earlier requests for authority to launch instant retaliatory attacks on Red China in event of a disastrous reverse or a Soviet attack and to withdraw Eighth Army from Korea for the defense of Japan at his discretion.[11]

The major change concerned the war objectives in Korea. Ridgway was to continue to "inflict maximum personnel and matériel losses on the forces of North Korea and Communist China operating within the geographical boundaries of Korea and the waters adjacent thereto." But the aim now was to "create conditions favorable to a settlement of the Korean conflict" which would, at a minimum:

• Terminate hostilities under appropriate armistice arrangements.
• Establish the authority of the Republic of South Korea over all Korea south of a northern boundary so located as to facilitate, to the maximum extent possible, both administration and military defense and in no case south of the 38th Parallel.

- Provide for the withdrawal by appropriate stages of non-Korean armed forces in Korea.
- Permit the building of sufficient ROK military power to deter or repel a renewed North Korean aggression.

In pursuit of those objectives Ridgway was authorized to conduct air and naval operations within the geographic boundaries of Korea and adjacent waters. However, he was specifically prohibited from conducting air and naval operations against Soviet territory, Manchuria, and the hydroelectric plants on the Yalu River. Air or naval operations would be carried out to seaward of a line twelve miles off the USSR territory on the Asian mainland and Manchuria. Aerial reconnaissance of North Korea would go no farther north than the Yalu River on the west coast and "short of Korean-Soviet" boundary on the east coast.

The limitations on ground operations reflected the Bradley-Haislip view, yet they were deliberately left vague:

You will obtain approval of JCS prior to undertaking any general advance beyond some [east-west] line passing approximately through the Hwachon Reservoir area. You are, however, authorized to conduct such tactical operations as may be necessary or desirable to insure safety of your command, to maintain contact, and to continue to harass the enemy. This includes authority to conduct guerrilla operations and limited amphibious and airborne operations in enemy rear areas.*

In response to Ridgway's repeatedly voiced concern about possible Soviet intervention in Korea, the language of the directive was more specific than the language of NSC-48/5. It specified:

- In event of open or covert employment of major Soviet units in Korea (including "volunteers") you will, subject to security of your forces, assume the defensive, make no move to aggravate the situation, and report to the JCS. This is not to be interpreted as a restriction on conduct of air and naval operations in Korea.
- If USSR announces in advance its intentions to reoccupy North Korea and gives warning either explicitly or implicitly that their forces should not be attacked, you will refer the matter immediately to the JCS.
- In event of an attempt to employ small Soviet units covertly in Korea, you should continue your current action.

---

*Bradley had declared Van Fleet's proposed amphibious landing at Tongchon "out of the question." The authorized amphibious and airborne operations referred to the numerous small-scale commando types of harassing or intelligence missions which had been mounted in North Korea for months.[12]

Along with the new directive, the JCS cabled Ridgway a position paper it had prepared earlier setting forth views on "conditions" for an "armistice." The JCS specified that an armistice arrangement:[13]

• Must be contingent upon the Communists' acceptance of a general agreement to end the aggression in Korea and to accede to basic terms of settlement satisfactory to the United States.

• Shall require all governments and authorities concerned, including North Korea and Communist China, to order a cessation of all acts of armed force; the establishment of a demilitarized area across Korea; and all ground forces to remain in position or be withdrawn to the rear except that all forces which may be in advance of the demilitarized area shall be moved to positions to its rear.

• Shall require an armistice committee to supervise the armistice with "free and unlimited access to the whole of Korea."

• Shall require all governments concerned to cease the introduction into Korea of reinforcing units or personnel and additional war equipment.

The chiefs amplified the details of the demilitarized zone (DMZ). It should be a zone "on the order of 20 miles in width, centered at or north of the 38th Parallel," the JCS wrote. "Its exact location shall be determined by the Armistice Committee on the basis of the position of the opposing ground units in combat at the time."[14]

*   *   *

Having finally and formally declared for a negotiated settlement in Korea, and believing the time had never been more opportune, Dean Acheson and his diplomats commenced all-out efforts to achieve it. Those efforts were mainly twofold:

• Calculated statements from the UN and Washington indicating a willingness to settle the war at or near the 38th Parallel.

• Secret diplomatic feelers designed to establish a communications link with Peking.

The first of these steps was taken in early June. Responding to a suggestion from Washington, UN Secretary-General Trygve Lie publicly announced on June 1 that a cease-fire "approximately along" the 38th Parallel would fulfill the main purposes of the UN in Korea, provided the cease-fire was followed by the restoration of peace and security in the area. Dean Acheson reinforced the Lie statement on the following day, June 2, during his testimony in the MacArthur hearings, which was released to the media by the committee censor that night. In response to a question by Republican Senator H. Alexander Smith, who asked whether or not the administration would settle for a cease-fire "at or near" the 38th Parallel, Acheson replied in the affirmative: "If you could have a real settlement, that would accomplish the military purposes in Korea." He elaborated: "That is, if the aggression would end and you had reliable assurances that it would not be resumed, then you could return to a peacetime status, and we would hope gradually to remove the troops from Korea, both Chinese troops and United Nations troops."[15]

Although both public statements were made with the best of intentions, the language employed was questionable. There were no adequate defensive positions "approximately on" or "on or near" the 38th Parallel. As Acheson and Lie knew, at that time Eighth Army, poised on Line Kansas, several miles north of the 38th Parallel in the center, was preparing to advance farther yet to Line Wyoming, which was almost twenty miles north of the parallel. Thus Lie and Acheson's public declaration of a willingness to negotiate a cease-fire at or near or along the 38th Parallel was at best deceptive and at worst false. The statements would return to haunt all parties concerned.

\* \* \*

The second step—renewed secret diplomatic feelers to Peking—was taken at about the same time. Like all prior attempts to reach Peking, these, too, at first failed. But a secret indirect approach to Moscow through George Kennan, then at the Institute for Advanced Study in Princeton, showed promise of bearing fruit.

At Acheson's request, Kennan made an informal call on the Soviet ambassador to the UN, Jacob Malik, on May 31. Malik received Kennan "cordially and pleasantly" at his home on Long Island. Kennan frankly stated that although he then had no official position in the U.S. government, he had come to "talk about a possible ceasefire in Korea" and he wondered if Malik might be willing to do so. Malik responded with the usual Communist propaganda lines (perhaps for the benefit of a tape recorder), but Kennan came away from the meeting with a feeling that further talks might be useful. The two men agreed to meet again on June 5.[16]

During the second meeting at Malik's home on Long Island, he made an electrifying statement. In a memo to Acheson, Kennan recorded the wording thus: "The Soviet government wanted peace and wanted a peaceful solution of the Korean question—and at the earliest possible moment." Kennan doubted that Malik would make such a statement to him without prior approval by Moscow and that therefore, Acheson should regard the statement "as a major policy statement of the Soviet Government."[17]

There was a hitch, however. Since the Soviet Union was not militarily engaged in Korea, Malik said, "it did not feel that it could take part in any discussion of the question of a ceasefire." Malik's "personal advice" was that Washington should "get in touch with the North Koreans and the Chinese Communists in this matter." Kennan interpreted this advice to mean that, as he wrote, "Soviet influence has already been brought to bear on the North Koreans and the Chinese Communists to show themselves amenable to proposals for a ceasefire." Kennan urged Acheson to "grasp at once the nettle of action."[18]

Acheson was willing to do so, but all avenues to Peking appeared to remain firmly closed. When the U.S. ambassador to Russia, former Admiral Alan G. Kirk, sent a representative to the Chinese Embassy in Moscow with a note, it was refused by an underling on the ground that "no diplomatic relations exist" between Peking and Washington. Acheson therefore was compelled to adopt a wait-and-see attitude.[19]

## III

The Eighth Army offensive Piledriver began officially on June 3. The principal objective was to advance in the center about twelve miles north, from Line Kansas to Line Wyoming, and dominate the Iron Triangle. A secondary objective was to advance the army front in the eastern zone about the same distance to the Punchbowl.[20]

Believing the CCF had been thoroughly crushed and was in total disarray, Van Fleet, who moved his advanced CP to Seoul, expected that Piledriver would be a fast, easy march. He was mistaken. It proved to be slow and arduous. Five factors significantly retarded Eighth Army's progress:

• A new rotation policy. Announced earlier, the policy began to take effect in May and June. Officers and enlisted men with the longest service in the front lines in Korea became eligible for individual rotation upon the arrival of a qualified replacement. The policy began stripping frontline units of their most experienced men. Many men who were eligible for rotation and awaiting replacements or soon to become eligible naturally became more cautious and chary of risk taking.

• Rumors of a cease-fire at the 38th Parallel. The public statements of Trygve Lie and Dean Acheson suggesting that the UN and Washington would settle for a cease-fire "approximately" along or "at or near" the 38th Parallel had reached Eighth Army. To many, Piledriver, which demanded an advance of about twenty miles north of the 38th Parallel, seemed pointless or worse. Why fight and die for real estate which was apparently to be returned to the CCF in a negotiated settlement?

• Miserable weather. Piledriver coincided with the onset of the rainy season in Korea. Monsoon-like torrents lashed the combat zone and rear areas.

Roads turned into "bottomless rivers of mud." Foxholes and slit trenches filled. Swollen rivers and streams washed out pontoon and treadway bridges. Trucks, artillery tows, and other heavy equipment bogged down.[21]

• Unexpectedly strong CCF resistance. The major elements of the CCF had withdrawn above the Iron Triangle. However, they had left very strong rear guards on key hills dominating the roads approaching Chorwon and Kumhwa. These CCF enclaves were stoutly dug into bunker networks, supported by mortars and machine guns and, in many places, by artillery and antitank guns.

• Fatigue. All divisions of I and IX corps had been engaged in heavy fighting or movement since May 21, when Van Fleet had launched Detonate. In I Corps Sladen Bradley's 25th Division had driven north about thirty-seven miles in ten days (May 21 to May 31). Shorty Soule's 3d Division had rushed halfway across the peninsula to help X Corps, then had rushed back to I Corps for Piledriver, with no intervening pause. Too many combat elements of Eighth Army were exhausted.

\* \* \*

Shrimp Milburn's I Corps was assigned the main responsibility for Piledriver. His forces were substantial: the ROK 1st Division, the newly organizing Commonwealth Division (British, Canadian, and Commonwealth brigades), the 1st Cav and 25th divisions, and the 3d Division (incorporating the reconstituted elements of the ROK 9th Division). The plan was that the ROK 1st and Commonwealth divisions would hold on the left at the Imjin River, while the 1st Cav, 3d, and 25th divisions crossed the Hantan River and took Chorwon and Kumhwa, the two towns forming the base of the triangle. Milburn would be supported on the right by Bill Hoge's IX Corps less the 24th division, which went into reserve.[22]

Of the three American divisions assigned by I Corps to Piledriver, the 3d had the most difficult and frustrating experience. Owing to washed-out bridges and muddy roads, its redeployment across the peninsula back to I Corps was seriously disrupted and delayed. The division was not fully ready for a major offensive on D day, June 3. Yet it prepared to attack as ordered.[23]

The 3d Division was inserted between the 1st Cav (attacking up the Uijongbu–Chorwon road) and the 25th Division, which moved right into terrain formerly occupied by the 24th Division. The 3d had first to cross the swollen Hantan River in about the same place the 25th Division had crossed it on April 21. Jim Boswell's 7th Infantry, first to arrive in I Corps, secured a bridgehead, after which engineers built a pontoon bridge. William Harris's Puerto Rican 65th Infantry moved into the bridgehead to help the 7th Infantry. Tom Yancey's 15th Infantry, last to arrive from X Corps, was placed in division reserve.

Led by the 7th and 65th regiments, the 3d Division attacked from the bridgehead at 6:00 A.M. on June 3. The division, its historian wrote, ran into "a hornet's nest." The 65th had a very rough time. The men of Saint St. Clair's 1/65, on the right, were forced to climb cliffs hand over hand to root out CCF. On the left Laurence Johnson's 2/65 was hit by a "vicious" CCF counterattack that disorganized the battalion and drove it back across the Hantan River. An armored probe by Wilson Hawkins's 64th Tank Battalion, on the division's right flank, encountered the first "serious" CCF antitank action of the war. Five Patton tanks were disabled by antitank guns; two, by mines.[24]

As a result of these setbacks, Shorty Soule was compelled to reorganize drastically the 3d Division's assault formation. He brought the depleted ROK 9th Division forward to screen the division's left sector. He pulled the shaken 65th Infantry back into division reserve, replacing it with Yancey's 15th Infantry. Sideslipping right to make room for the ROKs, Boswell's 7th Infantry linked with the 15th Infantry on a narrow front. When the division attack was resumed in earnest on June 8, the CCF drove the ROKs back one mile. And so it went.[25]

* * *

On the right of the 3d Division the attack of Sladen Bradley's 25th Division was only slightly less arduous. It was led by Gilbert Check's 27th Infantry on the left and Henry Britt's 24th Infantry on the right. These forces, Bittman Barth wrote, encountered "small but tenacious" CCF delaying troops dug in on hilltops. Barth himself saw only the opening phases of the action. On June 3 he was relieved by his exec, William Dick, and returned to the States. Promoted to two stars, Barth retired disabled in 1957.[26]

Henry Britt's 24th Infantry was again demoralized. On its long northward drive it had had a ghastly experience. It had uncovered the area where Harry Wilson's 5th Infantry and the 555th FAB had been ambushed in late April. Britt logged that it had been "a gruesome scene." The GIs had found the seven wrecked American tanks, "uncounted" vehicles, and "numerous friendly dead" scattered among the vehicles. The sight had not been one to lift spirits; the 5th Infantry had been one of the very best regiments in Eighth Army.[27]

There were other problems in the 24th Infantry. One was officer leadership, Britt noted candidly in his daily journal. Few, if any, officers in combat in Korea, he wrote, "retain effectiveness" beyond six months. In the 24th Infantry, he went on, it was less—"not over four months." Moreover, he wrote, the officer casualty rate in the 24th was "far greater" than any other regiment in Eighth Army. Yet Eighth Army seemed reluctant to send him replacements under the new rotation policy. He had some "intelligent" people, but they worried if they would ever get out. Their morale was "pretty low."[28]

The regiment had yet another new set of battalion commanders, none of them West Pointers. In the 1/24 Waldon C. Winston had relieved the Baron Baronowski. In the 2/24, Franklin W. McVay, had replaced George Clayton, who was rotated after having commanded the battalion for seven consecutive months—a regimental record. In the 3/24 John E. Boothe, Jr., had relieved the able Bill Mouchet, who went to the 27th Infantry as exec.[29]

Of the three battalion commanders, McVay was considered superior. He was a born leader who immediately won the respect of his black soldiers.[30]

Among his men was a platoon sergeant, Cornelius H. ("Connie") Charlton, in G Company. One of seventeen children of a West Virginia coal miner who had migrated to New York City, Charlton had enlisted in the Army when he was seventeen years old. After tours in Germany, the States, and Okinawa, he arrived in Korea with an engineer service unit. Bored with this rear-area job, in March 1951 Charlton, by then a sergeant, transferred to the 24th Infantry. His G Company commander, Gordon E. Gullikson, was so impressed with Charlton that he soon recommended him for battlefield commission.[31]

During the early phases of Piledriver, on June 2, the 24th Infantry ran up against fierce CCF resistance on Hills 1147 and 543, near the village of Chipom. McVay's 2/24 and Boothe's 3/24 took Hill 1147, but the 3/24 was repulsed on Hill 543. Britt ordered the 3/24 to withdraw and substituted McVay's 2/24. Connie Charlton's platoon led the attack on Hill 543 the following morning.

Early in this action the lieutenant leading the platoon was killed, leaving Charlton the senior man. Gathering up four men, Charlton led a frontal assault on a CCF machine-gun position. In the attack a CCF grenade knocked Charlton flat, but he got up, hurling his own grenades, and killed the CCF machine gunners. Bringing up the rest of the platoon, Charlton led another frontal assault on a second CCF machine-gun position. The CCF repelled the attack with grenades, one of which severely injured Charlton in the chest. Spurning aid for himself, Charlton sent his wounded to the rear, then led a third charge, directly into heavy CCF fire. Mortally wounded by a second grenade, Charlton staggered forward into the machine-gun position and killed the CCF before he himself died. His platoon followed, seizing Hill 543, only to be driven off that night by a CCF counterattack. Charlton was posthumously awarded the Medal of Honor. It was the second such award to a black (after William Thompson) in the 24th Infantry.

\* \* \*

Eighth Army closed on Line Wyoming "yard by weary yard, ridge by bloody ridge," as *Time* magazine put it. Van Fleet toured the front lines, still insistent that his corps and division commanders make lavish use of artillery. He declared that "no limitation" was to be placed on the expenditure of artillery ammunition without his specific knowledge and approval. He dressed down Bill Hoge one day because an eight-inch howitzer battery in IX Corps had fired only eleven rounds per gun. Notwithstanding the loss of all its artillery pieces in the May 16 CCF offensive, the ROK 9th Division (attached to the 3d Division) was to be provided a full issue of howitzers (eighteen 105-mms) to recreate an artillery battalion. Further, Van Fleet requested (via Ridgway) that the Pentagon send him ten more heavy artillery battalions: six 155-mm (one of them to be Long Tom guns) and four eight-inch.[32]

By June 9 the initial objectives of Piledriver were in sight. On the I Corps left the 1st Cav and 3d divisions reached the outskirts of Chorwon; on the right the 25th Division and the 7th Division (of IX Corps) were converging on Kumhwa. There were no triumphant bugles. The weather was still miserable. The Americans remained ill at ease, fearful of a sudden powerful CCF counterattack which could force yet another Eighth Army withdrawal in this interminable, no-win yo-yo war.

The divisions inched forward warily for several thousand more yards. By June 14 all four had reached Piledriver objectives on Line Wyoming. The 1st Cav and 3d divisions occupied deserted Chorwon; the 25th and 7th divisions, deserted Kumhwa. All units dug in, erected bunkers, strung miles of barbed wire, planted tens of thousands of mines, and zeroed in artillery. Behind them engineers and Korean laborers continued to reinforce Line Kansas, should another withdrawal become necessary.[33]

*　　*　　*

On Eighth Army's right flank Ned Almond's X Corps supported Piledriver with an attack toward the Punchbowl on June 4. It was carried out by the 1st Marine Division, flanked by the reconstituted ROK 5th and 7th divisions on the right and left, respectively.[34]

The Marines attacked with three regiments line abreast: First Marines on the left, the ROK Marine Regiment in the center, and the Fifth Marines on the right. Opposed by only the NKPA, the Marines ran into a brick wall. "For five days the fight raged with unabated fury," the Marine historian wrote. "The terrain limited the advance to a narrow front, so that the attack resembled the thrust of a spear rather than a blow from a battering ram." On June 8, Marine division commander Gerry Thomas was compelled to commit to the fight the reserve Seventh Marines, less the 3/7, which remained his sole division reserve. The Seventh Marines squeezed in between the First Marines and the ROKs in the division's left sector.[35]

The decisive breakthrough on that front was finally achieved by the ROK Marines. At two in the morning on June 11, adopting the NKPA tactic of a night attack, all three ROK Marine battalions fell on the sleeping NKPA "like an avalanche." The ROKs inflicted a brutal slaughter on the NKPA and gained a key terrain feature, which enabled the American Marine regiments to move onto Line Kansas, overlooking the Punchbowl. Gerry Thomas commended the ROKs: "Your seizure of objectives on the Kansas Line from a determined enemy was a magnificent dash of courage and endurance."[36]

\* \* \*

The Marine offensive to the Punchbowl and the advance of the ROKs to the east of it enabled the battered 2d Division to withdraw from the Inje area into IX Corps reserve, in accordance with Ridgway's orders. By that time the division was shattered; it was to remain in reserve for forty days, rebuilding and reorganizing and rotating those who had been in combat longest. During that period two regimental commanders, the 9th's Ed Messinger and the 23d's Jack Chiles, were rotated, being replaced by their execs, Olinto Barsanti and Frank Meszar, respectively. Before the division returned to combat, Barsanti (crippled with bursitis), Meszar, and the 38th's commander, John Coughlin, were rotated. Messinger went on to three stars, Chiles and Barsanti to two stars, Meszar to one star; Coughlin retired as a colonel in 1954.

The new commanders of the 9th, 23d, and 38th regiments were all young West Pointers. Command of the 38th went to the youngest of the three, Almond's G-3, Frank Mildren (West Point, 1939), who was given another X Corps staffer and Almond confidant, Edward L. Rowny (West Point, 1941) to be his exec. The X Corps assistant G-3, Joe Gurfein (West Point, 1941), was named exec of the 23d Infantry. Both Rowny and Gurfein would later rise to command their regiments. The appointments of these X Corps staffers to line positions appeared to confirm the story that Almond was running a "command nursery," giving choice jobs to the "teacher's pets." The long parade from X Corps to the 2d and 7th divisions to date included Nick Ruffner, Bill Quinn, Jack Chiles, Bill McCaffrey, Barsanti, Mildren, Rowny, and Gurfein.[37]

Most battalion commanders in the 2d Division were also rotated. These included James Nabors, commander of the 3/9, which remained segregated through the summer of 1951. After Nabors, command of the 3/9 became a revolving door. The 3/9 exec, Harris Pope, replaced Nabors, but Pope, suffering from a hernia, soon moved up to 9th Infantry exec. He was replaced in the 3/9 by the new 3/9 exec, Douglas Staggs, but Nick Ruffner put another man over Staggs, who reverted to exec. After a very brief stint Ruffner's man was replaced by a X Corps staff officer, James L. Culp. In the fall Culp and Staggs desegregated the 3/9.[38]

\* \* \*

Piledriver cooled Van Fleet's ardor for an all-out Eighth Army offensive deep into North Korea. The resistance had been far stronger than anticipated; the CCF might counterattack in massive force at any hour. On June

9 Van Fleet telexed Ridgway a situation report, recommending a general halt on the Kansas and Wyoming lines, limiting further Eighth Army action to hit-and-run raids designed to throw a possible CCF offensive off-balance.[39] On June 14 Ridgway, concurring with Van Fleet's overview, cabled the JCS a "concept of probable developments in Korea during the next 60 days":

Enemy lines of communication are over-extended. His supply situation is aggravated by heavy rainfall and air interdiction. Provided no general advance north of Kansas-Wyoming Line is made during this period, logistic support of Eighth Army will remain adequate. A general advance north of the Kansas-Wyoming area would tend to nullify Eighth Army's present logistic advantage over the enemy.

The enemy, due to his numerical superiority, has capability of retaining overall initiative, and of launching at least one major offensive during this period. However, the terrain along the general Kansas-Wyoming Line, when organized, can be strongly defended and used as base for limited offensive operations.

It is intended, therefore, to retain Eighth Army Forces along the general Kansas-Wyoming Line and continue to inflict maximum personnel and matériel losses by limited offensive operations. Examples of limited offensive operations which may be conducted, provided remunerative target of enemy troops or supplies are present, include seizure of Pyonggang and Kaesong by Task Forces and subsequent withdrawal of these forces to Kansas-Wyoming.[40]

At about this time Dean Acheson informed the JCS of the encouraging results of the Kennan-Malik talks. As Acheson remembered it, the chiefs in turn told Ridgway (probably on a back channel) that "an operation was on" and that he should "be prepared to advise on all relevant military matters and to conduct proceedings in the field as needed." In sum, notwithstanding the continued silence from Peking, an early cease-fire was now believed to be more than a possibility.[41]

Ridgway welcomed this top secret news. A cease-fire had been his overriding goal since his arrival in the Far East. Five years later he wrote:

My own conviction is that the magnificent Eighth Army could have driven the Chinese beyond the Yalu—if this country had been willing to pay the price in lives such action would have cost.

Personally, I strongly doubt that such a victory would have been worth the cost—particularly in light of the fact that our government seemed to have no firm policy on what steps to take thereafter. Seizure of the line of the Yalu and the Tumen would have been merely the seizure of more real estate. It would have greatly shortened the enemy supply lines and greatly lengthened our own. It would have widened our front from 110 miles to 420, and beyond that front would lie Manchuria and the whole mainland of Asia, in which all the wealth and manpower of this country could have been lost and dissipated.

So, it is useless to speculate on what might have been. I was not privy to the

# The Battle and Armistice Lines

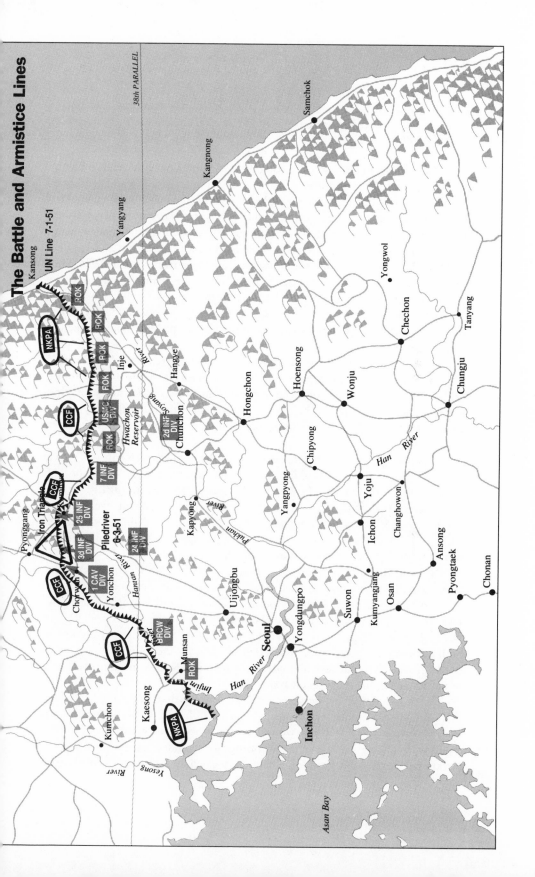

councils of our leaders at home when they decided to accept the Russian-sponsored overtures for a truce. But, in retrospect, I do not feel constrained to quarrel with that decision.[42]

The news from Acheson led Ridgway, Van Fleet, and the GHQ staff to study intently the many military factors entailed in a cease-fire and armistice. Of these factors, the most pressing and complex was the selection of a cease-fire line that would ensure the safety of Eighth Army in the event the negotiations never took place or broke down and the CCF mounted another major offensive. Complicating the selection of a cease-fire line was the earlier JCS stipulation that the opposing armies should be separated by a twenty-mile DMZ. This meant that after the cease-fire each of the opposing armies would have to withdraw ten miles to the rear of the "battle line."

After examining all the alternatives, Ridgway proposed the following concept. To ensure optimally its safety in the important Iron Triangle sector, Eighth Army required at minimum a heavily fortified line at Kansas, plus divisional OPLRs ten miles in advance of Line Kansas. Hence the "battle line" from which Eighth Army would withdraw ten miles (to create a twenty-mile DMZ) after the cease-fire must be not less than twenty miles north of Line Kansas. That would place the desired "battle line" on cease-fire day about eight miles north of Line Wyoming, almost directly in the center of the Iron Triangle.[43]

This concept was not in consonance with the public statements of Trygve Lie and Dean Acheson calling for a settlement "approximately" along or "on or near" the 38th Parallel. In Ridgway's concept, the line of OPLRs in the center sector (below the Iron Triangle) would actually be about twelve miles north of the 38th Parallel, very close to Line Wyoming. The line to which the CCF would withdraw from the "battle line" (to create a twenty-mile DMZ) would thus be about thirty-two miles north of the 38th Parallel.

Nor was that all. In order to ensure the safety of Eighth Army's extreme right flank, Ridgway had directed ROK I Corps to advance north along the coast to Songjong, about halfway between Kansong and Kosong. The ROK I Corps stop line was about thirty-five miles north of the 38th Parallel. If it were assumed that the stop line would become the "battle line" from which both sides would withdraw ten miles, that would leave the CCF forty-five miles north of the 38th Parallel in that sector and the ROKs in control of the important Kansong–Hongchon road.[44]

There was, however, one aspect of the concept that might tend to offset this considerable Eighth Army bulge above the 38th Parallel in the central and eastern sectors. In the extreme western sector, where Line Kansas bent southwesterly following the Imjin River, Ridgway would concede considerable terrain below the 38th Parallel, which he deemed largely indefensible. After the demilitarized zone had been established, the CCF line in that sector would be about ten miles south of the 38th Parallel and would include the ancient and symbolically important capital Kaesong.

\* \* \*

Van Fleet concurred with Ridgway's concept. In order to conform to it, he directed Shrimp Milburn to establish inside the Iron Triangle OPLRs which were twenty miles north of Line Kansas and about eight miles north of Line Wyoming. To support these OPLRs and ferret out CCF troops and throw them off-balance, Van Fleet also launched the first of his promised hit-and-run attacks on the CCF farther north.[45]

The most ambitious of these raids (Operation Goose) took place on June 13. The objective was Pyonggang, a town at the apex of the Iron Triangle. The raid was conducted by powerful armored elements of the 3d Division from Chorwon and the 25th Division from Kumhwa. It carried Eighth Army farther north than it had been for months or would ever go again and produced headlines. But the actual results were inconclusive and disappointing. Apparently the CCF elected to make a temporary tactical withdrawal rather than fight.[46]

The raid on Pyonggang and other probes and patrols led to the conclusion that the Iron Triangle had been "cleared" of the CCF and that the newly established OPLRs were relatively secure. Accordingly, Van Fleet issued orders for the 25th Division (and the Turks) to pull back into I Corps reserve for a well-deserved rest and remanning. During this respite all the senior commanders in the division, including Sladen Bradley, were rotated. Having won a second star, Bradley returned to routine assignments and retired disabled in 1956. Gerry Kelleher rose to one star. Gilbert Check and Henry Britt retired as colonels.[47]

The 24th Infantry remained segregated throughout the summer. Britt was succeeded by an able infantry officer, Richard W. Whitney (University of Akron, 1935), a paratrooper-commando who in World War II rose to command a regiment in the elite First Special Service Force. Whitney commanded for about two months, at which time he was promoted to 25th Division chief of staff, replacing Tom Dolvin, who was rotated and went on to three stars before retirement. Whitney was succeeded as commander of the 24th Infantry by the West Pointer (1935), the I Corps armor officer Thomas Gillis, who deactivated the unit on October 1, 1951.[48]\*

\* \* \*

---

\*The 24th Infantry was replaced on the line by the 14th Infantry, from Japan.

To accommodate the withdrawal of the 25th Division, Shrimp Milburn redeployed his forces on Line Wyoming. Shorty Soule's 3d Division shifted right to occupy the 25th Division sector. Charlie Palmer's 1st Cav relieved the ROK 9th Division elements on the left of the 3d Division. The ROK 9th, reconstituted as an independent division, shifted to the right of the 3d Division, tying in with the American 7th Division (of IX Corps) near Kumhwa.[49]

During these complicated shifts the CCF returned to occupy some strategically located hills in the Iron Triangle. When this was discovered, Van Fleet ordered Palmer and Soule to clear the hills to a point twenty miles north of Line Kansas, thereby maintaining a grip on the "battle line" Ridgway had decreed.

On June 22 Soule ordered Tom Yancey's 15th Infantry to clear Hills 682 and 717 in the dead center of the Iron Triangle. Yancey in turn gave the mission to Julius Levy's 1/15, which already had one company (A) outposting nearby Hill 528. It proved to be one of the toughest fights the 15th had yet encountered.[50]

Unavoidably delayed getting into position, Levy did not launch the attack until 9:30 A.M. He began with a two-company (B and C) attack on Hill 717. He met a "well-armed, well-led" enemy occupying "good defensive positions." It took most of the day to do it, but B and C companies finally cleared Hill 717 and dug in. Meanwhile, A Company, belatedly attacking from its positions on Hill 528, assaulted Hill 682. However, A Company got nowhere, and at 10:00 P.M. it was ordered to withdraw and join B and C companies in the 1/15 perimeter on Hill 717.

Later that evening the CCF on Hill 717 suddenly and violently counterattacked B and C companies. In close fighting in pitch-darkness, Levy's men fought heroically to repulse the attack and hold the hill. One private in B Company, Emory L. Bennett, mortally wounded, won a posthumous Medal of Honor. Four others in B Company and the C Company commander, Jack L. Dinkel, who was killed, won DSCs. Even so, the CCF drove B and C Companies from the hill. A Company, which had arrived too late to be of decisive help in the battle, covered the withdrawal.[51]

The shock of this encounter quickly dispelled the notion that I Corps had "cleared" the Iron Triangle of CCF. The enemy troops had obviously returned in force and meant to fight hard to hold at least the upper half of the triangle. They might even attempt to wrest back the lower half. Most forces on Line Wyoming were soon engaged in similar tough small-unit actions, fighting for control of various strategic hills in the Iron Triangle, a situation aptly described by one officer as a "fluid stalemate."[52]

During this standoff on Line Wyoming the Eighth Army rotation policy drastically denuded the 3d Division of its experienced subordinate leaders.

West Pointers William Harris and Saint St. Clair, of the Puerto Rican 65th Regiment, departed. Stripped of its experienced leadership and spirited volunteers, the 65th sank into a gradual decline that was to result, finally, in a scandalous bugout, after which the Army court-martialed ninety-two of its men. Tom Yancey and other veteran commanders in the 15th Infantry likewise were rotated. Clyde Baden, commander of the black 3/15, left in July. His replacement desegregated the outfit in October. Jim Boswell retained command of the 7th Infantry into the fall. Yancey rose to two stars, Harris and Boswell to one star, St. Clair and Baden retired as colonels.[53]

The 1st Cav Division was similarly denuded. The commander, Charlie Palmer, was rotated and went on (like his older brother, Williston) to four stars. The 5th Cav's crusty Marcel Crombez, then the oldest regimental commander in Korea (fifty), remained at his post until July. Having earned the distinction of commanding a regiment in Korea longer than any other officer, Crombez got one star before retirement in 1956. The 8th Cav's Bob Blanchard was also rotated in July and went on to one star. Ridgway's erratic protégé Dan Gilmer continued to command the 7th Cav for several more months until he was forced out by an inspector general's investigation. He retired in 1962, still a colonel.[54]

* * *

On the right of I Corps, in Bill Hoge's IX Corps sector, there were also some shifts on Line Wyoming. Babe Bryan's 24th Division, coming up from IX Corps reserve on June 23, replaced Buddy Ferenbaugh's 7th Division at Kumhwa, flanked on the left and right, respectively, by the ROK 2d and 6th divisions. Bryan remained in command of the 24th Division for many more months, but the 21st Infantry commander, Gines Perez, was rotated and went on to two stars. The 5th Infantry commander, Harry Wilson, was also rotated, replaced by Ridgway's planner and protégé Day Surles, who went to three stars. Wilson retired as a colonel.[55]

The 7th Division withdrew into IX Corps reserve at Line Kansas, above Chunchon, to rest and improve the Kansas Line fortifications. Ferenbaugh remained in command for many more months, but the 17th Infantry commander, Buffalo Bill Quinn, was rotated and went on to three stars. The 32d Infantry commander, Charles Mount, was rotated and rose to two stars. Almond's protégé Bill McCaffrey remained in command of the 31st Infantry for many more months and rose to three stars.[56]

## I V

Although Dean Acheson had been greatly encouraged by the Malik-Kennan talks, all efforts thereafter to establish a diplomatic channel to Peking failed. Lacking any positive contact with Peking or any further signals from Malik or any other Soviet source, the JCS, Ridgway, and Van Fleet began to think that perhaps Washington was being flimflammed; Malik had raised false hopes of a cease-fire merely to provide the CCF with time to regroup and launch another offensive. Accordingly, the military had second thoughts about the wisdom of Eighth Army permanently digging in on Lines Kansas and Wyoming.

Intense military planning discussions began in Washington, Tokyo, and Seoul. In the JCS Forrest Sherman still favored a northward advance of Eighth Army to a line from Pyongyang to Wonsan (the Korean waist). Joe Collins and Hoyt Vandenberg began to share that view. On June 20 the JCS asked Ridgway what he thought about a change in his directive which would remove "any undue restrictions upon your ability to exploit tactically the current situation" and asked for his military views for a deeper penetration into North Korea. In reply Ridgway agreed that the JCS restriction which limited Eighth Army at Lines Kansas and Wyoming should be removed. Meanwhile, Ridgway had directed Van Fleet to analyze all factors entailed in an advance to the waist along a line Pyongyang–Wonsan, with the "main effort" along the Seoul–Pyongyang axis. He also passed along Van Fleet's request for ten more 155-mm and eight-inch artillery battalions.[57]

\* \* \*

On Saturday evening, June 23, Jacob Malik made a scheduled address over the UN radio network. The occasion was prosaic and routine: the thirteenth broadcast in a UN-sponsored series entitled *The Price of Peace.* The few people monitoring the broadcast heard the usual Soviet propaganda diatribe about Washington's post-World War II policies and the usual sanctimonious defense of Moscow's policies, which merely sought "peaceful coexistence" with the West. But the concluding words of Malik's address brought the monitors to the edge of their seats.[58]

The Soviet Union will continue its struggle to strengthen peace and avert a new world war. The peoples of the Soviet Union believe that it is possible to defend the cause of peace. The Soviet peoples further believe that the most acute problem of the present day—the problem of the armed conflict in Korea—could also be settled.

This would require the readiness of the parties to enter on the path of a peaceful settlement of the Korean question. The Soviet peoples believe that as a first step discussions should be started between the belligerents for a cease-fire and

armistice providing for the mutual withdrawal of forces from the 38th Parallel.
Can such a step be taken?

I think it can, provided there is a sincere desire to put an end to the bloody
fighting in Korea.

I think that, surely, it is not too great a price to pay in order to achieve peace
in Korea.[59]

This part of the Malik speech was a public declaration of that which he
had told Kennan privately three weeks earlier. Since (as Acheson put it) Malik
would not dare extend the overture without prior Moscow clearance, Washington regarded his words "as official as it was possible to be." But owing to
the vitriol in the earlier part of the speech and the suspicion in the Pentagon
that it might be a flimflam, there was doubt about Moscow's sincerity.
Nonetheless, Acheson responded immediately with a cautious public statement, in the State Department's name:[60]

If Mr. Malik's broadcast means that the communists are now willing to end the
aggression in Korea, we are, as we have been, ready to play our part in bringing
an end to hostilities and in assuring against their resumption. But the tenor of Mr.
Malik's speech again raises the question as to whether this is more than propaganda. If it is more than propaganda, adequate means of discussing an end to the
conflict are available.[61]

The JCS got off an urgent message to Ridgway, passing along Malik's
remarks. Ridgway later wrote that he found the prospect of a cease-fire "not
unwelcome."[62] He sent his trusted planner Day Surles to Korea to confer with
Van Fleet about the details of the proposed "battle line" and demilitarized
zone and made plans to go to Korea for that purpose himself.[63] Meanwhile,
Ridgway was concerned that upon hearing the news, Eighth Army might let
down its guard. In a message to Van Fleet to be distributed to "all commanders," Ridgway said he knew nothing more than the gist of the Malik address.
However, "two things should be recalled," he cautioned the commanders:

One is the well-earned reputation for duplicity and dishonesty possessed by the
USSR, the other is the slowness with which deliberative bodies such as the [UN]
Security Council produce positive action. I desire that you personally assure
yourself that all elements of your command are made aware of the danger of such
a relaxation of effort and that you insist on an intensification rather than a diminution of the United Nations' action in this theater.[64]

Washington anxiously awaited a reaction to Malik's broadcast from Peking. It came within two days. Quoting a Peking newspaper editorial endorsing
the Malik proposal, Peking Radio stated, in effect, that "if the Americans
wanted peace they could accept all of the many offers made by the commu-

nists" (i.e., prior propaganda broadcasts demanding Formosa, a seat in the UN, etc.). The "tone" of the broadcast was reasonable and reassuring—far less strident and anti-American than the usual Peking broadcasts and Malik's speech. Yet when Ambassador Kirk attempted to communicate with the Peking Embassy in Moscow, he was again rebuffed, leaving the State Department baffled.[65]

If ever there was a time when direct, forceful, and continuous presidential direction of policy was required, this was it. Truman had approved NSC-48/5, but the available evidence suggests that he had been isolated from the vigorous follow-up measures to seek a negotiated settlement. For example, on the basis of his desk diary entries, there was a clear implication that he was not informed of the June 5 Malik–Kennan talk until June 21. "Had a session with the Sec. of State and Sec. of Defense," Truman wrote, "on a *most* important matter. Russians are tired of the Korean affair and want to quit. Well, we'll see."[66]

Truman, of course, had been diverted by the unprecedented public furor over the MacArthur firing and the challenges MacArthur had leveled at him in the MacArthur hearings and elsewhere. While the hearings were in progress, the White House had been busy leaking documents unfavorable to MacArthur, such as a transcript of the Wake Island meetings, in which the general had assured the president and the Washington contingent that the Chinese would not enter the Korean War but that if they did, he would slaughter them with air power. Totally absorbed in "winning" this important political contest with MacArthur, Truman may not have given the Malik peace overtures his utmost attention.[67]

Truman was in a feisty mood. In his view his administration had weathered the MacArthur challenge without fatal damage and, in fact, had "won" in the Senate hearings. The attempts by the right-wing elements to use MacArthur to beat up Truman were not working. Moreover, the emotional binge was subsiding. MacArthur "is now a 'drug on the market,' " Truman wrote with satisfaction in his diary on June 21. MacArthur's tour of Texas had been "a dud."[68]

Truman had several important speaking engagements on his calendar, the most important of which was the dedication of an Air Force research and development center in Tullahoma, Tennessee, on June 25, two days after the Malik radio broadcast. Although the Russian had concluded his broadcast with an olive branch of sorts, the earlier vitriol in his remarks had greatly angered Truman. So had a recent book-length speech by Joseph McCarthy, attacking Truman's idol George Marshall as a Communist traitor. As a result, Truman decided rather parochially to counterattack both the Russians and the Republicans in the same speech. "I'm going to tear the Russians and Republicans apart," he wrote his wife, Bess, who was in Independence. "Call a spade just what it is and tell Malik if Russia wants peace, peace is available and has been since 1945."[69]

He was as good as his word. Giving Malik tit for tat, he branded the rulers of the Soviet Union as "absolute tyrants" who were still trying to divide Washington from its allies and conquer the free world piece by piece. His right-wing Republican critics were scarcely better. The foreign policy they advocated, particularly for Asia, would abet the Soviet goal of separating Washington from its allies. The Republicans wanted the administration to "play Russian roulette with the foreign policy of the United States—with all the chambers of the pistol loaded." And so on.[70]

Considering that the Kremlin was apparently becoming the leading player in the tedious game of coaxing Peking to the negotiating table, Truman's critics would wonder at the appropriateness of these remarks. Where a statesmanlike pronouncement was clearly called for, Truman had delivered a childlike tantrum. But in fact, the remarks may have reflected a new and politically dangerous dilemma confronting the administration. It sincerely, perhaps desperately, wanted an end to the war in Korea, but in view of the fury of the right-wing Republican attacks, it dared not appear to be "soft on communism" or to engage in "appeasement."

Dean Acheson had apparently prevailed on Truman to include some sort of "response" to Malik's olive branch. Like Malik, Truman concluded his tantrum with a cautious overture:

We are ready to join in a peaceful settlement in Korea now, just as we have always been. But it must be a real settlement which fully ends the aggression and restores peace and security to the area and to the gallant people of Korea.

In Korea and in the rest of the world we must be ready to take any steps which truly advance us toward world peace. But we must avoid like the plague rash actions which would take unnecessary risks of world war or weak actions which would reward aggression.[71]

The next day, June 26, Dean Acheson pointedly repeated in public the administration's willingness to settle the war more or less at the 38th Parallel. Appearing before the House Foreign Affairs Committee in support of the foreign aid bill, he stated that Washington's military objectives in Korea would be satisfied if the Communists withdrew behind the 38th Parallel and gave adequate guarantees against a renewal of aggression. Acheson's statement appeared to be an aside, but no doubt it was a calculated signal aimed at Moscow and Peking.[72]

Meanwhile, Acheson had directed Ambassador Kirk in Moscow to call at the Soviet Foreign Office for certain "clarifications" of Malik's remarks. After meeting with Deputy Foreign Minister Andrei Gromyko late on June 27, Kirk, who believed Malik's remarks to be "a significant new turn in Soviet approach to Korea," cabled Acheson the gist of the talk. It appeared to be another Politburo signal.

Gromyko said that Malik's speech did indeed reflect official Soviet policy and insisted that the Soviet Union was sincere in desiring peace in Korea. The best way of achieving it, Gromyko suggested pointedly, was for the "belligerents" to meet on the battlefield and begin discussions. He advised that the conferees should limit such discussion to military matters only, avoiding "political or territorial" considerations.[73]

Even though Gromyko professed not to know Peking's attitude and his remarks were somewhat vague and evasive, Dean Acheson and his senior advisers were cautiously optimistic. Others, however, were not. Some continued to believe the Communists were buying time with all this talk of a possible armistice for the CCF to build up for another offensive. Still others, reflecting the fear of the administration's being again labeled "soft on communism," questioned whether it was wise or desirable to accept so eagerly what amounted to "Communist terms" for peace talks when the UN forces were gaining the dominant military position. It might be better to continue—or even to escalate—military force on the battlefield, enhancing Washington's bargaining position to the point that it could dictate its own "terms."

A few raised moral questions. The opposing military commanders might arrange a cease-fire and work out an armistice to include a truce "line," an exchange of POWs, a prohibition on reinforcements and other military matters, but what about the complex, unresolved political issues, such as Washington's long-term avowed aim of a free, unified, and democratic Korea? Was Washington now to abandon that high-minded political goal merely for the sake of an early end to the bloodshed? At the very least, what about an absolute political guarantee that neither the NKPA nor the CCF would again invade South Korea? Could military commanders also resolve that matter? If there were no such political guarantee, then the UN effort in Korea to date would have been largely in vain.[74]

Within the State Department, Arthur B. Emmons III, officer in charge of Korean affairs, summed up the case for caution and toughness:

I think it essential that, despite assurances from the communist side, we should be most reluctant to break off hostilities until as sound a basis as possible has been laid for the negotiation of a political settlement in Korea which will not prove a duplication of the fruitless efforts we have made in the past to accomplish our political objectives in Korea. Furthermore it seems to me that the United States, together with the United Nations, has an inescapable and grave moral responsibility to the people of Korea that from the tremendous sacrifices and destruction which has been occasioned to them by this war we will, to the best of our ability, provide for the realization of those aspirations for unification and independence which are, for them, of such overwhelming importance.[75]

By this time Dean Acheson's thirst to achieve a quick and simple end to the fighting in Korea was nearly insatiable. The Gromyko proposal seemed to offer the best bet. Gromyko had specifically ruled out "political and territorial" matters. So be it. The larger political issues could be thrashed out later, perhaps in some other forum. Acheson's position was tersely summed up by Dean Rusk in a memo: "There are advantages from the U.S. point of view in having the Korean problem settled for the short run on a military basis without involvement of a wide range of complex political issues now confronting us in the Pacific."[76]

Acheson and Rusk decided that the best way to "respond" to Gromyko's suggestions was to have Ridgway make a public statement, extending an invitation to the military commanders in Korea to meet at some mutually satisfactory place. On June 28 Rusk and the State Department director of Northeast Asian affairs, U. Alexis Johnson, met with the JCS to gain its approval for that course of action.[77] Omar Bradley and Joe Collins* concurred, but surprisingly, Hoyt Vandenberg registered very strong objections. Johnson's notes of the meeting recorded that:

General Vandenberg stated that he was "unalterably opposed" to . . . a message from General Ridgway to the opposing command. He felt that the US should use the Soviet proposal as a springboard to place the onus on the North Koreans and the Chinese, and that any message from Ridgway would, in effect, mean that we are asking for peace, instead of the communists. He stated that we are now hurting the communists badly and that any respite given them by an armistice would only permit them to build up to start fighting again. . . .

We should in no sense be put in the position of suing for peace at this point or stopping the fighting just when it was beginning to hurt the other side [and] we stand to lose more than we gain by the proposed statement by Ridgway.[79]

Bradley and Collins rebutted Vandenberg. Collins argued that Eighth Army was "now on a good defensive line in Korea and that we should take advantage of this apparently possible opportunity to stop the fighting." Stating that he believed the Soviets "mean this" and that Gromyko's proposal for a meeting limited to military commanders discussing only military matters was a face-saving device for Peking, Bradley also urged an end to the fighting. "Although an armistice might give the enemy a chance to build up," he said, and "we might continue to drain his resources by continued hostilities, we could not ignore the effect on the will of our people and other contributing UN member nations to continued support of the hostilities, if we in effect turned down what appeared to be an opportunity to end the hostilities."[80]

Neither Bradley nor Collins raised the subject directly, but both were influenced by the shocking human cost of the Korean War to date. American

---

*Forrest Sherman was absent—en route to Tokyo.[78]

Army statisticians had calculated that in the twelve months of war ending June 25, 1951, there had been a total of 1,960,354 battle casualties. They broke the total figure down thus:

| | |
|---|---|
| CCF: | 600,000 (dead, wounded, captured) |
| NKPA: | 600,000 (dead, wounded, captured) |
| ROK civilians: | 469,000 (170,000 dead) |
| ROK Army: | 212,554 (21,625 dead) |
| U.S.: | <u>78,800</u> (21,300 dead) |
| | 1,960,354[81] |

After further discussion the JCS unanimously approved the State Department proposal that Ridgway respond to the Communist broadcast. Thereafter JCS and State staffers drafted a preliminary version of the message. Later in the day the JCS met with George Marshall to revise and approve the message. The JCS transmitted the message to Ridgway the same afternoon to obtain his comments.[82]*

Ridgway had flown to Korea on June 26. He toured the front and later in the day met with Van Fleet, with whom Ridgway's planner Day Surles had been conferring about the possible cease-fire, the "battle line," the demilitarized zone, and other matters.[84]

By that time Van Fleet had nearly fulfilled Ridgway's desire to establish the "battle line" in the Iron Triangle twenty miles north of Line Kansas. That is, the 1st Cav and 3d division forces were engaged in a "fluid stalemate," fighting CCF forces for control of key hills in the center of the Iron Triangle which were about twenty miles north of Line Kansas. In addition, Van Fleet, complying with Ridgway's recent instructions, had studied a possible Eighth Army advance (to be code-named Overwhelming) to the Korean waist or to a Pyongyang–Wonsan line.[85]

All things considered, Van Fleet still did not then believe a further Eighth Army advance to the north was feasible or desirable. Intelligence indicated that while the CCF and NKPA had been very badly hurt in April and May, the Communist forces had recovered sufficiently to be able to inflict heavy casualties on Eighth Army. They still had 459,200 troops (248,100 CCF; 211,100 NKPA). Three CCF armies (Twenty-seventh, Thirty-ninth, and

---

*Acheson wrote incorrectly in his memoirs that the Pentagon was "most reluctant" to be "tagged with" the responsibility for initiating the cease-fire talks. The statement must have been based on his recollection of Hoyt Vandenberg's initial dissent. The JCS historian could find no evidence in the JCS files to support Acheson's recollection. To the contrary, Vandenberg excepted, senior Pentagon officials favored cease-fire talks and showed no evidence of ducking the responsibility for initiating them.[83]

Forty-second), comprising nine divisions, were at full strength and could counterattack Eighth Army almost at will. Moreover, the CCF was displaying every intention of firmly resisting any Eighth Army advance beyond the Iron Triangle. It was erecting a formidable line of fortifications (bunkers, tank traps, gun emplacements) all the way from Kaesong to Kumsong and bringing up unprecedented amounts of artillery. The CCF Air Force continued to grow; at any time it might be unleashed against Eighth Army. In sum, Van Fleet believed that unless there were a "major deterioration" of the enemy or an unexpected further withdrawal to the north, he would prefer that Eighth Army sit tight on Kansas–Wyoming.[86]*

Ridgway fully concurred. An all-out Eighth Army attack to the Korean waist under existing conditions would almost certainly incur a prohibitive cost in American casualties. Even a limited advance (five, ten, or twenty miles) to improve the army's defensive posture, disrupt a possible CCF counterattack, or gain an edge in the possible cease-fire arrangement would not be worth the cost in American blood. It would be difficult to justify any further casualties for territory that would almost certainly be returned in an armistice. Eighth Army would hold on Lines Kansas and Wyoming and see what developed on the "talking" front.[88]

Back in Tokyo, Ridgway met with the GHQ staff to analyze the statement he was to issue to the opposing CCF and NKPA military commanders. Ridgway suggested several revisions in the statement, which were discussed in a telecon with senior Pentagon and State officials in the evening of June 28, Washington time. One important goal was to word it in such a way that indicated the Communists, not the UN, had taken the initiative for the talks and yet do so without causing the Chinese to lose face. Omar Bradley believed that Ridgway's version was too tough, that "it unnecessarily involved questions of Communist Chinese prestige to a degree that might well jeopardize any possibility that there might be that armistice talks could be developed." After toning down the statement, the JCS did, however, include Ridgway's sensible suggestion that a specific place for the meeting be suggested.[89]

The final version of the statement, approved by President Truman, was transmitted to Ridgway shortly after noon on June 29, Washington time:

---

*Partly as a result of his own imprecise language in subsequent public statements, Van Fleet's exact views on taking Eighth Army farther north were often confused. To state these views simply, on May 28 he favored a deep penetration of North Korea (the amphibious landing of the 1st Marine Division at Tongchon and linkup with IX Corps) and believed it would destroy the CCF and NKPA, but by June 10 he preferred to stand on the Kansas and Wyoming lines unless the CCF withdrew or "deteriorated" or Eighth Army was heavily reinforced.[87]

Message to the Commander in Chief, Communist Forces in Korea. As Commander in Chief of the United Nations Command I have been instructed to communicate to you the following:

I am informed that you may wish a meeting to discuss an armistice providing for the cessation of hostilities and all acts of armed force in Korea, with adequate guarantees for the maintenance of such armistice.

Upon receipt of word from you that such a meeting is desired I shall be prepared to name my representative. I would also at that time suggest a date at which he could meet with your representative. I propose that such a meeting could take place aboard a Danish hospital ship [*Jutlandia*] in Wonsan Harbor.[90]

The JCS instructed Ridgway to release the statement almost immediately: by 6:00 P.M. on June 29, Washington time (8:00 A.M. on June 30, Tokyo time). Separate copies were transmitted directly to UN Secretary-General Lie and Ambassador Muccio in Seoul to give to Syngman Rhee.[91]

When the statement was issued, all UN governments with forces in Korea, save one, breathed a collective sigh of relief. The single exception, of course, was the ROK government in Seoul. Rhee was furious. When Muccio met with him and his senior officials, Rhee, employing "far fetched" and "irrelevant" language, threatened all manner of imprudent actions. Muccio was able to calm the group and to talk some sense by assuring that the proposed meetings would be purely "military," not "political," and that the ROKs would have a representative at the talks. Rhee finally consented to go along, provided that Washington agreed to five conditions, one of them being that the "actual front" (or current battle line), *not* the 38th Parallel, would be the ultimate line of demarcation between North and South Korea.[92]

## V

Within about thirty hours Peking Radio responded positively to the Ridgway statement. There were, in fact, several replies or what could be interpreted as replies. All were conciliatory, lacking the usual anti-American propaganda or conditions for talks, such as a seat in the UN or that Formosa be turned over to Peking.[93]

The several replies posed the problem of which should be adopted as the "official" one. Ridgway chose one and urged the chiefs to use it in their deliberations. He flashed the text of the Peking Radio broadcast to the Pentagon:

Peking. Here is important news from the Korean front. After consultations held today between General Kim Il Sung, Commander-in-Chief of the Korean Army, and General Peng Teh-huai, Commander-in-Chief of the Chinese People's Volunteers, a joint notice was sent to General Ridgway, Commander-in-Chief of the United Nations forces, in reply to the broadcast message from General Ridgway on June 30 in which he expressed willingness to dispatch delegates to hold ceasefire talks with our delegates. The contents of the notice are as follows:

General Ridgway, Commander-in-Chief of United Nations forces: Your broadcast message of June 30, regarding peace talks, has been received. We are authorized to tell you that we agree to suspend military activities and to hold peace negotiations, and that our delegates will meet with yours.

We suggest, in regard to the place for holding talks, that such talks be held at Kaesong, on the 38th Parallel.

If you agree to this, our delegates will be prepared to meet your delegates between July 10 and 15, 1951.

Signed, Kim Il Sung, Commander-in-Chief of the Korean People's Army, and Peng Teh-huai, Commander-in-Chief of the Chinese People's Volunteers.[94]

This message from Peking contained several features that Ridgway did not like. The most important of these was the clause "we agree to suspend military activities and to hold peace negotiations." In a follow-up cable to the JCS Ridgway stated: "Their intent is clear that military activities shall be suspended from the beginning of armistice negotiations." To Ridgway this raised the possibility that the Communists were not sincere, that the "talks" might be a smoke screen to buy time for the CCF to build up for a new offensive. In passing along the message, he told the JCS that a suspension of military activities to conduct talks "might gravely prejudice safety and security of UN forces," that he considered a suspension of hostilities "wholly unacceptable," and that "unless otherwise instructed," he would "categorically reject" that provision.[95]

To reinforce his case, Ridgway included ten recent intelligence tidbits indicating a continuing and substantial CCF military buildup. Some of these items were farfetched, such as an unverified report of a CCF "mechanized army" assembling near Koksan. Moreover, he argued, the proposed delay in the meeting to July 10 or 15 could give the CCF a further military advantage: rainy weather. He summarized his case this way:

Intelligence to date reveals a clearly developing pattern of capability to exercise an increasing offensive potential at any time from July 10 on. It is to be expected that, if exercised, optimum advantage would be taken of weather. It is further to be expected that enemy will intensify his efforts to increase this offensive potential throughout the period of negotiations, if conducted as he suggests they be conducted. If negotiations so conducted, we would be incapable of checking his military activities in Korea, particularly his preparations for major offensive action by ground and air.[96]

Ridgway closed his cable to the JCS with an urgent appeal that it support his rejection of a cease-fire. Upon receiving that approval, Ridgway said, he would broadcast a second message to Peking (rejecting a cease-fire) and "accepting Kaesong as the location," but "urging that the date be advanced."[97]

\* \* \*

The Truman administration now appeared to have within its grasp that which its allies and the vast majority of the American people wanted and that which it had adopted as official policy (in NSC-48/5). But actually to engage in negotiations posed or reposed new and old dangers. Among them:

• That, as Ridgway and others insisted, the proposed talks might be merely a CCF trick to throw Eighth Army off guard and to buy time to prepare for another major offensive.
• That even if the Communists were sincere in seeking an end to the fighting, they might use the negotiations as a propaganda forum to the detriment of the United States, dragging out the talks for months or even years, causing Washington to lose face among Orientals and others.
• That a negotiated settlement of the Korean War, as opposed to a clear-cut "victory," could be interpreted as "appeasement" of communism and weaken the resolve of the free world to "resist the spread of communism," thereby undermining America's rearmament program (per NSC-68) and the buildup of NATO forces.
• That notwithstanding the swelling opposition to the Korean War in the United States and elsewhere, a negotiated settlement was certain to draw renewed charges from right-wing critics that the Truman administration was "soft on communism" and had even "made a deal" with Communists.
• That negotiations with the Communists would be violently opposed by Syngman Rhee and his supporters, who might attempt to sabotage the talks or refuse to abide by the terms of a negotiated settlement.

For these reasons, and others, Washington approached the negotiations in an ambivalent frame of mind. On the one hand, it sincerely sought an end to the fighting. On the other hand, it was suspicious, distrustful, and cautious. Owing to the latter attitudes, its critics would argue that in the early stages it made two crucial blunders, which at the least soured the negotiations and at the worst doomed any hope of an early end to the fighting.[98]

First, it adopted Ridgway's position that the fighting must continue during the negotiations until a satisfactory armistice had been arrived at and signed, sealed, and delivered.

Secondly, it reneged on the public declarations by Dean Acheson and Trygve Lie of a willingness to settle the war on or near the 38th Parallel.

As to the first, the critics would contend that the decision to continue the fighting was a blunder because it did not in any sense give the Communists the benefit of the doubt. That is, it did not consider seriously the view that Peking had had enough in Korea and that it sincerely wanted to stop the fighting then and there. The critics would point out (in hindsight) that the Communist "buildup" proved to be purely "defensive," that they did not, in fact, ever again launch another major offensive. Hence the distrust of Communist motives in this respect was misplaced, and the decision to continue the fighting prolonged the bloodshed to little purpose and launched the negotiations in a needlessly belligerent atmosphere.

As to the second, the critics would contend that the decision to renege on a settlement at or near the 38th Parallel was a blunder because it failed to appreciate the important symbolic significance of the 38th Parallel to Peking and Pyongyang. The publicly expressed willingness of Washington and the UN to settle on or near the parallel may have decisively influenced the Communists to enter into negotiations. For Washington and the UN to promise to settle on the 38th Parallel and then to withdraw the promise, the critics argued, was not only stupid but also reprehensible. It placed the Communists in the position of having been tricked with such a great "loss of face" that it would be difficult, if not impossible, for them to negotiate in complete trust and without demanding at the least offsetting concessions.

Washington's case for reneging on a settlement at the 38th Parallel, the critics would argue, was weak and muddled. The main reason was to hold on to the "good defensive positions" above the parallel (Lines Kansas and Wyoming) so that after the armistice had been signed and American forces had withdrawn, the ROKs could create a Maginot Line from which to repel possible future CCF or NKPA attacks. But it was completely unrealistic to believe that no matter how well equipped or trained, ROKs alone could ever repel another determined CCF or NKPA invasion. In such an event Washington or the UN would again have to come to the rescue. Hence a modest UN or American police or "trip wire" force based at the 38th Parallel itself would have sufficed for purposes of deterring another Communist invasion.

\* \* \*

Upon receiving the various responses from Peking, Washington's first and most urgent task was to concur in Ridgway's recommendation to continue the fighting without creating such an issue over it that Peking would back off from the negotiations. This was achieved by complex semantic trickery. Rather than accept as "official" the Peking response calling for an immediate cease-fire that Ridgway had forwarded and recommended, Washington either found or concocted another "response" which did not specify an immediate cease-fire. The version selected as "official" was cabled to Ridgway with a confusing but pointed explanation:

The version transmitted in Mandarin from Peking, as translated in Washington before Peking broadcast in English, is in agreement with version later transmitted in English from Peking, and is accepted as official by State and Defense. It reads as follows:

Your statement of June 30 this year concerning peace talks has been received. We are authorized to inform you that we agree to meet your representative for conducting talks concerning cessation of military action and establishment of peace. We propose that the place of meeting be in the area of Kaesong on the 38th Parallel. If you agree, our representatives are prepared to meet your representatives between July 10 and 15, 1951.[99]

Along with this message the JCS cabled explicit instructions to Ridgway to continue the fighting. "There must be no relaxation in military effort on our part," the chiefs ordered, "until proper arrangements for cessation of hostilities have been agreed upon as contained in armistice terms." In framing his reply to Peking, Ridgway was not to "appear eager" to advance the date of the talks. He was to signal Washington's position on continuing the fighting with this sentence: "Since agreements on armistice terms has to precede cessation of hostilities, delay in initiating the meetings and in reaching agreement will prolong the fighting and increase the losses."[100]

Washington's second task was to find some way to soften the blow to be inflicted by its decision to renege on a settlement on or near the 38th Parallel. The JCS advised Ridgway that any mention of the 38th Parallel in connection with a meeting place "must be avoided." Furthermore:

If the communist commander refers to statements attributed to United States Government officials that the United States is prepared to accept a settlement on the 38th Parallel, you should take the position that such statements are not applicable to an armistice in the field but are properly the subject for governmental negotiations as to a political settlement. Further, you should state that in any event the military arrangements you propose involve certain areas under communist military control south of the 38th Parallel and certain areas under UN control north thereof. The net result, while military in character, does not prejudice political and territorial questions which would be for further consideration by appropriate authorities.[101]

Ridgway drafted a new message to Kim Il Sung and Peng Teh-huai for release in Tokyo at 2:30 P.M. on July 3. He proposed a preliminary meeting of "representatives" (or low-ranking liaison officers) to set the stage for the regular or more high ranking delegates: "I have received your reply to my message of 30 June. I am prepared for my representatives to meet yours at Kaesong on July 10, or at an earlier date if your representatives complete their preparations before that date. Since agreement on Armistice terms has to precede cessation of hostilities, delay in initiating the meetings and in reaching agreement will prolong the fighting and increase the losses.[102]*

Washington—and Ridgway—"won" the first round in the long-distance negotiations. In its reply the following day, July 4, Peking made no further reference to a cease-fire during the "talks." The "fighting," such as it was, would continue. Furthermore, Peking agreed to advance the date of the first meeting. The message from Peking stated:

General Ridgway, Commander-in-Chief of the U.N. Forces: Your reply of July 3 to us has been received. In order to guarantee effectively steps regarding various processes for the first conference of representatives of both sides, we agree to the dispatching of three liaison officers by each side to hold a preparatory conference in the Kaesong area as you proposed. If you agree to our proposal for setting the date for the conference of liaison officers as July 8, we will notify you of further business preparations for the meeting of liaison officers from both sides.[103]

Over the next two days, July 5 and 6, Ridgway and the two Communist leaders exchanged several more messages concerning the details of the time and place of the meeting of the liaison officers. All parties agreed that these low-level representatives would conduct a preliminary meeting on July 8 at Kaesong to arrange details for meetings of the senior delegates. Both sides also agreed to take steps to ensure the safe-conduct of the representatives.[104]

\* \* \*

As these cautious and preliminary steps proceeded, the Truman administration made what its critics described as another major blunder. Rather than send to Tokyo or Seoul a senior and expert political negotiator, skilled at dealing with Communists, such as George Kennan or Charles ("Chip") Bohlen, to operate freely behind the scenes and make on-the-spot decisions, it established an awesomely complex, inflexible, and virtually unworkable chain of command to conduct the negotiations. The UN negotiators in Korea would clear in advance all proposed bargaining positions and decisions with Ridgway. He would, in turn, clear all proposed positions and decisions with Washington. There the proposed positions and decisions would be thrashed out in joint meetings of the JCS and senior State Department officers. Then, finally, most of the proposed positions and decisions would be cleared by the White House and, in some instances, with other governments.

Although Ridgway ostensibly was to be merely a "relay station" in the cumbersome machinery, in fact, he would assume a far larger role. As the senior man "on the scene" he rightly believed his views on the proposed positions and decisions should be known and weighed in Washington. Accordingly, Ridgway himself established in Tokyo a special task force of his best and

---

\*The message concluded with details of exactly how Ridgway's liaison officers would go to Kaesong for this preliminary meeting.

brightest military advisers to review the incoming traffic from the UN negotiating team in Korea and to draft position papers and proposed courses of action for relay to Washington. This introduced yet another layer of bureaucracy and contributed substantially to what soon became an enormous flow of paperwork to and from Korea, Tokyo, and Washington.

In two wars Ridgway had proved to be beyond any doubt one of the great battlefield generals in American history. He also had had more experience than most general officers in "diplomatic" assignments: first in Latin America; later as an Army representative at the United Nations. In diplomatic settings he was suave, smart, and perfectly at ease. On the surface his battlefield and diplomatic experience suggested that Ridgway was ideally suited for the role he assumed during the negotiations.

This was not necessarily the case. The qualities that made Ridgway a great general—integrity, passion, idealism, awesome determination, force and drive, unflinching confidence in the correctness of his views—were not necessarily the qualities that made for a good negotiator. Ridgway was, in fact, utterly lacking in flexibility and the ability to compromise. Moreover, as he had demonstrated on several occasions in World War II, he would not hesitate to "lay his career on the line" to gain his way.

In his UN assignment in the postwar years Ridgway had often gone toe to toe in meetings with his Russian counterparts. This experience had transformed him into an implacable Communist hater, the most hawkish of hawks. He had found the Russians devious and dishonest and worse. His recent experience on the battlefield in Korea had intensified these feelings to the absolute limit. He still believed that Korea was merely the beginning of World War III, that the proposed negotiations were a Moscow trick, that at any instant the Russians might attack Eighth Army or even Japan. He was thus in no humor for compromise or conciliation. Since that was basically Washington's aim, Ridgway may have been the wrong man to have in Tokyo exerting influence over proposed positions and decisions.

On the eve of the first meeting of the senior delegates Ridgway drafted two documents, a "guidance" memo for the UN negotiators and a proposed press release.

In his guidance memo Ridgway stressed that the basic American premise was "implacable opposition to communism." The delegates were to lead "from strength not weakness"; at the same time they had to be very patient because "lengthy and frequent propaganda speeches would be inevitable." The wisest course would be to ignore them. However, delegates would take care not to cause the Orientals to lose face and would try to leave them a "Golden Bridge" of withdrawal. Whenever possible, delegates would exploit opportunities to "detach Communist China from the Soviet Union bloc" or "to increase tension between them." In conclusion he stated that if the delegates could cap the military defeat of the Communists in Korea with a successful armistice, "history may record that communist military aggression reached its high water mark in Korea, and that thereafter communism itself began its recession in Asia."[105]

The other document, the press release, was to be issued at the opening of the negotiations at Kaesong. It was MacArthuresque in tone. Its apparent purpose was to turn CCF soldiers and Chinese citizens against their Communist leaders and bring them back into the American orbit. Ridgway wrote:

In the long series of communist acts which have brought dissention, disaster, and death to the world, there had been none more tragic than the conflict which has set Chinese and American soldiers against each other. With its compelling fear of the truth, communist imperialism has sought repeatedly to obscure the long and loyal record of friendship between the Chinese and American peoples. To fabricate a pretext for sacrificing Chinese soldiers as instruments of their aggression in Korea, the communists have tried to convince the Chinese people that the United States planned an invasion of Chinese territory. The enormity of this falsehood is exceeded only by the sinister significance of the objective it was designed to cloak."

And so on for three more long, scathing paragraphs.[106]

It is doubtful that a less appropriate press release on the eve of these delicate negotiations could have been conceived. Fortunately Ridgway had sent it on to the JCS for prior clearance. The JCS rejected it promptly, explaining, "At the maximum, it might well lead to a breakdown of negotiations; at minimum, it would have undesirable domestic and international political repercussions." In any case, a statement of that type should be made only on "highest government level."[107]

This was merely a foretaste. In the coming days Washington was to discover that Ridgway could be as difficult as the Communists, and at times, more so. Washington therefore was to find it necessary to negotiate with not merely one stubborn adversary but two. The emergence of Ridgway as a strong "third party" greatly complicated and prolonged the negotiations and on some occasions very nearly led to their collapse.

\* \* \*

For UN ground forces, especially the U.S. Army, the first year of the Korean War had been a very tough—at times desperate—fight almost without respite. Seldom in modern Army history had American infantry fought for so long with so little in such miserable terrain and weather. The battle and non-battle casualties had been heavy. Had it not been for battlefield medical innovations (MASH units, air evacuation, R and R in Japan) both categories of casualties would have been far heavier.

The onset of the negotiations at the end of the first year marked a radical change in the character of the ground war. There would be no more dramatic events such as the Inchon landing or the withdrawal from the Chosin Reservoir. Nor would there be any grand, sweeping maneuvers. The war was to become a static affair, not unlike the trench warfare of World War I, with the opposing forces rooted near the 38th Parallel. The feats of UN airmen combating the ever growing CCF Air Force in MIG Alley would become the dominant news from Korea.

Notwithstanding the MacArthur hoopla, the majority of the American public turned firmly against the war. The lack of dramatic ground action—a stirring military resolution of the conflict—and the complex and tedious negotiations probably turned others against it. Not a few simply became bored with the war—or non-war—and turned their attention to other matters at home. The Korean conflict was gradually to slip from the front pages and, in due course, the public consciousness. It was to become The Forgotten War.

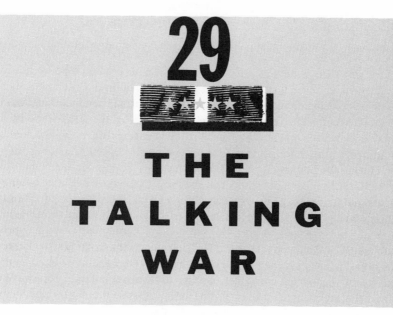

# THE
# TALKING
# WAR

## I

The senior delegates met for the first time at Kaesong on July 10. The UN team, headed by Ridgway's naval chief, Turner Joy, included Joy's deputy chief of staff, Arleigh Burke; the Eighth Army deputy chief of staff, Hank Hodes; FEAF vice commander Laurence C. Craigie; ROK I Corps commander Paik Sun Yup; and others. They confronted two senior CCF generals—Hsieh Fang and Teng Hua—and three senior NKPA generals: the NKPA chief of staff Nam Il, and Lee Sang Cho, and Chang Pyong San.[1]

Right off, the UN team realized it had been a mistake to agree to meet behind enemy lines at Kaesong. Although Ridgway had insisted that Kaesong be declared a "neutral zone," it was hardly that. The place teemed with armed CCF and NKPA soldiers. The UN members coming by road through Communist lines had to fly white flags and go through CCF checkpoints; those arriving by helicopters were met and escorted to the meetings by armed NKPA soldiers. The Western press was barred from Kaesong; the Communist press had free access. The Communist propaganda goal was clearly to create the impression that the UN had come to Kaesong, hat in hand, to surrender or to sue for peace.

The first task of the delegates was to establish an agenda. In keeping with Gromyko's advice to avoid political and territorial matters, Admiral Joy and his team came prepared to discuss three cardinal points: a truce line, exchange of POWs, and machinery to guarantee enforcement of the armistice. The Communist agenda included those three items, plus one other: "withdrawal of all armed forces of foreign countries from Korea." Since the UN team rightly viewed this item as a "political" matter to be discussed by heads of government in some forum after the armistice, Admiral Joy vigorously opposed its inclusion. Ominously and more important, in opening discussions the Communists specified that the truce line would be the 38th Parallel. Joy likewise vigorously opposed any specific line, insisting that the agenda wording be limited to the more general term "truce line."

During the first two days of discussions, July 10 and 11, the Communists were militarily precise and proper in the meetings, but their troops continued to manipulate access to Kaesong in order to milk the situation of maximum propaganda. The Western press remained barred; UN team members continued to be subjected to annoying procedural harassments. With approval from the JCS, Ridgway instructed Joy that unless the Communists corrected this situation instantly, he was to recess the talks. On July 12, when a UN press contingent was barred entry to Kaesong, Joy walked out, and Ridgway supported the action by denouncing the Communists in a radio broadcast from Tokyo. In response, the Communists backed down and admitted the Western press. The talks resumed on July 15.[2]

During the next several days the Communists pressed to keep the "withdrawal of foreign troops from Korea" on the agenda. Already hostile to the Communists, Ridgway requested permission from the JCS to break off the talks permanently if that particular item was not immediately struck. Shaken, the JCS instructed Ridgway to cool down, to do nothing to jeopardize the talks, and, if necessary, to counterpropose some vague, distant "machinery" to accommodate the point. In return, Ridgway hotly insisted to the JCS that Washington stop hedging and vacillating and stick firmly behind its announced public positions. "To undermine this in the slightest degree by any concession of any kind at this stage of our discussions would be instantly recognized and seized upon as a fundamental weakness and exploited to the fullest." In response, Washington backed down. Dean Acheson declared publicly that withdrawal of non-Korean troops was not an appropriate item for talks between military men. The JCS authorized Ridgway to stand firm and, if the talks did break down, to make certain the onus fell on the Communists.[3]

Foul weather prevented the UN team from reaching Kaesong on July 20. When the talks resumed the following day, the Communists exhibited a reluctance to get down to business. They proposed a recess until July 25, in order that "each side could reconsider the views presented by the other side." When he heard this news, Ridgway was again upset and suspicious. Believing that "unrelenting" military pressure might be required to keep the Communists at the bargaining table, he requested permission from the JCS to launch a highly publicized all-out bombing attack (140 bombers; 230 fighters) on Pyongyang. Somewhat aghast, the JCS denied permission, but when Ridgway appealed,

MacArthur-like, on the ground that the denial impinged on his responsibility to provide for the "security of UN forces," the JCS backed down and authorized the strike, although without publicity.[4]

Meanwhile, the talks resumed on July 25. That day the Communists agreed to drop the withdrawal of foreign troops from the agenda. In its place they proposed a more benign wording: "recommendations to the governments of the countries concerned on both sides." Viewing this as a substantial concession, Admiral Joy and Ridgway accepted it, as did Washington.[5]

When the conferees met again on July 26, the revised agenda was approved. It consisted of four main items: truce line, exchange of POWs, machinery for enforcing the armistice, and recommendations to governments. In view of the rocky beginnings, the UN team and Ridgway were heartened by this "progress." Passing the agenda on to Washington with some satisfaction, Ridgway concluded that the Communist delegation "desires to continue the negotiations as rapidly as possible."[6]

Washington, too, was pleased at the progress, but Seoul definitely was not. Syngman Rhee evidently had not expected any kind of agreement to emerge from the talks and was thus surprised and angry by the speedy adoption of the agenda. He instructed his delegate, Paik Sun Yup, to boycott further talks. Ambassador Muccio called on Rhee and persuaded him to get in line. Rhee agreed that Paik could return to the talks "for the time being," but Muccio cabled Acheson: "Whole incident is further indication President Rhee on blindly emotional grounds is attempting to sabotage armistice."[7]

While Paik was absent on July 27, the delegates began detailed discussions on the first item on the agenda, the truce line. In prior discussions the Communists had stressed that they would consider no other truce line than the 38th Parallel. Admiral Joy launched the formal discussions with a "rebuttal" of the Communist position and offered a map outlining a truce line running more or less along the existing battle line, from which a twenty-mile-wide DMZ would be established.[8]

It was obvious to the Communists from the detailed nature of Joy's presentation that the UN proposal was no mere bargaining position, but rather a reneging on publicly stated positions. When the delegates resumed talks the following day, the chief Communist spokesman, Nam Il, clearly shocked and angry, described the UN proposal as "incredible," "naive and illogical," and "absurd and arrogant." In a long speech laced with anti-West propaganda he denounced the UN military actions in Korea, then reproposed a truce line at the 38th Parallel, to include a twenty-kilometer-wide DMZ. In rebuttal, Joy characterized Nam Il's remarks as "inappropriate," "irrelevant," "discourteous," and "rude and groundless." Passing along the gist of that day's meeting to Washington, Ridgway commented: "Although it is too early to predict, the possibility exists that discussions may deadlock on the issue of the 38th Parallel.''[9]

He was correct. Day after day Nam Il and Admiral Joy made lengthy speeches, Nam Il arguing for the 38th Parallel, Joy for the existing battle line. Neither side would yield an inch. In keeping with his policy of maintaining "unrelenting" military pressure on the Communists, on July 30 Ridgway launched the JCS-approved unpublicized mass air attack on Pyongyang. Four hundred and forty-five FEAF and Marine aircraft took part in the raid, which inflicted enormous damage on the North Korean capital.[10]

The raid did nothing to advance the negotiations. Possibly in retaliation, on August 4 the Communists permitted (or initiated) a flagrant violation of the "neutral zone" at Kaesong. A full company of heavily armed CCF soldiers, marching in single file, passed within 300 yards of the UN team quarters. Furious, Ridgway ordered Joy to break off the talks, and he drafted a scathing denunciation of the Communists, demanding of them absolute guarantees that corrective action would be taken before he would permit Joy to return. The JCS approved the recess but instructed Ridgway to tone down his language in the radio broadcast. In response to Ridgway's broadcast, the Communists said the incident was inadvertent, assured Ridgway they would take corrective action "in order that our conference will not be obstructed by accidental side issues," and hoped he would instruct Joy to return.[11]

Ridgway was still not satisfied. He cabled the JCS that "indications multiply" that the Communists were deliberately using the armistice talks "for the purpose of gaining time in which to prepare for and to increase chance of success of major offensive action." He went on:

The discussions are between soldiers; half of them are Communists who understand only what they want to understand; who consider courtesy as concession and concession as weakness; who are uninhibited in repudiating their own solemn obligations; who view such obligations solely as a means for attaining their ends; who attained to power through murderous conspiracy and who remain in power by that and other equally infamous practices. To sit down with these men and deal with them as representatives of an enlightened and civilized people is to deride one's own dignity and to invite the disaster their treachery will inevitably bring upon us.

He would advise the UN team to meet the enemy on its own terms and "to employ such language and methods as those treacherous savages cannot fail to understand, and understanding, respect."[12]

Ridgway had prepared yet another broadcast, again denouncing the Communists and insisting that the Kaesong neutral zone be patrolled by a six-man UN-Communist team. If the Communists did not agree to this joint inspection team, he would "insist upon a new site" for the talks. Again aghast at Ridgway's anger and hawkishness, the Joint Chiefs of Staff told Ridgway that it seemed to them the Communist broadcast had met his demands and that it disapproved any talk of a new site: "To impose new conditions now would be difficult to justify in many important quarters."[13]

The war of words over "incidents" escalated. On August 8, while the talks were still in recess, the Communists accused the UN of two deliberate provocations. They claimed first that a ROK patrol had approached and fired at unarmed Communist soldiers in a neutral zone and, secondly, that a FEAF aircraft had attacked and destroyed a truck of the CCF delegation which was well marked with white panels and flags. Following a careful investigation, Ridgway correctly but hotly dismissed these charges as "completely without validity."[14]

The following day the Communists extended an olive branch, again urging Ridgway to instruct Joy to resume the talks. Inasmuch as they had taken steps to guarantee the neutrality of the zone at Kaesong, it was "inconceivable" that there would be any further violations unless Ridgway "should deliberately fabricate incidents as an excuse to terminate the armistice negotiations." For their part, the Communists piously claimed, they definitely would not "terminate the negotiations rashly and irresponsibly without going through the procedural steps of protest, investigation, consultation and settlement, should a similar failure on your part occur." The Communists concluded: "We continue to hope that you instruct your delegates to come to Kaesong to resume the conference."[15]

The talks resumed on August 10. The Communist insistence on a truce line at the 38th Parallel deadlocked the sessions. Admiral Joy, Ridgway told the JCS, "delivered firm speech rejecting 38 Parallel." The Communist response was a speech, "repeating well worn arguments for 38 Parallel," concluding that their position was "absolutely unshakable." An extraordinary scene ensued. Having reached a complete impasse on this issue, the two teams of delegates sat across the table in stony silence for two hours and eleven minutes.[16]

Again boiling mad, Ridgway recommended to the JCS that unless the Communists agreed to yield on the 38th Parallel and accept the present battle line (or to bypass that agenda item for another), the talks should be terminated within seventy-two hours.[17]

The JCS hastened to remind Ridgway that negotiations with Communists required time and utmost patience and that under no circumstances should he "break off" or even "indefinitely recess" the talks.

There is reason to believe [the JCS continued] that Communists expected us to agree on 38th Parallel, based upon Malik statement and public discussions here and elsewhere prior to Malik's statement [i.e., Acheson and Lie statements]. It will take time for Moscow and Peking to amend their position; we cannot yet assume that difference between your proposals and 38th Parallel is breaking point for Communists. . . . UN position on rejection of 38th Parallel remains entirely firm and you should anticipate no change in your instructions on that point.[18]

The delegations met daily at Kaesong from August 10 to August 22. The issue of the truce line remained the sole topic on the table, with neither side budging. On August 16, in an effort to break the deadlock, the senior delegates appointed a "subdelegation" to explore possible solutions. Hank Hodes and Arleigh Burke represented the UN. On August 21, when it was clear that the subcommittee itself might deadlock, the UN team proposed (for negotiating purposes) a Washington-approved "concession": The UN would accept the Communist proposal for a twenty-kilometer-wide DMZ rather than the JCS proposal for a twenty-mile-wide DMZ. Inasmuch as this would leave the Communist forces much closer to the 38th Parallel than the JCS proposal, they seemed to exhibit interest, leaving the UN team cautiously optimistic.[19]

The optimism was almost immediately dashed. On August 23 the Communists abruptly broke off the talks. The stated reason was that a FEAF aircraft had bombed the Kaesong neutral zone, causing the "unlawful murder" of a CCF platoon leader. Invited to investigate these charges, UN airmen could find no convincing evidence whatsoever of a FEAF attack. The UN investigators concluded that "the incident was unquestionably staged by the Communists" as an "excuse to bring an end to the negotiations."[20]

For Ridgway this turn of events was both infuriating and baffling. After the UN side had made what he believed to be a major "face-saving" concession to the Communists (on the width of the DMZ), they had responded not only by breaking off the talks but also by attempting to place the onus for the breakdown on the UN with a faked FEAF "bombing." Why? No one knew. Speculations centered on two possibilities, one negative, one positive. Finally realizing that Washington had firmly reneged on the 38th Parallel issue, the Communists were no longer willing to negotiate an armistice, or they were willing to concede on the 38th Parallel but needed time to clear the concession through Peking, Pyongyang, and possibly Moscow.[21]

After a thorough investigation of the "bombing," Ridgway issued a statement rightly declaring the Communist accusations "utterly false" and "preposterous" fabrications and placed the onus for breaking off the talks on them. However, in compliance with directives from Washington, he left the door ajar, adding that when the Communists were ready to "terminate suspension of the negotiations," he would instruct the UN team to return to the talks.[22]

The talks remained suspended for two full months.

## II

While the negotiators haggled at Kaesong, Ridgway, in pursuit of his policy of maintaining "unrelenting" military pressure on the Communists, ordered ground as well as air action.

This policy suited Van Fleet just fine. He had become deeply concerned about the combat readiness of Eighth Army. The onset of the talks had, of course, raised the possibility that an armistice might be reached at any hour. Few in Eighth Army wanted to take chances and be the "last man killed." Moreover, the rotation policy had changed the face of the army: The old hands were being replaced by thousands of newcomers who were green to combat. Signs went up: DRIVE CAREFULLY! THE MAN YOU HIT MIGHT BE YOUR REPLACEMENT. An inexperienced, static army imbued with caution and indifference could rapidly become a vulnerable army. As Van Fleet later put it, "A sitdown army is subject to collapse at the first sign of enemy effort. . . . I couldn't allow my forces to become soft and dormant."[23]

Van Fleet and his planners conceived a number of aggressive offensive operations. These included revised versions of Overwhelming (an all-out Eighth Army attack to the Korean waist on a line Pyongyang–Wonsan) and a new plan Wrangler (an amphibious landing of the Marines at Tongchon to link with IX Corps). However, these large-scale operations were ultimately rejected by either Van Fleet himself or Ridgway because they would be too risky or costly in casualties or because they might cause the Communists to lose too much face and jeopardize the negotiations. Instead, Van Fleet substituted a series of "limited objective" offensives, which, notwithstanding the torrential rains, would be carried out more or less consecutively by the three new corps commanders.[24]

These operations began in the eastern sector of Eighth Army's front near the Punchbowl, still held by X Corps, which was now commanded by West Pointer (1920) Clovis E. Byers, fifty-one. Coming out of a long period in reserve, Nick Ruffner's remanned and reequipped 2d Division relieved the Marine 1st Division near the Punchbowl on July 15. Flanked east and west by the ROK 5th and 7th divisions and supported by the ROK 8th Division, the 2d Division had the limited objective mission of advancing Line Kansas slightly to the north of the Punchbowl, into dominating terrain held by the NKPA.[25]

Thus began another agonizing and bloody chapter in the history of the 2d Division in Korea. The NKPA troops had not rotated; they were veterans of months of fighting in the X Corps sector. By this time they had dug an interlocking system of heavy bunkers on the hilltops and had been resupplied with artillery, mortars and machine guns, small arms and grenades. They were determined not to yield a yard, and they repelled repeated and determined attacks day after day, week after week. The 2d Division historian described the miserable and very tough fighting on the aptly named Bloody Ridge and Heartbreak Ridge:

Sweating, heart-pounding heavy-footed soldiers dragged their throbbing legs up these tortured, vertical hills. Those who succeeded in grasping their way close to the bunkers were greeted by the crump and shower of black smoke, dirt and sharp steel as grenades were tossed down on them. Dirty, unshaven, miserable, they backed down, tried again, circled, climbed, slid, suffered, ran, rolled, crouched and grabbed upward only to meet again the murderous fire, the blast of mortar and whine of bullets and jagged fragments. Minutes seemed like hours, hours like days, and days like one long, terrible, dusty, blood-swirled nightmare.[26]

After the Communists had broken off the armistice talks on August 23, Van Fleet stepped up military pressure in the X Corps sector. On August 26 he recommitted Gerry Thomas's Marines to the line on the right (or east) of the 2d Division, displacing ROKs. "It was to a very large extent a new 1st Marine Division," the historian wrote. "Very few veterans of the [Chosin] Reservoir campaign were left, and even the Marines of the hard fighting in April and May had been thinned by casualties and rotation." The Marines were soon embroiled in equally tough, miserable fighting. In their first four-day fight for a hill the Marines incurred about 600 casualties, including attached ROKs.[27]

The Marines were shocked by the fierceness of the opposition from these heretofore lackluster NKPA soldiers and by the new and heavy enemy firepower. The Marine historian wrote that NKPA artillery "almost equalled the firepower provided by the organic Marine artillery and the guns of attached U.S. Army units. NKPA strength in mortars and machine guns also compared favorably with that of Marines."[28]

The addition of the Marines to the X Corps battle line substantially assisted the 2d Division, and in due course X Corps succeeded in slaughtering uncounted thousands of the NKPA and advancing to its "limited objective," a new line north of the Punchbowl. But the cost to make these minor improvements in the X Corps line was shocking. The 2d Division and attached ROKs incurred 2,700 casualties in capturing Bloody Ridge and 3,700 American casualties in capturing Heartbreak Ridge. Concluding it was "unprofitable to continue the bitter operation," Van Fleet told corps commander Clovis Byers to "firm up his line" and "plan no further offensives."[29]

*  *  *

The next major operation took place on Eighth Army's left flank. Called Commando, it was carried out by I Corps, now commanded by W. ("Iron Mike") O'Daniel, fifty-seven, the legendary commander of the 3d Division in World War II. The strategic aim of Commando was to keep "unrelenting" pressure on the enemy; the tactical aim was to push the UN line about six miles northwest from Wyoming to Jamestown, in order to keep CCF artillery fire off the Seoul–Chorwon–Kumhwa railroad, which was being developed into a primary supply line behind that sector of the front. Five reinforced divisions would participate, left to right: the ROK 1st, the newly created British Commonwealth Division (commanded by A. J. H. Cassels), the 1st Cav, Shorty Soule's 3d Division, and the 25th Division of Bill Hoge's IX Corps.[30]

Operation Commando commenced on October 3. The right- and left-flank forces in I Corps advanced to the new line without undue hardship or casualties, but in the center the 1st Cav Division, now commanded by West Pointer (1925) Thomas L. Harrold, forty-nine, ran up into the dug-in CCF Forty-seventh Army, which was determined not to yield an inch. Ghastly fighting like that on Bloody and Heartbreak ridges took place on or near hills dominated by Old Baldy.[31]

It took about sixteen days of hard, bloody fighting for the 1st Cav Division to advance six miles to Line Jamestown. During this period practically the entire division was engaged. The four division artillery battalions fired an astonishing 380,856 rounds. I Corps incurred about 4,000 casualties, about 2,900 of which were in the 1st Cav. The historian described the carnage:

The 1st Cavalry Division was engaged almost constantly in the most bitter fighting of the entire Korean campaign. The effort required in driving an entire Chinese Army from an excellent defensive line was so great as to almost defy description. One of the regiments reported that fully two-thirds of its rear area personnel had been sent up to frontline units to fill the gaps left by an unprecedented number of casualties. Survivors of companies joined with remaining fragments of other companies to return and assault again the positions that had previously all but wiped them out. This maximum, around-the-clock exertion extended to every unit and every man in the division.[32]

After the 1st Cav had finally reached Line Jamestown, the I Corps commander, Iron Mike O'Daniel, issued orders for the corps to hold that line and dig in. There would be no more major offensives. As the British historian wrote, "future operations would be confined to those necessary to maintain existing positions." One month later the battered 1st Cav was withdrawn from Korea and returned to Japan, replaced by the 45th (Oklahoma National Guard) Division, which had arrived in Japan the previous spring. Having originally embarked for an amphibious landing and mopping-up operations at Inchon, which had been expected to take no longer than about six weeks, the 1st Cavalry Division had spent sixteen terrible months in Korea.[33]

\* \* \*

These operations and others along Eighth Army's front during the recess in the talks in August, September, and October inflicted severe punishment on the enemy. Van Fleet estimated enemy casualties from all causes at about 234,000. While this figure was probably far too high, even half that would have significantly hurt the CCF and NKPA units engaged. During the same period the UN incurred a total of about 60,000 casualties, 22,000 of which were American, raising total American casualties in the Korean War to about 100,000.[34]

The shocking numbers of new American casualties incurred in the August to October fighting for the seemingly inconsequential ridges had finally and conclusively turned most Americans against the war. A poll taken in October found that only 33 percent disagreed with the proposition that the affair in Korea "was an utterly useless war." Omar Bradley rightly became deeply concerned about this dramatic loss of public support; it intensified Washington's quest for an early armistice.[35]

## III

During the fall fighting Washington continued to seek ways and means of reopening the talks. The liaison officers of both sides met from time to time at Panmunjom (five miles east of Kaesong) to discuss issues informally or to lodge charges of new "incidents." On a higher level Ridgway and the Communist leaders continued to hurl charges and countercharges by radio broadcast or formal notes, each blaming the other for the breakdown in the negotiations.

Ridgway remained hostile and hard-line. He continued to distrust and detest the Communists for their lies and deceits and propaganda. He deeply regretted UN "concessions" because he believed they signaled weakness. Of the UN concessions, the one he regretted most was the agreement to meet at Kaesong. During the early hiatus in the talks he made up his mind that should the Communists indicate a willingness to resume the talks, the UN team absolutely would not return to Kaesong. A new, truly neutral site, policed by both sides, would have to be found.

Ridgway announced his position to Washington in a strongly worded cable on September 3. He requested authority to "insist upon a new and satisfactory" site and specifically to "refuse any further negotiations within the Kaesong area." The JCS sympathized with Ridgway's reasons for seeking a new site but it believed that a categorical refusal to return to Kaesong was unwise. It might produce "a final break" in the talks "without at the same time fixing clear responsibility for failure on Communists or involving an issue which would receive fullest possible support of our allies." Therefore, the JCS authorized Ridgway cautiously to seek a new site but not to issue any statement that could be construed as an "ultimatum."[36]

Several days passed with no response from the Communists. During that time Ridgway became more irate; Kaesong festered in his mind. He concluded that since there were no talks going on at Kaesong and the Communists were probably utilizing the neutral zone to hide a troop buildup, it was pointless to continue the neutrality of Kaesong. He therefore proposed on September 11 to the JCS that he be granted authority to capture Kaesong militarily, both to "remove one more basis for Communist stalling tactics and to deprive the enemy of the distinct military advantage he now enjoys." He would give the Communists twenty-four hours' advance notice of the proposed operation but, at the same time, impose no conditions which could in any way be construed as suspending or terminating the talks.[37]

These plans were rudely shattered that very same day by an unintentional FEAF blunder. The Communists charged that in the early hours of September 10 FEAF had bombed the Kaesong neutral zone. This time the charge proved to be true. An aircraft of the 3d Bomber Wing had evidently strayed off course and had mistakenly strafed Kaesong. No physical damage had occurred, but inasmuch as the attack was "real," Ridgway felt compelled to issue an apology.

In view of this incident and the need for an apology, the JCS withheld approval for Ridgway to launch his proposed operation to capture Kaesong. That move, immediately following the apology, the JCS cabled, "would be used by Commies to support their charges that admitted violation was intentional and give color to past charges of UN violations in Kaesong area and of intentions to break off negotiations."[38]

A full week passed before the Communists replied to Ridgway's standing request for a new site. Their response was a long, scathing document which said, in effect, that if the UN would stop bombing Kaesong, that place would be a suitable meeting site. However, the message also contained an implication that the Communists might be ready to resume talks and for that reason Ridgway framed a restrained reply. After denying all but the one real bombing, he suggested that the liaison officers meet in Panmunjom to make arrangements to resume the talks. The Communists responded with another document, repeating old charges of UN treachery and deceit and stating, in effect, that there was no need for liaison officers to meet, that the senior delegates could resume talks in Kaesong. Again infuriated, Ridgway requested permission from the JCS to denounce the Communist allegations and for his liaison officer to meet the Communist liaison officer to press for a new site. If the Communists refused, he wanted authorization categorically to "refuse any further negotiations within the Kaesong area."[39]

This proposed ultimatum touched off a bureaucratic crisis in Washington.

The JCS sent Ridgway a "stopper" pending "high level consideration," then met with senior State Department officers. All agreed that since the refusal could lead to a permanent breakoff of the talks, under no circumstances should Ridgway categorically refuse to meet at Kaesong; nor should he press his case for a new site in such a way as to preclude a possible return to Kaesong. Moreover, while he was authorized to deny Communist allegations, he should cut out the "purple adjectives" and "truculent tone."[40]

The liaison officers met for two days, September 24 and 25, to discuss a new site and other issues. The Communists insisted that at the least the initial meeting be held in Kaesong. Believing that if even one meeting were held at Kaesong, all arguments for a change of site "would lose force," Ridgway dug in his heels. He repeated his request to Washington for authority to refuse categorically to return to Kaesong and to insist on a "new and satisfactory conference site."[41]

Ridgway's implacable position on Kaesong led to further urgent meetings in Washington. The State Department view was that Ridgway should not risk a "definitive breakdown" in the negotiations by refusing to return to Kaesong. The JCS was inclined to agree with Ridgway. Omar Bradley said: "We feel that General Ridgway should not be made to go back to Kaesong unless he is satisfied with conditions." Bradley was concerned, as was Ridgway, that the Communists might seize the UN delegates as hostages or otherwise harm them. But the moderate State Department view prevailed, and Joe Collins teleconned Ridgway to tell him of the decision.[42]

Ridgway still refused to budge one iota. In response to Collins's telecon, he again appealed to the JCS for support on his position, concluding by laying his career on the line: "I shall continue to do my utmost to execute faithfully your instructions, whatever be your decision on this issue of renewing delegation meetings in Kaesong. Unless, however, your decision should be to direct me to resume delegation meetings at Kaesong, I shall refrain from doing so."[43]

Ridgway's pronouncement that he would refuse to obey a direct order to return to Kaesong caused an uproar in Washington. If the order were issued and he refused to comply, President Truman would have no alternative but to sack him, as he had sacked MacArthur. However, the sacking of Ridgway at that time was simply unthinkable. He had "saved" Eighth Army and the UN positions in Korea. He enjoyed enormous worldwide prestige.

By happenstance, at this time there were significant changes in the Pentagon hierarchy. George Marshall, who was not in good health, resigned as secretary of defense. His deputy, Bob Lovett, a dedicated, loyal public servant, moved up to replace him. Lovett was an enormously capable inside executive, but he shunned the limelight and was thus virtually unknown outside the Washington bureaucracy. Upon the departure of Marshall, Truman persuaded Omar Bradley, who wished to go on the inactive list, to serve a second two-year term as chairman of the JCS, and Bradley, rather than Lovett, became Truman's closest military adviser.[44]

Bradley thought, not without good reasons, that Washington and Ridgway were drifting far apart in their views on the situation and about how to deal with the Communists. Bradley expressed it this way in a high-level Pentagon-State meeting: "When you are so close to those sons-of-bitches, you have different views. . . . I think General Ridgway has got away from the point that you can kick these fellows but still be polite to them. . . . Even if he is madder than hell, he should be polite."[45]

The divergence of views between Ridgway and Washington went beyond mere language and the Kaesong issue:

• On the basis of Ridgway's earlier cables and other sources, Washington was still under the impression that the Communists were benefiting militarily from the truce talks and for that reason were in no real hurry to conclude an armistice. It was thus to Washington's advantage to push hard for the earliest possible armistice, making further concessions if necessary. Contrarily, Ridgway now believed that the Communists were hurting militarily and did not wish to face another winter campaign, were eager for an armistice, and that absolutely no further concessions of any kind should be offered.

• On the basis of the seemingly favorable Communist reaction to the twenty-kilometer DMZ (introduced by the UN subdelegation on August 21), Washington believed that should the talks resume, that proposal should be reintroduced (in writing) as a formal proposal by the senior UN delegates. Viewing this as another major concession and sign of weakness, Ridgway argued contrarily that when negotiations resumed, the senior UN delegates should, in effect, start from scratch, holding to the earlier JCS-proposed twenty-mile DMZ. Washington believed that if Ridgway's recommendation on this issue were accepted, the Communists might very well revert to the 38th Parallel as the truce line, thereby putting everyone back to square one, perhaps prolonging the talks indefinitely.[46]

Even though Bradley had made plans for an important trip to Europe to confer on NATO matters, he decided that he should go at once to Tokyo to confer with Ridgway. At Bradley's suggestion, Dean Acheson agreed that State Department Sovietologist Chip Bohlen would go along, both to offer Ridgway the benefit of his long experience in negotiating with Communists and to examine more closely the Kaesong issue in behalf of State.[47]

\* \* \*

Bradley and Bohlen arrived in Tokyo on September 29. They conferred with Ridgway, Joy, and other GHQ senior officers and spent two days in Korea with Ridgway and Van Fleet, touring the battlefield and talking with corps, division, and regimental commanders. The visit dramatically narrowed the divergence of views between Washington and Tokyo:

- Bradley and Bohlen swung behind Ridgway's new view that the Communists were not benefiting militarily from the peace talks. "The military situation of the UN forces in Korea," Bohlen wrote, "was considerably more favorable" than it was believed to be in Washington, in fact, "extremely favorable for the UN." Bradley "had rarely seen combat forces in better shape from every point of view." All commanders in Eighth Army had "confidence bordering on absolute certainty" that any CCF offensive was "doomed to bloody failure." For that reason, Bohlen wrote, "There would appear to be no great need to hurry the talks and, indeed, the military situation would justify stringing them out, even in endless debate as to site." However, owing to the "important factor" of mounting American casualties, "we should, if possible, avoid a complete breakdown" in the talks and should "continue to attempt to achieve an armistice on acceptable terms."
- Bradley and Bohlen also swung behind Ridgway's refusal to return to Kaesong. While Bohlen thought the site controversy was "an artificial issue," now that it had been raised, he wrote, "There could be no question of forcing General Ridgway to return to that site under present conditions."
- Ridgway swung behind Washington's view that the twenty-kilometer DMZ at the battle line should be formally reintroduced by the senior UN delegates if the talks resumed. He did not, however, yield his position readily. "We found that General Ridgway and his negotiators felt . . . very strongly . . . they had made steady concessions to the Communists on procedural matters," Bohlen wrote, "and had thus possibly created an appearance of weakness which the military situation did not justify." Bradley and Bohlen tried to convince Ridgway that "this was not the impression" in the United States and the world, but, Bohlen wrote, "I do not believe we fully dissuaded him."[48]

\* \* \*

At about the same time the American ambassador to Moscow, former Admiral Kirk, was preparing to relinquish his post and retire. Kirk had not been able to see Stalin for two years, but he believed that upon his departure Stalin might grant a "farewell" interview, during which the ambassador could make certain points suggested by the State Department. State approved the idea and proposed that Kirk raise with Stalin "one outstanding issue, namely Korean armistice talks." Kirk should remind Stalin that it was Malik's speech that had "set off train of events leading to Korean negotiations," into which Washington had entered in good faith but which had now taken an "incomprehensible" turn. Washington wanted Kirk to persuade Stalin to instruct his Communist surrogates in Korea to resume negotiations.[49]

Kirk was not able to see Stalin, who was vacationing on the Black Sea, but on October 5 he conferred with Soviet Foreign Minister Andrei Vishinsky. Kirk told Vishinsky that Washington wanted Stalin to exert his "good offices and good will" personally to influence the Chinese and North Koreans to resume the talks. Speaking off the cuff, Vishinsky replied that the impasse was Ridgway's fault, that he (Vishinsky) "could not understand why Kaesong was not a suitable place for negotiations." Nonetheless, he assured Kirk that he would present Washington's case to Stalin.[50]

Kirk left Moscow before Vishinsky delivered Stalin's reply. The embassy chargé, Hugh S. Cumming, Jr., cabled Acheson the gist of the Soviet response:

US interest to end its war in Korea against Korean people understandable; USSR interest in end of war shown by its efforts in that direction; US responsible for delays in armistice talks; best way assure successful conclusion talks is instruct Ridgway not complicate matters with incidents or artificial difficulties such as relocation talks site; discussion armistice line military matter and must be included armistice talks. Soviet Union not participant negotiations but "all real efforts" toward successful conclusion negotiations "will meet in the present time, as in the past, with full and energetic support on part of Soviet Union."[51]

The liaison officers, meanwhile, had continued to meet occasionally at Panmunjom. On October 7, two days after the Kirk-Vishinsky talks in Moscow, the Communists yielded on Kaesong and proposed that the senior delegates resume the talks in Panmunjom. The following day Ridgway agreed to accept that proposal, provided the Communists would guarantee "equality of movement and control" at the new site. Over the next two weeks the liaison officers negotiated the size of the neutral zone and other security details.[52]

## IV

The senior delegates resumed the armistice negotiations at Panmunjom on October 25, after a hiatus of two months. The atmosphere remained unchanged: proper but cold, unsmiling, distrustful.

At the suggestion of the Communists, to which Turner Joy agreed, the subdelegates resumed discussions of the truce line. As directed by Washington, Hank Hodes and Arleigh Burke presented a written UN proposal and a map. The proposed truce line more or less traced the existing battle line except for two important details: UN forces would withdraw from positions along the east coast and at Kumsong, in return for a Communist withdrawal from Kaesong.[53]

Ridgway wanted Kaesong under UN control for several reasons: first, because the town was the ancient capital of Korea and had symbolic significance, which had increased during the war and the earlier negotiations; secondly, because UN forces had briefly held Kaesong before the negotiations and had withdrawn in good faith to provide a neutral zone for the talks (Ridgway viewed the UN withdrawal as a territorial concession for which it had received nothing in return, and therefore he wanted it back); thirdly, because Kaesong was an invasion "gateway" to Seoul, and Ridgway felt the UN should control it militarily; and fourthly, because Kaesong was (slightly) below the 38th Parallel and Syngman Rhee and the ROK government did not want to cede the Communists any territory south of the parallel.[54]

The subdelegates haggled all day. The Communists rejected the UN offer, objecting particularly to yielding Kaesong. In return, they proposed their own truce line. It yielded some indefensible terrain under Communist control on the Ongjin and Yonan peninsulas but retained Kaesong and required the UN to give up Bloody and Heartbreak ridges, the Punchbowl, and the UN forwardmost positions in the Iron Triangle at Kumhwa and Chorwon. Hodes, of course, rejected the Communist offer.[55]

What was significant in these opening gambits was that the Communists made no further mention of the 38th Parallel. Washington rightly viewed this as a major "breakthrough" in the negotiations, whether owing to the intervention of Stalin or to the UN military pressures or other reasons. Senior State Department officials viewed the opening positions of the subdelegates as "in the range of bargaining possibilities" and looked forward to a rapid series of compromises and a final settlement.[56]

It was not to be. Ridgway had gained the impression from Bradley and Bohlen that Washington would support his recommended hard-line approach, even if the negotiations dragged on indefinitely. He therefore instructed the UN team more or less to hold to its initial proposal as a "final offer," subject only to "minor changes," and, in no case, to give the Communists Kaesong. Inasmuch as the Communists had made it clear that they would not yield Kaesong, a deadlock again loomed.[57]

When word of Ridgway's position on Kaesong reached Washington, senior officials were deeply concerned. The JCS cabled Ridgway to say that he had got the wrong impression from Bradley and Bohlen. No one—not even Ridgway himself—had earlier agreed that the UN team should insist on gaining Kaesong. The UN's "minimum position," the JCS reminded Ridgway, was Line Kansas. "Thus certain adjustments, even in addition to those possible in the Chorwon–Kumhwa area, would appear to be practicable." The JCS concluded: "We recognize that it is difficult for Field Commander to surrender hard-earned ground and do not consider that you should do so unless negotiations seem likely to fail on an issue which does not involve our minimum position." In sum, be flexible and forget about Kaesong.[58]

Still believing the Communists were hurting and badly wanted an armistice and that the UN team had "momentum," Ridgway viewed these instructions from the JCS as at worst a betrayal and at least weak and vacillating. For several days he ignored Washington, instructing the UN team to continue to insist on gaining Kaesong. The Communists, in turn, continued to oppose the UN position, often vehemently. By November 3, when it was clear that holding Kaesong had become the "crux" of the Communist position, Ridgway instructed the UN team to yield—but only slightly. Hodes presented a new offer (or "concession"), which would place Kaesong in the middle of the DMZ, but the Communists vehemently opposed this scheme.[59]

On November 6, with another deadlock looming, the Communists appeared to grant the UN another major concession. They backed off their demands that the UN yield Bloody and Heartbreak ridges, the Punchbowl, and other terrain in the Iron Triangle. They proposed to accept the existing battle line as the final truce line, provided the UN would agree to it right then and there, even before the other items on the agenda had been resolved and the armistice been signed, and regardless of where the opposing forces might stand at the time of signing the armistice.[60]

Although this proposal appeared to contain major concessions, the UN team rejected it out of hand. Ridgway and Joy viewed it as possible treachery. It would, in effect, freeze Eighth Army in place (and short of Kaesong) and bring about an immediate cease-fire, but without agreement on the rest of the agenda. Ridgway described the proposal disparagingly to Washington as in effect a de facto cease-fire in which "the Communists would be insured against the effects of the UN military operations" while the other agenda items were under discussion. If this proposal were accepted, the Communists could drag out the negotiations for years without fear of UN ground forces' pressure.[61]

This was a possibility or perhaps even a probability, but it was not an easy one for the public to grasp. Viewed cursorily and uncritically, the Communists seemed to be offering what the UN delegation had sought for so many months: an end to the fighting, not at the 38th Parallel, as the Communists had originally insisted, but on the existing battle line, which guaranteed the UN Line Kansas. Considering the seeming uselessness of the stalemated war and the shocking American casualties in August, September, and October, the Communist offer seemed more than reasonable, and the public could not understand why Ridgway rejected it and continued to insist on gaining Kaesong and other "petty" concessions.

Nor could Washington. "Throughout," the JCS cabled Ridgway tartly, "we have taken as basic principle that demarcation line should be generally along battle line. Communists now appear to have accepted this principle. We feel that in general this adequately meets our minimum position re DMZ." As for Kaesong, the JCS would rather let the Communists keep it "than let negotiations break down or reach a stalemate." To judge from media reaction in the United States, the JCS continued, "it would be hard to make the people understand why negotiations broke down, if such should happen, over Kaesong in face of recent Communist concessions." Therefore, "early agreement along proposed Chinese-North Korean line in Kaesong area is advisable." To prevent the Communists from indefinitely dragging out debate on the other agenda items, Washington proposed a simple solution: a provisional acceptance of the Communist proposal, "qualified by a time limitation for completion of all agenda items."[62] But Ridgway vehemently disagreed. He insisted that the UN team continue to bargain for Kaesong and that it reject the latest Communist proposal.

At this time Soviet Foreign Minister Vishinsky intruded. In the course of a graceless speech before the UN General Assembly on November 8, excoriating the West, Vishinsky touched on Korea. He demanded that those nations engaged in the Korean War immediately cease military operations, conclude a truce, and withdraw their forces to the 38th Parallel "within ten days" and that all foreign troops and also all foreign volunteer forces withdraw from Korea "within a period of three months."

The Sovietologists in Washington and elsewhere were not certain how to interpret these remarks. Was it mere bombast? Or was it a signal to the Communists to rescind their latest offer and to revert to their original position on the 38th Parallel? Or was it a signal to the West to accept the latest Communist offer "within ten days" or face the possibility of a Communist reversion to the 38th Parallel?[63]

Whatever the case, public opinion and Washington officialdom swung behind the Communist proposal, dismissing Ridgway's objections to it and his insistence on gaining Kaesong as petty quibbling over side issues. On November 11 a *New York Times* editorial inquired rhetorically why the delegates were "backing and filling over a seeming trifle" when they had already agreed on the "big issues" regarding the truce line. Senior officials in both the State Department and the Pentagon agreed. On November 12 representatives from State and Defense (twenty-two men) met to settle the matter once and for all.[64]

The conferees were angry with Ridgway. Omar Bradley opened the discussion with this comment: "We told Ridgway the other day to agree on the present line as a final line if we can get the rest of the points agreed to in a short time. I am damned if I understand why they [the UN team] refuse to put that forward on the basis of say ten days in which to settle the other points. . . . We are not going anywhere on the ground. . . . I don't know why we are arguing about Kaesong. It doesn't mean anything to us." Joe Collins thought that the group should "be strong" and send Ridgway a "directive," or direct order, to accept the Communist proposal, stressing that "the President directs him or desires to have it done." Bradley and the others agreed to a directive, although Bradley did not want to insert the president's name least Ridgway get the wrong impression that the JCS agreed with Ridgway's view but had been overruled by the White House. Paul Nitze of State proposed that the time limit on the provisional agreement be extended to "a month." The other conferees concurred.[65]

The JCS cabled Ridgway their views in the early hours of November 13. He was to "press for an early settlement," stipulating to the Communists that the agreement would be valid for "approximately one month." In order to reach agreement "as promptly [as] possible," Ridgway would make "such concessions as are not significant," meaning give up his efforts to gain Kaesong. Unlike Ridgway, the JCS did "not consider" the provisional agreement a de facto cease-fire. UN ground actions could still continue "even though gains and losses would not be of significance to location of demarcation line if other items agreed to within time period." Moreover, UN air and naval action would not be affected by the agreement.[66]

Ridgway and Joy, indeed, all UN personnel concerned with the negotiations, were shocked. Ridgway responded with a protest and request for yet another reconsideration. The JCS position would probably "increase Communist intransigence" and weaken the UN posture on all other points, Ridgway insisted. He argued:

I have strong inner convictions that more steel and less silk, more forthright American insistence on the unchallengeable logic of our position, will yield the objectives for which we honorably contend. Conversely, I feel that the course you are directing will lead step by step to sacrifice our basic principles and repudiation of the cause for which so many gallant men have laid down their lives. We stand at a crucial point. We have much to gain by standing firm. We have everything to lose through concession. With all my conscience I urge we stand firm.[67]

Washington denied the appeal. On November 14 the JCS expressed appreciation of Ridgway's views but ordered him to do as he was told. The JCS repeated that it thought that the Communist proposal for the DMZ met the basic military requirements for the "defense" of Line Kansas and "protection" of Line Wyoming and was thus, in a broad sense, "no concession." Furthermore, it believed that "agreement on this agenda item, which [is] apparently of prime importance to Communists, might well expedite agreement on other items rather than retard them; particularly if we maintain military pressure."[68]

Ridgway made one final appeal to the JCS, but when this, too, was rejected, he reluctantly instructed Admiral Joy on November 15 to "press for early settlement" on the battle line. The offer would include the clear understanding that if all other items on the agenda had not been agreed to within "one month," the provisional truce line would no longer be valid. On November 21 the Communists agreed "in principle" but haggled over form and language and what actually constituted the battle line until November 27, when the delegates reached "final" agreement on the truce line. Should the negotiators fail to settle the other terms of an armistice, it would expire on December 27.[69]

Ridgway, meanwhile, had ordered Van Fleet to place Eighth Army in a position of "active defense." Van Fleet was authorized to seize terrain most suitable for defense, but he would limit offensive action to taking "outpost positions" not requiring more than one division. However, on November 27, when the delegates reached provisional agreement on the truce line, Van Fleet, without authorization from Ridgway, issued far more restrictive orders to Eighth Army. It should, he wrote, "clearly demonstrate a willingness to reach an agreement while preparing for offensive action if negotiations are unduly prolonged to this end. . . . Counterattacks to regain key terrain lost to enemy assault will be the only offensive action taken unless otherwise directed by this headquarters. Every effort will be made to prevent unnecessary casualties."[70]

These orders, the Army historian wrote, amounted to a cease-fire "if the enemy so desired." They made sense and were humane, but they were contrary to Ridgway's aim of continuing "relentless" ground pressure on the enemy until the other items on the agenda had been agreed to. Inevitably the orders leaked to the press, leading one correspondent to write that Van Fleet's order had "brought Korean fighting to a complete, if temporary, halt." Inasmuch as Van Fleet's orders and the press stories concerning them could undermine the UN negotiations at Panmunjom and had embarrassed the Truman administration, Ridgway was furious, cabling Washington that Van Fleet had "assumed a function entirely outside" his "field of responsibility." President Truman was likewise irate. He publicly denounced the stories as "fake," denying that Eighth Army had ceased offensive operations. To the contrary, Truman said, continued pressure by UN forces constituted the strongest incentive for the enemy to agree to an armistice. Chastened, Van Fleet ordered a resumption of local patrolling and stepped up artillery barrages, but these measures, the Army historian wrote, amounted to no more than "lip service."[71]

\* \* \*

In this way the truce line, believed to be the most important and controversial issue to both sides in the negotiations to end the Korean War, was settled. The agreement had been reached after five months of off-again, on-again talks and further shocking casualties on both sides. Although the UN had placed a one-month time limit on the truce line agreement, the time limit (as Ridgway gloomily predicted) was extended again and again, until the limit had no further meaning and was dropped as a consideration.

The truce line agreed to on November 27, 1951, thus became, after minor adjustments, the "final line" in the Korean War. Few would be satisfied with the "deal." The five months of talks had cost the UN an added 60,000 casualties, of which 20,000 were American. Administration critics were to argue that

Ridgway or Washington had needlessly prolonged the war; that the minor gains in the line had not been worth the cost in blood; and that a settlement on the 38th Parallel, as the Communists originally demanded, would probably have resulted in a "quick" armistice. Contrarily, hawks such as Ridgway were to contend that it was a grave mistake to diminish military pressure and to enter into a provisional agreement with the Communists before the other items on the agenda had been agreed to.

## V

At Panmunjom the senior delegates turned to the next two major items on the agenda: provisions for enforcing the armistice and exchange of POWs. The delegates negotiated these items more or less concurrently, and in due course the two became entwined.[72]

The principal UN objective on the first item was to prevent the secret introduction of Communist reinforcements into North Korea sufficient to overpower UN or ROK forces and reconquer South Korea. Unwavering in his hard-line position, Ridgway instructed the UN team to demand severe restrictions on the rotation of Communist troops and "free inspections" of virtually all of North Korea by joint UN-Communist ground and air teams. Viewing Ridgway's position on inspections as too rigid and possibly not attainable, Washington advised him to hold off in favor of a State Department proposal which eventually emerged as the "greater sanction" doctrine: the implication that should China or North Korea violate the armistice and reinvade South Korea, the UN forces in the Far East would retaliate directly at Red China, by air and sea.[73]

A secondary UN aim in these negotiations was to prevent the rehabilitation of certain militarily useful North Korean facilities, such as roads and railroads and especially airfields. At first, Washington assumed an extreme hard-line position on this issue, without offering reciprocal concessions, such as a moderation or suspension of its massive rehabilitation of South Korea. Upon review, however, the JCS concluded that Washington's position was overly harsh on the North Korean civilian population and probably not attainable anyway. It recommended that except for the airfields capable of accommodating jets, the rehabilitation of North Korean facilities should not be prohibited.

To this point President Truman had rubber-stamped most JCS or State positions in the armistice talks. On this issue, however, his dander rose. He demanded to know "why should we allow rehabilitation of roads, railroads and other facilities except for air fields? We have expended lives, tons of bombs and a large amount of equipment to bring these people to terms. They have been able to give us a bad time even in the crippled condition of their communications and they have been able to operate effectively even without air fields." When the JCS rejoined that "it would be impracticable to keep all of [North] Korea in a state of devastation," Truman backed down, and the JCS view prevailed.[74]

Following the policy review on the rehabilitation issue, the JCS cabled Ridgway new instructions. The UN team would demand prohibitions only on the rehabilitation or construction of jet-capable airfields. Inasmuch as the UN team offered no reciprocal agreement—rehabilitation and construction of jet-capable airfields in South Korea would continue—the Communists objected strenuously, and "airfield rehabilitation" soon became a major obstacle in reaching agreement on agenda item number three.[75]

*  *  *

In order to expedite the proceedings, on December 11 the UN team proposed concurrent negotiations over the next item on the agenda: exchange of POWs. Had Washington strictly abided by rules of the Geneva Convention pertaining to POWs, this agenda item might well have been settled in a matter of a few days, with an agreement to the customary all-for-all POW swap. However, for propaganda and humanitarian reasons Washington introduced several unprecedented and complicated conditions for the exchange of prisoners. The conditions infuriated the Communists, threw the negotiations into utter turmoil, led to bizarre twists and turns which enormously damaged the United States in the eyes of the world, and ultimately prolonged the Korean War for another year and a half, during which time United States forces suffered 37,000 more battlefield casualties.[76]

The factors which influenced Washington to depart from the usual all-for-all POW exchange were numerous and complex. Two factors were pivotal:

• Among the POWs held by the UN were about 20,500 Chinese. It was believed that a large number of them were former Nationalist Chinese soldiers who had defected or surrendered to the Communist forces during the China civil war. Inasmuch as these Chinese soldiers had, in effect, surrendered twice, they might be viewed by the Communists as unreliable or even traitorous. Upon repatriation, the Communists might punish them severely or even murder them. This situation suggested the radical idea that if these Chinese were so inclined, they might be repatriated, not to Red China but to Chiang Kai-shek on Formosa. If so, the refusal of these Chinese to return to Communist-controlled China might result in a substantial propaganda victory for Washington.[77]

• Among the POWs held by the UN were about 40,000 South Koreans who had been unwillingly impressed into the NKPA during its invasion of

South Korea and who had subsequently defected to or had been captured by UN forces. Many of these impressed ROKs had collaborated with UN forces. These collaborators and most other South Koreans had no desire to return to Communist control. Rightly believing these South Koreans were not actually "legitimate" POWs and that many, if not most, would be severely punished or murdered if returned to the Communists in a customary POW swap, Washington agreed with a request from the Rhee government that these 40,000 South Koreans should be "reclassified" and gradually released to return to their homes in South Korea.[78]

These ideas or concepts, the first harebrained, the second just and humane, gave rise to a larger and even more controversial and ill-advised notion which was in technical violation of the Geneva Convention:* that *all* POWs held by the UN would be polled to find out where they wanted to wind up. No POW held by the UN would be "forcibly" or "involuntarily" repatriated to the Communists.

The voluntary repatriation doctrine was hotly debated behind the scenes in Washington, Tokyo, and Seoul. Many senior American officials, including Ridgway and Joy, strongly opposed the doctrine as probably unworkable or illegal and as certain to be unacceptable to the Communists, thereby running a risk of prolonging the negotiations and war and possibly even leading to a complete breakdown of the talks. Its chief proponent was President Truman, who for political, propaganda, or high-minded moral reasons clung to it tenaciously. He proclaimed publicly that "we will not buy an armistice by turning over human beings for slaughter or slavery." He elaborated his position in his memoir: "Just as I had always insisted that we could not abandon the South Koreans who had stood by us and freedom, so I now refused to agree to any solution that provided for the return against their will of prisoners of war to Communist domination. . . . As far as I was concerned, this was not a point for bargaining."[79]

Of the many positions and decisions Truman took with respect to Korea and the war, his adamant stand for voluntary repatriation would be the most controversial and morally debatable. If, as its opponents predicted, it prolonged the negotiations and the war, American (and other) POWs held in

---

*Article 118 of the Geneva Convention of 1949, which the United States had signed but not yet ratified (but abided by and intended to ratify) stated: "Prisoners of war shall be repatriated without delay after cessation of hostilities." The "without delay" language had been incorporated into the article because the Soviet Union had retained thousands of German and Japanese POWs in slave-labor camps after the conclusion of World War II. That some POWs might not want to return to the country of their origin had not been anticipated, and no provision had been made in the convention for that contingency.

Communist captivity would have to endure many more months and perhaps years of cruel incarceration and possibly death. Moreover, it could further weaken the Eighth Army's will to fight, in that its soldiers, if captured, could not anticipate reasonable treatment or early release. Finally, it posed this trenchant question: Should American (and UN) soldiers fight and die or suffer wounds and injuries in order to give their former enemies, many of them traitors, freedom of choice over repatriation?[80]

\* \* \*

When the delegates opened discussions on the POW issue, the UN team did not at first reveal its position on voluntary repatriation. The UN delegates merely proposed an early "fair and equitable" exchange of POWs, the sick, wounded, and injured to be swapped first. Citing Article 118 of the Geneva Convention, the Communist delegates made their position unmistakably clear: They demanded an all-for-all swap without delay.[81]

Still concealing its position on voluntary repatriation, the UN team shifted to other ground: an exchange of POW lists. When both sides produced these lists on December 18, each team professed to be shocked. The Communist list contained a total of but 11,559 names, 7,142 ROKs and 4,417 non-ROKs, of which 3,198 were American. The UN list comprised 132,474 names, of which 95,531 were NKPA, 20,700 CCF, and 16,243 South Koreans impressed into the NKPA.[82]

Both sides cried foul. On the basis of NKPA radio boasts of having captured 65,000 ROKs in the early days of the war, and Eighth Army records which carried 88,000 ROKs and 11,500 non-ROKs as missing or captured, the UN team argued that the Communists were withholding about 88,000 names.\* On the basis of earlier UN POW lists provided to the Red Cross before the UN had begun to "reclassify" the 40,000 ROKs who had been impressed into the NKPA, the Communists argued that the UN was withholding about 44,000 names.[84]

\* \* \*

The charges and countercharges over the POW lists and allegedly withheld names dominated the talks through to the end of the year. During that time the one-month time limit on the truce line expired (December 27), but the delegates ignored that formerly important milestone and continued to ignore it in the weeks and months to come.

---

\*Owing to poor records and other factors, neither side actually had accurate figures on the other's POWs. Secretly, however, the UN did not believe the Communists were withholding 88,000 names. On October 27 Ridgway had cabled the Pentagon that he estimated the Communists held an "estimated maximum" of 6,000 non-ROKs and "about 28,000 ROKs."[83]

Soon after the New Year, on January 2, 1952, the UN team introduced the doctrine of voluntary repatriation into the talks. Not unexpectedly, the Communist reaction was complete shock and dismay. They labeled the doctrine "absurd" and too unreasonable to discuss. After days of acrimonious debate Admiral Joy concluded gloomily that the Communists would never concede on the issue, that it would indefinitely delay an armistice, and that furthermore, Washington was on "unsound ground in insisting on the principle." In his memoir Joy wrote that Washington's stubborn insistence on the voluntary repatriation doctrine "cost us over a year of war," during which the UN suffered 50,000 more casualties.[85]

Yet the Communists did not walk out. One reason was that in its all-out effort to "sell" the voluntary repatriation doctrine, the UN team consistently minimized its estimate of the number of UN POWs who would refuse to be repatriated to the Communists and at the same time softened its hard-line position on airfield rehabilitation and other issues relating to enforcement of the armistice. When, finally, the UN team unwisely and prematurely estimated that "only 16,000" UN POWs would refuse repatriation, the Communists appeared to soften their position and even tacitly approved a "screening" or poll of POWs in UN custody. At about the same time Washington conceived a dramatic "package deal" in which it would yield completely on the jet-capable airfield issue in return for a Communist concession on voluntary repatriation.[86]

The screen, or polling, of CCF and NKPA POWs began in early April 1952. The results astounded the United Nations. At the halfway mark in the polling of the 132,000 military POWs, the UN found that about 40,000 would resist repatriation to the Communists. On the basis of these figures, the UN projected that of the total 132,000 military POWs (plus 38,000 North Korean civilian internees), only a total of about 70,000 would elect to return to Communist control. This could be a great propaganda coup for the UN, but it also posed the danger that the Communists would lose face to such a degree that they would terminate the talks. Accordingly, the UN hurried along its "package deal."[87]

When the UN team presented its preliminary estimates on the number of UN-held POWs who would refuse repatriation on April 19, the Communists were thunderstruck. Again they felt they had been lied to and duped. Boiling mad, they bitterly denounced the UN team for treachery. A week later, on April 28, when the UN team presented its package deal, dropping its hard-line position on jet-capable airfields and softening on other unresolved issues pertaining to enforcement of the armistice, the Communists gave it scarcely a glance and walked out, recessing the talks indefinitely.[88]

* * *

After Washington had introduced the doctrine of voluntary repatriation into the negotiations in January 1952, the Communists launched a vicious and massive propaganda attack against the United States, in which POWs held by them and the UN became victims or instruments. This campaign consisted of three cunning and interrelated elements:

• *Germ warfare:* On February 2, 1952, Soviet Ambassador to the UN Jacob Malik accused the United States of employing bullets filled with "toxic gases" in Korea. Later that month, picking up and expanding this theme, Peking and Pyongyang and Communist organs worldwide charged that United States airmen and artillerymen had dropped and fired bacteria-infected insects and shellfish (beetles, lice, ticks, rats, fleas, clams, etc.) into North Korea. To substantiate these claims, the Communists created faked "exhibits," inaugurated a massive inoculation program, and finally, by torture and threats, forced two young Air Force POWs (and later, a senior Marine Corps pilot and thirty-five other Air Force pilots) to "confess" on film, on tape, and in press interviews that they had indeed been part of a huge United States germ warfare conspiracy. This wholly fabricated propaganda attack, supported by Communist-manipulated "demonstrations" all over the world, was astonishingly successful; Washington's slow-footed and righteous denials were not.[89]

• *Brainwashing:* Simultaneously with the germ warfare campaign, the Communists launched an "indoctrination" program of UN POWs, designed to turn them against the West and even refuse repatriation. The program included not physical torture but rather a form of mental torture: endless repetition of Communist slogans, phrases, and ideas and the exploitation of grievances, especially among black POWs. Although no POWs were directly threatened with grave harm or death, they knew that thousands of UN POWs had earlier been tortured and murdered, and partly as a result of this knowledge, this Communist campaign (which came to be known as "brainwashing") was also astoundingly successful. Postwar studies were to show that only about 12 percent of American POWs (Bill Dean among them) "actively and consistently" resisted the program. The great majority "cooperated in indoctrination and interrogation sessions in a passive sort of way, although there was a tendency to refuse to say anything obviously traitorous." Nonetheless, many UN POWs signed "peace petitions" and similar pro-Communist testimonials, which were distributed in the West. Ultimately, twenty-one Americans and one Briton were to refuse repatriation.[90]

• *POW riots:* Beginning in early 1952, the Communists allowed trained agents to be captured as POWs. These agents were instructed to organize the hard-core Communist POWs and foment riots and other disturbances inside UN POW compounds on the island of Koje and elsewhere, for the purpose of incurring UN punitive countermeasures, which the Communists could then exploit. Per plan, "riots" in UN POW compounds occurred on February 18 and March 13, 1952. In attempting to quell these riots, UN guards fired into the POWs, killing 89 and wounding 166. Having cunningly staged these incidents, the Communists then denounced the UN worldwide for "barbarous massacres" and "atrocities."[91]

After the Communists had broken off the talks on April 28, 1952, the POW "riots" intensified. On May 12, during one spectacular riot at Koje, Communists seized the American POW camp commander, Brigadier General Francis T. Dodd, who, in an attempt to negotiate with the rioters, got too close. The POWs "tried" Dodd and sentenced him to death. In an effort to save his own life, Dodd signed a document, agreeing to cease immediately the "barbarous behavior, insults, torture . . . [and] mass murdering" of POWs by UN guns, germs, poison gas, and atomic weapons and to halt the screening of POWs for the purpose of complying with the UN's "illegal and unreasonable" voluntary repatriation program. Sent to Koje to free Dodd by military force if necessary, the new I Corps chief of staff, Brigadier General Charles F. Colson, decided against using force and signed a document which he believed would gain Dodd's freedom. Colson conceded that numerous POWs had been killed and wounded by UN guards and that he would do all within his power "to eliminate further violence and bloodshed." He guaranteed "humane treatment" for UN POWs and agreed that there would be "no more forcible screening of any remaining POWs in this camp." Dodd got out, but the Communists exploited the two documents as further "proof" of UN "atrocities," humiliating the United States and Eighth Army and raising serious questions worldwide over the validity of the voluntary repatriation doctrine.[92]

*   *   *

All during the summer of 1952 the talks at Panmunjom remained deadlocked over the voluntary repatriation issue and devolved into an institutionalized propaganda forum, where the liaison officers or senior delegates met occasionally to lodge charges and countercharges. Neither side budged or offered any new proposals.[93]

The stalemated "war" also became institutionalized along the truce line. The opposing forces continued to hurl immense quantities of artillery shells and to send out patrols and occasionally attempted larger maneuvers to gain a hill. The Eighth Army staff conceived and from time to time urged larger operations, but these were canceled or postponed indefinitely. The unpopular draft continued in the United States. The Army sent scores of thousands of young Americans (20,000 to 30,000 per month) to the bunkers on the ridges in Korea, to put in about ten or eleven cautious and mostly boring months "at the front," after which they returned home for discharge, with no parades or other form of community thanks or recognition.

## V I

By 1952, a presidential election year, the Truman administration was under attack from many quarters. The war in Korea, which had cost more than 100,000 American casualties, remained an unresolved nightmare, mired in seemingly petty haggling at Panmunjom, while more Americans died and American POWs suffered physical and mental torture. McCarthyism was rampant and effective; millions of Americans did not doubt that the government, Dean Acheson's State Department in particular, was infested with Communist spies, pinkos, and fellow travelers. A number of Truman's cronies and appointees—including his senior Army aide, Harry Vaughan—had been caught with their hands in government cookie jars, creating an aura of impropriety and scandal. Public opinion polls gave Truman abysmally low approval ratings, averaging about 30 percent.[94]

Having decided earlier not to seek reelection, Truman began looking for a successor who could ride out the political and ideological storms and assure the Democratic party hold on the White House and Congress into the 1950s. His first choice was Dwight D. Eisenhower, still at NATO. Eisenhower was seriously considering a run for the presidency, but as a Republican. After Eisenhower, in effect, had declined Truman's offer, Truman turned to his friend and former secretary of the treasury Fred M. Vinson, whom Truman had appointed chief justice of the United States. When Vinson also declined, Truman offered the nomination to Illinois Governor Adlai E. Stevenson, who vacillated but finally accepted and, at the Democratic convention, chose Alabama Senator John Sparkman to run with him as vice presidential candidate.

The minority Republican party was sharply divided in 1952. The front-runner was right-wing, isolationist Senator Bob Taft, who had allied, as expected, with Douglas MacArthur. If the Taft-MacArthur ticket won, Taft promised to appoint Vice President MacArthur "deputy commander in chief of the armed forces." Fearing another resounding defeat, liberal Republicans (Thomas E. Dewey, Henry Cabot Lodge, and others) finally persuaded Eisenhower to run against the Taft-MacArthur ticket. Although Eisenhower was reluctant to campaign for delegates, he finally yielded and returned to the United States on June 1, 1952. In a tough convention fight he beat Taft and chose Richard M. Nixon for his vice presidential running mate.[95]

* * *

The NATO command Eisenhower gave up had become a prestigious and sought-after post. There was even talk of promoting Eisenhower's successor to five stars in order to outrank the deputy commander, British Field Marshal Bernard Montgomery, and other NATO generals. Omar Bradley, who had earlier hoped to persuade Truman to give the post to Joe Collins to make room for Ridgway as chief of staff of the Army, now changed his mind. Viewing the NATO post—and a possible five stars—as more prestigious than the chief of staff job, Bradley proposed Ridgway to succeed Eisenhower. Eisenhower wanted his NATO chief of staff, Al Gruenther, to succeed him, but the British preferred Ridgway over Gruenther (and other American Army candidates), and in the end Bradley's view prevailed. On May 12, 1952, Ridgway left Tokyo to relieve Eisenhower. Mark Clark, who had been contemplating retirement, replaced Ridgway in Tokyo; Joe Collins remained as Army chief of staff. Thus three West Point classmates (April 1917) held the three most powerful Army jobs in the world.[96]

Mark Clark assumed the Far East Command from Ridgway in the midst of the difficult POW riots in Koje in May 1952. Like Ridgway, Clark had often verbally fought with Communist negotiators as commander in postwar Trieste, and he assumed a hard-line position. Believing that only continuing UN military pressure would break the deadlock in the talks at Panmunjom, Clark drew up plans for greatly expanding ground operations to include deployment of Chinese Nationalist troops to Korea, UN amphibious landings behind the enemy in North Korea, and, where practicable, tactical use of atomic bombs against CCF and NKPA military targets and possibly even air and naval attacks on the China mainland.[97]

The ground plans were put on hold, but the JCS authorized Clark to mount renewed, massive bombing attacks on North Korea. The FEAF targets included not only the pitiable civilian populations of Pyongyang and seventy-eight smaller towns but also eleven North Korean hydroelectric plants and related facilities along the Yalu River and an oil refinery only eight miles from the Russian border. The attacks flattened what was left of Pyongyang, caused a two-week electrical blackout throughout all North Korea, and ignited worldwide protests, even by the governments in London and Paris. Clark dismissed the uproar and continued the FEAF bombing attacks in a vain hope to drive the Communists back to the negotiating table.[98]

By this time the chief UN negotiator, Admiral Joy, had been rotated to retirement and had been replaced by another West Pointer from the class of April 1917, William K. Harrison, Jr. Coordinating with Washington, Clark and Harrison conceived another voluntary repatriation "package offer," which would assure the Communists of 83,000 (rather than 70,000) returnees and other minor concessions. The new "package" was dramatically unveiled to the Communists on September 28, 1952, as a "final offer." When the Communists rejected the "package" on October 8, Harrison, per instructions from Washington, walked out. The senior delegates did not meet again for six months.[99]

Perhaps in retaliation, in early October 1952, the CCF commenced aggressive ground operations along the truce line in the Iron Triangle. In response, Van Fleet obtained permission from Clark for a limited counterattack. This resulted in bitter and costly fighting for several inconsequential hills (Jane Russell, White Horse, Pike's Peak) in the sector. It was during these actions that part of the Puerto Rican 65th Regiment bugged out. As a result the Puerto Ricans were also "desegregated" and scattered to other units.[100]

Inasmuch as neither side had sufficient ground forces or the will to overpower the other, these furious and futile actions gradually petered out and finally terminated, with neither side one whit better off. The fighting cost the UN forces another 9,000 casualties (mostly ROKs), and the CCF an estimated 19,000. As bitter cold weather set in—the third miserable winter of the Korean War—both sides again dug into bunkers along the truce line and again restricted ground action to patrolling and massive artillery duels. The vast expenditure of UN artillery shells seriously depleted theater and Eighth Army reserves. Van Fleet, who was increasingly frustrated and grief-stricken over the loss of his airman son who was lost on a FEAF bombing raid in April 1952,* complained bitterly of an "ammo shortage." His charges resulted in a sensational but inconclusive congressional investigation.[102]

Back in the States, the presidential campaign built up a full head of steam during this October fighting. The Korean War and the corruption and communism in the Truman administration emerged as the key issues. As for Korea, Eisenhower rejected the extremist views and promised vaguely to work firmly and prudently toward a just and lasting peace. This high-minded double-talk probably fell on deaf ears, but toward the end of the campaign, on October 24, Eisenhower electrified voters with a political stroke of genius, promising that "I shall go to Korea." When the votes were counted, Eisenhower had trounced Stevenson 442 electoral votes to 89.[103]

Fulfilling his promise, President-elect Eisenhower went to Korea, arriving on December 2 for a three-day tour, including a visit with his son, John, then serving as a battalion S-3 in the 15th Infantry. Mark Clark and Jim Van Fleet

---

*Of the many generals' sons serving in the Korean War, Don Faith and James A. Van Fleet, Jr., were the only ones killed in action. After completing 105 FEAF bombing missions, Hap Gay's son Hobart R., Jr., was killed in an aircraft accident in August 1952. Al Gruenther's son Richard had been severely wounded in northeast Korea. Mark Clark's son William, who rose to exec of the 9th Infantry, was wounded three times. The last time, in October 1951, on Heartbreak Ridge, he was hurt so severely that he was ultimately forced to retire. The sons of the 2d Division ADC George Stewart and Eighth Army engineer Pat Strong were wounded and physically disabled, respectively, and medically evacuated.[101]

attempted to present Eisenhower with superaggressive plans to win the war militarily, including the use of Chinese Nationalist troops and atomic bombs. But Eisenhower displayed little or no interest in these extreme proposals, leaving Clark and Van Fleet with the clear impression that Eisenhower would continue the Truman policy of seeking a negotiated solution.[104]

\* \* \*

The Eisenhower administration came to office in early 1953 with a clear mandate to end the damnable war in Korea honorably, but it possessed no magic solution. As a first step Eisenhower and his hawkish secretary of state, John Foster Dulles, turned to power diplomacy or what became known in journalese as "brinksmanship." First, they rescinded Truman's earlier orders which had neutralized Formosa, "unleashing Chiang Kai-shek" and raising the possibility that the Chinese Nationalist might attempt an invasion of the mainland. Secondly, they dropped discreet hints at Panmunjom, New Delhi, and elsewhere to the effect that if the deadlock in the peace talks were not soon broken, Washington might not confine the war to Korea and might employ atomic bombs in Asia. Thereafter, Eisenhower wrote in his memoirs, "the prospects for an armistice seemed to improve."[105]

The prospects may have been improved substantially by a stroke of fate. On March 5, 1953, Joseph Stalin died. Ten days later Stalin's successor, Georgi M. Malenkov, made a speech widely touted by Soviet propagandists, in which he seemed to extend an olive branch to the West. He declared that there was no existing dispute between Moscow and Washington that "cannot be decided by peaceful means, on the basis of mutual understanding." Although Dulles and others dismissed the speech as yet more Kremlin trickery, Eisenhower, over Dulles's objections, directly responded in a cautiously optimistic speech (entitled "The Chance for Peace"), in which he challenged Malenkov to match his words with specific deeds, including "an honorable armistice" in Korea.[106]

Whether at Moscow's specific direction or by pure coincidence, on March 28, two weeks after Malenkov's speech, the Communists suddenly responded favorably to an earlier proposal Mark Clark had made to exchange sick and wounded POWs. Not only that, but the Communists also said the exchange "should be made to lead to a smooth settlement of the entire question of prisoners of war, thereby achieving an armistice in Korea, for which people throughout the world are longing." This statement was followed several days later by pronouncements from Red China's Foreign Minister Chou En-lai and North Korea's Premier Kim Il Sung which appeared to soften the Communist stand against voluntary repatriation. Both Communist leaders expressed agreement to an earlier proposal to allow a "neutral state" (such as India or Switzerland) to supervise the exchange and interview Communist POWs who refused repatriation, to ascertain their true desires.[107]

These statements from Peking and Pyongyang appeared to presage the long-sought break in the peace talks deadlock. Even so, they were viewed cautiously and, in some instances, negatively in Washington. Two of the most powerful men in the Eisenhower cabinet, John Foster Dulles and the secretary of defense, Charles E. Wilson, argued to reject the overtures. Talking very toughly in the NSC on April 8, Dulles and Wilson urged a "much more satisfactory settlement in Korea," including a postarmistice political arrangement that would virtually unite Korea and leave it divided not at Line Kansas but much farther north, "along the waist" (Pyongyang–Wonsan). Believing this course could lead to an abrogation of the armistice and yet more fighting, which the American people would not tolerate, Eisenhower overrode Dulles and Wilson and cautiously approved the exchange of sick and wounded POWs—as a "test of good faith on the part of the Soviets."[108]

The Communist overtures were accompanied by a sudden and puzzling intensification of ground activity along the truce line, which resulted in a humiliating retreat from the hill Old Baldy by the U.S. 7th Division. These attacks were met by a new Eighth Army commander, Maxwell Taylor, whom Eisenhower had sent to Korea to relieve the restive and grieving Van Fleet, who retired with four stars, bitterly critical of Washington's conduct of the last two years of the Korean War. Taking command on February 11, 1953, Taylor—fresh from the Pentagon and fully alive to Eisenhower's desire for an end to UN casualties and an early honorable settlement of the war—dismissed the intensified CCF attacks as face-saving propaganda maneuvers and refused the 7th Division permission to counterattack Old Baldy.[109]

Notwithstanding stepped-up fighting all along the truce line, the swap of sick and wounded POWs, called "Little Switch," started on April 20 and continued to May 3. Governed by elaborate security measures, this extraordinary operation was accomplished without notable incident. The UN turned over a total of 6,670 POWs: 5,194 NKPA, 1,030 CCF, and 446 civilian internees. In return, the UN received a total of 684 POWs: 471 ROKs, 149 Americans, 32 Britons, 15 Turks, and 17 other UN personnel.[110]

\* \* \*

While Little Switch was going on, the senior delegates resumed talks at Panmunjom, after a hiatus of six full months. The delegates focused on the exchange of the main body of POWs and other unresolved issues. They soon mired in interminable debate over which "neutral" nation (or nations) would supervise the exchange of the main body of POWs and other petty issues. When these discussions devolved into bitter name-calling, the delegates recessed to explore alternatives, and Washington's hopes for an armistice seemed once again to be slipping away.[111]

Still believing that heavy military pressure was needed to force the Communists into an armistice, Mark Clark proposed, and the JCS approved, another massive FEAF air assault on the North Korean civilian population. The problem was there were no cities or towns left anywhere in North Korea. The complete absence of worthwhile targets led Clark's air chief, O. P. Weyland, to conceive a bold and galvanizing idea: FEAF would wipe out the North Korean rice crop (predicted to be 283,000 tons) and starve the Communists into submission.[112]

This FEAF campaign was launched on May 13 and continued over the next two weeks. The goal was to destroy a complex of earthen irrigation dams about twenty miles north of Pyongyang (Toksan, Chasan) and flood the interlocking rice paddies. Day after day large formations of FEAF F-84 jet fighter-bombers blasted away at the dams, not without success. The precise damage to the rice crop or the extent of starvation inflicted on the North Koreans was never determined, but FEAF reconnaissance photos showed sufficient flooding of the paddies and roads to enable Weyland to boast that this particular FEAF operation was "perhaps the most spectacular of the war."[113]

On May 25, possibly in retaliation, the Communists launched powerful offensives along the entire truce line. These attacks forced the American 25th Division into a humiliating withdrawal from hilltop outposts east of Panmunjom. But the main CCF force struck ROK-held positions in the central front near Kumsong. The offensive caused complete chaos and for a time posed grave dangers. Under the weight of the CCF attack, several ROK divisions broke and bugged out, leaving great gaps in the line. Max Taylor plugged the gaps with reserve ROK divisions and finally stopped the retreat. Typically, and fortunately, the CCF offensive soon ran out of steam and the situation stabilized.[114]

Amid the clamor of this bizarre war, the senior delegates at Panmunjom continued talking and making progress. By June 4 they had agreed on the mechanics of the main POW exchange, and most of the details of the armistice had been worked out. Four days later, June 8, both sides signed a repatriation agreement, clearing away the issue which had deadlocked the talks for eighteen months.[115]

Except for one large, nagging detail, peace seemed to be at hand. The final obstacle was posed not by the enemy but by an ally: Syngman Rhee. He had never relented in his efforts to sabotage the armistice. Throughout the talks he had demanded that no concessions whatsoever be granted the Communists, that the CCF be expelled from North Korea, that the NKPA be disarmed, and that all Korea be united under the ROK government. Now that the armistice appeared to be impervious to sabotage, Rhee declared that South Korea would not honor its terms and that he might detach the ROK Army from the UN command and continue the war alone.[116]

These were not idle threats. Beginning in mid-June, Rhee launched final, desperate efforts to sabotage the talks. First, on June 18 he directed ROK guards at the NKPA compounds to turn loose those men who did not wish to be repatriated. That night about 25,000 of 33,600 NKPA POWs in that category shed uniforms, fled through open gates, and melted into the South Korean population. Secondly, he imposed what amounted to martial law in South Korea and forebade all ROK Army personnel and civilians to continue working for the UN command. Thirdly, he alerted the senior ROK Army commanders to prepare to fight on, armistice or no armistice.[117]

These actions precipitated a crisis, but did not lead to the intended breakdown in the talks. Mark Clark and the chief UN negotiator, William Harrison, delivered to the Communists a written apology, which specifically blamed Rhee for the "escape" of the 25,000 NKPA. Meeting with Harrison on June 20, the Communists grudgingly accepted the apology. They suggested that Clark track down the "escapees" and reimprison them for a proper exchange, but knowing full well that this task would be impossible, they did not press the issue. Instead, they rightly posed the larger questions: What was to be done about Syngman Rhee? Could the UN command bring him under control? Would an armistice include the ROK government? If not, would the ROK government abide by its terms, or would it continue the war alone?[118]

President Eisenhower sent a task force to Korea to bring Rhee into line. Its members conceived a three-step strategy. In return for Rhee's cooperation on the armistice, they would first attempt to reason with Rhee by promising a long-term mutual defense treaty, full support for a twenty-division ROK Army, and untold billions in military and economic aid. If that failed, they would try a gigantic bluff. They would rescind those offers and threaten to withdraw all American forces from the peninsula, leaving South Korea to its fate. If the bluff also failed, they were prepared to stage a coup d'état (Operation Everready), replacing Rhee with a more amenable South Korean leader.[119]

Perhaps aware of the task force's strategy, the Communists initiated intense military measures, possibly designed to help bring Rhee into line. On June 26 they launched another massive offensive at ROK-held positions near Kumsong. Backed by heavy artillery, five CCF armies (fifteen divisions) swarmed out of the hills at the ROKs. Some ROKs bravely held, but too many panicked and abandoned their positions, fleeing to the rear. Responding to the crisis, Max Taylor shifted the American 2d and 3d divisions and substantial artillery into the ROK sector, to backstop the reeling ROKs. He finally managed to halt the flight at the Kumsong River, about six miles below the former ROK positions. In this action the ROKs suffered ghastly casualties; the Capital Division was utterly shattered.[120]*

---

*Total UN casualties incurred in the April through July fighting were 64,703. Most were ROK casualties sustained in the CCF offensive at Kumsong. During the same four-month period UN artillery fired an astounding 7,683,909 rounds.[121]

This humiliating ROK Army defeat, together with Washington's threats and promises, was apparently sufficient to bring Rhee back (or close) to his senses. On July 9, during the peak of the CCF offensive at Kumsong, Rhee agreed to cease his attempts to obstruct the armistice. Furthermore, he declared that his government would "endeavor to cooperate fully and earnestly" in what he believed would be a continuing effort by Washington and the United Nations to unify Korea by political action.[122]

\* \* \*

Having brought Rhee into line and resolved all other outstanding issues, the senior delegates met at Panmunjom at 10:00 A.M. on July 27. In a cold, wordless ceremony, witnessed by Western and Communist journalists and photographers, Generals Harrison and Nam Il each signed nine copies of the armistice. As set forth by its terms, twelve hours later, at 10:00 P.M., the guns fell silent along the front and the war in Korea was over. In the days following, the final exchange of POWs, called "Big Switch," proceeded. The Communists returned a total of 12,773 UN prisoners, including 3,597 Americans (Bill Dean among them), 7,862 ROKs, 945 British (mostly Gloucesters), 229 Turks, and 140 others. The UN returned a total of 75,823 Communist prisoners, including 70,183 of the NKPA and 5,640 of the CCF.[123]

\* \* \*

It had been a long and terrible war, the cost of which could never be accurately reckoned. The Pentagon estimated that military casualties on both sides came close to 2.4 million.\* Other sources estimated that North and South Korean civilian casualties were about 2 million. If these figures are approximately accurate, then about 4.4 million men, women, and children were killed, murdered, wounded, or otherwise incapacitated in the war. Both North Korea and South Korea were utterly ravaged. It would take decades for each nation to rise from the rubble.[124]

Americans paid a high price for President Truman's decision to "draw the line" in South Korea: 54,246 dead (33,629 killed on the battlefield; 20,617 military dead from other causes) and 103,284 wounded. The cost of the last two years of the talking war, in order to fix the DMZ at Line Kansas, to guarantee former enemies freedom of choice in repatriation, and to effect the release of 12,773 surviving UN POWs (including 3,597 Americans), was espe-

---

\*The Pentagon breakdown: Total UN killed, wounded, or missing: 996,937, of whom 850,000 were ROKs and 17,000 were other non-Americans. Total Communists killed, wounded, or missing: 1,420,000, of whom 520,000 were NKPA.

cially dear: 63,200 American casualties alone, 12,300 of whom were killed on the battlefield.[125]

Ironically, the United States did not ever withdraw its military presence from South Korea. The Eighth Army, comprised of about 40,000 men, fielding one combat division, is still there, serving as a trip wire force to back up the ROK Army at the DMZ. It stands as a reminder of and a living memorial to America's forgotten war.

# SOURCES
# AND
# ACKNOWLEDGMENTS

The seeds for this book may have been planted during the years 1950–1953 when I was the national security correspondent for *Time* and *Life* magazines in Washington. As such I reported on the Korean War, the MacArthur Hearings, the armistice negotiations, and the rearmament of the United States. I knew many of the Washington officials who appear in the foregoing pages. Their views and actions in those arduous times no doubt made a lasting impression.

The seeds lay dormant until 1979 when I renewed an acquaintanceship with the former Chairman of the Joint Chiefs of Staff, General of the Army Omar N. Bradley, who asked me to collaborate with him on his autobiography, *A General's Life.* The research for that book led to an immersion in the literature and history of the Korean War and to a renewal of many old Army acquaintances, including General Matthew B. Ridgway, one of the most re- markable battlefield leaders the Army has ever produced. A visit with Ridgway subsequently gave rise to the idea of a "battlefield biography" of Ridgway, focusing on his little-known but important role as founder and leader of America's elite airborne forces in World War II and as the dynamic comman- der of United Nations forces in the Korean War.

After completing Bradley's autobiography, my wife, Joan, and I began researching the Ridgway biography in 1982. To our surprise and disappoint- ment we found that notwithstanding the glamour and publicity attending the paratroopers of World War II there was no definitive history of their combat operations. Believing this interesting and vital story needed to be told, we

977

decided to break the Ridgway "battlefield biography" into two volumes, the first setting him in an authoritative history of airborne operations in World War II, the second in the Korean War. The first volume, *Ridgway's Paratroopers,* was published in 1985.

Returning to the history and literature of the Korean War, but this time with a greater need for authoritative battlefield narrative, we were again surprised and disappointed. Although there are many fine books on the origins, geopolitics, and politics of the Korean War (see below) and on Navy, Air Force, and Marine Corps operations, the official histories of United States Army operations in Korea are uneven, cursory, and incomplete.

The Army sent numerous staff historians to Korea to gather material for a grandly envisioned series, *United States Army in the Korean War.* But something went drastically wrong in the execution. The project resulted in merely one and a half volumes of combat narrative, Roy E. Appleman's *South to the Naktong, North to the Yalu,* which covers the action from June to November 1950, and Walter G. Hermes's *Truce Tent and Fighting Front,* which thinly covers action from July 1951 to July 1953, but which devotes half its space to the armistice negotiations. One volume of combat narrative, *Ebb and Flow,* which was designed to bridge the gap from November 1950 to June 1951 (between the Appleman and Hermes volumes), has only recently been completed but has not yet been published. A much needed single volume of Army operations in the Korean War, comparable to the James A. Field's *History of United States Naval Operations: Korea* and Robert F. Futrell's *The United States Air Force in Korea 1950–1953,* is not contemplated.

The uneven and unfulfilled characters of the histories of Army operations during the first year of the Korean War suggested to us the need for a book of larger scope than one focused strictly on Ridgway's command of Eighth Army. Hence our idea for a two-volume "battlefield biography" of Ridgway was again revised, this time to substitute a comprehensive history of the Army's first year in Korea, which would feature Ridgway prominently but not exclusively. The outcome of that decision is this book.

\* \* \*

In researching this book my wife and I began with a close reading of Roy Appleman's *South to the Naktong, North to the Yalu.* Called to active duty as a combat historian, Appleman went to Korea early in the action and began taking notes, a luxury hard-pressed fighters could not afford. He interviewed hundreds of the participants and walked or flew over the terrain. Later he submitted draft chapters of his book to many participants, eliciting hundreds of pages of "comments," many of which he incorporated into his book, but many of which he did not. These letters, which are on file at the Modern Military Records Branch of the National Archives, constitute a large and valuable body of primary source material. For the first six months of the war, our book owes much to Appleman's work and to the writers of these "comments."

Appleman was to write the second volume of combat narrative, *Ebb and Flow,* as a civilian under contract to the Army. But for various reasons this did not pan out and the volume was very slowly carried forward by other Army historians and brought to its final stages by Billy C. Mossman, an Army historian who had gone to Korea in 1950. The Army's chief of military history, Brigadier General William A. Stofft, and the chief of the histories division, Richard O. Perry, kindly permitted us to read *Ebb and Flow* in typescript (and to take notes), but only after we had finished our own work. This hurried reading was useful to us mainly as a check against errors in our own book, but it also clarified for us several combat actions which were either obscure or untold in the official records.

The other Army historians in Korea turned in a fairly large body of combat narrative. Some of it was used in the Appleman, Mossman, and Hermes volumes, but much of it was not. Some of it was collected in an official compendium, *Combat Actions in Korea,* edited by Russell A. Gugeler. Some of it was published elsewhere in military collections or periodicals, but much of it remains unpublished. Both the published and unpublished combat narratives are on file in typescript at the Army's Center of Military History in Washington, D.C. We read and drew from all of these documents.

Three other books which grew out of the work of the Army historians were of value to us. The first was *The River and the Gauntlet,* by S.L.A. Marshall, an editorial writer for the *Detroit News* and reserve Army colonel, who was an Army combat historian in World War II. Recalled to active duty, Marshall went to Korea not as a historian but as a technical analyst for the Army's Operations Research Office (ORO). This assignment led to a close look at the 2d Infantry Division immediately following the Chinese offensive at the Chongchong River on November 25, 1950. The technical research Marshall collected for the ORO reports served as the basis for *The River and the Gauntlet.* The second book was Roy E. Appleman's recent *East of Chosin.* Some of the material Appleman and other Army historians gathered in Korea for Appleman's aborted *Ebb and Flow* served as the basis for this work, but when he returned to civilian life, Appleman substantially enlarged the body of research and, as in the case of *The River and the Gauntlet,* wrote and published the book outside of official channels. The third book is the recent *Korea: The First War We Lost,* by Bevin Alexander (an Army combat historian in Korea), a fine, compact work, the first to make fullest use of the unpublished narratives by the Army combat historians and the Eighth Army and corps command reports to describe Army actions beyond Appleman into the spring of 1951.

In addition to the foregoing works by Army historians, five of the six Army divisions, two of the nineteen regiments, and one tank battalion serving in Korea produced "official" histories. The division (1st Cav, 2d, 3d, 24th, and 25th) and the tank battalion (89th) histories are devoted exclusively to the Korean War, the regimental histories (7th Cav, 187th Airborne) only partially. Although these division histories were written by amateur historians, and photographs received more space than the text, they proved to be useful to us in numerous ways. We consulted these hard-to-find volumes in the military libraries at the Army's Center of Military History in Washington; the Army's Military History Institute at Carlisle Barracks, Pennsylvania; and at the United States Military Academy at West Point. Through the kindness of the West Point librarian, Egon A. Weiss, and the chief of special collections, Robert E. Schnare, we were able to borrow these histories (and other books) on a long-term basis.

Only a few Army combatants produced memoirs of their service in Korea. Among the published works we found merely four volumes that were consistently useful: *General Dean's Story,* by William F. Dean as told to William L. Worden; *The Korean War* and (six brief chapters of) *Soldier,* by Matthew B. Ridgway; and *Puerto Rico's Fighting 65th U.S. Infantry,* by William W. Harris. Fortunately, during our research we came by seven unpublished memoirs bearing on the first year: "Tropic Lightning and Taro Leaf," by G. Bittman Barth; "Sabers and Safety Pins," by Paschal N. and Mary H. Strong; "My Service During the Korean War," by George C. Stewart; "Diary and Personal Adventures," by James H. Dill; an untitled memoir by W. B. Woodruff, Jr.; "Combat Duty in Korea," by Chester L. Bair; and "In a Higher Tradition," by David K. Carlisle and Charles M. Bussey.

A number of Army participants wrote articles or speeches relating to the first year of the war which were useful to us. Among the published articles: "The Lost Corps," by Robert C. Cameron; "The Winter of the Yalu," by James H. Dill; "Pitfalls in Logistic Planning," by Crump Garvin; "Flying Column," by Richard L. Gruenther; "The Naktong Crossings in Korea," by Emerson C. Itschner; "The Truth of Taejon" and "The Walking General," by Forrest K. Kleinman; and "Task Force Penetration," by James H. Lynch. Among the unpublished articles or speeches: "23d Infantry at Hangye, 17–18 May, 1951," by John H. Chiles; "Employment of Armor in Korea," by Welborn G. Dolvin; "Wonju through Chipyong," by Paul L. Freeman; and "Army Engineer in Korea," by Paschal N. Strong.

\* \* \*

With one exception the chroniclers of Army combat actions in Korea other than the onetime Army historians produced little of value. Most of these popular histories are more deeply indebted to Appleman, Gugeler, and Marshall than usually credited (if at all). The exception is the late Donald Knox's *The Korean War: An Oral History*. Although it is too heavily weighted to the Marine Corps and to the 3d Battalion, 5th Cav Regiment, to give a balanced view and peters out in early December 1950 (a second volume is said to be in the works), the book does contain new and informative interviews with or letters from Army combatants in Korea.

With the exception of a few oblique references or implications by Appleman, none of the published or unpublished works by the Army historians or former historians comes to grips with the eternally vital matter of battlefield leadership, which so importantly influenced the Army's first year in Korea. The corps, division, and regimental commanders are seldom even named, let alone described or evaluated. During our research we made a special effort to fill in that important gap, using a variety of sources, including official Army biographies obtained from the Army's Center of Military History, the brief service records contained in the West Point *Register of Graduates,* many obituaries published in the West Point magazine *Assembly,* the *Army Register,* and the biographies and evaluations contained in *The Papers of Dwight D. Eisenhower* (nine volumes).

\* \* \*

Our research took us to five major archives holding primary source material:

• The National Archives, downtown, Washington, D.C. Assisted by archivist John Taylor in the Modern Military Records Branch, we photocopied hundreds of pages of messages between the Joint Chiefs of Staff and GHQ, Tokyo. Most—but not all—of these documents were subsequently published in *Foreign Relations of the United States,* Vol. VII, 1951, parts 1 and 2. In addition, we obtained most of the photographs from the Still Pictures Branch (NNSP), which is now the custodian of U.S. Army Signal Corps photos taken during the Korean War.

• The National Archives depository at the Federal Records Center, Suitland, Maryland. The millions of pages of official reports and documents emanating from Eighth Army and its various components during the Korean War are housed at this facility. These range from high level strategic studies to typed transcripts of radio conversations between platoons and squads. We limited our research to the tactical narrative sections in the monthly command reports of Eighth Army, I, IX, and X corps, the six Army divisions, and the nineteen regiments. While these monthly summaries of combat actions and other activities contain obvious shortcomings and are duplicative as one moves up the chain of command, they were invaluable for gaining an overview of the war and its major battles, for lists of opposing formations, for weather reports and logistics and weaponry problems, for rosters of personnel, awards, and other information.

• The U.S. Army Military History Institute at Carlisle Barracks, Pennsylvania. Hospitably and intelligently assisted by archivist-historian Richard J. Sommers, we focused our research on three areas of this valuable Army archive: the Matthew B. Ridgway and Edward M. Almond papers, and the oral history collection. The well-organized Ridgway and Almond papers were indispensible to this book, as was the oral history collection, which include extensive interviews with Ridgway and Almond, Frank Pace, Charles L. Bolté, John E. Hull, Mark W. Clark, Maxwell D. Taylor, William M. Hoge, Hobart R. Gay, Paul L. Freeman, Harold K. Johnson, James K. Woolnough, and William F. Train.

• The MacArthur Memorial Archives in Norfolk, Virginia. Almost all of the important messages between MacArthur and the Joint Chiefs of Staff and Department of the Army have been published in *Foreign Relations of the United States,* Vol. VII, 1950, and the aforementioned Vol. VII, 1951, parts 1 and 2. The other important MacArthur papers have been thoroughly mined by D. Clayton James in his magisterial three-volume biography of MacArthur, of which Volume III, *Triumph and Disaster,* was indispensable to us. However, assisted by archivist David Boone, we located numerous other documents which proved helpful, especially numerous letters and telexes between MacArthur and Ridgway.

• The U.S. Marine Corps History (division) and Museum at the Navy Yard, Washington, D.C. Courteously assisted by its director, Brigadier General Edwin H. Simmons, who served in Korea and has published material about the war, we profited from our notes and photocopies from the following: The Aide-Mémoire and Flight Log of Major General Oliver P. Smith, Korea, 1950–1951; the Smith oral history; and the oral histories of Alpha A. Bowser (G-3, 1st Marine Division in Korea 1950–1951), Edward A. Craig (ADC of the 1st Marine Division in Korea), and Gerald C. Thomas, who succeeded Smith as commander of the 1st Marine Division. In addition we are indebted to General Simmons for official biographies of the foregoing and of numerous Marine regimental commanders in Korea, for division and regimental histories, and to him and the librarian, Major D. R. Smith, for the long-term loan of the five volumes comprising *U.S. Marine Corps Operations in Korea.*

In our earlier research for *A General's Life* and *Ridgway's Paratroopers* we conducted scores of taped interviews with various senior Army officers, including Ridgway, J. Lawton Collins, Mark W. Clark, Maxwell D. Taylor, and James M. Gavin among others. Some of this material pertained to the Korean War, notably our interviews with the members of Ridgway's inner circle who joined him in Korea: Frank W. Moorman, A. Day Surles, Walter

F. Winton, and Emory S. Adams. To these interviews we added scores more, including those with Ridgway, Charles D. Palmer, Garrison H. Davidson, thirty-one officers who commanded regiments in Korea, numerous infantry battalion commanders, tank battalion commander Welborn G. Dolvin, and many others. In addition, through the kindness of D. Clayton James, we obtained transcripts of his interviews (or oral histories) with John H. Chiles (whom we also interviewed) and Gines Perez, which are held (along with many other valuable interviews with MacArthur's associates in GHQ) in the Special Collection Department, Mitchell Memorial Library, Mississippi State University.

With the help of these interviews, the West Point *Register of Graduates,* veterans organizations, and other sources, we were able to track down by mail hundreds of other officers and men who served during the first year in Korea in both exalted and minor posts. Thus we began an enormous letter and telephonic exchange about combat actions in Korea which extended over three years. We are much indebted to these correspondents, many of whom conferred by letter or telephone with former associates in Korea (usually not identified to us) to check their own memories, in order to provide us with the most accurate information possible. These extremely helpful letters and/or telephone talks are acknowledged by name in the chapter notes, but we would like especially to thank the former Eighth Army deputy G-2, Robert G. Fergusson, whose interest in this project was unflagging, Rolfe L. Hillman, Jr., whose efforts to help us sort out the early senior command sequence and other matters in the 9th Infantry Regiment were unstinting, and David K. Carlisle, who first brought to our attention the flaws and bias in the Army's treatment of the blacks of the 24th Infantry in the official histories and who encouraged us to explore the black outfits in Korea in more detail.

\* \* \*

Finally, politics and geopolitics.

As we stated earlier—and it bears repeating—there are many fine studies which explore the origins of the Korean War, the decision of the Truman administration to enter the war, the political and geopolitical consequences of that decision, the Truman-MacArthur controversy, and the impact of the war on American military planning and society. In fact, the majority of books on the "Korean War" focus on these aspects to the neglect of the war itself. The many works that we have drawn from in that category are cited in the chapter notes.

Earlier, in our research for Bradley's autobiography, *A General's Life,* we thoroughly explored the military, budgetary, and political factors and controversies before and during the Korean War. We have incorporated some of that material in the opening section of this book, "Eve of War," adding more recent scholarship where appropriate, but our main goal in this book was to tell the story of the Army's first year on the battlefield.

For further background on the politics and geopolitics of the war we drew heavily upon memoirs of Truman, Acheson, MacArthur, Eisenhower, Ridgway, Collins, et al, plus the thousands of documents in the *Foreign Relations of the United States* series (described earlier) and five official government histories. These latter are: the first volume in the Army's Korean War Series, *Policy and Direction: The First Year,* by James F. Schnabel, and four volumes of the unpublished "The History of the Joint Chiefs of Staff," which are on file in the Modern Military Records Branch, National Archives. These volumes are: Vol. I (1945–47), by James F. Schnabel; Vol. II (1947–49), by Kenneth W. Condit; Vol. III (The Korean War, Parts 1 and 2), by James F. Schnabel and Robert J. Watson; and Vol. IV (1950–52), by Walter S. Poole. Volume III in the JCS series was, of course, the most useful to us. It occasionally has the text or a paraphrase of and exchange of messages between MacArthur or others and the Pentagon, which is not included in the *Foreign Relations* series, and hundreds of such cables for 1952 and 1953, which have not been published as of this writing by the Department of State.

In conclusion I wish to express my deepest gratitude to several people without whose support this book could never have come to fruition. First to my wife, Joan, who worked side by side with me in the various archives and during our many interviews and later, while I scribbled, transcribed countless tapes, handled the vast correspondence we engendered, edited and typed this huge manuscript several times, and performed hundreds—if not thousands— of other literary chores. Secondly, to our agent, Russell Galen of the Scott Meredith Literary Agency, Inc., who unfailingly provided the necessary resources and continuous encouragement. Thirdly, to our editor, Hugh O'Neill, who never wavered in his enthusiasm and support, and who carefully and thoughtfully edited the entire manuscript, line by line, and thereby improved it enormously.

# NOTES

## CHAPTER 1

1. Truman: Robert H. Ferrell, ed., *Dear Bess* (New York: W. W. Norton, 1983); Robert H. Ferrell, ed., *Off the Record: The Private Papers of Harry S. Truman* (New York: Harper & Row, 1980); Harry S. Truman, *Memoirs*, vol. I: *Year of Decision*, vol. II: *Years of Trial and Hope* (New York: Doubleday & Co., 1956); Margaret Truman, *Harry S. Truman* (New York: William Morrow, 1973) and *Bess W. Truman* (New York: MacMillan, 1986); Robert J. Donovan, *The Presidency of Harry S Truman*, vol. I: 1945–1948, *Conflict and Crisis;* vol. II: 1949–1953, *Tumultuous Years* (New York: W. W. Norton, 1977 and 1982).

2. Truman as commander in chief has not heretofore received the critical scholarly work the subject deserves. Richard F. Haynes has provided a useful survey in his *The Awesome Power: Harry S. Truman as Commander in Chief* (Baton Rouge: Louisiana State University Press, 1973), but his work lacks critical analysis or originality. In his soundly researched, admiring new biography, Donovan (*Tumultuous Years*, p. 57) merely approaches the subject: "President Truman occupies an important place in American history largely because he guided the United States to unprecedented international leadership in peacetime. He understood, for example, the significance of the Marshall Plan to that role. He seemed less clear in grasping the new requirements that international leadership imposed upon the American military structure, especially when it came to translating requirements into specific numbers of divisions, ships, and aircraft."

3. Merle Miller, *Plain Speaking* (New York: Berkley, 1973), pp. 164, 205, 287, 325. Miller's book has often been criticized as history, but these quotes have not been challenged and fairly represent Truman's views. During a private dinner with the former president, his daughter, and his son-in-law at the New York home of Robert Sherrod, Truman spoke at considerable length in a similar vein to the

author. In his memoirs (vol. I, p. 88), Truman wrote: "I knew . . . that Army and Navy professionals seldom had any idea of the value of money. They did not seem to care what the cost was. . . ." He added that the admirals were the "worst offenders."

4. *Dear Bess,* p. 286; rejected by West Point because of "flat eyeballs": *Harry S. Truman,* p. 47, p. 55. See also *Plain Speaking,* pp. 55, 84, 325.

5. *Dear Bess,* pp. 234, 257, 285, 290, 294–95. Some of this criticism, of course, may be ignored as the routine griping of a civilian soldier in the field; however, Truman's deep-seated contempt comes through vividly. Editor Ferrell comments: "Uncomfortable with Army regulations, Truman found himself equally annoyed with regular Army officers." In *Off the Record* (p. 7), Ferrell wrote that Truman had a "detestation of regular army officers and especially West Pointers, whom he considered absurd martinets concerned only with the currying of horses."

6. For example, *Dear Bess,* p. 479. Editor Ferrell comments on this period: "Regular officers frequently angered Truman with pretensions of professionalism. . . ." $15 billion: *Off the Record,* p. 164.

7. In an interview for his memoirs, conducted by William Hillman on January 22, 1954 (p. 8), Truman said that he was on the point of sending investigators from his Senate subcommittee to have a look at the "great plant constructions" in Tennessee and Washington, but that Secretary of War Henry L. Stimson asked him not to. "I can't tell you what it is," Truman quoted Stimson as saying, "but it's the greatest project in the history of the world. It's most top secret, and we'd appreciate it if you'd not go into the plants." Truman went on to say that it was not until April 13, 1945, the day after he assumed the office of president, "that I actually found out what it was all about." In his memoirs Stimson wrote that he went to the White House on April 24, 1945, "to discuss the atomic bomb with the President from whom the matter had hitherto been kept secret." In an oral history conducted from January 2, 1967, through June 30, 1970, Eben A. Ayers, special White House assistant in the Truman administration, said that Truman had told him essentially the same story that he told Hillman in "one rather long conversation" in May 1951. Truman's memory has been challenged, however. In an oral history on April 17, 1963 (pp. 451–52), Tom L. Evans, Kansas City businessman and longtime Truman confidant, stated that Truman had told him that Roosevelt had informed him about the A-bomb during a meeting on the White House lawn on August 18, 1944. In an oral history on April 16, 1969 (pp. 94–95), Walter Hehmeyer, a member of the wartime Truman Committee, stated that "just about every staff member on the Truman Committee knew about the development of the atomic bomb . . ." and that Army Chief of Staff George C. Marshall had personally briefed Truman on some of the details while Truman was chairing the committee. (Letter from George H. Curtis, Harry S. Truman Library, to author, April 30, 1986, with excerpts of aforementioned oral histories.) *Plain Speaking,* pp. 197–200; *Years of Decision,* p. 10.

8. Vaughan: *Tumultuous Years,* pp. 115–16 and ff.; *Bess W. Truman,* pp. 213, 259, 348–49.

9. Truman's postwar military force levels, war plans, budget policies, etc.: "The History of the Joint Chiefs of Staff," vol. I, 1945–1947, by James F. Schnabel; vol. II, 1947–1949, by Kenneth W. Condit; vol. IV, 1950–1952, by Walter S. Poole, all typescripts on file in the Modern Military Records Branch, National Archives (NA). In addition: Louis Galambos, ed., *The Papers of Dwight David Eisenhower,* vols. VI through IX (Baltimore: Johns Hopkins University Press, 1978), hereafter

*Ike Papers VI,* etc.; Walter Millis, ed., *The Forrestal Diaries* (New York: Viking Press, 1951); *Years of Trial and Hope;* General of the Army Omar N. Bradley and Clay Blair, *A General's Life* (New York: Simon & Schuster, 1983); Robert H. Ferrell, ed., *The Eisenhower Diaries* (New York: W. W. Norton, 1981); J. Lawton Collins, *Lightning Joe: An Autobiography* (Baton Rouge: Louisiana State University Press, 1979), and *War in Peacetime* (Boston: Houghton Mifflin, 1969); Demetrios Caraley, *The Politics of Military Unification* (New York: Columbia University Press, 1966); Paul Y. Hammond, *Organizing for Defense* (Princeton: Princeton University Press, 1961); James E. Hewes, Jr., *From Root to McNamara: Army Organization and Administration, 1900–1963* (Washington, D.C.: Center of Military History, 1975); Edward Kolodziej, *The Uncommon Defense and Congress* (Columbus: Ohio State University Press, 1966); Elias Huzar, *The Purse and the Sword: Control of the Army by Congress Through Military Appropriations 1933–50* (Ithaca: Cornell University Press, 1950); Clyde Edward Jacobs and John F. Gallagher, *The Selective Service Act: A Case Study of the Governmental Process* (New York: Dodd, Mead, 1968); William H. Riker, *Soldiers of the State: The Role of the National Guard in American Democracy* (Washington, D.C.: Public Affairs Press, 1957); Thomas H. Etzold and John Lewis Gaddis, eds., *Containment: Documents on American Policy and Strategy 1945–50* (New York: Columbia University Press, 1978); Barton J. Bernstein and Allen J. Matusow, eds., *The Truman Administration: A Documentary History* (New York: Harper & Row, 1966).

10. *Eisenhower Diaries,* p. 153. Eisenhower, referring to his days as chief of staff of the Army, wrote: "During 1946, 1947 and early 1948 I pleaded for a $15 billion budget. We never got it. . . ." Later (p. 159) he jotted: "One of our greatest troubles is inability to plan for a given amount of money. Some new authority always intervenes to cut it down in spite of prior commitment by the president himself. Once (in January 1947) he called me on the phone when I was in Coral Gables hospital to tell me he had to go back on a specific promise of $110 million for Army equipment (tanks and trucks). That was on advice of budget director James E. Webb, but generally the president does not tell me himself, we just get the bad news." Truman's goal of $6 or $7 billion: *Off the Record,* p. 133. In April 1948 Truman wrote: "When I took office our military budget was on the basis of 100 billions a year. It has come down to eleven billions. I had hoped to get it to six or seven."

11. *Off the Record,* p. 33. Ferrell wrote that Truman favored UMT in order to prevent the kind of unpreparedness the Army suffered between the world wars and for "another reason": UMT "represented essentially the citizen army idea rather than the old regular army viewpoint; the President believed that the defense of the nation rested upon civilian preparedness. He had seen regular army officers during the First World War and detested them." UMT and Pentagon budget: *Off the Record,* p. 133. Truman wrote: "Had UMT been authorized when I asked for it we might have succeeded" (in reducing the budget to six or seven billion).

12. *A General's Life,* p. 474.

13. *Off the Record,* p. 134. Truman wrote: ". . . the Navy as always is the greatest propaganda machine."

14. David Rosenberg, "The Hydrogen Bomb Decision," *Journal of American History,* vol. 66, no. 1 (June 1979).

15. *Forrestal Diaries.* See also the oral histories of Marx Leva and Louis H. Renfrow, Harry S. Truman Library, Independence, Missouri.

16. *Eisenhower Diaries,* pp. 150–60.
17. *A General's Life,* p. 489, and passim.
18. From 1950 to 1955 the author was *Time* magazine's national security correspondent and, as such, knew and reported extensively on Louis Johnson and other Pentagon leaders. See also: *Current Biography, 1949; Tumultuous Years,* pp. 61–62; *A General's Life;* Leva, Renfrow, and William H. Draper oral histories, Harry S. Truman Library.
19. *A General's Life,* p. 502.
20. Renfrow oral history. For Navy reaction, see the oral histories of Robert L. Dennison, Daniel V. Gallery, Malcolm Schoeffel, George Miller, John S. Thach, Fitzhugh Lee, Walter W. O. Ansel, David McDonald, D. D. Griffin, Charles Wellborn, Herbert Riley at the Naval Historical Center, Washington, D.C. At the Harry S. Truman Library, see oral history of John L. Sullivan. The "criminal" quote is from Paolo E. Coletta, "The Defense Unification Battle 1947–1950," *Prologue,* publication of the NA (Spring 1975). Additional background in author-John L. Sullivan interview, May 6, 1980.
21. Renfrow oral history.
22. Gordon Gray oral history, Harry S. Truman Library. Author-Gordon Gray interview, March 31, 1980. *A General's Life,* p. 503.
23. *Off the Record,* pp. 191–93.
24. *Tumultuous Years,* p. 62.
25. *Off the Record,* p. 192; Dean Acheson, *Present at the Creation: My Years in the State Department* (New York: W. W. Norton, 1969), p. 374; *A General's Life,* p. 503.
26. *Eisenhower Diaries,* p. 159.
27. The author recently coauthored Bradley's autobiography, *A General's Life.*
28. "No part": *Eisenhower Diaries,* p. 158.
29. The author knew Collins and Ridgway and interviewed Clark on numerous occasions, most recently on April 7, 1980. The author interviewed Collins in 1982; Ridgway in 1980 and 1984. For more background on the three men, see: Mark W. Clark, *Calculated Risk* (New York: Harper & Brothers, 1950) and *From the Danube to the Yalu* (New York: Harper & Brothers, 1954); Collins, *Lightning Joe* and *War in Peacetime;* Matthew B. Ridgway, *Soldier* (New York: Harper & Brothers, 1956) and *The Korean War* (New York: Doubleday, 1967). For biographies of Clark and Ridgway, see: Martin Blumenson, *Mark Clark* (New York: Congdon and Weed, 1984), and Clay Blair, *Ridgway's Paratroopers* (New York: Doubleday, 1985).
30. Author-Ridgway interview, October 31, 1984.
31. Various sources; Haislip: *Register of Graduates,* U.S. Military Academy (hereafter West Point *Register*).
32. "Different world": *Tumultuous Years,* p. 99.
33. "History of the Joint Chiefs of Staff," vol. IV, 1950–1952.
34. *Tumultuous Years,* pp. 101–02.
35. "Hydrogen Bomb Decision": *Tumultuous Years,* pp. 103–04.
36. *A General's Life,* pp. 507–09; *Tumultuous Years,* pp. 108–12.
37. *Tumultuous Years,* pp. 108–12.
38. *Foreign Relations of the United States* (hereafter *FRUS,* vol. number and year) (Washington, D.C.: Government Printing Office). The quotation here is from *FRUS IX,* 1949, pp. 376–78, 460–67.
39. Johnson conniving: *Off the Record,* p. 189. Editor Ferrell wrote: "Truman did not know it, but Johnson also intrigued in scandalous fashion against Secretary of

State Acheson, undercutting Acheson's China policy by allowing Assistant Secretary of Defense Paul Griffith to pass administration secrets to Nationalist Ambassador Wellington Koo." Truman did know, however, that Johnson was disloyal. Truman wrote (p. 192): "He had conferences with enemy Senators of mine—Wherry, McCarthy, Brewster, Taft, Hickenlooper—and made terrible statements to them."

40. *Present at the Creation*, pp. 371, 373–81.
41. *A General's Life*, p. 519.
42. *Present at the Creation*, pp. 373–74.
43. "Implemented": *Present at the Creation*, p. 374. Not implemented and "pig in a poke": "History of the Joint Chiefs of Staff," vol. IV, pp. 15–16.
44. Lloyd Norman, "Washington's War," *Army* magazine (June 1960). Norman was Pentagon correspondent for the *Chicago Tribune* in the late 1940s and early 1950s.
45. Bradley testimony: "Washington's War"; *War in Peacetime*, p. 71; "History of the Joint Chiefs of Staff," vol. IV, p. 21.
46. *A General's Life*, pp. 487–88.
47. "Washington's War."
48. Army force levels: James F. Schnabel, *Policy and Direction: The First Year*, in *United States Army in the Korean War* series (Washington, D.C.: Office of the Chief of Military History, 1972), p. 43 (hereafter *Policy and Direction*).
49. G. Bittman Barth unpublished monograph: "Tropic Lightning and Taro Leaf in Korea, July 1950–May 1951," in author's possession (hereafter Barth ms.). The Barth ms. is both a narrative account of his service in Korea until June 1951 and a history of the first year of the war. Although it focuses on the 25th Division and its artillery arm, it contains much valuable information on other units and numerous insightful asides.
50. *Policy and Direction*, pp. 45–46; *War in Peacetime*, p. 67; *Soldier*, p. 191.
51. "History of the Joint Chiefs of Staff," vol. IV, pp. 23, 32.

## CHAPTER 2

1. Postwar Japan: D. Clayton James, *The Years of MacArthur*, vol. III: *Triumph and Disaster 1945–1964* (Boston: Houghton Mifflin, 1985), hereafter *MacArthur III*.
2. William Manchester, *American Caesar 1880–1964* (Boston: Little, Brown, 1978), p. 3.
3. *MacArthur III;* Ronald H. Spector, *Eagle Against the Sun: The American War with Japan* (New York: Free Press/Macmillan, 1985), introduction.
4. *Off the Record*, p. 47; *A General's Life*, p. 542.
5. Almond: Almond oral history, conducted by his grandson, Thomas G. Fergusson, Almond papers, United States Army Military History Institute (USAMHI), Carlisle Barracks, Pa.; official biography. Author interviews with Chiles, December 21, 1982; Holden, July 25, 1985; Edward L. Rowny, May 25, 1984; letter to author, William P. Yarborough, July 28, 1984. Yarborough and Rowny served under Almond in Italy as senior officers; Rowny, Chiles, and Holden in Japan and Korea. Eisenhower rating in 1948: *Ike Papers IX*, p. 2252.
6. For further details of the 92d, see Chapter 6.
7. Edward Almond, Jr., and Galloway: West Point *Register* and letter to author from Almond's grandson (son of Galloway) Thomas G. Fergusson, March 24, 1985.

8. Mueller-Almond: *MacArthur III,* pp. 380–81. Collins-Almond antagonism: "Oral Reminiscences of Major General John H. Chiles," July 27, 1979, conducted by D. Clayton James, Special Collections Department, Mitchell Memorial Library, Mississippi State University, p. 40. Chiles said: "They hated each other's guts since they were young men at Fort Benning."

9. "Clear day": Paschal N. and Mary H. Strong, "Sabers and Safety Pins," manuscript kindly lent the author, p. 6. Strong was Eighth Army engineer, 1949–1951. Levy: *MacArthur III,* p. 62.

10. *MacArthur III,* p. 82 and passim.

11. Walker: West Point *Register,* official biography, *Time* magazine cover story, July 31, 1950, *Current Biography, 1950;* various interviews. Admirer quote: Author-Eugene M. Landrum (son of Walker's chief of staff, Eugene M. Landrum) interview, March 30, 1985, and his letter to author, February 25, 1985.

12. Service and friendship with Ike: Dwight D. Eisenhower, *At Ease: Stories I Tell to Friends* (Garden City: Doubleday, 1967), pp. 128–30, 169–74. With Marshall: Forrest C. Pogue with Gordon Harrison, *Education of a General 1880–1939* (New York: Viking Press, 1963), pp. 300, 317. Marshall then commanded the 5th Brigade, 3d Infantry Division, Vancouver Barracks, Washington. Walker left the 5th Brigade job for War Plans, where Gee Gerow was exec. Marshall followed Walker to Washington, first as chief of War Plans, then as deputy chief of staff, then (in 1939) as Chief of Staff. Gee Gerow succeeded Marshall as chief of War Plans and promoted Walker to be his exec. While house hunting, Marshall was a houseguest of the Walkers. Background on Gerow: official biography; *Ike Papers I,* p. 3.

13. *At Ease,* pp. 237–39. Stephen E. Ambrose, *Eisenhower,* vol. I: *Soldier, General of the Army, President-Elect 1890–1952* (New York: Simon & Schuster, 1983), pp. 124–25 (hereafter *Eisenhower I*).

14. "Of all . . .": quoted in *Time* magazine cover story, July 31, 1950. Patton diary: Martin Blumenson, *The Patton Papers, 1940–1945* (Boston: Houghton Mifflin, 1974), vol. II, pp. 616, 649. Hobart Gay, Patton's chief of staff, also kept a diary. On April 5, 1945 (*Patton Papers,* p. 680), Gay noted: "General Walker is always the most willing and cooperative. He apparently will fight any time, any place, with anything that the Army commander desires to give him." Eisenhower appraisal: *Ike Papers IV,* p. 2599.

15. "Pouter pigeon" and press relations: Author-James H. Polk interview, April 28, 1984. Polk was a senior armored task force commander under Walker in the ETO and in 1947 was assigned to MacArthur's G-2 section, after which he served in the Korean War as G-2 of X Corps.

16. Author-Thomas J. Marnane interview, October 2, 1984.

17. Author interviews with John H. ("Mike") Michaelis, April 28, 1984, and Marnane.

18. Korea background and Allied occupation: *Policy and Direction,* pp. 1–39; James F. Schnabel and Robert J. Watson, "The History of the Joint Chiefs of Staff," vol. III, pt. I and pt. II: "The Korean War," NA (hereafter "History of the JCS III"), pp. 1–48; Roy E. Appleman, *South to the Naktong, North to the Yalu* (Washington, D.C.: Office of the Chief of Military History, 1961), pp. 1–6, hereafter *South to the Naktong*; Robert K. Sawyer, *Military Advisors in Korea: KMAG in Peace and War* (Washington, D.C.: Office of the Chief of Military History, 1962); *MacArthur III,* pp. 388–402. For other background: Frank Baldwin, ed., *Without Parallel: The American-Korean Relationship Since 1945* (New York: Pantheon,

1973); Russell D. Buhite, *Soviet-American Relations in Asia: 1945–1954* (Norman: University of Oklahoma Press, 1981); Bruce Cumings, ed., *Child of Conflict: The Korean-American Relationship, 1943–1953* (Seattle: University of Washington Press, 1983), and *The Origins of the Korean War* (Princeton: Princeton University Press, 1981); Charles M. Dobbs, *American Foreign Policy, the Cold War and Korea 1945–1950* (Kent, Ohio: Kent State University Press, 1984); Burton I. Kaufman, *The Korean War: Challenge in Crisis, Credibility and Command* (Philadelphia: Temple University Press, 1986); Joyce and Gabriel Kolko, *The Limits of Power: The World and U.S. Foreign Policy 1945–1954* (New York: Harper & Row, 1972); I. F. Stone, *The Hidden History of the Korean War* (New York: Monthly Review Press, 1952); Callum A. MacDonald, *Korea: The War Before Vietnam* (New York: The Free Press/Macmillan, 1986).

19. MacArthur decree: *MacArthur III,* pp. 390–92. James wrote (p. 392) that the decree was "surely one of the most ill-advised documents of MacArthur's career. . . . " Retention of Japanese government and police: *MacArthur III; Origins of the Korean War,* pp. 138–39, examines the Korean reaction in impressive detail.

20. Hodge's withdrawal proposal: *Origins of the Korean War,* p. 211.

21. *MacArthur III,* p. 393.

22. *Origins of the Korean War,* pp. 356–81.

23. Patterson view: *Forrestal Diaries,* pp. 265, 273; *Ike Papers VIII,* p. 1660. JCS view: "History of the JCS III," pp. 13–14.

24. Marshall hesitation: *Forrestal Diaries,* pp. 273, 321–22; *Ike Papers IX,* p. 2100. Kennan view: *Containment,* p. 96.

25. JCS Staff Paper No. 1834, February 11, 1948, Bradley File, George C. Marshall Research Library, Lexington, Virginia.

26. "History of the JCS III," pp. 17–18.

27. Ibid., pp. 25–27.

28. S.L.A. Marshall, "Big Little War," *Army* (June 1960).

29. Kim: *Origins of the Korean War,* pp. 35–38; Rhee: Ibid., pp. 188–93.

30. *MacArthur III,* p. 395.

31. *South to the Naktong; Policy and Decision,* pp. 32–34; "History of the JCS III," pp. 13–18.

32. Hodge quoted: *MacArthur III,* p. 393.

33. *Military Advisors in Korea,* pp. 39, 96; *Policy and Direction,* p. 35; "History of the JCS III," p. 27.

34. *South to the Naktong,* pp. 7–9.

35. ROK Army: *Military Advisors in Korea,* pp. 41–48; *Policy and Direction,* p. 34; "History of the JCS III," pp. 21–28.

36. *South to the Naktong,* p. 13; *Military Advisors in Korea,* pp. 45–48.

37. *MacArthur III,* pp. 221–35; Michael Shaller, "Securing the Great Crescent: Occupied Japan and the Origins of Containment in Southeast Asia," *Journal of American History* (September 1982); George F. Kennan, *Memoirs 1925–1950* (Boston: Little, Brown, 1967).

38. JCS views on secret Japanese defense forces: *FRUS VII,* 1949, pp. 671–73; 885–86, 922–29. On March 1, 1949, the JCS recommended that "plans be made now for the eventual establishment of limited Japanese armed forces to maintain internal security and to assist in local defensive action in event of an emergency." The JCS further suggested that "strengthening and equipping of Japanese police and coastal patrols" be undertaken "with the secret ultimate objective in mind

of the use of these forces as a basis for the establishment of limited Japanese
military forces for the defense of Japan."

39. Landrum: Biographical information kindly provided by his son, Eugene M. Landrum, in letter to author, February 25, 1985, and in an interview, March 30, 1985.

40. *Eagle Against the Sun,* pp. 180–81; Forrest C. Pogue, *George C. Marshall, Organ-
izer of Victory 1943–1945* (New York: Viking Press, 1973), pp. 150–52, 155.

41. *A General's Life,* p. 262; *Lightning Joe,* pp. 209–10; *Ike Papers III,* pp. 1792,
2196–97.

42. Landrum letter, February 25, 1985. Collier: Official biography; for Patton criticism ("Collins and Bradley are too prone to cut off heads"), see *Patton Papers,*
p. 479. For another dissent, see Martin Blumenson and James L. Stokesbury,
*Masters of the Art of Command* (Boston: Houghton Mifflin, 1975), pp. 369–72.

43. Jim Mesko, *Armor in Korea* (Carrollton, Texas: Squadron/Signal Publications,
Inc., 1984). *Thrust,* The Story of the 89th Tank Battalion. "Employment of
Armor in Korea," by Welborn G. Dolvin, a lengthy speech delivered at VMI,
December 12, 1951—courtesy of Dolvin (hereafter Dolvin speech).

44. Division authorized strength, 1950: William Glenn Robertson, *Counterattack on
the Naktong, 1950* (Fort Leavenworth, Kan.: Combat Studies Institute, USA
Command and General Staff College, December 1985), pp. 3, 4, a study of the
24th Division in Korea, July–August 1950; *South to the Naktong,* p. 49; *Policy
and Direction,* p. 54; *War in Peacetime,* p. 67. Exact personnel figures vary. A
document in the Department of the Army (DA), dated June 27, 1950, in the
Matthew B. Ridgway Papers, Box 16, USAMHI, gives this rundown:

| | Authorized Strength | Actual Strength |
|---|---|---|
| 1st Cav Div.: | 12,510 | 11,357 |
| 7th Div.: | 12,513 | 11,371 |
| 24th Div. | 12,510 | 11,242 |
| 25th Div. | 13,650 | 13,080 |

45. Black market: Melbourne C. Chandler, *Of GarryOwen in Glory: The History of
the 7th U.S. Calvary* (Annandale, Va.: The Turnpike Press, 1960), p. 241, hereafter *Of GarryOwen in Glory.*

46. Author-Michaelis interview.

47. "Big Little War"; *War in Peacetime,* p. 67; Russell Weigley, *History of the United
States Army* (New York: Macmillan, 1967), p. 503. Marshall wrote that the
contraction to two battalions made the regiments "tactically rigid." Collins wrote
that the lack of infantry and artillery elements "in the early stages of the Korean
war, especially the shortages of reserve battalions, resulted in the loss, not only
of battles, but also of American soldiers' lives." Weigley wrote: "These reductions
were serious handicaps in a tactical system that assumed three-battalion regiments; in combat a regimental commander would have to fight with a single
battalion, if he desired a reserve, or put both battalions in the line and fight
without a reserve."

48. Author-Michaelis interview.

49. *Policy and Direction,* p. 55; Forrest K. Kleinman, "Truth of Taejon," *Army* (June
1960); *War in Peacetime,* pp. 66–67.

50. *Policy and Direction,* p. 55.

51. Author-Edgar R. Luhn interview, December 9, 1983.

52. *War in Peacetime,* p. 66.
53. West Point *Register;* Charles B. MacDonald, *A Time for Trumpets* (New York: William Morrow, 1985), p. 290, and passim.
54. *Military Advisors in Korea,* pp. 69, 98.
55. Various interviews—anonymity requested. For one official American view of corruption in the ROK Army, see Roberts's memo to all KMAG advisers, May 5, 1950, *FRUS VII,* 1950, pp. 93–96.
56. *Military Advisors in Korea,* pp. 60–63.
57. Ibid., p. 110.
58. Ibid., p. 76.
59. Ibid., pp. 107–10.
60. *South to the Naktong,* pp. 9–11.
61. *Military Advisors in Korea,* p. 73.
62. *Present at the Creation,* pp. 350–57.
63. *FRUS VII,* 1950, p. 42.
64. Ibid., pp. 64–66.
65. Ibid., pp. 67, 77.
66. *Military Advisors in Korea,* pp. 112–19; *FRUS VII,* 1950, p. 121. Aid bill: Ibid., p. 103.
67. *FRUS VII,* 1950, pp. 96–98. For an account of a typical VIP visit (by Philip C. Jessup), see *FRUS VII,* 1950, pp. 1–7, 18–23. Reporting on Jessup's visit, Muccio wrote Acheson (p. 19) that in a KMAG briefing Roberts "went on to paint a generally optimistic picture of the developments of the Korean security forces, especially of the Army. General Roberts expressed the view that the Korean Army had the capability of containing the North Korean forces in being. . . ."
68. Smith: *Hidden History of the Korean War,* pp. 61ff. Jessup: *FRUS VII,* 1950, p. 5. Knowland: "History of the JCS III," p. 42. Foster: *Policy and Direction,* p. 40. Hobbs: *FRUS VII,* 1950, p. 98. Gunther: *Hidden History of the Korean War,* p. 62.
69. *Time* (June 5, 1950), pp. 26–27. In a later issue, July 3, 1950, *Time* quoted Roberts as saying the ROK Army was the "best doggone shooting Army outside the United States."
70. Roberts: *Policy and Direction,* p. 39. Muccio: *FRUS VII,* 1950, pp. 48–51, 104–05. Drumright: *FRUS VII,* 1950, pp. 121–22.
71. *FRUS VII,* 1950, p. 5. Roberts stressed to Jessup in January 1950 "that five or ten bombers could come over and be absolutely unopposed and probably disrupt South Korea by the panic which would result from a raid on Seoul." Roberts told the Pentagon (*Policy and Direction,* p. 39) that the North Korean Air Force could give the ROKs a "bloody nose" and South Korea would be "gobbled up to be added to the rest of Red Asia." Muccio quoted from *FRUS VII,* 1950, p. 105. Many other *FRUS* entries, pp. 1–131, stress the potential of the NKPA Air Force and urge a ROK Air Force.
72. Training status: *Military Advisors in Korea,* p. 78. Corruption: *FRUS VII,* 1950, pp. 93–96 (Roberts memo to KMAG personnel). Ammo, trucks, etc.: *FRUS VII,* 1950, and *South to the Naktong,* p. 17; *Military Advisors in Korea,* p. 98.
73. "Not good tank country": *Military Advisors in Korea,* p. 100. Sawyer wrote: "The Americans did not include tanks . . . in part because of fiscal limitations and in part because the KMAG staff felt that the roads and bridges of South Korea did not lend themselves to efficient tank operations."
74. Here and below: Author-Darrigo interview, November 20, 1984; letter, Darrigo

to author, December 8, 1984; *South to the Naktong,* p. 23, and passim; letters, Darrigo to Appleman. These letters to Appleman may be found in the Modern Military Records Branch, NA, filed as "Background Papers" and "Supporting Documents" for Appleman's official history. These papers and documents, which include thousands of pages of interview notes and letters from key participants in the Korean War (many commenting on various drafts of the manuscript of the history) constitute a large and valuable collection of primary documents on the war. These documents and papers have been used extensively in this work, identified hereafter as Letter to Appleman or in some instances, Letter to the Office of the Chief of Military History (OCMH).

75. Border incidents: *South to the Naktong,* p. 6. NKPA evacuation of civilians: *Policy and Direction,* p. 64. Pyongyang propaganda: *FRUS VII,* 1950, pp. 98–104.
76. *Policy and Direction,* pp. 62–64.
77. Author-Darrigo interview. *Military Advisors in Korea,* p. 115, and *South to the Naktong,* p. 23, have brief accounts of Darrigo's experiences.
78. Paik-Rockwell: *South to the Naktong,* p. 22. Paik's age: *Time* (July 24, 1950).
79. NKPA and ROK tactical operations, here and below: *South to the Naktong,* pp. 21–30; *Military Advisors in Korea,* pp. 114–18.

## CHAPTER 3

1. UP story: *MacArthur III,* p. 419. Muccio cable: *FRUS VII,* 1950, p. 125. Time differential: *South to the Naktong,* p. 21n. Out of town: *Tumultuous Years,* pp. 188–91. Bradley's "bug": *A General's Life,* p. 530.
2. *Tumultuous Years,* pp. 188–91; *Present at the Creation,* pp. 404–05.
3. Speculation on Soviet intent and control of NKPA: *FRUS VII,* 1950, pp. 148–54 (State Department intelligence estimate); *A General's Life,* p. 535.
4. *FRUS VII,* 1950, p. 183.
5. *Tumultuous Years,* pp. 196–97, 202.
6. Ibid., p. 206. Donovan wrote: "Domestic political considerations also weighed heavily on Truman and Acheson."
7. *Present at the Creation,* pp. 404–05; *War in Peacetime,* p. 6.
8. Author's professional observation and social contacts with Pace 1950–1953. See also: *Current Biography, 1950* and Pace oral history, Harry S. Truman Library. The not "military expert" quote is from the oral history.
9. For earlier Ridgway marriages, see *Ridgway's Paratroopers,* ch. 1 notes, p. 530. He was divorced from his second wife, Margaret ("Peggy"), on June 30, 1947, in Reno, Nevada (letter Ridgway to author, July 3, 1984). Mary Princess ("Penny") Anthony was born on February 22, 1918, on a farm near Richmond, Virginia. Her parents died when she was a young girl. Penny and a sister, Myrl, were reared by their older sister, Lucy (Mrs. Morgan D. Kalbach), in Silver Spring, Maryland. On November 2, 1940, Penny married James Mackin Long in Washington, D.C. He served in the Army Air Forces in the Pacific, rising to the rank of master sergeant. Penny was divorced from him on June 11, 1947. Ridgway and Penny met in Washington in the postwar years at the Inter-American Defense Board, while he was director and she was head secretary. They were married at Fort Totten (Queens), New York, on December 13, 1947. (Martha Martin, "General Ridgway's Penny," *New York Sunday News,* August 31, 1952; Helen Worden Erskine, "Pretty Penny Ridgway—The General's Lady," *Collier's,* May 16, 1953.) Divorce records, U.S. District Court, Washington, D.C., #35694 (*Long*

v. *Long*); marriage records, New York City, courtesy the Honorable David Dinkins, clerk, by telephone, April 28, 1983. Matthew B. Ridgway, Jr., was born on April 27, 1949, in Panama: Ridgway Papers, Box 11, USAMHI. For whereabouts on June 25, 1950, see *Soldier,* p. 191.

10. *Soldier,* pp. 168–72. Ridgway's UN reports: See especially No. 8, Ridgway to Eisenhower, February 3, 1947, "Russian Objectives," Ridgway Papers, USAMHI (copy in author's possession).

11. *Soldier,* p. 192. "Immediate": Ridgway desk diary, June 26 and July 18, 1950, Box 16, Ridgway Papers, USAMHI.

12. *A General's Life,* pp. 532–33.

13. *FRUS VII,* 1950, p. 127.

14. Ibid., pp. 135–37 (telecon transcript).

15. Ibid., p. 137.

16. Ibid., pp. 165–66.

17. Ibid., pp. 157–61 (minutes of the meeting). Additional detail: Glenn D. Paige, *The Korean Decision* (New York: Free Press, 1968); *A General's Life; Present at the Creation;* "History of the JCS"; *Policy and Direction; War in Peacetime;* Beverly Smith, "The White House Story: Why We Went to War in Korea," *Saturday Evening Post* (November 10, 1951); "Record of Actions taken by the Joint Chiefs of Staff Relative to the United Nations Operations in Korea from 25 June to 11 April 1951, Prepared by Them," 107 pages, dated April 30, 1951, Modern Military Records Branch, NA, copy in author's possession (hereafter JCS "Record").

18. *A General's Life,* pp. 532–34. Text of MacArthur study: *FRUS VII,* 1950, pp. 161–65.

19. *A General's Life,* p. 535; *FRUS VII,* 1950, pp. 157–61.

20. JCS "Record."

21. *Tumultuous Years,* p. 209. *Time* (July 10, 1950). *Life* (July 7 and July 14, 1950).

22. *FRUS VII,* 1950, pp. 140, 237–38.

23. *South to the Naktong,* pp. 42–43; Church, "Memo for the Record," eleven pages, NA, supporting documents for Appleman's *South to the Naktong* (hereafter Church "Memo").

24. Church official bio. "Frail": Author-Marnane interview. "Sick": Oral history of Gines Perez, conducted by D. Clayton James, May 25, 1977, Special Collections Department, Mitchell Memorial Library, Mississippi State University. "Arthritis" and pain: Author-Garrison H. Davidson interview, September 27, 1984. Author-Ned D. Moore interview, May 24, 1984; Author-Michaelis interview.

25. *FRUS VII,* 1950, pp. 178–83 (minutes of meeting).

26. JCS "Record."

27. *South to the Naktong,* p. 43.

28. Church "Memo"; *South to the Naktong,* pp. 33–34.

29. Church "Memo."

30. Ibid.; *South to the Naktong,* pp. 43–44.

31. Church "Memo."

32. Douglas MacArthur, *Reminiscences* (New York: McGraw-Hill, 1964), p. 377; *MacArthur III,* p. 428.

33. Robert F. Futrell, *The United States Air Force in Korea 1950–1953* (New York: Duell, Sloan & Pearce, 1961), pp. 30–31.

34. *Reminiscences,* pp. 377–78; *MacArthur III,* p. 425.

35. Church "Memo"; *MacArthur III*, pp. 426–27. Higgins and several other reporters had flown from Tokyo to Kimpo Airfield on June 27. They went to KMAG HQ in Seoul but were soon driven out by the NKPA. Higgins crossed the Han River on a raft, returned to Japan by Air Force plane to file her story, then flew back to Suwon. MacArthur offered her a ride back to Japan on his plane. En route he gave her an interview. She quoted him as saying: "It is certain that the South Koreans badly need an injection of ordered American strength. The South Korean soldiers are in good physical condition and could be rallied with example and leadership. Give me two American divisions and I can hold Korea. The moment I reach Tokyo, I shall send President Truman my recommendation for the immediate dispatch of American divisions to Korea. But I have no idea whether he will accept my recommendations." (Marguerite Higgins, *War in Korea* [Garden City: Doubleday, 1951], pp. 33–34. Keyes Beech, *Tokyo and Points East* [Garden City: Doubleday, 1954], pp. 107–22.)

36. *MacArthur III; Eagle Against the Sun.*

37. Sherman quoted: "History of the JCS III," p. 117.

38. "Every unit . . .": Oral history, Harold K. Johnson, USAMHI. Johnson was a battalion and regimental commander in Korea and Army chief of staff, 1964 to 1968. The failure of most American divisions in combat baptism is seldom discussed in any detail by Army historians, but the problem is real. For example, see discussion in *A General's Life* re the failure of the 1st Armored Division and other units at Kasserine Pass; the 8th and 90th Infantry divisions in the Cotentin Peninsula. Ditto, *Ridgway's Paratroopers,* re failure of the 11th Armored division, the 17th Airborne Division, and the 75th and 87th Infantry Divisions in the Bulge counteroffensive and the 13th Armored Division in the campaign of the Ruhr Pocket.

39. *Eisenhower Diaries,* pp. 175–76.

40. Ridgway desk diary, Ridgway Papers, Box 16, USAMHI.

41. Ike and MacArthur: *Eisenhower,* pp. 91–92, 104–19. Comments on MacArthur: Ridgway desk diary. In another aside Eisenhower told Ridgway that he, Eisenhower, could be "useful" to the Pentagon because Truman had confidence in him and would confide in him "in a far greater degree than he would in Louis Johnson." However, Eisenhower did not see Truman on this visit to Washington.

42. *A General's Life,* pp. 537–38.

43. "History of the JCS III," pp. 103–25.

44. Airfields: *U.S. Air Force in Korea.*

45. "History of the JCS III," pp. 106–09; JCS "Record"; *Present at the Creation,* pp. 411–12; *War in Peacetime,* p. 19; *Years of Trial and Hope,* pp. 388–89.

46. *Years of Trial and Hope,* p. 388.

47. JCS "Record"; "History of the JCS III," p. 109.

48. "History of the JCS III," p. 106.

49. *War in Peacetime,* p. 20.

50. *FRUS VII,* 1950, pp. 248–50 (text).

51. *War in Peacetime,* pp. 20–21. Publicist: *Lightning Joe,* pp. 339–41.

52. *FRUS VII,* 1950, pp. 250–53 (text of telecon).

53. *War in Peacetime,* pp. 22–23; *Years of Trial and Hope,* p. 390; *A General's Life,* p. 539; "History of the JCS III," p. 117.

54. "History of the JCS III," p. 117; *A General's Life,* p. 539.

55. "History of the JCS III," pp. 117–18.

56. Ibid., pp. 121–22.
57. *Tumultuous Years,* pp. 217, 222.
58. Ibid., p. 217.

### CHAPTER 4

1. Letter, Hobart R. Gay, commanding general, 1st Cavalry Division, to Appleman. *South to the Naktong,* pp. 195–96, 488–89.
2. Letter, Colonel Donald McB. Curtis to editor, *Army* (July 1985).
3. Letter, Gay to Appleman; *South to the Naktong,* pp. 488–89.
4. "40 percent": Almond oral history, USAMHI.
5. Letter, Gay to Appleman; *South to the Naktong,* pp. 195–96, 488–89.
6. Ridgway oral history, pt. 3, pp. 73–74, Ridgway Papers, USAMHI.
7. Division readiness and strength: Department of the Army Memo, June 27, 1950, Ridgway Papers, Box 16, USAMHI. This document, which seems to overrate greatly divisional readiness, is in conflict with Almond's assertions that Eighth Army was only "40 percent" combat ready. It rates the Eighth Army division readiness thus:

| | |
|---|---|
| 1st Cavalry | 84 percent |
| 7th Infantry | 74 percent |
| 24th Infantry | 65 percent |
| 25th Infantry | 72 percent |

Disposition of 24th Division: William F. Dean, as told to William L. Worden, *General Dean's Story* (New York: Viking Press, 1954), p. 14. Transfer of 2,108 men: *South to the Naktong,* pp. 59, 195–96; *Of GarryOwen in Glory,* p. 243.
8. Dean's official bio; *General Dean's Story;* Forrest K. Kleinman, "The Walking General," a profile of Dean in *Army* (January 1986). (Kleinman was a former aide to Dean.) *Time* magazine cover story December 7, 1953.
9. *General Dean's Story,* pp. 5–11; "The Walking General." Son: West Point *Register.* Dean's book does not mention his wife's illustrious family. Kleinman alludes to the wealth but writes (mistakenly) that Dean married Dern's daughter.
10. *General Dean's Story,* pp. 5–11; "Walking General"; Army War College *Register.*
11. *General Dean's Story,* pp. 5–11; *Life* magazine profile of Dean, July 21, 1950; "Walking General."
12. *General Dean's Story,* pp. 11–13.
13. "Walking General."
14. Staff: 24th Division Records, NA (Suitland), RG 407, Boxes 3470, 3481, 3493, etc. At NA (Suitland) there are countless thousands of declassified documents on the Korean War. Most useful in this work were the monthly Eighth Army HQ Command Reports; corps Command Reports; division Command Reports; regimental Command Reports; battalion Command Reports, etc. These monthly reports usually include a roster of officers and narrative accounts of noteworthy actions or events. Where possible, personnel rosters were cross-checked with other sources, such as the *Army Register,* West Point *Register,* West Point *Assembly* obituaries, official biographies, and by interviews with or queries to participants. Personnel appraisals: Author-Davidson interview (Davidson was later ADC of the 24th Division). Additional information (and occasional appraisals) in the Barth ms.

15. Status of 34th: Letters, Lovless to Appleman, August 7 and 15, 1958, with attached letters from R. L. Wadlington, Harry E. Gallman, and Mrs. (Marge) Lovless; letters, Wadlington to Appleman, April 1 and June 23, 1953; letter, John J. Dunn to Appleman, June 17, 1955; letter, Harold B. Ayres to Appleman; letter, Richard W. Stephens to Appleman, April 17, 1952; letter, and interview notes, Charles E. Beauchamp to Appleman; letter, Jack E. Smith to Appleman, June 18, 1955. Letters, Lacy C. Barnett to author, January 7 and 16, 1985, enclosing officer roster; letter, Charles W. Menninger, Sr., to author, December 31, 1984; letter, Henry Leerkamp to author, February 4, 1985; letter, anonymous to author, January 12, 1985. Lovless biography: *Army Register,* and *A Time for Trumpets,* p. 134 and passim. Lovless relieved Hurley Edward Fuller as CO, 23d Regiment, 2d Infantry Division on June 16, 1944. Failure of prior commander: Letter, Lacy Barnett to author, February 16, 1985, and Wadlington to Appleman. Wadlington, formerly an Eighth Army inspector and war games umpire, wrote Lovless that he believed "the biggest trouble [with the 34th] was the fact that your predecessor had actually been derelict in his duty as CO of the regiment by not having given the unit supervised training." Lovless, who had been G-4 of the Eighth Army's IX Corps, which was disbanded in March 1950, wrote Appleman: "All officers were given new assignments. My original assignment was to Fifth Cavalry [regiment]. About this time Eighth Army was giving tests to combat units. My assignment was changed and I was ordered to command of the 34th Infantry Regiment. I was given to understand that the reason my assignment was changed was that the previous CO of the 34th had been relieved after the tests of that unit."

16. Letter, Stephens to Appleman, April 12, 1952.

17. Stephens: *Tokyo and Points East,* pp. 148–49; obituary, *Assembly,* March 1978; letters, Charles F. Mudgett to author, November 13, 1984, and February 5, 1985.

18. Letter, Smith to Appleman; letters, Mudgett to author; Mudgett biography.

19. *General Dean's Story,* p. 14.

20. Russell A. Gugeler, *Combat Actions in Korea* (Washington, D.C.: Combat Forces Press, 1954), pp. 3, 7. This useful book contains numerous battle narratives compiled by official Army historians (such as Martin Blumenson) during the fighting in Korea which for the most part were not used or used only in highly condensed form in the Army's official histories. The original manuscripts of these narratives, plus many other useful battle narratives which were not published, may be found at the U.S. Army's Center of Military History, Washington, D.C.

21. Martin: *Army Register;* Hugh Cole, *The Lorraine Offensive* (Washington, D.C.: Government Printing Office, 1950), p. 467. Wadlington and Ayres: Letters to Appleman. "Best battalion commander": William B. Caldwell III, taped self-interview. Ayres's DSC: *Army Register.*

22. Airborne limitations: *Ridgway's Paratroopers.*

23. Initial plan: *U.S. Air Force in Korea,* p. 73. Church "Memo." Church wrote that he got through to Ned Almond by telephone and Almond told him "two battalions" of the 21st Infantry would be flown to South Korea. Revised plan: *South to the Naktong,* p. 59.

24. Mudgett: Letters to author, November 13, 1984, and February 5, 1985; Smith: West Point *Register;* letter, Smith to Appleman; letter, Smith to author, September 15, 1984. Pryor: Letters, Mudgett to author; West Point *Register.*

25. *General Dean's Story*, p. 17; *South to the Naktong*, p. 60.
26. *U.S. Air Force in Korea*, pp. 73–74; *South to the Naktong*, pp. 60–61.
27. *General Dean's Story*, p. 18; *South to the Naktong*, p. 64.
28. *South to the Naktong*, pp. 63–64; letter, Mudgett to author, February 5, 1985.
29. *South to the Naktong*, p. 61.
30. Dean's plan: *South to the Naktong*, pp. 77–78; *General Dean's Story*, pp. 19–20.
31. *South to the Naktong*, pp. 77–78.
32. Barth: official biography; West Point *Register;* Barth ms.; *Lightning Joe*, pp. 209–10; *Ridgway's Paratroopers*, p. 282n. Barth commanded the 357th Regiment, 90th Division, until evacuated with battle wounds.
33. Author analysis of official biographies. "Roadbound": Various author interviews.
34. Barth ms., p. 1.
35. *Combat Actions in Korea*, pp. 3–19; *War in Korea;* various author interviews.
36. Barth ms., pp. 1–2.
37. Task Force Smith: *South to the Naktong*, pp. 61, 65–66.
38. HEAT: *South to the Naktong*, p. 68.
39. Ibid., p. 62.
40. Assembly, command, movement, and deployment of 34th Regiment: Ibid., pp. 77–79; letter to Appleman, per note 15.
41. Letter, with taped self-interview, Caldwell to author, January 24, 1985.
42. Letter, Dunn to Appleman, June 17, 1955.
43. Ibid.
44. Movement, deployment of 21st Regiment: Letters, Stephens and Brad Smith to Appleman. *South to the Naktong*, pp. 75–77, 88–89.
45. Letter, Lovless to Appleman, August 15, 1958, with enclosure from Ayres.
46. Task Force Smith action: *South to the Naktong*, pp. 68–75; Barth ms.
47. "Truth of Taejon."
48. Church "Memo." Church wrote in understatement: "Being [sic] their first action, some confusion and panic resulted from this daylight withdrawal and the battalion ceased to exist for several days as a unit."
49. "Truth of Taejon."
50. Letter, Caldwell to author, January 1, 1985.
51. Payne described: *War in Korea*, p. 60. Caldwell: Letter to author, January 24, 1985. Shadrick: *War in Korea*, p. 62; Higgins quoted: p. 63.
52. Letter, Lovless to Appleman, August 15, 1958.
53. *General Dean's Story*, pp. 21–22; letter, Lovless to Appleman, August 15, 1958.
54. Change in plan: Barth ms.; letters, Lovless, Dunn, Ayres to Appleman.
55. Ayres: Letter, Dunn to Appleman, June 17, 1955; letter, Caldwell to author, January 24, 1985.
56. *Combat Actions in Korea*, pp. 9–12.
57. Barth ms., p. 4.
58. Letter, Wadlington to Appleman, June 23, 1953.
59. *War in Korea*, p. 73.
60. *South to the Naktong*, p. 82; letter, Ayres to Lovless (to Appleman).
61. Letter, Ayres to Lovless (to Appleman).
62. Letter, Lovless to Appleman.
63. Letter, Dunn to Appleman. Seegers: West Point *Register;* obituary, West Point *Assembly*, Winter 1958. *War in Korea*.

64. Caldwell quoted in letter, Lacy C. Barnett (34th's historian) to author, February 16, 1985; letter, Menninger to author, December 31, 1984.
65. Letter, Lovless to Appleman.
66. Letter, Dunn to Appleman.
67. Ibid.
68. Ibid.
69. *South to the Naktong,* pp. 84, 87; letter, Menninger to author, December 31, 1984.
70. *General Dean's Story,* p. 25. Meyer: Letter, Barnett to author, January 7, 1985; Lantron: Letter, Leerkamp to author, February 4, 1985.
71. Walker in Korea: *South to the Naktong,* p. 109. Walker on Dean: Letter, Landrum to Appleman.
72. Visit to Chonan: *General Dean's Story,* pp. 25–26. Martin DSC: *South to the Naktong,* p. 87. Smith and Perry DSCs: West Point *Register.*
73. Dean on 34th: Letter, Stephens to Appleman, January 17, 1952.
74. Letter, Dean to MacArthur, July 8, 1950: *Policy and Direction,* pp. 84, 89.
75. Defense of Taejon: *South to the Naktong,* pp. 90, 110–11.
76. The 21st at Chonui-Chochiwon: *South to the Naktong,* pp. 90–100.
77. M-24 light tank: T. R. Fehrenbach, *This Kind of War* (New York: Macmillan, 1963), pp. 665–71, "Glossary of Weapons." Jim Mesko, *Armor in Korea: A Pictorial History* (Carrollton, Texas: Squadron/Signal Publications, 1984).
78. Stephens quoted: *South to the Naktong,* p. 93.
79. Letter, Stephens to Appleman, January 17, 1952.
80. Pryor: Letter, Mudgett to author, February 5, 1985.
81. Letter, Snee to author, September 15, 1985.
82. *South to the Naktong,* p. 95; *U.S. Air Force in Korea,* p. 86.
83. Appleman quoted: *South to the Naktong,* p. 98.
84. Stephens's DSC: West Point *Register.* Beech quoted: *Tokyo and Points East,* p. 149.
85. *South to the Naktong,* p. 100.

## CHAPTER 5

1. "History of the JCS III," pp. 178–80; Lynn Montross and Captain Nicholas A. Canzona, USMC, *U.S. Marine Operations in Korea 1950–1953,* vol. I: *The Pusan Perimeter* (Washington, D.C.: Historical Division, U.S. Marine Corps, 1954), pp. 47–54 (hereafter *U.S. Marine Operations in Korea I*).
2. "History of the JCS III," pp. 180–81.
3. Ibid., pp. 183–85.
4. Ibid. "Jolted," pp. 183, 185.
5. General Reserve: *Policy and Direction,* p. 44.
6. Eleven regiments: "History of the JCS IV," p. 38. Details: Various sources and author interviews. War plans, 5th RCT, 14th RCT, 65th RCT; 2d Division: Memos, July 5 and 22, 1950, Ridgway Papers, Box 16, USAMHI.
7. Eighteen infantry battalions: *Policy and Direction,* p. 90. Restated in *War in Peacetime,* p. 80.
8. *Policy and Direction,* pp. 105–08; *War in Peacetime,* pp. 81–85.
9. *Policy and Direction,* pp. 122–23; "History of the JCS IV," p. 43.
10. *Policy and Direction,* pp. 87–99. Ridgway Papers, Box 16, USAMHI; various author interviews. Ridgway made a personal crusade of getting 3.5-inch bazoo-

kas to Korea. On July 10, 1950, Ridgway memoed Collins that a three-man 3.5-inch rocket launcher team carrying twenty launchers and 1,600 rounds of ammo was "now en route" to the Far East "by air" and that "status of supply of additional launchers and ammo is satisfactory." In an interview with the author on October 31, 1984, Ridgway said: "I was riding herd on getting those things over there just as soon as possible. Normal channels would have taken maybe three weeks. But I assigned a special officer to follow the shipments from factory to the Far East, day by day, at each transshipping point, to make sure they got to the troops without delay."

11. "History of the JCS III," pp. 186–87; "History of the JCS IV," pp. 41–42. Supplemental "too high": Memo, July 18, 1950, Ridgway Papers, Box 16, USAMHI.

12. Memo, July 2, 1950, Ridgway Papers, Box 16, USAMHI.

13. Collins-Vandenberg trip here and below: *War in Peacetime,* pp. 115–16; *Policy and Direction,* pp. 105–08.

14. Revised Inchon landing plan: *South to the Naktong,* pp. 488–89.

15. Fire-fighting analogy: *Policy and Direction,* p. 107.

16. Eighth Army HQ: *South to the Naktong,* pp. 109–11. Dean: *War in Peacetime,* p. 84.

17. General situation: Summarized from *South to the Naktong.*

18. "Eastern" front: Ibid., pp. 106–07.

19. *War in Peacetime,* p. 84; *Policy and Direction,* p. 108.

20. Colonel Roy K. Flint, "The Tragic Flaw: MacArthur, the Joint Chiefs, and the Korean War," Ph.D. dissertation, Duke University, 1976; *Policy and Direction,* pp. 123–25, 159–60. Memo, Ridgway Papers, Box 16, USAMHI.

21. *Policy and Direction,* pp. 159–65, 169–71; "History of the JCS III," pp. 192–94.

22. 19th history: John K. Mahon and Romana Danysh, *Army Lineage Series: Infantry,* pt. 1 (Washington, D.C.: OCMH, 1972), pp. 413–25. Walker and the 19th: Official biography. Dean and the 19th: *General Dean's Story,* p. 27.

23. West Point *Register.* Obituary: West Point *Assembly,* Fall 1970.

24. *South to the Naktong,* p. 139.

25. Ibid., p. 135.

26. Ibid., pp. 124–25.

27. Ibid., p. 126.

28. Ibid., pp. 127–29.

29. Ibid., p. 129.

30. Ibid., pp. 130–33.

31. Ibid., pp. 131–33; map opposite p. 131.

32. Ibid., p. 135; casualties, p. 136. Letter, Elliott C. Cutler to author, December 29, 1984.

33. *South to the Naktong,* pp. 137–39. Letter, Meloy to Appleman. Meloy battle wound: *South to the Naktong,* p. 139n.

34. Miller to CO, 1/19: Letter, Cutler to author, December 29, 1984. Winstead killed in action, *South to the Naktong,* p. 139.

35. *This Kind of War,* p. 668.

36. *South to the Naktong,* p. 141; Logan to Appleman, July 30, 1950. Author-Mrs. Chandler interview, November 24, 1984.

37. *South to the Naktong,* p. 142; letter, Barszcz to Appleman.

38. *South to the Naktong,* p. 143; letter, Logan to Appleman; letter, Woods to author, March 9, 1985.

39. *General Dean's Story,* p. 27; *South to the Naktong,* p. 144.

40. *South to the Naktong,* pp. 148–50, 196.

41. Letters, Dean to Appleman, January 20, 1958, and Stephens to Appleman, January 17, 1952.

42. Letter, Stephens to Appleman, January 17, 1952. 3.5-inch bazookas: *South to the Naktong,* p. 157.

43. West Point *Register.* Author-Beauchamp interview, September 2, 1984.

44. Author-Beauchamp interview.

45. Letter, Beauchamp to Appleman.

46. Plan: *South to the Naktong,* pp. 150–51, 179.

47. Letter, Dean to Appleman, January 20, 1958.

48. *South to the Naktong,* pp. 152–54. Author-Beauchamp interview.

49. Author-Caldwell interview.

50. *South to the Naktong,* pp. 152–54. Pohl's glasses, transfer to 1/19: Letter, Cutler to author, November 29, 1984.

51. Author-Caldwell interview.

52. *South to the Naktong,* p. 155.

53. *General Dean's Story,* p. 29.

54. *South to the Naktong,* p. 156.

55. Ibid., p. 156; Author-Beauchamp interview.

56. *South to the Naktong,* pp. 157–58.

57. Ibid., pp. 159–61.

58. Ibid., pp. 160, 165.

59. Dean's mental state: Various author interviews. Dean's abandonment of his overall military responsibilities at this critical juncture to go on a "tank hunt" was to be criticized by participants and military historians. Details of "hunt": *South to the Naktong,* pp. 162–63; *General Dean's Story,* pp. 30–36. Dean later wrote (letter to Appleman, January 20, 1958) that the real reason for the "hunt" was to "inspire the men of the command in becoming tank killers. An unescorted tank in a city defended by infantry with 3.5-inch bazookas should be a 'dead duck' and I was trying to sell that idea to the command."

60. *South to the Naktong,* p. 164.

61. Ibid., p. 168. Dean later wrote (January 20, 1958) Appleman: "I may have given Colonel Beauchamp the impression that the 21st Regiment would move up to Taejon and protect the rear of the units in the city, although that was not my intention." Dean conceded that "the 21st Infantry Regiment should have been employed to secure the exit from Taejon" but he gave no such orders, and that "I alone am to blame for not having issued such an order."

62. Author-Beauchamp interview.

63. *South to the Naktong,* pp. 169–70. Dean wrote Appleman: "When I was told that Colonel Beauchamp had left the CP shortly after 1500, I concluded that he had personally gone forward to contact Ayres, and it was not until I was repatriated some three years later that I discovered this not to have been the case. . . . Later, at about 1700 I . . . inquired as to the whereabouts of Colonel Beauchamp. This was the first time that I realized that Beauchamp was no longer at the CP." Later Dean wrote, "When finding that Colonel Beauchamp had still not returned, I directed Colonel Wadlington to close station and move out." Notwithstanding Beauchamp's explanation of his whereabouts that afternoon, Dean, according to a 34th Regiment historian, Lacy C. Barnett, remained angry at Beauchamp in post-Korean years.

64. *South to the Naktong,* pp. 170, 173–75.
65. Sergeant Saul A. Stadtmauer, ed., *24th Forward: A Pictorial History of the Victory Division in Korea* (Tokyo: Toppan Press, 1953), hereafter *Victory Division in Korea.* Bruce Jacobs, *Korea's Heroes: The Medal of Honor Story* (New York: Berkley Medallion, 1961), pp. 205, 233.
66. *South to the Naktong,* pp. 170–71.
67. Ibid. Clarke and Tabor: *General Dean's Story,* pp. 30, 43–51, 54.
68. *General Dean's Story,* pp. 80–82; *South to the Naktong,* p. 177, 177n.
69. Medal of Honor to Mrs. Dean: *General Dean's Story,* photo section; Dean's quotes: Ibid., p. 3.
70. *South to the Naktong,* pp. 166, 171n; West Point *Register.* McDaniel was legally declared dead on December 31, 1953.
71. Author-Caldwell interview.
72. *South to the Naktong,* pp. 175–76.
73. Ibid., p. 179.
74. Ibid., p. 180.
75. Ibid., pp. 59, 179, 180.
76. Inchon plan again revised: Ibid., p. 489.

## CHAPTER 6

1. Official biography; West Point *Register.*
2. *A General's Life,* p. III and passim.
3. Letter, William W. Dick to author, December 14, 1984.
4. Official biography; Barth ms.
5. Letter, Dick to author.
6. 25th Division Records: NA (Suitland), RG 407, Boxes 3746, 3747, 3748, etc. Allan A. David, ed., *Battleground Korea: The Story of the 25th Division* (Tokyo: Toppan, 1952), hereafter *Battleground Korea.*
7. Author-Michaelis interview; West Point *Register.*
8. Author-Michaelis interview. *Ridgway's Paratroopers.* "Extraordinary": *Ike Papers IX,* p. 2253.
9. Author-Michaelis interview.
10. Ibid.
11. 25th Division records; *Battleground Korea.* Terry: Barth ms.; West Point *Register.* Check and Murch: Author-Michaelis interview; division records; *Army Register.*
12. Author-Michaelis interview.
13. 25th Division records; *Battleground Korea.* White: West Point *Register;* Preston: 25th Division records; Barth ms.
14. Here and below: Morris J. MacGregor, *Integration of the Armed Forces 1940–1965,* Defense Studies Series (Washington, D.C.: Center of Military History, 1981). Bernard C. Nalty, *Strength for the Fight: A History of Black Americans in the Military* (New York: Free Press, 1986). Mary Penick Motley, ed., *The Invisible Soldier* (Detroit: Wayne State University Press, 1975). Almond oral history, Almond Papers, USAMHI.
15. For a history of the 555th and further insights on racism and segregation in the Army, see Bradley Biggs, *The Triple Nickles* (Hamden, Conn.: Archon Books, 1986).

16. Almond oral history, Almond Papers, USAMHI. Almond said (side 1, tape 3, pp. 39–40): "The Negro is a useful individual; he is an American citizen, he should be employed in the defense of this nation, but to expect him to exercise characteristics that are abnormal to his race, is too much and not recommended by me. . . . The greatest problem that I can recall [in the 92d Division] was the undependability of the average [black] soldier to operate to his maximum capability, compared to his lassitude toward his performing a task assigned. While there are exceptions to this rule, the general tendency of the Negro soldier is to avoid as much effort as possible." Clark quoted: *Mark Clark,* p. 237.

17. *A General's Life,* pp. 484–86.

18. *Triple Nickles.*

19. 25th Division records; *Battleground Korea.* Author's interviews with 24th Infantry personnel.

20. Author-Ned D. Moore interview, May 24, 1984.

21. David K. Carlisle and Charles M. Bussey, "In a Higher Tradition," history of the 24th Infantry and 77th ECC in Korea, kindly lent author by Carlisle, pp. 20–21 (hereafter "Carlisle and Bussey ms."). In addition, numerous author-Carlisle interviews and extended correspondence. The 24th Infantry records, NA (Suitland), RG 407, unnumbered box, plus Boxes 3770, 3841, 3842, 3843, etc.

22. Carlisle and Bussy ms.; Carlisle correspondence; *Army Register.*

23. 25th Division records; 24th Infantry records; *Battleground Korea.*

24. Letter, Biggs to author, October 20, 1986.

25. Carlisle and Bussey ms.; Carlisle correspondence.

26. "Down payment": Carlisle and Bussey ms., p. 32; Carlisle correspondence. Dudley letter, copy courtesy Carlisle.

27. Lambert dispatch: *Los Angeles Examiner,* July 22, 1950; *Battleground Korea. Congressional Record,* July 24, 1950 (Congressman Thomas J. Lane of Massachusetts), and July 31, 1950 (Congressman Walter Judd of Minnesota).

28. *South to the Naktong,* pp. 190–91. Appleman's sneering and heretofore unchallenged account of Yechon has been used uncritically in some popular histories of the Korean War and intensified by some authors. See, for example, Joseph C. Goulden, *Korea: The Untold Story of the War* (New York: Times Books, 1982), p. 168. Goulden wrote with no other cited documentation that at Yechon, 24th Infantry troops "broke ranks and fled after only a few hours' fighting."

29. 25th Division records; *Battleground Korea.* Fisher: West Point *Register;* obituary, West Point *Assembly,* March 1985. Hogan: West Point *Register;* Barth ms.; letter, Hogan to author, July 15, 1986.

30. Historian: *South to the Naktong,* pp. 366–67, 367n. Berry quote: West Point *Assembly* obituary. Teeters: letter to author, October 30, 1984.

31. *Battleground Korea.* Wilkin: *South to the Naktong;* letter, Teeters to author; Army *Register.*

32. 25th Division records. *Battleground Korea.*

33. Various author interviews.

34. Letter, Hobart Gay to Appleman; *South to the Naktong,* pp. 488–89. Landing: 1st Cav Division records, NA (Suitland), RG 407, Boxes 4406–4409, etc. *Of GarryOwen in Glory,* p. 244. *The First Team: The First Cavalry Division in Korea* (Atlanta: Albert Love Enterprises, 1952), hereafter *First Team.*

35. Official biography; letter, Gay to Appleman. Loss of eye: Author interviews with Harris, September 30, 1984, and Clainos, September 28, 1984.

36. *Ike Papers II*, p. 1118; *Ike Papers IV*, p. 2538. *Patton Papers*, pp. 419–20. *Lorraine Campaign*, p. 525. Hobart Gay oral history, USAMHI.

37. *Patton Papers*, p. 680 (entry from Gay's diary).

38. West Point *Register*.

39. Silver cane: Author-Clainos interview. "Wasn't Patton": Author-Harris interview; letters, Holmes to author November 28, 1984, and September 20, 1985. Senior officer quoted: Author-Charles D. Palmer interview, September 6, 1984.

40. Captain Harry C. Butcher, *My Three Years with Eisenhower* (New York: Simon & Schuster, 1946), various entries. Author-Palmer interview. Genealogy lines and Williston B. Palmer; West Point *Register*, 1980 edition.

41. Division strength: *First Team*.

42. Division records; *First Team*. Palmer: Official biography; *Army Register*. Holmes: West Point *Register*. Kane and Field: *South to the Naktong*, pp. 196–200. Gay protest: *South to the Naktong*, p. 197; letter, Gay to Appleman.

43. Rohsenberger: Official biography; *Army Register*. Too old and deaf: Author-Palmer interview.

44. Division records; *First Team; South to the Naktong*, pp. 196–200. Harris: West Point *Register;* author-Harris interview.

45. Author interviews on June 16, 1987, with James M. Gibson and Harry A. Buckley, both in the 1st Battalion, 5th Cav.

46. *South to the Naktong*, pp. 198–200. *First Team*. Author-Field interview, June 14, 1987; author-Robbins interview, June 15, 1987. Author-Terry T. Feild interview (C.O., F Company, 2/8), June 14, 1987; author interview with Richard L. Cohen (S-3, 2/8), June 14, 1987. Rogers: West Point *Register*.

47. *First Team*.

48. 7th Cav: *Of GarryOwen in Glory*, p. 246. Nist: West Point *Register;* West Point *Assembly* obituary, September 1979. Heyer: *Army Register*.

49. Official biographies; author-Harris interview; author-Cochrane interview, June 13, 1987; letter, Holmes to author, December 7, 1984; other author interviews with 5th, 7th and 8th Cav officers.

50. *South to the Naktong*, p. 206.

51. Ibid., plus maps.

52. Author-Michaelis interview.

53. Ibid.; *South to the Naktong*, pp. 200–02.

54. Author-Michaelis interview.

55. Ibid. Press coverage of Michaelis and the Wolfhounds far exceeded that of any other commander and regiment.

56. *South to the Naktong*, pp. 193–94.

57. Ibid., p. 194.

58. Walden taped self-interview, March 5, 1987, courtesy Walden; author-Walden interview, June 13, 1987.

59. Letter, Biggs to author, October 20, 1986; Walden self-interview tape and author interview; Carlisle correspondence; "Carlisle and Bussey ms." For the harshest public condemnation of the 24th Infantry, see: Harold H. Martin, "How Do Our Negro Troops Measure Up?" *Saturday Evening Post*, June 16, 1951. Leon Gilbert: *South to the Naktong*, pp. 195, 195n; official court-martial records, courtesy Bussey.

60. *South to the Naktong*, p. 194.

61. Ibid.

62. Ibid. Movement of 1/35: p. 202.

63. Ibid., p. 206.
64. NKPA flanking attack: Ibid., pp. 210–13.
65. Ibid., p. 213.
66. Official biography; *Ridgway's Paratroopers,* p. 382 and passim; author-Moore interview; West Point *Register.*
67. Personnel: Letter, Cutler to author, December 29, 1984. Barszcz: Author-Moore interview.
68. Okinawa battalions: NA (Suitland), RG 407, Boxes 147, 743. *South to the Naktong,* pp. 214–15. Letters to Appleman from James E. Townes (S-4, 3/29); Tony J. Raibl (XO, 3/29); Sam C. Holliday (S-2, 1/29); George F. Sharra (CO, L Company, 3/29). Letters, Rupert D. Graves (CO, 29th Regiment on Okinawa) to author, November 10 and December 10, 1984.
69. *South to the Naktong,* pp. 215–21.
70. Ibid., pp. 222–24.
71. Ibid., pp. 205–07.
72. Ibid., pp. 206–07.
73. Ibid., p. 207.
74. Ibid. New Inchon plan: Ibid., p. 487. See also *MacArthur III,* p. 446.
75. *MacArthur III,* p. 446.
76. Tacit approval: *South to the Naktong,* p. 202. Gay's fear of encirclement: Ibid., p. 203. 24th bracketed: Ibid., pp. 192–93 (2/35) and 195 (1/35).
77. Ibid., pp. 205–09. Paraphrase of Walker talk: NA (Suitland), RG 407, Box 3746 (25th Division HQ diary, July 29, 1950).
78. *South to the Naktong,* pp. 225–50, 326–27.
79. Ibid., pp. 231–34. Moore DSC: Citation provided at author's request by Moore.
80. *South to the Naktong,* pp. 235, 248–49.
81. Ibid., pp. 248–49; *Battleground Korea.*
82. *South to the Naktong,* p. 251. Letter, Gay to Appleman. *First Team.*
83. *South to the Naktong,* pp. 253–55. Maps.
84. Indochina: Ronald H. Spector, *Advice and Support: The Early Years 1941–1960. The United States Army in Vietnam* (Washington, D.C.: Center of Military History, United States Army, 1983), p. 123.
85. Ibid., pp. 248–65.
86. Robert J. Lamphere and Tom Schachtman, *The FBI-KGB War* (New York: Random House, 1986), pp. 78–98 passim. FBI Special Agent Robert J. Lamphere has revealed that the deciphering by the Army code breaker Meredith Gardner of some old KGB messages in 1948 and 1949 led directly to the arrests of Soviet "atom spies" Klaus Fuchs, Julius and Ethel Rosenberg, Harry Gold, et al. In breaking these old KGB messages (dating from 1944 and 1945), Gardner made good use of an old Russian code book, captured earlier in Finland. Lamphere shared the information from these breaks with British code breakers and British intelligence and counterintelligence (MI-5 and MI-6), which were then penetrated by at least four top-level Soviet spies (Philby, Burgess, Maclean, Blount), who no doubt passed the news of the code breaks to Moscow. If Moscow had not already changed or strengthened the security of its codes in the postwar years, news of this break would surely have prompted it to do so in 1949 or 1950.
87. Wayne G. Barker, ed., *The Origin and Development of the National Security Agency* (Laguna Hills, Calif.: Aegeon Park Press, 1981). This monograph includes the so-called Brownell Report and other useful material. The North

Korea code-breaking "priority" listings are on p. 43. The report is summarized in James Bamford, *The Puzzle Palace* (Boston: Houghton Mifflin, 1982), pp. 46–55.

88. Letter, anonymous to author, February 21, 1985. Author-James H. Polk interview, May 28, 1984.

89. *South to the Naktong*, pp. 262–63. West Pointer (1932) James K. Woolnough (later a four-star general), who came to Eighth Army headquarters in early September for duty, remembered in his oral history (Woolnough Papers, USAMHI): "They had, of course, perfect intelligence. It all funneled in right there. They knew exactly where each platoon of North Koreans were going, and they'd move to meet it. . . . The Eighth Army commander . . . didn't have time to move the intelligence [to lower echelons so he] was moving squads [to meet the North Korean attacks]. . . . That was amazing, utterly amazing."

90. *South to the Naktong*, pp. 263–64.

91. Ibid., pp. 257–59, 262–65.

92. JCS "Record," p. 24; "History of the JCS III," pp. 506–09; *MacArthur III*, p. 453.

93. Major General Courtney Whitney, *MacArthur: His Rendezvous with History* (New York: Knopf, 1956), pp. 369–70; JCS "Record," pp. 24–25.

94. JCS "Record," p. 25.

95. "History of the JCS III," p. 509; *Tumultuous Years*, pp. 259–60.

96. JCS "Record," p. 26.

97. *MacArthur III*, p. 454; *A General's Life*, p. 549.

98. *Present at the Creation*, p. 422.

99. *MacArthur III*, p. 453; *MacArthur: His Rendezvous with History*, p. 371.

100. *Years of Trial and Hope*, p. 402.

101. *MacArthur III*, p. 454; *A General's Life*, pp. 549–50; *Tumultuous Years*, pp. 260–61.

102. *Present at the Creation*, p. 422; *MacArthur III*, p. 457.

103. JCS "Record," pp. 26–27.

104. *Years of Trial and Hope*, p. 403; *Plain Speaking*, p. 291.

## CHAPTER 7

1. Author-Moore interview; letters, Michaelis to Appleman, January 24 and September 29, 1953.

2. Letters, Michaelis to Appleman; *South to the Naktong*, p. 237.

3. *South to the Naktong*, p. 239. Dolvin: West Point *Register;* official biography; author-Dolvin interview, November 4, 1984. Dolvin speech.

4. *South to the Naktong*, pp. 241–41.

5. Ibid., p. 244.

6. Ibid., p. 243. An excellent account of this fight is presented by Harold H. Martin in the *Saturday Evening Post* (September 9, 1950): "The Colonel Saved the Day." See also *War in Korea*, pp. 116–30.

7. *War in Korea* and "Colonel Saved the Day."

8. Promotion: "Colonel Saved the Day." See also *Time* (September 3, 1950). Check's DSC: Author-Michaelis interview.

9. Author-Dolvin interview; Dolvin speech.

10. *South to the Naktong*, pp. 241–42.

11. *Tumultuous Years*, pp. 261–62; *MacArthur III*, p. 458. Francis H. Heller, ed.,

*The Korean War: A 25-Year Perspective* (Lawrence, Kan.: Regents Press of Kansas, 1977), p. 25 (hereafter Heller, *Korean War*).

12. *Policy and Direction,* p. 130, 145; "History of the JCS III," p. 195. Ridgway letter to a friend, Ridgway Papers, Box 16, USAMHI.
13. Harriman report on the trip: *Years of Trial and Hope,* pp. 397–404 (extracted in *FRUS VIII,* 1950, pp. 542–44). Cable, Ridgway to Walker, August 6, 1950, Ridgway Papers, Box 16, USAMHI.
14. Harriman report.
15. Ridgway desk diary entries, August 15 and 16, 1950. Ridgway memos, August 8 and August 9, 1950, reproduced in *FRUS VII,* 1950, pp. 540–42 ("Conference with General MacArthur"). Report of Ridgway's senior aide, Frank W. Moorman, August 9, 1950, including report of Colonel Eckert (AGF), Ridgway Papers, Box 16, USAMHI. Moorman's report was approved by Ridgway.
16. Bartlett's three senior assistants were William C. Bulloch, Robert H. Booth, and Logan Clarke, all West Pointers from the classes of 1929 and 1930. Letters to author from Bulloch, April 9, 1985, and William F. Train (G-3 section), December 2, 1984, with enclosures; West Point *Register.*
17. Knight: *Ridgway's Paratroopers,* p. 6. Respect for MacArthur: *Soldier,* p. 223; Ridgway, *Korean War,* various entries. "Genius": Ridgway oral history, pt. 3, pp. 74–75, USAMHI.
18. Ridgway memo, August 15, 1950. Ridgway oral history, pt. 3, p. 84. Harriman, Norstad view: Heller, *Korean War,* p. 35.
19. In his oral history (pt. 3, p. 84) Ridgway said that Norstad told him that MacArthur had told him, Norstad, that "he wanted to see Ridgway in command of Eighth Army."
20. Ridgway report, August 8, 1950; *FRUS VII,* 1950, and Box 16. Ridgway addendum to August 8, 1950, memo on August 11, 1950, Box 16, USAMHI.
21. Moorman, Eckert reports; Ridgway memo, August 9, 1950.
22. "Asset": Ridgway addendum to memo of August 8, 1950, Box 16, USAMHI.
23. Heller, *Korean War,* p. 35. Ridgway oral history, pt. 3, p. 84.
24. *Policy and Direction,* pp. 131–33, 148–49.
25. Ridgway desk diary, August 15 and 16, 1950, Box 16, USAMHI. Gruenther: West Point *Register;* official biography.
26. Ridgway memo, August 16, 1950, Box 16, USAMHI.
27. Heller, *Korean War,* p. 35.
28. *South to the Naktong,* pp. 266–67.
29. Ibid., p. 270. Pierce: 24th Infantry records. Thompson: *South to the Naktong,* p. 270n.; *Battleground Korea; Korea's Heroes,* p. 233.
30. Champeny: Official biography; *Army Register.* Appleman misspells Champeny as "Champney" throughout *South to the Naktong.*
31. Official biography. Italian service: John Ellis, *Cassino: The Hollow Victory* (New York: McGraw-Hill, 1984), various entries. Korean occupation: *Military Advisors in Korea,* various entries.
32. Carlisle and Bussy ms.; Carlisle correspondence.
33. Corley: West Point *Register;* official biography; obituary, West Point *Assembly,* December 1984; various author interviews. Replacing Pierce: 24th Infantry records (officer rosters), unnumbered box, NA (Suitland).
34. *South to the Naktong,* pp. 271–72.
35. West Point *Register;* obituary, West Point *Assembly,* Summer 1970. Ordway promotion: Letter, Ridgway to Eisenhower, July 2, 1949, Ridgway Papers, Box 10, USAMHI.

36. *South to the Naktong,* pp. 271–72.
37. *U.S. Marine Operations in Korea I,* pp. 49–51.
38. Official bios, courtesy U.S. Marine Corps History and Museums, Navy Yard, Washington, D. C. (hereafter USMC History); *U.S. Marine Operations in Korea I.*
39. Marine advances: *U.S. Marine Operations in Korea I. South to the Naktong,* pp. 274–76.
40. Heckemeyer: West Point *Register.* 3/5 action: *South to the Naktong,* p. 286.
41. 5th RCT here and below: Barth ms.; *South to the Naktong,* pp. 276–86. Letters, Ordway to Appleman, February 8, 1955, and to R. W. Stephens, November 11 and November 18, 1957.
42. Corley and 3/24: *South to the Naktong,* p. 285.
43. *South to the Naktong,* p. 284; *U.S. Marine Operations in Korea I,* p. 148; Barth ms.
44. *U.S. Marine Operations in Korea I,* pp. 150–51.
45. *South to the Naktong,* pp. 275, 287–88; *U.S. Marine Operations in Korea I,* pp. 139–41.
46. *South to the Naktong,* p. 286.
47. Throckmorton: West Point *Register;* official biography; Author-Throckmorton interview, November 8, 1984.
48. Author-Throckmorton interview.
49. *South to the Naktong,* p. 286; Ordway letter to Appleman, November 21, 1957; Author-Throckmorton interview.
50. Author-Throckmorton interview.
51. Tactics and action here and below: *South to the Naktong,* pp. 289–318; *Counterattack on the Naktong* (see Chapter 2, note 44). The 111-page Robertson monograph, based on 24th Division, regimental, and battalion reports, and other sources, is without doubt the finest official Army account of any battle in Korea. Clearly and concisely written, meticulously documented, thoughtful in analysis, and containing excellent maps, it sets new standards for such works.
52. Author-Darrigo interview.
53. Perez: *Army Register;* Gines Perez oral history, Special Collections Department, Mitchell Memorial Library, Mississippi State University, courtesy D. Clayton James.
54. Ibid.
55. Clarke C. Munroe, *The Second United States Infantry Division in Korea, 1950–1951* (Tokyo: Toppan Printing Co., 1951), hereafter *Second Division in Korea.* Author-Jack W. Rudolph interview, February 15, 1985. Rudolph (West Point, 1933) commanded the 38th in 1948 and 1949.
56. Keiser: West Point *Register;* official biography; obituary, West Point *Assembly,* Summer 1970. Author-Gerald G. Epley interview, September 12, 1984. Letters, Epley to Appleman, October 26 and December 6, 1979, kindly provided by Epley.
57. Bradley: West Point *Register;* official biography; author interviews with Epley and with Paul F. Freeman, September 23, 1984; Freeman oral history, USAMHI. Haynes: official biography; author interviews with Freeman and Epley; Freeman oral history. Tully: West Point *Register;* author-Epley interview.
58. Author interviews with Michaelis, Epley, and other senior 2d Division personnel and Eighth Army personnel.
59. Sloane: West Point *Register;* obituary, West Point *Assembly,* December 1984.

Author-Mrs. Charles C. Sloane interview, September 25, 1984. *Life* (May 22, 1950).

60. Hill: West Point *Register;* official biography; obituary, West Point *Assembly,* 1980. Son: West Point *Register* and 7th Cav records.
61. Various author interviews with 9th RCT senior officers.
62. McMains official biography. McMains letters to author November 19 and December 28, 1984, and September 12 and 30, 1986. Evaluation: Author interviews with Barberis; Julius W. Becton, Jr., September 29, 1986; Harris M. Pope, September 22, 1986. Letter, William R. Ellis to author, April 15, 1985. Other author interviews with 9th Infantry personnel.
63. McMains correspondence. Frazier: *Army Register.*
64. 3/9 to Yonil: *South to the Naktong,* pp. 325–26; McMains correspondence.
65. Londahl and Harrison: Letters to author from, and interviews with, 9th Infantry personnel.
66. Harrison leg and Walker: Author-Barberis interview; letters to author from, and interviews with, 9th Infantry personnel.
67. Letter, Ellis to author.
68. 3/27: Author-Michaelis interview. De Chow: *Army Register.*
69. Author-Freeman interview; official biography. Freeman oral history, USAMHI.
70. Messinger: West Point *Register;* obituary, West Point *Assembly,* September 1976. The dual-command setup in the 23d was described in author-Barberis interview. He said: "While we were getting ready to sail, the decision was made from above to send in new regimental commanders. To my personal knowledge, I know that General Dutch Keiser fought that decision from the Pentagon. He wanted to retain his incumbent regimental commanders. . . . In the case of the Twenty-third Infantry, Colonel Paul Freeman came in, and General Keiser put him in as RCT commander, leaving Ed Messinger as the regimental CO. This did not work out too well, as you can imagine, since the RCT had no staff, etc. However, this is the organization that we sailed with." Freeman defense of Keiser: Author-Freeman interview. 23d well trained: Freeman oral history, p. 98. Richardson: *Second Division in Korea;* letter, Mrs. Richardson to author, February 2, 1985, with enclosures.
71. West Point *Register;* official biography. Author-Barberis interview.
72. Author-Barberis interview. *Counterattack on the Naktong.*
73. Donald Knox, *The Korean War: An Oral History* (New York: Harcourt Brace Jovanovich, 1985), p. 93.
74. Author-Barberis interview.
75. Collier: official biography; letter, Collier to Appleman. Collier was Walker's XX corps chief of staff in World War II and rose to brigadier general but reverted to colonel in postwar years.
76. *U.S. Marine Operations in Korea I,* pp. 173–206.

## CHAPTER 8

1. *South to the Naktong,* pp. 10, 193, 195, 205, 342, 469–70.
2. Ibid., p. 336 (map).
3. Author-Palmer interview.
4. Crombez: Official biography; West Point *Register.* Positive views: Author-Palmer interview; author-Peter D. Clainos interview, September 28, 1984; Harold K. Johnson oral history, USAMHI. Negative views: Author interviews with

Billy Harris, Buckley, Victor L. Fox and John C. Barrett Jr., June 15, 1987. "Brave, yes . . ." from Buckley interview; "sonofabitch" from Barrett interview.

5. *South to the Naktong,* pp. 380–81. Author interview with Rodgers, July 12, 1987. All three tank battalions came to Korea from California on the same ship.
6. Author-Rodgers interview.
7. Ibid.
8. *South to the Naktong,* p. 339; *First Team.*
9. Author-Buckley interview.
10. Author-Gibson interview; author-Buckley interview.
11. *South to the Naktong,* p. 339.
12. West Point *Register;* author-Clainos interview.
13. *South to the Naktong,*, pp. 340–42.
14. Ibid., pp. 342–44.
15. Letter, Gay to Appleman; author interviews with James H. Lynch, Harris, and Dolvin.
16. West Point *Register;* author-Harris interview.
17. *South to the Naktong,* pp. 344–45.
18. Ibid., pp. 345–47.
19. Clifford: West Point *Register;* author-Mrs. Paul T. Clifford interview, June 14, 1987; author-Mrs. Claude E. Allen interview, June 14, 1987 (Allen was exec of the 2/5). Author interviews with Buckley and Gibson, and other 5th Cav personnel.
20. *South to the Naktong,* p. 347. Appleman wrote that Crombez relieved the 2/5 commander "because he had lost control of his units and did not know where they were." However, all sources insist that Clifford brought the 2/5 to Korea from Japan and remained in command for months.
21. Ibid., p. 347.
22. Ibid. Knox, *Korean War,* p. 95.
23. *South to the Naktong,* pp. 347–48.
24. Ibid., pp. 337, 354.
25. Ibid., pp. 319–33.
26. Ibid., pp. 330–31, 351–54; *U.S. Air Force in Korea,* pp. 131–32. James A. Field, *History of United States Naval Operations: Korea* (Washington, D.C.: Government Printing Office, 1962), pp. 146–49.
27. *South to the Naktong,* pp. 345–47.
28. Ibid., pp. 353–54, 356, 358.
29. Ibid., pp. 356–57.
30. Ibid., p. 358, 411.
31. Ibid., p. 358.
32. Ibid., pp. 362–63; *Second Division in Korea;* 23d Infantry operations report, August 1950, courtesy Paul Freeman.
33. *South to the Naktong,* pp. 331–32.
34. *War in Peacetime,* p. 121.
35. *South to the Naktong,* p. 382. Allen: Official biography; *A General's Life,* p. 102 and passim.
36. Official biography; letters, Dabney to author, November 4 and November 27, 1986. At the University of Kentucky Dabney was Phi Beta Kappa, was graduated cum laude, and was the ROTC "honor graduate." He kept the "artillery clique" in the G-3 section—Bullock, Clarke, and Booth—in place. The section

was strengthened by the addition of West Point (1931) infantryman William F. Train, a veteran of ETO fighting.

37. *War in Peacetime,* p. 122.
38. *South to the Naktong,* pp. 379–84.
39. Ibid., pp. 393–96.
40. Ibid., p. 389.
41. 24th Division records, NA (Suitland), RG 407, Boxes 3481, 3493. Menoher was "medically evacuated" as a nonbattle casualty on August 25, 1950. Davidson reported for duty on August 26, 1950. Davidson: official biography; author-Davidson interview.
42. 24th Division records, NA. Author interviews with Kinney, September 27, 1984, and Moore. Kinney and Moore correspondence with author. Letter, Kenneth J. Woods (34th Infantry) to author, March 8, 1985. Naudts: *Army Register.*
43. 34th Strength: Letters, Barnett (and others) to author. Walker decision: Author interviews with Beauchamp, Moore, Kinney, and Throckmorton. *South to the Naktong,* p. 389.
44. *South to the Naktong,* p. 389; various author interviews.
45. *South to the Naktong,* p. 389. Growdon: Official biography; West Point *Register.* United Press profile, dated March 23, 1951, and other material kindly provided by Growdon's daughter and son-in-law, Mr. and Mrs. Robert Foister, in a letter to the author, October 7, 1986.
46. Robert Debs Heinl, Jr., *Victory at High Tide: The Inchon-Seoul Campaign* (Philadelphia: J. B. Lippincott, 1968), pp. 24–30; *History of U.S. Naval Operations: Korea,* pp. 177–78; *Policy and Direction,* pp. 146–47.
47. *War in Peacetime,* pp. 126–27; *Victory at High Tide,* p. 43.
48. See, for example, *Victory at High Tide,* p. 3.
49. *A General's Life,* p. 510.
50. *War in Peacetime,* p. 125. Collins wrote that "Admiral Sherman seconded my suggestion" for Kunsan.
51. *MacArthur: His Rendezvous with History,* p. 379; *MacArthur III,* p. 460. James wrote that MacArthur sent his message to the VFW on August 20, 1950.
52. *Policy and Direction,* p. 158; *South to the Naktong,* p. 490. Schnabel wrote that MacArthur asked the Pentagon for authority to activate X Corps on August 21, 1950. At that time Collins and Sherman were en route to Tokyo by air. The Pentagon granted approval on August 22, 1950, while Collins and Sherman were in Korea.
53. John H. Chiles oral history, Special Collections Department, Mitchell Memorial Library, Mississippi State University, p. 41.
54. *Policy and Direction,* pp. 155–57. August 7, 1950, MacArthur's GHQ G-3, ("Pinky") Edwin K. Wright, proposed that MacArthur utilize Shepherd's Marine HQ in Honolulu for planning and executing Inchon.
55. *Victory at High Tide,* pp. 40, 43. Doyle: Official biography.
56. Exclusion: *Victory at High Tide,* p. 40. According to Heinl, Shepherd remarked: "Marines weren't *persona grata* in Tokyo in those days." Shepherd official biography. Shepherd support of MacArthur: *Victory at High Tide,* p. 17. Almond alienation of Smith, etc.: Oral history and aide-mémoire, Korea, Oliver P. Smith, USMC History.
57. No one at the meeting took notes, nor was a transcript made. This account follows those of Schnabel, Appleman, Heinl, MacArthur, Collins, and James.
58. *MacArthur III,* pp. 461–62.

59. *Present at the Creation,* pp. 423–24; *Tumultuous Years,* pp. 263–64.
60. *Tumultuous Years,* pp. 264–65; "History of the JCS III," pp. 516–18.
61. *Reminiscences,* p. 388; *Tumultuous Years,* p. 265.
62. *Years of Trial and Hope,* pp. 405–06.
63. *Off the Record,* p. 193.
64. James H. Dill, "Personal Adventures" in Korea, manuscript, courtesy Dill. Dill also kept a diary in Korea (hereafter Dill diary). Letters, Dill to author, February 7 and 23, 1985.
65. *A General's Life,* pp. 552–53.
66. "History of the JCS III," p. 211; *War in Peacetime,* p. 127.
67. "History of the JCS III," pp. 211–12; *War in Peacetime,* p. 127.
68. Here and below: *A General's Life,* pp. 557–62; *Present at the Creation,* pp. 445–47, 451–52; *War in Peacetime,* pp. 143–46; *Tumultuous Years,* pp. 268–73. For various official documents relating to the debate see *FRUS VII,* 1950, pp. 567–708.
69. Truman's September 1 radio address: *Years of Trial and Hope,* p. 409.
70. Allen S. Whiting, *China Crosses the Yalu: The Decision to Enter the Korean War* (Santa Monica, Calif.: Rand Corporation, 1960).

## CHAPTER 9

1. *South to the Naktong,* pp. 392–93.
2. Ibid., pp. 394–95.
3. Ibid., p. 395. Dropping 87th Regiment in Seoul area: pp. 459, 510.
4. Ibid., pp. 417–18 (photo of jeep).
5. Author-Lynch interviews, May 24 and 26, 1984.
6. Letter, Woods to author, March 8, 1985.
7. *South to the Naktong,* , pp. 439–41.
8. Ibid., pp. 368–75. Casualties and personnel: 24th Infantry records (August 1950), NA (Suitland), RG 407, unnumbered box.
9. Correspondence and author interviews with Carlisle, Biggs, and Walden.
10. *South to the Naktong,* p. 441.
11. Author-Walden interview and Walden taped self-interview.
12. *South to the Naktong,* p. 441.
13. Ibid., pp. 479–80.
14. Ibid., pp. 479–80.
15. Ibid., p. 482. Kean's recommendation to disband the 24th: p. 486.
16. Author-Walden interview and Walden self-interview.
17. Walter G. Hermes, *Truce Tent and Fighting Front* (Washington, D.C.: Office of the Chief of Military History, 1966), pp. 64–67 (hereafter *Truce Tent*); letter, Ryan to James A. Van Fleet to Matthew B. Ridgway, December 30, 1951, Box 19, Ridgway Papers, USAMHI; related documents dated November 5, 1950, and January 3, 1951, in Boxes 18 and 19.
18. 24th Infantry Records, NA. Corley relieved Champeny on September 7, 1950. Corley age: West Point *Register.* Battlefield promotion: Corley obituary, West Point *Assembly,* September 1984.
19. 24th Infantry records, NA. *Army Register.* Blair: Biographical note to a magazine article by Blair, "I Send Your Son into Battle," *Saturday Evening Post* (June 23, 1951). The note states that Blair, son of a Kansas railroad engineer, tried twice for West Point and failed. He enlisted in the Army and won a com-

mission in World War II and fought with Merrill's Marauders in Burma, where he won the DSC, Purple Heart, two Bronze Star Medals, and other medals. Also, article, *San Francisco Chronicle,* January 14, 1958.

20. David K. Carlisle, "America's First Korean War Victory," article ms., courtesy Carlisle.
21. 1/29 to 3/35: *South to the Naktong,* p. 365.
22. Ibid., pp. 441–43.
23. Ibid., pp. 472–73.
24. Ibid., pp. 472, 478.
25. Freeman oral history, p. 102, USAMHI.
26. *South to the Naktong,* pp. 446–47.
27. Ibid., pp. 444–45.
28. *Second Division in Korea;* Robert Manning, ed., *Above and Beyond: A History of the Medal of Honor from the Civil War to Vietnam* (Boston: Boston Publishing Co., 1985), pp. 256–59, 337; author-Murphy interviews, August 20 and August 22, 1986.
29. West Point Korean War casualties: West Point *Register,* 1980 edition, pp. 822–23. See also *Newsweek* (June 18, 1951).
30. *South to the Naktong,* pp. 448–51; 23rd Infantry operations report, September 1950, courtesy Freeman; *Second Division in Korea;* Freeman oral history, USAMHI; author-Freeman interview.
31. *Second Division in Korea,* p. 11. The 38th arrived at Pusan on August 20, 1950. Peploe: West Point *Register;* official biography.
32. Letter, Skeldon to author, February 12, 1985; author interview with a former senior commander, 2d Division, who requested anonymity. Author-Hodges interview, June 22, 1987.
33. *South to the Naktong,* pp. 467, 469–70.
34. Ibid., p. 450.
35. Letter, Freeman to author, March 26, 1986.
36. Ibid.
37. Author-Holden interview, July 25, 1985.
38. Freeman oral history, USAMHI; author-Freeman interview; 23d Infantry operations report, September 1950; *South to the Naktong,* p. 469.
39. *South to the Naktong,* pp. 452–53. Walker quoted in 23d Infantry operations report, September 1950.
40. *South to the Naktong,* pp. 454, 496; *Marine Operations in Korea I,* pp. 210–11; *Victory at High Tide,* pp. 61–64.
41. *South to the Naktong,* p. 496. Walker "extremely excited": *Policy and Direction,* p. 165.
42. Oliver P. Smith oral history and Smith, aide-mémoire, both at USMC History. Letter, Smith to Appleman. *Victory at High Tide,* p. 62.
43. Smith oral history.
44. *South to the Naktong,* pp. 496–97; *Policy and Direction,* pp. 164–65.
45. "Tell Walker": *South to the Naktong,* p. 496.
46. Extension to September 5: *Marine Operations in Korea I,* p. 236.
47. *South to the Naktong,* p. 464; *Marine Operations in Korea I,* pp. 212–36.
48. *Marine Operations in Korea I,* pp. 228–29.
49. *South to the Naktong,* p. 466.
50. William B. Hopkins, *One Bugle No Drums: The Marines at Chosin Reservoir* (Chapel Hill: Algonquin Books, 1986), p. 23.

51. Promotion, retirement: West Point *Register;* official biography; letter, John G. Hill, Jr., to author, March 20, 1986, enclosing further biographical material.
52. Author-Barberis interview.
53. The action of the 1st Cav in defense of Taegu, September 1 to September 15, 1950: *South to the Naktong,* pp. 411–36; *First Team;* author interviews, as noted.
54. Treacy: West Point *Register.* 3/5 background: *Army Lineage Series,* p. 346; Knox, *Korean War,* pp. 311–12.
55. Author-James H. Lynch interview, September 9, 1986. West Point *Register.* Lynch's father, George A. Lynch (West Point, 1903), a classmate of MacArthur's, retired in 1941 a major general. His older brother, George E. (West Point, 1929), a decorated regimental commander in World War II, was then on the staff of the National War College.
56. Official biography; West Point *Register;* Johnson oral history, USAMHI; profile, Martin Blumenson, "Most Remarkable Man," *Army* (August 1968); Bruce Palmer, Jr., *The 25-Year War* (New York: Touchstone, 1985), pp. 25–26.
57. Johnson oral history.
58. Author interviews with 5th Cav personnel: Victor Fox, June 15, 1987; John C. Barrett, June 15, 1987; and Harry A. Buckley and James M. Gibson. Letters, Norman Allen, CO, I Company (3/5), to his mother from Korea; Allen ms. The latter are excerpted in Knox, *Korean War.* Fox, who has copies but could not make them available to the author owing to a prior publishing commitment with Knox for a proposed sequel to his *Korean War,* stated that Allen's letters and ms. make clear the deep resentment in the 3/5 for Crombez, and describe the problems between Crombez and Treacy. On Treacy's death, see below.
59. *South to the Naktong,* pp. 411–36.
60. Spoiling attack: Ibid., p. 411.
61. Ibid., pp. 412–13.
62. Ibid.; *Of GarryOwen in Glory,* pp. 259–67.
63. *South to the Naktong,* pp. 419–20; *Combat Actions in Korea,* pp. 39–46. Hitchner killed: *Of GarryOwen in Glory,* p. 263. Callaway: *Of GarryOwen in Glory,* p. 267, and West Point *Register.*
64. *South to the Naktong,* pp. 414, 419.
65. Ibid., p. 421.
66. Ibid., pp. 422–29.
67. General withdrawal: Ibid., p. 415.
68. Panic in Taegu: Ibid., pp. 415–16, 421–22. Walker quoted: p. 417.
69. "Existence": *First Team.* Robbins and Cohen: Author interviews with Robbins and Cohen.
70. Casualties in 3/8: Johnson oral history, USAMHI. DSC awarded for action on September 4, 1950: "Most Remarkable Man." Palmer sickened: Letter, Holmes to author.
71. *South to the Naktong,* p. 432. Hill 314: Ibid., pp. 432–35. Author-Lynch interview.
72. *South to the Naktong,* p. 435. Walton: *Army Register,* and author interviews with Feild and Cohen.
73. *South to the Naktong,* p. 432; Knox, *Korean War,* p. 352.
74. *South to the Naktong,* pp. 395–96.
75. ROK order of battle: Ibid., p. 399 (map).
76. Ibid., p. 544.

77. Assignment of Coulter: Ibid., p. 398. Coulter: Official biography.
78. D. Clayton James, *The Years of MacArthur: Volume I, 1880–1941* (Boston: Houghton Mifflin, 1970); *Cassino.*
79. *South to the Naktong,* pp. 398–400; Tychsen official biography; Tychsen ms., Tychsen papers, USAMHI.
80. *South to the Naktong,* pp. 402–04.
81. Ibid., pp. 404–06.
82. Coulter relieved: Ibid., p. 405; Tychsen ms.
83. *South to the Naktong,* pp. 407–10.
84. Ibid., pp. 491–92, 547.
85. JCS concern: "History of the JCS III," p. 213; *War in Peacetime,* p. 128.
86. "History of the JCS III," pp. 212–13.
87. *Reminiscences,* pp. 399–400.
88. *Years of Trial and Hope,* p. 409; "History of the JCS III," p. 214; *War in Peacetime,* p. 129.

## CHAPTER 10

1. *South to the Naktong,* pp. 501–02; *Victory at High Tide,* p. 73.
2. *South to the Naktong,* p. 502.
3. Ibid.; *Victory at High Tide,* pp. 73–75; *MacArthur III,* p. 474.
4. *South to the Naktong,* p. 502; *History of U.S. Naval Operations: Korea,* pp. 185–90.
5. *South to the Naktong,* p. 503; *Victory at High Tide,* pp. 80–82; *History of U.S. Naval Operations: Korea,* pp. 191–92.
6. *Victory at High Tide,* p. 80; *History of U.S. Naval Operations: Korea,* pp. 183, 193.
7. *Victory at High Tide,* p. 84; *History of U.S. Naval Operations: Korea,* p. 193.
8. *Victory at High Tide,* pp. 76, 87.
9. *MacArthur: His Rendezvous with History,* pp. 356–58.
10. *Victory at High Tide,* pp. 90–97; *History of U.S. Naval Operations: Korea,* p. 197. Frank Gibney in *Time* (September 25, 1950).
11. *Victory at High Tide,* pp. 97–108.
12. Author-Henry G. Walker interview, November 15, 1985; Bell quoted in *Time* (September 29, 1950); Higgins quoted in *Victory at High Tide,* p. 102.
13. Author-Walker interview.
14. *Victory at High Tide,* pp. 105, 116; author-Walker interview.
15. *Victory at High Tide,* pp. 108–17.
16. Ibid., pp. 119–20.
17. *MacArthur III,* p. 478; *Policy and Direction,* p. 173.
18. *South to the Naktong,* pp. 509–10.
19. NKPA in Inchon-Seoul area: *South to the Naktong,* pp. 395; 495, 500, 506, 508, 513, 519, 523, 538; *Victory at High Tide,* pp. 30, 66, 94, 97, 146.
20. *Victory at High Tide,* various.
21. "Five days": *South to the Naktong,* p. 515. "So obsessed": Letter, Smith to Appleman, NA.
22. O. P. Smith, aide-mémoire, pp. 604–10. Chiles: West Point *Register;* Chiles oral history. Author-Walker interview. Almond oral history, USAMHI.
23. Chiles oral history; author-Chiles interview. Bypassing Smith: *Victory at High Tide,* p. 213.

24. *South to the Naktong,* p. 512.
25. Official biography.
26. *Present at the Creation,* pp. 305–06; "History of the JCS II," pp. 429–72.
27. Wedemeyer quoted in *Forrestal Diaries,* p. 383. Letter, Paddock to author, December 3, 1984. Author-Davis interview, June 9, 1986.
28. Barr's reluctance to serve at Inchon: Author-Herbert B. Powell interview, September 8, 1986. X Corps view of Barr: Author-William J. McCaffrey interview, May 23, 1984; letter, anonymous to author, April 8, 1986. Letter, Paddock to author.
29. West Point *Register;* official biography; author-Powell interview. Paddock letter: Russell Weigley, *Eisenhower's Lieutenants* (Bloomington, Ind.: Indiana University Press, 1981), p. 323.
30. *Policy and Direction,* pp. 165–68. Letter, Paddock to author, kindly enclosing personal diary for July–August 1950.
31. Strength: *South to the Naktong,* p. 512. Quality of ROKs: Letter, Barr to Appleman. See also *South to the Naktong,* pp. 386–89; *Policy and Direction,* p. 167.
32. Interviews with numerous 7th Division officers and enlisted men, including Francois (Februay 15, 1986) and Davis (June 9, 1986). Additional background on the 31st and 32d: Letter to author and unpublished ms., "Combat Duty in Korea," by Chester L. Bair. 31st surrender on Bataan: *Army Lineage Series,* p. 547. "Foreign Legion": Ripley "Believe It or Not" item, circa 1953.
33. *South to the Naktong,* pp. 512–13. Author-Beauchamp interview.
34. Ibid.; *Victory at High Tide,* p. 157.
35. *South to the Naktong,* p. 513.
36. *Victory at High Tide,* p. 168; *MacArthur III,* p. 479.
37. *South to the Naktong,* p. 519; *Policy and Direction,* p. 174.
38. *MacArthur III,* p. 479.
39. *South to the Naktong,* pp. 497, 542. "History of the JCS III," p. 214.
40. *Patton Papers,* p. 502.
41. *South to the Naktong,* pp. 542–45 (Map V).
42. Train oral history, USAMHI; letters, Train to author, December 2, 1984, and June 3, 1986.
43. Walker quoted: Letter, Landrum to Appleman.
44. West Point *Register;* official biography; *Ike Papers IV,* p. 2597; *Eisenhower's Lieutenants,* p. 556 and passim.
45. Author-Rinaldo Van Brunt interview, September 15, 1984.
46. Fear of flying: Letter, Tarkenton to author, November 7, 1984. Dog: Letter, Mrs. (Libby) Milburn to Appleman. Author-Van Brunt interview.
47. Tychsen ms., USAMHI.
48. *South to the Naktong,* pp. 545–47.
49. Ibid.
50. *Of GarryOwen in Glory,* p. 271.
51. Ammo shortage: *South to the Naktong,* p. 542; Paul Freeman oral history. Bridging shortage: *South to the Naktong,* p. 543; *Policy and Direction,* pp. 175–76.
52. *South to the Naktong,* pp. 568–71.
53. Ibid., pp. 548–52; *Second Division in Korea;* 23d Infantry operations report, September 1950; Freeman oral history; author interviews with Freeman and Barberis; letter, McMains to author.

54. Letters to author from McMains. Author-Becton interview, September 24, 1986; letter, Becton to author, October 8, 1986; official biography.

55. Frazier and Harlan: Letter, McMains to author, December 28, 1984; *Army Register.* Letter, Harlan to author, February 11, 1985. Author-Becton interview. Performance of McMains and 3/9: Letters, John E. Ellis to author, April 15, 1985.

56. *Second Division in Korea.* Commanders: Letters to author from Peploe, February 4, 1985, and Skeldon, February 12, 1985.

57. *Second Division in Korea,* p. 42. The historian wrote that "a critical shortage of bridging existed throughout the Army area and this shortage seriously hampered units of the division." He went on to say that "every foot of bridge in the division" was directed to the 38th Regiment sector. See also: Freeman oral history.

58. *South to the Naktong,* pp. 552–58, 560–64; *Of GarryOwen in Glory,* pp. 268–72.

59. 2/7 casualties: *South to the Naktong,* p. 563.

60. Knox. *Korean War,* pp. 316–61. Fox quoted on p. 347.

61. Ibid., pp. 374–75.

62. *South to the Naktong,* p. 555, photo of Kumho ford, p. 557.

63. Ibid., p. 562; *Of GarryOwen in Glory,* pp. 269–70.

64. *Victory at High Tide,* p. 147; *South to the Naktong,* p. 571; *Policy and Direction,* pp. 175–76.

65. *Policy and Direction,* pp. 175–76.

66. Continuing amphibious plans: *South to the Naktong,* p. 610; *A General's Life,* p. 568.

67. *Victory at High Tide,* p. 188.

68. *Victory at High Tide,* p. 189; O. P. Smith oral history; Chiles oral history; author-Chiles interview.

69. For a damning critique of X Corps, see *Victory at High Tide,* pp. 259–61. Ruffner: Official biography. Haig, McCaffrey, Quinn, Rowny: West Point *Register;* official biographies; author interviews with McCaffrey, Rowny, and Quinn.

70. Author interviews with McCaffrey, Rowny, other X Corps senior officers, and James Y. Adams, September 25, 1984.

71. *Victory at High Tide,* p. 210.

72. Smith versus Smith: E. B. Potter, *Nimitz* (Annapolis, Md.: Naval Institute Press, 1976) pp. 305–09; *Eagle Against the Sun,* pp. 313–16.

73. *Victory at High Tide,* p. 211; *South to the Naktong,* pp. 527–28.

74. *South to the Naktong,* pp. 520–23.

75. Ibid. Letter, Paddock to author.

76. Reserve: *South to the Naktong,* p. 539n; Arch E. Roberts, *RAKKASANS!: History of the 187th Airborne Regiment* (Nashville, Tenn.: Benson Printing Company, n.d.).

77. West Point *Register;* letter, Ovenshine to author, October 22, 1984.

78. Letter, Ovenshine to author.

79. *South to the Naktong,* pp. 524–26; *Victory at High Tide,* pp. 213–25.

80. *South to the Naktong,* pp. 529–30.

81. *Victory at High Tide,* p. 220.

82. *South to the Naktong,* pp. 529–31; *Victory at High Tide,* pp. 220–21.

83. *Ridgway's Paratroopers.*

84. *Victory at High Tide,* p. 221.

85. Letters, Beauchamp to Appleman, Barr to Appleman, Paddock to author; *Victory at High Tide,* p. 261.

86. *South to the Naktong,* p. 534; *Victory at High Tide,* p. 239.
87. Thompson quoted in *Victory at High Tide,* p. 242. For street fighting, see *South to the Naktong,* pp. 531–36; *Victory at High Tide,* pp. 225–51.
88. *South to the Naktong,* pp. 538–39; *RAKKASANS!*
89. *South to the Naktong,* pp. 538–39. Letters to author from Olson, June 27, 1986; the 31st S-2, Carl S. Witte, June 16, 1986; two other 31st officers, George A. Rasula, April 22, 1986, and May 28, 1986, and Richard F. Mitchell, October 6, 1986.
90. *South to the Naktong,* p. 539n. Letter, Ovenshine to author; author interviews with Powell and Davis.

### CHAPTER 11

1. *South to the Naktong,* pp. 571–72.
2. Ibid., p. 570; Barth ms.
3. Barth ms.
4. *South to the Naktong,* p. 574 and map X.
5. Ibid., pp. 575–77; author-Dolvin interview; Dolvin speech.
6. Author-Dolvin interview; Dolvin speech.
7. *South to the Naktong,* p. 577.
8. Ibid., p. 579; Barth ms.
9. *South to the Naktong,* pp. 579–80.
10. Freeman oral history, pp. 104–07, USAMHI; author-Freeman interview; *Second Division in Korea.*
11. Freeman oral history; letter, Sherrard to author, February 2, 1985.
12. *South to the Naktong,* pp. 579–80; *Second Division in Korea;* 23d Infantry operations report, September 1950.
13. Freeman oral history.
14. Ibid.
15. Letter, Sherrard to author, March 24, 1986.
16. *South to the Naktong,* p. 581; *Second Division in Korea;* Freeman oral history; letter, Sherrard to author.
17. Letters, Sherrard to author, February 2, 1985, and March 27, 1986.
18. Author-Freeman interview; Freeman oral history. Author-Hodges interview.
19. *South to the Naktong,* p. 581.
20. *Second Division in Korea.*
21. *South to the Naktong,* p. 553.
22. Ibid., pp. 562–63, 566.
23. Ibid., p. 554.
24. Strong bio: West Point *Register;* "Sabers and Safety Pins"; letter, Strong to author, July 19, 1986.
25. *South to the Naktong,* p. 557; "Sabers and Safety Pins"; Strong speech to the Corps of Engineers, circa December 1951, "Army Engineer in Korea," kindly provided to author by Strong (hereafter, Strong speech).
26. Strong speech.
27. Ibid.
28. *South to the Naktong,* pp. 565–66; *Of GarryOwen in Glory,* pp. 269–71.
29. *South to the Naktong,* p. 566.
30. Here and below: Author-Harris interview.
31. Author-Clainos interview.
32. Letter, Webel to author, October 14, 1985.

33. *South to the Naktong,* p. 566; *Of GarryOwen in Glory,* pp. 272–81; James H. Lynch, "Task Force Penetration," *Combat Forces Journal* (January 1951); author-Lynch interview.
34. *South to the Naktong,* pp. 589–90.
35. Ibid., p. 588.
36. Ibid., p. 562.
37. West Point *Register;* official biography; author-Edson interview, May 25, 1984. The other three spare regimental commanders were: Ashton H. Manhart (West Point, 1932); James K. Woolnough (West Point, 1932); and William Belke.
38. Johnson oral history, USAMHI.
39. West Point *Register.*
40. *South to the Naktong,* pp. 582–83; C. N. Barclay, *The First Commonwealth Division* (Aldershot: Gale & Polden, 1954), pp. 19–21.
41. *South to the Naktong,* pp. 584–85.
42. Ibid., p. 586.
43. Ibid., p. 587.
44. Ibid., pp. 587–88.
45. Ibid., pp. 590–97; "Task Force Penetration"; author interviews with Harris and Lynch.
46. *South to the Naktong,* p. 593; author-Edson interview.
47. *South to the Naktong,* pp. 592–93.
48. Ibid., p. 593; author-Edson interview; Johnson oral history.
49. *South to the Naktong,* p. 595.
50. Author-Edson interview; Johnson oral history; *South to the Naktong,* p. 594.
51. *South to the Naktong,* p. 595.
52. Author-Edson interview; Johnson oral history.
53. ROK operations: *South to the Naktong,* pp. 567–68, 598–600.
54. Walker quoted: Ibid., p. 595.
55. Ibid., p. 604.
56. Ibid., p. 537; *MacArthur III,* pp. 482–83.
57. X Corps casualties: *Victory at High Tide,* p. 257. Eighth Army casualties: *South to the Naktong,* p. 604.
58. Awards: *MacArthur III,* p. 484.
59. Ibid.
60. Letter, Ridgway to MacArthur, September 27, 1950, Ridgway Papers, Box 16, USAMHI. Ridgway wrote Walker a similar letter: "Well done. The full fruits of the gallantry and indomitable perseverance of you and your forces through the dark days of withdrawal and defense seem now about in your grasp. They will, I think, attest a performance unsurpassed in our military annals—a proper permanent tribute to our dead and maimed. Congratulations from the heart."

## CHAPTER 12

1. *Tumultuous Years,* pp. 268–80; *Present at the Creation,* pp. 451–55; *War in Peacetime,* pp. 143–46; *A General's Life,* pp. 557–62. William Stueck, *The Road to Confrontation: American Policy Toward China and Korea, 1947–1950* (Chapel Hill: University of North Carolina Press, 1951), reprinted in *Child of Conflict.* James I. Matray, "Truman's Plan for Victory: National Self-Determination and the Thirty-eighth Parallel Decision in Korea," *Journal of American History* (September 1979). Pertinent documents: *FRUS VII,* 1950, pp. 502–693;

for JCS views, see ibid., pp. 502–510 and 528–35; for midsummer CIA views (later revised), see ibid., pp. 600–03; for dissenting views of George Kennan, see ibid., pp. 623–28.

2. Text of NSC-81: *FRUS VII,* 1950, pp. 685–93. JCS cable to MacArthur containing gist of NSC-81: JCS "Record." *Policy and Direction,* p. 180.

3. "Truman's Plan for Victory"; "History of the JCS III," pp. 240–45; *U.S. Air Force in Korea,* p. 188.

4. *Road to Confrontation.*

5. Ibid. Some historians—notably William Stueck—make the case that Truman and Acheson made a tragic error in failing to respond to these unusual Soviet overtures. The initial tough Soviet terms, they argue, may well have been merely bargaining positions which might have been softened considerably in behind-the-scenes negotiations.

6. *Policy and Direction,* pp. 187–90; *South to the Naktong,* pp. 608–12.

7. Assumptions: Ridgway oral history, pt. 3, pp. 75–76. "Walker assumed," Ridgway remembered, that after Inchon "X Corps would pass to his control." Walker sent a message to MacArthur in regard to his plans for X Corps, but Ridgway remembered, "He got back a very curt reply from MacArthur, very abruptly and curtly turning that down. He said he had other plans for X Corps." For a probing and dispassionate analysis of these decisions, see: Martin Blumenson, "MacArthur's Divided Command," *Army* (November 1956).

8. Owing to subsequent events, in most histories of the Korean War the plan for X Corps to play the dominant role in the capture of Pyongyang by this "flanking" attack is understressed. That it was to be the dominant force, with Eighth Army playing a secondary role, is clear from the priorities accorded X Corps and a statement by MacArthur to Truman at Wake Island on October 15. There MacArthur (*FRUS VII,* 1950, p. 949) said that he would land X Corps at Wonsan and that it would "take Pyongyang in one week."

9. Ridgway oral history, pt. 3, pp. 75–76.

10. "MacArthur's Divided Command."

11. Opposition to the Wonsan plan: Letter, Barr to Appleman, May 25, 1954; Barr wrote: "I urged that in lieu of planned operation that the 7th and 1st Cav Divisions be grouped into a corps and be given the mission of immediately pursuing in the direction of Pyongyang." Malcolm W. Cagle and Frank A. Manson, *The Sea War in Korea* (Annapolis, Md.: U.S. Naval Institute, 1957), p. 119, quotes Barr as preferring "to take the high road" from Seoul to Wonsan rather than carry out an amphibious landing. This was apparently his second choice. O. P. Smith's reservations: Letter, to Appleman. Turner Joy: *Sea War in Korea,* pp. 118–19. Joy said: "None of us at Commander, Naval Forces Far East, could see the necessity for such an operation, since the X Corps could have marched overland to Wonsan in a much shorter time and with much less effort than it would take to get the corps around to Wonsan by sea." Joy's deputy chief of staff, Arleigh A. Burke (later CNO), stated: "As events developed we objected to an amphibious assault as being unnecessary. It would take a lot of troops out of action for a long time when the enemy was already on the run. We felt the same objective—to seize the port of Wonsan—could be achieved by marching the X Corps up the road leading from Seoul to Wonsan." (*Sea War in Korea,* p. 119.)

12. *Sea War in Korea,* pp. 118–120. Letter, Almond to W. H. Tunner, July 25, 1963, Almond Papers, USAMHI. Almond's proposed D day of October 15:

Lynn Montross and Captain Nicholas A. Canzona, USMC, *U.S. Marine Operations in Korea 1950–1953,* vol. III: *The Chosin Reservoir Campaign* (Washington, D.C.: Historical Division, U.S. Marine Corps, 1962), p. 11 (hereafter *U.S. Marine Operations in Korea III*).

13. *FRUS VII,* 1950, pp. 781–82, 785; *Policy and Direction,* pp. 182–83; "History of the JCS III," p. 230.
14. "History of the JCS III," pp. 236–37; *Reminiscences,* pp. 407–08.
15. *A General's Life,* pp. 567–68; *War in Peacetime,* p. 160; Ridgway, *Korean War,* p. 44.
16. *Present at the Creation,* p. 453; "History of the JCS III," p. 238.
17. *Policy and Direction,* p. 183; "History of the JCS III," pp. 242–43.
18. "History of the JCS III," p. 243; *South to the Naktong,* p. 608.
19. *South to the Naktong,* p. 615.
20. "History of the JCS III," p. 244; *FRUS VII,* 1950, pp. 903–06.
21. Whitney, *MacArthur,* p. 108; *FRUS VII,* 1950, p. 852; *South to the Naktong,* pp. 758–59, 608.
22. *Policy and Direction,* pp. 198–99; "History of the JCS III," pp. 260–61.
23. Author-Polk interview.
24. *South to the Naktong,* pp. 750–51, 766–69; *U.S. Marine Operations in Korea III,* p. 91. For a close-up view of Lin Piao and Communist guerrillas in action in World War II, see Theodore F. White, *In Search of History* (New York: Harper & Row, 1981).
25. *FRUS VII,* 1950, pp. 935–38. The assessment was formally submitted on October 12, 1950.
26. *South to the Naktong,* p. 613.
27. *Reminiscences,* p. 408.
28. *South to the Naktong,* p. 614; *First Commonwealth Division,* p. 21.
29. Knox, *Korean War,* pp. 374–78.
30. Ibid., pp. 380–81.
31. *South to the Naktong,* p. 623; "History of the JCS III," p. 244; *FRUS VII,* 1950, p. 903.
32. *MacArthur,* p. 115; *FRUS VII,* 1950, pp. 914, 931; "History of the JCS III," p. 249.
33. *South to the Naktong,* p. 759.
34. Ibid., p. 623.
35. Ibid., pp. 624–25.
36. Ibid., pp. 625–26; *Of GarryOwen in Glory,* p. 282.
37. Author interviews with Harris, Clainos, and Lynch.
38. Ibid.; *South to the Naktong,* pp. 626–28.
39. *South to the Naktong,* p. 622.
40. Ibid., p. 630; maps, pp. 624 and 641.
41. Ibid., maps, pp. 624 and 641.
42. Knox, *Korean War,* pp. 382, 384, 397, 406.
43. *South to the Naktong,* pp. 616–17.
44. *U.S. Marine Operations in Korea III,* pp. 27–28; *Sea War in Korea,* pp. 121–47; *History of U.S. Naval Operations: Korea,* pp. 230–37.
45. *Policy and Direction,* pp. 205–06; *Sea War in Korea,* pp. 120–21; *History of U.S. Naval Operations: Korea,* pp. 225–26; *U.S. Marine Operations in Korea III,* pp. 22–23.

46. Joy's objections: *Sea War in Korea,* pp. 120–21; *History of U.S. Naval Operations: Korea,* pp. 225–26.
47. Iwon alternative: *Sea War in Korea,* p. 120.
48. *South to the Naktong,* pp. 620–21; *U.S. Marine Operations in Korea III,* pp. 24–25. George C. Stewart ms. in two parts, "Korea: August 1950–December 15, 1950" and "My Service with the Second Division During the Korean War" (hereafter Stewart ms.), courtesy Stewart.
49. *South to the Naktong,* pp. 631–33.
50. *War in Peacetime,* p. 142.
51. *Tumultuous Years,* p. 284.
52. *Present at the Creation,* p. 456; Pace oral history, pp. 91–92. For State Department objections, see memo by Philip C. Jessup, *FRUS VII,* 1950, pp. 915–16.
53. *MacArthur III,* p. 502. Press: *Reminiscences,* p. 410.
54. *MacArthur III,* pp. 504–05; *Tumultuous Years,* pp. 284–85.
55. *FRUS VII,* 1950, pp. 948–60 (minutes compiled by Omar Bradley).
56. Ibid., p. 953.
57. Ibid., p. 954.
58. *MacArthur III,* p. 508.
59. Ibid., pp. 512–13; *Reminiscences,* p. 413.
60. *MacArthur: His Rendezvous with History,* pp. 118–19; *South to the Naktong,* pp. 766–68.

## CHAPTER 13

1. "History of the JCS III," pp. 273–74; *South to the Naktong,* pp. 684–86; *War in Peacetime,* p. 177.
2. "History of the JCS III," p. 274.
3. Letter, Gay to Appleman, January 23, 1954.
4. Ibid.
5. *South to the Naktong,* p. 647.
6. Airborne RCT firepower: *Ridgway's Paratroopers; RAKKASANS!;* various author interviews. The firepower had been increased significantly since World War II with the development of techniques for dropping 105-mm howitzers (and other heavy weapons) from the yawning rear door of the new troop carrier aircraft, the C-119 "Flying Boxcar." However, compared to a conventional RCT, an airborne RCT's firepower was far less and the airborne RCT depended on uncertain air drops for replenishment.
7. *South to the Naktong,* pp. 642–42.
8. Ibid., p. 642. Letter, Harris to Appleman.
9. Letter, Harris to Appleman.
10. Author-Harris interview; letter, Crombez to Appleman.
11. *South to the Naktong,* p. 643; letters, Harris and Crombez to Appleman. Author-Harris interview.
12. Author-Harris interview; *Of GarryOwen in Glory,* p. 351. Woolnough: West Point *Register.*
13. Letter, Gay to Appleman. Woolnough oral history, Woolnough Papers, USAMHI. Author-Cochrane interview; other author interviews with 7th Cav officers.
14. *South to the Naktong,* pp. 643–45; *First Commonwealth Division,* p. 22.
15. *South to the Naktong,* p. 646; letter, Clainos to Appleman; author-Clainos inter-

view. Appleman gives the number of NKPA captured as 1,700 men; Clainos
insists it was 2,500.

16. Author-Clainos interview.
17. *South to the Naktong,* p. 647.
18. Ibid.
19. Ibid., p. 648; letter, Gay to Appleman.
20. Letters, Gay and James B. Webel to Appleman.
21. Letter, Gay to Appleman.
22. Author interviews with Harris and Lynch. *Of GarryOwen in Glory,* p. 285; *First Commonwealth Division,* p. 22.
23. *South to the Naktong,* pp. 648–49.
24. Ibid., pp. 649–50.
25. Ibid., pp. 651–52. Citation: Silver Star Medal to Growdon, courtesy his daughter Mrs. Nancy Foister, October 7, 1986.
26. *South to the Naktong,* p. 652; Knox, *Korean War,* pp. 611–14.
27. Knox, *Korean War,* pp. 611–14.
28. Ibid., p. 413.
29. Author-Harris interview; *Of GarryOwen in Glory,* pp. 285–86; Woolnough oral history, USAMHI; Johnson oral history, USAMHI.
30. *U.S. Air Force in Korea,* pp. 196–97; *South to the Naktong,* p. 654; *RAKKA-SANS!;* author-Arthur H. Wilson interview, September 13, 1984. Other information on the 187th kindly provided by Major General Harvey J. Jablonsky (CO 187, June 1948–June 1950); Lieutenant General Thomas J. H. Trapnell (CO 187, after Bowen); William E. Weber, president *RAKKASANS!* Alumni group; Noel B. Nyquist of the 674th Airborne FAB and others.
31. *Ridgway's Paratroopers; RAKKASANS!*
32. Bowen obituary, West Point *Assembly,* December 1977; West Point *Register.* Author interviews with or letters from various 187th senior commanders.
33. 187th roster of commanders; *RAKKASANS!;* West Point *Register.*
34. *U.S. Air Force in Korea,* pp. 196–97.
35. *South to the Naktong,* pp. 654–55.
36. *U.S. Air Force in Korea,* pp. 196–97. MacArthur: *South to the Naktong,* p. 658.
37. *South to the Naktong,* p. 655; *RAKKASANS!*
38. *South to the Naktong,* pp. 655–56; *RAKKASANS!*
39. 187th roster; West Point *Register.*
40. *RAKKASANS!; South to the Naktong,* p. 657.
41. *South to the Naktong,* p. 658.
42. Ibid., pp. 659–60; *RAKKASANS!*
43. *South to the Naktong,* pp. 659–60; *First Commonwealth Division,* p. 23.
44. *South to the Naktong,* pp. 662–63.
45. *RAKKASANS!;* 187th Records, RG 319, Box 627, Modern Military Records Branch, NA. Author interviews with Wilson, September 13, 1984, and September 20, 1986; Gerhart, September 20, 1986; Munson, September 20, 1986.
46. *South to the Naktong,* pp. 664–65; *First Commonwealth Division,* p. 23.
47. JCS "Record," pp. 51–55; "History of the JCS III," pp. 274–76; *South to the Naktong,* p. 670.
48. "History of the JCS III," p. 275.
49. Ibid., pp. 275–76.
50. *War in Peacetime,* pp. 180–81.
51. "History of the JCS III," p. 276.

52. *South to the Naktong*, pp. 635–36, 684; *Marine Operations in Korea III*, pp. 30–31.
53. *South to the Naktong*, pp. 685–87.
54. *Marine Operations in Korea III*, pp. 30–31.
55. *South to the Naktong*, pp. 632, 635–37. Bair ms.
56. *Marine Operations in Korea III*, pp. 39–45.
57. *South to the Naktong*, pp. 636–37.
58. Official biography; author-Powell interview, September 8, 1984.
59. Author-Powell interview; West Point *Register*.
60. Author-Powell interview.
61. Ibid.; *South to the Naktong*, p. 637; *Marine Operations in Korea III*, p. 75.
62. *South to the Naktong*, pp. 606, 684–85.
63. *Marine Operations in Korea III*, p. 99; *South to the Naktong*, pp. 732–33.
64. Author-Powell interview. Richard L. Gruenther, "Flying Column," *Armed Forces Chemical Journal* (April 1951), a detailed account of the 1/17's operations from Iwon to Pungsan to the Ungi River, October 29, 1950, to November 5, 1950.
65. Here and below: "Flying Column."
66. *South to the Naktong*, pp. 672, 681.
67. *South to the Naktong*, pp. 681–82; *First Commonwealth Division*, pp. 23–24.
68. *South to the Naktong*, pp. 681–82; *First Commonwealth Division*, pp. 23–24. Snow flurries: *South to the Naktong*, p. 676. Author-Dolvin interview; Dolvin speech.
69. *South to the Naktong*, p. 682; Gines Perez oral history.
70. *South to the Naktong*, pp. 682–83; letter, Brad Smith to author, September 5, 1985.
71. *South to the Naktong*, p. 683; author-Throckmorton interview.
72. Author-Throckmorton interview.
73. *South to the Naktong*, p. 683.
74. Author-Davidson interview.
75. *South to the Naktong*, p. 683; author interviews with Throckmorton and Davidson.
76. Ibid.
77. *South to the Naktong*, pp. 675–76, 718.
78. Ibid., pp. 676–77.
79. Ibid., pp. 672–74.
80. Ibid., pp. 674–75.
81. Ibid., pp. 686–87.
82. Ibid., p. 687.

## CHAPTER 14

1. GHQ and Willoughby views here and below: *South to the Naktong*, pp. 757–65. Letters, Landrum and Dabney to Appleman. Letter, William C. Bullock to author, April 9, 1985.
2. Chiles oral history; author-Chiles interview. In both Chiles stated that Willoughby falsified intelligence reports.
3. *South to the Naktong*, p. 761. Willoughby's trip to Korea and comments on CCF POWs derived from an interview or oral history with the 1st Marine Division G-3, Alpha A. Bowser, quoted in Dr. Alvin D. Coox, "Lessons Learned in

Korea," a paper delivered on October 28, 1976, to the Fifteenth Annual U.S. Army Operations Research Symposium, Fort Lee, Virginia, copy in Almond Papers, Correspondence 1970s, USAMHI. According to Coox, Bowser stated that when Almond told Willoughby he had CCF POWs, Willoughby said: "I don't believe you!" Bowser went on: "Almond said, 'Well, would you like to come down and look at them?' . . . He did. He was then convinced. He said words to the effect [however] that they still could be stragglers or volunteers." Almond wrote Coox that his paper was "very complete and factual."

4. Numerous author interviews. Without exception interviewees noted the "fear" Willoughby inspired and then critized or ridiculed him as an incompetent sycophant. Typical of the ridicule was Chiles's comment: "Sir Charles was very dramatic and cultivated a German accent. He always smelled like formaldehyde, like he was dead. I don't know what he was chewing. . . ."

5. Letter, Tarkenton to author, November 7, 1984. After his death, further correspondence from his son, Scott Tarkenton, October 5, 1985, and April 27, 1986, enclosing detailed biographical and duty information (DA Form 66).

6. Letters, Fergusson to author, February 21 and May 3, 1985, and several letters in 1986 and 1987, kindly providing information on Eighth Army staff and personnel and related matters.

7. *South to the Naktong,* pp. 754–55, 677; *FRUS VII,* 1950, pp. 1013–14, 1018.

8. *South to the Naktong,* pp. 751, 764; *FRUS VII,* 1950, p. 1022.

9. Dabney: Letter to Appleman. Train: Oral history, USAMHI; letter to author, December 2, 1984.

10. *South to the Naktong,* pp. 675–78; *Of GarryOwen in Glory,* pp. 286–87; *Second Division in Korea,* pp. 51–53; *Policy and Direction,* p. 235.

11. *South to the Naktong,* p. 679; *Of GarryOwen in Glory,* p. 286.

12. *South to the Naktong,* p. 690; letter, Thompson to Appleman, September 5, 1954.

13. *South to the Naktong,* pp. 679–80.

14. Ibid., p. 689; Johnson oral history, pp. 35–36.

15. Johnson oral history.

16. *South to the Naktong,* pp. 689–90.

17. Ibid., p. 690; letter, Gay to Appleman.

18. *South to the Naktong,* p. 690.

19. Ibid., p. 691; letter, Johnson to Appleman.

20. *South to the Naktong,* p. 719; *Marine Operations in Korea III,* pp. 89–93.

21. *South to the Naktong,* pp. 691–94.

22. Ibid., p. 694; *Second Division in Korea,* pp. 51–53.

23. *South to the Naktong,* pp. 695–700; author-Edson interview.

24. *South to the Naktong,* pp. 700–04.

25. Ibid., pp. 704–05; letter, Harris to Appleman; author interviews with Harris and Clainos.

26. *South to the Naktong,* pp. 705–07.

27. Ibid., pp. 707–08; author-Edson interview.

28. Author-Edson interview; Johnson oral history.

29. Letter, Johnson to Appleman; Knox, *Korean War,* pp. 439–44.

30. Letter, Harris to Appleman; author-Lynch interview.

31. *South to the Naktong,* pp. 709, 713–14; *First Commonwealth Division,* p. 27; Perez oral history.

32. *South to the Naktong,* p. 709.

33. Ibid., pp. 711–13; author interviews with Moore and Kinney; letter, Cutler to author, May 5, 1986.
34. *South to the Naktong,* p. 711.
35. Letter, Barberis to S.L.A. Marshall, August 2, 1954, courtesy Mrs. Barberis.
36. *South to the Naktong,* pp. 714–15.
37. Ibid., pp. 755–56.
38. Letter, Williamson to author, March 28, 1986.
39. *South to the Naktong,* pp. 734, 740; *Marine Operations in Korea III,* p. 131. Max Dolcater, *History of the Third Infantry Division in Korea* (Tokyo: Toppan Printing Co., 1954), p. 73; hereafter *Third Division in Korea.*
40. *Marine Operations in Korea III,* p. 135; *South to the Naktong,* p. 744; Knox, *Korean War,* p. 474.
41. O. P. Smith aide-mémoire; Smith oral history and letter to Appleman.
42. *South to the Naktong,* pp. 743–44; *Marine Operations in Korea III,* pp. 110–19.
43. O. P. Smith letter to Appleman.
44. *South to the Naktong,* pp. 733, 737.
45. Official biography; West Point *Assembly* obituary, January 1955; author-Beauchamp interview.
46. *South to the Naktong,* pp. 734, 737. Letter, Powell to author, April 3, 1986. Reilly: 7th Division Records, NA (Suitland), Boxes 3172–3176, West Point *Register;* letters to author from 31st Infantry members Olson, Rasula, Mitchell, Witte, and Oliver W. Robertson (3/31), July 5, 1986. Copy of letter, John J. Z. Zitzelberger to Eric Hammel, June 18, 1984, courtesy Zitzelberger. Author interviews with Davis (aide to Barr, was transferred to the 2/31), and Gerard A. Francois (3/31), February 15, 1986.
47. *South to the Naktong,* pp. 734, 737. 7th Division Records. Author-Beauchamp interview; letter, Beauchamp to author, March 25, 1986.
48. *South to the Naktong,* pp. 754, 762; *FRUS VII,* 1950, p. 1055.
49. *South to the Naktong,* p. 768.
50. "History of the JCS III," p. 289; JCS "Record," p. 55.
51. JCS "Record," p. 56.
52. *Policy and Direction,* p. 235.
53. Ibid., pp. 235–36.
54. *FRUS VII,* 1950, p. 953; *U.S. Air Force in Korea,* pp. 209–10.
55. *U.S. Air Force in Korea,* pp. 209, 212.
56. Ibid., p. 207.
57. "History of the JCS III," pp. 291–92.
58. Ibid.
59. *FRUS VII,* 1950, pp. 1055–57; *Present at the Creation,* pp. 463–64; *Years of Trial and Hope,* p. 427; "History of the JCS III," p. 292; JCS "Record."
60. *A General's Life,* p. 585; *Reminiscences,* pp. 419–20.
61. *Reminiscences,* pp. 420–21.
62. "History of the JCS III," pp. 293–94 (text); *FRUS VII,* 1950, p. 1058.
63. "History of the JCS III," p. 294; *A General's Life,* p. 585.
64. *Tumultuous Years,* pp. 295–98.
65. Robert Leckie, *Conflict: The History of the Korean War* (New York: Putnam, 1962), p. 181 (text).
66. "History of the JCS III," pp. 294–95; *A General's Life,* pp. 585–87.
67. *FRUS VII,* 1950, p. 1106.
68. *A General's Life,* p. 558.

69. *FRUS VII,* 1950, pp. 1075–76 (text); "History of the JCS III," pp. 294–95.
70. "History of the JCS III," p. 295n.
71. *FRUS VII,* 1950, p. 1076 (text); "History of the JCS III," pp. 295–96; *Policy and Direction,* p. 245; *Present at the Creation,* p. 465.
72. *Present at the Creation,* p. 465; *Policy and Direction,* p. 248; *A General's Life,* pp. 588–89.
73. *A General's Life,* p. 589.
74. *FRUS VII,* 1950, pp. 1117–21.
75. *South to the Naktong,* p. 771.
76. *FRUS VII,* 1950, pp. 1097–98.
77. Ibid., pp. 1107–10 (text).
78. *Tumultuous Years,* pp. 295–96, 298.
79. *FRUS VII,* 1950, pp. 1117–21.
80. *A General's Life,* pp. 593–94; *Years of Trial and Hope,* pp. 431–33; "History of the JCS III," pp. 304–06.
81. *A General's Life,* pp. 587, 594; *Present at the Creation,* p. 466.
82. Richard E. Neustadt, *Presidential Power* (New York: John Wiley & Sons, 1960), p. 94.
83. *U.S. Air Force in Korea,* pp. 211–14.
84. Ibid., pp. 214–17.
85. *FRUS VII,* 1950, pp. 1175–76.
86. *South to the Naktong,* pp. 667–69, 771–72; "Sabers and Safety Pins"; *Sea War in Korea,* pp. 152–62.
87. *Policy and Direction,* pp. 257–58; "History of the JCS III," p. 322.

## CHAPTER 15

1. *Third Division in Korea,* pp. 53–63; 3d Division records, NA (Suitland), Boxes 2889, 2891, 2894, etc.
2. Official biography; *Third Division in Korea,* pp. 19, 95–96; author-James Y. Adams interview, September 25, 1984.
3. Swing: Official biography; West Point *Register; Ridgway's Paratroopers,* pp. 17–18; author-Harry Wilson interview; *Third Division in Korea,* p. 57. Soule assumed command on August 10, 1950.
4. Swinton quoted in *Third Division in Korea,* pp. 95–96; author-Robert M. Blanchard interview, September 30, 1984.
5. Author interviews with James O. Boswell, September 25, 1984, and John S. Guthrie, January 25, 1987, and Blanchard.
6. Mead and Newman: Official biographies; West Point *Register.* Simpson staff: Dwight D. Eisenhower, *Crusade in Europe* (New York: Doubleday, 1948); *A General's Life.* Regimental commander quoted: Author-Guthrie interview.
7. *Army Lineage Series,* pp. 36–37. William W. Harris, *Puerto Rico's Fighting 65th U.S. Infantry* (San Rafael, Calif.: Presidio Press, 1980); hereafter *Fighting 65th.* Author-William W. Harris interview, September 22, 1984.
8. *Fighting 65th,* p. 1.
9. Ibid., pp. 4, 9.
10. Ibid., p. 104.
11. Ibid., pp. 69, 104. Stella, Dawalt: West Point *Register;* letter, John E. Slaughter (Dawalt's successor) to author, February 8, 1985.
12. *Third Division in Korea,* p. 351. Letter, Bradley Biggs to author, October 20,

1986. Biggs was one of the first members of the 785th in World War II; in Korea he left the 24th Infantry to rejoin the 64th Tank Battalion. Bartlett: West Point *Register;* West Point *Assembly* obituary, Fall 1971.

13. *Fighting 65th,* p. 84; West Point *Register.*
14. *Fighting 65th,* pp. 85–87.
15. *Newsweek* (October 13, 1952, and January 19, 1953); *Time* (January 19, 1953).
16. *Fighting 65th,* pp. 90–100; *Third Division in Korea,* pp. 69–70.
17. *Fighting 65th,* p. 108.
18. *Third Division in Korea.* Moore and Neely: West Point *Register.*
19. Author interviews with Thomas R. Yancey (XO, 15th), October 9, 1986; Blanchard, September 30, 1984; Allen L. Peck, October 11, 1986; Russe, September 29, 1984.
20. Author interviews with Yancey, Blanchard, and Peck. Peck quoted.
21. Blanchard, Peck: West Point *Register;* author interviews.
22. Huston official biography; letters, Huston to author, July 15, August 26, October 3, October 9, 1986; January 12, 1987. The last two contain a complete and valuable account of the 3/15 July–November 1950, including officer rosters.
23. Huston correspondence.
24. Ibid.
25. Ibid., including text, Moore letter of commendation.
26. Letter, Abrams to author, April 28, 1986.
27. *Third Division in Korea,* p. 78.
28. Author-Blanchard interview, plus Blanchard unpublished ms. on his career, courtesy Blanchard.
29. Trent: West Point *Assembly* obituary, July 1955; West Point *Register; One Bugle No Drums,* pp. 78–79.
30. Letter, Huston to author, January 31, 1987; *Third Division in Korea,* p. 386.
31. Letters, Huston to author, January 12 and January 31, 1987; author interviews with Peck and Yancey; Huston biography.
32. Guthrie: Official biography, West Point *Register;* letter to author, November 13, 1984; author-Guthrie interview. Downing: West Point *Register.*
33. Official biography; Guthrie interview.
34. Letter, Guthrie to author, November 3, 1984, and interview.
35. Author interviews with Guthrie; Boswell, September 25, 1984; O'Neil, September 24, 1984. West Point *Register.* Letters, Samuel G. Kail (XO, later CO, 2/7) to author, October 30 and December 9, 1984, May 28 and June 11, 1986.
36. Author-Guthrie interview.
37. *Third Division in Korea,* p. 73.
38. *Policy and Direction,* pp. 260–61.
39. Smith letter to Cates; Smith aide-mémoire, November 15, 1950.
40. *Policy and Direction,* pp. 262–63.
41. Ibid., pp. 262–64.
42. Here and below: 17th Infantry action, *South to the Naktong,* pp. 734–36; "Flying Column," author-Powell interview.
43. Temperatures: Dill diary (near Pungsan): "The temperature was recorded on the powder thermometers, highly accurate instruments carried by each gun section to measure variation from standard firing table temperature of gunpowder."
44. *South to the Naktong,* p. 737; *Policy and Direction,* p. 265.

45. "Flying Column"; *South to the Naktong*, p. 735 (group photo); author-Walker interview. "Hallowed ritual": Letter, 7th Division G-3, John Paddock, to author, April 6, 1986.
46. *South to the Naktong*, pp. 736–37; author-Powell interview.
47. Letter, Bowman to author, April 22, 1986; author-Bowman interview, April 22, 1986.
48. *South to the Naktong;* author-Beauchamp interview; letter, Beauchamp to author, March 25, 1986.
49. Kingston: Official biography; letter, Kingston to author, April 28, 1986. Task Force Kingston: *Masters of the Art of Command*, pp. 87–99.
50. *Masters of the Art of Command*, pp. 87–99; Kingston biography.
51. *Policy and Direction*, pp. 165–66; *U.S. Marine Operations in Korea III*, p. 145.
52. Letter, Paddock to author, April 6, 1986.
53. Here and below: 7th Division records. Letters to author from Robertson, Rasula, Beauchamp, Powell, Paddock, and others. Letter, Zitzelberger to Hammel. Author-Davis interview. Dill diary, November 20 to November 29, 1950. *Combat Actions in Korea*, pp. 62–87.
54. E Company, 2/31, "frozen, etc.": Dill diary, November 19, 1950, and Dill article, "The Winter of the Yalu." In the latter artilleryman Dill wrote: "Company E of the 31st Infantry came down into our [31st FAB, B] battery position about dark after a hard march over the mountains [in deep snow]. The company commander told us he had no way of carrying anyone who fell out, and since anyone who did would either die in the snow or be killed by the enemy, he took a drastic step. The First Sergeant marched at the rear and was ordered to use rifle sling as a whip. Any man who fell was lashed until he got up and kept going. . . ."
55. Dill diary, November 26, 1950, and "Yalu."
56. *Third Division in Korea.*
57. *Fighting 65th*, pp. 115–18.
58. Ibid., pp. 114–15.
59. *Third Division in Korea*, p. 83.
60. J. H. Williams, "No Advance Beyond Chosin," *Military History* (April 1985).
61. *South to the Naktong*, pp. 756–57; Letter, Smith to Appleman.
62. *FRUS VII*, 1950, p. 1161.
63. Ibid., pp. 1126, 1143–45 (Acheson instructions to Ambassador Warren Austin at UN).
64. *MacArthur: His Rendezvous with History*, pp. 141–43; *Tumultuous Years*, p. 301.
65. "History of the JCS III," p. 314; *FRUS VII*, 1950, pp. 1204–08.
66. "History of the JCS III," pp. 324–26; *FRUS VII*, 1950, pp. 1204–08.
67. "History of the JCS III," p. 326n. *FRUS VII*, 1950, pp. 1222–24.
68. *FRUS VII*, 1950, pp. 1231–33.

## CHAPTER 16

1. The dispositions and actions of Eighth Army units during its offensive—and afterward—as depicted in this and succeeding chapters are derived from numerous sources. Chief among these are the Eighth Army Command Reports (see especially "Narrative of Operations" and "War Diary G-3 Section") for November and December 1950. These reports (hereafter Command Report, month) are

on file at NA (Suitland), RG 407, Boxes 1122 (November narrative), 1132 (November G-3 War Diary), and 1134 (December narrative). Other sources: (1) The Army's second volume, chronologically, in the Korean War series, *Ebb and Flow,* by Billy C. Mossman. This volume picks up the combat action where the Appleman volume, *South to the Naktong,* stops, in November 1950, and continues to July 1951. Long overdue, the volume is scheduled for publication in 1988 by the Army's Center of Military History, Washington, D.C. It was made available to the author in typescript for reading and note taking in May 1987, through the courtesy of the Army's chief of military history, Brigadier General William A. Stofft, and the chief, Histories Division, Lieutenant Colonel Richard O. Perry, and is hereafter cited as *Ebb and Flow.* (2) Official histories of the American 1st Cav, 2d, 24th, and 25th divisions and the British Commonwealth Division, loc. cit. (3) *Of GarryOwen in Glory* and *RAKKASANS!* and the 23d Infantry operations report, loc. cit. (4) The Barth ms., the Strong ms., the Carlisle and Bussey ms., loc. cit. (5) The oral histories of Harold Johnson, Paul Freeman, and Gines Perez, loc. cit. (6) Author interviews with Charles Palmer, Garrison Davidson, Paul Freeman, William Harris, John Throckmorton, John Michaelis, Ned Moore, Welborn Dolvin, Oliver Kinney, Cesidio Barberis, and others. (7) Correspondence to author from numerous participants, in response to specific queries. (8) S.L.A. Marshall, *The River and the Gauntlet* (New York: Morrow, 1953); hereafter cited as *River and the Gauntlet.* Marshall, military editor of a Detroit newspaper (and an Army historian in the ETO in World War II), was called to active duty with the rank of colonel in November 1950. He went to Korea to write and edit a series of classified reports on tactics, weapons, enemy, etc., for the Army's Operations Research Office (ORO). The popularly published *River and the Gauntlet* derived from his interviews of Eighth Army personnel (mainly in the 2d Division) for the ORO, immediately after the battle, November–December. (For more on Marshall's tour in Korea see his autobiography, *Bringing Up the Rear* [San Rafael, Calif.: Presidio Press, 1979], hereafter cited as *Bringing Up the Rear*.) Although *River and the Gauntlet* was praised as a classic of its kind upon publication, and it was a valuable resource in many respects, the book is difficult to read and is not without flaws. Marshall's ORO mission to Korea apparently required that he focus on squad-, platoon-, and company-level actions. Hence the reader only rarely has a glimpse of the big picture—at theater, army, corps, division, regimental, and battalion levels. There are numerous errors in times and dates, and Marshall is careless about names. Senior commanders are not fully identified. Several battalion commanders are incompletely identified, or misidentified, or their names are misspelled. (9) Robert C. Cameron, "The Lost Corps," *Military Review* (May 1953). Cameron, KMAG adviser to ROK II Corps, gives a good account of its action.

2. *River and the Gauntlet,* p. 19.
3. *South to the Naktong,* pp. 754, 763; *Policy and Direction,* pp. 259, 273.
4. *Policy and Direction,* p. 273. MacArthur put NKPA "fragments" at 50,000. See *FRUS VII,* 1950, p. 1237.
5. United Press wire service story, November 23, 1950, published in *Green Bay Press Gazette;* Knox, *Korean War,* pp. 466, 469. Whiskey: Various interviews.
6. Knox, *Korean War,* pp. 464–65. Awards ceremonies in the 7th Cav were delayed to November 26, 1950, according to *Of GarryOwen in Glory,* p. 288, and author-Harris interview.
7. Freeman oral history, USAMHI.

8. *MacArthur III,* p. 534; *MacArthur: His Rendezvous with History,* p. 416; *Reminiscences,* pp. 423–24.
9. Cameron, "The Lost Corps."
10. *Time* (December 4, 1950); unidentified "wire service" story published in *Green Bay Press Gazette,* November 24, 1950.
11. AP story, *Green Bay Press Gazette,* November 24, 1950; *Reminiscences,* p. 424.
12. *MacArthur III,* pp. 534–35.
13. "Tragic Flaw," p. 374.
14. *South to the Naktong,* p. 746.
15. Command Report, November 1950.
16. *River and the Gauntlet,* pp. 210–11.
17. Rangers: Author-James Y. Adams interview, September 25, 1984. Adams helped train Ranger companies at Fort Benning and went to Korea to check on their fighting. Barth ms.
18. *River and the Gauntlet,* pp. 188–89. Barth ms.
19. Command Report, November 1950. Names from 24th rosters, NA (Suitland), Box 3770. Barth ms.
20. *Second Division in Korea;* author-Freeman interview.
21. *River and the Gauntlet,* pp. 25–26; *Second Division in Korea.* Wolfe (and, below, his successors): courtesy 2d Division historian Robert Arrington, telephone interview September 11, 1987. Wolfe appraisal: author-Barberis interview.
22. Personnel: letter, Peploe to author, February 4, 1985; letter, Skeldon to author, February 12, 1985. Author interviews with Warren D. Hodges and William E. Manning, June 22, 1987.
23. Command Report, November 1950.
24. Ibid.
25. Barth ms.
26. *River and the Gauntlet,* pp. 24–26, 55, 80–81.
27. Ibid., pp. 94, 98–105.
28. Command Report, November 1950.
29. Ibid.; *River and the Gauntlet,* passim.
30. *River and the Gauntlet,* pp. 188–89; Barth ms. Desiderio's story is also told in *Korea's Heroes.*
31. *River and the Gauntlet,* pp. 197–98, 213.
32. Ibid., pp. 212–13; author-Walden interview and Walden taped self-interview. Letter, Sloane to Corley, December 11, 1950, courtesy McMains.
33. *River and the Gauntlet,* pp. 24–26, 55, 76, 80–81.
34. Author-Barberis interview.
35. Hill for Wolfe: Letters from various 9th Infantry commanders; author-Arrington interview.
36. *River and the Gauntlet,* pp. 19, 24, 29, 32–38. Awards: *Second Division in Korea.*
37. *River and the Gauntlet,* p. 83.
38. *Second Division in Korea;* 23d Infantry operations report; author-Freeman interview.
39. Knox, *Korean War,* pp. 622–25.
40. Ibid. Letters to author from Kean, July 17, 1986, and Marks, July 24, 1986.
41. *Second Division in Korea; River and the Gauntlet,* pp. 53–54; 23d Infantry operations report; Freeman oral history.

42. *River and the Gauntlet,* p. 54.
43. Pittman award: *Second Division in Korea,* p. 207.
44. *River and the Gauntlet;* author-Barberis interview.
45. Letter, Sloane to Corley.
46. *River and the Gauntlet,* p. 94.
47. Author-Barberis interview.
48. *River and the Gauntlet,* pp. 106–10.
49. Ibid., pp. 120–30. Imrie DSC: *Second Division in Korea,* p. 210.
50. *River and the Gauntlet,* pp. 152–63, 172–73.
51. "The Lost Corps."
52. *River and the Gauntlet,* p. 178.
53. *Ebb and Flow,* Chapter IV, p. 19.
54. *Policy and Direction,* p. 171.
55. Command Report and G-3 diary, November 1950.
56. Command Report, November 1950.
57. *River and the Gauntlet,* pp. 169–70. Author-Michaelis interview.
58. *Ebb and Flow,* Chapter IV, pp. 30–31.
59. Command Report, November 1950; Barth ms.; *Second Division in Korea;* 23d Infantry operations report; author-Freeman interview.
60. *Second Division in Korea;* author interviews with Barberis and Becton; letters to author from McMains and Harlan (January 6, 1985).
61. *River and the Gauntlet,* pp. 214, 231.
62. Ibid., pp. 234, 240, 243–45.
63. Ibid., p. 246; Barth ms.
64. *Second Division in Korea;* 23d Infantry operations report.
65. *Second Division in Korea;* 23d Infantry operations report.
66. Author-Barberis interview.
67. Ibid.
68. Forney: "Sabers and Safety Pins"; West Point *Register.*
69. Command Report, November 1950. *Ebb and Flow,* Chapter VI, pp. 10–11; author-Freeman interview.
70. Command Report, November 1950; author interviews with Garrison Davidson, Throckmorton, and Moore.
71. Letter, Cutler to author, May 5, 1986; author-Throckmorton interview.
72. Disposition and operations of X Corps forces from November 27, 1950, to evacuation at Hungnam are derived from numerous sources. Among these: (1) X Corps, "Special Report on Operations in the Chosin Reservoir Area, 27 November to 10 December 1950," at NA (Suitland) and also Marine Corps History. (2) Almond daily war diary and oral history, Almond Papers, USAMHI. (3) *U.S. Marine Operations in Korea III;* "No Advance Beyond Chosin"; O. P. Smith aide-mémoire and oral history; Alpha Bowser oral history. (4) The Army's 7th Division Command Reports for November and December 1950, NA (Suitland), Boxes 3174 and 3176; a special report on the Chosin Reservoir operations, November 27 to December 15, 1950, NA (Suitland), Box 3172; and extracts from the 7th Division War Diary, NA (Suitland), courtesy George A. Rasula. (5) *Ebb and Flow,* Chapters V and VII. (6) Dolcater, *Third Division in Korea.* (7) Martin Blumenson, "Chosin Reservoir," Chapter 7 in Gugeler, *Combat Actions in Korea,* and Blumenson's original manuscript, with attachments (cataloged as Document 8-5.1a BA43) at the Army's Center of Military History. (8) Chester Bair, "Combat Duty in Korea," ms. (9) Harris, *Fighting 65th.*

(10) James Dill diary. (11) Author interviews with John Chiles, William McCaffrey, William Quinn, Joseph A. Guerfein, Edward L. Rowny, and James H. Polk of X Corps; Charles Davis, Herbert Powell, Charles Beauchamp, Lenoise Bowman, Charles L. Peckham, Thomas Gregory, Carl G. Witte, John J. Zitzelberger, and Gerard A. Francois of the 7th Division; John Guthrie, James Boswell, Thomas O'Neil, Samuel Kail, William Harris, Henry P. Russe, and Robert Blanchard of the 3d Division. (12) Letters to the author from Powell, Beauchamp, John Paddock, Paul F. Oswald, Bowman, George A. Rasula, William R. Lynch, Oliver W. Robertson, Witte, Wesley J. Curtis, Richard F. Mitchell, Francois, Bair, and Zitzelberger of the 7th Division. (13) Knox, *Korean War;* Hopkins, *One Bugle No Drum;* Andrew Geer, *The New Breed: The Story of the U.S. Marines in Korea* (New York: Harper and Brothers, 1954); Eric Hammel, *Chosin: Heroic Ordeal of the Korean War* (New York: Vanguard Press, 1981), hereafter cited as *Chosin;* W. J. Davis, *Chosin Marine* (San Diego: privately printed, 1986); Roy E. Appleman, *East of Chosin* (College Station, Texas: Texas A&M University Press, 1987), hereafter cited as *East of Chosin;* Robert M. Coombs, "Changjin (Chosin) Reservoir Korea 1950: A Case Study of U.S. Army Tactics and Doctrine," thesis, U.S. Army Command and General Staff College, 1975 (hereafter Coombs thesis).

73. *Chosin,* p. 6. In letter to author, February 18, 1986, Hammel said the Ruffner quote was derived from a letter from Ruffner to Hammel, no date, now on file in Marine Corps History.

74. *East of Chosin,* p. 11. Appleman's book, a meticulous and exhaustive piece of research, is a remarkable and invaluable resource. While it is principally concerned with operations of Task Force MacLean, it deftly sets the larger scene.

75. *U.S. Marine Operations in Korea III,* p. 352. Shift of CCF Forty-second Army: *South to the Naktong,* p. 768. For more detail on CCF forces, see *East of Chosin,* pp. 50–56.

76. Details of Task Force MacLean from Blumenson, "Chosin Reservoir," in *Combat Actions in Korea,* and his manuscript; special report on 7th Division operations at the Chosin Reservoir, with attached statements from Robert E. Jones, Robert E. Drake, Robert J. Kitz, and Richard S. Luna; *East of Chosin;* Coombs thesis. Where sources conflict, Appleman is used.

77. Almond war diary. That he passed Task Force MacLean elements is inferred.

78. *U.S. Marine Operations in Korea III,* p. 152 and ff.; "No Advance Beyond Chosin"; Knox, *Korean War,* pp. 469–615. "Unenthusiastic": Brigadier General Edwin H. Simmons (director, USMC History), "China Steps In," in chapter 4 of David Rees, ed., *The Korean War: History and Tactics* (New York: Crescent Books, 1984), pp. 46–59.

79. Strength of Task Force MacLean: Appleman analysis and Coombs thesis.

80. *U.S. Marine Operations in Korea III; Chosin;* Knox, *Korean War;* "No Advance Beyond Chosin."

81. *Third Division in Korea,* pp. 86–87.

82. *East of Chosin,* pp. 98–99.

83. Ibid., pp. 77–85.

84. Ibid., pp. 86–98.

85. Almond war diary; Smith aide-mémoire; *U.S. Marine Operations in Korea III,* pp. 188–89, 205.

86. Almond quoted by Blumenson, "Chosin Reservoir," in *Combat Actions in Korea,* pp. 69–70.

87. "Raise morale:" *Ebb and Flow,* Chapter V, p. 15; *East of Chosin,* p. 107.
88. Blumenson, *Combat Actions in Korea,* pp. 69–70; *East of Chosin,* pp. 107–08.
89. *East of Chosin,* pp. 123–32.
90. *FRUS VII,* 1950, pp. 1237–38, 1239n.
91. *A General's Life,* p. 598; "History of the JCS III," p. 338.
92. *Tumultuous Years,* pp. 305–06.
93. *FRUS VII,* 1950, pp. 1242–49 (minutes).
94. *Reminiscences,* pp. 422–23; *FRUS VII,* 1950, p. 955 (Wake Island).
95. *FRUS VII,* 1950, p. 1247.
96. "History of the JCS IV," pp. 70–71; Truman formally approved NSC-68 (which became NSC-68/4) "as a working guide for the purpose of making an immediate start" on December 14, 1950. NSC-68/4 stated that owing to the "crisis" created by CCF intervention in North Korea, "Our military buildup must be rapid . . . a greatly increased scale and tempo is required . . . [and] we must also proceed at once to establish a production and mobilization base that will permit a very rapid expansion to full mobilization."
97. "History of the JCS IV," pp. 46, 75–77.
98. *Policy and Direction,* pp. 278–79; Major General Charles A. Willoughby and John Chamberlain, *MacArthur 1941–1951* (New York: McGraw-Hill, 1954), pp. 399–400; *MacArthur: His Rendezvous with History,* p. 423.
99. *Policy and Direction,* p. 279.
100. Ibid., p. 279; *Third Division in Korea.*
101. "History of the JCS III," pp. 342–43.
102. *FRUS VII,* 1950, p. 1253.
103. JCS "Record"; *FRUS VII,* 1950, pp. 1253–54; "History of the JCS III," pp. 343–44.
104. *FRUS VII,* 1950, pp. 1259–60.
105. Ibid., p. 1259.
106. Ibid., p. 1260.
107. "History of the JCS III," pp. 345–46.
108. Ibid., pp. 346–47; JCS "Record," p. 68.

## CHAPTER 17

1. Disposition and actions of Eighth Army: See note 1, Chapter 16.
2. Barth ms.
3. *Ebb and Flow,* Chapter VI, pp. 13–15.
4. "How Do Our Negro Troops Measure Up?"
5. T. H. Pettigrew, Jr., *The Kunu-ri Incident* (New York: Vantage Press, 1963).
6. *Ebb and Flow,* Chapter VI, p. 14.
7. Pettigrew gives the date of Blair's relief as December 2, 1950. 24th Infantry Records (NA, Suitland, Box 3770) confirm that Blair left the regiment in early December and by December 25, 1950, was in the 25th Division G-2 section. Retirement: *Army Register; San Francisco Chronicle,* January 14, 1958.
8. *Saturday Evening Post* (June 23 and December 22, 1951). Robbery, trial, and imprisonment: *The San Francisco Chronicle,* January 14, 15, 16, 17, 23; February 1, 7; March 29; April 22, 1958; and May 13 and June 21, 1959.
9. Letters to author from David Carlisle.
10. *River and the Gauntlet,* pp. 261–62.
11. Ibid.

12. Ibid., p. 263. Becker report: *Ebb and Flow,* Chapter VI, p. 23. "Fled the battlefield": Author-Freeman interview.
13. *River and the Gauntlet,* p. 265.
14. Command Report, November 1950. *Ebb and Flow,* Chapter VI, pp. 16, 19. *First Commonwealth Division,* p. 34.
15. Command Report, November 1950. *Ebb and Flow,* Chapter VI, pp. 23–24. *Second Division in Korea;* 23d Infantry operations report; author interviews with Freeman and Barberis; *River and the Gauntlet,* p. 269. Hill wounded, replaced by Henckley: correspondence from Rolfe L. Hillman, Jr.; author-Arrington interview.
16. Relief of Sloane: Author-John Murphy interview, August 22, 1986. After winning a DSC and recovering from his wounds, Murphy was made 9th Infantry S-2.
17. *River and the Gauntlet,* p. 270; author-Barberis interview; letter, Barberis to author, September 28, 1986. Citation, Silver Star Medal, provided on author's request by Barberis. As for the Medal of Honor, Barberis wrote: "Oh well, you can't take it with you, so what the hell? I know what I did. . . . I can still look at myself in a mirror and not be ashamed."
18. Author-Harris M. Pope interview, September 22, 1986. Harris was CO of I Company, 3/9, later the 3/9 S-3, exec, and finally CO.
19. Author-Barberis interview; letter, Barberis to S.L.A. Marshall, July 29, 1954, courtesy Mrs. Barberis. Citation, DSC, CheuMon Lee: *Second Division in Korea.*
20. *River and the Gauntlet,* pp. 280–81.
21. 38th strength and order of march: Ibid., p. 273 and passim.
22. Ibid., p. 274.
23. Ibid., p. 280.
24. Ibid., p. 281.
25. Ibid., pp. 281–87.
26. Ibid., p. 284.
27. Author-Manning interview.
28. Letter, Jones to author, December 18, 1985.
29. Letter and tape, Hillman to author, November 26, 1986.
30. Author-Pope interview.
31. *River and the Gauntlet,* p. 315.
32. Ibid., p. 309.
33. Ibid., pp. 303–04. Citation, Skeldon DSC: *Second Division in Korea.*
34. *River and the Gauntlet,* p. 304. *U.S. Air Force in Korea,* pp. 237–38.
35. *River and the Gauntlet,* pp. 320–24, 331–33. Silver Star Medal: *Second Division in Korea.*
36. *River and the Gauntlet,* pp. 306–07.
37. Ibid., pp. 318–20.
38. Ibid., p. 327.
39. Ibid., pp. 331–32.
40. Ibid., pp. 335–61. *Combat Actions in Korea,* pp. 53–61, contains the story of Harrelson and the 17th FAB.
41. *River and the Gauntlet,* p. 339.
42. *Second Division in Korea; Ebb and Flow,* Chapter VI, pp. 31–35. "Combat Losses of Artillery Weapons," a report of the Eighth Army artillery officer, January 17, 1951, at NA (Suitland), Box 1149. Lavell: West Point *Register.*

43. *River and the Gauntlet,* p. 337.
44. Casualties: Ibid., p. 360; letter, Hillman to author, November 26, 1986.
45. 23d Infantry operations report; *U.S. Air Force in Korea,* p. 244.
46. Freeman oral history; author-Freeman interview.
47. Author interviews with Freeman and Epley. Letters, Epley to Appleman, October 26 and December 6, 1979, commenting on Appleman's unpublished book on the Korean War covering the period November 1950 to July 1951, kindly provided by Epley. *Ebb and Flow,* Chapter VI, p. 37, citing a letter from Bradley to Appleman, states that at 4:00 P.M. Bradley approved Freeman's plan.
48. *River and the Gauntlet,* pp. 327–28. Epley letters to Appleman.
49. Freeman oral history; author-Freeman interview. De Shazo: West Point *Register.*
50. Report of the Eighth Army artillery officer, January 17, 1951. Many sources incorrectly report the total loss of artillery pieces in the 2d Division that day as sixty-four.
51. Letter, Ellis to author, April 15, 1985.
52. *River and the Gauntlet,* pp. 328–31; 23d Infantry operations report; author-Freeman interview.
53. *River and the Gauntlet,* p. 328.
54. *Of GarryOwen in Glory,* pp. 289–90.
55. Knox, *Korean War,* pp. 656–57.
56. Ibid., p. 640.
57. *Of GarryOwen in Glory,* pp. 289–91.
58. Ibid., p. 291.
59. Knox, *Korean War,* pp. 655, 658.
60. *Of GarryOwen in Glory,* p. 291.
61. Author interviews with Harris and Lynch.
62. *Ebb and Flow,* Chapter VI, p. 39.
63. *Bringing up the Rear,* pp. 181–83.
64. Ibid., pp. 184–85.
65. Official biography; USNA *Register of Alumni; Lightning Joe,* p. 135 and passim.
66. Albert C. Wedemeyer, *Wedemeyer Reports!* (New York: Henry Holt, 1958), pp. 208 and passim, 325, 331; Barbara Tuchman, *Stilwell and the American Experience in China: 1911–45* (New York: Macmillan, 1977), pp. 429, 502.
67. Messinger and Coughlin: *Second Division in Korea,* p. xix (command chart); West Point *Register.* Messinger: West Point *Assembly* obituary; author interviews with Freeman and Meszar, September 10, 1984; letter, Peploe to author, February 4, 1985.
68. *Bringing up the Rear,* pp. 188–89.
69. Letter, anonymous to author, January 2, 1986; author-Epley interview.
70. Stewart ms. Son: West Point *Register.*
71. Letter, Charles A. Strong to author, February 14, 1987.
72. Command Report, December 1950.
73. *Ebb and Flow,* Chapter VIII, pp. 1–2.
74. "Sabers and Safety Pins"; Strong speech and an unpublished article, "Notes from Eighth Army's Engineer in Korea," courtesy Strong.
75. "Sabers and Safety Pins."
76. Knox, *Korean War,* pp. 658–59. *Time* (December 11, 1950) wrote: "Dull explosions rocked the city as Allied commanders blew up ammunition and supply dumps."

77. John G. Westover, *Combat Support in Korea* (Washington, D.C.: Combat Forces Press, 1955), p. 132. This book is a collection of vignettes about officers and men of Eighth Army's support units (medics, engineers, ordnancemen, MPs, etc.). Some vignettes are derived from official reports or letters; some were compiled by Army combat historians in Korea.

78. Ibid., pp. 133–35.

79. Ibid., p. 135. Author-Walker interview. The Army historian wrote that the destruction of Eighth Army material and supplies at Pyongyang had been authorized, if not encouraged, by GHQ, Tokyo. The authority was conveyed to Walker by Pinky Wright, who visited Walker's forward CP on December 2. The Eighth Army G-4, Albert K. Stebbins, later estimated that if Eighth Army had held another seventy-two hours at Pyongyang, it could have saved 8,000 to 10,000 tons of supplies. (*Ebb and Flow,* Chapter VIII, pp. 2, 7.)

80. Almond war diary. Dispositions and actions of X Corps: See Note 72, Chapter 16.

81. *U.S. Marine Operations in Korea III; Chosin,* pp. 171–81, 200–10. *"At all costs":* *Chosin,* p. 178.

82. For operations of Task Force MacLean, see Note 76, Chapter 16.

83. *East of Chosin,* p. 144.

84. Ibid., pp. 145–48.

85. Ibid., pp. 158–59.

86. *FRUS VII,* 1950, pp. 1259–60.

87. *Third Division in Korea; Chosin,* pp. 212–13. Hammel wrote: "Corps was not making sense. Beginning on the afternoon of November 29, after issuing no plans or directives for two critical days, X Corps issued a series of plans and directives and recommendations that were so at variance with one another and with objective reality as to render them utterly meaningless." *Fighting 65th,* pp. 119–20. Harris wrote that in a period of three days, November 30 to December 2, he received four sets of orders from X Corps to 3d Division, each tending to reverse the other. "Since no explanation was given for these changes, I must admit that I was a mite confused; the troops must have thought that we were all out of our minds, for they had been marching and countermarching like yo-yos."

88. Almond war diary; Smith aide-mémoire; *East of Chosin,* pp. 180–81.

89. Blumenson, "Chosin Reservoir," in *Combat Actions in Korea.*

90. *East of Chosin,* p. 176.

91. *Chosin,* p. 199.

92. *Combat Support in Korea,* pp. 206–07 (an account by Rosen).

93. *East of Chosin,* p. 186.

94. West Point *Register.* Senior staffer quoted: Letter, Richard F. Mitchell to author, October 6, 1986. Author-Davis interview.

95. West Point *Register;* author-Gurfein interview, May 26, 1984.

96. Gurfein quoted in *East of Chosin,* pp. 162–63. Gist repeated in author-Gurfein interview.

97. Army forces at Koto: Research kindly provided the author by George A. Rasula, Francis S. Obradovich (CO, C Company, 185th Engineers), and John J. Zitzelberger (of the 2/31) in 1986 and 1987. In addition, Obradovich article in "Chosin Few" (1985), a newsletter published by survivors of operations at the Chosin Reservoir.

98. Author-Gurfein interview.

99. *East of Chosin,* pp. 188–94.

100. The definitive account of the "breakout" of Task Force Faith on December 1 is contained in *East of Chosin*, pp. 195–277. The summary here and below relies almost entirely on Appleman's account.
101. Author-Gregory interview, March 26, 1986.
102. Foster: West Point *Register*. Ransome: Knox, *Korean War*, p. 552.
103. Blumenson, "Chosin Reservoir," in *Combat Actions in Korea*, p. 78.
104. Marshburn: West Point *Register*.
105. Shelton: Ibid.
106. Chester Bair ms.
107. Blumenson, "Chosin Reservoir," in *Combat Actions in Korea*.
108. *U.S. Marine Operations in Korea III*, pp. 243–45.
109. George A. Rasula taped interview with Escue, October 18, 1981, transcript courtesy Rasula. The survivors rescued by Escue may have been included in the totals reported by the Marines.
110. *East of Chosin*, p. 291.
111. Ibid., pp. 300–04.
112. DSCs: *East of Chosin* and MacLean's obituary in *Assembly*. Faith Medal of Honor: Department of the Army General Order 59, August 2, 1951, copy courtesy Ridgway. See also *Korea's Heroes*. Omar Bradley presented the medal to Faith's wife, Barbara, on June 21, 1951.

## CHAPTER 18

1. *Published Papers of the President of the United States: Harry S. Truman, 1950*, pp. 724–28; *FRUS VII*, 1950, pp. 1261–62; *Tumultuous Years*, pp. 309–10; *Green Bay Press Gazette*, November 30, 1950.
2. *MacArthur: His Rendezvous with History*, pp. 446–49; *MacArthur III*, pp. 540–41; *Tumultuous Years*, pp. 315–16. *Green Bay Press Gazette*, December 1, 1950, carried excerpts of MacArthur's remarks in the Baillee story and *U.S. News & World Report* interview.
3. "Shooting": *Harry S. Truman*, p. 493.
4. Ibid.; *MacArthur III*, p. 541.
5. Poll: Ibid., p. 539.
6. *A General's Life*, p. 602; *MacArthur III*, p. 542.
7. *FRUS VII*, 1950, pp. 1276–81, 1310–13, 1312–13, 1323–34, 1336–39, 1345–47. There were two major meetings at the Pentagon on December 1 and 3, 1950, involving all senior officials of Defense and State, plus Averell Harriman at the December 1 meeting. On Saturday, December 2, Truman and the Pentagon contingent rode in a special train to Philadelphia to keep a long-standing date to attend the Army-Navy football game. During the train trip up and back there were further conferences, and after returning to Washington that night, Acheson, Marshall, and Bradley conferred with Truman for two hours or more at the White House. (See *A General's Life*, p. 605 and 605n.) Smith's comment: *FRUS VII*, 1950, p. 1279.
8. *FRUS VII*, 1950, p. 1311.
9. Ibid., p. 1280.
10. Ibid., pp. 1320–22 (complete text MacArthur to JCS, December 3, 1950).
11. Ibid., pp. 1345–46.
12. Collins to Far East: *FRUS VII*, 1950, p. 1278. Stay there: *FRUS VII*, 1950, p. 1313. Take battlefield command: *FRUS VII*, 1950, p. 1345.
13. *FRUS VII*, 1950, pp. 1323–24 (minutes); "History of the JCS III," pp. 355–63.

14. Letter, Ridgway to Roy Appleman, March 6, 1978, Almond Papers, USAMHI.
15. *Korean War,* pp. 61–62.
16. "History of the JCS III," p. 362.
17. Ibid., p. 364.
18. *War in Peacetime,* p. 229; Ridgway memo on Collins trip, December 8, 1950, Ridgway Papers, Box 16, USAMHI. *Ebb and Flow,* Chapter VIII, pp. 15–16.
19. Author-Walker interview.
20. *War in Peacetime,* p. 230; *Policy and Direction,* p. 283.
21. *War in Peacetime,* pp. 229–30; *FRUS VII,* 1950, p. 1521. *Ebb and Flow,* Chapter VIII, pp. 15–16.
22. *U.S. Marine Operations in Korea III,* pp. 280–83, 335–39, 346; author interviews with Powell and Beauchamp.
23. *War in Peacetime,* p. 234.
24. Ibid.; *Policy and Direction,* p. 283.
25. The "line": *War in Peacetime,* p. 235.
26. "History of the JCS III," p. 369; *Sea War in Korea,* p. 181.
27. *War in Peacetime,* pp. 229–32; *Policy and Direction,* p. 295; JCS "Record"; Ridgway memo, December 8, 1950, Ridgway Papers, Box 16, USAMHI.
28. *War in Peacetime,* p. 232.
29. Ibid., pp. 232–33; *A General's Life,* p. 607.
30. *FRUS VII,* 1950, pp. 1352 ff.; "History of the JCS III," pp. 370–78; *Policy and Direction,* pp. 288–93; *Tumultuous Years,* pp. 316–19.
31. *U.S. Marine Operations in Korea III.*
32. Almond war diary; Smith aide-mémoire.
33. Smith oral history.
34. *U.S. Marine Operations in Korea III,* p. 307 (breakdown of forces at Hagaru and Koto), pp. 381–82 (casualty tables). Correspondence Rasula to author, including a copy of a long letter from Rasula to a friend, dated February 4, 1951, explaining the command setup of the "provisional 31st Regiment" and its operations from Hagaru to Koto to Hamhung (hereafter Rasula-friend letter); author-Witte interview.
35. *U.S. Marine Operations in Korea III;* Rasula-friend letter.
36. *U.S. Marine Operations in Korea III; Ebb and Flow,* Chapter VII, pp. 19–20.
37. *Third Division in Korea,* pp. 86–87, 90. Author interviews with 3d Division commanders Guthrie, Boswell, Harris, and others. Letters, Samuel Kail (CO, 2/7) to author, October 30 and December 9, 1984.
38. *U.S. Marine Operations in Korea III,* pp. 281–82; "No Advance Beyond Chosin," *Time* (December 18, 1950).
39. *U.S. Marine Operations in Korea III,* pp. 288–93.
40. Ibid., pp. 294–95; *Chosin,* pp. 329–30.
41. Rasula-friend letter.
42. *U.S. Marine Operations in Korea III,* pp. 295–99; author-Witte interview; Rasula-friend letter.
43. *U.S. Marine Operations in Korea III,* pp. 296–98; *Sea War in Korea,* p. 177; Rasula-friend letter.
44. Drake in rear guard: Rasula-friend letter; author interview with Drake, July 12, 1987.
45. *Third Division in Korea,* pp. 92–93.
46. Ibid., pp. 92–93; *Fighting 65th,* p. 125; *U.S. Marine Operations in Korea III,* p. 308.
47. Author-O'Neil interview, September 24, 1984.

48. Letter, Kail to author, December 9, 1984.
49. *Chosin,* pp. 361, 363–64. Letter, Obradovich to Zitzelberger, January 17, 1986, courtesy Obradovich; Obradovich article on Koto forces in "Chosin Few" newsletter; author-Gurfein interview.
50. *U.S. Marine Operations in Korea III,* pp. 317–18; Rasula-friend letter.
51. *U.S. Marine Operations in Korea III,* pp. 320–23.
52. Author-Drake interview.
53. Rasula correspondence; letter, Mitchell to Zitzelberger, February 26, 1986, courtesy Zitzelberger; Obradovich article in "Chosin Few" and letter to author, May 27, 1986.
54. *Life* (December 25, 1950); David Douglas Duncan, *This Is War* (New York: Harper, 1951). Army anger at Duncan and postal stamps: Letter, Zitzelberger to author, April 5, 1986, with various enclosures; Obradovich article in "Chosin Few"; Rasula correspondence.
55. Rasula-friend letter; *Third Division in Korea; U.S. Marine Operations in Korea III,* p. 327; author-O'Neil interview; letter, Zitzelberger to Hammel, June 18, 1984, courtesy Zitzelberger; author-Zitzelberger interview, February 15, 1986.
56. Childs: West Point *Register;* Childs letter to author, November 12, 1984. *Fighting 65th,* pp. 135–36. *Third Division in Korea,* p. 388 (Nieves medal); *U.S. Marine Operations in Korea III,* pp. 327–28; *Chosin,* pp. 357–58, 403; *Above and Beyond; Korea's Heroes.* N. A. Canzona and John C. Hubbel, "The Twelve Incredible Days of Colonel John Page," *Reader's Digest* (April 1956).
57. *U.S. Marine Operations in Korea III,* pp. 333–41; *History of U.S. Naval Operations: Korea,* p. 295.
58. *U.S. Marine Operations in Korea III,* p. 330.
59. *Third Division in Korea;* author interviews with Guthrie, Harris, Beauchamp, and Powell; correspondence from Guthrie, Beauchamp, and Powell; *Fighting 65th.*
60. *U.S. Marine Operations in Korea III,* pp. 331–55.
61. Ibid., pp. 355–56.
62. *Third Division in Korea,* p. 108.
63. Ibid., pp. 94–96.
64. *Time* (January 1, 1951). Sutton Silver Star: *Third Division in Korea,* p. 386.
65. *History of U.S. Naval Operations: Korea,* pp. 300–02; *Sea War in Korea,* p. 188; *U.S. Marine Operations in Korea III,* pp. 342–44.
66. *Fighting 65th,* p. 129.
67. *History of U.S. Naval Operations: Korea,* pp. 295–96.
68. Ibid., pp. 296, 302; *Third Division in Korea,* p. 102.
69. *History of U.S. Naval Operations: Korea,* pp. 302–04; *Third Division in Korea,* pp. 102–05; *Time* (December 25, 1950).
70. *History of U.S. Naval Operations: Korea,* pp. 296, 304; *Time* (December 25, 1950).
71. *Sea War in Korea,* p. 183.
72. *Third Division in Korea,* p. 104.
73. Command Report, December 1950. *Ebb and Flow,* Chapter VIII, pp. 1–10, 18–20.
74. Barth ms.; Knox, *Korean War,* p. 664.
75. Fisher obituary: West Point *Assembly,* March 1985. Barth ms.; letter, Teeters to author, November 5, 1985.
76. Kelleher: Official biography. Corley: Official biography; West Point *Register;* West Point *Assembly* obituary.

77. Author-Van Brunt interview.
78. 24th Infantry records, NA (Suitland), Box 3770.
79. Barth ms.; 25th Division records, NA (Suitland), Box 3766.
80. 25th Division records, Box 3766. Author interviews with Michaelis and Dolvin. Letter, William Dick to author.
81. Author interviews with Davidson, Moore, and Kinney. Correspondence from Moore, Kinney, and Cutler. Stephens versus Davidson: Letter, Cutler to author, May 5, 1986.
82. Command Report, December 1950. *Ebb and Flow,* Chapter VIII, p. 22.
83. Johnson oral history, USAMHI. Palmer: *Army Register.*
84. Knox, *Korean War,* p. 675.
85. Letter, Clainos to author, April 6, 1986.
86. *Of GarryOwen in Glory,* p. 294.
87. Author-Clainos interview.
88. Harold H. Martin, "The Greeks Know How to Die," *Saturday Evening Post* (July 7, 1951). Letter, Arbouzis to author, October 12, 1985.
89. *Of GarryOwen in Glory,* p. 294; author-Harris interview; letters to author from Clainos, April 6, 1986, and Webel, October 14, 1985.
90. Replacements: *Policy and Direction,* p. 295.
91. Command Report, December 1950. *Ebb and Flow,* Chapter VIII, p. 25. *FRUS VII,* 1950, p. 1521 (Muccio to Acheson, December 11, 1950).
92. "History of the JCS III," p. 389.
93. Ibid.
94. *FRUS VII,* 1950, pp. 1570–73; "History of the JCS III," p. 390.
95. "History of the JCS III," p. 391.
96. *FRUS VII,* 1950, pp. 1574–1619. Acheson's and Truman's views: Ibid., p. 1601. Marshall: Ibid., p. 1571.
97. Muccio cables: *FRUS VII,* 1950, pp. 1548–49, 1565.
98. Ibid.; *Ebb and Flow,* Chapter VIII, p. 25.
99. Command Report, December 1950. Muccio: *FRUS VII,* 1950, p. 1586.
100. *Second Division in Korea.*
101. "Sabers and Safety Pins," pp. 381–82.
102. *First Commonwealth Division,* pp. 39–40; author interviews with Moore and Davidson.
103. *Time* (January 1, 1951); telex (official version of accident), Ridgway to MacArthur, February 2, 1951, MacArthur Archives.
104. Telex, Ridgway to MacArthur.
105. *Pacific Stars and Stripes,* December 26 and 27, 1950. Four stars: West Point *Register.* Sam: West Point *Register.*
106. *Policy and Direction,* p. 305; Barth ms.; 25th Division records, NA (Suitland), Box 3766.
107. *War in Peacetime,* p. 236.
108. Ibid., p. 236; Ridgway, *Korean War,* pp. 79–80.

## CHAPTER 19

1. Author interviews with Ridgway, his aides and his cohorts. See also magazine profiles: *Time* cover stories, April 2, 1945, March 5 and July 16, 1951; and *Newsweek* cover stories, January 8 and April 30, 1951; *Life* cover story, May 12, 1952.

2. Author-Walter F. Winton interview, November 6, 1982.
3. Author-Ridgway interview; Ridgway oral history, USAMHI; *Soldier.*
4. Official biography; West Point *Register;* Command and General Staff School and Army War College records; Ridgway oral history.
5. *Soldier,* pp. 33–34; Ridgway oral history. Paucity of Spanish-language officers: Author-Maxwell D. Taylor interview, November 18, 1982.
6. Various speeches and writings, Ridgway Papers, USAMHI.
7. Ridgway oral history; James Michener, "A Tough Man for a Tough Job," *Life* (May 12, 1952).
8. Memory: Ridgway oral history; "A Tough Man."
9. Ridgway marriages: See Chapter 3, note 9.
10. Chapter 3, note 9. Controversy: Various author interviews.
11. Ridgway oral history.
12. Author-Ridgway interview.
13. *Ridgway's Paratroopers,* pp. 1–24.
14. Ibid.; battle wound described, p. 469.
15. Gavin quoted: James M. Gavin, *On to Berlin* (New York: Bantam [Trade edition], 1985), p. 221. Eisenhower quoted: *Ike Papers IV,* p. 2216, and *Ike Papers VI,* p. 79.
16. *Soldier,* pp. 196–97.
17. Ridgway Papers, Box 16, USAMHI.
18. Ibid.
19. Coterie: See *Ridgway's Paratroopers.* Eaton: West Point *Register.*
20. Official biographies; West Point *Register.* Author-Moorman interview, November 6, 1982, and subsequent letters. "Safe line": Ridgway interview by Maurice Matloff, April 19, 1984, Department of Defense History (hereafter Matloff interview).
21. *Soldier,* p. 197. Extra socks: Letter, Ridgway to Gavin, December 28, 1950, Ridgway papers, Box 17, USAMHI.
22. *Soldier,* pp. 199–200.
23. Official biographies; West Point *Register.* Author-Winton interview and subsequent letters.
24. *Soldier,* pp. 201–02.
25. Frederick A. Hetzel and Harold L. Hitchens, "An Interview with General Matthew B. Ridgway," *Western Pennsylvania Historical Magazine,* vol. 65, No. 4 (October 1982), hereafter "Interview."
26. Ibid.; Ridgway official biography; MacArthur official bio and *MacArthur I,* pp. 266, 293.
27. Ridgway notes on the conference in "Special File," Ridgway Papers, Box 20, USAMHI.
28. Ridgway, *Korean War,* p. 81, report, Ridgway Papers, Box 20, USAMHI.
29. "Interview," p. 296.
30. Cable, Ridgway to Collins, December 29, 1950, Ridgway Papers, Box 22, USAMHI.
31. Ibid.
32. Report, Ridgway Papers, Box 20.
33. Ibid.
34. Ibid.
35. *Soldier,* p. 201; "Interview," p. 285.
36. Almond oral history, USAMHI.

37. Ridgway, *Korean War,* p. 83.
38. *Soldier,* p. 202.
39. Ridgway Papers, Box 20, order of December 26, 1950. Also in Command Report, December 1950.
40. *Soldier,* p. 203.
41. "Deplorable": Matloff interview. "174,000": *Soldier,* p. 205.
42. The figure 350,000 (*U.S. Air Force in Korea,* p. 251) seems about right for the Eighth Army field forces. Lynn Montross, Hubbard D. Kuokka, and Norman W. Hicks, *U.S. Marine Operations in Korea 1950–1953, vol. IV, The East-Central Front* (Washington, D.C: Historical Division, U.S. Marine Corps, 1962; hereafter *U.S. Marine Operations in Korea IV*), p. 24, puts the number of "UN Forces in Korea" (in January 1951) at 444,336, including FEAF, all naval forces, and the ROK Army infrastructure. Eighth Army order of battle: Command Report, January 1951.
43. Ridgway on ROK Army: Interview of Ridgway by Major Matthew P. Caulfield, USMC, and Colonel Robert M. Elton, USA, August 29, 1969 (hereafter "Caulfield interview").
44. Ibid.
45. *Soldier,* pp. 203–04.
46. Here and below, Ridgway's movements in Korea: HQ or command diary, Box 22, Ridgway Papers, USAMHI (hereafter Diary). The diary lists Ridgway's main stops, personnel seen and, often, subjects discussed.
47. *Soldier,* pp. 204–5.
48. Johnson oral history, USAMHI, p. 53.
49. Ridgway views on corps and division commanders: Ridgway, *Korean War,* pp. 88, 90 (p. 88: "The leadership I found in many instances sadly lacking, and I said so out loud"; p. 90: "The lack of aggressiveness in our Corps and Division commanders . . ."). See also memo, "Leadership Problems" (for discussion with Collins), Special File, January 11, 1951, Box 20; letters, Ridgway to MacArthur, January 7, 1951, Box 17, USAMHI, and to Collins, January 8, 1951, Box 20; Diary, January 10, 1951; letter, Beiderlinden (G-1, GHQ) to Brooks (G-1, Department of the Army), January 11, 1951, re Ridgway's "still pressing for the younger brigadier generals"; letter, Ridgway to Haislip, February 24, 1951, Box 20; Ridgway oral history, pt. 2, p. 118; pt. 3, pp. 53–56.
50. Author-Ridgway interview. Coulter official biography. Coulter was relieved on January 31, 1951. Tychsen was relieved the same day, per message Ridgway to Beiderlinden of that date (MacArthur Archives). See also official biography and Tychsen ms., USAMHI.
51. Author-Ridgway interview. Ridgway oral history, pt. 2, p. 117 (Milburn not named, but implied); pt. 3, pp. 75–76 (Almond named).
52. Author-McCaffrey interview, May 23, 1984.
53. Diary, January 11, 1951 (handwritten entry); Ridgway oral history, pt. 3, p. 12, re Moore. Current duty: Official biographies.
54. Official biographies.
55. Letter, Gavin to Ridgway, December 28, 1950, Ridgway Papers, Box 17; author-Gavin interview.
56. Slap on wrist: Ridgway oral history, pt. 3, pp. 85–86. Letters, Beishline to Ridgway, February 10, 1951, Ridgway Papers, Box 18. Letter, Ridgway to Haislip, February 24, 1951, Ridgway Papers, Box 20, USAMHI.
57. Official biographies; West Point *Register;* West Point *Assembly* obituaries for Harrold and Ladue.

58. Letter, Louis A Walsh to author, November 28, 1983, and many other sources. The Jeter story was famous. In his oral history Ridgway, recalling the incident (but not naming Jeter) said he was "shocked" by the G-3 plans and "chewed them out."

59. Author-Jeter interview, June 9, 1986.

60. Ibid., Letter, Jeter to author, February 25, 1985; letter, Charles M. Peeke to author, December 6, 1984; author interview with Thomas D. Gillis, September 26, 1984.

61. Ridgway, *Korean War,* p. 84.

62. Ibid., Appendix, p. 263.

63. Ibid., p. 84.

64. Caulfield interview.

65. Ridgway oral history, pt. 2, pp. 109–10.

66. Diary, December 28, 1950. Command report, December 1950.

67. Ridgway oral history, pt. 2, p. 102. "Combat Losses of Artillery Weapons," NA (Suitland), Box 1149.

68. Official biographies; West Point *Register.*

69. *Soldier,* p. 206; Diary, December 28, 1950. "Combat Losses of Artillery Weapons."

70. Johnson oral history, p. 56.

71. FEAF morale and withdrawal plans: *U.S. Air Force in Korea,* pp. 251–52.

72. *History of U.S. Naval Operations: Korea,* p. 311; *U.S. Marine Operations in Korea IV,* p. 14–15.

73. Command Report, December 1950; *U.S. Air Force in Korea,* p. 254.

74. Command Report, December 1950.

75. Almond oral history.

76. *U.S. Marine Operations in Korea IV,* p. 19.

77. Ridgway oral history, pt. 3, p. 77.

78. Smith oral history, Bowser oral history, Smith aide-mémoire, December 30, 1950, and January 7, 1951, are all at USMC History. Bowser official biography.

79. *U.S. Marine Operations in Korea, IV,* pp. 18–19.

80. Ibid., pp. 11–13.

81. Smith oral history; Bowser oral history.

82. Ridgway, *Korean War,* p. 85. The tour is described on pp. 85–89 and in *Soldier,* pp. 204–07.

83. Author-Lynch interview; letters, Smith to author, April 24, October 5, November 7, 1983, and September 15, 1986.

84. *Soldier,* p. 204.

85. Ridgway, *Korean War,* pp. 86–87.

86. See note 49, above.

87. Ridgway oral history, pt. 3, pp. 69–71; memo, March 14, 1951, Box 20, USAMHI.

88. Author-Davidson interview.

89. Ibid.

90. Official biography; West Point *Register.* For 13th Infantry action in Ruhr, see *Ridgway's Paratroopers,* p. 484.

91. Author interviews with Moore, Kinney, and letters from Mudgett. Perez oral history. Official biography and West Point *Assembly* obituary of Stephens.

92. Author interviews with Ridgway and Palmer. *Lightning Joe,* p. 185 and passim; *Ridgway's Paratroopers,* p. 417. Post: Official biography; West Point *Register.*

93. Author interviews with Clainos and Harris; Johnson oral history.

94. Official biography; West Point *Register. Ike Papers III,* pp. 1684–85. Letter, Paddock to author, December 3, 1984.
95. *Eisenhower's Lieutenants,* p. 128 and passim; author-Van Brunt interview. Ferenbaugh official biography.
96. Author-Davis interview.
97. Letter, Paddock to author, December 3, 1984; author-Powell interview; letters to author from Huston, and Holmes, December 7, 1984.
98. Hinds official biography; West Point *Register.*
99. Here and below: Distilled from *Soldier;* Ridgway, *Korean War;* Diary; oral history; speeches, and other sources in Ridgway Papers, USAMHI.
100. Letter, Smith to author, October 5, 1983; cable, MacArthur to Ridgway, December 20, 1950, Ridgway Papers, Box 17, USAMHI.
101. Stephen E. Ambrose, *Eisenhower,* vol. II: *The President* (New York: Simon & Schuster, 1984), pp. 495–96, 503–40 (hereafter *Eisenhower II*). "History of the JCS IV," pp. 179–221.
102. *FRUS VII,* 1950, pp. 1588–1626. See especially Dean Rusk memo, pp. 1588–90; Battle memo, pp. 1600–04; CIA estimate, December 27, 1950, pp. 1605–10; Battle memos, pp. 1614–16. The JCS directive to MacArthur of December 29, 1950, is on pp. 1625–26. For additional insights, see "History of the JCS III," pp. 394–98.
103. *Reminiscences,* pp. 430–31; MacArthur: *His Rendezvous with History,* p. 431.
104. Text of MacArthur reply, *FRUS VII,* 1950, pp. 1630–33.
105. *A General's Life,* p. 616.

## CHAPTER 20

1. Here and below: Command Report, December 1950; *Ebb and Flow,* Chapter IX, pp. 6–24; Command Report, January 1951, NA (Suitland), Box 1143. *Soldier,* pp. 209–10; Barth ms.
2. Command Report, January 1951; "Combat Losses of Artillery Weapons," NA (Suitland), Box 1149.
3. *Soldier,* p. 210.
4. Command Report, January 1951; *Soldier,* p. 210; similar account in Ridgway, *Korean War,* pp. 93–94.
5. Diary, January 1, 1951, Ridgway Papers, Box 22, USAMHI.
6. *First Commonwealth Division,* p. 40; Ridgway, *Korean War,* p. 94.
7. Diary, January 1, 1951; Ridgway, *Korean War,* p. 94.
8. Command Report, January 1951.
9. W. B. Woodruff, manuscript on Korean War (hereafter Woodruff ms.), courtesy Woodruff.
10. Command Report, January, 1951; Barth ms. (and maps); *Of GarryOwen in Glory,* p. 295; *First Commonwealth Division.*
11. Command Report, January 1951.
12. *U.S. Air Force in Korea,* pp. 256–58; *U.S. Marine Operations in Korea IV,* p. 27. "Largest" and 700 plus sorties: Command Report, January 1951.
13. *Soldier,* p. 211; Ridgway, *Korean War,* p. 95; Command Report, January 1951.
14. Diary, January 2, 1951; Command Report, January 1951.
15. *Ebb and Flow,* Chapter X, pp. 2–3.
16. Refugees described in cables Muccio to Acheson, *Foreign Relations of the United States,* vol. VII, 1951: *Korea and China,* pt. 1, pp. 2–3, 30–31 (hereafter

*FRUS VII,* 1951, pt. 1). See also *Time* (January 15, 1951), pp. 23–24; "Sabers and Safety Pins."
17. "Sabers and Safety Pins."
18. Ibid.
19. Diary, January 2, 1951.
20. Caulfield interview.
21. Diary, January 2, 1951; *Soldier,* pp. 210–11.
22. *Second Division in Korea,* pp. 88–89; *Soldier,* p. 211; Command Report, January 1951.
23. *Second Division in Korea;* 23d Infantry operations report; Freeman oral history.
24. *Second Division in Korea;* Freeman oral history; 23d Infantry operations report.
25. Author interviews with Freeman and Meszar.
26. Command Report, January 1951.
27. Ridgway to MacArthur, January 2, 1951, MacArthur Archives.
28. Ridgway to Collins, January 3, 1951, Ridgway Papers, USAMHI.
29. Ridgway order to Milburn, Coulter, dated January 4, 1951, "confirms verbal instructions," MacArthur Archives; Command Report, January 1951.
30. Command Report, January 1951; *Soldier,* p. 212; Ridgway, *Korean War,* pp. 95–96; author-Palmer interview.
31. DUWKs best: "Sabers and Safety Pins."
32. Command Report, January 1951.
33. *First Commonwealth Division,* pp. 41–43.
34. Ridgway memo, January 3, 1951, Ridgway Papers, Box 22, USAMHI.
35. Command Report, January 1951; *First Commonwealth Division,* p. 40; *Of Garry-Owen in Glory,* p. 295.
36. *Soldier,* p. 213.
37. Ibid., p. 214.
38. *First Commonwealth Division;* "Sabers and Safety Pins"; *Ebb and Flow,* Chapter XI, p. 4.
39. Ridgway directive, January 2, 1951, Ridgway Papers, Box 21, USAMHI.
40. *U.S. Air Force in Korea,* p. 258.
41. Command Report, January 1951.
42. *Second Division in Korea,* p. 90.
43. Command Report, January 1951; *Second Division in Korea; Third Division in Korea.* "Sixteen trainloads": Barth ms.
44. Command Report, January 1951.
45. Ibid.
46. *Soldier,* p. 214.
47. Memo, January 8, 1951, Ridgway Papers, Box 20, USAMHI.
48. Letter, Ridgway to Collins, January 8, 1951, Ridgway Papers, Box 20, USAMHI.
49. Author-Michaelis interview.
50. Author-Dolvin interview.
51. Command Report, January 1951.
52. Command Report, January 1951; Barth ms.; author-Michaelis interview.
53. Barth ms. Keyes: 25th Division records, *Army Register.* Keyes had replaced George De Chow, who went to the 25th Division staff.
54. Command Report, January 1951.
55. *Third Division in Korea,* pp. 127–28.
56. Author interviews with Boswell, Blanchard, William Harris, and Guthrie.

57. Guthrie: Official biography; author interviews with Guthrie and Boswell.
58. West Point *Register;* official biography.
59. Author-Boswell interview.
60. Weyand: Official biography; characterized by his contemporary, Bruce Palmer, Jr., in *25-Year War,* p. 133.
61. Various author interviews with 65th Infantry personnel.
62. Various author interviews with 3d Division commanders.
63. Here and below: Author-Blanchard interview; Blanchard ms.; Blanchard correspondence with author, especially letter of September 8, 1986.
64. Command Report, January 1951; *Second Division in Korea.*
65. Letters, Almond to Ridgway, January 9, 13, and 14, 1951, Ridgway Papers, Box 20, USAMHI.
66. Command Report, January 1951.
67. *Second Division in Korea,* p. 91.
68. "Second only": Almond oral history, USAMHI.
69. Freeman oral history.
70. Ibid.; Almond oral history.
71. Freeman oral history.
72. Ibid.; *Second Division in Korea,* pp. 91–92.
73. *Second Division in Korea,* p. 92.
74. Letters to author from McMains; from Thomas W. Mellen, April 1 and May 2, 1985; from Gaylord M. Bishop, March 14, 1985. Author-Barberis interview.
75. Author-Barberis interview.
76. Letter, Mellen to author, April 1, 1985.
77. Author-Barberis interview; roster, 2/9, January 20, 1951, courtesy Robert Arrington.
78. Author interviews with Pope and Becton. Letters to author from McMains, and from Gaylord M. Bishop to author, March 14, 1985.
79. See note 65.
80. Letter, Ridgway to MacArthur, January 17, 1951, Ridgway Papers, Box 20, USAMHI.
81. Author-Holden interview.
82. Cable Department of the Army to Ridgway, January 16, 1951, Ridgway Papers, Box 17, USAMHI: "Press here has played up relief of McClure. With return of Barr and Church already scheduled plus possibility of Gay and Kean, Haislip fears if not handled skillfully may result in Congressional investigation. . . ." For press coverage, see, for example, *Time* (January 22, 1951).
83. McClure biography.
84. Collins debt to Richardson and probably Ruffner: *Lightning Joe,* pp. 105–06, 134.
85. Author interviews with Chiles, Freeman, Epley. Revocation of "beard order": *Time* (January 22, 1951).
86. Command Report, January 1951; author interviews with Powell and Beauchamp. Gavin: Official biography; West Point *Register.* Duty with 3/65 and promotion: *Fighting 65th,* p. 69. "Sharp gentleman": letter, George A. Rasula ("Acting S-3," 31st Infantry, in January 1951) to author, April 22, 1986.
87. Sink: Official biography; West Point *Register. Ridgway's Paratroopers,* p. 223.
88. Letter, Paddock to author, December 3, 1984; author-anonymous interview.
89. Quinn: Official biography; West Point *Register.* Author-Quinn interview, September 18, 1984.

90. Author-Epley interview. Billy Harris of the 7th Cav (in author-Harris interview) concurred with Epley's conclusion.
91. Author-Quinn interview. Quinn kindly provided a diary and scrapbook containing photos and newspaper clippings and a monograph, "The Buffaloes," a history of the 17th Infantry (which, however, erroneously dates the regiment from 1812 rather than 1861, per *Army Lineage Series*).
92. Letters to author from Huston, October 31, 1986, and from Powell, September 26, 1986.
93. Letter, Powell to author, September 26, 1986.
94. Command Report, January 1951; *Second Division in Korea;* 7th Division records; *RAKKASANS!*
95. *Second Division in Korea,* pp. 92–93; 23d Infantry operations report.
96. *Second Division in Korea,* p. 92.
97. Command Report, January 1951.
98. Diary, January 8, 1951. *U.S. Marine Operations in Korea IV,* p. 29.
99. *U.S. Marine Operations in Korea IV,* pp. 29–30.
100. Diary, January 9, 1951.
101. Ibid.
102. Bowser oral history.
103. "Lowest": "History of the JCS III," p. 412.
104. *FRUS VII,* 1950, pp. 1625–26, 1633; *War in Peacetime,* p. 247.
105. "History of the JCS III," p. 402.
106. Memo, January 5, 1951, Box 20, Ridgway Papers, USAMHI; Train oral history, USAMHI.
107. Letter, Ridgway to MacArthur, January 6, 1951, Box 20, Ridgway Papers, USAMHI.
108. Ibid.
109. ROK Army, government, and police totals and dependents: *FRUS VII,* 1951, pt. 1, p. 104 (report of Joe Collins). Schnabel, in *Policy and Direction,* p. 313, gives the figures as ROK Army, 260,000; ROK government, 36,000; and ROK police, 600,000. The last figure must be a typo for 60,000. If so, the total would be 356,000. He estimated dependents at 400,000, for a grand total of 756,000. Letter, Ridgway to MacArthur, January 6, 1951, Box 20, Ridgway Papers, USAMHI.
110. MacArthur to Ridgway, January 7, 1951, Box 20, Ridgway Papers, USAMHI.
111. "History of the JCS III," pp. 403–06; *FRUS VII,* 1951, pt. 1, pp. 71–72 (text by Sherman per "History of the JCS III," p. 417).
112. "History of the JCS III," pp. 404–06.
113. Ibid., pp. 416–17.
114. MacArthur's case: *Policy and Direction,* p. 329.
115. Vandenberg quoted in David Rees, *Korea: The Limited War* (New York: St. Martin's, 1964), p. 276.
116. *FRUS VII,* 1951, pt. 1, pp. 70–72; "Other papers" cited on pp. 80–81.
117. *FRUS VII,* 1951, pt. 1, pp. 41–43; "History of the JCS III," pp. 408–10.
118. *MacArthur: His Rendezvous with History,* pp. 434–35.
119. *FRUS VII,* 1951, pt. 1, pp. 55–57; "History of the JCS III," pp. 410–11.
120. "History of the JCS III," pp. 412, 440; *Present at the Creation,* p. 515; *A General's Life,* p. 619.
121. Letter, Ridgway to Haislip, Box 17, Ridgway Papers, USAMHI.
122. *FRUS VII,* 1951, pt. 1, pp. 69–70; "History of the JCS III," p. 415.

123. Cheju: *FRUS VII,* 1951, pt. 1, pp. 104–05 (Joe Collins report).
124. Collins and Vandenberg: *FRUS VII,* 1951, pt. 1, pp. 57, 60, 61, 67–69. Smith: *FRUS VII,* 1951, pt. 1, pp. 58, 70. Bolling: *Time* (January 22, 1951).
125. "History of the JCS III," pp. 415–16; *FRUS VII,* 1951, pt. 1, p. 69n.
126. Acheson proposal: "History of the JCS III," p. 415. Bradley veto: *FRUS VII,* 1951, pt. 1, p. 61.
127. *FRUS VII,* 1951, pt. 1, pp. 77–79, "History of the JCS III," pp. 419–21; *Years of Trial and Hope,* pp. 493–95.

## CHAPTER 21

1. "History of the JCS III," pp. 421–31; *Present at the Creation,* pp. 512–13; *U.S. Air Force in Korea,* p. 263.
2. Command Report, January 1951; Ridgway orders, Diary, January 14, 1951.
3. Diary, January 14, 1951. Letter, Ridgway to Milburn, January 15, 1951, Ridgway Papers, Box 17, USAMHI.
4. Letter, Ridgway to friend, Box 34E, Ridgway Papers, USAMHI; Ridgway, *Korean War,* p. 98.
5. Author interviews with Van Brunt, James Lynch, Day Surles, and William McCaffrey.
6. Command Report, January 1951; *Third Division in Korea,* pp. 131–32.
7. Ridgway oral history, pt. 3, pp. 69–71; Command Report, January 1951. Musical chairs: 24th Infantry records, NA (Suitland), Box 3841.
8. Command Report, January 1951; Barth ms.
9. *Third Division in Korea,* pp. 131–32; Command Report, January 1951.
10. Command Report, January 1951; Barth ms.
11. Ibid.
12. Command Report, January 1951.
13. Here and below: "Report of Eighth Army Armor Section, January 1951," with attached document entitled "Lessons on Tank Design from the Campaign in Korea," NA (Suitland), Box 1149. Numerous I Corps armor afteraction reports and armor combat lesson bulletins for the period January–June 1951, kindly provided by the I Corps armor officer, Thomas D. Gillis; letter, Ridgway to Department of the Army, January 14, 1951 (requesting organic tank companies for the 1st Cav, 7th, 24th, and 25th divisions), and (negative) reply of the Department of the Army, January 25, 1951, both in Box 17, Ridgway Papers, USAMHI; author interviews with Dolvin and Gillis, and with William M. Rogers (CO, 70th Tank Battalion and chief, Eighth Army armor section, January–June 1951) and Robert E. Drake (CO, 31st Tank Company).
    The Pershing heavy tank, introduced at the tail end of World War II to compete with the heavily armed German tanks (eighty-eight-mm guns or larger), was declared a flop even then, Dolvin and Rodgers asserted, and in the postwar years had been withdrawn from the Army's active inventory. Its "belly" armor was too thin to ward off mines, and there were problems with the gun traversing system. Its biggest problem, however, was mechanical unreliability. One prime defect, Rodgers remembered, was a "Rube Goldberg" fan belt system, which had "five belts operating off one pulley." If one belt broke, the other four also had to be replaced. "In Korea," Rodgers said, "we had to follow behind our 'monument Pershings' with a whole truckload of fan belts." The "lousy tank" quote is from Dolvin interview; "complete flop" from Rodgers interview.

14. "History of the JCS III," pp. 432–33; *War in Peacetime,* p. 252.
15. *War in Peacetime,* pp. 254–55; *MacArthur: His Rendezvous with History,* pp. 438–39.
16. "History of the JCS III," p. 433; *FRUS VII,* 1951, pt. 1, p. 105.
17. "History of the JCS III," p. 433.
18. Diary, January 15, 1951.
19. Melvin B. Voorhees, *Korean Tales* (New York: Simon & Schuster: 1952), pp. 101–10. American order of battle: Newspapers and *Time* (July–December 1950).
20. S.L.A. Marshall, *Infantry Operations and Weapons Usage in Korea (Winter 1950–51)* (Baltimore: Johns Hopkins University Press, 1953), pp. 116–19 (hereafter *Infantry Operations*).
21. *Korean Tales,* pp. 105–06.
22. Whitehead story, datelined New York, January 13, 1951, courtesy Rolfe Hillman scrapbook.
23. Command Report, January 1951, p. 74; *The New York Times,* January 15, 1951; *War in Peacetime,* p. 253; *FRUS VII,* 1951, pt. 1, p. 96.
24. Collins-Ridgway rivalry: *Ridgway's Paratroopers.*
25. *Ridgway's Paratroopers; War in Peacetime,* p. 253; author interviews with Collins and Ridgway.
26. Diary, January 15, 1951. Promotion dates: official bios.
27. *Second Division in Korea,* pp. 91–93; 23d Infantry operations report.
28. Command Report, January 1951.
29. Visit: Diary, January 15, 1951.
30. Kunzig: Official biography; West Point *Register.* Perez oral history, Special Collections Department, Mitchell Memorial Library, Mississippi State University.
31. Diary, January 15, 1951, and aide-mémoire re division commanders.
32. Hull: Ms.; USAMHI; official biography; *Lightning Joe,* pp. 100–07 and passim. Bolté: Official biography; author-Bolté interview, November 19, 1982; Bolté oral history, USAMHI. Bolté's sons: West Point *Register* and author-Phillip Bolté interview, August 17, 1987. Eisenhower rating for Hull and Bolté: *Ike Papers IX,* p. 2252.
33. Letter, Collins to Ridgway, May 24, 1951, Box 20, Ridgway Papers, USAMHI.
34. *U.S. Air Force in Korea,* p. 262; *Policy and Direction,* p. 327; *FRUS VII,* 1951, pt. 1, p. 104.
35. Diary, January 16, 1951. Letter, E. M. Landrum to author, February 25, 1985.
36. Diary, January 16, 1951.
37. *War in Peacetime.* Jokes: E. J. Kahn, Jr., *The Peculiar War* (New York: Random House, 1952), p. 6.
38. Diary, January 17, 1951.
39. *FRUS VII,* 1951, pt. 1, p. 103.
40. Ibid.
41. *War in Peacetime,* pp. 253–54.
42. *A General's Life,* pp. 622–23.
43. *War in Peacetime,* p. 255.
44. Ibid.
45. *FRUS VII,* 1951, pt. 1, pp. 102–03; *War in Peacetime,* p. 255.
46. *Second Division in Korea,* pp. 94–95.
47. Letter, Mellen to author, April 1, 1985.
48. Author-Barberis interview.
49. Letter, Mellen to author, April 1, 1985.

50. *Second Division in Korea,* p. 94; author-Barberis interview.
51. *MacArthur: His Rendezvous with History,* p. 459.
52. Text in *Soldier,* pp. 207–08; Ridgway, *Korean War,* pp. 204–05. Harold F. Harding, ed., *The Age of Danger: Major Speeches on American Problems* (New York: Random House, 1952), pp. 138–40.
53. Letter, Dill to Harry G. Summers, Jr., November 26, 1984, courtesy Dill.
54. Command Report, January 1951; Johnson oral history, USAMHI.
55. Command Report, January 1951; *Third Division in Korea.*
56. Johnson oral history, USAMHI.
57. Command Report, January 1951; *First Commonwealth Division,* p. 50.
58. Command Report, January 1951; Barth ms.
59. Command Report, January 1951.
60. *U.S. Air Force in Korea,* pp. 265–66.
61. Ibid., pp. 267–68.
62. Order, Box 17, Ridgway Papers, USAMHI.
63. Ridgway oral history, pt. 3, pp. 67–69.
64. Bolté to MacArthur, December 12, 1950, and MacArthur to Department of the Army, December 24, 1950, both in MacArthur Archives. Ridgway oral history, pt. 3, pp. 67–69.
65. Ridgway oral history, pt. 3, pp. 67–69.
66. Command Report, January 1951.
67. *U.S. Naval Operations in Korea,* pp. 323–24.
68. Command Report, January 1951.
69. Order of attack: Ibid.
70. *U.S. Air Force in Korea,* p. 263; *Soldier,* p. 216.
71. Command Report, January 1951.
72. Barth ms.
73. *Thrust! History of the 89th Tank Battalion,* courtesy Dolvin.
74. Woodruff ms.
75. Letter, Ridgway to MacArthur, January 26, 1951, Ridgway Papers, Box 17, USAMHI. Diary, January 26, 1951. Kelleher promotion: Letter, Ridgway to Department of the Army, Ridgway Papers, Box 17, USAMHI.
76. Command Report, January 1951; Barth ms. ("400 killed"); *Infantry Operations,* pp. 104–05.
77. *Infantry Operations,* p. 105.
78. Ridgway to MacArthur, January 26, 1951, Box 17, Ridgway Papers, USAMHI.
79. Command Report, January 1951; *Of GarryOwen in Glory,* pp. 295–96.
80. 1st Cav Division records, NA (Suitland), Boxes 4419, 4438, etc.
81. *Of GarryOwen and Glory,* pp. 295–96.
82. Ibid.
83. Ibid., p. 296.
84. *First Team; Korea's Heroes.*
85. Johnson oral history; 1st Cav Division Records, NA (Suitland), Box 4438. Author interviews with Harris, Palmer, Clainos and Robert Blanchard.
86. Command Report, January, 1951; *Third Division in Korea,* pp. 135–36.
87. Diary, January 28, 1951, *FRUS VII,* 1951, pt. 1, p. 146 and 146n.
88. Diary, January 28, 1951; 25th Division records.
89. *Third Division in Korea,* pp. 135–36.
90. Ibid.; Command Report, January 1951.
91. Command Report, January 1951.

92. *Third Division in Korea,* p. 137.
93. Ibid.
94. *Fighting 65th,* pp. 146–47.
95. Command Report, January 1951.
96. *Of GarryOwen in Glory,* pp. 296–97.
97. Diary, January 28 and 29, 1951.
98. *Victory Division in Korea;* profile, *Pacific Stars and Stripes,* August 14, 1951; various author interviews.
99. Letter, Mudgett to author, October 15, 1986.
100. Author interviews with Moore and Kinney.
101. Letter, Cutler to author, October 6, 1986.
102. Dispositions: 21st at Yoju; *Combat Actions in Korea,* map p. 91. Command Report, January 1951. Author-Kinney interview.
103. Diary, February 1, 1951; telex, Ridgway to all commands, February 21, 1951.
104. Command Report, January 1951; *Second Division in Korea,* pp. 95–96; 23d Infantry operations report.
105. *Combat Actions in Korea,* pp. 88–107; Paul Freeman, "Wonju Through Chipyong" (with detailed maps), courtesy Freeman; Freeman oral history, USAMHI.
106. Russell: 2d Division records; *Army Register.*
107. "Wonju Through Chipyong."
108. Stewart ms.
109. "Wonju Through Chipyong."
110. Freeman oral history; Harold H. Martin, "Who Said the French Won't Fight?" *Saturday Evening Post* (May 5, 1951); Caulfield interview; Ridgway, *Korean War,* p. 107.
111. "Wonju Through Chipyong."
112. Stewart ms.
113. *Second Division in Korea,* pp. 95–96.
114. "Wonju Through Chipyong"; Freeman oral history.
115. "Wonju Through Chipyong"; Stewart ms.
116. "Wonju Through Chipyong."
117. Diary, February 9, 1951; Caulfield interview; Ridgway, *Korean War,* p. 107. Citations: *Second Division in Korea,* pp. 221–23.

## CHAPTER 22

1. Ridgway telex to MacArthur, February 3, 1951, MacArthur Archives, paraphrased in *Policy and Direction,* pp. 334–35.
2. Command Report, February 1951, NA (Suitland), Box 1154.
3. Ibid.
4. Ibid.
5. Ridgway telex to MacArthur, February 3, 1951.
6. Ibid.
7. *MacArthur: His Rendezvous with Destiny,* pp. 460–61.
8. MacArthur telex to Ridgway, February 4, 1951, MacArthur Archives; *Policy and Direction,* p. 336; *MacArthur: His Rendezvous with Destiny,* pp. 460–61.
9. Ridgway, *Korean War,* p. 107.
10. Command Report, February 1951.
11. Ibid.; Barth ms.

12. Barth ms.
13. Letters, Woodruff to wife, February 11, 1951, courtesy Woodruff, and to author, November 10, 1986.
14. Command Report, February 1951; Barth ms.
15. Author Dolvin interview; Dolvin speech.
16. Dolvin speech.
17. Ibid.
18. Ibid.
19. Author-Dolvin interview. Fowler: *Third Division in Korea.*
20. Dolvin speech; author-Dolvin interview.
21. Dolvin speech.
22. *Korea's Heroes,* pp. 168–83.
23. *Third Division in Korea,* pp. 138–42 (and map).
24. 9th FAB: *South to the Naktong,* p. 413n and passim; 999th FAB: *Third Division in Korea,* p. 138.
25. *Third Division in Korea,* p. 138. Letters, to author from John D. Howard, February 28, 1987, and from George L. Ball, March 26, 1987.
26. *Third Division in Korea.* Letter, Hahn to Huston, February 9, 1951, courtesy Huston. *Time* (March 12, 1951) again featuring Sutton.
27. Letters, to author from Howard, February 28 and April 20, 1987, and from Ball, March 26, 1987.
28. Letters, to author from Howard, April 20, 1987, and from Abrams, May 28, 1986.
29. *Third Division in Korea,* pp. 138–40; various author interviews. Weyand: Author-Boswell interview.
30. *Fighting 65th,* pp. 156–57.
31. Command Report, February 1951; *First Team; Victory Division in Korea.*
32. *First Team; Of GarryOwen in Glory,* pp. 300–01. Hallden: Author-James Lynch interview.
33. Command Report, February 1951. Adams: *Korea's Heroes.* Diary, February 7, 1951.
34. 5th Infantry records, NA (Suitland), Box 5237.
35. Letter, Cutler to author, August 3, 1986.
36. Author-Kinney interview; letter, Kinney to author, August 6, 1986. Various author interviews.
37. Official biography; West Point *Register.* Letter, Cutler to author, October 6, 1986, kindly enclosing 1936 *Howitzer* excerpt and other material on Garland.
38. Official biography. 76th Division: *Eisenhower's Lieutenants,* p. 520 and passim. Russians: photo, courtesy Cutler.
39. Letter, Woods to author, October 9, 1986.
40. *U.S. Marine Operations in Korea IV,* pp. 41–57.
41. Ibid., p. 58.
42. Command Report, February 1951.
43. Dolvin speech.
44. Command Report, February 1951.
45. Ibid.; Dolvin speech.
46. Dolvin speech.
47. Command Report, February 1951; Barth ms.
48. *Ebb and Flow,* Chapter XIII, p. 14; *Third Division in Korea,* pp. 140–43; *Fighting 65th,* pp. 162–63.
49. *Fighting 65th,* pp. 170–71. Order dated February 15, 1951.

50. Letter, Bradley to Ridgway, February 12, 1951, Ridgway Papers, Box 17, USAMHI.
51. "History of the JCS III," pp. 444–50.
52. Ibid., pp. 460–61.
53. Telex, Taylor to MacArthur, February 10, 1951, MacArthur Archives. "History of the JCS III," p. 451; *Policy and Direction,* p. 338.
54. MacArthur to Taylor, February 11, 1951, MacArthur Archives; *Policy and Direction,* p. 338.
55. Diary, February 13, 1951. Fruitcake: Letter, Ridgway to Mrs. MacArthur, February 13, 1951, Ridgway Papers, Box 17, USAMHI.
56. *Strength for the Fight,* pp. 258–59; *MacArthur III,* p. 568.
57. Letter, Peeke to author, December 6, 1984; author-Dolvin interview. Corley medals: West Point *Register.* Corley obituary: West Point *Assembly.* Corley's eight Silver Star medals earned him an entry in the *1967 Guinness Book of World Records.*
58. Author-Michaelis interview.
59. *Policy and Direction,* p. 339 and 339n; *MacArthur III,* pp. 581–82.
60. Command Report, February 1951. Combat Notes No. 9, "The Battle of Hoengsong" (with maps), X Corps G-3 Section, foreword by Edward M. Almond, courtesy Thomas W. Mellen. *Second Division in Korea,* pp. 98–99.
61. Reinforcements to Chipyong: "Wonju Through Chipyong"; *Combat Actions in Korea,* pp. 108–33. Combat Notes No. 11, "Defense of Chipyong-ni" (with maps), X Corps G-3 Section, courtesy Thomas W. Mellen. 23d Infantry operations report. Author-Freeman interview.
62. Command Report, February 1951; author-Fergusson interview, August 17, 1986.
63. Details to Almond: Author-Fergusson interview.
64. Command Report, February 1951.
65. Letter, Peploe to author, February 4, 1985; official biography; *Second Division in Korea,* p. xix.
66. West Point *Register* (class of 1932 graduates and 1935 nongraduates); author interviews with William E. Manning, Warren D. Hodges, and James Y. Adams (a classmate and friend of Robert Lee Coughlin).
67. Author interviews with Hodges and Manning.
68. Command Report, February 1951; X Corps report; *Second Division in Korea.*
69. Command Report, February 1951.
70. Here and below: Command Report, February 1951; X Corps report; *Second Division in Korea; Ebb and Flow,* Chapter XIV, pp. 1–31.
71. Stewart ms.
72. Citation: *Second Division in Korea,* pp. 223–24.
73. Casualties: X Corps report.
74. Telex, Ridgway to MacArthur, March 9, 1951, Ridgway Papers, Box 17, USAMHI.
75. Command Report, February 1951.
76. X Corps report.
77. Letter, Bowman to author, April 22, 1986.
78. X Corps report; *Ebb and Flow* chapter XIV, pp. 16–26.
79. Command Report, February 1951.
80. Distilled from Diary, February 12 to 15, 1951; "Special File," Box 20, Ridgway Papers, February 12, 1951 (re I Corps attack across Han east of Seoul into "rear" of the CCF); Command Report, February 1951; Barth ms.; 1st Cav Division

records; *First Commonwealth Division*, pp. 50–51; *U.S. Marine Operations in Korea IV; Of GarryOwen in Glory;* etc.

81. Barth ms.; *First Commonwealth Division*, p. 56; *Of GarryOwen in Glory*, p. 310.
82. Telex, Ridgway to MacArthur, February 16, 1951, MacArthur Archives; Kean official biography.
83. 25th Division records.
84. Author-Michaelis interview.
85. *Second Division in Korea*, pp. 105–09; X Corps report (and maps).
86. Stewart ms.
87. Ibid.
88. *Second Division in Korea*, pp. 106–07; Command Report, February 1951.
89. Stewart ms.
90. *Second Division in Korea*, p. 107.
91. Stewart ms.
92. *Second Division in Korea*, p. 107.
93. *Ebb and Flow*, Chapter XIV, p. 27.
94. Diary, February 13 and 14, 1951; author-Chiles interview.
95. Stewart ms.
96. Ridgway oral history, pt. 3, p. 76, USAMHI.
97. X Corps report.
98. Quirk: Letter, Ridgway to Walter Annenberg, Box 17, Ridgway Papers, USAMHI. John Cooney, *The Annenbergs* (New York: Simon & Schuster, 1982). Memo, Quirk to Ridgway, March 17, 1951, HQ Diary, Box 22, Ridgway Papers, USAMHI.
99. Here and below: *Combat Actions in Korea*, pp. 108–33; "Wonju Through Chipyong"; Freeman oral history; 23d Infantry operations report; *Second Division in Korea*, p. 106 and passim; *Ebb and Flow*, Chapter XV, pp. 15–33. Harold H. Martin, "The Two Terrible Nights of the 23rd," *Saturday Evening Post* (May 19, 1951); X Corps Combat Notes No. 11 (Chipyong-ni), courtesy Thomas W. Mellen.
100. *Ebb and Flow*, Chapter XV, p. 31.
101. Here and below: "Wonju Through Chipyong."
102. *Combat Actions in Korea*, p. 115.
103. "Wonju Through Chipyong."
104. Letter, Freeman to author, August 23, 1986. Freeman stated that the implication in his oral history that he was wounded on February 15, 1951, is wrong.
105. Author-Chiles interview; West Point *Register*. Haste, "teacher's pet," from Stewart ms.
106. Stewart ms.
107. Letters to author from Freeman, August 23, 1986, and Chiles, August 26, 1986.
108. Task Force Crombez: *Combat Actions in Korea*, pp. 134–44.
109. "Wonju Through Chipyong."
110. *Third Division in Korea*, pp. 145–46.
111. *Fighting 65th*, pp. 166–67; *Third Division in Korea*.
112. *Fighting 65th*, p. 168.
113. Barth ms.; *First Commonwealth Division; Of GarryOwen in Glory*, pp. 304–05.
114. Author-Phillip Bolté interview.
115. Here and below: *Of GarryOwen in Glory*, pp. 304–07 (and map).
116. "Special File," February 12, 1951, Box 20, Ridgway Papers, USAMHI.
117. Command Report, February 1951; Diary, February 15, 1951.

118. *Combat Actions in Korea,* pp. 134–44.
119. "Wonju Through Chipyong."
120. Ibid.
121. Task Force Crombez: *Combat Actions in Korea,* pp. 134–44; 1st Cav Division records, February 15, 1951, NA (Suitland), Box 4438.
122. Letter, Freeman to author, August 23, 1986; author-Freeman interview; Freeman oral history; Diary, February 15, 1951.
123. Text in 1st Cav Division records, February 15, 1951, NA (Suitland), Box 4438.
124. Action details here and below: *Combat Actions in Korea;* 1st Cav Division records; *Ebb and Flow,* chapter XV, pp. 15-33.
125. West Point *Register;* author-Barrett interview.
126. Author interviews with Barrett, James Gibson, and Victor Fox. In the last, Fox, also relying on the substance of the letters of the 3/5 company commander, Norman Allen, to his mother, reconstructed much the same scene.
127. Treacy's frame of mind: Author-Barrett interview.
128. Author-Barrett interview.
129. Ibid.
130. *Combat Actions in Korea.*
131. "Psychological": Crombez report, 1st Cav Division records, February 15, 1951, NA (Suitland), Box 4438. Casualties: *Ebb and Flow,* Chapter XV, p. 32.
132. Author-Barrett interview. Casualties: *Combat Actions in Korea.*
133. Author-Barrett interview. "Disobeyed": 1st Cav Division records, February 15, 1951.
134. Author-Barrett interview.
135. Tactical criticism: *Combat Actions in Korea.* Ridgway praise: *Ebb and Flow,* Chapter XV, p. 33. DSC and star: West Point *Register.* Notwithstanding Ridgway's support, Crombez held no other major commands and retired in 1956.
136. Author interviews with Clainos and Blanchard. Letter, Blanchard to author, July 15, 1986.
137. Author-Blanchard interview.
138. *Of GarryOwen in Glory,* p. 310.
139. Command Report, February 1951.
140. Barth ms.
141. Ibid.
142. Ibid.
143. Diary, February 17, 1951; author-Chiles interview.
144. Diary, February 18, 1951.
145. Ibid.
146. *U.S. Air Force in Korea,* pp. 263–64.
147. Letter, Bradley to Ridgway, February 23, 1951, Box 17, Ridgway Papers, USAMHI; *A General's Life,* p. 608.

## CHAPTER 23

1. Diary, February 18, 1951; Command Report, February 1951.
2. Author interviews with Winton, Surles, Moorman, Lynch, Fergusson, and Adams. Letters to author from Smith, September 15, 1986; Surles, September 24, 1986; Fergusson, October 2, 1986; and Adams, October 3, 1986. Ridgway oral history, pt. 3, pp. 53–56, USAMHI.

3. Ridgway "Memo for Record," in Diary, February 24, 1951. Command Report, February 1951.
4. Command Report, February 1951.
5. Marine air wing: *U.S. Air Force in Korea,* pp. 314–18; *U.S. Marine Operations in Korea IV,* pp. 15–18, 63–65, 76–78.
6. "Sabers and Safety Pins."
7. Ibid.
8. Here and below: Dabney's paper: *Ebb and Flow,* Chapter XVI, p. 4; author-Ridgway interview; Ridgway, *Korean War,* pp. 104–05; and various author interviews. Regarding the defeatism in the Eighth Army staff, Surles said: "When I arrived at the Eighth Army CP in Taegu, I went to the G-three section, where I was told to report. Ridgway was not in Taegu. He rarely was in Taegu. He refused to come back there because he thought they were defeatist and too far behind the lines. The chief of staff [Lev Allen] wouldn't move them up. The first briefing I got from Bill Train, who was [later] the chief of plans, was on the withdrawal plan from the present front line back to Pusan. They had it all drawn out. . . . I told Ridgway when I first saw him and he had an apoplectic attack. . . . There was a tremendous number of people in the headquarters and some very fine people. General Allen, General Hodes—a brilliant man . . . Dabney. . . . But they were beaten." Moorman said: "Everybody on the Eighth Army staff had that bugout fever. They gave me this staff paper recommending withdrawal. I said I knew General Ridgway wouldn't approve it. Sure enough, he didn't. I got hold of the original on which he had written across the top 'Disapproved' and decided to keep it. One night I told him about it. He said he had agonized for hours over that. There was the whole Eighth Army staff telling him to withdraw. I gave him the paper, and he still has it."
9. Diary, February 19, 1951, and "Memo," February 24, 1951; *U.S. Marine Operations in Korea IV,* pp. 65–66.
10. Smith oral history.
11. Diary, February 20, 1951; International News Service account of MacArthur visit in *Pacific Stars and Stripes,* February 21, 1951.
12. MacArthur's remarks in *Stars and Stripes,* February 21, 1951. Ridgway's comment: Diary, February 23, 1951, and Ridgway, *Korean War,* pp. 109–10. In his book, Ridgway substituted "offensive" for "initiative," but the diary has "initiative."
13. Command Report, February 1951.
14. Ibid.
15. *U.S. Marine Operations in Korea IV,* pp. 84–88.
16. "Memo," February 20, 1951, Special File, Box 20, Ridgway Papers, USAMHI.
17. Command Report, February 1951.
18. *U.S. Marine Operations in Korea IV,* p. 68.
19. Diary, February 21, 1951; *U.S. Marine Operations in Korea IV,* p. 68.
20. *U.S. Marine Operations in Korea IV,* p. 70.
21. Here and below: Mildren official biography; West Point *Register;* author-Mildren interview, September 11, 1984.
22. Stewart ms.
23. Relief of Edwards: Letter, Chiles to author, August 26, 1986. Wohlfeil: *Second Division in Korea;* West Point *Register.*
24. Letters, to author from McMains, December 28, 1984, and from Gaylord Bishop, March 14, 1985; author-Pope interview. *Second Division in Korea; Army Register.*
25. Author-Pope interview.

26. Ibid.; author-Becton interview.
27. Ladue: Memo, March 14, 1951, Special File, Box 20, Ridgway Papers, USAMHI.
28. Gerot replaced: Letter, Rolfe Hillman to author. Barsanti: Official biography.
29. Letter, McCullough to author, November 30, 1984.
30. Official biography; author interviews with Mildren and Meszar.
31. *South to the Naktong,* p. 43n; official biography.
32. Letter, Mellen to author, May 2, 1985.
33. *Second Division in Korea,* p. 113.
34. Ibid.; 23d Infantry operations report.
35. Author-Barberis interview. Letters, to author from Ellis, April 5, 1985; from Mellen, May 2, 1985; and from Robert Arrington, May 25, 1986.
36. *U.S. Marine Operations in Korea IV,* pp. 61 (map, p. 70).
37. *Second Division in Korea,* p. 113.
38. 31st "slow": Diary, February 23, 1951. Other: Command Report, February 1951.
39. Command Report, February 1951; 1st Cav Division records, NA (Suitland), Box 4441; *First Commonwealth Division,* pp. 53, 73.
40. Author interviews with Ridgway and Surles.
41. Official biography. Details of crash: "Memo," Box 17, Ridgway Papers, USAMHI; O. P. Smith aide-mémoire, February 24, 1951.
42. Diary, February 24, 1951.
43. West Point *Register;* Hoge biography; Hoge obituary, West Point *Assembly,* June 1981; author-George F. Hoge (son) interview, September 5, 1986.
44. Author-Ridgway interview; Ridgway quoted in West Point *Assembly* obituary.
45. Author-Ridgway interview.
46. Haislip to Ridgway, February 25, 1951, and Ridgway Memo, February 28, 1951, Box 17, Ridgway Papers, USAMHI.
47. Smith oral history and aide-mémoire, February 25, 1951. Diary, February 26, 1951.
48. Telex, Ridgway to MacArthur, February 25, 1951, MacArthur Archives.
49. Command Report, February 1951; Diary, February 25 and 26, 1951; Smith aide-mémoire, February 25 and 26, 1951.
50. *Present at the Creation,* p. 517; *FRUS VII,* 1951, pt. 1, pp. 189–94.
51. *War in Peacetime,* pp. 265–66; *FRUS VII,* 1951, pt. 1, pp. 202–06.
52. *FRUS VII,* 1951, pt. 1, pp. 232–34.
53. Ridgway, *Korean War,* p. 116.
54. Telex, Ridgway to MacArthur, March 22, 1951, MacArthur Archives; *FRUS VII,* 1951, pt. 1, pp. 246–47.
55. Ridgway, *Korean War,* pp. 116–17.
56. *FRUS VII,* 1951, pt. 1, p. 247.
57. Ibid., pp. 202–03.
58. Ibid., pp. 203, 234.
59. Command Report, February 1951; Smith aide-mémoire, February 25, 1951.
60. Ridgway, *Korean War,* p. 113.
61. Smith aide-mémoire, February 25 and 26, 1951.
62. Diary, February 26, 1951. Smith aide-mémoire, February 26, 1951.
63. Smith aide-mémoire, March 1, 1951.
64. Dam: *Sea War in Korea,* p. 240. Flooding details: Telex, Ridgway to Strong, February 28, 1951, and reply, Box 17, Ridgway Papers, USAMHI.
65. Attempted bombing: *U.S. Air Force in Korea,* p. 347.
66. Diary, February 26, 1951.

67. *History of U.S. Naval Operations: Korea,* p. 330.
68. Smith aide-mémoire, March 1 and 4, 1951; Command Report, March 1951. "Relief": Author-Van Brunt interview.
69. Gillmore: Official biography; letter, Gillmore to author, November 20, 1984. Wilson: West Point *Register.*
70. Diary, March 5, 1951.
71. Ibid.
72. Command Report, March 1951, NA (Suitland), Box 1166.
73. Ibid.; Barth ms. (and map).
74. Barth ms.; author-Carlisle interview and correspondence.
75. Barth ms.; 27th Infantry Command Report, March 1951, NA (Suitland), Box 3851.
76. Corley: 24th Infantry Command Report, March 1951, NA (Suitland), Box 3841. (Corley was evacuated on February 20, 1951.) Corley obituary: West Point *Assembly.*
77. Letter, McMains to author, December 28, 1984. Britt: 24th Infantry Command Report, NA (Suitland), Box 3841; West Point *Register;* author-Michaelis interview.
78. Ridgway, *Korean War,* p. 110; telex, Ridgway to MacArthur, March 5, 1951, MacArthur Archives and Ridgway Papers, Box 17, USAMHI.
79. Diary, March 6, 1951. Memo, "Special File," March 8, 1951, Box 20, Ridgway Papers, USAMHI.
80. Command Report, March 1951; Barth ms.
81. "Armor Combat Lesson Bulletin No. 9," courtesy Thomas Gillis.
82. Ridgway, *Korean War,* p. 112.
83. Barth and Woodruff mss. Author-Michaelis interview.
84. Woodruff ms.
85. Ibid.; *Combat Actions in Korea,* pp. 145–51.
86. Carlisle and Bussey ms.; 35th Infantry Command Report, March 1951, courtesy Woodruff.
87. 24th Infantry Command Report, NA (Suitland), Box 3841; Carlisle and Bussey ms.; C. L. Rishel, "We Crossed the River Han," *Tropic Lightning Flashes* (April 1952). The latter confuses the order of batallion crossings.
88. Barth ms. 27th and 35th regimental records, NA (Suitland), Boxes 3851 and 3859. Additional 35th Infantry records and order of 35th crossing, courtesy Woodruff, letter to author, February 23, 1987. Citation for the 3/27: *Battleground Korea.* Hatch: West Point *Register.*
89. Ridgway, *Korean War,* pp. 112–13.
90. Barth ms.; 24th Infantry records, NA (Suitland), Box 3841.
91. Barth ms.
92. Command Report, March 1951; *U.S. Marine Operations in Korea IV,* pp. 80–81; *Second Division in Korea.*
93. *U.S. Marine Operations in Korea IV,* p. 70; *Time* (March 12, 1951); telex, Ridgway to MacArthur, March 9, 1951, and Quirk memo to Ridgway, March 17, 1951, both in Box 17, Ridgway Papers, USAMHI. Den Ouden: Diary, March 8, 1951.
94. *Time* (March 12, 1951).
95. Diary, March 7, 1951. Candy: Letter, Ridgway to MacArthur, March 8, 1951, Box 17, Ridgway Papers, USAMHI. Conversation: Memo, "Special File," Box 20, Ridgway Papers, USAMHI.

96. Diary, March 7, 1951. *Of GarryOwen in Glory,* pp. 311–13.
97. Author-Billy Harris interview.
98. Here and below: 1st Cav Division records, NA (Suitland), Box 4441. Author interviews with 5th Cav members John Barrett, Harry Buckley, James Gibson, Richard L. Irby (June 14, 1987), and Victor Fox. In addition, author interviews with Mrs. Paul Clifford and Mrs. Claude E. Allen and Mrs. Allen's daughter, Mrs. Betty Allen Mauney, on June 14, 1987. Letter, Mrs. Mauney (who is researching her father's career and death) to author, June 15, 1987. Clifford's awards: West Point *Register.*
99. Author-Buckley interview.
100. Diary, March 7, 1951; *MacArthur III,* p. 592 (picture of MacArthur reading statement).
101. *Conflict: The History of the Korean War,* pp. 265–66.
102. Command Report, March 1951.
103. Barth ms. and map.
104. "Secure": Barth ms.
105. Command Report, March 1951; letter, Ridgway to Marshall, March 12, 1951, Box 17, Ridgway Papers, USAMHI.
106. Diary, March 13, 1951; author interviews with Surles, Winton, and Moorman.
107. Dabney sacked: Author-Ridgway interview; letter, Bullock to author, April 9, 1984. Ridgway dislike of Dabney: Author-Moorman interview ("For some reason I don't know, Dabney and Ridgway were mortal enemies"). DSM and efficiency report: Letter, Dabney to author, October 15, 1984.
108. Official biography; West Point *Assembly* obituary, June 1974; letter, Charles Mudgett to author, February 5, 1985.
109. Train oral history; letter, Train to author, December 2, 1984; author-Surles interview.
110. Gertrude Samuels, "Ridgway—Three Views of a Soldier," *New York Times Magazine,* April 22, 1951.
111. Diary, March 12, 1951.
112. "Tremendous victory": *FRUS VII,* 1951, pt. 1, pp. 229, 244. Other: *Conflict,* pp. 266–67.
113. *FRUS VII,* 1951, pt. 1, p. 234.
114. *U.S. Marine Operations in Korea IV,* pp. 83–84.
115. Command Report, March 1951.
116. Bair ms.
117. Gavin "cold fish" and sacked: Various interviews or letters requesting anonymity.
118. Author-McCaffrey interview, May 23, 1984; West Point *Register;* letter, Mitchell to author, October 6, 1986.
119. Author-McCaffrey interview; letter, McCaffrey to author.
120. Author-Beauchamp interview. Mount: West Point *Register.*
121. *FRUS VII,* 1951, pt. 1, pp. 244–46.
122. Diary, March 15, 1951.
123. *FRUS VII,* 1951, pt. 1, pp. 244–46.
124. Ibid., p. 245.
125. Ibid., p. 245; memo, "Special File," March 15, 1951, Box 20, Ridgway Papers, USAMHI.
126. Command Report, March 1951; Barth ms.
127. Letter, Ridgway to USMA Cadet Stan Bayley, October 30, 1968, Box 17, Ridgway Papers, USAMHI.

128. *Time* (March 5, 1951 and April 2, 1945).
129. Letter, Marshall to Ridgway, February 27, 1951, G. C. Marshall Library. Cable, Eisenhower to Ridgway (via GHQ, Tokyo), March 8, 1951; letter, Bradley to Ridgway, February 5, 1951; and letter, Rusk to Ridgway, March 3, 1951. Cable and both letters are in Ridgway Papers, Box 17, USAMHI.
130. *FRUS VII,* 1951, pt. 1, p. 229; *War in Peacetime,* p. 261; Ridgway, *Korean War,* pp. 110–11.

## CHAPTER 24

1. Command Report, March 1951; *First Commonwealth Division,* p. 56.
2. *Third Division in Korea,* pp. 154–56; *Fighting 65th,* p. 175.
3. *Fighting 65th,* p. 175.
4. *Third Division in Korea,* p. 156. Carney: Ibid., p. 419.
5. Ibid., p. 156; *Fighting 65th,* pp. 185–86.
6. "Sabers and Safety Pins"; *Time* (March 26, 1951).
7. "Sabers and Safety Pins"; Barth ms.; author-Davidson interview.
8. "Sabers and Safety Pins" and Strong speech.
9. *U.S. Marine Operations in Korea IV,* p. 85.
10. Ibid., p. 88; *First Commonwealth Division,* pp. 315–17; *Second Division in Korea,* pp. 116–17.
11. Command Report, March 1951; *Second Division in Korea,* pp. 115–16.
12. Diary, March 17, 1951. Diary notes, March 17, 1951, Special File, Box 20, Ridgway Papers, USAMHI.
13. Ridgway, *Korean War,* pp. 122–23.
14. Ibid., p. 123.
15. Diary notes, March 17, 1951, Special File.
16. Smith oral history, quoted in *MacArthur III,* pp. 575–76.
17. Diary notes, March 17, 1951, Special File.
18. Ibid.
19. Letter, Beishline to Ridgway, October 22, 1951, Box 18, Ridgway Papers, USAMHI.
20. Smith oral history, quoted in *MacArthur III,* pp. 575–76.
21. Command Report, March 1951; *First Commonwealth Division,* p. 54.
22. Command Report, March 1951; author-Adams interview.
23. *RAKKASANS!*
24. Command Report, March 1951; *U.S. Air Force in Korea,* p. 324.
25. Ridgway, *Korean War,* p. 115.
26. Command Report, March 1951; Diary, March 19, 20, and 21, 1951; author-Adams interview.
27. *Tumultuous Years,* p. 352.
28. *FRUS VII,* 1951, pt. 1, pp. 298–99.
29. Ibid., p. 251.
30. *MacArthur III,* p. 645; *American Caesar,* p. 637.
31. *MacArthur III,* pp. 588–89.
32. Ibid.
33. *FRUS VII,* 1951, pt. 1, p. 294.
34. Ibid., pp. 255–56.
35. Ibid., p. 258.
36. MacArthur to Ridgway, March 22, 1951, MacArthur Archives.

37. Ridgway to MacArthur, March 22, 1951, MacArthur Archives.
38. Ibid.
39. Command Report, March 1951; Barth ms.
40. Command Report, March 1951; Ridgway to corps commanders, March 22, 1951, Special File, Box 20, Ridgway Papers, USAMHI.
41. Command Report, March 1951; *Third Division in Korea,* pp. 158–59.
42. Ridgway oral history, pt. 2, pp. 27–28; Caulfield interview.
43. MacArthur to Ridgway, March 23, 1951, MacArthur Archives.
44. "History of the JCS III," p. 473; *Policy and Direction,* pp. 361–63.
45. *U.S. Air Force in Korea,* pp. 325–26; *RAKKASANS!* Ranger Companies: *Ebb and Flow,* Chapter XVIII, p. 1.
46. Author interviews with Munson, Wilson, and Gerhart. Gerhart afteraction report, Modern Military Records Branch, RG 319, Box 627.
47. *U.S. Air Force in Korea,* p. 326.
48. Ibid., pp. 325–26; author-Wilson interview.
49. Author-Adams interview.
50. *U.S. Air Force in Korea,* p. 326; Gerhard afteraction report; Ridgway oral history, pt. 2, pp. 6–7; author interviews with Wilson, Munson, and Gerhart.
51. Author-Wilson interview.
52. Ibid.
53. *U.S. Air Force in Korea,* p. 326; Gerhart afteraction report; memo, March 23, 1951, Special File.
54. Author-Lynch interview; Diary, March 23, 1951.
55. Author-Gerhart interview; Gerhart afteraction report; memo, March 23, 1951, Special File.
56. "Task Force Growdon," I Corps "Armor Combat Lesson No. 18" (with maps), courtesy Thomas Gillis. AP, UP, INS press dispatches; *Time* (April 2, 1951); *Life* (April 9, 1951); *Pacific Stars and Stripes,* March 24, 1951. *Third Division in Korea,* p. 158.
57. *Pacific Stars and Stripes,* March 24, 1951; *Life* (April 9, 1951); wire service reports. Commendations: Letters, Milburn to Hoge, April 2, 1951; Milburn to Growdon, April 2, 1951; Hoge to Bryan, April 6, 1951; Bryan to Growdon, April 15, 1951, courtesy Growdon's daughter, Mrs. Robert Foister, who also kindly provided some press reports.
58. *U.S. Air Force in Korea,* p. 325; *RAKKASANS!*
59. Command Report, March 1951; *Third Division in Korea,* pp. 158–60.
60. Diary, March 24, 1951.
61. *Fighting 65th,* p. 171.
62. *Third Division in Korea,* p. 154. Tagalog: Author-Boswell interview.
63. *Fighting 65th,* pp. 171–72.
64. Ibid., p. 172.
65. Author-Boswell interview; Diary, March 24, 1951.
66. *FRUS. VII,* 1951, pt. 1 pp. 265–66.
67. Ibid., p. 265; *Present at the Creation,* pp. 518–19.
68. *Harry S. Truman,* p. 513.
69. *FRUS VII,* 1951, pt. 1, pp. 266–67; *War in Peacetime,* p. 270.
70. *FRUS VII,* 1951, pt. 1, p. 267; *Present at the Creation; Years of Trial and Hope,* p. 501; *War in Peacetime,* p. 270.
71. "History of the JCS III," p. 529; *War in Peacetime,* p. 271.

72. *FRUS VII,* 1951, pt. 2, pp. 1608–09, 1616–19.
73. Command Reports, March and April 1951.
74. Command Report, April 1951, NA (Suitland), Box 1179; *U.S. Air Force in Korea,* p. 335.
75. Command Report, April 1951.
76. *U.S. Air Force in Korea,* p. 327; Gerhart afteraction report.
77. *RAKKASANS!*
78. *Third Division in Korea,* pp. 164–65.
79. *Third Division in Korea,* p. 165; *RAKKASANS!*
80. Barth ms.
81. Morale: 24th Infantry records, NA (Suitland), Box 3842.
82. Ridgway oral history, pt. 3, pp. 69–71; Diary, March 14, 1951, and memo, March 14, 1951, Special File, Box 20, Ridgway Papers, USAMHI.
83. Barth ms.
84. Ibid.
85. Ibid.
86. *First Commonwealth Division,* p. 55.
87. Author-Throckmorton interview.
88. Author-Wilson interview; West Point *Register.*
89. Command Report, March 1951.
90. Command Report, March and April 1951.
91. Ibid.
92. Command Report, March 1951.
93. Dill diary, March 25 to April 1, 1951.
94. Command Report, March 1951; *FRUS VII,* 1951, pt. 1, p. 372; Diary, March 28, 1951.
95. Command Report, April 1951.
96. *Policy and Direction,* p. 364.
97. *FRUS VII,* 1951, pt. 1, p. 271.
98. Ibid., pp. 291, 317.
99. *Policy and Direction,* p. 364.
100. *FRUS VII,* 1951, pt. 1, pp. 295–96.
101. Ibid., p. 313n.
102. Diary, April 1, 1951.
103. Almond oral history; Diary, April 1, and April 4, 1951.
104. Command Report, April 1951; *Third Division in Korea,* p. 166; *First Commonwealth Division,* p. 56.
105. Command Report, April 1951. 937th: Barth ms.; Diary, April 11, 1951.
106. Command Report, April 1951; *Of GarryOwen in Glory,* p. 319; *U.S. Marine Operations in Korea IV,* pp. 94–95.
107. Diary, April 3, 1951.
108. Ibid.; Memo April 3, 1951, Special File.
109. Memo, April 3, 1951, Special File.
110. Letter, Komosa to author, November 1, 1983.
111. Ibid.
112. Ibid.; Diary, April 3, 1951.
113. *Policy and Direction,* p. 363.
114. MacArthur to Marshall, April 6, 1951, Box 17, Ridgway Papers, USAMHI. Official biographies.

## CHAPTER 25

1. *FRUS VII,* 1951, pt. 1, p. 298.
2. *Tumultuous Years,* p. 352.
3. *Years of Trial and Hope,* p. 507; *Present at the Creation,* p. 521; *A General's Life,* p. 631; Heller, *Korean War,* p. 235.
4. *A General's Life,* pp. 631–31; *Off the Record,* pp. 210–11.
5. *Off the Record,* pp. 210–11.
6. *A General's Life,* p. 632.
7. Ibid.
8. Ibid., p. 633.
9. Ibid.
10. Ibid.
11. Ibid., p. 634.
12. Ibid., pp. 634–35; *MacArthur III,* pp. 594–95, quotes a similar but earlier draft of the reasons.
13. *War in Peacetime,* p. 283.
14. *A General's Life,* p. 635; "History of the JCS III," p. 543.
15. *A General's Life,* pp. 630–31; *FRUS VII,* 1951, pt. 1, p. 309; "History of the JCS III," pp. 485–86, 535.
16. *Tumultuous Years,* p. 354.
17. Pace oral history. Details of Pace visit: MacArthur Archives, February 29, 1986, RGs 5 and 9, SCAP File, CinC Appts, secretary memos, and photo albums, etc., courtesy Edward Boone.
18. Almond calls on MacArthur: Courtesy Edward Boone, MacArthur Archives. MacArthur's records show that Almond saw MacArthur on April 4, 1951, at 1:15 P.M. and April 8, 1951, at 5:45 P.M. In his oral history Almond mistakenly puts the second visit on April 9.
19. Pace oral history.
20. Command Report, April 1951; *Third Division in Korea,* pp. 165–66.
21. *Third Division in Korea,* pp. 166–68.
22. Command Report, April 1951; Barth ms.; Woodruff ms.
23. Barth ms.
24. Command Report, April 1951; author interviews with Wilson and Throckmorton.
25. Command Report, April 1951.
26. Ibid.
27. Diary, April 9, 1951.
28. Ibid.
29. Command Report, April 1951; Diary, April 9, 1951. *U.S. Marine Operations in Korea IV,* p. 95 and maps no. 8 and no. 10.
30. Command Report, April 1951; *Of GarryOwen in Glory,* p. 320.
31. *Of GarryOwen in Glory,* p. 320.
32. Ibid. Hoge furious: *Ebb and Flow,* Chapter XIX, p. 18.
33. *Of GarryOwen and Glory,* pp. 372–72; author-Harris interview.
34. Letter, Ridgway to Gilmer, Ridgway Papers, Box 17, inviting him to Korea, holding out prospect of a promotion to brigadier general. Diary, March 29, 1951. Various author interviews with Ridgway confidants.
35. West Point *Register;* Ray Cline, *United States Army in World War II, The War Department, Washington Command Post: The Operations Division* (Washington,

D.C.: Office of the Chief of Military History, 1951), p. 182n and appendix. *Ike Papers IX,* p. 1919.

36. *Ike Papers III,* pp. 1940–41.
37. *Ike Papers IX,* pp. 1919, 2253.
38. Author interviews with Harris and others. Letter, Henry F. Daniels (Battalion CO, 7th Cav) to author, November 13, 1984.
39. *Second Division in Korea,* pp. 121–22.
40. Command Report, April 1951; *Second Division in Korea,* pp. 121–22; 23d Infantry operations report on "Swing."
41. Command Report, April 1951; Dill diary.
42. Command Report, April 1951; *U.S. Marine Operations in Korea IV,* pp. 100–01.
43. *U.S. Marine Operations in Korea IV,* p. 100.
44. Diary, April 10, 1951; Pace oral history.
45. Pace oral history. Private: Memo, Diary, April 12, 1951, Box 20, Special File, Ridgway Papers, USAMHI.
46. *MacArthur III,* p. 597. Pace deadline: *FRUS VII,* 1951, pt. 1, pp. 300–01.
47. *Tumultuous Years,* p. 355.
48. Leak and flap: *A General's Life,* p. 636; *MacArthur III,* p. 597; *Tumultuous Years,* pp. 356–57.
49. Power failure: Pace oral history. Mechanical difficulty: *FRUS VII,* 1951, pt. 1, pp. 300–01.
50. "History of the JCS III," pp. 545–46.
51. Texts, *MacArthur III,* pp. 597–98.
52. Pace oral history.
53. *MacArthur III,* pp. 598–99.
54. Ibid., p. 600.
55. Command Report, April 1951.
56. Ibid.; *Third Division in Korea,* pp. 168–69; *Fighting 65th,* pp. 176–77; Barth ms.
57. Barth ms.
58. Carlisle and Bussey ms.; letter, Carlisle to Lieutenant General Willard W. Scott, Jr., superintendent, USMA, September 16, 1985, courtesy Carlisle.
59. 24th Infantry records, NA (Suitland), Box 3843.
60. Letters, Carlisle to author, May 24, 1986, and to Scott, September 16, 1985, courtesy Carlisle.
61. Various correspondence, Carlisle to author.
62. Command Report, April 1951.
63. Pace oral history; Diary, April 11, 1951.
64. Pace oral history; Ridgway, *Korean War,* pp. 157–58.
65. Diary, April 11, 1951; Pace oral history.
66. Pace oral history; Diary, April 11, 1951; author-Throckmorton interview.
67. Pace oral history.
68. Diary, April 11, 1951; John E. Hull oral history, conducted by James W. Wurman, 1973, USAMHI; Pace oral history.
69. Author-Ridgway interview. Hull: Ridgway oral history, pt. 4, p. 33. Swing and Brooks: Letter, Ridgway to Joe Collins, May 8, 1951, Ridgway Papers, Special File, Box 20, USAMHI, nominating Swing, Brooks, or Hull as "standby commander" for Eighth Army. Brooks in Pace party: *MacArthur III,* p. 599.
70. Cable, Ridgway to Marshall, April 11, 1951, Marshall Library.
71. Ridgway memo, April 12, 1951, Special File, Box 20, Ridgway Papers, USAMHI.
72. *Soldier,* p. 223.

73. Ridgway memo.
74. *Bess W. Truman,* pp. 99–100 and passim.
75. Ridgway oral history, pt. 3, p. 81.
76. Ridgway memo.
77. Ibid.
78. Author-Surles interview.
79. Records of the JCS, CCS 383.21 Korea, RG 213, Modern Military Records Branch, NA (hereafter JCS NA). See also *Policy and Direction,* pp. 378–79.
80. JCS NA.
81. *U.S. Air Force in Korea,* pp. 293–94; *Korea: The Limited War,* p. 193.
82. Diary, April 12, 1951; Ridgway oral history, pt. 4, pp. 1–2.
83. Ridgway memo, April 12, 1951, Special File.
84. Ridgway memo, April 14, 1951, Special file.
85. Diary, April 14, 1951; *Soldier,* pp. 223–24.
86. Command Report, April 1951; Diary, April 13, 1951.
87. Diary, April 13, 1951.
88. Ridgway memo, April 13, 1951, Special File.
89. Official biography; West Point *Register; Howitzer 1915.*
90. *Howitzer 1915. A General's Life,* p. 34.
91. Official biography; West Point *Register.*
92. *War in Peacetime,* p. 294; *A General's Life,* pp. 64, 263.
93. *Lightning Joe,* p. 204 and passim; *A General's Life,* p. 263 and passim. *Ridgway's Paratroopers,* pp. 259–65.
94. *Ridgway's Paratroopers,* pp. 479–87; *Eisenhower's Lieutenants,* p. 709 and passim; *Ike Papers VI,* pp. 79, 427.
95. "History of the JCS II," p. 41; *Ike Papers IX,* pp. 2185–86.
96. "History of the JCS II," pp. 25–59.
97. Ibid.
98. Ibid. Van Fleet: Official biography.
99. Diary, April 14, 1951; *Time* (April 23, 1951); *Newsweek* (April 23, 1951).
100. Ridgway oral history, pt. 4, pp. 1–2; Ridgway telex to Van Fleet, April 19, 1951, JCS NA.
101. Diary, April 14, 1951.
102. Ridgway memo, April 14, 1951, Special File.
103. JCS NA.
104. *MacArthur III,* p. 603; Diary, April 15, 1951.
105. *MacArthur III,* p. 603. Hickey for Almond: Author-Surles interview. Allen: Author-Phillip Bolté interview. Recovered from his battle wound, Bolté became Allen's aide-de-camp.
106. *MacArthur III,* pp. 611–12.
107. Ibid., p. 611.
108. *MacArthur: His Rendezvous with History,* p. 482.
109. *A General's Life,* pp. 638–39.
110. *MacArthur III,* pp. 612–13; *A General's Life,* p. 639.
111. *MacArthur III,* p. 613.
112. Text of speech: "General Douglas MacArthur's Address to Congress," MacArthur Archives; *Congressional Record,* vol. 97, pt. 3, p. 4123.
113. *MacArthur III,* p. 616.
114. *Time* (April 30, 1951).
115. *MacArthur III,* p. 621; *Tumultuous Years,* p. 362.

116. *A General's Life,* p. 652.
117. *MacArthur III,* p. 617.
118. Van Fleet published two long articles in *Life* magazine (April 11 and April 18, 1953), recounting some of his experiences in Korea and his dissenting views on the conduct of the war. Quote here is from April 11 issue.
119. *Life* (April 11, 1953).
120. Command Report, April 1951.
121. Ibid.; author-Throckmorton interview.
122. Command Report, April 1951.
123. Interview with Ridgway; Ridgway memo on Dulles, April 17, 1951, Special File; Ridgway oral history, pt. 4, p. 3.
124. Ridgway to JCS, April 17, 1951; JCS to Ridgway, April 19, 1951; both in JCS NA.
125. Ridgway telex to air, naval, and ground chiefs (and correction), April 19, 1951, JCS NA. Slightly inaccurate excerpts in "Tactical Operations," Command Report, April 1951.
126. *A General's Life,* p. 640.

## CHAPTER 26

1. Diary, April 21, 1951; Command Report, April 1951.
2. Barth ms.; "Sabers and Safety Pins"; Hoge oral history.
3. Van Fleet in *Life* (May 11, 1953). The Eighth Army historian wrote (Command Report, April 1951, "Plans and Preparations") that Van Fleet's determination to hold Seoul "was a departure from the tactical concept of the two previous army commanders that Seoul was not a valuable target for tactical purposes."
4. Ridgway memo, April 21, 1951, Special File, Ridgway Papers, Box 20, USAMHI.
5. Ridgway oral history, pt. 3, pp. 86–87.
6. Van Fleet in *Life* (May 11 and May 18, 1953).
7. Ridgway to JCS, April 25, 1951 (enclosing directive of April 22, 1951), NA JCS; excerpts in Ridgway, *Korean War,* pp. 166–68.
8. Command Report, April 1951.
9. Ibid.
10. *U.S. Air Force in Korea,* pp. 175–77.
11. Command Report, April 1951.
12. Ibid. George Forty, *At War in Korea* (New York: Bonanza Books, 1985), p. 83; *Combat Actions in Korea,* p. 163.
13. Van Fleet, *Life* (May 18, 1953).
14. Ibid.
15. *U.S. Marine Operations in Korea IV,* pp. 101–02; official biographies, courtesy USMC History.
16. *U.S. Marine Operations in Korea IV,* p. 102.
17. Ibid., pp. 101–02.
18. Command Report, April 1951; *U.S. Marine Operations in Korea IV,* pp. 103–04.
19. Barth ms.; *Third Division in Korea,* p. 194. Babe Bryan's alert: *Ebb and Flow,* Chapter XX, p. 21.
20. The actions of Eighth Army in the CCF offensive here and below are derived from numerous sources, chiefly: (1) Eighth Army, I and IX corps Command Reports of April and May 1951. (2) Army, division and regimental records for April and May 1951, at NA (Suitland). (3) Histories of the Army's 1st Cav, 2d, 3d, 24th,

and 25th divisions, the 1st Marine Division, Commonwealth Division, and the 7th Cav and 187th and 65th regiments. (4) Johnson oral history and Barth ms. (5) *Ebb and Flow,* Chapters XXI through XXIV. (6) Author interviews and correspondence with participants. (7) *Time* and *Newsweek* (April 30 and May 7, 1951). For details of the actions of the British and Commonwealth Brigades, in addition to *First Commonwealth Division, Third Division in Korea, Korea: The Limited War,* and *At War in Korea,* see: *The Korean War: History and Tactics,* Chapter 7, "The Chinese Counterattack," by Bryan Perrett, pp. 74–85. For further background on the Gloucesters, see: W. J. Harris, "English Country Regiments," *This England* (Summer 1986).

21. Quoted in *Korea: The Limited War,* p. 249. From: Anthony Farrar-Hockley: *The Edge of the Sword* (London: Frederick Muller, 1954).
22. *Third Division in Korea,* pp. 195–96; *First Commonwealth Division,* p. 63.
23. Barth ms.
24. *Fighting 65th,* pp. 181–82.
25. Ibid. Command Report, April 1951.
26. *Third Division in Korea,* pp. 197–98.
27. Ibid.; Barth ms.
28. *Time* (April 30, 1951).
29. 24th Infantry records, NA (Suitland) Box 3843; Barth ms.
30. Barth ms. Barth alone among sources consulted mentions T-34 tanks.
31. Letter, Dick to author.
32. Command Report, April 1951.
33. Ridgway to JCS, May 1 and May 5, 1951 (quoting Eighth Army investigations), JCS NA; Command Report, April 1951; *Life* (May 18, 1953).
34. *Life* (May 18, 1953).
35. Command Report, April 1951, "Tactical Operations," p. 113. Much later, in *Life* (May 18, 1953), Van Fleet, arguing for a buildup of ROK forces, reversed himself and wrote with exaggeration: "I saw nothing disgraceful about the 6th Division's defeat. . . . These 10,000 lightly armed soldiers had run right into the noose of a mass Chinese attack; they had collided with no less than four full Chinese armies advancing full tilt . . . [and] the [survivors] had no choice but to flee."
36. *First Commonwealth Division,* p. 67.
37. Ridgway to JCS, May 5, 1951, JCS NA; *Combat Actions in Korea,* p. 163; *U.S. Marine Operations in Korea IV,* p. 111; *Ebb and Flow,* Chapter XXI, pp. 6–9.
38. *Combat Actions in Korea,* pp. 162–73; *U.S. Marine Operations in Korea IV,* pp. 109–11.
39. Command Report, April 1951; *Ebb and Flow,* Chapter XXI, pp. 11–12.
40. *U.S. Marine Operations in Korea IV,* p. 110 (map).
41. Ibid., pp. 108–09, 112 (map).
42. Command Report, April 1951 ("Plans and Operations," p. 19).
43. *First Commonwealth Division,* pp. 55–56; *At War in Korea,* pp. 83–85.
44. Command Report, April 1951; *First Commonwealth Division,* p. 67; *At War in Korea,* pp. 83–92.
45. *First Commonwealth Division; At War in Korea.* 72d: *Second Division in Korea,* p. 122.
46. Command Report, April 1951.
47. Ibid.; *U.S. Marine Operations in Korea IV* (maps); *Second Division in Korea.*
48. Command Report, April 1951.
49. Ibid.

50. Ibid.
51. *Second Division in Korea,* pp. 123–24.
52. Diary, April 24, 1951.
53. *First Commonwealth Division; At War in Korea;* Perrett in *Korean War: History and Tactics.*
54. Command Report, April 1951.
55. I Corps "Armored Combat Lesson Bulletin No. 22," courtesy Thomas Gillis. The report stated: "The counter-attack should have started about four hours prior and should have been of Regimental strength, supported by the entire battalion of tanks, instead of a battalion [of ROK infantry] and a company of tanks."
56. Author interviews with Yancey and Peck. Letter, Howard to author, February 28, 1987.
57. Johnson oral history.
58. Command Report, April 1951. Belgians exhausted and not employed: *Ebb and Flow,* Chapter XXIII, pp. 3–7.
59. *Ebb and Flow,* Chapter XXIII, p. 39.
60. Ibid., pp. 3–9.
61. Ibid., p. 8.
62. Command Report, April 1951.
63. *Ebb and Flow,* Chapter XXIII, pp. 9–11.
64. Command Report, April 1951; *First Commonwealth Division; At War in Korea.*
65. Ibid. Ray Stuart, "A Classic Diggers Battle," *Canberra Times,* May 25, 1979.
66. *At War in Korea; Ebb and Flow,* Chapter XXII, pp. 7–15. The latter is the source for the bugout of the American engineers.
67. *At War in Korea,* pp. 89–91; *Ebb and Flow,* Chapter XXII, pp. 17–18.
68. *Second Division in Korea,* p. 123; West Point *Register;* letter, Miller to author, November 19, 1986, with enclosures, including *Canberra Times* cited above.
69. Hoge oral history, USAMHI. No doubt exaggerating an amusing "war story," Hoge said of the Anzac party: "The first thing I knew, the whole line had disappeared. . . . Those Australians are wonderful fighters and so are that Anzac outfit, the [New Zealand] artillery, but they'd drawn off. Their commander had taken them off to celebrate Anzac Day and they left this great big hole. . . . Fortunately I got hold of the 5th Cav and threw them in there."
70. *Second Division in Korea,* pp. 224–25 (citation).
71. *U.S. Marine Operations in Korea IV,* pp. 113–15; *Combat Actions in Korea.*
72. *Combat Actions in Korea,* pp. 162–73.
73. *U.S. Marine Operations in Korea IV; Combat Actions in Korea.*
74. *Combat Actions in Korea,* p. 172.
75. Command Report, April 1951.
76. Ibid.; *Life* (May 11 and May 18, 1953).
77. Command Report, April 1951.
78. Van Fleet quoted: Harry J. Middleton, *The Compact History of the Korean War* (New York: Hawthorn Books, 1965), p. 189, and *Korea: The Limited War,* p. 251. In the Command Report for May 1951 (NA, Suitland, Box 1192) the Eighth Army historian wrote ("Tactical Narrative," p. 85): "The Army Commander also directed that artillery be used lavishly and that he wanted his commanders 'to expend bullets rather than flesh and to remember that artillery is the greatest close-in weapon available.' He reiterated that he wanted massed artillery expended on the next CCF attack." Later, (p. 88) he quoted Van Fleet as saying: "I want to stress again that my idea of obstacles and fire power is vast. We must

expend steel and fire, not men. I want to stop the [enemy] here and hurt him. I welcome his attack and want to be strong enough in position and fire power to defeat him. I want so many artillery holes that a man can step from one to another. This is not an overstatement; I mean it!"

79. Thomas official biography and oral history, USMC History.
80. *U.S. Marine Operations in Korea IV,* p. 118; Smith biography.
81. Letter, Almond to Appleman, September 27, 1978, Almond Papers, USAMHI.
82. Ridgway to JCS, April 25, 1951, JCS NA. Statement issued at 10:00 P.M., April 24, 1951, Tokyo time.
83. Command Report, April 1951; *Ebb and Flow,* Chapter XXIII, pp. 15–16.
84. *Ebb and Flow,* Chapter XXIII, p. 24.
85. *First Commonwealth Division; At War in Korea;* Perrett in *Korean War: History and Tactics.*
86. *Ebb and Flow,* Chapter XXIII, pp. 16–17.
87. Ibid., p. 18 (1/24 "scattered"); Barth ms.
88. Woodruff ms.
89. *Ebb and Flow,* Chapter XXIII, p. 19.
90. Ibid., p. 26; *Fighting 65th,* pp. 182–83.
91. *Fighting 65th,* p. 183; Johnson oral history.
92. *Ebb and Flow,* Chapter XXIII, pp. 25–26.
93. Ibid.
94. Ibid.; *Fighting 65th,* p. 183.
95. *Ebb and Flow,* Chapter XXIII, pp. 26–27; *Fighting 65th,* p. 183.
96. *At War in Korea;* Perrett in *Korean War: History and Tactics.* Forty states that 46 Gloucesters escaped; Perrett says 63, the Army historian 40, a figure that is in the Command Report of April 1951 (p. 101). Hannum's tankers reported rescuing 43 Gloucesters, per I Corps "Armor Combat Lesson Bulletin No. 22," dated May 22, 1951. There are similar conflicts in the total number of Gloucesters. Farrar-Hockley says 800; Forty, 622; the Army historian, 773. *Ebb and Flow,* Chapter XXIII, p. 35, provides this breakdown: 28 officers; 671 men; 28 artillerymen; 46 men in the mortar battalion. Total: 773.
97. "Nearly 1,000" from *Ebb and Flow,* see note 96. The Army historian wrote that 21 officers (8 of them wounded) and 509 enlisted men (145 wounded) of the Gloucester Battalion were captured and that two officers and 24 enlisted men died in captivity. Perrett wrote that 30 Gloucesters died in captivity.
98. Citation: *First Commonwealth Division,* p. 67; Van Fleet quoted in *Korea: The Limited War,* p. 250.
99. Letter, Ridgway to Van Fleet, May 7, 1951, Ridgway Papers, Box 18, USAMHI. *Ebb and Flow,* Chapter XXIII, pp. 38–39.
100. *Third Division in Korea,* pp. 203–04.
101. *Combat Actions in Korea,* pp. 152–61.
102. Ibid. Medals of Honor for Essebagger and Goodblood: *Korea's Heroes,* pp. 232–33; *Above and Beyond,* p. 337. Citations: *Third Division in Korea,* pp. 374–75. Middleman DSC: *Third Division in Korea,* p. 202 (citation). Wounds: *Combat Actions in Korea.*
103. 1/7 Presidential Unit Citation: *Third Division in Korea,* pp. 395–96 (attached units listed).
104. Medals of Honor: *Korea's Heroes,* pp. 232–33; *Above and Beyond,* p. 337. (No mention of these awards in *Third Division in Korea.* )
105. *Third Division in Korea,* pp. 203–04.

106. Barth ms.
107. *First Commonwealth Division,* pp. 70, 72, 74.
108. Command Report, April 1951.
109. Here and below: *Ebb and Flow,* Chapter XXIII, pp. 20–23; Barth ms.
110. Command Report, April 1951 (p. 101), describes ambush of the 5th RCT tersely (and deceptively): "Then the 5th Infantry in late afternoon began its withdrawal through the new positions. While en route, it engaged an enemy battalion covering a road block; as darkness was closing in, this regiment disengaged and used an alternate route to move to an assembly area behind the 21st Infantry."
111. *U.S. Marine Operations in Korea IV,* p. 117.
112. Command Report, April 1951.
113. *U.S. Marine Operations in Korea IV,* p. 120.
114. Command Report, April 1951. *U.S. Marine Operations in Korea IV.*
115. *U.S. Naval Operations: Korea,* pp. 347–48; *Sea War in Korea,* pp. 240–41.
116. *Sea War in Korea.*
117. Command Report, April 1951; *Third Division in Korea,* p. 204; Barth ms.; *Time* (May 7, 1951).
118. *U.S. Air Force in Korea,* pp. 336–37.
119. Ibid., pp. 275–77, 338.
120. *Third Division in Korea,* p. 204.
121. Command Report, April 1951; *Ebb and Flow,* Chapter XXIV, pp. 1–2.
122. ROKs: I Corps "Armor Combat Lesson Bulletin No. 22," courtesy Thomas Gillis; Kelleher: Barth ms. *Ebb and Flow,* Chapter XXIV, pp. 12–13.
123. Command Report, April 1951.
124. Ibid.
125. *Ebb and Flow,* Chapter XXIV, pp. 12–13.

## CHAPTER 27

1. Command Report, April 1951.
2. Command Reports, April and May 1951.
3. Command Report, April 1951.
4. Command Report, May 1951.
5. Letter, Huston to author, October 3, 1986.
6. Ridgway to JCS, April 27, 1951, Ridgway Papers, Box 20, Special File, USAMHI; *FRUS VII,* 1951, pt. 1, pp. 385–86.
7. JCS to Ridgway, April 28, 1951, Ridgway Papers, Box 20, Special File, USAMHI; *FRUS VII,* 1951, pt. 1, pp. 386–87.
8. Guard divisions: *Policy and Direction,* p. 385. Japanese police reserve: Letter, George Marshall to Truman, May 1, 1951, Truman Papers, Secretary File, Truman Library.
9. *Policy and Direction,* p. 383; *War in Peacetime,* pp. 298–300.
10. *Policy and Direction,* pp. 382–87, 395–96; *War in Peacetime,* pp. 298–302. Letter, Ridgway to Bolté, May 10, 1951, Ridgway Papers, Box 18, USAMHI.
11. Diary, May 3, 1951; Command Report, May 1951.
12. Command Report, May 1951; *U.S. Marine Operations in Korea IV,* p. 122; *Policy and Direction,* p. 387.
13. Command Report, May 1951.
14. Ridgway to JCS, May 5, 1951, JCS NA; Command Report, May 1951; *Policy and Direction,* pp. 388–89.

15. *FRUS VII,* 1951, pt. 1, p. 419n. "Criminal waste": *Ebb and Flow,* Chapter XXII, p. 21.
16. Ridgway, *Korean War,* p. 177.
17. *FRUS VII,* 1951, pt. 1, pp. 419–20.
18. Ibid., p. 420 n.
19. *Time* (May 28, 1951); *Life* (May 18, 1951).
20. Ridgway to JCS, May 1, 1951, JCS NA.
21. OPLR: Command Report, May 1951.
22. Author interviews with Billy Harris, Robert Blanchard, William J. Cochrane (7th Cav S-2), and Frank J. Culley (October 1, 1984), who relieved Gilmer as CO, 7th Cav, and with other 1st Cav Division or Eighth Army officers who requested anonymity. The description of the ringmount and "silliest thing" quote is from the Cochrane interview. The condemnation of Gilmer was universal and, owing principally to the misery he caused his men and what was viewed as "needless casualties," the criticism was often more heated and bitter than depicted in the text. Some believed that Gilmer was actually a "mental case."
23. Barth ms.
24. Ibid.; *Third Division in Korea,* pp. 206–07.
25. Telex, Eisenhower to MacArthur, March 8, 1951; Ridgway to MacArthur, March 9, 1951; both in MacArthur Archives. Author-Michaelis interview; official biography.
26. *Of GarryOwen in Glory,* p. 322.
27. Command Report, May 1951; *Policy and Direction,* pp. 388–89.
28. Command Report, May 1951; *U.S. Naval Operations in Korea,* p. 351.
29. Command Reports, April and May 1951.
30. Command Report, May 1951; *Third Division in Korea,* pp. 206–07.
31. Ridgway, *Korean War,* pp. 192–93.
32. Ibid.
33. *Integration of the Armed Forces,* pp. 442–43.
34. Ibid., pp. 392, 440–44.
35. Ibid., p. 445.
36. Command Report, May 1951.
37. Ibid.
38. Ridgway to JCS, May 12, 1951, JCS NA; *Policy and Direction,* p. 389.
39. *Third Division in Korea,* pp. 206–07.
40. Barth ms.
41. Ibid.
42. Command Report, May 1951.
43. Ibid.
44. Ibid. The Van Fleet statement released to the press is reproduced on pp. 121–22 of the "Tactical Narrative."
45. The details of X Corps combat for the period May 15 to about May 30, 1951, are drawn from the Eighth Army Command Report, May 1951, and more particularly, from a X Corps special report on the May 16 offensive against X Corps entitled "The Battle of the Soyang River" (hereafter "Battle"), which was kindly provided to the author by Thomas Mellen. "Battle" is a voluminous and well done study which includes afteraction reports of X Corps and the 9th, 23d, and 38th regiments as well as numerous highly detailed maps which show the positions of enemy and friendly forces, including artillery units, day by day. In addition the author consulted *Second Division in Korea, Third Division in Korea, U.S. Marine*

*Operations in Korea IV, Combat Actions in Korea, Combat Support in Korea,* a formal critique of the battle by John Chiles, kindly provided by Chiles, and the Almond oral history.

46. "Battle"; letters to author from Bishop, March 14, 1985, and Mellen, May 2, 1985.
47. "Battle."
48. "Battle"; *Combat Actions in Korea,* pp. 174–90 (story of the 3/38 action, May 16–19).
49. "Battle."
50. *Combat Actions in Korea,* pp. 174–90.
51. *Second Division in Korea,* pp. 124, 127–32.
52. Author-Mildren interview.
53. Ibid.; author-Polk interview.
54. *Second Division in Korea,* p. 130.
55. "Battle"; *Second Division in Korea; Combat Actions in Korea.*
56. "Battle." Command Report, May 1951; letter, Komosa to author, October 18, 1986, with enclosures.
57. "Battle."
58. *Second Division in Korea;* Stewart ms.
59. "Battle."
60. Ibid.; letter, Chiles to author, December 1, 1986, enclosing a transcript of his critique of the battle.
61. "Battle" (maps detail the 23d deployment); Chiles critique.
62. Chiles critique.
63. Wound: letter, Chiles to author, December 1, 1986. French: Chiles critique.
64. "Battle"; *Second Division in Korea.*
65. *Combat Actions in Korea,* p. 180.
66. "Battle."
67. Ibid.
68. *Second Division in Korea,* p. 132; "Battle"; *Newsweek* (May 28, 1951), noted Ruffner's crash.
69. "Battle"; Command Report, May 1951.
70. Almond oral history.
71. Ibid.
72. Ibid.
73. "Battle"; Command Report, May 1951; *Third Division in Korea,* p. 208.
74. Command Report, May 1951.
75. Ibid.
76. "Battle"; *Second Division in Korea.*
77. "Battle."
78. Ibid. Letter, Chiles to Andre Fontaine, April 23, 1959, defending malicious and unfounded accusations that the 23d had bugged out, courtesy Lloyd Jenson.
79. 23d action, here and below: "Battle"; letter, Chiles to Fontaine; Chiles critique; author interviews with Chiles and Meszar.
80. Barth ms. puts the 38th casualties at 1,600. In author's interview with Frank Mildren, he said the 1/38 and 2/38 were "clobbered" and "chewed up" badly.
81. "Battle"; *Combat Actions in Korea,* pp. 186–88.
82. Diary, May 19, 1951. Ridgway had been promoted to four stars on May 11, 1951.
83. "Battle"; Command Report, May 1951; Ridgway to JCS, May 20, 1951, JCS NA; *Time* (May 28, 1951); *Life* (May 11 and 18, 1953).

84. "Battle"; Command Report, May 1951; *Third Division in Korea,* p. 208; *U.S. Marine Operations in Korea IV,* p. 125–26.
85. Ridgway to JCS, May 20, 1951, JCS NA.
86. Almond oral history.
87. Ibid.; *First Commonwealth Division,* pp. 75–76.
88. "Battle." Ridgway to JCS, May 20, 1951, JCS NA; Command Report, May 1951; Barth ms.; *Policy and Direction,* p. 389; Ridgway, *Korean War,* pp. 177–78; *War in Peacetime,* p. 297.
89. Ridgway to JCS, May 20, 1951, JCS NA.
90. Command Report, May 1951.
91. *Combat Actions in Korea,* p. 189.
92. "Battle"; *Third Division in Korea,* p. 208; author-Yancey interview.
93. Almond oral history.
94. Author-Yancey interview.
95. Almond oral history.
96. Ibid.
97. The 3/9 problem: letter, Thomas W. Mellen to author, May 2, 1985.
98. Author-Yancey interview.
99. "Report of the Third Battalion, 15th Infantry, Counterattack on Pungam-ni," by John D. Howard, courtesy Howard.
100. "Battle"; *Third Division in Korea,* pp. 208–11.
101. "Battle."
102. Command Report, May 1951; Dill diary, May 20 and 21, 1951; telex, Van Fleet to Ridgway, May 22, 1951, Ridgway Papers, Box 20, Special File, USAMHI.
103. Diary, May 19 and 20, 1951; Ridgway, *Korean War,* p. 178; memo, Ridgway to Joe Collins (re Chung), May 23, 1951, Ridgway Papers, Special File, Box 20 USAMHI.
104. Ridgway, *Korean War,* p. 179; *U.S. Air Force in Korea,* pp. 350–51. *Time* (June 4, 1951); *Newsweek* (June 4, 1951). Official biographies.
105. *Time* (May 28, 1951); *Newsweek* (May 28, 1951). Pentagon figures: *FRUS VII,* 1951, pt. 1, p. 445.
106. Ridgway to JCS, May 20, 1951, JCS NA.
107. Command Report, May 1951; Barth ms.
108. Woodruff ms.
109. Command Report, May 1951.
110. "Battle."
111. Ibid.; *Second Division in Korea,* pp. 136–37; *U.S. Marine Operations in Korea IV,* p. 130.
112. "Battle"; *Third Division in Korea,* pp. 211–12.
113. *Fighting 65th,* pp. 188–89.
114. "Battle"; *U.S. Marine Operations in Korea IV,* p. 130.
115. Ridgway to JCS, May 24, 1951, JCS NA.
116. Ibid.
117. Ibid.; memo, Ridgway Papers, Box 17, USAMHI. Ladue obituary, West Point *Assembly,* January 1957. Omar Bradley wrote that Ladue was "a thinker with imagination, who always exercises good judgment" and was "capable of performing tasks of any magnitude."
118. Here and below: *Combat Actions in Korea,* pp. 191–200 (the 187th's story on May 24); "Battle"; X Corps, "Combat Notes No. 12," a special report on Task Force Baker, with maps, courtesy Thomas Mellen.

119. *Combat Actions in Korea,* p. 194.
120. Ibid., p. 195.
121. Ibid., p. 198.
122. "Battle."
123. Ibid.; *Second Division in Korea; Third Division in Korea,* pp. 212–13.
124. *Second Division in Korea,* p. 127.
125. "Battle."
126. Ibid.; X Corps "Combat Notes No. 12."
127. Command Report, May 1951; *U.S. Marine Operations in Korea IV,* pp. 132–33.
128. Ridgway oral history.
129. Diary, May 28, 1951.
130. Command Report, May 1951; Barth ms.; *First Commonwealth Division,* pp. 74–79; "Battle."
131. Command Report, May 1951; "Battle." 24th Division POWs: *Combat Support in Korea,* p. 199. 7th Division POWs: Command Report, May 1951.
132. Command Report, May 1951; "Battle"; *Third Division in Korea,* p. 229; Barth reported advance elements of the 3d Division began arriving in I Corps on May 28. "Battle" states that on May 28, 1951, the 3d Division was "recalled to [Eighth] army reserve."
133. The landing was canceled on May 29, 1951, twenty-four hours after Van Fleet proposed it, *U.S. Marine Operations in Korea IV,* p. 133; Command Report, May 1951.
134. X Corps "Combat Notes No. 12"; "Battle." The latter states that on May 30, 1951, Task Force Baker advance to Kansong was halted. ROK I Corps to Kansong: "History of the JCS III," p. 501.
135. *Second Division in Korea,* p. 138. The division began its withdrawal into IX Corps reserve on June 5, 1951.
136. Van Fleet estimate: Command Report, May 1951. 2d Division: *Second Division in Korea,* p. 138; regimental afteraction reports in "Battle"; 23d Infantry operations report.
137. Van Fleet quoted: *Sea War in Korea,* p. 309; *Life* (May 11 and 18, 1953); *Policy and Direction,* p. 399n. Almond quoted: Oral history.
138. Diary, May 30, 1951.
139. *Time* (May 28, 1951).
140. Command Report, May 1951.
141. Ridgway to JCS, May 30, 1951, JCS NA.

## CHAPTER 28

1. See, for example, *Time* and *Newsweek* magazines, issues of April 30; May 7, 14, 21, and 28; and June 4, 1951.
2. For a succinct and well-balanced survey of the MacArthur hearings, see *MacArthur III,* pp. 621–40.
3. *MacArthur III,* pp. 623–24; *A General's Life,* pp. 639–40.
4. *A General's Life,* p. 640.
5. The censored portions of the transcript have been released and are on file in the National Archives. They reveal little of value to the central arguments.
6. Casualties: *Newsweek* (June 11, 1951). Bradley on public reaction to war: *FRUS, VII,* 1951 pt. 1, p. 568.
7. Heller, *Korean War,* pp. 140–70.

8. JCS: *FRUS, VII,* 1951, pt. 1, pp. 295–96. NSC-48/5: *FRUS VI,* 1951, *Asia and the Pacific,* pt. 1, pp. 33–63.
9. *FRUS, VII,* 1951, pt. 1, pp. 470–72.
10. Ibid., pp. 487–93; JCS to Ridgway, May 31, 1951, JCS NA; *Policy and Direction,* p. 396.
11. *FRUS, VII,* 1951, pt. 1, pp. 487–93; JCS to Ridgway, May 31, 1957, JCS NA.
12. *FRUS, VII,* 1951, pt. 1, pp. 470–71.
13. Ibid., pp. 285–88.
14. Ibid., p. 287.
15. *"History of the JCS III,"* p. 563; *Years of Trial and Hope,* p. 516; *Present at the Creation,* p. 531; *FRUS, VII,* 1951, pt. 1, pp. 497, 538; *The New York Times,* June 2 and 3, 1951.
16. *FRUS, VII,* 1951, pt. 1, pp. 460–62, 483–86.
17. Ibid., pp. 507–11.
18. Ibid.
19. Ibid., p. 545.
20. Command Report, June 1951 (NA, Suitland, Box 1206); Barth ms.; *Third Division in Korea,* pp. 229–330.
21. Command Report, June 1951; *Third Division in Korea,* p. 229.
22. Command Report, June 1951.
23. *Third Division in Korea,* pp. 229–330.
24. *Fighting 65th,* pp. 193–95; *Third Division in Korea,* p. 230; Command Report, June 1951.
25. *Third Division in Korea,* pp. 230–31.
26. Barth ms.; letter, Dick to author.
27. 24th Infantry records, NA (Suitland), Box 3845.
28. Ibid.
29. Ibid. Clayton commanded the 2/24 from October 28, 1950, to May 27, 1951.
30. Carlisle and Bussey ms., p. 112.
31. *Korea's Heroes,* pp. 184–89; *Above and Beyond.*
32. Command Report, June 1951; *Time* (June 18, 1951).
33. Ibid.
34. *U.S. Marine Operations in Korea IV,* p. 146; map 15, p. 140.
35. Ibid., pp. 147–51.
36. Ibid., p. 147.
37. *Second Division in Korea,* pp. 138–87, command charts, xix. West Point *Register.* Author interviews with Chiles, Meszar, Mildren, and James Y. Adams. Letter, John M. Lynch to author, February 19, 1985. Adams (West Point, 1935) took command of the 23d Infantry; Lynch (West Point, 1936), the 9th.
38. Letter, Lynch to author, February 19, 1985; author-Pope interview.
39. *Policy and Direction,* pp. 398–99.
40. Ridgway to JCS, June 14, 1951, JCS NA.
41. *Present at the Creation,* pp. 531–32; "History of the JCS III," p. 564. Schnabel and Watson report no written evidence could be found that Acheson informed Ridgway.
42. *Policy and Direction,* p. 399, citing Ridgway article in the *Saturday Evening Post* (February 25, 1956).
43. *Policy and Direction,* pp. 400–01.
44. Ridgway to JCS, May 30, 1951, JCS NA.

45. Command Report, June 1951; *Of GarryOwen in Glory,* p. 325; *Third Division in Korea,* p. 233.
46. Command Report, June 1951; *Third Division in Korea,* p. 233.
47. Command Report, June 1951; *Third Division in Korea,* p. 233; 27th Infantry records, NA (Suitland), Box 3854. Bradley, Kelleher, and Check: Official biographies and author interviews with peers.
48. Letter, Whitney to author, November 9, 1984; author-Gillis interview; Gillis diary; 24th Infantry records, NA (Suitland), Boxes 3846, 3847, 3848. Ray V. Porter brought the 14th Infantry to Korea; he was replaced by the 25th Division chief of staff, Whitney.
49. Command Report, June 1951; *Third Division in Korea,* p. 233.
50. *Third Division in Korea,* pp. 234–35.
51. Bennett citation: Ibid., pp. 373–74. DSCs: Ibid., pp. 235–37.
52. "Fluid stalemate": *Time* (June 11, 1951).
53. *Fighting 65th;* author interviews with Harris, St. Clair, Boswell, Yancey, and Tom O'Neil. Subsequent troubles in the 65th: *The New York Times,* January 28, 1953. Official biographies. O'Neil (returned from emergency leave) replaced Yancey as the 15th Infantry commander.
54. Official biographies; West Point *Register;* author interviews with Palmer and Blanchard. Gilmer: Various author interviews with 1st Cav senior officers.
55. Command Report, June 1951. Official biographies; author interviews with Wilson and Surles.
56. Command Report, June 1951. Official biographies; West Point *Register;* author interviews with Quinn and McCaffrey. Of the fifty-one Army officers who commanded infantry regiments during the first year of the Korean War, two were killed (Robert Martin, 34th Infantry, and Allan MacLean, 31st Infantry). Six rose to general (four stars): Johnny Johnson (5th and 8th Cav), Paul Freeman (23d Infantry), Herb Powell (17th Infantry), Johnny Throckmorton (5th Infantry), Guy Meloy (19th Infantry), and Mike Michaelis (27th Infantry). Three rose to lieutenant general (three stars): Ed Messinger (9th Infantry), Bill Quinn (17th Infantry); Bill McCaffrey (31st Infantry). Eleven rose to major general (two stars): Billy Harris (7th Cav), Olinto Barsanti (9th Infantry), Jack Chiles (23d Infantry), George Peploe (38th Infantry), John Guthrie (7th Infantry), Tom Yancey (15th Infantry), Charles Beauchamp (34th and 32d regiments), Charles Mount (32d Infantry), Ned Moore (19th Infantry), Dick Stephens (21st Infantry), and Gines Perez (21st Infantry). Eleven rose to brigadier general (one star): Marcel Crombez (5th Cav), Hal Edson (8th Cav), Bob Blanchard (8th Cav), John Hill (9th Infantry), Frank Meszar (23d Infantry), Jim Boswell (7th Infantry), William Harris (65th Infantry), Richard Ovenshine (31st Infantry), Art Champeny (24th Infantry), John Corley (24th Infantry), Gerry Kelleher (35th Infantry). Eighteen were not promoted to general: Carl Rohsenberger (5th Cav), Cecil Nist (7th Cav), Dan Gilmer (7th Cav), Ray Palmer (8th Cav), Pete Clainos (8th Cav), Charles Sloane (9th Infantry), John Coughlin (38th Infantry), Dinty Moore (15th Infantry), Tom O'Neil (15th Infantry), John Gavin (31st Infantry), Godwin Ordway (5th Infantry), Harry Wilson (5th Infantry), Ollie Kinney (19th Infantry), Pete Garland (19th Infantry), Jay Lovless (34th Infantry), Horton White (24th Infantry), Gilbert Check (27th Infantry), Hank Fisher (35th Infantry).
57. *Policy and Direction,* pp. 400–01; *War in Peacetime,* p. 308.
58. FRUS, VII, 1951, pt. 1, pp. 546–47.
59. Ibid., p. 547.

60. "Official": *Present at the Creation,* p. 533.
61. *FRUS,* VII, 1951, pt. 1, p. 547.
62. Ridgway, *Korean War,* p. 181.
63. Ibid.
64. "History of the JCS III," p. 565; *Policy and Direction,* p. 402.
65. *FRUS,* VII, 1951, pt. 1, pp. 552–53, 558, 548–49.
66. *Off the Record,* p. 212.
67. Leaks: *Time* (April 30, 1951).
68. *Harry S. Truman,* pp. 517–18; *Off the Record,* p. 213.
69. *Harry S. Truman,* p. 519; *Off the Record,* pp. 213–14.
70. *Years of Trial and Hope,* p. 517.
71. *FRUS,* VII, 1951, pt. 1, p. 547.
72. *Truce Tent,* citing *The New York Times* of June 22, 1951.
73. *FRUS,* VII, 1951, pt. 1, pp. 551, 560–61.
74. Ibid., pp. 571–73.
75. Ibid., p. 573.
76. Ibid., pp. 569–70.
77. Ibid., pp. 566–71.
78. Diary, June 29, 1951; Ridgway, *Korean War,* p. 182.
79. *FRUS,* VII, 1951, pt. 1, pp. 567–68.
80. Ibid., p. 568.
81. *Policy and Direction,* p. 405.
82. "Unanimous": *FRUS,* VII, 1951, pt. 1, p. 597. Other: Ibid., pp. 569, 577; "History of the JCS III," pp. 566–67.
83. *Present at the Creation,* pp. 553–54; "History of the JCS III," p. 566n.
84. Diary, June 26, 1951; Command Report, June 1951.
85. Overwhelming: *Truce Tent,* pp. 74–75.
86. Command Report, June, 1951. *Truce Tent,* pp. 76–77 (as of July 1, 1951). *FRUS,* VII, 1951, pt. 1, p. 558; *Policy and Direction,* p. 403; *War in Peacetime,* p. 307; Ridgway, *Korean War,* p. 181.
87. Van Fleet in *Life* (May 11, 1953), p. 132. To "clarify" his various confusing public statements, Van Fleet wrote: "The enemy recovered quickly from the beating we gave him in May and entrenched again by June 10. This is the reason I concurred with General Ridgway—as has been reported in rebuttal against my belief that the enemy was on the run—that a 20-mile advance which was being considered at that time would 'cost us too many casualties.' There was no similarity between the conditions of June 26 and the opportunities that had existed 30 days earlier— or between the value of a final defeat to the enemy and a limited 20-mile advance."
88. *Policy and Direction,* p. 403.
89. *FRUS,* VII, 1951, pt. 1, pp. 583–87.
90. Ibid., pp. 586–87.
91. Ibid.
92. Ibid., pp. 601–07.
93. Ridgway to JCS: Ibid., pp. 609–10.
94. Ibid.
95. Ibid.
96. Ibid.
97. Ibid.
98. See, for example, Bevin Alexander, *Korea: The First War We Lost* (New York: Hippocrene Books, 1986), pp. 429–33.

99. *FRUS,* VII, 1951, pt. 1, pp. 612–13.
100. Ibid., p. 613.
101. Ibid., pp. 600, 612.
102. Ibid., p. 616.
103. Ibid., p. 623.
104. Ibid., pp. 623–24.
105. *Truce Tent,* pp. 18–19.
106. *FRUS,* VII, 1951, pt. 1, pp. 637–38.
107. Ibid., p. 639.

## CHAPTER 29

1. Chief sources for the negotiations in this chapter are: *FRUS VII,* 1951, pt. 1, pp. 636–1473; "History of the JCS III," pt. 2, pp. 563–1059; *Truce Tent. FRUS* contains lengthy daily reports on the negotiations from Ridgway and most JCS messages to Ridgway, until December 31, 1951. Other sources: Ridgway, *Korean War; War in Peacetime; Compact History of the Korean War; Korea: The Limited War; Korea: The First War We Lost;* C. Turner Joy, *How Communists Negotiate* (New York: Macmillan, 1953); *From the Danube to the Yalu.*
2. *FRUS VII,* 1951, pt. 1, p. 671.
3. Ibid., pp. 703–06, 713.
4. Ibid., pp. 719–20, 731.
5. Ibid., pp. 727–29.
6. Ibid., p. 737.
7. Ibid., pp. 738–39 (Muccio to Acheson).
8. Ibid., pp. 737–49.
9. Ibid., p. 748.
10. Ibid., p. 401.
11. Ibid., pp. 778–88.
12. Ibid., pp. 787–88.
13. Ibid., p. 789.
14. Ibid., pp. 794–95.
15. Ibid., pp. 798–99.
16. Ibid., p. 801.
17. Ibid., pp. 810–11.
18. Ibid., p. 812.
19. Ibid., pp. 814–47. "Subdelegation": Ibid., p. 828. UN truce line concession: Ibid., pp. 846–47.
20. Ibid., pp. 848–49, 850–52.
21. Ibid., pp. 852–53.
22. Ibid., p. 854.
23. Division histories; *U.S. Marine Operations in Korea IV,* p. 173. Van Fleet: *Truce Tent,* p. 81.
24. *Truce Tent,* pp. 80, 98.
25. Ibid., p. 82. Byers: West Point *Register. Second Division in Korea,* pp. 161–64.
26. *Second Division in Korea,* p. 165; mss. "Bloody Ridge" and "Action on Heartbreak Ridge," compiled by Army combat historian, on file at the U.S. Army Center of Military History.
27. *U.S. Marine Operations in Korea IV,* pp. 171–80.
28. Ibid.

29. *Truce Tent,* pp. 86, 96. Van Fleet order: *U.S. Marine Operations in Korea IV,* p. 199.
30. *Truce Tent,* pp. 98–99; *First Team; Third Division in Korea,* p. 254 and ff. O'Daniel: Official biography.
31. *Truce Tent,* p. 102; *Of GarryOwen in Glory,* p. 333.
32. *First Team; Of GarryOwen in Glory,* pp. 327–34.
33. *First Commonwealth Division,* p. 109; *First Team.*
34. "History of the JCS III," p. 625; *Present at the Creation,* p. 652. Acheson puts American casualties from June 1950 to June 1951 at 78,800; "History of the JCS III" puts American casualties from June 1951 to November 1951 at 22,000.
35. Poll: Heller, *Korean War,* p. 147. Bradley: *FRUS VII,* 1951, pt. 1, p. 862.
36. *FRUS VII,* 1951, pt. 1, pp. 811, 882–85.
37. Ibid., pp. 900–01.
38. Ibid., pp. 901–03.
39. Ibid., pp. 906–10, 917, 924, 926.
40. Ibid., pp. 927, 931.
41. Ibid., pp. 938–39.
42. Ibid., pp. 939–45.
43. Ibid., pp. 952–55.
44. *A General's Life,* p. 648.
45. *FRUS VII,* 1951, pt. 1, pp. 957–58.
46. "History of the JCS III," p. 603.
47. *FRUS VII,* 1951, pt. 1, pp. 960, 965.
48. Ibid. (Bohlen report), pp. 990–95.
49. Ibid., pp. 970–71.
50. Ibid., pp. 1001–02.
51. Ibid., pp. 1042–47 (full text).
52. Ibid., pp. 1005–07.
53. Ibid., pp. 1061–63.
54. Ibid., pp. 900, 1101.
55. *Truce Tent,* pp. 114–15.
56. *FRUS VII,* 1951, pt. 1, p. 1074n.
57. Ibid., p. 1072.
58. Ibid., p. 1074.
59. Ibid., p. 1068.
60. Ibid., p. 1091.
61. Ibid., p. 1099.
62. Ibid., pp. 1092–93.
63. Ibid., p. 1104.
64. *The New York Times:* "History of the JCS III," p. 617. November 12, 1951 meeting: *FRUS VII,* 1951, pt. 1, pp. 1121–22.
65. *FRUS VII,* 1951, pt. 1, pp. 1122–24.
66. Ibid., p. 1126.
67. *Truce Tent,* p. 118; *FRUS VII,* 1951, pt. 1, pp. 1128–30.
68. *FRUS VII,* 1951, pt. 1, p. 1131.
69. Ibid., pp. 1136, 1159–61, 1186–87.
70. *Truce Tent,* pp. 176–77.
71. Ibid., p. 177; "History of the JCS III," p. 622; *FRUS VII,* 1951, pt. 1, pp. 1199–1200.

72. *FRUS VII*, 1951, pt. 1, pp. 1189–1473; "History of the JCS III," pp. 654–72; *Truce Tent*, pp. 135–74.
73. *Korea: The First War We Lost*, pp. 450–51.
74. "History of the JCS III," p. 659.
75. Ibid., p. 664.
76. UN December 11, 1951, proposal: *FRUS VII*, 1951, pt. 1, pp. 1297–98, 1305–06. Casualties: See note 34.
77. "History of the JCS III," pp. 675–77.
78. *FRUS VII*, 1951, pt. 1, pp. 1049, 1068.
79. Opposition: "History of the JCS III," pp. 677–79. Truman quoted: *Years of Trial and Hope*, pp. 521–23 (full text).
80. *Korea: The First War We Lost*, pp. 452–53.
81. *Truce Tent*, p. 140.
82. Ibid., p. 141.
83. *FRUS VII*, 1951, pt. 1, p. 1069.
84. "History of the JCS III," pp. 697–98.
85. *Truce Tent*, pp. 144–45. Joy: Ibid., p. 149.
86. Ibid., pp. 169–72.
87. Ibid.
88. Ibid., p. 174.
89. *Compact History of the Korean War*, pp. 209–11; *Korea: the First War We Lost*, p. 456.
90. *Compact History of the Korean War*, pp. 211–14.
91. *Truce Tent*, pp. 233–39.
92. Ibid., pp. 243–62.
93. Ibid., pp. 263–82.
94. Truman's approval rating: Heller, *Korean War*, p. 145 and passim. In mid-May 1951 Truman's approval rating was 24 percent. Joseph Goulden wrote in *The Korean War* (p. 600) that in the last two years of Truman's presidency, his approval rating "never rose above 32 percent and at times dipped as low as 23 percent."
95. *Tumultuous Years*, pp. 392–401; *Eisenhower I*, p. 516 and passim.
96. Bradley's views on Collins, Ridgway, Gruenther, and NATO job: Letters, John R. Beishline to Ridgway, October 27 and December 6, 1951, January 20, February 29, and April 5, 1952, Ridgway Papers, Box 18, USAMHI. Ike views on Gruenther: Letter, Beishline to Ridgway, December 6, 1951.
97. *Truce Tent*, pp. 249, 310–11, 332–33, 366–67; "History of the JCS III," pp. 857–58, 930–34. Clark asked the JCS for two Chinese Nationalist divisions on May 27, 1952. On September 29, 1952, Clark wrote Joe Collins to say that Washington had failed to get an armistice "because it had not placed enough military pressure on the enemy." On October 9 and 16, 1952, Clark asked that he be authorized to use atomic bombs in his war plan, OPLAN-52.
98. *Truce Tent*, pp. 320–22, 324–25; *U.S. Air Force in Korea*, pp. 480–93.
99. *Truce Tent*, p. 265. Harrison took over on May 22, 1952. Harrison: West Point *Register*. "Package": *Truce Tent*, pp. 276–82.
100. *Truce Tent*, pp. 303–18. Puerto Rican bugout: Ibid., p. 310, 310n; *New York Times*, January 28, 1953.
101. West Point *Register*. William Clark: Letter, John M. Lynch (CO, 9th Infantry) to author, February 19, 1985.

102. *Truce Tent,* pp. 317–18. Ammo "shortage": pp. 224, 324–25, 336–37, 356. See also *War in Peacetime,* pp. 318–22; *Life* (May 18, 1953).

103. Ambrose, *Eisenhower I,* pp. 550–72; *Tumultuous Years,* pp. 398–401. Ambrose (p. 569) wrote that "Korea, not crooks or Communists, was the major concern of the voters." However, see Heller, *Korean War,* p. 155, quoting a University of Michigan postelection survey which concluded the Korean War had been a "minor factor" in the election. Subsequent discussion in Heller tends to support Ambrose's view. See also the "History of the JCS III," p. 911: "The national policy toward Korea came under intense scrutiny as a major issue in the campaign. . . ."

104. "History of the JCS III," pp. 934–36; Dwight D. Eisenhower, *The White House Years: Mandate for Change: 1953–1956* (Garden City: Doubleday 1963), pp. 130–34; *From the Danube to the Yalu,* pp. 232–39; *A General's Life,* pp. 657–59.

105. *Eisenhower II,* pp. 47–48, 98. *Mandate,* pp. 180–81; Eisenhower repudiated Truman's Formosa policy in his State of the Union address, February 2, 1953; *Truce Tent,* p. 409.

106. *Eisenhower II,* pp. 91–92, 94–97; *Truce Tent,* p. 412.

107. *Truce Tent,* pp. 412–13.

108. *Eisenhower II,* p. 97.

109. *Truce Tent,* pp. 393–95.

110. Ibid., pp. 415–19, 514–15.

111. Ibid., pp. 419–29.

112. Ibid., pp. 460–61; *U.S. Air Force in Korea,* pp. 623–37.

113. *U.S. Air Force in Korea,* p. 627.

114. *Truce Tent,* pp. 462–70.

115. Ibid., pp. 429–32.

116. Ibid., pp. 436–48; "History of the JCS III," pp. 983–94.

117. *Truce Tent,* pp. 449–51.

118. Ibid., pp. 452–53.

119. Ibid., pp. 454–58. Everready: "History of the JCS III," pp. 990–92. Task force: Ibid., pp. 999–1019.

120. *Truce Tent,* pp. 470–77.

121. Ibid., p. 477.

122. "History of the JCS III," pp. 1020–30.

123. *Truce Tent,* p. 490, 514–15.

124. Pat Meid and James M. Yingling, *U.S. Marine Operations in Korea, vol. V, Operations in West Korea* (Washington, D.C.: Historical Division, U.S. Marine Corps, 1972), pp. 531–32; *Korea: The First War We Lost,* p. 483; other sources. Total casualty figures in the Korean War vary significantly.

125. *Present at the Creation,* p. 652.

# INDEX

*This is a general subject and name index. An index of military units follows on page 1124.*

1085

# INDEX OF
# MILITARY UNITS

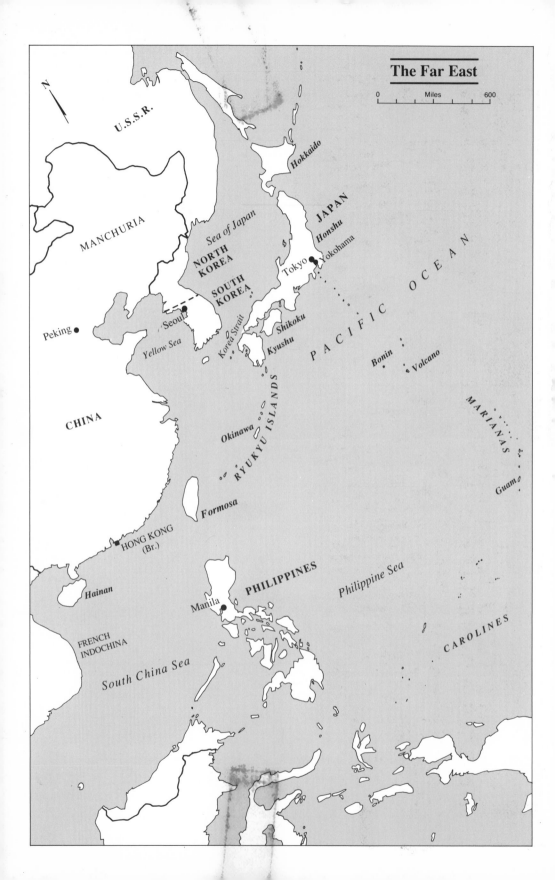

## The Far East

N

Miles
0          600

U.S.S.R.

MANCHURIA

Hokkaido

Sea of Japan

JAPAN

NORTH
KOREA

Honshu

SOUTH
KOREA

Tokyo   Yokohama

Seoul

Shikoku

Peking

Korea Strait

Kyushu

Yellow Sea

PACIFIC   OCEAN

Bonin

Volcano

CHINA

MARIANAS

Okinawa

RYUKYU ISLANDS

Guam

Formosa

HONG KONG
(Br.)

Hainan

PHILIPPINES

Philippine Sea

Manila

CAROLINES

FRENCH
INDOCHINA

South China Sea